THE AMERICAN
AND
CANADIAN WEST

Clio Bibliography Series No. 6

Abstracts from the periodicals data base of the
American Bibliographical Center

Eric H. Boehm, Editor
Joyce Duncan Falk, Executive Editor
Pamela R. Byrne, Managing Editor
Users of the Clio Bibliography Series may refer to current issues of
America: History and Life *and* Historical Abstracts
for continuous bibliographic coverage of the subject areas
treated by each individual volume in the series.

1.
The American Political Process
Dwight L. Smith and Lloyd W. Garrison
1972   LC 72-77549   ISBN 0-87436-090-0

2.
Afro-American History
Dwight L. Smith
1974   LC 73-87155   ISBN 0-87436-123-0

3.
Indians of the United States and Canada
Dwight L. Smith
1974   LC 73-87156   ISBN 0-87436-124-9

4.
Era of the American Revolution
Dwight L. Smith
1975   LC 74-14194   ISBN 0-87436-178-8

5.
Women in American History
Cynthia E. Harrison
1979   LC78-26194   ISBN 0-87436-260-1

6.
The American and Canadian West
Dwight L. Smith
1979   LC 78-24478   ISBN 0-87436-272-5

THE AMERICAN AND CANADIAN WEST

A BIBLIOGRAPHY

Dwight L. Smith
Editor

Ray A. Billington
Introduction

Santa Barbara, California
Oxford, England

Smith, Dwight La Vern, 1918-
    The American and Canadian West.

    (Clio bibliography series; 6)
    Includes index.
    1. The West—History—Bibliography.
2. The West—History—Abstracts. 3. Northwest,
Canadian—History—Bibliography. 4. Northwest,
Canadian—History—Abstracts. I. Title.
Z1251.W5S64   [F591]   016.978   78-24478
ISBN 0-87436-272-5

© 1979 by ABC-CLIO, Inc.

American Bibliographical Center—Clio Press, Inc.
2040 Alameda Padre Serra
Santa Barbara, California

European Bibliographical Center—Clio Press
Woodside House, Hinksey Hill
Oxford OXI 5BE, England

Design by Don French, from a 19th century engraving.
Printed and bound in the United States of America

CONTENTS

HISTORIOGRAPHY
Entries concerned with historiography of the American and Canadian West are located along with the other entries in this bibliography under the appropriate subject matter headings.

INDIANS
Archaeology, anthropology, ethnology, tribal histories, and other exclusively Indian items are not included in this bibliography. Indian items related to other aspects of Western Canadian and American history, such as missionary activity, fur trade, and settlement, are classified under the appropriate headings, with the exception of Indian Wars, which is a separate category under military history. Complete coverage of Indian items is made in a previous volume in this series. See Dwight L. Smith, ed., *Indians of the United States and Canada* (Santa Barbara: ABC-Clio, Inc., 1974).

PREFACE

Interest in Western history is enduring. The volume of literature on the subject is beyond the capacity of ordinary mortals to digest. The continuous outpouring of published materials is prodigious and sustained. Even specialized libraries and collectors strain their capacities and resources to acquire and catalog all of these books and articles. Important efforts are making notable contributions toward some semblance of bibliographic order and control over the published literature.

The American and Canadian West is an effort in that direction. This volume is concerned with the periodical literature of history and the social sciences of the world published from 1964 through 1973. Updating is projected in a second volume to cover another five years of publication of AMERICA: HISTORY AND LIFE.

Previous volumes in the *Clio Bibliography Series* concern either a particular subject or a chronological period. *The American and Canadian West* deals with a region or geographic area. The selection of materials included and their classification are sometimes more arbitrary than in the previous volumes of the series. The scope needs careful definition.

The American and Canadian West is concerned with Western history within chronological and spatial bounds. Items of prehistory and developments after 1945 are generally excluded. Geographically it includes the trans-Mississippi West and the trans-Shield Canadian West. Except for those with a westward orientation, items that deal with the history of the states on the west bank of the Mississippi River are not included. For Canada the division is made by the Ontario-Manitoba provincial boundary. In the Southwest, the Mexican-American boundary usually determines the selection. In Alaska and the Canadian North, only items that are more Western than Arctic have been included.

Finally, studies more concerned with national or non-Western topics are eliminated even though they fulfill the chronological and spatial definitions. An item about the founding of the United Nations in San Francisco, for example, does not fall within the scope of this volume. Likewise, articles about the Vancouver press coverage of the sweep of the United Farmers of Ontario in the 1919 provincial election or about the Spanish-American War veterans of Idaho are beyond present interest. Such articles are included only if they are primarily concerned with the impact of these external matters on the course of Western history. On the other hand, such subjects as parliamentary action in Ottawa to aid settlement in Alberta or the participation of Georgia prospectors in the Colorado gold rush are included.

The omission of a special category for Indians, a principal subject in any bibliographic treatment of the Canadian and American West, is deliberate. Indians is itself the subject of a previous volume in this series where full coverage is given (*Indians of the United States and Canada*, 1974). Since some of the material in the Indian volume is related to other aspects of Western Canadian and American history — missionary activity, the fur trade, military history, settlement, and Indian-white relations, in general — its omission here would make a fundamental distortion. It is included, therefore, in the present volume. Archaeology, anthropology, ethnology, tribal affairs, and other exclusively Indian items are *not* included. Historiography is another standard category for historical bibliographies. Those items which are couched in terms of the frontier or the Westward movement or the West without any particular spatial moorings are not used here. Those which do have particular reference to the subject matter of this volume are located under the appropriate subject matter headings. Such items as bibliographies and other research aids are treated in the same way.

The American and Canadian West is the product of the sustained interests and efforts of many. Hundreds of scholars throughout the world have faithfully digested the periodical literature to prepare the abstracts that constitute the unparalleled historical data bank of AMERICA: HISTORY AND LIFE (see list of abstracters). It is from these some 33,400 entries of its first ten volumes that I have selected 4,157 abstracts that are the entries in the present volume.

When an author completes a manuscript he seeks a publisher. Usually, when a manuscript has been accepted for publication, an editor is assigned to work with the author. The editor guides the author through cutting, enlarging, revising, making stylistic changes, rewriting, or accomplishing whatever other modifications are desirable to prepare the manuscript for publication. Beyond that, the actual physical production of the book is of minor concern to the author and editor.

The principals and their functions involved in the publication of a project of this sort, however, are more intimately related. The intellectual contributions are not confined to the bibliographer, subject to modifications by an editor. The magnitude and the special nature of the project require the editorial efforts of several people, not only those normally considered as editors, but also systems analysts and data processing specialists.

The intellectual aspects filter from the bibliographer, through the editors, to the technicians, who make utilization of the computerized data bank possible. The involvement flows in the other direction also. The technical aspects of tapping the data bank must be sufficiently understood by the editors and appreciated by the bibliographer so that the manuscript can be prepared in the proper form for the technicians to process.

Of necessity, the editors for this project are bibliographers, as well as in-house editors in the usual sense. They are also knowledgeable practitioners in the ways of satisfying the needs of computer data banks and of exploiting their rich resources.

In a word, THE AMERICAN AND CANADIAN WEST is a team effort. The several aspects of the preparation of the manuscript are so closely intertwined and interrelated that they cannot each be described discretely.

I assumed responsibility as bibliographer and editor for THE AMERICAN AND CANADIAN WEST while on assignment as consultant to the American Bibliographical Center during the summers of 1977 and 1978 and for other briefer periods in Ohio. I screened the data bank of AMERICA: HISTORY AND LIFE to select and classify the entries for this project. From the early planning stages to the final conception, Joyce Duncan Falk, Director of the American Bibliographical Center and Executive Editor of the series, gave definition and clarity to the project.

Pamela R. Byrne, Managing Editor, Clio Bibliography Series, coordinated the many facets of the project throughout, from data selection to final production. Her patience and good humor, as well as her editorial skills and management, kept the team effort functioning efficiently. Editorial assistants Linda Press, Stanton Richards, and Elizabeth Schools, edited and indexed the entries of the bibliography. This assignment was tedious and intellectually demanding. The utility of the thousands of items in this bibliography is enhanced by their indexing.

The technical services performed by Systems Analyst Doug Farmer, Director of Data Processing Services Ken Baser, and the production staff involved retrieval of the abstracts from the data bank of AMERICA: HISTORY AND LIFE and sophisticated correction processes. Their willing consultation smoothed the intellectual and technical demands of the project, and their efforts brought the text of these volumes to the form necessary for publication.

We are fortunate that Ray A. Billington, Senior Research Associate at The Huntington Library and dean of historians of the American West, has written the introductory essay for THE AMERICAN AND CANADIAN WEST. Billington is a bibliographer of the West in his own right. His introduction gives perspective and utility to this bibliography, a reflection of the scholarship as it appears in the periodical literature.

Finally, I wish to acknowledge indebtedness to the scores of historians who have written the abstracts that serve as annotation to the bibliographic citations in this volume. Their names appear in a special listing at the end of the volume, as well as with each of the abstracts they have written.

DWIGHT L. SMITH

Miami University
Oxford, Ohio

INTRODUCTION

Ray Allen Billington, The Huntington Library

Those of us whose memories reach back over the decades can recall with nostalgic longing the days when the literature of American history was scant enough to be easily manageable even to the novice, when virtually all articles on the subject were printed in the journals of the state historical societies or such standard quarterlies as the *American Historical Review* and the *Mississippi Valley Historical Review*, and when the yearly output of books and articles, numbering some three thousand at the most, could be conveniently listed in the annual volume of *Writings on American History* (including those on Canada and Latin America) compiled by the indefatigable Grace Gardner Griffin and distributed without charge to all members of the American Historical Association who had paid their five-dollar dues. There, a half century ago, the expert in the period from 1789 to 1829 could eagerly open the volume for 1928 and find that eight books and articles on his subject had appeared. There the demographer could be pleased to note that publications on population and race required less than a single page for their listing. Those were the days when scholars could boast with some assurance that they had "mastered" a subject.

The horse-and-buggy bibliographies of that era have been long-since outmoded, the victims of two inevitable trends in modern historical scholarship. One has been the explosion of knowledge, and with it the phenomenal proliferation of scholarly journals where that knowledge can be recorded. These have invaded our libraries in overwhelming numbers during the past two decades, usually in the modest garb of a mimeographed "newsletter" at first then after a year or so as a substantial quarterly publication, complete with footnoted articles, a gallery of specialized reviews, and a price tag that has sent librarians into hair-pulling despair.

Nor does there seem any end to this multiplication as scholars devise new approaches to traditional subjects or discover the significance of new ones. One imaginative statistician has projected the current rate of growth into the future, to emerge with the alarming prediction that by the end of the century a million scholarly journals will be circulating, by the year 2050 no less than ten million, and by 2100 nearly one hundred million. Even discounting the fact that liars do figure, there can be no question that bibliographical techniques geared to the past must be revolutionized to make this Everest of information usable.

No less fatal to the simple techniques of yesteryear has been the broadening worldwide interest in American Studies. Since World War II Americanists have multiplied by the hundreds in Europe, Asia and Africa, in the Pacific Basin, most of them ardent investigators who publish their findings in a mushrooming number of journals overseas. No single library in the United States could hope to subscribe to all, yet buried in their pages are kernels of information essential to our understanding of the American past. How can this body of learning be made available to investigators in the United States?

During the past few decades, numerous serial bibliographical aids have attempted to grapple with this problem, but one succeeded beyond all others: *America: History and Life*, founded in 1964 by that dedicated enthusiast, Eric H. Boehm. During the intervening years that publication has grown from a modest pamphlet-size listing appearing three times yearly to a formidable series of volumes requiring no less than 540 tightly packed, triple columned pages (in 1977) simply to index articles and reviews abstracted or cited on its pages. Essential as this finding aid has proven itself, it is already reaching the magnitude when the specialist in one aspect of the American past must spend an undue amount of time searching its pages for information in his own field.

Realizing this, the American Bibliographical Center has undertaken a series of volumes that extract from *America: History and Life* all references to subjects of special interest to scholars. This fine, handsome volume on *The American and Canadian West*, skillfully edited by Dwight L. Smith, offers ample evidence of the importance of this innovation in the field of historical scholarship. For here, conveniently arranged, the specialist in American or Canadian Western frontier studies, will find listed over 4,000 articles on his subject published in 310 historical and social science journals from all over the world between 1964 and 1973. The citations are accompanied by brief abstracts that are descriptive rather than evaluative. Best of all, a second volume is already being compiled to continue the story, with the promise of still more to come.

The usefulness of any bibliography depends on two things: its completeness and its usability. This work passes with high grades on both points. The periodicals abstracted for its pages include every pertinent journal printed in the United States and Canada and throughout the world. What other bibliography would list articles published by *Ûji Lariohaar* (German Federal Republic), *Seiryo Shigaku* (Japan), or *Jahrbuch für Amerikastudien* (German Federal Republic), in addition to a whole galaxy of geographic, economic, sociological, literary, and scientific journals?

This work also passes the usability test with flying colors. The thousands of articles are classified under chronological, topical, and geographical headings, ranging from "The Spanish and Mexican Years," through "Exploration and Travel," "Military History," "Economic Activity," "Transportation and Communication," "Society," "Culture," and "Religion," to sections on regionalism dealing with "The Great Plains," "The Rocky Mountains and Intermontane Provinces," and "The Pacific Coast States."

An investigator will note that these headings are, in turn, subdivided under other rubrics which more accurately reflect the particular emphases in the periodical literature. Under "Economic Activity," for example, the bibliographic entries are grouped into "Fur Trade and Indian Trade," "Mining and Oil," "Labor," "Agriculture," and "Business History." Further refinement occurs under "Agriculture" where the breakdown headings are "Cattle and Sheep," "Public Land and Homesteading," "Speculation," and "Conservation." The range of subject matter under any of these is diverse. The sixty some entries under "Cattle and Sheep" include such subject matter as: Arkansas to California cattle drives, British investment in Wyoming cattle, ranching on Indian reservations, sheep ranching in Oregon, Negro cowboys, a cattlemen's frontier bibliography, sheep drives and trails in Nevada, cattalo experiments, and "Hip Pocket Businessmen: The Cattle-Trailing Contractors." Besides the 170 some entries listed under "Agriculture," other appropriate agricultural references can be easily located through the index.

The subject matter of the article determines its location in this bibliography. Unless its focus pertains to the history of a particular locale rather than to the topical subject matter in general, the bibliographic entry is listed under the appropriate topic (Section II). When the subject matter of the article is principally concerned with the history of an area, it is in regional or geographic divisions (Sections III-IV). Under "Pacific Coast States," the abstracts of articles are located under the subheadings of Washington, Oregon, and California. As an illustration, Oregon's entries run from imprints to the efforts of an Oregon publicist, from the role of Willamette Valley vegetation in its economic development to the biography of a territorial judge, and from a local election to Methodist activities in pre-territorial provisional government.

Since *The American and Canadian West* is a report of the state-of-research as it is reflected in the periodical literature during 1964-1973, its classification system labels and groupings are, in turn, determined by that literature. A simple topical breakdown, therefore, for "The Spanish and Mexican Years" (Section I) into "Exploration," "The Mission and Presidio Frontier," and "Colonization" is quite adequate. A geographic arrangement for "The Canadian West" (Section IV), subdivided under provincial headings, is appropriate. "The Alaskan Scene" (Section V) is most satisfactorily arranged on a chronological basis: "Russian America," and "Pre-Statehood Alaska, 1867-1959." Finally, "The Post Frontier West, 1890-1945" is divided into topical categories.

Equally helpful is the skillful way in which the editor has avoided duplication, always a time-consuming problem for users of bibliographies. Certain categories are omitted entirely: thus articles on western historiography are listed under the various subjects with which they deal rather than in a separate section, while those on Native Americans have already been gathered in another volume published in the Clio Bibliography Series, *Indians of the United States and Canada* (ABC-Clio, Inc., 1974), and are not duplicated here. Works concerned primarily with pre-history or with the period after 1945 are also largely omitted, as are those about non-Western topics even though they describe events taking place in the West. This then, is a specialized bibliography geared to the needs of students of the American and Canadian Wests, uncluttered by extraneous items not pertinent to the subject.

To assure the ultimate in easy use, the volume has a thorough topical and subject index. This allows the elimination of duplicate items and lessens the necessity of "see also" references in the bibliography itself. Thus, an abstract appears only once in this bibliography, under the most appropriate section, but a user has access to it from several points in the index. For example, many of the articles listed in the section "Mormonism" will be indexed under both "Mormonism" and "Utah" but do not appear in the Utah section of the bibliography.

Here is a bibliography, then, that has been meticulously prepared and carefully planned with the needs of the user always in mind. Intelligently structured, worldwide in its coverage of the periodical literature, and equipped with every possible device to assure usability, it is a tool that students of the American frontier will find essential to their needs, no matter how specialized their interests. The American Bibliographical Center and Dwight Smith have performed an invaluable service to frontier historical studies in making it available.

RAY ALLEN BILLINGTON
The Huntington Library

List of Abbreviations

A	Author-prepared Abstract
Acad	Academy, Académie, Academia
Agric	Agriculture, Agricultural
AIA	Abstracts in Anthropology
Akad	Akademie
Am	America, American
Ann	Annals, Annales, Annual, Annali
Anthrop	Anthropology, Anthropological
Arch	Archives
Archaeol	Archaeology, Archaeological
Art	Article
Assoc	Association, Associate
Biblio	Bibliography, Bibliographical
Biog	Biography, Biographical
Bol	Boletim, Boletín
Bull	Bulletin
c	century (in index)
ca	circa
Can	Canada, Canadian, Canadien
Cent	Century
Coll	College
Com	Committee
Comm	Commission
Comp	Compiler
DAI	Dissertation Abstracts International
Dept	Department
Dir	Director, Direktor
Econ	Economy, Econom-.
Ed	Editor, Edition
Educ	Education, Educational
Geneal	Genealogy, Genealogical, Généalogique
Grad	Graduate
Hist	History, Hist-.
IHE	Indice Histórico Español
Illus	Illustrated, Illustration
Inst	Institute, Institut-.
Int	International, Internacional, Internationaal, Internationaux, Internazionale
J	Journal, Journal-prepared Abstract
Lib	Library, Libraries
Mag	Magazine
Mus	Museum, Musée, Museo
Nac	Nacional
Natl	National, Nationale
Naz	Nazionale
Phil	Philosophy, Philosophical
Photo	Photograph
Pol.	Politics, Political, Politique, Político
Pr	Press
Pres	President
Pro	Proceedings
Publ	Publishing, Publication
Q	Quarterly
Rev	Review, Revue, Revista, Revised
Riv	Rivista
Res	Research
S	Staff-prepared Abstract
Sci	Science, Scientific
Secy	Secretary
Soc	Society, Société, Sociedad, Società
Sociol	Sociology, Sociological
Tr	Transactions
Transl	Translator, Translation
U	University, Universi-.
US	United States
Vol	Volume
Y	Yearbook

Abbreviations also apply to feminine and plural forms.
Abbreviations not noted above are based on *Webster's Third New International Dictionary*
and the *United States Government Printing Office Style Manual*.

1. THE SPANISH AND MEXICAN YEARS

General

1. Bannon, John Francis. HERBERT EUGENE BOLTON - WESTERN HISTORIAN. *Western Hist. Q. 1971 2(3): 260-282.* The rural Wisconsin-born Bolton attended the State university where he came under the influence of Frederick Jackson Turner. His graduate studies were completed at the University of Pennsylvania in 1899. After various teaching stints, Bolton accepted a position at the University of Texas in 1901 in European history. Location and other favorable circumstances soon attracted him into study of the Spanish Borderlands. In 1909 he went to Stanford University to teach in the same area of his research interests; he moved on to the University of California at Berkeley and its Bancroft Library two years later. Here Bolton inspired thousands of undergraduates, trained hundreds of graduates, and published his major works. He was a western American historian in a continental rather than a narrow nationalistic sense. Illus., 25 notes, biblio. D. L. Smith

2. Bannon, John Francis. A WESTERN HISTORIAN - HOW HE GOT THAT WAY. *Western Hist. Q. 1970 1(3): 242-248.* The author recounts the educational background that prepared him for the Jesuit priesthood and his professional training in Western history. The 17th-century mission frontier of Sonora, Mexico, was his early specialization, from which he progressed into New Spain and the Borderlands, and New France and Louisiana. Several of his books have surveyed or explored facets of the Spanish Borderlands. His most persistent theme is that the American West has been studied too much from the Anglo point of view rather than the Spanish or French. "The Anglo-Americans so very seldom were really pioneers" because their way was often paved by the other two groups. Bannon asserts that Western historiography's greatest needs are bibliographies, more publishing outlets for scholarship, and broader views that go beyond localized antiquarian preoccupation. D. L. Smith

3. Beggs, Beatrice. THE DIARY OF RAFAEL GOMEZ: MONTEREY IN 1836. *Southern California Q. 1963 45(3): 265-269.* The diary of a Mexican lawyer who immigrated to California in 1831 and served as legal advisor or "assessor" to the government. Thirty-one entries cover events of 1836 and part of 1837. A biographical sketch of Gómez is appended. A. K. Main

4. Bonney, David. THE INDIAN AND THE HORSE. *Am. Hist. Illus. 1966 1(5): 44-54.* The emergence of the horse on the American Continent, his crossing into Asia, and reintroduction by Spaniards are traced. Emphasis is on the impact of the horse on the Plains tribes and the methods of catching, training, and equipping him. 3 photographs, 4 drawings. E. Brown

5. Brinckerhoff, Sidney B. THE LAST YEARS OF SPANISH ARIZONA, 1786-1821. *Arizona and the West 1967 9(1): 5-20.* The efforts of the Spanish to terminate the expanding war with the Apache in Arizona and northern Sonora were discouraging. Not infrequently the undermanned Spanish garrisons along the northern frontier were forced on the defensive. A new policy was inaugurated in 1786 designed to break the Apache will to resist and to make them dependent on the Spanish. Strong, coordinated, and continued military pressure with peace rewarded with gifts, food, and supplies, it was hoped, would induce the Indians to settle on reservations near the presidios. Agricultural pursuits, liquor, and antiquated firearms should corrupt them and keep them under control. If the Indians did not subscribe to this program they were to be hunted down and killed. In these twilight years of Spanish control the Apache menace was sharply reduced by large-scale military expeditions, the missionaries stepped up their Christianization, and mining, ranching, and farming foundations in Arizona were laid. Peace continued after the end of the Spanish period for another decade, until the restless Apache once again went on the warpath. The Mexican Government accepted the Spanish system but financial stringency and problems of stabilizing the new government left much of the control in the hands of the local presidial officers. And, by their very nature, the Apache were not to be

content very long in a sedentary and agricultural situation. 4 illus., map, 35 notes. D. L. Smith

6. Brunn, Stanley D. and Wheeler, James C. NOTES ON THE GEOGRAPHY OF RELIGIOUS TOWN NAMES IN THE U.S. *Names 1966 14(4): 197-202.* An examination of religious town names in the United States. A religious place name is defined here as the name of a town or individual mentioned in the Bible or a saint's name. Heaviest concentrations of religious town names appear in the east central area extending from Pennsylvania to Missouri and in California and along the gulf coast from Texas to Florida. Salem, Lebanon, and Athens occur most frequently. California, Ohio, Pennsylvania, Illinois, and Missouri, in that order, show the largest number of religious town names. Based on 1960 US Census and Biblical concordances and dictionaries; 9 notes. D. Lindsey

7. Bush, Alfred L. THE SPANISH SOUTHWEST AND THE MORMONS AT PARKE-BERNET. *Manuscripts 1967 19(2): 29-32.* On 28 March 1967 the Parke-Bernet Galleries offered for sale a large group of distinguished manuscripts from America's Spanish Southwest. The prices for almost all items were much below their estimated value and the 38 lots fetched some 67,590 dollars when the estimated bids had totaled 113,100 dollars. With the exception of three Spanish manuscripts the only sales of the evening beyond their estimates were five lots of Mormon manuscripts. Many of the items are described and their prices given. C. J. Allard

8. Caughey, John W. HERBERT EUGENE BOLTON. *Am. West 1964 1(1): 36-39, 79.* The author's personal student-day memories and his present estimate of Herbert Eugene Bolton as an historian. Bolton is best known for his concept of the Spanish borderlands and for his idea that history which reaches beyond the confines of political boundaries is the most observable and understandable. Although his dream for hemispheric history has not been accepted, his writings are durable and will not soon need to be redone. A man of "prodigious stature," a foremost trainer of Western and Latin Americanists, "he is ripe for legend as the Paul Bunyan of western historians." D. L. Smith

9. Chavez, Angelico. THE UNIQUE TOMB OF FATHERS ZARATE AND DE LA LLANA IN SANTA FE. *New Mexico Hist. R. 1965 40(2): 101-115.* Unusual history of the twin stone casket of Fathers Asencio de Zarate and Geronimo de la Llana, who died in the mid-17th century. Their tomb with epitaphs is perhaps the only such survivor from the colonial period in New Mexico. D. F. Henderson

10. Christiansen, Paige W. THE APACHE BARRIER. *Rocky Mountain Social Sci. J. 1966 3(2): 93-108.* An outline of the role played by the Apache as a barrier to Spanish, and later Anglo-American, occupation of the Southwest. The Apache entered the Southwest by 1100 A.D., secured territory, and underwent a change from hunters to predators. The author dwells upon Apache-Spanish conflicts, correcting what he considers the omissions of earlier historians. 37 notes. R. F. Allen

11. Coker, William S. and Holmes, Jack D. L. SOURCES FOR THE HISTORY OF THE SPANISH BORDERLANDS. *Florida Hist. Q. 1971 49(4): 380-393.* Approximately 140 thousand pages of material for Spanish Louisiana have been microfilmed, and an index is available from Loyola University, New Orleans. A guide to the microfilmed diocesan records of Louisiana and the Floridas, 1576-1803, is available from the University of Notre Dame. The Mississippi Department of Archives and History, Jackson, has the microfilm negative of the Natchez chancery court records of 1781-97. Microfilm copies of 20 thousand pages of documents relating to Spanish Alabama, 1780-1813, are available at the Universities of Alabama in Birmingham and Tuscaloosa; the University of West Florida, Pensacola; and the University of Florida, Gainesville. Photostats and typescripts from archives in Madrid relating to Tennessee and the Old Southwest are available at the Lawson McGhee Library, Knoxville, Tennessee. Memphis State University has microfilmed materials from Mexico City, Seville, Madrid, Cuba, and Santa Fe. Cabildo records

of New Orleans, 1769-1803, are available on microfilm from the New Orleans Public Library. The Wisconsin Historical Society has copies of Spanish archival material for 1766-1805. In the Library of Congress are the Woodbury Lowery Collection for 1551-1660, the East and West Florida Papers, and the Jeannette Thurber Connor Papers. The most comprehensive collection of material from Spanish archives, 1565-1763, is at the University of Florida. Information on copying of French materials can be obtained from the Coordination Center of the Manuscript Division, Library of Congress.   R. V. Calvert

12. Coughlin, Magdalen. CALIFORNIA PORTS: A KEY TO DIPLOMACY FOR THE WEST COAST, 1820-1845. *J. of the West 1966 5(2): 153-172.* Commercial interests desired a port on the Pacific to use in trade with the Orient. American diplomacy entered the struggle, and, after the Monroe Doctrine, competition was mainly between the United States and England. France also dreamed that the coast might be hers, but started late and had no concrete claim. The first major diplomatic effort of the United States began when John Quincy Adams instructed the newly appointed American ambassador to Mexico to try to purchase Texas and, if possible, the California ports. Under Jackson the effort continued. That the British were also interested was well known. This contributed to the California ports' becoming the key to American diplomacy in the 1840's. Polk pledged to get Texas and Oregon but his real objective was California. This desire resulted in war with Mexico. Thus, an interaction of economic investment in the Oriental trade evolved into a diplomatic contest for control of the Pacific and the necessary California ports. Documented from published sources; 78 notes.   D. N. Brown

13. Cutter, Donald C. HARBOR ENTRY AND RECOGNITION SIGNALS IN EARLY CALIFORNIA. *California Hist. Soc. Q. 1970 49(1): 47-54.* In the last decade of the 18th century, the Spanish Royal Navy employed two young Americans, John Kendrick, Jr., and Joseph Burling O'Cain, as pilot and apprentice pilot respectively, to solve the Spanish problem of a lack of naval personnel in the Pacific Northwest and California coasts. Both performed their duties, but Spanish officialdom decided that employing Americans in the Spanish Navy was too risky a proposition. Since the Americans upon discharge took with them their knowledge of entry and recognition signals for admission into Spanish harbors, the Spanish Government found it necessary to create a new set of signals, which went into effect in 1797. The author notes that both O'Cain and Kendrick eventually returned to the west coast and took part in clandestine trade operations, thus profiting from their training in the Spanish Navy. Based on documents in the Archivo General de la Nación and on published sources; illus., photos, 13 notes.   A. Hoffman

14. Duffield, Lathel F. THE TAOVAYAS VILLAGE OF 1759: IN TEXAS OR OKLAHOMA? *Great Plains J. 1965 4(2): 39-48.* Reviews the background and the events of Colonel Don Diego Ortiz Parilla's campaign of 1759 against the Comanches in northern Texas. Using Parilla's descriptions, present geographical conditions and archaeological evidence, the author concludes that the Indian village of Taovayas, where the climax of the campaign occurred, was on the north bank of the Red River in present Oklahoma rather than in Texas as is generally believed. Maps. Based on both primary and secondary sources listed at the end.   O. H. Zabel

15. Dunn, Fabius. THE CONCERN OF THE SPANISH GOVERNMENT OF TEXAS OVER UNITED STATES EXPANSIONISM, 1805-1808. *Louisiana Studies 1965 4(1): 47-61.* Lieutenant Colonel Manuel Antonio Cordero y Bustamente was appointed ad interim governor of the province of Texas in July 1805. He served as acting governor in Texas from 9 September 1805 until 7 November 1808. The essay reviews the concern of his administration with the expansionist tendencies of the United States, and implies that the Spanish, from their viewpoint, had just reasons for fear.   G. W. McGinty

16. Ellinwood, Sybil. CALABASAS. *Arizoniana 1964 5(4): 27-41.* The Sobaipuri Indians farmed on this beautiful spot before the 17th century. Here Father Eusebio Kino established a ranch to support his mission at nearby Guebabi. "Calabasas became successively a fortified hacienda in Mexican times, a U.S. military encampment after the Gadsden Purchase, and finally a bustling town, envisioned as a hub of the cattle and mining industries." The action of the Court of Private Land Claims in 1894 voiding all Spanish land grants along the border decided against the Boston investors in Calabasas. Since the buildings burned in 1927 only a few bricks and adobes mark the site. Illus., biblio.   E. P. Stickney

17. Evans, Edward G. and Morales, Frank J. FUENTES DE LA HISTORIA DE MEXICO EN ARCHIVOS NORTEAMERICANOS [Sources of Mexican history in U.S. archives]. *Hist. Mexicana 1969 18(71): 432-462.* A guide to and description of Spanish and Mexican manuscripts concerned with Mexico and the Southwestern United States in U.S. archives. The guide is intended to encourage anthropologists and ethnologists to use primary material and is limited to manuscripts produced prior to 1750. The collections are listed alphabetically by states, then by institution. Biblio.   W. H. Beezley

18. Evans, G. Edward. A GUIDE TO PRE-1750 MANUSCRIPTS IN THE UNITED STATES RELATING TO MEXICO AND THE SOUTHWESTERN UNITED STATES, WITH EMPHASIS ON THEIR VALUE TO ANTHROPOLOGISTS. *Ethnohist. 1970 (1/2): 63-90.* "The nature and location in the United States of pre-1750 Spanish manuscript materials, as these relate to Mexico and the American Southwest, are outlined. The discussion and a bibliography are offered as an encouragement to anthropologists to avail themselves of such primary sources."   J

19. Figueroa y Melgar, Alfonso de. LINAJES QUE FORJARON LA HISPANIDAD [Families who forged Spanish America]. *Hidalguía [Spain] 1967 15(83): 497-524.* Outlines a book, soon to be published, which gives the genealogical history of the illustrious families who seeded the lands of America from Tierra del Fuego to the Spanish regions of North America. Includes aborigines, colonizers, and discoverers.   A. de F. (IHE 67424)

20. Forbes, Jack D. BLACK PIONEERS: THE SPANISH-SPEAKING AFRO-AMERICANS OF THE SOUTHWEST. *Phylon 1966 27(3): 233-246.* Considers the prominent part played by Africans and Spaniards of part-African ancestry in the exploration and colonization of the Spanish empire in America. A study of records of Spanish-speaking towns in California leads the author to conclude that persons of part-Negro ancestry constituted at least 20 percent of the population in 1790. Over half of the population of such towns was non-Spanish. The records also suggest that as the status of persons improved in the community their race was sometimes changed from Negro to mulatto or from mulatto to Spaniard. This fact together with continuing miscegenation tended to obliterate both the memory and the physical characteristics of Negro ancestry in Spanish California. Racial attitudes of European and Anglo-American immigrants in the 19th century encouraged neglect of this theme and contributed to the myth of Castilian heritage among the upper class in California. Based largely on unpublished records of Spanish settlements in late 19th-century California in the Bancroft Library, 30 notes.   S. C. Pearson, Jr.

21. Forbes, Jack D. RACE AND COLOR IN MEXICAN-AMERICAN PROBLEMS. *J. of Human Relations 1968 16(1): 55-68.* Demonstrates the fact that the reactions of white Americans to Mexican-Americans since the 1830's have been complicated by racist attitudes. In spite of this, the myth persists that "Mexican-Americans are 'Whites with Spanish Surnames' and that their problems are little if any different from those of Polish-Americans or Italian-Americans....Color prejudice against brown-skinned Mexican-Americans and Indian-Americans will not completely disappear, in the writer's opinion, until the brown-skinned Negro is also made a social equal of the white." Based on primary and secondary sources; 16 notes.   D. J. Abramoske

22. Geiger, Maynard, ed. and trans. SPREADING THE NEWS OF THE CALIFORNIA CONQUEST, 1769-1770. *Southern California Q. 1965 47(4): 395-407.* Demonstrates the time element involved in relaying the news of the conquest of California back to official headquarters. José Gálvez planned the conquest from Mexico, but even after it had been accomplished by Gaspar de Portolá, it was a year and a half before Gálvez and Viceroy de Croix learned of its completion. Two letters from Portolá are printed. 40 notes.   A. K. Main

23. Grey, Don. NOTES ON WYOMING HISTORY, A SPANISH SWORD BLADE FROM DAYTON, WYOMING. *Ann. of Wyoming 1963 35(2): 207-210.* Discusses the finding of a 17th century Spanish sword blade at Dayton, Wyoming during 1961, and the efforts made to determine the date and origin of it. Includes sketches of the blade, an inscription upon it, and several types of sword handles.

R. L. Nichols

24. Gronet, Richard W. THE UNITED STATES AND THE INVASION OF TEXAS, 1810-1814. *Americas 1969 25(3): 281-306.* U.S. policy toward the Spanish colonies at the start of their independence struggle was influenced by fear of encroachment by other European powers, by commercial interest, and by expansionism as well as ideological sympathy. William Shaler, appointed in 1810 as Special Agent to Mexico, had a previous record of "revolutionary and commercial activities" in Spanish America which "must have been known" to the U.S. Government; thus, the author doubts the thesis of some authors that Shaler's eventual role in Texas involved unauthorized filibustering. In 1812, from Louisiana, he helped organize the invasion of Texas by Mexican insurgent José Bernardo Gutiérrez de Lara (1778-1814). The expedition was initially successful, the capital city San Antonio having been taken, but excesses of Gutiérrez and dissension among Mexican insurgents and with U.S. participants ultimately caused its failure. Meanwhile, the disastrous course of the U.S. war with Britain forced the United States to abandon its "Mexican policies of aid and penetration." Based on Special Agents correspondence in the U.S. National Archives, and on published primary and secondary sources; 69 notes.

D. Bushnell

25. Haines, Francis. HORSES FOR WESTERN INDIANS. *Am. West 1966 3(2): 4-15, 92.* That the Plains Indians had been horsemen from time immemorial is historically inaccurate. The advent of horses to the western United States is comparatively recent. The hypothesis that bands of stray horses from the expeditions of Hernando De Soto (1539-42) and Francisco Coronado (1540-42) furnished the parent stock is untenable. With only minor adaptations, the Indians borrowed the entire horse-culture complex from the Spanish New Mexican colony between 1650 and 1700. The manner in which this was accomplished and the spread of the horse frontier into the Great Plains grassland areas and into the Pacific Northwest are explained. Map, illus., biblio. note.

D. L. Smith

26. Haines, Francis. HOW THE INDIAN GOT THE HORSE. *Am. Heritage 1964 15(2): 16-21, 78-81.* Legend has it that the Indian acquired the horse by capturing strays from De Soto or Coronado or both. The author shows why this cannot be true and then proposes that the Indians acquired them from the Spaniards by various means later, in the 17th century. Illus.

C. R. Allen, Jr.

27. Holmes, Jack D. L. SHOWDOWN ON THE SABINE: GENERAL JAMES WILKINSON VS. LIEUTENANT-COLONEL SIMON DE HERRERA. *Louisiana Studies 1964 3(1): 46-76.* An explanation of a showdown in 1806 of the century-old question of where Louisiana ended and where Texas began. Events that brought the armies of Spain and the United States facing each other on the Sabine and resulted in a compromise known as the Neutral Ground Treaty are described. This compromise, perhaps, postponed the Mexican War 40 years. 81 notes.

G. W. McGinty

28. Ives, Ronald L. THE LOST DISCOVERY OF CORPORAL ANTONIO LUIS: A DESERT CURE FOR SCURVY. *J. of Arizona Hist. 1970 11(2): 101-114.* Although there is voluminous evidence to support the generally accepted idea that the Spanish were remiss in seeking a preventive or cure for scurvy, there is documentary proof that there was some awareness of the cause of this disease. Although the specific scurvy preventive, ascorbic acid, commonly called vitamin C, was not isolated and recognized until 1932, Spanish discovery of a powerful antiscorbutic was a byproduct of the disastrous Vizcaíno Expedition of 1602-03. With several dead from scurvy and several seriously ill from the disease, the expedition put in at the Mazatlan Islands. Going ashore to help bury the dead, Corporal Antonio Luis sampled *tuna*, fruit of the prickly pear cactus or opuntia. The healing properties worked immediately and he shared it with his shipmates. Knowledge of these antiscorbutic properties became widely known in Sonora and Baja California, especially in one port that was established as a relief station for the Manila Galleons.

Sonoran and Californian documents show a widespread knowledge of the medicinal value of cactus fruits until the time of the Jesuit expulsion in 1767. After that this knowledge seemed to die out. 3 illus., 24 notes.

D. L. Smith

29. Ives, Ronald L. MANJE'S MERCURY MINES. *J. of Arizona Hist. 1965 6(4): 165-176.* To find the precise location of some mercury mines described by Juan Mateo Manje in 1697, the author uses his scientific and engineering background in combination with his avocation of history. He demonstrates, by placing them in Yuma County, Arizona, how a man of his varied skills can, on the basis of available evidence, be quite accurate in solving such mysteries. 3 maps, 12 notes from published sources.

J. D. Filipiak

30. Jenkins, Myra Ellen. TAOS PUEBLO AND ITS NEIGHBORS, 1540-1847. *New Mexico Hist. R. 1966 41(2): 85-114.* A summary of the encroachments on lands claimed by the Taos Indians from the visit of Hernando de Alvarado in 1540 to the transfer of the lands to the United States in 1847. Based on printed sources and the Spanish Archives of New Mexico, Series I, Bureau of Land Management; 80 notes.

D. F. Henderson

31. Kessell, John L. CAMPAIGNING ON THE UPPER GILA, 1756. *New Mexico Hist. R. 1971 46(2): 133-160.* Provides a background to the campaign of 1756, and an account by Chaplain Bartolomé Sáenz, S.J., of the campaign against the Gila Apache in 1756. Over 300 fighting men (60 under Captain Bernardo Antonio de Bustamante y Tagle, from Chihuahua, the remainder under Captain Gabriel Antonio de Vildósola from Sonora) made their base camp at Todos Santos, near present-day Cliff, New Mexico. The campaigners killed some Apache warriors and captured Apache women and children, but failed to deter future Apache raiding. 78 notes.

D. F. Henderson

32. Lecompte, Janet. DON BENITO VASQUEZ IN EARLY ST. LOUIS. *Bull. of the Missouri Hist. Soc. 1970 26(4): 285-305.* Chronicles the successes and failures of Vasquez (1738-1810) as a merchant, soldier, and fur trader in the Louisiana Territory during the periods it was alternately under Spanish, French and American rule. Before 1800, Vasquez enjoyed considerable commercial success and was regarded one of the more prominent citizens of the region. Thereafter, his fortunes and prestige declined. Discusses the fur trade while France and Spain controlled the Mississippi Valley. Based on primary and secondary sources; table, 108 notes.

H. T. Lovin

33. Lillard, Richard. SCIENCE AND ART IN THE SOUTHWEST: TWENTIETH-CENTURY TECHNOLOGY EXPLODES IN THE LAND OF ENCHANTMENT. *Am. West 1972 9(4): 4-11, 63-64.* The pueblo villages of 1530 are the most culturally coherent communities of the American Southwest desert country. Even though some alteration has occurred with the coming of the Spanish- and English-speaking conquerors and settlers, the pueblos today have the longest-lasting, most virile, and most artistic of the civilized traditions of the Southwest. At the same time, the architectural styles, household furnishings, religious carvings, and other cultural aspects of the descendants of the early Spanish colonists are much in evidence. While Anglo Americans have sought to revive and to perpetuate the cultural traditions of the earlier groups, the staggering scientific achievements of recent years and the vaunted American standard of living have made significant impact on the face of the Southwest. Even though the life of the Southwest has changed, 20th-century man can ill afford to lose sight of the rich heritage of the area. Adapted from a forthcoming book. 12 illus.

D. L. Smith

34. Lutz, Paul V. GOVERNMENT LOSES SUIT FOR DOCUMENTS. *Manuscripts 1967 19(4): 9-11.* In a decision that is cause for collectors to rejoice, a U.S. District Court jury supported Kenneth D. Sender against a U.S. Government complaint that certain documents purchased by Sender in good faith were in fact the property of the Government. The Government had sought title to 313 historical documents, all in Spanish, dated between 1697 and 1846, and pertaining to New Mexico. Judge Elmo B. Hunter's definition of a "public record" will set a precedent unless overruled by a higher court. His definition: A public record is "a document or writing made or received by a government official in connection with his official duties and retained or required to be retained as government property either by virtue of law or by virtue

of custom and practice observed in the area." The Government plans to appeal the decision.

C. J. Allard

35. Monahan, Forrest D., Jr. THE KIOWAS AND NEW MEXICO, 1800-1845. *J. of the West 1969 8(1): 67-75.* The Kiowa moved into the southern Plains country in the late 18th-century. Their hunter economy depended heavily on trade with the Spanish New Mexicans and later the Anglo-American traders. For three quarters of a century government gifts and private trade brought changes in Kiowa culture. 67 notes.

D. L. Smith

36. Morris, Wayne. THE WICHITA EXCHANGE: TRADE ON OKLAHOMA'S FUR FRONTIER, 1719-1812. *Great Plains J. 1970 9(2): 79-84.* Surveys the heyday of Wichita Indian trade with whites in the 18th century. Beginning in 1719 the French, both from New Orleans and the Illinois villages, traded with the Wichita on the Arkansas River. One French purpose was to establish trade, also, with Spanish Santa Fe. The French helped the Wichita form a trade alliance with the Comanche in 1747. Osage attacks then forced the Wichita to join their kinsmen on the Red River. After that they generally were known as Taovaya, and the center of trade became Nachitoches. Louisiana was transferred to the Spanish in 1763, but strict Spanish trade policies could not prevent considerable Taovaya trade with French contraband traders. After the Louisiana Purchase (1803) Americans traded until roughly 1812 with the Taovaya, who then moved south into Texas because of Osage marauding. 25 notes.

O. H. Zabel

37. Nasatir, A. P. INTERNATIONAL RIVALRY FOR CALIFORNIA AND THE ESTABLISHMENT OF THE BRITISH CONSULATE. *California Hist. Soc. Q. 1967 46(1): 53-70.* Paper read at the Western History Association meeting, Oklahoma City, 29 October 1964. When "effective occupation" became the criterion for national ownership on the Pacific Coast, California was pushed into the forefront of international politics. The rivalry, especially that of Great Britain, the United States, and Mexico, for control of trade in California is traced in detail through the 1830's and 1840's. The first British consul in California formally appointed was James Alexander Forbes who held the post from 1843 to 1851. His reports in the Public Record Office show that "he tried to thwart the Americans from taking over California." Based on the author's work in the Public Record Office, London.

E. P. Stickney

38. Nasatir, Abraham. THE SHIFTING BORDERLANDS. *Pacific Hist. R. 1965 34(1): 1-20.* Describes efforts of the Spanish to maintain their empire, especially in the Mississippi-Missouri and Santa Fe regions, against the encroachments of first the British and later the Americans.

J. McCutcheon

39. Nunis, Doyce B., Jr. BOOKS IN THEIR SEA CHESTS. *Am. West 1965 2(3): 74-79.* Books and literacy in Spanish California were not found far beyond missions or an occasional ranchman's private library. Books were usually restricted in nature by the dictates of the Catholic Church. Mexican independence, a more liberal attitude by the clergy, the establishment of printing, and the development of the hide and tallow industry changed this, especially the latter. Merchants began to appear in California's ports in increasing numbers. Many were New England-based. Boredom and the monotony of long sea voyages and of the gathering of the hide and tallow cargoes for the return voyage led some of the sailors to carry books in their sea chests. Many of these volumes became "an indelible but unfathomed legacy" for Alta California. Biblio. note.

D. L. Smith

40. Paredes, Américo and Foss, George. THE "DECIMA CANTADA" ON THE TEXAS-MEXICAN BORDER: FOUR EXAMPLES. *J. of the Folklore Inst. 1966 3(2): 91-115.* A discussion of four songs representative of the *décima* tradition on the Texas-Mexican border. Tape-recorded by Américo Paredes in 1954 with musical transcription and analysis by George Foss, each song "represents a category - the religion, the philosophical and the comic...." Although some influence has crept in from other Latin-American peoples, the Texas-Mexican border *décima* is mostly indigenous, is still composed and sung, and "may even outlast the *corrido....*" Documented.

J. C. Crowe

41. Paredes, Américo. THE "DECIMA" ON THE TEXAS-MEXICAN BORDER: FOLKSONG AS AN ADJUNCT TO LEGEND. *J. of the Folklore Inst. 1966 3(2): 154-167.* An analysis of the origin, development, and characteristics of the *décima* on the Texas-Mexican border. An important folksong type in Spanish cultures, the *décima* "acquired both secular and religious function, serving as vehicle for ballad, lyric, and flyting." Religion has exerted great influence on the *décima's* development, but it is more adaptable to secular themes. After being settled in 1749, the Lower Rio Grande country had created *décimas* by 1850. Although their creation was general certain families have been proficient in composition and preservation. Documented.

J. C. Crowe

42. Posner, Russell M. A BRITISH CONSULAR AGENT IN CALIFORNIA: THE REPORTS OF JAMES A. FORBES, 1843-1846. *Southern California Q. 1971 53(2): 101-112.* Concerns the reports of James Alexander Forbes (1804-81), who was "the first and only official British representative in the [California] territory during the Mexican period." Forbes served as vice consul of Queen Victoria's government in California from 1843 to 1846 and kept his superiors informed about the misgovernment and intrigues there during the last years of Mexican control. He believed that Californians wanted to be free from Mexico, but he did not want to see them annexed by the Americans; rather, he desired a British protectorate over the area. In 1845 Forbes reported that the Mexican-controlled government in California had been replaced by one composed of native Californians, but to his disappointment the new government did not declare itself free from Mexico nor ask for a British protectorate. After the American acquisition of California, Forbes stayed on as Great Britain's diplomatic representative until 1850. Although he was mildly anti-American he remained in California until his death. Based primarily on British Foreign Office papers; 31 notes.

W. L. Bowers

43. Reno, Philip. REBELLION IN NEW MEXICO - 1837. *New Mexico Hist. R. 1965 40(3): 197-214.* For a short time during August and September 1837, a successful revolt by northern New Mexico's village poor, aided by Pueblo Indians, vested New Mexico governmental authority first in a revolutionary canton, then in a *Junta Popular,* or "People's Assembly," with José Gonzales of Taos named governor. The revolt was smashed and the rule of law reestablished in September 1837. While the rebels, except in matters of taxation, hoped to carry on under the same government and laws as before, they did make two modifications in the focus of political power: first, governmental power was to reside in the village leaders, second, the Pueblo Indians were to be included in councils on government policy. 33 notes.

D. F. Henderson

44. Riley, Carroll L. EARLY SPANISH-INDIAN COMMUNICATION IN THE GREATER SOUTHWEST. *New Mexico Hist. R. 1971 46(4): 285-314.* Attempts to answer the question, "how did the European manage to establish meaningful contact with the aborigine?" After analyzing the method of solving the language problems in the expeditions of Cortés, Nuño de Guzmán, Friar Marcos de Niza, and Coronado, concludes that from the documentary and archeological evidence "it seems clear that there was ample contact between North and West Mexico and the Greater Southwest, and contact from the lower Colorado River region to New Mexico and probably beyond. No single favored trade language can be absolutely demonstrated, but Pima seems a good candidate." Theorizes that "there may have been some knowledge of either Nahuatl or Tarascan in the Pueblo area, the result of *pochteca* activity." 81 notes.

D. F. Henderson

45. Ronan, Charles E. OBSERVATIONS ON THE WORD "GRINGO." *Arizona and the West 1964 6(1): 23-29.* Although a commonly accepted etymology of the word "gringo" is that Mexicans fabricated it from hearing American soldiers in the Mexican War singing the popular melody of "Green Grow the Rushes, O!" but the word is much older. Scholars are not in agreement as to its correct origin, but "gringo" appears in a pre-1750 dictionary. Beginning in the 1830's it is frequently used in travel accounts, dictionaries, and in Spanish and Spanish-American literature. After the Mexican War its popularity increased. Until the mid-19th century it referred to unintelligible language and to foreigners who spoke Spanish with an accent. In northern South America, Central America, and Mexico, it refers only to North Americans. 31 notes.

D. L. Smith

46. Rossi, Paul A. THE WESTERN STOCK SADDLE. *Am. West 1966 3(3): 22-26.* The standardized western stock saddle of today evolved from the saddles used by the Spanish as they conquered Mexico in the 16th century. This evolution is traced in detail. The Spanish war saddle (1530) was a modified version of the Moorish war saddle. The Mexican ranchero saddle (1770) was developed to handle wild or half-wild stock. The California mission saddle (1800) emerged as the vaqueros worked the mission herds. The Mexican ranchero saddle (1827) was a further adaptation of the vaqueros, principally in California. The Texas saddle (1850) was basically of American design. The Mother Hubbard saddle (1870), used during the boom years of the post-Civil War range cattle industry, represented a high point in western saddlery. The California center-fire saddle (1905) was evolving in the Far West about the time the Mother Hubbard was moving north with the cattle drives. The swell-fork plains saddle (1920) represents a blending of the previous two. The eight labels and dates are those of the specific illustrations for the article.

D. L. Smith

47. Rubio Mañé, Ignacio. ITURBIDE Y SUS RELACIONES CON LOS ESTADOS UNIDOS DE AMERICA [Iturbide and his relations with the United States of America]. *Boletín del Archivo General de la Nación [Mexico] 1964 5(2): 333-376, 1965 6(1): 63-126, (2): 251-408.* Part I. Discusses Agustín de Iturbide (1783-1824) and his relations with the United States. Focuses on the period of the struggle for Mexican Independence, 1814-15. Reviews the activities of rebel leaders José Manuel de Herrera and José María Morelos. Traces Mexican relations with the United States and rebel bids for foreign military aid. Gives an account of the first days of the Provisional Government (1821) created in conformance with Iturbide's Plan of Iguala. 58 notes. Part II. Reviews Europe's politically reactionary atmosphere at the time and discusses its effect on events in Mexico. Contrasts the policies of Presidents James Madison and James Monroe in regard to rebellion in Spanish possessions. Records discussions of the Mexican Congress and the Commission of External Relations on regulations governing Mexican emissaries, and official expression of Mexico's goodwill toward the United States. 82 notes. Part III. Focuses on the internal problems confronting the new Mexican Government, such as the presence of Spanish troops in Mexico, the difficulties of organizing the military, and concern with American colonization of Texas. Describes the events leading to Iturbide's coronation as emperor (1822). Records American congressional discussions of titles and rules of succession. Reveals the mixed reaction of the US Congress to Iturbide's coronation, and the opposition of its Republican members. Publishes records of congressional discussion on the proposal that a Subsecretariate of State and Internal and Exterior Relations be created. 72 notes.

L. Cashman

48. Santos, Richard G. AN ANNOTATED SURVEY OF THE SPANISH ARCHIVES OF LAREDO AT SAINT MARY'S UNIVERSITY OF TEXAS. *Texana 1966 4(1): 41-46.* The previously lost archives, rediscovered in 1934, comprise approximately 25 hundred documents, primarily provincial in nature, issued by Spain for Nuevo Santander, and by Mexico for Tamaulipas, in the period from 1749 to 1868. The documents are described.

W. Elkins

49. Santos, Richard G. THE QUARTEL DE SAN ANTONIO DE BEXAR. *Texana 1967 5(3): 187-202.* Uses military records and land office records to establish the existence of this historic site. These barracks were originally ordered built by the Texas governor in 1805, but were not erected for five years. The quartel was used to raise troops in the revolution against Spain and to raise counterrevolutionary troops in 1811 and 1813. It was apparently destroyed in 1836, when Travis and his followers chose the Alamo. The original intended floor plan has been found, and according to what are believed to be the remains, this plan was followed closely. It has been recommended that the site be restored and recorded as a Texas Historic Landmark. Illus., 75 notes.

W. A. Buckman

50. Simmons, Marc. TLASCALANS IN THE SPANISH BORDERLANDS. *New Mexico Hist. R. 1964 39(2): 101-110.* The Indians of Tlascala served the Spaniards in several capacities: 1) as formal colonizers clustered around mission centers where they functioned as teachers and exemplary farmers to Indian neophytes, 2) as free laborers in the new mining regions, 3) as auxiliary soldiers, and 4) as individual servants and assistants to Spanish explorers and friars going North. Tlascalans are mentioned at Zacatecas, San Luis Postosí, and Saltillo, Mexico; San Juan

Bautista and the Seno Mexicano region of Texas; and Santa Fe and Analco, New Mexico.

D. F. Henderson

51. Smith, R. A. INDIANS IN AMERICAN-MEXICAN RELATIONS BEFORE THE WAR OF 1846. *Hispanic Am. Hist. R. 1963 43(1): 34-64.* Detailed accounts of Apache, Navajo, Ute, Comanche, and Kiowa Indian raids into northern Mexico in the 1830's and 1840's. The author carefully traces the plunder trails used by the Indian tribes, and discusses the Indian strategy of capturing horses, other animals, and women and children. As treaties signed with the Indians were not honored, it is shown that the Mexican federal and state governments could evolve no more effective solution to the problem than to resort to the Spanish colonial practice of providing payment for Indian scalps. The raids increased in severity in the early 1840's as the Indians in general, and the Comanches in particular, took advantage of worsening relations between Mexico and the United States. No solution had been found when war came in 1846.

B. B. Solnick

52. Troike, Rudolph C. A PAWNEE VISIT TO SAN ANTONIO IN 1795. *Ethnohist. 1964 11(4): 380-393.* Edits and interprets relevant portions of a document in the Archivo General, Mexico, recording a visit to the seat of government for the Spanish province of Texas of a group of Pawnees and other plains tribes in February 1795. Spanish-U.S. border rivalries and tribal disruption and pressures resulting from the westward movement are linked with the incident; tribes and chieftains are identified.

H. J. Graham

53. Vigness, David M. A DEDICATION TO THE MEMORY OF CHARLES WILSON HACKETT, 1888-1951. *Arizona and the West 1965 7(1): 1-4.* Charles Wilson Hackett was a Latin Americanist of the Herbert Eugene Bolton school. His efforts led to the establishment of the massive collection of Latin Americana at the University of Texas. His principal contribution to scholarship was the considerable body of source materials which he translated, edited, and published. He served in an editorial capacity on several professional journals. His activities included government assignments and the pursuit of scholarly concerns abroad. Hackett was acclaimed "a constant source of inspiration and academic enthusiasm to a host of students." Appended with a selected list of his publications relating to the Spanish borderlands; illus.

D. L. Smith

54. Voght, Martha. HERBERT EUGENE BOLTON AS A WRITER OF LOCAL HISTORY. *Southwestern Hist. Q. 1969 72(3): 313-323.* Bolton's principal contribution to history is usually regarded as the concept of hemispheric unity. The "Bolton thesis" is synonymous with the history of the Americas and its indivisibility. Generally overlooked is that his initial contributions were in local history, that he reached his synthetic positions through the study of local history, and that he believed the true value of local studies can be realized only by seeing them in the perspective of the wider view. His career is "an active refutation" of the disrepute with which local history is often stigmatized. 50 notes.

D. L. Smith

55. West, Elizabeth Howard. THE RIGHT OF ASYLUM IN NEW MEXICO IN THE SEVENTEENTH AND EIGHTEENTH CENTURIES. *New Mexico Hist. R. 1966 41(2): 115-153.* After noting the history of the right to safety or asylum in a place of worship, the author discusses in detail the 32 recorded cases in New Mexico, the first of which occurred in 1685, the last in 1796. Analysis of the cases revealed that crimes of violence predominated, followed by theft or fraud, neglect of duty, political offenses, and resistance to official authority. Persons involved were from all classes, and one was a woman. The larger number of instances occurred in the cities of Santa Fe, Albuquerque, and Santa Cruz. Originally published in the *Hispanic American Historical Review,* 1928 8(3). Based on the Spanish Archives of New Mexico; 21 notes.

D. F. Henderson

56. Wolff, Thomas. THE KARANKAWA INDIANS: THEIR CONFLICT WITH THE WHITE MAN IN TEXAS. *Ethnohist. 1969 16(1): 1-32.* "The Karankawa Indians, whose aboriginal homeland was on the east coast of Texas, were first encountered by non-Indians when Alvar Nuñez Cabeza de Vaca and his men came upon them soon after A.D. 1528. From then until the demise of the Karankawa in 1858 the relationship between these Indians and Spaniards, Frenchmen, English-

men, Mexicans and Anglo-Americans passed through various phases, all of which are outlined here." J

57. —. 1964 SERRA AWARD OF "THE AMERICAS." *The Americas 1965 21(4): 399-408.* Consists principally of the address by Dr. France V. Scholes at the presentation of the Serra Award to Dr. George P. Hammond, director of the Bancroft Library, Berkeley, California. The speaker describes Hammond's contributions as teacher, research scholar, and administrator, especially in relation to Spanish Southwest and colonial Latin American studies. Also printed is Hammond's acceptance address, in which he discusses mainly his work (since 1946) at the Bancroft Library. D. Bushnell

Exploration

58. Barthol, Johannes. A WESTERN EXPLORER'S GUIDE TO SAN MIGUEL ISLAND. *Western Explorer 1965 3(3): 3-24.* An encyclopedic discussion of a tiny windswept island, westernmost of the Santa Barbara Channel Islands which lie scattered off the coast of southern California. Approximately 37 square miles of desolate beauty, San Miguel Island was discovered in 1542 by Juan Rodriguez Cabrillo, a Portuguese in the employ of Spain. The Canaliño Indians were the only inhabitants until the early 1800's when they moved to the mainland. For nearly 50 years the island was uninhabited, but in 1848 the United States acquired it from Mexico and between 1850 and 1946 leased it to cattle and sheep raisers. Since 1946 the U.S. Navy has owned the island. The author was an employee of one of the last lessees of the island and lived and worked there for some time. He describes in detail the history, physical features, and wildlife of the island. W. L. Bowers

59. Bartroli, Tomás. EXPLORACIONES, AVENTURAS Y DESVENTURAS DE LOS ESPAÑOLES EN EL PACIFICO NORTE [Explorations, adventures, and misfortunes of the Spanish in the northern Pacific]. *Hist. y Vida [Spain] 1969 2(19): 98-118.* During the decline of the Spanish Empire in America, there arose for Spain various problems of "rivalry," discovery, and colonization of territories situated north of California. The presence of Spain in these territories consisted in the creation of the establishment at Nootka Island (in what is today British Columbia) and in some journeys made north of this place, starting from Mexico. The method of settling the ownership of these territories and the treaties made for this purpose with England showed once more that the presence of Spain in the new continent was to be of short duration and that its influence before the world was already eclipsed. 17 illus.
T. M. S. (IHE 76019)

60. Buchanan, William J. LEGEND OF THE BLACK CONQUISTADOR. *Mankind 1968 1(5): 21-25, 93.* In 1539 Estevancio de Dorantes, the Negro slave of a Spanish master, wandered through the lands of Nueva España. The folklore of the Zuñi Indians contains a legend pertaining to his last journey: One of the survivors of the ill-fated Narvaez expedition of 1528, he wandered across Texas and New Mexico with Cabeza de Vaca. During the eight-year period of wandering, Estevan learned to speak at least six Indian languages. In the spring of 1539, Estevan was sent to the North to discover the "Cities of Gold." He soon began to assert himself at the expense of the friar with whom he was traveling. Now adorned with brightly colored plumes and practicing the weird ritual of a medicine man, he began to tell the Indians he met that he was a god, and he attracted a group of followers. From each group of new Indians which he met, he demanded and received women and gifts. Success clouded his judgment, and his arrogance with the Indians of Zuñi led to his death in 1539. Illus. P. D. Thomas

61. Burlingame, Robert. MORE THAN WE HAD THOUGHT: CABEZA DE VACA, HANIEL LONG, AND OUR DAY. *Southwest R. 1968 53(4): 360-373.* A comparison of Cabeza de Vaca's *Naufragios,* now usually termed the *Relación* (1542) and Haniel Long's Interlinear to Cabeza de Vaca (1936), now called *The Power within Us.* "What would . . . de Vaca think were he to encounter the more luminous and idealized Spaniard depicted in Long's book? Would he recognize the literary projection, the symbolic personage mutated from the original life?" D. F. Henderson

62. Carter, George F. CALIFORNIA AS AN ISLAND. *Masterkey 1964 38(2): 74-78.* Considers the notion of early Spanish explorers that California was an island, pointing out that radiocarbon dates from the Salton Sea (then filling the Imperial Valley and draining into the Gulf of California) show it existing at just about the same time that primary explorations were carried out. Journals of the first explorations refer to California repeatedly as an island, perhaps understandable in view of the fact that those first explorers came up the Gulf of California and met the Colorado River outflow, then sailed up it - perhaps into the Salton Sea. Based upon secondary sources; 1 note. C. N. Warren

63. Cutter, Donald C. EARLY SPANISH ARTISTS ON THE NORTHWEST COAST. *Pacific Northwest Q. 1963 54(4): 150-157.* From 1783 through 1802, Spanish artists ("photographers of the age") accompanying explorers and scientific expeditions to the Pacific Northwest seacoasts made sketches and portraits of sights and natives observed in the region. Brief accounts describe the graphic work of Thomás de Surfa, José Cardero, Atanasio Echeverría, and others. Locations of some of the original sketches and maps are indicated. C. C. Gorchels

64. Faulk, Odie B. NOW FOUND - FATHER KINO'S 1710 MAP. *Pacific Historian 1966 10(1): 30-34.* Discusses the influence of Father Eusebio Francisco Kino, S.J., on the cartography of the Western world. Active in Spanish colonizing efforts in Baja California after 1681, Kino spent much time exploring, converting the natives, and teaching agricultural methods, in addition to making 18 known maps. His maps of California were reproduced widely without citation, and even Alexander Humboldt used his 1710 map. Ernest J. Burrus. S.J., has recently published the fruits of Kino's work in his *Kino and the Cartography of Northwestern New Spain* (Tucson: Arizona Pioneers' Historical Society, 1965). Documented with the published studies of Kino's work, illus., map. T. R. Cripps

65. Garrahy, Stephen T. and Weber, David J. FRANCISCO DE ULLOA, JOSEPH JAMES MARKEY, AND THE DISCOVERY OF UPPER CALIFORNIA. *California Hist. Q. 1971 50(1): 73-77.* Whether Ulloa discovered Upper California in 1540 and died there, or whether he returned to Mexico, remains a subject of historiographical controversy. The standard account by Henry R. Wagner asserted that Ulloa returned to Mexico. However, Joseph J. Markey, an Oceanside physician, has made a lifelong avocation of attempting to prove that Ulloa died on the expedition and that his ship sank in Pacific waters. The basis of Markey's argument is a document recording the testimony of one of the expedition's survivors. Markey claims to have obtained a copy of this document from a Spanish archive, but searches by historians have failed to locate the original. Markey's views have enjoyed wide publicity, and he has promised to publish a book in the near future. Perhaps Markey's document will be made available for scholarly inquiry so that the argument can be resolved. 15 notes. A. Hoffman

66. Gibson, Jon L. THE DE SOTO EXPEDITION IN THE MISSISSIPPI VALLEY: EVALUATION OF THE GEOGRAPHICAL POTENTIAL OF THE LOWER OUACHITA RIVER VALLEY WITH REGARD TO THE DE SOTO-MOSCOSO EXPEDITION. *Louisiana Studies 1968 7(3): 203-212.* Discusses the report of the US De Soto Expedition Commission (1939) and an appraisal of its findings. An attempt is made to locate Anilco and other places named in the lower Ouachita River valley. Some of the places, descriptions, and distances could be reconciled with present-day geography, but others could not. The main emphasis is on the feasibility of the findings of the commission "in areas south of the regional scope of the Lower Mississippi Valley Survey." Map, 25 notes. G. W. McGinty

67. Holland, Francis Ross, Jr. A BRIEF HISTORY OF CABRILLO NATIONAL MONUMENT. *J. of the West 1968 7(2): 256-269.* Outlines the problems in carving out the present monument near San Diego from the military reservation. The history of the statue of Cabrillo which now stands on the monument grounds is given. Its acquisition was somewhat illegal. R. N. Alvis

68. Hunt, John Clark. SIR FRANCIS DRAKE VISITS CALIFORNIA. *Am. Hist. Illus. 1967 22(8): 46-53.* Emphasizes Drake's stopover in California during his voyage seeking a Northwest Passage in 1578. During his around-the-world voyage on the *Golden Hind,* Drake sailed

along Latin America, plundering Spanish ships. Sailing northward and encountering stormy weather, Drake found a "convenient harbor" in northern California where his ship was repaired. Drake and his crew met and befriended aborigines. From the various accounts and available evidence it is most likely that Drake's ship was repaired in either the San Francisco Bay area or 50 miles north in the Drake Bay area.

G. H. Skau

69. Ives, Ronald L., ed. RETRACING THE ROUTE OF THE FAGES EXPEDITION OF 1781. *Arizona and the West 1966 8(1): 49-70 and (2): 157-170.* Part I. As early as 1540 the Yuma crossing on the Colorado River was known. Its economic and strategic importance increased as it developed as a gateway on the trail from Sonora, Mexico, through Arizona to Alta, California. Two mission-presidio settlements were established at the crossing in 1780, but the Yuma Indians soon became disgruntled and massacred all but the women and children in July 1781. Don Pedro Fages, a veteran infantry officer with extensive service in California and Sonora, was sent from Sonora to Yuma to rescue the captives, execute the leaders of the rebellion, and restore peace with the other Indians. Highly literate and competent, Fages kept a diary of his 106-day, 980-mile expedition over the difficult terrain of the desolate Sonoran frontier. The Fages diary places the Yuma relief expedition of 1781 in a much clearer historical perspective. Although its existence has been known by historians for some time, the itinerary of the expedition has remained elusive and vague because few of the sites mentioned by Fages appear on modern maps. The editor has solved the mystery to a large extent by personal field investigations. 2 maps, 60 notes. Part II. The expedition led by Don Pedro Fages in the late summer of 1781 from Pitic near present Hermosillo, Sonora, Mexico, to Yuma, Arizona, was to rescue captives, punish the participants of the massacre of the Yuma mission-presidio-settlements, and to restore peace. It is traced from the rest retreat at Sonoyta back to Yuma to search for the Franciscan martyrs, and the subsequent return back to Pitic. The manuscript is in the Bancroft Library. 2 maps, 20 notes.   D. L. Smith

70. Kessell, John L. ANZA, INDIAN FIGHTER, THE SPRING CAMPAIGN OF 1766. *J. of Arizona Hist. 1968 9(3): 155-163.* Discusses Juan Bautista de Anza's ability as an Indian fighter by describing in detail his spring campaign of 1766. Born in 1735 in a frontier outpost as the son of an Indian-fighting captain, Anza seemed predestined to be a soldier. Enlisting in the Spanish Army at 16, he became a lieutenant at 19 and obtained his own command as a captain at 24. In 1766, after six years' experience as a captain, he led an expedition against the hostile Apache Indians in the mountains south of the Gila River. Anza succeeded, by hard marching and various strategems, in killing or capturing 40 Apache. However, he was able to recover few of the horses previously stolen by the Apache. This affair proved significant only as a training exercise for Anza and his men. Based largely on Anza's report in the Biblioteca Nacional; illus., map, 22 notes.   R. J. Roske

71. Moreno Echevarría, José María. ALVAR NUÑEZ CABEZA DE VACA, EXPLORADOR A LA FUERZA [Álvar Núñez Cabeza de Vaca, explorer by force]. *Hist. y Vida [Spain] 1969 2(12): 92-101.* Sketches the life of Cabeza de Vaca. Pays special attention to Cabeza's adventures and discoveries in Texas and Mexico (1527-36), giving little importance to the last stage of his life, in Hispanic America and Spain. 12 illus.

T. M. S. (IHE 73609)

72. Nasatir, Abraham P. JUAN RODRIGUEZ CABRILLO. *Western Explorer 1964 3(2): 3-12.* Depicts the life of the Portuguese navigator in the employ of Spain who is known as the "discoverer of California." Cabrillo was the first to use the name "California" to identify the area; however, the author contends that he is described more accurately as the "discoverer and explorer of the Pacific Coast" for this places him and his work in truer historical perspective. During the year 1542 Cabrillo led an exploratory expedition up the Pacific coast as far north as Cabo de Pinos near where Fort Ross later stood. Cabrillo died on San Miguel Island on 3 January 1543, but his expedition had discovered most of the capes and harbors of Lower and Upper California between the 29th and 42nd parallels. Later Spanish explorers and the paucity of information about Cabrillo have detracted from his discoveries and fame. Biblio.

W. L. Bowers

73. Rey, Agapito. A DEDICATION TO THE MEMORY OF HERBERT INGRAM PRIESTLEY, 1875-1944. *Arizona and the West 1964 6(3): 187-190.* Herbert Ingram Priestley was a student, associate, and successor of Herbert Eugene Bolton at the University of California and its Bancroft Library. Long years of close collaboration made them leaders in the study of the Spanish borderlands. Priestley's particular interest was Mexico and extended to early Spanish explorers of California and the West. Appended with a selected list of his writings related to the Spanish borderlands; illus.   D. L. Smith

74. Romer, Margaret. ABOARD SHIP ON DRY LAND. *J. of the West 1969 8(4): 606-612.* Tells of the experience of the *Bruja*, a 25-ton sailing schooner which became grounded some 200 yards from the eastern bank of the Colorado River some distance above its mouth, on 21 July 1826. The expedition was led by Lieutenant R. W. H. Hardy, formerly of the Royal British Navy, who was in the employ of the General Pearl and Coral Fishing Association of London. He had been commissioned to search for new pearl oyster beds in the Gulf of California. He ran low on supplies and was attempting to sail up the Colorado River to find fresh water and friendly Indians from whom he might purchase food. After many anxious days and experiences with the local Cocopa Indians, the tide lifted the vessel, which then returned to the Gulf of California.

R. N. Alvis

75. Servín, Manuel P. SYMBOLIC ACTS OF SOVEREIGNTY IN SPANISH CALIFORNIA. *Southern California Q. 1963 45(2): 109-121.* "Symbolic acts of sovereignty" refers to actions, such as religious ceremonies and planting flags, by which early explorers attempted to establish the sovereignty of their rulers over discovered land. The first such act concerning California was undertaken on 3 May 1535 by Hernán Cortés in Baja California, when he claimed possession of that land and all other connecting lands for Spain and for himself as governor. In 1539 Cortés' lieutenant, Francisco de Ulloa, solemnly took possession of the mouth of the Colorado River, and afterwards of various parts of Baja California. Covered also are the possession-taking activities of Juan Rodríguez Cabrillo, Sir Francis Drake, Sebastián Vizcaíno, Gaspar de Portolá, and numerous others. 36 notes.   A. K. Main

76. Spaulding, Edward S. *Noticias 1966 12(2): 1-25.* Discusses early historical references to Point Conception, located in the southwestern corner of Santa Barbara County. In 1542 when Juan Rodríguez Cabrillo sailed this area, then known as Cape Galera, the sea at the point was known as a mariners' grave. In 1602 Vizcaino sailed the Santa Barbara Channel and renamed the point Purísima Concepción. Vancouver, as he passed down the coast, Anglicized the name to the present version. The author recounts his own trip to the point in January 1966. He discusses the geographical layout, the natural wildlife, and the aesthetics of the point. 20 photos.   M. J. McBaine

77. Spaulding, Edward S. POINT CONCEPTION. *Noticias 1966 12(2): 1-25.* An account of a recent trip to Point Conception on the southwest corner of Santa Barbara County. This dangerous cape was first noted in 1542 by Juan Rodriguez Cabrillo. In 1602 Sebastián Vizcaíno sailed through the Santa Barbara Channel and gave the point the name it bears today. The lighthouse was lit for the first time in 1856; the prisms of the lenses had been ground in Paris. Illus.   E. P. Stickney

78. Strout, Clevy Lloyd. FLORA AND FAUNA MENTIONED IN THE JOURNALS OF THE CORONADO EXPEDITION. *Great Plains J. 1971 11(1): 5-10.* Summarizes Francisco Vázquez de Coronado's exploration of the southwestern United States in 1540-41. Details all references in the journals to flora and fauna. Because "the writers of the documents were soldiers, not trained biologists," specific identification of some items is not possible. The expedition was interested mainly in finding gold and converting the natives, but was charged also with ascertaining whether the area was suitable for colonization. Therefore, considerable attention was paid to resources such as plants and animals. Based largely on documents in the Seminary of Medieval Spanish Studies; map, 109 notes.   O. H. Zabel

79. Treutlein, Theodore E. THE PORTOLA EXPEDITION OF 1769-1770. *California Hist. Soc. Q. 1968 47(4): 291-313.* The 1769 expedition under Don Gaspar de Portolá, governor of Lower California, had as its original objective the exploration of the port of Monterey and

its occupation for the Crown by the founding of a presidio and mission. Fray Junípero Serra was a member of the expedition; many of the members were Indian or part Indian. On the trip north they at first failed to identify Monterey. After reaching San Francisco they returned to search for Monterey which they found in April 1770 and formally occupied 3 June 1770. "The salient accomplishments of the year 1769 were the opening of a land route from Lower to Upper California, the founding of the San Diego Presidio and Mission..., the marking of a land trail from San Diego to the San Francisco Peninsula (in broad outline the beginning of *El Camino Real*), and the discovery of San Francisco Bay." Based on primary sources including the Bolton Papers, Bancroft Library, University of California, Berkeley; 22 notes.   E. P. Stickney

80. Wedel, Mildred Mott. J.-B. BENARD, SIEUR DE LA HARPE: VISITOR TO THE WICHITAS IN 1719. *Great Plains J. 1971 10(2): 37-70.* A biography of Jean-Baptiste Bénard, Sieur de la Harpe (1683-1765). Emphasizes his three explorations in French Louisiana, 1718-23. In the first, he explored the Red River where he contacted the Wichita Indians; in the second, the Gulf coast to Galveston Bay; and in the third, the Arkansas River. His reports to his employers, John Law's Company of the West (later the Company of the Indies), and his memoirs and other writings, provide a great deal of information on the Indians and the terrain of the areas explored. Discusses the French-Spanish conflict for control of the Trans-Mississippi West. Map, 111 notes.
O. H. Zabel

81. Wedel, Waldo R. AFTER CORONADO IN QUIVIRA. *Kansas Hist. Q. 1968 34(4): 369-385.* The legendary Quivira visited by Coronado in 1541 has interested students for years. Some have argued that Quivira was located near the great bend of the Arkansas River. Since 1940 the Smithsonian Institution has been excavating Indian sites in this region. Historical and archaeological evidence suggests that the sites designated as the Little River focus, the Great Bend aspect, and the Paint Creek culture were among the Indian villages visited by Coronado. The evidence indicates that this central Kansas phase of Wichita culture was not affected by the coming of the white man. The culture, which disappeared in the 18th century before the arrival of French explorers, may have been destroyed by the Osages, the Apaches, or weather changes. The evidence shows that the inhabitants were in contact with Pueblo Indians in the Rio Grande drainage basin, and the artifacts found at the sites provide guidelines for working into both the prewhite past and ethnohistoric present. Based on articles and books; illus., 14 notes.
W. F. Zornow

82. Wedel, Waldo R. CORONADO'S ROUTE TO QUIVIRA 1541. *Plains Anthropologist 1970 15(49): 161-169.* "The oft-discussed historical question as to Coronado's route of march in 1541 from the Rio Grande pueblos to the settlements of Quivira is re-examined in light of documentary research, hitherto unpublished, by the late J. R. Swanton of the Bureau of American Ethnology. A collation of all available narratives casts strong doubt on Schroeder's 1962 theory that the expedition at no time traveled south of the Canadian River, and instead supports older interpretations by Hodge, Bolton, and others who maintained that the expedition separated far south of that stream. The documentary evidence, like that from archaeology, supports the view that the 16th century province of Quivira was the home of ancestral Wichita Indians residing in central Kansas along the great bend of the Arkansas River."   J

83. Wiecek, William M. IMAGINARY GEOGRAPHY, A RARE MAP OF ANOTHER GREAT SALT LAKE: DATED 1703. *Am. West 1971 8(5): 10-12.* Many nonexistent places were indicated on maps produced in the first two centuries of the cartographic history of North America. A notorious source of corruption was the 1703 book of the traveler-storyteller Louis-Armand de Lom D'Arce, baron de Lahontan. His *Nouveaux Voyages* told of his expedition into the heart of the continent. Westward of the Straits of Mackinac, however, his trip was wholly imaginary. His details bedeviled American cartography for almost a century. William Delisle, the greatest of the early 18th-century French cartographers, was known for his scientific accuracy. When he prepared a new *Carte du Canada,* however, Delisle uncharacteristically accepted details of Lahontan's account and incorporated them into otherwise blank places on his own. For the first time on the maps of Europeans there appeared a "lake of salty water." Lahontan's fiction and Delisle's conjectural location of a salt lake beyond a western mountain range, a bit of

imaginary geography, were legitimatized over a century later with the discovery of the Great Salt Lake. Map.   D. L. Smith

84. Williams, Tennant S. THE DE SOTO EXPEDITION IN THE MISSISSIPPI VALLEY: ARMADA ON THE MISSISSIPPI, 1543. *Louisiana Studies 1968 7(3): 213-227.* An account of what happened to the De Soto expedition after his death 21 May 1542 at the Indian village of Guachoya on the Mississippi River. The new commander Luis de Moscoso decided to get the expedition out of North America as quickly as possible. On 5 June 1542, he led his men westward in an attempt to reach Vera Cruz. The expedition wandered through northwestern Louisiana and eastern Texas until he decided to retrace his steps in October. He reached Anilco, 10 miles west of Guachoya, in December and then traveled to Aminoya. Here they spent the winter, expropriating the food supply of the natives. Seven brigantines, each 50 feet long, were constructed and supplied with food for the 300 Spaniards on their voyage to Vera Cruz. Moscoso's armada set sail down the Mississippi 2 July 1543. A virtual day to day account of the journey until it reached the Panuco River 52 days later is given. Based on the report of the De Soto Expedition Commission; 34 notes, map.   G. W. McGinty

85. Wood, Raymund F. FRANCISCO GARCES, EXPLORER OF SOUTHERN CALIFORNIA. *Southern California Q. 1969 51(3): 185-209.* Discusses the exploratory journey made in 1775-76 by Spanish missionary Francisco Tomás Hermenegildo Garcés (1738-81). On part of this journey, Father Garcés traveled from near present-day Tucson, Arizona, to Mission San Gabriel by way of the Mojave River (which he discovered) and through passes in the Tehachapi and San Bernardino Mountains. He returned by a route which took him to the Grand Canyon and through the Painted Desert. The journey was important because it opened a route between Spanish settlements in California and those in Arizona and New Mexico that was easier than the one through the sand dunes of the Colorado Desert west of Yuma. The author includes a brief account of Garcés' career prior to 1775 and of the events surrounding the so-called Yuma Massacre of 1781 in which he lost his life. Based on translations and secondary sources. 27 notes.   W. L. Bowers

The Mission and Presidio Frontier

86. Adams, Eleanor B. FRAY SILVESTRE AND THE OBSTINATE HOPI. *New Mexico Hist. 1963 38(2): 97-138.* The fame of Fray Silvestre Velez de Escalante, who lived in New Mexico from 1774 to 1800, rests chiefly on his exploration into Utah in 1776 in search of a land route to Monterey, California. The author concentrates on his unsuccessful attempt to convert the Hopi Indians in 1775. Fray Silvestre was shocked and disappointed by the actions and attitudes of the apostate Hopi. He recommended a show of force as the only means of setting them on the right track. A translation of the journal he kept during his stay with the Indians occupies the last 20 pages of the article.
D. F. Henderson

87. Adams, Eleanor B., ed. LETTER TO THE MISSIONARIES OF NEW MEXICO. *New Mexico Hist. R. 1965 40(4): 319-335.* Most of the writings of Fray Silvestre Velez de Escalante, an 18th-century Franciscan missionary and explorer, have been published. The *patente,* a letter to the missionaries of New Mexico, discovered in the archdiocese of Santa Fe is an exception. The letter reveals further evidence "of the progressive decline of the New Mexican missions" and also insight into the character and education of Fray Silvestre. A list of the writings of Fray Silvestre is included.   D. F. Henderson

88. Blick, James D. GEOGRAPHY AND MISSION AGRICULTURE. *Pacific Historian 1964 8(1): 3, 38.* Points out that mission agriculture in the Alta section of California was directly correlated with the geography of that region as evidenced by the fact that similar rainfall and climate in Spain and Mexico produced similar crops such as the staples wheat, barley, corn, and grapes.   T. R. Cripps

89. Bowman, J. N. THE BIRTHDAYS OF THE CALIFORNIA MISSIONS. *The Americas 1964 20(3): 289-308.* "A critical and analytical study of the founding dates" of the 21 Franciscan Indian missions in California. In discussing the discrepancies that have arisen and the defini-

tion of "founding," the article offers a review of the normal procedures (military-political as well as ecclesiastical) followed in the establishment of the missions. From archival and other sources.　　　　D. Bushnell

90. Bowman, J. N. THE NAMES OF THE CALIFORNIA MISSIONS. *The Americas 1965 21(4): 363-374.* Lists, and in some cases explains in greater or lesser detail, the different names by which the Spanish California missions have been known from their founding to the present, as found in mission records and popular usage. 9 notes.
　　　　D. Bushnell

91. Brown, Alan K. THE VARIOUS JOURNALS OF JUAN CRESPI. *The Americas 1965 21(4): 375-398.* Detailed analysis of the extant versions of the journals of the Franciscan friar Juan Crespí concerning his observations in California 1769-74, indicating differences and relationships among them. 58 notes.　　　　D. Bushnell

92. Brugge, David M. SOME PLAINS INDIANS IN THE CHURCH RECORDS OF NEW MEXICO. *Plains Anthropologist 1965 10(29): 181-189.* "The information found relating to four Plains tribes, Aa (Ae), Jumano, Kiowa and Pawnee, in the baptismal and burial records of the Catholic Church in New Mexico for the period from 1694 to 1875 is summarized in tabular form. A brief description is given of the circumstances resulting in these records and their possible significance to Plains history."　　　　J

93. Brugge, David M., ed. VIZCARRA'S NAVAJO CAMPAIGN OF 1823. *Arizona and the West 1964 6(3): 223-244.* José Antonio Vizcarra, Mexican governor of New Mexico (1822-25), negotiated a treaty with the Navajo in February 1823. This was an attempt to bring peace between the Navajo and New Mexicans whose expanding economies were based on livestock. In mid-June Vizcarra's 1,500-man army set out on a campaign to enforce the terms of the treaty. The elusive Navajo constantly retreated, scattered, and vanished into their hideouts. Translated and edited here are Vizcarra's journal with entries from 18 June through 31 August, and a diary report of an officer who led a detachment separate from the army with entries for 3-18 August. These documents detail the expedition on its march through west central New Mexico, across northeast Arizona, into southern Utah, and return. Map, 89 notes.
　　　　D. L. Smith

94. Burrus, Ernest J. KINO EN ROUTE TO SONORA: THE CONICARI LETTER. *Western Explorer 1964 3(2): 37-42.* The first published English translation of a letter (preserved in the Huntington Library, San Marino, California) sent from Conicari, Sonora, by Father Eusebio Francisco Kino, well-known Spanish missionary, to the Portuguese Duchess of Aveiro, wife of the Spanish Duke of Arcos and resident in Madrid. This was the last letter of Kino's extant correspondence with the duchess, who intervened repeatedly with the highest Spanish authorities to keep alive missionary activities among the Indian tribes of northwestern Mexico and Upper and Lower California. Introduction, 10 notes.　　　　W. L. Bowers

95. Chavez, Angelico. THE HOLY MAN OF ZIA. *New Mexico Hist. R. 1965 40(4): 309-318.* Biographical sketch of Fray Bernardo de Marta, for some years minister of Zia Pueblo, an Indian reservation. A Catalan by birth, he and his brother Juan joined the Franciscan Providence of Santiago in 1597, were ordained, and decided to go to the Indies. They arrived in the New World in 1606, where Fray Juan was allowed to proceed to the Far East. Fray Bernardo, however, was ordered to remain in America where he was in charge, successively, of Santo Domingo (a reservation), Galisteo, and finally of Zia. 16 notes.
　　　　D. F. Henderson

96. Chavez, Angelico. POHE-YEMO'S REPRESENTATIVE AND THE PUEBLO REVOLT OF 1680. *New Mexico Hist. R. 1967 42(2): 85-126.* The Pueblo Revolt of 1680 put to an end for a time the Spanish colony and the Franciscan missions in New Mexico. The causes were several, but the main rallying cry was the "ancient ones" of the pueblos versus the God and the saints of the Spaniards. In previous histories, the tactical genius of the revolt was thought to be El Popé of San Juan, but Governor Otermín and his captains felt at the time that El Popé could not have done it all alone. The interrogation of prisoners revealed that an "Indian representative of Pohé yemo" had ordered them to rebel. This

Indian was reported to be very tall and black with very large yellow eyes. In Pueblo mythology Pohé-yemo made the sun shine upon the people when they first came out upon the dark and dreary earth's surface. The tall black man with yellow eyes who was called the representative of Pohé-yemo was probably two people - Domingo Naranjo, the representative of Pohé-yemo in Taos, and Pedro Naranjo, carrying out his orders at San Felipe. Based on various records in the Biblioteca Nacional and the Archivo General de la Nación, Mexico, and the Spanish Archives of New Mexico; 80 notes.　　　　D. F. Henderson

97. Christiansen, Paige W. HUGH OCONOR'S INSPECTION OF NUEVA VIZCAYA AND COAHUILA, 1773. *Louisiana Studies 1963 2(3): 157-175.* Oconor, as commandant inspector, made a survey of the presidios and borders of the Internal Provinces of New Spain in order to strengthen them against the Indians. 50 notes.　　　　G. W. McGinty

98. Colley, Charles C. THE MISSIONIZATION OF THE COAST MIWOK INDIANS OF CALIFORNIA. *California Hist. Soc. Q. 1970 49(2): 143-162.* An account of the impact of Spanish civilization upon the Miwok Indians. First contacted by the Cermeño expedition in 1595, the Coast Miwok were among the most accessible of the California Indians to missionary work. The Mission San Francisco de Asís, established in 1776, served as an important base for Christianizing northern California Indians. The experiences of the Coast Miwok with mission life were mostly negative. Their language, culture, and freedom were ignored by the padres, who sought to impose an inhibiting, rigid code of Christian society upon them. Lashing was a frequent method of punishment. Mortality among the Coast Miwok ran high and many Indians became "fugitives" from the missions. Venereal disease was also spread. By the end of the mission period the Coast Miwok, the northern California tribe most exposed to the practices of the mission system, was decimated. Based on anthropological and historical writings; illus., map, 70 notes.
　　　　A. Hoffman

99. Curran, Francis J. INFLUJO MISIONERO EN LA FORMACION DE AMERICA SEPTENTRIONAL [The influence of the missionary in the shaping of North America]. *Estudios Centro Americanos [El Salvador] 1963 18(178): 7-11.* The history of the United States as well as the history of Christianity on the American continent are influenced by the missionary impulse of Catholicism. The humanity and religious concern of Spanish and Portuguese Catholicism stand clear against the callous indifference of English Protestantism. By the time the first English settlers had landed in Jamestown the Catholic missionaries had, from Georgia to California, won more than sixty thousand converts, while in the North the French "Black Robes" established the Catholic religion in over a third of a continent.　　　　T. B. Davis, Jr.

100. Daniel, James M. THE SPANISH FRONTIER IN WEST TEXAS AND NORTHERN MEXICO. *Southwestern Hist. Q. 1968 71(4): 481-495.* By the early 18th century the line of settlement of the Spanish frontier in the northern Mexico-Texas-New Mexico region was U-shaped. Delimited by missions, presidios, towns, and ranches, the line of the frontier ran approximately from San Antonio, Texas, southward to Saltillo, Coahuila, westward to Parral, Chihuahua, and then northward to El Paso, Texas, and Santa Fe, New Mexico. The Despoblado, or uninhabited area, within the U-shaped frontier was a funnel reaching deep into New Spain through which wave after wave of Plains Indians raided the colonial settlements. Spanish attempts to fill out the Despoblado were not successful and only occasional communications across its wide mouth were made through the colonial period. Mexican attempts toward independence dictated that the Spanish concentrate on more urgent matters than the northern frontier. Regular communications from San Antonio to El Paso were not established until the American period. Map, 59 notes.
　　　　D. L. Smith

101. Di Peso, Charles C. and Matson, Daniel S. THE SERI INDIANS IN 1692 AS DESCRIBED BY ADAMO GILG, S.J. *Arizona and the West 1965 7(1): 33-56.* Too little is known of Adamo Gilg and his work. This tireless priest was an ethnographer and linguist of considerable ability who served for nearly two decades on the northern frontier of New Spain. His principal work was with the heathen Seri Indians, a nomadic coastal people. His mission station was Santa Maria del Populo located in present central Sonora, Mexico. Numerous trips made him familiar with the country northward into southern Arizona. Gilg's letter of Febru-

ary 1692 is the earliest, and adjudged to be one of the best, ethnographic studies of the Seri. It is concerned with customs, items of material culture, and social organization. Father Gilg's map of Seriland which accompanied the letter gives information about mission districts and other pertinent data not available elsewhere. Primitive sketches of a Seri group are included. The map is reproduced from the original in the Jesuit Archives in the Vatican. The letter is translated from the published 1726 German version. 93 notes.   D. L. Smith

102. Dumke, Glenn S. THE MASTERS OF SAN GABRIEL MISSION'S OLD MILL. *California Hist. Soc. Q. 1966 45(3): 259-265.* Indicates the range and character of the people who once owned or used the Old Mill of San Gabriel Mission. The Franciscan friar, José María de Zalvidea, who built the mill (probably in 1816), through his leadership and enterprise made the Mission San Gabriel known as the "richest of the missions." There were many owners of the mill until, in 1962, it was deeded to the city of San Marino to be used as a historic monument. The author delivered this speech 24 October 1965 at the ceremony of the presentation of the keys to El Molino Viejo to the California Historical Society. Illus.   E. P. Stickney

103. Eckhart, George B. SOME LITTLE-KNOWN MISSIONS IN TEXAS (PARTS I AND II). *Masterkey 1962 36(4): 127-136; 1963 37(1): 9-13.* Attempts to identify six missions in Texas and Mexico near the confluence of the Rio Conchos and the Rio Grande. "Unfortunately no remains of even the ruins of these missions are to be found today." Based on secondary sources; biblio.   C. N. Warren

104. Eckhart, George B. SPANISH MISSIONS OF TEXAS 1680-1800. *Kiva 1967 32(3): 73-95.* Discusses explorations and expeditions in Texas from 1519 to the founding of the first mission (El Paso) in 1680. The 38 missions are described, located, and dated; their founders are named and present status given. 5 maps.   M. W. Machan

105. Evans, William E. THE CONFIRMATION CONTROVERSY OF 1779, SERRA VS. NEVE: A RATIONALE. *Southern California Q. 1969 51(2): 85-96.* A discussion of "possibly the most important controversy between Church and State" during the tenure of Felipe de Neve, Spanish governor of the Californias from 1774 to 1782. In 1768 the Franciscan missionary Junípero Serra discovered a copy of a papal bull authorizing the Jesuits to administer the sacrament of confirmation and he asked that the privilege be given to Franciscans in California since the Jesuits had been expelled. The Pope granted the authority for 10 years beginning in 1774, but the documents giving the concession did not actually reach Serra until 1778. Neve as governor sought to have the authority taken from Serra and the Franciscans in 1779. The author believes that Neve did not make this policy but only followed the orders of his protemporal superior, Teodoro de Croix, who after 1776 was commandant general of the Interior Provinces. The plan of Croix, the author thinks, was to secularize the missions but he did not succeed. In 1781, with only three years of the allotted time remaining, Croix and Neve were forced to acknowledge the authenticity of Serra's right to confirm. Based largely on secondary sources although utilizing a nunber of published quotations from original sources; 31 notes.   W. L. Bowers

106. Faulk, Odie B. and Brinckerhoff, Sidney B. SOLDIERING AT THE END OF THE WORLD. *Am. West 1966 3(3): 28-37.* The mission, the major agency of frontier colonization in the Spanish push northward from Mexico City into the American Southwest, had failed to civilize, Hispanicize, and Christianize the Indians. The Royal Regulation of Presidios in 1772 inaugurated a new program intended to bring about pacification of the natives by force of arms here in the region often referred to as *el fin del mundo* the end of the world. The equipment, living conditions, discipline, morale, and fighting techniques of the less than a thousand soldiers stationed in 15 to 20 presidios scattered throughout the northern tier of provinces of New Spain designated as the Interior Provinces, an area larger than most of Europe, are described and discussed. All the necessary ingredients were present for a successful military pacification of the Indians, but Spanish officials failed to make proper use of them. This policy was replaced by another in 1786. Illus., biblio. note.   D. L. Smith

107. Faulk, Odie B. SPANISH-COMANCHE RELATIONS AND THE TREATY OF 1785. *Texana 1964 2(1): 44-53.* The Spanish Government had little trouble with the eastern and northern Indian tribes of Texas. The Lipan Apache gave trouble when the Spanish forces were occupied elsewhere than with them. The Comanches were the greatest Indian adversaries to the Spanish. The Spanish learned that neither Hispanicizing in missions nor coercion worked with the Comanches. The Spanish turned to making treaties with them. Reproduces a report from Pedro de Nava, Commandant-General of the Interior Provinces, to Viceroy Miguel Joseph de Azanza, dated 23 July 1799. This document gives the terms of the Treaty of 1785 and illustrates the continuing menace of the Comanches and a desire by some Spanish officials to return to the policy of coercion. 18 notes.   W. A. Buckman

108. Fireman, Bert M., ed. KINO ON THE ARIZONA BORDER. *Am. West 1966 3(3): 16-21, 94-95.* Eusebio Francisco Kino, Jesuit missionary, explorer, map maker, and chronicler of Pimería Alta (Sonora, Mexico, and Arizona) from 1687 to 1711, made important contributions to the knowledge of geography of the region and thus paved the way for Spanish occupation of Alta California. On a memorable journey in 1698 he marched to the northwestern frontier of New Spain, to the Gila River. On the return, in a southwestward direction, he was within eyesight of the mouth of the Colorado River. This and other journeys in the vicinity established the fact that California was not an island, but that it was a part of the mainland of the continent. The 1698 Kino diary has been published in book form (Fay Jackson Smith, John L. Kessell, and Francis Fox, *Father Kino in Arizona.* Arizona Historical Foundation, Phoenix). Published here are excerpts from the book with interpolated editorial comments. The original manuscript is in the Archivo General de la Nación, Mexico. Illus., maps.   D. L. Smith

109. Geiger, Maynard. BIOGRAPHICAL DATA ON THE MISSIONARIES OF SAN FERNANDO COLLEGE SERVING THE CALIFORNIA MISSIONS IN 1817 AND 1820. *California Hist. Soc. Q. 1969 48(2): 125-151.* A new translation of two Spanish documents giving biographical information and an evaluation of the merit of the Franciscan missionaries administering the 19 California missions. The reports were submitted in 1817 by Commissary Prefect Fray Vicente Francisco de Sarría and in 1820 by Sarría's successor, Fray Mariano Payeras. Based on documents in the Santa Barbara Mission Archives; 78 notes.   A. Hoffman

110. Geiger, Maynard. BIOGRAPHICAL DATA ON THE CALIFORNIA MISSIONARIES (1769-1848). *California Hist. Soc. Q. 1965 44(4): 291-310.* Of the 142 bona fide Franciscan missionaries in Upper California, 58 died in service and quite a large number suffered from ill health. Even though all were required by civil law to serve at least 10 years at the College of San Fernando itself or in its missions, 56 spent less than 10 years in the missions. Twenty-eight spent 30 or more years. All made a sacrifice and deserve to be remembered for their contribution to the development of an uncultivated wilderness. The article is based on research done for a biographical dictionary waiting publication. The sources include archives in Rome, Seville, and the Franciscan provinces of Spain; in Mexico; and in California in the Santa Barbara Mission Archives; the Archbishop's Archives, San Francisco (The Alexander Taylor Collection); the Bancroft Library; and the various mission registers; 12 notes.   E. P. Stickney

111. Geiger, Maynard. THE BUILDING OF MISSION SAN GABRIEL: 1771-1828. *Southern California Q. 1968 50(1): 33-42.* Details, as adequately as the records permit, the building activity at San Gabriel Mission between 1771 when the mission was founded and 1828 when the last mention of construction activities was made in the annual mission reports. Building went on for over 50 years partly because the mission occupied two different sites and partly because repairs had to be made after two earthquakes. No buildings of stone or adobe were constructed at the original location on the southernmost limits of San Gabriel Valley, but between 1775, when the mission was moved to its present location, and 1828 a number of buildings of stone and sun-dried brick were constructed. Based mainly on annual reports of the San Gabriel missionaries in the Mexican National Archives; illus., 32 notes.   W. L. Bowers

112. Geiger, Maynard, ed. and trans. A DESCRIPTION OF CALIFORNIA'S PRINCIPAL PRESIDIO, MONTEREY, IN 1773. *Southern California Q. 1967 49(3): 327-336.* A translation of about one-fifth of a letter written by Captain Pedro Fages, commandant of the

Monterey presidio, to the viceroy Antonio María Bucareli 29 November 1773. The letter was an official report of his activities in Upper California and the part translated here describes the presidio at Monterey in considerable detail, giving measurements, directions, and the uses of all rooms and buildings as well as other pertinent information about the fortification. The original document upon which the translation is based is in the Mexican National Archives. Illus., 29 notes.   W. L. Bowers

113. Geiger, Maynard. THE FIRST EXPANSION OF THE MISSION FIELD IN CALIFORNIA, 1770-1771. *Southern California Q. 1966 48(2): 187-194.* Annotated translation of two letters from the Marqués de Croix to Fray Junípero Serra and Comandante Pedro Fages concerning the initiation of missionary activity in the vicinity of San Diego and Monterey. The original documents are in the Archivo General de la Nación in Mexico City; photocopies are in the Santa Barbara Mission Archives.   H. Kelsey

114. Geiger, Maynard. FRAY ANTONIO RIPOLL'S DESCRIPTION OF THE CHUMASH REVOLT AT SANTA BARBARA IN 1824. *Southern California Q. 1970 52(4): 345-364.* A translation and edition of Franciscan missionary Antonio Ripoll's report (5 May 1824) to Vincente Francisco Sarría, acting president of the Missions, concerning the Chumash Indian uprising at Santa Barbara Mission in late February 1824. The Indians, mistreated by the soldiers at the presidio, revolted against them rather than the missionaries. Ripoll's report reveals that he was a compassionate advocate of the Indians and was angry with the military authorities for creating the occasion for the uprising. Part of the document has been translated in Zephyrin Engelhardt's *Santa Barbara Mission,* but the second half, in which Ripoll gave his reactions to the uprising, was previously untranslated. Based on a copy of Ripoll's report in the Santa Barbara Mission Archive Library; 97 notes.   W. L. Bowers

115. Geiger, Maynard. FRAY RAFAEL VERGER, O.F.M., AND THE CALIFORNIA MISSION ENTERPRISE. *Southern California Q. 1967 49(2): 205-231.* A translated and edited letter by Rafael Verger, Guardian of the College of San Fernando in Mexico City, written to Don Manuel Lanz de Casafonda, the Spanish royal attorney 3 August 1771. "Clearly discernible throughout the document are the tensions existing between the religious and political arms of the conquest." Verger described in detail the problems faced by the Franciscans in their efforts to establish missions to convert the Indians of upper and lower California. In particular, he criticized the policies of José Gálvez, the *real patronato,* whom he considered too dictatorial and short-sighted. Verger, cautious and pessimistic, did not share the outlook of some of the fathers at the missions, especially that of Padre Junípero Serra who was working with the Indians at Monterey and San Diego. Based on a photocopy of Verger's letter in the Santa Barbara Mission Archives; the original letter is in the Biblioteca del Museo Nacional, Mexico City; illus., 50 notes.   W. L. Bowers

116. Geiger, Maynard, ed. and trans. MISSION SAN GABRIEL IN 1814. *Southern California Q. 1971 53(3): 235-250.* An English translation of replies given by missionaries at San Gabriel Mission in 1814 to a questionnaire sent to all existing California missions by the Spanish Government in 1813. The responses to the 36 questions, although brief, convey useful Indian ethnological information and "throw some light on the Mission Indians as the several missionaries in daily contact with their neophytes knew them." A translation of these answers from San Gabriel Mission, without the questions, was published previously by Father Zephyrin Engelhardt, O.F.M., in 1927. Based on a document in the Santa Barbara Mission Archives; 23 notes.   W. L. Bowers

117. Geiger, Maynard. NEW DATA ON MISSION SAN JUAN CAPISTRANO. *Southern California Q. 1967 49(1): 37-45.* The Santa Barbara Mission Archives contain biennial and annual reports prepared by missionaries and sent to the president of the missions for all 21 missions built by the Spanish between 1769 and 1823 except the famous San Juan Capistrano. The author has found most of the missing reports in the Mexican Archives. Since much data about Mission San Juan Capistrano has been obtained from other sources, the newly-found reports are important chiefly for supplying missing information about building activities between 1778, the year the mission was moved to its present site, and 1795, the date from which details on building have already been traced.

Reports are complete except for the years 1778, 1780, 1784, and 1785, but fortunately the report for 1783 traced building progress since 1778. The documents indicate that the original site of the mission was not the one generally claimed, although the author does not indicate the first site except to state that it was about halfway between the ocean and the present location. Data in the reports also make it clear that the mission was moved to the new site in 1778 and that two churches were built there between 1778 and 1795, the original one in 1778 and a second one in 1782. Based on documents in the Mexican Archives. 21 notes.   W. L. Bowers

118. Geiger, Maynard. NEW DATA ON THE BUILDINGS OF MISSION SAN FRANCISCO. *California Hist. Soc. Q. 1967 46(3): 195-206.* Traces the history of the church buildings at Mission San Francisco between 1776 and 1791 and summarizes the development of other buildings in connection with these churches.   E. P. Stickney

119. Geiger, Maynard. SAN DIEGO'S SPURIOUS 1773 WATER RIGHTS DOCUMENT. *Southern California Q. 1969 51(3): 211-220.* Concerns a bogus document in the Hubert Howe Bancroft Collection at the University of California, Berkeley. The document "grants to Mission San Diego, the presidio and the people of the future pueblo rights to the water of the San Diego River in perpetuity." It is addressed to Fray Junípero Serra, President of the California Missions, dated 17 December 1773, and purportedly signed by Antonio María Bucareli y Ursúa, Viceroy of New Spain, and by Julla Ramón Mendoza, "Second Secretary of the Castle." The author considers the document spurious because the Spanish used is atrocious; the signature of the Viceroy seems partially traced and not like other copies of his signature; the office Mendoza claimed to occupy did not exist; there is no such name as "Julla" in Spanish; Mendoza's signature should not have been on the document and certainly not above that of the Viceroy's as it was; and, there is no record of the document in Bucareli y Ursúa's correspondence. The author conjectures that the document was fraudulently composed during the 1850's and presented to the Private Lands Commission by someone who was concerned about San Diego's future. 21 notes.   W. L. Bowers

120. Geiger, Maynard J. THE STORY OF CALIFORNIA'S FIRST LIBRARIES. *Southern California Q. 1964 46(2): 109-124.* Libraries arrived in California with the coming of the missions in 1769; until 1823 there were organized collections of books in all 21 missions. The Franciscans came to California through the College of San Fernando in Mexico City. In 1808 permission was granted that when a missionary died his books might remain in his mission instead of being sent back to the motherhouse. The books were numbered by shelf position within broad categories. Volumes related to such varying subjects as theology, preaching, ascetic life, sacred and profane history, agriculture, music, medicine, geography, biography, and architecture. Documented.   E. P. Stickney

121. Gerald, Rex E. PORTRAIT OF A COMMUNITY: JOSEPH DE URRUTIA'S MAP OF EL PASO DEL NORTE, 1766. *Am. West 1966 3(3): 38-41.* Following the Seven Years' War (1756-63), an investigation was made of the military situation along the northern borders of New Spain. Present Ciudad Juarez, Chihuahua, Mexico, was then a presidio-mission station. A 1766 map drawn by Joseph de Urrutia and a diary of Nicholas de Lafora, who were members of the inspection team, give a social and economic portrait of the El Paso, Texas, and Juarez areas that also helps to explain the present cities. The map is reproduced from the British Museum. Illus., biblio. note.   D. L. Smith

122. Gordon, Dudley C. A DEDICATION TO THE MEMORY OF JOHN GILMARY SHEA, 1824-1892. *Arizona and the West 1964 6(1): 1-4.* Jesuit-trained John Dawson Shea changed his middle name to Gilmary, meaning "follower of Mary." In his most productive years, he was regarded as "the greatest living Catholic historian" in the United States. His field of research was the history of the Catholic Church in America, and his best work was concerned with the pioneering efforts of the Jesuit missionaries in the French, English, and Spanish colonies, especially with the Indians. His prolific pen produced nearly three hundred multivolume histories, translations, linguistic studies, edited documents, textbooks, devotional works, and numerous unsigned articles. For many years he was editor in chief of the Frank Leslie publications. His scholarship gained international recognition. Illus., biblio.   D. L. Smith

123. Goss, Robert C. THE PROBLEM OF ERECTING THE MAIN DOME AND ROOF VAULTS OF THE CHURCH OF SAN XAVIER DEL BAC. *Kiva 1972 37(3): 117-127.* "Little evidence has been uncovered regarding the facts of construction of the church of San Xavier del Bac [in Arizona], aside from the letters of Father Francisco Inturralde which reported in 1797 that construction and decoration were complete (Fontana 1963). Judgments concerning the methods of the church builders and artisans must be based on our knowledge of the technology used in New Spain and by the medieval cathedral builders of Europe. Occasionally the church itself yields visual clues to methods of its construction. Such was the case with respect to several holes found in the walls of the nave and main dome, shedding light on the problem of determining how domes over the crossing and sacristy and the low roof vaults were erected. This paper considers several visual clues in the church structure pointing to alternative methods of dome and vault construction and explaining the builders' solution to the problem of constructing a round dome over San Xavier's square transept crossing." J

124. Habig, Marion A. MISSION SAN JOSÉ Y SAN MIGUEL DE AGUAYO, 1720-1824. *Southwestern Hist. Q. 1968 71(4): 496-516.* A Franciscan mission in East Texas was a casualty of the French thrust westward from Louisiana in 1719. With the Spanish retreat there was a pullback to the newly founded halfway station of San Antonio. There, in 1720, Mission San José y San Miguel de Aguayo was established. The mission flourished until the last quarter of the century. Rapid decline into poverty came thereafter. The complete secularization decree of the Mexican Government was applied to San José in 1824. After more than a century of neglect, Mission San José was restored during the 1930's. In 1941 it was dedicated as a national historic site. 75 notes.
D. L. Smith

125. Halpin, Joseph. MUSICAL ACTIVITIES AND CEREMONIES AT MISSION SANTA CLARA DE ASIS. *California Hist. Q. 1971 50(1): 35-42.* One of the more prosperous missions in the California system, Santa Clara featured an Indian choir and orchestra. The Indians learned music from Father Magín Catalá and Father José Viader. They learned two-part and four-part singing and participated in the singing at Masses, religious festivals, and special services. Musical instruments included violins, small drums, triangles, and flutes. Following secularization, Mission Santa Clara de Asís declined rapidly; the Indians scattered, and most of the musical instruments were lost or stolen. Based on secondary sources; photo, 20 notes.
A. Hoffman

126. Hays, Alden. THE MISSING CONVENTO OF SAN ISIDRO. *Palacio 1968 75(4): 35-40.* Excavations at Gran Quivira National Monument were conducted by the National Park Service from 1965 to 1967. The work resulted in evidence that the mission of San Isidro had been built at the large Pueblo village of Las Humanas by Fray Francisco Letrado in 1629. Another Franciscan, Fray Diego de Santander, returned to this mission, abandoned by Letrado in 1632, and built a larger structure dedicated to San Buenaventura. Documented, illus.
S. A. Eger

127. Hefter, J. and Ferrer-Llull, Francisco. SPANISH TEXAS HUSSARS, CA. 1803. *Military Collector and Historian 1965 17(4): 118-120.* Describes the dress of this unusual military unit *(Usares de Texas)* which temporarily replaced the century-old Cuera Dragoons in 1800. The radical changes in the Spanish frontier military organization, tactics, dress, and armament were made by Ramón de Murillo. Original manuscripts, including Murillo's *plan demostrativo,* are cited. Illus., 3 notes.
C. L. Boyd

128. Heric, Thomas M. RANCHO LA BREA: ITS HISTORY AND ITS FOSSILS. *J. of the West 1969 8(2): 209-230.* Traces the history of Rancho La Brea from its first sighting by Father Juan Crespi, who accompanied Portola in 1769, down to the present day. Centers on the fossil excavations, particularly as they relate to the Department of Paleontology at the University of California, Berkeley, and the Los Angeles County Museum. Includes several photographs showing the Hancock home at the Rancho, excavations in progress, and George Allan, Ida, and Major Henry Hancock. J

129. Hillebrand, Timothy S. TENTATIVE SUMMARY OF ARCHAEOLOGICAL FINDINGS AT THE PRESIDIO CHAPEL SITE. *Noticias 1967 13(4): 18-23.* Summarizes archaeological finds on the Spanish presidio chapel site of Santa Barbara, California. The "dig's" main aim "was to determine the exact location of the Chapel." Describes positions of the test trenches. Of the 109 recorded burials, three were located. A pink layer, possibly a plaster floor, was found and dated as post-1884. The exact width and length of the chapel were determined and the eastern sacristy positively located. For reconstruction there is already a choice of a pre- or post-1797 design; but more excavation should be done when funds are available. Note.
T. M. Condon

130. Hutchinson, C. Alan. THE MEXICAN GOVERNMENT AND THE MISSION INDIANS OF UPPER CALIFORNIA, 1821-1835. *Americas 1964 21(4): 335-362.* Efforts to promote the development of California inevitably involved the status of the Indian missions, which had been adversely affected by the Mexican war of independence but whose Indian charges provided the main labor force. Measures for gradual secularization, with a view to converting the Indians into independent farmers, were followed in 1833 by a law for full, immediate secularization. But the latter left unsettled the disposition of the mission lands, which became a subject of considerable confusion and debate. Based on a wide variety of primary (including unpublished) and secondary sources. 126 notes.
D. Bushnell

131. Hutchinson, Charles E. JUAN CRESPI, DIARIST. *California Historian 1968 14(3): 89-92.* The pathfinder Fray Juan Crespi deserves recognition for helping to open up the State of California. Not much is known about the Franciscan monk except that he wrote of the difficulties that were encountered in establishing missions in California. In his diary he told of finding a new harbor, San Francisco Bay, wrote down interesting observations about the natives on the coast between Ventura and Santa Barbara and took readings of the latitude at important points along the journey. The father was appointed missionary at Monterey and his last great venture was the exploration of the territory north of San Francisco on board of the frigate *Santiago.* After the Alaskan voyage, Father Crespi made his home at Mission San Carlos Borromeo at Carmel. His diaries are valuable in understanding the development of early California settlements.
O. L. Miller

132. Ives, Ronald L. THE BELL OF SAN MARCELO. *Kiva 1963 29(1): 14-22.* "Legends concerning the supposed bell of San Marcelo Sonoitac on the Arizona-Sonora border are reviewed and the history of the Wellton bell is reconstructed. The latter bell is found to be unrelated to San Marcelo which, despite legend, may never have possessed a bell." J

133. Kessell, John L. ANZA DAMNS THE MISSIONS: A SPANISH SOLDIER'S CRITICISM OF INDIAN POLICY, 1772. *J. of Arizona Hist. 1972 13(1): 53-63.* Because of reaction to charges that the mission administration of Sonora needed spiritual and temporal overhauling, a full-scale investigation was set in motion in 1772. As captain of the garrison at Tubac in southern Arizona, Juan Bautista de Anza (1735-88) prepared a report which is here reproduced in translation. Paternalism of the missionaries, he asserted, stifled the rapid assimilation of the Indians. He urged administrative reform. 14 notes.
D. L. Smith

134. Kessell, John L. DOCUMENTS OF ARIZONA HISTORY: A PERSONAL NOTE FROM TUMACACORI, 1825. *J. of Arizona Hist. 1965 6(3): 147-151.* Tumacacori, now a national monument, was one of eight pioneer missions in the Pimeria Alta established by the Franciscan order. Quoted here is a letter from Fray Ramon Liberos, then serving as resident missionary, to an unknown friend, dated 20 November 1825. The letter comments on church and Indian affairs and is believed to be the last letter from the last Franciscan at the mission. Introduction and 20 notes, many from Spanish and Mexican archives.
J. D. Filipiak

135. Kessell, John L. FATHER EIXARCH AND THE VISITATION AT TUMACACORI, MAY 12, 1775. *Kiva 1965 30(3): 77-81.* "This official account of conditions in 1775 at Mission San José de Tumacácori, while teasingly vague in some respects, does provide a small beam into the hazy first decade of Franciscan administration in Pimería Alta. A biographical sketch of the capable missionary Father Thomás Eixarch precedes the document." J

136. Kessell, John L. FATHER RAMON AND THE BIG DEBT, TUMACACORI, 1821-1823. *New Mexico Hist. R. 1969 44(1): 53-72.* Relates the attempt by the Padre of Tumacácori, Father Ramón Liberós, to obtain payment from the sale of four thousand head of cattle by his predecessor, Father Juan Bautista Estelric, to Lieutenant don Ignacio Perez. The cattle were sold in 1821 to raise money for church construction. The debt was eventually paid, although the church was not completed when Father Ramón and other Franciscans were banished in 1828. 37 notes. D. F. Henderson

137. Kessell, John L. THE MAKING OF A MARTYR: THE YOUNG FRANCISCO GARCES. *New Mexico Hist. R. 1970 45(3): 181-196.* A brief biographical sketch of Father Francisco Garcés, killed by the Yuma Indians at Yuma Crossing, New Mexico, on 17 July 1781. Born in 1738 in Aragon, Spain, he was educated at the convent of San Crístobal de Alpartir. Inspired by two friars from a missionary college in Mexico, he left Spain in 1763, survived a shipwreck, and arrived in Mexico late in 1763. After five years at the college, he volunteered to serve in Sonora. 44 notes. D. F. Henderson

138. Kessell, John L. THE PUZZLING PRESIDIO SAN PHELIPE DE GUEVAVI, ALIAS TERRENATE. *New Mexico Hist. R. 1966 41(1): 21-46.* Traces in minute detail the history of the presidio from its establishment in 1742 until its demise in 1775. Located on a spot known locally as San Mateo de Terrenate, in Sonora, Mexico it was designated by at least six different names during its first 10 years, thus creating a puzzle about its true location. It was an outpost of defense against Apache raids, especially for the Guevavi Mission in what is now Arizona. Based on both printed and various archival materials. D. F. Henderson

139. Kessell, John L. SAN JOSE DE TUMACACORI - 1773: A FRANCISCAN REPORTS FROM ARIZONA. *Arizona and the West 1964 6(4): 303-312.* Franciscan Father Bartholomé Ximeno was sent as a missionary to the Pima Indians in Pimería Alta on the far northwestern frontier of New Spain and stationed at Tumacácori in present southern Arizona. His tenure there was for a little over a year. The forced Jesuit exodus and their replacement by Franciscans was part of a reform program in Tumacácori and elsewhere in New Spain. The missionaries were requested in 1772 to contribute their suggestions for a new plan for temporal and spiritual government of the missions. Father Ximeno took full advantage of this opportunity to express himself in a report of 5 March 1773 to his superior. The report, translated, edited, and reproduced here, constitutes the earliest account of conditions at Tumacácori by a Franciscan. It is also a commentary on the Apache-harrassed frontier of northwestern New Spain. Based on microfilm copy, University of Arizona Library, facsimile Library, and reproduction of a 1772 Ximeno burial record; map, 23 notes. D. L. Smith

140. Ladd, Ellen. FATHER SERRA STILL TEACHING. *California Historian 1964 10(3): 77-78.* Celebration of Serra's 250th birthday and dedication of his birthplace in Petra, Majorca as a historic and religious shrine. S

141. Lavender, David. BUILDING A NEW WORLD: THE WHITE MAN'S MIGHTY EFFORT TO CIVILIZE THE FIRST CALIFORNIANS. *Am. West 1971 8(6): 36-41, 60-61.* Missionaries were principal instruments of Spanish policy in the extension of New Spain into California in the second half of the 18th century. Peripatetic missionaries ministered to sedentary and submissive Indians in their native villages. More generally in California, however, the Indians were neither sedentary nor submissive, and distances from Mexico precluded adequate military protection. The Indians were lured into mission compounds or stations with promises of free-food, wondrous trinkets, music, and pageantry. Spiritual teaching was but a part of a larger program including lessons in agriculture and handicrafts. The missionaries were, in effect, political as well as spiritual agents. Saving souls was the religious goal, but it also became necessary to substitute "civilized" Indians for European colonists who failed to come to New Spain in sufficient numbers to populate the new territories. Eventually the mission population reached 20 thousand. Mexican law of 1824 secularized mission property. By the time of the 1849 gold rush, the great majority of these Indians were absorbed into agricultural peonage on California's ranches. 4 illus. D. L. Smith

142. Leutenegger, Benedict, ed. and trans. NEW DOCUMENTS ON FATHER JOSÉ MARIANO REYES. *Southwestern Hist. Q. 1968 71(4): 583-602.* Franciscan Father José Mariano Reyes, apparently well-loved by the Indians with whom he worked, was a poor manager of mission affairs and conducted business and correspondence with ecclesiastical and political superiors directly rather than through prescribed channels. He was transferred from mission to mission in Texas. Charges were brought against him repeatedly and some of his actions were reversed. The four translated and edited letters, two from Reyes himself, are concerned with some of these matters. They reveal the character of Reyes and give a view of some of the internal problems of the mission system. 52 notes. D. L. Smith

143. Leutenegger, Benedict. [TWO FRANCISCAN DOCUMENTS ON EARLY SAN ANTONIO, TEXAS]. *Americas 1968 25(2): 191-206.*
SAN ANTONIO AND FATHER ANTONIO DE OLIVARES, O.F.M., 1716, *pp. 191-199.* Presents a biographical sketch of [San Buenaventura y] Olivares, who was long active in Franciscan missionary work in Mexico as well as in Spanish Texas, and who was among the founders of San Antonio in 1718. The author provides in translation a report of 1716 by Olivares to the Viceroy of New Spain. It describes the region of San Antonio and its Indian inhabitants in generally optimistic terms.
SAN ANTONIO AND FR. BENITO FERNANDEZ, *pp. 199-206.* Provides a letter in translation by Texas missionary Benito Fernández [de Santa Ana], which was written in 1740. The letter describes the region and inhabitants, expressing satisfaction with the progress of the work of conversion. Both documents are from the Biblioteca Nacional, Mexico City. Based mainly on primary and secondary published sources; 52 notes. D. Bushnell

144. Marín H., Miguel. UN MISIONERO POBLANO EN LA PIMERIA ALTA [A colonizing missionary in "Pímeria Alta"]. *Abside [Mexico] 1968 32(4): 404-425.* Refers to the Franciscan friar Ignacio Ramírez de Arellano (Puebla, 1770-1805). In letters he sent to his brother Joaquín and other relatives, he gave some data on the Indians among whom he worked for a brief period. Based on letters in the possession of the author, a descendant of the Ramírez Arellano family. T. G. (IHE 72242)

145. McGloin, John Bernard. A DEDICATION TO THE MEMORY OF PETER MASTEN DUNNE, S.J., 1889-1957. *Arizona and the West 1963 5(2): 96-100.* Peter Masten Dunne, Jr., a Jesuit scholar whose formal training was in early modern European history emphasizing the Renaissance and Reformation, became "the foremost interpreter" of the Jesuits in colonial New Spain after his mentor and doctoral adviser, Herbert Eugene Bolton. In the classroom and in his writings, he stressed the interrelation of Latin American and European cultures. Illus., biblio. listing of Dunne's writings. D. L. Smith

146. Meadows, Don. THE ORIGINAL SITE OF MISSION SAN JUAN CAPISTRANO. *Southern California Q. 1967 49(3): 337-343.* In a response to the Reverend Maynard Geiger's article which proved the existence of an earlier site for Mission San Juan Capistrano than the present one, the author seeks to pinpoint the exact original location. Using bits of information gleaned from a number of sources, he concludes that the first mission which existed from 1776 to 1778 was located where the home of Pierre Lacouague now stands. This places the original site in San Juan Canyon two miles east-northeast of its present location, on a knoll on the south side of San Juan Creek. Based on published documents, diaries, and U.S. Geological Survey maps; 10 notes. W. L. Bowers

147. Moriarty, James Robert, III. HISTORIC SITE ARCHAEOLOGY AT MISSION SAN DIEGO DE ALCALA. *Masterkey 1969 43(3): 100-108.* The recent excavation of the Mission of San Diego was the pilot project for the newly formed graduate and undergraduate level course, "Historic Sites Methods," established in August 1966 at the University of San Diego as a joint endeavor by the History and Anthropology Departments. Discusses reasons behind the course, present work, and goals. 5 photos. C. N. Warren

148. Quinn, Robert M. SPANISH COLONIAL STYLE: THE ARCHITECTURAL ORIGINS OF THE SOUTHWESTERN MISSIONS. *Am. West 1966 3(3): 56-66, 93, 94.* All other arts served in accessory and subservient roles to architecture in New Spain. However it was modified by local tradition and techniques, it was nonetheless Spanish. The stylistic taproots of Spanish architecture are traced back to Moslem and Christian art forms and cultural influences. The Spanish blend was brought to the New World soon after the conquest and adapted to new and strange conditions as it spread into the American Southwest. The architecture of the frontier missions is the most northerly penetration of this art form and is one of Spain's lasting contributions to the area's cultural life. Illus., biblio. note. D. L. Smith

149. Ruiz, Juanita. FAREWELL, BATUC - A LOST HISTORIC SITE. *J. of Arizona Hist. 1965 6(3): 152-154.* Batuc, a mission established by Spanish Jesuits as early as 1629, was inundated by water in 1964, the backup from the El Novillo dam. The author describes her visit to the scene after the facade of the mission had been removed, and before it was covered by water. Illus., biblio. J. D. Filipiak

150. Servín, Manuel P. COSTANSO'S 1794 REPORT ON STRENGTHENING NEW CALIFORNIA'S PRESIDIOS. *California Hist. Soc. Q. 1970 49(3): 221-232.* A translation of Don Miguel Costansó's report to the Marqués de Branciforte, the Viceroy of New Spain. An astute and enlightened observer, Costansó urged the Spanish Government to strengthen its Alta California colony militarily, economically, and socially. He suggested "Hispanicizing" of the colony by bringing in people of Spanish and Spanish-Indian blood, by supplying farming equipment from the Crown, and by greater attention to the potential of the California seaports. Had Costansó's ideas been implemented, Manifest Destiny would have encountered a California quite different from the isolated province it was. 16 notes. A. Hoffman

151. Smith, Watson and Fontana, Bernard L. RELIGIOUS SACRAMENTALS FROM AWATOVI. *Kiva 1970 36(2): 13-16.* "In 1966 a 17th Century metal crucifix was discovered near the nave of the church of San Bernardo at Awatovi [in Arizona]. It is similar in style to religious medals associated with graves beneath the floor of the nave." J

152. Speiss, Lincoln Bunce. CHURCH MUSIC IN SEVENTEENTH-CENTURY NEW MEXICO. *New Mexico Hist. R. 1965 40(1): 5-21.* Indicates that church music did reach a surprising state of development in 17th-century New Mexico, but the actual music used has not been found. D. F. Henderson

153. Stephens, W. Barclay. TIME AND THE OLD CALIFORNIA MISSIONS. *California Historian 1968 14(4): 127-136.* Describes the efforts of the Spanish to establish two missions in the present State of California. The author describes some of the difficulties, hardships, heartaches, and dependence on ships. The story centers around Junípero Serra, a Franciscan monk who, in 1749, set sail for Mexico to work in the missionary field. Soon afterward Serra and other missionaries were sent to California by King Carlos of Spain to open new missions at San Diego and Monterey. The author discusses their efforts to do so, emphasizing the problems of the frontier including the need for accurate time measurement such as a chronometer, a calender and sun dials, or mechanical timepieces. The article closes with a description of the timepieces used in the California missions. O. L. Miller

154. Warner, Ted J. DON FELIX MARTINEZ AND THE SANTA FE PRESIDIO, 1693-1730. *New Mexico Hist. R. 1970 45(4): 269-310.* Between 1693 and 1710 Don Félix Martínez established a satisfactory record as a soldier in the ranks and as commander of the garrison in New Mexico. In 1710 he was sent to Mexico City, armed with power of attorney from the soldiers. During his stay, he took no effective action to help the soldiers; instead, he used his stay to seek personal preferment. In September 1715 he was named governor ad interim of New Mexico, a position he held until January 1717 when he was summoned to Mexico City, arrested, and confined for the next 8 years. Upon release, Martínez was given permission to return to New Mexico to enlist support to win final vindication. The testimony he obtained was eventually turned over to the viceroy, but there is no record of viceregal action. Based on various records in the Archivo General de las Indias (Seville), Archivo General de la Nación (Mexico), and the Spanish Archives of New Mexico; 127 notes. D. F. Henderson

155. Warner, Ted J. FRONTIER DEFENSE. *New Mexico Hist. R. 1966 41(1): 5-20.* Traces the establishment of Spanish dominion in the vast expanse of northern Mexico, including the southwestern borderlands of the United States. "By 1725 a line of frontier presidios extended in an irregular arc across two thousand miles from Sonora to Eastern Texas." The 16 posts were garrisoned by a total force of only 806 officers and men. The New Mexico presidios, important links in the chain of outposts, were El Paso (established in 1683) and Santa Fe (established in 1693). Based on printed sources and material from the Archivo General de la Nación, México, and the Archivo General de Indias, Seville. 26 notes. D. F. Henderson

156. Weber, Francis J. THE CALIFORNIA MISSIONS AND THEIR VISITORS. *Americas 1968 24(4): 319-336.* The isolation of upper California was gradually lessened as foreign vessels began to frequent the area in the late 18th century. The published observations of foreign visitors gave both detailed information and widely varying viewpoints on the Franciscan mission system. In chronological order, the work of 24 authors is briefly discussed, each of whom "noticeably influenced later chroniclers and historians of the period." Based on published writings of the authors in question and on later historical and bibliographical literature; 119 notes. D. Bushnell

157. Weber, Francis J. CALIFORNIA'S SERRANA LITERATURE. *Southern California Q. 1969 51(4): 325-342.* A bibliographic essay concerned with the published writings (1787-1969) by and about Fray Junípero Serra, "the Golden State's most outstanding historical and religious pioneer." Nearly 60 primary and secondary works are discussed. Excluded are most periodical articles and newspaper stories normally available in libraries. W. L. Bowers

158. Weber, Francis J. THE DEVELOPMENT OF ECCLESIASTICAL JURISDICTION IN THE CALIFORNIAS. *Records of the Am. Catholic Hist. Soc. of Philadelphia 1964 75(2): 93-102.* Traces the evolution of episcopal authority in the Californias from the background of the viceroyalty of New Spain in the 16th century to the 12 units of ecclesiastical jurisdiction in California in the 20th century. 3 tables. W. J. Grattan

159. Weber, Francis J. JOHN THOMAS DOYLE, PIOUS FUND HISTORIOGRAPHER. *Southern California Q. 1967 49(3): 297-303.* John Thomas Doyle was a lawyer and scholar who figures prominently in early California history. Born in New York City in 1819, he led a varied life which included residence and schooling in Ireland, work in Nicaragua, a position on the first Board of Regents of the University of California, service as a trustee of the San Francisco Law Library, a term as a State Commissioner of Transportation, interest in viniculture, and activity aimed at promoting the collection and preservation of original documents. It was in his role as lawyer and historiographer that he did important work concerned with the Pious Fund case. This fund, formed by charitable Catholics during the Spanish colonial period to further the conversion and civilization of Indians in California, was secularized and incorporated into the Mexican treasury in 1842 and the case involved the Church's effort to get annuities from Mexico. Doyle prepared evidence used in two successful court battles and gathered together the documents and publications relating to the case. Nineteen of these are listed with brief annotations for each. Based on secondary sources; 18 notes, biblio. W. L. Bowers

160. Weber, Francis J. MISSION SAN GABRIEL'S BICENTENNIAL. *Southern California Q. 1971 53(3): 179-183.* Traces the Spanish missionary effort in Lower and Upper California. Such work was a prime factor in Spanish colonial success in the New World. Mission San Gabriel, now 200 years old, was typical of Spanish missions in the Californias in that it performed a Christianizing and civilizing function among the Indians. Based on secondary sources; 15 notes. W. L. Bowers

161. Weber, F. J. THE PIOUS FUND OF THE CALIFORNIAS. *Hispanic Am. Hist. R. 1963 43(1): 78-94.* From funds originally raised to permit the Society of Jesus to colonize California, the capital of the Pious Fund grew to over one million dollars. Seized by the Spanish crown after the expulsion of the Jesuits in 1767, the Fund passed to the Mexican government when Mexico won its independence. In 1842 President Antonio Lopez de Santa Anna took the assets of the Fund, but unsold proper-

ties were restored to the Church in 1845. The Bishops of California took the case to the Mixed Claims Commission on land titles, which ruled for them and against Mexico in 1875. Other aspects of the case, taken before the Hague Tribunal, saw a ruling favorable for the Church in 1903. A detailed account of the legal maneuvers, and of the disbursement of the funds received is followed by comments on the current status of the Fund, for no monies have been realized since 1913. B. B. Solnick

162. Weber, Francis J. SAN FERNANDO MISSION: AN HISTORICAL GLANCE. *Records of the Am. Catholic Hist. Soc. of Philadelphia 1965 76(3): 174-187.* Traces the operations, growth, formalities of ownership, and architecture of Mission San Fernando Rey de España since its foundation in 1797, as well as its decline following the American seizure of California. 31 notes. J. M. McCarthy

163. Weber, Francis J. THE STATIONS AT MISSION SAN FERNANDO. *Masterkey 1965 39(1): 7-12.* Traces the succession of moves of the 14 stations of the Cross which originated at Mission San Fernando around 1800 and are now claimed by Mission San Gabriel. The author urges their return to their rightful home. Based on primary and secondary sources; illus., biblio. C. N. Warren

164. Weber, Francis J. THE UNITED STATES VERSUS MEXICO: THE FINAL SETTLEMENT OF THE PIOUS FUND OF THE CALIFORNIAS. *Southern California Q. 1969 51(2): 97-152.* The Pious Fund was a charitable trust formed by Catholics during the Spanish colonial period to further missionary work in the Californias. In 1842 the Mexican Government took control of the trust and incorporated it into the national treasury. This is a detailed discussion of the long struggle by the Catholic Church in California to gain annual payments derived from the fund from the Republic of Mexico. High points of the complicated litigation included: 1) the arbitral decision of the Mixed Claims Commission in 1875 which awarded annual payments of 43,050.99 dollars (Mexican) to the California Church for the years between 1848 when California became a part of the United States and 1868 when Mexico agreed to submit the dispute to the Commission; 2) the decision of the Hague Tribunal in 1902 which extended the application of the earlier award and required Mexico to pay a lump sum for the 33 years of unpaid annuities and the annual payments in perpetuity; 3) Mexico's refusal to make payments after 1914 because of deteriorating relations with the United States and because of American refusal to abide by an arbitral decision in 1911 which required the return to Mexico of the Chamizal, 823 acres of land detached from Mexico at El Paso, Texas, when the Rio Grande River created a new channel in 1864; and, 4) the final settlement of the Pious Fund case reached in August 1967, when the California Church waived perpetual payments for a lump sum payment. Based on original and secondary sources; 205 notes. W. L. Bowers

165. Weber, F. J. VERSATILE FRANCISCAN LINGUIST. *Masterkey 1968 42(4): 153-156.* Felipe Arroyo de la Cuesta arrived at Mission San Juan Bautista in 1808 where he served as administrator for 25 years. During this time he made extensive notes on the languages, history, colonization, exploration, and settlement of the area. The ethnological accomplishments of Father Arroyo on the California frontier certainly deserve more than the scant recognition afforded him. 16 notes. C. N. Warren

166. Weber, Francis J. ZEPHYRIN ENGELHARDT, O.F.M., DEAN OF CALIFORNIA MISSION HISTORIANS. *Southern California Q. 1965 47(3): 235-243.* Zephyrin Engelhardt was born at Bilshausen, Hanover, Germany, 13 November 1851, and came to America the following year. He studied in Covington, Kentucky, Quincy, Illinois, and St. Louis, and was ordained in 1878. He first taught at St. Joseph's College in Cleveland, then was sent to do missionary work in the Midwest, New York, and California. In 1900 he returned to California, working for a period at Banning's Indian Boarding School before transfer to Mission Santa Barbara, where he spent most of the rest of his life. In addition to his numerous publications (many described here), he organized and added to the now famous historical collections in the Santa Barbara Mission Archives. He died in 1934 in Santa Barbara. 40 notes. A. K. Main

167. Weddle, Robert S. THE SAN SABA MISSION: APPROACH TO THE GREAT PLAINS. *Great Plains J. 1965 4(2): 29-38.* Deals primarily with failure of the Spanish attempt to maintain a northern military and religious outpost at the San Sabá Mission (now Menard, Texas) from 1757 to 1770. The failure resulted from vacillating Spanish policies and the power of the Plains Indians - especially the Comanches. It marked the turning point for the Spanish Empire in Texas. Based on both primary and secondary sources listed at the end. O. H. Zabel

168. Whiting, Alfred F. FATHER PORRAS AT AWATOVI AND THE FLYING NUN. *Plateau 1971 44(2): 60-66.* "An account of flying visits to New Mexico in the 17th century made by a Spanish nun (or two) and the effects of these visits upon the men who built at Awatovi the first mission church among the Hopi." J

169. Yates, Richard. LOCATING THE COLORADO RIVER MISSION [OF] SAN PEDRO Y SAN PABLO DE BICUNER. *J. of Arizona Hist. 1972 13(2): 123-130.* A perpetuated error places the location of the mission of San Pedro y San Pablo de Bicuner downriver from Yuma at Pilot Knob on the California side of the Colorado River. A careful reading of the Spanish documents, however, places the mission upstream from Yuma near present-day Laguna Dam. Since the site is now bisected by a canal, archeological confirmation of this location is no longer possible. The mission was destroyed in the Yuma Indian uprising of 1781. Map, 16 notes. D. L. Smith

170. —. MISSION SAN GABRIEL ARCANGEL, A PICTORIAL PORTFOLIO. *Southern California Q. 1971 53(3): 251-279.* Includes 27 photographs from the Santa Barbara Mission Archives depicting Mission San Gabriel Arcángel from the first painting of it in 1832 to recent times. W. L. Bowers

Colonization

171. Adams, Eleanor B., and Algier, Keith W. A FRONTIER BOOK LIST—1800. *New Mexico Hist. R. 1968 43(1): 49-59.* A book list which appeared in the inventory of the belongings of Joaquín de Amézqueta, a Basque merchant who arrived on the Northern frontier of New Spain sometime during the second half of the 18th century. 38 titles. D. F. Henderson

172. Becker, Robert. DISEÑOS [Sketch maps]. *Am. West 1967 4(1): 55-64, 92-95.* An 1824 colonization law, further clarified by an 1828 regulation, was the basic instrument for the establishment of land titles in Mexican California. It provided for the method of disposing of the public domain. Its provisions were construed to mean that an individual could receive up to 11 leagues, about fifty thousand acres, in a single grant for the purpose of cattle raising. The specified process began when a petitioner submitted a *diseño* to the governor with a request for title to the tract of land he wished. The sketch map was a pencil, ink, crayon, or even watercolor production, sometimes quite primitive and at other times quite sophisticated, and frequently similar to 16th- and 17th-century Mexican maps. The accompanying petition cited the petitioner's Mexican citizenship, any services he may have rendered his country, and described the land as vacant and available. Included is a description of the follow-through from presentation of the petition to its grant and some of the legal problems involved when California became American territory. Illus., biblio., note. D. L. Smith

173. Benson, Nettie Lee, ed. and trans. A GOVERNOR'S REPORT ON TEXAS IN 1809. *Southwestern Hist. Q. 1968 71(4): 603-615.* As a result of reform in the wake of the Napoleonic invasion of Spain, New Spain sent a representative to sit on the governing junta in Spain. Texas Governor Manuel María de Salcedo y Quiroga prepared a detailed report on the state of affairs in his province for the instruction and information of New Spain's junta representative. Dated 8 August 1809, the document deals with economic, demographic, political growth potential, Indian and American affairs. 45 notes. D. L. Smith

174. Bradfute, Richard W. THE LAS ANIMAS LAND GRANT, 1843-1900. *Colorado Mag. 1970 47(1): 26-43.* Traces the history of the Las Animas Grant in Colorado, which was made by the Mexican Government in 1843 prior to conquest by the United States. The author con-

cludes that the grant illustrates the problems caused by congressional indecision in its attempts to determine property rights. Congress delayed action upon property claims and made no consistent rules for deciding them. Results included fraud, substantial litigation which reached the U.S. Supreme Court several times, and the clouding of land titles. Not until 1900 was the struggle over the land claims concluded. Illus., maps, 69 notes.   O. H. Zabel

175. Bridges, Katherine and DeVille, Winston, trans. and ed. NATCHITOCHES AND THE TRAIL TO THE RIO GRANDE: TWO EARLY EIGHTEENTH-CENTURY ACCOUNTS BY THE SIEUR DERBANNE. *Louisiana Hist. 1967 8(3): 239-259.* Two descriptions of Louisiana and Texas by François Dion Deprez Derbanne, an early settler in Atchitoches, and a biographical sketch of Derbanne. The first account was written by Derbanne at Dauphin Island on 1 November 1717. "Journey of the Canadians, Graveline, Derbanne, LaFrésniè and DeBeaulieu, to the Rio Grande River [sic] 1716-1717," translated from Pierre A. Margry, *Découvertes et Etablissements des Français (1614-1754),* 6 Vols. (Paris, 1877-86). The second is Derbanne's "Relation du poste de Natchitoches," prepared in New Orleans 22 October 1723, translated from a copy located in the Newberry Library. 74 notes.
                                                    R. L. Woodward

176. Brody, J. J. and Colberg, Anne. A SPANISH-AMERICAN HOMESTEAD NEAR PLACITAS, NEW MEXICO. *Palacio 1966 73(2): 11-20.* The authors describe the excavation of a New Mexico homestead. Because the written records of early New Mexico colonists are scarce or nonexistent, the authors discuss methods of reconstructing the daily life of the colonial New Mexican by combining archeology with historical research. 3 photos, table, 10 notes, biblio.   S. A. Eger

177. Carranco, Lynwood. ANZA'S BONES IN ARIZPE. *J. of the West 1969 8(3): 416-428.* Outlines the career of Juan Bautista de Anza (1735-88), a central figure in the settlement of California. He led a large company of men, women, and children on his second expedition to California in 1776, and founded a colony at San Francisco Bay. After returning to Mexico he was made governor of New Mexico (which then embraced what is now California, Arizona, New Mexico, Texas, and northern Mexico), serving from 1777 to 1787. In 1963 his bones were discovered in the cathedral of Nuestra Señora de Asunción in Arizpe, situated in a picturesque valley in the Sierra Madre Mountains in Sonora. Included are photographs of the cathedral and Anza's bones.
                                                    R. N. Alvis

178. Chaban, Ruth. THE ACEQUIA MADRE OF SANTA FE, NEW MEXICO. *Historic Preservation 1971 23(2): 10-14.* Discusses efforts to trace and reestablish the Acequia Madre (mother ditch) of the old Spanish irrigation system of Santa Fe. The acequia was constructed "shortly after 1610" and can still be seen in the southern side of the city. Notes that "even today the Acequia Madre is governed by the age-old Spanish laws, with a mayordomo de acequia and three commissioners to supervise its upkeep." Recently a survey of its course has been completed and the Acequia Madre is now a historic site in the New Mexico State Register of Cultural Properties. Photos.   J. M. Hawes

179. Collins, Karen Sikes, ed. FRAY PEDRO DE ARRIQUIBAR'S CENSUS OF TUCSON, 1820. *J. of Arizona Hist. 1970 11(1): 14-22.* Fray Pedro Antonio de Arriquibar, chaplain of the Royal Presidio of San Agustin del Tucson, in 1820 compiled the earliest known detailed listing of Tucson residents. His count lists by name the heads of households and their wives, and enumerates the other members of the household. Of special interest are the names of soldiers and civilians, many of whom are direct ancestors of present-day southern Arizona families. Statistical observations can be deduced from this enumeration of Fray Pedro's 395 parishioners. Includes the census. Illus., 15 notes.   D. L. Smith

180. Coughlin, Magdalen. BOSTON SMUGGLERS ON THE COAST (1797-1821): AN INSIGHT INTO THE AMERICAN ACQUISITION OF CALIFORNIA. *California Hist. Soc. Q. 1967 46(2): 99-120.* The inability of Spain to cope with the needs of far-removed colonies on the California coast gave American ships an opportunity. They supplied the necessary service by smuggling, since the official Spanish policy was one of tight control of trade. By 1803-04, four ships were putting into California ports. The beginning of the Spanish-American Wars of Inde-

pendence in 1816 made the Californians almost completely dependent on the New Englanders. "With the coming of Mexican independence the Spanish mercantilistic policy was overthrown and a new liberal commercial system adopted." Hides and tallow became prominent items of trade. 66 notes.   E. P. Stickney

181. Din, Gilbert C. PROPOSALS AND PLANS FOR COLONIZATION IN SPANISH LOUISIANA, 1787-1790. *Louisiana Hist. 1970 11(3): 197-213.* Encouraging Americans to migrate to Spanish Louisiana, Governor Esteban Miró cooperated with private immigration agents such as Agustin Macarty, William Fitzgerald, Mauricio Nowland, James Kennedy, Peter and Bryan Bruin, John Leamy, Peter Paulus, and George Morgan. Royal Orders of 1787 and 1788 provided a friendly legal base for such migration. "Rather than continue to exclude them, and thus risk invasion, the Spanish government permitted them to enter and to establish themselves in supervised settlements with Irish priests and small detachments of soldiers." Many colonization schemes resulted, "yet not one immigration agent was able to stimulate a massive movement of people to Louisiana. In spite of the open door to Americans, comparatively few chose to take advantage of it." Population growth in Kentucky and Tennessee during the period was much greater. Based on Spanish archival records and published works; 29 notes.   R. L. Woodward

182. Egan, Ferol. TWILIGHT OF THE CALIFORNIOS. *Am. West 1969 6(2): 34-42.* In response to the Russian movement southward along the Pacific coast from Alaska, Spain took steps in 1769 to Christianize and colonize California. Because of the relative geographic isolation from Mexico, California's Spanish settlers soon developed a culture of their own. The system of land holding, the status of missions, the stratification of society, and the gracious living of the Californios are described. This way of life was doomed with the discovery of gold in 1848 and the influx of Yankee gold seekers. Anti-Mexican attitudes, legal connivance, brazen land squatters, the 1862 smallpox epidemic, and the drought of 1863-64 closed the era of the Californios. Their culture and way of life could not compete with Yankee industry, politics, and money. 7 illus.
                                                    D. L. Smith

183. Englekirk, John E. THE PASSION PLAY IN NEW MEXICO. *Western Folklore 1966 25(1): 17-33.* Attempts to explore the background and origin of the Passion Play, one of 10 clearly independent religious Spanish folk plays in New Mexico. There is evidently no written copy of the play. A mixture of primary and secondary sources.
                                                    J. M. Brady

184. Faulk, Odie B. THE COMANCHE INVASION OF TEXAS, 1743-1836. *Great Plains J. 1969 9(1): 10-50.* Traces the background of the Spanish conflicts with the Indians on their northern frontier prior to 1743. After that date the major concern was with the Comanche Indians who were expanding into Texas. The author traces in some detail the gradual withdrawal of the Spanish until, by 1821, the population of Texas, "exclusive of Indians, was 3,500, or half of what it was reported to have been fifteen years earlier." One of the reasons Anglo-Americans petitioned the Mexican Government to make Texas a separate province in 1833 was the failure of Coahuila to provide aid against the Comanche. By the end of the Spanish and Mexican era in 1836, the Comanche were still in control of the plains and were raiding San Antonio and areas below the Rio Grande. Only years later did "an advancing technology and increasing numbers of settlers...bring defeat to this tribe and confine it within a reservation, bringing permanent peace." 119 notes.
                                                    O. H. Zabel

185. Faulk, Odie B. LAW AND THE LAND: THE LEGAL HERITAGE OF THE AMERICAN SOUTHWEST. *Am. West 1970 7(1): 14-16, 57.* Anglo-American frontiersmen found a fully developed legal structure in the European sense in the former Spanish colonial areas. It was based on Roman law and was modified to fit the exigencies of the New World. Mining, farming, and ranching were the principal economic pursuits in the Southwest and, when the United States took legal control of the region, the legislation already on the books concerning these matters was simply adopted. To a lesser extent, vestiges of the Spanish criminal code and other aspects of its legal structure are still in use today. In general, the transition from Indian to Spanish to Mexican to American legal jurisdiction was orderly.   D. L. Smith

186. Faulk, Odie B. RANCHING IN SPANISH TEXAS. *Hispanic Am. Hist. R. 1965 45(2): 257-266.* An examination of the growth of the cattle industry in Spanish Texas. Included are details of attempts to regulate and tax cattle ranching, protests by ranchers and clergy, and problems with the Indians of the area. By the late 18th century cattle had proved to be a source of revenue for the government and for the ranchers as they were exported eastward to Louisiana - illegally after Louisiana became part of the United States. Based on materials in the Béxar Archives of the University of Texas. Documented, 33 notes.

B. B. Solnick

187. Fireman, Janet R. and Servín, Manuel P. MIGUEL COSTANSO: CALIFORNIA'S FORGOTTEN FOUNDER. *California Hist. Soc. Q. 1970 49(1): 3-19.* Costansó (1741-1814) was a military engineer who accompanied Junípero Serra and Gaspar de Portolá on the expedition to colonize Alta California in 1769. Costansó rendered service as a cartographer, and he was the first man to compose a map of San Francisco Bay. In later years, Costansó, an intelligent and enlightened servant of the Crown, offered plans and advice for the settlement of Alta California. These plans included integration of the Spanish and Indian societies, the importation of settlers under favorable inducements, and the training of the Indians by artisans. These suggestions, and Costansó's condemnation of Church ownership of large areas of land, drew opposition from the Franciscan clergy. Costansó also served his monarch through his work in designing fortification, churches, and monuments; as an engineer he assisted in the project to supply water to Mexico City. In spite of his enormous contributions, Costansó has been almost entirely neglected by historians who have preferred perpetuating the Portolá-Serra viewpoints in the settlement of Alta California. Based on archival material, memoirs, contemporary documents, and secondary works; illus., photo, 57 notes.

A. Hoffman

188. Geiger, Maynard. ANTONIO MARIA BUCARELI'S CHRISTMAS OF 1776. *Southern California Q. 1968 50(4): 427-443.* Concerns two letters written by the Viceroy of New Spain Antonio María Bucareli on Christmas Day 1776. One was an eight-page letter to Junípero Serra, president of the California missions, and the other was a 28-page letter to Felipe de Neve, newly-appointed Governor of California. In both messages Bucareli "outlined his policy, revealed his plans, and spelled out his wishes for the betterment of Alta California." Translated and edited versions of the letters are presented. Bucareli's letter to Serra is in the Santa Barbara Mission Archives and a certified copy of the letter to Neve (dated 20 March 1777) is in the Mexican National Archives in Mexico City. Illus., 34 notes.

W. L. Bowers

189. Greenleaf, Richard E. ATRISCO AND LAS CIRUELAS 1722-1769. *New Mexico Hist. R. 1967 42(1): 5-25.* A case study of the battle between two branches of the Durán y Chavez family at Atrisco for the possession of Las Ciruelas. The dispute illustrates the multitude of land-holding problems in 18th-century New Mexico, including the subdivision of land, nebulous boundaries, questionable titles, and costly litigation. Based on documents in the Archive General de la Nación, Mexico; 38 notes.

D. F. Henderson

190. Guest, Florian F. THE INDIAN POLICY UNDER FERMIN FRANCISCO DE LASUEN, CALIFORNIA'S SECOND FATHER PRESIDENT. *California Hist. Soc. Q. 1966 45(3): 195-219.* That the policy of the Spanish government was one of peace toward the California Indians is clear from the correspondence of the viceroys of New Spain and the governors of New Spain. These peaceful intentions are also illustrated in the matter of legal punishments for Indian delinquents and criminals. Unfortunately, Junípero Serra, Fermín Francisco de Lasuén and their successors followed the cruel practices of punishment which were common in Europe and in New Spain for over two centuries but which the Enlightenment at home was at the time decrying. A crisis at San Francisco in 1796 showed that the Indians were overworked and underfed. Lasuén made two visits to investigate. He exonerated two missionaries (Danti and Landaeta) of crimes of which they had been accused but recommended more moderate punishment, lighter work, and cooked rations. Based chiefly on the Archive of California, Bancroft Library; the Archivo General de la Nación, Mexico; and Lasuén's writings; 88 notes.

E. P. Stickney

191. Guest, Francis F. MUNICIPAL GOVERNMENT IN SPANISH CALIFORNIA. *California Hist. Soc. Q. 1967 46(4): 307-336.* Presents evidence that municipal government in California in the Spanish period was one of military domination, a condition natural when the towns existed only to serve a military purpose. The townsmen had to do their trading under unjust conditions, with nothing to buy in return for their grain, and with fixed prices whether the harvest had been good or bad. The military regime under which the towns lived insured order and dispensed justice, but it stifled initiative and subjected townsmen to economic injustice. 120 notes.

E. P. Stickney

192. Hawgood, John A. A PROJECTED PRUSSIAN ACQUISITION OF UPPER CALIFORNIA. *Studies in Internat. Hist.: Essays Presented to W. Norton Medlicott (London: Longmans, 1967),* pp. 103-118.

193. Hawgood, John A. A PROJECTED PRUSSIAN COLONIZATION OF UPPER CALIFORNIA. *Southern California Q. 1966 48(4): 353-368.* In 1842 Baron Christian von Bunsen, Prussian minister in London, conceived the idea of purchasing and colonizing California which won the enthusiastic support of Friedrich von Roenne, Prussian minister in Washington. There was an indication that the Mexicans might be willing to sell the area, but the German Government in Potsdam rejected the scheme, apparently on the advice of Alexander von Humboldt who was recognized as the leading European authority on New Spain and the Mexican Republic. The author suggests that the Potsdam policymakers may also have realized that the United States would never accept the acquisition of California by a European power. Events later in the 1840's bear this out. Based on primary and secondary sources; 35 notes.

W. L. Bowers

194. Ives, Ronald L. FROM PITIC TO SAN GABRIEL IN 1782: THE JOURNEY OF DON PEDRO FAGES. *J. of Arizona Hist. 1968 9(4): 222-244.* The first completely annotated printing of Lieutenant Colonel Pedro Fages' 1782 journal covering his expedition from Sonora to coastal California. Fages, a Catalan minor noble, was born about 1745. Joining the army, he began his military career in Spain and then served in Mexico. In 1769 he led a segment of the original expedition sent to settle Alta California. Upon his arrival Fages became the military commander of the province. In 1774 he was relieved of his post, largely because Father Junípero Serra wanted a more capable commander. Returning to Mexico in 1782, Fages was assigned to lead a party to Alta California over the Camino del Diablo. This was a demanding chore since the land link between Alta California and Mexico had been severed by the Yuma Massacre of 1781. Leaving Sonora in late February, Fages safely led a party of 40 people by way of Yuma and the Salton Sink to Mission San Gabriel. Based on field work in Sonora, Arizona, and California, as well as published and unpublished documents; illus., 3 photos, 3 maps, 38 notes.

R. J. Roske

195. Jackson, Helen Hunt. ECHOES IN THE CITY OF THE ANGELS. *J. of the West 1968 7(3): 381-396.* This story of life in Los Angeles before the advent of American settlement is reprinted from *Century Magazine,* December 1883. Miss Jackson describes the founding of the city and the life of the early settlers in romanticized terms. She then goes on to relate anecdotes of Spanish acquaintances she had in Los Angeles in the latter half of the 19th century. Illus.

R. N. Alvis

196. Mathes, W. Michael. A BIOGRAPHICAL NOTE ON ISIDRO DE ATONDO Y ANTILLON, ADMIRAL OF THE CALIFORNIAS. *California Hist. Soc. Q. 1969 48(3): 211-218.* Efforts to colonize 17th-century California by private enterprise having proved abortive, a colonizing attempt combining secular and ecclesiastical resources was proposed in the 1670's. Atondo, a veteran Spanish soldier, petitioned and received the appointment to head the expedition. Atondo was the Governor and Captain General of Sinaloa; his career has been neglected in favor of his more famous contemporary, Eusebio Francisco Kino. In 1683, after four years of preparation, the Atondo expedition crossed the Gulf of California to the Baja California peninsula. Plans included establishment of a permanent settlement and the locating of pearl beds. Several camps were established, with hopes of a permanent colony at San Bruno. The lack of arable land prompted Atondo and Kino to cross the peninsula, the first Europeans to do so. The problems of supplying the colony and the failure to find arable land led to San Bruno's abandonment in 1685.

Despite the hopes of Atondo and Kino, the colonization attempt was suspended, chiefly because of Indian revolts occurring at this time. Atondo continued his service to the Crown and received the Order of Santiago for his efforts. Based on archival materials in the Archivo General de Indias in Seville; 28 notes.   A. Hoffman

197. Mathes, W. Michael. EARLY CALIFORNIA PROPAGANDA: THE WORKS OF FRAY ANTONIO DE LA ASCENCION. *California Hist. Q. 1971 50(2): 195-205.* A Carmelite friar, Fray Antonio de la Ascención (1573-1636), served on Vizcaíno's expedition to California in 1602-03. He joined Vizcaíno in submitting enthusiastic reports on California's possibilities for harbors, landmarks, and other advantages. Vizcaíno's plans, however, were rejected by the viceroy, who favored searching for a port on some yet-undiscovered mid-Pacific island. Despite this and other setbacks, Fray Antonio maintained his interest in California. In 1620 he submitted a report praising California's fertility, mineral resources, ports, and location, and he also remarked on a lake of gold and the Strait of Anian. Although his report received no official recognition, it was acclaimed by contemporary writers. An *audiencia,* held in 1627 to determine the feasibility of settling California in connection with pearl fishing rights, requested the padre to submit his views. He submitted two documents reiterating his opinions on California's possibilities. Fray Antonio's early writings on California stand as an important contribution to the literature on California as an attractive place for settlement. The writings influenced later writers who used Fray Antonio's work as a source of information on California. Based on archival sources in Spain and Mexico, and on published documents; 44 notes.
                                                   A. Hoffman

198. McGloin, John Bernard. WILLIAM A. RICHARDSON, FOUNDER AND FIRST RESIDENT OF YERBA BUENA. *J. of the West 1966 5(4): 493-503.* Commentators on the history of San Francisco generally emphasize the role played by the military and the missionaries in the founding process. The author contends that the city developed more from the civil pueblo of Yerba Buena than from either the presidio or the mission. William A. Richardson, founder of the pueblo, is little remembered. He was an English sailor who arrived at the port in 1822, became port captain, and married the daughter of the comandante. In 1835 he erected a tent at what is now Grant Avenue and Clay Street. Around this tent there grew up Yerba Buena which is San Francisco's most important component. Richardson deserves recognition as the founder of this community. Based on published sources; 19 notes.
                                                   D. N. Brown

199. Moriarty, James Robert, and Campbell, Walton. THE INDIANS SHALL HAVE NO WEAPONS OR HORSES. *Western Explorer 1966 4(2): 1-8.* A discussion of the beginnings of the horse-oriented culture of the Plains Indians of the southwest and of the reasons for the slow acceptance of the horse by southern California Indians. The authors challenge the conventional theory that the horses used by American Indians came from the natural increase of horses lost by early Spanish expeditions. They see the Indian acquisition of the horse as the product of the later Spanish colonial period when Pueblo Indians in the Santa Fe area drove out the Spaniards in 1680. As the Pueblo people traded horses taken from the vanquished Spanish colonists to tribes farther to the north, a distinctive horse-oriented culture was created on the plains. Indians in southern California accepted the horse more slowly because their food-gathering and nonnomadic habits required little travel, and because they were either isolated from Spanish influence by being so far inland or they were so much under Spanish control at the presidios and missions that they had no opportunity to develop their own well-defined horse culture. Based on primary and secondary sources, 5 illus., biblio.
                                                   W. L. Bowers

200. Murphy, Lawrence R. THE BEAUBIEN AND MIRANDA LAND GRANT 1841-1846. *New Mexico Hist. R. 1967 42(1): 27-47.* Detailed history of the grant given by Governor Manuel Armijo in 1841 to Carlos Beaubien and Guadalupe Miranda to the vast tract in what is today northern New Mexico and southern Colorado. Although Beaubien was unable to develop the area, he laid the groundwork for the later settlement by his sons-in-law, Jesús G. Abreu and Lucien B. Maxwell. Based on various records in the Mexican Archives of New Mexico, Santa Fe; on the Beaubien and Miranda Land Grant Papers, Bureau of Land Management; and on Records of Private Land Claims, adjudicated by the U.S. Surveyor General; 66 notes.   D. F. Henderson

201. Murray, Edward P. TUCSON, GENESIS OF A COMMUNITY. *Hist. Today [Great Britain] 1967 17(12): 835-844.* A sketch of the settlement of southwest Arizona, 1538-1848. The subjects discussed are the Spanish explorers, the settlements of the Jesuit missionaries, Indian problems, the decay of settlements after Mexico's independence, the transfer of Arizona from Mexico to the United States, and the resettlement. Illus.   L. A. Knafla

202. Myres, Sandra L. THE SPANISH CATTLE KINGDOM IN THE PROVINCE OF TEXAS. *Texana 1966 4(3): 233-246.* A study of the Spanish attempts to raise cattle on the grazing lands of Texas shows that many ranching practices associated with the American West in the 19th century had their origin during the days when Texas was a Spanish province. Among the problems the Spanish cattle raisers faced were those arising from the few civilian settlers, inadequate government control, and the frequent Indian attacks. The author calls this field of Texas research one that demands further detailed study. Based on Spanish archival material in the Archives of the University of Texas and printed documents; 38 notes.   R. J. Roske

203. Nielsen, George R., ed. BEN MILAM AND UNITED STATES AND MEXICAN RELATIONS. *Southwestern Hist. Q. 1970 73(3): 393-395.* A letter written in 1825 from Benjamin Rush Milam, an early Anglo-American in Texas, to Joel Poinsett, U.S. Minister to Mexico, regarding the drawbacks of the land market in Texas. Milam also described the frontier problems resulting from Indian raids and a growing number of refugee slaves and outlaws, suggesting the possibility of a reciprocal arrangement between Mexico and the United States for their return. No further communication between the two has been found to date.   R. W. Delaney

204. Nuttall, Donald A. THE GOBERNANTES OF SPANISH UPPER CALIFORNIA: A PROFILE. *California Hist. Q. 1972 51(3): 253-280.* A comparative study of the nine *gobernantes* (men who held direct responsibility of a region, and, after 1777, the governorship as well) of California for the Spanish colonial period, 1769-1822. The nine men shared many similarities in their background, qualifications, performance, and personality. Most were peninsular Spaniards; five of the nine were Basques or Catalans; all but one were of noble birth. All had extensive military experience and averaged 50 years of age on becoming *gobernante.* Three died while in office. The nine men devoted an average of 60 percent of their lives to the royal service. They were courageous in combat and for the most part were successful in dealing with their military subordinates and with the Franciscans. The various problems and controversies should not detract from the *gobernantes'* accomplishments, which had a fair degree of efficiency and dedication. Provides profiles of each of the *gobernantes.* Based on material from Mexican archives and on secondary sources; 36 notes.   A. Hoffman

205. Peterson, Charles E. CALIFORNIA BREA ROOFS. *Masterkey 1965 39(3): 114-118.* A review of the use of tar (Spanish brea) for the roofing of houses in California in the 18th and 19th centuries. Based on primary and secondary sources.   C. N. Warren

206. Pourade, Richard F. THE DAYS OF THE DONS. *California Historian 1964 10(5): 140-144.* Gives an account of the transition from the mission period to the rancho period in the 1830's and 1840's in southern California, a time of "turmoil and lawlessness." The gold rush days in San Diego are included.   E. P. Stickney

207. Reeve, Frank D.; Adams, Eleanor B., ed.; and Kessell, John L., ed. NAVAHO FOREIGN AFFAIRS, 1795-1846. *New Mexico Hist. R. 1971 46(2): 101-132, (3): 223-251.* Part I. Details the efforts by Spanish authorities to negotiate successful treaties with the Navaho Indians. The period of relative peace from 1720 to 1770 was ended by violence in the 1770's and early 1780's. A treaty in 1786 preserved calm until 1796. The new trouble stemmed partly from New Mexico's rising population and the need for more land. A compromise effected in 1808 by Governor Real Alencaster permitted the Navaho to remain at peace with the New Mexicans for the next several years. Based on records at the Archivo General de la Nacion, the Spanish Archives of New Mexico, and the Mexican Archives of New Mexico; 67 notes. Part II. After two years of trouble, a new Governor, don Facundo Melgares, undertook a major military campaign against the Navaho in October 1818. The 49-day campaign

failed to produce significant results. The following year, Melgares launched a more successful campaign that brought about a formal treaty, signed at Santa Fe on 21 August 1819. The resulting peace lasted but two years, and by 1821 the Navaho again were raiding. During 1822 several individuals exercised civil or military authority, or both. The confusion prevented effective action against the Indians. Finally in 1823 Bartolomé Baca became the political chief; Colonel José Antonio Vizcarra became the military chief. Vizcarra took to the field for ten weeks, from 18 June to 31 August, with considerable success. On 20 January 1824, 14 articles of peace were signed at Jémez. Based on various manuscript collections; 56 notes. Article to be continued.   D. F. Henderson

208. Ressler, John. INDIAN AND SPANISH WATER-CONTROL ON NEW SPAIN'S NORTHWEST FRONTIER. *J. of the West 1968 7(1): 10-17.* A discussion of irrigation in the Northwest frontier of New Spain ("pre-Gadsden Purchase Sonora, Baja California, and Alta California as far north as it was missionized—just north of San Francisco Bay") from 2500 B.C. to the 19th century A.D. The article centers on the interaction between the technology of the irrigation system and who built or used it—this interaction produces an "irrigation landscape." The author concluded that "from a landscape dominated by natural vegetation and landforms, the Northwest frontier of New Spain was transformed by its inhabitants into a landscape in which manifestations of culture, if not dominant, were extremely evident." Based on secondary sources; 19 notes.   E. A. Erickson

209. Robinson, W. W. LOS ALAMITOS: THE INDIAN AND RANCHO PHASES. *California Hist. Soc. Q. 1966 45(1): 21-30.* Discusses the Indian and rancho phases of Los Alamitos, a seven and one half acre parcel within the city limits of Long Beach. It includes a charming house and garden dating from Spanish days and was the site of an important Indian village, a community sometimes called Pubuna, of Shoshonean-speaking Indians who were fishermen. Father Geronimo Boascana, who served as missionary there from 1814 to 1826, wrote down their beliefs and traditions. In 1784 Manuel Perez Nieto of Sinaloa, Mexico, secured from Governor Pedro Fages a large land concession which included Los Alamitos. By 1790, Perez Nieto had settled in fertile land near Whittier, where he had large cattle operations. In a sense, the rancho period continued until 1952. Illus., 20 notes.   E. P. Stickney

210. Robinson, W. W. OUR SPANISH-MEXICAN HERITAGE. *Masterkey 1965 39(3): 104-113.* Reviews highlights dating from 1781, in the Spanish-Mexican heritage of Los Angeles, and presents a guide to several interesting historic spots in the area, with historical anecdotes. 2 illus.   C. N. Warren

211. Simmons, Marc. AN ALCALDE'S PROCLAMATION: A RARE NEW MEXICO DOCUMENT. *Palacio 1968 75(2): 5-9.* Presents a translation of the proclamation of Alcalde Don Ignacio Maria Sanchez Vergara, dated 25 April 1813, which represents an important contribution to understanding the local government in New Mexico during the colonial period. The document provides information on master-servant relations, irrigation practices, and the kind of protection provided for the Indians' farm land from the grazing livestock of the Spanish colonists. 6 notes.   S. A. Eger

212. Spell, Lota M. and Cerna, Santiago, trans. SAMUEL BANGS, IMPRESOR PIONERO EN MEXICO Y TEXAS [Samuel Bangs, pioneer printer in Mexico and Texas]. *Humanitas [Mexico] 1966 7: 441-451.* An account of Bangs's contribution to the creation of a popular press in Texas and northern Mexico from 1817 to 1847. Documented from primary source materials in the Mexican National and other archives; 44 notes.   R. G. Paulston

213. Stark, Richard. [NATIVITY PLAYS]. *Palacio 1966 73(4): 5-22.*
LOS PASTORES, *pp. 5-17.* Presents an example of the 19th-century Nativity plays, *Los Pastores.* This version of *Los Pastores* is given in both Spanish and English.
JOURNEYS OF THE SHEPHERDS, *pp. 18-22.* Discusses the music from the Nativity plays, *Los Pastores,* which were popular in New Mexico during the 19th century. The music of *Los Pastores* reveals a part of the cultural life of the rural Spanish settlers in New Mexico. Map, photo.   S. A. Eger

214. Tanner, John D., Jr. and Lothrop, Gloria R. DON JUAN FORSTER, SOUTHERN CALIFORNIA RANCHERO. *Southern California Q. 1970 52(3): 195-230.* An edition of data given in a personal interview in 1877 by John Forster, pioneer rancher of Southern California, to Thomas Savage, who was doing research for historian Hubert Howe Bancroft. Forster, known as Don Juan to early Californians, discussed the period from his arrival in Mexican California in 1832 to 1847. Forster came to California from England, started as a trader, married the sister of Don Pío Pico, last governor of Mexican California, and later became a prominent rancher. Much of the data concerns the political situation in California prior to 1846 and subsequent military activities there when hostilities began in that year between the United states and Mexico. Based on Savage's interview data in the Bancroft Library at the University of California, Berkeley; illus., 51 notes, 3 appendixes.   W. L. Bowers

215. Timmons, W. H. TADEO ORTIZ AND TEXAS. *Southwestern Hist. Q. 1968 72(1): 21-33.* Disillusioned over the prospects of Spain's New World colonies being adequately represented in the provisional government resisting Napoleonic rule in 1811, Tadeo Ortíz de Ayala espoused the cause of Mexican independence. Increasingly he became aware of the potential and importance of Texas to the over-all scheme of Mexican and Latin-American independence. Off and on, primarily through colonization schemes, Ortíz attempted to get official endorsement for involvement in Texas from the new Mexican government. Anglo-American colonization was progressing at an alarming rate. Ortíz was one of the exponents of the idea of counter-colonization with Mexicans and Europeans. An 1833 appointment as director of colonization in Texas and a scheme to bring 200 European families to Texas to counter the growing independence trend there were cut short by death from cholera as he was en route to New York to carry out his commission. 42 notes.   D. L. Smith

216. Tyler, Daniel. GRINGO VIEWS OF GOVERNOR MANUEL ARMIJO. *New Mexico Hist. R. 1970 45(1): 23-46.* Relates the views of various Anglo-Saxons about Manuel Armijo, governor of New Mexico from 1827 to 1829 and again for all but 18 months between the years 1837-46. The views presented are diverse, some extremely critical, others favorable. The Americans cited include George Wilkins Kendall, Charles Bent, James Josiah Webb, and James W. Magoffin. 68 notes.   D. F. Henderson

217. Vigness, David M. DON HUGO OCONOR AND NEW SPAIN'S NORTHEASTERN FRONTIER, 1764-1776. *J. of the West 1967 6(1): 27-40.* After the Coronado and De Soto expeditions the heroic age of Spanish exploration of the area north of Mexico ended. The northern movement slowed because the Great Plains were physically unattractive and their inhabitants hostile, but the area had to be defended in order to keep foreign powers at a far distance from New Spain's heartland. The Spanish avoided the Great Plains, however, until the Treaty of Paris of 1763 realigned intercolonial claims of Europeans in America. Now that aggressive English settlers were on their northeastern frontier, the Spanish began to look to their northern defenses. A key figure in the execution of the changing policies was the Irish-born Don Hugo Oconor. He left Ireland after the failure of a rebellion against the English. Entering the Spanish Army, he was sent to Cuba in 1763. He rose rapidly in Spanish service. In the fall of 1765 the viceroy sent him to northern New Spain to inspect the area's defensive establishment. The author traces the role played by Oconor as he moved to combat the Indian problem, cope with foreign threats, and, in general, to develop the northern region of New Spain. Based largely on primary sources; 39 notes.   D. N. Brown

218. Want, Marguerite Taylor. THE CRUMBLING ADOBES OF CHAMBERINO. *New Mexico Hist. R. 1964 39(3): 169-180.* Following the Treaty of Guadalupe Hidalgo, 1848, several New Mexicans moved to Mexico in order to remain under Mexican control. The Mexican government encouraged this by establishing colonies of immigrants from New Mexico and granting land to them. In 1852 the civil colony of Refugio was founded, which included the tiny village of Chamberino. Under the Gadsden [Purchase] Treaty of 1853, the area became US territory. Reflections on schools, irrigation projects, floods, and Dutch immigrants are included. Undocumented.   D. F. Henderson

219.   Weber, David J.   SPANISH FUR TRADE FROM NEW MEX-
ICO, 1540-1821.   *Americas 1967 24(2): 122-136.* While a Spanish colony, New Mexico "carried on a lively trade" in hides and some of the
coarser furs. The potential for trade in "fine" furs was little developed,
in considerable part because of the limited market for them in Mexico and
Spain. However, the existing trade became an "integral part of New
Mexico's economy." It also served as a stimulus to Spanish exploration
in both the Rockies and plains, while within the colony itself "hides and
pelts were used as clothing, as a medium of exchange, and on at least one
occasion as food during...severe famine." Based mainly on published
sources; 68 notes.   D. Bushnell

220.   Wilder, Mitchell A.   SANTOS.   *Am. West 1965 2(4): 37-46.*
Santos is the religious folk art of the New Mexican frontier, one of the
very few indigenous American arts. Its cultural isolation explains the
tenacity of its vigor and form. This picture essay is concerned with the
rather unusual figures of the New Mexican version of the Third Order of
St. Francis, Los Hermanos Penitentes. Abstracted from a book on the
same subject. Illustrations from the Taylor Museum, Colorado Springs
Fine Arts Center.   D. L. Smith

221.   —.   [FRANCE VINTON SCHOLES].   *The Americas 1971
27(3): 223-232.*
Greenleaf, Richard E.   FRANCE V. SCHOLES: HISTORIAN OF
    NEW SPAIN,   *pp. 223-227.* A tribute to Scholes as a dedicated
    teacher and productive scholar specializing in the history of colo-
    nial Yucatan, New Spain, and New Mexico. He was a pioneer in
    the field of Mayan ethnohistory, and he did comparable work on
    New Mexico. In the course of his career he has collected and
    published - or otherwise shared - a great quantity of historical

documents, while emphasizing the role of meticulous archival research in the historical discipline.
Adams, Eleanor B.   THE HISTORICAL SOCIETY OF NEW MEX-
    ICO HONORS FRANCE VINTON SCHOLES FOR OUT-
    STANDING ACHIEVEMENT IN SPANISH COLONIAL
    HISTORY,   *pp. 228-232.* Underscores the contribution made by
    Scholes to historical and anthropological studies of New Mexico,
    from which he branched out more broadly into Spanish American
    colonial history. Notes his collaboration with, and the inspiration
    he provided to, other generations of researchers, as well as teaching
    and administrative positions held. Reprinted from *New Mexico
    Historical Review* 1970 45(3): 245-250.   D. Bushnell

222.   —.   THE SAN CARLOS.   *California Historian 1968 14(3): 85-
87.* Describes the activities of the *San Carlos,* the tiny flagship of the
Spanish fleet on the Pacific coast of the Americas. This ship and the *San
Antonio* were used in 1769 to establish new colonies in Alta California
at San Diego and Monterey. The *San Carlos* in 1775 "played another
dramatic part in California history" by sailing into San Francisco harbor
and charting the region for further development. The author closes by
stating that "California will remember the little *San Carlos* as a pioneer
on the pacific coast."   O. L. Miller

223.   —.   A SIDELIGHT ON THE SANTA FE TRADE, 1844.
New Mexico Hist. R. 1971 46(3): 261-264. Presents a letter from Samuel
Wethered, Jr., to Manuel Álvarez, along with an 1844 invoice. Álvarez,
a Spanish-born merchant and U.S. consul at Santa Fe, was one of several
merchants who discovered the advantages of importing goods directly
from Europe. The invoice, one of a number that have survived, illustrates
the scale on which Álvarez was doing business.
                                                      D. F. Henderson

2. THE AMERICAN WEST: TOPICS

General

224. Aberbach, Alan D. A SEARCH FOR AN AMERICAN IDENTITY. *Can. R. of Am. Studies [Canada] 1971 2(2): 76-88.* Following the Declaration of Independence "came a deliberate and intentional design to create a culture and a heritage that would replace the British and European traditions..." One of the chief actors in this effort was Samuel Latham Mitchill (1764-1831), a Jeffersonian from New York City who served in Congress, 1800-12. "He was concerned with one over-riding desire - to create a distinct American identity in whatever way he could and through whatever means were at his disposal." During the early years of the American Republic Mitchill "achieved an international as well as a national reputation as a chemist (he pioneered the introduction of the Lavoisierian system of nomenclature), geologist, botanist, physician, ichthyologist, professor, politician and humanitarian." Mitchill believed with Jefferson that American independence gave man "the opportunity to develop to the fullest extent of his potentiality," but with Hamilton he believed in a strong state. He worked closely with Jefferson and helped to secure passage of the Louisiana Purchase and approval for the Lewis and Clark expedition. Mitchill was dissatisfied with the term "United States" and preferred the name "Fredonia," which he derived from "free" and "done." Mitchill sought the acceptance of this and related terms for over 20 years. He urged American writers to take up American themes and avoid the failings and pitfalls of Shakespeare. In 1807 he published a guide book for New York City. 24 notes. J. M. Hawes

225. Albright, Horace M. JACK ELLIS HAYNES - A TRIBUTE. *Ann. of Wyoming 1963 35(1): 85-87.* A eulogy which describes the life and career of Jack Haynes from 1884 to 1962 as the leading concessioner of Yellowstone National Park with emphasis on his efforts to assist the national park service. R. L. Nichols

226. Allen, Robert V. RUSSIAN DOCUMENTS ABOUT THE UNITED STATES. *Q. J. of the Lib. of Congress 1964 21(3): 217-233.* Surveys briefly materials, preserved in Soviet archives, relating to US history and Russian-American relations 1800 to date. Four periods are covered in the discussion: 1) "Early Russian-American relations and the Russian American Company" (including events and diplomacy of the War of 1812, exploration, fur trade, China trade); 2) mid-19th century (including the US Civil War); 3) the 1890's to 1917; 4) 1917 to the present. Soviet monographs, articles, library reading lists and major edited official document series, all of which are cited, afford the bases for the descriptions and annotations. Publishing policies are characterized, and probable continuations noted. H. J. Graham

227. Athearn, Robert G. A DEDICATION TO THE MEMORY OF COLIN BRUMMITT GOODYKOONTZ, 1885-1958. *Arizona and the West 1971 13(3): 216-220.* Indiana-born frontier historian Goodykoontz was trained under Herbert Eugene Bolton and Frederick Jackson Turner. His academic career was spent at the University of Colorado. He was an active participant in professional associations, including the presidency of the Pacific Coast Branch of the American Historical Association. His research and writing primarily was concerned with the controls which were evident in the westward movement. Illus., biblio. D. L. Smith

228. Atherton, Lewis E. WESTERN HISTORICAL MANUSCRIPTS COLLECTION - A CASE STUDY OF A COLLECTING PROGRAM. *Am. Archivist 1963 26(1): 41-49.* A study of the collection program of the University of Missouri in Western Americana. S

229. Billington, Ray A. A DEDICATION TO THE MEMORY OF JAMES BLAINE HEDGES, 1894-1965. *Arizona and the West 1968 10(2): 104-110.* Missouri-born James B. Hedges received his doctoral degree under Frederick Jackson Turner at Harvard University. After several years at Clark University, he spent the remainder of his teaching career at Brown University. His principal writings were pioneer studies in the role played by railroads in the colonization of the West, in the economic history of the Canadian West, and in the biography of an important Eastern mercantile family. He is remembered more, however, as a teacher with rigid and difficult standards, but as one who was rated one of the most popular teachers at Brown University. Illus., appended with a selected list of Hedges' writings. D. L. Smith

230. Billington, Ray Allen. THE FRONTIER AND I. *Western Hist. Q. 1970 1(1): 4-20.* The author briefly traces his student and early professional career and his eventual commitment to western history. After explaining the motivation for each of his several volumes, the major portion of the essay is devoted to an auto-historiographical discussion of *America's Frontier Heritage* (New York: Rinehart and Winston, 1967), which the author regards as his most significant work to date. This book was designed to proselytize as well as to enlighten. He is disturbed, however, that the general public and the young, social science-oriented historians have not been influenced. Unless the American people, he asserts, seriously study the frontier, they will neither understand their past nor recognize the distinctive features of their own culture. The very future of frontier history as a field of historical scholarship is at stake. Illus. D. L. Smith

231. Blake, Forrester. BIBLIOGRAPHY FOR WESTERNERS. *Rendezvous 1967 2(2): 33-42.* A list of books for writers using Western subjects. In a short preface the author separates this list and others that are to follow from the "classics" on the subject as well as those in the huge specialized collections like the Huntington Library's collection in San Marino or the Bancroft Library's collection in Berkeley. Another list is made from libraries in smaller cities, towns, and crossroad hamlets. The lists are not designed to exhaust these sources or catalog them all but to call the writer's attention to the breadth, quantity, and quality of these sources that have not yet found their way into standard library catalogs. H. F. Malyon

232. Bloom, Jo Tice. CUMBERLAND GAP VERSUS SOUTH PASS: THE EAST OR WEST IN FRONTIER HISTORY. *Western Hist. Q. 1972 3(2): 153-167.* Frederick Jackson Turner suggested Cumberland Gap (Tennessee) and South Pass (Wyoming) as, respectively, 18th- and 19th-century observation posts from which to view the same procession of westward expansion. "To Turner and to most Americans born in the nineteenth century, the terms *frontier* and *west* were synonymous." Frontier characteristics attributed by the popular mind and by many historians only to the trans-Missouri West should, in the interests of accuracy, be attributed also to the cis-Missouri West. "It is time for western historians to begin writing with maturity the history of the 350 years of the American frontier. If we continue to draw distinctions between a regional and a national concept, the frontier will lose relevance in our classrooms and research....Let us expand our horizons. Let us bring together our knowledge of all the frontiers and pass on the heritage of Daniel Boone and Jim Bridger, of George Rogers Clark and Stephen Watts Kearney, of the Moravian minister and the Franciscan friar, of Cumberland Gap and South Pass." 20 notes. S

233. Brennan, John A. THE UNIVERSITY OF COLORADO'S WESTERN HISTORICAL COLLECTIONS. *Great Plains J. 1972 11(2): 154-160.* The University of Colorado's history faculty, especially Professor James F. Willard (head of the Department of History from 1907 to 1935), began to collect source documents on the American West in 1903. The Historical Collection, later renamed the Western Historical Collections, was established in 1918. From 1918 to 1959, the history department and university library shared responsibilities. Since 1959, the library has administered the collections and continued to acquire materials. The collections have numerous manuscript holdings as well as newspapers, photographs, local and regional pamphlets, and reference books. 2 notes. O. H. Zabel

234. Carter, Harvey L. A DEDICATION TO THE MEMORY OF ARCHER BUTLER HULBERT, 1873-1933. *Arizona and the West 1966 8(1): 1-6.* Archer Butler Hulbert, historian of the American frontier, was a student and close friend of Frederick Jackson Turner. Although he

did not modify Turner's essential thesis in any way, Hulbert did as much as Turner himself to explain and amplify it. He tended, like Turner, to make sweeping assertions without sufficient proof. Both discriminated insufficiently between cause and effect. As Turner might be credited as the one who formulated the concept of the significance of the frontier, Hulbert interpreted and popularized that concept. Hulbert's prodigious efforts were concerned primarily with the trials by which the frontier moved westward. His first historic work, in 16 volumes, *Historic Highways of America,* is illustrative. He is as well known for many other works that came from his prolific pen. Appended with a selected list of his works relating to the American frontier; illus.   D. L. Smith

235. Case, Leland D.   THE WESTERNERS: TWENTY-FIVE YEARS OF RIDING THE RANGE.   *Western Hist. Q. 1970 1(1): 63-76.* The Westerners, a nearly stag organization, is "somewhere between a scholarly historical society and a Lions Club." A local group is usually dubbed a "corral," but "posse" is sometimes used and there are a few other variations. In 25 years, 33 units have been established, five in Europe. The Chicago corral was launched in 1944, followed soon by one in Denver. Their programs, traditions, publications, and activities are varied and challenging. The Westerners are credited with helping to make the cowboy the chief symbol of Americanism throughout the world, a symbol that is beginning to eclipse Uncle Sam. 42 notes.
                                                                        D. L. Smith

236. Castel, Albert.   THOMAS HART BENTON - CHAMPION OF THE WEST.   *Am. Hist. Illus. 1967 2(4): 12-19.* A biographical summary of Senator Thomas Hart Benton of Missouri, noted expansionist, father-in-law of General John C. Frémont, and one of the quartet - Calhoun, Clay, and Webster were the others - who dominated the U.S. Senate in the 1820-50 period. More than any other individual he was responsible for our aggressive expansion policy.   J. D. Filipiak

237. Catton, Bruce.   THE MOMENT OF DECISION.   *Am. Heritage 1964 15(5): 48-53.* Examines presidential decisions to purchase Louisiana (Thomas Jefferson, 1803), defy South Carolina's attempt to nullify the Federal tariff (Andrew Jackson, 1832), issue the Emancipation Proclamation (Abraham Lincoln, 1862), prosecute the Northern Securities Company (Theodore Roosevelt, 1902), and order the use of the atomic bomb (Harry S. Truman, 1945). The ultimate decision is a lonely responsibility. Illus.   H. F. Bedford

238. Dahl, Victor C.   GRANVILLE STUART: AUTHOR AND SUBJECT OF WESTERN HISTORY.   *Pacific Hist. R. 1970 39(4): 493-511.* A study of the historical effect of the published diaries (1925) of Stuart (1834-1918), *Forty Years on the Frontier, as seen in the Journals and Reminiscences of Granville Stuart, Goldminer, Merchant, Rancher and Politician,* Paul C. Phillips, ed. (New York: American Book Company). These memoirs, along with Stuart's book *Montana As It Is* (Glendale, California: Arthur H. Clark Co., 1967), have provided the raw material for inspiration to historians and novelists of the frontier period who subsequently considered Stuart an authority on frontier life and society. 47 notes.   E. C. Hyslop

239. Davies, Thomas M.   THE RIO GRANDE TREATY OF 1933: A PRELUDE TO SETTLEMENT.   *New Mexico Hist. R. 1965 40(4): 277-292.* A persistent difficulty between the United States and Mexico has been the Rio Grande boundary and the ownership of the plot of land known as El Chamizal, between El Paso, Texas and Ciudad Juarez, Chihuahua. In minute detail the origin, negotiation, and ratification of the Rio Grande Treaty of 1933, which provided for straightening the channel and construction of a flood retention dam, are discussed. Unfortunately the treaty specified that work should begin at Monument Fifteen on Cordoba Island, one mile east of Chamizal. Not until 1963 was the Chamizal problem solved. Documented, 57 notes.
                                                                        D. F. Henderson

240. Davis, W. N., Jr.   WILL THE WEST SURVIVE AS A FIELD IN AMERICAN HISTORY? A SURVEY REPORT.   *Mississippi Valley Hist. R. 1964 50(4): 672-685.* A survey based on questionnaires sent to history departments in 1962. The movement for modification would adjust the focus to emphasize economic, social, and cultural history. The Turner thesis will long remain a profitable point of departure, but instructors are "utilizing recent scholarly production to bring the history of the

West down to the present, to relate the West to the present, to relate the West to the nation of the 1960's." Turner himself was always concerned with the past as illuminating the present. The surveyor believes that "the grand Turnerian hypothesis will survive a while longer"; the current is only beginning to run out. Departments dropping the course did so because of lack of faculty interest and departmental planning and thought, not lack of student demand. 16 notes.   E. P. Stickney

241. DeLapp, Mary.   PIONEER WOMAN NATURALIST.   *Colorado Q. 1964 13(1): 91-96.* The story of Martha Maxwell (1831-81), Colorado naturalist of the 1860's, who is credited with being the first taxidermist to place animals and birds in their natural settings.
                                                                        A. Zilversmit

242. Deutsch, Herman J.   THE WEST IN PAPERBACKS.   *Pacific Northwest Q. 1963 54(3): 113-123.* Annotated list of paperback books relating to the history of the western United States.
                                                                        C. C. Gorchels

243. Diggins, John P.   THE FRONTIER HERITAGE: AMBIGUOUS LEGACY.   *Am. West R. 1967 1(2): 15-23.* Discusses the book *America's Frontier Heritage* (New York: Holt, Rhinehart and Winston, 1966) by Ray Allen Billington. Billington can be labeled as a Turnerian revisionist and in this volume of the *Histories of the American Frontier* series he surveys all facets of frontier writings, including the anti-Turner element in US history. The reviewer finds the book has only one fault. "In a book as broad and bold as Billington's, a few vulnerable generalizations are bound to emerge." He goes on to explain these "generalizations," and adds the book "has brilliantly evaluated the frontier heritage in all its complexity."   O. L. Miller

244. Dodds, Gordon B.   A DEDICATION TO THE MEMORY OF HIRAM MARTIN CHITTENDEN, 1858-1917.   *Arizona and the West 1963 5(3): 182-186.* After graduation at West Point, Hiram Martin Chittenden went on to advanced study in applied engineering. Tours of duty in the West, including two in Yellowstone Park (1891-93, 1899-1904), kindled his interest in history and conservation. His works on the Yellowstone, the fur trade, and on Missouri River steamboating were long recognized as definitive, but his study of Father Pierre Jean de Smet was not as highly regarded. His style was formal, clear, and undramatic. His works contain a mass of detail. He was typical of the Progressive era of American history in his strong belief in progress and in "the divine mission of the Anglo-Saxon." Illus., biblio. of Chittenden's works concerning the American West.   D. L. Smith

245. Eggleston, Edward.   GEORGE W. NORTHRUP: THE KIT CARSON OF THE NORTHWEST.   *North Dakota Hist. 1966 33(1): 5-21.* Called by the Dakota Indians "The-Man-That-Draws-the-Handcart," George W. Northrup by the age of 18 had mastered the Dakota tongue and customs. After having served as a trader's clerk in the Yankton country for three years he outfitted himself with a handcart of supplies and attempted to go from St. Cloud, Minnesota, to Fort Benton and on to the Pacific Coast alone, traveling 36 days before Sioux attackers forced him to seek a trading post. During the next few years as he guided several parties in the Upper Great Plains and narrowly escaped death from Yankton and Teton Indians, he became a skilled naturalist. During the Civil War he served in the Union Army first as a scout in the Army of the Cumberland and later in Brackett's Battalion in suppressing the Sioux on the frontier in 1864. In the Battle of Killdeer Mountain, 28 July 1864, he was killed at the age of 27 years. Illus., 29 notes.
                                                                        I. W. Van Noppen

246. Emmonds, David M.   MORETON FREWEN AND THE POPULIST REVOLT.   *Ann. of Wyoming 1963 35(2): 155-173.* Discusses the actions and views of Moreton Frewen, an English speculator in Wyoming cattle lands from 1879-1900. Shows that although at first Frewen opposed the settlers in the Johnson County War, economic reverses and an awareness of social problems caused him to adopt many Populist ideas. He later backed free silver and bimetallism, attacked Wall Street bankers, demanded that the government aid the citizens by controlling corporate business, and denounced the Jews. Based on range cattle industry materials, Colorado State Historical Society resources, newspapers, and published state materials.   R. L. Nichols

247. Finneran, Helen T. RECORDS OF THE NATIONAL GRANGE IN ITS WASHINGTON OFFICE. *Am. Archivist 1964 27(1): 103-111.* Traces the history of the Grange from its conception by Oliver Hudson Kelley. Records in Washington, D.C. include Kelley's Papers (1865-69), William Saunders' Papers (1867-99), and records maintained by the Grange's Washington office since 1919, the national master, legislative representative (a discontinued post), and director of youth activities. Other records are scattered throughout the nation. Suggests topics in which the Grange was concerned.   D. C. Duniway

248. Foner, Eric. THE WILMOT PROVISO REVISITED. *J. of Am. Hist. 1969 56(2): 262-279.* In 1846 a group of Van Burenite Democrats, largely New Yorkers, sponsored the Wilmot Proviso, an attempt to stop the expansion of slavery into territories to be purchased from Mexico. The move was defensive in nature, an attempt to protect northern Democrats from the charge of acquiescing in a slave conspiracy to add more slave States. In New York especially, abolitionist sentiment was growing and Democrats were already under fire for supporting the South in the matter of the gag rule. Southerners would make no compromise to allow northerners to vote for Texas annexation and Van Buren came to believe that the northern Democrats were betrayed by Polk. Pushed by southern "aggression," Van Buren felt that the fragile coalition of his party was endangered. If accepted, he felt the Proviso might allow the party to survive. 67 notes.   K. B. West

249. Frantz, Joe B. WESTERN IMPACT ON THE NATION. *Western Hist. Q. 1970 1(3): 249-264.* The West has been a factor in national development "ever since the first drunk turned outward instead of homeward at Jamestown." Many claims can be made to the effect that numerous facets of the national character originated in the westering experience in American history; but, it is here asserted that the impact of the West is principally a matter of space and natural resources, which, together spell opportunity. Despite the fact that the West is the Nation's most urbanized region, it still has the most space. Given this situation, "something just has to happen periodically." The natural resources of the region are like "a self-renewing lottery ticket." When one opportunity ends, a new intoxicating opportunity arises elsewhere, presently in Alaskan oil. The impact is basically philosophical, commingling despair with blind optimism. Like the old prospector, the West is less interested in moving intelligently than hopefully. Progress is unplanned, accidental, and miraculous. 2 notes.   D. L. Smith

250. Freeze, Alys H. THE WESTERN HISTORY COLLECTION OF THE DENVER PUBLIC LIBRARY. *Great Plains J. 1972 11(2): 101-115.* Beginning in 1929 and first advised by Professor Archer Butler Hulbert of Colorado College, the Denver Public Library has acquired a comprehensive collection of books and source materials related to the Rocky Mountain region. In 1934 the collection was organized as a separate Western History Department. Its materials and staff serve researchers and seekers of information on the West. Details the indexes and finding aids, the holdings of microfilm newspapers, the major types of subjects among the nearly 300 thousand photographs, lithographs, paintings, etc., the rare book and document collection, the frontier theater collection, and notable collections of private papers. The collection emphasizes the Rocky Mountain region, but includes materials about all States west of the Mississippi.   O. H. Zabel

251. Friend, Llerena. POSSES ALL OVER THE PLACE: PUBLICATIONS OF THE WESTERNERS. *Lib. Chronicle of the U. of Texas 1965 8(4): 58-65.* In March 1944 Chicago Westerners were organized "to investigate, discuss, and publish facts relative to the background of the West and preserve a record of the Western region." They do this through the publication of Brand Books. The organizations are now worldwide, each with its own publication.   D. Brockway

252. Fritz, Henry E. NATIONALISTIC RESPONSE TO FRONTIER EXPANSION. *Mid-America 1969 51(4): 227-243.* With emphasis on the Jacksonian era, documents the formation of an American frontier mythology which tended to unite all sections of the nation, and which correlated natural rights philosophy with the mythical reality of a powerful democratic nation with a mission to expand its frontiers amidst a hospitable natural environment. The Lockean philosophical implications of the image of an American "Empire" in the West indicate the European heritage of this idea. However, the frontier seemed to promote democratic principles of self-government and of laissez-faire economic opportunities and provided a unique American nationalism which the author investigates with respect to the Turnerian frontier hypothesis. Based primarily on newspapers; 43 notes.

J. F. Scaccia

253. Glaab, Charles N. THE DOCUMENTS BOOK: A REVIEW ARTICLE. *Wisconsin Mag. of Hist. 1964 47(3): 261-263.* Discusses three recent anthologies (1963) of historical documents, on the trans-Mississippi West, the age of Jackson, and the new industrial society. A critique of the documents approach to textbooks.   S

254. Grant, Ellsworth S. GUNMAKER TO THE WORLD. *Am. Heritage 1968 19(4): 4-17, 86-91.* Samuel Colt (1814-62) was, perhaps, the leading American industrialist of his era. Tradition suggests that his observation of a ship's wheel led to the development of a multishot pistol. After several failures, he got family and friends to finance him and lived the life of a tycoon. The plant closed after five years and shortly a family scandal occurred. Meanwhile, Colt maintained interest in his own work and received a naval subsidy to develop a waterproof cartridge. He also helped S. F. B. Morse by laying the wire for Morse's telegraph from Washington to Baltimore. His reputation zoomed when his pistol won the praise of Texas Rangers. Military orders for weapons followed when the Mexican War began. Colt, ever the innovator, developed tachniques to machine produce 80 percent of his weapons. Colt continued to mass produce and promote his products as he won new friends in Europe and the United States. He later married into the upper-class Jarvis family of Connecticut and founded the gigantic Colt Armory near Hartford. Colt finally died prematurely of exhaustion and personal family frustration in 1862. He left an estate of more than 15 million dollars. Based on primary and secondary sources; 6 illus., 2 photos.   J. D. Born, Jr.

255. Green, Norma Kidd. FOUR SISTERS: DAUGHTERS OF JOSEPH LA FLESCHE. *Nebraska Hist. 1964 45(2): 165-176.* Briefly relates through the life stories of four daughters of Joseph La Flesche, the last recognized chief of the Omaha tribe, how they made their place in a new culture and became competent and accepted citizens in the white man's society.   R. Lowitt

256. Hafen, LeRoy R. A WESTERNER, BORN AND BRED. *Western Hist. Q. 1972 3(2): 128-135.* The author was born of a Mormon polygamous family in a small village in southern Nevada in 1893. After marriage to Ann Woodbury, who became a Western American historian in her own right and with whom he collaborated on several projects, he attended Brigham Young University and taught high school. After earning a master's degree in Mormon history at the University of Utah he achieved a doctorate under Herbert E. Bolton at the University of California at Berkeley. For 30 years he served as State historian of Colorado, edited the *Colorado Magazine,* and usually taught a course at the University of Denver. The most ambitious product of these prolific writers were the 15-volume series, *The Far West and the Rockies, 1820-1875* (Glendale, Calif.: Arthur H. Clark Co., 1954-62). Most of his works and those written jointly with his wife were monographic or were edited source materials and documents on Western American history. Photo, appendix.

D. L. Smith

257. Haines, Francis. THE NEZ PERCE TRIBE VERSUS THE UNITED STATES. *Idaho Yesterdays 1964 8(1): 18-25.* Reviews the history of relations between white settlers and Indians in the United States from the first settlements, with particular emphasis on treaty negotiations with the Nez Perce Indians of north Idaho, dating from 1855. The author explains the problems of rights to Indian lands following the discovery of gold on Orofino Creek in 1860. He traces the negotiations with representatives of the Nez Perce tribe following the passage by Congress of the Indian Claims Commission Act of 1946 to the final settlement of the Nez Perce claims in 1957.   M. Small

258. Handlin, Oscar. RECONSIDERING THE POPULISTS. *Agric. Hist. 1965 39(2): 68-74.* The Populists had a mistrust of social and cultural authority, which led to a total reliance upon common sense and a rejection of standards maintained by the dominant groups of the nation.

W. D. Rasmussen

259. Hanna, Archibald, Jr. ADDITIONS TO THE BEINECKE COLLECTION OF WESTERN AMERICANA. *Yale U. Lib. Gazette 1965 39(3): 135-136.* Notes that the Beinecke Collection is strong in material on Aaron Burr and on the Mexican War. In both these fields the new acquisitions include important additions. The manuscripts recently added related principally to California and the Southwest, dating from the 17th century to the middle of the 19th century.   E. P. Stickney

260. Hanna, Archibald, Jr. SHREDS FROM HENRY WAGNER'S MANTLE. *Am. West 1964 1(1): 59-64, 78.* Surveys the extent of bibliographical studies of western Americana, indicates the magnitude of what needs to be done, and suggests some ways in which this might be accomplished. [Wagner was the author of works on exploration and particularly of a two-volume annotated bibliography, *The Spanish Southwest* (r. ed. 1937)].   D. L. Smith

261. Hanna, Archibald, Jr. [TEN BOOKS ON WESTERN AMERICANA]. *Scholarly Publishing 1972 3(2): 117-124.* Discusses 10 books dealing with western America. The works described are neither the 10 rarest nor necessarily the 10 most important on this area, but they are both significant and representative. Lists, for each book, the contents, availability, and bibliographical data.   J. A. Casada

262. Hanna, Archibald, Jr. WESTERN AMERICANA COLLECTION: RECENT ACQUISITIONS. *Yale U. Lib. Gazette 1971 46(1): 41-43.* Discusses notable acquisitions for 1970 to Yale's Western Americana Collection. Supplies more details to Beinecke librarian Herman W. Liebert's annual report in the *Gazette* 1971 45(4): 133-179.   D. A. Yanchisin

263. Hansen, Klaus J. THE MILLENNIUM, THE WEST, AND RACE IN THE ANTEBELLUM AMERICAN MIND. *Western Hist. Q. 1972 3(4): 373-390.* Persistent themes throughout the course of American history have included: the notion that the millennium would begin in this country, the sanctity of the "errand into the wilderness" as a continuing fulfillment of the symbolic significance of the American West, and the racial self-image of whites and the white image of blacks and Indians. Although these themes usually impinged upon one another, they achieved a particularly tragic juxtaposition in the years before the Civil War. This convergence had profound implications for the assumptions and codes of American romanticism that heretofore have largely been implicit in cultural and intellectual history. An examination of the areas of overlap of these familiar themes reveals the insecurity of the dominant Anglo-Saxon element and helps to explain the victimization of the black and the Indian. 33 notes.   D. L. Smith

264. Hare, Stella D. JEDEDIAH SMITH'S YOUNGER BROTHER IRA. *Pacific Historian 1967 11(3): 42-52.* Ira Gilbert, Jedediah Smith's younger brother, served as "Diah's" executor after General William Ashley, the original executor, but eventually left Saint Louis before settling the accounts. Moving to the east coast, he went into business, then returned to the West and later to Ohio. After a term of farming he moved with his second wife to the goldfields of California in 1849. The author concludes with a detailed description of the family's descendants. Documented with letters from several collections in Missouri and California, court records, and published accounts; illus.   T. R. Cripps

265. Harrison, Lowell H. JOHN BRECKINRIDGE AND THE ACQUISITION OF LOUISIANA. *Louisiana Studies 1968 7(1): 7-30.* An explanation of John Breckinridge's role in the purchase of Louisiana. The background of Breckinridge's rise to power and his influence with President Jefferson are given. As Senator from Kentucky, he assumed the role as champion of the interests of the people of Kentucky as well as those of the West. His ability attracted the attention of Jefferson, who sought his advice in purchasing and providing a government for Louisiana. He was rewarded for this service in 1805 by appointment as attorney general of the United States. Based on correspondence, newspapers and official documents; 70 notes.   G. W. McGinty

266. Hicks, Jimmie. EDWARD EVERETT DALE: A BIOGRAPHY AND A BIBLIOGRAPHY. *Chronicles of Oklahoma 1967 45(3): 290-306.* Eminent historian of the American West, Oklahoman Edward Everett Dale's achievements are as notable as his longevity. He has been a cowhand, sheriff, country school teacher and administrator; earned a Harvard University doctorate in early middle age; was a long-time professor (University of Oklahoma, 1914-19, 1922-52, and other visiting appointments until 1959), popular lecturer, humorist, and author (a 10-page bibliography is appended). He continues to produce. 25 notes.   D. L. Smith

267. Hicks, Jimmie. THE FRONTIER AND AMERICAN LAW. *Great Plains J. 1967 6(2): 53-67.* Traces the transfer of English common law to the American colonies and to ever expanding frontiers and examines the development of law particularly in Texas and California. In the latter, a kind of Western common law was developed in the miners' codes. Similar developments can be found in "cow custom" on the Great Plains. The author concludes that while American law is of mainly English ancestry, it was adapted to fit frontier conditions. Influences of American law include "a lack of respect for law merely because it is law," "a profound faith in laws as a sovereign cure-all for all economic, social and political ills," and "a kind of perpetual vigilantism in American life." Based mainly on secondary materials, 40 notes.   O. H. Zabel

268. Hitchcock, Catherine E., comp. THE TRANS-MISSISSIPPI WEST IN "AMERICAN HERITAGE": AN ANNOTATED BIBLIOGRAPHY. *Arizona and the West 1970 12(1): 63-94.* One hundred and sixty-three articles from çAmerican Heritage for the period 1949-69 deal with the Trans-Mississippi West. This accounts for one of every 10 published in the magazine. 1952 was the most popular year, and 1951 was the least. The annotations in this bibliography are capsule short-paragraph summaries. They are presented in the order in which the articles were published. The principal emphases have been oil, mining, lumber, trapping, Indians, artists, politics, exploration, and transportation.   D. L. Smith

269. Hollingsworth, J. Rogers. COMMENTARY: POPULISM, THE PROBLEM OF RHETORIC AND REALITY. *Agric. Hist. 1965 39(2): 81-85.* Urges a study of the institutions and class structure of the society in which Populism was important, and illustrates his point with comments on Populists in Kansas.   W. D. Rasmussen

270. Ives, Ronald L. GEOGRAPHY AND HISTORY IN THE ARID WEST. *Am. West 1964 1(2): 54-63.* "Traditional" history and geography ignored the contributions that each discipline can contribute to the other. Modern environmental geography—physical geography, geomorphology, climatology, meteorology, plant ecology, and logistics—will augment and clarify the historical documentary records of western America. In examining historical accounts of trails and sites using this science of environments, the relative determinant value of the water barrel and canteen seems greater than that of the repeating rifle and the scalping knife. Man's response to changes in the psychological, social, and physical environment is man's history.   D. L. Smith

271. Jacobs, Wilbur R., ed. FREDERICK JACKSON TURNER'S NOTES ON THE WESTWARD MOVEMENT, CALIFORNIA, AND THE FAR WEST. *Southern California Q. 1964 46(2): 161-168.* Turner wrote: "The Westward Movement can be rewritten on its East Coast and West Coast side; but there is less for the normal development . . . in the Middle West. . . ." He observes that the interior functions as a support for the Far West, that the Colorado basin is a hinterland for Los Angeles, and that the Mountain states are partly a backlash from the Pacific Coast. He points out the importance in southern California of the process of transition "from Spanish society to American." Prints memoranda in the Huntington Library written when Turner was a research associate there.   E. P. Stickney

272. Jenkins, John W. GATEWAY TO THE WEST. *Am. West 1964 1(1): 52-58.* Describes the Jefferson National Expansion Memorial in St. Louis, now under construction and, especially, the 12 interpretative units of exhibits that will compose the Museum of Westward Expansion.   D. L. Smith

273. Krenkel, John H. BANCROFT'S ASSEMBLY LINE HISTORIES. *Am. Hist. Illus. 1967 1(10): 44-49.* Hubert Howe Bancroft does not rightfully deserve the acclaim he gave himself by having his publishing company use his name as the author for his famous 39-volume history of the Pacific States. He better deserves the titles of editor and general manager. The author provides biographical sketches of 11 of Bancroft's

assistants and notes that it is their contributions that make the series valuable today.   J. D. Filipiak

274. Lacour-Gayet, Robert.   NAPOLEON AGRANDIT LES ETATS-UNIS [Napoleon enlarged the United States]. *R. de Paris [France] 1968 75(1): 50-56.* Discusses the sale by Napoleon I of the Louisiana Territory to the United States in 1803. The author concentrates on the effect of the sale on Franco-American relations, referring to antagonisms caused by the separate peace with England in 1783, the excesses of the French Revolution, President Washington's neutrality policy, the undeclared war and the XYZ Affair, and the possible threat to the United States of a strong France in control of the Mississippi estuary. He attributes Napoleon's willingness to sell to his loss of Santo Domingo and to his desire to avoid forcing the United States into seeking the protection of the British navy. The author defends Napoleon's actions because the sale removed a major cause of antagonism between the two countries and opened the way to the Anglo-American War of 1812.

W. F. Spencer

275. Lamar, Howard R.   HISTORICAL RELEVANCE AND THE AMERICAN WEST. *Ventures 1968 8(2): 62-70.* The historian's attempt to present an understanding of the past relevant to his own time has posed difficulties for specialists of the American West. Dominated by Frederick Jackson Turner's frontier hypothesis through the first four decades of this century, by the 1940's the critics of the theory had forced a new treatment of the West such that the West was no longer considered in the mainstream of American history. However, more recent interpretations tend to incorporate and reorder the materials of Western history rather than reject them. And, even the debate over various implications of the Turner thesis continues to stimulate insights into the national history. There are also revisions of such basic stereotypes as mountain men, cowboys, and debt-ridden farmers, their characters being neither so rough-hewn nor individualistic as legend asserted. The circumstances which produced such imagery, and the reality behind it, are only now being appraised. Since one cannot really compartmentalize segments of American history, the author sees the history of the trans-Mississippi West as relevant to this age in that it is the model for studying the interrelation of an expanding population with limited environment and resources. A good part of the essay surveys the historiography of the American West, mostly since 1948. 30 notes.   R. J. Wurtz

276. Lord, Clifford L.   A DEDICATION TO THE MEMORY OF REUBEN GOLD THWAITES, 1853-1913. *Arizona and the West 1967 9(1): 1-4.* Yale-educated (American literature and history) Wisconsin journalist Reuben Gold Thwaites was handpicked by Lyman C. Draper in 1886 to be his successor as secretary of the State Historical Society of Wisconsin. During his 26 years in this capacity he became one of the outstanding historical editors with a prodigious output: *Jesuit Relations* in 73 volumes, *Early Western Travels* in 32 volumes, *Original Journals of the Lewis and Clark Expedition* in eight volumes. There were dozens of others. Thwaites authored 15 books. He applied advanced business methods to all his scholarly endeavors - to the library, the museum, his editorial work, and writing, although he personally edited his documentary works and wrote the drafts for his books. He added valuable collections to the already famous Draper manuscripts, built a new and still used historical society and university library, helped Wisconsin communities obtain Carnegie libraries, helped establish many local historical associations, and launched the forerunner of the American Association for State and Local History. Appended is a selected list of his works; illus.

D. L. Smith

277. Martin, Curtis.   IMPACT OF THE WEST ON AMERICAN GOVERNMENT AND POLITICS. *Colorado Q. 1964 13(1): 51-69.* The West fostered not only the individualism that Frederick Jackson Turner saw, but also "empirical collectivism, practical cooperation, and anti-monopoly sentiments." Many of the characteristics of westerners were the product not of physiography but of the fact that most westerners were farmers and represented the business interests of farming. "The most significant way in which the West differed (and differs) politically from the rest of the country was with respect to the element of flexibility." The significance of the West for American government is that it provided a seedbed for the resolution of the inner conflicts that troubled the nation.

A. Zilversmit

278. McCorison, Marcus A.   DONALD MC KAY FROST - A COLLECTOR OF WESTERN AMERICANA. *Western Hist. Q. 1972 3(1): 67-76.* Frost (1877-1958), of Charleston (South Carolina) and Boston (Massachusetts) was a prominent and successful lawyer. He abandoned his active practice of the law in 1924 to pursue his avocational interests in collecting Western Americana. Frost began to accumulate books on the American West apparently in the early 1920's. He was a discriminating collector and took the finest care of his acquisitions. The Frost collection of well over four thousand volumes with Frost Fund additions is deposited in the American Antiquarian Society, Worcester, Massachusetts.

D. L. Smith

279. McKee, Jesse O.   THE RIO GRANDE: THE POLITICAL GEOGRAPHY OF A RIVER BOUNDARY. *Southern Q. 1965 4(1): 29-40.* In the treaties of 1848, 1884, 1905, 1933, and 1963 the United States and Mexico undertook to define their common boundary along the Rio Grande. The treaty of 1963 settled the last serious dispute over the boundary along the river.   D. A. Stokes

280. Mering, John V.   A DEDICATION TO THE MEMORY OF FRANK HEYWOOD HODDER, 1860-1935. *Arizona and the West 1972 14(2): 108-112.* Educated at the University of Michigan and at Göttingen and Freiberg in Germany, Hodder spent most of his active years as a professional historian at the University of Kansas. His scholarship was devoted to the pursuit of the idea that the pre-Civil War discord in the United States was primarily over the status of the western Territories. Slavery was secondary. He argued the importance of railroads in the Dred Scott case, the Compromise of 1850, and the Kansas-Nebraska Act. This was his principal theme, whether in his presidential address to the Mississippi Valley Historical Association, a high school government text, or his articles. Illus., biblio.   D. L. Smith

281. Moffat, Charles H. and Hanrahan, Edward S., eds.   LIFE OF A WANDERER: THE MEMORIES OF EDWARD STEPHENSON III. *West Virginia Hist. 1967 28(2): 73-100.* These reminiscences relate the career of Edward Stephenson III who was born at Parkersburg in western Virginia about 1802. They continue the story of his life as a wanderer until 1869. Beginning as a Methodist circuit rider, Stephenson served his church briefly in Pennsylvania and western Virginia. After forsaking the ministry he practiced law intermittently in such places as Wheeling, Key West, Florida, Texas, and Mexico. A rudimentary knowledge of several foreign languages enabled him at various intervals to teach school in such diverse places as Kentucky, South Carolina, Louisiana, Texas, and Monterey, Mexico. His versatility was also demonstrated as a carpenter in a number of the Southern States. His witty account of his travels shows an observant eye and is useful for his commentary on the areas which he visited.   D. N. Brown

282. Moore, R. Laurence.   THE CONTINUING SEARCH FOR A SOUTHWEST: A STUDY IN REGIONAL INTERPRETATION. *Arizona and the West 1964 6(4): 275-288.* Seeks to determine if there is a Southwest, and, if so, how it can be defined or measured or recognized by distinguishable characteristics. Although, with some justification, the concept can be considered as an all-things-to-all-people proposition, the author confines himself to four criteria as a means of testing the homogeneity of a hypothetical Southwestern region. As to geography, a first index to homogeneity, it is concluded that there is one common factor - the climate. The second criterion, historical experience, is difficult to determine, because even the most universal and persuasive influences have not survived well into the present, and many of the impressions expressed about Southwestern history are either not unique to the area or are untrue. The third measure of a regional consciousness, contemporary economic patterns, gives a more satisfactory measurement in that increasing urbanization sets the area apart from many others in the West. The final index, the people, is not so satisfactory because most of those who live there do not have roots that give them distinctive characteristics. In the last analysis, the author concedes that unscientific measurements must be used. That there is a feeling that approaches true poetry about a Southwestern identity is perhaps the only measurement. 10 notes.

D. L. Smith

283. Morrill, Allen C. and Morrill, Eleanor D.   THE MEASURING WOMAN AND THE COOK. *Idaho Yesterdays 1963 7(3): 2-15.* Tells of the work of anthropologist Alice Cunningham Fletcher and her com-

panion Jane Gay among the Nez Perce Indians of North Idaho from May 1889 to September 1892. Sent by the US government to measure and allocate land to the Indians under the provisions of the Dawes Act of 1887, the two women worked to overcome the hostility of the remnants of Chief Joseph's band. The authors depend largely on the letters of Jane Gay in the Women's Archives at Radcliffe College and on the published works of missionary Kate McBeth.   M. Small

284. Nash, Gerald D. BUREAUCRACY AND REFORM IN THE WEST: NOTES ON THE INFLUENCE OF A NEGLECTED INTEREST GROUP. *Western Hist. Q. 1971 2(3): 295-305.* The Federal Government alone has invested over 300 billion dollars in the peopling and development of the trans-Mississippi region since 1850. More than 50 billion dollars have been expended by the States. Distribution and disbursal was accomplished through a complicated network of administrative agencies staffed by thousands of Federal, State, and local officials. One of the important functions of these public administrators was their crucial role in the formulation of reform programs in economic, political, and social spheres. Particularly this bureaucracy exerted power through the execution of policies in their domain, and these civil servants were prime sources of legislation adopted by the State and Federal Governments. Bureaucrats have affected the promulgation of economic reforms in the areas of disposition of land, irrigation, reclamation, agriculture, transportation, business, banking, and labor. Their influence in shaping public policies has been subtle and one of the most potent upon western life since the middle of the last century. Historians need to focus on these civil servants to gain a more realistic understanding of the functioning of government policies in the trans-Mississippi West. 23 notes.
D. L. Smith

285. Nordholt, J. W. Schulte. MANIFEST DESTINY EN IMPERIALISME [Manifest destiny and imperialism]. *Internationale Spectator [Netherlands] 1967 21(9): 665-681.* Discusses U.S. expansion, first on the continent of America and then into the Pacific Ocean and the Caribbean. The author describes the manifest destiny policy and its expansion into an imperialist policy and indicates that there was strong opposition on the part of an antiexpansionist element. It was not, however, a conflict of idealists with realists. Both sides were idealistic, but they differed on their basic assumptions. The success of the expansionists forced the United States to become a world power. Based on 19th-century American writings; 33 notes.   W. S. Reid

286. Nordin, Dennis S. A REVISIONIST INTERPRETATION OF THE PATRONS OF HUSBANDRY. *Historian 1970 32(4): 630-643.* Uses the printed records of at least a dozen State Granges, the proceedings of individual lodges, farmer newspapers, and the memoirs of such leaders as Oliver H. Kelley to demonstrate that Solon J. Buck's classic history from 1913, *The Granger Movement* (Lincoln: U. of Nebraska Press, 1963), is too narrow in that it ignores developments in the East and concentrates too much on commerce, independent political parties, and fights against economic monopolies. The movement endured for a decade longer and was more complex than Buck apparently realized. The adult education program overshadowed every other aspect of Grangerism. Finds ample evidence to support the assertion of contemporary Grange leaders that the order was primarily a social and educational fraternity for American farmers and their families. 49 notes.   N. W. Moen

287. Oliva, Leo E. OUR FRONTIER HERITAGE AND THE ENVIRONMENT. *Am. West 1972 9(1): 44-47, 61-63.* Without denying the accomplishments of the pioneers who conquered the American West, and without destroying their image as courageous and heroic individuals, it must not be overlooked that these same pioneers indulged in wasteful and destructive practices. Frontiersmen began the rape of the land causing disappearance of forests and wildlife, erosion of soil, and poisoning of air and water. Many then escaped the destruction they had wrought by moving on to a new frontier. Those who thus suffered the hardships and the hard work of the conquest of nature did not appreciate the long-range consequences of their actions and should not be condemned. When it came to polluting they were rank amateurs. It would take their practices plus industrial technology and much greater population density to bring the environmental crisis. The despoiled land, the lost species, and the barren hillsides cannot be restored. What remains is part of our heritage. Biblio.   D. L. Smith

288. Parish, Peter J. DANIEL WEBSTER, NEW ENGLAND, AND THE WEST. *J. of Am. Hist. 1967 54(3): 524-549.* Unlike many of his contemporary New England politicians, Daniel Webster did not fear the movement of population to the West and the development of that section. Undoubtedly partially motivated by his presidential aspirations, Webster was amiably disposed to farm life and consciously strove to attract Western support by endorsing policies which he felt would contribute to the development of the West and of the nation as a whole. He argued that a high tariff, modified by reciprocal trade agreements, would benefit Western agriculture; he supported Federal aid to internal improvements (including land grants to railroads) in order to develop Western markets; and, most strikingly, he endorsed a liberal land policy, including graduation, preemption, and, by 1850, homestead legislation. His stand on land policy estranged him from John Quincy Adams and other Whigs, but endeared him to Stephen A. Douglas and Lewis Cass.
K. B. West

289. Paul, Rodman W. THE NEW WESTERN HISTORY: A REVIEW OF TWO RECENT EXAMPLES. *Agric. Hist. 1969 43(2): 297-300.* A review of *The Eastern Establishment and the Western Experience: The West of Frederic Remington, Theodore Roosevelt, and Owen Wister* (New Haven: Yale U. Press, 1968) by G. Edward White, and of *The Cattle Towns* (New York: Alfred A. Knopf, 1968) by Robert R. Dykstra. While the two books are unrelated, except that both deal with western history of the later 19th century, they are good examples of modern research, methodology, and interpretation under optimum conditions. The salvation of the much-criticized field of Western history will come through the cumulative effect of competent scholars taking up the major topics, one by one, and subjecting each to a reflective examination that is based not only on more extensive research than hitherto, but also on fresh insights and new approaches. These books are examples of the kind of work needed.   W. D. Rasmussen

290. Pickens, Donald A. OKLAHOMA POPULISM AND HISTORICAL INTERPRETATION. *Chronicles of Oklahoma 1965 43(3): 275-283.* During the 1930's historians explained Populism as the forerunner of the New Deal, as liberalism. More recently Richard Hofstadter in *The Age of Reform: From Bryan to F.D.R.* (New York: Vintage Press, 1955) characterized Populists as anti-Semites, militant racists, and superpatriots whose political descendants supported McCarthyism. The author believes that Hofstadter was making a psychological analysis without proper documentation, and cites other historians who have criticized Hofstadter's judgment, including C. Vann Woodward amd Walter T. K. Nugent. Populism in the Middle West and particularly in Oklahoma is examined, and the conclusion is that Populism was a response to a very real need of the farmer, since economics was a major factor in the life of the farmer. He then traces the transfer of many Populists in Oklahoma from Populism to Socialism. There was no other party for them to join after the collapse of the Populists. They needed a party of reform and the Socialist Party was available. 35 notes.   I. W. Van Noppen

291. Pollack, Norman. FEAR OF MAN: POPULISM, AUTHORITARIANISM, AND THE HISTORIAN. *Agric. Hist. 1965 39(2): 59-67.* Populism was not retrogressive, seeking to recreate the past, but forward-looking with the aim of adapting to an industrialized society.
W. D. Rasmussen

292. Pomeroy, Earl. WHAT REMAINS OF THE WEST? *Utah Hist. Q. 1967 35(1): 37-55.* Challenges several widely-accepted conclusions about the history of the Western frontier. The author questions the beliefs that frontiersmen received little aid from the U.S. Government or from Eastern capitalists, that their farms were subsistence rather than commercial in character, that there was little urban influence in the Western communities, and that the effects of the frontier were restricted to the period of early settlement. Presented at a meeting of the Utah State Historical Society in September 1965.   S. L. Jones

293. Pratt, Grace Roffey. THE GREAT-HEARTED HUTTONS OF THE COEUR D'ALENES. *Montana 1967 17(2): 20-23.* A small investment in a northern Idaho silver mine brought a fortune to Levi W. and May Hutton during the early years of this century. They invested in Spokane real estate and established substantial charities for homeless children. Mrs. Hutton was active in politics and in the feminist movement. Illus.   S. R. Davison

294. Riggs, John A. AMERICAN HISTORY IN THE HARVARD COLLEGE LIBRARY. *Harvard Lib. Bull. 1967 15(4): 387-400.* Harvard's American history collection, excelled in overall strength only by that of the Library of Congress, has developed largely from gifts. In 1818 Harvard acquired its first significant holdings of Americana, when it received a gift of books and maps relating to New World and Colonial history. Subsequent benefactions have enabled Harvard to expand the collection generally and to amass as well materials on special topics, e.g., the Civil War, Mormonism, Western America, Lincoln, and Theodore Roosevelt. Only in 1910 did Harvard earmark endowed funds specifically for American history; systematic purchase of current imprints was not provided for until 1950. In 1965, however, the library inaugurated a program of acquisitions, mostly in microfilm, to eliminate gaps in the then-existing collection and to supply the current research needs of its American history scholars. 17 notes. J. D. Byrum

295. Ripich, Carol A. JOSEPH W. WHAM AND THE RED CLOUD AGENCY, 1871. *Arizona and the West 1970 12(4): 325-338.* The Sioux, among the most warlike of the Plains Indians, roamed the vast expanse between the Platte and Yellowstone rivers, the Upper Missouri, and the Rockies. This area was astride the path of westward American expansion and emigrant roads, stage and freight lines, and a transcontinental railroad. In addition, the Dakota and Montana gold fields were in the area. By an 1868 treaty the western half of present South Dakota was to be a Sioux reservation, the Bozeman Trail and military posts were to be abandoned, agencies were to feed and clothe the Indians, and the Government promised to educate the Sioux and train them to become self-supporting farmers. In March 1871 Joseph Washington Wham was sent as a Government agent to the Oglala band of Sioux to implement the treaty as it pertained to them. Charismatic Red Cloud, principal chief of the Oglala, was more than agent Wham could handle. Problems of locating the agency, the presence of whiskey traders, the matter of rations to the Indians, the temptation to raid the herds of Wyoming ranchers, gold in the Black Hills, and other thorny problems plagued Wham's efforts. A November scandal at the agency exposed Wham's inefficiency and contributed to his dismissal in mid-January 1872. Although he had been unequal to the situation, he had managed somehow to maintain peaceful relations with the Oglala Sioux. Illus., map, 36 notes. D. L. Smith

296. Ryan, Pat M. JOHN P. CLUM, "BOSS-WITH-THE-WHITE-FOREHEAD." *Arizoniana 1964 5(3): 48-60.* The 22-year-old Clum was appointed agent on the San Carlos Apache Reservation of Arizona, arriving 8 August 1874. He had an embattled three-year career, being at odds with the U.S. Army. In 1877 he refused to "submit to inspection by the army." His colorful career included being a lawyer, newspaper editor, postmaster, and city auditor at Tombstone; 20 years with the Office of Post Office Inspectors, traveling extensively; a spectacular part in the Klondike Gold Rush of 1898; and lecturer on the West to promote tourism for the Southern Pacific Railway. Illus., biblio. E. P. Stickney

297. Scheiber, Harry N. TURNER'S LEGACY AND THE SEARCH FOR A REORIENTATION OF WESTERN HISTORY: A REVIEW ESSAY. *New Mexico Hist. R. 1969 44(3): 231-248.* Reviews *The American West: A Reorientation* (U. of Wyoming Publications, XXXII, 1966), edited by Gene M. Gressley. The editor organized the volume with a view toward "eschewing 'stubborn provincialism' and breaking with the excessive emphasis on the orthodox 'Turnerian' approach that still dominates so heavily in western historiography." The book, however, does not provide a fully developed alternative to Frederick Jackson Turner's unifying framework. 36 notes. D. F. Henderson

298. Scott, Hollis J. LEROY R. HAFEN, 47 YEARS AS CHRONICLER OF WESTERN AMERICANA. *Utah Hist. Q. 1966 34(3): 243-254.* Surveys and analyzes Hafen's studies in Western history from the writing of his master's thesis on "Handcart Migration to Utah" at the University of Utah in 1919 to 1966. Considerable emphasis is given to his collaboration with his wife Ann Woodbury Hafen in several of his publications. A bibliography of the works which he and his wife have written and edited is included. S. L. Jones

299. Smith, Alice E. A DEDICATION TO THE MEMORY OF JOSEPH SCHAFER, 1867-1941. *Arizona and the West 1967 9(2): 102-108.* Wisconsin-born and educated Joseph Schafer spent 20 years (1900-20) at the University of Oregon before returning to his native State as superintendent of its historical society for another 20 years. Careful scholarship and penetrating analysis were his hallmarks. He was interested in the latest methods and developments in historical research. A product of the frontier and a student of Frederick Jackson Turner, Schafer became an ardent disciple and remained a strong defender of the Turner theory for the rest of his life. He was a founder and a president of the Agricultural History Association, and active in other professional organizations. Appended with a selected list from the hundreds of books and articles that came from his pen relating to the American West; illus. D. L. Smith

300. Snell, Joseph W., ed. DIARY OF A DODGE CITY BUFFALO HUNTER, 1872-1873. *Kansas Hist. Q. 1965 31(4): 345-395.* The daily events in the life of Henry H. Raymond between 11 November 1872 and 25 November 1873 are summarized in two, three or four lines. The diary is not only a source of information about Dodge City's first year and a manual on the method and technique employed in hunting buffalo, it is also a source of information about the Masterson brothers, (William B. "Bat", Edward J., and James P.), who went on from their earlier association with Raymond as buffalo hunters to achieve a lasting fame as western gun fighters. The diary is reproduced with a few explanatory notes and brief identifications of the principal persons appearing in it. The author's misspellings and poor grammar remain unaltered. W. F. Zornow

301. Swaim, Elizabeth A. TWO WESTERN NARRATIVES DATED. *Papers of the Biblio. Soc. of Am. 1972 66(2): 171-174.* Argues from internal evidence that Austin S. Clark's *Reminiscences of Travel* and F. A. Isbell's *Mining and Hunting in the Far West,* both publications undated but commonly presumed to be from 1870 and 1871, were more nearly printed in 1897 and 1899 respectively. 8 notes. C. A. Newton

302. Tutorow, Norman E. SOURCE MATERIALS FOR HISTORICAL RESEARCH IN THE LOS ANGELES FEDERAL RECORDS CENTER. *Southern California Q. 1971 53(4): 333-344.* A "descriptive inventory" of holdings of the Los Angeles Federal Records Center which are "valuable from an historical perspective." Records are those of governmental agencies dating from 1853 to 1968 and are useful research sources for those studying local, State, regional, and national history. The best inventoried materials at present are the extensive records of judicial agencies. These include various court records and the reports and records of the Immigration and Naturalization Service, the Bureau of Prisons, and the Bureau of Narcotics and Dangerous Drugs. Records of the agencies and departments of the executive branch of the national government provide "a veritable gold mine of information for the social historian." Department of Interior records include, for example, condemnation proceedings for various Federal projects, statistics on fish catches, histories of oil wells, and correspondence related to Indian affairs. Department of Agriculture records at the center contain materials from the experiment stations of the Far West and the Forest Service. Treasury Department records include materials such as reports from the customs offices at San Diego and San Pedro and the Coast Guard offices at Long Beach and Wilmington. Weather and climatology records, Army, Navy, and Air Force reports, and Food and Drug Administration files are among the records from the Departments of Commerce, Defense, and Health, Education, and Welfare. W. L. Bowers

303. Ulph, Owen. THE LEGACY OF THE AMERICAN WILD WEST IN MEDIEVAL SCHOLARSHIP. *Am. West 1966 3(4): 50-52, 88-91.* A reply to Lynn White, Jr., "The Legacy of the Middle Ages in the American Wild West," *American West.* White's article is "irrelevant to the problems of the American West" and "an example of the legacy of the undisciplined West in medieval scholarship." His historical logic is faulty and shallow and the evidence he marshals to support his thesis is not appropriate. Following his method to its ultimate application would produce different conclusions from those he has reached. The author asserts that the medieval legacy in the United States is almost nil, the experiments to introduce medieval institutions in Canada collapsed, and the "bastardized medieval practices" that gained some foothold in Mexico remain essentially regressive. A meaningful conclusion about the

relationship between the Middle Ages of Europe and the American West is not to be found in "the sterile concept of a linear legacy." Of considerable potential, however, is the recognition that societies that demonstrate similarities in social conditions have a tendency to produce similar techniques and value structures that are independent of any direct lines of cultural inheritance. Herein is a sophisticated approach that should bear fruit. Biblio., note.

                                                                    D. L. Smith

304. Unger, Irwin. CRITIQUE OF NORMAN POLLACK'S "FEAR OF MAN". *Agric. Hist. 1965 39(2): 75-80.* Pollack ascribes to the Populists an ideology not current among them.

                                                                    W. D. Rasmussen

305. Van Alstyne, Richard W. CALIFORNIA AND THE "NORTH AMERICAN ROAD TO INDIA." *Pacific Historian 1969 13(1): 1-7.* The United States for a long time dreamed of developing North America as a land bridge between the Orient and Western Europe, hoping to serve as a commercial middleman. Thomas Jefferson and Thomas Hart Benton advocated such a course. Individuals such as John Ledyard, Perry McDonough Collins, Charles Wilkes, Matthew Calbraith Perry, and John Rodgers worked to make it possible. The Civil War diverted US attention from these efforts, however, and the opening of the Suez Canal insured that European-Oriental commerce would remain more direct, despite completion in the United States of a transcontinental railroad and preparations to link it to a trans-Pacific steamship service. For a time, Americans considered a Russian-American entente for the mastery of the North Pacific and of Northeast Asia, but relations cooled. By 1904, the US Government entered into a silent partnership with Japan to drive Russia from Manchuria, though relations with Japan also cooled when Japan appeared unwilling to allow the United States to share in the exploitation of Manchuria. American efforts to become the moral and economic leader of China from the 1880's through the presidency of Woodrow Wilson provide a perfect illustration of the Protestant ethic with its alliance of business, religion, and government. Based on primary sources; 7 notes.

                                                                    F. I. Murphy

306. Villegas, Daniel Cosío. BORDER TROUBLES IN MEXICAN-UNITED STATES RELATIONS. *Southwestern Hist. Q. 1968 72(1): 34-39.* Border frictions are one of the major determinants in Mexican-American relations. Six themes dominate the subject: the westward movement as it affected the international border before 1848; the establishment of the official borderline between the two countries; American concern for the border when France dominated Mexico in 1864-65; problems caused by Indian and cattle thieves' raids and the flight of fugitive criminals over the border; American-based Mexican subversive or revolutionary movements; and confrontation of the two cultures throughout Mexico, especially in the border zone. Some bibliographical data is included for each. 5 notes.

                                                                    D. L. Smith

307. Warner, Ezra J. A BLACK MAN IN THE LONG GRAY LINE. *Am. Hist. Illus. 1970 4(9): 30-38.* Henry Ossian Flipper (1856-1940) was the first Negro graduate of West Point (class of 1877). He spent some years in frontier duty in the Southwest. He was accused of embezzlement, tried by court-martial, and dismissed from the service for a lesser charge in 1882. Being fluent in Spanish, he went to Nogales, Arizona, and set up business as a civil engineer who surveyed public lands in Mexico. In 1893 he was appointed special agent of the US Department of Justice to aid in determining the validity and boundaries of various Spanish and Mexican land grants within U.S. territory. Raises serious question about the real reason for Flipper's dismissal from the Army. Based on Flipper's own autobiography, newspapers, and interviews; illus.

                                                                    E. P. Stickney

308. White, Lynn, Jr. THE LEGACY OF THE MIDDLE AGES IN THE AMERICAN WILD WEST. *Am. West 1966 3(2): 72-79, 95.* Argues that a study of the mental, emotional, and technical equipment of the pioneers who pushed the American frontier westward, rather than the frontier "challenge"-American life "response" explanation approach suggested by Frederick Jackson Turner, is the key to understanding the history of the American West. Originality and creative adaptation are rare when man finds himself in new circumstances. What the American frontiersmen did was to choose and to elaborate on the tradition and heritage they brought with them. This legacy came, in large measure, from the medieval world of Europe in the form of gadgetry, such as the

windmill, gunpowder, and barbed wire; and patterns of preference - for example, for whiskey over beer and wine, for gambling with cards rather than with dice, and hanging by rope over other forms of execution. Our image of the medieval world is fragmentary and distorted; our recognition of the vast accumulation of things on the American frontier which had their roots in the Middle Ages is less than it should be. It is asserted that the continuity between the history of medieval Europe and the United States is "detailed and massive." Illus., 51 notes. Reprinted from *Speculum*, April 1965.

                                                                    D. L. Smith

309. Wiggins, Robert A. "WESTERN AMERICANA" AND ITS AUDIENCE. *Am. Q. 1966 18(4): 705-708.* Reviews five books which range from "a valid survey kind of approach" to the West to more restricted studies of specific subjects within narrower geographical limitations. The cumulative effect of the volumes tends to remind readers of past follies and raises the question of why so little of the knowledge learned of these follies has been applied. The books are: W. Eugene Hollon, *The Great American Desert* (New York: Oxford U. Press, 1966); Holway R. Jones, *John Muir and the Sierra Club: The Battle for Yosemite* (San Francisco: Sierra Club Books, 1965); William R. Goetzmann, *Exploration and Empire* (A. A. Knopf, 1966); Robert I. Burns, S.J., *The Jesuits and the Indian Wars of the Northwest* (New Haven: Yale U. Press, 1965), and Alvin M. Josephy, Jr., *The Nez Percé Indians and the Opening of the Northwest* (New Haven: Yale U. Press, 1965).

                                                                    R. S. Pickett

310. Williams, Burton J. THE TWENTIETH CENTURY AMERICAN WEST: THE OLD VERSUS THE NEW. *Rocky Mountain Social Sci. J. 1969 6(2): 162-167.* Argues that the ruling theory of Frederick Jackson Turner has imposed its dogma on the historical profession far too long, and that historians ought to discard cumbersome tradition and begin anew with fresh methods and hypotheses. 9 notes.

                                                                    R. F. Allen

311. Wilson, Major L. IDEOLOGICAL FRUITS OF MANIFEST DESTINY: THE GEOPOLITICS OF SLAVERY EXPANSION IN THE CRISIS OF 1850. *J. of the Illinois State Hist. Soc. 1970 63(2): 132-157.* Analyzes the positions adopted by Whigs, Democrats, and Free Soilers on the issue of slavery in the territories, and concludes that the Compromise of 1850 did not remove the major elements of conflict which this issue embraced. Based mainly on materials drawn from the *Congressional Globe*.

                                                                    S. L. Jones

312. Wiltsey, Norman B. THE GREAT BUFFALO SLAUGHTER. *Mankind 1968 1(6): 32-44.* Surveys the destruction of the great buffalo herds that once roamed North America. The buffalo was always an object of interest to American explorers from the first description given by Alvar Núñez Cabeza de Vaca until their systematic hunting by parties of "sportsmen" from the East in the 19th century. With the coming of the railroads, the markets for buffalo hides opened up. In 1881, 50 thousand hides were shipped by rail; in 1882, 200 thousand; but by 1885 hides were so rare that each was selling for 75 dollars. By 1889 only 541 buffalo were known to be alive in the United States. The great herds had been destroyed. Illus.

                                                                    P. D. Thomas

313. Winkler, A. M. DRINKING ON THE AMERICAN FRONTIER. *Q. J. of Studies on Alcohol 1968 29(2): 413-445.* "Many Americans inhabiting the western frontier during the 19th century drank whisky freely and frequently as they struggled to cope with a hostile environment. The trappers who opened each successive area in the movement toward the Pacific, the miners, the cattlemen and the pioneer farmers who followed later, all drank substantially greater quantities than did those who remained in the east. Nineteenth-century Americans throughout the country drank with less restraint than had their forebears. The frontier environment acted as the force which dislodged the last barriers against intemperate consumption. Crude surroundings provided the shock which drew certain widely prevalent tendencies into bold relief. In colonial America widespread disapproval of intoxication kept drinking habits from getting out of hand, even among those who drank regularly in public and private. After the Revolution, however, the social atmosphere in the country began to change and societal restrictions and limitations were less strictly observed. Per capita consumption increased steadily until the mid-19th century. Travelers, missionaries, soldiers and forty-niners who recorded their impressions all commented on the extensive American

consumption, while comparable accounts indicate no such excesses during either the preceding or succeeding centuries. Whisky, the most popular beverage after 1790 when distillation was found to be an economical way of transporting grain to market, became an expected part of all social intercourse and excessive drinking became a problem. Nonetheless, many observers commented that, even though intoxicated, drinkers were able to function fairly well. The drinking habits which developed among the various frontier groups were related to the patterns of daily activity. The trappers were unable to carry liquor with them and consequently drank explosively whenever they gathered together at the rendezvous for 1 month each year. The cowboys could not drink while they were on the trail, but they more than compensated for these dry periods when they reached the 'cow towns.' The western miners lived in crude communities where alcohol was readily available and they drank heavily throughout the year to help ease their loneliness for the families they had frequently left behind. Their habits became even more intemperate in the winter when the weather severely limited their activity. Western soldiers drank whisky so excessively that Congress in 1832 suspended their liquor ration; but the excessive drinking continued. The Indians were encouraged to drink by the fur traders and when drunk became violent and uncontrollable. The farmers, the last and by far the most moderate inhabitants of each frontier area, were interested in cultivating the soil and developing the land. They built settlements and frequently enjoyed some form of primitive community organization. Their drinking patterns reflected their relative stability: though they drank more than their eastern counterparts, they were seldom violently drunk and even when intoxicated were able to perform their simple daily tasks. During the 19th century temperance and abstinence sentiment and organization grew sporadically, but real support came primarily from the larger urban centers. In the sparsely settled rural areas clergymen encouraged abstinence, but not until a territory was fairly well populated and reasonably structured communities had begun to develop could the reformers hope to make much progress. [Bibliography of 68 items.]"   J

314. —. GRENVILLE MELLEN DODGE: SOLDIER-ENGINEER. *Palimpsest 1966 47(11): 433-480.*
Mauck, Genevieve Powlison. DESTINY BECKONS WESTWARD, *pp. 433-449.* Traces the life of General Dodge from his birth in Massachusetts in 1831 to the end of the Civil War when he was commander of all U.S. forces in Kansas, Nebraska, Colorado, and Utah.
—. HIS GREATEST ACCOMPLISHMENT, *pp. 450-459.* Resigning his commission in 1866 Dodge joined the Union Pacific Railroad as chief engineer. At the same time he had been elected to Congress from the Fifth District of Iowa. It was his work that was essential for the routing and building of the transcontinental railroad.
GENERAL DODGE BUILDS A HOUSE, *pp. 460-464.* In 1869 Dodge started construction on a 14-room Victorian mansion in Council Bluffs. His house was to be "without ostentation" but to have "dignity and graciousness." The 35 thousand dollars he spent on his house was a large sum for that day.
LAST DAYS IN COUNCIL BLUFFS, *pp. 465-475.* After several years in business in New York City, Dodge returned to Council Bluffs in 1907 to write and to spend his last days. He died on 3 January 1916 at the age of 84.
Petersen, William J. AS OTHERS VIEWED HIM, *pp. 476-480.* Petersen feels the years have not dimmed the memory of Dodge, but in fact, have added new luster to his name. Many illustrations including several color photographs of General Dodge's home which is now a museum.   D. W. Curl

315. —. [WALTER STANLEY CAMPBELL]. *Arizona and the West 1965 7(2): 87-104.*
Swain, Dwight V. A DEDICATION TO THE MEMORY OF WALTER STANLEY CAMPBELL, 1887-1957, *pp. 87-90.* Walter Stanley Campbell, whose nom de plume was Stanley Vestal, sprang from the pioneer West to become a Rhodes scholar and to achieve fame as a teacher of professional writing courses. Hiw own works included biography, history, textbooks, novels, short stories, essays, juveniles - a total of 24 books - besides uncounted articles, reviews, and magazine and newspaper copy. He believed, practiced, and taught that scholarship should be linked with enthusiasm and fact with passion. Appended with a selected list of Campbell's writings related to the American West. Illus.

Berthrong, Donald J. WALTER STANLEY CAMPBELL: PLAINSMAN, *pp. 91-104.* Except for the years at Oxford, service in World War I, and a few years as a high school English teacher in Kentucky, Walter Stanley Campbell spent most of his life among the Plains Indians and as an English professor at the University of Oklahoma. In his writing he drew upon his intimate knowledge of the Indians to correct the warped and distorted image of them held by most writers. His most successful books were concerned with the Sioux and their resistance to white advance in the Northern Plains. The author treats of Campbell's research methods and the contents of some of his studies. Present day historians value Campbell's writings not as sources in Western history, but for apt characterizations and incidents in Western history. Based on the Campbell Papers in the University of Oklahoma Library and Campbell's published works; 3 illus., 25 notes.   D. L. Smith

Exploration and Travel

316. Allen, John L. AN ANALYSIS OF THE EXPLORATORY PROCESS: THE LEWIS AND CLARK EXPEDITION OF 1804-1806. *Geographical R. 1972 6(91): 13-39.* "Geographical exploration is a process that has objectives, courses of action, and results. These are all strongly conditioned by the nature of the geographical knowledge available at the time exploration takes place. The Lewis and Clark Expedition of 1804-1806 is an excellent example of such conditioning. The expedition's goal—the discovery of a water route through western North America to the Pacific—was founded on faulty geographical concepts of the interior. As exploration proceeded, the course of the expedition was changed as the preconceived notions were gradually recognized to be inconsistent with the knowledge derived from field observations and experiences. It was primarily because of their ability to recognize inadequate data, to replace it with more accurate frameworks, and to adjust their behavior accordingly, that Lewis and Clark returned with the information which substantially changed the nature of geographical lore about the American Northwest."   J

317. Allen, John L. LEWIS [AND] CLARK ON THE UPPER MISSOURI: DECISION AT THE MARIAS. *Montana 1971 21(3): 2-17.* Meriwether Lewis and William Clark had advance information about the upper Missouri River, but none concerning the Marias, in northern Montana. At the mouth of this tributary, they were puzzled as to which was the true Missouri, and were not certain until they reached the Great Falls, above the junction. New significance is seen in this correct decision by the leaders, who staked their prestige in selecting the southern fork despite the belief among the enlisted men that the Marias was the major stream. Based primarily on the edited editions of the expedition's journals; illus., maps, 36 notes.   S. R. Davison

318. Andrews, Thomas F. SATIRE AND THE OVERLAND GUIDE: JOHN B. HALL'S FANCIFUL ADVICE TO GOLD RUSH EMIGRANTS. *California Hist. Soc. Q. 1969 48(2): 99-111.* Describes a guidebook for those afflicted with gold fever. Unlike most others of the genre, Hall's guidebook was satirical. Hall, a Boston printer, never went to California; instead, he "borrowed" his material from newspaper anecdotes, particularly one account which appeared in the *Missouri Republican* of 28 December 1848. The author correctly dates the publication of Hall's guidebook as 1851 and presents a selection from the guidebook. Based on a copy of the guidebook in the Henry E. Huntington Library, San Marino; illus., map, 26 notes.   A. Hoffman

319. Appleman, Roy E. LEWIS AND CLARK: THE ROUTE 160 YEARS AFTER. *Pacific Northwest Q. 1966 57(1): 8-12.* A look at the Lewis and Clark Trail today. The author shows the unchanged landmarks as well as the developments which substantially changed the characteristics of the trail, showing effects of the damming of rivers and the construction of railroads and highways.   C. C. Gorchels

320. Appleman, Roy E. THE LOST SITE OF CAMP WOOD: THE LEWIS AND CLARK WINTER CAMP, 1803-04. *J. of the West 1968 7(2): 270-274.* From William Clark's field notes we are given a picture of camp life at Camp Wood during the winter preceeding the expedition into the Louisiana Territory. The location of that camp is surmised to be

on the west bank of the Mississippi River in Missouri. The changes in the channels of the Mississippi, Missouri, and Wood Rivers are discussed in connection with the location of the camp. The notes were found in a Saint Paul attic in 1953 and published in 1964 by the Yale University Press after editing by Ernest Staples Osgood.   R. N. Alvis

321. Arrington, Joseph Earl. "SKIRVING'S MOVING PANORAMA": COLONEL FREMONT'S WESTERN EXPEDITIONS PICTORIALIZED. *Oregon Hist. Q. 1964 65(2): 133-172.* Called "a romantic example of nineteenth century visual education," Skirving's Moving Panorama was a composite painting of about 80 scenes of western United States exhibited particularly in eastern cities and in Great Britain during 1849-51. Historical background is included on the expeditions of John C. Frémont (on whose journeys many of the scenes were based). Biographical sketches are given of John Skirving, Joseph Kyle, Jacob A. Dallas, and other contributing artists. Numerous representative scenes are described.   C. C. Gorchels

322. Bailey, Lynn R. LT. SYLVESTER MOWRY'S REPORT ON HIS MARCH IN 1855 FROM SALT LAKE CITY TO FORT TEJON. *Arizona and the West 1965 7(4): 329-346.* The 1854 presence of U.S. troops in Salt Lake City, Utah, was for a two-fold purpose. The first, to solve the suspected Mormon-inspired ambush murder of an army officer, was soon taken care of. The second was to mark a shorter route through the Great Basin to the Pacific for troop movements. Two routes were to be explored. Lieutenant Sylvester Mowry, later prominent in Arizona affairs but at the time persona non grata with Mormon officials for his seduction of a married niece of Brigham Young's, was placed in command of a detachment of dragoon recruits to explore the more difficult route. Mowry's very life was in danger until he passed beyond Mormon territory. His route approximated U.S. highway 91 from Salt Lake City to Los Angeles, California, across Utah and southern Nevada. From Los Angeles he marched northward on the principal interior route to his destination, Fort Tejon. Based on the National Archives; 2 maps, 57 notes.   D. L. Smith

323. Barry, Louise, ed. CHARLES ROBINSON—YANKEE '49ER. HIS JOURNEY TO CALIFORNIA. *Kansas Hist. Q. 1968 34(2): 179-188.* A journal covering some of the experiences that physician Charles Robinson and his 50 associates of the Congress and the California Mutual Protective Association had in Kansas during their trip from Boston to the California gold fields in 1849. Robinson's journal-narrative is drawn from a pamphlet *Nebraska and Kansas. Report of the Committee of the Massachusetts Emigrant Aid Co.* published in Boston in 1854; a letter he published in the *Worcester* (Massachusetts) *Spy* in 1854; *The Kansas Conflict,* which he published in 1892. The journal-narrative contains much information about Kansas geography, Indians, missions, and Kansas City. 10 notes.   W. F. Zornow

324. Baydo, Gerald. OVERLAND FROM MISSOURI TO WASHINGTON TERRITORY IN 1854. *Nebraska Hist. 1971 52(1): 65-87.* Carefully recounts the journey of the Jacob Ebey family of Plum Grove Place, Missouri, to Whidbey Island, Washington Territory, in 1854. Relies heavily on the diary of one of his sons, Winfield Scott Ebey. The family traveled 2,192 miles in 169 days.   R. Lowitt

325. Benjamin, Theodosia. THE AUDUBON PARTY - NEW YORK TO CALIFORNIA, 1849. *Pacific Historian 1968 12(4): 7-27.* An account of an expedition led by John Woodhouse Audubon, the naturalist's son, from New York to California via Mexico in 1849. The expedition, which at one time numbered 98 men, started as the California Company of Colonel Henry L. Webb, with Audubon as second in command. Owing to the ravages of cholera in Texas, Webb decided to abandon the expedition; Audubon, at the urging of some of the expedition's members, became the new leader. After some delay the group struck out for Mexico. They encountered accidents, more cholera, stealthy nocturnal forays by the Indians, four weeks of uninterrupted rain, and swollen streams. Through it all, Audubon delighted in the flowers and new species of birds, but regretted that he had no time to collect specimens or to paint. Once in California, the party had little success in mining for gold. Many of its members later made important contributions to the development of California, including Robert Simson, member of the Board of Trustees of the College of California (later the University of California), and Dr. John B. Trask, California's first State Surveyor and first State Geologist. Based on *Audubon's Western Journal: 1849-1850;* 8 illus., map, 36 notes.   F. I. Murphy

326. Betts, William J. ROUTE TO MOUNT RAINIER. *Beaver [Canada] 1965 296(Summer): 18-23.* An attempt to retrace the path taken by Dr. William Fraser Tolmie (1812-86) from Nisqually House to Mt. Rainier in 1833. He was the first white man to approach the mountain and the first to botanize the Cascades on the western approaches. Excerpts from his diary of the journey. Illus.   L. F. S. Upton

327. Bidlack, Russell E. and Cooley, Everett L., eds. THE KINTNER LETTERS: AN ASTRONOMER'S ACCOUNT OF THE WHEELER SURVEY OF UTAH AND IDAHO. *Utah Hist. Q. 1966 34(1): 62-80 and (2): 169-182.* Ten letters written by Charles Jacob Kintner of Ann Arbor, Michigan, from Utah and Idaho between 14 May and 28 November 1877. Kintner had an appointment as assistant astronomer in the Geographical Survey West of the One Hundredth Meridian, headed by First Lieutenant George M. Wheeler of the Corps of Engineers. Though Kintner in one of his early letters promised a description of Mormon society, he writes little about the Mormons. Mostly the letters deal with the terrain which he observed and the details of the camp life of the expedition. The letters were published in 1877 in the *Ann Arbor Register* and are reprinted here as they appeared in that newspaper. Illus., 43 notes.   S. L. Jones

328. Bishop, Z. C. LETTERS OF ZEBULON C. BISHOP, AMERICAN TRAVELER. *Oregon Hist. Q. 1965 66(2): 161-170.* Five letters written on a journey in Oregon and other lands, with observations concerning early settlers of Oregon and climate, 1850-1856.   C. C. Gorchels

329. Brinckerhoff, Sidney B. PASSPORT TO MEXICO. *J. of Arizona Hist. 1967 8(1): 54-59.* Provides a biographical sketch of Captain Isaac Harding Duval who, with his party, traveled through the Southwest and Mexico to the goldfields. There is a reproduction of his passport issued in June 1849.   J. D. Filipiak

330. Brodhead, Michael and Unruh, John D., Jr. eds. ISAIAH HARRIS' "MINUTES OF A TRIP TO KANSAS TERRITORY" IN 1855. *Kansas Hist. Q. 1969 35(4): 373-385.* Isaiah Morris Harris was one of 11,356 Ohioans who settled in Kansas territory before 1860. His "minutes" contain a summary of the events that happened on all but two of the days between 29 October and 15 November 1855, when he traveled by steamer from Cincinnati to Kansas. He recorded his impressions of the people he met and the towns visited during the trip and recounted his first experience at meeting Indians in Kansas. He touched briefly on the slavery agitation that rocked Kansas territory at the time, but it is evident that he came to Kansas to farm rather than to participate in the struggle. Based on newspapers, articles, local histories, and the diary which is in the possession of a granddaughter, Vida A. Harris, of Manhattan, Kansas; illus., 43 notes.   W. F. Zornow

331. Brogan, Phil F. OREGON GEOLOGY: THE CENTURY OLD STORY. *Oregon Hist. Q. 1966 67(1): 5-40.* The unique and spectacular geological features of Oregon are depicted in context with historical explorations. The roles of outstanding geologists, such as Joseph Silas Diller, Israel Cook Russell, and Thomas Condon, are described, and their writings are listed. The objectives and characteristics of current geological studies are indicated. Illus.   C. C. Gorchels

332. Brown, D. Alexander. BLACK BEAVER. *Am. Hist. Illus. 1967 2(2): 32-41.* "Sikitomaker," or Black Beaver, the anglicized name he chose, was a Delaware Indian and a famous scout for military and scientific explorers in the West. In the 1830's he was a trapper for the American Fur Company, and in the late 1840's he served in the Mexican War. Respected by both white men and Indians, Black Beaver was the last chief of the Delaware.   J. D. Filipiak

333. Brown, D. Alexander. A GIRL WITH THE DONNER PASS PARTY. *Am. Hist. Illus. 1966 1(6): 42-48.* Virginia Elizabeth Reed, 12 years old, and her family left Illinois in 1846 for California. Virginia wrote letters of her impressions to a cousin, in which she described their daily activities, hardships, and her excitement. Part way through the journey they joined the ill-fated Donner party. Because of killing a man, even though in self-defense, Virginia's father James Reed was banished from the wagon train and sent ahead alone to seek help at Sutter's Fort. The party reached the Sierra too late in the winter to pass and was halted by

the weather. Although several of the members of the party resorted to cannibalism, Virginia wrote "thank God we have all got thro, and we did not eat human flesh." On 19 February 1847 a relief party from Sutter's Fort arrived. James Reed had made it through the mountains and gotten help. Of the original party of 87, 36 had died in the Sierra snows. Based on the original letters of Virginia Reed; 5 illus., map.

M. J. McBaine

334. Brown, Terry. AN EMIGRANTS' GUIDE FOR WOMEN: MAKING THE NECESSARY PREPARATIONS FOR THE ARDUOUS FIVE-MONTH JOURNEY ALONG THE OREGON TRAIL. *Am. West 1970 7(5): 12-17, 63.* Guidebooks for the Oregon Trail were written "by men for men." They pictured a romantic West and were made more to sell and to attract settlers westward than they were to guide. The present piece is "a fictionalized facsimile of an 1850 guidebook written [in 1970] by a woman for women." In contrast to the half-truth misinformation of the guidebooks contemporary to the trail itself, this one is "accurate and well-researched." It is concerned mainly with questions of interest to wives and mothers, and deals with preparations for the journey, medical supplies, major problems en route, notable sights on the way, the travel train code of conduct, and a typical day on the trail. Illus., map.

D. L. Smith

335. Bryan, Charles W., Jr. FROM MARTHASVILLE TO MARYSVILLE IN 1850. *Bull. of the Missouri Hist. Soc. 1963 19(2): 115-126.* Tells of the experiences of a group of gold seekers who left their homes in Missouri and survived the 2,100-mile journey from Fort Leavenworth to Marysville, California. Details are given about the two families that composed the party, where they later settled, and what type of work they undertook. Letters between family members describe the daily hard activities of miners.

D. H. Swift

336. Camp, Truman W. THE JOURNAL OF JOSEPH CAMP, 1859. *Nebraska Hist. 1965 46(1): 29-38.* A portion of Camp's Journal, describing his trip from Iowa to Nebraska, including his visit to Omaha in June and July 1859, is presented with the original spelling and punctuation retained.

R. Lowitt

337. Carley, Maurine. BRIDGER TRAIL TREK: TREK NO. 17 OF THE HISTORIC TRAIL SERIES. *Ann. of Wyoming 1967 39(1): 108-128.* Discusses the three-day trek over the Bridger Trail in July 1966 sponsored by the Wyoming State Archives and Historical Department and the Wyoming Historical Society. The trekers retraced the old trail by car. The report includes a journal and eight short papers describing such places as Poison Spider Country, Bridger Trail Ford, and Neiber Stage Stop which figured in the history of the trail. A list of trekers is appended. Illus.

R. L. Nichols

338. Carley, Maurine. CHEYENNE-DEADWOOD TRAIL TREK: TREK NO. 15 OF THE EMIGRANT TRAIL TREKS. *Ann. of Wyoming 1965 37(1): 75-109.* Discusses the two-day trek over the Cheyenne-Deadwood Trail in June 1964 sponsored by the Wyoming State Archives and Historical Department and the Wyoming State Historical Society. The object was to retrace the old trail by car. Includes 15 descriptions of places and things which figured in the history of the trail, such as Pole Creek Ranch, Isaac Bard Stage Station, and the George Lathrop monument.

R. L. Nichols

339. Carley, Maurine. THE FIRST FIFTY MILES OF THE OREGON TRAIL IN WYOMING. WYOMING'S EASTERN BORDER TO WARM SPRINGS. *Ann. of Wyoming 1970 42(1): 77-103.* Discusses the 20th annual trek over a historic trail in Wyoming (July 1969). Sponsored by the State Historical Society, the trip by car followed portions of the Oregon Trail in eastern Wyoming. The author mentions the activities of the party and includes brief papers about 15 sites of interest. A list of the trekers is appended. Illus., photos.

R. L. Nichols

340. Carley, Maurine, comp. OREGON TRAIL AND CALIFORNIA-MORMON TRAILS: FORT BRIDGER TO WYOMING'S WESTERN BORDER. *Ann. of Wyoming 1969 41(1): 113-130.* A brief discussion of Trek 19 sponsored by the Wyoming State Historical Society and other interested groups in the State. On 13-14 July 1968 the participants drove over about 75 miles of the Oregon, California, and Mormon trails which passed west from Fort Bridger to the western border of Wyoming.

R. L. Nichols

341. Carley, Maurine SECOND SEGMENT OF THE OREGON TRAIL: COLD SPRING TO FORT FETTERMAN. *Ann. of Wyoming 1970 42(2): 252-274.* Continued from a previous article. A description of the 21st annual trek over a historic trail in Wyoming in July 1970. Sponsored by the State Historical Society of Wyoming, the journey, by car, followed portions of the old trail whenever possible. The discussion includes a description of group activities and eight brief papers read to the travelers about prominent points or events on the trail. A list of the 166 participants is included.

R. L. Nichols

342. Carley, Maurine. THIRD SEGMENT OF THE OREGON TRAIL, DOUGLAS TO INDEPENDENCE ROCK: TREK NO. 22 OF THE HISTORICAL TRAIL TREKS. *Ann. of Wyoming 1971 43(2): 270-295.* Presents a log of a trek over a historic Wyoming trail. Traveling by automobile in July 1971, the group retraced portions of the Oregon Trail between Douglas and Independence in east-central Wyoming. Includes 10 brief papers about historical sites along the route. Illus.

G. R. Adams

343. Caughey, John W. THE TRANSIT OF THE FORTY-NINERS OR WHY, OH WHY, DID THEY EVER LEAVE WYOMING. *U. of Wyoming Pub. 1971 37: 17-27.* In 1849 some 25 to 30 thousand men crossed Wyoming heading for gold fields. Describes what these travelers saw and did during their brief journey through Wyoming. Gives attention to trails, travel conditions, geographical features, settlements, food, recreation, etc. This group of migrants had little impact on Wyoming, but they still were part of its history. Based primarily on travel diaries; 106 notes.

H. B. Powell

344. Chandler, M. G. SIDELIGHTS ON SACAJAWEA. *Masterkey 1969 43(2): 58-66.* With the vast amount of territory obtained by the Louisiana Purchase, it became necessary to explore and occupy this new land. The author describes the advance preparations made by the explorers chosen by President Jefferson to lead the first expedition into the Far West - Meriwether Lewis and William Clark. After outfitting the group in St. Louis, they made their way up the Missouri to a Minitaree village where they took on Toussaint Charbonneau and his pregnant 14-year-old Shoshone slave girl, named Sacajawea (Bird Woman) by the Minitaree. As the Shoshone were a hostile tribe, Sacajawea was not only a godsend as a guide, but also insured the expedition's safe conduct through Shoshone territory. In later life Sacajawea left Charbonneau and married a Comanche warrior. The son she bore while on the expedition, Jean Baptiste, and a nephew she adopted while in Shoshone country, Bazil, were educated in Europe at Clark's expense. Both boys returned to the Wind River Shoshone Reservation to be joined later by the widowed Sacajawea, who died on 9 April 1884 in her mid-90's. Based primarily on discussions with C. A. Eastman, noted Sioux Indian authority.

C. N. Warren

345. Chandler, W. B., ed. SOME PIONEER EXPERIENCES OF GEORGE CHANDLER. *Oregon Hist. Q. 1965 66(3): 197-207.* Autobiographical reminiscences of George Chandler, edited by his son. Includes his experiences in traveling from Missouri to Baker, Oregon, in 1862 and descriptions of early Indian violence in Baker until 1878.

C. C. Gorchels

346. Conrad, David E. THE WHIPPLE EXPEDITION ON THE GREAT PLAINS. *Great Plains J. 1963 2(2): 42-66.* Briefly explains why the 32nd Congress (1852-53) authorized exploration of four transcontinental railway routes. The author gives a brief biography of Lt. (later General) Amiel Weeks Whipple (d. 1863) who commanded the 35th parallel survey. A description follows of the selection of personnel and supplies and the experiences of the party in the summer and autumn of 1853 as it moved westward across the Great Plains from Fort Smith up the valleys of the Washita and Canadian Rivers to the Pecos. The remainder of the journey is only mentioned. Sources include *Journal of Lt. Whipple* and *Pacific Railway Survey*, Vol. III.

O. H. Zabel

347. Conrad, David E. THE WHIPPLE EXPEDITION IN ARIZONA, 1853-1854. *Arizona and the West 1969 11(2): 147-178.* From mid-July 1853 to late March 1854, Lieutenant Amiel Weeks Whipple conducted an exploring and survey expedition from Fort Smith, Arkansas, to Los Angeles, California, along the 35th parallel. A feasible transcontinental rail route was the principal object of the expedition,

although a substantial amount of ethnological and scientific data was an important by-product. The party moved across present Arizona during the months of December, January, and February, which proved to be a challenging and trying experience. U.S. Highway 66 and the Santa Fe Railroad have approximated the Whipple route across the Southwest, especially in Arizona. Scientists on the expedition named scores of new plant and animal species and geological formations. The report made on the Indian tribes that were encountered was long considered as a standard reference. 5 illus., map, 58 notes. D. L. Smith

348. Cortambert, Louis; Myer, Mrs. Max W.; and Chapman, Carl H., eds. JOURNEY TO THE LAND OF THE OSAGES, 1835-1836: BY LOUIS CORTAMBERT. *Missouri Hist. Soc. Bull. 1963 19(3): 199-229.* A biographical sketch accompanies this account by an educated young French immigrant, Louis Cortambert, of his travels to and in the Osage Indian country just west of Missouri and the Arkansas Territory. The account gives some description of the area and its inhabitants, but the informative material is subordinated to the author's provocative personal reactions and reflections on the frontier, Indian life, religion, French society, American society, philosophy and history. Also included are short comments on some major American cities and on other Indian tribes to which he paid a brief visit - chiefly the Creeks and Cherokees. R. J. Hanks

349. Crampton, C. Gregory. F. S. DELLENBAUGH OF THE COLORADO: SOME LETTERS PERTAINING TO THE POWELL VOYAGES AND THE HISTORY OF THE COLORADO RIVER. *Utah Hist. Q. 1969 37(2): 214-243.* An introduction and the texts of a group of letters regarding Colorado River explorations and other matters of Western history written by Frederick S. Dellenbaugh to Raymond T. Stites, Russell Frazier, and Charles Kelly between 1926 and 1934. Dellenbaugh, who had been a member of the second Powell expedition down the Colorado (1871-72), subsequently published many books about the West and its history. The letters printed here are in the Utah State Historical Society, the New York Public Library, and the Arizona Pioneers' Historical Society, Tucson. S. L. Jones

350. Cutright, Paul Russell. THE JOURNAL OF PRIVATE JOSEPH WHITEHOUSE A SOLDIER WITH LEWIS AND CLARK. *Bull. of the Missouri Hist. Soc. 1972 28(3): 143-161.* A commentary about a document discovered in 1966 that relates to the western explorations of Meriwether Lewis and William Clark in 1804-06. This newly-found document is a journal concerning Joseph Whitehouse's activities while he was a member of the Lewis-Clark expedition. The journal covers a period of several months that were not treated in an earlier Whitehouse journal published in 1916. The recently-discovered Whitehouse journal adds little of significance to existing knowledge about the Lewis-Clark expedition, but it contains "items of interest and a few of intrinsic worth." Hence, the newly-found Whitehouse journal merits "a report." 24 notes. H. T. Lovin

351. Cutright, Paul Russell. LEWIS AND CLARK AND DU PRATZ. *Missouri Hist. Soc. Bull. 1964 21(1): 31-35.* Provides historical information on the copy of the 1774 edition of *The History of Louisiana,* by Antoine Simon Le Page Du Pratz, which was carried by Lewis and Clark on their western expedition (1803-06) and which has been discovered in the possession of the Library Company of Philadelphia. Facsimile copies of two pages. 6 notes. R. J. Hanks

352. Cutright, Paul Russell. LEWIS AND CLARK BEGIN A JOURNEY. *Missouri Hist. Soc. Bull. 1967 24(1): 20-35.* The early days of the Lewis and Clark expedition, on the Missouri River from the Mississippi to the Kansas River, established the procedures and patterns they were to follow for most of their journey. In this, their instructions from President Thomas Jefferson were regarded as articles of faith. Careful examination of the data they collected reveals that they were much more than explorers and army officers. Interested in geography, meteorology, mineralogy, botany, zoology, and ethnology, they soon became "keen-eyed observers, disciplined inquirers, and meticulous chroniclers." 59 notes. D. L. Smith

353. Cutright, Paul Russell. LEWIS AND CLARK INDIAN PEACE MEDALS. *Missouri Hist. Soc. Bull. 1968 24(2): 160-167.* Giving medals to prominent Indians had been the practice from early colonial days. The Lewis and Clark expedition used them to promote peace and friendship. The Indians valued the medals highly. The circumstances of presentation and a description of the six medals and the one accompanying certificate which are known to have survived are included. 8 illus. D. L. Smith

354. Cutright, Paul Russell. MERIWETHER LEWIS: ZOOLOGIST. *Oregon Hist. Q. 1968 69(1): 5-28.* Depicts Meriwether Lewis as an observer of fauna as shown in the journals of the Lewis and Clark Expedition in 1804-06. The author concludes that for his time Lewis was a surprisingly competent zoologist with an objective, systematic approach that set a pattern for future naturalists. C. C. Gorchels

355. Cutright, Paul Russell. THE ODYSSEY OF THE MAGPIE AND THE PRAIRIE DOG. *Missouri Hist. Soc. Bull. 1967 23(3): 215-228.* President Thomas Jefferson had instructed Meriwether Lewis and William Clark, among numerous other things, to give close attention to the animals in the country they explored, especially those unknown in the United States. Specimens of all sorts were sent back to Jefferson. One unprecedented shipment included six live animals: four magpies, one sharp-tailed grouse, and a prairie dog. This cargo left Fort Mandan on 7 April 1805. One magpie and the prairie dog survived the trip to Washington. They were scrutinized and studied by naturalists, artists, and museum personnel, as well as the President. 35 notes. D. L. Smith

356. Darrah, William C. JOHN WESLEY POWELL AND AN UNDERSTANDING OF THE WEST. *Utah Hist. Q. 1969 37(2): 146-151.* Summarizes Powell's career, emphasizing his scientific concerns and contributions. S. L. Jones

357. Davidson, Marshall B. CARL BODMER'S UNSPOILED WEST. *Am. Heritage 1963 14(3): 43-65.* "The rediscovery of a Swiss artist's paintings...re-creates the image of America in the 1830's." S

358. Dewing, C. E. THE WHEELER SURVEY RECORDS: A STUDY IN ARCHIVAL ANOMALY. *Am. Archivist 1964 27(2): 219-227.* Traces the history of records relating to topographical and incidental field work under Lt. George M. Wheeler, 1871-79. Some were lost prior to 1929, when the Geological Survey included "one ton" of "old notebooks" in a list of useless papers submitted to the Librarian of Congress for review before submission to Congress. At this point, Francis P. Farquhar obtained their transfer to Stanford University. While at Stanford some were given to other western universities, some to individuals, and the remainder have now been returned to the National Archives. Forty-eight volumes were recently purchased by Yale University. D. C. Duniway

359. Edwards, Clinton R. WANDERING TOPONYMS: EL PUERTO DE LA BODEGA AND BODEGA BAY. *Pacific Hist. R. 1964 33(3): 253-272.* Traces the confusing history of the name of the Bodega-Tomales region in California. Ironically notes that today Bodega y Quadra's name is affixed only to a shallowly indented bay he mentioned only in passing, and to a lagoon he never saw. J. McCutcheon

360. Egan, Ferol. JORNADA DEL MUERTO [Journey of death]. *Am. West 1969 6(4): 12-19, 61-63.* Colonel Henry L. Webb, a veteran of the Mexican War, and John Woodhouse Audubon, an accomplished artist who was seeking new animals and birds to paint in the tradition of his famous father, led a company of 80 men to the California gold fields. About half the size of the Webb-Audubon party, the Hampden Mining Company of Westfield, Massachusetts, set out on a similar mission. Some 50 greenhorns from New York City formed the Kit Carson Association (no connection with the famed mountain man) to accomplish the same results. These three outfits used the El Dorado Trail during the 1849 California gold rush. They all traveled by ship to a Texan or Mexican gulf port. From there they planned a hoped-for easy trek across northern Mexico, along the Gila River of southern Arizona, and across the southern California desert to El Dorado. The incredible hardships of their "jornada del muerto" exacted high tolls before they reached their destination. Adapted from a forthcoming book. 3 illus., map, biblio. note. D. L. Smith

361. Elder, Clara A. TWO GOLD RUSH LETTERS. *New York Hist. 1970 51(1): 71-76.* James Elder (1828-52) left New York to seek his fortune in the California gold fields. His two letters to his wife describe the perils of the sea journey to California. He died in a shipwreck while on the last leg of his journey. 4 illus. G. Kurland

362. Elliott, Mary Joan. THE 1851 CALIFORNIA JOURNAL OF M. V. B. FOWLER. *Southern California Q. 1968 50(3): 227-265.* Continued from a previous article. Reproduces entries from Matthew Van Benschoten Fowler's journal for 6 April to 6 May 1851, when the journal ends. During this period Fowler journeyed on foot through the Santa Clara Valley in search of a suitable farm, observed the State Legislature in session at San Jose, became discouraged with his prospects in California, and left for his home in New York State. Based primarily on a document held by the University of California, Los Angeles; 72 notes, biblio. W. L. Bowers

363. Ewers, John C. PLAINS INDIAN REACTIONS TO THE LEWIS AND CLARK EXPEDITION. *Montana 1966 16(1): 2-12.* Although the Northwest Plains Indians had earlier met white men, their contact with Lewis and Clark was decisive in establishing a hostile attitude, especially toward Americans. Diplomacy apparently was the least successful aspect of the expedition. Published sources. S. R. Davison

364. Faulk, Odie B., ed. A LETTER FROM JOHN R. BARTLETT AT CAMP YUMA, 1852. *J. of Arizona Hist. 1965 6(4): 204-213.* A letter written 11 June 1852 by the US Boundary Commissioner John Russell Bartlett. It is valuable for its description of the route from San Diego to Camp Yuma, California, on the Colorado River and his account of the killing of Colonel Louis Craig by two army deserters. A sketch of Bartlett's life and the work of the boundary commission is added by the editor. J. D. Filipiak

365. Faulkner, Mont E. EMIGRANT-INDIAN CONFRONTATION IN SOUTHEASTERN IDAHO, 1841-1863. *Rendezvous 1968 2(2): 43-58.* Seeks to explain the causes of violence between the Shoshone and Bannock tribes with the white emigration to and through southeastern Idaho from 1841 to 1863. The author cites as causes: first, the nature of tribal political organization was toward an extreme individualism as opposed to a national loyalty, so that decisions by chief spokesmen were not binding upon the whole; second, the settlers and emigrants pastured the best grass land (bottomland), thereby destroying the basis of Indian wealth and power in raising horses; third, the lack of central authority in the emigrant trains west of Fort Laramie caused them to break up into small groups averaging 2.5 wagons per group. H. F. Malyon

366. Flanagan, Vincent J. GOUVERNEUR KEMBLE WARREN, EXPLORER OF THE NEBRASKA TERRITORY. *Nebraska Hist. 1970 51(2): 171-198.* Discusses the expeditions led by Lieutenant Warren in 1855, 1856, and 1857 into the far reaches of the Nebraska Territory and their significance for the future growth and development of the region. R. Lowitt

367. Fleming, L. A. and Standing, A. R. THE ROAD TO "FORTUNE": THE SALT LAKE CUTOFF. *Utah Hist. Q. 1965 33(3): 248-271.* Relates how Samuel J. Hensley with a party of men and horses found the shortcut on the California Trail, known as the Salt Lake Cutoff, and analyzes why it became important in the migration to California. Described is where the trail ran as related to highways, towns, and other features in the existing landscape as discovered by the authors in personal explorations of the terrain. Illus., 38 notes. S. L. Jones

368. Gaither, Gerald H., ed. and Finger, John R., ed. A JOURNEY OF STEPHEN STONE: OBSERVATIONS ON KANSAS IN 1881. *Kansas Hist. Q. 1971 37(2): 148-152.* Stone was typical of the young men who went west to make their fortune. Four entries in his journal for the period 9-22 March 1881 cover those phases of his trip from Wisconsin to Arizona during which he went from Dubuque, Iowa, to the western border of Kansas. In addition to the usual comments on the countryside and experiences during brief stops in Kansas City and Topeka, Stone's journal contains information on ticket prices, the cost of rooms and meals, and property valuation - the sort of information that does not usually find its way into diaries. The journal is in the Grace Stone Beuher collection at the University of Tennessee. Illus., 14 notes. W. F. Zornow

369. Garrard, Lewis H. IN THE LODGE OF VI-PO-NA: A VISIT TO THE CHEYENNE. *Am. West 1968 5(4): 32-36.* Narrates his travels and observations of his 1846 trip over the Santa Fe Trail and the Southwest, first published in 1850 as *Wah-to-Yah and the Taos Trail.* The present narrative is excerpted from a 1968 facsimile reproduction of the 1936 edition. It describes Garrard's visit to a Cheyenne village on the Purgatoire River where he was hospitably received by Chief Vi-Po-Na. Recorded are numerous ethnographic details. Illus. D. L. Smith

370. Goetzmann, William H. L'EXPLORATION DES REGIONS DE L'OUEST EN RETROSPECTIVE: LE ROLE DE L'EXPLORATEUR ET DU SAVANT SUR UNE "FRONTIERE" SOUS-DEVELOPPEE [The exploration of the West in retrospect: the role of the explorer and scientist in an underdeveloped "frontier"]. *Cahiers d'Hist. Mondiale [France] 1964 8(4): 707-731.* Points out the value of studying the Western explorers as early, and much neglected, contributors to American science. Documented. M. Cherno

371. Goodwin, Victor O. DEVELOPMENT OF THE EMIGRANT ROUTES OF NORTHERN NEVADA. *Nevada Hist. Soc. Q. 1965 8(3/4): 27-40.* A review of the early history of Nevada and some of the trails to California not commonly known to readers outside Nevada. The author gives some highlights in the lives of some of the early travelers. W. J. Brooks

372. Gordon, Dudley. RETRACING LUMMIS' FOOTSTEPS IN ARIZONA AND NEW MEXICO. *Masterkey 1963 37(4): 147-158.* Reports on a trip by the author and others, taken in 1963, retracing much of the route taken by Charles Fletcher Lummis on his celebrated walking trip through Arizona and New Mexico in 1884. The author is Lummis' biographer. Based on personal experience; 5 illus. C. N. Warren

373. Griffin, Walter R. GEORGE W. GOETHALS, EXPLORER OF THE PACIFIC NORTHWEST, 1882-84. *Pacific Northwest Q. 1971 62(4): 129-141.* Goethals, best known as the supervisor of the construction of the Panama Canal, 1907-14, had active years as US Army engineer officer assigned to Vancouver Barracks in Washington Territory, 1882-84. Traces Goethals' assignments in exploring and mapping territory in the Pacific Northwest region, particularly in the Colville Valley. As a result of his work, according to Goethals' annual report of 1 October 1883, his office issued a total of 487 maps during the preceding year. Based primarily on official reports of the US Army Chief of Engineers and Goethals' official reports on deposit in the National Archives; 2 maps. C. C. Gorchels

374. Guthrie, Blaine A., Jr., and Guthrie, Mitchell R. CATFISH, CORNMEAL AND THE BROAD CANOPY OF HEAVEN: THE JOURNAL OF THE REVEREND GUERDON GATES DESCRIBING HIS TRIP QN THE RED RIVER OF LOUISIANA AND TEXAS, 1841-1842. *Register of the Kentucky Hist. Soc. 1968 66(1): 3-34.* Reproduced in full, this newly-discovered journal throws added light on the early settlement of Texas in the 1840's. Written by an educated Baptist minister, the leader of a group of Kentuckians who were drawn to Texas by offers of free land, the Reverend Guerdon Gates describes his journey and the many hardships encountered. Often his group relied only on an occasional catfish and cornbread for food and slept in the open under "the broad canopy of heaven." Gates encountered considerable difficulty in navigating the Red River into Texas. The trip was made more unpleasant by "a variety of dispositions, tempers and habits" in his small group. The editors used mainly contemporary newspapers and secondary sources. 28 notes. B. Wilkins

375. Haines, Francis, Jr. GOLDILOCKS ON THE OREGON TRAIL. *Idaho Yesterdays 1965 9(4): 26-30.* An account of various attempts by Indians to trade horses for blond children of the pioneers traveling on the Oregon Trail. Indian relations with the pioneers are detailed in three exacting tales of warfare and travel after reaching Oregon. D. H. Swift

376. Hale, Douglas D. FRIEDRICH ADOLPH WISLIZENUS: FROM STUDENT REBEL TO SOUTHWESTERN EXPLORER. *Missouri Hist. R. 1968 62(3): 260-285.* Wislizenus was a physician who came to the United States in 1836 after a six-year association with the student rebellion in Germany and the nationalistic movements that swept

Europe during the period. He came to St. Louis in 1839 to practice medicine but was soon attracted to the Far West. His journey over the Oregon Trail in 1839 and his trip to Santa Fe and the Southwest in 1846-47 are described in detail. The second trip was intended as a geological and botanical expedition, but Wislizenus' scientific work was interrupted by the outbreak of war with Mexico. Based largely on Wislizenus' reports of his journies, *A Journey to the Rocky Mountains in the Year 1839* (1912) and *Memoir of a Tour to Northern Mexico* (1848), and Wislizenus' papers now in the possession of Mrs. Dee Eades of St. Louis. Illus., 81 notes.   W. F. Zornow

377. Hardeman, Nicholas P., ed. CAMP SITES ON THE SANTA FE TRAIL IN 1848 AS REPORTED BY JOHN A. BINGHAM. *Arizona and the West 1964 6(4): 313-319.* John A. Bingham left Independence, Missouri, in 1848, probably bound for gold and adventure in California. Traveling over the Santa Fe Trail, he wrote a letter, here reproduced, on 12 July 1849 to a friend back in Missouri. The mileage chart which makes up the bulk of the letter lists check points and camp sites that are lacking in such detail in most other first-hand accounts. Editorial comments are derived largely from papers in the possession of the editor and of the Bingham family. Map, 18 notes.

D. L. Smith

378. Harlan, Gilbert Drake, ed. A WALK WITH A WAGON TRAIN: A TEEN-AGE CIVIL WAR VETERAN STROLLS INTO THE WEST. *J. of the West 1964 3(2): 141-162.* After returning from Civil War service with the First Minnesota Heavy Artillery, Wilson Barber Harlan, still only 18 years of age, decided to leave his home in Minnesota to seek his fortune in the Montana gold fields. He learned that Captain Robert E. Fisk was organizing a wagon train with Helena as its destination. He paid Fisk one hundred dollars for the privilege of walking the entire distance alongside the wagons. Harlan kept a diary of his experience in which he faithfully recorded the mileage made by the train each day. He also made notes as to the richness of the soil, water supplies, types of vegetation, and abundance of game, as the train moved through Minnesota, Dakota Territory, and Montana Territory. Illus., map, 16 notes.   D. N. Brown

379. Harris, Everett W., ed. THE YAGER JOURNALS: DIARY OF A JOURNEY ACROSS THE PLAINS. *Nevada State Hist. Soc. Q. (2): 18-39, (3): 26-48, (4): 26-52, 1971 14(1): 26-54, (2): 33-54.* Part I. The Yager Journals were kept by James Pressley Yager, a native of Kentucky born on 21 February 1834 who crossed the plains in 1863. The Yager Journals represent one of the few descriptions of Nevada still available of the closing year of Nevada's Territorial Period. This section of the journals begins on 22 April 1863 in Louisville, Kentucky, where the journey began. By train and river steamer the party went to St. Louis and St. Joseph in Missouri, then to Nebraska City, Nebraska, where the actual wagon trip began. Covers the wagon trip from 14 May to 20 June 1863 along the California Trail to a point near present-day Casper, Wyoming. Photos, 44 notes. Part II. Covers 21 June-10 July 1863, from near present-day Casper through South Pass and on to Echo Creek in Utah, west of Fort Bridger and about four days from Salt Lake City. Yager described the region, including abandoned pony express stations and telegraph communications. The telegraph provided warning of Indian and outlaw dangers. Mentions Army outposts. Map, 28 notes. Part III. Covers the journey along the Mormon Trail from Echo Creek to Camp Thousand Springs Valley northeast of present-day Wells, Nevada. The dates of the trek were 10 July-7 August 1863. From 15 to 17 July the party rested in Salt Lake City, and Yager observed the Mormons and their city. The Yager party struck out north from Salt Lake City, went past the Great Salt Lake to the City of Rocks, an important landmark on the California Trail, and thence traveled southwest to Camp Thousand Springs. Map, photo, 21 notes. Part IV. Begins on 7 August 1863 in the Thousand Springs Valley of Nevada and ends on 29 August 1863 at Boiling Springs, just east of Reno. Yager described the trip across Nevada on the California Trail. In his entry for 13 August, Yager discussed the party's experiences with the various Indian tribes from early on in the trip. In his entries for 18 and 19 August Yager discussed problems of crossing extensive alkali and salt flats. Intermittently, for the next 10 days, he encountered additional alkali and salt flats. Photo, 33 notes. Part V. Covers 30 August-21 October 1863. The Yager party crossed the Forty Mile Desert near what is now Wadsworth, Nevada. This is one of the most difficult stretches of the Humboldt Trail and was strewn with evidence of the

difficulties encountered by previous pioneers. Wagon parts, water barrel hoops, the bones of oxen, broken bottles, and many other items littered the area. Progress on the last parts of the desert was impeded by very heavy sand. After the desert crossing, the Yager party followed the Truckee River canyon to a point near Truckee (now Reno). From this point the party split; Yager and several companions headed for Virginia city, and the remainder turned south to California. Yager and his group reached Virginia City, then moved on to Carson City, stopping only long enough to earn some money cutting timber. In mid-October, Yager moved on to Placerville, California, via the Carson River route. Yager and his party camped about 20 miles northwest of Stockton. Photo, 83 notes. Part VI. This last segment of the Yager Journals begins on 28 October 1863 and ends with 31 December 1863. Records the travels and observations of Yager and his companions in the California gold fields and in the Sierras along the California-Nevada border. Yager's observations throughout the journals appear to be accurate and of surprising depth considering the rough circumstances in which he lived and traveled. 63 notes.   E. P. Costello

380. Holzhueter, John O., ed. FROM WAUPUN TO SACRAMENTO IN 1849: THE GOLD RUSH JOURNAL OF EDWIN HILLYER. *Wisconsin Mag. of Hist. 1966 49(3): 210-244.* After a short introduction to Hillyer's life and the gold rush of 1849, the text of the journal is given with only repetitious portions deleted. It concludes with the author's arrival in Sacramento, California. The journal has several unique features: 1) it is one of the few journals chronicled by an 1849 immigrant that includes details of an Indian slaying; 2) it records a route taken by a minority of forty-niners (beginning at Council Bluffs, Iowa); and 3) because of Hillyer's education and interest in writing, it contains sufficient detail to make the journal "fresh and exciting." 3 photos, 13 drawings, map, 38 notes.   H. A. Negaard

381. Howard, Helen Addison. THE MYSTERY OF SACAGAWEA'S DEATH. *Pacific Northwest Q. 1967 58(1): 1-6.* Summarizes some of the controversial assumptions, books, and articles relating to the role and life span of the young Indian woman Sacagawea who accompanied Lewis and Clark as an interpreter on their expedition through the regions of the Rocky Mountains in 1805. Documented.

C. C. Gorchels

382. Hufford, Kenneth. TRAVELERS ON THE GILA TRAIL, 1824-1850, PART I. *J. of Arizona Hist. 1966 7(1): 1-8.* The Gila Trail, the famous southernmost of the overland trails to California, is indicated as having had little use before the Gold Rush of '49. The few significant users are here described with comments on the routes they used. Documented, map, biblio. To be continued.   J. D. Filipiak

383. Hufford, Kenneth. TRAVELERS ON THE GILA TRAIL, 1824-1850 PART II: AN ANNOTATED BIBLIOGRAPHY. *J. of Ariz. Hist. 1967 8(1): 30-44.* An annotated bibliography of 63 published original accounts of Gila Trail travelers from 1824 to 1850. Major categories are: Early Explorers, 1824-1836; Military Expeditions, 1845-1849; and the largest, Emigrant Journals of the Gold Rush, 1849-1850.

J. D. Filipiak

384. Jackson, Donald. HOW LOST WAS ZEBULON PIKE? *Am. Heritage 1965 16(2): 10-15, 75-80.* Summarizes the Pike expedition so as to evaluate two frequently made charges regarding Zebulon Pike: 1) that Pike was acting on behalf of General James Wilkinson and that the expedition was a ruse for a spying mission, and 2) that Pike was never really lost when he was arrested by Spanish soldiers. The author dismisses both charges and says about the latter that Pike was lost twice, not once. The significance of the expedition is judged to be high in importance but less than that of Lewis and Clark. Illus., map.   J. D. Filipiak

385. Jackson, Donald. THE MYTH OF THE FREMONT HOWITZER. *Missouri Hist. Soc. Bull. 1967 23(3): 205-214.* John Charles Frémont took "the Frémont howitzer" with him on his second western expedition in 1843. Bitter weather in January 1844 forced him to abandon it somewhere on the eastern slope of the Sierra Nevada. One of the several legends that have grown up around the howitzer was the concoction of Frémont, his wife, and his father-in-law, Senator Thomas Hart Benton of Missouri. This version has long enjoyed acceptance by historians. The author now shows it as "an absolute fiction" fabricated to cover the

official censure of Frémont for the "hasty and ill-advised manner" in which he obtained the weapon. 13 notes. D. L. Smith

386. Jackson, Donald. ON READING LEWIS & CLARK. *Montana 1968 18(3): 3-7.* A summary, not intended to be comprehensive, touches most classes of writing on the subject: juvenile, specialized, fictional and serious generalization. "My best advice to anyone interested in Lewis and Clark: read everything you can lay your hands on. It cannot possibly be dull, and much of it will be very rewarding." S. R. Davison

387. Jackson, Donald. THE PUBLIC IMAGE OF LEWIS AND CLARK. *Pacific Northwest Q. 1966 57(1): 1-7.* Conjecture, based on research, on how much accurate knowledge the general public has about the Lewis and Clark expedition, including observations about material in textbooks for school children. Four common fallacies about the expedition are analyzed. C. C. Gorchels

388. Jackson, Donald. SOME ADVICE FOR THE NEXT EDITOR OF LEWIS AND CLARK. *Missouri Hist. Soc. Bull. 1967 24(1): 52-62.* Not only did Meriwether Lewis and William Clark maintain journals on their expedition, but so did every literate member of the group. From 1807 on they began to appear in print. Their publishing history has produced numerous works of varying degrees of quality and in a bewildering quantity. A new standard edition is sorely needed. Three special problems any future editor will have to address himself to are: completeness of the record uncovered to date; duplication in several journals; and the manners, times, and places in which the journals were produced. 18 notes. D. L. Smith

389. Jackson, Donald. ZEBULON M. PIKE "TOURS" MEXICO. *Am. West 1966 3(3): 67-71, 89-93.* James Wilkinson, commanding general of the U.S. Army, sent Zebulon Pike westward from Saint Louis, Missouri, in 1806 to explore the upper reaches of the Arkansas River and thence to return down the Red River to an American post in Louisiana. Pike got lost and mistakenly descended the Rio Grande. He was intercepted by the Spanish, questioned in Santa Fe and Chihuahua, and then escorted back to American territory. It has frequently been charged that when Pike missed the Red River he did so deliberately because Wilkinson had sent him on a private mission vaguely connected with the Aaron Burr conspiracy. The author examines the evidence and concludes that Pike had an oral understanding with Wilkinson as to what he was supposed to do on the mission, but that Pike was not involved in Wilkinson's private schemes. Illus., map, biblio. note. D. L. Smith

390. Jackson, Donald. ZEBULON PIKE AND NEBRASKA. *Nebraska Hist. 1966 47(4): 355-369.* Recounts the councils in 1806 between Zebulon Pike and the Pawnee and affirms that the site of the meeting was in Nebraska and not in Kansas as some scholars had assumed. Also suggested is the significance of Pike as a western explorer. R. Lowitt

391. Jackson, Sheldon G. AN ENGLISH QUAKER TOURS CALIFORNIA: THE JOURNAL OF SARAH LINDSEY, 1859-1860, PART III. *Southern California Q. 1969 51(3): 221-246.* Continued from a previous article. Reproduces entries from Sarah Lindsey's diary for the period 19 September 1859 through 18 August 1860. During this time the Lindseys again ministered to miners in the San Francisco and Sacramento areas and visited Quakers in the Pacific Northwest and Hawaii. In addition to religious aspects of their California travels, Mrs. Lindsey described the people and their living conditions. The Lindseys departed from California for Australia on 18 August 1860. Based mainly on a manuscript in the Devonshire House Library, London; 21 notes. W. L. Bowers

392. Jackson, Sheldon G., ed. AN ENGLISH QUAKER TOURS CALIFORNIA; THE JOURNAL OF SARAH LINDSEY, 1859-1860, PARTS I AND II. *Southern California Q. 1969 51(1): 1-33, and (2): 153-175.* Entries from the journal of an English Quaker minister, Sarah Lindsey, who accompanied her husband to California in 1859-60. Sarah was the wife of Robert Lindsey, wealthy industrialist and Quaker minister who devoted much of his life to a worldwide ministry. The Lindseys ministered to California gold miners, and visited the giant redwoods and San Francisco. Besides relating the religious aspects of their journey, Mrs.

Lindsey gives a description of the countryside and some glimpses of the life of the people living there. Based on a manuscript in the Devonshire House Library, London, and a number of secondary works; 31 notes. To be continued. W. L. Bowers

393. Jacobs, Elijah L. A MAGIC JOURNEY. *Am. West 1967 4(3): 50-51, 75-77.* When a small boy, the author's family journeyed from their homestead in Oklahoma Territory to visit their former home in Kansas and then returned to Oklahoma. The trip was made in a covered wagon. The reminiscing includes descriptions of sod busting, towns, and other sights, as well as anecdotes connected with the journey. D. L. Smith

394. Jamison, Samuel M. DIARY. *Nevada Hist. Soc. Q. 1967 10(4): 3-27.* In 1850, Samuel M. Jamison traveled overland to participate in the California gold rush. Entries from 19 April to 18 September chronicle the cross-continental trek from Independence, Missouri, to Georgetown, California, and his gold-searching attempts. D. L. Smith

395. Johnson, Leland R., ed. AN ARMY ENGINEER ON THE MISSOURI IN 1867. *Nebraska Hist. 1972 53(2): 253-291.* Provides the text of the journal kept by Brevet Major Charles W. Howell, Army Corps of Engineers, during an examination of the Missouri River from 28 June to 27 September 1867. Howell was ordered to conduct an examination of the river from its mouth to the head of navigation to plan its improvement for the benefit of navigation. R. Lowitt

396. Johnston, Francis J. SAN GORGONIO PASS: FORGOTTEN ROUTE OF THE CALIFORNIOS? *J. of the West 1969 8(1): 125-136.* The San Gorgonio Pass is the natural gateway between the fertile coastlands of California and the deserts of the California hinterland, Arizona, and Sonora. It has been commonly accepted that little use of the pass was made after it was opened by Juan Bautista de Anza in 1774. Evidence indicates otherwise. Although it was not the primary and official route, it was used by many Californios into the 1850's. Sufficient numbers used it to fasten semiofficial place names to some of its more prominent natural features. 61 notes. D. L. Smith

397. Keenan, Jerry. EXPLORING THE BLACK HILLS: AN ACCOUNT OF THE CUSTER EXPEDITION. *J. of the West 1967 6(2): 248-261.* Despite the Laramie Treaty of 1868, which guaranteed the Sioux that their sacred Black Hills would not be violated by the white man, General Philip Sheridan received permission to send a scouting expedition into the area. On 2 July 1874 a large force led by Lieutenant Colonel George Custer left Fort Abraham Lincoln. Accompanying the expedition were two geologists, a zoologist, a botanist, a photographer, a mapmaker, and two veteran miners. The expedition was to learn as much of the region as possible. The information gathered triggered a massive rush of miners into the area. This invasion of the Black Hills angered the Indians and was an important factor in the Sioux War of 1876. Based on published sources, illus., 4 notes, biblio. D. N. Brown

398. Landsverk, O. G. NORSE MEDIEVAL CRYPTOGRAPHY IN AMERICAN RUNIC INSCRIPTIONS. *Am.-Scandinavian R. 1967 55(3): 252-263.* Considers the Kensington Stone with its runic inscription an authentic 14th-century artifact. It and other runic inscriptions reveal that Norsemen, early in the 11th century, were in New England and had traveled as far west as present-day Oklahoma. According to the Kensington Stone, Norsemen came to Minnesota about 1362. Authority for these assertions lies in the recent discovery of a solution to Norse cryptograms which has been reportedly forgotten for 500 years. The complex cryptogram hidden in the Kensington runic inscription records the name of the stone carver and the runic inscriber as well as the year 1362. The purpose of the runic cryptogram was to conceal a specific calendar date. The solution to the cryptograms in the Heavener, Oklahoma, runic inscriptions shows Norsemen reached eastern Oklahoma 25 December 1015 and 30 December 1022. Based on research analyzing runic inscriptions which are reproduced along with calendar tables used to verify the dates in the cryptograms. J. G. Smoot

399. Larson, T. A., ed. ACROSS THE PLAINS IN 1864 WITH GEORGE FORMAN. *Ann. of Wyoming 1968 40(2): 267-281.* Continued from a previous abstract. George Forman's travels across Nebraska,

Wyoming, and Montana during 1864 are chronicled in his journal. He describes the scenery, weather, diet, Indians, bridges, and trails along the route to Virginia City and complains about prices there. He discusses his unsuccessful prospecting in the Northern Rockies and concludes with a brief narrative of his return to Denver. Based on government reports, reminiscent accounts, and secondary material; 8 notes.

R. L. Nichols

400. Levitin, Sonia. FIRST HISTORIC TREK ACROSS THE WILD LAND TO CALIFORNIA. *Smithsonian 1971 2(8): 68-73.* The story of the first party from the United States to reach California overland, in 1841. Organized by a Missouri schoolmaster, John Bidwell, the party had originally included 500 people. Finally 68 people gathered at Sapling Grove, Missouri, to make the trip. At that time no one knew the way to California. A fraudulent map and advice from a settler in California, John Marsh, however, seemed to indicate that the journey would be relatively easy. Before departing the California group joined with some missionaries (led by Father Pierre Jean De Smet) who were going to Oregon. Together they would follow the Oregon Trail to Soda Springs, where the groups would split. They crossed the plains, where they met a "prankish" Indian party and shot buffalo. When the group reached Soda Springs, 33 of the original 68 decided to go to California. They had no guide, and their map was in error. They found the Humboldt River and followed it to the Sierra Nevada. The mountains proved to be the most difficult obstacle to their journey. There they killed and ate their livestock. In November 1841 all 33 persons reached John Marsh's ranch. Based on diaries and memoirs; illus.

J. M. Hawes

401. Lottich, Kenneth V., ed. MY TRIP TO MONTANA TERRITORY, 1879. *Montana 1965 15(1): 12-25.* Charles French Kellogg migrated from Kansas to Montana in 1879. His life was commonplace, but his diary provides details of the trip and of conditions in Butte and Missoula during the years when civilization was replacing the frontier in this area.

S. R. Davison

402. Mahoney, Donald, ed. END OF AN ERA: THE TRAVEL JOURNAL OF MARY MAHONEY. *Nebraska Hist. 1966 47(3): 329-338.* A day-by-day report of a 1901 covered wagon journey by seven farm families from western Nebraska to Colorado looking for better land, written by Mary Mahoney, the wife of one of the leaders of the expedition.

R. Lowitt

403. Marston, O. Dock. THE LOST JOURNAL OF JOHN COLTON SUMNER. *Utah Hist. Q. 1969 37(2): 173-189.* Daily entries in the journal of Sumner, a member of the party accompanying Powell on his first expedition down the Colorado from 24 May to 28 June 1869.

S. L. Jones

404. Mattes, Merrill J. ON THE TRAIL OF LEWIS AND CLARK. *Montana 1966 16(3): 6-22.* A series of 42 recent photographs, with captions derived from the Lewis and Clark journals and from incidents of the trip when the pictures were taken in the summer of 1965. The route was along the Missouri River, where relatively few miles have not been inundated by reservoirs.

S. R. Davison

405. Mattison, Ray H., ed. THE FISK EXPEDITION OF 1864: THE DIARY OF WILLIAM L. LARNED. *North Dakota Hist. 1969 36(3): 208-274.* In 1864 James W. Fisk led a wagon train from Minnesota through the western Dakota Territory, trying to open a new and shorter route to Bannack and Virginia City, Montana Territory. The Fisk train was the only one of eight trains of the 1860's that had serious Indian trouble along the route to the gold fields. William L. Larned and his family were members of the expedition. Larned kept a diary of the trip starting on 29 June 1864 and concluding 31 January 1866. The Indian trouble is recorded by Larned beginning with the entry of 2 September 1864. The diary is taken from a typed copy owned by the Minnesota Historical Society; the original has been lost. Illus., photos, 37 notes.

E. P. Costello

406. Mayer, Robert W. WOOD RIVER, 1803-1804. *J. of the Illinois State Hist. Soc. 1968 61(2): 140-149.* Deals with the question of locating the exact point from which the Lewis and Clark expedition started up the Missouri River when leaving Illinois Territory. It is concluded that the coordinates of their camp site are Latitude 38 50' 45" North, Longitude

90 07' 11" West, a point now on the Missouri bank but in 1803-04 on the Illinois bank of the Mississippi River.

S. L. Jones

407. McDermott, John Francis. LOST MANUSCRIPTS OF WESTERN TRAVEL. *Arizona and the West 1969 11(4): 315-326.* Citing many examples, the author asserts that "irretrievably lost" manuscripts probably have only disappeared from sight; that manuscripts are sometimes found in unexpected places and circumstances; that "lost" diaries are published every year, and further discoveries will continue indefinitely; and that western travel manuscripts that yet remain "lost" abound in a great variety and wealth. Sleuthing experiences and techniques continue to be productive. Several suggestions are made of possible travel manuscripts that should be confirmed and ferreted out. 3 illus., 18 notes.

D. L. Smith

408. Meschter, Daniel Y., ed. SIXTY DAYS TO AND IN YELLOWSTONE PARK. *Ann. of Wyoming 1972 44(1): 5-23.* Presents an edited version of five letters which Wyoming dairyman Henry A. Kirk (1836-1904) wrote to the *Carbon County Journal* in Rawlins in 1892. The letters describe a thousand-mile round trip which Kirk, his two sons-in-law, and their families made by horse and wagon from Rawlins to Yellowstone National Park in July and August 1892. Kirk's account is appealing because he made the trek for pleasure rather than for scientific purposes. Based on primary and secondary sources; illus., 24 notes.

G. R. Adams

409. Mihm, Friedrich. INTERESTING ACCOUNTS OF THE TRAVELS OF ABRAHAM ABRAHAMSOHN TO AMERICA AND ESPECIALLY TO THE GOLD MINES OF CALIFORNIA AND AUSTRALIA. *Western States Jewish Hist. Q. 1969 1(3): 128-145.* Abrahamsohn was born in Pomerania. He married; and being unsuccessful in business, left his wife and children in 1849 to seek his fortune in America. He came to America, peddled for a while in New York, became a glazier, and went to California in 1851. He observed business conditions in San Francisco, entered business there for a while, lost his goods in a fire, and then went to the mountains to prospect for gold. Article to be continued.

R. E. Levinson

410. Mihm, Friedrich. INTERESTING ACCOUNTS OF THE TRAVELS OF ABRAHAM ABRAHAMSON TO AMERICA AND ESPECIALLY TO THE GOLD MINES OF CALIFORNIA AND AUSTRALIA. *Western States Jewish Hist. Q. 1969 1(4): 182-195, 2(1): 44-61, 1970 2(2): 106-116.* Continued from a previous article. Part II. Abrahamson, in gold-rush California, became a wheelwright, tailor, *mohel*, restaurant owner, and clothing store clerk, all the while witnessing gold fever, robberies, murders, gambling, bull-bear fights, and lynchings. In May 1852 he sailed for Australia to find better opportunity. He predicted, "California will become a really blessed land once the gold fever has abated,..." Part III. After a voyage of nine weeks, Abrahamson arrived in Port Jackson, New South Wales. He sailed to Melbourne and went to the gold fields, where he encountered aborigines. He panned for gold with four others, but Abrahamson and another left after the other three were caught withholding gold from the common share. Abrahamson then panned a thousand dollars' worth of gold on his own. After warning from a a friendly aborigine, he eluded an attack by another aborigine who was bent on murder. He took up the still more profitable work of baking bread in the mining camp and prospered. Part IV. After 11 months of baking, Abrahamson sailed home to Germany in 1853 and rejoined his family.

S

411. Miller, David H. THE IVES EXPEDITION REVISITED: A PRUSSIAN'S IMPRESSIONS. *J. of Arizona Hist. 1972 13(1): 1-25.* The outbreak of the Mormon War gave added meaning to the already launched steamboat exploring-surveying expedition of Lieutenant Joseph Christmas Ives (1828-68) on the Colorado River. He was now to ascend the river to determine the feasibility of transporting troops and supplies to the mouth of the Virgin River, and thence by land to Utah. Balduin Möllhausen, a Prussian with experience on southwestern Army surveys and other expeditions, served as artist, assistant naturalist, and unofficial diarist for Ives. Möllhausen's descriptions, observations, and illustrations of the journey and Indians met on it, published in two volumes as *Reisen in die Felsengebirge Nord-Amerikas* (Leipzig, 1861), are the basis for the present study of the 1857-58 expedition up the Colorado River from the Gulf of California in Mexico to the Black Canyon between Arizona and

Nevada, somewhat short of what was mistaken as the stipulated destination. 7 illus., map, 48 notes.

D. L. Smith

412. Munkres, Robert L. ASH HOLLOW: GATEWAY TO THE HIGH PLAINS. *Ann. of Wyoming 1970 42(1): 5-42.* Describes Ash Hollow, which was a prominent resting place for users of the Oregon Trail. Lying between the South and North Platte rivers, it provided welcome water, fuel, game, and grass. The author includes travelers' comments and notes the danger that pioneers encountered from the descent into the hollow as well as from occasional Indian depredations. Based on published travel accounts, diaries, and filmed manuscript material from the Newberry Library, Chicago; illus., photo, 175 notes.

R. L. Nichols

413. Munkres, Robert L. INDEPENDENCE ROCK AND DEVIL'S GATE. *Ann. of Wyoming 1968 40(1): 23-40.* This is a description of the geographic formations Independence Rock and the Devil's Gate, prominent landmarks on the Oregon Trail. The former is an isolated granite outcropping at the end of the Sweetwater Valley in Wyoming. The latter is a gorge through which the Sweetwater River flows, and is about five miles above Independence Rock. The article discusses travelers' descriptions of the two formations, as well as how they served as landmarks and places to leave messages or news. Based on manuscripts, published journals, and reminiscent accounts; illus., 76 notes.

R. L. Nichols

414. Munkres, Robert L. THE PLAINS INDIAN THREAT ON THE OREGON TRAIL BEFORE 1860. *Ann. of Wyoming 1968 40(2): 193-221.* Examines 66 diaries of travelers using the Oregon Trail between 1834 and 1860 to determine the actual danger from Indian attack on that route. The vast majority of diarists studied encountered no overt threat of attack in either Nebraska or Wyoming. Indian harassment of travelers was mainly through begging, demanding tolls, and theft of livestock. These acts occurred more often than did physical attack. Carelessness of the travelers induced some Indian harassment. Based on printed and manuscript diaries kept by travelers on the Oregon Trail; 87 notes.

R. L. Nichols

415. Munkres, Robert L. SODA SPRINGS: CURIOSITY OF THE TRAIL. *Ann. of Wyoming 1971 43(2): 215-235.* Describes the reactions of more than two dozen mid-19th-century diarists to Soda and Steamboat Springs on the Oregon-California Trail between Forts Bridger and Hall. Invariably curious about these mineral springs, passing travelers often conducted experiments regarding the taste, temperature, and pressure of the water and the smell of gases escaping from the earth. The gas nauseated most, and the water generally had a purgative effect. Only the Indians consistently used the springs for practical purposes. They made dye from the water of some springs and utilized the white clay in the vicinity as a cleansing agent. Although some travelers predicted that the springs would become a famous resort area, the springs are now covered by the Soda Point Reservoir. Based on primary and secondary sources; 131 notes.

G. R. Adams

416. Munkres, Robert L. WIVES, MOTHERS, DAUGHTERS: WOMEN'S LIFE ON THE ROAD WEST. *Ann. of Wyoming 1970 42(2): 191-224.* Claims that the usual discussions of opening the West omit half of the story by concentrating entirely on male activities and ignoring the role of women on the frontier. The author describes the travel conditions experienced by female pioneers and their responses to these. Overland travel was physically demanding and the usual difficulties of cooking and related household chores were intensified by the crude or missing facilities on the overland trail. Clothing, diet, health, and constant hardship of travel posed problems. However, healthy, well-prepared travelers might enjoy a wide variety of food and have an interesting, if not enjoyable journey. Based mainly on numerous manuscript and published diaries kept by female pioneers; 158 notes.

R. L. Nichols

417. Myers, Lee. POPE'S WELLS. *New Mexico Hist. R. 1963 38(4): 273-299.* John Pope had little more success in finding artesian wells on the Llano Estacado than he had against Robert E. Lee at the battle of Second Manassas. In 1854 Brevet Captain Pope explored the 32nd parallel route for a railroad to the Pacific. The principal obstacle on the route was the lack of water. Backed by a Congressional appropriation of 100 thousand dollars, Pope began to drill for artesian wells in 1855 - a task

which would encounter numerous difficulties and end unproductive in 1859.

D. F. Henderson

418. Nichols, Roger L., ed. THE CAMP MISSOURI-CHARITON ROAD, 1819: THE JOURNAL OF LT. GABRIEL FIELD. *Missouri Hist. Soc. Bull. 1968 24(2): 139-152.* When the 1819 Yellowstone Expedition failed to reach its objective, the troops settled down in temporary quarters at Camp Missouri, Nebraska. It became imperative that land communications be established with settlements further down the Missouri River. It was Lieutenant Gabriel Field's assignment to survey for a road to Chariton in Missouri. Field's Trace, as it came to be known, connected Camp Missouri with the town of Chariton and further on to Franklin. For several years it functioned as a major overland route through northwestern Missouri. His 31 October-27 November 1819 journal, herein edited, is a starkly realistic picture of the tiresomely routine and harsh life of the frontier soldier. 28 notes.

D. L. Smith

419. Nichols, Roger L., ed. GENERAL HENRY ATKINSON'S REPORT OF THE YELLOWSTONE EXPEDITION OF 1825. *Nebraska Hist. 1963 44(2): 65-82.*

420. Nichols, Roger L. STEPHEN LONG AND SCIENTIFIC EXPLORATION ON THE PLAINS. *Nebraska Hist. 1971 52(1): 51-64.* Examines Long's expeditions of 1819 and 1820, the first American efforts to explore the Great Plains in a scientific manner and the only significant Army explorations between the War of 1812 and the 1840's. The expeditions should not be considered failures which harmed America, but rather expeditions that included the most significant explorations of the period after the War of 1812.

R. Lowitt

421. O'Leary, James L., Mrs. HENRY CHATILLON. *Bull. of the Missouri Hist. Soc. 1966 22(2, pt. 1): 123-142.* Discusses the life of Henry Chatillon (d. 1873), Francis Parkman's guide on the Oregon Trail in 1846. Four letters written for him to Parkman, 1847-67, still exist. The author also quotes from Parkman's correspondence with Frederic Remington about illustrating *The Oregon Trail* in 1892. 39 notes.

T. M. Condon

422. Olsen, Robert W., Jr. THE POWELL SURVEY KANAB BASE LINE. *Utah Hist. Q. 1969 37(2): 261-268.* Describes the establishment of a base line at Kanab by measurements conducted by members of Powell's second expedition down the Colorado and the markers which were erected at the base line.

S. L. Jones

423. Osgood, Ernest S. CLARK ON THE YELLOWSTONE 1806. *Montana 1968 18(3): 9-29.* A summary of selected incidents of the Lewis and Clark trip, with emphasis on Clark's eastbound journey from Lolo to the Dakota line, and particularly his adventures in the Yellowstone Valley. Largely paraphrased from the Thwaites edition of the explorers' journals; illustrated with recent photographs showing the terrain.

S. R. Davison

424. Paulson, Norman, ed. A LETTER FROM HORATIO H. LARNED TO KATE LARNED ALEXANDER. *North Dakota Hist. 1969 36(3): 275-278.* Horatio H. Larned was the son of William L. Larned and accompanied his father on the 1864 Fisk Expedition from Minnesota to Montana Territory. The part of the Horatio Larned letter that is published in this article provides additional details on the expedition. This letter is dated 1 July 1910. Illus., photos.

E. P. Costello

425. Peebles, John J. ON THE LOLO TRAIL: ROUTE AND CAMPSITES OF LEWIS AND CLARK. *Idaho Yesterdays 1965 9(4): 2-15, and 1966 10(2): 16-27.* Part II. Continues the author's study of the explorers' overland journey from the Missouri to the Clearwater. Includes excerpts from the journals of Meriwether Lewis (1774-1809) and William Clark (1770-1838) between the spring of 1805 and the winter of 1805-06. Part III. Follows the trail and campsites of Lewis and Clark on their return through Idaho during the spring and summer of 1806. The explorers left Fort Clatsop 23 March 1806, traveled down the Columbia to the Dalles, then moved eastward by land. They crossed the Snake and Clearwater, traversed the mountains, continued down the Missouri and arrived in St. Louis 3 September 1806. Illus., maps.

B. B. Swift

426. Peebles, John J. RUGGED WATERS: TRAILS AND CAMP-SITES OF LEWIS AND CLARK IN THE SALMON RIVER COUNTRY. *Idaho Yesterdays 1964 8(2): 2-17.* An account of the course and campsites of the Lewis and Clark expedition through northern Idaho, from 9 August to 4 September 1805. The author, an engineer, has used the journals of members of the party, Clark's compass traverse notes, and Clark's maps to reconstruct this portion of their journey. Contains detailed maps and recent photographs of the places the author has determined to be the campsites.   M. Small

427. Petersen, William J. THE LEWIS AND CLARK EXPEDITION. *Palimpsest 1964 45(3): 97-144.* In three short articles the author discusses the Lewis and Clark expedition in its passage along the western edge of what was to be the state of Iowa. The complete Journal of Sergeant Charles Floyd, a member of the expedition, is published for that portion of the trip through the state (pp. 132-143).   D. W. Curl

428. Peterson, Ernst. REV. SAMUEL PARKER AND THE SOUTHERN NEZ PERCE TRAIL. *Montana 1966 16(4): 12-27.* The Protestant missionary Samuel Parker, passed through the southwestern tip of present Montana in 1835, en route to the homeland of the Nez Percé Indians, who were his escort on this occasion. The author attempts to identify the trail they followed. Based on Parker's published account, supported by the author's field reconnaissance and illustrated with his recent photos.   S. R. Davison

429. Povlovich, Charles A., Jr., ed. WILL DEWEY IN UTAH. *Utah Hist. Q. 1965 33(2): 134-140.* Provides editorial comment on and the text of five letters written by Will Dewey to his brother after a sudden, unannounced departure from his home in Missouri. His destination was Utah. The letters contain a lively account of his adventures with white settlers and with the Indians.   S. L. Jones

430. Reid, Russell. SAKAKAWEA. *North Dakota Hist. 1963 30(2/3): 101-113.* North Dakota claimed that Sakakawea, the bird woman, young Indian wife of Charbonneau and member of the Lewis and Clark expedition, was the Snake squaw who died in 1811 at the age of 25 in South Dakota. This claim is based on the journal of John Luttig, a clerk of Manuel Lisa's Missouri Fur Company. Wyoming accepts the claim of Dr. Grace Raymond Hebard in her book *Sacajawea* (1933) (the accepted spelling in Wyoming), that the Indian woman was a Shoshone who lived to the age of 100 years and died in Wyoming in 1884. Map and illus.   I. W. Van Noppen

431. Rusho, W. L. FRANCIS BISHOP'S 1871 RIVER MAPS. *Utah Hist. Q. 1969 37(2): 207-213.* Explains how Bishop's maps, which have been lost, were made during the second expedition conducted down the Colorado by Powell and tells how Bishop's tracings of sections of these maps survived to become part of Bishop's papers, which are now located in the Utah Historical Society.   S. L. Jones

432. Rusho, W. L. RIVER RUNNING 1921: THE DIARY OF E. L. KOLB. *Utah Hist. Q. 1969 37(2): 269-283.* Provides an explanatory introduction and the edited text of a diary kept by Ellsworth Kolb between 3 September and 13 October 1921 when he and his brother were the boatmen in an expedition to map Cataract Canyon on the Colorado River. The diary describes the progress of the work and the life in the river camps from day to day.   S. L. Jones

433. Sears, Stephen W. TRAIL BLAZER OF THE FAR WEST. *Am. Heritage 1963 14(4): 60-64, 80-83.* Traces Jedediah Strong Smith's (1799-1831) contributions to the exploration and mapping of the American West in a series of expeditions from 1823 to 1831. Map.   C. R. Allen, Jr.

434. Shafer, Gladys. EASTWARD HO! EZRA MEEKER MEMORIALIZES THE OREGON TRAIL, 1905-1910. *Am. West 1968 5(6): 42-48.* Ezra Meeker, 1852 Oregon Trail pioneer, whose life missed the century mark by two years, sought adventure to the last of his days. At 76, for example, he set out to revive the fame of the almost forgotten and "scantily acknowledged" Oregon Trail. He cannibalized three old trail wagons to put together a prairie schooner and acquired a team of oxen. In January 1906 he left his home in Washington to follow the old trail in reverse. Lecturing, inspiring erection of over a hundred wooden and granite monuments, selling postcards and an account of his journey, he reached trail's end at the Missouri River. Here his goal was extended to the national capital as a means of publicizing the Oregon Trail and petitioning government support. Two years later the battered old trail wagon passed through the gates of the White House to receive the enthusiastic welcome of President Theodore Roosevelt and his warm endorsement of Federal support to mark and memorialize the trail properly. Meeker made another ox wagon trek in 1910 locating uncertain stretches of the trail. 5 illus.   D. L. Smith

435. Shirk, George H. A TOUR ON THE PRAIRIES ALONG THE WASHINGTON IRVING TRAIL IN OKLAHOMA. *Chronicles of Oklahoma 1967 45(3): 312-331.* In 1832, Washington Irving and others spent a month on the plains of Oklahoma, an account of which he gave in *A Tour on the Prairies* (reprinted 1955 by the University of Oklahoma Press). In 1956, the Oklahoma Historical Society issued a detailed route guide following Irving's trail. New highways, a reservoir, and other changes have made the 1956 guide out of date. The route guide is herein updated to conform to 1967 highways. Biblio. note.   D. L. Smith

436. Smith, Alson J. JEDEDIAH SMITH AND THE HONOURABLE COMPANY. *Beaver [Canada] 1964 295(Summer): 28-39.* Jedediah Strong Smith (1799-1831) ranked as an explorer of the American West second only to Lewis and Clark. On two fur trading expeditions, in 1824 and 1828, he encountered the men of the Hudson's Bay Company in the Oregon Country. He spent the winter of 1828-29 at Fort Vancouver as a refugee from an Indian massacre; his stolen goods were collected for him by the Company's men. Impressed by the hospitality he had received, Smith withdrew his trappers east of the Rockies where they competed with the Hudson's Bay Company. Illus.   L. F. S. Upton

437. Snell, John W., ed. BY WAGON FROM KANSAS TO ARIZONA—THE TRAVEL DIARY OF LYDIA E. ENGLISH. *Kansas Hist. Q. 1970 36(4): 369-389.* Lydia E. English was one of 13 adults and an unspecified number of children who traveled from Concordia, Kansas, to Prescott, Arizona, between 20 September and 6 December 1875. Her diary ran in the 18 and 25 February and the 3 and 10 March 1876 issues of the Concordia *Empire,* the source for the present edition of the diary. English described the countryside, towns, and inhabitants she encountered. The diary interests was it was written when most settlers were moving to central Kansas rather than from it, and because it blends contemporary situations into a background provided by the earlier history of the Southwest. This happened because the party followed both the Santa Fe Trail and parts of the older trails established by Spanish priests. Based on articles, local histories, and manuscripts in the Kansas State Historical Society; illus., 44 notes.   W. F. Zornow

438. Sommer, Jane Hamill. OUTFITTING FOR THE WEST, 1849. *Missouri Hist. Soc. Bull. 1968 24(4, pt. 1): 340-347.* Through correspondence and excerpts from other documentary material, Independence, Missouri, was advertised as the best jumping-off place for Oregon and California. Particulars as to the equipment needed and the probable cost are also indicated. 5 notes.   D. L. Smith

439. Spring, Agnes Wright. WESTERN TOURISM OF SAMUEL MALLORY. *Montana 1965 15(3): 68-79.* Annotated diary of a trip down the Missouri River by barge and steamboat from Fort Benton to St. Louis in 1864. Also, Mallory's account of his return trip overland in 1868 is included with summary paragraphs on his later years at the family home in Danbury, Connecticut.   S. R. Davison

440. Standford, Lyle. MAN'S TENDENCY TO IGNORE HIS HERITAGE AND TO DESTROY IT. .. .A REVIEW ESSAY. *Idaho Yesterdays 1964 8(4): 29-32.* Reviews *The Natural History of the Lewis and Clark Expedition* (East Lansing: Michigan State U. Press, 1961), edited by Raymond Darwin Burroughs. Burroughs based his study on the Lewis and Clark journals. The value of the study increases as the reader gives "attention to the original journals using the suggestions implied through Burroughs' selections from the findings." The book has its place in the history of conservation and is giving perspective to our modern position. It points out the lesson of man's tendency to ignore his heritage and to destroy it.   B. B. Swift

441. Stearns, Harold G. LEWIS AND CLARK TRAIL: AMERICA'S HISTORIC AVENUE. *Montana 1964 14(1): 53-58.* Outlines tentative plans for establishing a Lewis and Clark Memorial Trail, possibly as a chain of state parks and monuments along the route.
L. G. Nelson

442. Steele, Harriet. GOLD RUSH LETTERS COPIED FROM AN OLD LETTER BOOK. *Pacific Historian 1964 8(1): 43-52.* Harriet Steele, an Englishwoman, crossed the American continent by wagon in 1852 and 1853. Three letters describe her new experiences as a pioneer, the hazards of the journey, and the customs of the Americans (especially the Mormons). The letters also include a careful comparison of English and American prices and wages in gold rush Placerville and San Francisco.
T. R. Cripps

443. Stevens, Harriet F. ONE OF THE MERCER GIRLS: A JOURNAL OF LIFE ON THE STEAMER CONTINENTAL. *Ann. of Wyoming 1963 35(2): 214-228.* The journal of Harriet F. Stevens, one of the "Mercer Girls" - single girls living in the eastern United States whom Asa Shinn Mercer persuaded to emigrate to Washington Territory in 1866. The journal describes living conditions aboard the ship *Continental*, fellow passengers, crossing the equator, several Latin American ports, and coastal scenery. It is now in the collections of the Wyoming State Archives and Historical Department.
R. L. Nichols

444. Stevenson, Elizabeth. MERIWETHER AND I. *Virginia Q. R. 1967 43(4): 580-591.* In the perspective of a visit to her childhood home at Great Falls, Montana, the author expertly reviews a segment of the Lewis and Clark journey to the Pacific. She also suggests that the economic and political views of the West have changed little since her childhood while the South is in ferment.
O. H. Zabel

445. Stiles, Helen J. DOWN THE COLORADO IN 1889. *Colorado Mag. 1964 41(3): 225-246.* Frank Mason Brown planned to construct a railroad following the Colorado River from Grand Junction, Colorado, to the Gulf of California and from there to San Diego. It was to be a water-level road on which Colorado products could be carried to California, and tourists attracted by the scenery. Frank C. Kendrick, a Denver mining engineer, was employed to make the survey of the route from Grand Junction to the mouth of the Green River. Kendrick kept a notebook account, day by day, from 18 May to 27 May, of the first party of record to run this 160 mile stretch of the Colorado (then the Grand) River. Brown's accidental death on 25 May halted the railroad project. Kendrick's notebook is reproduced here. It is the property of the State Historical Society of Colorado.
I. W. Van Noppen

446. Strong, Douglas H. SEQUOIA NATIONAL PARK: DISCOVERY AND EXPLORATION. *Western Explorer 1966 4(2): 9-27.* Details the discovery and exploration of the Sequoia National Park region from the first recorded sighting of the Sierra Nevada by the Spaniard Pedro Fages in 1772 to the establishment of the park in 1890. The first American to visit the area was Jedediah Smith in 1827. Hale D. Tharp, in 1858, was the first white man to discover the giant sequoia forest. The first permanent white settlement was established in 1851. No one ventured into the High Sierra until 1864 when the California State Geological Survey directed by Josiah Dwight Whitney undertook an expedition. The survey party discovered the highest peak in the United States outside Alaska which it named for its director. Naturalist John Muir visited the region during the 1870's and became interested in its preservation. Prospectors, sheepmen, and loggers also took part in the exploration of the area and the latter two groups left their mark on the region by their overgrazing and deforestation practices. However, the giant sequoias were not immediately threatened and by the time they were a movement to protect and preserve them had arisen. Based on primary and secondary sources, newspapers, and government documents; 7 illus., 102 notes.
W. L. Bowers

447. Stucker, Gilbert F. HAYDEN IN THE BADLANDS. *Am. West 1967 4(1): 40-45, 79-85.* The pioneering explorations of Ferdinand Vandeveer Hayden were the principal foundations of present day understanding of the geology of the trans-Mississippi West. Twenty-three year old Hayden began his geologic studies in South Dakota's Badlands in 1853 with an assignment to prospect for the fossil remains of prehistoric animals. On this and successive expeditions in 1855 and 1866 he found bones and fossils and observed geologic formations. He cataloged, collected, analyzed, interpreted, and systemized what he found and observed. He worked out the broad geologic outlines of the Black Hills and filled in many of the details. Although his interpretations have not escaped revision his general concept remains and his reports are still basic sources on Badlands geology. Appended are two lengthy excerpts from Hayden's published writings, one from his field journal of the 1855 expedition, and the other, from his reflections on the paleontological aspects of the area, written following his 1866 explorations. Illus., biblio., note.
D. L. Smith

448. Stull, John O. THE LAST PATHFINDER: GENERAL EDWARD F. BEALE, U.S. NAVY (RETIRED). *U.S. Naval Inst. Pro. 1966 92(2): 76-83.* Biography of a U.S. Naval officer who became a scout and pathfinder during the American acquisition of California. Naval Lieutenant Beale resigned his commission, but soon had the Army rank of brigadier general bestowed upon him by the governor of California. Beale built up major holdings in California and participated in survey expeditions. The author describes him as "the last of the pathfinders." Undocumented, illus.
W. C. Frank

449. Swanner, Charles D. RICHARD HENRY DANA, JR.: AN EARLY VISITOR TO ORANGE COUNTY. *California Hist. 1968 15(1): 21-25.* Discusses the life of Richard Henry Dana, Jr., the author of *Two Years Before the Mast* (1840). Dana entered Harvard University in 1831, but due to eye problems was forced to leave in 1834. From 1834 to 1836 he served as a common seaman. His well-known book, an account of a voyage to California, brought him fame but not fortune. The author offers an account of Dana's ancestors in America from 1640.
O. L. Miller

450. Townshend, F. Trench. TRAVEL, SPORT AND ADVENTURE. *Ann. of Wyoming 1970 42(2): 183-189.* A reprint of two chapters from the author's book, *Ten Thousand Miles of Travel, Sport and Adventure* (London, 1869). The narrative describes cross-country travel by train to Fort Saunders and the overland trek through Wyoming and Colorado. It includes comments about lawless activities in Laramie, the work of the local vigilantes, travel through the Rockies to North Park in Colorado, and hunting experiences.
R. L. Nichols

451. Tucker, John M. MAJOR LONG'S ROUTE FROM THE ARKANSAS TO THE CANADIAN RIVER, 1820. *New Mexico Hist. R. 1963 38(3): 185-219.* Although Long's route southward from the Arkansas in search of the Red River has never been accurately traced, until now no attempt had been made to correlate the observations of Dr. Edwin James, botanist and geologist for the expedition, to existing terrain. The author, with the assistance of several geologists familiar with the southwest, has done this. While the author's findings are a major addition to the history of the expedition, he calls for "even more searching analysis...-[to] clarify other details which are as yet obscured."
D. F. Henderson

452. Tyler, Ronnie C., ed. EXPLORING THE RIO GRANDE: LT. DUFF C. GREEN'S REPORT OF 1852. *Arizona and the West 1968 10(1): 43-60.* Lieutenant Duff C. Green was in command of an escort party for the U.S. Boundary Survey Commission in 1852. The expedition to which he was attached explored uncharted Rio Grande country from Presidio del Norte south to Eagle Pass, Texas, traveling considerably in the States of Chihuahua and Coahuila of Northern Mexico. The 18-page manuscript in the National Archives, dated 16 December 1852, is Green's report of his tour of duty from 11 June to 24 November. The document records the examination and exploration of the rugged canyon country of the Rio Grande, a parley with hostile Indians, the weakness of Mexican frontier defense, a rare account of military escort life with the commission, and an explanation of a part of the stormy and controversial history of the commission. 3 illus., 2 maps, 67 notes.
D. L. Smith

453. Webb, Henry J. THE LAST TREK ACROSS THE GREAT SALT DESERT. *Utah Hist. Q. 1963 31(1): 26-33.* Recounts the retracing in Trackmaster vehicles by author and others in August 1962, of the Donner-Reed trail. At many places the ruts of the old trail were still discernible. Pioneer artifacts were found. Additional information was discovered on controversial points concerning the exact route of the trail.
S. L. Jones

454. Webster, Donald B. FREMONT AND HIS FRIEND. *Am. Hist. Illus. 1966 1(5): 32-36.* The travels of a mountain howitzer, carried at great difficulty on the second expedition (1843-44) of John C. Frémont exploring the Rockies, into southern Oregon, and across the Sierras into Mexican California. The little canon was abandoned in a snowdrift, discovered years later, moved around several times, and is believed by some to be the one at the Nevada State Museum in Carson City. 3 photos, drawing.   E. Brown

455. West, Helen B. OUR NATIONAL EPIC. *Montana 1966 16(3): 3-5.* Increasing public interest in the expedition suggests that people are finding in it an ideal American undertaking which they can join vicariously by reading its history and tracing out its route. "The American nation wants to re-live the celebrated trek."   S. R. Davison

456. White, Helen McCann. CAPTAIN FISK GOES TO WASHINGTON. *Minnesota Hist. 1963 38(8): 216-230.* Between 1862 and 1865 Captain James Liberty Fisk, soldier, propagandist for western emigration, lobbyist and leader of four overland expeditions from Minnesota to the Montana gold fields, made four trips to Washington, D.C. in an effort to get federal funds and support for a scheme to blaze and then fortify a road from eastern Minnesota to the Rocky Mountain gold fields. He never achieved this ultimate goal, partly because of alleged personality defects and partly because of the power shift in Washington after Lincoln's assassination. The three earlier trips to the capital, however, produced the funds necessary to convey and give some protection to relatively small parties of emigrants on their westward trip.
P. L. Simon

457. Williams, Burton J., ed. OVERLAND TO THE GOLD FIELDS OF CALIFORNIA IN 1850: THE JOURNAL OF CALVIN TAYLOR. *Nebraska Hist. 1969 50(2): 125-149.* Presents a portion of the Taylor journal devoted primarily to crossing the territory now included in the State of Nebraska. It begins with his departure from Saint Joseph on 26 May and concludes with his arrival at Fort Laramie 33 days later.   R. Lowitt

458. Wilson, William E. and Mueller, George. HOBOING IN THE WEST IN THE 1880'S. *Montana 1968 18(2): 36-51.* Recollections, as of 1930, of a walking trip by two young men through the heart of the Sioux country in 1881, while the area was still dangerous after the military action of recent years. Adventures with Indians, soldiers, wild animals, and weather enlivened the journey. A prologue and an epilogue by George Mueller supply further data on Wilson, crediting him with discovery of gold in the area around Gilt Edge, Montana, in limestone formations generally believed never to contain precious metals. Illus.
S. R. Davison

459. Yates, Ted. SINCE LEWIS AND CLARK. *Am. West 1965 2(4): 22-30.* The author was commissioned to produce and direct a recreation of the Lewis and Clark Expedition for a television film for the National Broadcasting Company. Lewis and Clark contended with "a total wilderness" of undetermined size and danger, inhabited by wild animals and primitive Indians. Relentless civilization has despoiled and altered the country so much that the Lewis and Clark journals "seem to be a myth, a romantic fiction." The many "travesties" of a century and a half have rendered the land to a "just plain hideous" state. Instead of being "a spectacle of beauty," the Lewis and Clark country is "a debacle of neglect and abuse." Maps, illus.   D. L. Smith

460. Zullo, Janet Lewis. ANNIE MONTAGUE ALEXANDER: HER WORK IN PALEONTOLOGY. *J. of the West 1969 8(2): 183-199.* After a brief biographical sketch of Alexander (1867-1950) up to 1905, presents her personal account of the saurian expedition of 1905 to the Humbolt mountain range in Nevada. Observes the methods of discovering fossils and their excavation and the beauties of the country, and describes her companions. The author describes some of Alexander's later expeditions.   J

461. —. NOTES OF A TOURIST THROUGH THE UPPER MISSOURI REGION. *Bull. of the Missouri Hist. Soc. 1966 22(4, pt. 1): 393-409.* A microfilm reproduction of an article in four parts which originally appeared in a St. Louis weekly, *The Missouri Saturday News,* published for only one year (from 6 January 1838 to 19 January 1839),

dated 25 August, 1 September, 8 September, and 15 September 1838. Apart from his signature (Jacques), the author is unknown. The State Historical Society of Wisconsin at Madison has the complete file of this obscure paper. Jacques described a tour of the Upper Missouri region by a party of unknown explorers. He was convinced that the Indian is "an idler and a savage." All attempts on the part of the government to assist the Indians to become an agricultural people had been unsuccessful. "Let an attempt therefore be made to induce the border tribes to become herdsmen, and in case of the success of the plan, their own immediate wants will not only be supplied, but they will soon become a wealthy people." Jacques said that although Indian children neglected their parents, parents seldom or never neglected their children; that true courage was not a trait of Indian character; that most Indian women were beautiful, and that "their faces do not belie their hearts."
D. D. Cameron

Military History

General

462. Anderson, Harry H. THE BENTEEN BASEBALL CLUB: SPORTS ENTHUSIASTS OF THE SEVENTH CAVALRY. *Montana 1970 20(3): 82-87.* Losses suffered at Custer's fight on the Little Big Horn in June 1876 are often described, but rarely mentioned is the damage to the baseball team fielded by Captain Frederick W. Benteen's "H" Company. Four men in the starting lineup were killed or wounded in the battle. Yankton newspapers preserved details of the team and its members' style of play during the season or two before the disastrous engagement in Montana.   S. R. Davison

463. Austin, William T. ACCOUNT OF THE CAMPAIGN OF 1835 BY WILLIAM T. AUSTIN, AIDE TO GEN. STEPHEN F. AUSTIN AND GEN. EDWARD BURLESON. *Texana 1966 4(4): 287-322.* A descriptive narrative of the campaign, in the vernacular. The account deals with an army of Texas soldiers, led by Stephen Fuller Austin and Burleson, between October and December 1835. Describes Stephen Austin's election as commanding officer, paraphrases some of his speeches to the troops, recounts an early engagement with the Mexican force under General Cos near Gonzales in October and a later, more serious battle at San Antonio in December, which resulted in the capitulation of the Mexicans. Mentions the efforts by Sam Houston and William H. Wharton to prevent Austin's troops from encountering the Mexican force until Houston himself could assume command. Notes the activities of other prominent officers in the Texan force, including Colonel James Bowie, Erastus (Deaf) Smith, Benjamin Rush Milam, and Lieutenant Colonel William Barret Travis. From the Austin Papers in the University of Texas Archives.   J. E. Findling

464. Avillo, Philip J., Jr. FORT MOJAVE: OUTPOST ON THE UPPER COLORADO. *J. of Arizona Hist. 1970 11(2): 77-100.* The Mexican War and the discovery of gold in California inspired a heavy migration from the eastern United States to the Southwest and the Pacific Coast. This necessitated protection to the emigrants from the hostile Indians and intensified the need for adequate roads. Numerous Army posts were soon established throughout the Southwest to guard the routes of travel. One of these, Fort Mojave, Arizona, was founded in 1859 along a wagon route from Fort Defiance, New Mexico, at a crossing of the Colorado River from Arizona into California to the north of Needles. By 1865, with the Indians generally pacified and with the road to California well established, Fort Mojave had virtually fulfilled its purpose. Life at the post became very uneventful and settlers lived unmolested in the vicinity. The Army abandoned the fort in 1890. 3 illus., map, 67 notes.
D. L. Smith

465. Baker, Galen R. EXCAVATING FORT MASSACHUSETTS. *Colorado Mag. 1965 42(1): 1-16.* Excavation of the first permanent American military post in Colorado has been valuable chiefly in revealing the design for the fort and the materials used in construction, plus a few Indian artifacts.   I. W. Van Noppen

466. Baker, Galen R. EXCAVATING FORT MASSACHUSETTS. *Colorado Mag. 1968 45(2): 143-161.* An archaeological study of Fort Massachusetts based on excavations made in 1964-66 which give considerable information about the construction and design of the post. Artifacts discovered during the excavation reveal something of the life led by frontier troops of the period. Illus., 7 notes. O. H. Zabel

467. Baker, Galen R. PRELIMINARY EXCAVATION AT FORT VASQUEZ. *Colorado Mag. 1964 41(2): 158-164.* The Colorado State Historical Society and the Trinidad State Junior College made excavations to study the possible destruction of prehistoric material by the building of a new visitor center and museum at the site of the old fort. The tested areas indicated a lack of any important archaeological materials but did afford insight into the change of the surface and underlying ground levels. I. W. Van Noppen

468. Beckham, Stephen Dow. LONELY OUTPOST: THE ARMY'S FORT UMPQUA. *Oregon Hist. Q. 1969 70(3): 233-257.* Originally established in 1856 to serve a military role in preventing clashes between Indians of the Oregon Pacific coast and newly-arrived white miners and settlers, Fort Umpqua had a short and unsatisfactory existence. Events in the early years of the Civil War and reduction of Indian aggressiveness brought official closure of the fort in 1862. C. C. Gorchels

469. Birrer, Ivan J. LETTER OF INSTRUCTIONS. *Military. R. 1965 45(8): 59-62.* Reproduces, as a classic example of clear and concise orders which leave much to the discretion of the recipients, a facsimile of the "letter of instructions" on 15 February 1856 by Secretary of War Jefferson Davis to the commanders of Fort Leavenworth and Fort Riley, directing these two commanders to conduct counterinsurgency operations in Kansas. At the bottom of this letter, Davis addressed a note to the Kansas territorial governor, advising him of the instructions he had issued. "Given the hindsight of more than 100 years, it is hard to see how the letter of instructions could have been improved. All the elements that make up the good field order were quite precisely enunciated. In addition, the peculiar circumstances of the operation were appropriately emphasized. The almost providential use of the term 'insurgent' long before it came into popular vogue is striking." Photo, note. D. D. Cameron

470. Blackburn, Forrest R. ARMY FAMILIES IN FRONTIER FORTS. *Military R. 1969 49(10): 17-28.* Discusses the problems encountered by military dependents at frontier forts in the American West in the 1860's. Mentions high food prices, weather hazards, diseases and epidemics, Indians, and dugout homes. 4 photos, 8 notes. G. E. Snow

471. Bloom, Mary Geneva. SOLDIERS WESTWARD: WHERE ARE THEIR OWN STORIES? *Pacific Historian 1964 8(1): 39-41.* A plea for the need of historians to seek out the letters of the western pioneers and soldiers, for most of the literature of western history consists of memoirs and other works published from the distance of time. In three periods: 1) the California gold rush and the Mexican War, 2) the Civil War, and 3) the period of Indian warfare, there was great excitement, but historians find a dearth of sources from the pens of common soldiers. The question is asked: "Did any of these men keep diaries of those decisive years of the seventies and eighties?" T. R. Cripps

472. Bogart, Charles H. THE WARSHIP THAT SANK BEFORE BEING LAUNCHED—USS CAMANCHE. *Warship Int. 1969 6(4): 50-53.* In response to demands from the California legislature that the Federal Government provide naval protection to the State, the monitor USS *Camanche,* completed in 1863, was ordered to San Francisco. Before launching, the vessel was disassembled and transshipped on board the *Aquila.* The latter vessel was damaged in a gale while moored in San Francisco Bay in November 1863 and sank at Hathaway Wharf. The *Camanche* was finally raised in 1864 and made her maiden voyage in 1865. She was decommissioned in 1866 and sold for scrap in 1899 without ever firing a shot in anger. Biblio. A. S. Birkos

473. Brinckerhoff, Sidney B. METAL UNIFORM INSIGNIA OF THE U.S. ARMY IN THE SOUTHWEST, 1846-1902. *J. of Arizona Hist. 1965 6(2): 71-84.* Relying on such materials as have been found in Arizona, the author emphasizes the historical importance of metal uniform insignia in four sections: buttons, branch insignia, buckles, and epaulettes. 20 illus., 19 notes. J. D. Filipiak

474. Brinckerhoff, Sidney B. MILITARY HEADGEAR IN THE SOUTHWEST 1846-1890. *Arizoniana 1963 4(4): 1-16.* The 1889 version of the white summer fatigue helmet was the result of 44 years experience gained from southwestern army duty and of copying directly French and German military styles. "Thirty years of Indian fighting and extremely adverse weather conditions were required before the army command fully realized the need for practical and specialized military headgear." Bibliography of published and unpublished sources. Illus. E. P. Stickney

475. Burke, Charles T., ed. LETTERS FROM THE WILD WEST *Montana 1969 19(1): 8-23.* Presents the letters of Frank Burke written to his family in Massachusetts in the early 1880's from posts in western and central Montana where he was stationed as a corporal in the Army Signal Corps and attached to the Weather Service. He witnessed some of the vigilante activity around Fort Maginnis when local ranchers were dealing with horse thieves. The editor supplies a biographical sketch of the author of the letters, who was his uncle. Illus. S. R. Davison

476. Clarke, Dwight L. SOLDIERS UNDER STEPHEN KEARNEY. *California Hist. Soc. Q. 1966 45(2): 133-148.* Sketches the lives and later careers of five men who served under General Kearney in the so-called Army of the West and who exerted the first American influence on California. 1) Captain Henry Smith Turner, whose letters and journal are important historical sources, in the 1850's was a banker in San Francisco and later in St. Louis. 2) Lieutenant William Hemsley Emory served on the two boundary commissions for surveying the Mexican-U.S. line. 3) John Mix Stanley, artist, had a series of minor tragedies and narrow escapes. He was the first to photograph the American Indian. All but five of his many paintings were lost in the Smithsonian Institution fire of 1865. 4) Captain John Strother Griffin, a surgeon, resigned his commission in 1854 to become a leader in civic, business, and educational affairs in Los Angeles. 5) Philip St. George Cooke was the leader of the Mormon Battalion. The defection to the South of most of his family made him an object of suspicion. Illus. E. P. Stickney

477. Conway, Walter C., ed. COLONEL EDMUND SCHRIVER'S INSPECTOR-GENERAL'S REPORT ON MILITARY POSTS IN TEXAS NOVEMBER, 1872-JANUARY, 1873. *Southwestern Hist. Q. 1964 67(4): 559-583.* Gives a brief account of the inspector-general's duties and reprints the text of the report, which covered seven posts: the San Antonio Arsenal, Fort McIntosh, Ringgold Barracks, Fort Brown, Fort Clark, Fort Duncan, and the post at Austin. Schriver (1812-99) gave individual reports on the subsistence, quartermaster's, and medical departments of each post. He gave a general account of his inspection trip and cited three major problems: transportation, communications, and lack of post histories. He recommended that annual post history reports be sent to the Adjutant-General of the Army and that telegraph lines be constructed. He advocated rectification of four transportation difficulties: overloading of trains, lack of proper care of animals, harness, and wagons by teamsters, driving at improper seasons, and misuse of forage. 5 notes. W. A. Buckman

478. Day, Daniel S. FORT SEDGWICK. *Colorado Mag. 1965 42(1): 16-35.* From 1864 to 1871 Fort Sedgwick, at first named Camp Rankin, served as a protector of travelers, settlers, and stage lines from depredations of hostile Indians. Comments on the life of the camp and activities of the troops. I. W. Van Noppen

479. Egan, Ferol. THE BUILDING OF FORT CHURCHILL: BLUEPRINT FOR A MILITARY FIASCO, 1860. *Am. West 1972 9(2): 4-9.* Fort Churchill was erected to the east of Carson City, Nevada, in the wake of the Paiute War of 1860, to protect silver miners, ranchers, and overland travelers from potential Paiute attacks. Construction materials had to be hauled in, some from the Pacific coast; the going rate for labor was high in competition with the Comstock Lode boomtowns; and the consequent total cost was seemingly excessive. Duty was unexciting and uncomfortable, but the Army maintained the elaborate fort until the completion of the transcontinental railroad in 1869. A brief attempt was made in the 1930's to restore Fort Churchill from the ruins. Today it is a State park. 6 illus. D. L. Smith

480. Ewy, Marvin. THE UNITED STATES ARMY IN THE KANSAS BORDER TROUBLES, 1855-1856. *Kansas Hist. Q. 1966 32(4): 385-400.* U.S. forces in Kansas during the troublesome days that preceded the Civil War tended to follow a policy of neutrality in most cases. Three explanations are offered. Policy decisions were made in Washington where the authorities insisted upon a policy of strict neutrality by men in the field. Military officers in Kansas were aware that much of the trouble was motivated more by a desire for profit than by a desire to advance either freedom or slavery, and so they were very careful to see that the civilians who stood to profit did not provoke hostilities. Most of the professional soldiers in Kansas were devoted to the United States, and so they were able to rise above sectional interests or love for their own States to follow a policy that advanced national interests. Based on secondary works and material in the Kansas Historical Collections; 41 notes.
W. F. Zornow

481. Fite, Gilbert C. THE UNITED STATES ARMY AND RELIEF TO PIONEER SETTLERS, 1874-1875. *J. of the West 1967 6(1): 99-107.* In the summer of 1874 the twin disasters of drought and grasshoppers destroyed a large portion of the crops between Fort Worth, Texas, and St. Paul, Minnesota. Thousands of settlers verged on starvation. Largely as the result of a report made by General James Brisben on conditions in southwestern Nebraska, General E. O. C. Ord at Omaha wrote the Adjutant General requesting permission to distribute rations. When refused he continued to bombard his superiors in Washington with requests for help. Secretary of War Belknap informed President Grant of the situation and recommended that the Army be authorized to distribute clothing. The request was granted and during the winter the Army gave clothing and blankets to needy settlers, mainly in western Kansas and Nebraska, but to some in Dakota and Minnesota. As a result of continued agitation, Congress in February 1875 appropriated funds to provide needed food. This was likewise distributed by the Army, the best equipped government agency to handle relief. Based on government documents, 32 notes.
D. N. Brown

482. Frazer, Robert W. CAMP YUMA - 1852. *Southern California Q. 1970 52(2): 170-184.* An edition of the report by Inspector General George A. McCall concerning his inspection of Camp Yuma in 1852. An introduction gives the early history of the military outpost which was located at the junction of the Colorado and Gila rivers between 1851 and 1883. At the time McCall visited the post it had only recently been reestablished after being abandoned during the previous year. McCall's report "presents a description of an important western military post early in its career and indicates some of the problems and difficulties with which the army had to cope in order to maintain a post on the lower Colorado." Based chiefly on the Inspector General's report and other government documents; 46 notes.
W. L. Bowers

483. Frazer, Robert W. FORT BUTLER: THE FORT THAT ALMOST WAS. *New Mexico Hist. R. 1968 43(4): 253-270.* In 1860 the military department of New Mexico was completely reorganized. Of 13 existing forts, cantonments, and garrisoned positions, only three were to be retained, but four new forts would be established. One of the new forts was designated Fort Butler, intended to control the Comanche and Kiowa Indians and serve as a general depot for the department. Although a site was selected and approved, the rapid approach of the Civil War caused the plans to be abandoned. Based on Record Groups 92, 94, and 98, National Archives. 59 notes.
D. F. Henderson

484. Friend, Llerena, ed. STILL IN TEXAS. *Southwestern Hist. Q. 1968 72(2): 223-239.* Hugh E. Dungan was stationed at Fort Brown, Texas. Three of his letters of 1851-52 contain a typical soldier's reactions to army life, homesickness, and unhappiness with his assignment. 32 notes
D. L. Smith

485. Goodale, Roy, ed. A CIVILIAN AT FORT LEAVENWORTH AND FORT HAYS. EXTRACTS FROM A DIARY OF EPHRIAM GOODALE. *Kansas Hist. Q. 1967 33(2): 138-155.* The diary covers the period from 7 April 1878 to 24 September 1879. The state of the weather, attendance at church, and local events are the diarist's major concerns. Illus., 23 notes.
W. F. Zornow

486. Gould, C. E. SOLDIERING ON THE FRONTIER. *Ann. of Wyoming 1963 35(1): 83-84.* Gould's letter to his brother was written in September 1858 to describe his duties as a U.S. Army enlisted man serving at Fort Bridger. It includes a sketch plan of the post.
R. L. Nichols

487. Grange, Roger R., Jr. DIGGING AT FORT KEARNEY. *Nebraska Hist. 1963 44(2): 101-121.* Examines various phases in the construction of Fort Kearney and discusses archaeological work at the site and findings made in 1960 and 1961.
R. Lowitt

488. Hacker, Nancy A. and Landrum, Francis S., eds. ALEXANDER PIPER'S REPORTS AND JOURNAL. *Oregon Hist. Q. 1968 69(3): 223-268.* The background and activities of Alexander Piper, first lieutenant in the US Army, with particular reference to his expedition into the Klamath country of Oregon and northern California in the summer of 1860. Migrants to that area had reported troubles with the Indians over a span of years. Following an introduction are the official letters of Piper to his superior officer and the facsimile pages of the "Journal of the March of Lt. A. Piper from Ft. Umpqua to the Vicinity of Klamath Lake, 1860."
C. C. Gorchels

489. Hamlin, Percy G. DOCUMENTS OF ARIZONA HISTORY: AN ARIZONA LETTER OF R. S. EWELL. *J. of Arizona Hist. 1966 7(1): 23-26.* Richard S. Ewell (later a Confederate lieutenant general), captain and commander of one of the four companies commissioned to establish the first U.S. Army post in the vicinity of present-day Tucson, arrived in the area, recently acquired by the Gadsden Purchase, in November 1856. The letter is to his sister in Virginia, mentions the Mission of San Xavier del Bac near Tucson but is mostly about family matters. 6 notes.
J. D. Filipiak

490. Hanft, Marshall. THE CAPE FORTS: GUARDIANS OF THE COLUMBIA. *Oregon Hist. Q. 1964 65(4): 325-361.* Detailed account of acquisition and placement of artillery forts established for military control of the mouth of Columbia River, 1863-65. Descriptions of artillery pieces as well as emplacement methods are included, with many photographs and maps. Numerous footnotes show scholarly use of primary sources: mostly official documents and letters.
C. C. Gorchels

491. Hawkins, C. S. OLD FORT POINT. *California Historian 1968 15(1): 15-17.* Discusses the efforts of the thousand-member Fort Point Museum Association to promote the restoration of the fort as a museum and the placing before Congress of three bills that would name the fort a National Historic Site. When completed in 1861 it was "a classic example of the brick forts built by the US Army Engineers to guard the seacoast of the United States during the 1800's." The fort was declared obsolete in 1906.
O. L. Miller

492. Holt, Daniel D. "IT...BELONGS TO THE OLD REGIME" - EUGENE F. WARE WRITES FROM FORT KEARNEY, 1864. *Nebraska Hist. 1965 46(3): 235-243.* Realistic description of Fort Kearney with comments about men famous in the raging Civil War who had been stationed there, written in 1864 by the future literary and public figure, then a lieutenant with the 7th Iowa Cavalry.
R. Lowitt

493. Innis, Ben, ed. THE FORT BUFORD DIARY OF PVT. SANFORD. *North Dakota Hist. 1966 33(4): 335-378.* Wilmot P. Sanford volunteered and served five years in the U.S. Infantry, most of it at Fort Buford at the junction of the Yellowstone and Missouri Rivers. He never received a promotion, but he was intelligent and observant. Day by day he noted in a diary the weather, his food, activities, the books he read, his services as librarian, his correspondence with numerous females, and his eagerness to complete his term of enlistment. The diary, covering nine months, was published in the centennial year of the establishment of the fort. Illus., 48 notes, many based on Fort Buford records.
I. W. Van Noppen

494. Jenkins, John H. THE TEXAS NAVY: LOS DIABLOS TEJANOS ON THE HIGH SEAS. *Am. West 1968 5(3): 35-41.* Not only is the role of the Texas Navy generally unknown by the lay public, it is usually overlooked by "land-oriented" historians. The first battle of the Texas revolution was a naval engagement and the last battle before annexation into the United States was naval as well. The author asserts that the extraordinary record of the naval forces explains Texan success in her

revolution and her continued independence until annexation. With annexation, the Texas Navy was incorporated into that of the United States. An abridged history of *Los Diablos Tejanos* [The Texan Devils] on the high seas is submitted to support these contentions. 4 illus.

D. L. Smith

495. King, C. Richard. JAMES CLINTON NEILL. *Texana 1964 2(4): 231-252*. Account of various incidents in the life of James Clinton Neill, colonel in the Texas revolutionary army. As commander at San Antonio he disobeyed orders from Houston to destroy the Alamo. A leave of absence removed him from the Alamo before its fall. Later at Gonzales, Houston took over Neill's command and ordered the retreat to San Jacinto. Neill was commander of the artillery at San Jacinto, but was wounded in the hip by the first shot fired by the Mexican artillery. Neill always seemed to just miss the opportunity to be a hero. 61 notes.

W. A. Buckman

496. Knuth, Priscilla. "PICTURESQUE" FRONTIER: THE ARMY'S FORT DALLES. *Oregon Hist. Q. 1966 67(4): 292-346, 1967 68(1): 4-52*. In a detailed study divided into two parts, the author covers the history of the reconstruction or "transformation" of the frontier military post of Fort Dalles in the Columbia River gorge in Oregon from a very small post to an unusually fine and large military headquarters and supplies depot. A relatively expensive construction project in its day, yet justified by the commanding officer with sound arguments, the fort's primary role was one of serving as a supply depot to the outposts of Fort Walla Walla and Fort Simcoe. Its importance is shown by the fact that more than 250 civilian workers were employed at one time to carry out the numerous jobs under the supervision of military personnel. The activities of Captain Thomas Jordan and architect Louis Scholl are shown in the historical setting of Indian wars and migrant wagon trains crossing the territory. Illustrations include drawings, plans, large maps, photographs of buildings, and portraits of principals at the fort. Appendixes show expenditures, numbers of military troops in the region, and details of labor costs.

C. C. Gorchels

497. Lord, Walter. MYTHS & REALITIES OF THE ALAMO. *Am. West 1968 5(3): 18-25*. Great events have their myths and legends, especially the most famous battle of the Texan Revolution. Since the garrison was slaughtered, firsthand accounts are scarce. Except for one, the small number of eyewitnesses were not immediately interviewed. Five years later the first serious student of the Alamo visited the site, but he did not record his account until many years after that. The supposed "sole adult Anglo survivor" was not interviewed by a historian until nearly 40 years after the catastrophe. Legend filled in the story of this epochal event. An 1889 romantic novel fabricated details, it was used as the basis for an oration, and the snowballing was on. A 1931 doctoral thesis perpetuated rather than exposed much of the mythology and thus gave it new authority. Texan pride is another formidable obstacle in the way of removing the considerable fiction that encrusts the Alamo story. The author destroys the fabric of folklore, thread by thread. Although the Alamo was "anything but a successful holding operation," he maintains it did outrage America and brought a massive flow of aid that assured the ultimate freedom of Texas. 4 illus.

D. L. Smith

498. Maul, David T. A MAN AND HIS BOOK. *Register of the Kentucky Hist. Soc. 1967 65(3): 212-229*. Sparked by the inscription of "Major Theodore Talbot, U.S.A." in William Hardee's *Rifle and Light Infantry Tactics* (1855) in the author's possession, he has endeavored to write a biography of Major Talbot and the story of his book. Talbot, the son of a U.S. Senator from Kentucky, played one of the innumerable secondary roles in history. He was present on John C. Frémont's second and third expeditions to the West, served in the Mexican War, saw duty in Oregon and Florida, and in 1860 was attached to Major Robert Anderson's command at Ft. Sumter. In 1862 he died of heart disease in Washington, D.C. Based on Talbot's diary and government records, 59 notes.

B. Wilkins

499. McDermott, John Dishon. CRIME AND PUNISHMENT IN THE UNITED STATES ARMY: A PHASE OF FORT LARAMIE HISTORY. *J. of the West 1968 7(2): 246-255*. After a brief account of the hierarchy of military procedure, the author describes a number of crimes and their punishments at Fort Laramie. These ranged from drunkenness to murder and desertion.

R. N. Alvis

500. McDermott, John D. and Chappell, Gordon. MILITARY COMMAND AT FORT LARAMIE. *Ann. of Wyoming 1966 38(1): 4-48*. Includes a brief discussion of the men commanding Fort Laramie from 1849 to 1890. It also has four lists which contain the dates each man exercised his command, his rank, full name, regiment, other military titles (brevet or volunteer ranks), and whether or not the officer graduated from West Point. Based on records in the National Archives. Illus., notes.

R. L. Nichols

501. McNitt, Frank. FORT SUMNER: A STUDY IN ORIGINS. *New Mexico Hist. R. 1970 45(2): 101-117*. Discusses the reasons a military post was established at Bosque Redondo (on the Pecos river), and the reasons that post was made the center of a reservation for Navajo and Apache Indians. Various military surveys are analyzed, including those by Brevet Colonel John Munroe in 1850 and Brevet Major James H. Carleton in 1852 and 1854. A post was finally established at the Bosque in November 1862. In 1863, Carleton, now a general and commander of the Military Department of New Mexico, converted the post into a reservation for 400 Apache, which accommodated over 40 thousand Navajo the following year. Based on various U.S. Army Records in the National Archives; 29 notes.

D. F. Henderson

502. Mears, Mildred Watkins. THE THREE FORTS IN CORYELL COUNTY. *Southwestern Hist. Q. 1963 67(1): 1-14*. Traces briefly the establishment of three forts near Gatesville, Texas: Fort Gates (1849), South Fort Hood (1942), and North Fort Hood (1943).

J. A. Hudson

503. Moore, Marc A. MARINES OF THE TEXAS REPUBLIC. *Southwest R. 1967 52(2): 164-176*. From December 1835, when the first recorded Marine operation occurred, until June 1846, when the Texas Navy was turned over to the United States, Texas had a Marine Corps. Marines participated in the capture of several Mexican vessels, the illegal capture of a British vessel, and a mutiny.

D. F. Henderson

504. Mozer, Corinne C. A BRIEF HISTORY OF FORT FILLMORE, 1851-1862. *Palacio 1967 74(2): 5-18*. Fort Fillmore, established in southern New Mexico 40 miles north of El Paso, played a prominent part in that region's history. Originally the post was intended as a check against raiding Navajo and Apache bands and for patrolling the border with Mexico. In 1861, Union troops fought and lost the Battle of Mesilla to Confederate troops. After their defeat, the Union troops abandoned Fort Fillmore and fled east toward Fort Stanton, but were captured near San Augustine Springs where they surrendered. The fort was briefly reoccupied in 1862 by the California Volunteers, and was finally officially abandoned on 3 November 1862. Based primarily on primary and secondary sources in the National Archives; illus., 51 notes, biblio.

S. A. Eger

505. Murray, Robert A. THE HAZEN INSPECTIONS OF 1866. *Montana 1968 18(1): 24-33*. In the autumn of 1866 General William B. Hazen inspected the military posts along the Bozeman Trail and on to Fort Benton. His report is the only impartial description of the forts and their state of readiness, matters about which later writers have differed. Hazen was especially critical of the utilization of military supplies and manpower. He also expressed harsh views about Indians and about the West as a place for settlement. His cartographer on this trip was Ambrose Bierce. Based mainly on official reports printed in Congressional Executive Documents; illus., 2 maps, 14 notes, biblio.

S. R. Davison

506. Murray, Robert A. PRICES AND WAGES AT FORT LARAMIE, 1881-1885. *Ann. of Wyoming 1964 36(1): 19-21*.

507. Murray, Robert A. THE UNITED STATES ARMY IN THE AFTERMATH OF THE JOHNSON COUNTY INVASION. *Ann. of Wyoming 1966 38(1): 59-75*. Discusses the reaction of the Federal government, through the Army, to the so-called Johnson County War of 1892. First the Army merely reported the difficulties. Then, upon presidential orders, U.S. troops moved to the scene, stopped the fighting, accepted the surrender of the invaders, and escorted them to Fort McKinney near the town of Buffalo. After the Army released the prisoners to state authorities, the state officials demanded and got more troops moved into Johnson County to maintain order. Based on the Records of the Office of the Adjutant General, and the Records of the Department of the Platte at the National Archives. 67 notes.

R. L. Nichols

508. Myers, Lee. MILITARY ESTABLISHMENTS IN SOUTH-WESTERN NEW MEXICO: STEPPING STONES TO SETTLE-MENT. *New Mexico Hist. R. 1968 43(1): 5-48.* Historical sketch of the following military camps and forts established by the US Army in Southwestern New Mexico between 1851 and 1866: Cantonment Dawson, Fort Webster, Gila Depot, Burro Mountain Camp, Fort McLane, Fort West, Camp Mimbres, Fort Cummings, and Fort Bayard. 149 notes.

D. F. Henderson

509. Myers, Lee. MUTINY AT FORT CUMMINGS. *New Mexico Hist. R. 1971 46(4): 337-350.* According to one version of the mutiny, a company of black soldiers developed a well-planned plot to kill their officers, loot the post, and carry off the officers' wives as slaves. The plot was revealed to the officers by a maidservant. The officers assembled the conspirators, unarmed, on the parade ground while a detachment of white soldiers of the 3rd Cavalry secretly occupied the blacks' barracks, secured their arms, and positioned themselves at the windows. Unfortunately, this version is pure fiction. A mutiny did occur in December 1867, but the maidservant, instead of revealing the plot to the officers, was the cause of the trouble. Secondly, the mutineers assembled armed, and thirdly, the detachment from the 3rd Cavalry was not present or even assigned to the garrison. Based on Records of the Office of the Judge Advocate General, General Courts Martial, 1812-1938, National Archives, Record Group 153; 33 notes.

D. F. Henderson

510. Nichols, Roger L. MARTIN CANTONMENT AND AMERI-CAN EXPANSION IN THE MISSOURI VALLEY. *Missouri Hist. R. 1969 64(1): 1-17.* Martin Cantonment was a small installation on the Missouri River about 20 miles north of Leavenworth, Kansas. The author gives an account of its construction and its role as a supply base for a grandly conceived plan to extend American influence into the West by means of a military expedition up the Missouri River in 1818. Martin Cantonment fulfilled its role as a supply depot and gave the soldiers stationed there some experience for the later phases of the expedition. The failure of the expedition demonstrated that before the Mexican War most military activities in this valley were limited and temporary. Based on books, articles, and archival material in the National Archives, the State Historical Society of Missouri, and Yale University; illus., photos, map, 13 notes.

W. F. Zornow

511. Nichols, Roger L. SCURVY AT CANTONMENT MISSOURI, 1819-1820. *Nebraska Hist. 1968 49(4): 333-347.* Surveys and analyzes the outbreak of scurvy among the troops at Cantonment Missouri during the winter of 1819-20, the first recorded epidemic within the confines of what became the State of Nebraska. This epidemic "killed or weakened nearly one tenth of the entire army" and indicates "how little attention governmental and army leaders paid to the welfare of American frontier soldiers."

R. Lowitt

512. Oates, Stephen B. THEY DID RIGHT BECAUSE IT WAS RIGHT. *Southwest R. 1963 48(4): 387-395.* Brief narrative of the experiences of John S. Ford's company of Texas Rangers from 23 August 1849, when they were sworn into the service of the United States, to 23 September 1851, when they were mustered out. The mission of the Rangers was the protection of residents between the Nueces and Rio Grande Rivers from renegade Comanches and Mexican outlaws who had terrorized the area.

D. F. Henderson

513. Parmalee, Paul W. FOOD ANIMALS UTILIZED BY THE GARRISON STATIONED AT FORT FILLMORE, NEW MEXICO 1851-1862. *Palacio 1967 74(2): 43-45.* Excavations at Fort Fillmore were conducted by the Museum of New Mexico. From bone remains unearthed from various parts of the fort, it was determined that the principal source of meat was beef, supplemented by sheep, goats, and hogs. Analyzes other bone remains from other sources, principally wild game, which was relatively inconsequential in the soldiers' diet. Compares the typical diet, determined by bone remains, with the diet of soldiers at other forts in the United States, including colonial ones. Documented, biblio.

S. A. Eger

514. Robinett, Paul M. and Canan, Howard V. THE MILITARY CAREER OF JAMES CRAIG. *Missouri Hist R. 1971 66(1): 49-75.* Craig came to Missouri in 1843. At the outbreak of the Mexican War he raised a company and saw service in Indian country. After a trip to

California during the gold rush, he returned to St. Joseph, Missouri, to practice law. In 1862 he became a brigadier general of volunteers in the Department of the Mississippi. In this capacity he was charged with the responsibility for policing 300 of the 500 miles of the combined overland mail and telegraph lines to the Far West. Later in the Civil War he returned to St. Joseph as a brigadier general of the Enrolled Missouri Militia (E.M.M.), and in this capacity finished out the war fighting against guerrilla bands in northern Missouri. Based on articles, secondary sources and on manuscripts in the National Archives and the Archives of the Adjutant General of Missouri, Jefferson City; illus., 66 notes.

W. F. Zornow

515. Ruhlen, George. EARLY NEVADA FORTS. *Nevada Hist. Soc. Q. 1964 7(3/4): 3-63.* An alphabetical account of the 20 military camps, 10 forts, two temporary fortifications, one post and one reservation in Nevada. Each has a brief sketch indicating their period of existence and approximate location with an individual bibliography and some documentation. A general bibliography, including map sources, is provided.

J. D. Filipiak

516. Ryan, Garry D. CAMP WALBACH, NEBRASKA TERRITORY, 1858-1859: THE MILITARY POST AT CHEYENNE PASS. *Ann. of Wyoming 1963 35(1): 4-20.* Discusses the location of a temporary army camp at Cheyenne Pass, Wyoming, to guard the Fort Riley-Bridger's Pass Road and to protect supply lines for the Army of Utah. Gives a description of guard details, building projects, and disciplinary measures at the post. Suggests the camp was closed when the military road was abandoned and the Mormon War ended. Based on camp and unit records in the National Archives.

R. L. Nichols

517. Sachse, Nancy D. FRONTIER LEGEND; BENNINGTON'S MARTIN SCOTT. *Vermont Hist. 1966 34(3): 157-168.* Farm boy Scott served a year in New York during the War of 1812 and soon reenlisted. He rose from second lieutenant to colonel, 1818-46; served in the Fort Snelling-Fort Mackinac area and died storming Chapultepec. A sharpshooter, horse lover, and unsuccessful land speculator, he dueled with a Virginian and participated in the 1819 Yellowstone expedition and Stephen Long's 1823 Red River expedition. Thousands attended his interment behind Bennington's First Church.

T. D. S. Bassett

518. Sacks, Ben. THE ORIGINS OF FORT BUCHANAN: MYTH AND FACT. *Arizona and the West 1965 7(3): 207-226.* The Gadsden Purchase from Mexico added land south of the Gila River to the territory of New Mexico, which area is primarily within the present-day State of Arizona. The principal threat to the peace and security of settlers and travelers in the 1853 purchase were the wild Apache Indians. Not until 1856 were troops dispatched to the troubled region. In June of 1857 they established Fort Buchanan south of the Gila at the head of the Sonoita Creek Valley. The fort continued in existence until it was evacuated and destroyed in July 1861. The author untangles the confusion, misinformation, conflicting accounts, and mistaken conclusions drawn concerning the evacuation of the Mexican military from the Gadsden Purchase, the arrival and establishment of American military authority, and the antecedents and early history of Fort Buchanan. 72 notes.

D. L. Smith

519. Sibbald, John R. CAMP FOLLOWERS ALL. *Am. West 1966 3(2): 56-67.* Camp followers are defined as to include the three groups of women sanctioned by scattered references in army regulations: wives and daughters of officers, servants, and laundresses. While the females of Soapsuds Row were usually wives of enlisted men, some were civilian wives or single women. Excluded from the present use of the term "camp followers" are the ladies of easy virtue who lived in nearby settlements and were frowned upon by the War Department. The ubiquitous army camp followers managed to string their bloomers on the clotheslines of almost every western American frontier garrison in the four decades following the outbreak of the Civil War. From their letters and diaries, the author determined that their major concerns were the effect of the elements on their complexions, the problems of keeping household goods, the education of their children, the loss of contact with their home churches, and the constant moves which were the lot of army personnel. At least one officer's wife set up housekeeping at 19 different locations. Map, illus., biblio. note.

D. L. Smith

520. Sibbald, John R. FRONTIER INEBRIATES WITH EPAULETS. *Montana 1969 19(3): 50-57.* Recounts the futile attempt of Colonel Philippe R. De Trobriand to suppress excessive drinking among the officers of his command in Dakota Territory in 1867. Although violations were flagrant and the evidence abundant, the colonel was unable to gain convictions in courts martial or to enforce discipline by other means. The apparent reasons for his failure were the loyalty among West Point "brothers" and the political influence of the offenders. Illus., 10 notes, largely from De Trobriand's published journal. S. R. Davison

521. Sibley, Marilyn McAdams, ed. LETTERS FROM THE TEXAS ARMY, AUTUMN, 1836: LEON DYER TO THOMAS J. GREEN. *Southwestern Hist. Q. 1969 72(3): 371-384.* Leon Dyer served as an officer in volunteer forces during the Texan Revolution. When the commanding officer turned to politics, he left the volunteers under Dyer and instructed Dyer to keep him informed of events in the army. In eight letters to his general, Dyer describes personalities and problems in the Texas army in late 1836 and early 1837. 35 notes. D. L. Smith

522. Smythe, Donald. JOHN J. PERSHING: FRONTIER CAVALRYMAN. *New Mexico Hist. R. 1963 38(3): 220-243.* General Pershing spent four and a half years in the Western cavalry. The author makes a detailed exposition of these years, interspersing anecdotes with comments, as one on Pershing, "(few people ever looked better astride a charger)." D. F. Henderson

523. Smythe, Donald. JOHN J. PERSHING AT FORT ASSINIBOINE. *Montana 1968 18(1): 19-23.* John J. Pershing, future commander of the American Expeditionary Force in World War I, was stationed in 1895 at Fort Assiniboine in northern Montana. As lieutenant of a troop of the 10th Cavalry, a Negro regiment, he carried out orders to gather and deliver to the international border a number of Cree Indians for deportation to Canada. His management of this difficult assignment won commendation from his superiors. 16 notes. S. R. Davison

524. Stansbury, Howard. THE BANNOCK MOUNTAIN ROAD. *Idaho Yesterdays 1964 8(1): 10-15.* Report to the US Army in regard to the establishment of a wagon-road from Fort Hill Hall (in southeastern Idaho) to the Great Salt Lake. The author, an army captain, concluded after a journey through the area, that the project was entirely practicable without waiting for road-builders to make improvements.

M. Small

525. Storey, Brit Allan, ed. AN ARMY OFFICER IN TEXAS, 1866-1867. *Southwestern Hist. Q. 1968 72(2): 242-251.* Four letters of Adam Kramer, an American officer on duty in Texas, 1866-67, are commentaries on the Army in Texas and Texas history. 33 notes.

D. L. Smith

526. Taylor, Morris F. FORT MASSACHUSETTS. *Colorado Mag. 1968 45(2): 120-142.* Using army records, the author gives a detailed account of events, officers, and units in the short-lived Fort Massachusetts. The fort, located some 92 miles north of Taos, New Mexico Territory, now in the State of Colorado, was built in 1852 and abandoned in 1858. "More than anything else, a poorly-chosen location made its moment in history relatively brief." Illus., map, 129 notes.

O. H. Zabel

527. Taylor, Morris F. FORT WISE. *Colorado Mag. 1969 46(2): 93-119.* Describes the building of Fort Wise on the upper Arkansas River near Bent's New Fort in the fall of 1860. The establishment of the fort was influenced by the outbreak of the Civil War, the Confederate threat to the Southwest, and the transfer of troops to the East. The fort, named for the former Virginia governor and Confederate officer Henry Wise, was renamed Fort Lyon in 1862. Here the Cheyenne and Arapaho, in the Treaty of Fort Wise (1861), accepted a reservation. Illus., 133 notes.

O. H. Zabel

528. Thompson, Erwin N. THE NEGRO SOLDIERS ON THE FRONTIER: A FORT DAVIS CASE STUDY. *J. of the West 1968 7(2): 217-235.* Gives an account of the Negro soldiers stationed at Fort Davis, Texas. The fort was established in 1854 and abandoned in 1862 during the Civil War. The first regulars to return in 1867 were Negroes. Between 1867 and 1885 all the regular colored units were stationed at Fort Davis at one time or another. Both their accomplishments as fighters and some comments on the social record are offered. Photographs of Fort Davis and a Remington sketch of an Apache scout and a Negro cavalryman are included. R. N. Alvis

529. Utley, Robert M. ARIZONA VANQUISHED: IMPRESSIONS AND REFLECTIONS CONCERNING THE QUALITY OF LIFE ON A MILITARY FRONTIER. *Am. West 1969 6(6): 16-21.* Before the arrival of the railroad in the 1880's, Arizona was regarded as the most odious assignment that a soldier could receive. As much as one-fifth of the entire U.S. Army was stationed there at times. A mass of reminiscent and contemporary literature produced by military officers and their wives record impressions and feelings about their residence in Arizona. In general, it was regarded as an intolerable place in which to live. The scorched and malarial valleys of the Gila River and its tributaries were the basis of the Army's impression of Arizona. The Indians, chiefly the Apache, were respected for their skill and prowess; the Mexicans received no more than passing notice from these observers; and the white civilian Arizonans were viewed as parasites on the Army. Nostalgia, nevertheless, does pervade the reminiscences of most of the Arizona veterans; some of it is characteristic of the things for which Arizona is noted today. 12 illus.

D. L. Smith

530. Utley, Robert M. THE PAST AND FUTURE OF OLD FORT BOWIE. *Arizoniana 1964 5(4): 55-60.* The legislation creating Fort Bowie National Historic Site is the successful culmination of a campaign that goes back a quarter of a century. In 1963 Senator Barry M. Goldwater and Representative Morris K. Udall introduced identical bills in Congress which resulted in Public Law 88-15 (signed into law on 30 August 1964). Fort Bowie commanded the eastern entrance to Apache Pass. "From 1858 until the outbreak of the Civil War the famed Butterfield Company ran its stagecoaches over the rocky slopes of the Pass." In 1861 the pass was the scene of Lieutenant George N. Bascom's attempt to arrest Cochise. Fort Bowie was established in July 1862. Illus.

E. P. Stickney

531. Vandenbusche, Duane. LIFE AT A FRONTIER POST: FORT GARLAND. *Colorado Mag. 1966 43(2): 132-148.* This fort, constructed in 1858, replaced Fort Massachusetts which had been established in 1852 to protect the "cradle of Colorado history" settlements in northern New Mexico, recently acquired from Mexico. Fort Garland, one of the most important of the frontier posts, protected settlers from the Ute, Apache, and other Indian tribes. Kit Carson was commandant, 1866-67, from which time the Indians were relatively peaceful until 1879, when the Meeker Massacre caused the strengthening of the garrison to 1,500 men. After 1881 the troops were reduced to a skeleton force and in 1883 the fort was abandoned. I. W. Van Noppen

532. Walker, Henry P. THE RELUCTANT CORPORAL: THE AUTOBIOGRAPHY OF WILLIAM BLADEN JETT. *J. of Arizona Hist. 1971 12(1): 1-50, (2): 112-144.* Part I. Jett (1858-1941) typed his autobiography shortly before his death. Selects the remembrances of Jett's life as a noncommissioned Army officer in the frontier towns of Phoenix and Tempe in Arizona Territory. He enlisted in the cavalry on 9 April 1881. Jett was a good soldier, but because he was so highly critical of those with whom he associated in the Army, he was a poor and reluctant noncom. 7 illus., 62 notes. Part II. Jett was discharged from the Army in 1886 after service in Colorado, New Mexico, and Arizona. After a stint as a civilian teamster for the Army in Arizona and a try at cattle ranching, Jett went to Phoenix and hired out as a teamster for a lumber yard. After conversion in a local Methodist service and close association with another church in Tempe where he had been transferred by his employer, Jett returned to Virginia in 1888 to pursue a formal education and to enter the ministry. 2 illus., 24 notes. D. L. Smith

533. Wallace, Andrew. GENERAL AUGUST V. KAUTZ IN ARIZONA, 1874-1878. *Arizoniana 1963 4(4): 54-65.* Kautz "represents in the American Southwest the highest kind of self-sacrificing character which the Army occasionally sent to the frontier." He was a steadying influence and the instrument of orderly progress and law. His troubles with the Apaches, the Indian Office, and politicians are surveyed. Based on a preliminary study for a doctoral dissertation at the University of Arizona. Illus. E. P. Stickney

534. Weigley, Russell F. HEROES AND HORSE-SOLDIERS. *Am. West R. 1967 1(2): 11, 29-31.* Reviews five books concerning the US Cavalry and Western development. They are *Grenville M. Dodge: Soldier, Politician, Railroad Pioneer* (Bloomington: Indiana U. Press, 1967) by Stanley P. Hirshson; *Spurs to Glory: The Story of the United States Cavalry* (Rand, McNally, 1966) by James M. Merrill; *The yellowlegs: The Story of the United States Cavalry* (Garden City: Doubleday, 1966) by Richard Wormser; *Stephen Harriman Long, 1784-1864: Army Engineer, Explorer, Inventor* (Glendale, Calif.: Arthur H. Clark, 1966) by Richard G. Wood; and *Custer's Gold: The United States Cavalry Expedition of 1874* (New Haven: Yale U. Press, 1966) by Donald Jackson. The discussion first centers on Grenville Dodge, pointing to his good and bad exploits. "Dodge was enough of a rascal that Jay Gould seems an appropriate colleague," but one also must remember him as an able corps commander in the Civil War. Dodge believed that success depended on "brains, push and combinations." He bestirred himself only when a profit was evident. The reviewer found both *Spurs to Glory* and *The Yellowlegs* of a limited use historically. They tell the history of the cavalry in a succession of good stories, nothing more. Very little is said about cavalry tactics and the response of American cavalry to changes in warfare. The biography of Stephen Harriman Long pictures the man as "the noblest Roman of them all" and tends to build an image of a hero. *Custer's Gold* is basically a sound book and "can be recommended heartily."
O. L. Miller

535. Whilden, Charles E. LETTERS FROM A SANTA FE ARMY CLERK, 1855-1856. *New Mexico Hist. R. 1965 40(2): 141-164.* Seven letters from Charles E. Whilden, clerk in the Commissary Department, Third Infantry, to his brother and sister-in-law, William G. and Ellen Whilden of Charleston, South Carolina. The letters "describe the exciting experiences Charles Whilden had with the wagon train on the way west - inquisitive Indian chiefs, stampeding cattle, and prairie fires - and paints a clear picture of a relatively quiet but interesting existence in the city of Santa Fe."
D. F. Henderson

536. Wilson, John P. EXCAVATIONS AT FORT FILLMORE. *Palacio 1967 74(2): 27-41.* An archeological site report of the excavations of Fort Fillmore conducted by the Museum of New Mexico. Describes the shape and method of construction of several of the fort's buildings, and further details the nature of the artifacts unearthed in the refuse areas. Documented, illus., biblio.
S. A. Eger

537. Wilson, Rex L. ARCHEOLOGY AND EVERYDAY LIFE AT FORT UNION. *New Mexico Hist. R. 1965 40(1): 55-64.* Chronicle of the discovery and restoration of old Fort Union, New Mexico. Stresses the importance of sinks and water closets as repositories for substantial quantities of artifacts.
D. F. Henderson

538. Wilson, Rex L. TOBACCO PIPES FROM FORT UNION, N. MEXICO. *Palacio 1966 73(1): 32-40.* Describes tobacco pipes found during the excavations at Fort Union National Monument. The clay, porcelain, briar, and wooden pipes found at the fort reflect the types of smoking equipment available at the fort between 1863 and 1891. Based on secondary sources; map, 4 photos, 7 notes.
S. A. Eger

539. Wood, C. E. S. PRIVATE JOURNAL, 1878-79. *Oregon Hist. Q. 1969 70(1): 5-38; (2): 138-170.* Part I. Observations and comments of a young lieutenant in the US Army as recorded in his personal journal while in Oregon and the territories of Washington and Idaho in 1878. A wide range of experiences is covered, including association with many people (actresses, soldiers, pioneer settlers, Indians, and boatmen). Part II. Tells of his experiences in going from Vancouver to Walla Walla and vicinity for important meetings with Indians (1879). The journal reflects a wide range of experiences - from the "monotony and melancholy" of February days in Goldendale (covered with 27 inches of snow) to life-and-death Indian problems. Included are reports of negotiations among J. H. Wilbur, Indian Agent at the Yakima reservation, Indian Chief Moses, and Lieutenant Wood which led to the US Government's decision to create for Chief Moses a new Indian reservation.
C. C. Gorchels

540. —. DIARY OF A FORT FILLMORE DRAGOON. *Palacio 1967 74(2): 42, 47-48.* This partial diary was originally published in the *San Antonio Express* by a soldier stationed at Fort Fillmore in 1851. It provides some interesting commentary on local news and on events in Mexico.
S. A. Eger

541. —. FORT STEVENS. *Colorado Mag. 1966 43(4): 302-307.* Presents a number of documents relating to Fort Stevens. These documents may be found in *Commands, Department of the Missouri,* R.G. 98, National Archives. The fort was never completed because two months after it was established in 1866 it was decided that a post was not required at that point. It might appropriately be called Colorado's forgotten fort. 2 illus., 10 notes.
I. W. Van Noppen

542. —. [FREMONT AND THE CALIFORNIA BATTALION.] Giffen, Helen S. THE CALIFORNIA BATTALION'S ROUTE TO LOS ANGELES. *J. of the West 1966 5(2): 207-224.* Traces the route followed by the California Battalion, commanded by Lieutenant Colonel John C. Frémont, from San Juan Batista to Los Angeles in late 1846. The purpose of the march of some four hundred men with their animals, ordnance, and equipment was to recapture Los Angeles from the rebellious citizenry. The author details the march through difficult terrain and records the numerous problems encountered. Upon arrival it was found that Los Angeles had already fallen to the forces of Commodore Stockton and General Kearny. The march is noteworthy primarily as an endurance contest. Documented from materials located in the Bancroft Library and in the library of the Society of California Pioneers, illus., map, 27 notes. Outland, Charles F. FREMONT SLEPT WHERE? *J. of the West 1966 5(3): 410-416.* Challenges Helen S. Giffen's interpretation of the route followed by Frémont's California Battalion on that part of the march in the Santa Clara Valley in Southern California. The author assigns different sites for some of the places where Miss Giffen maintained that Frémont camped. Documented from published sources, 12 notes.
D. N. Brown

The Mexican War

543. Allen, John Houghton. ALWAYS A BRAVE RIVER. *Southwest R. 1965 50(4): 345-354.* Reflections on the history of the region between the Nueces and Rio Grande rivers of Texas. The inhabitants, "a rude independent horseback people," did not desire independence from Spain, and were shocked to be claimed by the Republic of Texas. They wanted to be left alone, but instead became the "bone of contention and the direct cause of the Mexican War and a principal battlefield." The people suffered under "gringo" rule until Juan Nepomuceno Cortina took over and controlled the region between 1859 and 1874. Cortina was displaced, not by the Texas Rangers, but by Porfirio Díaz who made him a political prisoner and exiled him to Mexico City. Undocumented.
D. F. Henderson

544. Baker, Sima and Ewing, Florence. WILLIAM BROWN IDE, PRESIDENT OF THE CALIFORNIA REPUBLIC. *California Historian 1968 13(3): 101-103.* Presents a sketch of William Brown Ide (1796-1852), President of the California Republic, and of the events that transpired in the Mexican War that resulted in the acquisition of California by the United States. After the war Ide caught the "gold fever" and soon entered politics to serve in different elected positions. He died in Monroeville of smallpox.
O. L. Miller

545. Beirne, Charles J. THE THEOLOGY OF THEODORE PARKER AND THE WAR WITH MEXICO. *Essex Inst. Hist. Collections 1968 104(2): 130-137.* Sketches Parker's background and theology in order to understand his attitude toward the Mexican War, which he opposed "intuitively" because it was another link in the chain enslaving the Negro. 28 notes.
J. M. Bumsted

546. Bell, Patricia. GIDEON PILLOW: A PERSONALITY PROFILE. *Civil War Times Illus. 1967 6(6): 12-19.* Covers some of Pillow's activities during the Mexican War as well as during the Civil War. Conceited and quarrelsome, Pillow met with only minor successes on the battlefield and earned the enmity of all with whom he served. A portrait is included.
R. N. Alvis

547. Brack, Gene M. MEXICAN OPINION, AMERICAN RACISM, AND THE WAR OF 1846. *Western Hist. Q. 1970 1(2): 161-174.* Mexican officials were well aware of the inadequacy and weakness of the nation's army and the emptiness of the treasury in the 1840's. They

believed that Texas could not be recovered, that it was in the best interests of Mexico to preserve peace, and that war with the United States would be disastrous. Public opinion, however, was hostile to the United States and opposed the ceding of territory to her - the alternative to war. Mexicans closely related American expansionism to racism, being aware of the state of the Indian and Negro in the United States. Knowing that Americans looked upon Mexicans as inferior, they feared the loss of Texas and California, as well as of other Mexican territory which would soon follow. For two decades the press had fed Mexicans a steady diet of American racism. The cumulative effect was a public opinion so rigidly opposed to American expansion that it forced Mexico into a war in 1846 that would not likely be won. 55 notes.   D. L. Smith

548. Chamberlin, Eugene Keith. NICHOLAS TRIST AND BAJA CALIFORNIA. *Pacific Hist. R. 1963 32(1): 49-63.* Reviews the Mexican War campaigns and diplomacy relating to Baja California. Absolves Trist for not securing the area because at no time was the area ever formally demanded by the United States.   J. McCutcheon

549. Farnham, Thomas J. NICHOLAS TRIST AND JAMES FREANER AND THE MISSION TO MEXICO. *Arizona and the West 1969 11(3): 247-260.* Nicholas Trist was sent on a diplomatic mission to Mexico in 1847 to negotiate for peace. When he forwarded a Mexican proposal to Washington to establish the international boundary at the Nueces River rather than at the Rio Grande, President James K. Polk ordered his recall. With the collapse of Mexican military resistance the new interim government urged Trist to ignore his recall and to begin negotiations. He refused and prepared to return to the United States. On the eve of his departure James L. Freaner, a newspaper correspondent and his closest companion in Mexico, paid Trist a call. Freaner pursuaded him to violate his recall instructions and to remain in Mexico to conclude the peace, despite the consequences that might result to his professional career and reputation. The alternative, Trist believed, was continued war or extended military occupation of Mexico. Within two months of the fateful meeting of 4 December 1847, Trist had negotiated the Treaty of Guadalupe Hidalgo based on his original instructions but not on the military situation of the moment. 2 illus., 29 notes.   D. L. Smith

550. Gracy, David B., II and Rugeley, Helen J. H., eds. FROM THE MISSISSIPPI TO THE PACIFIC: AN ENGLISHMAN IN THE MORMON BATTALION. *Arizona and the West 1965 7(2): 127-160.* Persecuted in Missouri, the Mormons moved west again. Five hundred men and boys were enlisted to serve in a Mormon battalion under General Stephen W. Kearny in the Mexican War. At Fort Leavenworth, Kansas, two English youths enlisted. One, Robert W. Whitworth, kept a diary account of the battalion's march to Santa Fe, New Mexico, and on across the Southwest to the final muster near Los Angeles, California. The diary, here reproduced and edited, contains an introductory narrative, daily entries from 13 August 1846 to 16 July 1847, and pen and ink sketches. This account is especially valuable because it is one of a very few similar battalion diaries, its descriptions are fresh impressions of many things which the other diarists overlooked or took for granted, and the author, who was not a Mormon, gives a more detached view on the march. The diary is privately owned. 65 notes.   D. L. Smith

551. Harstad, Peter T. and Resh, Richard W. THE CAUSES OF THE MEXICAN WAR: A NOTE ON CHANGING INTERPRETATIONS. *Arizona and the West 1964 6(4): 289-302.* In the wake of the Mexican War the abolitionist-inspired explanation of the conflict was that it represented the culmination of a long conspiracy on the part of the South to gain more land for slavery expansion and additional slave States. Subsequent interpretations, whether favorable or unfavorable to the Polk administration, couched in patriotic terms or advanced from some other point of view, were to be affected or colored by the abolitionist rationale. Not until the early years of the present century when they were conditioned by the debate over imperialism and the role of America in world affairs did historians in general discard the conspiracy thesis in favor of Manifest Destiny and the extension of national boundaries as the principal cause of the war. American historians still have not made any radical departure from this approach. Since, it is asserted, assumptions of historians are influenced by the society in which they live and by their own personalities, only future generations will be able to determine to what extent a new emphasis on economic and commercial factors as an explanation of the Mexican War reflect the attitudes of our own times. 33 notes.
D. L. Smith

552. Hatheway, G. G. COMMODORE JONES'S WAR, 1842. *Hist. Today [Great Britain] 1966 16(3): 194-201.* U.S. Commodore Thomas ap Catesby Jones sailed into Monterey, California, on 19 October 1842, and captured it for the American government, only to learn shortly thereafter that there was no war between Mexico and the United States. The confusing state of California affairs with Mexico, France, and England in the 1840's is sketched, together with some of the embarrassing details of Jones' surrender. Though recalled and dismissed, Jones was able to escape with his ship for a year's vacation at Hawaii before returning to be relieved of command.   L. A. Knafla

553. Hugh, James. JONES AT MONTEREY, 1842. *J. of the West 1966 5(2): 173-186.* Commodore Thomas ap Catesby Jones, commanding a naval squadron in the Pacific, sailed into the Mexican harbor of Monterey, California, in 1842 and seized it during peacetime. He held the port for 30 hours before realizing he was mistaken in his belief that the nations were at war. His action caused a diplomatic furor and Jones was relieved of his command but was not punished. The author maintains that the vague orders given to Jones by Secretary of the Navy Upshur were of such latitude that the commodore was virtually a free agent. He may have been alarmed at reports that a French squadron was bound for California or he may have feared British objectives there. He was likewise convinced that Mexico and the United States were probably at war and it was his duty to seize and hold California. On 19 October 1842, he demanded and received surrender of Monterey. It was occupied the following day and was held until 22 October when Jones was convinced there was no war. Undocumented, illus.   D. N. Brown

554. Johnson, Robert Erwin COMMODORE AND VIRGINIA PLANTER. *Virginia Cavalcade 1967 16(3): 4-11.* A biographical sketch of Thomas Ap Catesby Jones (1790-1858). A naval officer for almost 50 years, he saw only 14 years of sea duty and is remembered largely for his participation in the Battle of Lake Borgne during the War of 1812 and for his error in forcing the surrender of Monterey in California in 1842, under the mistaken assumption that the United States were at war with Mexico. In 1819 Jones inherited a plantation, Sharon, in Fairfax County, Virginia, and he combined supervision of his plantation with his naval assignment during his periods of shore duty in Washington. Illus.   N. L. Peterson

555. Jones, Oakah L., Jr. THE PACIFIC SQUADRON AND THE CONQUEST OF CALIFORNIA, 1846-1847. *J. of the West 1966 5(2): 187-202.* The conquest of California from Mexico would have been impossible had U.S. naval forces not been present and argues that the naval contingents were largely successful because of their land operations. Marines and sailors formed the nucleus of the makeshift Army of the United States in California. Together with the forces of Frémont and Kearny they succeeded in winning control after the Navy closed all ports. The author details the part played by the forces of Commodore Sloat on land and sea. Also covered are the actions of Commodore Stockton who replaced Sloat. The army of Stockton and Frémont moved on Los Angeles in December 1846 and occupied it in January 1847. The author maintains that the naval squadron present on the Pacific coast had made possible the annihilation of all effective enemy action. Without the Navy, Frémont could not have been supplied, U.S. land forces would have been inferior in numbers, and Monterey and San Francisco could not have been held. Thus, the Navy was the decisive factor in the conquest of California. Documented from published sources, illus., 60 notes.
D. N. Brown

556. Katz, Irving. CONFIDANT AT THE CAPITAL: WILLIAM W. CORCORAN'S ROLE IN NINETEENTH-CENTURY AMERICAN POLITICS. *Historian 1967 29(4): 546-564.* William W. Corcoran, wealthy Washington, D.C., investment banker, philanthropist, and patron of the arts, was an important power behind the scenes and exerted tremendous influence in both Democratic and Whig administrations from the early 1840's to the Civil War. Important members of the administration were frequent guests at his home, and Daniel Webster, John C. Calhoun, and Stephen A. Douglas, among others, used his services as a banker. His firm floated a large loan to the government during the Mexican War of 1846-48. He favored the South and supported James Buchanan, but lost favor with the advent of Lincoln. 28 notes.
F. J. Rossi

557. Lavender, David. THE MEXICAN WAR: CLIMAX OF MANIFEST DESTINY. *Am. West 1968 5(3): 50-64.* "Manifest destiny" is regarded by the author as a latter-day label for American expansionism that started as early as the French were expelled from the continent in the middle of the 18th century. In a thumbnail sketch he traces the westward movement from the penetration of trans-Appalachia to its "ultimate expression" in the Mexican War. This fulfills manifest destiny. "Premonitory shadows" of the Civil War are not recognized in its afterglow. 15 illus., 4 maps and battle plans. D. L. Smith

558. Lee, John D. DIARY OF THE MORMON BATTALION MISSION. *New Mexico Hist. R. 1967 42(3): 165-209.* When trouble developed with Mexico in 1846, President Polk authorized the recruitment of 500 Mormon volunteers to accompany an expedition to California. Following the death of Captain James Allen, the Mormon leaders decided that John D. Lee and Howard Egan should overtake the battalion and go on with them to Santa Fe. "The diary here published is Lee's account of his trip, with notes on the terrain, the happenings in camp, and the general condition of the army." The diary begins on 30 August 1846 and ends on 20 September 1846. 54 notes. To be continued. D. F. Henderson

559. Lee, John D. DIARY OF THE MORMON BATTALION MISSION. *New Mexico Hist. R. 1967 42(4): 281-332.* Continued from a previous article. Five hundred Mormon volunteers accompanied an expedition to Santa Fe during trouble with Mexico in 1846. This part of Lee's diary begins on 21 September in New Mexico and ends on 19 November in Atchison County, Missouri. Included is a description of Las Vegas and a somewhat moralistic account of Santa Fe following American occupation. 103 notes. D. F. Henderson

560. Lofgren, Charles A. FORCE AND DIPLOMACY, 1846-1848: THE VIEW FROM WASHINGTON. *Military Affairs 1967 31(2): 57-64.* Assays the strategic alternatives open to the United States during the Mexican War and concludes that the Polk administration saw in military operations a means of convincing Mexico that coming to terms was less costly than not doing so. Based on published documents and studies; 28 notes. K. J. Bauer

561. Manders, Eric I. and Colwell, Wayne A. CALIFORNIA BATTALION OF MOUNTED RIFLEMEN, 1846. *Military Collector and Historian 1966 18(1): 14-15.* Describes the diverse dress and arms of the emigrants, sailors, mountain men, "Bear Flaggers," and Indians who were organized into a battalion of volunteers by Brevet Captain John Charles Frémont for the purpose of "liberating" California from Mexico. Published sources, illus., 6 notes. C. L. Boyd

562. Mannix, Richard. ALBERT GALLATIN AND THE MOVEMENT FOR PEACE WITH MEXICO. *Social Studies 1969 60(7): 310-318.* Analyzes and explores the various reasons for Gallatin's opposition to U.S.-Mexican warfare, with the main basis for opposition being the tremendous debt which would result. Gallatin held pro-war sentiments during the War of 1812 when he was Secretary of the Treasury. 41 notes. L. R. Raife

563. Merk, Frederick. DISSENT IN THE MEXICAN WAR. *Massachusetts Hist. Soc. Pro. 1969 81: 121-136.* Reprinted in *Dissent in Three American Wars* (Cambridge, Mass.: Harvard U. Press, 1970). Concentrates chiefly on political opposition to the Mexican War with some reference to the dissent of literary figures such as Ralph Waldo Emerson, Henry David Thoreau, and James Russell Lowell. The political dissenters included conservative Whigs who criticized President James Knox Polk but voted supplies for the prosecution of the war; "conscience" Whigs and radical Democrats convinced that the administration hoped to spread slavery into Mexico and Central America; and Southern Democrats such as John Caldwell Calhoun, who doubted that a cause for war existed. Concludes that the dissent prevented the treaty of peace with Mexico from being even more harsh than it was. Based chiefly on newspapers and Federal and State documents; 24 notes. J. B. Duff

564. Meyer, Howard N. WHY ARE WE IN TEXAS (AND ELSEWHERE)? *Minority of One 1968 10(7-8): 14-17.* Study of the pretexts for war with Mexico in 1846-48 with comparisons to the Vietnam War of today. The war with Mexico was brought on by the appetite for slave territory by the South as well as by the ambitions of President James K. Polk for control of California. War was declared hastily on the basis of unexamined evidence. Polk forced on Congress the dilemma of supporting his position or being accused of refusing to rescue imperiled American troops. During the war, Polk's effort to prop up Santa Anna in Mexico proved a fiasco. Opposition to the war did develop, not only in the United States, but among American troops in Mexico as well. P. W. Kennedy

565. Nunis, Doyce B., Jr. NOTES AND DOCUMENTS: SIX NEW LARKIN LETTERS. *Southern California Q. 1967 49(1): 65-103.* Six letters of Thomas Oliver Larkin, prominent early California settler and businessman, are reproduced. They were found in the Faxon Dean Atherton collection in the possession of the California Historical Society. Addressed to Atherton, Larkin's lifelong friend, they were written between 1842 and 1853. Five of the letters are published for the first time and they complete George P. Hammond's edition of the known Larkin letters *(The Larkin Papers,* 10 volumes, Berkeley and Los Angeles: U. of California Press, 1951-65). The six letters published here concern the capture of Monterey by American Commodore Thomas ap Catesby Jones in 1842, the "Bear Flag Revolt" of 1846, and the activities of many American traders in California during the 1840's. 117 notes. W. L. Bowers

566. Oates, Stephen B. LOS DIABLOS TEJANOS [The Texas Devils]. *Am. West 1965 2(3): 41-50.* "The Texas Devils," so dubbed by the frightened populace of Mexico City, were the Texas Rangers who served in the Mexican War with Zachary Taylor and Winfield Scott. Although they were responsible for Taylor's brilliant victory at Buena Vista and for the defeat of Mexican guerrillas that bothered Scott, their seemingly insatiable appetites for revenge, blood, and trouble caused anxiety and brought shame to the American military record of deportment in the war. Usually whitewashed or overlooked by other writers, the author reluctantly allows the possibility that the Rangers regarded war as "one occupation in which man could strip himself of all compassion, all diplomacy, and fight with uninhibited fury, as the violent nature of his soul dictated." Illus., note, biblio. D. L. Smith

567. Payne, Darwin. CAMP LIFE IN THE ARMY OF OCCUPATION: CORPUS CHRISTI, JULY 1845 TO MARCH 1846. *Southwestern Hist. Q. 1970 73(3): 326-342.* The incursion of General Zachary Taylor's army into Mexico was the first instance of U.S. regular troops becoming engaged in conflict on foreign soil. Thus the prior seven-month encampment in Corpus Christi, itself an unknown and largely unexplored territory, came to be viewed as a significant testing ground for the physical and psychological adaptations and tendencies of men quartered in an environment which demanded readjustments. The first joys and delights of a temperate but invigorating climate, wild game, excellent fishing, and breathtaking vistas soon turned to near despair as bad weather, illness, and boredom became the pervasive elements, alleviated only by the influx of traders and the erection of theaters, shops, and bars. The experience, nevertheless, induced a toughening of the regulars that was to well prepare them for their first war in another country. R. W. Delaney

568. Pruyn, Robert N. A CONFEDERATE VETERAN'S RECOLLECTIONS OF CAMPAIGNING THROUGH MEXICO WITH "OLD ROUGH AND READY." *Civil War Times Illus. 1963 2(6): 10-15.* Reminiscences of a 12-year-old drummer boy during the Mexican American War. The author portrays camp life at Fort Brown, Texas, as General Zachary Taylor prepared his troops for the coming conflict. Although the force was small, some three thousand regulars, they were well trained. The author briefly remarks on the march to Mexico City. Based on a personal interview with Pruyn and retold by Major General James E. Edmonds; 8 illus. M. J. McBaine

569. Romer, Margaret. "LEAN JOHN" RIDES FOR HELP. *J. of the West 1966 5(2): 203-206.* Los Angeles fell to American forces on 13 August 1846 but a month later the citizens, chafing under the puritanical rule of Lieutenant Archibald Gillespie, besieged the American garrison atop Fort Moore Hill. Lack of supplies worried the Americans more than it did the Californians. A man named John Brown got through the rebels' line and made an epic ride for assistance. Punishing his mounts he managed to ride the almost 500 miles to San Francisco in four days. Commodore Stockton immediately ordered a ship to sail to the relief of the beleaguered garrison but it arrived too late. Starvation rations and the

need of continual vigilance had sapped the strength of the Americans so Gillespie accepted the terms of General José Flores and left the town. The ride of John Brown had been in vain. D. N. Brown

570. Smith, Ralph A. THE "KING OF NEW MEXICO" AND THE DONIPHAN EXPEDITION. *New Mexico Hist. R. 1963 38(1): 29-55.* Story of a little known guide of a little known expedition during the Mexican War. Irishman James Kirker - known to the Mexicans as Don Santiago Querque, and to the Americans as Don Santiago Kirker - worked as fur trader, politican, and had contracted at intervals for a decade with the government of the Mexican state of Chihuahua to scalp hostile Indians. Kirker joined Colonel Doniphan's Expedition, 1846, serving as scout, interpreter, etc., to the successful capture of El Paso and Chihuahua. Trusted by neither the Mexicans nor the Americans, he had a 19 thousand dollar reward on his head when he joined the expedition. Kirker died leading a wagon train to California in 1853.
D. F. Henderson

571. Stonesifer, Roy P., Jr. GIDEON J. PILLOW: A STUDY IN EGOTISM. *Tennessee Hist. Q. 1966 25(4): 340-350.* An evaluation of Pillow's personality and its effects on his actions in the Mexican and Civil Wars. Commissioned by his friend President Polk, Pillow attempted to blame his failures on his superiors, Winfield Scott in the Mexican War and Leonidas Polk in the Confederate forces at Belmont, Missouri. At Fort Donelson he went over the head of his immediate superior General John B. Floyd to persuade Albert Sidney Johnston to attempt the defense of the fort. Although the Confederate position was indefensible, he hoped to get public acclaim by defeating the Union forces. Floyd's inability to give orders and Pillow's unwillingness to take them lost the chance of victory or withdrawal. Personal animosities prevented the adoption of new plans of escape and the army surrendered. Based on official records, personal papers, and secondary sources; 53 notes. C. F. Ogilvie

572. Sullivan, Wilson. THE MEXICAN WAR AND VIETNAM. *Mankind 1968 1(7): 7-9.* A comparison of domestic opposition to two of the nation's unpopular wars. The political figures who opposed and supported the Mexican War of the 19th century are examined.
P. D. Thomas

573. Tanner, John D., Jr. CAMPAIGN FOR LOS ANGELES - DECEMBER 29, 1846, TO JANUARY 10, 1847. *California Hist. Soc. Q. 1969 48(3): 219-241.* After the defeat of Stephen Watts Kearny's forces at the Battle of San Pascual on 6 December 1846, the survivors of the Kearny detachment joined with Commodore Robert Field Stockton's sailors in a campaign march against the Californians. Under the command of Stockton, with Kearny as aide-de-camp, the army marched from San Diego to Los Angeles, a distance of about 145 miles, in 13 days. The author traces the route of the army, its encampments, and encounters with the Californians under José María Flores. Culminating battles were fought on the banks of the San Gabriel and Los Angeles rivers, resulting in the retreat of the Californians. Stockton's combined force of soldiers and sailors entered the Pueblo de Los Angeles on 10 January 1847, physically worn out but with high morale. Three days later the Capitulation of Cahuenga was signed, ending the war in California. Based on diaries, memoirs, documents, and published sources. 69 notes.
A. Hoffman

574. Tyler, Ronnie. THE RANGERS AT ZACUALTIPAN. *Texana 1966 4(4): 341-350.* An account of the final engagement of the Mexican War for Colonel John Coffee Hays' Texas Rangers, on 25 February 1848. In the town of Zacualtipan, 140 miles north of Mexico City, Hays' force of about 380 encountered the Mexican guerrilla band of Padre Jarauta, inflicting large numbers of casualties and effectively pacifying the area. The article is principally composed of reports of the engagement, written by Colonel Hays, Major William H. Polk, a cavalry commander, and Major Alfred M. Truett, commander of a small mounted attack force. The author notes the special effectiveness of the Colt revolver in this engagement. Based on secondary sources; 23 notes.
J. E. Findling

575. Viola, Herman J. ZACHARY TAYLOR AND THE INDIANA VOLUNTEERS. *Southwestern Hist. Q. 1969 72(3): 335-346.* General Zachary Taylor censured an Indiana regiment in his official

report on the Battle of Buena Vista, but he commended the regiment's commander for gallantry in this crucial battle of the Mexican War. Except for its commander and a few of his men, the Hoosiers had retreated at a critical moment in the battle. Taylor's report angered Indiana. The retreat was a fact; but when it was later revealed that the regiment's commander had ordered the retreat himself, Taylor refused to correct his report. Historians have held this report largely responsible for Taylor's loss of Indiana in the presidential election of 1848. Analyses of the voting patterns in the "volunteer" counties of Indiana do not bear this out. 44 notes. D. L. Smith

576. Wallace, Lee A., Jr. THE FIRST REGIMENT OF VIRGINIA VOLUNTEERS 1846-1848. *Virginia Mag. of Hist. and Biog. 1969 77(1): 46-77.* In November 1846, Virginia was asked to provide a regiment of infantry for immediate service in the Mexican War; it was quickly recruited and John Francis Hamtramck was named colonel. The regiment joined Major General Zachary Taylor's army in northern Mexico early in 1847 after active campaigning there had ceased. It spent most of its service in garrison duty and was mustered out of service following its return to Virginia in July 1848. Based on official records, private papers, and newspapers; 107 notes. K. J. Bauer

577. Weber, R. B., ed. THE MEXICAN WAR: SOME PERSONAL CORRESPONDENCE. *Indiana Mag. of Hist. 1969 65(2): 133-139.* Presents letters written by Captain Thomas Ware Gibson, leader of the Clark County Volunteers (Indiana) during the Mexican War. In Mexico Clark's group joined Major General Zachary Taylor's troops. Gibson's letters reveal chauvinism and a basic Protestant orientation. These letters - one to his wife, one to his brother-in-law, and one from his wife - provide valuable insights into the men fighting the war and the people at home waiting for them. The letters contain comments on battlefield conditions, food rationing, habits of enemy soldiers, the Battle of Buena Vista, and the often-repeated allegation that the Indiana troops showed cowardice in the field. Based on primary sources; 11 notes. N. E. Tutorow

578. Weinert, Richard P. THE "HARD FORTUNE" OF THEODORE O'HARA. *Alabama Hist. Q. 1966 28(1/2): 33-43.* Discusses the unsuccessful military career of Theodore O'Hara in the Mexican War and the Civil War. His forced resignation in 1856 to avoid court-martial is suggested as a possible cause of his later failure in the Confederate Army. O'Hara is remembered for a single poem "The Bivouac of the Dead" (1847). E. E. Eminhizer

The Civil War

579. Altshuler, Constance Wynn. MILITARY ADMINISTRATION IN ARIZONA: 1854-1865. *J. of Arizona Hist. 1969 10(4): 215-238.* Traces the Army administration from the first American possession of the Gadsden Purchase in 1854 until the close of the Civil War in 1865. During this period the Department of New Mexico administered the area called Arizona. At the start of the Civil War the U.S. regulars left Arizona; in 1861 Confederate troops occupied Tucson. The California column, led by Colonel James H. Carleton, started from Fort Yuma by late spring of 1862 and recaptured Tucson after some skirmishes. A District of Arizona was created; it consisted only of a rather narrow strip of territory from the Colorado River in the west to the Rio Grande in the east and extended only as far north as the Gila River. The California troops eventually left Arizona, only to be replaced by New Mexico volunteers and a company of regulars. The district continued to report to the Department of New Mexico until 7 March 1865, when it was attached to the Department of the Pacific, which had headquarters in California. During the Civil War civilians steadily complained that they were inadequately protected from the Apache Indians. Based on primary and secondary sources; 2 maps, 54 notes. R. J. Roske

580. Ashcraft, Allan C., ed. A CIVIL WAR LETTER OF GENERAL STEELE, CSA. *Arkansas Hist. Q. 1963 22(3): 278-281.* The general in command of Fort Smith, Arkansas and of Confederate Indian Territory, wrote to Acting Brigadier General S. P. Bankhead, recently named commander of the Northern Sub-District of Texas. The letter, dated 11 July 1863, discussed overall conditions of Steele's command, offered some information concerning the Union's strength and probable

future plans, and dealt with common problems of western Arkansas, southeastern Indian Territory, and northern Texas.

E. P. Stickney

581. Ashcraft, Allan C. CONFEDERATE INDIAN DEPARTMENT CONDITIONS IN AUGUST, 1864. *Chronicles of Oklahoma 1963 41(3): 270-285.* Confederate relations with the Indians have seldom been given sufficient consideration. With the coming of secession the Confederate States Government made strong attempts to win the support of the Indians residing within its borders. Eventually a dozen Indian regiments fought for the Confederacy. But the care of the nonmilitary tribal member caused a serious problem. The basis of this article is a report in August 1864, by R. W. Lee, Assistant Superintendent of Indian Affairs, CSA, delineating the problems in supervising the various tribes. He had continued difficulty in obtaining food and supplies for the Cherokee, Creek, Osage, Seminole, Chickasaw, Choctaw, and "Reserve Indians." There was also the problem of maintaining amicable relations among the tribes. Supply depots were established. Looms, spinning wheels, wagon shops, and blacksmith shops were provided for the subsistence of the Indians. The number of the Indians of each tribe needing subsistence were listed and the need for schools was emphasized. The Indians were exempted from taxation. 12 notes.

I. W. Van Noppen

582. Ashcraft, Allan C. CONFEDERATE INDIAN TERRITORY CONDITIONS IN 1865. *Chronicals of Oklahoma 1965 42(4): 421-428.* For four years the Indian Territory experienced the horrors of the Civil War. Military conditions in 1865 are delineated in Inspector General reports on the state of affairs in Indian Territory. 12 notes.

I. W. Van Noppen

583. Ashcroft, Allan C. CONFEDERATE INDIAN TROOP CONDITIONS IN 1864. *Chronicles of Oklahoma 1964 41(4): 442-449.* Captain B. W. Marston was sent to inspect the regiments and companies of General Douglas H. Cooper's Indian Division. Discipline was lax. Arms and equipment were poor. The Indians had to disperse to their homes because there were no houses or food for them. Many white men were in the Indian regiments to get out of service. Marston urged the removal of the causes of disorganization. He stated that General Cooper had no command over the men. Cooper asked permission to separate the white soldiers from the Indian troops. By 1865 Captain Marston was in command of a separate battalion in the Indian Division. The division was lacking in basic military attributes. Leadership and command were weak, yet the individual soldiers had an interest in "the cause." 11 notes.

I. W. Van Noppen

584. Banks, Dean. CIVIL WAR REFUGEES FROM INDIAN TERRITORY, IN THE NORTH, 1861-1864. *Chronicles of Oklahoma 1963 41(3): 286-298.* Describes the plight of the Upper Creek and Seminole Indians who fled from the Indian Territory into Kansas because they were loyal to the Union. They were attacked, pursued, and arrived in Kansas naked and without supplies. They froze, starved, suffered, and many died. Food, clothing, and medical care supplied by the Federal Government were inadequate in quality and quantity. Many braves, however, enlisted in and fought for the Union Army. In 1864, these loyal Indians were able to return to thier homes. 41 notes.

I. W. Van Noppen

585. Barr, Alwyn, ed. THE BATTLE OF BAYOU BOURBEAU, NOVEMBER 3, 1863: COLONEL ORAN M. ROBERTS' REPORT. *Louisiana Hist. 1965 6(1): 83-91.* Major General Nathaniel P. Banks' surprise attack by sea at Sabine Pass was defeated 8 September 1863. A second Union effort at the conquest of Texas was halted at Opelousas. The Confederate commander, Major General Richard Taylor, ordered Colonel Oran M. Roberts to join Brigadier General Thomas Green in pursuing and harassing the Federal troops. The ensuing battle of Bayou Bourbeau was represented in the *Official Records* by only one short summary report from the Southern side. Roberts' report of 6 November 1863, here published from the Archives of the University of Texas Library, amplifies the accounts previously available. 24 notes.

E. P. Stickney

586. Barr, Alwyn. THE BATTLE OF BLAIR'S LANDING. *Louisiana Studies 1963 2(4): 204-212.* An account of the attempt by the Confederates to capture the flotilla of Union gunboats on the Red River following General Banks defeat at Mansfield, 8 April 1864. The gunboats had advanced to the mouth of Loggy Bayou, about 20 miles south of Shreveport when news of the defeat reached them on 10 April. Units of dismounted Texas calvary caught up with the fleet on 12 April, and made a spirited effort, with a few pieces of light artillery and muskets, to capture it.

G. W. McGinty

587. Barr, Alwyn. CONFEDERATE ARTILLERY IN THE TRANS-MISSISSIPPI. *Military Affairs 1963 27(2): 77-83.* Description of the various types of artillery pieces used by Confederate forces west of the Mississippi River.

K. J. Bauer

588. Bearss, Edwin C. THE CONFEDERATE ATTEMPT TO REGAIN FORT SMITH, 1863. *Arkansas Hist. Q. 1969 28(4): 342-380.* Narrates the maneuvering and engagement of Union and Confederate troops in western Arkansas and in Indian Territory in fall 1863. The objective was Fort Smith, essential to control of the Arkansas River Valley above Little Rock, and to the security of western Arkansas. Map, photos, 83 notes.

B. A. Drummond

589. Bearss, Edwin C. FEDERAL GENERALS SQUABBLE OVER FORT SMITH, 1863-1864. *Arkansas Hist. Q. 1970 29(2): 119-151.* Details the confused situation resulting from a general order of the War Department that detached Fort Smith and Indian Territory from the Department of Arkansas and assigned them to the Department of Kansas. Conflicting claims of subordinates of Major Generals Samuel Ryan Curtis and Frederick Steele handicapped the defense of northwest Arkansas, complicated provisioning of troops, and contributed to delay of the Red River campaign. Photos, 84 notes.

B. A. Drummond

590. Bearss, Edwin C. THE FEDERALS CAPTURE FORT SMITH, 1863. *Arkansas Hist. Q. 1969 28(2): 156-190.* An account of the Union offensive in Indian Territory in the summer of 1863, which culminated in the occupation of Fort Smith on the Arkansas River. This campaign, together with the subsequent occupation by another Union Army, virtually eliminated Confederate activity north of the Arkansas River. Illus., maps, 72 notes.

B. A. Drummond

591. Bearss, Edwin C. THE FEDERALS RAID VAN BUREN AND THREATEN FORT SMITH. *Arkansas Hist. Q. 1967 26(2): 123-142.* An account of the military activity in northwestern Arkansas from August 1862 through the raid by Federal troops on Van Buren in late December 1862. At stake were the overland routes from Fort Smith to Missouri through the Boston Mountains and the Arkansas River from Van Buren and Fort Smith west into Indian Territory. Based on the *Official Records* and monographs. 2 maps, 48 notes.

B. A. Drummond

592. Bearss, Edwin C. GENERAL WILLIAM STEELE FIGHTS TO HOLD ONTO NORTHWEST ARKANSAS. *Arkansas Hist. Q. 1966 25(1): 36-93.* Brigadier General William Steele's six months' command of Confederate forces in Fort Smith proved a difficult assignment. Supplies and troop morale were low. Operations such as these against Union troops at Fayetteville in April and at Fort Gibson in Indian Territory in July, illustrate the futility of Confederate efforts for a victory in this arena without better support.

P. M. McCain

593. Bidlack, Russell E. ERASTUS D. LADD'S DESCRIPTION OF THE LAWRENCE MASSACRE. *Kansas Hist. Q. 1963 29(2): 113-121.* A brief biographical sketch of Erastus D. Ladd, who migrated to Kansas in 1854 as a member of the second party of the Emigrant Aid Company, provides a background for the introduction of his description of Quantrill's attack on Lawrence. His description of the raid appeared in a hitherto unexamined Michigan newspaper, the Marshall *Statesman,* in the form of a letter to his father on 30 August 1863. Ladd suggests that it is the duty of the citizens of Marshall, Michigan to aid in relieving the distress of the Lawrence victims.

W. F. Zornow

594. Brophy, A. Blake. FORT FILLMORE, N.M., 1861: PUBLIC DISGRACE AND PRIVATE DISASTER. *J. of Arizona Hist. 1968 9(4): 195-218.* Traces the events of July 1861 which caused the fall of Union-held Fort Fillmore in the New Mexico Territory to a small force of Confederates led by Colonel George Baylor. With 300 Texans, Baylor

occupied Mesilla, a settlement across the river from Fort Fillmore. Thereupon, the Union commander, Major Isaac Lynde (1804-86) unsuccessfully sent 380 regulars from the fort to dislodge them. When the Confederates were lightly reinforced, Major Lynde hastily abandoned Fort Fillmore and attempted to retreat. The clouds of dust quickly betrayed this Union maneuver and the Confederates pursued. When his water supplies seemed inadequate, Lynde lost heart and unconditionally surrendered his 700 troops to the numerically inferior southerners. The Confederates paroled the Union troops because there were no supplies to feed the northern prisoners. Major Lynde's conduct in these events came under attack and he was dropped from the Union Army rolls in November 1861. After the war, Lynde launched a successful campaign to rehabilitate his reputation. The army simultaneously restored him to his rank and retired him in November 1866. Based largely on the published official records of the Civil War and archival material of the Federal Government; 2 maps, 94 notes.   R. J. Roske

595. Brown, D. Alexander. THE BATTLE OF WESTPORT. *Civil War Times Illus. 1966 5(4): 4-11, 40-43.* Describes the unsuccessful Confederate raid into Kansas, climaxed by the Union victory at Westport, 23 October 1864. The Confederate defeat "virtually closed out the war in the Kansas-Missouri border country." Undocumented, illus., maps.
                                    W. R. Boedecker

596. Brown, D. Alexander   THE MILLION DOLLAR WAGON TRAIN RAID. *Civil War Times Illus. 1968 7(6): 12-20.* Tells of a Confederate raid on a rich Union supply train of 205 wagons in Indian Territory on 18 September 1864. The 29th and 30th Texas regiments, plus an Indian brigade, numbered about two thousand men. The force was commanded by Brigadier General Stand Watie, a three-quarter-blood Cherokee Indian, Acting Brigadier General Richard M. Gano, and Colonel Charles DeMorse. The wagon train, under Major Henry Hopkins, had about 800 men. Meeting at Cabin Creek Stockade, the Union soldiers were driven off and the Confederates captured the wagon train. Casualties were light on both sides. The Texans were to have made a raid into Kansas to draw off Union forces from Sterling Price who was launching an invasion of Missouri. Had they done so, the Confederates "might have gained a great deal more than the spoils of a rich wagon train."
                                    R. N. Alvis

597. Browne, P. D. CAPTAIN T. D. NETTLES AND THE VALVERDE BATTERY. *Texana 1964 2(1): 1-23.* Timothy Dargan Nettles participated as a private in the Battle of Valverde, New Mexico, 21 February 1862. A new Confederate battery was formed with the Union artillery captured in this battle. Nettles soon became first lieutenant and then captain of this unit. The Valverde battery saw effective action in Louisiana, Texas, and Arkansas throughout the Civil War. Captain Nettles was apparently a quiet, efficient man who made few friends. Traces the artillery pieces to their present locations. An appendix gives the muster roll of the Valverde Battery as of 31 December 1862 and the specifications on three cannons. Illus., 67 notes.   W. A. Buckman

598. Canan, Howard V. THE MISSOURI PAW PAW MILITIA OF 1863-1864. *Missouri Hist. R. 1968 62(4): 431-448.* Membership in the Enrolled Missouri Militia was limited to loyal men. The State finally authorized the formation of two regiments of "disloyal" men. These regiments were assigned to home guard duty on the Northwestern frontier of Missouri where it was not expected that they would have to fight any Confederates. Personal prejudices usually dictated an author's estimate of the value of these so-called Paw Paw regiments. The documents in the *Official Records* support the position that the Paw Paw regiments were of great value in protecting the lives and property of citizens in Northwest Missouri. They were good enought to drive off marauding bands of Kansas "Redlegs," but they proved unable to cope with Confederate forces or organized guerrillas. The task of protecting the Northwestern frontier of Missouri could have been done more effectively by regular troops. Illus., 47 notes.   W. F. Zornow

599. Canan, Howard V. WHEN YANK FOUGHT YANK: AN INCIDENT ON THE KANSAS BORDER. *Civil War Hist. 1966 12(2): 143-155.* Description of an unauthorized raid against Missouri Unionists by a gang of Kansas Unionists in November 1862. Although the raid caused great physical damage and made more difficult the task of keeping loyal Missourians loyal, the culprits went unpunished because of the

sympathetic attitude of the commander of the Department of the Missouri toward them. It was another illustration of the bitter feelings Kansans still held dating back to the "border ruffian" depredations of the middle fifties. Many Kansans felt the Civil War afforded them an excellent chance to get even with Missouri, and, operating on the theory that all the people in that state had been "ruffians," they plundered and stole from them indiscriminately. The Kansas-Missouri rivalry remained a headache for departmental commanders and high political figures. Based on the *Official Records*.   E. C. Murdock

600. Castel, Albert. CIVIL WAR KANSAS AND THE NEGRO. *J. of Negro Hist. 1966 51(2): 125-138.* The reputation of Kansas for radicalism concerning questions of abolition and Negro rights is only partially deserved. While a minority of settlers went to Kansas to assure its becoming a free State, most were either indifferent or hostile to the Negro. Kansas was the first State to raise Negro troops but it did so despite considerable opposition. After the war some Kansas communities had segregated schools, and it was not until 1884 that the word "white" was removed from the voting provisions of the State constitution. Kansans were more willing to support the national program of Radical Republicanism than to implement progressive racial policies within the State's own borders.   L. Gara

601. Castel, Albert. ORDER NO. 11 AND THE CIVIL WAR ON THE BORDER. *Missouri Hist. R. 1963 57(4): 357-368.* General Thomas Ewing's Order no. 11 of 25 August 1863 forced many families to leave their homes in designated areas on Missouri's western border. The order has been criticized and praised without analyzing the background of the order or studying its long-range effects. Artist George Caleb Bingham criticized the order. His picture depicted Ewing's brutal enforcement of it. Attention is called to Ewing's Order no. 10, transferring many families to Arkansas. This was answered by Quantrill's attack on Lawrence, Kansas, which was followed by Order no. 11. The author agrees with Bingham that Ewing had political ambitions and hoped to satisfy a demand for revenge in Kansas, but points out that the order was designed to deprive the guerrillas of their supplies and was anticipated by Ewing's superiors. Order no. 11 was modified to the point that it probably did not prevent a repetition of the Lawrence affair. New Kansas defenses and a change in the interest of the guerrillas were probably responsible for the peace in Kansas. Based on newspapers and documents in Missouri, as well as the O. R.   W. F. Zornow

602. Castel, Albert. QUANTRILL'S BUSHWHACKERS: A CASE STUDY IN PARTISAN WARFARE. *Civil War Hist. 1967 13(1): 40-50.* An analysis of Quantrill's guerrilla activity as a model for the study of partisan warfare today. Quantrill was familiar with the six essentials of guerrilla fighting as set down by "that modern-day master of partisan war" Mao Tse-tung: 1) a climate of public opinion adverse to the government; 2) a tough, hard nucleus of rebels ready to die for their beliefs; 3) a dynamic and outstanding leader; 4) tactics of surprise, or hit and run; 5) a sanctuary; and 6) a supply of arms. After citing examples of these elements, the author concludes with the observation that had modern American military leaders known more about Quantrill's methods "they might not have committed so many mistakes and experienced so many unpleasant surprises attempting to cope with the disciples of Ho Chi Minh." Primary and secondary sources.   E. C. Murdock

603. Castel, Albert. THEY CALLED HIM "BLOODY BILL." *J. of the West 1964 3(2): 233-242.* Bill Anderson was a guerrilla leader in Missouri during the Civil War. At times he was a member of Quantrill's raiders, but he often led his own band of cutthroats known as The Clay County Boys. He was guilty of perpetrating atrocities in Kansas and Missouri during the war. His group, of which the James brothers were members, murdered and mutilated Union troops whenever the opportunity afforded. Anderson was killed on 26 October 1864 when he led a charge against a superior Union force. His life reveals the viciousness of the Civil War on the western border. Documented from published sources, 34 notes.   D. N. Brown

604. Clendenen, Clarence C. A CONFEDERATE SPY IN CALIFORNIA: A CURIOUS INCIDENT OF THE CIVIL WAR. *Southern California Q. 1963 45(3): 219-233.* In July 1864, when the Civil War had been raging for three years and things were going poorly for the Confederacy, a certain Captain H. Kennedy, CSA, landed in San Francisco. He

was to attempt to enlist sympathy, aid, and soldiers from California, whose population was largely southern in origin. Kennedy proceeded to Virginia City, Nevada, where he attempted to organize a group of Confederate sympathizers and desperate men to march south, take Arizona and New Mexico, and thus open a way for the Confederacy to California. Union intelligence discovered the plot, however. The author also details several other plots designed to enlist aid in California or even to bring the whole State into the Confederacy. 24 notes.   A. K. Main

605.   Clendenen, Clarence C.   MEXICAN UNIONISTS: A FORGOTTEN INCIDENT OF THE WAR BETWEEN STATES. *New Mexico Hist. R. 1964 39(1): 32-39.* In 1864 a group of 1500 soldiers, with artillery, under command of General Juan Nepomuceno Cortina, crossed the US-Mexican border to evade French Imperialist forces and to surrender to US federal forces. Colonel Day, the federal commander, dispatched Major E. J. Noyes to accomplish the surrender and disarm the soldiers, although he might allow them to retain or resume their arms for defense. When the Confederates attacked Noyes' force, the Mexicans were rearmed, and probably used their artillery in the resulting skirmish. Unfortunately 12 Mexican soldiers were captured, which precipitated a rash of correspondence between the local Union and Confederate commanders. General U. S. Grant closed the matter in a brief decision: "If Cortina's men came into the United States, there was no law against it. The Imperialists had the same right."   D. F. Henderson

606.   Crook, Carland Elaine.   BENJAMIN THERON AND FRENCH DESIGNS IN TEXAS DURING THE CIVIL WAR. *Southwestern Hist. Q. 1965 68(4): 432-454.* In 1862, Benjamin Théron, consular agent for France in Galveston, wrote identical letters to General Sam Houston and to Francis Richard Lubbock, Governor of Texas. Questions put by the French official led the Governor to conclude that it represented "an incipient intrigue" and to so notify the Confederate administration. Charges were made by the Confederacy that France had designs on Texas. There was fear that neither the North nor the South could resist foreign encroachments and that this might be the first step in that direction. Most of the controversy and apprehension were eventually quieted with the French Government's disapproval of Théron's letters and by the fact that Napoleon III did not commit his troops to make Texas a protectorate. Théron frequently used his consular prerogatives and official titles indiscreetly. His letters to Houston and Lubbock may well have been another example of Théron's indiscretions. 78 notes.   D. L. Smith

607.   Currin, Jean McCulley.   WHY INDIAN TERRITORY JOINED THE CONFEDERACY. *Lincoln Herald 1967 69(2): 83-91.* Presents evidence that the pro-Southern and proslavery proclivities of the Five Civilized Tribes coupled with the withdrawal of Federal troops and general misunderstanding of Indian attitudes in the Territory by the Union government at the beginning of the War enabled Confederate agents to draw the Indians into an alliance in 1861.   S. L. Jones

608.   Danziger, Edmund J., Jr.   CIVIL WAR PROBLEMS IN THE CENTRAL AND DAKOTA SUPERINTENDENCIES: A CASE STUDY. *Nebraska Hist. 1970 51(4): 411-424.* Examines the work of the Office of Indian Affairs during the Civil War in protecting and caring for the friendly Indians of Kansas, Nebraska, and Dakota, and in pacifying the hostiles while pioneers pushed up the Kansas, Platte, and Missouri rivers, trespassing on Indian lands and destroying game.   R. Lowitt

609.   Danziger, Edmund J., Jr.   THE OFFICE OF INDIAN AFFAIRS AND THE PROBLEM OF CIVIL WAR INDIAN REFUGEES IN KANSAS. *Kansas Hist. Q. 1969 35(3): 257-275.* The poor care provided by the Office of Indian Affairs for its charges became even poorer during the Civil War. Thousands of Indians driven into Kansas from Indian Territory during the war faced a grim future. No one wanted them in Kansas, but no one could guarantee their safety in Indian Territory. For more than three years they were allowed to wander or were herded back and forth across the border. The Office of Indian Affairs was hampered by corruption, jurisdictional quarrels, low morale, administrative weaknesses, inordinate demands imposed by the war, and the inability to anticipate how many Indians would become refugees because of the war. Based on books, articles, annual reports of the Commissioner of Indian Affairs, records of the Department of the Interior, of the War

Department, and of the Southern Superintendency, and material in the National Archives; illus., map, photos, 71 notes.   W. F. Zornow

610.   Davison, Stanley R. and Tash, Dale.   CONFEDERATE BACKWASH IN MONTANA TERRITORY. *Montana 1967 17(4): 50-58.* Throughout the sixties Montana territorial politics reflected feelings arising from the Civil War. Extreme viewpoints clashed as Radical Republicans in the Union League of America confronted unreconciled Democrats with a strong anti-Negro bias. The often cited pro-Southern majority is found to have been a fact. Based on newspapers from the period; illus.   A

611.   Debo, Angie.   THE LOCATION OF THE BATTLE OF ROUND MOUNTAINS. *Chronicles of Oklahoma 1963 41(1): 70-104.* Marshals and evaluates the evidence, oral and written, concerning the site of the Battle of Round Mountains. The Creek Indians with Union sympathies were seeking to emigrate to Kansas with all their household belongings. They were pursued by Confederate troops and caught near the Round Mountains at the mouth of the Cimarron and above Tulsa. There is much controversial evidence concerning the location. From fragments of dishes, cooking pots, and a buggy step, the author presents conclusions concerning the location of the battle.   I. W. Van Noppen

612.   Dyer, Brainerd.   CALIFORNIA'S CIVIL WAR CLAIMS. *Southern California Q. 1963 45(1): 1-24.* Union troops to fight the Civil War were raised almost entirely by the State governments, whose officials supervised recruiting, arming, equipping, and officering. The Federal Government took steps to reimburse the States for their trouble and expenses, Congress passing a bill on 27 July 1861 to cover disbursement of necessary funds. By 1873, 23 States had been reimbursed nearly 40 million dollars. California was slow in presenting its claim, missing the original deadline of 30 June 1864. By 1930, nearly 15 million dollars more had been paid out, but California has never been reimbursed. The claim, which is still being pressed over 100 years after the war it concerns, has become involved in a tremendous legislative and judicial tangle; 99 notes.   A. K. Main

613.   Edwards, G. Thomas   HOLDING THE FAR WEST FOR THE UNION: THE ARMY IN 1861.   *Civil War Hist. 1968 14(4): 307-324.* A review of military and political events in the Department of the Pacific (chiefly in California) from January through September 1861. General Albert Sidney Johnston (1803-62), was in command in the early months. He ruled wisely and impartially, but was removed in late April because of his southern connections and rumors of disunionist plots. The principal mission of the new commander, General Edwin Vose Sumner (1797-1863), was to check the secessionist movement. Exploiting Unionist feelings, cowing the disunionists by a show of military power, yet carefully respecting the civil rights of all, Sumner successfully executed his assignment. The loyalty of the Far West was established without serious incident. Based on official records and secondary sources.

E. C. Murdock

614.   Edwards, John.   AN ACCOUNT OF MY ESCAPE FROM THE SOUTH IN 1861.   *Chronicles of Oklahoma 1965 43(1): 58-89.* Never before published, this narrative by a Presbyterian missionary begins on 11 May 1861 when a vigilance committee visited the Choctaw Reservation to check the allegiance of the missionaries and to warn those who were not willing to fight for the Confederacy to leave the Indian Territory. They believed that John Edwards was an abolitionist and threatened to hang him, but he convinced them that he had no objection to slavery so they merely commanded him to leave the Territory. Later, word came to him that the vigilance committee of Texans was coming to hang him. Most of the narrative relates the events of his escape as he and his family traveled first on horseback, then by wagon, boat, and train, eventually reaching Bath, New York. After the war he returned to minister to the Choctaw.   I. W. Van Noppen

615.   Faulk, Odie B.   CONFEDERATE HERO AT VAL VERDE. *New Mexico Hist. R. 1963 38(4): 300-311.* Tom Green is an often overlooked, but not forgotten hero of Texas and the Confederacy. After a brief sketch of Green's pre-war exploits, the author traces his Confederate career from the battle of Val Verde, New Mexico to his death, toward the end of Dick Taylor's campaign against Banks, in west Louisiana.

D. F. Henderson

616. Finch, Boyd. SHEROD HUNTER AND THE CONFEDER-ATES IN ARIZONA. *J. of Arizona Hist. 1969 10(3): 139-206.* Traces the prominent part Sherod Hunter played in the short-lived Confederate occupation of Arizona. Hunter was born about 1824 in Robertson County, Tennessee. In 1857 he was living in Mesilla, New Mexico, and later in Mowry City, New Mexico, where he farmed. Hunter and disaffected Arizona politicians who hoped to cut off a long east-west strip of the New Mexico territory and call it Arizona joined the Confederate cause in early 1861. When Lieutenant Colonel John R. Baylor led a force of Texans into the New Mexico Territory, Hunter joined them and helped to capture Fort Fillmore and its Union garrison. He became a second lieutenant in a company of Arizona Rangers raised from Confederate sympathizers in southern New Mexico. Soon the rangers fought not only the Union troops but the Apache as well. After Brigadier General Henry Hopkins Sibley reinforced Baylor's forces in the Mesilla area, the Confederates planned offensive operations to wrest additional territory from Union control. One prong of the Confederate attack was to strike into western Arizona; Hunter commanded 75 men in this effort. From Tucson Hunter pushed west to the Pima villages to negotiate a treaty with the Indians. Meanwhile, the main Confederate thrust northward toward Fort Union was turned back at the Battle of Glorieta Pass. Unaware of this Confederate setback, Hunter attempted to hold Tucson against an advancing Union column from California. The result was the "westernmost battle" - really a skirmish - at Pichacho Peak, 40 miles west of Tucson. Although Hunter won this engagement, the superior Union forces soon outflanked him and he retreated east from Tucson. Reunited on the Rio Grande with the main Confederate force, the starving and disheartened army retreated all the way back to San Antonio, Texas. Although many Arizonans deserted the fleeing Confederates during the long retreat, Hunter continued with the Southern forces into the interior of Texas. In the fall of 1862 he became a major in the Texas cavalry, seeing action in both Texas and Louisiana. However, when the Confederacy became disorganized in 1865, Hunter dropped from view; his ultimate fate is unknown. Based largely on contemporary documents and newspapers; 130 notes, appendix.   R. J. Roske

617. Fischer, LeRoy H. and Rampp, Lary C. QUANTRILL'S CIVIL WAR OPERATION IN INDIAN TERRITORY. *Chronicles of Oklahoma 1968 46(2): 155-181.* By the time of the Civil War, William Clarke Quantrill had established a reputation as a vagrant criminal. Disliking regular soldiering, he gathered a band of army deserters and assorted criminals and became a Confederate specialist in guerrilla fighting in Missouri, Kansas, and Indian Territory. His reputation for ruthlessness and revenge paralyzed Union offensive operations. Although he was unreliable, Quantrill was useful to the Confederate cause. 6 illus., map, 53 notes.   D. L. Smith

618. Geise, William. MISSOURI'S CONFEDERATE CAPITAL IN MARSHALL, TEXAS. *Missouri Hist. R. 1963 58(1): 37-54.* Reprint of an article appearing in the *Southwestern Hist. Q.* 1962 66(2). The relations between Southern sympathizers in Missouri and the Confederate government are described in detail. The major item of consideration is Thomas C. Reynold's effort to establish a capital for Missouri in Texas, a development which the author compares to the mid-20th century manifestation of "governments-in-exile."   W. F. Zornow

619. Gibson, A. M. CONFEDERATES ON THE PLAINS: THE PIKE MISSION TO WICHITA AGENCY. *Great Plains J. 1964 4(1): 7-16.* Describes the Confederacy's interest in Indian Territory and General Albert Pike's mission there in August 1861. He was successful in treating with both the civilized tribes in the east and the Comanches in the west. He was unable to meet with the Kiowas, the most hostile toward neighboring Texas. About one-half of the article is composed of two long quotations from Pike's report to the Confederate government. Published government records and some unpublished letters provide the main additional sources. 13 notes.   O. H. Zabel

620. Goldman, Henry H. SOUTHERN SYMPATHY IN SOUTHERN CALIFORNIA, 1860-1865. *J. of the West 1965 4(4): 577-586.* Prior to the Civil War most of the population arriving in Southern California had come from the slave States and were sympathetic to the southern cause. Disunion sentiment flourished there as early as 1860 and in 1861 secret secessionist societies were organized. One, the Knights of the Golden Circle, planned to seize government forts and take the southern

counties out of the Union. The editor of the *Los Angeles Star*, Henry Hamilton, campaigned for secession and attacked the Lincoln administration. Hamilton and members of the Knights actively campaigned for the reelection of the Democratic governor John G. Downey but to no avail. The Democrats did win the offices in Los Angeles city and county. Continued expressions of southern sentiment led General E. V. Sumner to order reinforcements into the Los Angeles area. Former U.S. Senator William Gwin was arrested and held in prison for two years, and other political arrests were also made. Most secessionist activity, however, was below the surface and the Army was able to maintain full control. Based on newspapers and other published sources, 63 notes.
                                                           D. N. Brown

621. Hall, Martin Hardwick. THE MESILLA TIMES: A JOURNAL OF CONFEDERATE ARIZONA. *Arizona and the West 1963 5(4): 337-351.* The *Mesilla Times* was founded in 1860 in Mesilla, Territory of Arizona (present State of New Mexico), not only to keep the people of the eastern part of the territory informed but also to publicize to the nation Arizona's economic potential and its political problems. Because of its location on the principal Texas-California route, its position in a rich agricultural region, and its nearness to rich copper, gold, and silver mines, the future of Mesilla and its paper looked rosy. The author traces the vicissitudes of the paper as it became a self-appointed voice of the Confederacy and champion of the freedom of the press. One of the editors used the *Times* to feud with the officer in charge of Confederate troops in the area and became the mortal victim of one of the colonel's bullets. The demise of the paper itself apparently came about the same time as the Confederate evacuation of Arizona in mid-1862. Based on files and fragments of the *Times* and other miscellaneous sources. 63 notes.
                                                           D. L. Smith

622. Hall, Martin H. NATIVE MEXICAN RELATIONS IN CONFEDERATE ARIZONA, 1861-62. *J. of Ariz. Hist.* Discusses the warm reception which the invading Confederate forces initially received from the native Mexican population living in what was called the Confederate Territory of Arizona. The first Confederate commander was Colonel John R. Baylor, who was very popular with the native population, but his successor General Henry Hopkins Sibley with his East Texas troops proved to be much less understanding of the Mexican inhabitants. Soon many acts of robbery and abuse completely alienated the natives. As a result, when the Confederates abandoned Arizona and West Texas in June 1862, they left behind a native population which welcomed the Federal forces. Based on contemporary newspapers and records in the National Archives; illus., map, 16 notes.   R. J. Roske

623. Hall, Martin Hardwick. PLANTER VS. FRONTIERSMAN: CONFLICT IN CONFEDERATE INDIAN POLICY. *Essays on the Am. Civil War* (Austin: U. of Texas Pr., 1968): 45-72. Describes the controversy over Colonel John Paul Baylor's "Indian Order" in 1862-63. Baylor, an old Indian fighter, was in command of Confederate troops in West Texas-Arizona, an area which had been badly victimized by Apache Indians. Under the mistaken impression that the Confederate Government had authorized a policy of Indian extermination, Baylor issued an order that all adult Apaches be killed and the children enslaved. When Jefferson Davis learned of the order, he demanded an explanation from Baylor, who replied that all those familiar with Apache atrocities against whites would heartily approve his order. Unconvinced, Davis revoked Baylor's commission. The author holds that Baylor's "Indian Order" was representative of frontier thinking and that his dispute with Richmond reflected a breakdown in communications between those who had battled Apache Indians all their lives and those who had never seen an Indian. Based on primary sources, newspapers, and the *Official Records*.
                                                           E. C. Murdock

624. Harrison, Jeanne V. MATTHEW, CONFEDERATE AGENT AT THE WICHITA AGENCY INDIAN TERRIT0RY. *Chronicles of Oklahoma 1969 47(3): 242-257.* Matthew Leeper served as both the U.S. Government agent and the Confederate agent to the Comanche Indians. A native of North Carolina, Leeper was educated at Chapel Hill. He and his family moved often, living in Georgia, Tennessee, Mississippi, and Arkansas where he served as Receiver of the Public Moneys. President Buchanan offered Leeper the position of Consul to Smyrna (in the Mediterranean) or Cuba, but Leeper did not want to leave the United States, so he was given the job of Indian agent. When the Civil War began,

Leeper was reappointed to the same job by the Confederate government. In the massacre which occurred at the Wichita Agency in Indian Territory on 23 October 1862, Leeper was feared slain. He escaped, however, and was aided by some friendly Comanche. This account is based on the memory of the author, Mr. Leeper's daughter; illus., 12 notes.

K. P. Davis

625. Heath, Gary N. THE FIRST FEDERAL INVASION OF INDIAN TERRITORY. *Chronicles of Oklahoma 1967 44(4): 409-419.* The Battle of Pea Ridge, Arkansas, 6-8 March 1862 was the turning point of the war for Indian Territory. The Confederates were defeated, the Union forces were in the ascendancy, and Union commanders decided to invade Indian Territory, with victorious results. The defeated men spread fear and panic and caused the disintegration of Confederate alliances with the Indians. Many sought refuge within Federal lines. 33 notes.

I. W. Van Noppen

626. Hood, Fred. TWILIGHT OF THE CONFEDERACY IN INDIAN TERRITORY. *Chronicles of Oklahoma 1964 41(4): 425-441.* A description of the Battle of Honey Springs and the capture of Fort Gibson and Fort Smith. The Confederates were badly armed, clothed, fed, and were defeated and scattered. Stand Waties raided near Fort Gibson and up the Neosha Valley but was defeated. These Confederate defeats impaired relations with their Indian allies. General Kirby Smith assured Watie that the Confederate position would be strengthened. There was friction between Generals Cooper and Steele. General Maxey was sent to take command and he found the army demoralized. He sought to make full use of the Indians. Stand Watie captured a steam ferryboat and a wagon train of 300 wagons with over one million dollars worth of Federal supplies. In November 1864 Indian troops had still not been armed. Few Federal troops were left. Cooper was finally placed in command of the Indian Territory just a month before Lee surrendered. 49 notes.

I. W. Van Noppen

627. Huff, Leo E. THE UNION EXPEDITION AGAINST LITTLE ROCK, AUGUST-SEPTEMBER, 1863. *Arkansas Hist. Q. 1963 22(3): 224-237.* Under the command of Major General Frederick Steele the Union forces began the expedition to Little Rock from Helena, Arkansas on 11 August 1863. The Confederate commander of the District of Arkansas was Major General Sterling Price. The decisive battle was fought 10 September; Steele outmaneuvered Price, but the latter saved his army. The expedition was significant because it resulted in: 1) the loss of Missouri and Indian Territory as Confederate recruiting grounds, 2) the loss to the Confederacy of a large portion of Arkansas and its capital, and 3) the further isolation of the Confederate Trans-Mississippi Department.

G. B. Dodds

628. Hunt, Aurora. THE CIVIL WAR ON THE WESTERN SEABOARD. *Civil War Hist. 1963 9(2): 178-186.* The importance of the Pacific Squadron lay in maintaining peace in an ocean travelled by ships of all nations; this despite numerous tense situations. In 1862 the Army of the Pacific secured the West Coast from invasion by victories at Glorieta and Apache Canyon. The navy dealt not only with Confederate-initiated crises but also with threats from the Russians, Japanese, and French.

L. Filler

629. James, Parthena Louise. RECONSTRUCTION IN THE CHICKASAW NATION: THE FREEDMAN PROBLEM. *Chronicles of Oklahoma 1967 45(1): 44-57.* The Dawes Commission destroyed the Chickasaw Nation in 1894 by appropriating the land to individual tribal members. It was at this time that the problem of Chickasaw freedmen was solved. From the Civil War to 1894 much confusion existed with regard to the status of the freedmen. This made law and order in the Chickasaw Nation difficult. This confusion could have been avoided if the United States had acted to remove the freed slaves as the Chickasaw elected to have done under the treaty of 1866. But after the freedmen settled and built in the Nation they no longer wanted to move. The Chickasaw, however, were equally determined to move the black men for fear of losing control of their Nation. Fortunately for the Chickasaw, other Reconstruction problems were not so difficult. 50 notes.

K. P. Davis

630. Jones, V. C. THE BATTLE OF GALVESTON HARBOR. *Civil War Times Illus. 1967 5(10): 28-38.* An account of a coordinated land and sea attack by Confederate forces which temporarily broke the Union blockade of the island port. Superior numbers and surprise were the decisive elements in the engagement. Map, illus.

W. R. Boedecker

631. Kajencki, Francis C. THE LOUISIANA TIGER: SULAKOWSKI. *Polish-Am. Studies 1966 23(2): 82-88.* An account of Colonel Valery Sulakowski's services in the Polish Brigade which saw action in the Peninsular Campaign in Virginia in 1862. Also described is Colonel Sulakowski's contribution to the Confederacy on the Texas front where he served as an engineering expert. The author concludes with an account of Sulakowski's attempt to recruit thirty thousand volunteers in Poland for the Confederacy following the collapse of the Polish revolt of 1863. Based on newspaper articles and military records.

S. R. Pliska

632. Kellersberger, Getulius. THE FIRST (AND LAST) ROCKET BATTERY OF THE CONFEDERATE ARMY IN TEXAS. *Civil War Times Illus. 1963 2(3): 26-27.* Illus.

633. Kibby, Leo P. CALIFORNIA, THE CIVIL WAR, AND THE INDIAN PROBLEM: AN ACCOUNT OF CALIFORNIA'S PARTICIPATION IN THE GREAT CONFLICT. *J. of the West 1965 4(2): 183-209, (3): 377-410.* Part I. California entered the Union as a State in 1850 and during the remainder of that decade made remarkable progress despite the lack of competent executive leadership. The strong sectional disturbances of the 1850's extended into the State. The election of 1860 did not show clearly what would occur in the event of division between North and South. When war came, California became an objective of both sides. Early gains by the Confederacy in New Mexico and Arizona Territories, plus the fact that there were groups sympathetic to the Confederacy at work in California, indicated the State might soon be dominated by the South. When Union troops won battles at Apache Canyon and Glorieta Pass in March 1862 the eventual status of California was determined. The State made material contributions to the Union during the remainder of the war. 99 notes. Part II. When Federal troops were withdrawn from western territories, President Lincoln authorized volunteers to be recruited to protect the vacated region. The California volunteers proceeded to Arizona and New Mexico where they performed valuable service. Units of the volunteers also were assigned to protect the overland route to California and others to protect supply lines from Indian uprisings and depredations. Three of every four volunteers spent the full period of enlistment in the struggle with the Indians. Peace was finally restored in late 1864 when a treaty was concluded. By October 1866 all California soldiers had been returned to civilian life. Based on official records and other published material. 205 notes, biblio.

D. N. Brown

634. Kibby, Leo P. PATRICK EDWARD CONNOR, FIRST GENTILE OF UTAH. *J. of the West 1963 2(4): 425-434.* Patrick Edward Connor was the Commanding General of the Third California Infantry between 1861 and 1865. His unit was sent to Utah during the Civil War to protect overland mail routes. What might have been a relatively routine assignment of guarding Utah and Nevada Territories from Indians and Rebels with only one regiment was complicated by the presence of the Mormons. The Latter-Day Saints, led by Brigham Young, had settled near the Great Salt Lake in 1847 and had not been on friendly terms with the Federal Government since the United States won the Mexican War. Brigham Young and Patrick Connor took an instant dislike to each other and proceeded to open a verbal battle which often verged on physical violence and did not end until Connor left Utah. Young disliked what he felt was interference by Federal troops, and Connor characterized Young as disloyal to the United States. The author concludes, however, that the two men did eventually develop a grudging admiration for each other. The efforts of Connor were beneficial in that he protected mail routes, lessened the Indian menace and encouraged immigration to Utah. Based on secondary sources and primarily on *The War of the Rebellion* series of records on the Civil War; 75 notes.

K. P. Davis

635. Kibby, Leo P. UNION LOYALTY OF CALIFORNIA'S CIVIL WAR GOVERNORS. *California Hist. Soc. Q. 1965 44(4): 311-321.* Discusses the evidence contradicting Baron de Stoeckl, Russian chargé d'affaires, who in April 1865 informed the Russian Foreign Office that California had made "only small financial contributions" and had not supplied "a single man during the entire war." As a matter of fact, about 16 thousand volunteers served, and about 185 million dollars in

gold was shipped from San Francisco alone. California contributed her share of the direct tax imposed by Congress. The two war governors, Leland Stanford and Frederick F. Low, are shown to have been loyal to the Union. Based largely on official records, 59 notes.

E. P. Stickney

636. King, James T., ed. THE CIVIL WAR OF PRIVATE MORTON. *North Dakota Hist. 1968 35(1): 8-19.* Thomas F. Morton was with a Minnesota volunteer infantry regiment on "The Sioux Expedition" on the Dakota frontier in the summer of 1863. In a letter written when his contingent halted for supplies, Morton deplores its inefficiency and mismanagement; and, if the Union armies on the Civil War fronts were no better, the cause of the Confederacy was assured. Nor does his estimate change very much in a subsequent letter before he hears news of three successful engagements against the Sioux. 5 illus., 28 notes.

D. L. Smith

637. King, Jerlene. JACKSON LEWIS OF THE CONFEDERATE CREEK REGIMENT. *Chronicles of Oklahoma 1963 41(1): 66-69.* A full-blooded Creek Indian, Jackson Lewis was six years old when his tribe was removed from Alabama and Georgia to Oklahoma. Earning the respect of his people as he grew up, he became an excellent doctor, a Baptist deacon, a Mason, and a member of the House of Warriors. He served as a doctor in the Army of the Confederate States in Company K of the Second Regiment Creek Indian Volunteers. He died in 1910.

I. W. Van Noppen

638. Kornweibel, Theodore, Jr. THE OCCUPATION OF SANTA CATALINA ISLAND DURING THE CIVIL WAR. *California Hist. Soc. Q. 1967 46(4): 345-357.* On 1 January 1864 Federal troops occupied Santa Catalina Island, off the coast of Southern California, for the purpose of securing the island for use as an Indian reservation. The purpose was never announced; local opinion concluded that the action was taken to forestall a Confederate attempt to seize the island for a privateer base, and this unfounded idea continued to be repeated in history books. The author disproves the Confederate base theory and shows the series of circumstances that prevented the use of the island for an Indian reservation for tribes from the north. The War Department was cool toward the plan; accordingly the Department of the Interior, after sounding out the Bureau of Indian Affairs, which was negative, defeated the proposal. When it was certain that the island would not be used for a reservation, it was evacuated on 14 September 1864. By removing most of the population of miners from the island, the occupation "served only to prolong its isolation." Based largely on Army records; 45 notes.

E. P. Stickney

639. Langsdorf, Edgar. PRICE'S RAID AND THE BATTLE OF MINE CREEK. *Kansas Hist. Q. 1964 30(3): 281-306.* The battle of Mine Creek occurred during the closing stages of General Sterling Price's unsuccessful effort to invade Missouri and Kansas in 1864. It is important because it was the largest Civil War battle in Kansas and marked the end of the Price raid. It was the last major battle fought in the trans-Mississippi theater of operations. The Union victory yielded many prisoners and kept Price from carrying out his objective to attack Fort Scott, Kansas. Based on the official records.

W. F. Zornow

640. Larson, Gustive O. UTAH AND THE CIVIL WAR. *Utah Hist. Q. 1965 33(1): 55-77.* Concentrates on the relationship which developed between the Mormons and the Northern governnent. Though Utah was disposed to be friendly to the North, the hostility and suspicion of territorial governors and Federal troops stationed in the Territory occasionally created severe stress between the settlers and Lincoln's government. Lincoln tried to retain Mormon friendship by adopting a hands-off policy regarding such issues as polygamy. The last governor he appointed (James Duane Doty) adopted a conciliatory policy, and by the end of the war amicable relations prevailed. Based on Brigham Young letters in the Coe Collection at Yale University, the Territorial Papers of Utah Territory in the National Archives, and the *Official Records;* illus.

S. L. Jones

641. Lemley, Harry J. LETTERS OF HENRY M. RECTOR AND J. R. KANNADAY TO JOHN ROSS OF THE CHEROKEE NATION. *Chronicles of Oklahoma 1964 42(3): 320-329.* Henry M. Rector, Governor of Arkansas, wrote to John Ross, principal chief of the Chero-

kee Nation, urging the Cherokee to side with the Confederacy. J. R. Kannaday, commander of Fort Smith, wrote Ross asking the intentions of the Cherokee in the war. Ross answered that their treaties were with the U.S. Government but that he would advise the Cherokee to be neutral. There follow sketches of the lives of Rector and Ross. After the Confederate victories at the first Battle of Manassas (Bull Run) and the Battle of Wilson Creek, Ross and the Cherokee signed a treaty uniting the Cherokee Nation with the Confederate States. After the Confederate defeat at Locust Grove, Chief Ross went north and favored the Union. 4 notes.

I. W. Van Noppen

642. Mayhall, Mildred E. CAMP COOPER - FIRST FORT IN TEXAS TO FALL, 1861, AND EVENTS PRECEDING ITS FALL. *Texana 1967 5(4): 317-343.* Account of affairs on the West Texas frontier just before the Civil War. The people on the frontier were concerned about a wave of Comanche raids. The inhabitants of East Texas were concerned with the issues of slavery and secession. When the Texas legislature moved to secede, State troops moved on Camp Cooper, the key Federal fort on the frontier near the Brazos River. The fort was surrendered peaceably on 20 February 1861, almost two months before Fort Sumter's surrender. Presents the letters exchanged in the surrender. 36 notes.

W. A. Buckman

643. McNeil, Kinneth. CONFEDERATE TREATIES WITH THE TRIBES OF INDIAN TERRITORY. *Chronicles of Oklahoma 1965 42(4): 408-420.* Early in the war the Confederate Congress established a Bureau of Indian Affairs and appointed a commissioner to negotiate alliances with the tribes of the Indian Territory. Many Indians resented their removal in the 1830's, others wished to remain neutral. Treaties were concluded with the Choctaw, Seminole, Chickasaw, with one faction of the Creek, with a number of small tribes, and with the Plains Indians. After the Confederate victory at Wilson's Creek on 10 August 1861, the Cherokee joined the Confederate alliance on 7 October. The Confederacy was to be the protector of each tribe and it assumed the payment of all money Washington owed the tribes. The Indians promised to furnish troops to protect the Indian Territory. There was proposed, and rejected, a provision for ultimate statehood. The treaties gave official recognition to slavery. The Confederate government was unable to meet its obligations to the tribes but they remained loyal. 44 notes.

I. W. Van Noppen

644. Miller, Robert Ryal. THE "CAMANCHE": FIRST MONITOR OF THE PACIFIC. *California Hist. Soc. Q. 1966 45(2): 113-124.* In 1861 with the outbreak of the Civil War, mobile defenses in San Francisco were needed because parts of the bay were out of range of existing forts. In 1862 after the battle of the *Monitor* and the *Merrimack*, James T. Ryan, California State senator, formed a partnership to prefabricate vessels in New Jersey to be transported to San Francisco and assembled there. The difficulties encountered in building and launching the *Camanche* were many, and by the time the ship was ready for service the need for a floating battery no longer existed. It was decommissioned at Mare Island in 1866 only a year after the commissioning. The *Camanche* (larger than its prototype) never fired a shot except in practice or as a salute, but she functioned for many years as a warehouse, barracks, training ship, and coal barge until junked in the 1920's. Based on official records and newspapers, 31 notes.

E. P. Stickney

645. Mink, Charles R. GENERAL ORDERS, NO. 11: THE FORCED EVACUATION OF CIVILIANS DURING THE CIVIL WAR. *Military Affairs 1970 34(4): 132-136.* In an attempt to control guerrillas and to prevent vengeance attacks from Kansas, Brigadier General Thomas Ewing, Jr. ordered most inhabitants banished from four counties in Missouri. The evacuation had limited effectiveness against the guerrillas and engendered such strong opposition that it contributed little to the outcome of the war. Based on printed documents, newspapers, and monographs; 25 notes.

K. J. Bauer

646. Mitchell, Leon, Jr. CAMP GROCE, CONFEDERATE MILITARY PRISON. *Southwestern Hist. Q. 1963 67(1): 15-21.* Describes and traces the history of Camp Groce, from June 1863 until its abandonment in December 1864. Camp Groce, near Hempstead, Texas, was the first Confederate military prison west of the Mississippi River.

J. A. Hudson

647. Neet, J. Frederick, Jr. STAND WATIE: CONFEDERATE GENERAL IN THE CHEROKEE NATION. *Great Plains J. 1966 6(1): 36-51.* A discussion of Cherokee support for the Confederacy during the Civil War. The main leader of the Indians throughout the war was Brigadier General Stand Watie, CSA. Watie campaigned with considerable success in Indian Territory, Arkansas, and Missouri against Federal forts, troops, and supply trains. When General Watie surrendered on 23 June 1865 he was probably the last Confederate General to do so. Photo, 28 notes. O. H. Zabel

648. Niepman, Ann Davis. GENERAL ORDER NO. 11 AND BORDER WARFARE DURING THE CIVIL WAR. *Missouri Hist. R. 1972 66(2): 185-210.* On 25 August 1863, Jackson, Cass, Bates, and parts of Vernon counties in Missouri were depopulated by General Order no. 11. General Thomas Ewing (1829-96) said there was a threat of retaliation by Kansans against Missouri for the sack of Lawrence on 21 August. Both Ewing and his immediate superior, General John Schofield, agreed that only by depopulation or by an increase of military personnel could widespread loss of life be averted along the border. Since no additional troops were available, the depopulation approach was the only possible one. The decision might have been sound, but Ewing was unwise in the methods used to enforce the order. Schofield had prohibited Kansas and Missouri troops not in US service from crossing the border without special orders, but Ewing used Kansas troops in Missouri without special orders and even gave their commanders a discretionary right to cross the border at will. 9 illus., 84 notes. W. F. Zornow

649. Oates, Stephen B. TEXAS UNDER THE SECESSIONISTS. *Southwestern Hist. Q. 1963/1964 67(2): 167-212.* Traces Texas' participation in the Civil War from adoption of the ordinance of secession on 16 February 1861 to surrender of the Confederacy's Trans-Mississippi Department on 22 May 1865. J. A. Hudson

650. Plummer, Mark A. MISSOURI AND KANSAS AND THE CAPTURE OF GENERAL MARMADUKE. *Missouri Hist. R. 1964 59(1): 90-104.* The interminable conflict that raged between Kansas and Missouri during the Civil War was dramatized by numerous incidents, but no incidents better reflect this continuing hostility than those associated with General Sterling Price's raid in Missouri during 1864. One of his division commanders, General John S. Marmaduke, was the central figure in one of these incidents. A newspaper report that Marmaduke was captured at Mine Creek by a boy belonging to a Kansas regiment, provoked a protest that the capture was effected by a group of Missourians. After a rebuttal from Kansas, the facts came out that the capture was made by a member of the Third Iowa. The highlights of Price's invasion are also summarized. Based on local newspapers and the *Official Records.* W. F. Zornow

651. Ragan, Cooper K., ed. THE DIARY OF CAPTAIN GEORGE W. O'BRIEN, 1863. *Southwestern Hist. Q. 1964 67(3): 413-433.* Continued from 1963 67(1): 26-54 and 1963 67(2): 235-246. Traces O'Brien's activities as a member of the 11th (Spaight's) Battalion, Texas Volunteers from 4 October 1863 to 29 December 1863, while the battalion was engaged in a campaign in Louisiana during the Civil War. R. L. Williamson

652. Rampp, Lary C. INCIDENT AT BAXTER SPRINGS ON OCTOBER 6, 1863. *Kansas Hist. Q. 1970 36(2): 183-197.* Baxter Springs was a Union base astride the military road from Fort Leavenworth, Kansas, to Texas. Loss of this base would jeopardize Union operations in the Southwest. As he retreated into Texas after sacking Lawrence, Kansas, William Clarke Quantrill almost succeeded in doing this when he came very close to annihilating the garrison. Quantrill's brief victory did not affect the course of the war, but it did impede Union operations in the Department of Kansas, and it led to the removal of the pursuing commander General James G. Blunt for having failed to prevent Quantrill's attack. The entire action brought no overall credit to either side, but it was distinguished by many instances of individual valor. Based on books, articles, unpublished theses, and official records; illus., 33 notes. W. F. Zornow

653. Rampp, Lary C. NEGRO TROOP ACTIVITY IN INDIAN TERRITORY, 1863-1865. *Chronicles of Oklahoma 1969 47(1): 531-559.* Negroes in Indian Territory, primarily the First Kansas Colored

Volunteers Infantry Regiment, acquitted themselves well during the Civil War. They benefited, too, by learning to accept authority and responsibility. Some learned to read and write while in the service. Desertion in black units was only seven percent as compared with 19 percent by their white counterparts. One result of this service was to change in part the attitude of the white men toward the black. The first engagement in Indian Territory in which Negroes participated was the battle of Cabin Creek on 2 July 1863. The Union force of 900 men under Colonel James M. Williams beat off a serious attack of nearly 2,200 Confederates. The blacks proved their worth as fighters in a tough situation. Two weeks later the Union troops battled with a superior force at Elks Creek and defeated the Confederates decisively, following up with a victory over the retreating rebels at Honey Springs. The courage of the blacks in battle aided the Union cause substantially. In a brief skirmish the next summer, the blacks again defeated the Confederates at Iron Bridge in the Choctaw Nation (15 June 1864). The last major engagement of the war, however, was fought in the fall of the year. On 16 September a major force of two thousand Confederates moved against a Union haying operation at Flat Rock. Only four of 200 black troops survived, but two days later at Cabin Creek the rebel forces were defeated. Based on the *War of the Rebellion* series of official documents, plus secondary sources; illus., map, 44 notes. K. P. Davis

654. Rezneck, Samuel. HORSFORD'S "MARCHING RATION" FOR THE CIVIL WAR ARMY. *Military Affairs 1969 33(1): 249-255.* In 1864 the scientist Eben N. Horsford proposed that the Army adopt a concentrated "marching" ration of his design. Although initially rebuffed by the Army's investigators, Horsford secured a recommendation for a trial of the ration from General U. S. Grant. This led to a contract for five hundred thousand rations in February 1865. Delivered after the end of fighting, they were tested by troops in Texas with universal disapproval. Based primarily on official records; 15 notes. K. J. Bauer

655. Richards, Edward Moore. "PRICE'S RAID," PERSONAL REMINISCENCES OF THE AMERICAN CIVIL WAR, KANSAS, OCTOBER 1864. *Irish Sword [Ireland] 1966 7(28): 234-240.* A personal account of Edward Moore Richards, member of the Kansas militia, when he was called to help repulse a raid on Kansas by General Sterling Price of the Confederate Army. Many details of activities of the Kansas troops during this encounter are provided. H. L. Calkin

656. Rittenhouse, Jack. AN 1862 CONFEDERATE HANDBILL. *Palacio 1967 74(1): 5-9.* Relates the finding of a Confederate handbill printed in Santa Fe, New Mexico, on 29 March 1862, which praised the Texan forces for their part in the Battle of Glorieta. Traces the Civil War campaign in New Mexico and outlines the skirmishing prior to the battle at Glorieta and the major fighting at the battle itself. The battle was significant, because the Confederates abandoned Santa Fe and withdrew to the South, ending the war in the West. Includes a facsimile of the handbill. Based mainly on secondary sources; biblio. S. A. Eger

657. Robertson, James I., Jr. THE CONCISE ILLUSTRATED HISTORY OF THE CIVIL WAR. *Am. Hist. Illus. 1971 6(2): 3-64.* A narrative of the Civil War. Discusses overview, causes, secession, advantages and disadvantages of the United States and the Confederacy, military campaigns (1861, 1862 in East, 1862 in West, 1863 in East, 1863 in West, 1864 in East, 1864 in West, 1865 in East, 1865 in West), navies, and the heritage of the war. 147 illus., biblio. D. B. Dodd

658. Sacconaghi, Charles D., ed. A BIBLIOGRAPHICAL NOTE ON THE CIVIL WAR IN THE WEST. *Arizona and the West 1966 8(4): 349-364.* An annotated bibliography of 121 items, with particular emphasis on articles and books, concerning the military phases of the Civil War in the trans-Mississippi West. Most of the items were written during the centennial years and have not appeared in other guides in annotated form. As there is no volume which gives comprehensive coverage of the fighting in the West, the editor suggests that the best approach is through bibliographies. Eight specific reference tools are suggested. D. L. Smith

659. Sawyer, William E. THE MARTIN HART CONSPIRACY. *Arkansas Hist. Q. 1964 23(2): 154-165.* Hart obtained a commission as captain in the Confederate Army in Greenville, Texas in June 1861. The

next that is known of him is the application at Springfield, Missouri, of Hart and his little group of followers for commissions in the Union Army and for permission to operate against the Confederate forces in northern Arkansas. Hart had recruited a rabble whose sole motive was to destroy the well-to-do whites around Charleston, Arkansas. He and Hays, a leader of a guerrilla band associated with Hart, were convicted of murder and hanged at Fort Smith in January 1863. Illus., 44 notes.

E. P. Stickney

660. Shirk, George H. A CONFEDERATE POSTAL SYSTEM IN THE INDIAN TERRITORY. *Chronicles of Oklahoma 1963 41(2): 160-218.* Numerous letters and documents are cited to show the extent of the Confederate postal system in Indian Territory during the Civil War. The Confederacy sought to continue the postal system of the United States. Many mail contractors and postmasters continued to serve. Prior to the formal advertisement for bids by John Reagan, the Confederate Postmaster General, temporary service was continued. Difficulty was experienced in obtaining mail carriers. Many men made bids for mail contracts with the hope of being exempted from military service. General Kirby Smith generally did not approve their exemptions. Much mail was carried by the Army courier service. Local postmasters in the Indian nation made heroic efforts to transmit the mail. Stamps of the Confederate States of America were actually printed in the Indian Territory. 7 illus., plates, maps, 27 notes.

I. W. Van Noppen

661. Shirk, George H. THE PLACE OF INDIAN TERRITORY IN THE COMMAND STRUCTURE OF THE CIVIL WAR. *Chronicles of Oklahoma 1968 45(4): 464-471.* The area of Indian Territory, present Oklahoma, was included in the regional organizational structure of both the Union and Confederate Armies during the Civil War. The changes in jurisdictional theaters, their commanding personnel, and the general orders directing the changes are indicated for both armies for the years of 1861-65.

D. L. Smith

662. Speierl, Charles F. PATCHOGUE'S KANSAS BRIGADE. *Long Island Forum 1971 34(11): 242-245, (12): 260-262.* Part I. Relates the formation of Patchogue's Kansas Brigade (of Company C in the Twelfth New York Regiment) in the spring of 1861. Patchogue's was the only brigade raised on the village level in Suffolk County. Illus. Part II. The brigade participated with distinction in the Battle of Gaines' Mill (27 June 1862). After the war, the majority of the men returned to Patchogue. Map.

G. Kurland

663. Stinson, Dwight E. THE BLOODIEST ATROCITY OF THE CIVIL WAR. *Civil War Times Illus. 1963 2(8): 42-46.* An account of the butchery at Lawrence, Kansas by the Confederate "Colonel" William C. Quantrill whose guerilla band was outlawed by the US Government. Illus.

S

664. Stotts, Gene. THE NEGRO PAUL REVERE OF QUANTRILL'S RAID. *Negro Hist. Bull. 1963 26(5): 169-170.* Relates the story of an 18-year-old Negro servant's five-mile walk from a farmhouse to Eudora, Kansas, 20 August 1863, to warn the settlers there that a large Confederate raiding party was headed for Lawrence. Henry, the servant, accomplished his mission but two riders sent to warn Lawrence failed to reach their destination and the town was burned.

L. Gara

665. Taylor, Morris F. CONFEDERATE GUERRILLAS IN SOUTHERN COLORADO. *Colorado Mag. 1969 46(4): 304-323.* The Civil War had repercussions in Colorado and New Mexico. The author discusses the "pro-Southern operations that may be regarded as irregular warfare of a more or less predatory nature." In 1861 some 40 alleged guerrillas were captured near Fort Wise. In 1862 a force of guerrillas under George Mattison operated in southern Colorado with some apparent official Confederate approval. The aim of this group was to destroy Government wagon trains and public (not private) property. In 1863 a group of alleged guerrillas operated in the vicinity of Fort Lyons. In 1864 a group under James Reynolds raided along the Santa Fe Trail and elsewhere in southern Colorado, but acted more as outlaws than as bonafide guerrillas. Reynolds and some of his group were taken prisoner and were shot by soldiers, perhaps on the order of Colonel John M. Chivington. Illus., 99 notes.

O. H. Zabel

666. Thane, James L., Jr. THE MYTH OF CONFEDERATE SENTIMENT IN MONTANA. *Montana 1967 17(2): 14-19.* Contends that there is little truth in the conventional account of strong Confederate feeling among the Democratic majority in early territorial Montana. Previous historians have relied too exclusively on one newspaper, the *Montana Post,* which reflected the Radical Republican viewpoint of its owners during the 1864 election campaign. Citations are largely from this newspaper. Illus., 18 notes.

S. R. Davison

667. Tyler, Ronnie C. AN AUSPICIOUS AGREEMENT BETWEEN A CONFEDERATE SECRET AGENT AND A GOVERNOR OF NORTHERN MEXICO. *Am. West 1972 9(1): 38-43, 63.* On 26 June 1861, Confederate secret agent José A. Quintero talked with Governor Santiago Vidaurri of the northern Mexican states. Quintero proposed a reciprocal agreement covering trade, fugitives, and raiding across the Rio Grande. The Confederacy could ill afford to station troops along the international border to accomplish these ends by force. Vidaurri proposed that Coahuila join the Confederacy. Membership in an "enlightened" states' rights republic, new markets for Mexican raw materials, and security by alliance with a powerful neighbor were attractions. Confederate foreign policy with Mexico had been badly bungled by its envoy in Mexico City, so a shift was made and Quintero was made permanent representative and emphasis was shifted to further negotiations with Vidaurri. Although the Confederacy rejected the annexation offer, international cooperation along the Rio Grande border during the Civil War enabled Texas and surrounding States to continue fighting after most southerners were exhausted and their supplies depleted from increasing effectiveness of the Union blockade. Excerpted from a forthcoming book. 7 illus., note.

D. L. Smith

668. Tyler, Ronnie C. COTTON ON THE BORDER, 1861-1865. *Southwestern Hist. Q. 1970 73(4): 456-477.* During the Civil War, when the Confederacy chose to prohibit the shipment of cotton to England in the hope of provoking its intervention, southern cotton merchants received permission to ship cotton to Mexico in exchange for consumer goods and war material. By wagon and ox cart cotton was hauled over hundreds of miles through barren, desolate, desert country to its destination in Matamoros, from whence it was transferred to ocean-going vessels. Mexican officials, speculators, profiteers, and Union threats on land and sea all posed continual hazards to the sellers, but the commerce thrived. Even the French occupation of Mexico did not seriously interrupt the commerce in cotton. When the war ended, the economic foundations for future fortunes were laid on both sides of the border.

R. W. Delaney

669. Utley, Robert M. KIT CARSON AND THE ADOBE WALLS CAMPAIGN. *Am. West 1965 2(1): 4-11, 73-75.* The Santa Fe Trail was the only supply and communication line to the Federal troops stationed in Santa Fe during the Civil War. They were guarding against the possibility of another Confederate threat to New Mexico similar to the one in 1862. The long, richly-laden supply trains along the trail were a temptation to the southern Plains Indians. Kiowa and Comanche raiding accelerated throughout the summer of 1864. With approaching winter, when the Indians preferred peace so that they could spend the time gathering food, the American offensive was prepared. Colonel Christopher Carson led New Mexico and California volunteer troops and friendly Ute Indian auxiliaries on a campaign highlighted 25 November 1864 by the Battle of Adobe Walls on the South Canadian River in the Texas Panhandle. Carson's victory lessened the hostile forays along the Santa Fe Trail the following summer, but also proved to be the opening of a decade of intermittent warfare that ended with the Red River War of 1874-75. Illus., map, biblio., note.

D. L. Smith

670. Walker, Henry P., ed. SOLDIER IN THE CALIFORNIA COLUMN: THE DIARY OF JOHN W. TEAL. *Arizona and the West 1971 13(1): 33-82.* Private John W. Teal (ca. 1820-80), a native of Canada, served in the California cavalry during the Civil War. Working as a miner at the outbreak of the war, he enlisted on 24 September 1861. Presents Teal's diary, a "worm's eye view" of the march of the California Column from California, its service in New Mexico, its return to California, service on the San Bernardino-Fort Mohave road, and Teal's return to Canada after his discharge. Includes nearly 30 short biographical notes on members of his company that Teal appended to the diary. 2 maps, 156 notes.

D. L. Smith

671.　Warren, Hanna R.　RECONSTRUCTION IN THE CHERO-KEE NATION. *Chronicles of Oklahoma 1967 45(2): 180-189.* The Ridge faction of the Cherokee Nation in Oklahoma joined the Confederacy in the Civil War. After 1863, the Ross faction repudiated their Southern commitments, freed their slaves, and supported the Union. When the Ross faction confiscated the Ridge faction's property during the war, the long-standing bitterness between the two groups increased. This hampered Federal treatymaking efforts and caused considerable hardship to the Indians in the winter of 1865-66. The Northern group signed the Reconstruction Treaty of 1866 and the Southern element accepted the terms without signing. It was a year later before harmony was restored and 1870 before all the legal technicalities were resolved. The status of their former Negro slaves remained a touchy question. 40 notes.
　　　　　　　　　　　　　　　　　　　　D. L. Smith

672.　Weinert, Richard P.　CONFEDERATE BORDER TROUBLES WITH MEXICO. *Civil War Times Illus. 1964 3(6): 36-43.* Describes the dealings of Confederate Brigadier (later Major) General Hamilton Prioleau Bee (1822-97) with the Mexicans at Fort Brown, Texas. The long Rio Grande border with Mexico was the only Confederate frontier not controlled by the Union. Across this border came guns and supplies in exchange for Southern cotton.
　　　　　　　　　　　　　　　　　　　　R. N. Alvis

673.　West, Larry L.　DOUGLAS H. COOPER, CONFEDERATE GENERAL. *Lincoln Herald 1969 71(2): 69-76.* Outlines developments in Indian Territory during the Civil War. Emphasis is placed on Cooper's role and his emergence in 1865 as military commander of Indian Territory, which had been designated as a separate department.
　　　　　　　　　　　　　　　　　　　　S. L. Jones

674.　Westphall, David.　THE BATTLE OF GLORIETA PASS: ITS IMPORTANCE IN THE CIVIL WAR. *New Mexico Hist. R. 1969 44(2): 137-154.* Maintains that a Confederate victory in the battle at Glorieta Pass (1862) "would have meant not only the addition of New Mexico to the Confederacy, but would also have opened the way for the Confederate conquest of the American West, including Colorado, Utah, Nevada, and California." A brief description of the Confederate campaign, including the battle at Valverde (1862) and the destruction of the Confederate supply train at Johnson's ranch is included. 35 notes.
　　　　　　　　　　　　　　　　　　　　D. F. Henderson

675.　Willey, William J.　THE SECOND FEDERAL INVASION OF INDIAN TERRITORY. *Chronicles of Oklahoma 1967 44(4): 420-430.* Following the first invasion of Indian Territory, Union commanders organized a second invasion under Brigadier General James E. Blunt. Union forces conquered northwest Arkansas. On 17 October 1862 General Blunt defeated Brigadier General Douglas H. Cooper at Old Fort Wayne, a disaster for the Confederacy. Union forces seized Fort Gibson on 18 April 1863 in the Creek Nation. Using this as a base, U.S. commanders seized control of the whole Indian Territory. The largest battle of the war in the Indian Territory took place at Elk Creek, near Honey Springs, on 17 July. General Cooper and his force of six thousand men were defeated. These Federal successes were due chiefly to superior arms. The deciding factor was ammunition. Many Confederate units were useless because of wet gunpowder. On 22 August General Blunt advanced, defeated the Confederates at Perryville, and captured Fort Smith. The Battle of Honey Springs was decisive in the contest for the Indian Territory. The Confederates were badly armed, the Indian troops were undisciplined, and there was intense rivalry between Generals Cooper and William Steele. 30 notes.
　　　　　　　　　　　　　　　　　　　　I. W. Van Noppen

676.　Williams, Burton J.　QUANTRILL'S RAID ON LAWRENCE: A QUESTION OF COMPLICITY. *Kansas Hist. Q. 1968 34(2): 143-149.* An examination of the circumstantial evidence that links a Lawrence, Kansas, banker William H. R. Lykins with the charge that certain persons supplied Confederate guerrilla William C. Quantrill with valuable information about Lawrence before he sacked and destroyed the town on 21 August 1863. Lykins was a Southerner who moved to Kansas from Missouri. He knew some of Quantrill's men. His house escaped damage while virtually all of the others in his neighborhood were destroyed. Lykins' life was spared, although the heaviest casualties occurred in his neighborhood. These facts are not offered as proof that Lykins collaborated with the raiders; they are offered only to indicate that an impressive case can be made to show that he or other residents might have

given Quantrill information. Based on papers in the Kansas State Historical Society and the Kansas Methodist Historical Library, Baker University; illus., 18 notes.
　　　　　　　　　　　　　　　　　　　　W. F. Zornow

677.　Williams, James C.　THE LONG TOM REBELLION. *Oregon Hist. Q. 1966 67(1): 54-60.* Even though most of Oregon's residents were loyal to the Union cause during the War Between the States, 1861-65, small clusters of secessionists were scattered throughout the state. Shortly after the end of the war in 1865, a small group of Confederate sympathizers in Eugene caused the "Long Tom Rebellion" which led to the arrest and incarceration of Henry Mulkey, a ringleader.
　　　　　　　　　　　　　　　　　　　　C. C. Gorchels

678.　Wright, Muriel and Fischer, LeRoy H.　CIVIL WAR SITES IN OKLAHOMA. *Chronicles of Oklahoma 1966 44(2): 158-215.* For the Civil War Centennial the Oklahoma Historic Sites Committee in 1958 listed 557 historic sites. In this survey 86 historic sites relating to the Civil War are listed. Of these, 29 are combat sites and 57 are war-related. The significance of each location is cited. It is thought that this study will be used more for reference than as a narrative. The arrangement of sites is alphabetical by counties. 19 illus., biblio.
　　　　　　　　　　　　　　　　　　　　I. W. Van Noppen

679.　—.　KANSAS AND THE CENTENNIAL OF THE CIVIL WAR. *Kansas Hist. Q. 1965 31(1): 62-66.* In 1963, the Civil War Centennial Commission in Kansas assisted in an observance of the Lawrence raid of 1863. James I. Robertson of the U.S. Civil War Centennial Commission was the principal speaker. The Baxter Springs massacre of 6 October 1863 was also commemorated. Dr. Robertson also particpated in the 1964 commemoration of the Battle of Mine Creek, the climactic battle of the war in Kansas on 25 October 1864. The text of his speech is reproduced.
　　　　　　　　　　　　　　　　　　　　W. F. Zornow

The Indian Wars

680.　Adams, Donald K., ed.　THE JOURNAL OF ADA A. VOGDES, 1868-1871. *Montana 1963 13(3): 2-17.* A young army wife relates the experiences and sensations encountered during residence at Fort Laramie and Fort Fetterman, deep in the country of hostile Indians. The observations of this sensitive white woman on such matters as Indian dress and behavior, and primitive social life at these remote posts, are stressed in these selections from the original diary which is held in the Henry H. Huntington Library.
　　　　　　　　　　　　　　　　　　　　L. G. Nelson

681.　Alcorn, Rowena L. and Alcorn, Gordon D.　AGED NEZ PERCE RECALLS THE 1877 TRAGEDY. *Montana 1965 15(4): 54-67.* Josiah Redwolf, now 93, recalls incidents of the Nez Percé War, which he witnessed as a boy of five. His comments confirm that the Indian retreat was led by others than Chief Joseph, who is traditionally credited.
　　　　　　　　　　　　　　　　　　　　S. R. Davison

682.　Alcorn, Rowena L. and Alcorn, Gordon D.　OLD NEZ PERCE RECALLS TRAGIC RETREAT OF 1877. *Montana 1963 13(1): 66-74.* Suhm-Keen, an Indian lad of ten, witnessed most of the action in the Nez Perce War, including the battles at Clearwater, the Big Hole, and Canyon Creek, before the surrender at Bear Paw. He escaped into Canada with his parents, where Sitting Bull and other Sioux refugees befriended them. Now 95 years old, and known as Sam Tilden, this Nez Perce recounted these episodes for the authors in 1962, surely one of the last interviews with survivors of this war.
　　　　　　　　　　　　　　　　　　　　L. G. Nelson

683.　Alexander, Thomas G. and Arrington, Leonard J.　THE UTAH MILITARY FRONTIER, 1872-1912: FORTS CAMERON, THORNBURGH AND DUCHESNE. *Utah Hist. Q. 1964 32(4): 330-354.* Describes how problems arising between Indians and Utah frontiersmen caused the U.S. War Department to establish Fort Cameron 200 miles south of Salt Lake City and Forts Thornburgh and Duchesne. The author deals primarily with the relationships which developed among the settlers, the Indians, and the U.S. military forces and emphasizes the contributions made by these military installations to the economic growth of the settlements adjacent to them. Based mainly on materials derived from the reports of the U.S. War Department, reports of Congress, and Utah newspapers.
　　　　　　　　　　　　　　　　　　　　S. L. Jones

684. Anderson, Harry A. INDIAN PEACE TALKERS AND THE CONCLUSION OF THE SIOUX WAR OF 1876. *Nebraska Hist. 1963 44(4): 233-254.* Examines the role of influential leaders among the agency Sioux, notably Spotted Tail, who traveled in the winter of 1876-77 to the hostile Indian camps and after extensive talks with the fighting chiefs, persuaded them to come in and surrender to the military authorities.
R. Lowitt

685. Anderson, Harry H., ed. STAND AT THE ARIKAREE. *Colorado Mag. 1964 41(4): 337-342.* A letter from Major S. Brisbane of the Second U.S. Cavalry describing the battle of Beecher Island, 17-25 September 1868, one of the most spectacular of a long series of conflicts with Plains Indians. Major George A. Forsyth with a company of 50 enlisted scouts was attacked by a much larger number of Cheyennes and Sioux. Five of Forsyth's company were killed, and 16 wounded. Indian losses were greater.
I. W. Van Noppen

686. Ball, Eve. THE APACHE SCOUTS: A CHIRICAHUA APPRAISAL. *Arizona and the West 1965 7(4): 315-328.* An intra-Apache power struggle led to an 1883 Mexican-based raid into New Mexico resulting in the massacre of a white couple and the taking of their child into captivity. This status assertion incident provoked General George Crook to swiftly organize an expedition against the offenders. He enlisted a band of Apache scouts to guide his troops. Subsequently other Apache enlisted and the scouts were used in various capacities for Crook, even against the Apache themselves. The author interviewed some of the scouts and their descendants and found, contrary to the generally accepted notion, that the Chiricahua hold nothing but contempt for those who served as scouts. Based extensively on personal interviews; 5 illus., 62 notes.
D. L. Smith

687. Barrett, Francis A. THE GREATEST RIDE IN WYOMING HISTORY. *Ann. of Wyoming 1966 38(2): 223-228.* Describes briefly the Fetterman massacre and the weakness of the remaining garrison at Fort Philip Kearny in December 1866. In this situation, John "Portugee" Philips, a civilian employee, agreed to ride to Fort Laramie 236 miles away asking for aid. This he did in four days, traveling through snow and below zero cold, hiding from hostile Indians, and eating only a few biscuits. Based on published secondary material, illus., 30 notes.
R. L. Nichols

688. Barsness, John and Dickinson, William. THE SULLY EXPEDITION OF 1864. *Montana 1966 16(3): 23-29.* General Alfred Sully's campaign against the Sioux in Dakota and Montana demonstrated the effectiveness of a large force and adequate arms, including cannon, in making war against the plains tribes. His column not only routed a concentration of warriors but safely escorted a wagon train en route from Minnesota to Montana's newly opened gold mines. Undocumented, illus., map.
S. R. Davison

689. Bate, Walter N. EYEWITNESS REPORTS OF THE WAGON BOX FIGHT. *Ann. of Wyoming 1969 41(2): 192-202.* Disputes the small number of Indian casualties in the Wagon Box Fight at Fort Phil Kearny on 2 August 1867. Using the published reports and memoirs of both white and Indian participants, the author tries to determine actual Indian losses. Estimates vary from five to 1,500, but none of the participants give a figure below 180. By comparing the various white and Indian reports of the battle, and using a ratio of two wounded to one dead, the author concludes that Chief Red Cloud's report of between 1,100 and 1,300 Indian casualties is accurate. Based on archival material, published reminiscences, and secondary sources; illus., photos, 13 notes.
R. L. Nichols

690. Bean, Geraldine. GENERAL ALFRED SULLY AND THE NORTHWEST INDIAN EXPEDITION. *North Dakota Hist. 1966 33(3): 240-259.* Reviews the almost unnoticed Battle of White Stone Hill near present Ellendale, North Dakota, on 3 September 1863 when General Sully and troops of the Northwest Indian Expedition decisively defeated some 1,500 Sioux warriors. Fears of the settlers were somewhat calmed and some who had abandoned their farms returned. Land companies had enticed settlers since 1861 when Dakota Territory was created. Gold discoveries in Montana had boosted activities in the Upper Missouri country. Major General John Pope, who had been placed in charge of military operations on the northwest frontier after his defeat at Bull Run

in 1862, had devised a pincers movement, one column commanded by Colonel Henry H. Sibley and the other by Sully. While Pope fumed at Sully's slow progress, he was pleased with the outcome of the battle. Other officials disagreed as to its effectiveness, as the Dakota Territory was not freed of the Indian menace. Illus., 51 notes, biblio.
I. W. Van Noppen

691. Bell, Gordon L. and Bell, Beth L. GENERAL CUSTER IN NORTH DAKOTA. *North Dakota Hist. 1964 31(2): 101-113.* Discusses the campaign of the Seventh Cavalry led by General George Armstrong Custer against Chief Sitting Bull and his tribes. The expedition left Fort Abraham Lincoln on 17 May 1876 with 1,200 men and 150 wagons. A day-by-day account is given of the progress of the march until 3 June 1876, just 22 days before the Battle of the Little Big Horn. Attention is given to the events leading up to this confrontation, particularly the settler expansion into the sacred Indian grounds of the Black Hills. The author discusses some of the more important diaries and personal accounts of Custer's years in North Dakota. Based on primary and secondary sources; photo, map.
M. J. McBaine

692. Bell, William Gardner. A DEDICATION TO THE MEMORY OF JOHN GREGORY BOURKE, 1846-1896. *Arizona and the West 1971 13(4): 318-322.* Of Irish heritage and equipped with a classical education, 16-year-old John Gregory Bourke falsified his age to volunteer for service in the Civil War. He decided on a military career and received an appointment to the US Military Academy. After graduation in 1869, Bourke received frontier duty. Geographically and militarily his western service spanned the Indian Wars of the 1870's and 1880's, much of it as a trusted aide-de-camp of General George Crook. Bourke systematically compiled field notes upon which Crook relied heavily in his command and in preparation of offical reports. Bourke's extensive diaries became the raw data base for his subsequent writing career - historic and scientific books, monographs, and articles. This literary outpouring began as early as 1874 and continued through and beyond his 1886-91 Washington years of detached service and subsequent active duty in the West again. Not only was Bourke widely acclaimed for his chronicles of the campaigns in which he participated, but he produced much ethnological data and scientific observation of the Plains Indians. His classic *On the Border with Crook* assured posterity for his commander. Illus., biblio.
D. L. Smith

693. Bigler, David L. THE CRISIS AT FORT LIMHI, 1858. *Utah Hist. Q. 1967 35(2): 121-136.* Describes how units of the Nauvoo Legion, the volunteer militia of Utah Territory, under the command of Lieutenant Colonel Benjamin Franklin Cummings moved northward from the Utah Valley to rescue a Mormon missionary and colonizing group in Oregon Territory from Indian attack. This article is a chapter from a study "Massacre at Fort Limhi, Early Mormons in Oregon Territory, 1855-58."
S. L. Jones

694. Brimlow, George F., ed. TWO CAVALRYMEN'S DIARIES OF THE BANNOCK WAR, 1878. *Oregon Hist. Q. 1967 68(3): 221-258.* Biographical sketches and diaries of a second lieutenant and a private who participated in a military campaign against Indians in Oregon and Nevada in 1878. Details include descriptions of the countryside, experiences on marches, and reports of minor conflicts.
C. C. Gorchels

695. Brinckerhoff, Sidney B. "STEADFAST" GREGG IN ARIZONA. *Arizoniana 1964 5(2): 31-37.* Following service with General Winfield Scott during the Mexican War and with a cavalry brigade in the Army of the Potomac, Colonel J. Irvin Gregg came to Arizona Territory as commander of the Eighth Cavalry. Here he became measurably involved in Indian affairs and campaigns in the Fort Whipple area and, subsequently, at Churchill Barracks, Nevada.
W. Unrau

696. Brown, D. Alexander. THE BATTLE OF THE ARICKAREE. *Am. Hist. Illus. 1967 2(8): 4-11, 55-57.* Describes the battle of the Arickaree (Beecher's Island) in September 1868 between Major [later Colonel] George Alexander Forsyth's Army forces and Indians led by Roman Nose, a Cheyenne. The Indians wished to stop the encroachment of whites and the Kansas Pacific Railroad. Forsyth and his band of 50 scouts pursued roughly 600 Cheyenne north from Fort Wallace (Kansas) to the Arkansas River in the eastern Colorado Territory. The Indians then

pinned them down for nine days. Relief troops from Fort Wallace saved the survivors. Frederick Beecher, nephew of Henry Ward Beecher and a veteran of the battle of Gettysburg, died during this battle, which was later named in his memory. Roman Nose also was killed during this battle.
G. H. Skau

697. Brown, D. Alexander. THE GHOST DANCE AND BATTLE OF WOUNDED KNEE. *Am. Hist. Illus. 1966 1(8): 4-16.* Summarizes the Ghost Dance movement among the American Plains Indians that climaxed with the battle known as Wounded Knee, between Chief Big Foot's band of Sioux and the 7th U.S. Cavalry. The immediate events leading to the battle on 29 December 1890 are given in detail. Illus.
J. D. Filipiak

698. Brown, Mark. THE JOSEPH MYTH. *Montana 1972 22(1): 2-17.* Challenges the common belief that Chief Joseph was solely instrumental in the Nez Perce resistance in 1877 and that he was the military leader in charge of their flight across Montana. Evidence reveals that hostilities were begun by a band other than Joseph's, that he participated only reluctantly in the Idaho maneuvers, that he tried to surrender at the outset of the march, and that he had little part in subsequent actions and decisions. Further, a well-known speech of surrender attributed to Joseph is at best a garbled or greatly edited version of a message sent by him through an interpreter some hours before he himself came in. There was no oratory by Joseph. 25 notes.
S. R. Davison

699. Brown, Mark H. YELLOWSTONE TOURISTS AND THE NEZ PERCE. *Montana 1966 16(3): 30-43.* Summarizes the encounters between fleeing Nez Percé Indians and several groups of tourists and prospectors in Yellowstone National Park in 1877. Varied treatment of the whites reflected Nez Percé uncertainty after the Big Hole battle, where settlers joined troops in attacking the unwary fugitives. Undocumented, illus.
S. R. Davison

700. Brown, Mark K. CHESSMEN OF WAR. *Idaho Yesterdays 1966 10(4): 22-29.* "An analysis of the strategy of troop movements in the Nez Perce War of 1877." The author compares the game of chess with the war, where the positions of U.S. troops dictated the final outcome of the conflict. General Oliver Otis Howard (1830-1909) requested reinforcements from all three geographic divisions of the Continental Army to contain the movements of the Nez Perce under the leadership of Chief Joseph (1840-1904). Included are the engagements from the Battle of White Bird Canyon to the final confrontation by Colonel Nelson Appleton Miles in northeast Montana. 6 illus.
D. H. Swift

701. Byars, Charles, ed. GATEWOOD REPORTS TO HIS WIFE FROM GERONIM0'S CAMP. *J. of Arizona Hist. 1966 7(2): 76-81.* A letter from First Lieutenant Charles B. Gatewood in Arizona to his wife, written 26 August 1886, describing Geronimo's agreement to surrender to the military forces. Gatewood had been selected by General Nelson Miles to follow Geronimo into Mexico to try to obtain his surrender. The editor supplies a biographical sketch of Gatewood and 8 notes.
J. D. Filipiak

702. Carley, Maurine. BOZEMAN TRAIL TREK: TREK NO. 14 OF THE EMIGRANT TRAIL TREKS. *Ann. of Wyoming 1964 36(1): 43-77.* Discusses the two-day trek over the Bozeman Trail in July 1963, sponsored by the Wyoming State Archives and Historical Department, the Wyoming State Historical Society and several county societies. The object was to retrace the old trail by car and make observations along the route. Includes 19 brief descriptions of such historic sites as Fort Phil Kearny, the Tongue River Battle, the Fetterman Fight, and Lake De Smet, which figured in the history of the trail.
R. L. Nichols

703. Casanova, Frank E., ed. GENERAL CROOK VISITS THE SUPAIS: AS REPORTED BY JOHN G. BOURKE. *Arizona and the West 1968 10(3): 253-276.* In November 1884 General George Crook, commanding officer at Whipple Barracks, Arizona, led a party to visit the Havasupai Indians who lived in Cataract Canyon, a tributary of the Grand Canyon. Captain John Gregory Bourke, then Acting Inspector General of the Department of Arizona, detailed the journey in his diaries. His meticulous and perceptive observations, herein edited, describe the terrain, the perilous trails, inscriptions on the walls, vegetation, and matters of ethnology such as food, dress, shelter, weapons, crops, and trade. 4 illus., map, 74 notes.
D. L. Smith

704. Chaput, Donald. GENERALS, INDIAN AGENTS, POLITICIANS: THE DOOLITTLE SURVEY OF 1865. *Western Hist. Q. 1972 3(3): 269-282.* In March 1865 Senator James Rood Doolittle (1815-97) of Wisconsin was appointed chairman of a joint congressional committee to investigate the condition of the Indian tribes and their treatment from American civil and military authorities. The Sand Creek massacre of November 1864 was merely the latest of the evidences that Indian affairs "were in a mess." The committee of Congressmen sent out questionnaires and personally visited scores of Indians, soldiers, agents, and politicians. Analyzes the responses to the questionnaire and the extent of their correspondence to the recommendations which the Doolittle committee report made. Legislation which Doolittle suggested failed to pass, but the findings of the survey secured the Indian Bureau in the Department of the Interior. The report is a prime source of midcentury Indian conditions, through the eyes of Army officers, Indian agents, and superintendents. 62 notes.
D. L. Smith

705. Clough, Wilson O. MINI-AKU, DAUGHTER OF SPOTTED TAIL. *Ann. of Wyoming 1967 39(2): 187-216.* Examines the sources from which the story of the death and burial of Spotted Tail's daughter Mini-Aku at Fort Laramie, Wyoming, in 1866 has developed. The author discusses the original accounts of the incident, traces the additions, and shows the sources for later secondary descriptions. He concludes that Mini-Aku was one of Spotted Tail's elder daughters, that she was about 18 when she died and was buried at Fort Laramie, and that she probably helped persuade her father to remain at peace. Based on Indian Office records, military reminiscences, and secondary material; illus., 30 notes, biblio.
R. L. Nichols

706. Cullens, J. CUSTER'S LAST STAND. *Army Q. and Defence J. [Great Britain] 1965 90(1): 104-109.* Describes the Battle of Little Big Horn and the subsequent skirmishes with the Indians. No other single event in American history has captured public imagination more completely. It is rather like the charge of the Light Brigade at Balaclava in that both were exercises in military futility which led to disaster and a place in history. Maps.
K. James

707. Davis, Jane S. TWO SIOUX WAR ORDERS; A MYSTERY UNRAVELED. *Minnesota Hist. 1968 41(3): 117-125.* Following the Sioux uprising of 1862 over three hundred of the defeated Indians were tried by a military tribunal under General Henry H. Sibley and sentenced to death. The approval of President Lincoln was necessary for their execution. For over a century the Minnesota Historical Society prized a Lincoln manuscript letter ordering the execution of only 39. Recent research by the author in the National Archives indicates that this was only a preliminary draft and was never actually mailed. A facsimile of the letter that was actually sent, showing slight variations, is included.
P. L. Simon

708. Delaney, Donald J. THE CATLIN PORTRAIT OF GENERAL LEAVENWORTH. *Kansas Hist. Q. 1971 37(4): 345-350.* Describes a miniature recently presented to the Fort Leavenworth museum by Dorothy Kershaw Keena of Tacoma, Washington, a great-great-great-granddaughter of General Henry Leavenworth. This picture in watercolor on ivory was painted by George Catlin in 1834 at Fort Gibson in Indian territory, near present-day Tulsa, a few weeks before General Leavenworth died on an expedition against the Comanche and Pawnee. The miniature was only identified as Catlin's work when an observant officer at Fort Leavenworth spotted the artist's signature minutely penciled on the picture. Describes two peace medals dated 1801 and 1866 that came to the museum from the general's family. Illus., 3 notes, biblio.
W. F. Zornow

709. Dippie, Brian W. THE SOUTHERN RESPONSE TO CUSTER'S LAST STAND. *Montana 1971 21(2): 18-31.* Southern newspapers presented the George Armstrong Custer incident (1876) as the result of Republican blunders, chiefly of keeping too many troops in the South while Indians slaughtered the outnumbered forces on the western frontier. Much was made of President Ulysses Simpson Grant's responsibility, and of the assignment of his son, Lieutenant (later Major General) Frederick Dent Grant, to safe military positions in the East. The journalists seemed willing to forgive Custer for his service in the Union Army during the Civil War, and to adopt him as a regional hero and martyr. Based on contemporary newspapers; illus., 61 notes.
S. R. Davison

710. Dozier, Jack. 1885: A NEZ PERCE HOMECOMING. *Idaho Yesterdays 1963 7(3): 22-25.* Describes the return in 1885 of the remnants of Chief Joseph's band of Nez Perce Indians to the region from which they had been driven during the Nez Perce War of 1877, with particular attention to the organized efforts of local citizens (Lewiston, Idaho) to prevent their return.   M. Small

711. Drake, John M. THE OREGON CAVALRY. *Oregon Hist. Q. 1964 65(4): 392-400.* Continued from a previous article. Recollections of the author, dated 17 January 1906, on the establishment and role of voluntary cavalry in Oregon (while army regulars were transferred to fight in the Civil War), 1861-63. This account completes Drake's recollections published in the *Oregon Historical Quarterly,* 1964 65(1).
    C. C. Gorchels

712. Ege, Robert J. ISAIAH DORMAN: NEGRO CASUALTY WITH RENO. *Montana 1966 16(1): 35-40.* The Indians who overran Major Reno's original position in the Little Big Horn Battle were surprised to find the body of a Negro civilian. Sitting Bull identified him as Azimpa, a runaway slave who had married a Sioux woman and lived at times among her people. Later he worked around frontier army posts, where he was known as Isaiah Dorman. Apparently he had accompanied General Terry's command as a guide and interpreter, in the hope of meeting old friends among the Sioux.   S. R. Davison

713. Ege, Robert J. LEGEND WAS A MAN NAMED KEOGH. *Montana 1966 16(2): 27-39.* Fictionized biographical sketch of Myles Walter Keogh, stressing his dramatic death with Custer in 1876.
    S. R. Davison

714. Ellis, Richard N. AFTER BULL RUN: THE LATER CAREER OF GENERAL JOHN POPE. *Montana 1969 19(4): 46-57.* Following an undistinguished campaign in Virginia in 1862, General John Pope was transferred to a post in Minnesota with orders to chastise the Indians responsible for recent massacres in that area. Success during the next two years restored Pope's military reputation, and most of his remaining career consisted of important assignments on the frontier. His observation of Indian problems led him to advocate new policies toward hostile tribes. His enlightened program failed largely because of incompetent subordinates and because of political pressures to retain the old methods of treaties and annuities. Illus., 28 notes.
    S. R. Davison

715. Ellis, Richard N. COPPER-SKINNED SOLDIERS: THE APACHE SCOUTS. *Great Plains J. 1966 5(2): 51-67.* A detailed description of the use of Apache scouts by the U.S. Army between 1871 and 1886. General George Cook inaugurated the practice. He and his successors, even the skeptical General Nelson Miles, found them essential in dealing effectively with hostile Apaches. In spite of their exceptional loyalty, the loyal Indians were removed to Florida with the hostiles and not until 1913 were the survivors allowed to return to New Mexico. Biblio.   O. H. Zabel

716. Ellis, Richard N. GENERAL JOHN POPE AND THE SOUTHERN PLAINS INDIANS, 1875-1883. *Southwestern Hist. Q. 1968 72(2): 152-169.* As commander of the Department of the Missouri, Major General John Pope had put down the hostilities of the Kiowa, Comanche, and Southern Cheyenne. With the conclusion of hostilities in 1875, Pope entered into a protracted struggle with the Bureau of Indian Affairs to maintain the peace and to treat the Southern Plains Indians with humanity. He believed that ultimate assimilation was the proper goal but that the process of conversion must be one of sympathetic firmness and instruction in white ways. He insisted that they could not be permitted to starve. Pope's continuous battle with the bureau over the treatment of the Indians brought little improvement before he was transferred to another command in 1883. 47 notes.   D. L. Smith

717. Ellis, Richard N., ed. GENERAL POPE'S REPORT ON THE WEST, 1866. *Kansas Hist. Q. 1969 35(4): 345-372.* Presents a report dated 25 February 1866 prepared by John Pope (commanding general of the Division of the Missouri) for his superior William T. Sherman (commanding general of the Division of the Mississippi). Pope described the geography, economy, and settlement of his vast command that reached from Texas to Canada and from Wisconsin to the Rockies. He also described the northern, central, and southern routes of transportation and commerce through his command. Pope's report contained elaborate recommendations on the placement of troops and revisions in the Government's Indian policies. He favored transferring control of Indian affairs to the War Department, abandoning the unrealistic treaty system, and setting up new trade regulations. Based on books, articles, congressional reports, and the Official Records; illus., 2 maps, 25 notes.
    W. F. Zornow

718. Ellis, Richard N. THE HUMANITARIAN GENERALS. *Western Hist. Q. 1972 3(2): 169-178.* During the Indian wars, Army officers were generally characterized as "glory-seeking exterminationists." Indian Bureau officials, reformers, and some politicians believed that the Army looked for the slightest pretext to fight the Indians. The military did have a difficult position caught between the demands of settlers and the friends of the Indians, punishing criminals from both races, organized for war and trying to maintain peace, and faced with the guerrilla tactics of the Indians. Some officers manifested a great deal of compassion and conducted early-day pacification programs. Oliver Otis Howard, George Crook, John Pope, Ranald S. Mackenzie, Benjamin Grierson, and Nelson Appleton Miles were truly humanitarian generals. They were sincere and benevolent men who were neither hawks nor doves, neither exterminationists nor sentimentalists. 27 notes.
    D. L. Smith

719. Ellis, Richard N. THE HUMANITARIAN SOLDIERS. *J. of Arizona Hist. 1969 10(2): 53-66.* Agrees that in the 20 years after the Civil War, despite the detractions of civilian critics, many Army officers actually favored a humanitarian policy toward the western Indians. Officers such as Major General George Armstrong Custer and Lieutenant General Nelson Appleton Miles sought glory and were not responsive to the legitimate needs of the Indians, but General George Crook, Major General Oliver Otis Howard, Brigadier General Benjamin Henry Grierson, and Major General John Pope did regard the Indians sympathetically. They fought the Indians as they had to, but felt compassion for a proud, conquered people. 4 photos, 24 notes.
    R. J. Roske

720. Ellis, Richard N. POLITICAL PRESSURES AND ARMY POLICIES ON THE NORTHERN PLAINS, 1862-1865. *Minnesota Hist. 1970 42(2): 42-53.* Places on Major General John Pope (1822-92), commander of the Division of the Missouri, much of the blame for the Army's failure to soundly defeat the Sioux Indians during the Powder River campaign in Wyoming and Montana in the summer of 1865. Ignoring the reports of his subordinates, Pope yielded to pleas from Minnesotans, including former Governor Henry Hastings Sibley (1811-91), and diverted his ablest field commander, Brigadier General Alfred Sully (1821-79), and Sully's forces from the Powder River area to Dakota Territory to protect Minnesota's western frontier. Minnesotans had been calling for increased military aid and protection since the Sioux uprising of 1862; Pope finally bowed to their unfounded fears of a new Indian outbreak largely because of the influence of Sibley who had defended Pope against political attack in 1863 and 1864. Based on primary and secondary sources; illus., map, 33 notes.   G. R. Adams

721. Ellis, Richard N. VOLUNTEER SOLDIERS IN THE WEST, 1865. *Military Affairs 1970 34(2): 53-55.* One of the major reasons for the failure of the 1865 campaign against the Sioux and the Cheyenne was the insubordination of many of the troops who were volunteers awaiting demobilization following the Civil War. 11 notes.   K. J. Bauer

722. Enochs, James C. CLASH OF AMBITION: TAPPAN CHIVINGTON FEUD. *Montana 1965 15(3): 58-67.* Indian fighting on the plains during the Civil War was complicated by a feud between John M. Chivington and Samuel F. Tappan, commanders of the troops in eastern Colorado. Based on correspondence of the two men, and on newspapers and other printed sources. Photograph portraits.   S. R. Davison

723. Ewers, John C. A CROW CHIEF'S TRIBUTE TO THE UNKNOWN SOLDIER. *Am. West 1971 8(6): 30-35.* Chief Plenty Coups, a Crow, was probably the last surviving war chief to have earned his rank in the intertribal wars on the northern Great Plains in the 1870's. He was the representative of all Indians at the burial service ceremonies for the Unknown Soldier at Arlington National Cemetery, 11 November 1921.

During graveside ceremonies, Plenty Coups removed his own historic eagle-feathered war bonnet and decorated coup stick and placed them on the edge of the sarcophagus. Unexpectedly he delivered a short un-scheduled dedication. Today his coup stick and bonnet rival the world's highest military honors for attention of visitors to the Arlington trophy room. 5 illus., biblio.

D. L. Smith

724. Feraca, Stephen E. and Howard, James H.　THE IDENTITY AND DEMOGRAPHY OF THE DAKOTA OR SIOUX TRIBE. *Plains Anthropologist 1963 8(20): 80-84.* The authors discuss the cultural, linguistic, and historical situation of the Dakota or "Sioux" Indian tribe (first mentioned by white explorers ca. 1640), who lived in a region just west of the Great Lakes. By 1750, the westernmost groups had begun to cross the Missouri River and filter into the Black Hills region. Until after the War of 1812, the Dakota were allies of the British. In 1862, the eastern or Santee bands rose against the whites in what is called the Minnesota uprising. Defeated by government forces, many of the Santee sought refuge in Manitoba and Saskatchewan, Canada. Those remaining in the United States were placed on reservations further west, though some were allowed to stay, or filtered back, into Minnesota. "The dialect of the Eastern or Santee division is *Dakota,* that of the Middle or *Wiciyela* division *Nakota,* and that of the Teton division *Lakota.*" 5 notes, biblio.

D. D. Cameron

725. Filipiak, Jack D.　THE BATTLE OF SUMMIT SPRINGS. *Colorado Mag. 1964 41(4): 343-354.* Tall Bull led a band of Cheyennes and Sioux in a last stand against encroachments of white men and railroads. From 1 May to 2 June 1869, they raided in the Saline and Solomon River Valleys. Appeals of settlers for protection led to the Republican River Expedition of eight undermanned companies of the Fifth Cavalry commanded by Brevet Major General Eugene A. Carr and a battalion of Pawnee Indian scouts led by Major Frank J. North, with "Buffalo Bill" Cody as the chief scout. This was the last conflict with Plains Indians in Colorado Territory. It was reenacted as the climax to Cody's Wild West Show for years.

I. W. Van Noppen

726. Fisher, John R.　THE ROYALL AND DUNCAN PURSUITS: AFTERMATH OF THE BATTLE OF SUMMIT SPRINGS, 1869. *Nebraska Hist. 1969 50(3): 293-308.* An account of the futile searches by the Fifth Cavalry under Major William Bedford Royall for refugee bands of Cheyenne and Sioux Indians in the Republican River valley of southern Nebraska in 1869 following the Battle of Summit Springs. After reaching Fort McPherson, Thomas Duncan replaced Royall as commander of the Republican Valley Expedition. The Battle of Summit Springs "had been a major defeat of hostile Indians of the central plains," and the expeditions of Royall and Duncan "made it plain to the Indians that it was not a chance encounter. ...The military intended to keep the Indians and the plains in a semblance of order." 42 notes.

R. Lowitt

727. Fleming, Elvis Eugene.　CAPTAIN NICHOLAS NOLAN: LOST ON THE STAKED PLAINS. *Texana 1966 4(1): 1-13.* Captain Nicholas Nolan, in search of marauding Comanches, led a detachment of Negro cavalrymen and a group of buffalo hunters into the Staked Plains of Northwest Texas and Eastern New Mexico in the summer of 1877. Although the expedition became lost and suffered from lack of water, it indirectly removed the last major Indian impediment to settlement of the area.

W. Elkins

728. Fowler, Don D., ed.　NOTES ON THE EARLY LIFE OF CHIEF WASHAKIE TAKEN DOWN BY CAPTAIN RAY. *Ann. of Wyoming 1964 36(1): 34-42.* Discusses the importance of such documents for the anthropologist and historian. "Notes" were taken by Captain Patrick Henry Ray during the 1890's and are in the form of a reminiscence. Describes a Shoshoni Council with American Peace Commissioners in 1851 and the Indians' rejection of peace with their enemies, the Cheyennes and Blackfeet. The "Notes" show the chief's attitudes toward raiding and warfare and his participation in such events. The document is located with other Shoshoni materials at the Bancroft Library.

R. L. Nichols

729. Gage, Duane.　BLACK KETTLE: A NOBLE SAVAGE? *Chronicles of Oklahoma 1967 45(3): 244-251.* An examination of the conflicting opinions concerning the character and performance of the Cheyenne Indian chief Black Kettle, the circumstances under which he

was compelled to act, leads to the conclusion that he was a victim of the times in which he lived. Black Kettle was a powerful and controversial figure in the post-Civil War Indian wars on the Great Plains. Illus., 22 notes.

D. L. Smith

730. Gordon, Dudley, ed.　LUMMIS AS WAR CORRESPONDENT IN ARIZONA. *Am. West 1965 2(3): 4-12.* Charles F. Lummis was sent by the Los Angeles *Times* to cover the army campaign under General George Crook against the Apaches under Geronimo. For months in 1886 this assignment took him through Arizona, New Mexico, Sonora, and Chihuahua. Printed here is the Lummis field report about the pursuit and surrender of Geronimo on 17 March 1886, written at Fort Bowie, Arizona Territory. Also included are a short notice from the *Times* of Lummis' assignment and editorial comments on Lummis, Geronimo, and Crook. The holographic field report is in the Southwest Museum. Illus.

D. L. Smith

731. Grange, Roger T.　TREATING THE WOUNDED AT FORT ROBINSON. *Nebraska Hist. 1964 45(3): 273-294.* Presents the surgeons' reports prepared after treating the wounded, both white and Indian, after the Cheyenne outbreak at Fort Robinson in 1879 and analyzes medical practice and knowledge of the time.

R. Lowitt

732. Gray, John S.　ARIKARA SCOUTS WITH CUSTER. *North Dakota Hist. 1968 35(2): 442-478.* The Fort Berthold Reservation in North Dakota supplied some of the most effective Indian scouts the US Army could obtain in the Indian wars in the West. Published in 1912 as The Arikara Narrative (State Historical Society of North Dakota Collections, VI), O. G. Libby records data he collected from nine survivors of the Sioux campaign of 1876 in which George A. Custer was defeated at the Little Bighorn. The National Archives has microfilmed the "Register of Enlistments of Indian Scouts, 1866-1914." Two tables of names and data on the scouts are compiled from these two sources and biographical information is gleaned from other sources. 15 illus., 30 notes.

D. L. Smith

733. Gray, John S.　LAST RITES FOR LONESOME CHARLEY REYNOLDS. *Montana 1963 13(3): 40-51.* A year before scout Reynolds died in the Battle of the Little Big Horn in 1876, he met and became a close friend of Philetus W. Norris, later to be superintendent of Yellowstone National Park. On learning of Reynolds' death, and of the superficial burial given to bodies on that field, Norris made the trip to Montana, found the shallow grave, and retrieved the few bones he was able to collect. It is assumed that Norris buried these remains in his own family plot at Ann Arbor, which has itself been obliterated.

L. G. Nelson

734. Gray, John S.　WHAT MADE JOHNNIE BRUGUIER RUN? *Montana 1964 14(2): 34-39.* Adventures of a Sioux half-breed scout with General Nelson A. Miles in his dealings with Sitting Bull from 1876 to 1890.

S. R. Davison

735. Gray, John S.　WILL COMSTOCK, SCOUT: THE NATTY BUMPO OF KANSAS. *Montana 1970 20(3): 2-15.* Identifies frontier scout William Averill Comstock (1842-68) as the child of a prominent Michigan family and as a grandnephew of James Fenimore Cooper. Orphaned early, Will Comstock became an Indian trader in Nebraska before he was 18 years old. In the Indian troubles of the 1860's he served as an army scout, including some service under George A. Custer in Kansas. He died while on a peace mission to the Cheyenne Indians in 1868. Derived from published material and U.S. Census records; illus., 23 notes.

S. R. Davison

736. Greenfield, Charles D.　LITTLE DOG, ONCE-FIERCE PIE-GAN WARRIOR. *Montana 1964 14(2): 23-33.* From 1840 to 1866 Little Dog led his people in war against enemy tribes but was friendly to the whites.

S. R. Davison

737. Greenway, John.　THE GHOST DANCE: SOME REFLECTIONS, WITH EVIDENCE, ON A CULT OF DESPAIR AMONG THE INDIANS OF NORTH AMERICA. *Am. West 1969 6(4): 42-47.* Religion is explained as the formulation and articulation of the unreasonable hope of a culture threatened with extinction that is manifested when all reasonable hope has vanished. A nativistic prophet or leader emerges

who maintains that his credentials and charge to lead his people are divinely given. Natural selection determines whether his endeavor will succeed and survive the competition of other similar movements of the same time. This happened "scores" of times among American Indians. The most important, according to the author, was the Ghost Dance despair cult which first appeared briefly (1870-73) among the Ute in western Nevada. It resurfaced at the same place in 1889 under the leadership of a Paiute named Wovoka, otherwise known as Jack Wilson, who steadfastly maintained the divinity of his mission. The Ghost Dance cult combined primitive Indian beliefs and Christian conceptions. It spread rapidly from tribe to tribe, although its acceptance was not universal by all of the groups in the Plains and Rockies area. The cult is herein documented by accounts of competent white ethnographers on the scene. It came to an end in December 1890 with the massacre committed by the U.S. 7th Cavalry at Wounded Knee, South Dakota. 3 illus.

D. L. Smith

738. Hagemann, E. R. SCOUT OUT FROM CAMP MC DOWELL. *Arizoniana 1964 5(3): 29-47.* Captain George B. Sanford with four officers and 91 men, left Camp McDowell 27 September 1866 in pursuit of Apaches. His report 10 days later was highly commended by General McDowell. By the end of November *The Arizona Miner* was fulsome in its praise of Sanford for having killed 15 men and taken many prisoners. The Third Legislative Assembly passed a resolution, "Thanking the Arizona Volunteers." Sanford "had committed the Army to a war with the Apaches that the Federal Government could not henceforth disavow and which would last for more than twenty years." Sanford led many more scouts until the regiment was transferred in 1873. Illus., map, 48 notes.

E. P. Stickney

739. Hagemann, E. R., ed. "THOU ART THE MAN": AN ADDRESS ON THE INDIAN QUESTION IN 1892 BY COLONEL GEORGE BLISS SANFORD. *J. of Arizona Hist. 1968 9(1): 33-38.* After a distinguished career with the Sixth Cavalry, serving both in the Civil War and on the western frontier, Colonel Sanford retired and gave this address to the Litchfield Scientific Association in the winter of 1892. In this speech, Colonel Sanford described the customs and life patterns of the Pima and Apache Indians. He felt strongly that the Indians, especially the Pima who had long been allies of the Americans, had become the innocent victims of white aggression. He added that it was not only the Government, but also the people of the United States who, in a very real sense, broke treaties and displaced the Indians. He closed his address by appealing for justice for the Indian and "an equal share" in this country. Based on a privately owned manuscript; 7 notes.

R. J. Roske

740. Hampton, H. D. POWDER RIVER INDIAN EXPEDITION OF 1865. *Montana 1964 14(4): 2-15.* In response to popular demand, General Patrick E. Connor was given responsibility for clearing hostile Indians from the Oregon Trail in Wyoming. Connor accompanied one of three columns marching against the Sioux, Cheyennes and Arapahoes. Hampered by unseasonable cold, "incompetent guides and vague maps," and with forces largely made up of recruits and unwilling Civil War veterans, the campaign accomplished little. Indicated sources are Congressional documents and standard published accounts.

S. R. Davison

741. Harrison, Lowell H. INDIANS VS. BUFFALO HUNTERS AT ADOBE WALLS. *Am. Hist. Illus. 1967 2(1): 18-27.* The Texas Panhandle was the locale of a fight between Comanche Indians and a small settlement housing nearly 30 people. The author provides the background of the battle, including the development of a new tanning process which encouraged the buffalo hunters to venture into territory claimed by the Indians. The major battle took place 27 June 1874, and there were brief exchanges for a few days afterward before the Indians departed to make other attacks to the south. Retaliation came with a military campaign in 1874-75 under Generals Nelson A. Miles and Ranald S. Mackenzie.

J. D. Filipiak

742. Hart, Newell. RESCUE OF A FRONTIER BOY. *Utah Hist. Q. 1965 33(1): 51-54.* Tells how Shoshone and Bannock Indians in Utah carried off a 10-year-old boy, Reuban Van Orman, after killing his parents and of how his uncle Zachias, with the help of Federal troops, recovered him two years later. Based on records of Zachias Van Orman in the Oregon State Historical Society and the *Official Records.*

S. L. Jones

743. Hill, Burton S. THE GREAT INDIAN TREATY COUNCIL OF 1851. *Nebraska Hist. 1966 47(1): 85-110.* Discusses the great gathering of over ten thousand Indians from numerous tribes near Fort Laramie, Wyoming where they assembled to confer with white officials, numbering, with troops, less than 300 men, on problems vexing them at the time emanating from loss of forage and game owing to heavy traffic on the Oregon Trail. The treaty that emerged from the council was amended by the Senate and did not insure the harmonious relations the negotiating commissioners hoped would follow.

R. Lowitt

744. Hofling, Charles K. GEORGE ARMSTRONG CUSTER: A PSYCHOANALYTIC APPROACH. *Montana 1971 21(2): 32-43.* Analyzes Custer's character and personality for clues to his performance in the disastrous campaign against the Sioux and Cheyenne in 1876. Traces his career in terms of frequent reverses mingled with occasional brilliant successes, all with indications of instability and a desire to attract attention. Custer had reasons to feel both guilt and resentment, leading to an urge to accomplish spectacular feats. Inner conflict may have dulled his judgment and led him to the fatal errors that insured the annihilation of his command. Based mainly on secondary sources; illus., 9 notes.

S. R. Davison

745. Hopkins, Richard C. KIT CARSON AND THE NAVAJO EXPEDITION. *Montana 1968 18(2): 52-61.* An account of Kit Carson's campaign against the Navaho in the Canyon de Chelly region in 1864. With Captain Albert H. Pfeiffer, Carson broke the Navaho power by a series of raids against their villages and fields, leading to their early surrender. Based on military correspondence among officers concerned.

S. R. Davison

746. Howard, Helen Addison. THE STEPTOE AFFAIR. *Montana 1969 19(2): 28-36.* Summarizes events leading to and including the "Steptoe Massacre" of 1858 near Spokane. An explanation is furnished for the mysterious shortage of ammunition for the besieged soldiers: a civilian teamster forgot to bring the packs. Emphasis is placed on the assistance given the troops by Timothy, a Nez Percé chief and convert to Christianity. Illus., biblio.

S. R. Davison

747. Hughes, Willis B. THE FIRST DRAGOONS ON THE WESTERN FRONTIER, 1834-1846. *Arizona and the West 1970 12(2): 115-138.* The mounted volunteers who were pressed into service for the Black Hawk War (1832) were unsatisfactory and the mounted rangers who succeeded them were merely a stopgap measure to reckon with the fast-moving horse Indians. Congress created the elite First Dragoon Regiment which patrolled the thousand-mile frontier between the Red rivers of Minnesota and Texas, with Colonel Henry Dodge (1782-1867) as its commander from 1834 to 1836, and General Stephen Watts Kearny (1794-1848) as his successor from 1836 to 1846. With nine major expeditions over much of the Great Plains and as many treaties to its credit, the regiment fulfilled its mission with great success. Escort duty down the Santa Fe trail, assistance in settling removal-emigrant Indians, and contacting and overawing Plains tribes were the principal activities. The dragoons maintained this peace on the western frontier for 12 years without a single battle with the Indians, an amazing feat in itself. The experiences of the period also schooled the army in campaigning on the Great Plains, lessons that were to serve it well in later years. 4 illus., 2 maps, 57 notes.

D. L. Smith

748. James, Rhett S., ed. BRIGHAM YOUNG-CHIEF WASHAKIE INDIAN FARM NEGOTIATIONS, 1854-1857. *Ann. of Wyoming 1967 39(2): 245-256.* Presents a series of six letters from Brigham Young to Shoshone Chief Washakie during the years 1854 to 1857. These demonstrate Brigham Young's desire to live peacefully with the Indians, as well as his realization that the Indians had to become farmers if they were to survive. Based on the Brigham Young Papers, Church Historian's Office, Salt Lake City, Office of Indian Affairs material in the National Archives, and published material; 39 notes.

R. L. Nichols

749. Johnson, Dorothy M. CUSTER RIDES AGAIN. *Montana 1967 17(2): 53-63.* Informal description of present-day reenactments of the Battle of the Little Big Horn, where General George A. Custer was killed in 1876. Since the 50th anniversary observance in 1926, celebrations have become annual affairs, sponsored by the Crow tribe. These Indians

were not heavily involved in the battle, but it was fought on their land. Based on standard published accounts, illus., 15 notes.

S. R. Davison

750. Jones, Oakah L., Jr. THE ORIGINS OF THE NAVAJO INDIAN POLICE, 1872-1873. *Arizona and the West 1966 8(3): 225-238.* The warlike Navajo who returned from military imprisonment in New Mexico in 1868 to a northeastern Arizona reservation were finding it difficult to change suddenly to a peaceful agrarian way of life. Recurrent drought and poor crops, unsatisfactory reservation boundaries, and irregular distribution of government rations served only to intensify their predicament. Soon mounted Navajo bands were raiding settlements in New Mexico and stealing livestock from the ranches. Both civilian and military observers believed that the Navajo could be guided into useful citizenship if a Navajo regulatory body replaced the present military guardianship. The lean winter of 1871-72 and imminent starvation provoked the Indians to increasingly uncontrollable raids on horse, sheep, and cattle herds. At an August Navajo-Apache peace conference the Navajo warchief Manuelito himself openly proposed the establishment of a native police force. Manuelito became the captain of the Navajo Indian Police, a force of 100 men. They provided their own horses, but were uniformed and equipped by the Army. The Navajo Police were so efficient and effective in returning stolen property and discouraging further incidents that they were dissolved in late 1873. There is evidence, however, that a similar arrangement was continued for some time on an informal basis by the Indian agent to maintain law and order. This experiment was an important forerunner of a later general governmental policy for administering Indian reservations through native police forces. Based in part on Bureau of Indian Affairs records in the National Archives; 2 illus., 27 notes.

D. L. Smith

751. Jordan, Weymouth T., Jr. LIEUTENANT C. D. COWLES AT NORTH PLATTE STATION, 1876. *Nebraska Hist. 1971 52(1): 89-91.* An 1876 letter from Lieutenant Calvin Duvall Cowles (1849-1937) to his father, written at the height of the Sioux campaign. Cowles mentioned his personal affairs and the "indian news."

R. Lowitt

752. Josselyn, Daniel W. INDIAN CAVALRY. *Great Plains J. 1963 2(2): 77-79.* Based on Theodore R. Davis' account of his personal experiences following Custer in Kansas as an artist for *Harper's New Monthly Magazine.*

S

753. Karnes, Thomas L. GILPIN'S VOLUNTEERS ON THE SANTA FE TRAIL. *Kansas Hist. Q. 1964 30(1): 1-14.* Mexican War caused a breakdown of defense on the Santa Fe Trail, but Major William Gilpin organized a "Separate Battalion of Missouri Volunteers" to restore peace along the trail. Gilpin was successful in keeping the northern tribes from cooperation with the southern, but he was unable to do more than postpone the Indian struggles for a short time. The entire operation in 1847-48 was characterized by dishonest and humorous events. Many of Gilpin's subordinates proved thoroughly unreliable; there were accusations of murder, horse stealing and indiscipline. One man even enrolled his mistress as a "private." Based on material in the National Archives.

W. F. Zornow

754. Kelly, Lawrence C. WHERE WAS FORT CANBY? *New Mexico Hist. R. 1967 42(2): 49-62.* From June 1863 until October 1864 New Mexican volunteers used Fort Canby as a headquarters camp in their campaign against the Navajo Indians. Previous historians placed the site of Fort Canby at Pueblo, Colorado, but the author, by a careful reading of military correspondence, locates the correct site at Fort Defiance. Based on records in the National Archives, Record Group 98; 19 notes.

D. F. Henderson

755. Kelsey, Harry. BACKGROUND TO SAND CREEK. *Colorado Mag. 1968 45(4): 279-300.* Asserts that politics offers a fertile field for research on the background of the Sand Creek Massacre (1864). Discussed are the activities of three "totally unqualified political appointees" who served as Indian agents in Colorado Territory prior to the massacre. The inept Samuel G. Colley, cousin of the newly named Commissioner of Indian Affairs William P. Dole, was appointed to the Upper Arkansas Indian Agency in 1861. There is some evidence that his son, Indian trader Dexter Colley, traded and sold Indian "annuity" goods. John W. Wright, crony of John P. Usher, secretary of the interior, re-

ceived a lucrative contract to survey lands on the Upper Arkansas reservation and also to serve as special agent to the Caddo Indians. After completing a useless survey opposed by Governor John Evans, Wright attacked Evans by linking him with the causes of the Indian wars. The third agent was Simeon Whiteley, friend of Simon Cameron and Senator James R. Dolittle, who was appointed agent to the Middle Park Indian Agency apparently with the main function of organizing support for the Lincoln administration in the West. Largely to blame for the "scandalous state of affairs in the Indian service" in the 1860's was Commissioner William P. Dole who accommodated "political cronies, greedy relatives, well-meaning amateurs and conniving rascals" in the Indian service. Illus., 89 notes.

O. H. Zabel

756. King, James T. "A BETTER WAY": GENERAL GEORGE CROOK AND THE PONCA INDIANS. *Nebraska Hist. 1969 50(3): 239-256.* Discusses the background of the 1879 case *United States ex rel. Standing Bear vs. Crook* wherein, through the efforts of General Crook and others, Standing Bear and his Ponca tribesmen were allowed to remain on their Nebraska lands and were not forced to return to lands set aside for them in the Indian Territory. For the Ponca, the affair showed that justice was not impossible within the white man's law.

R. Lowitt

757. King, James T. FORGOTTEN PAGEANT - THE INDIAN WARS IN WESTERN NEBRASKA. *Nebraska Hist. 1965 46(3): 177-192.* An interpretative survey of the military frontier in Nebraska emphasizing the period (1854-90) when the Indian-fighting army was most closely associated with the people of western Nebraska.

R. Lowitt

758. King, James T., ed. FORT MC PHERSON IN 1870: A NOTE BY AN ARMY WIFE. *Nebraska Hist. 1964 45(1): 99-107.* Reminiscences written in 1910 by Mary Magwire Carr, wife of Brevet Major General Eugene A. Carr, of the two years she spent at Fort McPherson, Nebraska from October 1869 to November 1871.

R. Lowitt

759. King, James T. GEORGE CROOK: INDIAN FIGHTER AND HUMANITARIAN. *Arizona and the West 1967 9(4): 333-348.* General George Crook enjoyed a well-earned reputation as a vigorous fighter who campaigned tirelessly through most of the major Indian wars of the trans-Mississippi West. He is probably best remembered as "conqueror of the Apaches." Often overlooked is that the olive branch, as well as implements of war, was carried in the talons of the American eagle. This is epitomized in General Crook who conceived and executed one of the most enlightened Indian policies in American frontier history. Much of his humanitarian program rested upon his experiences in Arizona Territory, especially during his second tour of duty, 1882-86. Possessed with a remarkable ability to replace war's ruthlessness with humanity in peace, Crook was willing to treat the Indian with decency and fairness. On his first assignment to Arizona in 1871, he found that American cruelty and viciousness had attained "exquisite perfection" aimed toward literal extermination. He felt that in such circumstances the Indian would have to be conquered before he could be pacified. A further innovation was to enlist friendly natives as scouts, not only for the intelligence value they could offer but also as a demoralizing factor against the hostiles. Implementation was delayed until his second Arizona tour because less satisfactory programs were imposed from the Federal Government. Meanwhile his voice was heard increasingly as a champion of justice for the Indian. Granted unusual freedom of action upon his return to the Southwest in 1882, Crook was determined to give the Apache the opportunity to adjust himself to a civilized sedentary culture and to treat him as an equal. A steady barrage of letters, articles, and speeches supplemented his military actions. Unfortunate policy differences with superiors led to Crook's resignation from the Arizona command before fulfillment of his dreams. He remained, nevertheless, an active champion of Indian rights. Illus., 34 notes.

D. L. Smith

760. King, James T. NEEDED: A RE-EVALUATION OF GENERAL GEORGE CROOK. *Nebraska Hist. 1964 45(3): 223-235.* Calls for a new biography of General Crook and examines the 1876 campaign against the Sioux. The author contends that Crook was not always a consummate military commander and was overly concerned with his public "image." He failed not only in his objective of defeating the Indians but even of meeting them.

R. Lowitt

761. Kircus, Peggy D. FORT DAVID A. RUSSELL: A STUDY OF ITS HISTORY FROM 1867 TO 1890 WITH A BRIEF SUMMARY OF EVENTS FROM 1890 TO THE PRESENT. *Ann. of Wyoming 1969 41(1): 83-111.* Continued from a previous article. Discusses health and dietary problems at the post. Unsanitary conditions and poorly constructed living quarters caused high rates of sickness and lowered efficiency and morale. The author then examines the role of troops from the fort in the Indian wars on the northern plains against the Sioux, Cheyenne, and Ute tribes, as well as their participation in the battle at Wounded Knee (1890). Briefly traced are the activities at the post since the close of the Indian wars. During the ensuing decades the Army used the post to house units during peacetime, as a regional processing center during war, and most recently as a missile base. Based on published journals, government records, and secondary accounts; 94 notes.
R. L. Nichols

762. Kivett, Marvin F. ALONG THE TRAIL. *Nebraska Hist. 1964 45(2): 217-220.* Discusses the historical potentials of Fort Robinson and calls for a program of detailed research and planning that will further develop them over a period of years. The Red Cloud Agency site, located less than two miles from the fort, should also be developed. Recreational and natural history values are mentioned as worthy of development along with the historical.
R. Lowitt

763. Knuth, Priscilla, ed. CAVALRY IN THE INDIAN COUNTRY, 1864. *Oregon Hist. Q. 1964 65(1): 5-118.* All but nine pages of this article consist of the "Private Journal" of Captain John M. Drake describing an army cavalry expedition from Fort Dalles, Oregon, into eastern Oregon Indian country. The editor states that two "editions" of Drake's journal were used, one version believed to be the original (kept in the Coe Collection at Yale University) and the second version, a typewritten copy (held at the Oregon Historical Society). The journal gives many details of the business of a small military detachment trying to locate hostile Indians. Drake's observations are candid and personal, such as (in speaking of any army officer), "He fills my mind's eye precisely of a stiff, aristocratical old fool, morbid in his sensibilities and uncivil and contemptible in his intercourse with others." There are no battles with the Indians. Strife (bloodless) is limited to the criticisms and misunderstandings among the members of the expedition and military superiors and residents of Oregon. The journal covers the period of 20 April to 11 October 1864.
C. C. Gorchels

764. Kroeker, Marvin. COLONEL W. B. HAZEN IN THE INDIAN TERRITORY. *Chronicles of Oklahoma 1964 42(1): 53-73.* Deals with Hazen's career as a special military agent at Fort Cobb, 1868-69. Following the Congressional Act of 1867 Hazen sought to bring the peaceable Southern Indians - Kiowa, Comanche, Kiowa Apache, Wichita, Cheyenne, and Arapaho - in to restricted reservations and to teach them an agricultural mode of life. Treaties had been made with these Indians at Medicine Lodge in 1867. Congress failed to appropriate sufficient funds. The Indians were destitute and resentful. Generals Sheridan and Sherman were in command of the military. Hazen had the task of separating the friendly from the hostile Indians. He refused to deal with the Cheyenne and Arapaho tribes who were considered hostile by Sherman and Sheridan, and he urged these tribes to make peace. His funds were inadequate to provide for eight thousand Indians, some of whom raided in Texas. Too few troops were available to restrain these malcontents. Strenuous efforts were made to introduce farming. Hazen's services as special agent were concluded in 1869. He had only partially succeeded in establishing a reservation system but he had prepared the way to lead the Indian on the white man's road. 90 notes.
I. W. Van Noppen

765. Langley, Harold D., ed. THE CUSTER BATTLE AND THE CRITIQUE OF AN ADVENTURER. *Montana 1972 22(2): 20-33.* Reproduces a letter written to a Congressman in July 1876, commenting on the Battle of the Little Big Horn (25 June 1876). The author was Charles F. Henningsen (1815-77), a professional soldier and world-wanderer. Henningsen stressed the incompetence of regular troops in fighting Indians, the superiority of local "border men" for such duty, the guilt of Army officers in stimulating Indian wars, and the hypocrisy of the clamor for more military posts, wanted by the frontiersmen mainly for the money spent around these forts. Henningsen analyzed Custer's battlefield tactics, less than a month after the event. 23 illus., 22 notes.
S. R. Davison

766. Lass, William E. THE "MOSCOW EXPEDITION." *Minnesota Hist. 1965 39(6): 227-240.* An account of the Moscow Expedition of 1863. Following the Sioux uprising of the previous year and the removal of most of the Indians to the Dakota Territory, it became necessary to provide them with food, clothing and other supplies. Two businessmen named James B. Hubbell and Clark W. Thompson contracted to transport the supplies overland, through 292 miles of wilderness, with the help of a troop of soldiers who almost proved to be more hindrance than help. The whole affair turned into a farce with political overtones and is another sordid chapter in the story of the poor treatment of the Indians by the white man. Based on letters and newspapers in the Minnesota Historical Society.
P. L. Simon

767. Lass, William E. THE REMOVAL FROM MINNESOTA OF THE SIOUX AND WINNEBAGO INDIANS. *Minnesota Hist. 1963 38(8): 353-364.* Following the great Sioux uprising of 1862, the US government bowed to local pressure and took steps to remove all Indians from southern Minnesota - the relatively peaceful Winnebago as well as the Sioux. They were to be removed beyond the limits of the state to an area along the upper Missouri. Steamboats were chosen to transport them since it was felt this would be cheaper for the government and easier on the Indians than an overland trek. The trip was difficult and uncomfortable. There was considerable over-crowding and insufficient food and water. The white missionaries who accompanied their charges were so appalled by the treatment of the Indians that one wrote to his Bishop, "...if I were an Ind[ian] I would never lay down the war club while I lived." Based largely on Indian Office *Reports* and newspaper accounts.
P. L. Simon

768. Liberty, Margot. "I WILL PLAY WITH THE SOLDIERS." *Montana 1964 14(4): 16-26.* During the Ghost Dance excitement of 1890, two young Cheyennes deliberately murdered a white youth and prearranged their own deaths by announcing the time and place of their attack against US troops at Lame Deer, on the Northern Cheyenne Reservation. In view of almost the entire Cheyenne tribe, assembled for distribution of rations, the two charged down a hillside, firing at the waiting soldiers, and were killed by volleys of rifle fire. Their exploit has become a tribal legend, and primitive stone markers have been placed to indicate the site. Derived from recent testimony of elderly Indians who witnessed the event, and early published accounts.
S. R. Davison

769. Lyon, Juana Frazer. ARCHIE MC INTOSH, THE SCOTTISH INDIAN SCOUT. *J. of Arizona Hist. 1966 7(3): 103-122.* A biographical sketch of an Indian scout who was the son of a Hudson's Bay Company employee and a Chippewa woman, in part educated in Scotland, who served as a valuable scout for General George Crook in the campaigns against the Apache Indians in Arizona.
J. D. Filipiak

770. Madaus, H. Michael. THE PERSONAL AND DESIGNATING FLAGS OF GENERAL GEORGE A. CUSTER. *Military Collector and Historian 1968 20(1): 1-14.* Before the advent of modern communications, flags were used to mark out the locations of units and commanders. The author deals with the personal and unit banners associated with General Custer during the Civil War. The flashy cavalryman was something of a trend setter in the creation of personal battle flags. The designs which Custer worked out and used are re-created. It is suggested that the flags carried at Little Big Horn (at present not known) were probably quite similar to those illustrated here. 9 plates, photo, 24 notes.
D. C. Oliver

771. Madsen, Brigham D. SHOSHONI-BANNOCK MARAUDERS ON THE OREGON TRAIL, 1859-1863. *Utah Hist. Q. 1967 35(1): 3-30.* Shows how the Shoshoni and Bannock Indians in their traditional territories north and west of Utah were disturbed by the overland migration to Washington, Oregon, and California and recites the stories of various hostile encounters between these Indians, the overland migrants, and U.S. military forces sent into the area to protect white settlers. Mormon leaders are described as favoring a pacific policy of feeding and clothing the Indians rather than fighting them, but the narrative reveals that Mormon settlers were not always prepared to follow such a policy. Based in part on Records of the Bureau of Indian Affairs in the National Archives, contemporary newspaper accounts, and *The War of the Rebellion.*
S. L. Jones

772. Marsh, Richard E. A LIMITED HISTORICAL REVIEW OF THE JICARILLA APACHES DURING THE EVENTFUL YEARS, 1848-1855. *Southwestern Lore 1969 35(3): 42-53.* "From 1848 to 1855 the Jicarilla, which means 'basket-makers,' Apaches were extremely treacherous and warlike. Launching incessant raids against the New Mexican settlers, their energetic activities forced the United States Army to maintain an almost continuous attack against them in order to establish limited peace. With the constant efforts of the army during 1854 and 1855, the Jicarillas were subdued but not without considerable expense and loss of lives. The geographic area and fundamental cultural components of Apache culture which contributed to this situation are examined, and the history of their activities during this time period is recounted."
AIA (1:2:88)

773. McCann, Frank D., Jr. GHOST DANCE: LAST HOPE OF WESTERN TRIBES. *Montana 1966 16(1): 25-34.* In the late 1880's the Ghost Dance religion arose among the Paiutes and spread to other western tribes. Based on the teachings of Wavoka the Prophet, with elements derived from earlier mystic cults and from several Christian denominations, the religion later added a variety of Indian innovations. The Sioux version contributed to the disorders which ended in the Wounded Knee episode, after which the movement soon faded away. Based on publications of the U.S. Bureau of Ethnology and other professional papers.
S. R. Davison

774. McDermott, John D. FORT LARAMIE'S SILENT SOLDIER - LEODEGAR SCHNYDER. *Ann. of Wyoming 1964 36(1): 4-18.* Discusses the army career of Ordinance Sergeant Schnyder at Fort Laramie from 1848 until 1886 when he was ordered to New Bedford, Massachusetts. The article traces events such as the gold rush to the Black Hills and Indian attacks on the post, through Schnyder's career. Shows how Schnyder solved financial difficulties by becoming fort postmaster while continuing as ordinance sergeant. Based on records at Fort Laramie, published government documents, and state histories.
R. L. Nichols

775. McDermott, Louis M. THE PRIMARY ROLE OF THE MILITARY ON THE DAKOTA FRONTIER. *South Dakota Hist. 1971 2(1): 1-22.* Describes the role of the Army in the settlement of the West. Describes Indian warfare from 1860 to 1890. Discusses the characteristics of officers and men in the Army and the Indian battles fought in the Department of Dakota. 12 illus., 48 notes.
D. H. Swift

776. McNitt, Frank. NAVAJO CAMPAIGNS AND THE OCCUPATION OF NEW MEXICO, 1847-1848. *New Mexico Hist. R. 1968 43(3): 173-194.* A narrative of two expeditions against the Navajo following the American occupation of New Mexico. The expedition of 1847, led by Major Robert Walker, nearly ended in a disaster, and failed completely to force the Navajo to cease their raids on New Mexican livestock. The expedition of 1848, under Colonel Edward W. B. Newby, resulted in the "second American treaty with the tribe which . . . was never ratified and was not much worse or better than the treaties that preceded it." Based on Record Group 94, National Archives, and various newspapers; 26 notes.
D. F. Henderson

777. Mehren, Lawrence L., ed. SCOUTING FOR MESCALEROS: THE PRICE CAMPAIGN OF 1873. *Arizona and the West 1968 10(2): 171-190.* The restive Mescalero Apache, neither happy with a new reservation created for them in southeastern New Mexico in mid-1873 nor with the regular rations allotted to them, continued to steal large quantities of horses, mules, and cattle from ranchers in the vicinity. Apparently, in addition to other reasons, the Mescalero believed that the whites owed them tribute in the form of horses and mules. Major William Redwood Price, experienced in recovering stolen stock from other Apache, was assigned to recover the considerable loot accumulated by the Mescalero and to see that they settled peacefully on the reservation. In four reports, herein edited, Price and his principal officers detail the fall campaign of 1873, in which the Mescalero were pursued in the mountains of southeastern New Mexico and into Texas. He succeeded in driving them from New Mexico but failed both to keep them on the reservation and to recover the stolen stock. 2 illus., map, 66 notes.
D. L. Smith

778. Meyer, Roy W. THE ESTABLISHMENT OF THE SANTEE RESERVATION, 1866-1869. *Nebraska Hist. 1964 45(1): 59-97.* Traces the history of the Santee Sioux, chiefly by examining government policies and actions, from their exile from Minnesota in 1863, as a result of the Sioux uprising in 1862. The focus is on their disheartening experiences in Nebraska where they were brought in 1866 to the Niobrara River. Concludes that by 1869 the Santee Sioux "were on their way back from the nadir of their history."
R. Lowitt

779. Millbrook, Minnie Dubbs. THE WEST BREAKS IN GENERAL CUSTER. *Kansas Hist. Q. 1970 36(2): 113-148.* George Armstrong Custer's first year on the Great Plains was not a success. His actions did not bear out his superiors' impressions that he was a born leader and fighter. During a lengthy campaign against the Indians from March to September 1867, Custer complained about the food and weather, showed little interest in fighting, cracked down with unnecessary severity on deserters, and at one point even left his command in the field to rush back to his family and civilization. This final offense brought Custer before a court-martial that found him guilty and suspended him from service for a year. When he returned to his regiment, Custer responded with vigor to every opportunity to show that he was a good soldier and became a skilled member of the Indian fighting army. Based on books, articles, Government publications, newspapers, and manuscripts in the National Archives and Kansas State Historical Society; illus., 129 notes.
W. F. Zornow

780. Mueller, Oscar O. THE NEZ PERCE AT COW ISLAND. *Montana 1964 14(2): 50-53.* Corrects the common belief that soldiers made no effort to protect goods seized by the Indians during the Nez Perce retreat of 1877.
S. R. Davison

781. Munn, Fred. MEMOIRS OF A CAVALRY VETERAN. *Montana 1966 16(2): 50-64.* Reminiscences recorded in 1937 by one of the last survivors of the campaigns against the Sioux in 1876 and Nez Percés in 1877. He was among the first to view the scene of the Custer battle. The next year, under General O. O. Howard, he witnessed the Camas Prairie fight in Idaho. Undocumented, illus.
S. R. Davison

782. Murray, Robert A. THE LONG WALK OF SERGEANTS GRANT AND GRAHAM. *Ann. of Wyoming 1966 38(2): 137-141.* Discusses the hardships encountered by Sergeants George Grant and Joseph Graham while walking 90 miles from Fort Philip Kearny to Fort C. F. Smith during February 1867. The men faced problems of cold, lack of food, loss of direction, and Indian pursuit, but succeeded in reopening communications between the two posts. In 1871 Sergeant Grant received the Congressional Medal of Honor for his part in this event. Based on materials in the War Records Branch of the National Archives, 30 notes.
R. L. Nichols

783. Murray, Robert A. THE WAGON BOX FIGHT: A CENTENNIAL APPRAISAL. *Ann. of Wyoming 1967 39(1): 104-108.* Discusses past research on the Wagon Box Fight in August 1867 near Fort Philip Kearny. The author examines the Wagon Box Fight from the usually neglected manuscript reports of that engagement submitted by Captain James Powell and by Major Benjamin F. Smith, both participants. Major Smith's unit frightened the Indian attackers and rescued the surrounded troops under Captain Powell. As a result of this attack, the troops received more organized target practice and gained confidence in their units and firepower. Based on correspondence in Record Group 98, National Archives, and secondary material; 11 notes.
R. L. Nichols

784. Murry, Robert A. THE CUSTER COURT MARTIAL. *Ann. of Wyoming 1964 36(2): 175-185.* Discusses General George A. Custer's actions during the Indian campaign of the summer of 1867 which led to his court martial on a charge of being absent from duty. Includes the charges, findings, and sentence of the court. Based on archival records of the War Department.
R. L. Nichols

785. Myers, Lee. THE ENIGMA OF MANGAS COLORADAS' DEATH. *New Mexico Hist. R. 1966 41(4): 287-304.* Leader of the Copper Mine band of Apache Indians, Mangas Coloradas was killed while under guard of soldiers at abandoned Fort McLane, sometime during the night of 18 January 1863. Four versions - all supposedly by eyewitnesses - are presented. Documented, 26 notes.
D. F. Henderson

786. Myers, Lee. FORT WEBSTER ON THE MIMBRES RIVER. *New Mexico Hist. R. 1966 41(1): 47-57.* First located at Copper Mines, now Santa Rita, and later moved to the Mimbres River, Fort Webster was the first post established to combat the Apache menace in southwestern New Mexico. The location of the second site has remained in doubt. After a careful analysis of several reports and a comparison of mileage, Myers believes that the Horace Bounds ranch site was the location of old Fort Webster. Based on printed sources and materials in the National Archives; 20 notes. D. F. Henderson

787. Nalty, Bernard C. and Strobridge, Truman R. CAPTAIN EMMET CRAWFORD, COMMANDER OF APACHE SCOUTS, 1882-1886. *Arizona and the West 1964 6(1): 30-40.* Civil War veteran Emmet Crawford was assigned to cavalry duty against the Indians in the West in late 1870. In 1882, as military commandant of the San Carlos reservation in Arizona Territory, he enlisted Apache and trained them for service as scouts. In his efforts to work with civilian authorities to maintain peace and to make the Indians self-sustaining, and in his leadership of the scouts on campaigns with General George Crook throughout northern Mexico, Arizona, and New Mexico, Crawford earned the respect of soldiers and Indians alike. In pursuit of a Geronimo-led renegade band in northern Mexico in January 1886, Crawford was asked for a truce. Mexican irregulars came upon the scouts, and, in the confusion as to their identity, Crawford was mortally wounded by a Mexican bullet in a brief skirmish. Geronimo, who was prepared to surrender, was further pursued for several months before he finally capitulated. 2 illus., 40 notes. D. L. Smith

788. Nalty, Bernard C. and Strobridge, Truman R. THE DEFENSE OF SEATTLE, 1856: "AND DOWN CAME THE INDIANS." *Pacific Northwest Q. 1964 55(3): 105-110.* Describes the aggressiveness of Indians against the small settlement of Seattle in 1856 with details of the important role of the warship *Decatur*. Bibliography includes mostly primary sources. C. C. Gorchels

789. Nalty, Bernard C. and Strobridge, Truman R. EMMET CRAWFORD, PENNSYLVANIA VOLUNTEER TURNED INDIAN FIGHTER. *Pennsylvania Hist. 1966 33(2): 204-214.* Crawford entered the Union Army as a private and frequently saw action, particularly during the Peninsular Campaign and at Antietam. After the war, he was commissioned a second lieutenant in the Regular Army. With the Third Cavalry, he helped to round up the Apache in 1871, chased Cheyenne at the Kansas-Nebraska border in 1875, and saw action in the Sioux War of 1876. Promoted to captain in 1879, he became provost marshal at the San Carlos Apache Reservation in 1882, where he became known as a friend of the Indian. On 10 January 1886, he had succeeded in routing Geronimo's renegades and had received a peace feeler from the famed Apache leader. That night Mexican scalp-hunters attacked Crawford's scouts, and the captain was killed signaling to the Mexicans that his Apache were scouts. Had Crawford lived, the authors argue, Geronimo would have surrendered with little delay. Based largely on primary sources; 43 notes. D. C. Swift

790. Nichols, Roger L. THE ARMY AND THE INDIANS 1800-1830 - A REAPPRAISAL: THE MISSOURI VALLEY EXAMPLE. *Pacific Hist. R. 1972 41(2): 151-168.* A critique of the position that the Army played a major role in America's frontier advance. Using the experience of the military in the Missouri Valley as an example, the author concludes that the Army was generally unsuccessful in its relationship with the Indians. There was inability either to establish physical control of the region or to maintain peace among the tribes and between the Indians and whites. Evidence has not been presented to support the claim that the military was "an orderly purveyor of civilization." 55 notes. E. C. Hyslop

791. Nieberding, Velma. THE NEZ PERCE IN THE QUAPAW AGENCY. *Chronicles of Oklahoma 1966 44(1): 22-30.* After the famous two thousand mile retreat of Chief Joseph and the Nez Percé warriors, they surrendered in 1877 and were brought to the Quapaw Agency in 1878, staying there for a year. Chief Joseph and his people wanted to return to their tribal lands in Idaho or Oregon but General William T. Sherman was vengeful and they were sent to die in a malarial camp at Fort Leavenworth. Agent Hiram Jones was severe with the Nez Percé because Chief Joseph appealed directly to Washington. The Nez

Percé relinquished all claims to their lands and were transported to their new home in the Ponca Agency. Chief Joseph was a symbol of the heroism of his people who wanted only peace and a place where they could live as they had always lived. 24 notes. I. W. Van Noppen

792. Olmstead, Merle C. JOHN W. COMFORT: PORTRAIT OF A U. S. REGULAR, 1865-1892. *Military Collector and Historian 1968 20(4): 126-127.* A veteran of the Civil War, Comfort was in and out of the Regular Army until 1892. He served along the border and in the Indian campaigns. While in Texas he was awarded the Congressional Medal of Honor. Photographs show Comfort in the raffish costume of the 5th Cavalry and in the German-style dress cavalry uniform. 6 notes. D. C. Oliver

793. Olson, James C. THE "LASTING PEACE" OF FORT LARAMIE. *Am. West 1965 2(1): 46-53.* Despite the inconclusive army campaign of 1865 in its attempt to clear the Sioux and Cheyenne from the Powder River road to the Montana gold fields, army and Indian Bureau officials were hopeful of getting the Indians to quit the warpath and to agree to "a lasting peace." A June 1866 peace conference at Fort Laramie appeared to be making progress until the arrival of an army colonel in advance of a contingent of troops. This apparently upset a principal Sioux chief who withdrew from the council with his band. The treaty that was negotiated in 1868 was assented to by Indians who really had no stake in the Powder River area. Those concerned with the Powder River road stepped up their attacks on the army, culminating in a December massacre, the worst defeat the army had yet suffered in warfare with the Indians. Derived from a forthcoming book. Illus., biblio., note. D. L. Smith

794. Onstad, Preston E. CAMP HENDERSON, 1864. *Oregon Hist. Q. 1964 65(3): 297-302.* Description of a brief military expedition of the First Oregon Volunteer Cavalry against the Snake Indians in rugged countryside of eastern Oregon, 1864. C. C. Gorchels

795. Onstad, Preston E. THE FORT ON THE LUCKIAMUTE: A RESURVEY OF FORT HOSKINS. *Oregon Hist. Q. 1964 65(2): 173-196.* Detailed description of location and function of the US Army military establishment in Oregon, said to have been constructed to protect the native Indians from the white men. A "fort" in name only, the post was generally sparsely manned throughout its history, from 1857 to 1866, and was never the scene of any warfare. The most noted army officer stationed at the post was Philip H. Sheridan. Included are contemporary letters which describe the physical features and paraphernalia of the post. C. C. Gorchels

796. Parker, Henry S. HENRY LEAVENWORTH - PIONEER GENERAL. *Military R. 1970 50(12): 56-68.* Discusses the life and career of Brigadier General Henry Leavenworth in conjunction with the first observance of Founder's Day at Fort Leavenworth. Sketches Leavenworth's career and states his significance as a tireless worker for peace with the Indians, a strict disciplinarian, and founder of Fort Leavenworth, Kansas. G. E. Snow

797. Peters, Joseph P. MARCH OF THE MONTANA BATTALION. *Montana 1965 15(2): 38-51.* Résumé of an unofficial diary kept by Colonel Albert G. Brackett as he led four cavalry companies from southwestern Wyoming to Fort Ellis (Bozeman), Montana Territory in 1869. S. R. Davison

798. Pfaller, Louis "ENEMIES IN '76, FRIENDS IN '85 - SITTING BULL AND BUFFALO BILL. *Prologue: J. of the Nat. Archives 1969 1(2): 16-31.* Primarily discusses two episodes involving Sitting Bull and William F. Cody - the Chief's highly successful participation in Buffalo Bill's "Wild West Show" in 1885, and Cody's attempts to restrain Sitting Bull from causing trouble and to deliver him to the Army late in 1890 during the Indian "messiah craze." James McLaughlin, Indian agent, was deeply involved in both events. McLaughlin initially refused requests to exhibit Sitting Bull, fearing that publicity might make the Chief unmanageable. However, he later relented, hoping that exposure to civilized life might induce Sitting Bull to persuade his followers to pursue both education and farming. Because of the Chief's obnoxious behavior, however, upon returning to the reservation after the 1885 tour during which he had befriended Annie Oakley and during which he had met President Grover

Cleveland, McLaughlin refused to allow him to accompany later shows. During the 1890 craze, McLaughlin, fearing violence, was chiefly responsible for thwarting Cody's attempts to reach Sitting Bull. Based on records in the National Archives, the James McLaughlin Papers at Assumption Abbey Archives in Richardton, North Dakota, and some secondary sources; 8 illus., 43 notes.   W. R. Griffin

799. Pfaller, Louis L., ed. THE GALPIN JOURNAL: DRAMATIC RECORD OF AN ODYSSEY OF PEACE. *Montana 1968 18(2): 2-23.* In 1868 Father Pierre-Jean DeSmet traveled from Fort Rice, North Dakota, to the camp of hostile Sioux in southeastern Montana, to induce tribal leaders to attend a peace conference. Charles Galpin, a Fort Rice trader, served as guide and interpreter. To supplement his own notes, DeSmet asked Galpin to keep a record of the journey; this diary, discovered in Europe in 1924, provides the body of this article. In addition to extensive verbatim reports of speeches by Sitting Bull and other prominent Sioux, the document also supplies information on the land as it then appeared, circumstances of travel, habits of the Indians, and the personality of the missionary priest. Illus., map.   S. R. Davison

800. Pfaller, Louis. ROY P. JOHNSON. *North Dakota Hist. 1963 30(1): 5-16.* Beginning at age 46 to write historical articles with an account of the Battle of the Little Bighorn, Johnson became a storehouse of information about North Dakota's past. Prior to that time he had served in the US Navy during World War II, been a telegraph operator, and then a reporter for the *Fargo Forum.* His speech, "Digging for History," is quoted in full.   I. W. Van Noppen

801. Pfaller, Louis. SULLY'S EXPEDITION OF 1864 FEATURING THE KILLDEER MOUNTAIN AND BADLANDS BATTLES. *North Dakota Hist. 1964 31(1): 25-77.* The author admits that this account of the battles is a bit "white-flavored" since it was based on the diaries of white men who participated. After General Alfred Sully's indecisive campaign against the Sioux in 1863, he was determined to bring the tribes under control in 1864, and at the campaign's close he expressed satisfaction. Small Indian bands of raiders continued to harass white settlers, but as a unit they were no longer a threat. 16 illus., 4 maps, 150 notes.   I. W. Van Noppen

802. Rector, William G. THE RENO-BENTEEN DEFENSE PERIMETER. *Montana 1966 16(2): 65-72.* Modern research shows that some soldiers in Major Marcus A. Reno's command at the Little Big Horn were deployed in a position allowing only a limited field of fire. Casualty figures suggest that the Indians took advantage of this situation to sneak in close enough for effective shots at troops on the opposite side of the defense circle. Based on examination of the site, with some reference to standard printed sources.   S. R. Davison

803. Reese, J. W. OMV'S FORT HENRIETTA: ON WINTER DUTY, 1855-56. *Oregon Hist. Q. 1965 66(2): 133-160.* History of the construction of a military fort on the Umatilla River in Oregon and its use by the Oregon Mounted Volunteers during the Yakima Indian War of 1855-56. Incidents at the fort and nearby territory show harrassing actions of Indians.   C. C. Gorchels

804. Richards, Kent. ISAAC I. STEVENS AND FEDERAL MILITARY POWER IN WASHINGTON TERRITORY. *Pacific Northwest Q. 1972 63(3): 81-86.* Conflict occurred between Isaac Ingalls Stevens (1818-62), Governor of Washington Territory, and military officials in attitudes and activities toward Indians, 1854-57. Hostilities between newly-arriving white settlers and Indians in the Territory involved Stevens in treatymaking and close association with military men. Stevens was not successful in his efforts to accomplish peaceful accord because he lacked the capacity for cooperation, moderation, and compromise. Based mainly on letters in University of Washington libraries; 27 notes.   C. C. Gorchels

805. Rickey, Don, Jr. THE BATTLE OF WOLF MOUNTAIN. *Montana 1963 13(2): 44-54.* Relates the tactical details of a minor skirmish, important only because it marked the end of Sioux and Cheyenne resistance which had continued since the Custer Battle the previous summer. On 8 January 1877, Colonel Nelson A. Miles led a small infantry force against the winter camp of Chiefs Crazy Horse and Big Crow on the Tongue River near present Birney, Montana. Casualties amounted to

two or three dead on each side and a few wounded. Routing of the Indians from their camp and loss of their supplies, coupled with the demoralizing effect of Big Crow's death, led to the band's surrender within the next few weeks. Principal source is official reports, augmented by unpublished first-hand accounts.   S. R. Davison

806. Rickey, Don, Jr. MYTH TO MONUMENT: THE ESTABLISHMENT OF CUSTER BATTLEFIELD NATIONAL MONUMENT. *J. of the West 1968 7(2): 203-216.* Gives a brief description of the action between the 7th Cavalry and the Sioux on 25 June 1876 which resulted in the death of Custer and five companies of cavalry under his command. Sentiment for a national memorial to Custer and his men began within weeks after the action, but it was not until 1940 that it was set aside as a part of the National Park System (it had been a National Cemetery since 1879).   R. N. Alvis

807. Rowen, Richard D., ed. THE SECOND NEBRASKA'S CAMPAIGN AGAINST THE SIOUX. *Nebraska Hist. 1963 44(1): 3-53.* A journal, a diary, and a series of drawings, all previously unpublished, by the colonel in command, a corporal, and a private, respectively, illuminate the activities of the Second Nebraska Volunteer Infantry in 1863 in Dakota Territory in the campaign to crush the Sioux uprising.   R. Lowitt

808. Schoenberger, Dale T. CUSTER'S SCOUTS. *Montana 1966 16(2): 40-49.* Accounts for the action of each of the 39 scouts who went into the Little Big Horn battle with Custer in 1876. In general, their conduct was praiseworthy. Undocumented.   S. R. Davison

809. Shearer, George M. THE BATTLE OF VINEGAR HILL. *Idaho Yesterdays 1968 12(1): 17-21.* The author's eyewitness account of the defeat of the mounted infantry high on a ridge removed from water. Held down by the Sheepeater Indians, the soldiers had only vinegar to drink, but they escaped in the night after a 14-hour siege. This defeat of the Army in Idaho led to a general court-martial for the commanding officer. Shearer considered him a "coward," and "totally unfit to take command of any body of troops."   G. Barrett

810. Sidwa, Anne H. JOSEPH KARGE: 1823-1892. *New Jersey Hist. Soc. Pro. 1963 81(4): 247-255.* Political activities after his university years resulted in his fleeing from Poland to New York in 1851. In 1861 he was assigned as Lieutenant Colonel to the first New Jersey cavalry. He was severely wounded in August 1862 but returned to the field and fought in the Valley of the Shenandoah and at Fredericksburg. He continued to see successful service in the field until November 1865. In 1867 he took post command of Camp Winfield Scott in Nevada, where his tact in dealing with the Indians won their affection. In 1870 he was called to Princeton University to teach continental languages. Documented.   E. P. Stickney

811. Sievers, Michael A. SANDS OF SAND CREEK. *Colorado Mag. 1972 49(2): 116-142.* Discusses the readily accessible important works on the "Sand Creek Massacre" of 1864 as they relate to the controversies over certain key topics. Argues that "most historians have been concerned primarily with the conspiracy-hostility theory, the peacefulness of the Indians at Sand Creek, rational explanations for 'atrocities,' Sand Creek as the cause of a general uprising, and who and what should be held responsible for the whole affair." The recent trend is for professional historians, removed in space and time and influenced by a growing concern for minority history and emphasis upon multicausation, to use more freely the records of the Bureau of Indian Affairs and the War Department. Based on secondary sources; 7 illus., 44 notes.   O. H. Zabel

812. Smith, Cornelius C., Jr. CROOK AND CRAZY HORSE. *Montana 1966 16(2): 14-26.* Two indecisive battles, fought in the same year and in the same vicinity as Custer's famous fight, contributed to that disaster. A victory by troops under General George Crook at either the Powder River or Rosebud battles in the spring and summer, respectively, of 1876, would have prevented the Custer affair.   S. R. Davison

813. Smith, Ralph A. THE SCALP HUNTER IN THE BORDERLANDS, 1835-1850. *Arizona and the West 1964 6(1): 5-22.* From the late 18th century Apache and Comanche Indians crossed the present

U.S.-Mexico boundary to terrorize much of northern Mexico. Destruction of life and property was probably greater in the 1840's than in any other decade. There were over 10 major plunder trails used by the marauders to transport the stolen livestock and other loot. The Mexican states of Sonora, Chihuahua, Coahuila, and Durango launched extensive scalp bounty systems to eliminate the raiders or to cow them into a cessation of their activities. The scalp industry boomed, especially as some unemployed Americans during the Panic of 1837 seized this opportunity for quick riches. James "Don Santiago" Kirker was the most famous of these entrepreneurs, making a systematic business out of it, even working at times for the Indians against the Mexicans. There was a reward of several thousands of dollars posted a number of times for Kirker's scalp. Ironically, during the Mexican War when Mexican authorities were unable to pursue the bounty system because of involvements with American armies, the Yankee enemy gave the Mexican countryside more security from the Indians than it had had for many years. When not battling Mexicans the Americans found sport in fighting the Indian marauders. Although Mexico continued to have troubles with these Indians until the 1880's, the scalp bounty industry phase ended almost completely in the spring of 1850. The source of supply had been seriously decimated and "unethical" practices were making it unhealthy for American bounty hunters. Illus., map, 41 notes.   D. L. Smith

814.   Stevens, Robert C.   THE APACHE MENACE IN SONORA, 1831-1849.   *Arizona and the West 1964 6(3): 211-222.* Civil strife weakened Sonora, Mexico, economically and militarily to such an extent that the state was unable to organize an effective defense against Arizona and New Mexico-based Apache raiders in the 20 years following Mexican independence. The Apache swept down on Sonora from their north-of-the-border mountain retreats, raiding and pillaging almost at will. No relief was forthcoming from Mexico City. The devastation of the marauders was so appalling and furious that the line of settlement in the state receded southward while other parts of the nation were gaining rapidly in settlement. Attacks continued almost unchecked until the 1850's when Apache enmity shifted to westward advancing Anglo-Americans. 33 notes.   D. L. Smith

815.   Stewart, Edgar I.   THE CUSTER BATTLE AND WIDOW'S WEEDS.   *Montana 1972 22(1): 52-59.* The families of the men killed in the Battle of the Little Big Horn in 1876 were left destitute. Since the 7th Cavalry had been nearly wiped out, little help could come from the customary source of donations from within the regiment. A month after the battle, the *Army and Navy Journal* started a drive for funds to provide emergency support. Men throughout the Army responded generously, as did some Navy personnel and a number of civilians; several corporate donations were for major amounts. Yet the total of 14 thousand dollars was small in terms of the need. A count showed 24 widows and twice as many children, about 15 of the families being those of enlisted men. There is evidence that Mrs. Custer and two other widows whose officer husbands had carried insurance offered to forego their shares of the fund in favor of soldiers' survivors. Based on files of the *Army and Navy Journal.*   S. R. Davison

816.   Stewart, Edgar I.   THE LITTLE BIG HORN: 90 YEARS LATER.   *Montana 1966 16(2): 2-13.* Factual and interpretive summary of events culminating in the Battle of the Little Big Horn on 25 June 1876. Lt. Colonel George A. Custer and five companies of his 7th Cavalry were annihilated, while a secondary command under Major Marcus A. Reno and Captain Frederick W. Benteen suffered heavy losses in a separate engagement a few miles away. Almost at once, controversy developed over several aspects of the affair, and none of the questions seemed near settlement as the 90th anniversary approached. Illustrated with portraits and photographs.   S. R. Davison

817.   Stewart, Edgar I.   A PSYCHOANALYTICAL APPROACH TO CUSTER: SOME REFLECTIONS.   *Montana 1971 (3): 74-77.* The author, a historian, takes exception to the psychiatrist's findings that early childhood influences determined Custer's performance in the Sioux War of 1876. Discusses factual matters involved in the attack by Custer's men and the ensuing battle in which the whole command was killed.
                                    S. R. Davison

818.   Stewart, Kenneth M.   A BRIEF HISTORY OF THE MOHAVE INDIANS SINCE 1850.   *Kiva 1969 34(4): 219-236.* "Descriptions of

Mohave culture in the middle of the nineteenth century are contained in such writings as [R. B.] Stratton's account of the captivity of the Oatman girls [*The Captivity of the Oatman Girls,* 1857], the reports of railroad surveyors ([Lorenzo] Sitgreaves and [Amiel Weeks] Whipple) and accounts of the steamboat captains ([Joseph C.] Ives). The long period of intertribal warfare was ending, but the apprehensive Mohave fought the white intruders on several occasions before they were finally subdued. Reservations were established, but the Mohave had to undergo many hardships before making a better adjustment to changing times."   J

819.   Tate, Michael L.   FRONTIER DEFENSE ON THE COMANCHE RANGES OF NORTHWEST TEXAS, 1846-1860.   *Great Plains J. 1971 11(1): 41-56.* Surveys the various attempts to protect the northwest Texas frontier during the first 15 years of statehood (1846-60). Describes the ineffectiveness of the US Army and its frequent augmentation with State rangers. Treaty attempts and establishment of reservations were also ineffective. Solution of the situation did not occur during the period. However, an attempted offensive policy and certain logistical information acquired then made termination of Indian domination in northwest Texas possible in the 1870's. Based on primary and secondary sources; 58 notes.   O. H. Zabel

820.   Taylor, Morris.   ACTION AT FORT MASSACHUSETTS: THE INDIAN CAMPAIGN OF 1855.   *Colorado Mag. 1965 42(4): 292-310.* A reinterpretation of the Indian campaigns of 1855 throughout southern Colorado, using heretofore overlooked primary sources - the personal letters of DeWitt Peters (assistant surgeon attached to the campaigns) and observations of Rafael Chacon (a participant in the campaigns). They were successfully directed against the Moache Utes and Jicarilla Apaches, leading to the cessation of hostilities by these two tribes against the white people.   R. Sexauer

821.   Taylor, Morris F.   CAMPAIGNS AGAINST THE JICARILLA APACHE, 1854.   *New Mexico Hist R. 1969 44(4): 269-291.* Examines the Jicarilla Apache raids in 1854 - their background and the reactions to them. The trouble began in February with a raid on cattle belonging to Samuel B. Watrous, and ended with a massacre of the inhabitants of a small fur traders' post, Fort Pueblo, on Christmas Day. Military units from Fort Union pursued the Indians and fought several engagements without decisive results during 1854. Based on documents in the National Archives; 70 notes.   D. F. Henderson

822.   Taylor, Morris F.   CAMPAIGNS AGAINST THE JICARILLA APACHE, 1855.   *New Mexico Hist. R. 1970 45(2): 119-136.* Describes the spring 1855 campaign against the Mohuache Ute and the Jicarilla Apache Indians. Colonel Thomas T. Fauntleroy, First Dragoons, was given command of the campaign and was assisted by both regular army troops and a battalion of New Mexican Volunteers under the command of Lieutenant Colonel Ceran St. Vrain. St. Vrain's volunteers never inflicted a defeat on the Jicarilla of sufficient certitude to end their depredations. Colonel Fauntleroy and his mixed force, however, dealt the Mohuache Ute heavy blows so that they quickly became peaceful. Treaties were eventually signed with both Indian groups, but were not ratified by the U.S. Senate. 59 notes.   D. F. Henderson

823.   Taylor, Morris F.   KA-NI-ACHE.   *Colorado Mag. 1966 43(4): 275-302, 44(2): 139-161.* Part I. Surveys the origins of a skirmish between the Moache Utes under Ka-ni-ache and the U.S. Cavalry under Colonel A. J. Anderson at Trinidad on 3 October 1866. The author presents a history of the Moache tribe and a biographical sketch of Ka-ni-ache. He suggests that the chief cause of this skirmish was the raids the Moaches, compelled by hunger, had been making. Illus., 19 notes. Part II. Traces the activities of Ka-ni-ache, the leading chief of the Moache Utes from 1866 until his death in 1880. Pressures for the removal of the Utes to reservations were mounting, and, while a treaty for such a purpose was negotiated in 1868, the government did not have its way until 1877. Such questions as the size and location of the reservation and the terms of the treaty were constantly disputed. In 1874 a new treaty was made and the chiefs agreed to a reduction of their former claims. 7 illus., 141 notes.
                                    I. W. Van Noppen

824.   Taylor, Morris F.   THE MAIL STATION AND THE MILITARY AT CAMP ON PAWNEE FORK, 1859-1860.   *Kansas Hist. Q. 1970 36(1): 27-39.* An account of the military forces that provided protec-

tion for the U.S. mails moving along a 150-mile stretch of the Santa Fe Trail during the Kiowa and Comanche uprising during 1859-60. This protective measure is shown to have been largely ineffective because of bad weather conditions, an insufficient number of troops along the portion of the trail being protected, a lack of escort from Pawnee Fork eastward to Council Grove, and the uncertainty of making connections with patrols coming northward from Fort Union in New Mexico Territory. Based on books, articles, local newspapers, and records of the Office of Indian Affairs, Office of the Adjutant General and U.S. Army Command, and Department of Missouri records in the National Archives; 57 notes.
                                                    W. F. Zornow

825.   Thane, James L., Jr.   THE MONTANA "INDIAN WAR" OF 1867.   *Arizona and the West 1968 10(2): 153-170.* In the spring of 1867, a rumor started with the Army at Fort C. F. Smith in Montana Territory that an all-out uprising of 11 thousand Sioux Indians was being planned. Territorial officials barraged Washington with letters and telegrams demanding that the Regular Army take the field. Meanwhile steps were taken to raise a local volunteer force to protect the threatened settlements until the Army should arrive. The confusion and breakdown in communications between territorial and Federal officials resulted in a so-called "Indian War." Only a few minor raids occurred in the summer of 1867. Four Indians were killed. Montana Territory expended over a million dollars in its efforts. The Federal Government eventually reimbursed Montana for about half of the amount. 7 illus., 42 notes.
                                                    D. L. Smith

826.   Thetford, Francis.   BATTLE OF THE WASHITA CENTENNIAL, 1968.   *Chronicles of Oklahoma 1968 46(4): 358-361.* Some 3,500 spectators observed the 1968 reenactment of Custer's attack on Black Kettle's small Cheyenne village. The "nucleus of the pageant's attacking force was an organization of young Californians operating out of Los Angeles County under the formal name of U.S. 7th Cavalry Association, Grand Army of the Republic, Reactivated." Later in the afternoon came the solemn Indian burial service of the remains of an unknown Indian, "in commemoration of Chief Black Kettle and the Cheyenne tribal members who lost their lives in the Battle of Washita." The services were directed by an ordained Mennonite minister, himself a Cheyenne and a member of the Oklahoma Indian Affairs Commission. Illus.
                                                    E. P. Stickney

827.   Thrapp, Dan L.   DAN O'LEARY, ARIZONA SCOUT: A VIGNETTE.   *Arizona and the West 1965 7(4): 287-298.* Dan O'Leary's youth and last days are shrouded in mystery and obscurity. During his prime, however, he was an outstanding figure of the Southwest. Arriving in Arizona sometime in the 1850's or 1860's, he acquired guide and scout experience, probably for the Army. He scouted for the Army against hostile Indians, was a guide to a railroad survey across northern Arizona, freighted for the Army and local merchants, piloted wagon trains through dangerous areas, tracked Indian thieves, became a friend and confidante of unfortunate Indians, probably named Tombstone, and traveled over much of the Southwest. Many of these items can be authenticated, although some of the stories about O'Leary are probably legend. 38 notes.
                                                    D. L. Smith

828.   Tyler, Barbara Ann.   COCHISE: APACHE WAR LEADER, 1858-1861.   *J. of Arizona Hist. 1965 6(1): 1-10.* The frequently explored "Bascom affair" - an incident named after Lieutenant George N. Bascom which resulted in a number of dead, both soldiers and Indians - is presented as an event which brought Cochise to the front rank of Apache leadership. Relying on recent reexaminations by other historians, the writer emphasizes that "the Bascom affair merely gave Cochise a motive for revenge," and did not transform him into a hostile, for he had raided American settlements prior to February 1861, when the altercation with Lieutenant Bascom occurred. A few footnotes to published sources, one to government (National Archives) sources.
                                                    J. D. Filipiak

829.   Unrah, William F.   INDIAN AGENT VS. THE ARMY: BACKGROUND NOTES ON THE KIOWA-COMANCHE TREATY OF 1865.   *Kansas Hist. Q. 1964 30(2): 129-152.* It is too easy to see the Indian problem of 1865 as a simple one to be solved either by military force or treaties and civilian control. The debate over whether the War or Interior Department should control Indian affairs was complicated by such factors as the difficulty and cost of conducting military operations

in an era when men were tired of war and anxious to economize, an era of corruption, illicit livestock trade, land claims, town rivalries, and railroad speculation. The army was not anxious to fight, and other interests demanded peace. Jesse Leavenworth (1807-85) negotiated the treaty. The army criticized him, but actually his treaty gave military men time to build up their forces for a later war and, in the meantime, saved the country much added expense. Based on records from the National Archives.
                                                    W. F. Zornow

830.   Utley, Robert M., ed.   CAPTAIN JOHN POPE'S PLAN OF 1853 FOR THE FRONTIER DEFENSE OF NEW MEXICO.   *Arizona and the West 1963 5(2): 149-163.* Brevet Captain John Pope of the Corps of Topographical Engineers worked on mapping missions, surveying boundaries, and making railroad surveys on the western military scene during the 1850's. After more than two years in New Mexico he was so concerned with the Indian problems that plagued the territory that he formulated an unsolicited plan to solve them. His observations were "acute" and his solutions were "well-reasoned." Pope's recommendations concerning communications, defense, deployment of troops, relations with the Indians, and other details were never adopted. Map, 26 notes.
                                                    D. L. Smith

831.   Utley, Robert M.   CUSTER: HERO OR BUTCHER?   *Am. Hist. Illus. 1971 5(10): 4-9, 43-48.* Summarizes the image of Major General George Armstrong Custer with a focus on his career as an Indian fighter from 1867 to June 1876. Historians have had as much difficulty in judging Custer as his contemporaries did. There are still those who are either Custerphobes or Custerphiles, although the current emphasis on Red History and the Vietnam War is not likely to improve the image of an Indian-fighting cavalryman. Other field commanders deserved equal or greater recognition but they lacked the distinctive personal style that captures popular fancy - and an autobiography, and wife-biographer. Yet Custer's attitudes that Indians should be civilized under Army guidance, combined with his admiration for many Indian customs as well as their physical proficiencies, were contradictions shared by most frontier commanders. Based on primary and secondary sources; 11 illus.
                                                    D. B. Dodd

832.   Utley, Robert M.   "PECOS BILL" ON THE TEXAS FRONTIER.   *Am. West 1969 6(1): 4-13, 61-62.* William R. Shafter had risen to the brevet rank of brigadier general in the Michigan Volunteers in the Civil War. Under the 1869 reorganization of the Army he was commissioned a lieutenant colonel of infantry. His assignment was to one of four Negro regiments garrisoning the little frontier forts of the West and fighting hostile Indians over the next three decades. Except for a brief period in Dakota, Pecos Bill Shafter's role in the opening of the West was played out largely on the sterile frontiers of Texas and Mexico. Ironically, one minority (black troops) was being used to subjugate another minority (Indians). This was compounded by the increasing employment of Indian scouts by the Army against the Indians. The use of black troops was "a calculated humiliation" against conquered Texans but it was turned to discrimination against the blacks who for nearly two decades were left to police the most disagreeable sectors of the American frontier. Tough, aggessive, and persevering, Shafter enjoyed the respect, if rarely the affection, of his troops and fellow officers. Although his racism was barely concealed, he still proved an effective commander of Negro troops. Shafter was one of the frontier Army's more effective leaders. Heretofore this has been larely unknown and his chief claim to fame has been that of a caricatured figure in the Spanish-American War. 7 illus., map, biblio. note.
                                                    D. L. Smith

833.   Utley, Robert M.   THE SURRENDER OF GERONIMO.   *Arizoniana 1963 4(1): 1-9.* In 1876, after the Federal Government moved the Apache Indians from the Chiricahua Mountains to San Carlos, a group of so-called "renegades" under Geronimo began a reign of terror that lasted three years. The successful attack upon them in 1886 was led by Brigadier General Nelson A. Miles in a difficult campaign demanding the utmost in endurance and perseverance from the men under his command because of the climate, terrain, and nature of the enemy. The details are based largely on Miles' *Personal Recollections* (1897) which included Capt. Leonard Wood's narrative. Illus.
                                                    E. P. Stickney

834.   Valputic, Marian E., ed. and Longfellow, Harold H., ed.   THE FIGHT AT CHIRICAHUA PASS IN 1869 AS DESCRIBED BY

L. L. DORR, M.D. *Arizona and the West 1971 13(4): 369-378.* In early October 1869 Apache murdered stagecoach passengers in southern Arizona, wrested control over a nearby herd of cattle, and began to drive the herd southward. While recovering the herd, Camp Bowie troops discovered what they believed to be an Apache stronghold near Chiricahua Pass. On 24 October a detachment of cavalry and a pack train rode eastward out of Camp Crittenden to strengthen the Bowie assault on the stronghold. Dr. Levi L. Dorr, who was with the Crittenden party, described the highlights of the expedition in a letter to a friend. Reproduced and edited here, the letter portrays the magnitude of the Apache menace in Arizona in 1869. Illus., map, 34 notes.   D. L. Smith

835.   Walker, Don D., ed.   COWBOYS, INDIANS & CAVALRY: A CATTLEMAN'S ACCOUNT OF THE FIGHTS OF 1884. *Utah Hist. Q. 1966 34(3): 255-262.* Contains an explanatory introduction and the text of a letter written by Harold Carlisle and published in the *Denver Republican* on 29 July 1884 describing a fight between several cattlemen and a group of Ute Indians near Durango, Colorado.

S. L. Jones

836.   Walker, Henry P.   BUGLER! NO PAY CALL TODAY! *Montana 1971 21(3): 34-43.* Conflict between President Rutherford Birchard Hayes and the Democrat majority in the House led to a deadlock over Army legislation in 1877 and to suspension of pay after 30 June, until mid-November. That was an active summer for the military, including the Nez Percé campaign in the Northwest and 18 engagements against the Nez Percé and other Indians. Despite the absence of pay, the Army continued to serve. "Certainly no clearer example could be found of the loyalty of the officers and men who carried on for some six months without pay or even a definite promise of pay. It is difficult to imagine the behavior of a factory worker or ribbon clerk under like circumstances, 95 years later!" Based on government documents and the writings of army personnel; illus., 33 notes.   S. R. Davison

837.   Walker, Henry P.   GEORGE CROOK: THE "GRAY FOX," PRUDENT, COMPASSIONATE INDIAN FIGHTER. *Montana 1967 17(2): 2-13.* Summarizes the career of George Crook, with some details of his campaigns and battles in Arizona, Wyoming, and Montana. The author rejects accusations that Crook was timid, and defends his record. Derived from standard published accounts of the Indian Wars, illus., 53 notes.   S. R. Davison

838.   Wallace, Ernest and Anderson, Adrian S.   R. S. MACKENZIE AND THE KICKAPOOS: THE RAID INTO MEXICO IN 1873. *Arizona and the West 1965 7(2): 105-126.* Indian hostilities increased steadily on the undefended Texas frontier after the Civil War. In response to mounting pleas that the distress be removed, the army established a line of posts across West Texas. This did not include what was called the Upper Rio Grande Border Region, an area from Laredo to Del Rio on the Rio Grande extending about 100 miles into Texas - a sparsely settled but well-stocked region. Forays made by Mexico-based Kickapoo Indians, with the connivance of Mexican officials, thoroughly terrorized the ranchers. In 1873 Cavalry Colonel Ranald S. Mackenzie was ordered to attack the Kickapoo villages some 35 miles across the border in the Mexican state of Coahuila. Although a jingoist Texas Congressman urged annexation of parts of northern Mexico and newspapers reported military plans of some magnitude on both sides of the border, the purpose of Mackenzie's expedition was to restore peace and order by removing the Kickapoo menace. The May 1873 raid destroyed the Kickapoo villages, forced them to remove to a reservation in the United States, and led to a revision of Mexican border policies. Based on government documents, Department of State files (microfilm), and newspaper accounts; illus., map, 65 notes.   D. L. Smith

839.   Watson, Chandler B.   RECOLLECTIONS OF THE BANNOCK WAR. *Oregon Hist. Q. 1967 68(4): 317-329.* Personal experiences of the author during a period of friction, 1877-79, with Indians in southern Oregon. Raids on cattle and depredation of settlements made living hazardous for the white man in the midst of unfriendly Indians, but actual violence was limited.   C. C. Gorchels

840.   Wells, Merle W.   THE NEZ PERCE AND THEIR WAR. *Pacific Northwest Q. 1964 55(1): 35-37.* Indians were in no sense engaged in warfare when US troops pursued fleeing Nez Percé 1,500 miles to the Canadian border in 1877. Individualism and relationship of warriors to chiefs is clearly expounded.   C. C. Gorchels

841.   Wertenberger, Mildred.   FORT TOTTEN, DAKOTA TERRITORY, 1867. *North Dakota Hist. 1967 34(2): 125-146.* A discussion of the history of Fort Totten, the most perfectly preserved military post on the Indian frontier. Founded in 1867 as a part of the military posts built for the protection of the overland route from southern Minnesota into western Montana, the fort went the way of many frontier posts when, after its abandonment in 1890, it became part of the Fort Totten Military Reservation for the Sioux Indians within the area. Today the fort is preserved as a historical site under the auspices of the North Dakota Historical Society. Included are photographs of individuals connected with the fort and of the fort as it stands today. Maps, photos, 45 notes.   R. Sexauer

842.   West, G. Derek.   THE BATTLE OF SAPPA CREEK (1875). *Kansas Hist. Q. 1968 34(2): 150-178.* A detailed account of a small engagement in Kansas on 23 April 1875 between some Cheyenne warriors and a small detachment of US regulars and civilians. Drawing upon the accounts written by four participants in the engagement, the author tries to show that the facts concerning the location of the battle, the size of the Indian encampment, the identity of the Indians involved, the number of Indian casualties, and the identity of the civilian participants have been incorrectly given by modern writers on Western lore who have relied on hearsay for their versions of the battle. Based on articles, books, and official records; illus., 71 notes.   W. F. Zornow

843.   White, Lonnie J.   THE BATTLE OF BEECHER'S ISLAND: THE SCOUTS HOLD FAST ON THE ARICKAREE. *J. of the West 1966 5(1): 1-24.* Indian depredations in Kansas and Colorado resulted in Major General Philip Sheridan's directing Major George A. Forsyth to employ 50 frontiersmen to be used as scouts against the hostiles. Securing his men, Forsyth, with Lieutenant Frederick Beecher as second-in-command, left Fort Wallace, Kansas, on 10 September 1868, in an attempt to locate the Indians. On 16 September the scouts camped on the Arickaree Fork of the Republican River in present Colorado. At daybreak on 17 September the scouts were attacked by several hundred Cheyenne, Arapaho, and Sioux. Retreating to a small island in the Arickaree, the scouts repulsed several charges by the Indians. Two scouts slipped through the Indian lines to seek assistance. On 21 September the main body of Indians withdrew, but the scouts remained on the island, subsequently named for Beecher who was killed in the fight, until a relief column reached them on 25 September. Because of its sensational nature, this battle became one of the best known Indian fights of all time. Based on material in the Kansas State Archives, illus., maps, 56 notes.

D. N. Brown

844.   White, Lonnie J.   FROM BLOODLESS TO BLOODY: THE THIRD COLORADO CAVALRY AND THE SAND CREEK MASSACRE.   *J. of the West 1967 6(4): 535-581.* Details the relations between Indians and whites in Colorado during the two years preceding the battle between the Third Colorado Cavalry and the Cheyennes on Sand Creek in November 1864 and concludes that the commander of the Third, Colonel John M. Chivington, may have been motivated by the hope that a decisive victory would advance his political fortunes. The author details the battle and the controversy which resulted from it, suggesting that the massacre might not have been so controversial had it not been for the political and personal animosities prevalent in Colorado at that time and had the Third not attacked a village that had seemingly been granted temporary immunity. He maintains that other politicians and military men, as well as all the white inhabitants of Colorado, must share the blame with Chivington if Sand Creek is to be condemned. He does not believe that the subsequent investigations of the affairs were thorough or objective. Based on newspaper and government reports as well as secondary sources, map, illus., 86 notes.   D. N. Brown

845.   White, Lonnie J.   THE HANCOCK AND CUSTER EXPEDITIONS OF 1867. *J. of the West 1966 5(3): 355-378.* Depredations of scattered bands of Cheyenne, Sioux, and Kiowa committed in 1865 and 1866 caused many frontiersmen and local military commanders to believe that the Indians would eventually embark on a full-scale war on the Southern Plains. Major General Winfield S. Hancock, commander of the Department of the Missouri, concluded the Indians meant to take the

warpath in the spring of 1867. To forestall this, Hancock led an expedition to convince the Indians that further hostile acts would be punished. Part of his command included four companies of the Seventh Cavalry under Lieutenant Colonel George Custer. The author gives a detailed account of the movement of this expedition. He concludes that neither Hancock's nor a subsequent expedition led by Custer succeeded in accomplishing its objectives. Hancock's unduly harsh attitude and rash actions provoked an Indian uprising rather than preventing one. Nor was Custer successful in punishing the Cheyenne and Sioux or in relieving pressure on the overland road. Based on published sources, illus., 37 notes.

D. N. Brown

846. White, Lonnie J. INDIAN BATTLES IN THE TEXAS PANHANDLE, 1874. *J. of the West 1967 6(2): 278-309.* In May and June of 1874 there began what was to be the last major Indian uprising on the Southern Plains. This Red River Indian War resulted from the dissatisfaction of the Kiowas, Comanches, and Cheyennes with the policies of the government and their concern over the continued slaughter of the buffalo by hidehunters. The most spectacular of the battles were fought in the Texas Panhandle. They included the Battle of Adobe Wells which was fought between hunters and representatives of five tribes in late June and early July; the first Battle of Palo Duro Canyon fought in late August; the Battle of Lyman's Wagon Train in early September; the Battles of Buffalo Wallow and Price's Fight in September; and the second Battle of Palo Duro Canyon which occurred late in that month. The author details all of these fights and some other minor skirmishes. The defeats suffered by the Indians ended their last stand in this area. Based on published sources, illus., 61 notes.

D. N. Brown

847. White, Lonnie J. WARPATHS ON THE SOUTHERN PLAINS: THE BATTLES OF SALINE RIVER AND PRAIRIE DOG CREEK. *J. of the West 1965 4(4): 485-503.* In 1867 Kansas was feeling the effect of raids conducted by bands of Sioux, Cheyenne, and Kiowa. Efforts were made by the U.S. Army to bring the hostiles under control, and this article details the result. In August 1867 cavalry units were attacked and defeated by the Indians in battles on the Saline River and Prairie Dog Creek in northwestern Kansas. The author concludes that the failure to punish the hostiles in 1867 made necessary Major General Philip H. Sheridan's winter campaign of 1868-69. Based principally on records in the War Department and National Archives, illus., map, 33 notes.

D. N. Brown

848. White, Lonnie J. WINTER CAMPAIGNING WITH SHERIDAN AND CUSTER: THE EXPEDITION OF THE NINETEENTH KANSAS VOLUNTEER CAVALRY. *J. of the West 1967 6(1): 68-98.* As a result of Indian forays in Kansas during the summer of 1868, General Philip Sheridan decided to conduct a winter campaign to punish the hostiles. Governor Samuel Crawford of Kansas offered to organize a regiment of volunteers which would augment the regular Army and, when the offer was accepted, resigned as governor to accept appointment as the regiment's colonel. Early in November the regiment, numbering slightly over twelve hundred men, was ordered to join the forces under Colonel George Custer at Camp Supply in Indian Territory. Due to the ineptitude of the guides, a raging storm, and the weak condition of the regiment's mounts, it arrived too late to participate in Custer's attack on Black Kettle's camp on the Washita. Later, however, the regiment marched with Sheridan and Custer through the western and southern part of the Indian Territory. The author concludes that, while the volunteers did not engage the Indians in combat, the additional strength they gave to Custer's expedition caused the hostiles to abandon any thought of resistance. Based largely on published sources, illus., 62 notes.

D. N. Brown

849. Wilson, John, ed. PRISONERS WITHOUT WALLS. *Palacio 1967 74(1): 10-28.* Reprints a report by Major Henry Davies Wallen (d. 1886) to the Assistant Adjutant General at Military Headquarters in Santa Fe, New Mexico. Wallen was the second commandant at Fort Sumner, assuming the post in November 1863. The letter describes in fairly accurate terms the social structure of the Navajo, who were then interned there, and of the Mescalero Apache. It provides a good deal of ethnographic information on these two Indian groups, and it is also helpful in understanding the Bosque Redondo chapter in the struggle between the Indians and the Anglo-Americans. Illus., biblio.

S. A. Eger

850. Wilson, Wesley C. THE U.S. ARMY AND THE PIEGANS - THE BAKER MASSACRE OF 1870. *North Dakota Hist. 1965 32(1): 40-58.* The massacre of 173 men, women, and children in their camp on a bitterly cold morning, by U.S. soldiers under Colonel Eugene M. Baker, was in retaliation for the murder of two white men by Piegan Indians. Baker was praised by his superior officers, but when public opinion in the East denounced the heartless affair a demand arose for a modified Indian policy, already put into planning by an Indian Commission appointed by President Grant. Because of the influence of humanitarians, several changes were made. Army officers were excluded from being Indian agents. Efforts were made to civilize the Indians, teach them skills, and prepare them for living in accordance with the standards of the white community. Treaties with tribes were discontinued and Indians were treated as individual members of society. The Piegan Massacre contributed impetus to the reform. 3 illus., 40 notes.

I. W. Van Noppen

851. Wiltsey, Norman B. PLENTY COUPS: CROW CHIEF. *Montana 1963 13(4): 28-39.* From early childhood, Plenty Coups showed the intelligence and adaptability that characterized his leadership of the Crow tribe in the years 1875-1932. Almost alone among Indian leaders, he chose a path of collaboration, appeasement and surrender, rather than one of resistance to the whites. This policy spared the Crows the wars and defeats that destroyed so many other tribes, and enabled his people to retain their traditional land as a reservation. Undocumented except for limited citation of newspaper dispatches covering one episode.

S. R. Davison

852. Woolworth, Alan. A DISGRACEFUL PROCEEDING. *Beaver 1969 299(spring): 54-59.* The dispersal of the Sioux that followed their Minnesota uprising in 1862 saw many of them as unwanted visitors in the Red River country. Two of the leaders, Little Six and Medicine Bottle, were kidnapped from there by American military men acting in concert with Canadian settlers. They were taken to Fort Snelling, Minnesota, where, after a lengthy trial, they were hanged for atrocities committed in the uprising. Illus.

L. F. S. Upton

853. Worcester, Donald E. SPOTTED TAIL: WARRIOR, DIPLOMAT. *Am. West 1964 1(4): 38-46, 87. Sinte Galeski* or Spotted Tail was a chief of the numerous and powerful horse and buffalo culture, Brulé Sioux of the High Plains. In 1854 he led a party that killed or fatally wounded all the 30 soldiers sent from Fort Laramie to arrest a Sioux who violated a treaty agreement which guaranteed emigrant safe passage across Sioux territory. Incarcerated at Fort Leavenworth he concluded it was futile for the Sioux to continue resisting the whites. Pardoned in 1856, he returned to his people and urged them to live in peace with the whites. The Sioux seemed justified in their hostility, and it was with considerable difficulty that Spotted Tail kept his friendly Brulés intact through the trying aggravations caused by Chivington and others. He resisted government efforts to convert his people to agriculture; and with several trips to Washington and other means, he gained concessions and slowed the process. He guided the Sioux through the difficult adjustment to reservation life and avoided open warfare that would have been disastrous. His death in 1881 at the hands of a rival did not end his policies and program. Illus., bibliographical note.

D. L. Smith

854. Wright, Peter M. THE PURSUIT OF DULL KNIFE FROM FORT RENO IN 1878-1879. *Chronicles of Oklahoma 1968 46(2): 141-154.* After the Battle of the Little Bighorn in 1876, American troops pursued and separated the Sioux and Cheyenne Indians into smaller groups. In the peace settlement that followed it was decided that the Northern Cheyenne should rejoin their southern kinsmen in Indian Territory. About half of the band, a faction led by Dull Knife, were restive and wanted to return to Sioux territory in the northern Plains. When they defied orders and fled in late 1878 they were pursued by Fort Reno-based troops. A network of troops, made possible by telegraph and rail communications, joined in efforts to stop the fleeing Indians. The Fort Reno troops were in pursuit into Nebraska. 53 notes.

D. L. Smith

855. Zimmerman, Jean L. COLONEL RANALD S. MACKENZIE AT FORT SILL. *Chronicles of Oklahoma 1966 44(1): 12-21.* Colonel Mackenzie, Indian fighter, was placed in command of Fort Sill to oversee the Kiowa-Comanche Agency. He believed moral restraint was superior to brute force. He faced three problems: Indians off the reservation, poor

administration of Indian affairs, and white thieves in Indian Territory. Mackenzie handled affairs with firmness, sympathy, and justice. 42 notes.

I. W. Van Noppen

856. —. ALL ABOUT COURTESY: IN A VERBAL WAR JOHN P. CLUM HAS A PARTING SHOT. *Arizoniana 1963 4(2): 11-18.* In 1877 the Indian agent Clum was ordered by the Commissioner of Indian Affairs to take Indian police, request military aid if needed, arrest marauding Indians at the Southern Apache Agency, remove them to the San Carlos Reservation and confine them there. During the carrying out of this order misunderstandings developed with General A. Kautz, commanding the Dept. of Arizona, who complained to his divisional commander about the agent's discourtesy.

M. Petrie

857. —. A BRITISH JOURNALIST REPORTS THE MEDICINE LODGE PEACE COUNCIL OF 1867. *Kansas Hist. Q. 1967 33(3): 249-320.* Henry Morton Stanley (who later found David Livingston in Africa) was a special correspondent for the St. Louis *Daily Missouri Democrat* during the 1867 campaign against the Plains Indians. His reports were published in the *Democrat* between 19 October and 2 November 1867. Some of them were later republished in greatly edited form in the first volume of his *My Early Travels and Adventures in America and Asia* (London: 1895). Given here are the articles pertaining to the peace negotiations as they appeared in the *Democrat.* Obvious errors have been corrected. Illus., 47 notes.

W. F. Zornow

858. —. IN MEMORIAM: LOUIS MC LANE HAMILTON, CAPTAIN 7TH U.S. CALVARY. *Chronicles of Oklahoma 1968 46(4): 362-386.* Hamilton, young grandson of Alexander Hamilton, lost his life in the Battle of the Washita, 27 November 1868. In 1869 General George Armstrong Custer wrote a long letter to the young man's mother, describing the situation and praising her son as exemplary in every respect. Pictures the grave of Louis McLane Hamilton and gives a transcription of the inscription on it. Illus., 2 notes.

E. P. Stickney

859. —. [SAND CREEK]. *Colorado Mag. 1964 41(4): 277-335.*
—. A CENTURY OF CONTROVERSY, *pp. 277-278.* Introduces the authors of these anniversary articles, a century after the Sand Creek Massacre or battle.
Carey, Raymond G. THE PUZZLE OF SAND CREEK, *pp. 279-298.* On 29 November 1864 Colonel John Chivington and the Third Regiment of Colorado Volunteer Cavalry, "hundred-daysters," attacked an encampment of one hundred Cheyenne lodges at Sand Creek. Figures vary as to the number killed. The "massacre" evoked nationwide disapproval and was studied by two congressional commissions and a military commission. Certain facts of the battle remain a mystery; how many were killed, whether the Indians were hostile, and whether the killed included a large number of women and children.
Unrau, William E. A PRELUDE TO WAR, *pp. 299-313.* The period 1860-63 in Colorado Territory was confused. Two successive territorial governors, two Indian agents serving concurrently, and a novice Indian commissioner in Washington tried to make satisfactory treaties with Cheyennes and Arapahoes, but they were unsuccessful, and war soon followed.
Lecompte, Janet. SAND CREEK, *pp. 314-335.* The Indian War in Colorado in 1864 was provoked by the political aspirations of Territorial Governor John Evans. The massacre cannot be justified. Evidence of the guilt of Evans and Chivington was suppressed in Colorado for one hundred years, while people there have continued to debate the propriety of the attack.

I. W. Van Noppen

860. —. SITTING BULL'S VERSION OF LITTLE BIG HORN. *Am. Hist. Illus. 1966 1(5): 27-31.* An account told in an interview with a correspondent of the *New York Herald* a year after the battle took place. Sitting Bull was in the village when Custer's force attacked, but took no part in the final destruction. What he knew was told him by other Indians. 2 photos, 2-page color painting of "Custer's Last Fight" by Gayle P. Hoskins.

E. Brown

Economic Activity

General

861. Arrington, Leonard J. INLAND TO ZION: MORMON TRADE ON THE COLORADO RIVER, 1864-1867. *Arizona and the West 1966 8(3): 239-250.* Before there was any certainty that a transcontinental railroad would ever be completed, Mormon leaders envisioned making the Colorado River the Mississippi of the West, i.e., the gateway into the heartland of the West. Steamboat navigation of the Colorado as far as the present Boulder Dam location would connect southern Utah and the Pacific coast. Freight and immigrants would thus be taken to within 500 miles of Salt Lake City, and the Mormons could more easily transport their own produce to markets in California and the East. A Mormon railroad from Salt Lake City to the river would further stimulate traffic and also encourage development of Utah's iron, cotton, and other industries. Urgent circumstances in 1864 provoked realization, in part, of these ideas: suspension of transcontinental railroad construction, prohibitive prices of provisions and equipment to Montana and Idaho mines because of the Civil War and freighting charges from the States, the long trip for church teams to pick up incoming Mormon immigrants at the Missouri River, and the need for a stimulus to the development of remote and isolated southern Utah. A church warehouse was erected at Callville, considered to be the highest practicable head of navigation on the Colorado. A road was built from St. George in southeastern Utah with settlements established enroute. A 6,500-acre plantation was purchased in Hawaii to produce sugar and long-staple cotton for Utah, in keeping with the desire to approximate self-sufficiency. During the years 1865-67, Mormon-supported ventures shipped lumber, agricultural machinery, general merchandise, and Hawaiian sugar and molasses by water from San Francisco to the mouth of the Colorado, by steamboat up the river, and by freight wagons overland to St. George, Salt Lake City, and as far as the Montana mine fields. Rapid construction of the Union Pacific Railroad and completion of the transcontinental line in 1869 rendered the Colorado River experiment unrealistic and unviable. Based in part on manuscripts in the Latter Day Saints Historian's Library, Salt Lake City, and the Utah State Historical Society; 2 illus., map.

D. L. Smith

862. Gambone, Joseph G. ECONOMIC RELIEF IN TERRITORIAL KANSAS, 1860-1861. *Kansas Hist. Q. 1970 36(2): 149-174.* Two relief campaigns preceded the one in 1860-61; the first came in 1854-55 during the territory's formative years, and the second came in 1856-57 during the time when national attention was fixed on "Bleeding Kansas." The third campaign was launched after a severe drought and an even more severe winter in 1859 threatened to depopulate Kansas. The aid that flowed in from other parts of the country not only met immediate needs but helped the settlers to plant a new crop after the starving times were over. Many contemporary observers insisted that the entire relief campaign was being manipulated to build the political reputations of some early Kansas leaders, and later writers usually accepted these slanders as true. Although not entirely rejecting the earlier idea that there was a close connection between local politics and the relief campaign, believes the relief campaign was foremost a vital element in the salvation of Kansas during a bitter economic crisis. Based on books, articles, newspapers, and manuscripts in the Kansas State Historical Society; illus., 91 notes.

W. F. Zornow

863. Granberg, W. J. JIM WARDNER: FINANCIAL WIZARD OF THE WEST. *Am. West 1964 1(4): 32-37.* James F. Wardner was one of the "fiddle-footed men" who helped to win the West by leaving roads where there were only trails before, towns where there had been nothing, and paying mines that had only existed in dreams. His gold-dust trail rambled over the American and Canadian West and South Africa, and left him on the beach at Nome. Rags to riches was his way of life involving him "with color and dash" in mining, banking, cornering the egg market, storekeeping, freighting, selling black cat pelts as "hood seal" furs, peddling synthetic butter, and anything else of interest or promise. An Idaho town and a British Columbia town bear his name. The biggest deal of his life came in the Bunker Hill and Sullivan activities in the Coeur d'Alene, possibly the world's largest lead mine. Derived primarily from Wardner's 1900 autobiography and contemporary newspaper files.

D. L. Smith

864. Gressley, Gene M. COLONIALISM: A WESTERN COMPLAINT. *Pacific Northwest Q. 1963 54(1): 1-8.* Throughout US history, the West has suffered and complained of economic exploitation and domination by the East. The Eastern-owned railways, mining companies, banks, and the government itself have been held responsible for higher cost of living and for retarding industrial development of the West. Many Westerners themselves, rather than resisting this, have abetted it by investing in the East and perpetuating the tradition of Eastern cultural superiority. As Texas and California have developed, it is the less populous mountain states which still especially resent this colonialism. Although it still exists, it is nevertheless being less complained of since industry and the center of population have moved westward, and Eastern travelers have swarmed through the West, many to settle down.
R. E. Wilson

865. Haines, Francis, Jr. BEST THICK GINGERBREAD WITH SWEETMEATS. *Idaho Yesterdays 1964 7(4): 30-32.* Investigates the large shipments of gingerbread to the Pacific Northwest from 1796 to the 1830's. Based on archives of the Hudson's Bay Company in London.
M. Small

866. McLaird, James D. RANCHING IN THE BIG HORNS: GEORGE T. BECK, 1856-1894. *Ann. of Wyoming 1967 39(2): 157-185.* Discusses the Wyoming rancher and businessman George T. Beck during the years from 1877 to 1894. The author examines Beck's economic activities as an example of the small-time frontier entrepreneur. These people, he claims, deserve more recognition than they have received for their part in developing the economy in frontier areas. Beck's career as a sheepman, cattle raiser, farmer, flour mill operator, prospector, town site promoter, and politician supports this thesis. Based on Beck's autobiography supplemented by manuscript, newspaper, and secondary material; illus., 87 notes.
R. L. Nichols

867. Nelson, Sharlene P. CAMP SIX: THE TACOMA LOGGING MUSEUM. *Forest Hist. 1966 9(4): 24-27.* The Western Forest Industries Museum, Inc., was originated by the Tacoma, Washington, Junior League and was subsidized by individuals and business firms. It was built on a 20-acre plot in Point Defiance Park, Tacoma, Washington. The museum's technological history of Washington logging begins with an 1882 donkey and continues with a Shay's geared locomotive, a high lead spar tree, tower skidders, and a five bunkhouse car camp. 4 photos and a drawing.
B. A. Vatter

868. Pethtel, Lillian. NAMES AND PLACES: NAME LORE AROUND KAMIAH. *Western Folklore 1965 24(4): 281-284.* Contains the names given to machines, men, and property by loggers and cattlemen in north central Idaho. Among the names given to trucks used in logging are "The Monster," "Old Asthma" and "The Road Runner."
J. M. Brady

869. Ridge, Martin. WHY THEY WENT WEST: ECONOMIC OPPORTUNITY ON THE TRANS-MISSISSIPPI FRONTIER. *Am. West 1964 1(3): 40-57.* The 1840's were a "watershed" dividing the rate and the nature of the economic growth of the trans-Mississippi West. The political boundaries of the contiguous continental territory of the country were rounded out in Oregon, Texas, and the Mexican Cession; Iowa was being filled in and Missouri was producing grain surpluses; trails to Oregon, California, Santa Fe, and Salt Lake were well established; fur hunters were finding sedentary pursuits more profitable; and gold was discovered in California. The public image of the West was changing and it was now regarded as hospitable and valuable. Economic factors of precious and base metals, land, and railroads, as well as a swelling tide of migration, transformed the trans-Mississippi West so rapidly that the Census Bureau announced the close of the frontier era in 1890. Illus., general bibliographical note.
D. L. Smith

870. Sprague, Marshall. THE DUDE FROM LIMERICK. *Am. West 1966 3(4): 53-61, 92-94.* Windham Thomas Wyndham-Quin, Fourth Earl of Dunraven, from County Limerick, Ireland, enamored by tales of the American West, made several extended hunting trips into the Colorado and Montana mountains in the 1870's and early 1880's. By methods in common use that violated the spirit of homestead laws, Dunraven set out to acquire the thousands of acres of the Estes Park country of Colorado as a private hunting preserve. Hordes of tourists, picnickers,

mountain climbers, squatters, and homesteaders who were also attracted to the area caused him to modify the whole idea. He decided to establish a summer resort and cattle ranch and to set up his own game preserve and lodge in another area far removed. Dunraven survived several lawsuits by those inhospitable to the foreign dude in their midst, leased his hotel, ranch, and herd in 1883, and finally sold out completely in 1907. Based on Dunraven's own autobiography and other writings and excerpted from a forthcoming volume; illus.
D. L. Smith

871. Wills, John W. BENJAMIN'S ETHICAL STRATEGY IN THE NEW ALMADEN CASE. *Q. J. of Speech 1964 50(3): 259-265.* Judah P. Benjamin, prominent 19th-century lawyer, relied primarily on ethical proof as he represented Andres Castillero in the *New Almaden Case* in California in 1860. Benjamin 1) sought to increase his own ethical appeal by demonstrating the characteristics which gained for him his prior reputation, 2) attempted to align his cause with the high ethical appeal of others (notably John C. Frémont), 3) attacked the character of the opposing counsel (primarily Jeremiah S. Black and Edmund Randolph), 4) used his own personal reputation in order to build and establish the character of his witnesses, and 5) sought to destroy the credibility of his opponents' witnesses. Chief source is *The United States vs. Andres Castillero, On Cross Appeal, Claim for the Mine and Lands of New Almaden, Argument of Hon. J. P. Benjamin,* reported by Sumner and Cutter (San Francisco, 1860). 21 notes.
M. A. Hayes

Fur Trade and Indian Trade

872. Albrecht, Dorothy E. JOHN LORENZO HUBBELL, NAVAJO INDIAN TRADER. *Arizoniana 1963 4(3): 33-40.* Of Spanish and Vermont ancestry, Hubbell was born and educated in New Mexico. He had homesteaded at Ganado where he later bought the trading post. His work with the Navajos was performed with understanding - he spoke the language - and he was instrumental in improving their turquoise jewelry and rug crafts. The Department of the Interior in recent years selected the Hubbell post as the best illustration of an Indian trading post. Documented, illus.
E. P. Stickney

873. Baird, Donald. SOME EIGHTEENTH CENTURY GUN BARRELS FROM OSAGE VILLAGE SITES. *Great Plains J. 1965 4(2): 49-62.* Asserts that a reliable historical picture of Indian trade guns of the 18th century may emerge from collecting and analyzing frontier gun barrels from Osage Indian sites in Missouri. The author provides information on cleaning and preserving the relics, manufacturing methods, markings, national origins and dating. Based on examination of the gun barrels and on secondary printed sources, illus., tables.
O. H. Zabel

874. Barry, Louise. THE RANCH AT WALNUT CREEK CROSSING. *Kansas Hist. Q. 1971 37(2): 121-147.* In 1855 a trading post was constructed at Walnut Creek Crossing on the Santa Fe Trail on the great bend of the Arkansas River, in Kansas. Until it was finally burned down by marauding Cheyenne and Arapaho in 1868, this ranch played an important role in supplying goods to traders moving along the trail and to military expeditions against the Indians. In 1969 the Kansas State Historical Society and Kansas Anthropological Association conducted excavations on the site of the old ranch. Illus., 101 notes.
W. F. Zornow

875. Boller, Henry A. JOURNAL OF A TRIP TO, AND RESIDENCE IN, THE INDIAN COUNTRY. *North Dakota Hist. 1966 33(3): 261-315.* From 1 September until 31 December 1858 Henry Boller, Upper Missouri fur trader, reported daily his preparation for his first trading expedition, the Assiniboine camp, his stock in trade, traveling experiences, Indian customs, descriptions of the country, the building of Fort Atkinson (a trading post) and life there, and the coming and going of the Indians to the fort. Boller and a rival trader, accompanied by assistants with ox-drawn wagons, went with the Gros Ventres as they moved on 30 October to their winter quarters where both traders had houses built for their stock. During November several trips were made back to Fort Atkinson for additional goods. Most of December was spent keeping store and hunting. Illus., 10 notes.
I. W. Van Noppen

876. Brandon, William. TWO THOUSAND MILES FROM THE COUNTING HOUSE: WILSON PRICE HUNT AND THE FOUNDING OF ASTORIA. *Am. West 1968 5(4): 24-29, 61-63.* With the Louisiana Purchase and the reports of the Lewis and Clark expedition, considerable Yankee attention focused on the Western beaver fur trade. John Jacob Astor, the leading American fur merchant, planned a chain of trading posts along the Lewis and Clark route, a monopoly of the trade with the Russians along the Pacific Northwest coast, and a vast trade cycle that would involve China, Europe, and New England. He was also aware of the political implications for the American position in the Oregon country. Two simultaneous expeditions were to set the plan in motion. The first was by sea to establish headquarters at the mouth of the Columbia River. The second was by land to win the confidence of the Indians and to determine proper locations for trading posts en route. Wilson Price Hunt commanded the overland expedition. As leader of the 1811 overland Astorians, he is credited with marking the route between the Snake River and the Columbia that later was to become an important link in the Oregon Trail. Hunt also founded and was in command of the post at Astoria, on the Oregon side of the mouth of the Columbia. Map, biblio. note.
D. L. Smith

877. Brooks, George R., ed. GEORGE C. SIBLEY'S JOURNAL OF A TRIP TO THE SALINES IN 1811. *Bull. of the Missouri Hist. Soc. 1965 21(3): 167-207.* Presents, with editorial introduction and notes, the journal of a man who, at the time, was chief factor in the new Indian trading post of Fort Osage up the Missouri River. Based on a letter to his father, Sibley's journal describes at considerable length the territory and Indian tribes in the area west and south of Fort Osage. He visited and described the Osage, Konsee, and Pawnee tribes and found further information about the earlier Zebulon Pike expedition. His was also the first account by a white man of the great salt deposits, or "Grand Salines," in what was later northern Oklahoma. 40 notes.
R. J. Hanks

878. Brooks, George R., ed. THE PRIVATE JOURNAL OF ROBERT CAMPBELL. *Missouri Hist. Soc. Bull. 1964 20(2): 107-118.* Continued from 1963 20(1): 3-24 (see abstract 1:167). The almost daily account - from 29 November through 31 December 1833 - of the affairs of the firm of Sublette and Campbell at its trading post, Fort William, on the upper Missouri River at its confluence with the Yellowstone River. The journal describes the difficult problems of construction, of supplies, of the Indians, and of employees - further complicated by constant and hostile competition from Kenneth McKenzie, chief clerk of the rival American Fur Company post at Fort Union. The last entry is a résumé of Campbell's activities in 1833.
R. J. Hanks

879. Brooks, George R., ed. THE PRIVATE JOURNAL OF ROBERT CAMPBELL. *Missouri Hist. Soc. Bull. 1963 20(1): 3-24.* A portion of the journal, with editorial introduction, of a prominent St. Louis fur trader and merchant, associated with William Sublette. Extensively footnoted by the editor, the journal covers the period of 21 September through 31 December 1833 - a portion of Campbell's residence at Fort William on the upper Missouri - and is a significant new source for that critical phase of the western fur trade which found Campbell and Sublette attempting to challenge the large American Fur Company of the Astors and Chouteaus. The journal contains considerable detail about the life, personalities and problems of a fur post. Article to be continued.
R. J. Hanks

880. Burns, Peter J. THE SHORT, INCREDIBLE LIFE OF JEDEDIAH SMITH. *Montana 1967 17(1): 44-55.* Biographical sketch of Jedediah Strong Smith, who at age 23 began trapping for the Ashley-Henry partnership in the northern Rocky Mountains. Soon entering the firm, he trapped and explored extensively, including two crossings of the Great Basin to the San Diego area, and a visit to the lower Columbia River. On an expedition to the Santa Fe country, he was ambushed and killed by Comanche Indians. Illus.
S. R. Davison

881. Carter, Harvey L. TOM TOBIN. *Am. West 1965 2(4): 91-94.* Thomas Tate Tobin went to Taos in 1837 to serve a general apprenticeship under his half brother in the ways of the frontier, particularly as a fur trapper and trader. He became a mountain man whose reputation rivaled that of Kit Carson's. His most famous exploit came in 1863 when he tracked down two bandits wanted by the Territory of Colorado for the wanton murder of more than a score of victims. He delivered the severed

heads of the murderers but never completely collected the reward offered by the territorial government. Illus., 19 notes.
D. L. Smith

882. Clayton, James L. THE GROWTH AND ECONOMIC SIGNIFICANCE OF THE AMERICAN FUR TRADE, 1790-1890. *Minnesota Hist. 1966 40(4): 210-220.* A synthesis of the dollar and cents value of the fur trade during the 19th century. The author lists the various types of fur-bearing animals involved as well as their relative value per pelt, and as a total in any given period. In addition, he tries to arrive at total values for the business of the various companies involved as well as for the types of fur. Based on Henry Poland's *Fur Bearing Animals* as well as the Records of the Hudson's Bay Company and other sources.
P. L. Simon

883. Dunn, Adrian R. A HISTORY OF OLD FORT BERTHOLD. *North Dakota Hist. 1963 30(4): 157-240.* Traces events from the migration of the three tribes, Mandans, Hidatsa, and Arikara to the Upper Missouri: the coming of fur traders, devastation of the three tribes by smallpox brought in with a steamboat cargo in 1837, building of Fort Berthold and establishment of a highly competitive fur trade there, the strife of the 1860's, the end of the Berthold trade in the 1870's, and efforts to educate the Indians and teach them useful trades. By 1880 the three tribes had lost half their reservation to the Northern Pacific Railroad and in 1884 individual allotments of land were made to heads of families for farms. The tribal culture was to be replaced with that of the white man. The balance of the tribal reservation was allotted to homesteaders. Seven chapters, illus., biblio.
I. W. Van Noppen

884. Elliot, Russell R. NEVADA'S FIRST TRADING POST: A STUDY IN HISTORIOGRAPHY. *Nevada State Hist. Soc. Q. 1970 13(4): 2-10.* Much confusion exists among Nevada historians as to whether the DeMont-Beatie-Blackburn party arrived in the Carson Valley of Nevada in 1849 or 1850. This party was credited with establishing the first trading post in Nevada. Historians have infrequently disputed the precise location of the post, the reasons for its founding, and the names of those who established it. The date has been in continuous dispute. The primary concern of the historian is still to establish truth. This article reviews the historiography of the dispute over the date - 1849 or 1850? Careful evaluation of all available evidence forces the conclusion that 1850 is the most plausible date of establishment of the first trading post in Nevada. Photo, 20 notes.
E. P. Costello

885. Ellis, Richard N., ed. BENT, CARSON AND THE INDIANS, 1865. *Colorado Mag. 1969 46(1): 55-68.* An introduction gives the setting for the report (27 October 1865) of William Bent and Kit Carson to General John Pope, commander of the Department of the Missouri. The report is reproduced. It recommends that Indians be controlled by the War Department and placed on reservations. Furthermore, it suggests that posts be garrisoned by regular troops and officers of "known discretion and judgment," that both white and Indian offenders be punished by law, and that strict regulations be enforced over trade with the Indians. Illus., 25 notes.
O. H. Zabel

886. Gilles, Albert S., Sr. WER-QUE-YAH, JESUS-MAN COMANCHE. *Southwest R. 1968 53(3): 277-291.* Captured and taken to Fort Sill in 1874 or 1875, Wer-que-yah became one of the Gilles' first customers at their trading store at Old Faxen, Oklahoma Territory. Reflections on the problem of Indian credit, conflict with the Government trader, and an explanation of the "grass payment" are included.
D. F. Henderson

887. Gilman, Rhoda R. LAST DAYS OF THE UPPER MISSISSIPPI FUR TRADE. *Minnesota Hist. 1970 42(4): 122-140.* Although the harvest of pelts in the upper Mississippi River region increased between 1830 and 1880, the great fur companies of the area virtually ceased to operate by 1854. A review of the organization and methods of these firms and their subsidiaries reveals that a dwindling Indian population and a trend toward diversification led to their decline. As white settlers flooded the upper Mississippi territory and Indians retreated to reservations, traders such as Henry H. Sibley, Henry M. Rice, and Pierre Chouteau, Jr., increasingly turned their attention from the fur trade to lumbering, banking, general merchandising, and land speculation. After the mid-1850's, pioneer farmers joined professional white and Indian trappers in supplying pelts to a new group of traders, including Joseph

Ullmann, who became Minnesota's leading fur dealer after 1870. Based on records of the American Fur Company, MSS. of the principal traders, and secondary sources; illus., map, 71 notes.   G. R. Adams

888.   Goetzmann, William H.   THE MOUNTAIN MAN AS JACK-SONIAN MAN. *Am. Q. 1963 15(3): 402-415.* Mountain Man exists as a figure of American mythology rather than history. To Irving in the 19th century he was Robin Hood. To the more discerning he has been a forlorn primitive out of the past. The author gives statistical tables of occupations based upon the lives of Mountain Men whose entrance into the Rocky Mountain fur trade during the period 1805-45 can be proven. In the complex character of the Mountain Man was a clearly discernible pattern - that of Jacksonian Man in search of respectability and success in terms of the society he had left behind. They clearly saw that the future of the Far West lay with the settlers rather than the trappers. Some were eager to see that the US (not the Mexican or the British) government be brought West and its institutions extended over the wild new land to protect the settler. This spirit may well have settled the Oregon question and brought on the Mexican War, for it was the spirit of Manifest Destiny. Based on contemporary sources and modern studies.   E. P. Stickney

889.   Greer, Charles and Scheffer, Victor B.   A 1715 PICTURE OF A FUR SEAL. *Pacific Northwest Q. 1971 62(4): 151-153.* The authors reprint the first unambiguous description of the fur seal as published in 1715 by Ryoan Terajima, a Japanese physician, and give an account of the known background information leading to the description. Included is a copy of the line drawing (and Oriental characters) of the fur seal, as taken from Terajima's *Comprehensive Pictorial Encyclopedia of Japan and China* (1715). Notes.   C. C. Gorchels

890.   Hafen, LeRoy R.   ETIENNE PROVOST, MOUNTAIN MAN AND UTAH PIONEER. *Utah Hist. Q. 1968 36(2): 99-112.* Reviews the information known about Etienne Provost's activities as fur trader, explorer, and entrepreneur in the Rocky Mountain West, with some emphasis on those movements which brought him into present-day Utah. Based on primary and secondary sources; notes.   S. L. Jones

891.   Hafen, LeRoy R.   FORT VASQUEZ. *Colorado Mag. 1964 41(3): 198-212.* During the 1830's fur men of the West turned from the beaverskin business to trade in buffalo robes. Four adobe forts were established in competition with each other on the South Platte River in Colorado for trade with the Cheyennes and Arapahoes. One of these, Fort Vasquez, was established in 1835 by Louis Vasquez and Andrew Sublette, both experienced fur traders, who shipped buffalo robes and tongues to St. Louis. In 1840 the fort was sold and when the new purchasers soon became bankrupt the place was abandoned. During the 1930's the WPA reconstructed the fort, mixing the old adobe remains with new materials. Based on letters, earlier accounts by the author, newspaper accounts, and memoirs.   I. W. Van Noppen

892.   Haines, Francis.   PIONEER PORTRAIT: ROBERT NEWELL. *Idaho Yesterdays 1965 9(1): 2-9.* "A mountain man who became one of the very first Idaho pioneers, Robert Newell was a friend of the Nez Perce Indians in the years of the fur trade and the gold rush." The author gives a brief biography of Newell's life and describes his adventures with other mountain men, his political activities, his success with various Indian tribes, and his several marriages. 2 photos.   B. B. Swift

893.   Haines, Francis, Jr.   FRANÇOIS PAYETTE. *Idaho Yester-days 1964-65 8(4): 12-21.* "One of the most successful and well known of all the voyageurs engaged in the fur trade of the Pacific Northwest, Payette spent much of his time in the Snake country of Idaho." Payette arrived in Astoria in 1812 and spent the next 32 years in the fur trade. He began with the Pacific Fur Company, transferred to the Northwest Company and then finished his career with the Hudson's Bay Company. The author describes Payette's activities during his 32 years in the fur trade. Payette was able to read and write: these advantages, along with his superior trapping and leadership abilities made him noticed by his superiors and lifted him from the obscurity that surrounds most of his fellow workers. He retired in 1844, returned to Montreal where he withdrew most of his savings (1,535 pounds) and disappeared from the known pages of existing history. Illus., 61 notes.   B. B. Swift

894.   Halliburton, R., Jr.   JOHN COLTER'S RUN FOR LIFE. *Great Plains J. 1963 3(1): 32-34.* Gives a brief biography of John Colter, the first "mountain man" and describes his narrow escape from the Blackfoot Indians in the upper Missouri area in 1808.   O. H. Zabel

895.   Hanson, Charles E., Jr.   RECONSTRUCTION OF THE BORDEAUX TRADING POST. *Nebraska Hist. 1972 53(2): 137-165.* Discusses the reconstruction of the trading post, 1956-67, with some account of its historical significance during 1846-72 when it was in operation. The post is about three miles east of Chadron, Nebraska.   R. Lowitt

896.   Jackson, Donald, ed.   JOURNEY TO THE MANDANS, 1809; THE LOST NARRATIVE OF DR. THOMAS. *Missouri Hist. Soc. Bull. 1964 20(3): 179-192.* Thomas, an obscure physician, still unidentified except for his last name, accompanied the 1809 expedition to the upper Missouri River sponsored by the St. Louis Missouri Fur Company. Apart from commercial purposes, one of the principal objectives of the expedition was to return safely to his village the Mandan chief, Sheheke (Shahaka), who had returned with the Lewis and Clark expedition and had been honored in Washington and the East. The account, from contemporary newspapers, consists primarily of descriptions of geography and of the Indians.   R. J. Hanks

897.   Johnson, Roy P.   FUR TRADER CHABOILLEZ AT PEMBINA. *North Dakota Hist. 1965 32(2): 83-99.* Discusses and summarizes the notebook of the North Dakota fur trader Chaboillez for the period 1797 to 1798. It is felt that this journal is the earliest record of human activity in North Dakota. The entries not only give a detailed description of the life of an early fur trader and the habits of his customers the Chippewa Indians, but they also "are a good mirror of life in Pembina in 1797-98." Based on primary and secondary sources; 2 illus., map, 15 notes.   M. J. McBaine

898.   Judge, W. James.   THE ARCHAEOLOGY OF FORT VASQUEZ. *Colorado Mag. 1971 48(3): 181-203.* From 1835 to 1840 or 1841 Fort Vasquez, on the South Platte River, served as an active fur trading post. After that it was occupied sporadically. In the 1930's it was partially reconstructed by the WPA. In 1958 the site became the property of the State Historical Society of Colorado and in 1964 a visitor's center was completed. From 1966 to 1970 considerable archaeological investigation of the site, to determine the structure and functions of the fort, occurred, especially under the direction of the author. After describing the archaeological evidence, the author asks why three other forts (St. Vrain, Jackson, and Lupton) were all built within 15 miles. He questions navigability of the South Platte and competition as adequate explanations. Rather, he suggests that the forts were not so much trading bases as supply points with traders going to the Indians. Also, the area provided both cottonwoods and ideal clay for adobe construction. Archaeologists and historians should cooperate to help explain why people behave as they do. Illus., tables, 25 notes.   O. H. Zabel

899.   Kroeber, Clifton B., ed.; Euler, Robert C.; and Schroeder, Albert H.   THE ROUTE OF JAMES O. PATTIE ON THE COLORADO IN 1826: A REAPPRAISAL BY A. L. KROEBER. *Arizona and the West 1964 6(2): 119-136.* James Ohio Pattie trapped the Gila and Colorado Rivers while on three expeditions in the years 1825-27. His *Personal Narrative,* first published in 1831, has appeared in several editions. Successive editors and other historians, while regarding Pattie's account as prime source material for the Southwest, have distrusted many of his dates, place names, identifications, and general reliability. The anthropologists whose notes are here published and edited by a historian had occasion, in connection with research for Indian claims cases, to study Pattie's account of the 1826 expedition. Pattie was with a "French" group of trappers down the Gila River. He joined an "American" expedition which ascended the Colorado River. These analyses correct Pattie and quarrel with him but, in general, give credence to the outline of his account of the 1826 venture as well as much of the specific information it contains. Map, 35 notes.   D. L. Smith

900.   Lattie, Alexander.   ALEXANDER LATTIE'S FORT GEORGE JOURNAL, 1846. *Oregon Hist. Q. 1963 64(3): 197-245.* Journal of an employee of Hudson's Bay Company, February to July 1846, while on duty at Fort George in Oregon Territory. The anonymous editor (proba-

bly Thomas Vaughan) gives a sketch of Lattie's life as river pilot and trader in the Pacific Northwest, 1831-49. Details in the journal include observations of weather, ship traffic, duties, and a few personal experiences.

C. C. Gorchels

901. Lavender, David. RAMSAY CROOK'S EARLY VENTURES ON THE MISSOURI RIVER: A SERIES OF CONJECTURES. *Missouri Hist. Soc. Bull. 1964 20(2): 91-106.* Explores the limited evidence concerning the early western career of a Scot who became after 1817 the most important director and executive of the western affairs of Astor's great American Fur Company and a prominent citizen of St. Louis. The early stage of his career was a period of changing and uncertain political, economic, and geographical circumstances in the fur trade from the Jay Treaty through the War of 1812. Trading routes, areas, and problems are described, as well as the intense competitive methods and conditions.

R. J. Hanks

902. Lavender, David. SOME AMERICAN CHARACTERISTICS OF THE AMERICAN FUR COMPANY. *Minnesota Hist. 1966 40(4): 178-187.* Points out the major changes of an American nature that came to the fur trade after John Jacob Astor entered the field. This had to do chiefly with the way the new fur company was organized - that is, the role of the various partners and their relationship with their field agents or winterers. In general, the American situation encouraged fragmentation rather than centralization and a considerable degree of lawlessness. Primary and secondary sources.

P. L. Simon

903. Lecompte, Janet. GANTT'S FORT AND BENT'S PICKET POST. *Colorado Mag. 1964 41(2): 111-125.* Locates and identifies three forts on the Arkansas River for trading with the Arapahoe, Cheyenne, Kiowa, and other Indians, two of which were known as Fort Cass and Fort William. Later all were supplanted by a great adobe trading post, Bent's Fort.

I. W. Van Noppen

904. Mattison, R. H., ed. HENRY A. BOLLER, UPPER MISSOURI RIVER FUR TRADER. *North Dakota Hist. 1966 33(2): 106-219.* Born in 1836 in Philadelphia, Boller early fell in love with the West, reading tales of Indian life during his youth. In the spring of 1858 he fulfilled his dreams and became a clerk for Frost, Todd and Company, an "opposition" company to the American Fur Company, which usually dominated the Upper Missouri trade. Most of his correspondence, which later enabled him to write *Among the Indians,* was penned during the years 1858 to 1860. The letters, printed here for the first time, are invaluable as a guide to the important events of the fading years of the Western fur trade. In addition, he was an avid observer of Indian customs and life during what was to be the last years of Indian freedom. Illus., 64 notes.

R. Sexauer

905. McPhillips, William. JED SMITH FINALLY MAKES HEADLINES. *Pacific Historian 1966 10(1): 21-24.* Reprints a news article in the *Los Angeles Times,* 20 December 1965, which attempts to show the relationship between the explorations of Jedediah Smith across the Mojave Desert into California to the discussion about building a public park on the land he traversed rather than see it immersed beneath a new dam. Conflict between the Department of Water Resources' project, the Feather River water reservoir, and local wishes to preserve trout streams and wild country was resolved through the planning of two young regional parks executives, Smith Falconer, Jr. and Peter Dangermond. The resulting project, a cooperative among Federal, State and private interests, will result in dams, power, and park land. Map, illus.

T. R. Cripps

906. Morgan, Dale L. THE FUR TRADE AND ITS HISTORIANS. *Am. West 1966 3(2): 28-35, 92-93.* Hiram Martin Chittenden has had a greater impact on the writing of western American history than either Frederick Jackson Turner or Walter Prescott Webb. The influence of his history of the fur trade can be seen in nearly everything that has been written concerning the history of the American West in the first half of the 19th century. While this monumental work at first furnished "a rationale by which a diffuse and refractory history was made intelligible," over the years it has come to exert a tyrannical conditioning force on the thinking of historians and students who regard its conclusions and observations as the gospel according to Chittenden. A plea is made for fresh studies and syntheses in the history of the fur trade. Several areas where the need is critical are indicated. Illus.

D. L. Smith

907. Morgan, Dale L. THE FUR TRADE AND ITS HISTORIANS. *Minnesota Hist. 1966 40(4): 151-156.* See previous abstract.

908. Morgan, Dale L. JEDEDIAH SMITH TODAY. *Pacific Historian 1967 11(2): 35-46.* An address by the author of *Jedediah Smith and the Opening of the West* (Indianapolis: Bobbs-Merrill, 1953) to the Jedediah Smith Society in which he suggests some of the problems of writing about a Western figure, especially the temptation to "heroize" the man. In discussing Smith the author argues from the man and his convictions rather than the better-known exploration exploits. He offers evidence to show how easily one might create an exaggerated mythical figure and concludes with a discussion of the growing canon of historical works on Smith and the increasing care with which Mexican archivists are treating California documents. Documented from published and manuscript sources; illus.

T. R. Cripps

909. Nunis, Doyce B., Jr. MILTON SUBLETTE, THUNDERBOLT OF THE ROCKIES. *Montana 1963 13(3): 52-63.* A biography of one of the Sublette brothers who were prominent in the fur trade. Milton took an active part in exploiting the fur trade of the Southwest and the transmontane West. He saw service with William H. Ashley, the firm of Smith, Jackson, and Sublette, and later as a partner with Thomas Fitzpatrick. He played an important role in the ventures of Nathaniel Wyeth. In 1834 his leg was amputated, an operation which greatly curtailed his career. While ill and crippled, he tried to resume his work in the mountains, but died at Fort Laramie in 1837. Based on published materials about the fur trade and on manuscripts in the collections of the Missouri Historical Society.

A

910. Oglesby, Richard E. PIERRE MENARD, RELUCTANT MOUNTAIN MAN. *Missouri Hist. Soc. Bull. 1967 24(1): 3-19.* Pierre Menard does not fit the stereotyped characterization of a frontiersman as one who lacked all the normal appurtenances of civilized brothers back East. Although he was a fur trader and trapper and an Indian fighter, he was also a public servant, a conservator of civilized life, and a patron of the arts. He fought the destructive tendencies of the primitive life by maintaining the ways of civilization in the hostile environment of the frontier. In 1809-10 he traveled to the Rocky Mountains as a member of the expedition of the St. Louis Missouri Fur Company, of which he was a business partner. Although realizing the tremendous potential for wealth in the area, the methods he had to use to achieve this goal were so distasteful he refused to go on another expedition. He was appalled at the cost of frontier enterprise and the loss of human dignity which it involved. 48 notes.

D. L. Smith

911. Peattie, Donald Culross. JEDEDIAH SMITH—TRAILMAKER EXTRAORDINARY. *Pacific Historian 1966 10(4): 4-8.* Chronicles the adult life of Jedediah Smith, taking him from Saint Louis in 1822 to his death at the hands of Indians in 1831. Smith was with General William Ashley's expedition to the Yellowstone trapping grounds in 1822. After attacks by grizzlies, Crow Indians, and more exploration to the Great Salt Lake, Smith, with William Sublette and David Jackson, formed his own company to seek beaver pelts. After hardships of mountain and desert and capture by the Spaniards, Smith explored up the west coast to the Klamath River. He returned to Saint Louis with a profit which he shared with the Methodist Church. Smith interrupted his early retirement to lead one last expedition to New Mexico where he died at the hands of Comanches on 27 May 1831.

T. R. Cripps

912. Pfaller, Louis. CHARLES LARPENTEUR. *North Dakota Hist. 1965 32(1): 5-17.* This French-born western fur trader kept a fascinating journal of the traders and their business methods. In spite of his good education and vivacious wit, he chose to go west in 1833 as a common hand for William Sublette and Robert Campbell's Rocky Mountain outfit. They built Fort William near the American Fur Company's well-stocked Fort Union and tried unsuccessfully to capture the Assiniboine trade. Larpenteur worked as a mule wrangler, cartwright, and horse guard. In the spring he was employed as a clerk at Fort Union, the beginning of a long career with that company. Among the exciting incidents he related were the Deschamps-Rem feud between two families of half-breeds, and the smallpox plague at Fort Union in 1837 which killed half of the Assiniboines. Larpenteur was sent in charge of trading outfits and finally was put in charge of a company post. There followed a

succession of failures, new appointments, efforts to become an independent trader, until finally in 1871 he settled on a farm in Iowa where he died in 1872. Illus., 22 notes.   I. W. Van Noppen

913. Pope, Polly. TRADE IN THE PLAINS: AFFLUENCE AND ITS EFFECTS. *Kroeber Anthrop. Soc. Papers 1966 34: 53-61.* Points to a relationship between Euro-American trade with the Plains Indians and changes in Plains Indian culture. The author includes specific examples of trading and their cultural effects among such Plains Indians as the Blackfoot, Kiowa, Omaha, Sioux, and Mandan. Based on secondary sources; 2 notes, biblio.   C. N. Warren

914. Prucha, Francis Paul. ARMY SUTLERS AND THE AMERICAN FUR COMPANY. *Minnesota Hist. 1966 40(1): 22-31.* Studies the competition between the American Fur Company and various U.S. Army sutlers, or trading post operators. The company tried a variety of methods in its efforts to crack the sutler ranks and preserve its monopoly of trade - especially in the Indian lands. The relationship of Samuel C. Stambaugh and Henry H. Sibley at Fort Snelling is used as an example of the larger struggle. In the end, the American Fur Company failed to control the sutler's business in the area of its trade.   P. L. Simon

915. Rowe, David C. GOVERNMENT RELATIONS WITH THE FUR TRAPPERS OF THE UPPER MISSOURI: 1820-1840. *North Dakota Hist. 1968 35(2): 480-505.* The fur industry based in the upper Missouri River country flourished in the 1820's and 1830's. Government intervention did not bother private individual trappers and traders, but company fur enterprises objected to government-operated trading houses. With any threat from the Indians or the British, however, the companies demanded governmental assistance and protection. The "fur barons" exerted considerable influence, and their success in getting governmental protection helped pave the way for the settlement of the West. 10 illus., 77 notes.   D. L. Smith

916. Sage, Donald. SWIRL OF NATIONS. *Beaver [Canada] 1963 293(Spring): 32-40.* Describes the role of the Hudson's Bay Company in the struggle between Russia, the United States, and Great Britain for control of the North Pacific. The Company had a post at Yerba Buena (San Francisco) from 1841 to 1846, and held on to Fort Vancouver until 1860. It also had an agency in Honolulu to provision the maritime fur trade. American settlement south of the 49th parallel decided the issue. Illus.   L. F. S. Upton

917. Saum, Lewis O. THE FUR TRADER AND THE NOBLE SAVAGE. *Am. Q. 1963 15(4): 554-571.* The philosopher or intellectual expressed his dislike of civilization by comparing it invidiously with savagery. "Having seen the savage, the fur trader had fallen from innocence." Fur traders did utilize the noble savage theme, essentially in order to air their grievances but also to offer sincere warnings of the evils of our civilization. "In either case first-hand experience in the crude realities of wilderness existence provided no absolute immunity from that intriguing and perennial passion, the ennobling of the savage." Based largely on published early travels of fur traders.   E. P. Stickney

918. Schusky, Ernest L. THE UPPER MISSOURI INDIAN AGENCY, 1819-1868. *Missouri Hist. R. 1971 65(3): 249-269.* Agency is often used as a synonym for reservation, but actually is a much more restricted enterprise dealing with trade. The Upper Missouri Agency developed during this half-century from essentially a paper organization that supplied many tribes with yearly presents to preserve peace and assist the fur trade, into a number of reservations where the Indians were confined and made dependent on the Federal government. Only the Sioux to the west remained strong; the tribes along the Missouri were reduced to living under agents who had great power over them and often little interest in their problems. Based on articles, books, and manuscripts in the National Archives; illus., 46 notes.   W. F. Zornow

919. Stevens, Harry R. A COMPANY OF HANDS AND TRADERS: ORIGINS OF THE GLENN-FOWLER EXPEDITION OF 1821-1822. *New Mexico Hist. R. 1971 46(3): 181-221.* On 5 August 1821, Hugh Glenn received a license from Major William Bradford to trade with Indians in the country beyond Fort Smith, Arkansas. Of the 18 men named in the license, only nine made the trip; 12 others joined them later. Several accounts of the expedition survive, including the

extensive *Journal of Jacob Fowler.* By delving into the background of eight of the men, in particular Hugh Glenn and Jacob Fowler, the author attempts to determine the origins of the expedition. 81 notes.
                                                        D. F. Henderson

920. Sunder, John E. FREDERICK G. RITER, FUR TRADER AND WEATHER OBSERVER. *North Dakota Hist. 1967 34(2): 157-169.* A monograph on the life of Frederick G. Riter, a Philadelphian who went west between 1853 and 1855 to regain his health. While in North Dakota he served as chief clerk at Fort Union, working for the American Fur Company. While there he kept a detailed meteorological record for the U.S. Patent Office and the Smithsonian Institution, between the months of August and November 1857 and during the month of January 1858. Having recovered his health, he returned to Philadelphia in 1862 where he lived until his death in November 1888. Documented from vital statistics dealing with Riter's life, including personal correspondence. Illus., 17 notes.   R. Sexauer

921. Tamony, Peter. "FROM FOFARRAW TO FOOFARAH!" *Pacific Historian 1966 10(2): 24-26.* Gives the history of the mountain man's word "foofarah," meaning frills, ostentation, braggadocio. The word probably derived from the French "fanfaron" or Spanish "fanfarron": braggart or blusterer.   T. R. Cripps

922. Weber, David J. MEXICO AND THE MOUNTAIN MEN, 1821-1828. *J. of the West 1969 8(3): 369-378.* Tells of the attempts by the Mexican Government to prevent the mountain men from trapping in what was then Mexico. A law was passed making it illegal for foreigners to trap in Mexico. The law was unenforceable since there were not enough troops. The quiet struggle between Mexico and mountain men contributed to the mutual contempt which Americans and Mexicans increasingly felt toward one another, and revealed Mexico's inability to effectively patrol and defend its vast northern frontier.
                                                        R. N. Alvis

923. Weber, David J., ed. WILLIAM BECKNELL AS A MOUNTAIN MAN: TWO LETTERS. *New Mexico Hist. R. 1971 46(3): 253-260.* Although Becknell is described as the father of the Santa Fe Trail, he did participate in at least one trapping venture in the Rocky Mountains. The two letters, the first written on 29 November 1824, a few days before his departure, and the second written probably in June 1825, describe the preparations for the expedition and the expedition itself. 9 notes.   D. F. Henderson

924. West, Helen B. ROBARE: ELUSIVE POST IN BLACKFEET COUNTRY. *Montana 1965 15(3): 44-57.* Montana's floods of 1964 washed away the last traces of early trading towns along the Blackfoot reservation's southern border. Robare, a center of whisky trade and other illicit business from 1874 to 1900, witnessed its share of fights, murders, and lynchings. Derived from letters and reports in archives of the Blackfeet Agency; illustrated with photographs and drawings.
                                                        S. R. Davison

925. —. SEÑOR DON MANUEL LISA. *Bull. of the Missouri Hist. Soc. 1966 23(1): 52-58.* This unsigned article originally appeared in the *Missouri Saturday News* on 10 March 1838. The writer described how Señor Don Manuel Lisa dealt fearlessly and successfully with the Indian tribes, such as the Osage and the Cheyenne, with whom he traded. Manuel Lisa formed the Missouri Fur Company and traded with the Indians extensively. Between 1809 and 1819 he was associated with John Dougherty in beaver trapping. In a confrontation with the Cheyenne chiefs, Lisa not only defied them but held a group of them as hostages. "Mr. Lisa retained the hostages he had confined, until his detached party reached the fort. His trade with the Cheyennes was subsequently conducted with the utmost circumspection, by exchanging commodities with them through a small opening in the wall of his trading house."
                                                        D. D. Cameron

Mining and Oil

926. Angelo, C. Aubrey. IMPRESSIONS OF THE BOISE BASIN IN 1863. *Idaho Yesterdays 1963 7(1): 5-13.* An eyewitness account of the Boise Basin gold rush of 1863, by a correspondent for the San Francisco *Daily Alta California,* reprinted with editorial footnotes. The author particularly stressed the hardships, the primitive conditions in the mining settlements, the ever-present problem of Indian attacks, the general lawlessness, and the greed of the miners and their associates. He described the claims, the quantity and quality of gold output, and the general economy of the mining settlements during the first months of the gold strike. M. Small

927. Arrington, Leonard J., and Hinton, Wayne K. THE HORN SILVER BONANZA. *U. of Wyoming Pub. 1966 32: 35-54, 147-151.* In September 1875 two prospectors discovered the Horn Silver Mine in the San Francisco Mountains of Southwestern Utah. With a striking resemblance to the famous Nevada Comstock Lode, the ore body projected into a funnel shape toward the surface. A principal handicap, however, was the inaccessibility of the mine. It was located 176 miles from the nearest railhead. Bankrupt Jay Cooke's famous organizational ability, Jay Gould's financial wizardry, stock subscription by the Church of Jesus Christ of Latter-Day Saints, and other elements combined to overcome this difficulty by mid-1880. Consolidated lines from Salt Lake City to San Francisco near the mine created the Utah Central Railway. The multimillion dollar stock subscription was taken up largely by Eastern capitalists. Jay Cooke's share in the enterprise was such that he was able to establish another fortune for himself. The management and production history of the Horn Silver Mine, an outstanding producer of lead, silver, zinc, copper, and some gold, is traced to the present. The rich ore has played out. Presently, the Horn dump is worked by an occasional person. 71 notes. D. L. Smith

928. Atherton, Lewis, ed. FIRE ON THE COMSTOCK. *Am. West 1965 2(1): 24-33.* Gideon Anthony Hamilton was an engineer in charge of milling machinery on the Comstock, Virginia City, at the height of its fame as a mining community. The Comstock suffered a catastrophic fire on 26 October 1875. Hamilton, an eye-witness to the occasion, described it to a friend in a letter here published with an editorial introduction. The Hamilton papers are in the Huntington Library, San Marino, California. Illus., biblio., note. D. L. Smith

929. Atherton, Lewis. THE MINING PROMOTOR IN THE TRANS-MISSISSIPPI WEST. *Western Hist. Q. 1970 1(1): 35-50.* The jack-of-all-trades image of the trans-Mississippi West mining frontier is probably overdrawn. Locators, promoters, and developers usually arrived early along with the prospectors and placer miners. Even experienced mine superintendents, professional mining engineers, and skilled deep-rock miners were early arrivals at most new mining discoveries after the Civil War. Mining was a matter of several specialties. Theodore J. Lamoreaux was a mining promoter from the 1880's to the 1920's, whose career is an effective illustration of specialization. He never gained the reputation for mining sagacity because he was never lucky enough to share richly in any bonanza strike. His operations on the fringes of the richest ore deposits and sources of investment capital do illustrate, however, "the outer limits of feasible mining promotion." He always had claims and mines for sale, more than could be marketed. Promoters learned to live in a market continuously glutted with every ingredient of production except capital. Lamoreaux fits the stereotype American mining promoter image that is common in American literature. 42 notes. D. L. Smith

930. Bakken, Gordon M. THE TAXATION OF MINERAL WEALTH AND THE NEVADA CONSTITUTIONAL CONVENTION OF 1864. *Nevada Hist. Soc. Q. 1969 12(4): 5-15.* In 1863 a proposed constitution for Nevada was soundly rejected by the voters primarily because of a provision that would tax all mines, productive or not. The mining tax was a crucial point before the delegates who reassembled in 1864 to redraft the constitution. The interest dispute between the mining faction and the cow county faction quickly became the chief stumbling block to a successful convention. Bitter debate finally produced a compromise which provided for taxation only on the proceeds of a mine or claim. The 1864 constitution was approved by the electorate. The Nevada experience became a pattern for other Rocky Mountain mining States, both in the factional arguments used and solutions applied to the mineral taxation problem. An appendix gives patterns of bloc voting in the 1864 Nevada Convention. Based on primary sources; 25 notes, appendix. E. P. Costello

931. Billington, Ray A. BOOKS THAT WON THE WEST: THE GUIDEBOOKS OF THE FORTY-NINERS & FIFTY-NINERS. *Am. West 1967 4(3): 25-32, 72-75.* Of all of the advertisers of the American West none were more extravagant in proclaiming the opportunities of the West and in stimulating and shaping westward migration than the guidebooks. The hundreds of 19th-century guides reveal that their authors were effective propagandists because they seemed to possess an unusual sensitivity to the social conditions of their day as well as a working knowledge of human psychology. This analysis is based on a study of 25 such guides published for use of emigrants to the California goldfields in 1848 and 1849, and of 17 which were for the edification of those in the Colorado rush of 1858-59. They all understated the cost of a journey to the goldfields, described the trail as shorter and easier than it was, and overstated the wealth awaiting the emigrants in the pot at the end of the rainbow. It is concluded that the guidebooks writers motivated a larger migration than events justified and that they were competent students of human motivation. The reactions of the users of the guidebooks were determined through examination of their diaries and reminiscences. Adapted from an address by the author at the opening of an exhibit of the Everett D. Graff Collection of Western Americana in the Newberry Library, Chicago; 7 illus., biblio. note. D. L. Smith

932. Burchardt, Bill. OSAGE OIL. *Chronicles of Oklahoma 1963 41(3): 253-269.* Discusses the murders of some oil-rich Osage Indians and the sensational trial of wealthy rancher W. R. Hale and his nephew Ernest Burkhart for these murders. Henry Roan, Anna Brown, and the Smith family had been murdered. Ernest Burkhart's wife was to inherit all their holdings. The U.S. Bureau of Investigation solved the murders and secured convictions in Federal court of Hale and Burkhart. These events serve as a springboard for the author to relate the history of the Osage Indians. In 1906 the reservation was broken up into 160-acre tracts. Each Osage received a "headright," meaning that he or she would receive an equal share of all mineral rights. After 1906 public lease auctions were held with oil companies bidding nearly two million dollars for each 160-acre tract. Oilmen and geologists came on special trains. Bootleggers, whiskey dealers, and criminals of all kinds flourished. Many Osage were murdered. Finally, after the U.S. Bureau of Investigation obtained convictions of Hale and Burkhart, the murders ceased. Documented, illus., biblio. D. L. Smith

933. Cantelon, Philip L., ed. THE CALIFORNIA GOLD FIELDS IN THE 1850'S: LETTERS FROM EPHRAIM THOMPSON, DAVIESS INDIANA. *Indiana Mag. of Hist. 1969 65(3): 157-172.* A series of letters from Thompson reflecting his disenchantment with California. Thompson wrote to his mother, father, and brother telling them how unpleasant his experiences in the gold fields had been and admonishing them to dissuade anyone from coming to "the diggings," if they could. Contains many insightful, firsthand descriptions of life in San Francisco and Sacramento. Based on primary sources; 9 notes. N. E. Tutorow

934. Clebsch, William A. GOODNESS, GOLD, AND GOD. *Pacific Historian 1966 10(3): 19-42.* "The California mining career of Peter Y. Cool, 1851-1852. A journal transcribed, edited, and introduced by...Clebsch." Cool, a New Yorker, came to the gold fields as a young man. As a missionary and miner he mixed piety and temperance with gold fever, ministered to the sick, and lectured on immorality. The journal describes the daily round of life of the miners, both at work and at rest. Reproduced are a photograph of Cool, two "typical pages" from the journal, a map of Calaveras County, and an alphabetized *personae.* Annotated. T. Cripps

935. Cornwall, Harry C. and Vandenbusche, Duane, ed. MY FIRST YEAR IN THE GUNNISON COUNTRY. *Colorado Mag. 1969 46(3): 220-244.* This selection from the memoirs of Cornwall, a young mining engineer, describes his first year in the Gunnison country. Cornwall recounts his 1879 trip from New York to Leadville by railroad and then by horseback to Ruby Camp. The remainder of the article deals with the characteristics and problems of the mining camp - speculation, food and

supplies, Indian scares, winter in the high mountains, travel, vigilante government, and mining claims. The editor, in an addendum, says Cornwall continued his engineering work in the Gunnison area until 1886 when he returned to the East permanently. Illus., 5 photos, 21 notes.

O. H. Zabel

936. Crockett, Norman L. FRONTIER DENTIST: THE LETTERS OF WALTHUS JEWELL WATKINS. *Colorado Mag. 1967 44(4): 277-292.* The development of Colorado was made evident by the coming of professional men. Walthus Jewell Watkins, dentist, came to Colorado in search of gold. He wrote more than one hundred letters to his brother in Missouri about the mining claims and his work as a dentist. These letters were written from various towns and mining camps—from Craig, Amethyst, and Steamboat Springs, Colorado; from Dixon and Baggs, Wyoming. They reveal conditions in the mining towns, the efforts of a dentist to make a living, and the uncertainties of mining claims. 3 illus., 16 notes.

I. W. Van Noppen

937. Cushman, Dan. GARNET: LAST BOOMING GOLD CAMP. *Montana 1964 14(3): 38-55.* Rise and decline of Garnet and neighboring gold camps in west central Montana, 1865-1890.

S. R. Davison

938. Davis, Robert Ralph, Jr., ed. AN OHIOAN'S LETTER FROM THE CALIFORNIA GOLD FIELDS IN 1850. *Ohio Hist. 1967 76(3): 159-163.* Contains the text along with an explanatory introduction and notes of a letter written by Philip John Hines of Van Wert, Ohio, from California to his family in October 1850. The letter describes his trip to California, the gold mining and related activities which he observed in California, and his own failure and resulting poverty. The letter and other Hines manuscripts are now in the possession of his great-great-great grandson, John Eugene Hines, Van Wert, Ohio.

S. L. Jones

939. Davis, William E., ed. GEORGE FORMAN, THE GREAT PEDESTRIAN. *Idaho Yesterdays 1966 10(1): 2-11.* "Entertaining and perceptive observations of Boise Basin during the gold rush." George Forman, an experienced miner in Australia, joined the Idaho gold rush in 1864. Forman walked most of the way from St. Joseph, Missouri, to Idaho and back again to his home in Michigan. The author provides an extensive account of the boisterous nature of Idaho City and the hard daily life of a miner in search of gold. 24 notes.

D. H. Swift

940. Day, Henry L. MINING HIGHLIGHTS OF THE COEUR D'ALENE DISTRICT. *Idaho Yesterdays 1964 7(4): 2-9.* Reviews the history of the development of the Coeur d'Alene mining district of northern Idaho from the discovery of gold in 1860 to the present.

M. Small

941. Greer, Richard A. CALIFORNIA GOLD - SOME REPORTS TO HAWAII. *Hawaiian J. of Hist. 1970 4: 157-173.* Presents extracts from letters and newspaper articles describing the California gold rush and its effects on Hawaii.

R. N. Alvis

942. Hartsock, D. Lane. THE IMPACT OF THE RAILROADS ON COAL MINING IN OSAGE COUNTY, 1869-1910. *Kansas Hist. Q. 1971 37(4): 429-440.* The Santa Fe railroad first built its line south from Topeka rather than northeast to Atchison because it wished to tap the coal fields of Osage County. Like most railroads, the Santa Fe wished to gain control of its own fuel supply. The Lawrence and Carbondale, Manhattan, Alma and Burlingame, and the Missouri Pacific also relied on Osage coal, but the principal developer was the Santa Fe. The penetration of the field by rails opened a wide market that was unhindered by competition. As long as the coal supply kept pace with demands, there was no incentive to develop other sources. Although it was the largest field west of the Mississippi, the Osage region eventually could not keep pace with rising demands. Even the Santa Fe was forced to seek other fuels in Kansas that would not only satisfy demands but also be cheaper and of better quality. Based on secondary sources; 4 illus., 2 maps, 3 tables.

W. F. Zornow

943. Hawgood, John A., ed. GENERAL SUTTER WRITES A LETTER: HERE PUBLISHED FOR THE FIRST TIME, IT SHOWS HIS IDIOSYNCRASIES AS WELL AS CALIFORNIA LIFE IN 1853. *Pacific Historian 1966 10(1): 34-41.* The first publication of a letter from John Augustus Sutter to Edward Kern, an artist. An introduction ex-

plains that Sutter lived a drifting life from Southwestern Germany, to Bern, then in 1834 to Le Havre, and finally to the Mexican province of Upper California in 1839 where he subdued Indians in the name of the Mexican Government. He found it easy to switch sides during the Mexican War and seemed to be on his way to prosperity after the discovery of gold at Sutter's Fort. But squatters, corrupt lawyers, and unfavorable court decisions ruined his fortune. The letter is a bitter tale of lost opportunities and a plea for justice. Documented from published sources; illus.

T. R. Cripps

944. Heite, Edward F. EXTRA BILLY SMITH. *Virginia Cavalcade 1966 15(3): 5-13.* An account of the life of William Smith, a Virginian whose adventurous life took him from the governor's mansion to the California gold fields and then back to Virginia to serve as a general in the Confederate Army. Illus.

R. B. Lange

945. Higley, Caroline. SUTTER'S GOLDEN EMPIRE. *Montana 1964 14(3): 26-36.* The discovery which started the Gold Rush of '49 was almost the only prosperous note in the life of John A. Sutter, who was ruined by trespassing miners.

S. R. Davison

946. Holliday, J. S., ed. ON THE GOLD RUSH TRAIL. *Am. West 1968 5(4): 38.* Three accounts of Fourth of July celebrations taken from diaries of Forty-Niners: William B. Swain's manuscript diary now in the Yale University Library; William J. Watson's *Journal, published in 1851;* and William B. Lorton's manuscript diary in the Bancroft Library.

D. L. Smith

947. Hyatt, L. Paul. J. M. ALEXANDER: A GOLD MINER'S LETTER, 1852. *California Hist. Soc. Q. 1970 49(4): 353-358.* Alexander's letter, written to his sister but intended for the rest of his family as well, describes his journey to California by sea, his success in prospecting for gold, and the high cost of living. When Alexander wrote the letter he had been in California about two weeks. Though he does not advise against making the journey, he cautions his friends about the dangers of disease and illness. 8 notes.

A. Hoffman

948. Hynding, Alan A. THE COAL MINERS OF WASHINGTON TERRITORY: LABOR TROUBLES IN 1888-89. *Arizona and the West 1970 12(3): 211-236.* Roslyn, perched on the isolated eastern arid slopes of the Cascades, and Newcastle, on the western slopes a few miles southeast of Seattle, were coal-mining towns of western Washington Territory where capital and labor wrestled in 1888 and 1889. With the rapid economic development of the 1880's, the frequent clashes between management and labor became violent. Managers of the coal mines were often unfair and ruthless, frequently taking the law into their own hands. Caught in the middle were the territorial authorities who were not sure whether they should maintain a scrupulous neutrality or support one of the sides in the disputes. By the time Roslyn and Newcastle became the focal points of the difficulties, a tradition of violence was firmly rooted in the territory, as was the employment of agents and strikebreakers by management. Management was victorious in the struggle. Better laws and better enforcement came with statehood in 1889. 3 illus., map, 35 notes.

D. L. Smith

949. Ives, Richard L. THE COCHRAN COKE OVENS. *J. of Arizona Hist. 1972 13(2): 73-81.* The five Cochran coke ovens are located along the Gila River almost due north of Tucson in southern Arizona. The area is virtually inaccessible today. Documentary evidence on the history of the ovens is nonexistent. Local folklore offers interesting explanations. The best oral information indicates that the ovens were built about 1890 to make mesquite charcoal which was used for smelting ores taken from mines north of the Gila River. This is further established as the probable explanation by the remains of trails, mines, and other artifacts in the area. The ovens themselves were ruggedly constructed and are excellently preserved stone relics. 3 illus., map, 7 notes.

D. L. Smith

950. Jackson, W. Turrentine. BRITISH IMPACT ON THE UTAH MINING INDUSTRY. *Utah Hist. Q. 1963 31(4): 347-375.* Traces the history of late 19th-century British investment in Utah mining ventures, concentrating on the boom period in silver mining in the early 1870's. The operations of several British syndicates are described in detail, greatest attention being directed to activities of local Utah agents whose manipula-

tions often resulted in severe losses by the British investor. The author concludes with a reference to the beginnings of British speculation in Utah gold and copper mining after 1895. Based in part on the records of the British syndicates available in the Bancroft Library, University of California, Berkeley. S. L. Jones

951. Jackson, William Turrentine. DAKOTA TIN: BRITISH INVESTORS AT HARNEY PEAK, 1880-1900. *North Dakota Hist. 1966 33(1): 22-63.* After capitalists took over gold mining operations following the gold rush, 1876-78, Harney Peak, highest mountain east of the Rockies, became the center for a tin mining promotion with British capital. Some mining journals in both England and America expressed skepticism as to the quantity of tin available in the claims attained by the Harney Peak Consolidated Tin Company, Ltd., while others maintained that the mines were of enormous extent and value. Professors in schools of mines and a tin mining authority from Cornwall encouraged the scheme, which turned out to be one of fraud and intrigue between vendors and promoters. With a supposed capital stock of 15 million dollars no more than 1,545 dollars worth of tin was produced. Yet the economic life of a portion of South Dakota for a period of 20 years was underwitten by this company in pretense of mining tin. I. W. Van Noppen

952. Jackson, W. Turrentine. HER BRITANNIC MAJESTY AND MONTANA'S SAPPHIRES. *Montana 1964 14(4): 57-67.* As early as 1883, sapphires of gem quality were recognized in the placer gold deposits near Helena. Speculators and investors showed interest after 1890, British capital especially being attracted. Over-optimism mingled with fraud led to failure of the first ventures. English sapphire companies later made some profit on stones of industrial grade from the Yogo area, which continues to be worked sporadically. Based on reports in newspapers and mining journals. S. R. Davison

953. Kalisch, Philip A. THE WOEBEGONE MINERS OF WYOMING: A HISTORY OF COAL MINE DISASTERS IN THE EQUALITY STATE. *Ann. of Wyoming 1970 42(2): 237-242.* Discusses the native origins of Wyoming coal miners, showing that Chinese laborers provided the bulk of the work force prior to the mid-1880's when violence forced them out of the State. Thereafter, Europeans comprised the majority of workers, with Russians, Italians, and Irish being the largest national groups represented. Describes the major mine disasters between that at Almy in March 1881 to the last one at Afton in February 1938. Concludes that little effort was made to prevent such accidents and that they were usually considered to be the responsibility of the miners. Based on newspaper accounts, U.S. Government investigations, surveys, reports, and published secondary material; 57 notes. R. L. Nichols

954. Kelley, Lawrence C. THE NAVAHO INDIANS: LAND AND OIL. *New Mexico Hist. R. 1963 38(1): 1-28.* The article meticulously traces the expansion of Navaho Reservation Land from 1868 to 1934. The discovery of oil in 1922 and a congressional decision in 1927 to uphold Indian title to the oil and to the land from which it came were the outstanding events of the 20th century. Although the oil revenues dwindled quickly, they proved enough to stimulate a reservation expansion program "which resulted in the present, apparently definitive boundaries of the reservation." D. F. Henderson

955. Kenn, Charles. A VISIT TO CALIFORNIA GOLD FIELDS. *Hawaiian Hist. Soc. Annual Report 1965: 7-16.* Translation of an account by the Reverend Lowell Smith, pastor of Kaumakapili Church, taken from *Ka Hae Hawaii* The Hawaiian Flag, a weekly newspaper edited by J. Pule, from 1 December 1858 to 19 January 1859. A photograph and biographical sketch of the Reverend Smith are included, as well as descriptions of San Francisco, San Jose, Sacramento, gold and quicksilver mining, and transportation in California. This paper was given before the Hawaiian Historical Society on 20 January 1965. R. N. Alvis

956. Kenny, William Robert. MEXICAN-AMERICAN CONFLICT ON THE MINING FRONTIER, 1848-1852. *J. of the West 1967 6(4): 582-592.* Discovery of gold in California brought thousands of American and Mexican citizens to the mining camps. Most Americans congregated in northern California while the Mexicans generally remained in the south. Where they came into contact in large groups there were exhibited open feelings of dislike and distrust. One reason was the

fact that the Mexican War had scarcely ended when gold was discovered. Other reasons include the different languages, the fact that the Mexicans were identified with a set of religious beliefs wholeheartedly despised in the United States and that the Mexicans were usually dark-complexioned individuals, which in itself indicates something sinister. All of this set the stage for open conflict. Murder, robbery, and other forms of violence were very common among the two groups. The imposition of a Foreign Miner's Tax by the California Legislature in 1850 resulted in Mexicans leaving the state. Although repealed in 1851, the Mexicans did not return to the goldfields. Based on newspaper accounts and published sources, 34 notes. D. N. Brown

957. Kersten, Earl W., Jr. THE EARLY SETTLEMENT OF AURORA, NEVADA, AND NEARBY MINING CAMPS. *Ann. of the Assoc. of Am. Geographers 1964 54(4): 490-507.* Considers the discovery, growth, regional economic influence, and subsequent decline of mining camps in the western Great Basin. Illus., maps, 59 notes. W. R. Boedecker

958. Kihn, Phyllis. CONNECTICUT AND THE CALIFORNIA GOLD RUSH: THE CONNECTICUT MINING AND TRADING COMPANY. *Connecticut Hist. Soc. Bull. 1963 28(1): 1-13.* The Connecticut Mining and Trading Company was founded in Hartford in December 1848 with one thousand shares at 25 dollars each. When the stock was all subscribed, the schooner *General Morgan* was purchased for 11 thousand dollars and the remainder was used for supplies and goods to be sold in California. A diary was kept of the voyage by Albert Lyman of Hartford. The trip to California from New York City took from 22 February to 5 August 1849. The second part of the diary as published described life in the diggings and covered the period 5 August to 1 January 1850. An account is given of the lives of some members of the company, including Jason F. Burr who died in 1920 at the age of 92, the last gold rush forty-niner resident of Hartford. Illus. E. P. Stickney

959. King, James T., ed. "I TAKE THIS OPPORTUNITY TO INFORM YOU...": THE GOLD RUSH LETTERS OF ANDREW CAIRNS. *California Hist. Soc. Q. 1967 46(3): 207-222.* Letters from an uneducated young farmer from New York State who decided in 1850 to go to California in search of gold. He went via the Isthmus of Panama from which his first letter was written. The letters document the familiar pattern of optimism, then bewilderment, and, after several years, discouragement and defeat. The last of the California letters was written from Yreka in 1854. The family lost track of him until 1862 when he wrote that he had become a farmer at Olympia, Washington. 55 notes. E. P. Stickney

960. Lapp, Rudolph M. THE NEGRO IN GOLD RUSH CALIFORNIA. *J. of Negro Hist. 1964 49(2): 81-98.* The gold rush brought several thousand slaves and free Negroes into California. They worked as miners, laborers, cooks and in other service occupations. Some of those who came as slaves earned enough to purchase their own freedom. The pioneer society of California permitted a degree of freedom for Negroes not known in most other parts of the country yet there were attempts to introduce slavery and to exclude free Negroes. In the courts Negroes were not allowed to testify against whites until 1863. Many of the California Negroes took advantage of the opportunities presented them for educational and economic advancement and they met in a number of conventions to demand improvement of their legal status. L. Gara

961. Larson, T. A., ed. ACROSS THE PLAINS IN 1864 WITH GEORGE FORMAN. *Ann. of Wyoming 1968 40(1): 5-21.* An edited account of Forman's trip from St. Louis to the Montana gold mines during the summer of 1864. Forman, an experienced logger and Mississippi River boatman, had participated in the Australian gold rush of 1852. In 1864 he crossed the plains traveling first as a teamster, and later in both small and large wagon trains. His journal discusses health and diet, general travel experiences, and rumors of Indian attacks. Based on government reports, reminiscent accounts, and secondary material; illus., 16 notes. To be continued. R. L. Nichols

962. Lavender, David. AVALANCHE AT THE BLACK BEAR. *Am. West 1965 2(3): 32-40.* With rising copper, lead, and zinc prices in 1925, the Black Bear mine near Telluride in the San Juan Mountains of

southwestern Colorado was reopened. A crew of 16 moved into the boarding and bunkhouse which was deliberately located away from the avalanche-prone path. Early in the morning on 2 April 1926, two slides occurred in rapid succession. The second overcame the first and the compression and pressure pushed the avalanche out of its normal chute. The boardinghouse was destroyed. All but two of the occupants miraculously survived. One of the survivors told the story to the author. Illustrated by photographs of the survivor.   D. L. Smith

963. Lavender, David. HOW TO SALT A GOLD MINE. *Am. Heritage 1968 19(3): 65-70.* Describes methods employed by the wily "prospectors" during the gold and silver rushes in the Far West. These old-time confidence men "salted" old mines by planting ore in obvious places, scattering handfuls of shredded silver dollars at the bottom of shafts, tamping minute fillings of dental gold into tiny rock cavities, painting a silver nitrate solution on the face of ore beds, squirting liquid into cracks with a syringe, or pelting the ore beds with a shotgun shell fill with coin shavings. New technological methods reduced the ease with which swindlers operated, but even today "the most a prospective buyer can hope for is that he will detect the fraud in time." Illus.
                    J. D. Born, Jr.

964. Lenon, Robert, ed. THE MINES OF GOLD BASIN, A REPORT OF 1883. *J. of Arizona Hist. 1967 8(4): 256-267.* An edited mining report of an otherwise unknown F. W. Speer, who wrote to interest Ohio investors in the "Gold Basin" region of northwest Arizona. Although Speer was optimistic about the amount of gold to be mined in the basin, later investors found only modest amounts of the precious metal when they tried it. Based on Speer's report and miscellaneous printed documents; map, 21 notes.   R. J. Roske

965. Lewis, Marvin. HOT CREEK AND THE WIDE GRAY VALLEY. *Nevada Hist. Soc. Q. 1970 13(2): 40-53.* A history of the most active period of Hot Creek, a mining camp in central Nevada. The story of Hot Creek is reconstructed principally from the diary of Martha James Gally, who arrived in Hot Creek with her family in 1866 and who recorded details of life in the isolated silver mining camp. Based on a diary, newspaper accounts, and official reports; map, 31 notes.
                    E. P. Costello

966. Leyendecker, Liston E. COLORADO AND THE PARIS UNIVERSAL EXPOSITION, 1867. *Colorado Mag. 1969 46(1): 1-15.* Points out that by the end of 1865 Colorado mining was a risky enterprise. In order to interest foreign investors, private persons organized a mineral display at the Paris Universal Exposition in 1867. Finances were limited and Joel Parker Whitney of Boston, who had Colorado mining interests, took over both the financing of the venture and its leadership as official Colorado Commissioner. His work was so well done that the Colorado ore exhibit was awarded a gold medal. The award helped convince wealthy Easterners that they should invest in Colorado mines. It also helped to assure Coloradans that their ores were worthy of more effort. Illus., 73 notes.   O. H. Zabel

967. Livingston-Little, D. E. THE BUNKER HILL AND SULLIVAN: NORTH IDAHO'S MINING DEVELOPMENT FROM 1885 TO 1900. *Idaho Yesterdays 1963 7(1): 34-43.* Traces the economic development of northern Idaho from 1885 to 1900, with particular reference to the Bunker Hill and Sullivan Mine, the largest, wealthiest, and most powerful corporation in the region. The author describes the creation of the company, the problems of finance and operation, and the violent labor disputes which marked the 1890's. He concludes that the pattern of development in northern Idaho followed closely that of most of the northernwestern states, and that the prosperity of the northern Idaho farmers was directly dependent upon the prosperity of the adjacent mining community. Based largely on the mining area press and on the letters and private papers of Simeon Gannett Reed (Reed College Project, 1940).   M. Small

968. Loose, Warren. AT BODIE. *Am. West 1968 5(4): 41-43.* Derived from local newspapers, this describes the 1880 Fourth of July celebration in a mining camp town.   D. L. Smith

969. MacDonald, Douglas. LOST HARDIN SILVER: ENIGMA OF THE BLACK ROCK DESERT. *Nevada Hist. Soc. Q. 1972 15(1): 20-26.* The story of the only search for a lost mine in the history of Nevada to set off a genuine rush, promote a town, and cause comments from mineralogists throughout the Nation. James Allen Hardin had discovered accidentally, and then lost, an apparently rich vein of silver in the Black Rock Desert of western Nevada about 1849. He discovered the vein while hunting for meat for a wagon train of which he was a member. He and his companion did not realize the magnitude of their discovery until about nine years later, after having settled in Petaluma, California. Hardin gathered a party to relocate the discovery, but could not find it. In 1866 some high-grade ore was found in the area. This fact, coupled with heavy reporting by newsmen, caused a rush to the area and the building of Hardin City. By the summer of 1868, much of the publicity had proved untrustworthy and the prospective empire in the Black Rock desert fell apart. The vein of silver that precipitated the renewed interest was never relocated, but Hardin had at one time the ore samples to prove it a lucrative strike. Photo.   E. P. Costello

970. Manley, Robert N. WEALTH BENEATH THE PRAIRIE: THE SEARCH FOR COAL IN NEBRASKA. *Nebraska Hist. 1966 47(2): 157-176.* Carefully surveys the search for coal from the 1850's through the first decade of the 20th century. This search, prompted by boomers who envisioned a glorious industrial future for the state, reached its height in the early 1870's and gradually gave way to the realization that, as one editor wrote, "Nebraska is an agricultural state, or it is nothing."   R. Lowitt

971. Marleau, Michael H. MINING IN THE SKY. *Pacific Historian 1969 13(1): 54-57.* An account of California's first silver mines and the events leading to the creation of Alpine County in 1864. Based on contemporary newspaper accounts; 2 illus., 20 notes.
                    F. I. Murphy

972. McCormick, Richard Cunningham. "THERE IS NO HUMBUG ABOUT THE GOLD." *Arizoniana 1964 5(3): 61-64.* In a letter to a friend in the East, McCormick wrote on 11 July 1864 showing interest in the coming presidential campaign; mentioning the progress of the new seat of government, Prescott, which he had himself named for the late eminent historian; and expressing the hope of acquiring wealth from the area's burgeoning gold placers. 8 notes.
                    E. P. Stickney

973. McFadden, Thomas George. "WE'LL ALL WEAR DIAMONDS." *Idaho Yesterdays 1966 10(2): 2-7.* "In 1865-1866 and again in 1892, the Owyhee region was the scene of a wild diamond hunting craze." The author presents articles from contemporary newspapers that helped publicize the diamond legend. The main impetus for the first rush was provided by Governor Caleb Lyon, whose reputation was described by the *Idaho Tri-Weekly Statesman* (1872) as "being not only a bilk, but a thief, who was as good as the best." Jackson L. Davis, nicknamed "Diamondfield Jack," was the only one of the 1892 diamond hunters to gain fame, if not fortune, from his persistence. Illus., 13 notes.
                    B. B. Swift

974. McKevitt, Jerry. "GOLD LAKE" MYTH BROUGHT CIVILIZATION TO PLUMAS COUNTY. *J. of the West 1964 3(4): 489-500.* Plumas County, situated high in the recesses of the northern Sierra Nevada, was not penetrated by white men until 1848. In 1848 Peter Lassen conducted an immigrant party through the area but the Lassen trail was difficult and little used after 1850. In that year, however, Thomas Stoddard claimed to have discovered a mountain lake near the headwaters of the Feather and Yuba Rivers whose shores were lined with nuggets of pure gold. Stoddard led one expedition in a fruitless search for the mythical lake and barely escaped lynching. Hundreds of other prospectors also rushed into the area. When the "gold lake" myth proved a disappointing reality, its drawing power was replaced by reports of actual discoveries on the Feather River. By late 1850 scores of mining camps had sprung up along this river and its tributaries. The author traces the establishment of the more important of these camps which were settled indirectly as a result of the hoax. Documented from published sources.
                    D. N. Brown

975. McMillan, A. C. GRANITE'S GLITTERING GLORY. *Montana 1964 14(3): 62-73.* Recollections of a clergyman who served the silver town of Granite, Montana, in its boom years around 1890.
                    S. R. Davison

976. Miller, Cincinnatus H. OLD BABOON. *Idaho Yesterdays 1967 11(4): 2-9.* Writes of the people that the author knew as an express-man in North Idaho. Provides a character sketch of a prospector in the Clearwater and Salmon River gold rushes and describes Lewiston, Idaho, in 1862. Discusses a secret gold strike in Baboon Gulch, how the gold was removed from the site, and how it was stolen by robbers. The robbers were caught and hung by the first Vigilance Committee of the North. 2 illus.
D. H. Swift

977. Miller, Nancy. MINING IN THE SAWTOOTHS: THE STORY OF VIENNA AND SAWTOOTH CITY. *Idaho Yesterdays 1965 9(1): 10-16.* "For a decade or so after the Bannock War of 1878, these two camps prospered in the beautiful country at the head of the Salmon River." The author describes the mining activities in the Sawtooth region, the major companies, the men involved, the quantities of money spent, and the profits. The *Ketchum Keystone* of 21 January 1888 attributed the failure of mining in the Sawtooths to the "indifferent ill management of properties" and "reckless and injudicious expenditure of money." At that time, successful means for economically processing the type of ores found in the area had not been developed. Photo.
B. B. Swift

978. Muldrow, William. ARTICLES OF AGREEMENT FOR AN EXPEDITION TO CALIFORNIA FOR GOLD, 1849. *Missouri Hist. Soc. Bull. 1963 20(1): 51-55.* Expresses the objectives, motives and hopes of a group of 12 to 14 persons organizing themselves as a "joint stock association" for the general purpose expressed in the title. The agreement covers specific provisions on such matters as expenses, period of the contract, and rights and obligations of the members. The document is in the Palmyra, Missouri Papers at the Missouri Historical Society Archives.
R. J. Hanks

979. Murray, Robert A. MINER'S DELIGHT, INVESTOR'S DESPAIR: THE UPS AND DOWNS OF A SUB-MARGINAL MINING CAMP. *Ann. of Wyoming 1972 44(1): 25-55.* Summarizes gold mining activity from 1860 to 1940 in western Wyoming's South Pass mining country and traces the history of a complex of mines collectively known as Miner's Delight. Compared to mining regions in other States, Miner's Delight produced little gold even during its peak years of 1865-80. Nevertheless, these early mining operations benefited Wyoming. The promise of gold attracted surplus labor which later helped to build the Union Pacific Railroad, brought additional permanent settlers to the Wind River Valley, and led the government to establish two military posts in the region. These posts, along with eastern investment dollars and local spending by mine operators, significantly boosted the area's economy. Never the roaring community described by some writers, Miner's Delight is now a ghost town, and few of the original buildings remain. Based on primary and secondary sources; 132 notes.
G. R. Adams

980. Nash, Gerald D. OIL IN THE WEST: REFLECTIONS ON THE HISTORIOGRAPHY OF AN UNEXPLORED FIELD. *Pacific Hist. R. 1970 39(2): 193-204.* Describes some of the major historical works on the western petroleum industry, suggesting further important research still to be done. Among the possibilities are biographical studies of industry leaders, history and analysis of scientific aspects (such as the influence of geological theories of the movement for oil conservation, including the economic, legal, and political aspects), studies of the U.S. Geological Survey, Bureau of Mines, or Department of the Interior, oil pollution problems, and oil policies overseas, including military and naval involvement. 20 notes.
E. C. Hyslop

981. Nunis, Doyce B., Jr. A CALIFRONIA GOLD RUSH LETTER FROM THE "HARTFORD COURANT." *Southern California Q. 1964 46(3): 265-279.* An anonymous letter dated 22 February 1850, printed in the 18 May 1850 issue of the *Hartford Courant.* It is an account of the writer's experiences in crossing the Colorado River, dealing with the Yuman Indians, crossing the "Great American Desert" to Los Angeles, and journeying up the San Joaquin Valley to Stockton and San Francisco.
J. Jensen

982. Oates, Stephen B. BOOM OIL! OKLAHOMA STRIKES IT RICH! *Am. West 1968 5(1): 11-15, 64-66.* The gold rush towns with their lawlessness and unrestrained individualism did not constitute the last American wild West frontier. All of the drama which attended the mining frontier was recast in the opening quarter of the present century and replayed on the red plains of Oklahoma. A series of spectacular oil discoveries, 1904-23, stirred the nation as nothing else had since the discovery of gold in California in 1848. The earlier "boomer" and "sooner" human stampedes into Oklahoma when the territory was opened paled in comparison. The author illustrates his generalizations with accounts of: Drumright, the hub of the great oil field; Ragtown, the bloodiest boomtown in the State's history; Burbank, where the unlucky Osage Indians became the wealthiest, per capita, people in the world and the victims of "hordes of white flies"; and Seminole City and Bowlegs, where the new hosts for oil field parasites were illiterate Seminole farmers. Although Oklahoma appeared to be completely victimized by oil boom crime, responsible oil companies came to realize the boomtown violence was not a necessary evil and introduced well regulated and planned company towns that mitigated the situation somewhat. The moral crusade of the Ku Klux Klan of the 1920's offered counterterrorism for righteousness and morality. Violence was not finally controlled, however, until the oil fields themselves declined and the lawless elements moved to the underground in large cities or to the last old-style oil boom in the Texas panhandle. 4 illus., biblio. note.
D. L. Smith

983. Oberbillig, Ernest. DEVELOPMENT OF WASHOE AND REESE RIVER SILVER PROCESSES. *Nevada Hist. Soc. Q. 1967 10(2): 3-43.* The methods used by the Spaniards in Mexico, Peru, and Bolivia to recover silver from ore were slow, crude, and laborious, predicated on a system of enslaved Indian labor. They were speeded up and mechanized for the Nevada mines from 1860 to 1900. Greater efficiency and lower cost were necessary so as to pay laborers a living wage and still leave a profit. Washoe and Reese River processes derive their names from the mining regions in Nevada where they were developed. From the Nevada silver country these perfected metallurgical innovations were copied widely throughout the world. 17 illus., 62 notes.
D. L. Smith

984. Oviatt, Alton B. PACIFIC COAST COMPETITION FOR THE GOLD CAMP TRADE OF MONTANA. *Pacific Northwest Q. 1965 56(4): 168-176.* Discovery and exploitation of gold fields in western Montana brought more than 11,000 people to Madison County within a year. Merchants and transportation companies quickly developed routes to deliver supplies to the miners, who were almost completely dependent upon outside sources for food, clothing, and equipment. The author summarizes the factors which brought success to Chicago and St. Louis merchants at the expense of those who depended on the Portland-Walla Walla-Mullan Road and other routes.
C. C. Gorchels

985. Pace, Josephine. KIMBERLY AS I REMEMBER HER. *Utah Hist. Q. 1967 35(2): 112-120.* Contains the author's reminiscences of her girlhood, when her father operated a hotel at the Kimberly gold mine, owned by the Annie Laurie Consolidated Gold Mining Company.
S. L. Jones

986. Parker, Watson. THE CAUSES OF AMERICAN GOLD RUSHES. *North Dakota Hist. 1969 36(4): 336-345.* Considers the gold rushes in Georgia in 1828, California in 1849, Colorado in 1859, the Black Hills in 1876, and Alaska in 1897. The author concludes that each of the areas was known as a gold-bearing area for years and even centuries before any large, well-publicized rush took place. The known presence of gold was never enough to trigger a rush. Two indispensable ingredients for a gold rush are: 1) a more than usually mobile population, and 2) a clever publicity program to stir and direct the laymen into a mad rush for gold. Based on a talk given by the author at the Northern Great Plains History Conference at the University of North Dakota in November 1968; illus., photos.
E. P. Costello

987. Parsons, John E., ed. NINE COUSINS IN THE CALIFORNIA GOLD RUSH. *New York Hist. Soc. Q. 1963 47(4): 349-397.* Six grandsons of the Irish patriot, Thomas Addis Emmet, along with three cousins, left New York by ship for the California gold fields in 1849. Many of their adventures are recounted in this series of letters written by one of the grandsons, William J. Emmet, and his cousin, Herman R. LeRoy. The letters cover the period from the voyage to California to the middle of 1850 and are published here for the first time.
C. L. Grant

988. Patterson, Edna B., ed. JOHN MC QUIG DIARY, 1869. *Nevada Hist. Soc. Q. 1963 6(2): 3-27.* Previously unpublished diary of a prospector (birth and death dates not given) relating his unsuccessful efforts and ending with his moving to Pennsylvania Gulch, California.
　　　　　　　　　　　　　　　　　　　　J. D. Filipiak

989. Paul, Rodman Wilson. IN SEARCH OF "DAME SHIRLEY." *Pacific Hist. R. 1964 33(2): 127-146.* Identifies the author of the Shirley letters from the Feather River, California mines, 1851-52, as Louisa A. K. S. Clapp, and recounts the methods used to discover her correct name. This frail young lady, born in New Jersey, connected probably with Julia Ward Howe and the New England Lees, came west with her husband, Fayette Clapp, A.B., Brown University. After spending many years in San Francisco as a school teacher and popular literary figure, she returned east and died at the age of 93. The author made use of college records and legal documents, in preparing this account for Radcliffe's forthcoming volume *Notable American Women, 1607-1950.*
　　　　　　　　　　　　　　　　　　　J. McCutcheon and S

990. Paul, Rodman Wilson. MINING FRONTIERS AS A MEASURE OF WESTERN HISTORICAL WRITING. *Pacific Hist. R. 1964 33(1): 25-34.* Surveys the apparent decline of interest in the frontier and submits that recent writing about the mining frontier, at least, is beginning to show the relevance of the frontier in the national as well as international framework.
　　　　　　　　　　　　　　　　　　　J. McCutcheon

991. Raymond, Rossiter W. STATISTICS OF MINES AND MINING IN THE STATES AND TERRITORIES WEST OF THE ROCKY MOUNTAINS. *Ann. of Wyoming 1968 40(2): 223-239.* A reprinted portion of a report to Congress first published in 1870, which discusses the mining operation in Wyoming Territory. The report includes the location, history, geology, and yield of each lode. It also describes the mills and heavy mining equipment which had been brought into the region.
　　　　　　　　　　　　　　　　　　　R. L. Nichols

992. Roske, Ralph J. THE WORLD IMPACT OF THE CALIFORNIA GOLD RUSH, 1849-1857. *Arizona and the West 1963 5(3): 187-232.* It is the author's assertion that the rush which followed the discovery of gold in California in 1848 "surpassed in world-wide significance anything that had happened in the history of any other American state." The exodus of California-bound gold seekers and the inflow of the bullion which they sent back home "profoundly affected" the major nations of the world. The majority consensus of bankers and businessmen of the time was that the new supply of gold meant prosperity, encouraged widespread speculation, and probably, of itself, raised prices in general. The California gold rush, along with the inventions and railroad construction of 1820-50, and the liberalized trade laws which resulted from the 1848 revolutions, may explain the commercial and industrial revolutions and the growth of democracy in the Western world in the last half of the 19th century. Country by country, starting with Hawaii which received the news first, throughout Latin America, Europe, and even Asia, the specific impact is outlined briefly. Based primarily on monographic studies, 250 notes.
　　　　　　　　　　　　　　　　　　　D. L. Smith

993. Roy, Jessie H. NEGRO JUDGES IN THE UNITED STATES. *Negro Hist. Bull. 1965 28(5): 108-111.* Sketches the career of Miflin Wister Gibbs, born a free Negro in 1823 in Philadelphia, who had his own contracting business in that city. Gibbs went to California during the gold rush and later joined the gold rush to British Columbia. After the Civil War he moved to Arkansas where, in 1873, he became the first Negro judge when he was appointed municipal judge of Little Rock.
　　　　　　　　　　　　　　　　　　　L. Gara

994. Rundell, Walter, Jr. TEXAS PETROLEUM HISTORY: A SELECTIVE BIBLIOGRAPHY. *Southwestern Hist. Q. 1963/64 67(2): 267-278.* An annotated bibliography of 63 significant volumes dealing with the Texas oil industry.
　　　　　　　　　　　　　　　　　　　J. A. Hudson

995. Schanck, Peter C. OF GREGORY, GOLD, AND GREELEY. *Q. J. of the Lib. of Congress 1969 26(4): 226-233.* Quotes the letter of 1859 in which John Hamilton Gregory from Georgia described his discovery of gold in Colorado, the direct cause of the great "Pike's Peak or Bust!" gold rush of 1859. Horace Greeley, sensing a good news story, set out for Colorado in the spring of 1859 and on 8 June was the opening speaker at the first mass meeting ever held in the Rocky Mountains (two or three thousand miners attended). At this meeting the miners formed the Gregory Diggings District, the enactments of which had a profound influence on Federal laws regulating the complex questions of claims boundaries and rights. Illus., 12 notes.
　　　　　　　　　　　　　　　　　　　E. P. Stickney

996. Shaw, Keith. VAN PELT'S MINE. *Alberta Hist. R. 1968 16(4): 11-16.* An account of mining claims staked when a portion of the former Blackfeet Indian Reservation in northern Montana was thrown open to prospecting in 1898. There is a detailed discussion of claims and other mining activities of Henry VanPelt.
　　　　　　　　　　　　　　　　　　　H. M. Burns

997. Shook, Robert W., ed. A LETTER FROM JOHN J. LINN. *Southwestern Hist. Q. 1968 72(2): 240-241.* Colonel John J. Linn, the leading mercantile agent of South Texas, saw an oil slick in the gulf waters of Texas in 1834 while traveling on a schooner. This letter reports the occurrence. 4 notes.
　　　　　　　　　　　　　　　　　　　D. L. Smith

998. Smalley, Eugene V. THE GREAT COEUR D'ALENE STAMPEDE OF 1884. *Idaho Yesterdays 1967 11(3): 2-10.* An account of the Coeur d'Alene gold rush (1884), first published in *Century Magazine,* October 1884. The author visited Coeur d'Alene in July 1884 and describes the country, gives the history of the area prior to his visit, tells of the various strikes he visited or learned about in his travels, and mentions the missions in the area. Illus.
　　　　　　　　　　　　　　　　　　　B. B. Swift

999. Smith, Duane A. COLORADO'S URBAN-MINING SAFETY VALVE. *Colorado Mag. 1971 48(4): 299-318.* Uses the Colorado mining frontier between 1859 and 1893 to test the safety valve theory of Frederick Jackson Turner. Gold and silver mining booms offered continuous opportunity for many classes of people and did minimize labor unrest. Illustrates the transitory nature of the culture and indicates the general absence of strikes in the metal-mining industry (in contrast to coal mining), until the 1890's when the safety valve had disappeared. Argues that "what existed in Colorado was a safety valve that was both urban and frontier at the same time. . . . This urban-mining safety valve significantly influenced the state's development for three decades." Illus., 57 notes.
　　　　　　　　　　　　　　　　　　　O. H. Zabel

1000. Smith, Duane A. GOLD, SILVER, AND THE RED MAN. *J. of the West 1966 5(1): 114-121.* Examines the impact of the mining frontier on the development of a systematic Indian policy and concludes that contemporary literature and journalism of that day contributed to the forming of adverse attitudes held toward the Indian by the pioneers, but that the polemics had little effect on government policy except as one facet of mounting general criticism. Thus, when the reaction of the miners toward the Indians is combined with other forces pressuring the national government, the indecision concerning the disposition of the Indian question in the 1860's and 1870's is more easily understood. Based on published sources, 12 notes.
　　　　　　　　　　　　　　　　　　　D. N. Brown

1001. Smith, Duane A. THE GOLDEN WEST. *Montana 1964 14(3): 2-19.* West of the Mississippi River, urban settlement typically began with mining activity.
　　　　　　　　　　　　　　　　　　　S. R. Davison

1002. Smith, Duane A., ed. PIKES PEAK FIFTY-NINER: THE DIARY OF E. A. BOWEN. *Colorado Mag. 1970 47(4): 269-311.* Describes the journey to the Colorado gold fields by Edwin A. Bowen (1831-1900), and provides a "straightforward narrative of his impressions and daily life." The entries from 23 February to 14 April 1859 relate the journey from LaSalle, Illinois, to St. Joseph, Missouri, by train and on to Denver, Colorado, by wagon. The diary illustrates several characteristics of the mining frontier, such as group effort, vigilante law, constant prospecting, land and claim trading, working the claims, and general disappointment for most miners. Bowen, a devout Baptist, did not work on the Sabbath, but remained in camp or attended religious services. The diary, now in the Huntington Library, covers the period from late February to early October 1859. Illus., map, 59 notes.
　　　　　　　　　　　　　　　　　　　O. H. Zabel

1003. Snyder, Charles M., ed. THOMAS BURROWES' CALIFORNIA, QUIET TIMES IN THE GOLD FIELDS. *California Historian 1967 13(4): 123-126, and 14(2): 53-57.* Thomas Burrowes arrived in California from Middletown, New Jersey, in 1854 by way of the Panama route, "on what was to become a four and one-half year venture in the gold fields." The Burrowes family was an adventurous one with brothers Edward and John T. herding cattle in Texas and brother Joseph panning gold in California. John was killed on a long cattle drive and Edward was killed while serving in the Confederate cavalry. While finding mining to be hard work and seasonal, Thomas dispatched a steady stream of letters to his family and friends in Middletown. He reported his personal experiences in the mining camps, his insights on methods of mining, his voyage to California, and general observations of Trinity and Shasta Counties. He also describes the weather, his job, and the politico-economic conditions in California during the 1850's.   O. L. Miller

1004. Stevens, Elmer E. THE CORNISH MINER. *California Historian 1964 10(5): 132-135.* Grass Valley's growth rested upon the introduction by General John Charles Frémont of miners from Cornwall who brought with them their deep-mining techniques as well as foods and customs. The Grass Valley Cornish Carol Choir, which has members of the fourth generation, is described. The Cornish pump was another important contribution. Their superstitions are also discussed.
E. P. Stickney

1005. Thompson, Thomas Gray. THE FAR WESTERN MINING FRONTIER: TRENDS AND UNSOLVED PROBLEMS. *Colorado Mag. 1964 41(2): 105-110.* Analyzes the historical writing on the subject of far western mining, revealing a wealth of material on prospectors and speculators, foreign capital and technological progress, and social and cultural aspects of the mining frontier. Author suggests facets that remain to be studied.
I. W. Van Noppen

1006. Todd, A. C. COUSIN JACK IN IDAHO. *Idaho Yesterdays 1965 8(4): 2-11.* Tells the story of the Cousin Jacks - miners from Cornwall - who left their exhausted Cornish mines for the mines of the United States. The author fills in the background of the Cornish emigration and describes the typical Cornish miner and his skills. One of these miners, Richard Thomas of St. Just, Cornwall, came to Idaho in the fall of 1904. Excerpts from 15 letters which he wrote home describe life in the silver and lead mines of Wardner and Burke from 1904 to 1906.
M. Small

1007. Townley, John M. EARLY DEVELOPMENT OF EL DORADO CANYON AND SEARCHLIGHT MINING DISTRICTS. *Nevada Hist. Soc. Q. 1968 11(1): 2-25.* The El Dorado-Searchlight area comprises two mining districts west of the Colorado River in the southern part of Nevada. Aboriginal mining is well authenticated, but as yet no evidence has been found of official activity during the Spanish and Mexican periods. The earliest documented visit to the El Dorado area was made in 1858 by an army expedition testing the navigability of the Colorado River. Itinerant prospectors had probably located surface high-grade silver ores a few years prior to this, but in the absence of transportation nothing could be done with them. Milling and other technical equipment was brought in during the 1860's. Although accurate and complete data are lacking, the El Dorado Canyon mining area flourished for the rest of the century. Development of the Searchlight district did not come until the 1890's, probably because of the surface barrenness of the veins and their indistinct outcrops. 3 illus., 64 notes.   D. L. Smith

1008. Townley, John. THE NEW MEXICO MINING COMPANY. *New Mexico Hist. R. 1971 46(1): 57-73.* Gold deposits in the Ortiz mountains were discovered in 1828. In 1833 Lieutenant don José Francisco Ortiz was granted some 1,500 linear feet along the Santa Rosalía outcrop. From 1833 to 1846 the Ortiz mine was the largest producer of bullion in the district. In 1853 John Greiner purchased the Ortiz grant from Maraquita Montoya, the widow of Ortiz. Greiner interested fellow politician Elisha Whittlesey in the properties, who in turn formed the New Mexico Mining Company which purchased the property from Greiner in August 1854. The mine was operated intermittently until 1870. 33 notes.   D. F. Henderson

1009. Turner, Justin G. ALL IS NOT GOLD THAT GLITTERS. *Am. Book Collector 1967 17(5): 19-22.* A transcription and commentary on a letter of 27 January 1850 written from California by Edward Floyd Jones, an engineer and surveyor, to his family. He describes the perils and hopelessness of gold mining, the constant rain, the Sacramento River flood, and the San Francisco fire. Illus.   D. Brockway

1010. Turner, Justin G. P. V. FOX OF MOKELUMNE HILL. *Pacific Historian 1966 10(3): 4-11.* Gives a brief introduction to two letters of P. V. Fox to his wife and to Louisa M. Newton, both of New York. The letters, in the possession of Turner, appear in their entirety and reveal the personal indebtedness that motivated Fox to move westward while also revealing the living conditions in Mokelumne Hill, California, where Fox mined for gold.   T. R. Cripps

1011. Vandenbusche, Duane. MARBLE: PAST TO PRESENT. *Colorado Mag. 1969 46(1): 16-39.* Discusses the history of quarrying in Marble, Colorado, source of the stone for the Lincoln Memorial, the Tomb of the Unknown Soldier, and various other memorials and buildings. The first white men in the Marble area were Spanish explorers and missionaries about 1800. The town was founded in 1881, and John C. Osgood established the Yule Creek White Marble Company. The first major contract was for the Colorado State Capitol in 1895. Channing F. Meek built the marble industry into a multimillion-dollar business by 1914. Marble suffered labor troubles, fires, and floods. In spite of the purchase of most of the marble operations in 1928 by the Vermont Marble Company, the quarries did not prosper and operations ceased in 1941. Today it is possible that recreation will bring more people to the area than the marble industry ever did. Illus., 68 notes.   O. H. Zabel

1012. Watkins, T. H. HOMESTAKE GOLD: 1971. *Am. West 1971 8(5): 24-31.* During the 1876 gold rush in the Black Hills the deposits of the Homestake Mine in Lead (South Dakota) were discovered. Within a few years it was transformed from a simple muscle-and-sweat endeavor into an enormous industrial complex. Today, Homestake is the largest, oldest, and richest gold mining operation in the United States. This 17-picture photo-essay illustrates the enterprise, which is a model of the application of machinery and computerized technology. Adapted from a forthcoming book.   D. L. Smith

1013. Webb, Warren F. and Brody, Stuart A. THE CALIFORNIA GOLD RUSH AND THE MENTALLY ILL. *Southern California Q. 1968 50(1): 43-50.* The gold rush of the 1850's played an important part in the development of care for the mentally ill in California. The sudden growth and expansion associated with the gold rush, as well as the unstable social environment it created, precipitated mental disorders which forced the California government to provide care and treatment. A hospital exclusively for the mentally ill was established at Stockton in 1853, the first of its kind in the West. An analysis is made of patient records of the Stockton State Hospital during the first 10 years of its existence which reflects characteristics of the population of early California. Based on contemporary state hospital records and secondary materials; 2 tables, 5 notes.   W. L. Bowers

1014. Wehrman, Georgia. HARSHAW: MINING CAMP OF THE PATAGONIAS. *J. of Arizona Hist. 1965 6(1): 21-36.* The history of Harshaw, in the extreme southern portion of Arizona, is seen as "a typical mining camp in many respects." The author tells of its early development, its height as a bonanza, and its eventual decline; its peak production was in the period 1879-87. Published and unpublished sources are cited; illus., map, 65 notes.   J. D. Filipiak

1015. Weinstein, Allen. THE BONANZA KING MYTH: WESTERN MINE OWNERS AND THE REMONETIZATION OF SILVER. *Business Hist. R. 1968 42(2): 195-218.* Writers of American history have been almost unanimous in presenting the idea that the Congressional demands for the remonetization of silver in the 1870's was inaugurated by large scale mining interests seeking a guaranteed market for their product. In analyzing the interrelationships between the owners of the large Bonanza mine and the Government coinage policies the author finds the idea that the "Bonanza Kings" supported remonetization of silver to be a myth. He found no evidence of a demand for remonetization by the so-called "Bonanza Kings."
J. H. Krenkel

1016. White, Gerald. CALIFORNIA OIL BOOM OF THE 1860's: THE ORDEAL OF BENJAMIN SILLIMAN, JR. *U. of Wyoming Pub. 1966 32: 1-32, 138-146.* Although the presence of oil had long been noted in California, its magnitude and potential value were not realized until the 1860's. Government sponsored surveys and scientific research of mineral wealth came into vogue on the Pacific coast as in the East in the 1850's. Within a few years after a Western Pennsylvania well ushered in the era of oil, California was experiencing its first oil boom. Eventually the wealth from gold would pale next to that obtained from the State's oil resources. The boom was triggered by the wildly enthusiastic consultative reports of an eminently noted Eastern professor of chemistry, geology, and mineralogy—Benjamin Silliman, Jr. His 1864-65 surveys of various California properties motivated entrepreneurial risks by Eastern investors, especially for oil. Challenged by certain scientists employed by California and others, Silliman's veracity, honesty, and reputation were questioned. A decade-long effort was carried on to force him from academic life and the scientific community. The boom subsided in 1867 when the developers were defeated by producing and refining problems. Silliman had made some error of judgment and he was also the victim of some unfortunate circumstances beyond his control. The subsequent development of the oil industry in California has vindicated Silliman to a considerable extent. 87 notes.   D. L. Smith

1017.   White, Gerald T.   THE CASE OF THE SALTED SAMPLE: A CALIFORNIA OIL INDUSTRY SKELETON.   *Pacific Hist. R. 1966 35(2): 153-184.* Traces the effect of a false oil sample on the development of the California oil industry. Benjamin Silliman, among others, was taken in by the sample. Silliman's enthusiasm was partially vindicated when California finally did become a leading oil producer.
J. McCutcheon

1018.   White, Gerald T.   THE SILLIMAN CONTROVERSY. *Huntington Lib. Q. 1966 30(1): 35-53.* Two distinguished scientists, Josiah Dwight Whitney and Benjamin Silliman, Jr., became embroiled in bitter controversy arising from the eager search for mineral resources, especially oil, in California. Whitney, insecure in the pioneer post of state geologist, suffered much frustration which exacerbated his somewhat suspicious and quarrelsome nature. Silliman, cheerful and ever optimistic, was far too enthusiastic as a consultant to mining firms. The result, at a time when geologists were still prone to sweeping statements on very limited evidence, was a vindictive campaign against Silliman's competence and ethics as a scientist. None of the principals in the affair appear as unperturbed seekers after truth.   H. D. Jordan

1019.   White, William.   WALT WHITMAN AND THE SIERRA GRANDE MINING COMPANY.   *New Mexico Hist. R. 1969 44(3): 223-230.* A note on Whitman's ownership of 200 shares of stock in the Sierra Grande Mining Company of Lake Valley, New Mexico. The stock was given to Whitman by Robert Pearsal Smith, a successful Quaker glass manufacturer, under the stipulation that the stock be returned to Smith on Whitman's death. The stock brought Whitman nine dividends of 50 dollars or less each. 6 notes.   D. F. Henderson

1020.   Williamson, Hugh P.   ONE WHO WENT WEST.   *Missouri Hist. R. 1963 57(4): 369-378.* Major James A. Tate of Callaway County, Missouri and some 60 other persons left Missouri on 5 April 1849 for the California gold fields. He kept a sketchy diary of the trip, which he undertook "to try and repair a ruined fortune." A copy of the diary is owned by Mrs. Roy Tucker of Fulton, and another is in the State Historical Society of Missouri. The original has been lost. Tate did not recoup his fortune but found only death in California.   W. F. Zornow

1021.   Wilson, Gladys Marie.   DISCOVERY OF THE COMSTOCK LODE.   *Am. Hist. Illus. 1967 2(6): 40-48.* The first significant silver ore discovery in the United States was made on 6 June 1859 in Western Utah Territory, at what was later to become Virginia City, Nevada. That it is named after Henry Thompkins Paige Comstock, a "loud-mouthed, bragging no-gooder" is a historical accident since the discovery was made by Patrick McLaughlin and Peter O'Riley. As early as 1848 emigrants on their way to California had found some gold on the site, but it was not until 1859 that the "blue earth" which miners had been throwing away was found to be loaded with silver (the first assay was 3,876 dollars to the ton). The shifting ownership and legal entanglements that followed are described.   J. D. Filipiak

1022.   Young, Otis E., Jr.   THE CRAFT OF THE PROSPECTOR. *Montana 1970 20(1): 28-39.* Discusses the techniques of early prospectors in the Rocky Mountains in making field determinations of the possible value of ore. The typical prospector is shown to have been better informed than he has been pictured, and to have not been so dependent on chance in finding and identifying profitable veins. Discoverers rarely stayed to

develop a mine, preferring to sell for a satisfactory price and to resume the search for another good strike. Based mainly on printed sources; 23 notes.
S. R. Davison

1023.   Young, Otis E., Jr.   A DEDICATION TO THE MEMORY OF THOMAS ARTHUR RICKARD, 1864-1953.   *Arizona and the West 1969 11(2): 104-108.* Born into an English family of mining engineers (his father and four uncles) and educated at the University of London and the Royal School of Mines, Thomas Arthur Rickard came to the United States at the age of 21 to serve an assayer apprenticeship for a Colorado mine. His professional stature was recognized in service as State geologist, from 1895 to 1901. His writing ability gained him editorship of several professional journals. He contributed so many unsigned pieces to these journals that it is impossible to compile a complete bibliography of them. Rickard wrote and edited numerous technical books and travel accounts relating experiences in the line of duty all over the world. In 1922 he retired to Victoria, British Columbia. His travels and writing still flourished. Increasingly he emphasized historical rather than technical subjects. One important retirement effort, *A History of American Mining* (New York: Johnson Reprint Corp., 1932), remains a definitive survey of nonferrous mining from colonial times. Illus., appended with a selected biblio.   D. L. Smith

1024.   Young, Otis E., Jr.   FIRE IN THE HOLE! EVOLUTION AND REVOLUTION ON THE WESTERN MINING FRONTIER. *Am. West 1970 7(4): 15-19.* The principal Stone Age mining technique, the "cold-mining" process, persisted until a few years before the 1848 discovery of gold in California. The use of muscle and simple hand tools to break solid rock, the use of maximum of brute physical force, and a minimum of skilled supervision, were not feasible on America's isolated frontier. The great distances over which the essentials for survival and livelihood had to be freighted made the costs prohibitive. With the development of gunpowder in early modern Europe, its application to mining was foreseen as a device for the excavation of ore. A principal difficulty in its use was the seeming inability to control the time of detonation. In 1831 a Cornwall miner invented an effective and dependable fuse, thus making blasting a practical reality in mining operations. The science of mining and tunneling was raised to an entirely different plane. When disaster hit the Cornish mines, the American mineral frontier was just opening, with an insatiable demand for skilled workers. And the Irish potato famine produced a ready supply of highly adaptable unskilled workers. Labor supply and demand coincided and, with the new fuse, produced a fabulous mining boom in the American West. New methods have evolved into the highly sophisticated techniques of today. Now, through the Plowshare Program, the Federal Government is trying to apply nuclear fission to unlock the mineral wealth from the earth. Taken from a forthcoming book. 6 illus., biblio. note.   D. L. Smith

1025.   Young, Otis E., Jr.   "SALTING" AND "HIGH GRADING": VICES OF THE MINERAL FRONTIER.   *Southern California Q. 1969 51(3): 247-268.* Discusses two vices which were prevalent in mining areas. "Salting" involved the "upgrading of dubious mining properties in a manner contrary to nature, with a view to profitable sale." "High grading" consisted of mine crews or quartz mill workers stealing bits of ore or amalgam. The author describes various methods employed to accomplish both of these vices. He suggests that "salting" was largely motivated by greed, but "high grading" was due in part to the low wages paid to miners. Based on contemporary and secondary sources; 59 notes.
W. L. Bowers

1026.   Young, Otis E., Jr.   THE SPANISH TRADITION IN GOLD AND SILVER MINING.   *Arizona and the West 1965 7(4): 299-314.* Despite the popular idea to the contrary, the Spaniards who came to the New World were steeped in mining experience and the theories of metallurgy. From Phoenician and Roman and earlier times the techniques of exploiting mineral riches had been carried on with diligence. Even the friars carefully quizzed the Indians and rewarded them for information or specimens that led to discoveries. The author describes the earmarks of a lode or deposit, the ways in which identification was made of the precious metal, the tools and equipment of the prospector, the use of Indian labor to dig out the ore, and the processes for extraction of the metal. The Spanish tradition in gold and silver mining and milling was employed from the beginning of the penetration into Mexico and adapted to the circumstances of the New World. It was transmitted to the American mining frontier chiefly in California. Although modifications of techniques were made on the American frontier by prospectors from Georgia, the Carolinas, and other non-Spanish areas the Spanish techniques persisted, especially among miners operating on a shoestring. As late as the Depression period of the 1930's the ancient Spanish "dry-washing" method was used by impoverished Americans turned prospectors. 4 illus., 39 notes.   D. L. Smith

1027. —. LETTERS FROM A STATEN ISLAND "FORTY NINER," 1850. *Staten Island Historian 1969 30(3): 23-25.* Letters of James Burger, who left Staten Island in 1849 to join the Gold Rush to California, describing life in San Francisco and the gold fields at the height of the California Gold Rush.   G. Kurland

1028. —. MONTANA COPPER. *Montana 1964 14(3): 56-61.* Condensed account of Butte's development by the "Copper Kings," William A. Clark, Marcus Daly, and F. Augustus Heinze, 1875-1900.

S. R. Davison

1029. —. MONTANA GOLD. *Montana 1964 14(3): 20-25.* Summary of important gold discoveries, 1852-1865.   S. R. Davison

Labor

1030. Bechtol, Paul T., Jr. THE 1880 LABOR DISPUTE IN LEADVILLE. *Colorado Mag. 1970 47(4): 312-325.* Analyzes the short-lived strike of 1880 in the Leadville area. The strike was typical of early labor disputes in the hard rock mines of the West. Various grievances triggered the walkout, which effectively closed down the mines. A union was organized to carry on early collective bargaining. The union leadership of Michael Mooney prevented vandalism and violence. Negotiations were unproductive and the union gradually scaled down its demands. When Governor Pitkin declared a state of martial law, the strike ended quickly and "essentially, the union agreed to return to work under the same conditions that prevailed before the strike began." The union organization did not survive the strike and permanent union representation in the Colorado mines was delayed until the organization of the Western Federation of Miners in 1893. 3 illus., 45 notes.   O. H. Zabel

1031. Black, Isabella. AMERICAN LABOUR AND CHINESE IMMIGRATION. *Past and Present [Great Britain] 1963 (25): 59-76.* Surveys 19th century and early 20th century American attitudes toward Chinese immigrants, with special reference to California. The Chinese aroused hostility out of all proportion to their numbers. Although they were from time to time defended by employers, Methodists, socialists, and even Mexican labor organizations, the defense was swamped by the patriotic and racist arguments of the opposition. Local violence and stringent federal legislation combined to render their lot unenviable.

A. W. Coats

1032. Davies, J. Kenneth. UTAH LABOR BEFORE STATEHOOD. *Utah Hist. Q. 1966 34(3): 202-217.* Shows that although Mormonism exerted considerable influence over unionism in Utah it did not prevent the invasion of major national organizations such as the Noble Order of the Knights of Labor and the railroad brotherhoods. Based on manuscript materials in the Latter-Day Saints Church Historian's Library, Salt Lake City, contemporary newspaper accounts, and monographic studies, notably masters' theses completed at the University of Utah.

S. L. Jones

1033. Gephart, Ronald M. POLITICIANS, SOLDIERS AND STRIKES: THE REORGANIZATION OF THE NEBRASKA MILITIA AND THE OMAHA STRIKE OF 1882. *Nebraska Hist. 1965 46(2): 89-120.* Examines the transition of the Nebraska militia system from 1879 to 1882 from a frontier outfit fighting Indians to a more "eastern" organization designed to curb industrial violence. The differences between the eastern militia and that of Nebraska and the use of the Nebraska organization in the Omaha strike of 1882 are examined.

R. Lowitt

1034. Grogan, Dennis S. UNIONIZATION IN BOULDER AND WELD COUNTIES TO 1890. *Colorado Mag. 1967 44(4): 324-330.*

Coal was discovered in Colorado in 1859 but not until the 1870's did the miners of Boulder and Weld Counties begin to form unions. There was a successful strike in 1871, but labor agitation was minimal before 1874. The economic depression caused operators to reduce wages. Local unions were organized. Some joined the Miners National Association but the national organization ceased to exist in 1876. In 1877 the Knights of Labor sought to organize the Colorado miners. Trouble resulted. The major coal producing areas were under local union control in 1880. In the 1880's the Boulder and Weld County mines were less prosperous, absentee ownership increased. Mine inspectors were appointed. The National Federation of Miners and Mine Laborers was organized. The Knights of Labor opposed the union. The loss of local union prestige caused the formation of a regional organization, the Coal Miners' Federation of Northern Colorado, in 1886. Political lobbying began, blacklisting was outlawed, mine inspectors had great power. In 1888 the Progressive Union of Miners and Mine Laborers was created, and in 1889 the United Mine Workers of America was founded. The Northern Colorado unions benefited, and the general strike was found to be effective. 5 illus., 66 notes.   I. W. Van Noppen

1035. Henderson, Patrick D. BRADSHAW BONANZA. *New Mexico Hist. R. 1963 38(2): 151-162.* Following a brief résumé of mining in Arizona and New Mexico, the author discusses in detail the Tiger strike of 1871 in the Bradshaw region of Arizona. From 1872 to 1875 activity centered around the Tiger, Eclipse, and Oro Belle mines. The town of Bradshaw saw its heyday in 1871, and declined rapidly thereafter.

D. F. Henderson

1036. Jones, Lamar B. LABOR AND MANAGEMENT IN CALIFORNIA AGRICULTURE, 1864-1964. *Labor Hist. 1970 11(1): 23-40.* Surveys the attitudes of California growers toward agricultural labor. First the Chinese, then the Japanese, and finally the Mexicans were viewed as a source of cheap labor to be utilized for short-term gains. This historical experience shaped the background for the present labor-management situation in California agriculture. Based on the *Pacific Rural Press;* 67 notes.   L. L. Athey

1037. Miller, Charlene. LOS GOLONDRINOS [Migratory farm workers]. *Kroeber Anthrop. Soc. Papers 1964 30: 51-71.* Traces the history of braceros, or golondrinos, who are migratory farm workers imported from Mexico. The author examines the effect of the individual bracero on Mexican cultural life, agricultural methods, and economy as well as the effect of imported labor on the local labor market in the United States. Various inequities and corruptions in the system of bracero labor, including the problem of wetbacks who are illegal entrants into the United States from Mexico are pointed out. The discontinuation of bracero labor poses many questions for the two countries. Based on primary and secondary sources and field investigation; 3 tables, 37 notes, biblio.

C. N. Warren

1038. Pawar, Sheelwant B. THE STRUCTURE AND NATURE OF LABOR UNIONS IN UTAH, AN HISTORICAL PERSPECTIVE, 1890-1920. *Utah Hist. Q. 1967 35(3): 236-255.* Concludes that Utah's labor unions developed in a pyramidal fashion, the base being composed of local unions which were established in Utah between 1860 and 1890; the midsection being composed of national or international unions uniting local unions in the same industry, a process which occurred in Utah between 1890 and 1920; while the top of the pyramid was occupied by a federation of national unions, a culmination realized in Utah only after 1920. The author deals primarily with the second state of development during which craft unions oriented toward conservative economic action are seen as winning domination over the union movement in Utah. The influence exerted by the Mormon Church in Utah was significant in moving the labor unions toward a conservative stance. The article is part of a doctoral dissertation prepared at the University of Utah and is based chiefly on handwritten minutes of several Utah unions now in the Archives of the Institute of Industrial Relations of the University of Utah.

S. L. Jones

1039. Reese, James V. THE EARLY HISTORY OF LABOR ORGANIZATIONS IN TEXAS, 1838-1876. *Southwestern Hist. Q. 1968 72(1): 1-20.* Most labor activity in pre-Civil War Texas was spontaneous in response to a specific problem or promising situation which lasted only for the duration of the situation. Occasionally grievances were aired in public meetings, petitions, or in ethnic society clubs. First steps toward bona fide labor organizations came in the fifties when ethnic groups formed workingmen's associations to encourage the development of trades, instruction in English and arithmetic, and other benevolent activities. There is no evidence of organized labor activity during the Civil War. With printers in the forefront, several unions were established in the postwar years, including a small number of Negro labor groups. Few, if any, however, had sufficient strength to sustain a successful strike. Unionization accelerated in the seventies. The climax came in violent railway strikes in 1877 which ushered Texas into a new era of militant unionism. Railroads had broken the frontier pattern of isolated and self-sufficient agricultural communities and started the State toward a modern, although still primarily agricultural, economy. 71 notes.

D. L. Smith

1040. Stegner, S. Page. PROTEST SONGS FROM THE BUTTE MINES. *Western Folklore 1967 26(3): 157-167.* From "New Songs for Butte Mining Camp," an extremely rare paperbound, undated booklet, nine songs are selected to illustrate the commentary they afford and the insight they give into the strikes and labor problems from the viewpoint of the labor organizers and the miners themselves. They are, in effect, social documents of this class, in the Butte, Montana, mining area. These songs were apparently not widely known in that area as no evidence suggests that they entered into the oral tradition. Although they cannot be considered folksongs, their importance to the folklorist and labor historian are significant. 6 notes.

D. L. Smith

1041. Watkins, T. H. REQUIEM FOR THE FEDERATION. *Am. West 1966 3(1): 4-12, 91-95.* In the 1860's, 1870's, and 1880's, hard-rock mining in the Rocky Mountain West grew into a formidable industry, complete with all the trappings: a massive labor force, absentee ownership, and the "peculiar convolutions" of investment capital. Substandard wages, long hours, the constant danger of the working environment, and the ever brutal contest between "the solid inertia of rock" and man's muscle were normal conditions. As eastern labor organized to resist the grinding exploitation of industry, the hard-rock miner also came to feel that unionism was his only hope. With the 1893 repeal of the Sherman Silver Purchase Act shutting down silver mines, mills, and smelters all over the West, hundreds of the unemployed miners streamed into the gold camp of the Cripple Creek, Colorado mining district and with them came the newly organized Western Federation of Miners. The new influx of labor drove wages down and lessened the miner's position. In one of the most violent confrontations in labor history, the federation challenged the power of the industrial capital that controlled the area. The federation overestimated its power and deliberately crossed the tenuous line between safety and disaster. It was class warfare in an ideological as well as a physical sense. A failure, the federation died by its own hand. Based on a forthcoming book; illus., map, biblio. note.

D. L. Smith

Agriculture

General

1042. Argersinger, Peter H. THE DIVINES AND THE DESTITUTE. *Nebraska Hist. 1970 51(3): 303-318.* Discusses the reaction of the churches to the crop failures and hard times that afflicted the Plains frontier in the 1890's. Churchmen at first were more concerned with the affect of hard times on themselves and their institutions. Only gradually did they shift their concern to the suffering.

R. Lowitt

1043. Baur, John E. CALIFORNIA CROPS THAT FAILED. *California Hist. Soc. Q. 1966 45(1): 61-68.* Soon after the Gold Rush, the success of several exotic crops, such as the eucalyptus, seemed to "vindicate the widespread belief that California's climate and soil were almost omnipotent." Until 1880, ignorance of climatology and agronomy was a handicap that led to many failures. Some of the failures were, in a later era, grown profitably, such as the cork oak, cotton, rice, dates, and avocados. Other tropical plants with which experiments were made were never commercially grown successfully, partly due to the dryness of the climate, partly to the cost of scarce human labor. Among such efforts here recounted in detail are those of growing tea, coffee, bananas, pineapples, quinine, and the opium poppy. Based on documents and newspapers; 91 notes.

E. P. Stickney

1044. Bennett, John W. ATTITUDES TOWARD ANIMALS AND NATURE IN A GREAT PLAINS COMMUNITY. *Plains Anthropologist 1964 9(23): 37-47.* "This is a description of rancher and farmer attitudes toward domestic and wild animals, and toward the natural environment of the region. With regard to the first topic, the important point is that the attitudes differ for different kinds of animals, although there is a general tendency to conceive of all animals in an emotionally neutral or indifferent fashion. Like all agriculturalists making the whole or part of their living from domestic animals which are sold for income, there is a tendency to conceive of cattle, in particular, as property, and not as fellow creatures or pets. Since most of the herd animals are regularly disposed of for slaughter, emotional attachments would be hazardous. Attitudes toward horses and domestic pets are somewhat different, but again, emotional attachments are rare or individualized, or sometimes concealed. With respect to Nature, differences between rancher and farmer attitudes are to be noted: the former idealizing Nature; the latter regarding it as a set of refractory but usable resources."

J

1045. Bonner, James C. PLANTATION AND FARM: THE AGRICULTURAL SOUTH. *Writing Southern Hist.: Essays in Historiography in Honor of Fletcher M. Green* (Baton Rouge: Louisiana State U. Pr., 1965): 147-174. A conscious determination to maintain white supremacy is, according to Ulrich Bonnell Phillips, the central theme of the South's history. The Phillips-Gray-Dodd planter-poor white thesis was first seriously challenged by Frank L. Owsley and his students at Vanderbilt University, who, using exhaustively the voluminous manuscript census records, showed that the great mass of nonslaveholders were undeserving of being called "poor white." This group not only called attention to the yeoman farmer but also made historians aware of the value of these census records as source material. Frederick Jackson Turner's frontier hypothesis is seen as an agricultural interpretation of American history at a time when the country was fast entering an urban-industrial age. Joseph Schafer has shown that the trans-Mississippi cattle business had its forerunner in the southern Piedmont in the Revolutionary period. 109 biblio., notes.

E. P. Stickney

1046. Cline, W. Rodney. SEAMAN ASAHEL KNAPP, 1833-1911. *Louisiana Hist. 1970 11(4): 333-340.* After a long career in agriculture and education in Iowa, Knapp moved to Lake Charles, Louisiana, in 1885 to participate in the land development enterprise of the North American Land and Timber Company promoted by Jabez Bunting Watkins. As assistant manager of the company, Knapp played an influential role in attracting settlers and developing the region as a major rice producer. He was less successful in promoting sugar, but was instrumental in fighting the boll weevil and in developing cotton production in eastern Texas. Few men have had such strong influence on the agricultural growth and development of a region as did Knapp. 3 photos., 25 notes.

R. L. Woodward

1047. Davis, Rodney O. BEFORE BARBED WIRE: HERD LAW AGITATIONS IN EARLY KANSAS AND NEBRASKA. *J. of the West 1967 6(1): 41-52.* Before the invention of barbed wire the enclosing of cultivated areas on the Great Plains was difficult and expensive. Various substitutes for wood fences were tried but were generally found to be ineffective. Increasingly, the remedy sought was a legal one, a herd law which would minimize fencing costs and protect crops by confining livestock at all times. The author maintains that this marked abandonment of tradition resulted from the lack of timber. He traces the development of the herd law agitation in Kansas and Nebraska during the 1860's and 1870's. By the latter part of the 1870's various herd laws had been enacted in both states. After the development of barbed wire the issue became less relevant as both farmers and ranchers found it advantageous to enclose. Yet, barbed wire merely ratified conditions already encouraged by the herd law's legalistic adaptation to the plains environment. Based on newspaper sources and government reports; 61 notes.

D. N. Brown

1048. Denevan, William M. LIVESTOCK NUMBERS IN NINETEENTH-CENTURY NEW MEXICO, AND THE PROBLEM OF GULLYING IN THE SOUTHWEST. *Ann. of the Assoc. of Am. Geographers 1967 57(4): 691-703.* Considers two different and conflicting theories for gullying in the American Southwest: one associating arroyo cutting, gullying with drought and poor vegetation cover and arroyo filling with higher rainfall and an improved vegetation cover; the other associating gullying with increased summer high-intensity rainfall.

Livestock numbers in the upper Rio Grande region during the entire period are examined, with particular attention to the Mexican period when ranges were heavily stocked with sheep but with little or no gullying. "The added perspective of livestock population history, uncertain as it is, suggests that probably neither one factor alone nor another but rather the combination of certain climatic events and overgrazing by man's livestock brought about severe modern gullying in the American Southwest." Map, 67 notes. W. R. Boedecker

1049. Dethloff, Henry C. RICE REVOLUTION IN THE SOUTH-WEST, 1880-1910. *Arkansas Hist. Q. 1970 29(1): 66-75.* An account of the origins of rice cultivation in the coastal prairies of Arkansas, Louisiana, and Texas. Photos, 31 notes. B. A. Drummond

1050. Duncan, Otis Durant. SOCIOLOGICAL ADJUSTMENTS IN GREAT PLAINS AGRICULTURE. *Great Plains J. 1963 3(1): 1-8.* The "Great Plains" area is defined; its socioeconomic characteristics described; and seven needed adjustments are enumerated and briefly discussed. These adjustments include the "number one" problem, water supply, as well as transportation, urban industrial development, control of hazards, discovery and development of indigenous resources, adjusted economic organization, and provisions for health, education and welfare. The needed physical and economic adjustments do not seem likely soon. O. H. Zabel

1051. Erdman, Loula Grace. THE DEVIL'S HAT BAND. *Am. West 1965 2(1): 39-45, 76-77.* Although several patents were issued for barbed wire in the first three quarters of the 19th century, the wire could only be produced slowly and laboriously by hand. An Illinois farmer, Joseph F. Glidden, patented a wire in 1874 (subsequently improved by substituting steel-drawn for galvanized wire) which could be mass produced. It is essentially the same as that in use today - two wires twisted into a cable with barbs set at intervals. Enthusiastic acceptance by the farmers of the Middle West came early. At first, on the Great Plains, most were skeptical of its practicality and desirability. Eventually, however, along with the windmill, the homesteader, and the railroads, it became a significant factor in changing the nature of the cattle industry and in the coming of the agricultural settlement of the Plains. "The Devil's Hat Band" was one of several uncomplimentary names given to barbed wire by its opponents. Illus., biblio., note. D. L. Smith

1052. Farquhar, Francis P. CALIFORNIA'S BIG TREES. *Am. West 1965 2(3): 58-64.* The discovery of the giant Sequoia trees of the Sierra Nevada, the history of the publicity ventures by which the species became known and was planted throughout the world, and the learned debate concerning the proper nomenclature are a chapter in a forthcoming book of regional history. Illus., biblio. note. D. L. Smith

1053. Fite, Gilbert C. DAYDREAMS AND NIGHTMARES: THE LATE NINETEENTH-CENTURY AGRICULTURAL FRONTIERS. *Agric. Hist. 1966 40(4): 285-293.* While many settlers on the western frontier were successful, others failed. Some underwent extreme deprivation. Drought, grasshoppers, and other natural disasters are responsible for most of the failures. Based on manuscripts in state collections. W. D. Rasmussen

1054. Forrest, Earle. THE FABULOUS SIERRA BONITA. *J. of Arizona Hist. 1965 6(3): 132-146.* The Sierra Bonita, founded in 1872 by Henry Clay Hooker and made famous in literature and drama, is still in the possession of the same family - the fifth generation - and is still the largest ranch in southern Arizona. Covers the ranch's history, with emphasis on its close association with nearby Camp (later Fort) Grant, and the founder's many friends, who included military leaders as well as Cochise, famous Apache Indian. Comments are also made about Hooker's daughter-in-law, Forrestine Cooper Hooker, a writer. 20 notes, some to Forrestine Hooker's reminiscences, now in the possession of her daughter, Mrs. Mary Hooker, one of the ranch's present owners. J. D. Filipiak

1055. Gease, Deryl V. WILLIAM N. BYERS AND THE COLORADO AGRICULTURAL SOCIETY. *Colorado Mag. 1966 43(4): 327-338.* William Newton Byers played an important role in the promotion of Colorado's agricultural industry. He did this in many ways, but one of the most important was the promotion of the Colorado Agricul-

tural Society. He began to promote an agricultural society and fair in 1860 but his efforts did not meet with much success until 1866 when the first fair was held. Byers provided most of the support for the society through editorials in the newspaper *Rocky Mountain News,* which he owned and edited. 25 notes. I. W. Van Noppen

1056. Gregory, Annadora F. CREATING THE FRUITED PLAINS. *Nebraska Hist. 1968 49(3): 299-321.* Recounts the early history of the Nebraska State Horticultural Society and then focuses on the career of Ezra F. Stephens (1844-1928), early Nebraska nurseryman, who left a rich heritage of well-planted orchards and attractive forest tree groves as a result of his 40 years' residence in Nebraska (1871-1911). R. Lowitt

1057. Higgins, F. Hal. THE CELEBRATED STEAM PLOW OF PHILANDER H. STANDISH. *Am. West 1966 3(2): 24-27, 91.* California's hard, durable wheat that could be shipped spoilage-free around the Horn was in rising demand all over the world in the late 1860's. Philander H. Standish, a Yankee mechanic who was lured to the West in 1851 by gold, witnessed the booming wheat industry. From a family background of inventing and practical engineering, he envisioned revolutionizing California agriculture with a self-powered plow that could rapidly and cheaply handle large acreages. Unveiled in 1868, his eight-ton rotary steam plow brought wide acclaim. Another more refined model gained even more admiration but no financial backing. Inordinate construction costs for the two models that made them more expensive to operate than conventional gang plows kept skeptical investment capital away from projected plans for mass production of the Standish steam plow. Illus. D. L. Smith

1058. Holbrook, Abigail Curlee. COTTON MARKETING IN ANTEBELLUM TEXAS. *Southwestern Hist. Q. 1970 73(4): 431-455.* Traces the development of cotton-growing activities in Texas from the 1820's to the Civil War, including the small, independent farmers and merchants and the larger plantation owners with their slaves, enticed into Texas by Stephen Austin. Follows the growth of Texas from a Mexican Province to a Republic and then a State, and identifies the men most responsible for creating a viable cotton economy in Texas. Describes the marketing, shipping, distribution, bankruptcies, and profits and losses and debts of the cotton growers, to illustrate how a frontier land soon became an integral part of an evolving industrial United States. R. W. Delaney

1059. Hoover, Herbert T. JOHN MILTON LEEPER: PIONEER FARMER. *Nebraska Hist. 1971 52(1): 31-44.* Examines the various moves of a pioneer farmer within the context of ideas expressed by Frederick Jackson Turner and the overall pattern of western agrarian development in the late 19th century. Observes that Leeper's odyssey presents a "safety valve" thesis in reverse. When Leeper found rural living conditions intolerable, he retreated to nearby towns to recoup his fortunes. R. Lowitt

1060. Jordan, Terry G. WINDMILLS IN TEXAS. *Agric. Hist. 1963 37(2): 80-85.* The scarcity of water due to low rainfall and a deep water table combined with high winds made windmills important to Texas. The railroads introduced windmills, probably in 1880, and within a few years they were numerous. With barbed wire fencing they brought about a revolution in livestock raising. Now electric pumps are displacing them. W. D. Rasmussen

1061. Kane, R. James. POPULISM, PROGRESSIVISM, AND PURE FOOD. *Agric. Hist. 1964 38(3): 161-166.* Farmers' interest in pure food laws stemmed from belief that their economic interests were damaged by food adulteration and misrepresentation. As early as 1881 the Farmers' Alliance advocated a pure food law. Edwin F. Ladd, chemist at the North Dakota Experiment Station, aroused farmers early in this century by convincing them that food manufacturers were "dumping" undesirable products in their state. The farmers' resentment became widespread in midwestern agricultural states and congressional representatives of these states gave active support to a federal pure food law, regardless of party affiliation. W. D. Rasmussen

1062. Kollmorgen, Walter M. THE WOODSMAN'S ASSAULTS ON THE DOMAIN OF THE CATTLEMAN. *Ann. of the Assoc. of*

Am. Geographers 1969 59(2): 215-239. Examines the settlement of the grassland area of the American West and emphasizes the economic aspects of the development. The settlement process is seen as a form of competition between two types of economic organizational forms, ranching and farming. The development of farming in the area was an effort to extend the characteristic economic form of the eastern woodlands into the grassland area, whereas the ranching activity which entered the area from the south was an importation from Spanish America. The intrusion was countered and ultimately thwarted by legislative acts proposed and supported by the American woodsman. The legislation which fixed the pattern of the final settlement of the area was the product of a variety of geographic misconceptions. 2 diagrams, 106 notes.

W. R. Boedecker

1063.　Manley, Robert N.　IN THE WAKE OF THE GRASSHOPPERS: PUBLIC RELIEF IN NEBRASKA, 1874-1875. *Nebraska Hist. 1963 44(4): 255-275.* Analyzes how Nebraska public opinion, in meeting the grasshopper invasions, traversed the cycle from private relief measures through state aid to federal assistance programs, which provided the only adequate relief most plague sufferers received.　R. Lowitt

1064.　Manley, Robert N.　A NOTE ON GOVERNMENT AND AGRICULTURE: A NINETEENTH CENTURY NEBRASKA VIEW. *Nebraska Hist. 1964 45(3): 237-252.* Notes Republican Senator Algernon S. Paddock as an example of Nebraska leaders who favored ideas that were later viewed as Populistic in origin: extension of federal authority in the interests of agriculture, and the regulation and even ownership of railroads. Suggests that Populism evolved in part from programs endorsed by Paddock and other Nebraska Republicans in preceding years.

R. Lowitt

1065.　Manley, Robert N.　SAMUEL AUGHEY: NEBRASKA'S SCIENTIFIC PROMOTER. *J. of the West 1967 6(1): 108-118.* Aughey was a Pennsylvania-born minister who migrated westward after his congregation became dissatisfied with his antislavery views. Always interested in natural science, he accepted a position at the new University of Nebraska in 1871. Thereafter, in speeches and writings he promoted the idea that a climatic revolution had resulted from planting trees and plowing the plains. He insisted that the region was now a farmer's paradise. The author concludes that Aughey's pseudoscientific arguments merely confirmed what the people wanted to hear. Aughey may have helped to attract settlers to Nebraska by contributing to the eradication of the myth of the desert, but he substituted in its place the myth that man possessed the ability to change the environment of the plains. Based largely on published sources; 44 notes.　D. N. Brown

1066.　Marvel, Tom.　AMERICAN WINES-GERMAN ACCENT. *Am.-German R. 1964 31(1): 19-21, 39.* Discusses the development of Rhine wines (especially Riesling and Sylvaner) in American viniculture. Most of these wines were developed by German vintners and became unpopular during World War I. Prohibition ruined many German firms. California and the Finger Lakes district of New York are the centers of a revival of German types of wines. 4 photos.　G. H. Davis

1067.　Nelson, Herbert.　THE VANISHING HOP-DRIERS OF THE WILLAMETTE VALLEY. *Oregon Hist. Q. 1963 64(3): 267-271.* Short sketch of the history of cultivation of hops in the world (for beer brewing), and early experiences, 1849-1930, of hop growers in Pacific Coast states.

C. C. Gorchels

1068.　Nichols, Roger L.　SOLDIERS AS FARMERS: ARMY AGRICULTURE IN THE MISSOURI VALLEY, 1818-1827. *Agric. Hist. 1970 44(2): 213-222.* Discusses agricultural operations at Fort Atkinson in eastern Nebraska. The troops stationed at the fort engaged in the first extensive American agricultural activity west of the Missouri. For the soldiers, farming meant a more varied and wholesome diet; for the country, these operations produced new, valuable information for future civilian settlement in the region; and for agricultural historians, this example of Army farming activity illustrates the potential value of military records in studying trans-Missouri agriculture in the 19th century. Based on primary sources, especially Army records; 32 notes.

D. E. Brewster

1069.　Olson, Gary D., ed.　RELIEF FOR NEBRASKA GRASSHOPPER VICTIMS: THE OFFICIAL JOURNAL OF LIEUTENANT THEODORE E. TRUE. *Nebraska Hist. 1967 48(2): 119-140.* The journal recounts the lieutenant's experiences in distributing Army clothing to needy settlers in Dawson County in the winter of 1875 who were left destitute by the 1874 grasshopper plague. True also prepared a list of needy people to receive food rations in Dawson and neighboring counties.

R. Lowitt

1070.　Richardson, C. Howard　THE NEBRASKA PRAIRIES: DILEMMA TO EARLY TERRITORIAL FARMERS. *Nebraska Hist. 1969 50(4): 359-372.* Examines major types of farming (crop and livestock farming, specialized crop farming, specialized livestock farming) in territorial Nebraska during the years 1855 and 1856. The author concludes that these early systems represented innovative adaptations. Farmers clung to mixed landscapes where wooded river valleys alternated with the upland prairies of eastern Nebraska. They either lived in communities close to a river valley or near a trail that provided easy access to one.

R. Lowitt

1071.　Rogers, William W., ed.　FROM PLANTER TO FARMER: A GEORGIA MAN IN RECONSTRUCTION TEXAS. *Southwestern Hist. Q. 1969 72(4): 526-529.* Thomas E. Blackshear was a member of a distinguished Georgia family, and was a planter, State legislator, and Major-General of the State militia during the Indian wars. When Georgia became more populated, Blackshear moved to Texas where he acquired sizable land holdings. He did not serve in the Civil War, but four of his sons served in the Confederate Army. This letter of 11 February 1867 shows Blackshear's racial bias, but it also shows that he realized the old plantation system could no longer continue. It is a lucid contemporary proposal for the revival of agriculture in postbellum Texas.

R. W. Delaney

1072.　Saum, Lewis O.　THE SUCCESS THEME IN GREAT PLAINS REALISM. *Am. Q. 1966 18(4): 580-598.* Examines the works of authors who have dealt with the farmer's struggle against the Great Plains. O. E. Rølvaag, Willa Cather, Hamlin Garland, and others provide a literature rich in details of the struggle. Only after the pioneer has conquered his environment does he taste bitterness and uncertainty. Based on citations from novels and literary criticism; 67 notes.

R. S. Pickett

1073.　Steward, Luther N., Jr.　CALIFORNIA COFFEE: A PROMISING FAILURE. *Southern California Q. 1964 46(3): 259-264.* Due to the high prices and the inferior quality of coffee imported into San Francisco in the 1870's, many farmers experimented in growing native California coffee plants or seeding foreign plants. By 1892, the experiments had ended, because frost destroyed seedlings even in Southern California. Uses published sources.　J. Jensen

1074.　Sultz, Philip W.　FROM SAGEBRUSH TO HAY AND BACK AGAIN. *Am. West 1964 1(1): 20-30.* A 15 photo picture essay of Wyoming's South Pass and Jackson Hole country. Visual evidence that nature's sagebrush easily takes over man's abandoned homestead buildings and hay fields. Illus.　D. L. Smith

1075.　Sztáray, Zoltán.　HARASZTHY ÁGOSTON A KALIFORNIAI SZŐLŐKULTURA ATYJA [Ágoston Haraszthy, the father of California's viticulture]. *Új Látóhatár [West Germany] 1964 7(6): 491-510.* A biography of Ágoston Haraszthy, a Hungarian who came to America in the middle of the last century. He was the author of two books, but most of his activities centered around the development of viticulture in California. Described is his adventurous life first in Wisconsin and later in California where he founded, in the area of Sonoma, what later became the grape production center of America. 44 notes.

P. Várkonyi

Cattle and Sheep

1076.　Adams, Ramon F.　THE COWMAN'S PHILOSOPHY. *Am. West 1965 2(4): 47-49, 95.* The old-time cowman was more than shop talk and profanity. Despite his wild and woolly reputation, he was "quicker of tongue than on the trigger." He was a philosopher whose keenness of observation and deduction, whose simplicity and humbleness, and whose humor were conditioned by long days of solitude and loneliness that gave him time to think deeply. The author illustrates these conclusions with gems collected over a lifetime of association with the cowman. Bibliographic note by Evelyn Oppenheimer. Biblio., illus.

D. L. Smith

1077. Atkinson, J. H. CATTLE DRIVES FROM ARKANSAS TO CALIFORNIA PRIOR TO THE CIVIL WAR. *Arkansas Hist. Q. 1969 28(3): 275-281*. Presents extant information about five cattle drives from Arkansas to California during the decade before the Civil War. Substantial documentation exists for only one of them. Photo, 3 notes.

B. A. Drummond

1078. Bennion, Glynn. A PIONEER CATTLE VENTURE OF THE BENNION FAMILY. *Utah Hist. Q. 1966 34(4): 315-325*. Reconstructs the cattle-grazing enterprises of the Bennion family in territorial Utah through the reminiscences told to the author by members of his family, particularly his father Israel Bennion. Emphasis is given to the tendency of the pioneer cattlemen to exhaust grassland resources by overgrazing.

S. L. Jones

1079. Berthrong, Donald J. CATTLEMEN ON THE CHEYENNE-ARAPAHO RESERVATION, 1883-1885. *Arizona and the West 1971 13(1): 5-32*. In 1883 seven cattle companies got approval from the Arapaho and Southern Cheyenne Indians to run stock on some three million acres of rented land on the reservation in western Oklahoma. The arrangements had the sanction of the Indian agent. The impact of this and other white incursions disturbed the Indians, especially a hard core of the Cheyenne. The Cheyenne Dog Soldiers, as they were called, led the opposition and were able to enforce their will on the agent, mixed-bloods, and the Indians who were succumbing to white institutions. A presidential order forced the cattlemen to leave the reservation. Cattlemen who hoped to get the order withdrawn spread rumors that the fierce Southern Cheyenne planned to raid southwestern Kansas in retaliation. In the summer of 1885, thousands of settlers fled to nearby towns in terror, abandoning their homes, livestock, and crops. The dissident Cheyenne had protected their reservation land by exercising traditional forms of control over their people. 10 illus., map, 50 notes.   D. L. Smith

1080. Brewster, Jane Wayland. THE SAN RAFAEL CATTLE COMPANY: A PENNSYLVANIA ENTERPRISE IN ARIZONA. *Arizona and the West 1966 9(2): 133-156*. Among the many investors who were attracted to Arizona Territory in the early 1880's was one Colin Cameron, astute businessman, experienced in land matters and animal husbandry. This scion of a prominent Pennsylvania family went to Arizona in 1882 and spent a year inspecting the lush valleys and hill country of southern Arizona. With cheap land and soaring beef prices Cameron decided on a large-scale enterprise. He and Pennsylvania associates chartered the San Rafael Cattle Company under the laws of New Jersey, and bought ostensible control of over 152 thousand acres of prime grazing land east of present Nogales, with 12 hundred head of cattle already ranging its grassy coverage. Cameron soon increased his cattle to some four thousand head. Despite skeptical Arizona cowmen, he successfully introduced pedigreed Herefords whose meat was much higher in the California markets than the Longhorns which most Arizona ranchers raised. Other refinements, such as thoroughbred Kentucky saddle horses, were soon added. Breeding brought improved strains and new markets made for bigger profits. Cameron astutely survived the threats of squatters, disputed land titles, unfavorable politicians and legislation, national cattle epidemics, droughts, the problems of grazing across the Mexican border, and other difficulties that eliminated many other range cattle industrialists. By 1900, the San Rafael Cattle Company had the largest registered herd of Herefords west of the Mississippi. In 1903 Cameron and San Rafael astutely sold their stock and improvements for 1,500,000 dollars. Illus., map, 62 notes.   D. L. Smith

1081. Burns, Robert H. BEEF MAKERS OF THE LARAMIE PLAINS. *Ann. of Wyoming 1964 36(2): 185-197*. An anecdotal account of cattle and sheep raising in Wyoming from 1880 to 1957. Discusses the operations of noted ranchers, cowboys and British investors. Based on one published article, the Corthell Collection, University of Wyoming, and personal reminiscences.   R. L. Nichols

1082. Burrill, Robert M. THE ESTABLISHMENT OF RANCHING ON THE OSAGE INDIAN RESERVATION. *Geographical R. 1972 62(4): 524-543*. "Ranching on the Osage Indian Reservation [in Indian Territory] was a vital link between the calf-raising country of Texas and the slaughterhouses of the upper midwest. The processes leading to the establishment of ranching resulted from interactions among many different groups of people with various motivations. These groups can be categorized as (1) cattlemen, whose major interests centered on cattle operations; (2) state and federal authorities, including politicians and bureaucrats, who wanted to resolve the most acute problems facing the majority of people at any given time; (3) settlers, who demanded free or cheap land; and (4) Indians, who were trying to maintain their cultural integrity. Careful examination of historical events and the effects these events had on the people in each category provides a means for comparative analysis and identification of the significant elements that led to the establishment of ranching in this area."   J

1083. Carlson, Alvar Ward. NEW MEXICO'S SHEEP INDUSTRY, 1850-1900: ITS ROLE IN THE HISTORY OF THE TERRITORY. *New Mexico Hist. R. 1969 44(1): 25-49*. Detailed analysis of the sheep industry of New Mexico, including methods of grazing, ownership, Indian difficulties, types of sheep, and marketing. By 1900, the sheep industry had changed from an open range industry to a sedentary sheep husbandry similar to that of the Midwestern States. This change was due in part to control of the range, preventive disease laws, the passing of the partido system, fences, private ownership of watering places, homesteading, and reclamation of thousands of acres. 81 notes.

D. F. Henderson

1084. Dobie, J. Frank. AB BLOCKER: TRAIL BOSS. *Arizona and the West 1964 6(2): 97-103*. Biographical anecdotes of Albert Pickens Blocker, an old-time trail boss whose fabled career took him over most of the cattle country of the Great Plains.   D. L. Smith

1085. Dobie, J. Frank. THE COWMAN WHO WAS MY FATHER. *Southwest R. 1967 52(4): 313-323*. Sketch of Jonathan Richard Dobie. The Dobie spread lay in Live Oak County, Texas, where as a rancher, the author's father did not fit the stereotype. He did not smoke, drink, or curse; he would not ride a pitching horse if he could avoid it; he did not carry a six-shooter; he seldom wore boots, never spurs; and he attended church regularly.   D. F. Henderson

1086. Dobie, J. Frank. HUNTING COUSIN SALLY. *Southwest R. 1963 48(3): 177-188*. Reminiscences of Colonel Ike T. Pryor as told to the author. Pryor claimed that his experiences in trying to find Cousin Sally (daughter of an aunt who raised Pryor for a brief period of time) during the turbulent Civil War years in Tennessee determined his successful life after the war. Pryor moved to Texas in the early 1870's, entered the cattle business, and quickly became a successful cattle buyer, land dealer, and rancher.   D. F. Henderson

1087. Durham, Philip and Jones, Everett L. NEGRO COWBOYS. *Am. West 1964 1(4): 26-31, 87*. More than five thousand Negro cowboys went up the trails from Texas in the years after the Civil War. Nearly all the pioneer cattlemen employed some Negroes. Like their white counterparts, thousands did their jobs and drew their pay without making even local history unless they got their names in the paper for disturbing the peace. Most of them disappeared when the trail drives were over and the dust settled. The Owen Wister-Zane Grey West includes whites of all kinds, Indians, and Chinese, but the Negro cowboy has been "fenced out." Anecdotal account excerpted from a forthcoming book of the same title. Biblio. note, illus.   D. L. Smith

1088. Durham, Philip and Jones, Everett L. SLAVES ON HORSEBACK. *Pacific Hist. R. 1964 33(4): 405-409*. Describes the life of the Negro cowboy in the Great Plains from 1850 to the 1870's. One in seven trailhands in the post-Civil War period was Negro.

J. McCutcheon

1089. Flanagan, Sue. CHARLES GOODNIGHT IN COLORADO. *Colorado Mag. 1966 43(1): 1-21*. A Texan for 30 years, Goodnight established the first extensive ranch in Colorado and became an international authority on the economics of the range industry. Beginning with Longhorns, Goodnight and his associate, John Wesley Iliff, bred them with

Herefords and Durhams. Plagued by desperadoes, Goodnight worked with law enforcement groups. The Panic of 1873 caused him heavy losses but he survived to carry on and to be praised by the writer J. Frank Dobie as more nearly approaching greatness than any other cowman in history.
I. W. Van Noppen

1090. Forsling, O. E. SHEEP TO CHEYENNE. *Idaho Yesterdays 1964 8(2): 26-32.* An unedited account of a trip made by the author in the summer of 1896, from Weiser, Idaho to Cheyenne, Wyoming with a flock of 6,800 sheep.
M. Small

1091. Frantz, Joe B. HOOF & HORN ON THE CHISHOLM TRAIL. *Am. West 1967 4(3): 15-20, 70-71.* The grass-covered plains between South Texas and Kansas linked the hordes of wild cattle in the former and the railroads that were snaking their way westward across the latter. The railroads, in turn, were projecting from the centers of the eastern cities where the industrial revolution was rapidly multiplying and concentrating the customers for the Texas beef. The first drive of cattle northward, in 1867, resulted in 20 carloads being shipped from Abilene, Kansas, to eastern slaughter houses. Thus was ushered in a new era in the American economy, dietary habits, and folklore. In 1871, it is estimated that 700 thousand cattle were driven northward. After this the numbers dropped drastically as the very nature of the western cattle industry changed. The Chisholm Trail was the collective name given the many variations of the route over which the cattle were driven. It originated wherever a herd was shaped up and ended wherever a market was found. 4 illus., biblio. note.
D. L. Smith

1092. Fritz, Henry E. THE CATTLEMEN'S FRONTIER IN THE TRANS-MISSISSIPPI WEST: AN ANNOTATED BIBLIOGRAPHY. *Arizona and the West 1972 14(1): 45-70, (2): 169-190.* Part I. Lists significant books and periodical literature, with imprint dates 1916-61, to explicate the main trends, shifts of emphasis, and omissions of the increasing literature on the trans-Mississippi cattlemen's frontier. Booster literature appeared from the mid-1870's to the end of the cattle boom in the mid-1880's, and the dime novels which embedded the cowboy myth in American folklore predominated over the next three decades. Scholarly treatment of the cattlemen's frontier began in 1916. Part II. Presents the significant books and articles with imprint dates 1952-70.
D. L. Smith

1093. Gard, Wayne. THE IMPACT OF THE CATTLE TRAILS. *Southwestern Hist. Q. 1967 71(1): 1-6.* The trail drives by which Texas longhorns were taken to the markets were major operations. Some ten million cattle were driven several hundred miles in probably the greatest migration of domestic animals in history. This solved a major problem by helping Texans recover from the impact of economic dislocation resulting from the Civil War. Booming expansion came to the trails-end, rails-end Kansas towns. The Great Plains were given a prolific source of folklore. Cattle ranching expanded into the central and northern sections of the Great Plains. The feeder cattle industry developed further east, principally in Illinois. New meat packing centers appeared. The trail drives hastened the western penetration of rail lines. Refrigeration and canning improvements expanded the market potential throughout the country and abroad. Map.
D. L. Smith

1094. Georgetta, Clel. SHEEP IN NEVADA. *Nevada Hist. Soc. Q. 1965 8(2): 15-38.* A partly firsthand account by a former sheepherder, the article emphasizes famous sheep drives and trails in Nevada. Many of the larger sheep owners are mentioned, and the author provides a light-hearted account of a sheepherder's diversions.
J. D. Filipiak

1095. Gibson, Arrell M. RANCHING ON THE SOUTHERN GREAT PLAINS. *J. of the West 1967 6(1): 135-153.* An account of the development of cattle ranching shows how topography and climate contributed to making the region a pastoral empire. Covered are the establishment of cattle towns, land tenure, bonanza ranching, and the numerous problems encountered by those hardy individuals seeking to make a living by raising the hardy longhorn. Based on published sources; 56 notes.
D. N. Brown

1096. Gossett, Gretta. STOCK GRAZING IN WASHINGTON'S NILE VALLEY: RECEDING RANGES IN THE CASCADES. *Pacific Northwest Q. 1964 55(3): 119-127.* History of changes in cattle-grazing in the mountain valley in central and western central Washington Territory and State over a span of a century, covering Indian activities, wars between cattlemen and sheepmen, and the encroachment of field agriculture. Activities in numerous valleys are described, and leading cattlemen are identified.
C. C. Gorchels

1097. Gould, Lewis L. FRANCIS E. WARREN AND THE JOHNSON COUNTY WAR. *Arizona and the West 1967 9(2): 131-142.* The Johnson County War of 1892 is probably "the most famous single episode" of Wyoming history. One of the major characters in the war was Francis E. Warren who was involved in public utilities, banks, railroads, and cattle in the State. He was also a politician and office holder at all levels of Territorial and State government. With "charming rascality" Warren used politics to enrich himself and to develop Wyoming. Persistent rustling in Johnson County in north central Wyoming was the casus belli which brought a stockmen-sponsored expedition to weed out the suspected thieves. This vigilante effort aroused the county whose citizens besieged the invaders and thus prompted the dispatch of Federal cavalry to their rescue. The Democrats immediately attempted to fix charges of complicity in the plans of the stockmen invaders, against the Republican administration including Senator Warren, nonpartisan in makeup though the expedition had been. It is clear from his papers, however, that Warren was unaware of the plotting and of the expedition - the event which unified his opponents, split the Republicans, and cost him his seat in the Senate. He was heavily involved in the cattlemen's cause, but it was rather in attempting to use Federal intervention to exterminate the rustlers in northern Wyoming, something the Johnson County War had not accomplished. This effort schooled Warren in techniques of persuasion and manipulation which served Wyoming well in his subsequent 1895-1929 tenure as a Senator. 4 illus., map, 31 notes.
D. L. Smith

1098. Gould, Lewis L. WILLIS VAN DEVANTER AND THE JOHNSON COUNTY WAR. *Montana 1967 17(4): 18-27.* Traces Van-Devanter's work as defense attorney for the ranchers accused in the Johnson County cattle war in Wyoming, and as a leader in minimizing damage to Republican Party prospects following that incident. Based on correspondence in the Library of Congress; illus.
S. R. Davison

1099. Hagan, William T. KIOWAS, COMANCHES, AND CATTLEMEN, 1867-1906: A CASE STUDY OF THE FAILURE OF U.S. RESERVATION POLICY. *Pacific Hist. R. 1971 40(3): 333-355.* The treaty which these two tribes signed with the United States in 1867 provided a reservation of 3 million acres closed to all white men. Relates the gradual encroachment of whites onto this land. First came the cattlemen, whose payment for the leasing of the lands was gradually welcomed by most of the Indians. Then potential settlers began to put pressure on the government for open land. In 1901 legislation opened a portion of the land to them, and brought to an end the cattleman's era. It was also the final blow to the principle of isolation inherent in the treaty. History might have been different had the government subsidized the experiment properly. 91 notes.
E. C. Hyslop

1100. Haines, Francis. HORSES AND THE AMERICAN FRONTIER. *Am. West 1971 8(2): 10-15.* The horse was central to much of the development of the frontier, especially for mining, the cattle industry, and the military. During the depression years of the 1890's, the Boer War relieved the surplus horse situation. Agents of the British Government bought thousands of horses from 10 Western States to ship to South Africa. With the end of the war and the return of prosperity, Western horses again supplied the national needs. Excerpted from a forthcoming book. 6 illus.
D. L. Smith

1101. Harrison, Lowell H. THE INCREDIBLE CATTALO. *Am. Hist. Illus. 1968 2(9): 32-35.* Between the 1880's and the early part of the 1900's, Charles Goodnight, a Texas Panhandle rancher, experimented in crossing the buffalo with domestic cattle, thus producing the cattalo. He hoped that the cross-breeding would combine the best features of both animals. Convinced that the cattalo were far superior to cattle, both as meat producers and as suitable to harsh winters, Goodnight lavished a small fortune upon the animals. However, his financial returns from the cattalo were negligible. After nearly 50 years of building up the cattalo herd, Goodnight was forced to sell. Shortly thereafter the cattalo disappeared from the Texas Panhandle. 4 illus.
R. V. McBaine

1102. Harrison, Lowell H. THOMAS SIMPSON CARSON, NEW MEXICO RANCHER. *New Mexico Hist. R. 1967 42(2): 127-143.* Carson, a native of Scotland, spent 30 years (1880-1910) in the United States, primarily in the Southwest. His meager capital was first invested in a ranch, which proved to be a financial disaster. Later endeavors included management of the Scottish Land and Mortgage Company's New Mexico property, and ranching again. Based on Carson's two books describing his adventures, *Ranching, Sport and Travel* (London, 1911) and *The World As Seen By Me* (London, 1923).

D. F. Henderson

1103. Hayes, Edward G. ZA ROUNDUP. *Colorado Mag. 1964 41(3): 213-224.* In 1887 when Edward Hayes operated the ZA Ranch near Colorado Springs with his partner Charles W. Codwise, Hayes wrote to his father in Canandaigua, New York, a spirited account of a roundup on the range which extended from Old Mexico to British America. He stated the purpose of the roundup, described the day-by-day life of the cowboys, and predicted the passing of the roundup as preemptions and homesteads were being scattered everywhere. The manuscript is in the Charles Leaming Tutt Library at Colorado College.

I. W. Van Noppen

1104. Hicks, Sam. GAMBLING MEN AND HONEST HORSES: A-WINTERING ON A WYOMING RANCH. *Am. West 1970 7(6): 40-47, 61.* Raised on a cattle ranch in the Jackson Hole country of Wyoming, the author describes his experiences, especially those concerning the care of livestock during the severe winters. It took both skill and luck for a rancher to successfully winter his cattle on the snow-country ranches. It was a gamble with the highest stakes. For the annual affair, the cattleman methodically bet everything he owned - cattle, horses, haystacks, and his family's future. 4 illus. D. L. Smith

1105. Holliday, J. S. THE LONELY SHEEPHERDER. *Am. West 1964 1(2): 36-45.* An outcast in the American West, little is known or has been written about the sheepherder. As late as 1920 the long standing war between cattlemen and sheepherders was serious. In his "reclusive bachelorhood" and with many hours in which only his attentive presence is required, the sheepherder whiles away his time with crafts as old as his profession. A previously overlooked pastime is found in the hundreds of carvings on the white barked aspen trees of the Wyoming-Colorado border high country. As illustrated, they are, in general, symbolic of thoughts of those lonely men - of women and whiskey. D. L. Smith

1106. Jager, Ronald B. THE CHISHOLM TRAIL'S MOUNTAIN OF WORDS. *Southwestern Hist. Q. 1967 71(1): 61-68.* In his *The Chisholm Trail* (Norman: U. of Oklahoma Press, 1954), Wayne Gard included a 323-item bibliography. On the Trail's centennial, a supplementary bibliography to the Gard listing is presented. The items are briefly annotated and classified as books, pamphlets, articles, and unpublished theses. 3 notes. D. L. Smith

1107. Jordan, Terry G. THE ORIGIN OF ANGLO-AMERICAN CATTLE RANCHING IN TEXAS: DOCUMENTATION OF DIFFUSION FROM THE LOWER SOUTH. *Econ. Geography 1969 45(1): 63-87.* Rejects the thesis of Webb that Americans brought no ranching tradition with them to Texas and learned the rudiments of ranching from Mexican ranchers. Develops an alternative proposition of a five-stage process of diffusion and blend of an Anglo-American and a Spanish-Mexican ranching tradition. This process took place to the east of the area in which Webb placed it. Supports this thesis by positing the existence of eight characteristics of 19th-century ranching in the coastal prairies of Texas in the period 1820-50, including open ranges, long drives to market, and management of cattle on horseback. Using Texas tax lists and the manuscript censuses of both the United States and Mexico, analyzes the birthplace and previous residence of cattle ranchers in this area at that time and establishes the lower southern origins of a large majority of them. Analyzing the cattle population of the lower South, the author supports the thesis that the entry of cattle ranching into Texas was an extension of the lower southern ranching belt. 2 tables, 8 figs.

W. H. Mulligan, Jr.

1108. Kenny, Jidith Keyes. EARLY SHEEP RANCHING IN EASTERN OREGON. *Oregon Hist. Q. 1963 64(2): 101-122.* Detailed activities of sheep ranchers in founding herds, providing for grazing, lambing, shearing, and marketing wool. C. C. Gorchels

1109. Kielman, Chester V. THE TEXAS AND SOUTHWESTERN CATTLE RAISERS ASSOCIATION MINUTE BOOK. *Southwestern Hist. Q. 1967 71(1): 91-108.* The basic document in the archives of the Texas and Southwestern Cattle Raisers Association (now preserved in the University of Texas Library) is the association's original minute book covering the years 1877-92. Kept with meticulous care and in great detail, it is "a veritable treasure house . . . on every phase of the cattle industry." Interlarded excerpts from the first decade and editorial comment are presented. Map, 35 notes. D. L. Smith

1110. Kollmorgen, Walter M. and Simonett, David S. GRAZING OPERATIONS IN THE FLINT HILLS - BLUESTEM PASTURES OF CHASE COUNTY, KANSAS. *Ann. of the Assoc. of Am. Geographers 1965 55(2): 260-290.* Describes the structure and processes of the large-scale grazing industry in the area. Although presently predominant, crop farmers are declining in numbers and influence because absentee, urban-owned, ranch-type operators control most of the good grassland. Illus., maps, tables, 40 notes. W. R. Boedecker

1111. Lehman, Anthony L. A CALIFORNIA HIDE TRADE LETTER, 1844. *Southern California Q. 1969 51(1): 57-61.* Publishes for the first time a letter from New England sailor John Girdler who was involved in the hide trade along the California coast during the 1840's. The letter "with its interesting description and decidedly Yankee viewpoint is probably typical of the correspondence sent homeward." Based on a letter in the possession of Frank Odom, Claremont, California; 12 notes.

W. L. Bowers

1112. Lewis, Theodore B. THE NATIONAL CATTLE TRAIL, 1883-1886. *Nebraska Hist. 1971 52(2): 205-220.* Examines the motives, chiefly of Texas cattlemen, to establish a national cattle trail, and the opposition the plan aroused among Northern cattlemen who by the 1880's opposed the competition of Texas cattle for a glutted market. Discusses the agitation for a national cattle trail, from conventions of cattlemen to the efforts of Texas Congressmen to secure enabling legislation. With the collapse of the range cattle industry, the trail became a dead issue.

R. Lowitt

1113. MacMillan, D. THE GILDED AGE AND MONTANA'S DHS RANCH. *Montana 1970 20(2): 50-57.* After Montana's Indian wars ended, cattlemen moved quickly to occupy the big ranges newly opened in the eastern two-thirds of the territory. Pioneer Granville Stuart (1834-1918), acting for financiers Andrew J. Davis (1820-90) and Samuel T. Hauser (1833-1914), preempted a choice ranch site northeast of present Lewistown. Hopes for prosperity were dimmed when the Army chose the same place for a new post, Fort Maginnis, in 1880. But the owners, all prominent in the Democratic Party, mustered enough political influence to have their ranch excluded from the boundaries of the military reservation. Based mostly on the correspondence of the principals; illus., 32 notes. S. R. Davison

1114. Osgood, Ernest S. I DISCOVER WESTERN HISTORY. *Western Hist. Q. 1972 3(3): 240-251.* The author has been interested in history since his grade school days. About 1900, his uncle, colonial American historian Herbert Levi Osgood, introduced him to the meticulous nature of historical research. After earning a degree in history at Dartmouth in 1912 and teaching for two years in an Ohio academy, the author accepted a high school teaching position in Montana. Here the history of the American West replaced his interests in medieval history. His doctoral dissertation at Wisconsin, which was published in 1929 as *The Day of the Cattleman,* was written under Frederick Logan Paxson. The author was professor of western history at the University of Minnesota from 1927 to 1957. Since retirement he has been a lecturer at the College of Wooster in Ohio. Illus. D. L. Smith

1115. Patterson, Edna. EARLY CATTLE IN ELKO COUNTY. *Nevada Hist. Soc. Q. 1965 8(2): 3-12.* A brief account of stock raising, cattle trails, and cowboys in Elko County, Nevada, with emphasis on noted personalities and legends related to the beef cattle trade.

J. D. Filipiak

1116. Porter, Kenneth O. NEGRO LABOR IN THE WESTERN CATTLE INDUSTRY, 1866-1900. *Labor Hist. 1969 10(3): 346-374.* Surveys the occupations which Negroes held or to which they could aspire in the cattle industry. Although seldom attaining the position of foreman or trail boss, the Negro laborer was probably less discriminated against in the cattle industry than in any other industry. The services of the eight or nine thousand Negroes were definitely needed for the success of the trail drives and the work of the ranches. Based on the archival files of J. Frank Dobie and on numerous primary and secondary sources; 91 notes.

L. L. Athey

1117. Poteet, Chrystabel Berrong. ON THE WICHITA-CADDO RANGE. *Chronicles of Oklahoma 1964 42(2): 55-61.* A narrative of "Big Jim" Walker, cattleman, and his nephew Hank Wilson. Hank had done well until his wife and baby died. Then when he took cattle to market in Kansas City, he forged his uncle's name and kept 43 thousand dollars. When he returned to visit the graves of his wife and baby before heading for California he was caught. His uncle gave him a thousand dollars and sent him on his way. Illus., 8 notes.

I. W. Van Noppen

1118. Rackley, Barbara Fifer. THE HARD WINTER 1886-1887. *Montana 1971 21(1): 50-59.* Anecdotes and personal observations of men directly involved in the loss of livestock during the notorious "hard winter." Overstocking of the range coincided with a dry summer and a winter of unusual severity, and delivered a death blow to the open-range cattle industry. Based on correspondence of individuals and firms concerned, and statistics from the War Department's Signal Corps, then the official agency for weather data; illus., 8 photos, 47 notes.

S. R. Davison

1119. Rogers, Jerry L. RESCUING RANCHING'S PAST. *Historic Preservation 1971 23(2): 4-9.* Discusses The Ranch Headquarters, an outdoor living museum of ranching history, near Texas Tech University in Lubbock. About 20 "significant historic buildings" are being assembled there, the oldest of which is the log cabin headquarters of the El Capote ranch, built in 1836. Other ranch houses and such secondary buildings as barns, bunkhouses, and offices will be included in the finished site. Completion date is 1976. Photos.

J. M. Hawes

1120. Rojas, Arnold R. THE VAQUERO. *Am. West 1964 1(2): 46-53.* Although used interchangeably, the terms cowboy and vaquero are not synonymous. The territory of the buckaroo (a Yankee corruption of vaquero) is west of the Rocky Mountains; that of the cowboy is east of the Rockies. The origin of the former term is Hispanic, the latter, African. They are unlike each other in "racial background, lingo, character, methods of working cattle, and conception of what a horseman should be." While the vaquero has been immortalized on canvas, very little prose has been devoted to him. Differences between the two are defined.

D. L. Smith

1121. Rostad, Lee. CHARLEY BAIR: KING OF WESTERN SHEEPMEN. *Montana 1970 20(4): 50-61.* Charles M. Bair (1857-1943) left home in Ohio at age 17 with 14 cents and seven green apples. "In Montana, 40 years later, he was the largest individual sheep grower on the continent." After some brief railroad work, he engaged in successful business ventures, including a trip to the Klondike during the gold rush to sell machines for thawing frozen ground. After building a fortune in sheep, he increased his wealth by investments in coal and oil properties. His friends included notables in the fields of politics and entertainment. Based mostly on family records; illus., 25 notes. S. R. Davison

1122. Sanderlin, Walter S., ed. A CATTLE DRIVE FROM TEXAS TO CALIFORNIA: THE DIARY OF M. H. ERSKINE, 1854. *Southwestern Hist. Q. 1964 67(3): 397-412.* Presents excerpts from a typescript of Michael H. Erskine's journal of a cattle drive from Texas to California, between April and November of 1854. Details of trail techniques and experiences are included. Significantly, there is little mention of Indian troubles.

R. L. Williamson

1123. Saum, Lewis O. THE MARQUIS DE MORES: INSTRUMENT OF AMERICAN PROGRESS. *North Dakota Hist. 1969 36(2): 140-161.* In 1882 the Marquis de Mores, Antoine de Vallombrosa (1857-96), arrived in the United States from France. With monetary backing from the father of his American-born wife, de Mores engaged in ranching and other endeavors in North Dakota and elsewhere in the Northwest. The man was either liked or hated, there was little middle

ground. He was a man of progress but, unfortunately, he never met with success in any of nis American ventures. De Mores tried large-scale ranching, slaughtering, and distribution of his own beef through a national consumers cooperative, but failed in all these ventures. To some he was a victim of the beef combines, to others the victim of his own inadequacies. Based on contemporary newspaper accounts; illus., photos.

E. P. Costello

1124. Savage, William M., Jr. PLUNKETT OF THE EK: IRISH NOTES ON THE WYOMING CATTLE INDUSTRY IN THE 1880'S. *Ann. of Wyoming 1971 43(2): 205-214.* Horace Curzon Plunkett (d. 1932), son of an Irish nobleman, came to Johnson County in 1879 in search of a dry climate in which to recuperate from tuberculosis. Settling on the EK Ranch, he entered partnerships with various Americans and Britons in both cattle and land development companies and was elected to membership in the Wyoming Stock Growers' Association. During his American sojourn, Plunkett experienced frequent difficulties with hostile cowboys, quarrelsome business associates, and depressed markets. Finally, after a prairie fire swept across much of his range land in the fall of 1886 and the severe winter of 1886-87 brought disaster to the entire northern plains cattle industry, Plunkett returned to Ireland in 1889 to manage family business affairs there. Based on secondary sources and Plunkett's diaries; 41 notes.

G. R. Adams

1125. Savage, William W., Jr. BARBED WIRE AND BUREAUCRACY: THE FORMATION OF THE CHEROKEE STRIP LIVE STOCK ASSOCIATION. *J. of the West 1968 7(3): 405-414.* Tells of the founding of the Cherokee Live Stock Association in response to a Federal order (1885) to remove fencing from the area known as the Cherokee Outlet. A loose organization had existed since 1879 for pooling cowboys and other mutual assistance, but the fencing issue brought things to a head.

R. N. Alvis

1126. Schapsmeier, Edward and Schapsmeier, Frederick. THEODORE ROOSEVELT'S COWBOY YEARS. *J. of the West 1966 5(3): 398-408.* Maintains that the years Roosevelt spent as a rancher in Dakota Territory occupy a significant part of the formative years of the future President. His adventure in the West taught Roosevelt that man could master his own fate, and this experience dominated his thinking and shaped his personality. Some of the events of his ranching days are related. Based on published sources, 44 notes. D. N. Brown

1127. Sharp, Paul F. BLACKFEET OF THE BORDER: ONE PEOPLE DIVIDED. *Montana 1970 20(1): 2-15.* In addition to the problems facing all Indians in the 19th century, the Blackfeet suffered because they straddled the invisible boundary between the United States and Canada. Uncertainty as to jurisdiction and responsibility led to neglect and harrassment on both sides of the line. The intrusion of stockmen into their dwindling reservation in 1875, and rivalry between the military and the Department of the Interior over control of the Indians brought a crisis. In 1882, after fruitless negotiations with Canada, the United States unilaterally forced across the border those deemed to be Canadian subjects. Since that time the United States has assumed responsibility of those remaining. Reprinted from the book *Whoop-up Country: the Canadian-American West, 1865-1885.* (Minneapolis: U. of Minnesota Press, 1955). Based primarily on correspondence, official reports, and published accounts; 39 notes.

S. R. Davison

1128. Sinclair, F. H. DOWN THE TRAIL WITH A RANGE RIDER. *Montana 1966 16(3): 57-64.* Biographical sketch of Dale Wilder, long-time manager of stockyards in Billings and a founder of the Montana Range Riders' Association Museum. The article consists largely of his reminiscences, covering his childhood in Texas and his early youth in Montana in the last years of the open range days. Illus

S. R. Davison

1129. Skaggs, Jimmy M. HIP POCKET BUSINESSMEN: THE CATTLE-TRAILING CONTRACTORS. *Great Plains J. 1970 10(1): 1-10.* Discusses the trailing of cattle north from Texas after the Civil War. More than half of the cattle were moved by contractors who did not own them. Some contractors combined trailing with speculation or cattle-buying; others depended on the delivery fee per head for their profits. Discusses the typical legal and physical arrangements for trailing and some of the hazards for both contractor and owner. The best source for

information is the 1925 book by John Marvin Hunter, ed., *The Trail Drivers of Texas* (New York: Argosy-Antiquarian, Ltd.). 36 notes.
O. H. Zabel

1130. Skaggs, Jimmy M.   JOHN THOMAS LYTLE: CATTLE BARON. *Southwestern Hist. Q. 1967 71(1): 46-60.* Impressed by the obviously expanding opportunites in the cattle industry in post-Civil War Texas, young John Thomas Lytle resigned as foreman of his uncle's ranch; leased a small pasture and stocked it with longhorns; and married into a prominent ranching family, acquiring at the same time an influential judge as a brother-in-law. His career spanned the history of the cattle industry in Texas from the days of the open range to the age of modern management. He started out in 1867 as a small rancher, became a trailing contractor, was involved in land and cattle speculation, moved into ranch developing, was a ranch executive, and finally became an influential pillar in the Texas Cattle Raisers' Association. By the time of his death he was regarded as the "Dean of Cattlemen." 64 notes.   D. L. Smith

1131. Smith, Helena Huntington.   THE "LORD" OF POWDER RIVER: A CATTLE KINGDOM IN WYOMING. *Am. West 1964 1(3): 58-63.* Englishman Moreton Frewen moved into the Powder River country of northern Wyoming and played a leading role as manager of one of the large British cattle corporations in the heyday of the cattle kingdoms. As principal in the Powder River Cattle Company he established himself in a palatial ranch house, married into the Lord Randolph Churchill family, and operated "ceaselessly" from Wyoming to New York to London. During the "euphoric haze of the cattle boom" his cattle numbered in the tens of thousands. With overstocking of the ranges and the decline of the boom, Frewen moved in all directions to prevent the decline: feeding and slaughtering in Nebraska to outflank Chicago meat-packers who were "victimizing" them; shipping live cattle direct to England from Lake Superior; appearing before the Privy Council to lift the quarantine on American cattle; scheming to transfer cattle ranching to the plains of Alberta. After the company folded, Frewen promoted a succession of incongruous causes and maintained contacts with prominent people. Taken from a forthcoming book. Illus., bibliographical note.
D. L. Smith

1132. Smith, Helena Huntington.   MYSTERY MAN OF THE JOHNSON COUNTY WAR. *Montana 1963 13(4): 40-49.* A summary of the little that is known about George Dunning, who accompanied the invading gunmen in the Wyoming cattle war of 1892. One Idaho resident among a group of Texans, he later claimed to be an infiltrating agent whose sympathies favored the small ranchers, the intended victims of the intruders. His story, labeled a "confession," was published in the Wyoming press, implicating prominent citizens in the murderous plot and furnishing material for Asa S. Mercer's *Banditti of the Plains,* a classic account of the episode. Briefly kept in protective custody, Dunning soon dropped out of sight, leaving unanswered the questions of his identity and true affiliations. Recent discovery of a packet of his letters, dated 1892, aroused new interest in him, and furnished some of the information for this article, along with earlier printed reports.   S. R. Davison

1133. Smith, Helena Huntington.   THE RISE & FALL OF ALEC SWAN. *Am. West 1967 4(3): 21-24, 66-68.* Alexander Hamilton Swan was one of the most famous western cattle kings. He created great ranches, imported purebreds, and was a prime mover in the stockyards industry. The Swan Land and Cattle Company controlled millions of acres of range and, in 1880, was capitalized at two and a half million dollars. Swan had moved to the raw Wyoming frontier in 1873 and started with three thousand head of cattle. The cattle boom gripped him like an infectious fever. His herds and holdings increased. He proliferated companies with eastern and foreign capital, and established major stockyards in Nebraska and Iowa. Then a series of misfortunes and misjudgments plagued his enterprises until by 1887 they were in a shaky condition. A 25 thousand dollar note which Swan had endorsed for a friend came due as he went to Europe on a business trip. This brought to light other notes which apprehensive holders pressed against the Swan empire. The resulting bankruptcy rocked the cattle kingdom and banks on two continents. Swan's faults of mismanagement were common to the big operators in the western cattle industry. It was the magnitude of the Swan enterprises that made his collapse so significant. 2 illus., biblio. note.
D. L. Smith

1134. Ulph, Owen C.   COWHANDS, COW HORSES, AND COWS. *Am. West 1966 3(1): 64-71.* Few cowhands, it is asserted, had the education, inclination, or talent to be their own press agents. Most sketches of range life are "hackneyed distortions peddled by scribbling hucksters whose knowledge of the elastic market for fanciful opiates and the magnitude of human gullibility far exceeds their knowledge of cowhands, cow horses, and cows." The author's depiction of these elements of range life, he claims, are more accurate because he has "the immediate, saddle-thumping perspective of the calloused buckaroo." He is a cow puncher as well as an academician. Illus.   D. L. Smith

1135. Unrau, William E.   JOSEPH G. MC COY AND FEDERAL REGULATION OF THE CATTLE TRADE. *Colorado Mag. 1966 43(1): 32-43.* Joseph McCoy, well-known as a cattleman instrumental in gaining railroad and cattle-raiser connections in Abilene, Kansas, also played a part in the entrance of the federal government into the economy of the West. He fought the Indian Department and labeled all agencies as corrupt. Because of his unremitting struggle, the cattlemen were able to continue their business with relatively few restrictions from Washington.   R. Sexauer

1136. Walker, Don D.   FROM SELF-RELIANCE TO COOPERATION: THE EARLY DEVELOPMENT OF THE CATTLEMEN'S ASSOCIATIONS IN UTAH. *Utah Hist. Q. 1967 35(3): 187-201.* Emphasizes the influence of national and state organization of cattlemen outside of Utah Territory and the leadership of Henry J. Faust in the establishment of the Territorial Stock Growers' Association of Utah at Salt Lake City in April 1885. A rival organization, the Utah Cattle and Horse Growers' Association, headed by William Jennings had been organized in January 1885. Efforts to unite the two organizations in April were not successful.   S. L. Jones

1137. Wilson, James A.   SOUTHWESTERN CATTLEMEN AND RAILROAD REGULATION: A MATTER OF DOLLARS AND SENSE. *Rocky Mountain Social Sci. J. 1970 7(1): 89-97.* Notes that Southwestern cattlemen came face-to-face with the "Age of Big Business" during the late 19th and early 20th centuries with the advent of the railroads. The author analyzes their grievances and protests, which led cattlemen to the discovery that organization and reliance on the National Government were their only effective defenses against aggrandizing corporations on whom they were forced to depend. 35 notes.
R. F. Allen

1138. Wilson, James A.   WEST TEXAS INFLUENCE ON THE EARLY CATTLE INDUSTRY OF ARIZONA. *Southwestern Hist. Q. 1967 71(1): 26-36.* From the late 1840's into the 1870's Texas stockmen drove their beef cattle over southern Arizona on the Texas-California trail. Even before the Civil War, Texans were impressed with the grazing possibilities offered by the Gadsden Purchase country of Arizona as well as other areas. By the last third of the century they were moving their herds into Arizona and establishing the range cattle industry there. Not only did the Texans contribute their proven range methods to the new grass country of Arizona but their problems as well. Texas rustlers brought lawlessness, poor management resulted in overstocking, and carelessness introduced destructive diseases. But these difficulties did force laws and associations in Arizona to curb and resolve them. The Anglo-American cattleman frontier in Arizona was an extension of the Texas experience. 38 notes.   D. L. Smith

1139. —.   THE CHISHOLM TRAIL. *Kansas Hist. Q. 1967 33(2): 129-137.* Commemorates the centennial of the opening of the Chisholm Trail. An introductory statement traces the general development of the trail from 1867 to the 1880's. Contemporary newspaper accounts give details of cattle drives on the trail. Quotations taken from four Kansas newspapers provide a frame for a lengthy excerpt from the 6 November issue of the New York *Daily Tribune.* This is described as "probably the best piece of contemporary journalism dealing with the cattle trade of 1867." Map, 6 notes.   W. F. Zornow

Public Land and Homesteading

1140. Alward, Dennis and Rolle, Andrew F. THE SURVEYOR-GENERAL EDWARD FITZGERALD BEALE'S ADMINISTRATION OF CALIFORNIA LANDS. *Southern California Q. 1971 53(2): 113-122.* Concerns a neglected aspect of the career of California pioneer Edward Fitzgerald Beale (1822-1903). Although best remembered as a naval officer during the time of American conquest of California and as Superintendent of Indian Affairs for the new State during the 1850's, Beale also served as Surveyor General of California and Nevada from 1861 to 1864. During those years Beale sought to do a difficult job in the face of Federal reluctance to fund his work adequately because of the Civil War which was raging at the time. By 1864 Beale despaired of his work as Surveyor General and tried to get reinstated in the armed forces, but his request for a military command was rejected and shortly thereafter he was fired from his job. Beale's political inexperience, resentment of "desk-bound duties," and blunt personality may have contributed to his release: however, his "awkward years as surveyor general . . . can be considered as quite reflective of the problems that faced the federal government in the settlement of the American West." Based on manuscript records in the National Archives; 25 notes. W. L. Bowers

1141. Beezley, William H. HOMESTEADING IN NEBRASKA 1862-1872. *Nebraska Hist. 1972 53(1): 59-75.* Analyzes the first decade of the operation of the Homestead Act (1862) in Nebraska. Concludes that "for many settlers the Homestead Act remained the promise of opportunity in Nebraska Territory." R. Lowitt

1142. Beezley, William H. LAND OFFICE SPOILSMEN IN "BLEEDING KANSAS." *Great Plains J. 1970 9(2): 67-78.* Discusses the Democratic appointees to the General Land Office in Kansas during territorial days (John Calhoun was surveyor general, Ely Moore was register, and Thomas C. Shoemaker, succeeded by William Brindle, was receiver). Their jobs were both administrative (surveying and transferring the public lands) and political (trying to ensure alignment of the territory with the Democratic Party). They failed in the latter function. In the former, however, considering the circumstances, they "completed surveys rapidly and handled entries efficiently." 36 notes. O. H. Zabel

1143. Braswell, Vernon S. THE OKLAHOMA FREE HOMES BILL 1892-1900. *Chronicles of Oklahoma 1967 44(4): 380-390.* The United States grew and developed because relatively free and cheap lands were available. Congress had a liberal land policy. The land ordinance of 1785 and the Homestead Law were significant. A settler who lived on land five years, cultivated it, and paid land office fees received his patent. Subsequent openings had a requirement that the settler pay an additional amount per acre. This was a departure from the provisions of the Homestead Law of 1862. From 1892 to 1900 Oklahomans agitated for free homes. Free Homes Leagues were organized. The Free Homes Bill (H.R. 996) was signed into law 17 May 1900. 22 notes. I. W. Van Noppen

1144. Chapman, Berlin B. LAND OFFICE BUSINESS AT LAWTON AND EL RENO. *Great Plains J. 1967 7(1): 1-25.* Discusses the opening to settlers by the Federal Government in 1901 of the Wichita, Kiowa, Comanche, and Apache reservations in Oklahoma, dealing not with the unique land lottery method used but with the opening and staffing of the land offices at Lawton and El Reno, the homesteaders who entered lands there, and the investigations carried out by land office personnel to ensure the legality of claims. Unfortunately, the records of these land offices were destroyed in 1928 as useless executive papers. 39 notes. O. H. Zabel

1145. Donahue, Francis. CUBAN VIEW OF THE OKLAHOMA RUN. *Chronicles of Oklahoma 1967 44(4): 362-364.* José Martí, Cuban national hero, writer, and revolutionary, wrote a vivid account of the "run." He described the homesteaders, the speculators, the masses of people in the towns, Arkansas City, and the torrent of 40,000 people pouring into the territory. The "Sooners" had gotten in early and laid out the town of Guthrie. I. W. Van Noppen

1146. Finley, Robert M. A BUDGETING APPROACH TO THE QUESTION OF HOMESTEAD SIZE ON THE PLAINS. *Agric. Hist.* *1968 42(2): 109-114.* Uses the traditional farm management budgeting technique to analyze how much land a homesteader on the Great Plains could have farmed by himself, using the tools and techniques of the times. Tables, based on accepted research studies, show the maximum days available for field work, the labor requirements for various crops, and the types of cropping systems. The author concludes that the homesteader could not have farmed more than 160 acres, so a larger homestead would not have necessarily solved his problems. Successful adjustments would still have waited until technology, experience, and the appropriate type of farming caught up. W. D. Rasmussen

1147. Gates, Paul W. THE CALIFORNIA LAND ACT OF 1851. *California Hist. Q. 1971 50(4): 395-430.* Challenges the view that land grant owners in California were cheated out of their holdings. Many of the opinions held regarding the law, the landowners, and the litigation are erroneous. Rather than a move to deprive Mexicans-turned-Americans of their property rights, the 1851 land law as adjudicated by the courts was more than favorable to the landowners, considering that boundaries were vague or nonexistent, that 56 grants were approved in the last seven months of Mexican rule and were incomplete according to Mexican law, and that the courts frequently accepted often-fraudulent evidence favoring the landowners. There were examples of landowners evicting settlers from patented lands after subsequent litigation found in the grantee's favor. Persons receiving grants included a large number of non-Mexicans who fought for their patents as tenaciously as did the Californios, into whose families they had often married. The Land Commission was under political control; Democrats replaced Whigs in 1853. Generalizations that Californio landowners lost their lands to Anglo-American land hunger must be seriously qualified as a result of careful investigation into contemporary source materials. Based on primary and secondary sources; 75 notes. A. Hoffman

1148. Gates, Paul W. PRE-HENRY GEORGE LAND WARFARE IN CALIFORNIA. *California Hist. Soc. Q. 1967 46(2): 121-148.* Agrarian warfare developed frequently on the frontier, but the California story is unique in that "it involved Spanish and Mexican land law, interpreted in United States courts by American lawyers and judges who . . . remolded it by the application of federal and state laws . . . Anglo-Saxon common law with its deep respect for property rights untempered by equity clashed with frontier conceptions of settlers' rights based on natural law." Discusses the squatter controversies that broke out in many counties of California. Many but not all claimants insisted on holding their grants intact, refusing to come to satisfactory terms with settlers. The failure to break up the great estates left by the Mexican Government, and the rapid rise in real estate values with the great influx of population to California, led Henry George to his solution of what he regarded as a developing land monopoly. 50 notes. E. P. Stickney

1149. Gates, Paul W. THE SUSCOL PRINCIPLE, PREEMPTION, AND CALIFORNIA LATIFUNDIA. *Pacific Hist. R. 1970 39(4): 453-471.* A study of the disposition of land grant claims inherited by the United States from Mexico following the California Land Grant Act of 1851. The Suscol claim, involving 81 thousand acres, was a major example of the legal confusion caused by claims for which the courts and lawyers were not prepared. The eventual outcome of this case led to legislation that permitted buyers of fraudulent claims to retain possession regardless of the size of their holdings, freeing them from the 160-acre limit, and permitted further legislation sanctioning land monopolization. 47 notes. E. C. Hyslop

1150. Hollon, W. Eugene. RUSHING FOR LAND: OKLAHOMA 1889. *Am. West 1966 3(4): 4-15, 69-71.* Much of Oklahoma was assigned to various Indian tribes. A part of the Seminole and Creek reservations, a two-million-acre tract in the center of Oklahoma, was never occupied. Popularly called "the District" it soon tempted land-hungry whites. The first "boomers" (the name given to trespassers who came in to boom the lands for settlement) who entered the area were probably hired by the customer-hungry railroads that crossed the District. As early as 1880 eviction troops were busy trying to prevent a forcible takeover. By April 1889 thousands of boomers, victims of recent droughts and blizzards, had collected along the southern border of Kansas. Some fifty thousand assembled at three designated places to participate in a run for the land because Congress had finally legalized the opening of the District to homesteaders, effective at noon on 22 April. By train, prairie schooner, wagon, carriage, buggy, bicycle, and even on foot, the race was on. Guthrie, for example, was settled, a government inaugurated, and the amenities of a frontier town established almost overnight. It also became the territorial capital. Based on photographic collections and other manuscript sources in the University of Oklahoma Library, contemporary articles in various national periodicals, and secondary histories; 19 illus., map, biblio. note.   D. L. Smith

1151. Holtz, Milton E.   EARLY SETTLEMENT AND PUBLIC LAND DISPOSAL IN THE ELKHORN RIVER VALLEY, CUMING COUNTY, NEBRASKA TERRITORY.   *Nebraska Hist. 1971 52(2): 113-132.* Examines public land disposal (1854-67) in a 22-section area of the Elkhorn River Valley. Stresses the noticeable pattern of elongated tracts fronting the river which enabled farmers to "share the wealth" of the valley.   R. Lowitt

1152. Judge, Frances.   CARRIE AND THE GRAND TETONS. *Montana 1968 18(3): 44-57.* Presents the reminiscences of a woman who had witnessed homesteading in the Jackson Hole area of Wyoming in the late 1890's, when she was about 10 years old. Included is biographical material about three generations of women—Carrie Nesbitt Dunn (the principal narrator), her mother, and her daughter who writes the supporting account. Illustrations are family photographs and portraits.
                                              S. R. Davison

1153. Mark, Irving.   THE HOMESTEAD IDEAL AND CONSERVATION OF THE PUBLIC DOMAIN.   *Am. J. of Economics and Sociol. 1963 (2): 263-278.* A detailed study of federal land policy from the Land Act of 1796 to the present. The disposal of land at low selling prices and in small parcels was opposed by Southerners who feared the spread of free-soil settlements, and Eastern manufacturers and land speculators who were disturbed by the economic impact of the westward movement. The Forest Reserve Act of 1891 brought conservation to the fore. The author concludes: "From the beginning of the Republic, the yearning to fulfill the homestead ideal has been a durable part of the national pattern. Into it the twentieth century has woven the desire to conserve the public domain."   B. E. Swanson

1154. Nash, Gerald D.   THE CALIFORNIA STATE LAND OFFICE, 1858-1898.   *Huntington Lib. Q. 1964 27(4): 347-356.* In disposing of eight million acres of state domain, California's ostensible goal was to create or at least encourage small family farms. In actual practice bad administration, careless drafting and large-scale corruption nearly nullified this intent.   H. D. Jordan

1155. Paulson, Howard W.   THE ALLOTMENT OF LAND IN SEVERALTY TO THE DAKOTA INDIANS BEFORE THE DAWES ACT.   *South Dakota Hist. 1971 1(2): 132-154.* Describes the allocation of land in severalty among Indians in the United States before the Dawes Severalty Act (1887). Explains the treaties and agreements designed to convert Indians to land ownership and agriculture advocated by white farmers. The Dawes Act did not solve the Indians' problem, but it was an attempt to stop encroachment on Indian land and to enable Indians to become self-sufficient. The greatest weakness of the Dawes Act was its application of general principles to varying conditions. 97 notes.
                                              D. H. Swift

1156. Socolofsky, Homer.   LAND DISPOSAL IN NEBRASKA, 1854-1906.   *Nebraska Hist. 1967 48(3): 225-248.* Presents new interpretations of the operation of the Homestead Law and other land laws by selecting cases in the General Land Office Records and adding to that material from other sources, such as county records and local newspapers. It is concluded that more persons who filed claims carried them through to patent than is often assumed.   R. Lowitt

1157. Socolofsky, Homer E.   SUCCESS AND FAILURE IN NEBRASKA HOMESTEADING.   *Agric. Hist. 1968 42(2): 103-107.* Pioneer farming in Nebraska was difficult whether the farmer was on a homestead, or a preemption, or on land purchased from a railroad or the State. Physical exhaustion and hazards to health and life took a heavy toll. Economic factors played an important part in both success and failure in homesteading or in successfully completing an extended sales contract for the purchase of land. About 43 percent of those trying to get land in Nebraska under the Homestead Act failed. However, it seems probable

that the rate of failure was nearly as high for those purchasing under extended contracts. Based upon manuscripts in the National Archives and the Nebraska State Historical Library.   W. D. Rasmussen

1158. Tatum, Donn B., Jr.   GENERAL WILLIAM S. ROSECRANS AND THE RANCHO SAUSAL REDONDO.   *Southern California Q. 1969 51(4): 275-312.* Concerns the struggle between Civil War General William Starke Rosecrans and others over land which is now a part of southwest Los Angeles. Conflict over the land arose because of the confused and inefficient way in which boundaries were established after California became American territory in 1848. Rosecrans came to California in 1867 and attempted to gain control of land which he believed was part of the public domain, but which the owner of an old Spanish rancho, Sausal Redondo, claimed was part of his property. Litigation between Rosecrans and the owner, Scotsman Robert Burnett, and between Rosecrans and squatters who settled on the land he sought to patent, continued until 1877. In the end Rosecrans won out and, while he personally made little from the land, his grandchildren gained considerable wealth from it. As for the Sausal Redondo, it was operated as a ranch and farm until 1887 when a part of it was acquired by promoters who made it a section of the city of Inglewood. Based on contemporary sources, Government documents, and secondary works; 111 notes.
                                              W. L. Bowers

1159. Taylor, Morris F.   CAPT. WILLIAM CRAIG AND THE VIGIL AND ST. VRAIN GRANT, 1855-1870.   *Colorado Mag. 1968 45(4): 301-321.* Discusses the relationship, from 1855 to 1870, of Captain William Craig to the huge Vigil and St. Vrain Grant made in 1843 by the Mexican Governor Manuel Amijo in what is now Colorado. Craig, a recent graduate of West Point, was first associated with Colonel Ceran St. Vrain in a campaign against the Utes and Apaches in 1855. From then on, despite inability to resign his US Army commission and a period of absence during the Civil War, Craig was associated with disposals and acquisitions of lands on the grant. The author views Craig's activities "against a background of great complexity, uncertainty, and highly questionable validity." In 1869 public surveys were extended to the grant, but controversy continued until 1900. Illus., maps, 104 notes.
                                              O. H. Zabel

1160. Taylor, Morris F.   A NEW LOOK AT AN OLD CASE: THE BENT HEIRS' CLAIM IN THE MAXWELL GRANT.   *New Mexico Hist. R. 1968 43(3): 213-228.* The history of the famous title case involving the Maxwell Land Grant Company's claim to nearly two million acres is well known, but the attempt by the heirs of Charles Bent to secure one-twelfth of the grant has generally been overlooked. The first attempt to validate Bent's claim came in 1859, the last in 1895, at which time the Supreme Court of New Mexico upheld a district court ruling in favor of the company. Defeat for the heirs of Charles Bent "resulted chiefly from their failure to convince the courts of any real fraud or imposition by Lucien B. Maxwell or anyone else." 66 notes.   D. F. Henderson

1161. Weaver, Glen D.   NEVADA'S FEDERAL LANDS.   *Ann. of the Assoc. of Am. Geographers 1969 59(1): 27-49.* An examination of the impact on the overall resource base of the State caused by Federal ownership of approximately 86 percent of the land area. Federal holdings have been influential in the development of virtually all sectors of the State's economy but particularly the range livestock industry. Much of the future economic growth of the State is related to recreational land development. "To a considerable extent, there is a need for reassessment of the roles which federal lands are to play in the state's economy." Illus., 5 maps, graph, 13 tables, 66 notes.   W. R. Boedecker

1162. White, Gifford.   THE LOST BOOK OF HARRIS COUNTY, TEXAS.   *Stirpes 1970 10(1): 10-15, and (2): 74-75.* Part I. Reprints the minutes of the Board of Land Commissioners of Harris County, Texas, 1838-39. Included is the testimony of early settlers claiming land ownership or desiring to obtain grants of land from the Republic of Texas and of witnesses in their support. The testimony is useful for tracing real estate holdings or locating early Texas settlers. Based on the manuscript in the General Land Office, Austin. Part II. Reprints testimony regarding land claims and personal experiences recorded by the Harris County, Texas, land commissioners. Included are dates of arrival in Texas, military experience, and size of family. The material is valuable for family historians. To be continued.   L. R. Murphy

1163. White, Gifford. THE LOST BOOK OF HARRIS COUNTY, TEXAS. *Stirpes 1970 10(3): 91-95.* Continued from a previous article. Part III. Contains entries copied from a land title book in the Texas General Land Office, Austin. Each lists the claims and evidence submitted by individuals holding title to real estate in the Houston area. Article to be continued. L. R. Murphy

1164. White, Gifford. THE LOST BOOK OF HARRIS COUNTY. *Stirpes 1970 10(4): 136-140, 1971 11(1): 7-13, (2): 76-78, (3): 99-104, (4): 127-129, 1972 12(1): 18-21.* Continued from a previous article. Part IV. Copies the testimony of Texans claiming land ownership in Harris County. Each entry contains biographical and genealogical data about the claimant. Part V. More testimony of Texans appearing before the Harris County Court in 1838 to secure land titles. Part VI. More applications for land, and testimony by witnesses. Part VII. Continues testimony. Part VIII. Lists further applicants and those vouching for them. Part IX. More applicants and witnesses. Article to be continued. L. R. Murphy and D. J. Engler

1165. White, Gifford. THE LOST BOOK OF HARRIS COUNTY. *Stirpes 1972 12(2): 68-69.* Continued from a previous article. Part X. Depositions of witnesses who vouched for land claimants in Harris County, April 1838. Several of the claimants fought at the battles of San Jacinto and San Antonio. Article to be continued. S

1166. Williams, R. Hal. GEORGE W. JULIAN AND LAND REFORM IN NEW MEXICO, 1885-1889. *Agric. Hist. 1967 41(1): 71-84.* George Washington Julian served from 1885 to 1889 as surveyor general of the territory of New Mexico. He was ordered to reform the administration of public land laws and in doing so became unpopular, particularly with those illegally monopolizing the land. Julian could not adjust his ideas of homesteads to the realities in New Mexico. Based on published contemporary accounts and presidential papers in the Library of Congress. W. D. Rasmussen

Speculation

1167. Bogue, Allan G. FORECLOSURE TENANCY ON THE NORTHERN PLAINS. *Agric. Hist. 1965 39(1): 1-16.* Methods of leasing and managing farms acquired through mortgage foreclosure are illustrated by a detailed account of the practices of Rockwell Sayre. As head of the Farmers Trust Company of Sioux City and Chicago, he administered the liquidation of its property after collapse of land values in the Dakotas during the 1880's and 1890's. By 1914 he had completed liquidation, and owned, himself, between 60 and 70 tracts of land in the Dakotas. He was still administering 59 of these in 1930. His system of tenancy differed considerably from that generally found in the more easterly of the midwestern states. Based on the Sayre Papers at State University of Iowa. W. D. Rasmussen

1168. Gates, Paul W. LAND AND CREDIT PROBLEMS IN UNDERDEVELOPED KANSAS. *Kansas Hist. Q. 1965 31(1): 41-61.* In no state was speculation a more important factor in its development than in Kansas. Even the slavery controversy and the clash between border ruffians and Jayhawkers did not disrupt the flow of capital to Kansas. The existence of Indian lands in Kansas also provided speculators with unusual opportunities. Absentee ownership and high interest rates were among the more important problems faced by Kansans. Usury laws, occupancy laws, and taxation were effective weapons in the struggle to force land improvements or transfers of titles to residents. There was little abatement in the land and credit problem of territorial days during the decade after the Civil War. This subject is discussed in greater detail in the author's *Fifty Million Acres: Conflicts Over Kansas Land Policy, 1854-1890* (Ithaca, 1954). W. F. Zornow

1169. Hershkowitz, Leo. "THE LAND OF PROMISE": SAMUEL SWARTWOUT AND LAND SPECULATION IN TEXAS, 1830-1838. *New York Hist. Soc. Q. 1964 48(4): 307-325.* Efforts of Samuel Swartwout and other New Yorkers to profit from land speculation in Texas are described. By 1835 speculation had become an obsession and contributed to the Panic of 1837. Not only were Swartwout's activities financially unsuccessful but he was forced to flee the country when it was discovered that he had defrauded the government of between one and two million dollars. C. L. Grant

1170. Schnell, J. Christopher. WILLIAM GILPIN: ADVOCATE OF EXPANSION. *Montana 1969 19(3): 30-37.* William Gilpin devoted his life to promoting plans for large-scale development of communities between Missouri and the west coast. Although many of his enterprises fell short of his hopes, he became wealthy on land speculations. As a promoter and briefly as territorial governor of Colorado he helped by his speeches and writings to erase the concept of a Great American Desert and to arouse favorable interest in the Southwest. Illus., 12 notes. S. R. Davison

1171. Stewart, William J. SETTLER, POLITICIAN, AND SPECULATOR IN THE SALE OF THE SIOUX RESERVE. *Minnesota Hist. 1964 39(3): 85-92.* Following the vicious Sioux uprisings that swept the Minnesota frontier in 1862, the Indians were forced to migrate beyond the line of white settlement, and their lands (totaling more than one half million acres) were sold. Speculators rather than small farmers grabbed up most of the choice land, with the help of powerful Minnesota politicians. Based largely on abstracts of public land sales. P. L. Simon

1172. Stewart, W. J. SPECULATION AND NEBRASKA'S PUBLIC DOMAIN 1863-1872. *Nebraska Hist. 1964 45(3): 265-272.* Carefully examines the extent and results of Nebraska land speculation, presenting figures as to numbers of entrymen, their residence, and amounts of land secured. Concludes that economic backwardness and tenancy were the chief results of the fact that Nebraska's public domain had been reduced by 800,000 acres during the decade 1863-72. R. Lowitt

1173. Taylor, Morris F. PROMOTERS ON THE MAXWELL GRANT. *Colorado Mag. 1965 42(2): 133-150.* The rise and fall of the Mountain City Industrial Company is a story typical of many of the land speculation companies started in the 1800's. Incorporated in 1887, a group of New Yorkers hoped that the company would lead them to success and fortune. The Maxwell Land Grant is southeast of Trinidad, Colorado, in an area where real estate dreams would have to be grandiose to be successful. The Company had its charter revoked in 1907 for nonpayment of taxes and soon sank into oblivion. R. Sexauer

1174. Williamson, Hugh P. JAMES ADDISON REAVIS: THE UNUSUAL REALTOR. *Missouri Hist. Soc. Bull. 1963 20(1): 38-44.* Focuses on the attempt in the late 19th century of a former St. Louis realtor to substantiate his fraudulently based and constructed claims to four-fifths of the present state of Arizona. In possession of papers purporting to uphold the validity of an 18th-century Spanish grant - the Peralta Grant - and assigning the grant to him, Reavis made a substantial fortune selling quit-claims until he was finally arrested and convicted of fraud in 1896. For a time he received support from very prominent lawyers. R. J. Hanks

Conservation

1175. Alexander, Thomas G. THE POWELL IRRIGATION SURVEY AND THE PEOPLE OF THE MOUNTAIN WEST. *J. of the West 1968 7(1): 48-54.* Discusses the role of John Wesley Powell (director of the Geological Survey) in a controversy over the methods to be used to improve irrigation in the Mountain West. Powell wanted the "federal government to control all the land and reservoir sites and to relinquish both in an orderly manner to private interests who would construct irrigation works for small settlers." He was opposed by people in the Mountain West who "wanted essentially *laissez faire* development in which the federal government controlled only the reservoir sites to guard against possible monopolization." Based largely on primary sources; 33 notes. E. A. Erickson

1176. Box, Thadis W. RANGE DETERIORATION IN WEST TEXAS. *Southwestern Hist. Q. 1967 71(1): 37-45.* West Texas is a part of the Great Plains complex. Under the migratory grazing of the buffalo, recurring fires, and periodic drought, a mixture of nutritious and palatable grasses evolved. Because of changing climatic conditions the grasses fluctuated in density, but there was sufficient quantity to provide the basis for the Western range cattle industry. From the time the first buffalo hunters arrived in 1873 to 1894 when domestic cattle perished by the thousands on the overgrazed grasslands, the virgin range was changed into a man-made desert. Today West Texas will not support a third of the number of animals the early cattlemen stocked it with. This "carrying capacity" took place in the first three decades of use. If the cycles of overstocking during good years and starvation during poor ones can be broken, range management principles can help prevent further deterioration. 49 notes.   D. L. Smith

1177. Carlson, Paul H.   FOREST CONSERVATION ON THE SOUTH DAKOTA PRAIRIES.   *South Dakota Hist. 1971 2(1): 23-45.* Traces the history of legislative efforts to conserve the forest regions from 1862 to the present. Examines all tree culture acts and their application and success in tree and land conservation. Statistics relating to the U.S. Department of Agriculture action in the Prairie States Forestry Project reveal excellent results during the 1930's. Tree planting programs have continued at a fairly even rate throughout the last quarter century. 10 illus., 6 tables, 33 notes.   D. H. Swift

1178. Clar, C. Raymond.   ONE THING LED TO ANOTHER. *Forest Hist. 1963 7(1/2): 2-9.* In researching his book *California Government and Forestry from Spanish Days until the Creation of the Department of Natural Resources in 1927* (Sacramento: State Printing Office, 1959), the author used these sources: manuscripts, old and new newspapers and periodicals, government reports, and college theses. Particularly valuable were private correspondence and onetime confidential files of men such as Governor George C. Pardee in the Bancroft Library and the California State Archives. Papers are in Spanish, French, Italian, Russian, and English. Illus., 8 notes.   B. A. Vatter

1179. Clark, Alfred.   THE SAN GABRIEL RIVER, A CENTURY OF DIVIDING THE WATERS.   *Southern California Q. 1970 52(2): 155-169.* Concerns the century-long history of San Gabriel River water division during the years 1868-1969. The first water divisions were made by neighboring farmers in 1868, but eventually "cities and water companies in a wide section of Southern California claimed and received part of the water." Users often struggled over the water, but sooner or later they agreed to compromises. Two of these compromises - one in 1889 and another in 1965 - "are even considered model solutions to water problems." Concludes that the history of San Gabriel water division shows the importance of water to Southern California and typifies the experience of water use in that section. Based on public records, newspaper accounts, and secondary sources; map, 74 notes.   W. L. Bowers

1180. Dick, Everett.   WATER: A FRONTIER PROBLEM. *Nebraska Hist. 1968 49(3): 215-245.* Surveys how settlers in Nebraska sought water from water-witches to wells to windmills. The account includes personal experiences.   R. Lowitt

1181. Dixon, Elizabeth I.   SOME NEW JOHN MUIR LETTERS. *Southern California Q. 1964 46(3): 239-258.* Twelve previously unpublished letters, 11 to Muir's younger brother Daniel and one to his mother, written from California between 1869 and 1876. These letters, full of delight in the wonders of Yosemite, were acquired by UCLA in 1961 from the daughter of Daniel Muir.   J. Jensen

1182. Dodds, Gordon B.   THE HISTORIOGRAPHY OF AMERICAN CONSERVATION.   *Pacific Northwest Q. 1965 56(2): 75-81.* Examination of the issues and men involved in conservation history - forests, fisheries, gas and oil, minerals, agriculture, and education, with excellent documentation. Arresting comments on the methodology and quality of modern historiography are included.   C. C. Gorchels

1183. Gease, Deryl V.   WILLIAM N. BYERS AND THE CASE FOR FEDERAL AID TO IRRIGATION IN THE ARID WEST. *Colorado Mag. 1968 45(4): 340-345.* As early as 1859 William N. Byers, editor and publisher of the *Rocky Mountain News*, was advocating Federal aid to irrigation in the arid West. In December 1864 an important Byers editorial suggested Federal land grants comparable to those used for encouraging railroad building for support of irrigation. It was not until the Carey Act (1894) and the Newlands Reclamation Act (1902) that the principle of Federal aid was accepted. Illus., 11 notes.
O. H. Zabel

1184. Kelley, Robert.   TAMING THE SACRAMENTO: HAMILTONIANISM IN ACTION.   *Pacific Hist. R. 1965 34(1): 21-49.* Recounts the 90-year struggle to halt the devastating flooding of the Sacramento River. Success was achieved only after local factionalism was replaced by cooperation between public agencies, including federal commissions, and private entrepreneurs.   J. McCutcheon

1185. Kidder, John.   MONTANA MIRACLE: IT SAVED THE BUFFALO.   *Montana 1965 15(2): 52-67.* During the years 1885-90 the American bison escaped extinction largely because two Montana stockmen, Michel Pablo and Charles P. Allard, bought a tiny herd from Samuel Walking Coyote and built it up to 300 head. This account traces the origin of this herd and its dispersal to provide stock for most of the bison preserves now in existence, including Yellowstone Park. Annotated, apparently based on contemporary accounts without specific citations.
S. R. Davison

1186. Korr, Charles P.   WILLIAM HAMMOND HALL: THE FAILURE OF ATTEMPTS AT STATE WATER PLANNING IN CALIFORNIA, 1878-1888.   *Southern California Q. 1963 45(4): 305-322.* The first efforts to control and develop the water resources of California were made in the years 1878 to 1888. William Hammond Hall, the first state engineer, was the major figure in the effort to establish public control over the State's water, and to plan its best use for all concerned. Though a very able man, his purposes and plans were repeatedly defeated by the State legislature, which, after creating the office and appointing him, would not appropriate the necessary money or enact the necessary legislation. 54 notes.   A. K. Main

1187. LeDuc, Thomas.   THE HISTORIOGRAPHY OF CONSERVATION.   *Forest Hist. 1965 9(3): 23-28.* The U.S. Constitution gives Congress the power to "dispose of and to make all needful Rules and Regulations respecting the . . . Property belonging to the United States," but " . . . we have had to buy compliance with soil conservation practices" on private lands, and even that was not possible until the New Deal. The most significant portion of all land was private land. The 19th century policies were clearly to sell the public domain, not to protect it from trespass and depredation, giving squatters preferential treatment in the purchase of the public domain. Conservation historians have been at fault for emphasizing corruption in disposal and use of the public domain, for failing to treat state history, for emphasizing legislative history to the neglect of administrative history, and for their failure to distinguish between resource stocks and flows. Both the Federal and State Governments have failed to use their legal powers to insure conservation.
B. A. Vatter

1188. Lewis, Christine.   THE EARLY HISTORY OF THE TEMPE CANAL COMPANY.   *Arizona and the West 1965 7(3): 227-238.* Early settlers in the Salt River Valley quickly realized that the key to development of the area was irrigation. Indeed, there was ample evidence of prehistoric use of the same technique. Individual enterprise was merely a temporary expedient until associations were formed to provide elaborate irrigation systems that could service thousands of acres. A typical large-scale venture, organized in December 1870, was the Tempe Irrigating Canal Company. Its stock became extremely valuable and the water it represented became appurtenant to the land. The territorial water code was loosely worded, and, by the 1880's, increased settlement and rival companies caused the water supply to dwindle. Court adjudication established the Tempe Canal's prior right to a substantial portion of water which secured extensive and productive agriculture for several years with a stable and efficient water system. 3 illus., map, 42 notes.
D. L. Smith

1189. Lilley, William, III and Gould, Lewis L.   THE WESTERN IRRIGATION MOVEMENT, 1878-1902: A REAPPRAISAL. *U. of Wyoming Pub. 1966 32: 57-74, 152-157.* By 1878, the most accessible irrigable land and water in the American West and the capital necessary to utilize them had been exploited. Henceforth the magnitude and complexity of the arid West posed formidable problems which required new approaches and solutions. The construction, maintenance, and operation of irrigation works required engineers and administrators beyond the pressures of local politics and the temptation of profits. The cost of necessary reservoir and ditch construction was beyond the means of private capital and the capacity of the Western State governments. Interstate authority was required to adjudicate disputes between States and to prevent intrastate abuses. While clearly only the Federal Government was adequate to these necessities and challenges, the West was a victim of its own convictions that irrigation should be the province of free enterprise alone. The authors reexamine the irrigation campaign of 1888-1902 and conclude that it does not demonstrate the evolution of Western attitudes culminating in the passage of the Newlands Reclamation Act in 1902, but rather the unchanging commitment of the West to a laissez-faire status quo. Only some enlightened politics of Nevada's Senator Francis G. Newlands and a like-minded President broke the old pattern. 48 notes.

D. L. Smith

1190. Miles, John G. THE REDWOOD PARK QUESTION. *Forest Hist. 1967 11(1): 7-11, 31.* In 1852 the California State legislature turned down a bill to create redwood reserves. Federal land disposal laws put the redwood forest into private hands. In 1902 California began a series of State appropriations to buy redwood land for parks. In recent years, proposals have been made to increase the land in State and Federal hands. 4 photos, 2 maps.

B. A. Vatter

1191. Moore, J. Cordell. A RIGHT TO DEVELOP BUT NOT TO WASTE: THE CONSERVATION OF GEOLOGICAL RESOURCES. *North Dakota Q. 1966 34(2): 32-37.* Argues that conservation must mean rational development of resources, not mere preservation. The author cites new uses of the mineral resources of North Dakota and urges their wise development, utilizing the history of the American oil industry as an example of conservation lessons learned the hard way.

J. F. Mahoney

1192. Munger, Thornton T. TREES IN HAZARD: OREGON'S MYRTLE GROVES. *Oregon Hist. Q. 1966 67(1): 41-53.* Sketch of the discovery of myrtle wood in Oregon in 1826, development of its use, and subsequent efforts of conservationists to forestall destruction of myrtle forests and groves, with special reference to the work of the Save the Myrtle Corporation, 1946-65.

C. C. Gorchels

1193. Murray, William C. GRASS. *Am. Heritage 1968 19(3): 30-47, 81-83.* Grass provided the raison d'être for the Great Plains, its buffalo, and its Indians. After the Civil War, pioneer farmers, cattle drovers, and stockmen combined their efforts in a personal, and sometimes impersonal, struggle to destroy the grasslands. This pictorial essay reveals the ecological problems of the Great Plains, and explains what the Federal conservation service has done to restore the balance of nature in that region. Based on primary and secondary sources; photos.

J. D. Born, Jr.

1194. Nash, Gerald D. THE CALIFORNIA STATE BOARD OF FORESTRY, 1883-1960. *Southern California Q. 1965 47(3): 291-301.* The history of the California State Board of Forestry mirrored that of public forestry throughout the nation particularly regarding the conflict between research and regulatory functions. 17 notes.

A. K. Main

1195. Olson, James C. ARBOR DAY - A PIONEER EXPRESSION OF CONCERN FOR ENVIRONMENT. *Nebraska Hist. 1972 53(1): 1-13.* Examines the background of concern in Nebraska for tree planting prior to the founding of Arbor Day. Discusses the careers of three men who played a major role in the tree planting movement in Nebraska from the 1850's to the end of the century: Robert W. Furnas, George L. Miller, and Julius Sterling Morton (1832-1902). Morton founded Arbor Day and later served as US Secretary of Agriculture.

R. Lowitt

1196. Potts, Merlin K. ROCKY MOUNTAIN NATIONAL PARK. *Colorado Mag. 1965 42(3): 217-223.* Enos Mills, "Father of Rocky Mountain National Park," probably conceived the idea of the preservation of the Long's Peak area as a national park in 1891 while on a survey party. He was successful in achieving its birth in 1914. The author traces its history since that time and touches briefly on major events, such as the Colorado-Big Thompson Water Project and Mission 66.

R. Sexauer

1197. Rasch, Philip J. THE TULAROSA DITCH WAR. *New Mexico Hist. R. 1968 43(3): 229-235.* Bordering the eastern marches of the White Sands, the small village of Tularosa (first settled in 1858) had only one problem - water. The only water supply was the Tularosa River, and attempts to dam the stream and use the water for irrigation were

constant sources of irritation. Several minor clashes between the villages and neighboring Indians and ranchers occurred in the 1870's. The final clash occurred in 1881 when several employees from the James West ranch annihilated a posse attempting to arrest them. The ranchhands were eventually arrested, indicted, but never convicted. 19 notes.

D. F. Henderson

1198. Reeves, Thomas C. PRESIDENT ARTHUR IN YELLOW-STONE NATIONAL PARK. *Montana 1969 19(3): 18-29.* A campaign to generate interest in Yellowstone Park led to an official tour in 1883 by 10 dignitaries including President Chester A. Arthur. Planning and leadership were entrusted to General Philip H. Sheridan, who organized a military-type expedition with a 75-man Army escort and a courier system to provide communication while the President toured the wilderness. President Arthur enjoyed the scenery, fishing, and camp life and seemed to improve in health. After crossing the park from south to north, they departed by train on 1 September. Increased appreciation of the park and its needs resulted from this well-publicized inspection.

S. R. Davison

1199. Sagaser, A. Bower. WINDMILL AND PUMP IRRIGATION ON THE GREAT PLAINS. *Nebraska Hist. 1967 48(2): 107-118.* Carefully discusses the mechanics and the implications of both windmill and pump irrigation on the Great Plains. Predicated on large bodies of underground water, after certain technological developments had occurred by 1910, pump irrigation began to surge ahead of windmills. Today it provides the chief source of water for agriculture on the Great Plains.

R. Lowitt

1200. Smith, Lowell and Deuel, Pamela. THE CALIFORNIA-NEVADA INTERSTATE WATER COMPACT: A GREAT BETRAYAL. *Cry California 1972 7(1): 24-35.* The history of the Truckee-Carson River water basin system. Pyramid Lake (Nevada), the Paiute Indians, and much wildlife all have been sacrificed to the agriculture interests of the Truckee-Carson Irrigation District. Now, only action by the US Congress can restore Pyramid Lake to its former water level.

R. Righter

1201. Sperry, James E., ed. JOHN WESLEY POWELL'S ADDRESS AT THE NORTH DAKOTA CONSTITUTIONAL CONVENTION. *North Dakota Hist. 1969 36(4): 369-380.* A short biography of Powell and a reprint of Powell's address to the North Dakota Constitutional Convention (1889). Powell warns the convention that, in drafting the State constitution, members should be certain that the waters of the State are held by the people and no one else. The right to hold property should be confined to land and in no circumstances be extended to personal or corporate ownership of the running streams. Powell's speech is quoted from the official report of the First Constitutional Convention of North Dakota. 8 notes.

E. P. Costello

1202. Strong, Douglas H. THE HISTORY OF SEQUOIA NATIONAL PARK, 1876-1926, PART III: THE STRUGGLE TO ENLARGE THE PARK. *Southern California Q. 1966 48(4): 369-399.* Continued (see abstract 4:819). When Sequoia National Park was established in 1890, it did not include the crest of the Sierra nor the Kern and Kings Canyons. It took 36 years to get the park enlarged to include Mount Whitney and Kern Canyon and another 14 years to have Kings Canyon National Park created. The delay was caused by the divergent views of "scenic conservationists" or preservationists and "utilitarian conservationists," the opposition of power companies, irrigationists, stockmen, lumbermen, hunters, and prospectors, and the general indifference of the American public. Many individuals and the Sierra Club, a national conservation organization, worked for scenic conservationists throughout the nation. Based on contemporary manuscript sources, government documents, publications of organizations, and newspaper accounts; 2 maps, 85 notes.

W. L. Bowers

1203. Strong, Douglas H. THE HISTORY OF SEQUOIA NATIONAL PARK, 1876-1926; PART I: THE MOVEMENT TO ESTABLISH A PARK; PART II: THE PROBLEMS OF EARLY YEARS. *Southern California Q. 1966 48(2): 137-167 and (3): 265-288.* Summarizes the events leading to the formulation of a national conservation policy, the ideological conflict between the Park Service and the Forest Service, and the first half century of the history of the park established to protect the giant sequoia. Illus., maps, notes.

H. Kelsey

1204. Taylor, Paul S.   RECLAMATION: THE RISE AND FALL OF AN AMERICAN IDEA. *Am. West 1970 7(4): 27-33, 63.* In the 1880's, organizing, financing, and constructing irrigation works in the West were accomplished by private enterprise. The projects were usually simple diversions of flowing waters and of comparatively modest proportions. As the potential and need were realized, questions of government involvement, of the public domain, and of the principal beneficiaries loomed large. By the 1890's the issues of speculative land monopoly and water monopoly were combined as land monopoly strove to overtake water monopoly. From 1891 to 1902 irrigation congresses and the U.S. Congress wrestled with these problems. National reclamation is presently concerned with some eight million acres of land which produce nearly two billion dollars worth of crops annually. About one-fourth of the Nation's population now resides in the Western reclamation States. The National Government has invested about 10 billion dollars in the reclamation enterprise. Despite the legal limitation of 160 acres of irrigated land by single ownership, however, the small farmer is victimized. The political power of giant landowners has taken precedence over the people, and protracted nonenforcement is the rule rather than the exception. 4 illus., biblio. note.   D. L. Smith

1205. Taylor, Paul S.   WATER, LAND, AND PEOPLE IN THE GREAT VALLEY—IS IT TRUE THAT WHAT WE LEARN FROM HISTORY IS THAT WE LEARN NOTHING FROM HISTORY? *Am. West 1968 5(2): 24-29, 68-72.* The San Joaquin, Tulare, and Sacramento Valleys watershed areas was designated the "Great Valley of California' by an 1873 congressional commission investigating irrigation possibilities. The principal problems, according to the report, were how to bring the land and water together, how to finance the costly canals and other structures to achieve this, and how to assure equitable distribution of irrigation benefits from monopoly of private ventures and speculation. The author traces the experience of the failure of the last in the "Great Valley" as a case history of one of the most important problems faced in the arid West. 2 maps, biblio., biblio. note.   D. L. Smith

1206. Teilmann, Henrick.   THE ROLE OF IRRIGATION DISTRICTS IN CALIFORNIA'S WATER DEVELOPMENT. *Am. J. of Econ. and Sociol. 1963 22(3): 409-415.* A description of the effect of a special tax structure by which revenue for maintenance and operation of irrigation projects was obtained in the Central Valley of California. This unique tax, passed in 1887, encouraged individual ownership of land in units of the most economic size and spurred development.
                                                       B. E. Swanson

1207. Walsh, Thomas R.   THE AMERICAN GREEN OF CHARLES BESSEY. *Nebraska Hist. 1972 53(1): 35-57.* Examines the career of Charles Edwin Bessey (1845-1915), long a professor of botany at the University of Nebraska, who carried the gospel of conservation and reforestation to all parts of the United States. Known as the "father" of the Nebraska National Forest, Bessey was also involved in the struggle to save the Calaveras Big Trees in the California Sierra and to establish, under the administration of the US Forest Service, Appalachian forest reserves extending from Maine to Georgia.   R. Lowitt

1208. Warren, Viola Lockhart.   THE EUCALYPTUS CRUSADE. *Southern California Q. 1962 44(1): 31-42.* Southern California was once almost barren of any kind of tree. The eucalyptus tree which came from Australia is now in abundance throughout California. The name "eucalyptus" is a combination of two Greek words meaning "well hidden." Ellwood Cooper, a modest educator and president of Santa Barbara City College, had planted a total of 50 thousand eucalyptus trees on his ranch by 1883. A campaign to plant this stately tree was in full swing over Southern California between 1875 and 1910. The hardwood specie did not fulfill the desires of a commercial product because it warped, twisted, and opened into huge cracks after being cut and cured. The great trees had accomplished the purpose of clothing a major portion of California with forest, relieving the monotony of the bare hillsides and uncultivated wastes.   D. H. Swift

1209. Watkins, T. H.   PILGRIM'S PRIDE. *Am. West 1969 6(5): 49-54.* Tourists began to arrive in the Grand Canyon area in the late 1880's by stagecoach from Flagstaff, Arizona. A couple of prospectors carved trails into the Canyon and provided guide service. By the late 1890's a complex of tourist facilities began to appear on the South Rim.

In 1908 a national monument was created and, in 1919, the Grand Canyon National Park was created. The Atchison, Topeka, and Santa Fe Railway had extended a line up from Flagstaff, and the Fred Harvey Company had gained the remunerative concessionaire's lease. The park quickly gained status as an American shrine and became the object of innumerable magazine articles, newspaper stories, books, paintings, travelogues, and many other forms of publicity. Adapted from a forthcoming book. 4 illus.   D. L. Smith

1210. Whitney, Charles Allen.   JOHN EASTWOOD: UNSUNG GENIUS OF THE DRAWING BOARD. *Montana 1969 19(3): 38-46.* Credits John Samuel Eastwood with the engineering concepts and designs which led to major water conservation programs for power and irrigation in the Southwest. Gifted as a planner of dams and related structures, he lacked business acumen and was cheated out of both the money and the recognition which should have been his reward. Note, biblio.
                                                     S. R. Davison

1211. Williams, Burton J.   TREES BUT NO TIMBER: THE NEBRASKA PRELUDE TO THE TIMBER CULTURE ACT. *Nebraska Hist. 1972 53(1): 77-86.* Describes efforts to encourage the planting of trees in Nebraska prior to the enactment of the Timber Culture Act of 1873. Though much was done to encourage tree planting, little was accomplished.   R. Lowitt

1212. —.   50 YEARS OF LEADERSHIP: THE NATIONAL PARK SERVICE. *Hist. News 1966 21(12): 240-242.* Yellowstone, Wyoming Territory, was set aside in 1872 as the first national park. Others were added as conservation became the vogue but were assigned to various governmental agencies. The complications caused by this practice and the accumulation of a body of regulatory legislation led to the creation of the National Park Service as a bureau of the Department of the Interior in 1916. Its purposes and jurisdiction have been enlarged so that it is not only concerned with the conservation of natural and scenic resources, but also in the preservation and interpretation of public sites and monuments of historical significance. By the beginning of 1966, the service was assigned 231 areas which include historical parks, monuments, military parks, battlefield areas, national cemeteries, a memorial park, national memorials, historical parkways, the White House, the National Capital Parks, and museums. Under the provisions of the Historic Sites Act the service identifies, classifies, and evaluates the principal historical and archaeological sites in the country. It is developing a comprehensive long-term plan for their preservation and use. 7 photos.
                                                       D. L. Smith

Business History

1213. Albrecht, Elisabeth.   VIGNETTES OF ARIZONA PIONEERS: ESTEVAN OCHOA: MEXICAN AMERICAN BUSINESSMAN. *Arizoniana 1963 4(2): 35-40.* Estevan Ochoa started in business at Mesilla in Mexico and supplied his several stores by the dangerous overland route, constantly fighting off Indians. When success allowed him to settle in Tucson, he promoted local industries, introduced sheep and cotton, financed schools, acted as mayor and president of the Board of Education and kept open a big, hospitable home. When the Confederates occupied Tucson for a short time he remained loyal to the Union cause and suffered temporary eviction and loss of property.
                                                        M. Petrie

1214. Amerine, Maynard A.   AN INTRODUCTION TO THE PRE-REPEAL HISTORY OF GRAPES AND WINES IN CALIFORNIA. *Agric. Hist. 1969 43(2): 259-268.* Outlines the history of wine in California, including comments on historical sources and a comprehensive bibliography. The author begins with the Mission period and its unfortunate legacy, the Mission grape, and continues with the contributions of such men as Agoston Haraszthy and Jean Louis Vignes. The wine industry expanded greatly from 1850 to 1918. Based on a survey of MSS and printed materials.   W. D. Rasmussen

1215. Armbruster, Henry C.   JOHN F. TORREY'S NEW BRAUNFELS YEARS. *Texana 1966 4(3): 201-212.* Studies the career of a Texas entrepreneur during the years when his activities were centered at the town of New Braunfels, a German immigrant community. A native of Connecticut, Torrey went to Texas as early as 1838 but did not place his base of operations in New Braunfels until 1846. In conjunction with various partners he built a trading house and grist mill there at that time. Torrey traveled around a great deal engaging in the Indian trade and even spent a year in California soon after the gold strike in that region. About 1850 Torrey built a blind and sash factory in New Braunfels. He avoided taking an active part in the Civil War but spent his time rebuilding and expanding his holdings which had been buffeted by fire, wind, and flood. In May 1873, after one of his partners had died, he liquidated all his facilities at New Braunfels and moved to Hood County where he became a farmer. Based on Torrey's manuscript collection in the University of Texas Library and contemporary newspapers; 89 notes.

R. J. Roske

1216. Arrington, Leonard J. SCIENCE, GOVERNMENT, AND ENTERPRISE IN ECONOMIC DEVELOPMENT: THE WESTERN BEET SUGAR INDUSTRY. *Agric. Hist. 1967 41(1): 1-17.* The sugar beet industry was established in the United States between 1888 and 1913. Much of the impetus came from U.S. Department of Agriculture. Successful small factories were established in Fond du Lac, Wisconsin, in 1866, and in Alvarado, California, in 1869. Later, Claus Spreckels and the Oxnard brothers established refineries in California, and the Oxnards in Nebraska. Activities in Utah were carried out by the Utah Sugar Company, financed by the Mormon Church. By the 1890's, it was obvious that successful beet cultivation would depend upon successful adaptation to irrigation. Various syndicates and the American Sugar Refining Company supplied capital. The author concludes that the industry depended upon contributions of science and engineering, government, entrepreneurship, and labor, rather than primarily upon tariffs or other protection against imports. Based on printed sources.

W. D. Rasmussen

1217. Arrington, Leonard J. UTAH'S PIONEER BEET SUGAR PLANT: THE LEHI FACTORY OF THE UTAH SUGAR COMPANY. *Utah Hist. Q. 1966 34(2): 95-120.* Studies the construction and operation of beet sugar factories, the experiments with sugar beet production, and the efforts to raise capital which preceded the opening of the Lehi factory in 1891. Major developments relating to the operation of that factory to the time of its closing in 1924 include problems in the growing of beets and the production oI beet seed. Based on manuscript collections in the Manuscripts Division of the Latter-Day Saints Church Historian's Library and the archives of Brigham Young University, from newspapers, and from monographic studies of Western economic development; photos.

S. L. Jones

1218. Bateman, Fred; Foust, James D.; and Weiss, Thomas J. LARGE-SCALE MANUFACTURING IN THE SOUTH AND WEST, 1850-1860. *Business Hist. R. 1971 45(1): 1-17.* Manuscript census records of 1850 and 1860 tentatively reveal that, first, "There is little hint that the West was about to become an important large-scale manufacturing region while the South remained dependent on agriculture. ...Second, though the regional variations were small, . . . southern large firms appear to have been more capital intensive than the western. . . .Third, in both regions the large firm had capital-labor ratios exceeding the U.S. average and had capital-output greater than the national norm. ...Finally, the growth of large firms in both the South and West between 1850 and 1860 lends credence to the contention that southern industrial development, already begun by 1860, was disrupted by the Civil War." 9 tables, 19 notes.

C. J. Pusateri

1219. Beckham, Stephen Dow. ASA MEAD SIMPSON, LUMBERMAN AND SHIPBUILDER. *Oregon Hist. Q. 1967 68(3): 259-273.* Biographical sketch of Simpson with emphasis on his lumbering and shipping interests on the Pacific coast of Oregon, Washington, and California. Activities of his offspring are sketched to show reasons for the decline of the Simpson empire.

C. C. Gorchels

1220. Bekeart, Philip Kendall. CALIFORNIA GUNSMITHS FOR THREE GENERATIONS. *Pacific Historian 1966 10(2): 4-14.* Frank Bekeart, of Flemish descent, migrated from London and was apprenticed to an American gunsmith, fought in the Mexican War, was wounded, came to gold rush California, panned gold, sold and repaired guns, and traded with the Indians in Coloma and San Francisco. By 1849 his son,

Philip Bekeart, worked for E. T. Allen, first repairing then selling guns in the Santa Clara Valley. The third generation of gunsmiths is represented by the author who kept the family company going from 1913 through 1965. Illus., photos.

T. R. Cripps

1221. Berg, Louis. PEDDLERS IN ELDORADO. *Commentary 1965 40(1): 63-67.* Numerous Jews accompanied the "forty-niners" in their trek west to the promised El Dorado. Some became miners but more often the Jew found more nuggets in peddling than in mining. The work was difficult and dangerous, the profits great. Many advanced from peddling to ownership of department stores, but enough turned to freighting to put that business largely in the control of Jews until the completion of transcontinental railroads. Most of the western peddlers found strict Orthodoxy too heavy a burden to carry in the wilderness. They encountered little prejudice in the equalitarian atmosphere of the frontier.

R. J. Moore

1222. Blake, Gordon J. GOVERNMENT AND BANKING IN TERRITORIAL NEBRASKA. *Nebraska Hist. 1970 51(4): 425-435.* Discusses the severe shortage of "hard currency" which existed throughout the territorial period (1854-76). Notes that the shortage created great difficulty in the conduct of economic affairs in the territory and led to the issuance of notes by banks which experienced little control or regulation during these years.

R. Lowitt

1223. Brown, John A., ed. BUSINESSMAN'S SEARCH: PACIFIC NORTHWEST, 1881. *Oregon Hist. Q. 1970 71(1): 5-25.* A diary of businessman Robert McConnell describing his efforts at the age of 52 to select a promising location for a store after leaving his home in Xenia, Illinois, in 1881 to seek fortune in the West. Details include observations about the weather, wages, and the price of food, brief descriptions of towns and the countryside, and comments on transportation facilities. 10 photos.

C. C. Gorchels

1224. Calvert, Robert A. NINETEENTH-CENTURY FARMERS, COTTON, AND PROSPERITY. *Southwestern Hist. Q. 1970 73(4): 509-521.* Although, in the post-Civil War period, cotton continued to be king of Texas' economy, the cotton farmer and worker benefited little: industrialization and the concomitant exploitation of the family farm had spelled the end of an era. Photos.

R. W. Delaney

1225. Chapman, Hank and Chapman, Toni. MIDAS OF NEW MEXICO. *Am. West 1971 8(1): 4-9, 62-63.* After a Jesuit education as a boy, an informal apprenticeship in his grandfather's fur and pelt shop in St. Louis, and two years with the American Fur Company, Lucien Bonaparte Maxwell (ca. 1818-75) went to Taos, New Mexico, in 1841 as a trapper. He signed on with three Charles Frémont expeditions as a hunter and married into the local Beaubien family. The Miranda and Beaubien families had received a vaguely described land grant in northeastern New Mexico from the Mexican governor. Maxwell's father-in-law stocked a ranch and gave him permission to use it as the base for a trading post and settlement. His trading post attracted Indians, served travelers on the Santa Fe Trail, and supplied provisions to American troops. He bought the Miranda share of the grant and, when his father-in-law died, bought out the other Beaubien heirs. Now named "Cimarron," the baronial Maxwell colony flourished and became the scene of a considerable gold rush. Selling the grant in 1870, Maxwell turned to banking for a few years and then went back to ranching until his death in 1875. The Maxwell Land Grant contained 1,714,764 acres, the largest individually owned tract in the continent. 7 illus., map, biblio. note.

D. L. Smith

1226. Colton, L. J. EARLY DAY TIMBER CUTTING ALONG THE UPPER BEAR RIVER. *Utah Hist. Q. 1967 35(3): 202-208.* Comments generally on the development and the economic purposes of the timber industry in Utah, Colorado, and Wyoming, but deals mostly with the construction and operation of a 30-mile flume on tributaries of the Bear River near Evanston, Wyoming, between 1872 and 1885. The author is a district ranger in the U.S. Forest Service and served for 10 years in the Evanston area.

S. L. Jones

1227. Cooley, Everett L. CLARION, UTAH, JEWISH COLONY IN "ZION." *Utah Hist. Q. 1968 36(2): 113-131.* Relates the attempts of Jews from Philadelphia and New York to establish an agricultural colony on arid lands in Utah. Though it quickly failed and most of the original settlers withdrew, the leader Benjamin Brown and a few others set up a poultry industry which has thrived and in 1967 as the Intermountain Farmers Association did a gross business of 9,125,000 dollars. Based on the papers of Utah Governor William Spry, records of the Utah State Land Board, correspondence and interviews by the author with original settlers of the Clarion colony, and "Clarion's Call," an unpublished manuscript by Barbara Vogel in the Utah State Historical Society.

S. L. Jones

1228. Coughlin, Magdalen. COMMERCIAL FOUNDATIONS OF POLITICAL INTEREST IN THE OPENING PACIFIC, 1789-1829. *California Hist. Q. 1971 50(1): 15-33.* The Manifest Destiny protagonists of the 1840's were preceded by the efforts of Boston-centered merchants who urged the acquisition of Pacific ports for the China trade. American agitation for these ports and for government sponsorship and protection was as old as the young Nation itself. The setbacks of the War of 1812 only postponed Federal endorsement of goals long hoped for by merchants who early recognized a tremendous profit potential in a China-Pacific trade. Actions taken following Andrew Jackson's election to the Presidency were based on the efforts of the merchants over the preceding four decades to inform the government and American people of the value of a window to the Pacific. The interests of the merchants constitute an important part of the expansion of the Nation. Based on government documents and on secondary sources; 73 notes.

A. Hoffman

1229. Davis, W. N., Jr. THE SUTLER AT FORT BRIDGER. *Western Hist. Q. 1971 2(1): 37-54.* William A. Carter was sutler at Fort Bridger in southwestern Wyoming from 1857 to his death in 1881. Not only did he provide all the real or fancied needs of the troops beyond those of government issue, but he was the all-purpose merchant for the Fort Bridger military community of civilian employees, camp followers, and others. Added to this was the considerable entrepreneurial opportunity of supplying miners, emigrants, railroads, Indians, and many others; Fort Bridger was strategically located on a high-road connecting the Great Plains and the Great Basin and points beyond. Carter also provided banking services, filled government contracts, and performed many other economic functions. His activities touched nearly every phase of the economic development of the Rocky Mountain and Great Basin country. 65 notes.

D. L. Smith

1230. Dillon, Richard H. MERIWETHER LEWIS, MANUEL LISA, AND THE TANTALIZING SANTA FE TRADE. *Montana 1967 17(2): 47-52.* Early plans for trading in Santa Fe involved such well-known Americans as Meriwether Lewis and Manuel Lisa. Lewis considered scouting the route into the Southwest while he was waiting to begin his own trip in 1804; this idea was squelched by Thomas Jefferson. Lisa in 1806 and again in 1812 went so far as to organize caravans intended for the Santa Fe trade. Indian hostility and treachery among his own men defeated his plans, leaving the way open for William Becknell to successfully pioneer the trade in 1821. Quotations from Lewis-Jefferson correspondence and from a Lisa letter.

S. R. Davison

1231. Donohoe, Joan Marie. AGOSTIN HARASZTHY: A STUDY IN CREATIVITY. *California Hist. Soc. Q. 1969 48(2): 153-163.* A brief account of the immensely varied life of a man who was by turns a European revolutionary, city developer in Wisconsin, gold rush argonaut, leading citizen of San Diego, State legislator, and metallurgist. Haraszthy eventually turned to viticulture, an occupation practiced by his family for hundreds of years. After careful investigation, Haraszthy purchased property in the Sonoma Valley and in 1857 established the Buena Vista Vineyard, the effective beginning of California's wine industry. The success of his efforts brought him into an association with financier William C. Ralston. The arrangement was less than satisfactory and Ralston forced Haraszthy out of the business. Haraszthy next turned to the direction of immigration policy, advocating programs to bring skilled people to California. With his advice ignored, he then embarked on an ambitious program of investments in Nicaragua. He died there in 1869, possibly eaten by a crocodile. His energy, vivid personality, and dedication to his adopted country's development are remembered in the title accorded him, "Father of California Viticulture." Based on newspapers and secondary sources; 28 notes.

A. Hoffman

1232. Ellis, Tuffly L. THE REVOLUTIONIZING OF THE TEXAS COTTON TRADE, 1865-1885. *Southwestern Hist. Q. 1970 73(4): 478-*

508. Although the gross production of cotton had declined during the Civil War years, what had been produced was successfully distributed through blockades or via the Mexican border. Following the war, the tremendous acceleration of technology, communications, transportation, and equipment procedures virtually revolutionized the Texas cotton trade. The Suez Canal together with the use of the telegraphic and cable systems created a one-world market; domestically, the great increase in railroads and waterway connections had the effect of creating competition between the large cities in the Midwest and East and the traditional cotton-trading centers of Galveston, Houston, and New Orleans. Texas soon gave way to the supremacy of the North and eastern interests as distribution and manufacturing centers, and thus ruled out the possibilities of a major capital urban area arising in Texas; the cause was the rapid revolutionizing of the cotton trade.

R. W. Delaney

1233. Fabry, Joseph and Knight, Max. ON THE RAISING OF OSTRICHES FOR LITTLE FUN AND LESS PROFIT: A SOUTHERN CALIFORNIA ADVENTURE IN ESOTERIC HUSBANDRY. *Am. West 1970 7(4): 22-26.* California and Arizona ranches experimented with ostrich raising in 1882-83. With ostrich feathers at prime prices all over the world to satisfy female fashion demands, and with what seemed as ideal environmental conditions for raising them, the birds were imported from South Africa. After three flocks were taken from Africa, the Capetown government, fearful of losing its monopoly, put on a 500-dollar export fee per bird. The American population of ostriches propagated to about six thousand. Their temperamental nature, the decline in fashion demands for the feathers, and the increasing demand for orange juice combined to end the ostrich venture. Ostrich ranches were replaced by orange groves. 7 illus.

D. L. Smith

1234. Fierman, Floyd S. THE DRACHMANS OF ARIZONA. *Am. Jewish Arch. 1964 16(2): 135-160.* Traces through the 1890's the career of a prominent Arizona commercial family founded by Philip Drachman (1833-89), who had immigrated to New York in 1852, and to Arizona in 1863.

A. B. Rollins

1235. Fierman, Floyd S. THE GOLDBERG BROTHERS: ARIZONA PIONEERS. *Am. Jewish Archives 1966 18(1): 3-19.* Continues the series on Jewish pioneers of the American Southwest. In addition to the Drachmans of Arizona, brothers Hyman and Isaac Goldberg pioneered in mining and merchandising activities. Hyman, prominent in Yuma, was elected to the lower house of the state legislature in 1874; Isaac joined with Philip Drachman in bold, if often futile, prospecting ventures as well as in running stores in Prescott and Tucson. At times, they were almost wiped out by such diasters as damaging cloudbursts and lost freight loads. Based on family records and contemporary newspaper sources.

J. Brandes

1236. Fierman, Floyd S., ed. SAMUEL J. FREUDENTHAL: SOUTHWESTERN MERCHANT AND CIVIC LEADER. *Am. Jewish Hist. Q. 1968 57(3): 353-435.* These reminiscences of Freudenthal (1863-1939) were written after he established a residence in California in 1932. The story concentrates on his experiences in Arizona and New Mexico in the 1880's and his long residency in El Paso, Texas. It is the story of a native American in a frontier environment who moved from economic self-interest to community spirit and long, honorable community service.

F. Rosenthal

1237. Fierman, Floyd S. THE SPIEGELBERGS: PIONEER MERCHANTS AND BANKERS IN THE SOUTHWEST. *Am. Jewish Hist. Q. 1967 56(4): 371-451.* A summary of the known data concerning the economic and financial activities of the Spiegelberg brothers during their sojourn in Santa Fe from 1846 to 1893. Nine appendixes contain previously unpublished materials which the author found in local and Army archives that have bearing on the growth of the Southwest and shed light on 19th-century business practices as well. Based on newspapers, family and business correspondence, and taxlists; illus.

F. Rosenthal

1238. Fracchia, Charles A. THE FOUNDING OF THE SAN FRANCISCO MINING EXCHANGE. *California Hist. Soc. Q. 1969 48(1): 3-18.* In the wake of the 1849 gold rush, San Francisco became the economic capital of California and the Far West. In the Comstock gold and silver fields of Nevada, discovered in 1859, the placer methods of individual miners were not adequate. Only expensive and large-scale mechanical techniques would suffice. San Francisco became the principal source of capital for the mining companies and the manufacturing center for the equipment which they used. Much of the profit from the Nevada mining operations produced the economic growth of San Francisco. The concomitant specialization which these economic changes brought to San Francisco's investment community resulted in the establishment, in 1862, of the San Francisco Stock and Exchange Board, later known as the San Francisco Mining Exchange. 9 illus., 35 notes.　　　D. L. Smith

1239. Freeman, Cheryl. WANTED: THE HONORABLE WILLIAM H. CUSHMAN. *Colorado Mag. 1972 49(1): 35-54.* Describes the career of Cushman, banker and developer in the mining town of Georgetown between 1867 and the failure of the bank in 1877. Illustrates the strong support of the Georgetown community for its most important citizen who not only helped develop local mines, roads, and utilities, but was an active member of the Colorado State Constitutional Convention of 1876. With the closing of the bank Cushman disappeared for three years. He was caught finally in 1880 and brought to trial for embezzlement in 1881 when the case was "argued and taken under advisement." The trial was never resumed and the Federal District Court docket book shows a *nolle prosequi* entry on 24 December 1883 after Cushman's case number. Concludes that the bank failure was probably due more to unwise loans than to intended fraud. Illus., 74 notes.　　　O. H. Zabel

1240. Fritzsche, Bruno. "ON LIBERAL TERMS": THE BOSTON HIDE MERCHANTS IN CALIFORNIA. *Business Hist. R. 1968 42(4): 467-481.* In *Two Years before the Mast* the author Richard Henry Dana (1815-82) claimed that enormous profits were made by trading vessels that set out from Boston to trade New England articles for the hides and tallow of California missions and ranches. Fritzsche attempts to show, with the aid of the account books of one such firm (William Appleton and Company) that Dana was incorrect. Based on the records, the conclusion is that the selling of imported goods was the more profitable part of the business, even when hides commanded a good price in Boston. When prices in Boston were low, purchasing hides in California and selling them in New England was not profitable. The trade was not as lucrative as Dana pictured. Based on company records; 4 tables, 22 notes.　　　C. J. Pusateri

1241. Gedosch, Thomas F. A NOTE ON THE DOGFISH OIL INDUSTRY OF WASHINGTON TERRITORY. *Pacific Northwest Q. 1968 59(2): 100-102.* Sketches the development of the dogfish oil industry in the Puget Sound region, 1850-92, with descriptions of catching the fish, processing for oil, uses of the oil in industry and medicine, and methods of marketing. Technical advances in the petroleum lubricants spelled the beginning of the eventual end of dogfish oil use in lubrication.　　　C. C. Gorchels

1242. Goldman, Henry H. A SURVEY OF FEDERAL ESCORTS OF THE SANTA FE TRADE, 1829-1843. *J. of the West 1966 5(4): 504-516.* Throughout the entire history of the trade with Santa Fe there were only five authorized military escorts. The first, under command of Major Bennett Riley, was in 1829. Following this initial effort another was ordered out in 1833 under Captain William N. Wickcliffe; one in 1834 under Captain Clinton Wharton; the fourth in 1839 under Lieutenant James N. Bowman; and the last in 1843 under Captain Philip St. George Cooke. There is some evidence that Missouri militiamen were also used along the trail. The chief value of the escorts lay in their morale-building effect, as the period of real Indian raiding came after the Mexican War when the escort system had been abandoned. Based on published sources, 74 notes.　　　D. N. Brown

1243. Goodrich, James W. IN THE EARNEST PURSUIT OF WEALTH: DAVID WALDO IN MISSOURI AND THE SOUTHWEST, 1820-1878. *Missouri Hist. R. 1972 66(2): 155-184.* Waldo made the first of several commercial trips to Taos, New Mexico, in 1828. He soon became accomplished at carrying on trade, obtaining credit for his ventures, buying trade goods, and collecting overdue notes. The profits from his commercial ventures were invested in Missouri land. After brief service in the Mexican War, Waldo returned to Missouri to resume his career as a farmer and land speculator. Soon he broadened his enterprises with the acquisition of a mail contract, a license to trade with the Indians, and a company to freight goods to western forts. Based on materials in

the National Archives, Jefferson City, Missouri, and the Missouri Historical Society, St. Louis; 11 illus., 89 notes.　　　W. F. Zornow

1244. Goodrich, James W. ROMULUS ESTEP CULVER: A SKETCH OF FRONTIER SELF-IMPROVEMENT AND TRAGEDY. *Missouri Hist. R. 1969 63(3): 329-344.* Culver is shown to have typified the strong desire for self-improvement and material gain that motivated the settlers moving into northwest Missouri after 1840. After building an extensive holding through a number of land purchases, Culver was drawn into the western trade that accompanied the Mexican War in 1846. His dealings with the armed forces and his trading expeditions to Bent's Fort and Santa Fe are described in detail. Culver's plan to make enough money through trading to purchase additional land in Missouri was cut short in Mora, New Mexico, where he and other traders were killed by the inhabitants. Based on county histories, local newspapers, articles, books, the Culver Papers in the State Historical Society of Missouri, records in the Clinton County courthouse, and land office records in Jefferson City, Missouri; illus., 60 notes.

W. F. Zornow

1245. Gregory, Ruth West. "THOSE GOOD PEAS," THE MORGAN CANNING COMPANY IN SMITHFIELD, UTAH. *Utah Hist. Q. 1968 36(2): 168-177.* Tells how the first canning plant of the Morgan Canning Company was established at Morgan, Utah, and relates the circumstances under which operations were extended to plants at Smithfield and Hyrum, Utah, and Franklin, Idaho. In 1928 the plants were sold to the Utah Packing Corporation (now the California Packing Corporation). The father of the author was a long-time employee of the company, and the material upon which this article is based was gathered with the aid of the founders and employees of the company.

S. L. Jones

1246. Gressley, Gene M. BROKER TO THE BRITISH: FRANCIS SMITH AND COMPANY. *Southwestern Hist. Q. 1967 71(1): 7-25.* Throughout the 19th century America was a favorite place for British investment. The pattern and structure of British investment were revolutionized by legislation in the 1860's which encouraged limited liability companies. Francis Smith, an American attorney and broker, determined to become a catalyst between British money and American opportunity. In 1875 his brokerage office, Francis Smith and Company, opened this door by securing the American agency for a British land mortgage company. In a few years unfavorable legislation forced Smith from the Middle West to the more profitable investment openings of the southern plantations. Branch offices mushroomed all over the South. Smith became especially intrigued with the lending possibilities in Texas. In the 1880's and 1890's Smith channeled an estimated 12 to 14 million dollars into Texas ranches and plantations. The firm, under a different corporate name, still flourishes in Texas. 68 notes.　　　D. L. Smith

1247. Halvorson, Ora Johnson. CHARLES E. CONRAD OF KALISPELL: MERCHANT PRINCE WITH GENTLE TOUCH. *Montana 1971 21(2): 56-67.* Biographical sketch of Charles Edward Conrad (1850-1902), with some attention to his brother, William G. Conrad (1848-1914). As displaced persons after the Civil War, they migrated to Montana, where they acquired fortunes in business and banking. Their interests centered in Fort Benton, Great Falls, and Kalispell, with extensions into Canada. Later activity in cattle and land led to the founding of the northern Montana town which bears their name. Both were known for their public spirit, generosity, and ethical business practices. Closely associated with the Indians during his trading days, Charles acted in their behalf throughout his life. He spent his later years in Kalispell, which likewise owed its founding to his investment and enterprise. Illus.

S. R. Davison

1248. Hamilton, Jean Tyree. ABEL J. VANMETER, HIS PARK AND HIS DAIRY. *Bull. of the Missouri Hist. Soc. 1971 28(1): 3-37.* Presents entries - dated March 1865 to May 1866 - from a diary kept by Vanmeter (1834-1920), a Missouri landholder and businessman. In 1865, Vanmeter journeyed to the booming Montana gold fields. The diary contains considerable information about travel on the Missouri River in 1865. Vanmeter's business activities are described in the diary. The diary also contains sketchy information about the gold mining camps in Montana in 1865. Provides some letters, dated 1865, to supplement some matters discussed in the diary. Based on primary and secondary sources; illus., 113 notes.　　　H. T. Lovin

1249. Henderson, James D.   MEALS BY FRED HARVEY. *Arizona and the West 1966 8(4): 305-322.* In 1850, Frederick Henry Harvey, an English lad of 15, arrived in New York with two pounds cash. Securing a two-dollar-a-week dishwashing job he began to accumulate restaurant business knowledge. By 1859 he had become an American citizen and had saved enough money to establish his own restaurant in St. Louis. Because a partner absconded with the restaurant funds, Harvey found employment in a variety of other occupations and gained valuable experience in railroading, ranching, and journalism. These forced him to travel about the country considerably. Impressed with the miserable facilities or even lack of them for travelers, he experimented briefly with two eating houses on the Kansas Pacific Railroad. In 1876 he sold the Atchison, Topeka and Santa Fe on his ideas and was soon revamping their two-year-old food service. The first Fred Harvey House was opened in Topeka, Kansas, and and was an immediate success. His first restaurant-hotel was opened in Florence, Kansas, in mid-1878. Others followed, and with his high standards and the surprise-inspection visit device Harvey was able to maintain near perfection. A fortunate move was the replacement of all male waiters by the "Harvey girls" who were uniformly dressed, well-trained and the essence of proficiency and politeness. Fred Harvey built America's first restaurant chain, with his 75 Harvey Houses placed at regular meal stops along the 12,000-mile Santa Fe system. Santa Fe officials pampered Harvey, to their mutual benefit. 5 illus., map.

D. L. Smith

1250.   Hermann, Robert K.   THE CHEROKEE TOBACCO CASE. *Chronicles of Oklahoma 1963 41(3): 299-322.* Following the Civil War Cherokees and Choctaws set up tobacco factories near the Arkansas line in Oklahoma. They believed their product was exempt from the U.S. excise tax. This contention was denied by the U.S. Supreme Court in 1871. The case was brought because E. C. Boudinot and Stand Watie believed that, according to the Cherokee Treaty of 1866 as a separate "nation," they were exempt from U.S. taxation. The 1871 Supreme Court decision erased any idea that an American "nation" could be preserved within U.S. borders. Illus., 21 notes.   I. W. Van Noppen

1251.   Hillman, Raymond W.   SPERRY BUILDING CAMPAIGN. *Pacific Historian 1968 12(4): 47-53.* Details an attempt to save the former Stockton, California, office of the Sperry Flour Mills, built in 1888. The Sperry Building Restoration Committee hoped to find new tenants for the building and to generate city-wide interest in saving the ornate structure. Should the building fall to a wrecking crew, Stockton and California will lose a tangible link to the days when grain products were an important California export. They will lose also an outstanding example of Victorian commercial architecture of the type that characterized buildings erected during California's first phase of urban development. 4 illus.

F. I. Murphy

1252.   Humphreys, Alfred Glen.   PEG-LEG SMITH: A HORSE TRADER ON THE OREGON TRAIL.   *Idaho Yesterdays 1966 10(2): 28-32.* A fascinating story of one of Idaho's pioneer merchants - and horsethieves. Until the 1849 California gold rush, Thomas L. Smith ran a trading post on Idaho's Bear River for Oregon and California immigrants. The author presents a brief sketch of some of Smith's adventures and of his contemporaries. Included is one illustration, entitled "A Herd of Wild Horses," by Idaho artist Charles Ostner.   B. B. Swift

1253.   Jensen, James M.   JOHN FORSTER - A CALIFORNIA RANCHERO.   *California Hist. Soc. Q. 1969 48(1): 37-44.* An account of the life of John Forster (1815-82), who at 15 years of age arrived in California from England and embarked upon a career as trader, rancher, and landowner. He married a sister of Pío Pico. Over a period of time Forster acquired more than 100 thousand acres of land, including Mission San Juan Capistrano, where for many years he and his family made their residence. Forster was successively a citizen of England, Mexico, and the United States, and he played an objective part in California's involvement in the War with Mexico. In the later years of his life his style of living brought him into debt. He tried several unsuccessful schemes to preserve his wealth and at his death his vast holdings were dissolved. Forster's life in California spanned the period from pastoral days to the new developments of the 1880's. Based on papers in the Bancroft Library and Huntington Library; 31 notes.   A. Hoffman

1254.   Jore, Léonce.   JEAN LOUIS VIGNES OF BORDEAUX, PIONEER OF CALIFORNIA VITICULTURE.   *Southern California Q. 1963 45(4): 289-303.* At the end of the Napoleonic Wars, the maritime merchants of Bordeaux began trading with the western coast of North America and the Pacific Islands. Jean Louis Vignes (1779-1862) went to the Sandwich Islands in 1827; the commercial venture of which he was part was a failure, and he procured work managing an American-founded distillery. The distillery was closed by the Hawaiian regent (under advice from missionaries) and Vignes went to California in 1831 to seek his livelihood. There he joined the small French colony and became one of the first major wine producers of California. His success attracted other French viticulturists, and several modern California wineries (including Paul Masson and Almaden) had their beginnings in this period. Vignes died in Los Angeles in 1862; his vineyard is now the site of Union Station, the great railway terminal of Los Angeles. 11 notes.   A. K. Main

1255.   Kahn, Edgar M.   PIONEER JEWISH SAN FRANCISCO STOCK BROKERS.   *Western States Jewish Hist. Q. 1969 1(2): 47-65.* Discusses the growth of professional stockbroking in San Francisco from the early days of that industry. Emphasizes Jewish stockbrokers who came from Germany, established firms, and helped form stock exchange groups that eventually became the Pacific Coast Stock Exchange. These companies dealt in mining stocks, as well as businesses that conducted their operations in San Francisco. Sets the story against the background of the national business scene and refers to boom and bust periods from the gold rush through World War I. 3 photos, 31 notes.

R. E. Levinson

1256.   Kensel, W. Hudson.   THE EARLY SPOKANE LUMBER INDUSTRY.   *Idaho Yesterdays 1968 12(1): 25-31.* The lumber industry started in Spokane in 1871, but did not develop as it did west of the Cascades because the coastal cities had the advantage of rail and sea shipping. The Spokane lumber industry depended on the local and eastern markets, and finished items became the most important. By 1910, freight rates and competition along with overproduction and price changes had weakened the Spokane lumber business. By this time, nevertheless, Spokane had become an important supply center for northern Washington and Idaho. 33 notes.   G. Barrett

1257.   Kortum, Karl and Olmstead, Roger.   IT IS A DANGEROUS-LOOKING PLACE - SAILING DAYS ON THE REDWOOD COAST.   *California Hist. Q. 1971 50(1): 43-58.* The lumber industry on the northern California coast in the latter part of the 19th century required a combination of skill, ingenuity, and luck. Storms, rocks, and other hazards made the loading and shipping of lumber from this region a dangerous business, yet it endured for over half a century. Elaborate chutes of wood and wire were constructed in numerous "dog holes," places where any opportunity to take on lumber could be utilized. 22 photos.   A. Hoffman

1258.   Lehman, Anthony L.   VINES AND VINTNERS IN THE POMONA VALLEY.   *Southern California Q. 1972 54(1): 55-65.* The era of grape-growing and wine-making in the Pomona Valley was 1884-92. Grapes were grown in the valley before the 1880's, but the first local winery was not built until 1884. Established when French viticulture was declining due to insect infestation, Pomona wine-making flourished and became an important aspect of the valley's economy. However, the ravages of phylloxera, an insect which attacked the root system of grapevines, and overproduction soon combined to bring about the demise of the local wine industry. By 1892, the major winery had closed and most grape growers had replaced their vines with citrus trees. Based chiefly on contemporary newspaper articles; 3 illus., 36 notes.   W. L. Bowers

1259.   Levinson, Robert E.   JULIUS BASINSKI: JEWISH MERCHANT IN MONTANA.   *Montana 1972 22(1): 60-68.* Basinski (1844-1926) came to the United States in 1866 as a Polish refugee. He migrated to Montana in 1870 with a small stock of merchandise, and engaged in trade at various places until 1894. During the Indian troubles of 1876 he daringly entered the area of hostilities and remained to become a leading merchant of Miles City. His later years were spent in the State of Washington, where he engaged in business at Tacoma and in the operation of apple orchards in the interior. His career was typical of many young Jews on the mountain-west frontier. Based on Basinski's reminiscences, in the University of Oregon Library at Eugene, and on early newspapers and family interviews; illus., 10 notes.   S. R. Davison

1260. Lomax, Alfred L. THE ALBANY WOOLEN MILL. *Oregon Hist. Q. 1966 67(1): 61-74.* History of the establishment of woolen mills in Albany, Salem, and other towns in Oregon, 1854-1907. Included are details about financing and coping with problems of developing markets and overcoming losses by fires and other unforeseen events.
C. C. Gorchels

1261. Lyon, William H. THE CORPORATE FRONTIER IN ARIZONA. *J. of Arizona Hist. 1968 9(1): 1-17.* Believes that lack of capital hindered the economic development of Arizona during the period 1854-94. Only the livestock industry was prospering. Newspapers and books shamelessly exaggerated the favorable financial aspects in order to woo elusive Eastern investors. The Arizona territorial government tried tax exemption and subsidies to attract industry. In the absence of private capital, the Federal Government provided economic help by building wagon roads and by maintaining a dozen army posts where soldiers were a ready market for various Arizona suppliers of goods and services. Some mining capital was contributed from California, the East, and the United Kingdom. After 1894, the impact of large corporations, such as Phelps-Dodge, United Verde, and the Southern Pacific and Santa Fe railroads, more successfully brought capital and technology to Arizona. Based on Government documents and contemporary newspapers; 47 notes.
R. J. Roske

1262. Maxwell, Robert S. LUMBERMEN OF THE EAST TEXAS FRONTIER. *Forest Hist. 1965 9(1): 12-16.* The East Texas region, a timber region as large as Maine, was exploited mainly from 1865 to 1900. The first cut was longleaf pine, followed by shortleaf and loblolly pine, which also provided a second growth before 1965. Owners, both absentee and immigrant, and managers of business firms were usually from the Northeastern United States and the Lake States, but the work forces were local whites and Afro-Americans. Henry J. Lutcher and G. Bedell Moore of Pennsylvania formed the L & M Company which invested in a variety of forest products and other industries between 1876 and 1965. John Henry Kirby invested in timber-related industries and organized the Kirby Lumber Company with the aid of eastern capital about 1900. William Joyce formed the Trinity County Lumber Company in 1890; by 1930, the company cut out and suspended East Texas operations, moving to the west coast and British Columbia. All three firms included railroad investment in their portfolio. The Texas lumber manufacturers organized themselves into a trade association. They cooperated on pricing and on political, legislative, labor, and wage policies without antitrust prosecution but violently and successfully opposed the organization of labor despite the best efforts of the Brotherhood of Timber Workers. 2 illus., 18 notes.
B. A. Vatter

1263. Maxwell, Robert S. RESEARCHING FOREST HISTORY IN THE GULF SOUTHWEST: THE UNITY OF THE SABINE VALLEY. *Louisiana Studies 1971 10(2): 109-122.* Discusses the timber barons who came south to exploit the magnificent forest of the Gulf Southwest, beginning in 1877. Concentrates on the operators of giant sawmills in the Sabine River Valley. Points out the economic and social impact. 23 notes.
G. W. McGinty

1264. McClintock, Thomas C. HENDERSON LUELLING, SETH LEWELLING AND THE BIRTH OF THE PACIFIC COAST FRUIT INDUSTRY. *Oregon Hist. Q. 1967 68(2): 153-174.* Sketches the productive activities of Henderson Luelling and his relatives in bringing to Oregon a "traveling nursery" of several hundred grafted trees including apple, pear, quince, plum, cherry, black walnut, and shell-bark hickory nut, plus a few grape vines and gooseberry and currant bushes in 1847, and their subsequent life. Through the horticultural skills and tireless work of the family, the growing of deciduous fruit had become a major industry on the Pacific coast by the end of the 19th century. Illus.
C. C. Gorchels

1265. McFadden, Thomas G. BANKING IN THE BOISE REGION: THE ORIGINS OF THE FIRST NATIONAL BANK OF IDAHO. *Idaho Yesterdays 1967 11(1): 2-17.* Explains community development in the Boise area upon establishment of a national bank in 1867. The basic functions of a 19th-century commercial bank were "1) to transfer funds, 2) to make loans and extend credit, 3) to receive special and general deposits, and 4) to issue notes, which, like Federal Reserve notes today, circulated as currency." The long struggle to secure a stable

and uniform currency is outlined in detail. Legal tender evolved from gold dust as the medium of exchange to greenbacks. 10 illus., 128 notes.
D. H. Swift

1266. McGinnis, Tony. ECONOMIC WARFARE ON THE NORTHERN PLAINS. *Ann. of Wyoming 1972 44(1): 57-71.* Traces the history of 19th-century intertribal warfare between the Crow Indians and their neighbors in the upper Missouri Valley region. While traditional horse stealing and an inherent desire for glory in combat often prompted these hostilities, much of the fighting resulted from encroachments by various tribes upon the rich land claimed by the Crows. Before 1850, the Blackfeet presented the most unrelenting challenge; after 1850, the Sioux, Cheyenne, and Arapaho became the Crows' chief enemies. Generally the Crows waged only defensive warfare and suffered severe losses of men and territory. The struggle ended only after most of the hostile Sioux were placed on government reservations in 1876-77. Based on statements by contemporary observers and on annual reports of the Commissioner of Indian Affairs; 70 notes.
G. R. Adams

1267. Nash, Gerald D. THE SUGAR BEET INDUSTRY AND ECONOMIC GROWTH IN THE WEST. *Agric. Hist. 1967 41(1): 27-30.* Businessmen took an active part in developing the Western sugar beet industry. Many of the first were immigrants from Europe. They made many constructive contributions, not only to the sugar industry, but also to the economic development. However, some groups, such as the Sugar Trust, suppressed competitors by cutthroat competition, forced sales, and monopolistic control of sugar markets. At the same time, the Sugar Trust contributed capital and provided needed technical direction.
W. D. Rasmussen

1268. Nielson, George R. TORREY'S FRONTIER POST NO. 2: A BUSINESS HISTORY. *Business Hist. R. 1963 37(3): 201-216.* This study of the Torrey Trading Post established during the 1840's on the Brazos River in Texas illustrates the problems and the economic role of the businessmen on the frontier during the 19th century.
J. H. Krenkel

1269. Packard, John C. SAN DIEGO'S EARLY HOTELS. *Southern California Q. 1968 59(3): 267-278.* Describes San Diego's leading hotels of the late 19th century. These included the Horton House built in 1870, the Florence Hotel constructed during the 1880's, the Hotel del Coronado built in the 1880's, Hotel Lakeside, La Jolla Park Hotel, and the Cliff Hotel, all of which were in or near San Diego. The author believes that these early hotels contributed to the financial and economic growth of southern California by attracting wealth which led to the agricultural and industrial development of the area. Based on contemporary and secondary sources; 2 illus., 19 notes.
W. L. Bowers

1270. Palmer, William R. EARLY MERCHANDISING IN UTAH. *Utah Hist. Q. 1963 31(1): 36-50.* Covers the period 1850-1870.

1271. Parker, Watson, ed. AN ILLINOIS GREENHORN IN BISMARCK, D. T. *North Dakota Hist. 1968 35(1): 20-27.* In May 1878 bank clerk George Watson Smith went to Dakota Territory to study the financial activities of the area and to investigate opportunities for profitable farm loans. The 16-30 May entries of his diary record these matters and his description of the country between Brainerd, Minnesota, and Fargo and Bismarck, North Dakota. He traveled by railroad. 5 illus.
D. L. Smith

1272. Rochlin, Fred and Rochlin, Harriet. TRACKING LEOPOLD EPHRAIM. *Western States Jewish Hist. Q. 1969 1(2): 75-84.* Leopold Ephraim (1850-1923) was a longtime merchant-businessman in Nogales. He was a merchant in the Southern United States, Montana, and San Francisco before coming to Southern Arizona between 1880 and 1882. After opening a general merchandise business in a tent in Nogales, Ephraim prospered. The Ephraim Building replaced the tent in 1905. Ephraim engaged in mining enterprises in Mexico and developed the first Nogales Water Company. He moved to Los Angeles in 1909 and died there. Based primarily on newspapers, local histories, and regional business directories; 3 photos, 24 notes.
R. E. Levinson

1273. Rothstein, Morton. A BRITISH FIRM ON THE AMERICAN WEST COAST, 1869-1914. *Business Hist. R. 1963 37(4): 392-*

415. Analyzes the contributions of Balfour, Guthrie and Company to the economic development of the Pacific coast region of the United States. The British firm supplied trading and shipping, merchant-banking, insurance, and other services, "in an area where they were in short supply."

J. H. Krenkel

1274. Schick, Robert. WAGONS TO CHIHUAHUA. *Am. West 1966 3(3): 72-79, 87-88.* The Chihuahua or Texas-Chihuahua Trail went from Indianola (now nonexistent) on the Gulf Coast of Texas to Ciudad Chihuahua in Mexico. It was one of the chief commercial routes between the United States and much of northern Mexico in the 1860's and 1870's. Wagon trains on this year-round freighters' trail transported the products of the mining industry of northern Mexico, large amounts of gold, silver, copper, and lead. Heavy loads of cowhides for American and overseas tanneries were often carried. In return their cargoes consisted of mining machinery, baled cotton, foodstuffs, and household items. The trail was 400 miles longer than the Santa Fe Trail, and the value of the goods carried over it was considerably greater. Eventually the iron horse replaced the mule-drawn wagons and the colorful days of the Texas-Chihuahua Trail were over. Map, illus., biblio. note. D. L. Smith

1275. Sears, Marian V. JONATHAN BOURNE, JR., CAPITAL MARKET AND THE PORTLAND STOCK EXCHANGE 1887. *Oregon Hist. Q. 1968 69(3): 197-222.* Part of a larger study of factors surrounding the establishment and contributions of more than two hundred local and regional stock exchanges started in the United States from 1860 to 1930, with material about only the Portland Stock Exchange founded in 1887 being presented here. With quickening economic development in the Pacific Northwest, aided by the completion of the Northern Pacific Railroad in 1883, Jonathan Bourne, Jr., and associates launched a stock exchange in Portland, Oregon, primarily as an exchange for mining stocks. Bourne's activities are traced, and details of early transactions on the exchange are given. Illustrations and references to source material are included. C. C. Gorchels

1276. Simons, Katherine. WILLIAM JACKSON PARISH, 1907-1964. *New Mexico Hist. R. 1964 39(4): 351-353.* Memorial tribute to Dean Parish, of the graduate school of the University of New Mexico, and author of *The Charles Ilfeld Company: A Study of the Rise and Decline of Mercantile Capitalism in New Mexico* (1951).

D. F. Henderson

1277. Smalley, Brian H. SOME ASPECTS OF THE MAINE TO SAN FRANCISCO TRADE, 1849-1852. *J. of the West 1967 6(4): 593-603.* The discovery of gold in California helped to revive the languishing commercial interests of the East. Ships recently inactive began to transport men and supplies to the goldfields. Almost nine percent of the 775 vessels which departed the east coast in 1849 embarked from Maine. The author gives an account of the voyage to California and shows why the ships from Maine ports declined in number after 1850. He concludes that the reason for this decline was that many of the vessels remained on the west coast after their initial trip. Based on newspaper and published sources, appendix, 30 notes, biblio. D. N. Brown

1278. Stanley, Gerald. MERCHANDISING IN THE SOUTHWEST: THE MARK I. JACOBS COMPANY OF TUCSON, 1867 TO 1875. *Am. Jewish Arch. 1971 23(1): 86-102.* Describes the Mark I. Jacobs retail store from its founding in 1867 until the retirement of its founder, Mark Israel Jacobs, in 1875, when his elder son assumed control. The store prospered with the growth of the Arizona Territory and the selection of Tucson as the territorial capital. The Jacobs family soon branched out into banking and became prominent in the political, social, and cultural life of Tucson. Based on primary and secondary sources; photo, 45 notes. E. S. Shapiro

1279. Stern, Norton B. ABRAHAM MOOSER - FIRST JEWISH BUSINESSMAN OF SANTA MONICA, CALIFORNIA. *Western States Jewish Hist. Q. 1969 1(3): 109-127.* Mooser (1842-1931) received his early education in Germany and he followed some relatives to America, arriving in 1858. After living in Nevada, he moved to California and settled in Santa Monica in 1891. He became an important grocery and clothing merchant, held leading positions in local lodges and organizations, and was active in Democratic Party affairs and the local Board of Trade. Seven of his children lived to adulthood. Photos, 71 notes.

R. E. Levinson

1280. Stern, Norton B., ed. MEMOIRS OF MARCUS KATZ - SAN BERNARDINO PIONEER. *Western States Jewish Hist. Q. 1968 1(1): 20-44.* Treats the multifaceted career of Katz (1820-99), a pioneer merchant and community leader of San Bernardino. Katz first came to San Bernardino in 1852, lived in San Diego briefly, and returned to San Bernardino in 1857. He engaged in business, served as Wells, Fargo and Company agent, and took part in local politics. His memoirs show that he used English, his adopted language, with felicity. He was active in local civic organizations and in the Jewish community. 2 photos, 31 notes.

R. E. Levinson

1281. Strong, Douglas Hillman. THE MAN WHO "OWNED" GRAND CANYON. *Am. West 1969 6(5): 33-40.* After reading an account of John Wesley Powell's 1869 boat trip down the Colorado River, a 19-year-old Boston department store employee headed west in 1883 to make his fame and fortune. Ralph Henry Cameron and his brother entered the mercantile business in Flagstaff, Arizona, where the Atlantic and Pacific Railway had reached, and they also operated a local sheep ranch. Robert Brewster Stanton's report of his 1889-90 survey for a water-level railroad route along the Colorado River provoked a rush of prospectors into the canyon. The Camerons joined the prospecting but were unsuccessful. Ralph Cameron launched into tourism, built a small hotel on the South Rim, and acquired a franchise for the toll "Cameron Trail," later to be known as Bright Angel Trail. When the Atchison, Topeka, and Santa Fe Railway moved in, in 1901, Cameron had a formidable adversary. By various machinations he was able to gain and keep control of key sites and to profit from the tourist business for over 30 years. Before it was over, Cameron was even elected U.S. Senator from Arizona. Finally, in 1926, after long legal and political maneuvering to delay a Supreme Court ruling against placer claims he had filed, his reputation was tarnished and he was not reelected for the U.S. Senate. He had, nevertheless, made notable contributions by exploring, building trails and tourist facilities, and opening mines. Derived from a forthcoming book. 6 illus. D. L. Smith

1282. Teiser, Ruth. SOCKEYE, CLING, AND THE GOLDEN STATE... OR, CALIFORNIA LABELED IN THE PANTRIES OF THE WORLD. *Am. West 1969 6(2): 20-25.* Foods grown on the Pacific coast were first commercially packed in 1858 or 1859. Commercial salmon pack started in 1864. An important segment for these California-based industries, as well as for the whiskey bottlers, the cigar boxers, and the patent-medicine producers, was the business of making labels. Max Schmidt, a young German sailor who came to San Francisco in 1871, gained a variety of experiences with lithography by working for a newspaper, a lithographic firm, and then a cigar-box maker. Adopting the latest methods he went into label making on his own. As other label makers disappeared he bought their stock and business. In 1880 he incorporated the Schmidt Label and Lithograph Company and soon dominated the market in the West. By adopting and perfecting letterpress techniques and offset presses his firm maintained its position of preeminence. In breadth of distribution, Schmidt labels are probably not exceeded as promotional literature portraying California as the earthly paradise in millions of pantries around the world. Based largely on interviews with members of the Schmidt family and firm; 24 illus. D. L. Smith

1283. Toole, K. Ross, and Butcher, Edward. TIMBER DEPREDATIONS ON THE MONTANA PUBLIC DOMAIN, 1885-1918. *J. of the West 1968 7(3): 351-362.* Tells of the struggles between the mining and railroad interests in Montana against the Federal Government over timber. The Free Timber Act of 1878 was poorly written and was interpreted strictly or loosely depending upon which political party was in power. A number of suits were pressed by the Federal Government, some of which were not finally settled until 1918.

R. N. Alvis

1284. Tweton, D. Jerome. THE MARQUIS DE MORES AND HIS DAKOTA VENTURE: A STUDY IN FAILURE. *J. of the West 1967 6(4): 521-534.* In 1882 the Marquis de Mores arrived in this country from France to learn the banking business. While doing so he became interested in the cattle business, and became convinced that a fortune was to be made by slaughtering cattle in the West and shipping the carcasses by refrigerator car to eastern markets. In 1883 he moved to North Dakota where he established the town of Medora, named for his wife. With two business partners he formed the Northern Pacific Refrigerator Car Com-

pany. The company acquired land, built holding pens, an abattoir, and an ice house. Within a short time a contract had been negotiated with the Northern Pacific Railroad to transport the beef. More locations were acquired from Portland to Chicago. The number of cattle slaughtered never met the hopes of the marquis nor did the market for dressed beef develop in the manner he had earlier forecast. Charges that the Medora company was selling diseased beef caused his New York retail system to collapse. In 1887 the abattoir was closed. Based on newspaper sources, 56 notes.
D. N. Brown

1285.   Unrau, William E.   THE COUNCIL GROVE MERCHANTS AND KANSA INDIANS, 1855-1870.   *Kansas Hist. Q. 1968 34(3): 266-281.* Reexamines "Bleeding Kansas" and the "Farmers' Last Frontier" in the light of recent studies demonstrating that small urban minorities often had more to do with frontier development than agrarian majorities. Council Grove merchants of this period are shown to have solved most of the land problems by keeping outside speculators from the area and to have kept the vital Indian trade in their own hands. Based on monographs, articles, newspapers, published Government records, and archives from the Kansas State Historical Society; illus., 81 notes.
W. F. Zornow

1286.   Watkins, Lee H.   JOHN S. HARBISON: CALIFORNIA'S FIRST MODERN BEEKEEPER.   *Agric. Hist. 1969 43(2): 239-248.* The honeybee was first introduced into Virginia about 1622, and spread rapidly to the Mississippi River. Their first successful introduction to California came in March 1853. A new era in California beekeeping began in 1857 when John Steward Harbison brought 67 colonies of bees to San Francisco. Harbison was an experienced beekeeper from a Pennsylvania beekeeping family. He quickly adopted the practical movable-frame hive, invented in 1851 by Lorenzo Lorraine Langstroth, and made improvements in it, particularly in inventing small comb sections for handling and marketing honey. Harbison made two successful large-scale introductions of bees into the Sacramento area, selling many of the hives for high prices. In 1869, Harbison moved to San Diego County, where he established records for honey production.
W. D. Rasmussen

1287.   White, Raymond E.   THE TEXAS COTTON GINNING INDUSTRY 1860-1900.   *Texana 1967 5(4): 344-358.* The Texas cotton industry was not destroyed in the Civil War because Texas was not a battlefield and it had an outlet for its crop, mainly Mexico. After the war it revived quickly, with the gin replacing slave labor. Production increased over six times in these four decades. Gives an account of the basic operation of the gin. Discusses financing of gins, manpower wages, the growth of market controls, particularly over bale quality, the beginnings of cooperatives, and the rise of the gin manufacturing industry. 31 notes.
W. A. Buckman

1288.   Winter, Frank H. and Sharpe, Mitchell R.   THE CALIFORNIA WHALING ROCKET AND THE MEN BEHIND IT.   *California Hist. Q. 1971 50(4): 349-362.* The idea of a rocket-powered harpoon compelled a number of men to seek ways to make such a weapon both feasible and profitable. One of the earliest methods was devised by Captain Thomas W. Roys, who died in poverty in 1877 after several unsuccessful attempts to perfect a workable rocket. California served as a natural locale for whaling rocket developers, as the Pacific whaling fleet used San Francisco as home port. Hugh Lamont, John N. Fletcher, and Robert L. Suits tried to improve the rocket's workability in the late 1870's, and they ran a series of tests in perfecting it. While a number of whaling ships used the rockets, a declining market for whale oil, the rockets' cost, and mariners' resistance to innovation resulted in the whaling rockets' failure as a business venture. Based on unpublished records in the National Archives and on secondary sources; photos, 29 notes.
A. Hoffman

1289.   Workman, William.   A LETTER FROM TAOS, 1826.   *New Mexico Hist. R. 1966 41(2): 155-164.* The letter, from William Workman, a merchant residing in Taos, to his brother David Workman of Franklin, Missouri, contains a request for materials to build a distillery, plus a comment on living in Taos. 31 notes.   D. F. Henderson

1290.   Wright, Marguerite J.   ECHOES FROM THE PAST: THE STORY OF THE ECHO FLOUR MILL.   *Utah Hist. Q. 1966 34(2): 161-168.* Relates the building of the original mill, its changes in owner-

ship, modifications in machinery and operation, and the final demolition of the mill in 1964. Based upon the reminiscences of the author and her father Arthur Marlow Jones, the last owner and operator of the mill. Photos.
S. L. Jones

Transportation and Communication

General

1291.   Aronson, Dennis.   THE POMONA STREET RAILWAYS IN THE SOUTHERN CALIFORNIA BOOM OF THE 1880'S.   *Southern California Q. 1965 47(3): 245-267.* In the 1880's there was a tremendous influx of tourists and settlers into southern California. One consequence of this boom was the growth of rail transportation in the area. At the height of the boom, five companies organized, built, and operated 10 miles of street railways in Pomona. The various lines and their influences on the city are described. Although most of them ceased to run in the early 1890's, they had considerable influence in promoting civic pride and improvement. Appendixes describe the rail companies in outline form and the location of proposed but unbuilt tracks. 82 notes.   A. K. Main

1292.   Bandy, William R.   MYSTERIOUS PARSONS BRIDGE.   *Montana 1963 13(4): 77-79.* One of the first substantial bridges in Montana was built across the Jefferson River near present Waterloo. Replacing a temporary toll ferry in 1865, the bridge served a road between Virginia City and Helena, accommodating a big volume of traffic in the gold-rush years. A small community, long since a ghost town, grew up around Parsons Bridge, with the usual stage station, road house, and general store. Interest was revived in the place in 1960 when legal action among three counties all cornering on the old bridge necessitated locating the exact site.   S. R. Davison

1293.   Barsness, Richard W.   LOS ANGELES' QUEST FOR IMPROVED TRANSPORTATION, 1846-1861.   *California Hist. Soc. Q. 1967 46(4): 291-306.* The gold rush centralized coastal shipping at San Francisco, thus relegating San Pedro to a minor position in commerce. In Southern California in the 1850's the major figure in transportation was Phineas Banning. He opened a new port named Wilmington. Banning became a leading entrepreneur in freighting operations over the 750-mile haul from Los Angeles to Salt Lake City by wagon road. In 1858 US Army camels made their local appearance. In the same year the Butterfield Stage Lines began service. In 1860 the telegraph link was completed between San Francisco and Los Angeles. Poor transportation and lack of capital deterred development of agriculture. To establish a broader economic foundation, major transportation improvements were needed. Thus, Southern California's first railroad, the Los Angeles and San Pedro, was promoted shortly after the end of the Civil War. Illus., 37 notes.
E. P. Stickney

1294.   Baughman, James P.   THE EVOLUTION OF RAIL-WATER SYSTEMS OF TRANSPORTATION IN THE GULF SOUTHWEST, 1836-1890.   *J. of Southern Hist. 1968 34(3): 357-381.* The pace and direction of railroad development in the Gulf Southwest (defined as the hinterland of the Gulf of Mexico between the Rio Grande and the Sabine River) prior to the 1870's was conditioned by patterns of interstate water-rail competition. Anticipating the coming of railroads, the shipping interests in the region accommodated to the challenge, and the "results by the 1890's were two great rail-water systems linking the Pacific and Atlantic coasts and the Mississippi Valley via the ports of the western Gulf of Mexico." The author details the five "competitive stages" in the evolution of these rail-water systems in their formative years between 1836 and 1890. Map, 45 notes.   I. M. Leonard

1295.   Carley, Maurine.   CHEYENNE - DEADWOOD TRAIL TREK: TREK NO. 16 OF THE HISTORIC TRAIL TREKS.   *Ann. of Wyoming 1966 38(1): 84-103.* Discusses the three-day trek over the Cheyenne-Deadwood trail in July 1965, sponsored by the Wyoming State Archives and Historical Department and the Wyoming State Historical Society. The object of the trek was to retrace the old trail by car.

Includes 14 brief descriptions of such places as Hat Creek Stage Station, Jenney Stockade, and Canyon Springs which figured in the history of the trail, as well as a map of the trek and a list of the participants. Illus.

R. L. Nichols

1296. Danker, Donald F. THE INFLUENCE OF TRANSPORTATION UPON NEBRASKA TERRITORY. *Nebraska Hist. 1966 47(2): 187-208.* Carefully surveys and analyzes the impact of transportation in territorial Nebraska (1855-67) along the Platte Valley and the Missouri River, which were the main highways to the West. Steamboating, wagon traffic, road building, and finally, railroad construction are all fully discussed, along with their effect on territorial development.

R. Lowitt

1297. DeGolyer, E., Jr. THE LIBRARY OF THE DEGOLYER FOUNDATION. *Technology and Culture 1964 5(3): 408-411.* "Consisting chiefly of the collections of the founder, but supplemented by important collections of drawings, manuscripts, pertaining to steam locomotives and steamships, the library is located . . . at Southern Methodist University. . . ."

C. O. Smith

1298. Elliott, Arlene. THE RISE OF AERONAUTICS IN CALIFORNIA, 1849-1940. *Southern Calif. Q. 1970 52(1): 1-32.* Discusses aeronautics in California from 1849, when an inventor advertised an "aerial locomotive" to take people to the gold fields, to 1940, when the North American Aviation Company sold its experimental fighter plane, the Mustang, to Great Britain. During the intervening years, Californians experimented with a variety of dirigibles, gliders, and engine-driven "heavier-than-air" craft. Some landmarks in California's aeronautical history were: an unmanned balloon airplane flight on 2 July 1869; a successful monoplane flight on 29 April 1905; the first international air meet in January 1909; the first licensed woman pilot in the country in 1911; pioneer hydroplane development; California location of the early airplane builders (Lockheed, Martin, Douglas, Ryan, and Northrop); leadership in the 1920's in the number of airports, licensed pilots, and mechanics; and establishment of many "firsts" for long-distance flights during the 1930's. Based mainly on contemporary periodical articles; 18 illus., table, 89 notes.

W. L. Bowers

1299. Ewing, Floyd F., Jr. THE MULE AS A FACTOR IN THE DEVELOPMENT OF THE SOUTHWEST. *Arizona and the West 1963 5(4): 315-326.* The Spanish mule, a new variety of mule stock to the trans-Mississippi moving American frontiersman, was developed for centuries for use in the semiarid highlands of Spain and Mexico. In the "mule years," 1820-60, this animal was rapidly adapted to many uses by the Americans. The mule came to be regarded as the equal of the prairie mustang and the Eastern horse for riding and as superior to them for packing and freighting. The seeming inexhaustible supply became a prime article of trade over such routes as the Santa Fe Trail. The mule played a significant role in mining, the range cattle industry, military engagements, and especially in rapid transportation across the rough and dry country of the Southwest. It was the most effective common denominator for all uses. Not universally preferred nor accepted, the mule nevertheless earned grudging respect for its contribution in the conquest of the American Southwest. Based on published sources and monographs; 53 notes.

D. L. Smith

1300. Fellows, Fred R. ILLUSTRATED STUDY OF WESTERN SADDLES. *Montana 1966 16(1): 57-83.* Drawings of 13 types of saddles used on the western frontier, with a page of descriptive comment on each, including its structure, design, origin, and area of use.

S. R. Davison

1301. Frizzell, John and Frizzell, Mildred. THE OKLAHOMA HISTORICAL SOCIETY STAGECOACH. *Chronicles of Oklahoma 1963 41(1): 3-8.* Discussion of the American stagecoach.

1302. Gendler, Carol. TERRITORIAL OMAHA AS A STAGING AND FREIGHTING CENTER. *Nebraska Hist. 1968 49(2): 103-120.* A careful analysis of Omaha as a staging and freighting center, handling passengers and mail and outfitting wagon trains, most of them headed west. Some attention is given to emigrant trains as well. The railroad meant the demise of all these functions, although Omaha remained an important transportation center serving westward regions.

R. Lowitt

1303. Goodwin, Victor. WILLIAM C. (HILL) BEACHEY: NEVADA-CALIFORNIA-IDAHO STAGECOACH KING. *Nevada Hist. Soc. Q. 1967 10(1): 3-46.* William C. Beachey, better known as Hill Beachey, was preeminent in the staging annals of northern Nevada, southern Idaho, and northern California. Particularly in those areas of Nevada and Idaho, Beachey's vision and energy in linking together their widely scattered and straggling mining camps and settlements was a major factor in their "dramatic flowering" in 1864-73. The Beachey staging empire waged a losing battle against the railroads. Considerable renown came to Hill Beachey when he apprehended the murderers of a close friend and his companions after relentlessly pursuing them over Idaho, Oregon, and northern California. Beachey had had a "blood-soaked dream" about the multiple-murder with all of the details weeks before the event. 67 notes, 4 illus.

D. L. Smith

1304. Gray, John S. THE NORTHERN OVERLAND PONY EXPRESS. *Montana 1966 16(4): 58-73.* The need for rapid mail service to the gold rush area of Montana led to an experimental horseback mail between Fort Abercrombie, North Dakota, and Diamond City, near Helena, Montana. The line operated in the latter half of 1867 but was withdrawn the next year because of the distance involved, the severe climate, and resistance by the Sioux Indians. Based on newspaper accounts and other contemporary sources.

S. R. Davison

1305. Hernandez, Richard A. FREDERICK MARRIOTT: A 'FORTY-NINER BANKER AND EDITOR WHO TOOK A "FLIER" IN PIONEERING AMERICAN AVIATION. *J. of the West 1963 2(4): 401-424.* Frederick Marriott was an editor and banker who emigrated from England to California in 1849. After little luck with mining, he turned again to newspaper editing and then to the invention of lighter-than-air craft. His "Avitor" flew a number of times and presaged the Zeppelin model by some years. Marriott also put 30,000 dollars into a heavier-than-air, steam-powered craft that was said to be able to carry four passengers, but when the U.S. Patent Office refused a patent in 1883 the project fell by the wayside. Based on newspapers and secondary sources; 46 notes.

K. P. Davis

1306. Hicks, Sam. APAREJO: THE PERFECT PACKSADDLE. *Am. West 1969 6(1): 28-32.* The *aparejo,* a packsaddle, consists of two rectangular pads stuffed with tough grass that are joined by an unfilled section of leather centered over the backbone of the burro. Hardwood sticks line the leading edge, bottom, and trailing edge of each pad. These sticks stiffen the *aparejo,* enabling the packer to pass his lash ropes under the corners of the pad and to cinch upward with a crushing pressure, binding the cargo in place. The grass-filled pads distribute the weight evenly over the animal's back. This packsaddle is tailored to the individual burro's need and is usually included with the animal on any change of ownership. 8 illus.

D. L. Smith

1307. Hilton, George W. DENVER'S CABLE RAILWAYS. *Colorado Mag. 1967 44(1): 34-53.* The heyday of the cable car in Colorado's largest city, Denver, coincided with the time of the great silver boom of the 1880's. Taking advantage of this, Denver received two installments of cable traction which gave that city the most complete coverage of any American metropolis. The author outlines the route of the cableway and the problems involved in such an extensive system, being the largest ever run from a single powerhouse. The first abandonment of the cable system came in 1891 as a result of complications from cable crossings. From that time until 1900 cable cars were gradually phased out of existence in Denver, in favor of the safer and more efficient electric car. Based on reports in contemporary newspapers; illus., map, 31 notes.

R. Sexauer

1308. Hood, Joseph F. ALL THE DARING YOUNG MEN: AVIATION COMES TO THE WEST. *Am. West. 1971 8(4): 10-15, 63-64.* Although there were earlier schemes and proposals, nothing came of aviation in the Far West until post-Civil War balloonists and parachute artists made barnstorming exhibitions. Chronicles the efforts of some of the balloon, parachute, dirigible, glider, and other airship stunts in California. The airplane had its California debut in 1910. Aviation history was made the next year by a two-month transcontinental flight to Pasadena, a landing on a battleship in San Francisco Bay, and demonstration of a seaplane at San Diego. 11 illus.

D. L. Smith

1309. Hutchings, James Mason. PACKING, IN THE MOUNTAINS OF CALIFORNIA. *Am. West 1965 2(3): 92-95.* A classic account of the mule packing train activities in the 1850's which transported supplies between such towns as Stockton, Marysville, Shasta, and Crescent City, and the isolated mining localities in the rugged and nearly inaccessible California mountains. This is an excerpt from the original article in *Hutchings' California Magazine* (December 1856), with an editorial introduction by Roger R. Olmsted. Illus.   D. L. Smith

1310. Hutchins, James S. ARMY SIX-MULE WAGON HARNESS OF 1875. *Military Collector and Historian 1966 18(3): 75-83.* Gives minute descriptions of the six-mule wagon harness which remained the standard from 1875 until the early 20th century. Although the quartermaster's department generally contracted with private freighters - they were less expensive - for the hauling of supplies to frontier posts where there were no railroads, the "Army six" wagon was an important means of transportaton especially during wars with the Indians. Documented with records from the National Archives, illus.   C. L. Boyd

1311. Jackson, W. Turrentine. A NEW LOOK AT WELLS FARGO, STAGECOACHES, AND THE PONY EXPRESS. *California Hist. Soc. Q. 1966 45(4): 291-324.* Surveys the history of Wells Fargo with emphasis on its contribution to western transportation. In 1852 in New York it was formed as a joint-stock association to take advantage of the business opportunities in California. From the start Wells Fargo engaged in banking and within two years it purchased three express companies. The author believes that the company's influence over finance and policy extended to all forms of communication including transportation. The company owned and operated at least four different pony express enterprises between 1852 and 1868 in California and Nevada and was responsible for the operation of the trans-Missouri Pony Express, from March to October 1861. Based primarily on the Minute Book of the Board of Directors of the Overland Mail Company which the author located in New York and some other documents hitherto unused; illus., 84 notes.   E. P. Stickney

1312. Jackson, W. Turrentine. WELLS FARGO STAGING OVER THE SIERRA. *California Hist. Soc. Q. 1970 49(2): 99-133.* Describes the stage line operations of Wells, Fargo and Company from the gold rush years through the 1860's. Throughout this period the company established regular schedules on several routes between Sacramento and Virginia City. Competition was heavy and Wells, Fargo and Company came to dominate the field by buying out smaller companies and consolidating its business with those of the smaller lines. For two years (1865-67) the company controlled the Pioneer Stage Company, with the public growing increasingly suspicious as to whether these companies were truly competitive. In December 1866 a "grand consolidation" was announced which left Wells, Fargo and Company the clear leader in stage line operation. The company paralleled the construction of the Central Pacific Railroad over the Sierras and, despite the obstacles of snow, mud, cold, and competition, the company efficiently delivered its mail, freight, and passengers. After the Central Pacific reached Reno, Wells Fargo withdrew from trans-Sierra operations to concentrate on the stretch between the Union and Central Pacific railroad construction and on the numerous feeder lines in the intermountain West. Based on newspapers and company records; illus., map, photos, 140 notes.   A. Hoffman

1313. Jackson, W. Turrentine. WELLS FARGO: SYMBOL OF THE WILD WEST. *Western Hist. Q. 1972 3(2): 179-196.* Wells, Fargo and Co. was launched in 1852 to take advantage of the California economic boom stimulated by the gold rush. Banking was unsupervised and half of the nearly 30 firms had already collapsed. Wells Fargo soon jumped to the leading position in gold shipments, and expanded its activities in scope and in area served. Recounts many stagecoach robberies and accidents. Today the nationwide operation includes computer services, securities clearance, leasing, real estate management businesses, and other interests. Wells Fargo's history is an integral part of the story of prerailroad transportation, the U.S. mails, the railway express, banking, and the economic history of the country. Wells Fargo also symbolizes American western history as a part of the national experience. 63 notes.   D. L. Smith

1314. Madsen, Brigham D. and Madsen, Betty M. THE DIAMOND R ROLLS OUT. *Montana 1971 21(2): 2-17.* Completion of the Union Pacific Railroad in 1869 brought rail service within 500 miles of the Montana gold fields. Relatively easy access made the Utah route to Montana competitive with steamboats to Fort Benton and with packstrings up from the Columbia River. The biggest firm to operate freight wagons north from Utah was the Overland Diamond R Freight Line, described here in terms of equipment, organization, and accomplishments. Mentions competing lines and individuals employed in the activity. Illus., 30 notes.   S. R. Davison

1315. Martin, Charles W., ed. A ROUND TRIP TO THE MONTANA MINES: THE 1866 TRAVEL JOURNAL OF GURDON P. LESTER. *Nebraska Hist. 1965 46(4): 273-313.* Following an overland stage coach route from Iowa to Montana and a water route on the Missouri River back to Iowa, Gurdon Lester gives a description of his travels in the year 1866. Traveling along the Platte River following severe Indian attacks and down the Missouri River at the height of the passenger traffic period, his diary conveys information about the trials and tribulations confronting travelers.   R. Lowitt

1316. Menefee, Arthur M. ARTHUR M. MENEFEE'S TRAVELS ACROSS THE PLAINS, 1857. *Nevada Hist. Soc. Q. 1966 9(1): 5-28.* Reproduction of a diary of a pioneer going from Missouri across the Western Plains to Carson City, Nevada. The diary contains many interesting observations.   W. J. Brooks

1317. Murray, Keith A. BUILDING A WAGON ROAD THROUGH THE NORTHERN CASCADE MOUNTAINS. *Pacific Northwest Q. 1965 56(2): 49-56.* An account of attempts to build a road across the mountainous area of northern Washington, showing special interst in the wagon road of 1880-96. Documented, map.   C. C. Gorchels

1318. Myers, Rex. TROLLEYS OF THE TREASURE STATE. *Montana 1972 22(2): 34-47.* Surveys the history of street railway lines serving Montana cities from the first in Billings (1882) to the last in Anaconda (1952). Most of the major cities saw a series of horse-drawn, steam-powered or electric conveyances, all of which suffered from poor patronage and enjoyed little financial success. Based on corporate papers and on secondary sources; 13 illus., 29 notes.   S. R. Davison

1319. O'Brien, Bob R. THE ROADS OF YELLOWSTONE 1870-1915. *Montana 1967 17(3): 30-39.* Summarizes efforts at road building in Yellowstone National Park in preautomobile days, stressing the work of Philetus W. Norris, superintendent in the late 1870's. Further improvement was done by Army Engineers between 1886 and 1905, largely directed by Hiram M. Chittenden. New park highways, accommodating modern traffic, have reverted to the straight, flat roads of Norris' time, in contrast to the winding, scenic style of Chittenden's designs. Based largely on official reports of park superintendents; illus.   S. R. Davison

1320. Olmsted, Roger R. THE FIRST CABLE CAR. *Am. West 1965 2(4): 14-17.* The first San Francisco cable car was tried, successfully, 2 August 1873. Reproduced for the first time is the original drawing by Andrew S. Hallidie, its inventor. Other early sketches and modifications are included. The text explains its operation and safety features as shown on the sketches. Illus., biblio. note.   D. L. Smith

1321. Peterson, Stacy. SILAS SKINNER'S OWYHEE TOLL ROAD. *Idaho Yesterdays 1966 10(1): 12-21.* "Describes the toll route established by Silas Skinner in 1866." The road extended from Silver City in the Owyhees down Jordan Creek 70 miles to Duncan's Ferry, Oregon. The route was built to provide a southwest outlet for the vastly rich mining district. The author discusses the development and problems of securing a franchise and of keeping the road in condition for all-weather travel. Skinner settled in the area and became a prominent citizen in Jordan Valley. The present highway follows the route of the old Skinner toll road. 56 notes.   D. H. Swift

1322. Pinney, Marie. CHARLES BECKER, PONY EXPRESS RIDER AND OREGON PIONEER. *Oregon Hist. Q. 1966 67(3): 212-256.* Biographical sketch of a pony express rider in the western United States. In his life (1834-1925) Becker had many other occupations which are recounted along with the historical atmosphere of the various places in which he lived, including Pennsylvania, Kansas, Utah, California, and, principally, Oregon. Illus.   C. C. Gorchels

1323. Rue, Norman L. PESH-BI-YALTI SPEAKS: WHITE MAN'S TALKING WIRE IN ARIZONA. *J. of Arizona Hist. 1971 12(4): 229-262.* Proposals for a telegraph system were prompted by the need of the Army for more efficient means of communication than the mail and special messengers within Arizona, because higher headquarters were on the Pacific coast during the Indian wars. Reconnaissance began at Prescott in mid-1873 to determine the route, and construction commenced a few weeks later. By mid-1877, Arizona was linked by military telegraph which eventually provided the territory with communications from the Pacific to the Gulf of Mexico. The telegraph served the Army well as an effective device for maintaining control over reservation Indians. As the railroad came to Arizona during the next few years it brought commercial telegraphy which gradually replaced the military lines. "Pesh-bi-yalti" was the Apache name for "the white man's talking wire." 8 illus., map, 90 notes.   D. L. Smith

1324. Shirk, George H. THE POST OFFICES OF OKLAHOMA: NOVEMBER 26, 1907-DECEMBER 31, 1965. *Chronicles of Oklahoma 1966 44(1): 31-90.* Although post offices had been listed for the Oklahoma Territory, when the territory became a state the Postmaster General reorganized his records and established a new index for Oklahoma, no longer listing designations such as "Cherokee Nation." This register was maintained until 1930 when it was deposited in the National Archives. The author compiled an index listing of post offices from 1907 to 1965 which is printed here.   I. W. Van Noppen

1325. Standing, A. R. THROUGH THE UINTAS: HISTORY OF THE CARTER ROAD. *Utah Hist. Q. 1967 35(3): 256-267.* Traces the career of a wagon road from the Union Pacific Railroad at Fort Bridger, Wyoming, to Fort Thornburgh, a military installation near Vernal, Utah. Established as a supply route for U.S. troops guarding settlers against Ute Indian attacks, it became a route for moving copper and other minerals from the Dyer Mine in Utah. A map and photographs of surviving remnants of the road are provided. Based in part on the reminiscences of William A. Carter, Jr., whose father established the road, these reminiscences are now in typescript at the Ashley National Forest, Vernal, Utah; map, photos.   S. L. Jones

1326. Stewart, George R. TRAVELERS BY "OVERLAND": STAGECOACHING ON THE CENTRAL ROUTE, 1859-1865. *Am. West 1968 5(4): 4-12, 61.* "Overland" herein refers to stagecoaching along the central route from Saint Joseph in Missouri, Leavenworth or Atchison in Kansas, via Salt Lake City, Utah, to California's Placerville or Folsom. Middle West business needs, growing Mormon settlements in Utah, and new gold discoveries in Colorado and Nevada necessitated and brought the forging of the last link in the transcontinental transportation chain. Staging ended completely when the railroad took over in 1869. Few passengers and little mail traveled the entire distance. Four accounts of those who did make the whole passage are the basis of this study to gain some impressions of the transcontinental venture that captured the imagination of contemporaries. Chronologically they span the development of stage travel from its beginnings to its culmination. Their experiences varied so greatly that the conception of "typical" does not apply. Horace Greeley, New York *Tribune* editor and public figure, sent letters back to his paper of his 1859 journey that were eventually collected into *An Overland Journey.* Richard Burton, famed traveler and later renowned translator of the *Arabian Nights,* made the passage in 1860 collecting material for his forthcoming *The City of the Saints.* Samuel Clemens, later known as Mark Twain, recounted his 1861 trip in *Roughing It.* In more than one sense of the word, the 1865 venture of Schuyler Colfax, speaker of the House of Representatives, and Samuel Bowles, editor of the Springfield, Massachusetts, *Republican,* was reported in letters and later in *Our New West.* 6 illus., map.   D. L. Smith

1327. Walker, Henry Pickering. FREIGHTING FROM GUAYMAS TO TUCSON, 1850-1880. *Western Hist. Q. 1970 1(3): 291-304.* Before railroads came to the Southwest in the 1880's, supplies for the area had to be freighted in by animals over long distances. Foodstuffs, clothing, hardware, and machinery were the essentials needed to support the American settlement in southern Arizona in the days of the big mining booms. During the Civil War, military supplies to support New Mexico and Arizona-based troops were a major concern. American-manufactured textiles and a wide range of other commodities from bacon to buttons became stock items of trade in the Tucson area. California and Texas coastal ports were too far away. Although Yuma, situated on the Colorado River, was reasonably close, sailing through the tricky upper Gulf of California and transshipment up the more difficult Colorado River added significantly to the freighting costs. Sonoran ports along the Gulf of California became attractive possibilities. Guaymas was the most favored and became the port of entry for southern Arizona. Among other considerations, as much as a month was cut from the shipping time of a cargo from San Francisco to Tucson. Political factors and government red tape, however, prevented development of the route to its full potential. Map, 39 notes.   D. L. Smith

1328. Watkins, T. H. THE REVOLOIDAL SPINDLE AND THE WONDROUS AVITOR. *Am. West 1967 4(1): 24-27, 69-70.* Rufus Porter, sometime editor of science and mechanics magazines, conceived the idea and issued a promotional booklet about an "Aerial Locomotive" to transport 1849 gold rushers from New York to California in three days. His steam powered revoloidal spindle or hydrogen gas-filled bag would carry two hundred passengers and all their baggage at 100 dollars per person. His airship was never built because he failed to sell enough stock to finance the venture. Englishman Frederick Marriott, a California newspaper owner with previous association in a transatlantic airship scheme, succeeded in raising sufficient capital to experiment with a similar idea. The 2 July 1869 maiden voyage of the "Avitor Hermes, Jr.," was America's "first powered flight of a lighter-than-air craft." It lasted about 10 minutes. Although it continued to perform on a demonstration basis and although some stock was subscribed, insufficient funds, wrecking of the Avitor, and the financial stringency of the 1870's deflated the project beyond recovery. Marriott later designed a heavier-than-air craft which he dubbed an "aeroplane" but was denied a patent in 1883 because his device was pronounced an "impossibility." 5 illus., biblio. note.
                                             D. L. Smith

1329. Whitham, Louise Morse. GREEN YEARGAIN AND STAR ROUTE 32024. *Chronicles of Oklahoma 1966 44(2): 147-157.* A great advance in postal service came in 1847 with prepaid postage stamps. Soon after, star routes were established. The Pony Express was begun in 1860 and operated until, a year later, telegraph lines carried messages faster. There are 12 thousand star routes in the United States. Star route mail comes directly to the contractor who has a postmaster's duties. The three stars stand for "celerity, certainty, and sincerity." Under the star route system the United States was divided into districts, each headed by a district contractor. He sublet to a local contractor the hiring of carriers. After 1878 Star Route 32024 was established to carry mail to Indian agencies. Green Yeargain was one of those employed to carry the mail. Generally he drove to the Sac and Fox Reservation, once to Las Vegas and back. Yeargain was Tulsa's first mail carrier. The first Tulsa U.S. Post Office was in the George Perryman farmhouse. The first post boxes still exist. They were large because the star routes carried both packages and letters. 5 notes, biblio.   I. W. Van Noppen

1330. Wilson, Gladys Marie. THE SAGA OF BUTTERFIELD'S OVERLAND MAIL. *Am. Hist. Illus. 1967 1(9): 14-23.* As the population expanded in the West, particularly in California, the settlers began demanding better mail and communication services. Reliable stagecoach runs were badly needed to traverse the dangerous wilderness. In 1858 John Butterfield (1801-69) established a stage service that went from Saint Louis to San Francisco in 24 days along a southern route. Butterfield's Overland Mail continued successfully until 1861 when Congress ordered it transferred to the central route. 5 illus., map.
                                             M. J. McBaine

1331. Winther, Oscar. THE TRAIL OF THE CONCORD COACH. *Am. West R. 1967 1(3): 13, 29.* Discusses Ralph Moody's *Stagecoach West* (New York: T. Y. Crowell, 1967). Each generation of writers has continued to publish matter concerning stagecoaching. Moody's book continues to ply this standard and he makes "no pretense of having made extensive use of original sources, save newspapers." The history of stagecoaching from early times is covered, but the book is solidly based in the trans-Mississippi West. The reviewer thinks "that Moody has presented his material in judicious and very readable fashion. . . . Though the book offers little information that is new to the professional historian, its substance is sober and sound."   O. L. Miller

Railroads

1332. Anderson, George L. A NORTH-SOUTH LINK: MISSOURI PACIFIC'S PROPOSAL: UNION PACIFIC'S ACHIEVEMENT, 1889-1910. *Kansas Q. 1970 2(3): 88-96.* Correspondence between two Kansas City men in 1889 proposed 10 branches for the Missouri Pacific Railroad. These branches were designed to integrate the Missouri Pacific's system and to take trade from the Atchison, Topeka and Santa Fe Railroad and from the Union Pacific Railroad. The Union Pacific in 1911 began passenger service over the only branch ever completed. Based largely on newspapers; 13 notes. B. A. Storey

1333. Arrington, Leonard J. THE TRANSCONTINENTAL RAILROAD AND THE DEVELOPMENT OF THE WEST. *Utah Hist. Q. 1969 37(1): 3-15.* Deals with the completion of the first transcontinental railroad route, which occurred in Utah in 1869, and the centennial of the event. The author shows how the concept of the transcontinental road developed, summarizes the major steps taken to finance and construct the railroads involved, and briefly reviews the major economic influences exercised by the transcontinental route on Western development. There is also a survey of the construction of the so-called "Mormon" lines, built to link Utah communities with the transcontinental system. S. L. Jones

1334. Athearn, Robert G. A BRAHMIN IN BUFFALOLAND. *Western Hist. Q. 1970 1(1): 21-34.* The 15-year-old Union Pacific Railway was in financial trouble because of over-expansion, increasing competition from other transcontinental lines, demands from the Government for repayment of loans, and the financial "milking" by such financiers as Jay Gould. One of the demands which the Senate Judiciary Committee made of the Union Pacific, in return for the cessation of Government pressure against the company, was that Charles Francis Adams, Jr. be elected as president. Elected to this position in 1884 the new president set out with characteristic energy to put the Union Pacific house in order. The Quincy (Massachusetts) Brahmin cleaned house in principal executive offices, attempted to mold public and editorial opinion, wrestled with the Knights of Labor, and established libraries at smaller towns along the line in an attempt to raise the moral level of the employees through education. With this and more, Adams failed to cure the ills of the Union Pacific. As his frustrations mounted, he became more sensitive to criticism. Jay Gould gained control of the railroad in 1890 and Adams resigned. 52 notes. D. L. Smith

1335. Athearn, Robert G. CONTRACTING FOR THE UNION PACIFIC. *Utah Hist. Q. 1969 37(1): 16-40.* Shows how Mormon leaders, finding their community facing a decline in the rate of economic growth and a high level of unemployment, eagerly accepted Union Pacific overtures to contract to prepare a road grade for the tracks which were to be laid on a section of the route through Utah. The author follows the story surrounding the difficulties experienced by the Mormons in getting prompt payment for work completed under the contract and of how in the resulting negotiations Mormon leaders maneuvered to get supplies and financial support for the Mormon branch lines they were building. The conclusion is that the results were mutually beneficial. Based primarily on manuscript materials in the Church of Jesus Christ of Latter-day Saints Historical Library, the Union Pacific Archives, and contemporary newspapers; illus. S. L. Jones

1336. Athearn, Robert G. THE FIREWAGON ROAD. *Montana 1970 20(2): 2-19.* Advances the thesis that the railroad was the primary force in subjugating western Indians - by bringing in overwhelming numbers of soldiers and giving them mobility, and by carrying in "hordes of settlers whose very numbers suffocated the Indian threat." It is shown that Government assistance to the railroads, often pictured as a swindle, was really an excellent investment, which was repaid abundantly in reduced rates for shipments and fares, and still further by donations of services which had never been widely publicized. An additional dividend came from the railroads' role in shortening the Indian wars, which were always costly. Derived from official records and newspapers of the period 1865-85; illus., 58 notes. S. R. Davison

1337. Athearn, Robert G. OPENING THE GATES OF ZION: UTAH AND THE COMING OF THE UNION PACIFIC RAIL-

ROAD. *Utah Hist. Q. 1968 36(4): 291-314.* Presents evidence contrary to widely held contemporary opinion that the Mormons in Utah greatly desired the building of the Union Pacific Railroad in their territory, and that they helped in various ways in planning and accelerating its construction. They had made significant plans for its use even before it reached them. Based primarily on the "Journal History" in the Church of Jesus Christ of Latter-Day Saints Historians Library, Salt Lake City, and contemporary newspaper accounts. S. L. Jones

1338. Athearn, Robert G. RAILROAD TO A FAR OFF COUNTRY: THE UTAH AND NORTHERN. *Montana 1968 18(4): 2-23.* Gives details of local politics and financial maneuvers involved in construction of a narrow gauge railroad, the Utah and Northern, from Utah to Montana between 1871 and 1881. Despite eagerness on the part of many Montanans, the line was built with no substantial help from that end of the project; actual resistance developed in those Montana towns not on the proposed route and those which preferred to await the Northern Pacific's standard gauge road. Forces in the territorial legislature prevented such subsidies as tax exemptions and county purchases of railroad bonds, the chief proposals of Utah and Northern's supporters. Illus., 101 notes. S. R. Davison

1339. Axelrod, Bernard. ROCKY MOUNTAIN CUSTOMS PORT OF ENTRY. *Colorado Mag. 1964 41(2): 126-134.* John Evans, Colorado's second territorial governor, pioneer educator, and successful businessman, envisioned Denver as the hub of a great railway system linking the Far East, South America, and the Great Lakes. He persisted in his effort to have Denver declared a customs port of entry until Congress passed such a law in 1882. I. W. Van Noppen

1340. Barsness, Richard W. IRON HORSES AND AN INNER HARBOR AT SAN PEDRO BAY, 1867-1890. *Pacific Hist. R. 1965 34(3): 289-303.* Reviews the efforts in San Pedro, California to construct a railroad linkup with deepwater shipping. Includes the work of the Corps of Engineers and the railroad war which led to domination of traffic by the Southern Pacific. J. McCutcheon

1341. Beebe, Lucius. THE OVERLAND LIMITED. *Am. Heritage 1963 15(1): 54-57, 87.* A sentimental history of one of the West's leading trains. Running between Chicago and San Francisco, it carried more important people than any other train with the possible exception of the New York Central's Twentieth Century Limited. Well illus., undocumented. C. R. Allen, Jr.

1342. Best, Gerald M. RENDEZVOUS AT PROMONTORY: THE "JUPITER" AND NO. 119. *Utah Hist. Q. 1969 37(1): 69-75.* Follows the history of the construction of the two locomotives which met at Promontory, Utah, on 10 May 1869, to mark the completion of the first transcontinental railroad and shows that the choice of these particular engines was mainly the result of accident rather than deliberate plan. Illus. S. L. Jones

1343. Bowman, J. N. DRIVING THE LAST SPIKE AT PROMONTORY, 1869. *Utah Hist. Q. 1969 37(1): 76-101.* Information about the preparations for the ceremonies held when the first transcontinental railroad was completed. Included are detailed descriptions of the several ceremonial spikes prepared for the occasion, the silver sledge, the laurel tie, the iron tie, and the wiring of the hammer and tie for nationwide broadcast over the Western Union wires. The author discusses the difficulty in finding sources which will provide reliable details, concludes that many questions remain unanswered because of the lack of adequate records, and bases his account primarily on contemporary newspapers. Illus. S. L. Jones

1344. Bray, Martha. PIERRE BOTTINEAU: PROFESSIONAL GUIDE. *North Dakota Q. 1964 32(2): 29-37.* Covers the career of a French-Indian guide in North Dakota during the 19th century. Bottineau, though occasionally a farmer or businessman, served primarily as guide to governmental, business and railroad parties crossing the northern plains. His career spanned development of the area from individual exploration to the railroad. J. F. Mahoney

1345. Carranco, Lynwood and Fountain, Mrs. Eugene. CALIFORNIA'S FIRST RAILROAD: THE UNION PLANK WALK, RAIL

TRACK, AND WHARF COMPANY RAILROAD. *J. of the West 1964 3(2): 243-256.* While gold first attracted men to Humboldt County, lumbermen soon followed. The first railroads were built in California to haul logs to the water's edge. Although the Sacramento Valley Railroad was incorporated in 1853, the Union Plank Walk, Rail Track, and Wharf Company Railroad was the first to be completed. Its wooden rails were in use by January 1855. Its name was later changed to the Arcata and Mad River Railroad. Initially the rolling stock was horsedrawn, but in the 1870's when passenger service was inaugurated the line converted to steam. The author traces the history of the railroad until 1955 when it was purchased by the Simpson Logging Company of Washington. It shows the importance of the line to the logging industry and to the entire economy of the area. Documented by interviews, files of the Northern Redwood Lumber Company, and newspaper sources; 77 notes.

D. N. Brown

1346. Clark, Earl. JOHN F. STEVENS: PATHFINDER FOR WESTERN RAILROADS. *Am. West 1971 8(3): 28-33, 62-63.* Self-trained civil engineer John Frank Stevens (1853-1943), experienced in locating the Canadian Pacific Railway through the Canadian Rockies, was hired in 1889 by James Jerome Hill to get his Great Northern Railway through the Rocky Mountains and the Cascade Mountains from Montana to Puget Sound. Stevens found the fabled Marias Pass across the Continental Divide in northwestern Montana and discovered Stevens Pass across the Cascades in central Washington. He moved on down the western slopes of the Cascades, and Hill's Great Northern reached Puget Sound in 1893. Stevens eventually became general manager of the Great Northern, later was chief engineer in charge of planning and construction of the Panama Canal, and then headed a post-World War I American mission to Russia to keep its railway system from collapsing. 8 illus., biblio.

D. L. Smith

1347. Clinch, Thomas A. THE NORTHERN PACIFIC RAIL-ROAD AND MONTANA'S MINERAL LANDS. *Pacific Hist. R. 1965 34(3); 323-335.* Recounts the history of the railroad's coming to Montana and the successful fight to preserve mineral lands from depredations by the Northern Pacific.

J. McCutcheon

1348. Cochran, John S. ECONOMIC IMPORTANCE OF EARLY TRANSCONTINENTAL RAILROADS: PACIFIC NORTHWEST. *Oregon Hist. Q. 1970 71(1): 26-98.* An account of the factors which brought railroads to Oregon, and the economic effects before, during, and after railroad development. Shows the influence of surveys, land grants, political considerations, and entrepreneurs on the location of routes. Such important activities of the region as wheat-growing, cattle-raising, and manufacturing are explored in relation to railroads. Specific lines are described, such as Northern Pacific, Union Pacific, and Oregon Pacific. Includes 22 pages of notes on sources; maps, photos, tables, diagrams.

C. C. Gorchels

1349. Combs, Barry B. THE UNION PACIFIC RAILROAD AND THE EARLY SETTLEMENT OF NEBRASKA 1868-1880. *Nebraska Hist. 1969 50(1): 1-26.* Examines the efforts of the Union Pacific to dispose of its Nebraska land grant by encouraging settlement in the State and then describes how the railroad benefited from the population growth.

R. Lowitt

1350. Cotroneo, Ross R. THE NORTHERN PACIFIC: YEARS OF DIFFICULTY. *Kansas Q. 1970 2(3): 69-77.* Traces early transcontinental railroad sentiment. Discusses the history of the Northern Pacific Railroad Company after it received a large land grant in 1864. Jay Cooke (1821-1905) was a major sponsor of the project until 1873, when his banking house had to close; in 1881 Henry Villard (1835-1900) gained control of the line. The line was rapidly completed, but Villard soon lost it. James Jerome Hill (1838-1916), after the failure of the Northern Pacific in the depression of 1893, joined forces with John Pierpont Morgan (1837-1913) and other friends to gain control of the Northern Pacific. Hill formed the Northern Securities Company to consolidate the operations of the Northern Pacific and the Great Northern, but in 1904 the courts dissolved the company. By that time the Northern Pacific was well-organized and able to survive easily on its own. Based largely on secondary sources; 45 notes.

B. A. Storey

1351. DeGolyer, Everett L., Jr. TEXAS RAILROADS: THE END OF AN ERA. *Southwestern Hist. Q. 1970 73(3): 356-380.* The centennial celebration (in May 1969) of the driving of the Golden Spike which completed the Overland Route was followed by a lesser but perhaps more nostalgic and disheartening occasion: the last Texas passenger train left the Dallas terminal on its final run. Traces the historical development, employment, and technical adaptations of the major Texas railroads over 100 years. Texas railroading has come to the end of an epoch. 17 photos.

R. W. Delaney

1352. Dillon, Richard H. FAITH TO MOVE MOUNTAINS. *Montana 1971 21(4): 61-66.* Tells of the devices used by builders of the Central Pacific Railroad in the mid-1860's to augment their Federal subsidy by misrepresenting the terrain west of the Sierra Nevada. Federal payment was larger for mileage in the mountains, and the scheme was to establish the western base of the Sierra only a few miles out of Sacramento, thus to include many flat miles within the section reported as mountainous. Undocumented.

S. R. Davison

1353. Drache, Hiram M. THE ECONOMIC ASPECTS OF THE NORTHERN PACIFIC RAILROAD IN NORTH DAKOTA. *North Dakota Hist. 1967 34(4): 320-372.* The Northern Pacific Railroad moved westward from Minnesota into Dakota Territory at Fargo in 1872. Given North Dakota's fertile land and favorable weather, coupled with a seemingly insatiable demand for wheat from the post-Civil War industrialization in the United States, the Northern Pacific became a highly significant factor in the rapid settlement and economic growth of the State. This conclusion is supported with 14 statistical tables of railroad construction, population growth, freight tonnage, wheat production, and related matters. 123 notes, 8 maps, appendix.

D. L. Smith

1354. Due, John F. THE CITY OF PRINEVILLE RAILWAY - A CASE STUDY IN GOVERNMENT ENTERPRISE. *Q. R. of Econ. and Business 1965 5(4): 63-81.* "The City of Prineville Railway [Oregon] is the only example in the United States of a railroad which was developed by and has been wholly owned and operated over a substantial period of time by a municipality. By the nature of its history, it provides an excellent case study of government operation of a commercial undertaking illustrating the dangers and pitfalls of such an undertaking as well as the benefits. The railroad also provides a good subject for benefit-cost analysis of a government project which has been in operation for a substantial period of time." Chart, 2 tables, 19 notes.

K. A. Chauvin

1355. Farnham, Wallace. RAILROADS IN WESTERN HISTORY: THE VIEW FROM THE UNION PACIFIC. *U. of Wyoming Pub. 1966 32: 95-109, 161-163.* A review of the historiography of the Union Pacific Railroad to 1964 finds that there were 13 books dealing at length with the subject. Although the authors represent a cross section of the literate and professional public, not one of them was a professional historian. Excepting in part for one book, they all appear to have been cooked up "from a single recipe"—early visions, belated legislation, troubled finance, melodramatic effort, final disgrace. Further, the sources thus far utilized are largely confined to bulky government documents, "spiced with an occasional memoir," which contain all the biases of their authors. Historians of the Union Pacific rely too readily on the limitations of the sources bequeathed to them; textbook writers and others who mention the subject borrow from them without question. Although the sources for research are limited by the fact that the Union Pacific archives have remained closed to historians, railroad history is not all buried in company archives. The masses of manuscripts that constitute the private papers and correspondence of the leading participants and the records of local and territorial governments through which the road ran are prime examples. If it is recognized that a railroad is more than a corporation with business records, that it is also an important part of the life of the nation, then it will be realized that sources are virtually unlimited. The author details some of the ramifications this can have for the historiography not only of the Union Pacific but of all Western history as well. 39 notes.

D. L. Smith

1356. Farnham, Wallace D. A STUDY OF HISTORICAL LEGENDS. *J. of Am. Hist. 1965 51(4): 632-650.* Attempts to reveal the facts from among the legends which exist in standard textbook accounts concerning the legendary role of Greenville Dodge in the building of the Union Pacific Railroad. The author finds the Dodge fables faulty and attributes their source to Dodge's published memoirs and Jacob R. Perkins' biography of General Dodge and the historian's susceptibility to romantic tales.

H. J. Silverman

1357. Farnham, Wallace D. "THE WEAKENED SPRING OF GOVERNMENT": A STUDY IN NINETEENTH CENTURY AMERICAN HISTORY. *Am. Hist. R. 1963 68(3): 662-680*. Examines the relations of the Union Pacific Railroad and federal and local government as a case study of the effects of the weakness of government during the 19th century. "It was not so much a government of limited powers, based on notions of laissez faire, as a government that failed to use the powers it had.... The task of government was left to private enterprise or a social compact, the use of which is a venerable part of American political behavior. Following this custom, the Union Pacific created its own law. But when the citizens of Omaha, the officers of the Central Pacific, and the speculators of Wall Street each in turn followed suit, the law of the social compact was found to resemble closely the law of the jungle. Corruption and robber barons were only the most fascinating results, the creations of an ungoverned people." Based on manuscript and printed sources.

M. Berman

1358. Frazer, Virginia Rust. DALLAS COUNTY RAILROAD BONDS. *Missouri Hist. R. 1967 61(4): 444-462*. A grand scheme was concocted in 1869 to build a railroad through Dallas County from Lebanon, Missouri, to Fort Scott, Kansas. The county court, which had no authority to do so, authorized bonds which were secured by the county's credit. When the Laclede and Fort Scott Railroad Company failed during the depression of 1873, the residents of Dallas County were left with a huge debt. After refusing to make any compromise in their obligation for many years, the residents of Dallas County finally agreed to a 20-year payment which allowed them to discharge their obligation for 10 cents on the dollar. A great bond burning ceremony was held on 4 July 1940. Based on newspapers, interviews with participants of their descendants, and the Western Historical Manuscripts Collection of the University of Missouri; illus., 69 notes.

W. F. Zornow

1359. Gagan, David P. THE RAILROADS AND THE PUBLIC, 1870-1881: A STUDY OF CHARLES ELLIOTT PERKINS' BUSINESS ETHICS. *Business Hist. R. 1965 39(1): 41-56*. Charles Elliott Perkins was a railroad man who rose through the ranks to eventually become the president of the Chicago, Burlington and Quincy Railroad in 1881. His business ethics were those which are typically associated with the "robber baron" or "captain of industry," though his business role held less glamour in the public eye. It may be succinctly stated thus: "public opinion cannot properly be said to have anything to do with commercial matters." He could not see the value of deliberately inviting public intervention in corporate affairs by laying open the corporate body and sincerely believed that the railroads were subject to the laws of trade and to no other regulating force. Capital was, however, responsible to the public to be fair and honest to protect their investment and invite further investment. To labor it owed only the encouragement to "sobriety, industry, and frugality," all other being left to the private charity of management if it so desired. Thus the natural law of trade represented his business ethics.

J. H. Krenkel

1360. George, Henry. WHAT THE RAILROAD WILL BRING US. *Am. West 1967 4(1): 66-69*. As the first transcontinental railroad was, in 1868, soon to be completed, the author contemplates the question of what the implications will be for Californians. He asserts that California is stagecoach-conditioned, that is, it is widely separated from the other parts of the world. Anticipation alone of the advent of the railroad, "the great settler of States and builder of cities" had reversed the postmining economic decline. Material prosperity - measured in terms of people, houses, farms, mines, factories, and ships - would increase beyond calculation. San Francisco was destined to become the second, perhaps the first, city of the continent. The author worries, however, about the price that a greater, richer, and more powerful California will have to pay under "the great law of compensation which exacts some loss for every gain." Examining the effect of wealth and power on older areas of the East and of Europe, he concludes that the consequences of the coming of railroads to California will be a mixed blessing. He bemoans that much that gave charm and character to California life and its people will be lost. While the future looked fair and bright, he warns in conclusion, that was the same outlook for the builders of the Tower of Babel. Reprinted from *Overland Monthly*, October 1869. Illus., map.

D. L. Smith

1361. Gilbert, Heather. THE UNACCOUNTABLE FIFTH: SOLUTION OF A GREAT NORTHERN ENIGMA. *Minnesota Hist. 1971 42(5): 175-177*. Advances a solution to the mystery of who besides George Stephen (1st Baron Mount Stephen), Donald Alexander Smith (1st Baron Strathcona and Mount Royal), James Jerome Hill, and Norman Wolfred Kittson held a one-fifth interest in the St. Paul and Pacific Railroad (later the Great Northern Railroad) after these individuals gained control of it in 1878. In a recently discovered Stephen letter in the Royal Archives at Windsor Castle, Stephen related that John S. Kennedy, agent for the Dutch bondholders who sold the railway, received the extra one-fifth interest from him. Based on the Stephen letter and on secondary sources; illus., 10 notes.

G. R. Adams

1362. Greiner, Jean M. THE GOLDEN, BOULDER, AND CARIBOU. *Colorado Mag. 1967 44(4): 307-323*. The Golden, Boulder, and Caribou Railway Company was chartered in 1878 to construct a railroad to haul coal from the Marshall Coal Mining Company and other mines. The road was completed in 1878 and was highly successful. In 1879 it was bought by the Union Pacific and its subsidiary the Kansas Pacific. It continued to prosper as coal was big business in Colorado in the 1880's —for eight and a half years. However, a more direct line was built between Denver, Marshall, and Boulder by the Denver, Marshall and Boulder Railway Company, chartered in 1885, completed in 1886. This line had been built to an unexploited area and had prospered, but it too was replaced by a more efficient route. 7 illus., 100 notes.

I. W. Van Noppen

1363. Grey, Alan H. DENVER AND THE LOCATING OF THE UNION PACIFIC RAILROAD, 1862-1866. *Rocky Mountain Social Sci. J. 1969 6(2): 51-59*. Discusses the decisionmaking process in the 1860's of route selection for the Union Pacific Railroad and its bypass of Denver, Colorado. Tha author challenges the assumption that routes were laid out primarily for distributing goods and services and believes they were based on engineering and operations criteria. Map, 17 notes.

R. F. Allen

1364. Grey, Alan H. THE UNION PACIFIC RAILROAD AND SOUTH PASS. *Kansas Q. 1970 2(3): 46-57*. Discusses the Union Pacific's reasons for ignoring South Pass, Wyoming, in crossing the Continental Divide. The original strong predilection of Union Pacific engineers and executives away from South Pass can be properly understood only when it is recognized that the Union Pacific was originally designed to make money from its construction and not from its later operation. Congress by 1866 made construction of the railroad potentially profitable and relinquished all save minor engineering controls over the construction of the railroad. Thomas C. Durant guided the group which proposed to profit from construction of the Union Pacific. Lines were chosen on the basis of cheap construction and mileage, since cheap construction provided maximum profits on fixed congressional loans. Routes were not determined by the economic potentialities of the area served. Based on primary and secondary sources; 46 notes.

B. A. Storey

1365. Harnsberger, John L. JAY COOKE AND THE FINANCING OF THE NORTHERN PACIFIC RAILROAD, 1869-1873. *North Dakota Q. 1969 37(4): 5-13*. Recounts the efforts of Jay Cooke to arrange European and American financing for the sale of bonds of the Northern Pacific Railroad, resulting in extensive advertising in the United States and establishment of a branch office in London. Despite all efforts, Cooke had little success in marketing the bonds and overextended his house in meeting overdrafts of the railroad. Cooke pioneered in the field of banking-industry relationships, but failed to understand fully the limits of a banker's ability to be also a promoter, and the danger of freezing his assets in the bonds of the Northern Pacific. Based on private papers and secondary sources; 35 notes.

J. F. Mahoney

1366. Hauck, Cornelius W. THE COLORADO RAILROAD MUSEUM. *Hist. News 1967 22(9): 198-200*. In 1958 two railroad enthusiasts who had modest collections of yesterday's outmoded railroad equipment and records established the Colorado Railroad Museum between Denver and Golden, Colorado, to preserve historic material from early day railroading in the State and the Rocky Mountain area. The large museum building, styled as an old-fashioned masonry station, is filled with displays, a library, and records. On the 12 acres of grounds are displayed trackage, locomotives and cars, water towers, and other pertinent items. Plans are afoot to effect an orderly transition of the museum from a closely-held private into a public institution under nonprofit foundation ownership. 6 illus. D. L. Smith

1367. Hidy, Ralph W. and Hidy, Muriel E. JOHN FRANK STEVENS, GREAT NORTHERN ENGINEER. *Minnesota Hist. 1969 41(8): 345-361.* Sketches the career of civil engineer Stevens (1853-1943) and details his contributions to the Great Northern Railway Company and associated rail lines between 1889 and 1911. Already well-known among railroad engineers, Stevens earned wide acclaim in December 1889 when he explored Marias Pass, Montana, and determined its practicability for a railroad. While with the Great Northern lines of James Jerome Hill (1838-1916), Stevens, an efficient administrator with technical skills and imagination, discovered Stevens Pass through the Cascade Mountains, set railroad construction standards in the Mesabi Range of northern Minnesota, and supervised construction of the Oregon Trunk Line, which was completed in 1911. Although during his distinguished career Stevens served two years as chief engineer of the Panama Canal and headed the American Railway Mission to Russia in 1917, he regarded his association with the Great Northern as his most satisfactory experience. Based on company records, Stevens' recollections, and contemporary periodicals; illus., maps, 40 notes. G. R. Adams

1368. Hutchinson, W. H. SOUTHERN PACIFIC: MYTH AND REALITY. *California Hist. Soc. Q. 1969 48(4): 325-334.* Challenges several generally accepted beliefs about the Southern Pacific Railway, labeling them myths. The author justifies the policy of land grants to railroads by noting that the nation was lacking in cash and credit while rich in lands, and that land grant legislation offered the most feasible means of bringing these vast lands under settlement. Though the price was high, the nation willingly paid it. In response to the idea that the Central Pacific brought the Chinese to California, the author notes the presence of 35 thousand Chinese in the State by 1860. Rather than view the Southern Pacific as strangling the State economically, the author cites the tremendous economic expansion that came with rail transportation. Lastly, he dismisses the idea that the "Espee" dominated the politics of the State. In actuality, the Espee controlled the legislature for only a brief period and, during the period of its so-called "dominance," the railroad actually lost numerous political battles. The author believes that California's tremendous growth has been due to developments in transportation, from the oxcart to the airplane, with the railroads possibly having the greatest effect. A. Hoffman

1369. Inkster, Tom H. JOHN FRANK STEVENS, AMERICAN ENGINEER. *Pacific Northwest Q. 1965 56(2): 82-85.* Sketch of the skillful work of John F. Stevens in surveying for cross-country railroads, especially in Washington, and in assuring progress in the construction of the Panama Canal. C. C. Gorchels

1370. Kaplan, Michael. OTTO MEARS AND THE SILVERTON RAILROAD. *Colorado Mag. 1971 48(3): 235-254.* Following service in the Union Army, Otto Mears, an immigrant from Kurland, Russia, became interested in the settlement and mineral development of the San Juan district of southwestern Colorado. He first built toll roads there and in the late 1880's turned to railroad construction. Describes Mears' building of the Silverton Railroad, completed in 1889, and of the Silverton Northern with its various extensions (1889-96 and 1903-05) to serve nearby mining areas. Mears was an "organizational genius" possessing "inventive wizardry" (snowsheds and adaptation of the automobile to rails), "ability to win respect, trust, and affection of his subordinates," and "courage and optimism in the face of the most discouraging circumstances." After World War I Mears' lines declined. In 1930 the Silverton Northern ceased operation and in 1942 the rolling stock, engines, rails, and other equipment were removed. Illus., maps, 85 notes.

O. H. Zabel

1371. Ketterson, F. A., Jr. GOLDEN SPIKE NATIONAL HISTORIC SITE: DEVELOPMENT OF AN HISTORICAL RECONSTRUCTION. *Utah Hist. Q. 1969 37(1): 58-68.* Records how Congress acted to establish the Golden Spike National Historic Site, which was placed in 1965 under the administration of the National Park Service, and describes the program now in progress to restore on the site the scene as it was in 1896 when the last spikes were driven. A visitor center is also planned, and an illustration shows the architect's concept of that center. Photos. S. L. Jones

1372. Kraus, George. CHINESE LABORERS AND THE CONSTRUCTION OF THE CENTRAL PACIFIC. *Utah Hist. Q. 1969 37(1): 41-57.* Provides a sketch of how the Chinese railroad workers lived and worked, how they managed the finances associated with their employment, and concludes that Central Pacific officials responsible for employing the Chinese, even those at first opposed to the policy, came to appreciate the cleanliness and reliability of this group of laborers. There are many quotations from accounts by contemporary observers. Illus. S. L. Jones

1373. Lavender, David. FOR SALE: AN EMPIRE, 1,500 DOLLARS DOWN. *Am. West 1969 6(3): 6-12, 29-32, 62-63.* Five men contributed 1,500 dollars each for stock in the Central Pacific Railroad to finance preliminary surveying in California and lobbying in Congress. This narrative account traces the machinations, politics, and other tactics of Collis P. Huntington, Theodore D. Judah, Mark Hopkins, Charles Crocker, and Leland Stanford in California, Nevada, and Washington to secure passage of the 1862 law by Congress establishing the first transcontinental railroad. 10 illus., biblio. note. D. L. Smith

1374. LeMassena, Robert A. THE "OTHER PROMONTORY": THE TRUE TRANSCONTINENTAL HOOK-UP. *Kansas Q. 1970 2(3): 66-68.* The Union Pacific-Central Pacific route was not a true transcontinental hookup since there was no bridge across the Missouri River at Omaha. Passengers and freight had to be ferried across the river. The true hookup was made 15 August 1870 at Strasburg, Colorado Territory, on the Kansas Pacific. 3 notes. B. A. Storey

1375. Mann, David H. THE UNDRIVING OF THE GOLDEN SPIKE. *Utah Hist. Q. 1969 37(1): 124-134.* Describes the ceremony which occurred in 1942 at Promontory where in 1869 the driving of the last spike had signaled the completion of the first transcontinental railroad. The rails at that point and for 123 miles of the abandoned "Old Line" railroad were to be salvaged for use in war production. Included is a brief summary of how Brigham Young had fought for a southern route which would pass through Salt Lake City, of how Union Pacific authorities chose the more northern Promontory route over his protests, of the difficulties encountered on the route, and of the completion in 1904 of a more southern cut-off across Great Salt Lake which led to the obsolescence of the Promontory line. S. L. Jones

1376. Marston, O. Dock. FOR WATER-LEVEL RAILS ALONG THE COLORADO RIVER. *Colorado Mag. 1969 46(4): 287-303.* Describes the two parts of a survey made in 1889 for the proposed Denver (Colorado) Canon and Pacific Railroad. Under the prompting of Frank Mason Brown, Frank Clarence Kendrick surveyed the Colorado River from Grand Junction to the mouth of the Green River in 1889. Later the same year Brown himself, Robert Brewster Stanton, and a surveying party attempted to continue the survey from the mouth of the Green River on down the Colorado. The attempt ended in failure and the loss of the lives of several of the party, including Brown's. Two surveyors' inscriptions near the mouth of the Green River are reminders of the survey's failure. Illus., 14 notes. O. H. Zabel

1377. Mason, David T. THE EFFECT OF O. AND C. MANAGEMENT ON THE ECONOMY OF OREGON. *Oregon Hist. Q. 1963 64(1): 55-67.* Sketch of management and disposition of forests granted to the Oregon and California Railway, as influenced by governmental legislation in 1866 and 1937. C. C. Gorchels

1378. McAfee, Ward M. A CONSTITUTIONAL HISTORY OF RAILROAD RATE REGULATION IN CALIFORNIA, 1879-1911. *Pacific Hist. R. 1968 37(3): 265-279.* The apparent inability of the California Legislature to effectively regulate railroad rates led the constitutional convention of 1878 to create a railroad commission empowered to set maximum rates. Not the first State to create such a commission, it was, however, the first to provide for one in its constitution. Other interesting features of the California Railroad Commission included immunity of its rate schedules from judicial review. A direct object of such a powerful commission was the monopolistic power of the Southern Pacific Railroad. The reform was rendered ineffective by a commission friendly to the railroad and court emasculation of regulatory legislation. Effective reform did not come until 1911 when changes were made by the progressives. These too were short lived. 76 notes. D. L. Smith

1379. Mercer, Lloyd J.   LAND GRANTS TO AMERICAN RAILROADS: SOCIAL COST OR SOCIAL BENEFIT? *Business Hist. R. 1969 43(2): 134-151.* Attempts by the use of econometrics to determine the values of railroad land grants of the 19th century to the railroads and to society as a whole. The author summarizes and criticizes previous treatments of this subject and then discusses his own findings. Using only the Central Pacific and the Union Pacific systems as the basis for his investigation, the author concludes that the railroad owners received unaided rates of return which substantially exceeded the private rate of return on the average alternative project in the economy during the same period. Thus the projects turned out to be profitable although it was generally expected by contemporary observers that the roads would be privately unprofitable without the land grant aid. The land grants did not have a major effect, increasing the private rate of return only slightly. Nevertheless, it is contended that the policy of subsidizing those railroad systems was beneficial for society since the social rate of return from the project was substantial and exceeded the private rate by a significant margin. Based on published materials; 6 tables, 30 notes.
C. J. Pusateri

1380. Miner, H. Craig.   BORDER FRONTIER: THE MISSOURI RIVER, FORT SCOTT & GULF RAILROAD IN THE CHEROKEE NEUTRAL LANDS, 1868-1870. *Kansas Hist. Q. 1969 35(2): 105-129.* An account of the controversy between the Cherokee Neutral Land League and James F. Joy when the latter tried to build a railroad from Kansas City to Galveston. The affair was marked by violence in the field, newspaper propaganda and tricky political maneuvering in Topeka and Washington. The league's opposition to Joy has been credited to concern over the legality of his title to the land and to the settlers' desire to purchase their holdings at the minimum price. It is argued here that Joy's title was never in question and the settlers were not overcharged by the line. The real problem came because Joy's system was too efficient. Because he wished to open the country and provide business for his line, Joy sold his lands on conditions that prevented speculation. This angered the settlers and others who wished to make money on land speculation. Based on material in the Detroit Public Library and the Kansas State Historical Society; illus., 145 notes.
W. F. Zornow

1381. Miner, H. Craig.   THE COLONIZATION OF THE ST. LOUIS AND SAN FRANCISCO RAILWAY COMPANY, 1880-1882: A STUDY OF CORPORATE DIPLOMACY. *Missouri Hist. R. 1969 63(3): 345-363.* Attempts to show that some of the railroad manipulation of the late 19th century was accomplished by diplomatic means rather than by cutthroat competition and rate wars which many writers have stressed as the only weapons of the "robber barons." The railroad empires had alliances, mother countries, and colonies. A tripartite alliance brought the St. Louis and San Francisco into a colonial status under the Atchison, Topeka and Santa Fe, an arrangement that benefited the mother line and also compensated the colony with traffic agreements, rate advantages, and other considerations. After 1881 the railroad empires of Jay Gould and Collis Huntington placed the St. Louis and San Francisco in a similar colonial status. Based on newspapers, biographies, county histories, monographs, records of the St. Louis and San Francisco Railway; illus., map, 57 notes.
W. F. Zornow

1382. Miner, H. Craig.   THE STRUGGLE FOR AN EAST-WEST RAILWAY INTO THE INDIAN TERRITORY, 1870-1882. *Chronicles of Oklahoma 1969 47(1): 560-581.* In September 1870, a survey team for the Atlantic and Pacific Railroad camped along the Arkansas River in Indian Territory. They prepared to survey a route westward to the Colorado River, but were stopped by orders of the Superintendent of Indian Affairs when various Indians protested. The issue thus drawn took 12 years to decide. It became a question of whether the Indian way of life and previous treaty guarantees would stand in the way of expanding industrial America. Most in Congress favored treating the Indians as wards and inferiors and viewed the national interest as the higher consideration. In the end, Congress passed a bill to allow the railroad construction to proceed. By the time Oklahoma became a State in 1907, it had more than five thousand miles of track. Based on documents in the Oklahoma Historical Society, on Congressional records, and on secondary sources; illus., map, 76 notes.
K. P. Davis

1383. Myrick, David F.   THE RAILROADS OF SOUTHERN ARIZONA: AN APPROACH TO TOMBSTONE. *J. of Arizona Hist.* *1967 8(3): 155-170.* Studies railroads, both projected and actual, from the date of the construction by Tom Scott of the first main line across Arizona until 1960, also tracing the story of the many local lines built in the southern part of the territory. Many were narrow gauge. They all had in common two characteristics: they were built in response to the needs of mining and then abandoned when those needs passed. The author emphasizes the struggle to build a branch railroad to the town of Tombstone. This feat was finally accomplished in 1903, and the railroad saw wildly fluctuating use until 1960. Based on contemporary newspapers; illus., map, 55 notes.
R. J. Roske

1384. Nash, Gerald D.   THE CALIFORNIA RAILROAD COMMISSION, 1876-1911. *Southern California Q. 1962 44(4): 287-305.* Californians of the Progressive era learned the fruits of hard-won experience in the regulation of railroads from 1876 to 1911. The Railroad Commission generally was not successful in imposing rigid regulations upon the Southern Pacific and other carriers under its jurisdiction. Two decades of trial and error convinced the commissioners that they required larger appropriations and larger staffs to pursue their work. John Morton Eshleman and Max Thelen undertook an exhaustive study of public utility regulations which resulted in the Public Utilities Act (1911). Jurisdiction of the commission extended not only to railroads, but also to express companies, sea-going vessels within the State, gas and electric plants, water systems, and warehouses. The act outlined the procedure of the commission with authority to issue administrative orders concerning rate levels, service, safety regulations, and the floating of securities. 36 notes.
D. H. Swift

1385. Odom, E. Dale.   THE VICKSBURG, SHREVEPORT AND TEXAS: THE FORTUNES OF A SCALAWAG RAILROAD. *Southwestern Social Sci. Q. 1963 44(3): 277-285.* The trials and tribulations of a small Southern railway after the Civil War.
D. F. Henderson

1386. Overton, Richard C.   WHY DID THE C. B. AND Q. BUILD TO DENVER? *Kansas Q. 1970 2(3): 3-17.* Discusses the pressures placed on the Chicago, Burlington and Quincy Railroad Company by Jay Gould through such railroad lines as the Union Pacific, the Kansas Pacific, the Wabash, and the Missouri Pacific. Charles Elliott Perkins was the major Burlington official who met the challenges Gould repeatedly threw at the Burlington as the key railroad in the Iowa Pool. The result was several years of tension between the Gould system and the Burlington system. Finally in 1881 the Burlington aggressively faced Gould, and in 1882 opened a line to Denver. The Union Pacific was forced to make major concessions to the Burlington and to the Iowa Pool. Based on primary and secondary sources; 87 notes.
B. A. Storey

1387. Ozawa, Jirō.   JŪKYŪ SEIKI CHŪYO AMERIKA SEIBU NO TETSUDŌ [Railroads in the West in the mid-nineteenth century]. *Seiyōshigaku [Japan] 1969 82: 1-27.* Describes the political and economic aspects of the construction and management of railroads in the mid-19th century. Fits railroad construction into the context of the history of the United States.
M. Sagara

1388. Pennington, Loren E.   COLLIS P. HUNTINGTON AND PETER STUDEBAKER: THE MAKING OF A RAILROAD REBATE. *Southern California Q. 1971 53(1): 41-53.* A "case study of the relationship of a nineteenth century railroad with one of its principal shippers." The Studebaker Brothers Manufacturing Company of South Bend, Indiana, shipped large quantities of its buggies and wagons via the Central Pacific Railroad, but disliked the rates charged and demanded better ones. In particular, the Studebakers objected to the refusal of the railroad to use a standard rate for mixed shipments of wagons, buggies, and unassembled parts. For more than three years (1881-84), Peter Studebaker carried on a correspondence with Collis Potter Huntington of the Central Pacific concerning the matter. He finally succeeded in getting a monthly rebate from the railroad by his persistence and by threatening to have the company withdraw its patronage of the Central Pacific in favor of the water route around Cape Horn. The rebate was "a simple solution to rather complex problems of both the railroad and its customer." Based largely on papers in the Collis P. Huntington Collection at Syracuse University; 47 notes.
W. L. Bowers

1389. Petrowski, William R. THE KANSAS PACIFIC RAILROAD IN THE SOUTHWEST. *Arizona and the West 1969 11(2): 129-146.* Simultaneously with the race in the 1860's of the Union Pacific and Central Pacific to complete the first transcontinental railroad, the Kansas Pacific lauched its own grandiose scheme. Originally known as the Union Pacific, Eastern Division, and intended as a feeder line to the transcontinental system, Pennsylvania Railroad interests and Missouri financiers transformed it into the Kansas Pacific Railway. Aggressive lobbying worked for Federal support to build a railway from Kansas City (Missouri) to Colorado, to dip down to the 35th parallel, and from thence to the Pacific. The intent was to make it a part of a network with connections to the east coast. Although its aggressive policies did not result in construction beyond Colorado the lobbyists did force the Union Pacific to build in haste. The Eastern backers found an alternative transcontinental system in the Union Pacific which in 1880 absorbed the Kansas Pacific. 3 illus., map, 42 notes.

D. L. Smith

1390. Petrowski, William R. THOMAS C. DURANT AND THE UNION PACIFIC, EASTERN DIVISION. *Kansas Q. 1970 2(3): 58-65.* Outlines Thomas C. Durant's relationship to the parties who controlled the Union Pacific, Eastern Division. In 1864 Durant became involved in the railroad through contracts with Samuel Hallett, a New York promoter who had eased John C. Frémont, his partner, out of the project. In 1863 Hallet brought John D. Petty of St. Louis into the railroad. Perry struggled to obtain financial support which finally came from Thomas A. Scott of Philadelphia. In the process Perry staved off the claims of Durant. Finally Perry eliminated Durant's influence; in the meantime Durant's divided energies caused him to lose control of the Union Pacific also. Based mainly on primary sources; 32 notes.

B. A. Storey

1391. Reinhardt, Richard. OUT WEST IN A PALACE CAR. *Am. West 1967 4(4): 26-33.* Reprinted here from the author's recent (1967) book, *Out West on the Overland Train*, are two selections. The first, by Frank Leslie himself, appeared in *Frank Leslie's Illustrated Newspaper* in 1877 as "Thirty-Three Hundred Miles in a Pullman Car." With it are included 12 of the illustrations. The second is the author's own "The Creme of the Automatic Buffet," an account of a 1967 trip which compares travel in the age of the Vend-O-Mat with that in "the bygone era of napkin rings."

D. L. Smith

1392. Reinhardt, Richard. OUT WEST WITH THE ROWDY BRAKEMAN: A RECOLLECTION FROM THE AGE OF STEAM. *Am. West 1970 7(3): 29-37.* Brakemen had one of the most dangerous jobs on the railroad in the days of the steam locomotive. However, that job inspired boys and young men to take up railroad careers. Probably nowhere else was the brakeman's life any more difficult than along the Kansas cattle frontier in the 1870's. Harry French worked on this frontier and had a flair for recounting his adventures. With an introduction by the author, a part of French's memoirs are included herein. Extracted from *Workin' on the Railroad: Reminiscences from the Age of Steam* by Richard Reinhardt, ed. (Palo Alto, Calif.: Am. West, 1970). 9 illus.

D. L. Smith

1393. Rolston, Alan. THE YELLOWSTONE EXPEDITION OF 1873. *Montana 1970 20(2): 20-29.* Describes the effort to locate a route for the Northern Pacific Railroad between Bismarck (North Dakota) and Bozeman (Montana). In the early 1870's the company sent out surveying parties and the Army furnished military escorts. Progress was hampered by weather and rough terrain, as well as by Indian resistance. The survey in 1873 particularly brought out the rivalry between the Army and the Department of the Interior concerning the scientific aspects of such an exploration, as well as conflicts over Indian policy. Based on contemporary reports and correspondence; illus., 14 notes.

S. R. Davison

1394. Seymour, Silas. THE GREAT UNION PACIFIC EXCURSION, 1866. *Nebraska Hist. 1969 50(1): 27-53.* An account of a trip sponsored by the directors of the Union Pacific to the end of the track which was west of Cozad, Nebraska, in October 1866. That point had been reached a year earlier. Many notables were members of the large party that participated in the excursion.

R. Lowitt

1395. Smith, Victor C. THE BURLINGTON AND KANSAS CITY: A CHAPTER IN RAILWAY STRATEGY. *Kansas Q. 1970 2(3):*

78-87. In 1869 the Chicago, Burlington and Quincy Railroad opened the first railroad line between Chicago and Kansas City by using the track of the Hannibal and St. Joseph. Charles Elliott Perkins, who controlled the CB and Q, always thought in terms of stability. When Jay Gould gained control of the "St. Joe" in 1871, Perkins became uneasy. In 1883 the CB and Q bought control of the "St. Joe." By that time there were lines competing with the CB and Q between Kansas City and Chicago, but the CB and Q had the best line. In 1886 the Santa Fe began plans for a competitive line from Kansas City, its terminus, on to Chicago. This line was completed in 1888, and the Santa Fe then had the best rail connections between those two key cities. Perkins had failed to prevent this competition because of his cautious approach to the threat of a competitive parallel line. Based on primary and secondary sources; 49 notes.

B. A. Storey

1396. Snell, Joseph W. and Wilson, Don W. THE BIRTH OF THE ATCHISON, TOPEKA AND SANTA FE RAILROAD. PART I. *Kansas Hist. Q. 1968 34(2): 113-142; (3): 325-356.* Part I. This part is divided into two sections. The first deals with the organization of the Atchison and Topeka Railroad in 1859 and the reorganization in 1863 as the Atchison, Topeka and Santa Fe. The role of both State and National government in the organization of the line, the officers, the awarding of contracts, and the planning of the route are the most important topics covered. The second section describes the construction of the line from Topeka to Emporia between 1868 and 1870. All of this is done by using the local newspapers in Atchison, Emporia, Topeka, and Lawrence and through extensive quotation from the papers' coverage of the day-to-day progress of the line. Illus., 12 notes. Part II. Between 1870 and 1872 the railroad was built northeast from Topeka to Atchison and along a generally western line from Emporia to the Kansas boundary. The "Newton General Massacre" during which five men were killed and six wounded, some minor shootings in Dodge City, threats of Indian uprisings, and the financing of the extensions of the line are covered by the authors. There is also a recapitulation of later corporate mergers and the construction of the line outside Kansas. Based on newspaper accounts; illus., 21 notes.

W. F. Zornow

1397. Snell, Joseph W. and Richmond, Robert W. WHEN THE UNION AND KANSAS PACIFIC BUILT THROUGH KANSAS. *Kansas Hist. Q. 1966 32(2): 161-186 and (3): 334-352.* Describes the construction of the Union Pacific, Eastern Division, from Wyandotte, Kansas, to Denver, Colorado, between 1863 and 1870. The account utilizes quotations from newspapers and a collection of telegrams in the archives of the Kansas State Historical Society.

W. F. Zornow

1398. Storey, Brit Allan. THE KANSAS PACIFIC SEEKS THE PACIFIC. *J. of the West 1969 8(3): 402-415.* Tells of the publicity and lobbying activities of the Kansas Pacific Railroad in its attempt to become a transcontinental line in competition with the Union Pacific. Discusses the activities of Thomas A. Scott and William Jackson Palmer. The Kansas Pacific failed in its attempts.

R. N. Alvis

1399. Storey, Brit Allan. WILLIAM JACKSON PALMER: THE TECHNIQUE OF A PIONEER RAILROAD PROMOTER IN COLORADO, 1871-1880. *J. of the West 1966 5(2): 251-262.* Born in Delaware in 1836, William J. Palmer became interested in railroads at an early age. In 1855-56 he studied engineering abroad. After his return to America he became the private secretary of J. Edgar Thompson, president of the Pennsylvania Railroad. In 1861 he entered the Army as a captain. By the end of the war he was a brevet brigadier general. After the war he moved west to work for a railroad. In 1869 he became director of the Kansas Pacific and was in charge of its construction into Colorado. He began his business activity in Colorado in 1869. In 1870 he resigned from the Kansas Pacific and went to London on his honeymoon. There he promoted the construction of the proposed Denver and Rio Grande which had been incorporated before he left Colorado. He decided to develop an empire-like arrangement of land, coal, town, and mineral companies which would support and benefit from his pioneer narrow-gauge railroad. Back in Colorado he promoted bond issues by various communities with the pledge that the railroad would connect with them. He engaged in the Royal Gorge War with the Santa Fe and won this battle in the courts. His techniques are considered typical of the railway barons of his time. Based on Palmer Papers in the Colorado State Historical Society and published sources; illus., 20 notes.

D. N. Brown

1400. Thompson, Gerald E., ed. RAILROADS AND MINES IN ARIZONA: THE CRAM MEMOIR OF 1858. *Arizona and the West 1968 10(4): 363-376.* A private group of Eastern investors organized the Texas Western Railroad Company to promote a railroad from the Mississippi River to the Pacific over a southern route. Captain Thomas Jefferson Cram, a topographical engineer experienced in civil engineering, was hired to survey and publicize the project. Including some current ideas as well as some of his own conclusions, Cram published a *Memoir* in 1858. He proposed a railroad from Texas to new silver mines at Tubac in southern Arizona. From there it would go south into Sonora, Mexico, to the Gulf of California seaport of Guaymas. Besides the advantages of any transcontinental line, this one had two special ones - it would encourage exploitation of the rich Arizona mines, and it would be the shortest of all transcontinental lines. The pamphlet, herein edited, was calculated to attract Eastern mining capital, Southern agriculturalists, Arizona territorial boosters, and Sonora annexationists. Illus., map, 39 notes.

D. L. Smith

1401. Trennert, Robert A. A VISION OF GRANDEUR: THE ARIZONA MINERAL BELT RAILROAD. *Arizona and the West 1970 12(4): 339-354.* The Arizona Mineral Belt Railroad was the dream of Colonel James W. Eddy, an Illinois lawyer, politician, and Civil War veteran who moved to Arizona Territory for fame and fortune. In the early 1880's the mining fields around Globe were booming, and the east-west Atlantic and Pacific Railroad was being built across northern Arizona on its way to the Pacific. Eddy's north-south railroad would haul timber and supplies to the mines at Globe and ore to the transcontinental Atlantic and Pacific Railroad for shipment to the East. He began to put the Arizona Mineral Belt Railroad together in 1881. Eventually, the scheme was projected to a total length of 785 miles from Lee's Ferry on the north to Nogales on the South, but not even the original route was completed. Insufficient financial backing and over-evaluation of the potential business it could command were the principal difficulties in the way of realization of the Mineral Belt Railroad. In 1893, except for 12 miles near Flagstaff used for logging, the line and scheme were abandoned. 6 illus., map, 40 notes.

D. L. Smith

1402. Williams, James C. HORACE GREELEY IN CALIFORNIA, 1859. *J. of the West 1969 8(4): 592-605.* In 1859 Horace Greeley ventured on an extended trip into the Western States. He spent five weeks of the five-month journey in California. Greeley's visit was probably instrumental in attaining the eventual construction of the transcontinental railroad. To this latter subject he devoted many speeches while he was in California. Includes a chronology of his trip. R. N. Alvis

1403. —. IMPACT OF THE TRANSCONTINENTALS. *Oregon Hist. Q. 1966 67(2): 101-178.*
Peterson, Robert L. THE IDEA OF THE RAILROADS: REGIONAL ECONOMIC GROWTH, *pp. 101-104.*
Baker, Abner. ECONOMIC GROWTH IN PORTLAND IN THE 1880'S, *pp. 105-124.*
Shroyer, Peter A. OREGON SHEEP, WOOL AND WOOLENS INDUSTRIES, *pp. 125-138.*
Carter, George E. THE CATTLE INDUSTRY OF EASTERN OREGON 1880-90, *pp. 139-159.*
Cox, Thomas R. LOWER COLUMBIA LUMBER INDUSTRY, 1880-93, *pp. 160-178.*
Following an introduction by Peterson in which he surmises the actual value of new railroads to Oregon's frontier economy in the 1880's, the articles by the other authors give details about aspects of the basic industries: manufacturing and wholesaling in Portland, fish, wheat, sheep, wool, woolen textiles, cattle, and lumber. Availability of loan money, the influence of absentee management, and the uncertainties of water transportation are discussed. Documented. C. C. Gorchels

Water

1404. Barsness, Richard W. RAILROADS AND LOS ANGELES: THE QUEST FOR A DEEP-WATER PORT. *Southern California Q. 1965 47(4): 379-394.* "More than anything else, it was railroad developments which changed the base of the Los Angeles area's economy from grazing to diversified agriculture, tourism, and trade, and provided the

foundation for the modern development of the city itself, including its harbor." The first railroad in southern California was built in 1869 between Los Angeles and its harbor, San Pedro, and was quickly bought by the Southern Pacific, which attempted by means of high fares to encourage direct rail shipping from San Francisco to Los Angeles, rather than shipping by sea to San Pedro. The establishment of transcontinental links and the encroachment of the Santa Fe and Union Pacific into the Los Angeles area prompted the railroads to attempt development of a modern harbor for the area. They advanced rival plans for rival sites. A bitter fight resulted both for city support and for Federal funds. The eventual winner was San Pedro which had been backed by influential voices in the city of Los Angeles, though not by the Southern Pacific which did, however, end up controlling the harbor until World War I when the city itself took it over. 43 notes. A. K. Main

1405. Bowdern, T. S. JOSEPH LABARGE, STEAMBOAT CAPTAIN. *Missouri Hist. R. 1968 62(4): 449-469.* An account of the career of a man who was both an employee and a competitor of the American Fur Company. LaBarge's trading activities on the Upper Missouri, the business ventures in which he became involved, the ships he built to carry out his own trading ventures, the ships on which he served as pilot or master, and the forts and trading posts at which he transacted his business are detailed. The 53 years that LaBarge was on the river spanned the half-century during which the Missouri River trade was at its peak. The good and bad years of the Missouri River steamboat trade are mirrored in the successes and failures of this man's career. Based on articles and the standard works on the Missouri River trade; illus.

W. F. Zornow

1406. Bryan, Charles W. ABOARD THE "WESTERN" IN 1879. *Missouri Hist. R. 1964 59(1): 46-63.* Basing his work on local newspapers and family archives, the author describes in detail some of the more interesting and important trips that his father and grandfather made up the Missouri River from Yankton, Dakota Territory during the season of 1879. The *Western,* which was one of the freight and passenger vessels of the Missouri River Transportation Company, had a profitable season for its owners. It carried more tons of freight than any other of the company's ships, experienced fewer delays and suffered less damage. The last point is important, since these steamers were of light construction and, therefore, likely to be damaged in the shallow river.

W. F. Zornow

1407. Bryan, Charles W., Jr. DR. LAMME'S GALLANT SIDEWHEELER "YELLOWSTONE." *Montana 1965 15(3): 24-43.* Attempting to open the Yellowstone River to commercial navigation, Dr. Achilles Lamme operated a steamboat on that tributary and the adjacent Missouri River in the years 1876-79. Shallow and shifting currents doomed the experiment which ended with the boat's sinking near Miles City. Based on newspaper accounts, supplemented by family records in the author's possession. Illus. S. R. Davison

1408. Chittenden, H. M. REPORT ON STEAMBOAT WRECKS ON MISSOURI RIVER. *Nebraska Hist. 1970 51(1): 17-23.* An 1897 report by the Secretary of the Missouri River Commission, containing a list of steamboat wrecks which occurred on the Missouri River from the opening of steamboat navigation in the 1850's to 1897. The causes of the wrecks are also analyzed in this report. Reprinted from *Nebraska History* 1925 8(January-March). R. Lowitt

1409. Dethloff, Henry C. PADDLEWHEELS AND PIONEERS ON RED RIVER, 1815-1915, AND REMINISCENCES OF CAPTAIN M. L. SCOVELL. *Louisiana Studies 1967 6(2): 91-134.* The first steamboat appeared on Red River in 1815, but the river had been an important artery of transportation for the white man with the canoe, flatboat, pirogue, and raft in use. The century of the steamboat was a period of tremendous growth and activity that changed the region from a subsistence, frontier economy to a plantation and commercial industrial economy. Steamboating on Red River looms large in the history of the Southwest. Captain M. L. Scovell's manuscript is a condensed history of steamboating on Red River. G. W. McGinty

1410. Faulk, Odie B. THE STEAMBOAT WAR THAT OPENED ARIZONA. *Arizoniana 1964 5(4): 1-9.* In 1866 Captain Samuel Adams took the *Esmeralda* from Yuma over 500 miles up the Colorado to

Callville, the Mormon settlement, after two unsuccessful attempts. The result was lower freight rates, opening of markets to farmers and stockmen, reduction of the costs at which merchants could sell goods and miners could sell ores, and a saving to the government of thousands of dollars in transporting military stores. Adams had bucked powerful interests during his fight with the opposing steamship company, and suffered economically, professionally, and personally. The earlier history of attempts to bring freight up the Colorado is narrated. Illus., biblio.

E. P. Stickney

1411. Havighurst, Walter. STEAMBOAT TO THE ROCKIES. *Am. West 1970 7(5): 4-11, 61-62.* Steamboats were introduced to the Missouri River in 1819 when the *Independence* carried a cargo of supplies from Saint Louis upriver for 250 miles, and when the *Western Engineer* and three other steamers of an Army exploration expedition headed for the Yellowstone River. Navigational problems of the river itself and the technological inadequacies of the steamboats were temporary aggravations. Exploration, collection of scientific data, fur resources, Indian trade, the movement of troops, the transporting of military and civilian supplies, and the migration of settlers were all compelling incentives to make the Missouri River the principal transportation artery of the trans-Mississippi West. The author traces the history of the trials and errors of steamboat navigation on the Missouri to 1885, when the *Missouri* made the last trip through to Fort Benton, Montana. 7 illus., biblio. note.

D. L. Smith

1412. Hunt, John Clark. STEAMBOATS ON THE PLAINS. *Am. Hist. Illus. 1966 1(4): 51-57.* After the Lewis and Clark expedition, the rivers became the main artery for opening up the West to travel and trade. The first vessels were the fur steamboats that carried supplies for trappers and traded with the Indians. The *Yellowstone* was the first steamboat to go all the way to the Upper Missouri (1831). These early boats were plagued with epidemics of cholera and smallpox. They were also slow because they had to search continually for firewood and were always having to be pulled off sandbars. Following the fur steamboats up the rivers were the mountain steamboats. These were much larger and could carry much more cargo. Sixty ships reached Fort Benton on the Upper Missouri in 1878. However, by 1890 the river traffic had died because of the advancing railroad. The Missouri steamboat traffic was extremely important during the 19th century for opening the West to increased trade. 4 illus.

M. J. McBaine

1413. Lass, William E. STEAMBOATING ON THE MISSOURI: ITS SIGNIFICANCE ON THE NORTHERN GREAT PLAINS. *J. of the West 1967 6(1): 53-67.* Of the many rivers of the Great Plains, only the Missouri could be navigated by boats for long distances. Commerce on the river was early confined to fur traders. It was the American Fur Company which employed the first steamboat on the river in 1831. After that year the use of such vessels expanded rapidly, and they played an important role in transporting people and supplies to the mining areas. The Army on the northern plains received much of its supplies by water. The advent of the railroads changed the pattern of commerce and resulted in a decline in the importance of the steamboat to the development of the region. Based largely on published sources, illus., 27 notes.

D. N. Brown

1414. Nichols, Roger L. ARMY CONTRIBUTIONS TO RIVER TRANSPORTATION, 1818-1825. *Military Affairs 1969 33(1): 242-249.* The series of Army expeditions up the Missouri River in 1818-25 contributed to the technology of river travel. The steamboat *Western Engineer* of 1819 combined a very shallow draft with one of the earliest installations of a stern wheel and in 1819-25 Colonel Henry Atkinson experimented with keelboats having manpowered paddle wheels. Based on official records, private papers, and published works; 23 notes.

K. J. Bauer

1415. Petsche, Jerome A. UNCOVERING THE STEAMBOAT BERTRAND. *Nebraska Hist. 1970 51(1): 1-15.* Describes the uncovering of the steamboat *Bertrand*, sunk on the Missouri River en-route from St. Louis (Missouri) to Fort Benton (Montana) in an area known as DeSoto Bend on 1 April 1865. The location and excavation of the cargo in 1968-69 ended periodic searches by others stretching back nearly a century.

R. Lowitt

1416. Watson, C. B. AN ADVENTURE IN THE SURF. *Oregon Hist. Q. 1965 66(2): 171-177.* The author's experiences as a participant in the rescue of men from the wrecked steamer *Tacoma* 1883. Illus.

C. C. Gorchels

1417. White, Wayne R. FACTORS ASSOCIATED WITH THE ERAS OF INLAND WATER CRAFT IN NINETEENTH CENTURY TEXAS. *Southwestern Social Sci. Q. 1964 45(2): 149-155.* Brief history of three eras of inland water transportation in Texas: era of the pirogue, 1800-20; keel and flatboat age, 1820-30; dominance of steamboats, 1830-90. Competition from railroads, reliance on one commodity - cotton, high insurance rates, and hazards posed by bridge building ended the steamboat age by the 1890's.

D. F. Henderson

Society

General

1418. Carstensen, Vernon. THE WEST MARK TWAIN DID NOT SEE. *Pacific Northwest Q. 1964 55(4): 170-176.* Examples of humor, often in the forms of irony and pathos, found in the life of pioneers and empire builders in the Pacific Northwest in the middle of the 19th century. Businessmen, legislators, newspapermen, and educators are among the men who demonstrated the humorous point of view.

C. C. Gorchels

1419. Davis, Ronald L. SOILED DOVES & ORNAMENTAL CULTURE: KANSAS COWTOWN ENTERTAINMENTS. *Am. West 1967 4(4): 19-25, 69-70.* The drama of the shoot-out and the pathos of the wages of sin have occupied most of the attention of pulp writers and historians of the West over the years. In striking contrast was the endemic yearning for respectability and refinement. A prime example of this was in the Kansas cowtowns where respectability versus moral anarchy was quite apparent. Abilene, Ellsworth, Newton, Wichita, and Dodge City all contained considerable numbers of solid citizens who were "moral to the point of prudery." Depravity usually flourished, despite efforts to control it, south of the railroad tracks and during nights of the summer months the title was one of the names given to the prostitutes who flourished on the south side of the tracks. Home-owned books, subscriptions to eastern magazines and newspapers, pianos in homes, and theaters (opera houses) that supported traveling performers as well as local amateurs were some of the more self-evident symbols of refinement. The dichotomy was not a complete one, however. There was an intermingling from both sides of the tracks and a pragmatic mutual tolerance. 5 illus., biblio. note.

D. L. Smith

1420. Dykstra, Robert R. TOWN-COUNTRY CONFLICT: A HIDDEN DIMENSION IN AMERICAN SOCIAL HISTORY. *Agric. Hist. 1964 38(4): 195-204.* Although scholars in all the social science disciplines have studied conflict between urban and rural communities, little attention has been paid to the conflict between towns and farmers. The existence of such conflict is illustrated by the relationships between the people of Kansas cattle towns and farmers of the surrounding areas in the 1870's and 1880's. Townspeople opposed seeking relief from the national government and from older communities for farm families in distress, fearing such an appeal would deter further settlement of the land. Based on newspapers of the period.

W. D. Rasmussen

1421. Egan, Ferol and Hutchinson, W. H. THE WEST OF "OUT OUR WAY." *Am. West 1970 7(3): 18-25.* The *Out Our Way* cartoons of James Robert Williams (1888-1957) were a vehicle to memorialize the humor of the West. His cast of characters portrayed people he had known. Sugar, the ranch cook who knew his way of life was ended, engaged in a symbolic struggle with Stiffy, the romantic cowhand who refused to concede that the only way of life he considered worthwhile was a thing of the past. The burlesque and exaggeration that Williams used as a basis for laughter were posited on the reality of his memory. *Out Our Way* of the 1920's, 1930's, and to the end of World War II, was "another last gasp" from the American West of yesterday. 11 cartoons.

D. L. Smith

1422. Larson, T. A. DOLLS, VASSALS, AND DRUDGES - PIO-NEER WOMEN IN THE WEST. *Western Hist. Q. 1972 3(1): 4-16.* Population in the Territory of Wyoming plummeted after the completion of the transcontinental railroad. In 1869 the half-bachelor territorial legislature passed a woman suffrage law. The most effective arguments in favor of this precedent were assurances that the Territory would thereby receive much free publicity and advertising and that it would promote immigration, including significant numbers of women. For varying reasons enough momentum developed so that the Western States, except New Mexico, had all granted the franchise to women by 1914. Kansas was the only State outside the western third of the country to enact such legislation. No simple explanation explains the West's priority in the matter of woman suffrage. One suffragette insisted that to deprive women the right to vote kept them from self-development. Keeping this opportunity from them made "dolls of society women, vassals of most wives, and hopeless drudges of the rest." Illus., 13 notes.   D. L. Smith

1423. Larson, T. A. WOMAN SUFFRAGE IN WYOMING. *Pacific Northwest Q. 1965 56(2): 57-66.* Evidence on why woman suffrage came to Wyoming first, with the history of events and people contributing to the successful enfranchising of women. One section gives the reasons for women enjoying voting rights without other political power in early days.   C. C. Gorchels

1424. MacCracken, Brooks W. THE CASE OF THE ANONY-MOUS CORPSE. *Am. Heritage 1968 19(4): 50-53, 73-77.* In 1878, 33-year-old John W. Hillmon, a resident of Lawrence, Kansas, married Sallie Quinn, a local waitress. Hillmon bought two 10-thousand-dollar life insurance policies and set out with a friend, John H. Brown, to find a suitable ranch. Following a preliminary search, Hillmon returned from Wichita, bought a third life insurance policy, and returned south where he was accidentally shot and killed by Brown at Medicine Lodge on 17 March 1879. Upon examination, insurance officials did not believe the dead man was Hillmon. Sallie disagreed and she pressed the matter in six court battles (1882-1903), two of which ended at the Supreme Court. The Supreme Court heard the case in 1892 (Insurance Company vs. Hillmon, 145 U.S. 285) and decided in favor of the insurance companies. With the Populist movement the case took on political overtones - Sallie became the victim of eastern money. Insurance firms eventually settled with her for 35 thousand dollars, including accumulated interest. Based on primary sources; 6 photos.   J. D. Born, Jr.

1425. Martin, Charles W. HERNDON HOUSE REGISTER, 1865-1866. *Nebraska Hist. 1967 48(1): 27-43.* A listing with brief biographical sketches of the important people who stayed at the Herndon House in Omaha in 1865 and 1866.   R. Lowitt

1426. McDonough, Marian M. QUEST FOR HEALTH, NOT WEALTH, 1871. *Montana 1964 14(1): 25-37.* Account of a family's migration from Chicago to Colorado, and settlement in the Colorado Springs area. Based on the diary of Mary Eliza Willard Young, whose illness occasioned the trip.   L. G. Nelson

1427. Poulsen, Ezra J. PARISIAN LIFE - WESTERN STYLE. *Idaho Yesterdays 1964 8(1): 2-9.* Memoirs of the author's boyhood at the turn of the 20th century in the small Mormon community of Paris, in southeastern Idaho. The author draws on the reminiscences of pioneers for the earliest history of the settlement. He places great emphasis on the social history of the small agricultural community.   M. Small

1428. Riley, Paul D., ed. RED WILLOW COUNTY LETTERS OF ROYAL BUCK, 1872-1873. *Nebraska Hist. 1966 47(4): 371-397.* Letters describing the first two years of a settlement at the mouth of Red Willow Creek. Comments on settlement, government, immigration, agriculture, Indians, buffalo, weather, and related topics present a picture of frontier conditions.   R. Lowitt

1429. Shumate, Albert. RINCON OR TELEGRAPH HILL: ROB-ERT LOUIS STEVENSON'S INTRODUCTION TO THE SOUTH SEAS. *California Hist. Soc. Q. 1967 46(3): 223-234.* Clears up the confusion as to the location of the home of Charles Warren Stoddard who introduced Stevenson to the South Seas. The evidence cited shows that the Stevenson-Stoddard meetings were on Rincon Hill not on Telegraph Hill. Illus., 27 notes.   E. P. Stickney

1430. Smith, Martha Browning. THE STORY OF ICARIA. *Ann. of Iowa 1965 38(1): 36-64.* An account of the communistic community established by the Icarian Society in Adams County, Iowa, in 1860. The society's origins and its unsuccessful ventures in Texas and Illinois are discussed. The Adams County community grew out of a schism in the Nauvoo settlement, with one group acquiring land near Corning, Iowa. By 1876 the land was paid for and the French community had acquired considerable assets. The same year saw a division in the community with the more conservative members establishing New Icaria one mile away. The group inhabiting the original site soon moved to California. New Icaria was dissolved in 1895 due to the desire of younger members to acquire personal property and pursue vocations of their choice. Illus., 22 notes.   D. C. Swift

1431. Spence, Clark C. KNIGHTS OF THE TIE AND RAIL - TRAMPS AND HOBOES IN THE WEST. *Western Hist. Q. 1971 2(1): 4-19.* The West was the favorite locale and the beneficiary of the peculiar contributions of the knight of the tie and rail. It was his land of milk and honey, adventure, scenery, and easy living. California was his particular paradise. The western vagabond came with the railroads and was a familiar sight in almost all parts of the West from the 1870's to World War II. By the 1880's he replaced the "redskin" in the public mind as a public menace, as an evil, shiftless, thieving beggar. In time he came to be regarded as a carefree, roving dreamer. While there were many forces that attracted or pushed him into such a situation, the ranks of the hobo (a migratory worker) or tramp (a migratory nonworker) expanded and contracted with the rise and fall of the national economy. The hobo laborer was found particularly in truck gardening, in fruit and hop harvesting through the Far West, and in the prairie wheat harvests of the Great Plains. Increasing refusal of western railroads to carry harvest labor free and mechanization-shortened harvest periods were principal factors in the decline of the hobo population. Improvements in railroad technology sorely reduced the hobo and tramp traffic. The knight of the tie and rail, with his marginal, reckless way of life, contributed to the tradition of mobility associated with the American frontier. Illus., note.   D. L. Smith

1432. Storke, Thomas M. A GLIMPSE OF SANTA BARBARA IN THE 1890'S. *Noticias 1966 12(4): 13-15.* Describes the social life of Santa Barbara in the 1880's and 1890's, which was centered around the Arlington Hotel. Tourists came especially in January, February, and March, and the clientele included east coast millionaires, Presidents, and a king. Fishing and riding were attractions, and so was poker, which the author played with mayors and sheriffs while "the three newspapers of the times had been carrying on a crusade against gambling." Photo.   T. M. Condon

1433. Sweetzer, Paul G. HISTORY OF SANTA BARBARA'S FIESTA "OLD SPANISH DAYS IN SANTA BARBARA." *Noticias 1966 12(3): 1-26.* The first fiesta in 1820 was occasioned by the dedication of Santa Barbara's mission. Richard Henry Dana in *Two Years Before the Mast* described a wedding celebration in 1836. The coming of California's first bishop, García Diego, to Santa Barbara in 1842 was marked by a celebration. There were many other occasions for fiestas through the years, but not until 1924 was the first "Old Spanish Days" held with its historical parade which has since become an annual event. Illus.   E. P. Stickney

1434. Tamony, Peter. MARTINI COCKTAIL. *Western Folklore 1967 26(2): 124-127.* The etymology, evolution, and history of the martini cocktail, the word and the drink, are traced. The author claims California as the matrix for the concoction and the 1860's as the probable time. 7 notes.   D. L. Smith

1435. Tamony, Peter. WESTERN WORDS. *Western Folklore 1965 24(2): 115-118.* Traces the development of the 10-gallon or Texas hat from the early sombrero to the hats which are given away by President Lyndon Johnson. Based on secondary sources.   J. M. Brady

1436. West, Elliott. OF LAGER BEER AND SONOROUS SONGS. *Colorado Mag. 1971 48(2): 108-128.* Investigates the history of temperance and prohibition sentiment and accomplishments in Colorado before 1900. Even in the earlier mining camps of the mountains there was considerable prohibition sentiment, institutionalized especially in the Independent Order of Good Templars. On the plains, colonies such as Greeley, Longmont, and Colorado Springs were limited to temperate members. Political and legal accomplishments of prohibitionists were few before 1900, limited mainly to the Scientific Temperance Instruction Act of 1887 and the "high license" law of 1889. This was so partly because political prohibitionists "preferred uncompromising high-mindedness to practical gains." However, "a foundation was laid for a broad temperance movement, which would produce majorities in the plains, mountains, and cities in the triumph of 1914." Illus., 117 notes.   O. H. Zabel

1437. Wilson, L. W., ed. REMINISCENCES OF JIM TOMM. *Chronicles of Oklahoma 1966 44(3): 290-306.* A biographical narrative by the Negro Jim Tomm who was born a slave near Muskogee in 1859. Tomm describes his parentage, life on the plantation, shoe and soap making, the log house with shake-shingle roof, grinding corn and wheat. He describes also many of the events and battles during the Civil War, the Green Peach War between the Spieche and Checote factions, tribal laws and courts, hauling freight, toll bridges and ferries, steamboats, saltworks, ranches, churches and schools, Indian cooking and crafts, allotments, railroads, and the Snake uprising. His narrative reveals much of the life and many of the homely conditions of the period. Illus., 4 notes.
I. W. Van Noppen

Immigration and Minority Groups

1438. Almaguer, Tomás. TOWARD THE STUDY OF CHICANO COLONIALISM. *Aztlan 1971 2(1): 7-21.* Analyzes the shifting nature of the Chicano as the object of Anglo colonialism. At the end of the Mexican-American War the Chicano in the Southwest was in the "classic colonial" situation, i.e., a Chicano majority in its homeland under the control of the Anglo conquerors. By the time of statehood this had shifted to an "internal colonial" situation, i.e., a Chicano minority governed as a colonial people by an Anglo majority. 22 notes, biblio.
G. L. Seligmann, Jr.

1439. Andrews, Thomas F. FREEDMEN IN INDIAN TERRITORY: A POST CIVIL WAR DILEMMA. *J. of the West 1965 4(3): 367-376.* In 1866 the Five Civilized Tribes and the United States concluded new treaties. During the Civil War factions of all these tribes had aided the Confederacy, and the United States forced the tribes to cede land for the use of other Indians and freedmen. Initially the Choctaw and Chickasaw asked that the ex-slaves be removed from their district and settled on ceded land. This was in accordance with the wishes of the freedmen, but in 1869 they held a meeting and expressed a desire to stay in the district. This was agreeable to the Choctaw and Chickasaw, but at a later date the Indian leaders sought to have the Negroes removed. In 1881 a Freedmen's Oklahoma Association was formed for the purpose of promoting colonization of surplus Indian land by freedmen. Little came of this, but in the 1880's the Choctaw adopted their freedmen as citizens with full tribal rights. The Chickasaw did not. The author maintains that the dilemma of the freedmen attracted the nation's attention to the unoccupied lands of Oklahoma and led to their settlement by whites. Based on Congressional documents and published sources, 56 notes.
D. N. Brown

1440. Archibald, Edith. SWEDISH FOLKLORE FROM THE IDAHO WHITE PINES. *Western Folklore 1965 24(4): 275-280.* Centers in northern Idaho, around Troy. Contains some of their songs, games, and stories of their difficulty with English.   J. M. Brady

1441. Bakanowski, Adolf. MY MEMOIRS - TEXAS SOJOURN (1866-70). *Polish Am. Studies 1968 25(2): 106-124.* Describes early life in Panna Maria, the first permanent Polish settlement in the United States and what is sometimes called the "Polish Jamestown." 14 notes.
S. R. Pliska

1442. Barth, Gunther. CHINESE SOJOURNERS IN THE WEST: THE COMING. *Southern California Q. 1964 46(1): 55-67.* The adaptation of the credit-ticket system to the passage between Hong Kong and San Francisco extended the physical and social framework of the Chinese world to California. "Chinese merchants utilized district companies and kinship organizations as instruments of extra-legal control and secured

the continuation of the pattern. The application of the traditional mode of Chinese emigration to the passage facilitated transplanting the system of oppression." Because they pursued the dream of returning home, these Chinese immigrants of the 1850's and 1860's remained apart from the flood of permanent immigrants. Documented.   E. P. Stickney

1443. Bell, Howard H. NEGROES IN CALIFORNIA, 1849-1859. *Phylon 1967 28(2): 151-160.* During the period between 1849 and 1859 Negroes accounted for about one percent of the population of California. Of activity by free Negroes prior to 1854 little is known, but a society composed of at least 37 members existed in San Francisco in 1849. Early in their California history the Negroes encountered discrimination. In 1855 the Mayor of Sacramento vetoed a measure to authorize a school for Negroes. The majority of the City Council overrode the veto and the press denounced the Mayor's action. Significant State conventions were held by Negroes in 1855, 1856, and 1857 in an effort to attack the problem of inequality before the law from the State level. Despite their protests little or nothing was accomplished in the matter of securing the right to testify in court. By the decade's end there were some hopeful signs. There was an indication of an organized effort to improve education in San Francisco. Still, Negroes had no right to testify in California courts and recognition of the right of suffrage was far in the future. Based on newspaper sources, 62 notes.   D. N. Brown

1444. Berneking, Carolyn E. THE WELSH SETTLERS OF EMPORIA: A CULTURAL HISTORY. *Kansas Hist. Q. 1971 37(3): 269-280.* Most of the Welsh settlers who arrived in Emporia after 1857 came to find land. Most liked their new home and became permanent residents. Cites a few families and individuals to show the nature of the Welsh settlement in Emporia. The settlers provided a valuable addition to the town's economic life, but their main contributions were in other areas. They were a deeply religious people, and their church organizations became the center of their cultural life in Kansas. Singing contests developed in connection with their congregations; solos, sight-reading contests, and chorus singing made for a number of festive occasions in Emporia. Based on secondary sources; 69 notes.   W. F. Zornow

1445. Berwanger, Eugene H. THE "BLACK LAW" QUESTION IN ANTE-BELLUM CALIFORNIA. *J. of the West 1967 6(2): 205-220.* Emigration of free Negroes into the western territories was often discouraged by the adoption of "Black Laws" which usually curtailed civil rights and sometimes prevented their residence. In California civil rights restrictions were enacted but attempts at Negro exclusion failed. The author traces the various restrictions imposed upon Negro residents and the effect they had on migration. The conclusion is that attempts at Negro exclusion failed because of fear of congressional opposition, the more weighty problem of Chinese immigration, and the diverse character of the population. Documented from newspapers and other published primary and secondary sources, 39 notes.   D. N. Brown

1446. Berwanger, Eugene H. WESTERN PREJUDICE AND THE EXTENSION OF SLAVERY. *Civil War Hist. 1966 12(3): 197-212.* An account of the attempts to establish slavery in Illinois, Indiana, Kansas, California, and Oregon, in the 45 years prior to the Civil War. These efforts failed not so much because of antislavery, as of anti-Negro sentiments. The author points out that in the old Northwest as well as the new Far West dislike of the Negro was widespread and the people did not want them around, either as slaves or free persons. And since slavery would bring the Negro in, the exclusion of slavery would keep him out. Many Republican leaders capitalized on this feeling with great success, and protection of white labor was a more important concern to the party than uplifting the Negro. Based on contemporary newspapers and numerous primary and secondary sources.   E. C. Murdock

1447. Beyer, George R. PENNSYLVANIA GERMANS MOVE TO KANSAS. *Pennsylvania Hist. 1965 32(1): 25-49.* Traces the extremely interesting story of immigration of Pennsylvania Germans in the late 19th century. Discusses the factors and motivations involved in their moving, the problems encountered, and the significant achievements of a few. Their move is viewed as part of a national trend in westward expansion rather than an isolated phenomenon.   W. B. Miller

1448. Bieter, Pat. FOLKLORE OF THE BOISE BASQUES. *Western Folklore 1965 24(4): 263-270.* Tells the hopes of the Basques, primarily those in Boise, Idaho, in coming to America. Also relates their attempts to keep alive their native culture. J. M. Brady

1449. Blodgett, Ralph E. THE COLORADO TERRITORIAL BOARD OF IMMIGRATION. *Colorado Mag. 1969 46(3): 245-256.* Traces the slow growth of Colorado's population in the 1860's and its rapid growth in the 1870's. The need for food products and the desire to achieve statehood, to develop Colorado's resources, and to broaden the tax base all encouraged promotion of settlement. While other agencies contributed to rapid settlement in the 1870's, "the Board of Immigration, created by the territorial legislature on February 9, 1872, was one of the most important." The Board collected information about the territory and distributed it in printed form through appointed agents in England, Germany and the United States. By statute, the Board went out of existence at the end of 1873 and was not re-created, although new agencies to promote immigration were set up in 1889 and 1909. Photo, 55 notes.
O. H. Zabel

1450. Braun, Florence S. JOHN STOLFA, SR.: FROM TISTIN, MORAVIA IN 1866 TO ARDMORE, OKLAHOMA IN 1966. *Chronicles of Oklahoma 1967 45(3): 307-311.* John Stolfa, Sr., migrated to the United States from his native Czechoslovakia in 1889. He settled in Texas as a tailor. Caught up in the panic of 1893, he moved to Indian Territory (present Oklahoma) where he engaged in a variety of business enterprises. He celebrated his 100th birthday in 1966. Written by his daughter, based on Stolfa's reminiscences and family records.
D. L. Smith

1451. Caldwell, Dan. THE NEGROIZATION OF THE CHINESE STEREOTYPE IN CALIFORNIA. *Southern California Q. 1971 53(2): 123-131.* White Californians between 1848 and 1890 systematically converted their image of the Chinese in their midst into that of the Negro. This "negroization" process involved seeing the Chinese as possessing the same characteristics as Negroes, e.g., degraded, filthy, intellectually inferior. Using articles and cartoons from magazines of the period, shows the evolution of the Chinese stereotype to the point at which it took on all aspects of the "negroid" stereotype. Based on contemporary sources; 5 illus., 32 notes. W. L. Bowers

1452. Chafe, William H. THE NEGRO AND POPULISM: A KANSAS CASE STUDY. *J. of Southern Hist. 1968 34(3): 402-419.* Seeking to explain why populism failed as a biracial movement, the author analyzes the "attitudes, aspirations, and concerns" of the Negro community in Kansas, and concludes that the Negro and white Populists actually did not share a common self-interest. Whereas whites were primarily concerned about economic issues, Negroes sought security against prejudice and violence as well as stability and status from the white community. This divergence of interest prompted Negroes to support the rich and wellborn white class that had traditionally befriended them. Thus, it is important "that historians concerned with Negro-white relations look at the Negro as an active participant instead of as a passive observer and recognize that the Negro's peculiar history and experience have given him a set of assumptions, perceptions, and interests which may be quite distinct from those of his white counterpart." 68 notes.
I. M. Leonard

1453. Chu, George. CHINATOWNS IN THE DELTA: THE CHINESE IN THE SACRAMENTO-SAN JOAQUIN DELTA, 1870-1960. *California Hist. Soc. Q. 1970 49(1): 21-37.* While most Chinese in California have lived in urban areas since 1900, an exception for many years was the Chinese who worked as tenant farmers and migrant laborers in the Sacramento-San Joaquin Delta region. From the 1870's on, large corporations controlled the land, while the Chinese "boss system" dominated the lives of the Chinese workers. As the business of agriculture developed, the various races working in the Delta region came to specialize in certain crops; asparagus became the specialty of the Chinese after 1900. Chinatowns flourished at Rio Vista, Courtland, Locke, Walnut Grove, and Isleton. Asparagus production peaked and then declined, followed closely by river Chinatowns. One by one the asparagus canneries closed; the Chinese workers grew old, left the region for the cities, or died, and no young Chinese replaced them. By 1960 little remained of the Chinese presence in the delta save a few hundred old men who, ironically, live under conditions remarkably similar to those which caused the original immigrants to leave the Pearl River Delta of China in the first place.

Based on government documents, reports, newspapers, personal interviews, and published works; illus., photos, 63 notes. A. Hoffman

1454. Cohen, Thomas. FIRST JEWISH COMMUNITY SITE - LOS ANGELES. *Western States Jewish Hist. Q. 1969 1(3): 89-108.* Describes the present status of the site of the Hebrew Cemetery. Also traces the origin of the Hebrew Benevolent Society of Los Angeles and the founding of the cemetery by the society in 1855. This site, the corner of Lilac Terrace and Lookout Drive, was acquired from the city council by the society, the first charitable organization in Los Angeles, and the deed was recorded 17 April 1855. Describes the dedication of the site as a State historical landmark in 1968. Illus., 3 photos, 72 notes.
R. E. Levinson

1455. Coleman, Marion Moore. KALIKST WOLSKI IN TEXAS. *Texana 1967 5(3): 203-214.* A Polish engineer educated in France, Kalikst Wolski came to America in 1852. In 1855 he led a group of colonists to a site near Dallas where they founded the colony of La Réunion. The author takes three stories from Wolski's memoirs, *Do Ameryki i w Ameryce - To America and In America* (Lemberg, 1876). The first is an account of a visit to a Galveston lighthouse. In the second Wolski relates stories he has heard of the hypnotic powers of rattlesnakes. Lastly, he tells the story of a woman saddened by the experience of having her daughter die in her arms from being scalped by Indians. 11 notes.
W. A. Buckman

1456. Coleman, Marion Moore, trans. and ed. NEW LIGHT ON LA REUNION, FROM THE PAGES OF "DO AMERYKI I W AMERYCE." *Arizona and the West 1964 6(1): 41-68, (2): 137-154.* Part I. French Socialist Victor Prosper Considérant formed a company and planned a colony in Texas for his Old World Followers. In 1853 he visited and designated a location on the Trinity River, a few miles to the west of Dallas, Texas. La Réunion was to be a utopian experiment in cooperative living, based principally on agriculture. Some 300 French, Belgian, Swiss, and German colonists arrived in 1855 and 1856. Disharmony, poor soil, and drought combined to wreck the experiment, and by 1857 many of the residents moved to Dallas, settled with Louisiana French in New Orleans, or returned to France. Among the first settlers at La Réunion was Kalikst Wolski, a Polish engineer who had fled to France when the 1830 Polish revolt against Russia crumbled and who became *persona non grata* in France following the 1851 coup d'état of Louis Napoleon. Wolski fled to the United States where he became proficient in English and studied a socialist utopian settlement in New Jersey. At the request of Considérant, Wolski went to New Orleans to become the guide and interpreter for a group of colonists who were coming from Europe to the new socialist community in Texas. In 1876 Wolski published the recollections of his experiences in Texas for the February-November 1855 period as several chapters in his *Do Ameryki i w Ameryce* To America and in America. This is one of few accounts of the founding and fate of the La Réunion experiment. Translated and edited here are four chapters of the 1877 Polish edition which describe the journey of the Wolski party by sea and land from New Orleans to La Réunion. Map, 50 notes. Part II. Contains comments and diary excerpts from Wolski's book concerned with conditions and personalities in the ill-fated colony. Map, illus., 29 notes.
D. L. Smith

1457. Coleman, Marion Moore. THE POLISH ORIGINS OF BANDERA, TEXAS. *Polish-Am. Studies 1963 20(1): 21-27.* Credits the true beginning of the town to 16 Polish families who settled there in 1844. Names some of the settlers and describes the early cypress shingle industry. The fact is lamented that even though Polish names appear in the community today, the Polish language of the founders is long gone.
S. R. Pliska

1458. Crouch, Barry A. and Schultz, Leon J. CRISIS IN COLOR: RACIAL SEPARATION IN TEXAS DURING RECONSTRUCTION. *Civil War Hist. 1970 16(1): 37-49.* Using Texas as an example, the authors analyze Comer Vann Woodward's theory that true racial segregation in the South did not emerge until the 1890's. With respect to segregated education, urban ghettos, harsh vagrancy laws, political and social disabilities, and violent treatment, Texas Negroes were "put in their place" during Reconstruction, not in the 1890's. E. C. Murdock

1459. Cutler, Lee. LAWRIE TATUM AND THE KIOWA AGENCY, 1869-1873. *Arizona and the West 1971 13(3): 221-244.* Iowa Quaker farmer Tatum became agent of the Kiowa Indian Agency in southwestern Indian Territory (Oklahoma) in the summer of 1869. He was to implement the new Federal Peace Policy by checking the raiding propensities of the Kiowa (whose culture was war-centered) by anchoring them to their reservation and by encouraging them to become sedentary farmers. His efforts resulted in construction of agency buildings, opening of a school, and introduction of full-scale cultivation. Tatum's Quaker reliance on peaceful measures to win the confidence of the Kiowa and Quaker rejection of the idea of use of the military force to keep them on the reservation only resulted in open scorn and defiance for his efforts. Frustrated and disillusioned over the Peace Policy, Tatum resigned and was replaced in early 1873 by another Quaker. 4 illus., 2 maps, 52 notes.
D. L. Smith

1460. Dahlie, Jorgen. OLD WORLD PATHS IN THE NEW; SCANDINAVIANS FIND FAMILIAR HOME IN WASHINGTON. *Pacific Northwest Q. 1970 61(2): 65-71.* Describes promotional efforts of the ethnic press and other agencies to bring immigrants, especially Scandinavians, to Washington. These efforts resulted in a fourfold increase in the State's population between the years 1890-1910. In the decade ending in 1910 the State's growth rate was six times that of the Nation as a whole, and 500 thousand inhabitants of foreign extraction were living in Washington. Allusions are made to experiences of individual immigrants and promoters.
C. C. Gorchels

1461. Davis, Charles K. A COLONY IN KANSAS - 1882. *Am. Jewish Arch. 1965 17(2): 114-139.* This account describes one of the attempts to settle East European Jewish immigrants on the land. Beersheba Colony, near Cimarron, Kansas, was assisted by Cincinnati's Hebrew Union Agricultural Society in order to provide better homes and livelihood than obtainable in the crowded tenement districts of eastern cities. Charles K. Davis of Cincinnati joined the Beersheba colonists to help guide them in farming; excerpts of his 1882 diary contains an appeal by the eminent Rabbi Isaac M. Wise for support of this settlement program as a major effort of the Russian Emigrants' Aid Society.
J. Brandes

1462. Dermigny, Louis. AUX ETATS-UNIS: "FRONTIERE" ET NOUVELLE "FRONTIERE" [In the United States: "frontier" and new "frontier"]. *Annales: Economies, Sociétés, Civilisations [France] 1963 18(3): 561-567.* Comment on an Italian translation of Francis Parkman, *The Oregon Trail,* and a French edition of Mario Einaudi, *The Roosevelt Revolution,* seeing them as examples of Italian interest in American history and the theme of the frontier, America being viewed as the frontier of Europe. There is also comment on the Supreme Court in connection with Jean-Pierre Lassale, *La Cour Suprème et le problème communiste aux Etats-Unis* (Paris, 1960) and on the Philippines in connection with George Fischer, *Un cas de décolonisation: Les Etats-Unis et les Philippines* (Paris, 1960).
R. Howell

1463. Douglass, William A. THE BASQUES OF THE AMERICAN WEST: PRELIMINARY HISTORICAL PERSPECTIVES. *Nevada Hist. Soc. Q. 1970 13(4): 12-25.* The Basque people are stereotyped as sheepherders in the eyes of many students of Western history. Most present-day sheepherders in the American West are Basques, but they are also heavily involved in the sheep industry as foremen, buyers, transporters, and ranch owners. For the past several centuries there has been a high rate of emigration of Basques from France and Spain. The Basques contributed greatly to Latin-American history and today are a business elite in many nations of Latin America. The most famous Basque in Latin-American history was Simón Bolívar. The Basques entered Nevada in the 1870's and immediately became excellent sheepherders. The Basques tend to do well in any profession to which they dedicate themselves, especially professions involving physical labor. The aim of most Basques who came to Nevada was to get into the business of owning sheep. Some succeeded, but others remained herdsmen. Photo, 9 notes.
E. P. Costello

1464. Drake, Donald E., II. MILITANCY IN FORTUNE'S NEW YORK AGE. *J. of Negro Hist. 1970 55(4): 307-322.* Timothy Thomas Fortune founded and edited *The New York Age* during the 1880's. This newspaper stood out as an uncompromising and independent voice of Negro militance in a period known for "accommodation" by the Negro community. Fortune built the *Age* into the leading Negro newspaper in the United States, but its circulation never exceeded ten thousand. The *Age* gave the Republican Party "its Civil War and Reconstruction dues," and supported the use of political power by Negroes whenever possible. Fortune opposed emigration to Africa; instead he supported the creation of a Negro State in the Oklahoma Territory. Strong emphasis on racial pride underscored most of the militance expressed in the *Age;* Fortune insisted that Negroes needed to develop their own separate culture. In his later years Fortune grew so disillusioned that he took up writing pamphlets for Marcus Garvey's Back to Africa Movement. 53 notes.
R. S. Melamed

1465. Earl, Phillip I. NEVADA'S ITALIAN WAR, JULY-SEPT., 1879 (SOMETIMES KNOWN AS THE "CHARCOAL WAR" OR THE "COAL BURNER'S WAR"). *Nevada Hist. Soc. Q. 1969 12(2): 47-87.* Recounts the events leading up to the killing of five Italian immigrant charcoal burners by a Sheriff's posse near Fish Creek, Eureka County, Nevada, on 18 August 1879. The author attempts to rectify misinterpretations of the causes of this event. The Eureka Mining District had 800 men employed as charcoal burners in 1877-79, of which 90 percent were of foreign extraction, primarily Italian. Charcoal burning was not a well-paying job and the living conditions of the burners were very poor. Attempts of the burners to raise charcoal prices aroused the animosity of the mine owners who were the sole customers. The burners desired to deal directly with the mine owners but the mine owners would deal only with the teamsters who hauled the charcoal to the mine smelters. Despite some support of the burners from the local population, the situation got out of hand. Responsibility for the shooting at Fish Creek cannot be fixed. The Eureka Mining District declined in the 1880's and 1890's and never recovered. Based on official reports, journals, and newspaper accounts; 165 notes.
E. P. Costello

1466. Eickenroht, Marvin. THE KAFFEE-KIRCHE AT FREDERICKSBURG, TEXAS, 1846. *J. of the Soc. of Architectural Historians 1966 25(1): 60-63.* A brief account of the octagonal church built in the German settlement of Fredericksburg, Texas, in 1846. A replica was constructed on a slightly different site in 1934-35. Based on histories of the early German settlements in Texas; illus.
D. McIntyre

1467. Ekman, Ernst. SWEDISH CONSULAR REPORTS FROM SAN FRANCISCO A CENTURY AGO. *Swedish Pioneer Hist. Q. 1968 19(3): 162-173.* The reports of consuls accredited by Sweden and Norway to the United States in the 19th century provide a great amount of information on Scandinavian immigrants in the United States. The reports that were filed by the consuls are currently stored in Stockholm, Sweden, and are available to scholars. Typical information contained in the reports includes suggestions on the trade possibilities for Scandinavian countries in California, descriptive material on California, reports on the doings of Scandinavian immigrants, and observations on the California and US political scene. 25 notes.
E. P. Costello

1468. Ewers, John C. WHEN RED AND WHITE MEN MET. *Western Hist. Q. 1971 2(2): 133-150.* It is more accurate to study the history of the Indians in the American West in a context of Indian-white confrontation than it is to consider this history as background material for understanding of one of the minority group problems which plague the country today. The Indians have always been different from any other of the ethnic minorities. A large and complex body of laws gives Indians certain rights and privileges shared by no other groups, whether minority or majority. The collective label is misleading: there were scores of independent villages or tribes of Indians, and no political, cultural, or linguistic unity. Most Indian groups distrusted one another as much as they distrusted the first white invaders. In the Indian-white confrontation, both races made substantial contributions, positive and negative, to total world culture. Historians and anthropologists should not try to expiate any sense of guilt about present-day problems by rewriting the history of the American West so that all Indians become "red knights in breechclouts" and all whites "pantalooned devils." Instead, all data should be weighed so that both sides can be given fair treatment. 19 notes. Banquet address, Tenth Annual Western History Association Conference, 9 October 1970.
D. L. Smith

1469. Faulk, Odie B. THE ICARIA COLONY IN TEXAS, 1848. *Texana 1967 5(2): 132-140.* The word Icaria suggests romance and distance. This was the name chosen by Etienne Cabet for his colony in Texas. Cabet was a French utopian-socialist. His attempt to bring his ideas to reality in Texas was a total disaster, mainly due to a misunderstanding in his acquisition of the land. The exact story of this attempt to found a colony is quite unclear, because the group was secretive, far from other settlements, and did not keep records. Uses this incident to illustrate some of the problems of historiography. 25 notes.   W. A. Buckman

1470.   Feld, Lipman Goldman.   NEW LIGHT ON THE LOST JEW-ISH COLONY OF BEERSHEBA, KANSAS, 1882-1886.   *Am. Jewish Hist. Q. 1970 60(2): 159-168.* Of the eight attempts to establish Jewish agricultural colonies in Kansas, Beersheba was the first and most success-ful. Sponsored by the Hebrew Union Agricultural Society in Cincinnati, the colony was established in 1882 and survived until 1885. Improper planning, insufficient training, and poor relations involving management and settlers, all caused the colony to fail. 27 notes.   F. Rosenthal

1471.   Fernandez, Ferdinand F.   EXCEPT A CALIFORNIA IN-DIAN: A STUDY IN LEGAL DISCRIMINATION.   *Southern Cali-fornia Q. 1968 50(2): 161-175.* An account of the legal discrimination practiced against California Indians. In the past, so-called "vagrancy laws" have bound Indians to forced labor for periods up to 15 years while other laws have denied them access to certain occupations. All California Indians were prohibited from buying and using liquor until 1953 and they could not legally possess firearms and ammunition between 1850 and 1913. California Indians were also the victims of social discrimination in the form of enforced segregation with respect to education. Moreover, they were denied citizenship and the concomitant rights to vote, hold office, and serve on juries until 1924. Only in the area of hunting and fishing have the laws been lenient. Here Indians have been exempted from the requirement of a license to hunt and fish, the prohibition upon the building of weirs in rivers to trap salmon, and other fish and game law provisions. The author closes on an optimistic note: while earlier legisla-tion concerning California Indians was often oppressive, today it is friendly and more just. Based on California statutes, other public docu-ments, and secondary sources; 96 notes.   W. L. Bowers

1472.   Fierman, Floyd S.   THE IMPACT OF THE FRONTIER ON A JEWISH FAMILY: THE BIBOS.   *Am. Jewish Hist. Q. 1970 59(4): 460-522.* Discusses the careers of members of the Bibo family and their role in the early history of New Mexico Territory in general merchandis-ing, sutlery, railroad extension, and both exploitation and protection of Indians. Emphasizes the careers of Nathan Bibo and his brother Solomon. Altogether, seven brothers and three sisters of the Bibo family left a lasting impression in their descendants, who were Indian and Roman Catholic, as well as Jewish. Based on original letters, reminiscences, and photographs; 8 photos, 40 notes, 12 appendixes.   F. Rosenthal

1473.   Friedmann, Robert.   THE RE-ESTABLISHMENT OF COM-MUNAL LIFE AMONG THE HUTTERITES IN RUSSIA (1858): A NEWLY DISCOVERED SOURCE.   *Mennonite Q. R. 1965 39(2): 147-154.* The communal life *(Gemeinschaft)* of the Hutterites, which had been established around 1530, began to fade away by the end of the 16th century in Europe and by the early 19th century in the Ukraine. The discovery of the account of Michael Waldner, the Hutterite brother who was chosen a preacher in 1858, throws light on the renewal of communal life. During an illness he had a vision which led to the restoration of communal living. In 1874, to escape military conscription in Russia, the group went to Bon Homme County, South Dakota. A year later Waldner returned to Russia and brought back several more families to America. Reproduces an account by his son.   E. P. Stickney

1474.   Geffen, Joel S.   JEWISH AGRICULTURAL COLONIES AS REPORTED IN THE PAGES OF THE RUSSIAN HEBREW PRESS HA-MELIZ AND HA-YOM.   *Am. Jewish Hist. Q. 1971 60(4): 355-382.* Considerable material on the almost 25 collective agricultural settle-ments in the United States appeared in the Russian Hebrew press in the 1880's. Ideological motivations and the constantly worsening situation in Russia made emigration necessary; thus the experiences in America aroused a great deal of interest, and the failure of most of these settlements caused much despair. The documents deal with Sicily Island (Louisiana), Alliance (South New Jersey), New Odessa (Oregon), and Winnipeg, Can-ada.   F. Rosenthal

1475.   Gilbert, Glenn G.   ENGLISH LOAN-WORDS IN THE GER-MAN OF FREDERICKSBURG, TEXAS.   *Am. Speech 1965 40(2): 102-112.* Deals with changes in grammar, pronunciation, and vocabulary as used by the Texas Germans. From the 1840's until the turn of the century, the German language became corrupted by its English environ-ment, whereupon a deliberate (even pedantic) effort was made to restore purity. World War I, however, cut short any German renaissance. The author presents many examples of changes and notes with surprise that these same changes occurred independently in other parts of the United States where German has been spoken for a long time. Based on personal experience; 38 notes.   R. W. Shoemaker

1476.   Goodwyn, Lawrence.   POPULIST DREAMS AND NEGRO RIGHTS: EAST TEXAS AS A CASE STUDY.   *Am. Hist. R. 1971 76(5): 1435-1456.* Decades of monoracial scholarship have imbedded a surprising amount of uninterpreted white supremacist material in schol-arly literature. Available sources of the details of interracial tension in the post-Reconstruction South, written by white politicians, law enforcement officials, and on occasion, by terrorists, generally reflect a strident bias. Recourse to Negro oral sources may impart new meaning to existing written sources. The article is a demonstration of the use of oral history techniques to supplement written sources. The area of inquiry concerns the forms of the destruction of an indigenous black Republican political structure that persisted in rural, cotton-producing Grimes County, Texas, for 35 years following the Civil War. Despite strenuous efforts by Demo-cratic partisans, the Grimes County People's Party, an interracial coali-tion of radical agrarian whites and black Republicans, repeatedly won elections through 1898. In 1899, defeated Democrats organized a new institution, the White Man's Union, to achieve political victory through the disfranchisement of blacks. A campaign of terrorism resulted in the murder of three Populist leaders, the exodus of a large number of third-party supporters, including approximately one-half of the county's black population, and Democratic political ascendancy within a vastly reduced electorate. The internal politics of the interracial coalition is assessed, as is the reputation of the White Man's Union as a civic enterprise for governmental reform.   A

1477.   Gressley, Gene M.   THE FRENCH, BELGIANS, AND DUTCH COME TO SALT CREEK.   *Business Hist. R. 1970 44(4): 498-519.* The "history of the Salt Creek oil field [in Wyoming], since its first recognition by the prospector, has been the scene of international corporate struggles, bitter claim disputes, unbelievable fraud, and wild political machinations." French, Belgian, and Dutch financiers were at-tracted partially by dishonest promotional activities and partially from the general financial "milieu existing in their countries in the early years of the twentieth century." They failed, however, "to send to Wyoming a cadre of managerial and technical talent" as they had to the Baku fields in Russia. "This failure, more than any other single factor, explains why the French, Belgians, and Dutch lost out in the scramble for dominance in the Salt Creek field," Nevertheless, they had "been a significant force in opening up one of the major oil fields in the United States." Based mainly on company records; 83 notes.   C. J. Pusateri

1478.   Gronowicz, Antoni.   PRELUDE IN AMERICA.   *Arizona Q. 1963 19(2): 127-134.* Helena Modjeska was induced to come to San Francisco with her husband and son, in response to letters from Henryk Sienkiewicz begging her to help the Polish immigrants in California found a center of Polish culture. The author describes in detail the events and circumstances leading up to her eventual signing of a two-year contract for a tour of the United States and Canada.   E. P. Stickney

1479.   Halvorsen, Helen Olson.   19TH CENTURY MIDWIFE: SOME RECOLLECTIONS.   *Oregon Hist. Q. 1969 70(1): 39-49.* Recol-lections of a woman who was born in Wisconsin in 1863, the daughter of Norwegian immigrants, dealing with domestic incidents of her life in Wisconsin, Minnesota, and Oregon. Emphasis is on her experiences as a midwife and as a mother of eight children of her own.

C. C. Gorchels

1480.   Hart, Charles Desmond.   SLAVERY EXPANSION TO THE TERRITORIES.   *New Mexico Hist. R. 1966 41(4): 269-286.* Born in Connecticut, educated at Yale and the Litchfield Law School, Truman Smith served in the Connecticut legislature, the U.S. House, and finally the U.S. Senate. When he arose on 8 July 1850 all the great speeches on the compromise had been delivered. The heart of his speech was a definitive statement that "the natural limits of slavery expansion" had been reached in New Mexico and Utah. Portions of the speech reproduced in the article were taken from the *Congressional Globe.* 24 notes.

D. F. Henderson

1481. Hess, Mary. PIONEERING IN KANSAS - EARLY HESSTON, I. *Mennonite Life 1971 26(3): 127-132.* In the late 19th century many Mennonites from Pennsylvania moved to Kansas. A number of them settled in Harvey County and founded the town of Hesston. Discusses the activities of these pioneers and the nature of life in early Hesston. 3 photos. Article to be continued. J. A. Casada

1482. Hill, Burton S. FRONTIER POWDER RIVER MISSION. *Ann. of Wyoming 1966 38(2): 214-222.* Discusses the efforts of the German Evangelical Lutheran Synod of Iowa to establish an Indian mission on the Powder River in 1859-60. The missionaries spoke only German, had little knowledge of Indian culture, and lacked adequate economic support, and their first efforts failed. Still, they did establish a headquarters at Deer Creek, and from there they worked among several tribes. They enjoyed a degree of success among the Cheyenne tribes, but apparently were not able to maintain their work because of Indian wars and U.S. Indian policy which moved the tribes to other areas. Illus.

R. L. Nichols

1483. Hill, Burton S. THOMAS S. TWISS, INDIAN AGENT. *Great Plains J. 1967 6(2): 85-96.* Twiss (1803-71), a graduate of the U.S. Military Academy at West Point (1826), taught at South Carolina College (1829-47), worked for industry (1847-55), and became a U.S. Indian Agent of the Upper Platte District in 1855 first at Fort Laramie and then at Deer Creek. He took an Ogalala wife, worked well with the Indians and supported more western military posts and the introduction of agriculture and Christianity to the Indians. He was charged with misusing government property and had difficulty cooperating with the military. In 1861, after Lincoln's election, he resigned but continued, for a time, to live at Deer Creek. His last years were spent at Nebraska City and Rulo, Nebraska. His wife and six children survived him. Two sons were scouts for General Crook in 1876 and one was among the first recruits for Carlisle Indian School in 1879. The name "Twiss" is still common among the Sioux. Illus. O. H. Zabel

1484. Hoglund, A. William. FINNISH IMMIGRANT FARMERS IN NEW YORK, 1910-1960. *In the Trek of the Immigrants: Essays Presented to Carl Wittke* (Rock Island, Illinois: Augustana Coll. Lib., 1964): 141-155. To replace the New England descendants who no longer stayed on the land, promoters tried to attract immigrant farm buyers to the hill country of Tioga, Chemung, and Tompkins Counties. The Finns who came were chiefly from the Finnish communities of Michigan, Wyoming, Pennsylvania, Minnesota, and Ohio, where they had been carpenters, miners, or steel workers. They began with dairying and raising chickens for the New York City market. But by 1957 barns were deteriorating on unused farms as they had before 1910, while immigrant institutions like the church and the cooperative declined. Only a few of the second generation took up farming. 55 notes. E. P. Stickney

1485. Humphreys, A. Glen. THE CROW INDIAN TREATIES OF 1868: AN EXAMPLE OF POWER STRUGGLE AND CONFUSION IN UNITED STATES INDIAN POLICY. *Ann. of Wyoming 1971 43(1): 73-89.* As a result of northern plains tribes' violent resistance to white encroachment upon Indian lands during the 1860's, Congress appointed an eminent commission in 1867 to arrange permanent reservations for the affected tribes. In contrast to the previous practice of conquest and destruction, the treaties proffered by the Indian Peace Commission represented a humanitarian approach to Indian policy. Several tribes accepted commission treaties, and the Mountain Crow signed after the commissioners promised to close Army forts on the Bozeman Trail and to protect the Crow from their traditional enemies, the Sioux. Although the senate ultimately ratified this treaty, the government displayed its usual inefficiency in dealing with Indians when a House-Senate dispute over control of Indian policy, and Congress' preoccupation with Reconstruction, prevented ratification of a similar treaty which a special agent had negotiated with the Prairie Crow. Based primarily on newspapers and government documents; 53 notes, biblio. G. R. Adams

1486. Hunt, John Clark. CALIFORNIA'S CHINESE CIVIL WAR. *Am. Hist. Illus. 1966 1(8): 56-58.* Describes what must be the most unusual battle ever fought in America—between two factions of Chinese in the California gold camp of Weaverville in 1854. The Cantons, or Young Woes, defeated the Hongkongs, or Ah Yous, but they used pistols to do it—the agreed-upon rules allowed only medieval pikes.

J. D. Filipiak

1487. Illick, Joseph E. "SOME OF OUR BEST FRIENDS ARE INDIANS...": QUAKER ATTITUDES AND ACTIONS REGARDING THE WESTERN INDIANS DURING THE GRANT ADMINISTRATION. *Western Hist. Q. 1971 2(3): 283-294.* Unlike Federal efforts and the attitudes of much of the mainstream of the American people, the Society of Friends was motivated by high ideals and achieved considerable success in dealings with the Indians. Occasionally the Quakers worked with and through government agencies. After the Civil War their slavery abolition energies were rechanneled to improve the conditions of the Indians of the trans-Mississippi West. They became the principal instruments for the operation of President Ulysses Simpson Grant's peace policy. For over a decade, 1869-85, they served as appointed agents on the various western reservations and superintendencies in a program of moral uplift and manual training. Their efforts to achieve acculturation failed because of reasons external to the experiment: frontier land hunger and Congressional patronage politics. With the collapse of government sponsorship, the Quakers quietly went to work outside the system. Biblio. D. L. Smith

1488. Jacobs, Wilbur R. THE FATAL CONFRONTATION: EARLY NATIVE-WHITE RELATIONS ON THE FRONTIERS OF AUSTRALIA, NEW GUINEA, AND AMERICA - A COMPARATIVE STUDY. *Pacific Hist. R. 1971 40(3): 283-309.* The real test of survival for a native group is the possession of the land. Compares the survival history of the American Indians, the Australian aborigines, and the natives of New Guinea, all of whom had similar civilizations in harmony with their surroundings before the advent of the white man. Only the Papuans have been able to maintain a strong identity with, and a great mass of, their land. On the contrary, the Indians and aborigines have been forced from their land with little or no regard for property rights. This pattern can continue unless the white man learns to understand and value native culture and rights. 85 notes.

E. C. Hyslop

1489. Johansen, Dorothy O. A WORKING HYPOTHESIS FOR THE STUDY OF MIGRATION. *Pacific Hist. R. 1967 36(1): 1-12.* Using Oregon and California as examples, the author postulates that "(1) Migrants who choose one destination over another alternative of approximately equal economic advantage have in common a range of value expectations which, insofar as they are realized or rationalized, are factors in the establishment of a differentiated community; and (2) the first settlers determine the character of a community and by communicating their value satisfactions or dissatisfactions to potential migrants, they, in effect, 'select' the migrants who will follow and thereby perpetuate the character of the differentiated community." 9 notes.

J. McCutcheon

1490. Jordan, Terry G. THE GERMAN SETTLEMENT OF TEXAS AFTER 1865. *Southwestern Hist. Q. 1969 73(2): 193-212.* Scholarly research of German immigration and colonization into Texas has largely emphasized the antebellum period, but "more Germans came to Texas after the Civil War...than came in the entire thirty-odd years of immigration before the war...." Perhaps this neglect may be due to the less romantic aspects of the postwar immigration: the Germans came not as pioneers, as they had in the antebellum years, but as secondary settlers of a market-oriented culture. Traces the German movements in all directions, citing the impetus of the railroads, the collapse of slave plantations which divided salable lands into small holdings, and the mobility of the Anglo-American settlers who pushed further west and thus allowed Germans to take up residence. After 1865, and particularly with the new waves of immigration in the 20th century, the urban German element developed rapidly. However, the influx of Latin Americans, Anglo Americans, and Negroes into the cities, as well as the scattering of the German population into different areas of the cities and suburbs, has led to a percentage decline of Germans in the cities and is also responsible for the disappearance of the previously common "German quarters."

R. W. Delaney

1491. Kelley, John P. and Timberlake, Charles E. IMPRESSIONS OF RUSSIAN PIONEERS IN THE WEST. *New Mexico Hist. R. 1967 42(2): 145-150.* Impressions of A. S. Kurbskii, "member of the Russian gentry," of the American West and the cowboy. Based on Kurbskii's book, *Russkii rabochii u severoamerikanskogo plantatora* [A Russian worker with a North American planter] (St. Petersburg, 1875).
D. F. Henderson

1492. Kempner, Isaac Herbert. MY MEMORIES OF FATHER. *Am. Jewish Arch. 1967 19(1): 41-59.* Excerpts from *Recalled Recollections* (Galveston, 1961) by the author whose father, Harris Kempner, came to America from Russian Poland in 1854. The senior Kempner established a thriving wholesale food business in Texas before the Civil War, later operating in Galveston. Details of life in Galveston in the 1870's and 1880's are coupled with accounts of a boarding school education in Virginia and New Orleans, then at Washington and Lee University. There is some discussion of the senior Kempner's philosophy as an immigrant, naturalized American, and religious Jew, including the principles of charity and personal liberty. In 1895 the elder Kempner died, and his son continued to build the family's business interests. Illus.
J. Brandes

1493. Kolehmainen, John I. SUOMALAISET AMERIKASSA: ASUTUS JA TYÖOLOT [The Finns in America: settlement and employment]. *Turun Historiallinen Arkisto [Finland] 1967 19: 257-268.* Describes various types of employment entered into by Finnish immigrants to the United States in the late 19th and 20th centuries. Mining was most important, followed by dock work on the Great Lakes, fishing on the Columbia River, lumbering, factory employment, and domestic service for women. Many immigrants later founded farms on marginal land, though much of this land is again deserted today. Job opportunities, rather than geographical preference, determined Finnish settlement patterns. The text is in English.
R. G. Selleck

1494. Lapp, Rudolph M. JEREMIAH SANDERSON: EARLY CALIFORNIA NEGRO. *J. of Negro Hist. 1968 53(4): 321-333.* Traces the movement and activities of Jeremiah B. Sanderson, a New Bedford free Negro. He went to California in 1854 where he became an outstanding leader as an educator and churchman. In the 1850's he was active in the Negro convention movement and after the Civil War he supported the movement for full civil rights. In all his activities he avoided controversy with other Negro leaders, working for harmony rather than dissension. He was killed in a railroad accident in 1875. Based on newspaper and manuscript sources; 49 notes.
L. Gara

1495. Lapp, Rudolph M. NEGRO RIGHTS ACTIVITIES IN GOLD RUSH CALIFORNIA. *California Hist. Soc. Q. 1966 45(1): 3-20.* The activities of the small Negro population in early California bear witness to the inaccuracy of the idea that the American Negro did little in his own behalf. Slavery was unconstitutional in the new state. The free Negro told his black brother that in California he had a legal chance for freedom. After several cases in court, it became apparent that, at least in San Francisco and Sacramento, the California Negro had an increasing number of white friends. In 1855, the California Negroes held their First Colored Convention, organized by the Franchise League and mainly concerned with testimony rights in civil and criminal cases where white men were also involved. An anti-Negro immigration bill died in 1858. The decade of the 1860's saw the rise of the fortunes of the California Negro. "By the time of the Fourth Colored Convention of 1865," the testimony laws having been revised, "the Negro leadership was turning itself to the problems of education and suffrage." Based on official sources; 63 notes.
E. P. Stickney

1496. Larn, Hubert. "FANTASTIC HILDA" - PIONEER HISTORY PERSONIFIED. *Swedish Pioneer Hist. Q. 1964 15(2): 63-76.* An interview with Swedish-born American pioneer Mrs. Hilda Erickson who, in 1963, celebrated her 104th birthday. Her story begins when she, her mother, and two of her brothers left Sweden in 1866 (the rest of the family followed later), sailed the Atlantic, rode from New York to Saint Joseph by rail, journeyed up the Missouri River to Omaha, and then joined a wagon train traveling to Grantsville, Utah. In Grantsville, Hilda later married John August Erickson and began a career which included roles as wife, mother, grocer, midwife, farmer, dentist, doctor to the Indians, and seamstress. Photo.
K. Chappell

1497. Larson, T. A. EMANCIPATING THE WEST'S DOLLS, VASSALS AND HOPELESS DRUDGES: THE ORIGINS OF WOMAN SUFFRAGE IN THE WEST. *U. of Wyoming Pub. 1971 37: 1-16.* Examines the reasons the Territories of Wyoming and Utah adopted woman suffrage in 1869. Expediency rather than liberal democratic attitudes moved both governments. Wyoming legislators wanted to gain free publicity, to attract a female population to their territory, to immortalize themselves, and to embarrass the Governor. In Utah the major reasons were a desire for equal justice for women and an attempt to counteract the campaign against polygamy. Older reasons such as chivalry, strengthening the home against transients and bachelors, and rewarding helpmates cannot be substantiated by facts. In every western State, different factors worked for woman suffrage. 85 notes.
H. B. Powell

1498. Lazar, Robert J. JEWISH COMMUNAL LIFE IN FARGO, N.D.: THE FORMATIVE YEARS. *North Dakota Hist. 1969 36(4): 346-355.* The first Jewish settlers arrived in Fargo in 1880 and were of the middle-class German reform Judaism. Later a large immigration of Eastern European Orthodox Jews who were attempting to escape oppression introduced a lower class of Jews. Smallpox, tornado damage, fire, and floods caused great damage to Jew and Gentile alike between the years 1890-1900. Three obstacles to the organization of Jewish religious life were the small numbers of Jews, the cultural differences between the German and East European settlers, and the great number of differences between the religious traditions. An Orthodox congregation was founded in 1896 in Fargo. By 1907 a synagogue was built and a school to educate Jewish youth was started. Above all else the early Jewish community attempted to retain their cultural heritage. Later they tended to evolve from an ethnic community into a status community, but only after some of the Jews gained the highest status and class position as the most privileged group among those with whom they lived. This is a modification of a general principle concerning conditions under which an ethnic community will change its original form. Based on newspaper, book, and documentary sources; illus., photos, 15 notes.
E. P. Costello

1499. Levinson, Robert E. JULIUS BASINSKI: PIONEER MONTANA MERCHANT. *Yivo Ann. of Jewish Social Sci. 1969 14: 219-233.* Describes the life of Julius Basinski, an immigrant Jew who settled in Montana in the last half of the 19th century. Discusses the fortunes and misfortunes of a business enterprise on the frontier. Basinski fitted into the pattern of immigrant Jews in the American West. "The majority of them were young, European-born merchants who followed the gold rushes and sold clothing, dry goods, mining equipment and tobacco, invested in the local economy and then settled in larger cities." 42 notes, biblio.
R. J. Wechman

1500. Lincoln, Evelyn. J. N. NORTON - NEBRASKA STATESMAN. *Swedish Pioneer Hist. Q. 1970 21(1): 31-40.* Discusses the sentiments drawn from a Fourth of July speech given by her father, Congressman John Nathaniel Norton, in a small Nebraska town. Some biographic data on the Norton family (the name was Anglicized from Nordeen) is given, beginning with emigration from Sweden and ending in Stromsburg, Nebraska, via Illinois. The patriotism expressed by Congressman Norton was drawn from his belief that an estate of worldly wealth is less of a bequest to sons and daughters than the estate of a good name, a Godly life, a respect for character, a thirst for knowledge, and a willingness to work. Based on personal reminiscences and family papers.
E. P. Costello

1501. Lindquist, Emory. PRÄRIEBLOMMAN: AN IMMIGRANT COMMUNITY IN CENTRAL KANSAS. *The Swedish Immigrant Community in Transition: Essays in Honor of Dr. Conrad Bergendoff* (Rock Island, Illinois: Augustana Hist. Soc. 1963), pp. 63-77. The story of Bethany College, Lindsborg, Kansas. The key factor in the founding of Lindsborg was the decision made by the Reverend Olof Olsson to emigrate to Kansas in 1869, after correspondence with C. R. Carlson, a former associate who was already in America. Approximately 250 people from parishes in Värmland, where Olsson was well-known and esteemed, joined his party. They were brought over by a land company with a contract with the Kansas Pacific Railroad. Originally the design was to develop a semicommunal colony based on Christian principles in McPherson and Saline counties. In Lindsborg the Swedes long maintained their identity and old loyalties. Their able leadership was also an important factor. 9 notes.
E. P. Stickney

1502. Lindquist, Emory. THE SWEDISH IMMIGRANT AND LIFE IN KANSAS. *Kansas Hist. Q. 1963 29(1): 1-24.* Territorial strife and the Civil War delayed Swedish immigration to Kansas. It was later stimulated by railroads, immigration companies, Swedish land companies, a State Bureau of Immigration, and the extensive publication of *Amerika breva,* which were the letters of immigrants to friends at home. The Swedes were afflicted with *hemlängtan* (defined loosely as "homesickness") because of the geographic and climatic contrasts between Sweden and Kansas and new customs in America. The Swedes published many papers in Kansas. Most of them were identified with the Republican Party and resisted the appeal of Populism, which was very strong in Kansas. The major motives for their immigration were economic conditions at home and a desire for religious liberty. Based on Swedish newspapers and literature.
W. F. Zornow

1503. Lurie, Nancy Oestreich. LADY FROM BOSTON AND THE OMAHA INDIANS. *Am. West 1966 3(4): 31-33, 80-85.* Alice Cunningham Fletcher was a pioneer anthropologist of widely recognized scholarly achievements. Little known is her role as an activist for Indian reform, resulting, in particular, in Federal legislation that established the earliest experiment in applied anthropology. In 1881, on her first field trip, she visited Indian reservations in Nebraska and South Dakota. At once Miss Fletcher became an outspoken critic of Indian policy and the injustices done to the Indians. She was the architect and moving spirit behind the Omaha Allotment Act of 1882 which became the model for the 1887 Dawes Severalty Act. By it, tribally held reservations were allotted into individually owned tracts. Unallotted lands were sold on the assumption that Indian population would continue to decrease. Within a decade, however, Indian disdain for the responsibilities of farming, depleted resources, increase in population, and other problems negated much of the hoped for reform from the allotment program. The author analyzes and evaluates the reasons for Miss Fletcher's misguided efforts. Based on a forthcoming essay on female American anthropologists, note, illus., biblio.
D. L. Smith

1504. Macleod, Celeste L. THE WESTERN JEWISH HISTORY CENTER. *Am. Jewish Hist. Q. 1968 (2): 271-277.* The story of the founding and early progress of this center is described. Located on the top floor of the Judah L. Magnes Memorial Museum in Berkeley, California, it houses a growing collection of materials on the history of the Jews in the Western United States.
F. Rosenthal

1505. MacPherson, Ian. BETTER BRITONS FOR THE BURLINGTON: A STUDY OF THE SELECTIVE APPROACH OF THE CHICAGO, BURLINGTON AND QUINCY IN GREAT BRITAIN, 1871-1875. *Nebraska Hist. 1969 50(4): 373-407.* A comprehensive account of the activities of the various agents of the Chicago, Burlington and Quincy in Great Britain seeking to recruit colonists for the railroad's Nebraska lands. Seeking at first only suitable people with an agricultural background, circumstances compelled the abandonment of this policy for one of recruiting any Briton moving westward, regardless of his experience or preparation.
R. Lowitt

1506. McGloin, John B. THOMAS CIAN, PIONEER CHINESE PRIEST IN CALIFORNIA. *California Hist. Soc. Q. 1969 48(1): 45-58.* A biographical sketch of a Chinese Catholic priest who deserves attention for his activities in gold rush California. As a young boy Cian went to Naples, Italy, to be trained for the Roman Catholic Church. Ordained a priest in 1853, he was called to California at the request of Father Joseph Alemany, Archbishop of San Francisco, who wanted a Chinese priest for missionary work among the newly arrived Chinese. Father Cian arrived in California in 1854. His efforts at converting his countrymen to the Catholic faith were relatively unsuccessful. The author attributes the failure to Cian's inability to speak the dialect of the majority of Chinese immigrants (though he was versed in Greek, Latin, Hebrew, and French); discouragement at the small number of Chinese Catholics and the large number of "heathens"; reluctance to engage in the basic missionary activities of visiting the mining camps and starting schools; and a desire to perform his missionary efforts in China rather than California. Cian served as an assistant pastor in a San Francisco church from 1856 to 1862, after which, for reasons not entirely clear, he left California. Concludes with a brief note on Cian's later years. Based on primary sources in the Archives of the Sacred Congregation de Propaganda Fide in Rome, Italy; 29 notes.
A. Hoffman

1507. McKenna, Jeanne. "WITH THE HELP OF GOD AND LUCY STONE." *Kansas Hist. Q. 1970 36(1): 13-26.* An account of the election of 1867 in Kansas with special emphasis on the unsuccessful effort to secure the ratification of two amendments enfranchising Negroes and women. Samuel Newitt Wood (1825-91), the leading personality in the State legislature, is shown to have played a key role in the campaign. He made his major effort in support of woman suffrage by organizing a Kansas Impartial Suffrage Association and bypassing the local Republicans to work directly with powerful suffrage interests in the East. His motives were mixed. He may have wished to build a national political following or to sell land to eastern suffragists. Whether his motives were personal gain or lofty idealism, Wood gave himself unstintingly to the campaign. Based on local newspapers and manuscripts in the Kansas State Historical Society and the Library of Congress; illus., 46 notes.
W. F. Zornow

1508. McLaughlin, Tom L. SECTIONAL RESPONSES OF FREE NEGROES TO THE IDEA OF COLONIZATION. *Res. Studies 1966 34(3): 123-134.* Examines the question of antebellum response of free Northern and Southern Negroes to the American Colonization Society's plans of settlement in Liberia in terms of Frederick Jackson Turner's "safety valve" theory as previously applied by George R. Woolfolk in his study of the migration of free Negroes into the general American West. The question is posed whether Negroes desired to migrate to Africa to escape oppressive conditions or regarded migration as a plan to purge the United States of free Negroes and so rejected the opportunity. Colonization was supported by Southern and Northern whites alike as a means of solving the social problem of unassimilated free Negroes. The response of Southern free Negroes was generally favorable, generally unfavorable on the part of Northern free Negroes. Although living conditions were equally oppressive for free Negroes in the North and the South, Northern free Negroes preferred to remain and strive for eventual freedom and social and economic equality for all Negroes within the United States. The historical background for contemporary racial problems is given. Based on secondary sources; 46 notes.
D. R. Picht

1509. Meier, Matt S. DISSERTATIONS. *J. of Mexican Am. Hist. 1971 1(2): 170-190.* An unannotated but selective bibliography of unpublished dissertations and M.A. theses dealing with Mexican American history. Those with titles which indicated an exclusive interest in sociology and education were excluded. 228 items.
G. L. Seligmann, Jr.

1510. Miller, Stuart Creighton. AN EAST COAST PERSPECTIVE TO CHINESE EXCLUSION, 1852-1882. *Historian 1971 33(2): 183-201.* Mary Coolidge's *Chinese Immigration,* first published in 1909, has been the standard work on the subject of the Chinese Exclusion Act of 1882, the first US restriction on open immigration to be made on ethnocultural grounds, and the first step leading to the much-criticized quota legislation of 1924. Coolidge emphasized the strength of anti-Chinese feeling in California and the important role of California politicians in persuading both major parties to include exclusionist planks in their platforms. Systematic study of editorials appearing in Northeastern newspapers for a considerable period before 1882 suggests that Chinese exclusion should be understood in the perspective of national cultural, racial, and public health fears rather than in terms of a narrow, California-based prejudice. 116 notes.
N. W. Moen

1511. Muir, Andrew Forest. HEINRICH THUERWAECHTER, COLONIAL GERMAN SETTLER. *Texana 1966 4(1): 33-40.* Heinrich Thuerwaechter, one of the first German emigrants in Texas, "had the unenviable distinction of never having had his name spelled correctly." He fought in the Battle of San Jacinto and, despite a reputation for being eccentric, won election as coroner of Harris County.
W. Elkins

1512. Myhrman, Anders. FINLANDSSVENSKA IMMIGRANTER I AMERIKA [Swedish-speaking Finnish immigrants in America]. *Historiska och Litteraturhistoriska Studier [Finland] 1966 41: 261-283.* Surveys the settlement patterns and organized activities of Swedish-speaking Finnish immigrants in North America, especially the United States. Most immigration occurred between 1885 and 1929, bringing large groups to New York City, Massachusetts, the upper Midwest, the Pacific Northwest, British Columbia and Ontario. Sickness insurance and temperance organizations began in the 1890's, both movements uniting in 1920 to form the still active Order of Runeberg. Lutheran, Baptist and Mission congregations have provided other points of contact. From 1897 the Swedish-language newspaper, *Finska-Amerikanaren - Norden* [The Finnish American - North], since 1935 appearing as *Norden,* has also been important. Since 1930 Americanization, and a shift to the English language, have been notable, with the inevitable decline of support for ethnically distinct activities. Undocumented.

R. G. Selleck

1513.   Nash, A. E. Keir.   THE TEXAS SUPREME COURT AND TRIAL RIGHTS OF BLACKS, 1845-1860.   *J. of Am. Hist. 1971 58(3): 622-642.* The five judges occupying the Supreme Court bench of Texas from 1845 to 1860 were libertarian in their attitudes toward black slaves as possessing human rights. They were harsh on whites who harmed or killed slaves, upheld the rights of blacks to competent counsel and to technically flawless trials, were sympathetic to blacks suing for freedom even when laws were ambivalent or seemed prejudiced to the defendant, and often reversed the convictions of those who attempted to abscond with slaves or who permitted slaves to carry guns. Such libertarianism from judges who were undeniably prosouthern in background and attitudes can perhaps best be explained in terms of judicial independence from popular opinion and the ability of judges to deal with slavery in specific individual terms rather than in general defensive terms. There is evidence that the Texas judges were not exceptions in the antebellum South. 100 notes.   K. B. West

1514.   Navarro, Joseph.   THE CONDITION OF MEXICAN-AMERICAN HISTORY.   *J. of Mexican Am. Hist. 1970 1(1): 25-52.* Places Mexican American history in a logical, historiographical framework. Defines terms, time period, and geographic location. Discusses the history of individuals of Mexican or Mestizo heritage in the United States since the Treaty of Guadalupe Hidalgo. Reviews the existing historical literature and finds gaps. 61 notes.   G. L. Seligmann, Jr.

1515.   Neighbours, Kenneth F.   THE GERMAN-COMANCHE TREATY OF 1847.   *Texana 1964 2(4): 311-322.* Account of the arrangement of a treaty between the Comanche Indians and a German land company. The land company, headed by J. O. Meusebach, needed to survey certain areas in the Comanche hunting grounds. Meusebach and his party, joined by Indian agent Major Robert S. Neighbors, met the Indians at their camp in February 1847 to make preliminary arrangements. A description of the encampment and the council was taken down by Doctor Ferdinand von Roemer, who accompanied Neighbors. The Comanche agreed to the survey on their lands for one thousand dollars. The treaty was signed on 9 May 1847 in the German town of Fredericksburg by the land company officers, the Indian agent, and the Comanche chiefs Santa Anna, Buffalo Hump, Old Owl, and Ketumse. 24 notes.

W. A. Buckman

1516.   Owen, Tom.   THE FIRST SYNAGOGUE IN LOS ANGELES. *Western States Jewish Hist. Q. 1968 1(1): 9-13.* Describes the events leading to the construction of Congregation B'nai B'rith Synagogue, the first synagogue in Los Angeles, in 1873, and some architectural details connected with the design and construction. Discusses other construction in Los Angeles designed by the architect of the synagogue, Ezra F. Kysor. Refers to the demolition of the synagogue building in 1896. Photo, 15 notes.   R. E. Levinson

1517.   Peoples, Morgan D.   "KANSAS FEVER" IN NORTH LOUISIANA.   *Louisiana Hist. 1970 11(2): 121-135.* A short, but lively, migration of freed Negroes from the lower Mississippi Valley to Kansas occurred in 1879-80. A US Senate committee investigated the mass immigration, but its conclusions simply reflected party-line positions. The Democrats blamed Republicans for luring the Negroes to States where they were fighting for continuance of Republican strength. The Republicans accused Southern white Democrats of imposing intolerable hardships upon the freedmen, forcing them to flee. The reasons for the exodus were several: blacks were ill treated, although their condition was better than in much of the rest of the South; white political domination had been achieved in 1878 by much terrorism of the blacks; a yellow fever epidemic in 1878 had added to the turmoil; blacks complained of sexual outrages against their women by the whites; educational facilities for the blacks were nonexistent or inadequate; propaganda encouraging the immigration was effective in Louisiana, sponsored by civil rights groups, the

railroads, and Kansas land interests. Negroes found Kansas as difficult as the South, and no more than a third of the immigrants remained there. A majority of those leaving returned to their old homes in the lower Mississippi Valley. Based principally on *Senate Reports* and Louisiana newspapers; 6 photos, 72 notes.   R. L. Woodward

1518.   Peters, Victor.   DIE HUTTERISCHEN BRUDERHÖFE IN AMERIKA   [The community farms of the Hutterian Brethren in the United States].   *Festschrift Percy Ernst Schramm zu seinem siebzigsten Geburtstag von Schulern und Freunden zugeeigt* (Wiesbaden: Franz Steiner Verlag GMBH, 1964): vol. 2, pp. 138-141. When the German settlers in Russia were made liable to military service, the Hutterites emigrated to the United States in 1874 and founded three community farms in the present State of South Dakota. A description of the settlement's social, economic, and cultural structure is given.

B. Altmann

1519.   Peterson, Hans J.   HILLDALE: A MONTANA HUTTERITE COLONY IN TRANSITION.   *Rocky Mountain Social Sci. J. 1970 7(1): 1-7.* Describes the development of the Hilldale Hutterite colony in historical perspective and delineates bills introduced into recent Montana legislative sessions that threaten the colony. 23 notes.

R. F. Allen

1520.   Plaut, W. Gunther.   JEWISH COLONIES AT PAINTED WOODS AND DEVILS LAKE.   *North Dakota Hist. 1965 32(1): 59-70.* Deals with two efforts to settle Russian Jewish immigrants on collective farms in Dakota Territory. The first, Painted Woods, was the project of Judah Wechsler, rabbi of St. Paul, in 1881. The colony failed because of crop failures, inexperience in farming, and contention within the community. Wechsler had to acknowledge defeat and the settlers drifted away. The second colony, at Devils Lake, was somewhat more successful but it, too, disintegrated by the 1920's.   I. W. Van Noppen

1521.   Pursinger, Marvin Gavin.   THE JAPANESE SETTLE IN OREGON: 1880-1920.   *J. of the West 1966 5(2): 251-262.* The first Japanese came to Oregon in 1834 as the result of a shipwreck. It was not until the 1880's that others came. The first was brought as a bride by a sea captain, and a few others came to engage in business. By 1890 only 25 Japanese were in the State, but after that the railroads brought in large numbers to build roadbeds. In 1900 some twenty-five hundred were in the State. Of these, thirteen hundred resided in Portland and others were scattered tnroughout the State. By 1904 they were largely engaged in agriculture. Their numbers increased due to some immigration and a high birth rate. Before 1920 there was an atmosphere of quiet reserve between the Japanese and their Caucasian neighbors which was not characteristic of the Pacific coast. Despite all efforts to earn acceptance into the socioeconomic complex of the region, their failure was evident when the legislature adopted punitive antialien land laws in 1923. Documented from published sources, 37 notes.   D. N. Brown

1522.   Quinn, Larry D.   "CHINK CHINK CHINAMAN"; THE BEGINNING OF NATIVISM IN MONTANA.   *Pacific Northwest Q. 1967 58(2): 82-89.* First attracted in large numbers by prospective opportunities in the gold mines of California, some Chinese immigrants moved to the gold fields in Idaho, Oregon, and Montana as these areas developed mining camps in the 1860's and 1870's. The author discusses the nativist sentiment against the Chinese in Montana, concluding that the strongest antagonists against them resulted from fears of economic competition.

C. C. Gorchels

1523.   Rolle, Andrew F.   THE ITALIAN MOVES WESTWARD. *Montana 1966 16(1): 13-24.* Among the many foreign-born pioneers in Montana, Italians were represented by several noted Jesuit missionaries. In later years, Italians were prominent in business and mining, but less so in agriculture. Based on contemporary newspapers and recent published sources.   S. R. Davison

1524.   Rosenbaum, Bella W.   IN MY LIFETIME.   *Am. Jewish Arch. 1967 19(1): 3-33.* The author was born in Kamenets Podolsk, on the Russo-Polish border, and spent her childhood in Winnipeg, Manitoba. She describes the life of Jewish immigrants in the western prairie lands during the 1880's, and later in Seattle, Washington. These reminiscences include personal observations of Indians in Manitoba and the Pacific

Northwest, as well as the commercial growth of Seattle stimulated by the Klondike gold rush. Mrs. Rosenbaum was the first woman to practice law in the State of Washington. By 1914, she moved to New York, where she was impressed with the congestion and suffering within the ghettos of East European immigrants. She comments on their willingness to work arduously under difficult circumstances, describing the sweatshops, small stores, and airless tenements. Illus.

J. Brandes

1525. Rudin, A. James. BEERSHEBA, KANS.: "GOD'S PURE AIR ON GOVERNMENT LAND." *Kansas Hist. Q.* 1968 34(3): 282-298. The character of Jewish migration to the United States changed after 1882 with the arrival of Orthodox Jews from East Europe and Russia as a result of the czar's anti-Semitic campaign. The Hebrew Union Agricultural Society helped to send a group of new immigrants to establish Beersheba, one of five short-lived agricultural communities in Kansas. Beersheba failed within four years because its location in Hodgeman County was poor, its inhabitants had little knowledge of farming as a science, its inhabitants preferred to follow the professions and trades they had followed in Europe, and its financial support was either uncertain or too costly. The venture may have set new forces in motion since, for the first time in America, Jews were called upon to aid other Jews through community action. Based on articles and the American Israelite; 51 notes.

W. F. Zornow

1526. Russell, Robert R. CONSTITUTIONAL DOCTRINES WITH REGARD TO SLAVERY IN TERRITORIES. *J. of Southern Hist.* 1966 32(4): 466-486. Discusses four doctrines held and argued in the years before the Civil War regarding slavery in the territories: 1) the traditional and early prevailing view that Congress had complete or almost complete legislative power in the territories; 2) the Free Soil doctrine that the fifth amendment prohibited slavery in territories; 3) the Calhoun doctrine of "nonintervention" that the Federal Government in the territories was only the trustee or agent of the several sovereign States, obliged not to discriminate among the states and hence incapable of forbidding the bringing into any territory of anything that was legal property in any State, and 4) the Cass or "squatter sovereignty" doctrine, later accepted by Douglas, that the residents of territories had the right to decide for themselves. These four doctrines are discussed in terms of the Dred Scott decision and the 1860 party platforms. 46 notes.

S. E. Humphreys

1527. Sachs, Howard F. DEVELOPMENT OF THE JEWISH COMMUNITY OF KANSAS CITY, 1864-1908. *Missouri Hist. R.* 1966 60(3): 350-360. Jewish merchants were in Kansas City before the Civil War; the first Jewish organization, a burial society, was formed in 1864. The first congregation, B'nai Jehudah, was formed in 1870. Within a year the congregation had formed a relief society; 10 years later it established a social club. The history of Kansas City's Jewish community after 1881 is marked by such developments as the establishment of a second congregation in 1883, a growing relief program for the immigrants from Eastern Europe and the friction between "German" and "Russian" Jews. Based on histories of Kansas City and a short monograph on the Jews in Kansas City published in 1908.

W. F. Zornow

1528. Saxton, Alexander. THE ARMY OF CANTON IN THE HIGH SIERRA. *Pacific Hist. R.* 1966 35(2): 141-151. The story of the Chinese contribution to the construction of the Central Pacific Railroad through the Sierras.

J. McCutcheon

1529. Schapsmeier, Edward L., and Schapsmeier, Frederick H. LINCOLN AND DOUGLAS: THEIR VERSIONS OF THE WEST. *J. of the West* 1968 7(4): 542-552. Although very similar in their desire to remove the roadblock of slavery from the path of American development, the two men's enunciations of their ideal for the West were quite different. Douglas took the approach of popular sovereignty with the belief that the West would not choose to have slavery in the States which would be created there. Lincoln appealed to the "higher law" and took the approach that slavery could not be permitted in the West. They were both dedicated to the preservation of the Union and, had it not been for Douglas' untimely death, he might have been able to serve Lincoln and the Nation in that preservation.

R. N. Alvis

1530. Schmidt, C. B. KANSAS MENNONITE SETTLEMENTS, 1877. *Mennonite Life* 1970 25(2): 51-58, 65-80. An English translation of a pamphlet written in 1878 to induce German Mennonite settlers from Russia and Germany to come and settle on the newly acquired land of the Atchison, Topeka and Santa Fe Railroad. The Mennonites who had settled in Kansas since 1874 were already happy and prosperous. Their farms were large and crop yields impressive. Problems connected with adjusting European patterns of life to the New World environment are discussed. Land prices were rising, but the Railroad still had 2,500,000 acres of "the best land" available. "Groups of ten to thirty families can still find land at reasonable prices some fifty to one hundred miles away from the large German settlements in Marion, Harvey, Butler, McPherson, and Reno counties." Illus.

D. J. Abramoske

1531. Schmidt, John F., ed. HEINRICH R. VOTH (1855-1931). *Mennonite Q. R.* 1966 40(3): 217-226. Presents the autobiographical account of Voth covering his early years in Russia, his emigration to Kansas in 1874, and his later matriculation at the Mennonite Institute in Wadsworth, Ohio. He became one of the pioneer Mennonite missionaries to the American Indians. 18 notes.

E. P. Stickney

1532. Schwartz, Lois Fields. EARLY JEWISH AGRICULTURAL COLONIES IN NORTH DAKOTA. *North Dakota Hist.* 1965 32(4): 217-232. A quarter of a million Jews came from Germany to the United States from 1815 to 1890, largely because of discrimination against them. Most of them settled in towns and cities and became assimilated into American life. Between 1881 and 1920 great numbers of Russian Jews migrated, victims of restrictive Russian laws. Philanthropists furnished money for their removal. Most of them found work in eastern cities in the clothing industries. However, some efforts were made to settle Jews in agricultural colonies in North Dakota. The Russian Jews were inexperienced at farming, crop failures and depression handicapped them, and most of them eventually drifted to the cities. 38 notes.

I. W. Van Noppen

1533. Schwartz, Mrs. David. OLDEST JEWISH CEMETERY IN THE WEST - STOCKTON, CALIFORNIA. *Western States Jewish Hist. Q.* 1969 1(2): 66-74. Surveys the history of the Jewish community of Stockton from the years of the gold rush, including the origin of the Jewish congregation in that city. Reprints, from local newspapers, several laudatory references to the Jewish community. Discusses Temple Israel Cemetery in Stockton, its origins and founders, and the manner in which the cemetery was restored after several years of neglect. Mentions the restoration project and official rededication ceremony. 2 photos, 20 notes.

R. E. Levinson

1534. Schwendemann, Glenn. THE "EXODUSTERS" ON THE MISSOURI. *Kansas Hist. Q.* 1963 29(1): 25-40. In 1879 many Negroes migrated to Kansas. It was difficult to find places for them to settle. Kansas City, Kansas refused to receive them, and Kansas City, Missouri was outside the state. Consequently they moved from St. Louis to Wyandotte, where they received cordially. Several local committees were established to assist them in finding permanent settlements and jobs. Many settled at Lawrence, Leavenworth, Topeka, and Atchison, although the latter town was criticized for not taking its share. The migration died down during the summer, but during the winter of 1879-80 the state was deluged by another crowd of immigrants from Texas. Based on local newspapers.

W. F. Zornow

1535. Shepperson, Wilbur S. IMMIGRANT THEMES IN NEVADA NEWSPAPERS. *Nevada Hist. Soc. Q.* 1969 12(2): 3-46. Discusses some of the more colorful characters and events in the early history of Nevada as reported in the press of the day. The focus is on the period 1870-1910, highlighting the contributions and problems of the large immigrant population that deluged Nevada during the boom days of the Comstock Lode. The author emphasizes the recurring American theme of the absolute requirement for cheap labor on the frontier and the social discrimination against those who provided it - in this case Orientals and South Europeans. The psychological impact of the loneliness and discrimination experienced by immigrants resulted in many destroyed lives. References to the bad and bawdy are numerous and are illustrative of the harsh, raw nature of life in frontier Nevada. Based on newspapers, books, and journals; illus., photo, 106 notes.

E. P. Costello

1536. Shuffler, R. Henderson. GERMANS WHO WENT WEST. *Am.-German R.* 1967 33(6): 10-13. Comments on the earliest German settlers in Texas. By 1840 there were 400 German voters and in 1843 a headquarters was established near what is now New Braunfels for a proposed mass immigration scheme. The inn built there has been restored as part of a historical preservation. Photo.   G. H. Davis

1537. Shumate, Albert.   AN EARLY ATTEMPT AT INTERNA-TIONAL GOODWILL.   *California Hist. Q. 1971 50(1): 79-83.* Gold-rush California's international flavor was reflected in the celebration following the fall of Sebastopol (1855) in the Crimean War. English, French, and Sardinian residents of San Francisco staged a grand celebra-tion, joined by sympathetic Americans, at South Park. A pavilion was erected and a banquet spread for the celebrants. Unfortunately, national spirit caused a number of people to ignore the dull speeches in favor of merriment. Disorder soon broke out as different anthems were sung, people stood on tables, and flags were seized. San Francisco's newspapers thought the affair disgraceful. Some sympathy in San Francisco was also displayed toward the Russian consul. Photos, biblio.   A. Hoffman

1538. Siemerling, A. and Geue, C. W., trans.   DIE LATEINISCHE ANSIEDLUNG IN TEXAS   [The Latin Settlement in Texas]. *Texana 1967 5(2): 126-131.* Account of an aristocratic and well-educated group whose members settled individually in the valley of Sisterdale about 50 miles northwest of San Antonio. The community became noted for its libraries, its cultural gatherings, its royal visitors, and its stand on slavery. The group was strongly abolitionist and used a San Antonio newspaper to expound its views. The community became most unpopular as the Civil War approached. They stood firmly by their views and many gave their lives in battle with Confederate troops. The nature of the settlement was completely changed shortly after the war.   W. A. Buckman

1539. Simundson, Daniel.   STRANGERS IN THE VALLEY: THE "RIO GRANDE REPUBLICAN," AND SHALAM, 1884-1891. *New Mexico Hist. R. 1970 45(3): 197-208.* Discusses the effect of newspa-per coverage on the colony of Shalam, inhabited by the "Faithists," as they preferred to be called. Largely financed by Andrew M. Howland and led by John B. Newbrough, the colony was located at Dona Ana near Las Cruces. Although the colony received rather favorable publicity in the Las Cruces *Republican* at first, the attitude of the paper later swung to apprehension and rejection. "By its silence, the *Republican* contributed to" the demise of the colony. 29 notes.   D. F. Henderson

1540. Stahler, Michael L.   WILLIAM SPEER: CHAMPION OF CALIFORNIA'S CHINESE, 1852-1857.   *J. of Presbyterian Hist. 1970 48(2): 113-129.* Traces the efforts of Speer (1822-1904) to help Chinese immigrants become assimilated in California during the Gold Rush. Chi-nese were greeted with hostility in California primarily because of their willingness to work for low wages. As a result discrimination against Chinese became a serious problem. Speer, a former China missionary, was sent to California by the Presbyterian Board of Foreign Missions to render a spiritual and material ministry to the Chinese. To this end Speer established a school, dispensary, and mission which helped Chinese adjust to America. Speer had little success in converting Chinese to Christianity but was a profound force working for political, economic, and social justice for the Chinese. He published the *Oriental,* which sought to ac-quaint Americans with the customs of the Chinese and thus to fight their oppression. Speer worked to secure equality under law for the Chinese from the California Legislature. He helped many Americans to become more tolerant and less oppressive of the Chinese. Based on primary and secondary sources; 69 notes.   S. C. Pearson, Jr.

1541. Starczewska, Maria.   THE HISTORICAL GEOGRAPHY OF THE OLDEST POLISH SETTLEMENT IN THE UNITED STATES. *Polish R. 1967 12(2): 11-40.* A detailed account of the first permanent Polish settlement in the United States at Panna Maria, Texas. It describes Texas as the Polish immigrants found it in 1854, and the Polish villages from which the settlers came. Sociologic and economic principles are interwoven into the historical account. Illus., maps, tables.
                                S. R. Pliska

1542. Stratton, David H.   THE DILEMMA OF AMERICAN EL-BOWROOM.   *Pacific Northwest Q. 1965 56(1): 30-35.* Using writings of Crèvecoeur, Emerson, Montesquieu, and others, the author examines some uncommon aspects of emigration to the open spaces of western United States covering the period of 1787 to the early 1900's. He theorizes

that space itself can be a detriment to pleasant living and that space is "an overhead cost-of-living, both socially and economically."
                                C. C. Gorchels

1543. Strombeck, Rita.   LEONARD STRÖMBERG; A SWEDISH-AMERICAN LITERARY PHENOMENON.   *Swedish Pioneer Hist. Q. 1972 23(3): 169-184.* Strömberg (1871-1941) wrote over 40 novels, published in both the United States and Sweden. During the 1920's and 1930's he was one of the most widely read Swedish authors. He was born in Arboga, Sweden. In 1892 he enrolled in the Methodist Theological Seminary at Uppsala. At his first mission he wrote his first novel. In 1895 he traveled to the United States. Attending the Methodist Conference, he was assigned to Concord, Nebraska. After serving at various Methodist churches he was sent to Oakland, Nebraska, in 1912. This was to be his home for the rest of his life. He received innumerable awards for his work as a writer, minister, and promoter of cross-cultural understanding. His writing represents an outlook similar to that of his fellow Swedish-Ameri-can emigrants with the theme of success based on hard work and Chris-tian principles. Based on primary sources; illus, 8 notes.
                                K. J. Puffer

1544. Szasz, Margaret Garretson.   INDIAN REFORM IN A DECADE OF PROSPERITY.   *Montana 1970 20(1): 16-27.* Examines the work of the Bureau of Indian Affairs under the administrations of Charles Burke (from 1921 to 1928) and his successor John Collier (from 1933 to 1945). The trend in the later years was away from the integration-absorption policy (in effect since the passage of the Dawes Act in 1887) and toward plans for preservation of the native culture and of the Indian's identity. Reformers are credited with some accomplishments and with the best of intentions, but "conditions on America's Indian Reservations have not improved a great deal in the last four decades...the battle for genuine improvement in the lot of the American Indian is yet to be won." Illus., 36 notes.   S. R. Davison

1545. Taketa, Henry.   "1969" - THE CENTENNIAL YEAR. *Pacific Historian 1969 13(1): 1-16.* Discusses the centennial of the Waka-matsu Tea and Silk Farm Colony of Gold Hill, El Dorado County, California. The ill-fated and short-lived colony (1869-71) marked the first Japanese emigration into the United States. Reproduces the 1870 census report on the colony. 8 illus.   F. I. Murphy

1546. Terbovich, John B.   RELIGIOUS FOLKLORE AMONG THE GERMAN-RUSSIANS IN ELLIS COUNTY, KANSAS.   *Western Folklore 1963 22(2): 79-88.* Discusses some of the religious folklore of an ethnic minority in central Kansas. Emphasis is on the folklore brought from Russia by the group in 1875.   L. J. White

1547. Turner, Justin G.   THE FIRST DECADE OF LOS ANGELES JEWRY: A PIONEER HISTORY (1850-1860).   *Am. Jewish Hist. Q. 1964 54(2): 123-164.* Based on earlier published material and manuscript and newspaper sources now available, the beginnings of Los Angeles Jewry are described. Eight pages of original photographs and 19 pages of documentation accompany the story.   F. Rosenthal

1548. Turner, Justin G. and Stern, Norton B.   MARCO ROSS NEW-MARK - 1878-1959: FIRST JEWISH HISTORIAN OF THE SOUTH-LAND.   *Western States Jewish Hist. Q. 1968 1(1): 3-8.* A tribute to Newmark, a descendant of an early Southern California Jewish family of prominence. Discusses the role of Newmark as historian of Southern California and as Jewish community leader. Lists the organizations with which he was connected in the general and the Jewish community. 4 photos.   R. E. Levinson

1549. Tweton, D. Jerome.   THREE SCANDINAVIAN IMMI-GRANTS IN THE AMERICAN WEST.   *Nebraska Hist. 1964 45(3): 253-264.* Surveys the careers of three Scandinavian immigrants in the American West. One was in Wisconsin in the 1840's, another was in Texas in the 1870's and the third settled in Nebraska in the 1880's. By examining their experiences, the author is able to offer generalizations on immigration and pioneering.   R. Lowitt

1550. Unrau, William E.   THE CIVILIAN AS INDIAN AGENT: VILLAIN OR VICTIM?   *Western Hist. Q. 1972 3(4): 405-420.* "Bug-ging the bureau" has been a continuing phenomenon of administration of

American Indian affairs almost from the time it came under civilian jurisdiction in 1849. The expensive military operations, the increasing annuity commitments, and the cumulative frustrations of the post-Civil War period failed to bring the Indian into the mainstream of American life and assured the antibureau crusade of continuity well into the present century. The negative is voluminously documented in the literature on depredations, massacres, assimilation, and the other failures. The Indian agent is usually portrayed as the most guilty of all those who subverted the government's good intentions. The fact remains, however, that the history of the Bureau of Indian Affairs remains largely unwritten. Several factors help to explain the biased "devil theory" of the Indian agent. The application of sound scholarship to the subject is the only way to determine the truth about the agent. 70 notes.   D. L. Smith

1551.   Unruh, John D., Jr.   THE BURLINGTON AND MISSOURI RIVER RAILROAD BRINGS THE MENNONITES TO NEBRASKA 1873-1878. *Nebraska Hist. Part I 1964 45(1): 3-30, Part II (2): 177-206.* Briefly examines Mennonite immigration to North America, chiefly from the Alexanderwohl congregation in Russia, and then focuses on the generous and successful efforts of the Burlington and Missouri River Railroad in bringing a portion of them to lands in Jefferson and Gage counties, where by early 1878 the Mennonites already owned approximately 40 thousand acres.   R. Lowitt

1552.   Urbach, William.   OUR PARENTS WERE RUSSIAN GERMAN. *Nebraska Hist. 1967 48(1): 1-26.* The author gives an autobiographical account of his childhood, including the history of his Russian-German parents and grandparents in Nebraska in the late 19th and early 20th centuries.   R. Lowitt

1553.   Weber, Francis J.   IRISH-BORN CHAMPION OF THE MEXICAN-AMERICANS. *California Hist. Soc. Q. 1970 49(3): 233-249.* Efforts of the Catholic Church to provide for the spiritual, social, and economic needs of Mexican immigrants to the United States were exemplified by the contributions of Los Angeles Archbishop John Joseph Cantwell. The Mexican Government's antireligious campaign caused thousands of Mexicans to come to the United States. The Los Angeles-San Diego Diocese was a center for the religious exiles, whose presence placed a strain on existing welfare agencies. Cantwell inaugurated a number of programs to assist Spanish-speaking Catholics, including an Immigrant Welfare Department, the Confraternity of Christian Doctrine, and other agencies. The diocese constructed religious edifices and met financial needs. Cantwell admonished priests in his diocese to learn the Spanish language. He also insisted that the ethnic backgrounds of Catholics not be a factor in determining welfare assistance. He thereby avoided prejudice from quarters opposing aid to Mexicans. Cantwell urged that the Church compete with equal energy with proselytizing from Protestant sects. Cantwell made a special effort to understand and remedy the problems of his Catholic parishioners from Mexico. By so doing he helped to build ties of friendship between Mexican and U.S. Catholic communities. Based on Los Angeles Archdiocese Archives and on published works; 54 notes.   A. Hoffman

1554.   Wenzlaff, Theodore C., ed. and trans.   THE RUSSIAN GERMANS COME TO THE UNITED STATES. *Nebraska Hist. 1968 49(4): 379-399.* Two articles, one appearing in 1909 and the other in 1924, that appeared in German-language newspapers are here presented with a brief introductory essay delineating the experiences and history of Russian-German groups in the United States with emphasis on those settlers in Nebraska and the Dakotas.   R. Lowitt

1555.   Widen, Carl T.   FROM SMALAND TO PALM VALLEY IN TEXAS. *Swedish Pioneer Hist. Q. 1967 18(3): 128-131.* Reprint of an address given by the author at the dedication of the Andrew Palm Family Memorial Church window, Round Rock, Texas, on 23 January 1966. The speech recounts much of the history of the Palm family in the 19th century.   E. P. Costello

1556.   Widen, Carl T.   A JULOTTA IN TEXAS - 1871. *Swedish Pioneer Hist. Q. 1970 21(1): 26-30.* The Julotta is the name of the traditional Swedish Christmas morning church service. The festivities began on Christmas Eve when the entire family gathered at the family home, ate a sumptuous meal, and exchanged gifts. At an early hour on Christmas morning the family attended the local church to sing hymns reserved

for Christmas. The Swedish Julotta came to Texas in 1848 but did not become an annual feature there until after the Civil War. The author describes a Julotta held in 1871 in a log church about 20 miles north of Austin. The story of this 1871 Julotta is quoted from the memoirs of the Methodist minister who conducted the service.   E. P. Costello

1557.   Wilhite, Ann L. Wiegman.   SIXTY-FIVE YEARS TILL VICTORY: A HISTORY OF WOMAN SUFFRAGE IN NEBRASKA. *Nebraska Hist. 1968 49(2): 149-163.* Surveys the struggle for woman suffrage in Nebraska from 1855 when Amelia Bloomer spoke in Omaha until 1920 when the Nebraska Woman Suffrage Association reorganized as the Nebraska League of Woman Voters and the women prepared to exercise their first voting privileges.   R. Lowitt

1558.   Wilson, Don W.   PIONEER JEWS IN CALIFORNIA AND ARIZONA, 1849-1875. *J. of the West 1967 6(2): 226-236.* Notes that Jewish contribution to the Far West has been largely ignored and endeavors to show how and where the role of the Jew in the West contrasted with that of the non-Jew. The author focuses on the Jews who were attracted to the West from Europe and the Atlantic Coast following the gold strike of 1848. He describes how and why they came and how they reacted to the new environment. It is concluded that the success of the pioneer Jew was greater than might be expected considering their relatively small numbers in the population. This is explained by the close kinship and cohesion of the migrant Jews and the fact that most were better financed for the western trip than were non-Jews. Based on material in the American Jewish Archives and published sources, 44 notes.   D. N. Brown

1559.   Winther, Oscar O.   THE BRITISH IN OREGON COUNTRY. *Pacific Northwest Q. 1967 58(4): 179-187.* Even though the boundary dispute in the Oregon country was settled against British interests in 1846, the interests of individuals from Britain were not impaired. Workers of the Hudson's Bay Company and other Britons are pinpointed as examples of successful reorientation. By 1850 it is said that 79.9 percent of the total of foreign-born whites living in the Oregon country were British. An appendix gives a breakdown of the Hudson's Bay Company employees south of the 49th parallel from January to June 1846 including place of origin, total number, and characteristics.   C. C. Gorchels

1560.   Winther, Oscar O.   THE ENGLISH IN NEBRASKA, 1857-1880. *Nebraska Hist. 1967 48(3): 209-223.* Discusses the English people in Nebraska, the role of individuals in encouraging emigration, the work of the railroads in facilitating and easing the process and the success and failure that beset the settlers on the Nebraska frontier.   R. Lowitt

1561.   Winther, Oscar O.   ENGLISH MIGRATION TO THE AMERICAN WEST, 1865-1900. *Huntington Lib. Q. 1964 27(2): 159-173.* The trans-Mississippi West, including Louisiana and Minnesota, received some 140 thousand English during the period 1865-1900. Economic changes in England and extensive discussion of the need and opportunity to emigrate laid the foundation for the active promotional activity of American railroads and other agencies. English newcomers, less numerous by far than Germans and Scandinavians and nearly as many as the Irish, contributed significantly to the development of the West.   H. D. Jordan

1562.   Winther, Oscar O.   ENGLISH MIGRATION TO THE AMERICAN WEST, 1865-1900. *In the Trek of the Immigrants: Essays Presented to Carl Wittke* (Rock Island, Illinois: Augustana Coll. Lib., 1964): 115-125. During the period 1865 to 1900, 139,579 English migrated to the West. The dominant elements were the farmers and those from the English lower middle classes; some were sons of lawyers, army officers, clergy, civil servants, and the younger sons of the landed gentry. A number of Cornish and Welsh workers eventually came to the western mines. "The English press found the West a constant and rich source for newscopy." *The American Settler*, published in London 1880-92, was influential; American inspired, it catered to intending emigrants and to Englishmen who had already made the move to western states. 48 notes.   E. P. Stickney

1563.   Wise, Isaac Mayer.   RABBI WISE: BY PARLOR CAR ACROSS THE GREAT AMERICAN DESERT. *Pacific Historian 1967 11(4): 17-27.* A first-hand account of Rabbi Wise's trip (1877) across

America by rail, which took him and his new wife from Peoria to Galesburg to Council Bluffs, Omaha, Kearney, and through the prairie to Salt Lake City. He found Jews in most of the communities along the way, but digresses at length only on Salt Lake City where he describes the Jews, the city, and its impressive natural surroundings. Upon reaching Eureka, Nevada, he was impressed by the Chinese community, the desert he had crossed, and the mining economy. Illus.   T. R. Cripps

1564. Woolfolk, George R. TURNER'S SAFETY VALVE AND FREE NEGRO WESTWARD MIGRATION. *Pacific Northwest Q. 1965 56(3): 125-130.* Analyzes the migration of Negroes from areas east of the Mississippi River to trans-Mississippi Spanish borderlands in the framework of Frederick Jackson Turner's "safety-valve" theory, principally between 1850 and 1860.   C. C. Gorchels

1565. Wortman, Roy T. DENVER'S ANTI-CHINESE RIOT, 1880. *Colorado Mag. 1965 42(4): 275-291.* The riot was caused by several factors - inflammatory and anti-Chinese articles in the *Rocky Mountain News;* the seizure of the Chinese issue in the Democratic Party as a tool against James A. Garfield, culminating in a Democratic procession the evening before the riot, and a general feeling by the laboring classes that the Chinese presented a grave threat to their jobs. A reaction against the violence was not enough to overwhelm the nativistic sentiment; sporadic actions against the Chinese continued and as late as 1902 they were not allowed to settle in Leadville. Documented.   R. Sexauer

1566. Zabel, Orville H. TO RECLAIM THE WILDERNESS: THE IMMIGRANT'S IMAGE OF TERRITORIAL NEBRASKA. *Nebraska Hist. 1965 46(4): 315-324.* Discusses efforts of Nebraska's territorial leaders to create an image attractive to the immigrant by stressing central location, abundant land, and presumed mineral resources. At the same time, they hesitated to spend territorial funds to develop this image and consequently met only limited success.   R. Lowitt

1567. —. EARLY DAYS: THE STORY OF SARAH THAL. *Am. Jewish Arch. 1971 23(1): 47-62.* Memoirs of Sarah Thal, who left Germany in the 1880's for Nelson County, North Dakota. Hardship and privation marked her years in the Dakota Territory. Schools, growing population, and the introduction of luxuries gradually made life on the plains more comfortable. Photo.   E. S. Shapiro

Demography

1568. Carlson, Alvar W. RURAL SETTLEMENT PATTERNS IN THE SAN LUIS VALLEY: A COMPARATIVE STUDY. *Colorado Mag. 1967 44(2): 111-126.* The San Luis Valley of Colorado, approximately 5,000 square miles, includes portions of five counties. The valley floor is between 7,000 and 8,000 feet above sea level and lies between mountain ranges. The author compares three methods of farming and patterns of settlement practiced there by several groups of people, Spanish Americans, Anglo-Americans, and Japanese Americans. Although each group practiced irrigation, its own cultural values determined its pattern of land utilization. Illus., 48 notes.   I. W. Van Noppen

1569. Edwards, Paul M. AN ANALYSIS OF SCOTTISH POPULATION. *Ann. of Wyoming 1969 41(2): 275-276.* From an examination of the Territorial census of 1869 and the Federal census of 1870 and 1880, shows that Scots comprised about 2 percent of the population of Wyoming and worked at 80 different occupations. Based on published secondary material and the census records; 3 notes.   R. L. Nichols

1570. Gregor, Howard F. SPATIAL DISHARMONIES IN CALIFORNIA POPULATION GROWTH. *Geographical R. 1963 53(1): 100-122.* Three patterns of population growth are seen to a higher degree in California than elsewhere: extreme concentration in a few centers; extensive urban sprawl within these centers; and - most critical of all - the location of most of the population in the drier parts of the state. Some of the disharmonies are: the location of the coastal population in the most active earthquake zone of the continental United States, the spread of cities over the alluvial fill with resultant flood control problems, strategic vulnerability, and air pollution. The urbanization of most of the prime agricultural lands along the coast has led to increased compensatory

production in the desert and the Central Valley. Illus., tables, 58 notes.   E. P. Stickney

1571. Hickman, Russell E. THE REEDER ADMINISTRATION INAUGURATED. PART 2. *Kansas Hist. Q. 1970 36(4): 424-455.* Studies the first territorial census of 1855. Shows the occupations of inhabitants, voters by district, previous homes of voters, age of territorial population, previous residence of territorial population, and a recapitulation of the sex, place of birth, color, and status as to slavery of the territorial population. Errors existed in previous opinions about the nature of territorial inhabitation; useful demographic information was previously lacking. Based on secondary sources; 91 notes.   W. F. Zornow

1572. Jordan, Terry G. POPULATION ORIGINS IN TEXAS, 1850. *Geographical R. 1969 59(1): 83-103.* "The manuscript census schedules of the early and middle nineteenth century, available on microfilm from the National Archives, contain valuable information on population origins that does not appear in the published censuses. By compiling county totals for surnames and place of birth, cultural and historical geographers can detect and map the ethnic patterns in any state. The present study attempts to show the usefulness of the census schedules through a detailed investigation of the patterns of population origin in Texas for the census year 1850. The distribution of various national, racial, and state nativity groups is presented, along with some suggestions of how these distributions are related to various facets of agriculture, urban development, and religion. Data on origins are fundamental to an understanding of the nature and processes of migration."   J

1573. MacDonald, Norbert. POPULATION GROWTH AND CHANGE IN SEATTLE AND VANCOUVER, 1880-1960. *Pacific Hist. R. 1970 39(3): 297-321.* A study of the similarities and differences in the population growth of the two cities. Tables indicate the population figures and distribution of birthplace of native and foreign-born populations of both cities. Describes immigration patterns along with the resulting distinctive population characteristics. 10 tables, 37 notes.   E. C. Hyslop

1574. Robbins, William G. OPPORTUNITY AND PERSISTENCE IN THE PACIFIC NORTHWEST: A QUANTITIVE STUDY OF EARLY ROSEBURG, OREGON. *Pacific Hist. R. 1970 39(3): 279-296.* Uses Roseburg as a representative community to study the relationship of population turnover and economic opportunity in the Pacific Northwest toward the end of the 19th century. The analysis is based on the figures of those who moved and those who stayed, showing the relation between wealth and persistence and the degree of change in the economic status of both groups. Results indicate that length of residence was directly proportional to economic standing and that after the first influx of settlers, improvement of economic standing depended on initial economic status. 12 tables, 45 notes.   E. C. Hyslop

1575. Wooster, Ralph A. WEALTHY TEXANS, 1860. *Southwestern Hist. Q. 1967 71(2): 163-180.* The Eighth Census of the United States reveals that some 263 Texans, including 15 women, were worth over a hundred thousand dollars in 1860. These plantation owners, lawyers, merchant capitalists, and railroad developers were a highly influential group. The census data of name, residence, age, nativity, occupation, value of real and personal property, and salaries are analyzed and some additional biographical information and other matters are introduced. 3 tables, 31 notes.   D. L. Smith

1576. Zimmerman, Carle C. THE HUMAN FACTOR IN GREAT PLAINS LIFE. *Great Plains J. 1966 6(1): 19-31.* Considers the adaptation of humans to the Great Plains in three respects. First, a diverse human population adapted itself to the semiarid plains during a period of machine production and agribusiness methods. Second, during the period that the area of the Great Plains was being occupied, a world population explosion has made safeguarding the soil a major national and world concern. Finally, a recently growing urban population has assumed U.S. political leadership which had been left largely in rural hands. "These three changing situations should be considered in any planning for the future of the Plains."   O. H. Zabel

Pioneer Life

1577. Barnes, Lela, ed. NORTH CENTRAL KANSAS IN 1887-1889. FROM THE LETTERS OF LESLIE AND SUSAN SNOW OF JUNCTION CITY. *Kansas Hist. Q. 1963 29(3): 267-323; (4): 372-428.* Part I. Leslie Snow came to Kansas to work at Junction City as an examiner for the US Bureau of Pensions. These are letters written to his fiancee, Susan Currier, in New Hampshire, and her letters to friends and family after becoming Leslie's wife. This installment contains only the letters written by Leslie to Susan which cover the period from 27 November 1887 to 18 June 1888. Most are written from Junction City, but Snow's occupation required him to travel constantly to investigate pension claims, and so many letters were written from such towns as Abilene, Salina, and Beloit. Aside from his expressions of loneliness, the letters are filled with Snow's descriptions of his life in Kansas. Part II. The concluding section contains letters written between 24 June 1888 and 27 May 1889. The first group consists of letters written by Leslie Snow to his sweetheart from such towns as Mankato, Hastings, Salem, Concordia, Glenn Elder, Council Grove, Cawker City, Abilene, and from his principal base of operations in Junction City. The letters are filled with descriptions of his own feelings, local news, and general observations on his job with the US Bureau of Pensions. On 4 December Susan Currier Snow wrote her first letter to her parents from her new home in Junction City. Her letters are filled with general comments on life in the West and careful descriptions of her own daily experiences.   W. F. Zornow

1578. Barry, Louise, ed. SCENES IN (AND EN ROUTE TO) KANSAS TERRITORY, AUTUMN, 1854: FIVE LETTERS BY WILLIAM H. HUTTER. *Kansas Hist. Q. 1969 35(3): 312-336.* William H. Hutter, editor of the *Easton [Pennsylvania] Argus,* visited Kansas Territory in 1854 in order to see Territorial Governor Andrew Horatio Reeder (1807-64), who also came from Easton and was related by marriage to the 29-year-old editor. The five letters were published in the *Easton Argus.* The first, which was sent from St. Louis on 27 October, deals mainly with the editor's experiences before reaching the West. The other four letters were sent from Leavenworth on 7 November and 29 November. The third and fourth letters concern the editor's experiences as he traveled from the eastern border of Kansas to Fort Riley and back. Having a newsman's keen eye for interesting details, Hutter revealed the rigors of frontier life on the eve of the years of Bleeding Kansas. Based on the *Easton Argus* file in the Easton Public Library; 12 notes.   W. F. Zornow

1579. Berry, Becky. GRANDMA BERRY'S NINETY YEARS IN OKLAHOMA. *Chronicles of Oklahoma 1967 45(1): 58-67.* Mrs. H. H. Berry of Norman, Oklahoma, was born in Boggy Depot, Indian Territory, in 1875. Some of her ancestors were fullblooded Choctaw Indians who lived in Mississippi and Alabama 150 years ago. In this article by her granddaughter, Grandma Berry reminisces about life in early Oklahoma. She attended the Baptist school at Atoka, Indian Territory, in 1888 and graduated from Kidd-Key College in Sherman, Texas, in 1894. She married Houston Henry Berry in 1903. Three sons and two daughters attended the University of Oklahoma. 21 notes, biblio.

K. P. Davis

1580. Bivans, Venola Lewis, ed. THE DIARY OF LUNA E. WARNER, A KANSAS TEENAGER OF THE EARLY 1870'S. *Kansas Hist. Q. 1969 35(3): 276-311, and 35(4): 411-441.* Part I. Luna Warner, her parents, and brother were among a group of 22 settlers who moved from the vicinity of Barre, Massachusetts, to claim homesteads on the Solomon River near Downs, Kansas. Only Walter Warner and his family remained in Kansas when the rest of the settlers later moved to California. Luna Warner remained at the homestead after her marriage in 1881 to Frank Lewis. The editor, Luna Warner Lewis' daughter, presents portions of her mother's diary that were written between 23 February 1871 and 31 March 1872. The entries vary in length from one sentence to a short paragraph. They contain some interesting comments on frontier life as seen through the eyes of a 15-year-old girl. Illus., 9 notes. Part II. This portion of the diary covers the period from 1 April 1872 to 31 December 1874. The entries vary in length from one sentence to a short paragraph. They contain comments on the author's family life and the daily routine on the Kansas frontier.   W. F. Zornow

1581. Chaffin, Glenn. AUNT TISH: BELOVED GOURMET OF THE BITTER ROOT. *Montana 1971 21(4): 67-69.* Appreciative account of Tish Nevins, born a slave in 1862, who went to Montana's Bitter Root Valley in 1899 as housekeeper for a motherless family. In later years she operated a boarding house in Hamilton, serving food whose fame extended beyond the State. Stresses the high character and lovable personality of a humble lady who recognized her limitations but refused to regard herself as "disadvantaged." Illus.   S. R. Davison

1582. Chandler, W. B. I WAS A THIRD GENERATION PIONEER. *Oregon Hist. Q. 1965 66 66(3): 208-217.* Description of the way of life of early settlers in eastern Oregon, with recollections of the author, including details about food, housing, entertainment, religion, and schools.   C. C. Gorchels

1583. Chapman, B. B. THE SOD HOUSE OF MARSHAL McCULLY: A LAST RELIC OF THE GREAT PLAINS HISTORY. *Chronicles of Oklahoma 1967 45(2): 211-216.* Marshal McCully established a homestead in the Cherokee Outlet and built a two-room sod house in 1894. This remained his residence until he built a frame structure in 1907. The sod house was then used as a general storage structure. It is now an Oklahoma Historical Society memorial. 3 illus.

D. L. Smith

1584. Coltharp, J. B. REMINISCENCES OF COTTON PICKIN' DAYS. *Southwestern Hist. Q. 1970 73(4): 539-542.* The author recalls the bittersweet days on a cotton farm: the drudgery, the cold, the backaches, mingled with the respites and the awesome excitement of a trip to the gin.   R. W. Delaney

1585. Davison, Stanley R. CHRISTMAS IN MONTANA. *Montana 1964 14(1): 2-9.* A synopsis of holiday celebrations in territorial times (1854-72), stressing the attempt to overcome limitations of the frontier environment. Drawn from pioneer reminiscences and newspapers of of the time.   L. G. Nelson

1586. Dick, Everett. SUNBONNET AND CALICO, THE HOMESTEADER'S CONSORT. *Nebraska Hist. 1966 47(1): 3-13.* An account of pioneer experience in the second half of the 19th century in the trans-Mississippi prairie and plains area as viewed by the homesteader's consort.   R. Lowitt

1587. Dole, Philip. THE CALEF FARM: REGION AND STYLE IN OREGON. *J. of the Soc. of Architectural Historians 1964 23(4): 201-209.* Analysis of the land planning and architectural features of the Elmer Calef farmstead, built in the Willamette Valley of Oregon 1872-73, which demonstrates that the builders followed closely another family farm at Washington, Vermont. Calef had left Vermont in 1855, but returned on a visit in 1872. His adoption of the New England style in Oregon illustrates what the author calls "a 'colonial' compulsion to reproduce the conventions of the earlier civilization from which the pioneer had migrated." Based on field study and family reminiscences.

D. McIntyre

1588. Fife, Austin E. JACK FENCES OF THE INTERMOUNTAIN WEST. *Folklore Internat.: Essays in Traditional Literature, Belief, and Custom in Honor of Wayland Debs Hand* (Hatboro: Folklore Associates, Inc., 1967): 51-54. Photographs and descriptions of six types of jack fences, mostly in the mountainous West. The type has persisted since Colonial days; is adaptable to use with various wires, and has been used as a snow fence, to corral livestock, as a property-line, and as a railroad fence. Its distinguishing feature is "the jack, which serves as the vertical member on which other fencing materials are mounted." 4 notes.

J. C. Crowe

1589. Fleckenstein, Opal. FIRST YEARS IN KANSAS. *Organon 1970 2(1): 11-18.* Describes life on the Kansas plains during the 1880's. Details life in the family home, the simple fare, the dangers of prairie fires, the incidence of blizzards, and the search for fuel. Money was scarce among these simple but proud people. The sod house school was a focal point in local affairs. Classes were held irregularly, but the school building served as a gathering place for social functions and other meetings.

P. W. Kennedy

1590. Greenfield, Elizabeth. A HORSE DRIVE TO MONTANA TERRITORY, 1881. *Montana 1963 13(3): 18-33.* At the age of 20, Henry Nelson came to the Sun River country with a drove of horses from Dakota. His adventures on that trip and during his career as a Montana rancher make up this story, related by his daughter and based on his reminiscences.
L. G. Nelson

1591. Haefker, Walther A. THEOBALD F. WALTHER. *Concordia Hist. Inst. Q. 1970 43(2): 51-58.* A biographical sketch of Theobald F. Walther (1846-1917), who was born in St. Louis, enlisted in the Union Army in 1862, took part in the battle at Harper's Ferry, and was ordained a Lutheran minister in 1870. Early in 1871, although he had been recently married and was then serving a church at Humbolt, Kansas, he disappeared and was not reunited with his family until 1878. Most of the rest of his life was spent in Nebraska where he worked as a railroad section hand and for the post office. Based on primary sources.
D. J. Abramoske

1592. Harlan, Gilbert Drake, ed. FARMING IN THE BITTERROOT AND THE FIASCO AT "FORT FIZZLE." *J. of the West 1964 3(4): 501-516.* The diary of Wilson Barber Harlan ended with the termination of his career as a prospector. This account of his later life is based largely on his reminiscences and newspaper sources. Harlan settled in the Bitterroot Valley of Montana as a farmer. In 1875 he married Mary Horn who had been teaching at Corvallis. To this union were born three children; one daughter still survives. In 1877 apprehension spread throughout the valley because the Nez Percé Indians under Chief Joseph were reported headed for the Bitterroot. Harlan joined a group of settlers who, in conjunction with the Army, built a fort in a canyon on the Lodo trail. Although the situation was tense, the Indians did not attack and after consultation left the valley. While Indian scares continued Harlan worked his Como ranch. Here he planted the first commercial apple orchards in Montana. He organized the Montana Horticultural Society and served as an officer of other farm societies. From 1887 to 1897 he served in the State legislature. He died at the Soldier's Home at Columbia Falls in 1935. Illus.
D. N. Brown

1593. Henning, Marion. COMIC ANECDOTES FROM SANTA. *Western Folklore 1965 24(4): 249-258.* A brief history of the John Renfro family, early settlers in the Santa, Idaho area. Also several comic stories by old-timers who still live there.
J. M. Brady

1594. Hess, M. W. BISHOP MIEGE, S.J.: A PAGE OF AMERICAN HISTORY. *Contemporary R. [Great Britain] 1967 210(1212): 36-39.* Jean-Baptiste Miège was a Savoyard who came to the United States as a missionary and was made Bishop of Kansas in 1850. His letters are a useful source for mid-19th-century American life and reveal that he was an American in spirit. Based on the Miège manuscript, translated by J. Neale Carman of the University of Kansas.
D. H. Murdoch

1595. Holding, Vera. A HERITAGE TO SHARE. *Chronicles of Oklahoma 1964 42(1): 2-6.* An epic account of the moving of the Cooke family to Custer County, Oklahoma, following the "run" into the Cheyenne-Arapaho country 19 April 1892. The narrative is told of Ida Cooke who traveled by covered wagon to cook for her father and brothers on the 14-day trip to their 160 acres and their 16 x 18-foot dugout with a sod roof. She attended school in a dugout house, but soon Mt. Olive Church was built of hewn logs. There Ida married Del Fancher and moved to his half-dugout of split logs chinked with mud. The earth floor was covered with braided rugs and Indian blankets. A photograph shows Ida Fancher with four generations of her descendants.
I. W. Van Noppen

1596. Holmgren, Virginia C. CHINESE PHEASANTS, OREGON PIONEERS. *Oregon Hist. Q. 1964 65(3): 229-262.* Biographical sketch of Owen and Gertrude Denny, with emphasis on their activities in bringing ringnecked pheasants from China to Oregon. After early failure, the efforts of the Dennys were successful, and pheasants multiplied for hunting and food throughout the country. Government publications and newspapers are sources for history of development of appropriate conservation laws and breeding farms for pheasants.
C. C. Gorchels

1597. Jervey, Edward D. and Moss, James E., eds. FROM VIRGINIA TO MISSOURI IN 1846: THE JOURNAL OF ELIZABETH ANN COOLEY. *Missouri Hist. R. 1966 60(2): 162-206.* Elizabeth Ann Cooley kept a diary from 1842 until her death in 1848. The first part of her journal covers the years in Virginia from 1842 to 1846; the second part covers her marriage to James W. McClure and her experiences in Texas and Missouri. The editors summarize the key points covered during the first portion of the journal. They reproduce the entire journal beginning with the entry of 15 March 1846 shortly after her marriage and just before her departure to the West. The diary is kept irregularly, and some of the entries are very brief. The diarist offers many observations on local events. The original journal is in the possession of Elizabeth Cooley McClure's descendants.
W. F. Zornow

1598. Johnson, Dorothy M. THE PATIENCE OF FRANK KIRKALDIE. *Montana 1971 21(1): 12-27.* Five years in the life of Franklin Luther Kirkaldie (1828-92), an undistinguished migrant to the Montana gold fields in the 1860's. Failing at mining, and doing little better at farming, he had to wait half a decade to amass enough money to send for his wife and children in Illinois. His letters to his wife reveal the hardships of those who established agriculture in the mountains. These letters are the basis for this story of frustration and eventual moderate success. Illus.
S. R. Davison

1599. Koch, William E. HUNTING BELIEFS AND CUSTOMS FROM KANSAS. *Western Folklore 1965 24(3): 165-175.* A list of beliefs and customs collected from oral tradition, classified: Animals, Birds, To Insure Luck, Safety, and Miscellaneous.
J. M. Brady

1600. Lehman, Leola. LIFE IN THE TERRITORIES. *Chronicles of Oklahoma 1963 41(4): 370-381.* A graphic account of the life of the author's mother in the Oklahoma and Indian Territories, and in the Oklahoma Panhandle where, at Nabisco, the family lived in a dugout. The neighbors were friendly and cooperative. A farmers' union was organized and a flour mill built. 4 illus.
I. W. Van Noppen

1601. Love, Rose Leary. GEORGE WASHINGTON CARVER - THE BOY WHO WANTED TO KNOW WHY? *Negro Hist. Bull. 1967 30(2): 15-18.* Traces Carver's school years at Neosha, Missouri, and Fort Scott, Kansas. Describes his jobs after high school in and around Minneapolis, Kansas. Carver bought a laundry but later decided to sell his interest and further his education. After an unsuccessful attempt to enter Highland University, he took out a land claim, built a sod house, and farmed 160 acres. He then worked at a hotel in Winterset, Iowa, and entered nearby Simpson College. He was then 25.
D. H. Swift

1602. McBurney, Laressa Cox. MY PIONEER HOME IN OLD GREER COUNTY. *Chronicles of Oklahoma 1964 42(1): 38-45.* A personal narrative of the covered wagon trail from Vernon, Texas, to Greer County, which was in Texas until the Supreme Court decision of 1896 gave it to Oklahoma. There were no trees, nothing but grass. Nearly every home had a dugout storm shelter. Included is an account of the first school in the county.
I. W. Van Noppen

1603. Metschan, Phil. CANYON CITY "FORT-UP," 1878. *Oregon Hist. Q. 1969 70(1): 56-59.* A letter describing violent troubles in Grant County, Oregon, in 1878, with Indians who left the Malheur Agency and pillaged and killed white men in the region.
C. C. Gorchels

1604. Pedersen, Lyman C., Jr. SAMUEL PIERCE HOYT AND HIS HOME ON THE WEBER. *Utah Hist. Q. 1965 33(2): 99-108.* Contains a brief account of Hoyt's movements and business activities in Utah but concentrates on the construction of his large home in the farm community of Hoytsville. Based on an interview with Hoyt's daughter, material in the Latter Day Saints Historian's Library at Salt Lake City, and contemporary newspaper accounts.
S. L. Jones

1605. Riley, Paul D., ed. NEIGHBOR TO THE MORTONS. *Nebraska Hist. 1972 53(1): 15-34.* Reminiscences of Kate Winslow Davis, writing in the 1920's, who in the 1860's became acquainted with the Julius Sterling Morton (1832-1902) family in Nebraska City. Her father managed Morton's farm for two years before moving in 1865 to a farm of his own.
R. Lowitt

1606. Roberts, R. Jay. THE HISTORY OF AGATE SPRINGS. *Nebraska Hist. 1966 47(3): 265-293.* Surveys the historical incidents that occurred in the vicinity of Agate Springs and the activities of the Cook family who developed a ranch there before it became Agate Fossil Beds National Monument in 1965.   R. Lowitt

1607. Sackett, Marjorie. KANSAS PIONEER RECIPES. *Western Folklore 1963 22(2): 103-106.* Collection of folk recipes which demonstrate the conditions of pioneer life.   L. J. White

1608. Schmidt, William F. THE LETTERS OF CHARLES AND HELEN WOOSTER: THE PROBLEMS OF SETTLEMENT. *Nebraska Hist. 1965 46(2): 121-137.* Letters deal with Wooster's experiences during the year 1872 when he settled in Nebraska, and his wife remained in Michigan while he prepared a home for her.
R. Lowitt

1609. Snell, Joseph W., ed. ROUGHING IT ON HER KANSAS CLAIM: THE DIARY OF ABBIE BRIGHT, 1870-1871. *Kansas Hist. Q. 1971 37(3): 233-268, (4): 394-428.* Part I. This portion of the diary contains the entries from 2 September 1870 to 30 June 1871. Abbie Bright (1848-1926) was from Pennsylvania. After visiting her brother Hiram in Indiana, she visited her brother Philip who was homesteading in Kansas. Abbie's account of her teaching in Indiana, her trip from Kansas City to Wichita, the daily routine of homesteaders, and her own experience as a homesteader in Kansas, provides illuminating if not entirely new glimpses of life on the frontier. Two copies of the diary are owned by the diarist's grandson, Donald G. Fairchild of Gladbrook, Iowa. Based primarily on the second and fuller version of the diary, although some material from the first version is incorporated when it provides supplementary information; illus., map, 26 notes. Part II. Covers entries for 2 July to 20 December 1871. Abbie Bright wrote about her brothers, neighbors, cooking, sewing, gardening, letter writing, illness, buffalo hunting, and other personal experiences and housekeeping chores. Illus., 44 notes.
W. F. Zornow

1610. Steele, Annie Laurie. OLD GREER COUNTY. *Chronicles of Oklahoma 1964 42(1): 27-37.* An account of pioneer life in Greer County depicts the first houses as dugouts; wood was scarce. Well water was so bitter that cisterns were constructed. The vicissitudes of the weather were extreme with storms, droughts, floods. Some settlers left but most of those who stayed prospered. Travelers were welcomed. Communal threshings and butcherings were held. Included is a description of pioneer life by Rosabel DeBerry, the author's aunt, containing tales of hardships, pets, accidents, and unusual events. 5 notes.   I. W. Van Noppen

1611. Swartz, Lillian Carlile. LIFE IN THE CHEROKEE STRIP, OKLAHOMA TERRITORY. *Chronicles of Oklahoma 1964 42(2): 62-74.* The author's father bought a tract of woodland in the Oklahoma Territory for 30 dollars and moved his family there from Hastings, Nebraska, in 1894. He built a 10-foot square log hut. Beds were made on the hut's dirt floor. Flowers, small animals, deer abounded, and they raised a pumpkin seven feet in circumference and melon weighing 80 and 90 pounds. Sorghum was grown for sugar. In June 1895 the Carliles built a new log house. The young people enjoyed parties and square dances. A Sunday school and a subscription school were started in 1894. Floods on the Cimarron and winter storms were hazards. The family cut, hauled, and sold wood for cash. The Reverend Mr. Swartz, a Methodist, organized a congregation and a church was built in 1899. Two Carlile sisters married Swartz brothers. 2 illus.   I. W. Van Noppen

1612. Swartz, Orvoe. A PIONEER'S SOD HOUSE MEMORIES. *Chronicles of Oklahoma 1964 41(4): 408-424.* A discussion of life on the sod house frontier in Oklahoma with praise for the hardihood of the pioneers. Described are the building of sod houses, the food, amusements, and crop failures.   I. W. Van Noppen

1613. Tschirgi, Frank. WHY A PIONEER? *Ann. of Wyoming 1968 40(2): 241-266.* A reminiscent account of pioneer life in Wyoming during the 1880-90 era. The author arrived in Wyoming as a teen-age boy in 1883, and there raised cattle and sheep. Later he moved into Sheridan to enter business. Included are descriptions of transportation, buildings, ranching, terrain, and animal life. Illus.   R. L. Nichols

1614. Tucker, Robert G. RICHARD EATON - PIONEER OF ILLINOIS AND TEXAS. *Stirpes 1971 11(2): 50-68.* Traces the Eaton family from Bourbon County, Kentucky, through Crawford and Clark Counties, Illinois, to Limestone County, Texas, 1796-1850. Discusses the role of the Eatons in settling land, fighting Indians, and establishing churches in each region. 11 notes, appendix.   L. R. Murphy

1615. Utley, Beverly. THEY MADE THE WEST WORTH WINNING. *Am. Hist. Illus. 1967 2(8): 27-35.* Describes the experiences of American pioneer women. Women trekked westward for love of man, God, and adventure. Mentions vignettes of pleasant times and of hardships such as extremes of weather, lack of food, Indian attacks, disease, etc.   G. H. Skau

1616. Waldorf, John Taylor. A KID ON THE COMSTOCK. *Am. West 1970 7(2): 11-17.* Waldorf wrote the memories of his 1873-86 boyhood in the Comstock mining boom of Nevada. Quotations from his account are captions for this 10-photograph essay. Taken from a revised edition of *A Kid on the Comstock: Reminiscences of a Virginia City Childhood,* originally compiled by his daughter.   D. L. Smith

1617. Wardle, Ralph M. TERRITORIAL BRIDE. *Nebraska Hist. 1969 50(2): 207-228.* Recounts the career of Emily Greenhow Doane as a young bride in the Territory of Nebraska and as a wife in the State of Nebraska. Stressed are social affairs in a frontier society. Based on Mrs. Doane's reminiscences which were recorded for the *Omaha Daily News* in 1919.   R. Lowitt

1618. Welsch, Roger L. THE NEBRASKA SODDY. *Nebraska Hist. 1967 48(4): 335-342.* Revisionist view that the technique and rationale of sod construction are quite complex and exacting. Sod houses could be comfortable and were better suited to prairie conditions than frame construction and consequently were and are used on into the 20th century.   R. Lowitt

1619. Welsch, Roger L. "SORRY CHUCK" - PIONEER FOODWAYS. *Nebraska Hist. 1972 53(1): 99-113.* Examines the homesteader's menu and investigates his home life, literature, and folklore. Though social pressure, for example, forced the abandonment of European foodways, it also prevented the borrowing of foods from the Plains Indians.   R. Lowitt

1620. Wilmot, Luther Perry. A PLEASANT WINTER FOR LEW WILMOT. *Colorado Mag. 1970 47(1): 1-25.* A personal account of the winter of 1860-61 which the author spent away from the diggings in Georgia Gulch, working in southeastern Colorado. Describes his trip to Bent's Fort to get a freight wagon from Majors' and Russell's camp, his brush with the Indians, his service as a hunter for Zan Hicklan's Ranch (where he met Kit Carson), and his observation of recruiting activities by both the Confederacy and the Union. Wilmot was especially proud of his success in target shooting, at which he won 740 dollars. Except for the Indian scare, "it was a pleasant winter for Lew Wilmot." Illus., 24 notes.
O. H. Zabel

Urbanization and Urban Life

1621. Allen, Florence A. YODER IN THE 1920'S. *Ann. of Wyoming 1967 39(2): 257-259.* Describes briefly the development of the town of Yoder in Goshen County, Wyoming, during the 1920's. The town resulted from construction policies of the Union Pacific Railroad Company and the activities of the Goshen Townsite Development Company. Jess Yoder helped to organize the original settlement, which accounts for its name. Included is a listing of prominent events and people. Based on plat books in the Goshen County Recorder's Office and names supplied by a local citizen; 7 notes.   R. L. Nichols

1622. Anderson, Harry H. DEADWOOD: AN EFFORT AT STABILITY. *Montana 1970 20(1): 40-47.* Often pictured as the wildest of Western cities, Deadwood actually had a functioning city government in its first full year, 1876. An outbreak of small pox led to the establishment of a "Board of Health and Street Commissioners" which also took jurisdiction in homicide cases by arranging for jury trials. The board led in organizing a formal city council without waiting for authorization by territorial officials. Delegates from this irregular council appealed successfully for the appointment of County Commissioners and for the establishment of a judicial district for the Black Hills. The provisional government then dissolved, its work completed. The author includes citations from the Deadwood *Pioneer* (1876).　　　　S. R. Davison

1623. Asplin, Ray.　A HISTORY OF COUNCIL GROVE IN OKLAHOMA. *Chronicles of Oklahoma 1968 45(4): 433-450.* Now a part of the Oklahoma City complex, Council Grove was the site of councils of Plains Indians. In 1858, Jesse Chisholm recognized the importance of the location and established a trading post there. Chisholm was a scout, trader, and interpreter of considerable renown. The contruction of a nearby ranch house about 1873 may have marked the arrival of Oklahoma's first permanent settlers. Later Council Grove's timber was set aside by the government for fuel, lumber, and fence posts for nearby Fort Reno. It was opened for general settlement in 1889. 2 illus., map, 76 notes.
　　　　D. L. Smith

1624. Baker, William J.　CHARLES KINGSLEY IN LITTLE LONDON. *Colorado Mag. 1968 45(3): 187-203.* The Victorian novelist, clergyman, and social reformer Charles Kingsley visited Colorado Springs in 1874. Kingsley's son Maurice had served as first assistant treasurer of the Denver and Rio Grande Railway and his daughter Rose visited Colorado Springs. In fact, in the early 1870's Colorado Springs was essentially an English colony, sometimes called "Little London." Kingsley had written a series of letters for the local newspaper *Far West.* Thus, when Kingsley sojourned in Colorado Springs from May until July 1874 he had both family and literary connections there. Illus., 50 notes.
　　　　O. H. Zabel

1625. Beebe, Lucius.　THE INDESTRUCTIBLE MRS. BROWN. *Am. West 1966 3(2): 48-53, 93-95.* "The Unsinkable Mrs. Brown," heroine of the *Titanic,* was Margaret Tobin Brown, wife of James J. Brown, a hard-rock miner whose employer gave him a substantial share in a lucrative Colorado mining venture. With the looks, charm, and culture of "an Irish washerwoman," Mrs. Brown was unable to buy her way into Denver's formal society. Her preposterous taste for furs, for example, earned here the name of "Colorado's unique fur-bearing animal." Her return on the *Titanic* from a tour abroad to seek recognition in Europe's less exclusive spas catapulted her into the limelight. She was, on that occasion, a veritable "heroine of a disaster." Her insatiable desire for attention after that "personified the essence of corn" and gained her no greater fame than that of an international eccentric. Appended with an autobiographical assessment of Lucius Beebe from the San Francisco *Chronicle,* 13 February 1966, and a Beebe vita; illus.
　　　　D. L. Smith

1626. Bogar, Gerald Dale.　OCOSTA-BY-THE-SEA. *Pacific Northwest Q. 1963 54(1): 29-32.* Rise and collapse of a community in southwestern Washington.

1627. Bowditch, Barbara.　PIONEER PORTRAITS - CHARLES COULSON RICH. *Idaho Yesterdays 1963 7(3): 18-20.* Biographical sketch of a Mormon leader (b. 1809) who founded Bear Lake settlement in southern Idaho (1863).　　　　M. Small

1628. Brier, Warren J.　TILTING SKIRTS AND HURDY-GURDIES: A COMMENTARY ON GOLD CAMP WOMEN. *Montana 1969 19(4): 58-67.* A gathering of anecdotes and editorial comments about wild women on the Montana frontier, particularly in Virginia City. Reform campaigns by editors and townspeople did not appear to succeed in closing the notorious hurdy-gurdy houses of the community. Interspersed with quotes from the Virginia City *Post.*　　　　S. R. Davison

1629. Broussard, Ray F.　SAN ANTONIO 1835-1845: UNA CIUDAD EN TRANSICION　[San Antonio, 1835-45: A city in transition]. *Humanitas [Mexico] 1964 5: 499-529.* Presents a detailed account of sociopolitical changes in San Antonio de Bexar during the 10-year period in which it was a part of the Republic of Texas. Based on primary sources; 78 notes, biblio.　　　　R. G. Paulston

1630. Brown, Wallace.　GEORGE L. MILLER AND THE BOOSTING OF OMAHA. *Nebraska Hist. 1969 50(3): 277-291.* Discusses the efforts of George L. Miller in advancing the prosperity of Nebraska in general and Omaha in particular from 1865, when he founded the Omaha *Herald.* Through the medium of his newspaper, Miller tried to attract settlers and investments by extolling the soil, low taxes, and excellent climate of Nebraska. He also exhorted Nebraskans to improve their State by promoting tree planting, agriculture, and stockraising. The author also discusses in detail Miller's fight to make Omaha the terminus of the Union Pacific and Central Pacific Railroads. 53 notes.　　　　R. Lowitt

1631. Burnett, Hugh and Burnett, Evelyn.　MADRID PLAZA. *Colorado Mag. 1965 42(3): 224-237.* A study of one of the numerous adobe villages of Colorado. The authors describe the founding of Madrid Plaza, a result of migration of Spanish-American people from New Mexico to the Purgatoire River Valley in Colorado in 1862. Included are extensive details of the construction of the adobe houses, with a sketch of the floor plan. Reasons for the abandonment of the plaza are outlined in the conclusion.　　　　R. Sexauer

1632. Burroughs, John Rolfe.　AS IT WAS IN THE BEGINNING. *Colorado Mag. 1969 46(3): 179-188.* A summary of late-19th-century problems in Denver which are similar to those of today. The author briefly discusses the city budget, police department, minority groups, traffic and transportation, public health, morals, and zoning. Based on Minute Books in the custody of the Denver City Clerk; illus., 4 photos, 25 notes.　　　　O. H. Zabel

1633. Byars, Charles.　THE FIRST MAP OF TUCSON. *J. of Arizona Hist. 1966 7(4): 188-195.* A map drawn in the fall of 1862 by John B. Mills, Jr., at the orders of Major David Fergusson of the California Volunteers. A full-page illustration of the map is provided, as well as a separate facsimile, and there is a bibliographical note.
　　　　J. D. Filipiak

1634. Chaffee, Eugene B.　BOISE: THE FOUNDING OF A CITY. *Idaho Yesterdays 1963 7(2): 2-7.* Analyzes the founding of Boise in 1863 and its early development, with particular attention to the Boise Basin gold rush and to the contributions of Major Pinkney Lugenbeel, businessman Henry C. Riggs, and newspaperman James S. Reynolds. Drawn largely from the *Official Records of the Union and Confederate Armies* and from manuscript sources in the possession of the Idaho State Historical Society.　　　　M. Small

1635. Chudacoff, Howard P.　"WHERE ROLLS THE DARK MISSOURI DOWN." *Nebraska Hist. 1971 52(1): 1-30.* Surveys the history of Omaha from 1854, when it was on the vanguard of the frontier, to 1920, when it was a thriving regional center beset by modern problems.
　　　　R. Lowitt

1636. Cogswell, Moses Pearson.　SAN FRANCISCO IN AUGUST, 1849. *Pacific Historian 1966 10(3): 13-18.* Excerpt from the diary of Moses Pearson Cogswell, partner in Cogswell and Rand, Boston merchants, while on a business trip in 1849 to the gold panning areas around San Francisco. The document records Cogswell's life and work, describes San Francisco conditions and compares them unfavorably with other places, yet predicts that the city will "become a great city, especially if a Railroad connecting it with some City on the Mississippi should be built." Includes a photo of Cogswell.　　　　T. Cripps

1637. DeHaas, John N. and DeHaas, Bernice W.　FOOTLIGHTS AND FIRE ENGINES. *Montana 1967 17(4): 28-43.* Sketches the construction, utilization, and demolition of the first civic center in Bozeman, Montana. After financial and legal troubles it was completed and dedicated in 1890, serving as a city hall, firehouse, and auditorium. In the next three decades the building saw heavy use as both touring and local attractions appeared on its stage; details are supplied about many of the plays and performers of that era. After 1927 the theater was abandoned, but the city government facilities remained. Earthquake damage in 1959 led to the building's replacement. It was razed in 1966. The authors, a professor of architecture and his wife, made photos during the demolition which are used here as illustrations along with architectural drawings. Based on newspapers of the period.　　　　S. R. Davison

1638. Dixon, Elizabeth I., ed.　EARLY SAN FERNANDO: MEMOIRS OF CATHERINE HUBBARD DACE. *Southern California Q.*

1962 44(3): 219-267. An oral history account of the development of the San Fernando Valley from a pastoral-rural setting to the present commercial-urban life. Charles Maclay was the founder of the City of San Fernando; he was a member of the California State Assembly and Senate from 1861 until 1873. Senator George K. Porter and his brother Benjamin F. Porter bought land in the valley and, in partnership with Maclay, developed the settlement of the entire valley of over one hundred thousand acres. The San Fernando Mission was occupied by Andres Pico's family from 1846 until purchased by the San Fernando Farm Homestead Association in 1869. The narrative is very rich in family accounts of prominent people in 19th-century southern California. 62 notes.

D. H. Swift

1639. Dobyns, Henry F. TUBAC: WHERE SOME ENEMIES ROTTED. *Arizona Q. 1963 19(3): 229-232.* Gives the history of the contemporary place name Tubac as an English borrowing of a Hispanicized form of an original northern Piman designation. The article is based on material gathered while the author was a research associate of the Arizona State Museum. 9 notes.

E. P. Stickney

1640. Feil, Lin B. HELVETIA: BOOM TOWN OF THE SANTA RITAS. *J. of Arizona Hist. 1968 9(2): 77-95.* The Santa Rita Mountains of Arizona, although rich in copper ores, were not mined until the mid-1870's. At that time, a Swiss miner gave the Latin form of his homeland - Helvetia - to the mining camp which sprang up there. This early boom died when copper prices fell in 1883. After almost a decade of dormancy, the Helvetia Copper Company of New Jersey began large-scale operations. By 1899 Helvetia was inhabited by 550 people, complete with connecting stage lines, branch stores of Tucson merchants, and a school. However, problems plagued the settlement. Water and coke, both essential ingredients in smelting operations, proved to be in short supply. In 1900 a spectacular fire gutted the smelter. Copper prices plummeted in 1902. By the end of that year the population had declined to only 100 people. In 1903, when the Helvetia Copper Company reorganized, it built a new smelter. Two other companies also began operations in the area. The new boom was short-lived and the town began a slow decline throughout the period ending in 1923. In that year the public school was finally closed and the last handful of stubborn settlers reluctantly abandoned the town. Based on printed sources, contemporary newspapers, and manuscript collections in the Arizona Pioneers' Historical Society; illus., 3 photos, 76 notes.

R. J. Roske

1641. Fritzsche, Bruno. SAN FRANCISCO IN 1843: A KEY TO DR. SANDELS' DRAWING. *California Hist. Q. 1971 50(1): 3-13.* The 1843 map of Yerba Buena by G. M. Waseurtz af Sandels, of whom little is known, has remained puzzling. Hubert H. Bancroft considered portions of Sandels' *A Sojourn in California* fictional, and doubt has been cast on the veracity of the map. The fault lies not with the map but with the key for it. A second key, based on corroborating evidence, accurately identifies 15 of the 17 buildings beyond doubt. Sandels' map is therefore an accurate depiction of San Francisco in 1843. Based on primary and secondary sources; map, 35 notes.

A. Hoffman

1642. Fronk, Ruth E. MEN, MONEY, AND MINERAL. *Idaho Yesterdays 1967 11(2): 8-15.* Describes the booms and recessions of Mineral City, a silver mining community near the Snake River in Washington County. Although previously explored for mineral deposits in the 1870's, the first profitable mines were not established until 1880. The author describes the furnishings of the miners' shanties and the many uses made of the frying pan. The growth of the community and its social life are illustrated. The author outlines the ups and downs through the years caused by the fluctuating price of silver. When production costs became greater than the income, the area collapsed and is now comatose. Illus., 14 notes.

B. B. Swift

1643. Fulton, Richard W. and Bahre, Conrad J., eds. CHARLESTON, ARIZONA: A DOCUMENTARY RECONSTRUCTION. *Arizona and the West 1967 9(1): 41-64.* Charleston, Arizona, nine miles west of Tombstone on the San Pedro River, was founded in 1878 to furnish labor for the stamp mills that crushed the silver ore from the mines of Tombstone. It was a typical western boom town. Charleston went into decline as the Tombstone mines were flooded and the local mills closed. By 1890 Charleston was a ghost town. Historical detective work has rescued the town from historical oblivion. Evidence from contempo-

rary maps, newspapers, manuscripts, county records, and study of the site itself enabled the editors to reconstruct a plat map, here printed. Other documentary information presented are a list of property transactions keyed to the plat map and a list of business firms. Any biographical and bibliographic information available is included in these lists. Finally there is added a list of the registered voters in 1882 when the town was at the height of its boom. This table includes registration number, name, age, occupation, and place of birth for each. 6 illus., 2 maps, 10 notes.

D. L. Smith

1644. Fulton, Richard W. MILVILLE-CHARLESTON, COCHISE COUNTY, 1878-1889. *J. of Arizona Hist. 1966 7(1): 9-22.* There were six towns along the banks of the San Pedro River in Cochise County, southeastern Arizona, soon after the silver strike of 1877. This is the tale of the founding, development, and eventual decline of two of them, Milville and Charleston, twin cities founded in 1878 and joined by a bridge in 1881. By 1881 they had reached their peak; the decline was noticeable after 1886. Documented, illus., map, 28 notes, biblio. note.

J. D. Filipiak

1645. Gilles, Albert S., Sr. DEATH'S FIRST VISIT TO OLD FAXON. *Chronicles of Oklahoma 1966 44(3): 307-312.* Describes life in the little town of Old Faxon which had 20 families, including the doctor's. Two women and an infant died in childbirth. Then men pitched in and made coffins and dug the graves. The women lined the coffins with quilting cotton and covered that with bleached muslin. A 20-year-old girl conducted the funeral service. Old Faxon had existed nine months when the deaths occurred. The Rock Island Railroad bypassed Old Faxon and the town ceased to exist. "The old townsite has been farmland for many years." Illus.

I. W. Van Noppen

1646. Gilles, Albert S., Sr. THE INLAND PRAIRIE TOWN. *Chronicles of Oklahoma 1965 43(3): 284-287.* Inland towns were established through the enterprise of one or more businessmen, not because of necessity. These towns, not on railroads, were night stopping places for travelers by horseback or wagon. The wagon yard furnished shelter for man and beast. Such a town usually had a saloon, a merchant, and, if there was a doctor, a drugstore. School and church services were provided. If the town fathers wanted to be on a railroad they had to pay the railroad a good price, otherwise a nearby town would be established on the railroad and the businesses would have to move to it.

I. W. Van Noppen

1647. Greene, A. C. THE DURABLE SOCIETY: AUSTIN IN THE RECONSTRUCTION. *Southwestern Hist. Q. 1969 72(4): 492-518.* Austin had a more stable and enlightened society during the Civil War and Reconstruction than did other cities in Texas. This was because Austin had opposed secession in 1861, was relatively stable economically, and was never endangered during the war. Also, with the complete collapse of civil government in Texas at the end of the war and the consequent looting by Confederate soldiers, Austin welcomed the return of U.S. rule and enjoyed good relations with Unionists and Federal troops. The customary acrimony toward Negroes and Radicals was not so evident in Austin, partly because the population was expanding and Austin enjoyed many local improvements including the building of sidewalks, bridges, and new buildings. In addition, the railroad and telegraph appeared during this time. Photos.

R. W. Delaney

1648. Guenther, Richard L. A HISTORY OF THE WELSH COMMUNITY OF CARROLL, NEBRASKA. *Nebraska Hist. 1965 46(3): 209-224.* Discusses the Welsh community of Carroll, Nebraska: its cultural, political and economic strivings, from its beginnings in the 1880's to the mid-1920's when its homogeneity began to break down.

R. Lowitt

1649. Hager, Anna Marie. A SALUTE TO THE PORT OF LOS ANGELES - FROM MUD FLATS TO MODERN DAY MIRACLE. *California Hist. Soc. Q. 1970 49(4): 329-335.* Surveys the transformation of San Pedro Bay from mud flats and islands to one of the Nation's most important seaports. Known as San Pedro since 1592, potentialities of the bay were recognized by a number of far-seeing men in the 19th century. Phineas Banning was active in the harbor's development for over 30 years. George H. Peck donated park lands. During the 1890's the "Free Harbor" contest occurred, with the forces favoring San Pedro, led by Senator

Stephen M. White, defeating the Southern Pacific-sponsored Santa Monica harbor for Federal funds. The development of the harbor caused social as well as geographical changes. The Brighton Beach resort area gave way to other, newer colonies of social activity. Islands were removed, breakwaters constructed, and new channels dredged. Skeletons and artifacts were unearthed by construction projects. Terminal Island was joined to the mainland. A part of the City of Los Angeles since 1909, San Pedro Harbor is now the site of shipyards, canneries, manufacturing firms, government installations, port facilities, and tremendous activity.
A. Hoffman

1650. Hahn, Harlan. THE LOST HISTORY OF BOOMTOWN: SOME INTERPRETATIONS FROM HAMLIN GARLAND. *Ann. of Iowa 1965 37(8): 598-610.* Concerns the writer Hamlin Garland's unsuccessful quest to discover in the Midwest a sense of continuity with the past. The historical nature of the Middle Border region is attributed to a preoccupation with the future. The rural town, having no past and not much present, looked only to the future. Pioneer restlessness and the changing world in which the towns developed accentuated the lack of a sense of history. Boosterism insured a large degree of conformity and was the major regional tradition. Obviously it too was future-oriented. Based largely on Garland's writings; illus., 36 notes.   D. C. Swift

1651. Hammer, Kenneth. TERRITORIAL TOWNS AND THE RAILROADS. *North Dakota Hist. 1969 36(4): 356-368.* The Dakota Territory, like so much of the West, is dotted with former towns, each of which were founded with high hopes of becoming the great town of the area. The original town pattern was determined largely by the distance that could be traveled in a day by cart. The railroad men laid out sidings at places where they hoped towns would be founded. Some railroad-instigated towns were populated from those who came from towns that were obviously by-passed by the railroads and thus doomed. Feuding between towns for the privilege of having the railroad come by often caused the demise of towns who paid too much for the privilege. By the 1880's the rail network was nearly set and the previous pattern of scattered communities had resolved into the more regular pattern dictated by the rail routes. Illus., photos, 11 notes.   E. P. Costello

1652. Henderson, Patrick D. BRADSHAW BONANZA. *New Mexico Hist. R. 1963 38(2): 151-162.* At its inception Bradshaw City was proclaimed the future capital of Arizona, but like numerous other mining camps, it was short-lived. The initial strike was made in 1869, the peak was reached in mid-1871. 30 notes.   D. F. Henderson

1653. Hill, Burton S. BUFFALO - ANCIENT COW TOWN, A WYOMING SAGA. *Ann. of Wyoming 1963 35(2): 125-154.* Discusses the frontier history of Buffalo, Wyoming from 1879 to 1900. Describes early settlers, the founding of banks and businesses, and the organization of early schools and churches. Shows the economic benefits brought to the town by Fort McKinney and how the growing cattle ranching industry aided town development. Discusses local political developments and the role of Buffalo citizens in territorial and early state affairs. Based on published state and local accounts.   R. L. Nichols

1654. Hill, Burton S. A GIRL CALLED NETTIE. *Ann. of Wyoming 1965 37(2): 147-156.* Discusses the activities of Nettie Wright in Buffalo, Wyoming. Includes biographical material on Mrs. Wright prior to her arrival in Buffalo, and describes her business activities as a saloon keeper and dance-hall operator in that community. Based on Johnson County Court House records and personal reminiscences of pioneer settlers. Illus.   R. L. Nichols

1655. Hill, Rita and Hill, Janaloo. ALIAS SHAKESPEARE, THE TOWN NOBODY KNEW. *New Mexico Hist. R. 1967 42(3): 211-227.* A description and history of a ghost town, first called "Mexican Spring," at the peak of its prosperity as a mining town "Ralston," and during its decline "Shakespeare." Silver was discovered in 1869, and in time several mines were opened. At some point in 1871 the city centered a diamond boom, which quickly turned into a diamond swindle. In 1879 a second silver boom began which lasted until the depression of 1893 closed the mines and ended the existence of the town. Based on newspapers; 84 notes.   D. F. Henderson

1656. Hochmuth, C. Arthur. FONTAINE QUI BOUILLE. *Colorado Mag. 1966 43(2): 114-120.* Traces the history of Manitou Springs, Colorado, from the first written references to the site, as "Fontaine qui Bouille," by French traders as early as 1815, until the name was changed in 1871. Illus., 16 notes.   I. W. Van Noppen

1657. Hornbein, Marjorie. DENVER'S STRUGGLE FOR HOME RULE. *Colorado Mag. 1971 48(4): 337-354.* From Denver's chartering in 1861 until 1889 it had essentially home rule. In 1889, however, Colorado created a board of public works and in 1891 a fire and police board for the city, but subject to the State. Traces the efforts for reform, including threats of violence, particularly in 1894 when troops and police faced each other in the streets. Reform demand grew and in 1903 the new Article XX of the Colorado constitution provided for home rule in Colorado cities and the merger of the city and county offices in Denver. There the local council replaced the legislature as the city's governing body, the city corporation gained "full power as to municipal ownership of public utilities," and "fire, police, and public works departments were placed under civil service." Full home rule was delayed, however, by charter revision and litigation until 1911. Illus., 112 notes.   O. H. Zabel

1658. Jackson, Pauline P. LIFE AND SOCIETY IN SAPULPA. *Chronicles of Oklahoma 1965 43(3): 297-318.* Describes the life and growth of Sapulpa, a county seat town in Oklahoma. Houses had gardens for homegrown food; hunting nearby was excellent. There was drinking and shooting on Saturday nights. There was one organ, a band, and two elocution teachers. Each Fourth of July was celebrated in a spectacular manner. Oil boom days brought the nickelodeon and the silent movies. County fairs were held after 1915. There were many women's and civic clubs. The Lucile Opera House was used for talent shows, benefit balls, recitals, graduation exercises, and convention meetings. The hard times of 1907-13 caused economic hardship, bank failures, and cessation of the growth of the town. "Today Sapulpa is a small but important industrial city." Appendix, 75 notes.   I. W. Van Noppen

1659. Johnson, J. R. COVINGTON: NEBRASKA'S SINFUL CITY. *Nebraska Hist. 1968 49(3): 269-281.* Recounts the brief, spectacular history of this Missouri River settlement across from Sioux City, Iowa, from its official beginnings in 1857 until it merged with South Sioux City, Nebraska, in 1893. At one time it was known as one of the "three wickedest places in the world."   R. Lowitt

1660. Judd, B. Ira. TUBA CITY, MORMON SETTLEMENT. *J. of Arizona Hist. 1969 10(1): 37-42.* The Mormon leader Jacob Hamblin founded Tuba City, to the north and slightly to the east of Flagstaff. In 1875 Chief Tuba of the Hopi tribe, in gratitude for help extended in irrigating his tribe's farms, gave Hamblin the townsite complete with a running spring. Soon Mormons from Utah joined Hamblin and Tuba City became a favorite stopping place for travelers. Fields were planted; with the help of an extensive irrigation system, field crops and fruit trees grew. In Janurary 1900 the Federal Government decided to erect a Navajo training school on the site. Negotiations went on for the next two years; by 31 December 1902 all settlers signed quitclaim deeds in exchange for a total of 48 thousand dollars for their lands and improvements. Today only tall boundary poplars remind one of the early settlement. Based on original records and secondary accounts; map, 7 notes.
R. J. Roske

1661. Kensel, W. Hudson. INLAND EMPIRE MINING AND THE GROWTH OF SPOKANE, 1883-1905. *Pacific Northwest Q. 1969 60(2): 84-97.* Even though the city was located relatively far from many of the mines in the Coeur d'Alene and Colville mining districts, Spokane cashed in on its claim to being the best place to get supplies for mining activities. Construction of transportation systems from Spokane, the development of rich mines in all directions from Spokane, and bumper crops south of the city confirmed the strength of the city. Even after large companies with headquarters in other cities gained financial control of the mines, Spokane continued to benefit from stock dividends and the sale and shipment of supplies.   C. C. Gorchels

1662. King, William F. EL MONTE, AN AMERICAN TOWN IN SOUTHERN CALIFORNIA, 1851-1866. *Southern California Q. 1971 53(4): 317-332.* Describes the early history of El Monte, which is "a neglected part of the chronicle of southern California." El Monte started during the 1850's as an area peopled chiefly by American farmers who came mostly from the South. Between 1851 and 1866, El Monte was a raw frontier town where vigilante activity was common. Reflecting their "strong southern heritage," many El Monte citizens were Democrats in their political allegiance and Baptists in their religious affiliation. During the Civil War there were also pro-Confederate activities. By 1866, El Monte was established as a highly successful agricultural center; this may have caused its slow growth during the next 75 years, for not until World War II did it change significantly. Based on primary and secondary sources; 2 illus., map, 81 notes.   W. L. Bowers

1663. Kircus, Peggy D. FORT DAVID A. RUSSELL: A STUDY OF ITS HISTORY FROM 1867 TO 1890. *Ann. of Wyoming 1968 40(2): 161-192.* Discusses the building and operations of Fort David A. Russell in Wyoming at present-day Cheyenne. Built to protect construction crews of the Union Pacific Railroad, it remained in use as a supply depot. Described are the post facilities, health and diet problems, and relations between the garrison and the nearby Cheyenne Indians. Based on published journals, government records, and secondary accounts; illus., 32 notes. To be continued.   R. L. Nichols

1664. Krenkel, John H. DEVELOPMENT OF THE PORT OF LOS ANGELES. *Am. Neptune 1965 25(4): 262-273.* Traces the transformation of Los Angeles harbor into one of the great seaports of the world, through federal expenditures beginning in 1870. The size and depth of the harbor were steadily extended through the late 19th and early 20th centuries by the building of breakwaters and the dredging of the offshore waters. Legislation and programs, with costs and chronology, are examined. The struggle over the choice between San Pedro and Santa Monica as a focus for the port and the role of Collis P. Huntington in that conflict are also assessed. Main source is government documents.
                                                             J. G. Lydon

1665. Krenkel, John H. THE DEVELOPMENT OF THE PORT OF LOS ANGELES. *J. of Transport Hist. [Great Britain] 1965 7(1): 24-33.* Los Angeles could not develop as a port until its estuary was deepened and the outer bay protected; these tasks could only be undertaken by the Federal government. Local pressure on the government ensured continuous development from 1871 to 1934. The U.S. government was prepared to spend large sums on Los Angeles both to facilitate trade for the Southwest and to develop a naval base. Documented mainly from U.S. Congressional documents; 53 notes.   D. H. Murdoch

1666. Kubicek, Earl C. SOLDIERS AND SINNERS AT LOMA PARDA. *Smithsonian J. of Hist. 1967 2(1): 43-54.* A difficult area of historical research is the documentation of the history of frontier towns, such as Loma Parda which was built in the territory of New Mexico in the second half of the 19th century. The author's research reveals that this small town dedicated itself to the entertainment of Army personnel from Fort Union, a lonely outpost guarding the Santa Fe Trail. The fortunes of Loma Parda prospered or failed along with the military establishment it served. 7 illus., 27 notes.   W. L. Willigan

1667. Larsen, Lawrence H. and Branyan, Robert L. THE DEVELOPMENT OF AN URBAN CIVILIZATION ON THE FRONTIER OF THE AMERICAN WEST. *Societas: A R. of Social Hist. 1971 1(1): 33-50.* By 1880 accepted eastern norms of urban services had been carried to the West by the settlers. Streets were rarely hard surfaced. Garbage was no serious problem. As to disposal of sewage, only San Francisco and Portland had advanced to levels comparable to the East. Police protection was on a level with that of the East, and San Francisco and Stockton were outstanding for their fire departments. All towns had public schools. Many had no parks, outstanding exceptions being San Francisco, Sacramento, Leavenworth, and Omaha. Most towns had cultural halls; San Francisco had 12 theaters. Most urban centers provided gas street lights; in 1880 Denver led the way with electricity. As the communities grew, public transportation became a need which was met either by an omnibus or by a horse railroad, or in San Francisco by cable cars. By the 1880's the newer cities of the West were no longer frontier outposts. 21 notes.
                                                             E. P. Stickney

1668. Lavender, David. THIS WONDROUS TOWN; THIS INSTANT CITY. *Am. West 1967 4(3): 4-14, 68-70.* Leadville, Colorado, became the instant center of a bonanza mining operation in the winter of

1878-79. In this heavily timbered upper valley of the Arkansas River, at high altitudes, the Leadville stampede developed, once it was realized what the probable potential was. In a methodical fashion corporate capital was beginning to exploit the region almost before the individualistic local placer miners knew what was afoot. For about three deceptive years the upper Arkansas gave all the appearances of a frontier myth fulfilled. If he worked hard and fast enough the poor man could make his fortune through the strength of his own hands. Almost any untrained man could strike ore almost anywhere on Carbonate Hill or Fryer Hill. Whether it was rich enough to pay was the suspenseful question. The frenzied growing pains of Leadville were typical for the mining frontier. The boom came to a screeching halt as the 20 million dollar Little Pittsburgh mine ran out of ore in early 1880. Soon others tumbled. Swiftly, by about 1882, Leadville changed from a frontier mining camp to a clearly recognizable eastern-type American city. Based on contemporary journalistic descriptions and later studies; 8 illus., biblio. note.   D. L. Smith

1669. Lee, Wayne. NAMES AND PLACES. *Western Folklore 1966 25(2): 122-124.* Concerns name changes of Nebraska towns.
                                                             J. M. Brady

1670. Madsen, Brigham D. and Madsen, Betty M. CORINNE, THE FAIR: GATEWAY TO MONTANA MINES. *Utah Hist. Q. 1969 37(1): 102-123.* Describes how anticipations developed that a construction camp along the line of the Union Pacific Railroad would become an important townsite because of its convenience as a transfer point to Montana mining operations and the availability of large quantities of fresh water from the Bear River on which it was located. Developments in the town of Corinne are described up to 1878 when it became clear that the anticipated growth was not to be realized. An additional factor of historical interest is derived from the predominantly non-Mormon makeup of the population of the community during this "boom" period. Derived mainly from contemporary newspaper accounts and published reminiscences of Western pioneers.   S. L. Jones

1671. McClenahan, Judith. CALL AND SEE THE ELEPHANT. *Idaho Yesterdays 1967 11(3): 11-13.* "Wyatt Earp joined the Coeur d'Alene gold rush of 1884 and established the White Elephant Saloon in Eagle City." The author describes Earp's efforts to break up some of the holdings of earlier locators and the protracted litigation caused thereby. The Earp brothers' true vocations were as saloon-keepers. Their short tenure of business in Idaho was in a tent they purchased for 132 dollars on 26 April 1884, complete with tables, chairs, bar equipment and stock. Illus.
                                                             B. B. Swift

1672. McLear, Patrick. ECONOMIC GROWTH AND THE PANIC OF 1857 IN KANSAS CITY. *Bull. of the Missouri Hist. Soc. 1970 26(2): 144-156.* In 1856, commerce in Kansas City grew rapidly due to westward expansion, to the city's strategic location as a trade center, and to the peace in neighboring Kansas that resulted when Governor John Geary successfully reduced the violence and turmoil that had accompanied the slavery controversy in Kansas. Immigration, too, contributed significantly to the urban development of Kansas City. The Panic of 1857 had little impact in Kansas City, scarcely slowing the pace of the city's growth or its commerce. Based primarily on secondary sources; 27 notes.   H. T. Lovin

1673. Mellinger, Philip J. FRONTIER CAMP TO SMALL TOWN: A STUDY OF COMMUNITY DEVELOPMENT. *Ann. of Wyoming 1971 43(2): 259-269.* Traces the 20-year transition of Hartville from a disorganized turn-of-the-century frontier camp into a small town with a well-defined political, social, and economic structure. Founded by prospectors in 1881, Hartville grew quickly during a mining boom in 1889 but retained its frontier characteristics. The community required two decades to assimilate its immigrant population and develop law and order, political stability, conventional revenue sources, public services, and a nonspeculative economy. These changes were hastened by realistic boosting from the local newspaper, an increase in family population, the formation of civic groups, and the realization that the once-anticipated unlimited economic expansion was impossible. The complex series of adjustments needed to transform Hartsville into an organized town demonstrates the necessity for additional study of community creation processes. Based chiefly on Hartville town records, the *Hartville Uplift,* and interviews with 20 early area residents; 25 notes.   G. R. Adams

1674. Miller, Nyle H. and Richmond, Robert W. SHERIDAN, A FABLED END-OF-TRACK TOWN ON THE UNION PACIFIC RAILROAD, 1868-1869. *Kansas Hist. Q. 1968 34(4): 427-442.* A graphic picture is painted of the wild doings in Sheridan, the end-of-track town for the Union Pacific, Eastern Division, from May 1868 to May 1870. The life of the town rose and fell with the bustle of railroad construction. The tempo of the town dropped off as track construction slowed down during the winter of 1868-69 and after January 1870, when construction had pushed more than 50 miles beyond the town. Illus.
W. F. Zornow

1675. Mitchell, Bruce. JUDGE BURKE'S WENATCHEE, 1888-93. *Pacific Northwest Q. 1965 56(3): 97-105.* Sketch of real estate speculations and development in the early days of the town of Wenatchee, Washington, with emphasis on the activities of Thomas Burke and the influence of railroad construction.
C. C. Gorchels

1676. Mulford, Prentice. CAMP - A GHOST TOWN IN THE MAKING. *Pacific Historian 1966 10(2): 39-43.* Describes the details of gold mining camp environment, stressing the ephemeral daily conditions of life in a frontier society and their transitory nature. Illus.
T. R. Cripps

1677. Murphy, Lawrence R. RAYADO: PIONEER SETTLEMENT IN NORTHEASTERN NEW MEXICO, 1848-1857. *New Mexico Hist. R. 1971 46(1): 37-56.* Discusses the establishment of a permanent settlement at Rayado on the edge of the Sangre de Cristo Mountains in what is now Colfax County. A huge tract of land including Rayado was granted in 1841 to Carlos Beaubien and Guadalupe Miranda. Miranda fled before the advancing American troops in 1846, leaving Beaubien full control over the grant. Beaubien then employed Lucien Bonaparte Maxwell to establish a foothold on the eastern side of the Sangre de Cristos. Mentions the problems of maintaining the settlement Maxwell founded in 1848, in particular defense against Indian attacks. After Maxwell's departure in 1857, Rayado diminished in importance. 56 notes.
D. F. Henderson

1678. Myers, Leel. AN EXPERIMENT IN PROHIBITION. *New Mexico Hist. R. 1965 40(4): 293-308.* Eddy, now Carlsbad, New Mexico was intended to be a model town. The founder, Charles Bishop Eddy, opposed the use of alcoholic beverages. He tried, through a provision in all deeds of lots sold which forbade the manufacture or sale thereon of intoxicating liquors to be used as a beverage, to free the settlement "of the frontier's iniquitous saloon." For 10 years the saloon men attempted in various ways to circumvent the regulation. This resulted in the founding of Phenix a mile and a half south of Eddy. Crime and violence flourished in Phenix to the dismay of the citizens of Eddy. In 1899, the first saloon moved back into Eddy. The restrictions had not been removed, "but the town had had enough of the experiment and it appears that all concerned tacitly decided to ignore them." Documented, 27 notes.
D. F. Henderson

1679. Myhra, Thomas J. THE SOCIAL SIGNIFICANCE OF EARLY BISMARCK. *North Dakota Hist. 1963 30(2/3): 72-46.* Bismarck, which for the first ten years of its existence displayed the characteristics of a frontier town, by 1881 had become an orderly city. Troops at Fort Abraham Lincoln and the railroad and steamboat employees kept the population fluid and caused people to tolerate vice. Largely because of the steamboat industry Bismarck experienced most of the social and economic influences that were being felt throughout the nation this period: sudden wealth alongside poverty; labor strife, strikes and picket lines, violence and murder, and a wide gulf in social position between management and labor. Illus., biblio.
I. W. Van Noppen

1680. Myres, Sandra L. FORT WORTH, 1870-1900. *Southwestern Hist. Q. 1968 72(2): 200-222.* Thriving Fort Worth, founded in 1849 in conjunction with an Army installation, declined during the Civil War to just another small settlement clinging to the edges of the Texas frontier. New civic-minded settlers and promotion people envisioned Fort Worth's potential and made a concerted effort to improve things. Not until 1876 did a railroad rescue the town from oblivion. By 1900 it was a flourishing West Texas marketing and trade center. 16 illus., 22 notes.
D. L. Smith

1681. Nash, Gerald. GOVERNMENT ENTERPRISE IN THE WEST: THE SAN FRANCISCO HARBOR, 1863-1963. *U. of Wyoming Pub. 1966 32: 77-93, 158-160.* Until the transcontinental railroad was completed in 1869, San Francisco was the most important Pacific coast entrepot for bulky goods and immigrants. Not until the present century was its supremacy as the leading harbor on the west coast seriously challenged. An 1853 California legislative investigation deplored the predatory use of the harbor by "capricious enterprise" and urged a development plan to save it from utter ruin. Sunken wrecks as well as rocks threatened navigation. Unauthorized wharves added to the difficulties. In 1863 the State assumed jurisdiction and inaugurated State ownership, one of the few cases of such in the country. This was a last resort measure because of the increasing neglect and deterioration under private auspices and because of the conflict of interest groups over the harbor properties. During the first 50 years public enterprise brought undoubted benefits to the San Francisco harbor. In the 20th century, however, these were offset by political corruption, lack of long range planning, inflexible finance procedures, and related difficulties. In 1957 the State legislature created a port authority to coordinate the increasing Federal participation in public transportation with State ownership and management of the harbor. Evaluation of this new development will have to await detailed qualitative appraisals of individual projects that will be the bases for statistical and quantitative studies of modern Western transportation. 32 notes.
D. L. Smith

1682. Nelson, Kitty Jo Parker. PRESCOTT: SKETCH OF A FRONTIER CAPITAL, 1863-1900. *Arizoniana 1963 4(4): 17-38.* This article appeared as Parts I and II of *Prescott's First Century, 1863-1964.* Before Prescott was founded its location was selected, Tucson being ruled out as a capital because of Confederate sympathies. The people, architecture, and cultural tone of the community were American and Yankee from the beginning. Prescott suffered economically from the removal of the capital to Tucson in 1867. Includes a guide to 75 historical landmarks of Prescott with an accompanying map. Illus.
E. P. Stickney

1683. Parker, Watson. SOME BLACK HILLS GHOST TOWNS AND THEIR ORIGINS. *South Dakota Hist. 1972 2(2): 89-114.* An essay on the 19th-century ghost towns in the Black Hills. Discusses the origins and bustling activity of the mining camps, 1870-1900. 21 illus., 64 notes.
D. H. Swift

1684. Pearson, Jim B. LIFE IN LA BELLE: A NEW MEXICO MINING TOWN. *New Mexico Hist. R. 1970 45(2): 147-158.* A social history of La Belle, a small New Mexico mining town of about one thousand, located on Comanche Creek 12 miles south of the Colorado-New Mexico border. Within six months of the news of a gold strike, 600 people crowded into La Belle. At its height it had a newspaper, eight general stores, a book and stationery shop, a drug store, a shoe shop, several hotels, and houses of ill repute. By 1897 the population began to drop and businesses moved out; by 1900 it had only 49 residents. Based on the La Belle *Cresset;* 51 notes.
D. F. Henderson

1685. Pedersen, Gilbert J. "THE TOWNSITE IS NOW SECURE": TUCSON INCORPORATES, 1871. [SIC]. *J. of Arizona Hist. 1970 11(3): 151-174.* After the Civil War, Tucson began to assume economic and political importance. The capital of Arizona Territory, it was also the mercantile center and commercial base as well as the location of an Army post which assured it some immunity from menacing Apache raids. By 1871 its population had reached perhaps three thousand. A principal handicap to growth, however, was that business adventurers could acquire some rights to the land only as "tenants by sufferance;" the land was Federal property. They thus lacked good title to the land and a mortgageable interest. The only exceptions were the few who could prove a continuous series of deeds dating back to original Spanish or Mexican authorities who were legally empowered to grant such deeds. Congressional acts in 1863 and 1864 granting town sites to proper local authorities, territorial legislation in 1871 regulating town sites and establishing procedures for land distribution, and completion of U.S. surveys in 1871 cleared the way. Procedures for obtaining legal titles were initiated, and the process began. At last, on 3 July 1874, the territorial delegate to Congress telegraphed that "full title to the Town Site is now secure" and the village of Tucson was officially established. It was incorporated as a city on 7 February 1877. 7 illus., 3 maps, 38 notes.
D. L. Smith

1686. Pool, Oran Jo. OLD HICO ON HONEY CREEK. *Southwestern Hist. Q. 1964 67(4): 485-490.* History of the founding, growth, and disappearance of an early settlement in Hamilton County. Old Hico was a typical frontier settlement with hand-hewn furnishings and simple diet. A petition for a separate county was granted in 1858, and for a post office in 1860. Also in 1860, the Hamilton County Minute Detachment of Mounted Texas Rangers was organized for defense against Comanche raids. Hico men served in at least two units during the Civil War. A major problem for Hico was transportation. By 1880 the Texas Central Railway was built across Hamilton county, two miles west of Hico. The townspeople completely relocated on the rail line. Every building was removed, except for a limestone mill which was torn down about 1940. A monument made from the old millstones was erected on the site in 1963 by the Hamilton County Historical Survey Committee. 22 notes.
W. A. Buckman

1687. Powell, Clarence Alva. EARLY OKLAHOMA SKETCH: KIOWA. *Arizona Q. 1965 21(1): 60-63.* A personal and literary comment on life in a small town (Kiowa, Oklahoma) in 1910-11.
J. D. Filipiak

1688. Remy, Caroline. HISPANIC-MEXICAN SAN ANTONIO: 1836-61. *Southwestern Hist. Q. 1968 71(4): 564-582.* San Antonio was the first Mexican town that travelers from the East encountered in Texas. This thumbnail sketch of the Hispanic-Mexican culture of the city is keyed to 12 illustrations. 33 notes.
D. L. Smith

1689. Savage, W. Sherman. GEORGE WASHINGTON OF CENTRALIA, WASHINGTON. *Negro Hist. Bull. 1963 27(2): 44-47.* Traces the career of George Washington (1817-1902), who was born in Virginia of a slave father and a white mother and who moved west as the ward of a white family, living for a time in Ohio, Missouri, and Illinois and finally settling in Washington, where he founded the city of Centralia. Documented.
L. Gara

1690. Schnell, J. Christopher and McLear, Patrick E. WHY THE CITIES GREW: A HISTORIOGRAPHICAL ESSAY ON WESTERN URBAN GROWTH, 1850-1880. *Bull. of the Missouri Hist. Soc. 1972 28(3): 162-177.* An essay about the growth of major American cities from Chicago and St. Louis westward to San Francisco and Seattle. Also treated are Kansas City, Minneapolis, Galveston, Houston, Denver, and Salt Lake City. Lists nine reasons which in varying combinations account for the growth of the cities mentioned. Based mainly on secondary sources; 38 notes.
H. T. Lovin

1691. Seale, William. SAN AUGUSTINE, IN THE TEXAS REPUBLIC. *Southwestern Hist. Q. 1969 72(3): 347-370.* Principally because of its strategic location on the San Antonio Road, San Augustine in East Texas flourished in the late 1830's and early 1840's. Its amenities included two colleges. East Texas was weakly governed under the Republic; and San Augustine with its road connections across the border to the Red River giving access to the gulf enjoyed the benefits of the unrestrained commercial intercourse which this location encouraged. Farming and speculation became the mainstays of its flourishing economy. Failure to adapt to changing external circumstances brought decline and oblivion for the town. 14 illus., 35 notes.
D. L. Smith

1692. Sites, George E., Jr. THE BRADFORD MAP OF NOGALES, ARIZONA. *J. of Arizona Hist. 1970 11(1): 1-13.* A natural pass through the desert mountains to and from Mexico was used as a camping area because of available forage, wood, and water. A trading post established there in 1880 soon grew into a small settlement called Issacson. Two years later it became the junction for the New Mexico and Arizona Railroad with the Sonora Railroad, linking the Mexican port of Guaymas with Arizona Territory towns. Issacson, renamed Nogales, soon prospered from rail activity, trade with Mexico, and development of nearby mines. Clamor for its incorporation, litigation to clear up the confusion in land titles, and uncertainty as to the precise location of the international boundary (it was situated on the boundary as a consequence of the Gadsden Purchase of 1854 by the United States from Mexico), caused conjecture and concern. Based on the survey that he made of the townsite, William Bradford, Jr., a civil engineer with the New Mexico and Arizona Railroad, prepared a map for the Nogales town council. It was adopted as the first official map of the town. It is still a basic reference item for

use by Nogales. Today it is stored in the Santa Cruz County Recorder's office. 2 illus., 21 notes.
D. L. Smith

1693. Sleeper, James D. PORTRAIT OF A SMALL TOWN: EIGHTY YEARS OF PROGRESS IN IRVINE, CALIFORNIA. *J. of the West 1967 6(4): 604-620.* Irvine, in Orange County, California, began in April 1887 when the estate of James Irvine deeded to the Santa Fe Railroad a depot site and right-of-way across the San Joaquin Rancho. Trains do not stop today in this community of 41 permanent residents, but it is not a town without a history. The author traces the development of the community as a shipping point for the agricultural products of the area. He recounts the development of the school system which became the center of the social and cultural life of the small community. Bypassed by major highways, the unincorporated town has been likewise bypassed by progress. It remains what it has always been, a sleepy, peaceful community. Illus.
D. N. Brown

1694. Smith, Duane Allan. MINING CAMPS: MYTH OR REALITY. *Colorado Mag. 1967 44(2): 93-110.* In the years after the "old" mining West ended, pulp writers and pseudohistorians created a never-never land, and a few refurbished camps are visited by tourists who interview natives who have a wealth of stories. On the other hand some scholars of stature are now studying the mining frontier, and more such scholars are needed. Urbanization was responsible for most of the problems of a mining town, such as sanitation, law and order, street maintenance, justice, advertising, railroads, high prices, isolation, and investment of profits. These and other problems are discussed as fields for research. 7 illus., 25 notes mostly from primary sources.
I. W. Van Noppen

1695. Smith, Helena Huntington. RAWLINS: PROFILE OF A RAILROAD TOWN. *Am. West 1969 6(3): 24-28.* Rawlins, Wyoming, was sired by the Union Pacific Railroad 102 years ago. It is on the Laramie-Green River sector, and, even today in the "twilight" of the railroads, 40 trains a day run through it. According to the author, whatever happened anywhere along the Union Pacific worthy of note, "happened bigger and better, or worse and more of it, in the vicinity of Rawlins." In this the author includes blizzards, holdups, and history. 3 illus.
D. L. Smith

1696. Sparger, Julia K. YOUNG ARDMORE. *Chronicles of Oklahoma 1965 43(4): 394-415.* From 1855 the Ardmore area was held communally by the Chickasaw Nation. From 1865 to 1900 a white person could settle there by marrying a Chickasaw or by buying land from Chickasaw citizens. In 1880 Alva Roth, who had married a Chickasaw, built the 700 Ranch on the site of Ardmore. In 1886 the railroad came and Ardmore was located on a map. Stores were built, ranches were important, by 1895 over a million dollars had come into the area from cotton, and coal mining was begun. The two "oil springs" became health resorts. There are descriptions of the lives of pioneer families and of the growth of Ardmore. There were the Robinson Opera House, shows, turkey shoots, dances. Ardmore was the site of the Federal court. By 1895 there were over a hundred lawyers out of a population of three thousand. After 1897 the Indians held land in severalty instead of communally. This caused a problem for those who had leased land. In 1898 telephones and electric lights were installed, in 1902 water mains were laid. Hargrove College was established in 1895. Oil was found in 1913 and the county filled up overnight. Biblio.
I. W. Van Noppen

1697. Stelter, Gilbert A. THE BIRTH OF A FRONTIER BOOM TOWN: CHEYENNE IN 1867. *Ann. of Wyoming 1967 39(1): 4-33.* Discusses the development of Cheyenne, Wyoming, as an example of the western cities built for the workers along the route of the Union Pacific Railroad. The author points out that the railroad chose the townsite and provided the short-term economic impetus for founding the settlement. Although local leaders encountered temporary difficulty with law enforcement and vigilante action, most of their efforts were spent on the problems of public health and sanitation, establishing a school, and developing a diversified economic base. Finally, a discussion of religion, journalism, and recreation is included. Based on newspapers, city archives, and secondary material; illus., 80 notes.
R. L. Nichols

1698. Steunenberg, A. K. FROM FRATERNITY TO PATERNITY: THE CALDWELL BROTHERHOOD OF BACHELORS.

Idaho Yesterdays 1966 10(4): 18-21. "Hilarious reports of organized bachelorhood in Caldwell entertained the community at the time Idaho became a state." The author provides selected editorial comments from a column in the Caldwell *Tribune,* playfully called the "Marriage Bureau." After three years the fraternity became known as the "Happy Fathers' Association." All of the original members, except five, had gotten married. 2 illus.   D. H. Swift

1699. Steunenberg, Bess.   EARLY DAYS IN CALDWELL. *Idaho Yesterdays 1966 10(4): 12-17.* "Recollections of what Caldwell was like, at least in the eyes of a child, at the turn of the century." The author describes his home town at the turn of the century, including the physical setting and prominent landmarks of the community. The College of Idaho was a factor in community growth and helped produce leaders in business, civic, and cultural endeavors. Caldwell was the central market for a large farming area. It also developed as a railroad shipping point for miners, wool growers, and cattlemen in Owyhee County. 5 illus.
                                                               D. H. Swift

1700. Storey, Brit Allan.   WILLIAM JACKSON PALMER, PROMOTER. *Colorado Mag. 1966 43(1): 44-55.* Traces the activities of William Jackson Palmer, the founder of Colorado Springs and Durango, Colorado. He promoted towns through which his Denver and Rio Grande Railroad passed, often at the expense and eventual demise of other towns in the area. Whatever his tactics, however, it cannot be denied that he was instrumental in the development of central Colorado. Documented from personal letters of Palmer.   R. Sexauer

1701. Studer, Jack J.   THE FIRST MAP OF OAKLAND, CALIFORNIA: AN HISTORICAL SPECULATION AS SOLUTION TO AN ENIGMA. *California Hist. Soc. Q. 1969 48(1): 59-71.* Unravels the mystery surrounding the first map of Oakland drawn by Pierre Portois in 1852. Referred to in court cases, no copy of it has ever been found. By investigating the circumstances around which the map was drawn, the author finds that a group of squatters with a vested interest in the land that came to comprise the City of Oakland engaged a surveyor, Julius Kellersberger, to survey the land and to draw a city map. The squatters, led by Horace W. Carpentier, needed legislative approval for the city's incorporation and were pressed for time in which to get it because the 1852 legislative session was nearing its end. When Kellersberger refused to hurry the survey, Carpentier hired Pierre Portois to draw a map, using Kellersberger's data. The Portois map served its purpose because the legislature approved the incorporation of the City of Oakland. Carpentier presumably burned the Portois map instead of filing it. Kellersberger's map came out later that year and was to serve as the reference for hundreds of deeds. Meanwhile, the Portois map maintained an enigmatic existence. Based on Contra Costa County deeds, State legislative journals, and secondary sources; 36 notes.   A. Hoffman

1702. Studer, Jack J.   JULIUS KELLERSBERGER: A SWISS AS SURVEYOR AND CITY PLANNER IN CALIFORNIA, 1851-1857. *California Hist. Soc. Q. 1968 47(1): 3-14.* Having come around the Horn in 1851, the Swiss-born surveyor Julius Kellersberger was first engaged in surveying and planning the town of Contra Costa, which was incorporated as the Town of Oakland and in 1854 as the City of Oakland. In 1855 Kellersberger was appointed US Deputy Surveyor. His first contract required great accuracy, expensive equipment, extensive loans, and organization of an expedition. The work was completed on time and forwarded to the General Land Office in Washington. This first job led to larger and more remunerative survey work. When Buchanan became President, under the spoils system all office-holders were changed, and thus Kellersberger lost his position. He then left a railway line or ship canal. Based on Julius Kellersberger's memoirs, the MSS of which is in the New York Public Library, and official records. 35 notes.
                                                              E. P. Stickney

1703. Swanson, Evadene Burris.   WHERE'S MANHATTAN? *Colorado Mag. 1971 48(2): 146-158.* Describes the May 1970 exploration, by history buffs, of the ghost town, Manhattan, in the Fort Collins area. Three men, all of whom had family connections with the all-but-vanished Manhattan, served as guides. Recounts aspects of local history. Illus., 12 notes.   O. H. Zabel

1704. Taylor, Morris F.   EL MORO: FAILURE OF A COMPANY TOWN. *Colorado Mag. 1971 48(2): 129-145.* Traces the history of the now-defunct settlement of El Moro, established as a rail-head town by the Denver and Rio Grande narrow gauge railroad and the Southern Colorado Coal and Town Company in 1876. For a time El Moro appeared to be a viable rival of Trinidad, four miles away. In 1878, however, the Atchison, Topeka and Santa Fe Railroad arrived in Trinidad and acquired control of Raton Pass. Moreover, Trinidad's growing importance as a coal center, a disastrous fire at El Moro in 1888, and the extension of Denver and Rio Grande to Trinidad all contributed to Trinidad's successful rivalry with El Moro. Illus., 91 notes.   O. H. Zabel

1705. Thompson, William D.   HISTORY OF FORT PEMBINA: 1870-1895. *North Dakota Hist. 1969 36(1): 4-39.* A tiny settlement at Pembina on the North Dakota side of the Red River became a stopping-off place between Saint Paul and Fort Garry, Canada, in the 19th century. When the rich lands of the valley began to attract settlers, Fort Pembina was constructed in 1870 to provide protection and stability. For two decades the post played a significant role, but its function was gradually absorbed by civil law enforcement officers. The garrison was phased out in the years 1891-95. 9 illus., map, 2 appendixes, 175 notes.
                                                               D. L. Smith

1706. Twichel, Thomas E.   FORT LOGAN AND THE URBAN FRONTIER. *Montana 1967 17(4): 44-49.* Between 1869 and 1880 a small military post, known first as Camp Baker and later as Fort Logan, provided limited protection to Montana's frontier in the Smith River area near present White Sulphur Springs. Although never effective for its purpose, the post is shown to have been a civilizing and stabilizing influence in the community. Citations include press items, government documents, and published accounts.   S. R. Davison

1707. Watkins, T. H.   GOLDEN DREAMS AND SILVER REALITIES: THE MECHANICS OF CIVILIZATION ON THE MINING FRONTIER. *Am. West 1971 8(3): 34-43.* Towns on the mining frontier were products of a society re-creating itself at a highly accelerated rate. That very condensation of history led to exaggeration and myth-making in the literature which it inspired. There was, however, a great deal more to the mining frontier than its flamboyance. Beneath the patina of legend it is possible to observe the dynamics of a transplanted society and something of the quality of the American character: after the first few months of a camp's existence in which an atmosphere of remarkable equality existed, the much-vaunted democracy of the mining frontier degenerated into a selectivity based on race and nationality. Vigilantism was not promoted out of any dedication to law and order; it simply became necessary because lawlessness reached a point where it could directly affect the miners personally. The mining frontier was, for the most part, an urban frontier. If the gold or silver deposits which inspired the birth of a mining camp showed any promise of permanence, the evolution from camp to town or city was remarkably brief. The single most telling difference of the town from its predecessor was civic improvement, an indication that its residents had acquired a stake in the area. Physical improvements and a more social and cultural order soon prevailed. 15 illus.   D. L. Smith

1708. Weinstein, Robert A.   THE MILLION-DOLLAR MUD FLAT. *Am. West 1969 6(1): 33-43.* San Pedro Bay, some 20 land miles south of Los Angeles, lacked all the natural requisites for a usable harbor. It was used early and often, nevertheless, as a port of entry. Eventually Yankee money and ingenuity made it one of the great ports of the world. In the early 19th century it provided one of the few entries for smuggling on the southern California coast as well as furnishing access to interior ranchos for the hide and tallow trade. As the pueblo of Los Angeles expanded its interests and energies, San Pedro, the only sea outlet within reach, developed to meet its needs. It all became official when Congress declared San Pedro an official port of entry in 1853 with a customs house and a collector of the port. Wharves, a breakwater, real estate development, railroad and other land transportation facilities, government subsidy, Army engineers, and other factors converted the mud flat into a major deep-water port. The completion of the Panama Canal was a further major impetus to business for the port and enhanced its position in transpacific trade. 16 illus., map.   D. L. Smith

1709. Wilson, Florence S. THE ADOBE FLORES. *Masterkey 1969 43(1): 4-21.* A detailed account of the ownership and tenants of a small house built on a large tract of land in southern California. The history of the land starts before the Mission San Fernando was secularized and follows all the various land transactions, showing how this land was to become the present day site of south Pasadena, Altadena, San Marino, and San Gabriel. Examines the legends and myths surrounding the small house now known as the Adobe Flores. Based on information obtained from historians, legal documents, and interviews; map, 2 photos, biblio.
C. N. Warren

1710. Wise, Isaac Mayer. RABBI WISE SEES SAN FRANCISCO: 1877. *Pacific Historian 1967 11(3): 10-25.* The rabbi was awed at the magnificence and rapidity of growth of San Francisco in the face of hardship. The time was 1877 and he was impressed by the number and size of hotels, warehouses, and the unique architectural style. His point of reference was Cincinnati with which he compared San Francisco's wage system and mode of dress. He noticed also the extremes of wealth and poverty in the gold producing region where bootblacks and bankers shared the city in unequal portions. Government loans went begging in the town where interest rates ran to 18 percent. He was struck also by the high proportion of Jewish businessmen, a rarity on the West Coast. On closer scrutiny he noticed the persistent prejudice and discrimination against the Chinese, yet he mentioned the anomaly of rich businessmen being in sympathy with the railroad strikers in the East. Photo.
T. R. Cripps

1711. —. COMSTOCK COUNTRY: LAND OF PROMISES. *Am. West 1970 7(5): 34-43.* Although settlement by the Mormons pre-dated the Comstock discovery of 1859, Nevada was essentially a no-man's-land crossed by gold seekers en route to the western slopes of the Sierra. Silver and gold rushes soon changed that. Burgeoning bonanza towns mushroomed almost overnight. The transcontinental railroads refined communications. Statehood gave the area political status. As the great mines gave out, dreams crumbled. Some towns have lasted to the present with new strikes and new attractions. Includes brief historical sketches of Reno, Virginia City, Carson City, Lake Tahoe, Sutro, and other towns. 16 illus., map.
D. L. Smith

1712. —. HISTORY OF VINITA. *Chronicles of Oklahoma 1969 47(3): 336-342.* Reproduced from an article in *The Indian Chieftain* dated 27 January 1898, the article gives the history of the town of Vinita. Founded originally as a station on the Missouri, Kansas and Texas Railroad, it was first called Downingville. First lots were sold in 1872 and the town was as rowdy as many western cities. It showed slow growth for the first ten years. The article closes by reciting all the progress and good features of Vinita. These assets include a freedom from racial prejudice, enterprising businesses, attractive residences and a good geographical location. Illus.
K. P. Davis

Recreation and Entertainment

1713. Bartlett, Richard A. "WILL ANYONE COME HERE FOR PLEASURE?" *Am. West 1969 6(5): 10-16.* With the setting aside of California's spectacular Yosemite area, first by congressional assignment to the State, and with the increasing publicity and public awareness of the wonders of the Yellowstone country, another congressional enactment in 1872 created Yellowstone as the country's first national park. With no funds for administration of the park it soon became a "reservation for the pleasures of despoilment." It was not until 1883 that significant numbers of sightseers began to frequent the park. Due to the contemplated completion of the transcontinental Northern Pacific Railroad, which would run within 60 miles of the park's entrance, tourist facilities mushroomed and promotional literature rolled off the presses. A branch rail line and road building were to make it more accessible. Although the 1883 season was not the expected bonanza, it was certainly profitable. The number of American and foreign dignitaries and celebrities who visited the park that year has never since been equaled. It was several years before the park saw such feverish activity again. 3 illus.
D. L. Smith

1714. Bennett, Mildred R., ed. THE INCOMPARABLE OPERA HOUSE. *Nebraska Hist. 1969 49(4): 373-378.* A letter by Willa Cather to the editor in chief of the Omaha *World-Herald* that appeared on 27 October 1929. It discussed early Nebraska opera houses and their impact on the social life of small towns.
R. Lowitt

1715. Boatright, Mody C. THE AMERICAN RODEO. *Am. Q. 1964 16(2, part 1): 195-202.* Current rodeo tradition stems from the search for a hero who could symbolize America's conquest over hostile environment. From its early days of local horsemanship contests to Buffalo Bill's Wild West Show extravaganza, the roundup, or rodeo, as the promoters came to describe it, became a means by which the image of a pioneering spirit replaced the actuality of boorish bumpkins and maverick ruffians. The cowboy took his place among the great horsemen of the world and comes down to us today as an embodiment of American heroism.
R. S. Pickett

1716. Budd, Louis J. TWAIN COULD MARK THE BEAT. *Midcontinent Am. Studies J. 1963 4(1): 39-44.* Enumerates with details a number of recorded occasions when Mark Twain indulged in social dancing which he loved and continued throughout his life. The first occasion known was when he was 23 years old. Episodes recounted include Carson City, Nevada; San Francisco; on shipboard at Yalta in 1867; and late in life in New York City. 17 notes, illus.
E. P. Stickney

1717. Cochran, Alice. THE GOLD DUST TRAIL: JACK LANGRISHE'S MININO TOWN THEATERS. *Montana 1970 20(2): 58-69.* Almost from the outset of the gold rush period, residents of the Rocky Mountain towns were supplied with theatrical entertainment. From 1859 to 1885 in the area north of Denver and Salt Lake City to the border, Irish actor John S. Langrishe led an outstanding touring company, offering a variety of plays ranging from original farces to Broadway favorites. The quality of the drama is indicated by the troupe's ability to attract good audiences in occasional swings through other parts of the country. But Langrishe was most appreciated in the mountain region. After his death a journalist wrote, "he furnished the only first-class amusement...the West had."
S. R. Davison

1718. Cochran, Alice. JACK LANGRISHE AND THE THEATER OF THE MINING FRONTIER. *Colorado Mag. 1969 46(4): 324-337.* Reviews the career of John S. (Jack) Langrishe - producer, director, star, and owner of many theaters in western mining towns. Arriving in Denver in 1860, he and his troupe were accepted as part of the community and were very successful in performing Shakespeare and melodrama until a decline in the mining boom after 1865 caused interest in the theater to lag. After a time in Chicago in the early 1870's, the Langrishe company toured Montana, Utah, and Wyoming, and spent three successful years in Deadwood, South Dakota. Discovery of silver at Leadville in 1878 drew Langrishe there, where a lavish opera house was built for him by H. A. W. Tabor. Langrishe later returned to Denver, but left in 1885 for Idaho where he edited a newspaper and participated in politics. It appears that he loved both the frontier and the theater and quit the theater "when the frontier passed because it had passed." Illus., 26 notes.
O. H. Zabel

1719. Deahl, William E., Jr. NEBRASKA'S UNIQUE CONTRIBUTION TO THE ENTERTAINMENT WORLD. *Nebraska Hist. 1968 49(3): 283-297.* Describes the development of the Wild West Show and the role of William F. "Buffalo Bill" Cody in developing it. The first successful show, presented in Omaha in 1883, is examined.
R. Lowitt

1720. Eby, E. H., ed. "AMERICAN SALMON," BY RUDYARD KIPLING. *Pacific Northwest Q. 1969 60(4): 177-182.* The article consists mostly of a copy of a sketch entitled "American Salmon" written by Rudyard Kipling in an edition of his book *American Notes*. Following this review of Kipling's experiences as a fisherman for salmon (fish also believed to be ocean-dwelling steelhead trout) in the Oregon country in 1889, the author includes comments on the circumstances of the fishing trip.
C. C. Gorchels

1721. Gohdes, Clarence, ed. HUNTING IN THE OLD SOUTH. *Georgia R. 1964 18(3): 255-265, (4): 463-478, 1965 19(1): 93-120, and (2): 226-238.* A new series inaugurated to illustrate the variety and method of hunting in the Old South. The stories, written by the hunters themselves, are selected for their "more or less authentic" qualities. The first selection describes hunting of deer in South Carolina, the second is a descriptive account of hunting turkey in Texas. The third, "The Virginian Canaan," is a description written by David Hunter Strother (1816-88) of "a gentleman's expedition into the Blackwater Falls wilderness" in West Virginia. This account was published in *Harper's New Monthly Magazine*, December 1853. In the fourth installment two selections of the hunters' original narratives describe wild cattle hunting in the swamp lands of Georgia. H. G. Earnhart and S

1722. Grimstad, Bill. SAND FLEAS AND SALAD DAYS. *Am. West 1966 3(2): 36-47.* A "gilded age" resort hotel constructed in 1887 on Coronado Island across San Diego Bay, "busted" before it boomed. In 1901 a wealthy sugar heir bought the defunct southern California venture and parlayed it into a resort area. The opulent Hotel del Coronado was surrounded by Coronado Tent City replete with all the trimmings - Victorian style entertainment and cultural goodies from polo for the men to billiards for the ladies, from Wagner to ragtime, from Fourth of July displays to deep-sea fishing. While some attribute the resort's decline to sand fleas, cockroaches, and unchaperoned post-midnight parties, the real cause was a shift to more "sophisticated" vacation gimmicks. Illus. from the photo archives of the Title Insurance and Trust Company of San Diego, California. D. L. Smith

1723. Hatch, Heather S., ed. THE BICYCLE ERA IN ARIZONA. *J. of Arizona Hist. 1972 13(1): 33-52.* The American bicycle craze of the 1880's and 1890's reached Arizona Territory. Pictures the European velocipede or boneshaker, high-wheeled ordinaries, smaller ordinaries, the safety bicycle, and tandems, as well as bicycle racing, cycling clubs, cyclists, repair shops, and an 1895 advertisement. Based on the collections of the Arizona Historical Society; 28 photos. D. L. Smith

1724. Hay, Robert Pettus. FRONTIER PATRIOTISM ON PARADE: WESTWARD THE GLORIOUS FOURTH OF JULY. *J. of the West 1966 5(3): 309-320.* Traces the frontier custom of celebrating the nation's birth from the early settlements in Kentucky and Ohio to the shores of the Pacific. Concludes that while some frontier methods of celebrating may have been crude, these citizens were no less patriotic than their more sophisticated cousins in the East. All Americans met on that day to glorify the nation's past, exult in its present, and to predict great things for the future. Based on published sources, 22 notes. D. N. Brown

1725. Hutchinson, W. H. THESEUS IN LEATHER LEGGINS. *Am. West R. 1967 1(2): 13,23.* Discusses the book *Bob Crosby: World Champion Cowboy* (Clarendon Press, 1967) by Mabel Crosby and Eve Ball. The rodeo is seen as "the last violent spasm in the national westering" which attracts millions of customers annually. Much of the history of the rodeo remains to be written. Crosby's story is a definite addition to the insight of rodeo life and history. It gives a clear account of his life and problems which does not impair "its contribution towards the history of Rodeo." O. L. Miller

1726. Jensen, Billie Barnes. ENTERTAINING THE 'FIFTY-NINERS.' *J. of the West 1966 5(1): 82-90.* Uses entertainment to show how institutions and customs of an older society were transplanted to the frontier but were conditioned by the frontier environment. Initially, the Colorado miners had only games, music, and hunting to occupy their leisure hours. When saloons were opened drinking and gambling became primary activities of the pioneer population. By the summer of 1859, the Cherry Creek settlements were growing rapidly and a theater was soon opened. The legitimate theater drew crowds in the last months of the year and so did another form of entertainment, the Negro minstrel show. Cultural organizations also flourished. In addition to lodges there were clubs established to provide entertainment and intellectual stimulus. Most residents found their social outlet in the bowling alleys and billiard saloons or at wrestling matches or horse races. These amusements helped the homesick miner to accept life on the frontier and to pass the long winter months when mining was impossible. Based on printed sources. D. N. Brown

1727. Lewis, Jim L. "BEAUTIFUL BISMARCK" - BISMARCK GROVE, LAWRENCE, 1878-1900. *Kansas Hist. Q. 1969 35(3): 225-256.* An account of some of the principal events that occurred at Bis-

marck Grove public park that was established on land belonging to the Union Pacific Railroad Company about two miles northeast of Lawrence. The park not only provided recreational facilities for the residents of nearby Lawrence, but it also provided a place for meetings and programs that drew audiences from other parts of Kansas and some of the other States. Bismarck Grove was the scene of many church encampments, temperance meetings, fairs, reunions, races, and parties, some of which the author describes briefly. Based on contemporary accounts in the newspapers of Topeka, Kansas City, Lawrence, and Leavenworth; illus., photos, 55 notes. W. F. Zornow

1728. MacDonald, Marie. "KID" FOSS AND THE BIRTH OF RODEO. *Montana 1971 21(3): 56-63.* Biographical sketch of Ralph Hjalmar Foss, setting forth his contributions to the rise of rodeo, largely in supplying bucking horses from his ranch in Montana's lower Yellowstone Valley. Identifies early participants in the sport, along with the names of the noted horses they attempted to ride. Discusses the period 1915-35. Photos. S. R. Davison

1729. McConnell, Virginia. A GAUGE OF POPULAR TASTE IN EARLY COLORADO. *Colorado Mag. 1969 46(4): 338-350.* Traces the fortunes of the Langrishe Theatrical Company, particularly in Denver. The author insists that, contrary to widely accepted belief, Denver and the Colorado mining camps preferred melodrama, low comedy, and farce to Shakespeare and opera. In a season-by-season and play-by-play discussion, the author shows that the death of the popular actor Mike Dougherty and the changing taste of Denver audiences caused the Langrishe Company to fall from the popularity it had enjoyed in the early 1860's. Illus., 30 notes. O. H. Zabel

1730. McDermott, Douglas and Sarlos, Robert K. THE WOODLAND "HERSHEY" OPERA HOUSE: THE END OF AN ERA IN CALIFORNIA THEATRE. *California Hist. Soc. Q. 1969 48(4): 291-306.* Woodland, California, the county seat of Yolo County, possesses a notable history of 19th-century theater. The town supported two opera houses in the last decades of the 19th century. In 1896, with the financial assistance of businessman David N. Hershey, an architecturally interesting opera house was built, replacing one that had been destroyed by fire four years earlier. From 1896 to 1913 the Woodland Opera House attracted plays, minstrel shows, musical recitals, political and religious meetings, and school graduations. Even motion pictures were shown. With the general decline of theatrical performances throughout the United States after 1910, the opera house closed its doors in May 1913. The authors contend that the opera house should be designated a historical landmark, and they call for its restoration and activation as an operating theater. Based on newspaper accounts and published works; illus., photos, 40 notes. A. Hoffman

1731. Olmsted, Roger R. THE MASTER MARINERS' REGATTA. *Am. West 1964 1(3): 24a-24h, 25-31.* One of the principal Fourth of July events in San Francisco for the years 1867-77, 1879, 1884-85, and 1891 was the regatta of the sailing freighters staged by the Master Mariners' Benevolent Association. Most of the illustrations for this picture essay were taken during the races of 1884 and 1885 and are from the J. P. Shaw collection, San Francisco Maritime Museum. Map, illus. D. L. Smith

1732. Ourada, Patricia K., ed. THE HAT SITTING BULL WEARS. *Ann. of Wyoming 1969 41(2): 272-274.* Andrew Fox, a son-in-law of Sitting Bull, relates how William F. Cody (Buffalo Bill) gave the Sioux chief a hat when he traveled with the Wild West show in 1885. Based on manuscripts, Government documents, and published secondary material; 15 notes. R. L. Nichols

1733. Perriog, Lynn I. RECREATION IN EARLY COLORADO MINING CAMPS. *Social Sci. 1965 40(2): 67-74.* Finds little evidence to support the legend of the Wild West in early Colorado mining camps. Although there were occasional outbursts of wayward conduct, the picture is one of "a wholesome place for the bringing up of children and the enjoyment of old age." Based on Denver and Central City newspapers, written reminiscences, and 1935 interviews with survivors. M. Small

1734. Pickett, Ralph H. FRIEDRICH VON HOLSTEIN'S HUNTING TRIPS, 1865-1866. *Kansas Hist. Q. 1966 32(3): 314-324.* A translation of five letters written to Ida and Alfred von Stuelpnagel by the former's cousin, Prussian and imperial German diplomat Friedrich von Holstein during two trips that he made from Washington to the Republican and Smoky Hill Rivers of Kansas. Two letters are devoted to each of the trips. The fifth letter to Alfred was written from Stuttgart. The author said he was sorry to miss the hunting but was pleased to miss the Indian uprising then in progress. The letters are filled with information about the excitement of a hunt.　　　　　　　　　W. F. Zornow

1735. Porter, Willard H. THE AMERICAN RODEO: SPORT AND SPECTACLE. *Am. West 1971 8(4): 40-47, 61-62.* The beginning of competitive rodeo is unknown, but dates perhaps as far back as Civil War days and originated probably in Texas. Cowboy competitions or "tournaments" were recorded at various places in the West as early as the 1870's. Competitive indoor rodeo started in the 1910's. Today rodeo is not only sport and spectacle, it is big business in Canada and the United States. 1970 statistics record nearly 550 approved shows, with over 11 million ticket buyers, and over four million dollars in prize money. 16 illus.
　　　　　　　　　D. L. Smith

1736. Rea, J. SEEING THE ELEPHANT. *Western Folklore 1969 28(1): 21-26.* "Seeing the Elephant" was a musical comedy which was revamped to a California setting by David G. Robinson as a burlesque ridiculing the 1849 gold rush, a farce in which carnival sharpers made innocents see nonexisting elephants. Its 4 July 1850 San Francisco premiere was so successful that "seeing the elephant" became a part of Western slang, and elephants soon became ubiquitous. The phrase assumed many meanings. No use of it after 1906 has been discovered. 37 notes.　　　　　　　　　D. L. Smith

1737. Russell, Don. CODY, KINGS, AND CORONETS: A SPRIGHTLY ACCOUNT OF BUFFALO BILL'S WILD WEST SHOW AT HOME AND ABROAD. *Am. West 1970 7(4): 4-10, 62.* Stage melodramatist William Frederick Cody was asked to get together an appropriate Fourth of July celebration in his home town of North Platte, Nebraska, in 1882. The unprecedented and unexpected success of the occasion inspired "Buffalo Bill's Wild West," not a "circus" or a "show" according to its promoters, but an "exhibition." Annie Oakley, Sitting Bull, and other famous names added luster to the exhibition. Cody's insistence on realism with Indians, wild animals, and all the other appropriate personnel and gadgetry he could employ gave his audiences vicarious thrills. European royalty and other assorted luminaries were his avid fans, adding their own luster to his performances. His European seasons were hard acts to follow, and his Canadian and American tours were successful. The 1893 season, near the entrance but not a part of the World's Columbian Exposition in Chicago, with profits near one million dollars, was the best year for Cody's extravaganza. Cody was copied and imitated by competitors, but he was never equaled. Adapted from a recent book; 8 illus.　　　　　　　　　D. L. Smith

1738. Schenck, Annie B. CAMPING VACATION, 1871. *Colorado Mag. 1965 42(3): 185-215.* An account by an eastern lady of a camping trip through the Colorado Rockies, 4-29 August 1871. Her daily journal entries present an unusual picture of the mountain wilderness of frontier Colorado. She includes accounts of visits to ghost and near-ghost mining towns in the higher elevations.　　　　　　　　　R. Sexauer

1739. Smith, Duane A. A STRIKE DID NOT ALWAYS MEAN GOLD. *Montana 1970 20(3): 76-81.* Pioneers of the trans-Mississippi West brought baseball with them. Even the mining towns found the necessary areas of flat ground, and the busiest miners seemingly could spare time for practice and play. Rough ground and lack of skill contributed to huge scores, one of 121 to 88 being reported. Drawn from newspaper accounts of the mining States from the 1860's to the 1880's.
　　　　　　　　　S. R. Davison

1740. Tamony, Peter. SANDLOT BASEBALL. *Western Folklore 1968 27(4): 265-269.* In 1860, San Francisco authorities dedicated several acres of a sand hill area to park purposes. The Sand Lot, as it was called, was the scene of meetings and recreational activities of a wide assortment. Variants of the place-name gradually emerged, with "sandlot" eventually denominating amateur and semiprofessional baseball on lots on the outskirts of towns. The San Francisco localism soon became standard, displacing other usages such as prairie baseball, dump lot baseball, and lot baseball. 9 notes.　　　　　　　　　D. L. Smith

1741. White, John I. RED CARPET FOR A ROMANOFF: 1872 HUNTING PARTY - WESTERN STYLE - IN HONOR OF RUSSIA'S GRAND DUKE ALEXIS. *Am. West 1972 9(1): 4-9.* In 1872, Grand Duke Alexis, son of Czar Alexander II of Russia, made a goodwill tour of the United States. His experiences included a lavish Nebraska prairie party hosted by General Philip Sheridan. Sheridan was assisted by Sioux Chief Spotted Tail and his entire village, General George Armstrong Custer, and William Frederick (Buffalo Bill) Cody. The highlight of Sheridan's 1872 party was history's most publicized buffalo hunt that has inspired many tall tales. The present account is derived from reports in a contemporary Nebraska newspaper that were subsequently published in book form. 3 illus.　　　　　　　　　D. L. Smith

1742. Young, Thomas Fox. HUNTING WILD GAME IN INDIAN TERRITORY, 1880. *Chronicles of Oklahoma 1969 47(1): 582-585.* The author was born in Fort Gibson, Cherokee Nation, in 1870. Son of a German immigrant, he learned to hunt from his father, a professional hunter and dog trainer. Game included turkey, prairie chicken, quail, rabbit, squirrel, beaver, otter, mink, raccoon, fox, oppossum and others. The author enjoyed deer hunting the most. His first kill came when he was 12 years old. His hunting partner at the time was Henry C. Brokmeyer. Based on a document from the Oklahoma Historical Society.
　　　　　　　　　K. P. Davis

Crime and Punishment

1743. Baenziger, Ann Patton. THE TEXAS STATE POLICE DURING RECONSTRUCTION: A REEXAMINATION. *Southwestern Hist. Q. 1969 72(4): 470-491.* The traditional view of historians has been that the story of the Texas State Police is one of the more unsavory chapters in the history of Reconstruction in Texas. This view is not a true one. The Texas State Police were organized to combat an alarming increase of lawlessness; they accomplished much that was good and had a better-than-average record. There is plenty of evidence to show that many Texans supported the Police, praised them, wanted the organization expanded, and felt they often owed their lives to the State Police. However, the Texas State Police became a symbol of Radical Reconstruction and aroused the resentment of many conservative southern Texans, and its fate was thus sealed. Most of the opposition was due to the fact that it was a racially integrated group. The opponents were determined to destroy the organization. After the abolition of the Police, there was more crime; no citizen was safe - including women and children. The Texas Rangers assumed many of the duties of the Police and some former Policemen became reputable Rangers.　　　　R. W. Delaney

1744. Beal, M. D. RUSTLERS AND ROBBERS: IDAHO CATTLE THIEVES IN FRONTIER DAYS. *Idaho Yesterdays 1963 7(1): 24-28.* Describes the "natural" evolution of cattle rustling from a legitimate attempt to round up unbranded cattle whose owners were unknown to organized brand-altering and deliberate theft. The author identifies numerous rustler rendezvous and describes the *modus operandi* of the chief Idaho rustlers during the last quarter of the 19th century. Drawn from regional histories, interviews, and unpublished manuscripts in Idaho State University and Idaho Historical Society collections.
　　　　　　　　　M. Small

1745. Bell, William Gardner. FRONTIER LAWMAN. *Am. West 1964 1(3): 4-13, 78.* Joseph Horner learned to ride, rope, and shoot on Texas cattle ranches after the Civil War. In the wake of establishing a reputation as an outlaw he disappeared from Texas as Joseph Horner and reappeared in Nebraska as Frank Canton. This is a classic illustration of the "history of interchangeability between law and lawlessness" in the American West. Apparently the lure of power, authority, and money sufficiently appealed to him to enlist his "guts and guns" on the side of the law. He enjoyed a long and checkered career as a western frontier peace officer, for several governmental jurisdictions and for the cattle barons. He was a central figure in the famous Johnson County (Wyoming) War. Data is derived principally from his autobiographical note books published as Edward E. Dale, *Frontier Trails*, (Boston, 1930). Illus., bibliographical note.   D. L. Smith

1746. Bensen, Maxine. PORT STOCKTON. *Colorado Mag. 1966 43(1): 22-29.* Attempts to untangle the truth from the untruths about Port Stockton, a desperado who died the fabled cowboy's death, with his boots on. Only questionable stories have survived about the first part of Stockton's life and there is no certainty as to where he was or what he really did during his early years. In 1880 he became marshal of Animas City, Colorado, but was soon dismissed by the townspeople because he was too quick on the trigger. He was killed in 1882 by a vigilance committee as a result of involvement in a Christmas Eve brawl.   R. Sexauer

1747. Blazer, Paul A. THE FIGHT AT BLAZER'S MILL: A CHAPTER IN THE LINCOLN COUNTY WAR. *Arizona and the West 1964 6(3): 203-210.* Blazer's Mill, Lincoln County, New Mexico, was the site on 4 April 1878 of an incident in the Lincoln County war. Andrew L. (Buckshot) Roberts was accused by some of having participated in the killing of a rancher. On the fateful day, Roberts inadvertently walked into a 13-member gang at Blazer's Mill. Single-handedly he routed the outlaws, but he was finally killed by one of their number, Billy the Kid (William H. Bonney). Based on verbal accounts and unpublished manuscripts of the author's father and grandfather who were present; 4 illus., 3 notes.   D. L. Smith

1748. Blew, Robert W. VIGILANTISM IN LOS ANGELES, 1835-1874. *Southern California Q. 1972 54(1): 11-30.* Discusses vigilante activity in Los Angeles between 1835 and 1874, the dates of the first and last recorded lynchings in the city. Vigilantism in Los Angeles involved no long-standing formal organization as in San Francisco, but was spontaneous in response to specific events. Newspapers were discreet in their references to participants, of whom many were the substantial men of the community. The more literate individuals in the city disapproved of "peoples' courts" but believed that existing conditions made them necessary. Newspaper editorials often prompted the formation of vigilance committees. Laxity in the administration of justice was generally cited as the justification for lynchings. 93 notes.   W. L. Bowers

1749. Brooks, Edward C. PRISON CHAPLAIN. *Colorado Mag. 1964 41(3): 253-260.* In 1885 the author, a young Methodist minister, was appointed chaplain of the newly-built Colorado Penitentiary at Canon City. Living within the walls of the prison for the next two years, he became well acquainted with the inmates and learned to respect them for their abilities. He soon organized groups such as a Chautauqua Literary and Scientific Circle, an evening school for illiterate prisoners, a choir, a glee club called the "Kentucky Warblers," and Wednesday evening entertainments. The author concluded that "society at large was in a great measure responsible for much of the crime" represented at the prison. Manuscript owned by Mrs. Don Secrist, daughter of Edward C. Brooks.   I. W. Van Noppen

1750. Burg, B. Richard. VIGILANTES IN LAWLESS DENVER: THE CITY OF THE PLAINS. *Great Plains J. 1967 6(2): 68-84.* Discusses the people's courts which developed in Denver in 1859 and 1860 to preserve peace and safeguard life and property. In spite of their effectiveness in a primitive society, the escape of a murderer resulted in the forming of a Vigilance Committee in the late summer of 1860. The secret trials held by this group initiated a lively controversy between the *Rocky Mountain News* and the *Rocky Mountain Herald* over the respective effectiveness of the people's courts and the Vigilance Committee's courts. With the creation of Colorado Territory on 28 February 1861, territorial courts were established and the people's courts passed out of existence. Based on newspaper accounts and secondary materials; map, 71 notes.   O. H. Zabel

1751. Day, Robert B. ELI AZARIAH DAY: PIONEER SCHOOLTEACHER AND "PRISONER FOR CONSCIENCE SAKE." *Utah Hist. Q. 967 35(4): 322-341.* Concentrates on Day's imprisonment for "polygamous cohabitation" and contains the texts of 11 letters written by Day to his families, two from Emery County in 1885 when he was in hiding from United States marshals, the others from Utah Territorial Prison in 1888-89, when he served a sentence of five months. His training at the University of Deseret and his career as a teacher in Utah are also reviewed.   S. L. Jones

1752. Degler, Carl N. A CENTURY OF THE KLANS: A REVIEW ARTICLE. *J. of Southern Hist. 1965 31(4): 435-443.* In the centennial year of the Ku Klux Klan, three books on its history were published. David M. Chalmers in *Hooded Americanism: The First Century of the Ku Klux Klan* (New York: Doubleday, 1965), combs the secondary literature and contemporary periodicals as no one has done before, but does little to analyze the myriad facts. He gives only one chapter to the Reconstruction period, the rest to the era since World War I. William Peirce Randel in *The Ku Klux Klan: A Century of Infamy* (New York: Chilton, 1965), devotes two-thirds of his book to the Reconstruction period, though omitting Alabama. His highly charged indignation over the Klan raises doubts as to the book's objectivity. Charles C. Alexander's *The Ku Klux Klan in the Southwest* (Lexington: U. of Kentucky Press, 1965), is a well-balanced, carefully documented study of the Klan in Arkansas, Texas, Louisiana and Oklahoma. The reviewer distinguishes between three different klans - that of the Reconstruction, the 1920's, and the present civil rights battle - and says it is wise to resist the temptation to lump them together.   S. E. Humphreys

1753. Dillon, Richard A. WELLS, FARGO'S "JEKYLL" AND HYDE: THE ELUSIVE EMBEZZLER WHO STUMPED THE COMPANY'S MASTER DETECTIVE. *Am. West 1971 8(2): 28-33, 59-60.* Charles Wells Banks was one of the ablest and most trusted Wells, Fargo and Company executives. The English-born Banks ran away to sea as a boy, worked in an American iron foundry, and served in the Civil War. In 1871 he went to California and became an assistant in the San Francisco banking firm. Within a few years he earned promotion to chief cashier of the company and had become one of the pillars of society. Banks mysteriously disappeared in 1886. He had embezzled probably 100 thousand dollars, possibly over several years. Investigation revealed that Banks had simultaneously lived another life, involving ownership of a brothel and associated details. He evaded the grasp of James B. Hume, the chief of detectives of Wells, Fargo, and escaped to the South Seas, where he spent the rest of his days in comfort and with considerable standing in his new community. 3 illus., biblio.   D. L. Smith

1754. Dillon, Richard H. J. ROSS BROWNE AND THE CORRUPTIBLE WEST. *Am. West 1965 2(2): 37-45.* Preposterous and persistent myth has it that the West was peculiarly different from the rest of the United States, that an "aberrant individualism" characteristic of the strong and the silent was necessary to conquer this area, and that the settlement process was, therefore, a struggle of evil versus good. The author maintains that westward-moving Americans were a mixture who were simply motivated by the hope of finding something better than they had left behind them. Of greater concern is "a phenomenon hardly touched by chroniclers to date." Within five years after the discovery of gold in California, the raw frontier was metamorphosed into "a super-sophisticated society" in many respects. For one, as the nature of mining changed from a venture of individuals to capitalistic enterprise, adventurous westerners turned to mine the public treasury in "a veritable carnival of corruption." John Ross Browne, a talented essayist and reporter, a dedicated civil servant, was dispatched to conduct a thorough investigation. In this capacity he uncovered the fraud in the mints, customs houses, Indian agencies, land offices, and other federal agencies. Through the 1850's and 1860's Browne's recommendations for reforms were implemented and fraud decreased considerably. Derived from confidential reports to the secretary of the treasury and extracted from a forthcoming book. Illus.   D. L. Smith

1755. Dinges, Bruce J. THE COURT-MARTIAL OF LIEUTENANT HENRY O. FLIPPER: AN EXAMPLE OF BLACK-WHITE RELATIONSHIPS IN THE ARMY, 1881. *Am. West 1972 9(1): 12-17, 59-61.* Henry Ossian Flipper was the first black graduate of the US Military Academy, class of 1877, and the only black officer in the US Army. He demonstrated an unusual degree of ability and was given considerable responsibility in service on the frontier. A change of command, a transfer of duties, and an unexplained disappearance of commissary funds, however, led him to conclude that a systematic campaign of persecution had been launched against him. Convinced of Flipper's innocence, acquaintances raised sufficient funds to cover the missing sum. Even though full restitution was made, his personal effects were still held and he was court-martialled on charges of embezzlement. Even though the proceedings in 1881 at Fort Davis, Texas, found Flipper not guilty of embezzlement, he was declared guilty of "conduct unbecoming an officer and gentleman" and sentenced to dismissal from the Army. The defense maintained that the real question, which repeatedly surfaced during the trial, was whether a black would be permitted to serve as an officer in the Army. 6 illus., note.   D. L. Smith

1756. Egan, Ferol. INCIDENT AT TRAGEDY SPRINGS: AN UNSOLVED MYSTERY OF THE CALIFORNIA TRAIL. *Am. West 1971 8(1): 36-39.* In mid-1848, Mormon Battalion veterans of the Mexican War made their way back from the Sacramento Valley of California to Utah. Their three scouts who had disappeared were later discovered in shallow graves with badly mutilated bodies. Clues were scattered about to make it appear that the scouts had been murdered by Indians. A close scrutiny of the unconvincing evidence, however, verifies that the culprits were not the Indians of the vicinity and perhaps not Indians at all. The murder mystery at Tragedy Springs is, and will probably remain, unsolved. Illus.   D. L. Smith

1757. Godbold, Mollie Moore. COMANCHE AND THE HARDIN GANG. *Southwestern Hist. Q. 1963 67(1): 55-77, and 67(2): 247-266.* Part I reviews the activities of the Texas outlaw, John Wesley Hardin, in Comanche, Texas in the mid-1870's. Part II continues the review from the mid-1870's until his death in 1895.   J. A. Hudson

1758. Gower, Calvin W. VIGILANTES. *Colorado Mag. 1964 41(2): 93-104.* The murder case of James Gordon is significant because it "involved such broad issues as prejudice against Germans in mid-nineteenth century America, the inability of a territorial government properly to rule its western portions, and the operation of a 'vigilante court.'" Gordon escaped and fled from Denver to Leavenworth, Kansas Territory, was captured and eventually was returned to Denver for trial by a vigilante court.   I. W. Van Noppen

1759. Grover, Dave. DIAMONDFIELD JACK: A RANGE WAR IN COURT. *Idaho Yesterdays 1963 7(2): 8-14.* An account of the bizarre Idaho murder case in the 1890's, which involved a colorful accused killer (Diamondfield Jack Davis), the range war between sheepmen and cattlemen, and a legal battle between two of Idaho's greatest lawyers, William E. Borah and James H. Hawley. Based on court records and on newspaper files of the Idaho Historical Society.   M. Small

1760. Hogan, William F. ADOLPH GEORGE BUTTNER: TUCSON'S FIRST CHIEF OF POLICE. *Arizoniana 1964 5(2): 26-31.* Biographical sketch of Tucson's first chief of police, who after a somewhat clouded career as an enlisted man during the Civil War was instrumental in bringing about justice and local government improvements to frontier Arizona.   W. Unrau

1761. Hogan, William F. JOSEPH SEXTON HOPLEY, DISPENSER OF JUSTICE. *Arizoniana 1963 4(3): 41-45.* Hopley "traversed Arizona terrain during its territorial years as a United States cavalryman, rancher, and lawman." A 15-year veteran of Indian warfare, he was discharged at Tucson in 1885. He began a business life as a dairyman and worked at cattle raising 30 miles east of Tucson. For eight years he operated a mail stage and express line. As marshal of Tucson for four terms, he effectively enforced antigambling legislation and new antiliquor laws. Documented, illus.   E. P. Stickney

1762. Hughes, Albert H. OUTLAW WITH A HALO. *Montana 1967 17(4): 60-75.* Summarizes the numerous film versions of the Jesse James story, with considerable detail as to studios, actors, and directors. The scripts varied from overdramatized biographies to near fiction, all with a tendency to glamorize this bandit. Illustrated with stills from various films.   S. R. Davison

1763. Jeffrey, John Mason. THE BIZARRE BAZAAR. *J. of Arizona Hist. 1970 11(3): 202-217.* The formidable and disreputable maximum security prison of Arizona Territory was located at Yuma, 1876-1909. Even though there were many work opportunities and tasks for the prisoners, there was not enough work to go around. From modest beginnings with their jackknives and cigar boxes, the prisoners expanded their leisure activities into whittling, carving, engraving, hammering, braiding, and painting. They utilized native woods and other local materials. A substantial handicraft industry evolved that inadvertently became a successful forerunner of today's prison rehabilitation programs. Soon

the prisoners had established a thriving manufacturing and sales business which became well known to the traffic on the southern trade route which passed through Yuma between California and the East. The handicraft projects did not take the place of regular work programs, but manufacture of sale items by some of the prisoners became a welcome leisure adjunct to their daily activities. The frontier's most "bizarre bazaar" was a beneficial contact for the prisoners with the society that had imprisoned them. 9 illus., 21 notes.   D. L. Smith

1764. Jeffrey, John Mason. DISCIPLINE IN THE ARIZONA TERRITORIAL PRISON: DRACONIAN SEVERITY OR ENLIGHTENED ADMINISTRATION? *J. of Arizona Hist. 1968 9(3): 140-154.* The Arizona Territorial Prison in Yuma during the period 1876-1910 acquired a reputation for being a place as hellish as Andersonville during the Civil War. The author argues that this reputation was unjustified. A myth that gained wide credence was that no convict ever successfully escaped. According to the official records, at least 20 inmates succeeded in fleeing the prison. Cruel or unusual disciplinary practices were not employed and no one was ever executed there. The only convict punishments allowed - the ball and chain and an isolation cell - were standard features of prison life in 19th-century America. Prison regulations at Yuma were humane and generally in advance of the customary practices of the period. Based largely on printed prison reports and secondary accounts; illus., 3 photos, 28 notes.   R. J. Roske

1765. Johnson, Dorothy M. THE HANGING OF THE CHIEFS. *Montana 1970 20(3): 60-69.* Attempts to identify those responsible for the hanging of two or more Indians charged with kidnapping and other crimes, in the Fort Laramie area in 1865. The author concludes that all accounts are questionable, even as to the number of Indians executed and the details of charges against them. Based on published sources, including official documents; 16 notes.   S. R. Davison

1766. Johnson, Jerome W. MURDER ON THE UNCOMPAHGRE. *Colorado Mag. 1966 43(3): 209-224.* A discussion of a seemingly insignificant pair of murders which took place in Colorado in 1880 and had statewide repercussions. Before the murderers were brought to trial there was widespread fear of the possibility of an Indian war, agitated by the Utes in retaliation for the murder of the chief's son; the event had become an issue in the state election of 1880, and both the state and the Federal government had become involved in a jurisdictional dispute which threatened to precipitate a clash between state militia and the U.S. Army. The author traces the incident to illustrate the additional conflicts between the Indian and white man of the 1870's and 1880's, leading to lynch law justice, the exploitation of the Indian problem by politicians, and the constant encroachment on the Indian lands by the whites. Based mainly on newspapers published at the time, especially the *Denver Daily News;* illus., map, 53 notes.   R. Sexauer

1767. Jones, Brian. JOHN RICHARD, JR., AND THE KILLING AT FETTERMAN. *Ann. of Wyoming 1971 43(2): 237-257.* Examines the circumstances and consequences of the murder of an Army corporal at Fort Fetterman on 9 September 1869 by John Richard, Jr. (ca. 1844-72), an Indian trader and half-Sioux. Although Richard claimed self-defense, the author suggests that behind the act lay a series of conflicts with military authorities, a personal quarrel with the murdered soldier, and a penchant for hard liquor. After the shooting, Richard went to live with the Oglala Sioux, and the press erroneously feared that he would inspire an antiwhite alliance between the mutually antagonistic Sioux and Crow tribes. Recognizing Richard's potential influence among the Sioux, however, various military and Indian Office officials and Wyoming merchants successfully prevented his prosecution. When Richard killed Chief Yellow Bear in another drunken fit in 1872, though, he did not go unpunished: the chief's friends took the murderer's life on the spot. Based on Indian Office and military records and secondary sources; 61 notes.
                                                    G. R. Adams

1768. Kvammen, Lorna J. PRISONERS, POPULATION, AND THE ECONOMY. *California Anthropologist 1971 1(1): 25-36.* "This paper examines the utilization of prisoners in relationship to economic and demographic factors over a range of historical periods. It then examines the relationship between these factors in penal procedures in the United States from Colonial times to the present. Special emphasis is given to practices in California. The third section tests the hypothesis against information available on the disposition of prisoners in the USSR, an underpopulated nation with an expanding economy."

(AIA 3:3:1093) J

1769. Ladd, E. Robert. VENGEANCE AT THE O. K. CORRAL. *Arizoniana 1963 4(2): 1-10.* In 1897, at Tombstone, the rancher Colonel William Cornell Greene shot "Judge" James Burnett because he held him responsible for the death from drowning of his small daughter. In the subsequent famous trial he was able to rally all his friends and swing the jury's verdict to not guilty. In the following years he increased his holdings to 400 thousand acres.   M. Petrie

1770. Lehman, Leola. A DEPUTY U.S. MARSHAL IN THE TERRITORIES. *Chronicles of Oklahoma 1965 43(3): 289-296.* Deals chiefly with the career of William Bartley Murrill as a deputy U.S. Marshal in Oklahoma, but in doing so depicts the problems of law and order in a territory where no U.S. courts existed. The Indian had their own courts and law enforcement officers, but those had no jurisdiction over white men. Consequently Oklahoma was the hideout of many gangs of outlaws, including some women. The terrain of eastern Oklahoma enabled such gangs to hide out easily. There were entire settlements of outlaws, such as the "Dogtown Settlement," although after the coming of law-abiding citizens to the territory such became a thing of the past. Outlaws continued to have headquarters in the territory, however, and train robberies and bank holdups were not uncommon. The outlaws were tough and lawmen had to be tough, too. 13 notes.   I. W. Van Noppen

1771. Limbaugh, Ronald H. RAGGED DICK IN A BLACK HAT. *Idaho Yesterdays 1967 11(4): 9-13.* An authentic account of one of early territorial Idaho's more improbable officials. In 1866 Horace C. Gilson embezzled 42 thousand dollars of Federal money meant for the creditors of Idaho territory. A lawsuit did not recover the money and Congress finally paid off the creditors. The case was characterized by dishonest officials, a frustrating sectional hostility, and a weak legal system. 19 notes.   D. H. Swift

1772. Littlefield, Daniel F., Jr. and Underhill, Lonnie E. NEGRO MARSHALS IN THE INDIAN TERRITORY. *J. of Negro Hist. 1971 56(2): 77-87.* It is little known that several of the lawmen in Indian Territory (now Oklahoma) during the late 19th century were Negroes. Their duties pertained to the regions occupied by the Five Civilized Tribes - the Cherokee, Choctaw, Creek, Chickasaw, and Seminole - and were used by the Indian Police and the U.S. Marshal's office. The Indians preferred the black law officers, who unlike the white officials had lived all or most of their lives among the Indians and Indian freedmen. A fee system and the lack of available courts also made the Indians distrust white officers. Based mostly on Indian newspapers of the region, and on secondary sources; 45 notes.   R. S. Melamed

1773. Malin, James C. SOME RECONSIDERATIONS OF THE DEFEAT OF SENATOR POMEROY OF KANSAS, 1873. *Mid-America 1966 48(1): 47-57.* Many circumstances surrounding the "exposure" of Senator Samuel C. Pomeroy for bribery and vote buying have not heretofore been brought to light. This study relates how two young residents of Fort Scott, Kansas, unexpectedly became involved in the dramatic events.   L. D. Silveri

1774. Metz, Leon C. PAT GARRETT: ANOTHER LOOK AT A WESTERN GUNMAN. *Montana 1971 21(4): 70-80.* Expands the conventional biography of Pat Garrett (1850-1908), usually known only as the slayer of Billy the Kid (William Bonney) in 1881. Garrett remained prominent as a law officer, a promoter of irrigation and land projects, and holder of appointive office. Under appointment by Theodore Roosevelt, he served as U.S. Customs Collector at El Paso. Failure in most of his undertakings is attributed to a quarrelsome and sarcastic personality. He was mysteriously shot to death in 1908 in New Mexico. Illus.
S. R. Davison

1775. Moorman, Donald R. HOLM O. BURSUM, SHERIFF 1894. *New Mexico Hist. R. 1964 39(4): 333-344.* Evidently a chapter from the author's doctoral dissertation, "A Political Biography of Holm O. Bursum, 1899-1924," relates in detail the three principal problems of a New Mexican territorial sheriff: law enforcement, finances, and politics. The

most taxing was law enforcement. The sheriff not only had to deal with ordinary criminals, but also with Indian depredations. Financially the sheriff had difficulty collecting rewards, obtaining just claims from the territorial legislature for mileage, and extracting money from the federal government for prisoners kept in the county's jail. The sheriff was also an important political figure; Bursum used the position as a stepping stone into the US Senate.   D. F. Henderson

1776. Myles, Myrtle T. THE LAST OF THE WEST'S BADMEN. *Idaho Yesterdays 1967 11(3): 14-21.* Discusses "the Nevada career of Diamondfield Jack Davis." Jackson Lee Davis (1863-1949) was an active participant in the Owyhee diamond rush of 1892 where he gained his nickname. In 1896 he became the principal figure in Idaho's most famous sheep and cattle war. He was released from prison in 1902 and, with the aid of influential friends like John Sparks and Judge O. W. Powers, he made considerable profits in the Nevada goldfields. He later became involved in industry and labor disputes throughout the Western States. Illus.   B. B. Swift

1777. Newman, Simeon H., III. THE SANTA FE RING: A LETTER TO THE "NEW YORK SUN." *Arizona and the West 1970 12(3): 269-288.* The Republican Santa Fe Ring controlled New Mexico after the Civil War through political patronage, bribery, and coercion. Its members rigged elections, maneuvered legislative proceedings, and ran the bar association. The ring was composed of patent attorneys in land disputes. They took land in lieu of fees, gaining millions of acres of mineral-rich real estate. In 1875 the ring bought the 96,000-acre Maxwell Land Grant in Colfax County, maneuvered it into a claim for some two million acres, and brought eviction proceedings against numerous settlers who occupied the excess area which the ring was trying to obtain. Backing a candidate for Congress, the ring hoped to gain Federal recognition of the enlarged grant. Simeon Harrison Newman, a Democratic journalist who had fled the wrath of the ring into neighboring Colorado, wrote a letter to the New York *Sun* detailing strong indictments of these territorial politicians. Based on the letter of 31 July 1875 and certain other documents concerning ring activities; 4 illus., 29 notes.   D. L. Smith

1778. Olmsted, Roger. COLLECTOR'S CHOICE: A FIRST FOR LAW AND ORDER. *Am. West 1970 7(1): 11-13.* In the early 1850's, San Francisco-produced letterheads depicted a great variety of scenes of life or notable events in California and provided space for personal messages to the folks back home in the States. One, reproduced here, is a sketch of José Forner y Brugada (1820-52) in prison chains, containing a brief biographical sketch and his confession. Forner was executed in 1852 for murder. His was the first legal execution in California, and was witnessed by some ten thousand spectators. Illus.   D. L. Smith

1779. Olmsted, Roger. SAN FRANCISCO AND THE VIGILANTE STYLE. *Am. West 1970 7(1): 6-11, 63-64, and 7(2): 20-27, 60-62.* Part I. After a criminal assault on a merchant, a "Committee of Vigilance" was formed in 1851 by a group of San Francisco citizens who despaired the long-standing inadequacy of the machinery of legal redress. Corrupt judges, a defective system of jury selection, the seeming inability of the courts to convict known criminals, and legal corruption of many sorts abounded. When civic leaders were sufficiently fed up, the ad hoc San Francisco vigilance committee formed and was soon in communication with similar committees springing up in all of the major towns in California. The explicitly stated purpose of the San Francisco group was the deportation of scoundrels. In the 1851 reign of the committee, criminals were convicted and hanged, hoodlums were deported, suspicious characters were not permitted to land, and others were rescued from miscarriage of justice. The vigilance group did not insure honest government, however, because the System was hopelessly corrupt. 5 illus. Part II. San Francisco's growth and prosperity were the product of the gold rush in California. Decline in gold production ended the boom and resulted in a bank panic and general business depression in 1855. A newspaper was started by James King of one banking house that failed. He used it as a vehicle to assault corruption, from the ballot box stuffer to the most prominent businessmen and politicians. His attacks inflamed and took advantage of the growing popular discontent with the prevailing corruption. King was assassinated in 1856 by James P. Casey who had a criminal record and who was currently editor of an obscure paper and a practicing corrupt politician. With antecedents from the 1851 "Committee of Vigilance," the "Great" Committee of Vigilance of 1856 was created on an ad hoc basis. "Absolute obedience, [and] absolute secrecy" were its modus operandi. The committee enlisted some five thousand men, tried Casey and another unconvicted murderer, and hanged both. It further ferreted out, tried, and deported a score of the most notorious political scoundrels. In an altercation with California Supreme Court Judge David Terry, an outspoken critic of the committee, Terry "spitted" a member of the committee through the neck with his Bowie knife. The vigilantes now had a prisoner they could not convict nor release. Terry's trial was drawn out to see if the victim would recover. He did, and Terry was convicted and released. Apparently fearing Federal intervention, the committee adjourned, permanently. 7 illus., biblio., note.   D. L. Smith

1780.   Ophus, John.   THE LAKE COUNTY WAR, 1874-75. *Colorado Mag. 1970 47(2): 119-135.* Discusses a feud between two men in Lake County which turned into mob violence. When Elijah Gibbs was acquitted of the murder of George Harrington, a vigilance committee was formed which took over the county government. Pressure was brought upon Gibbs' supporters to leave the county. Several murders, including that of Judge John L. Dyer, resulted. Lacking troops, the territorial governor was powerless and a major breakdown in legal machinery occurred. Illus., 77 notes.   O. H. Zabel

1781.   Owens, Kenneth N.   JUDGE LYNCH IN WASHINGTON TERRITORY.   *Pacific Northwest Q. 1964 55(4): 177-178.* Inspired by a short letter found in the archives of a university library revealing that a "murderer" was enjoying freedom in a mining camp of 1862, the author of this article philosophizes on the difficulty of bringing law-enforcement to the western mining frontier during the latter half of the 19th century.
                                                              C. C. Gorchels

1782.   Pedersen, Gilbert J.   THE DRAGOON WHO TURNED HORSE THIEF: THE BENTLEY SAGA RECONSIDERED. *Arizoniana 1964 5(4): 49-54.* Reviews the story in the (Tubac) *Weekly Arizonian* of 3 March 1859 about Alenson Bentley, a horse thief and army deserter. Quotations are given from later issues of the same weekly, telling of his escape from the guardhouse, his recapture, and later sentencing and cruel punishment. His eventual fate when Fort Defiance was evacuated in 1861 is uncertain unless we can believe the not too probable account given by Captain James H. Tevis in his *Arizona in the 50's* (Albuquerque: U. of New Mexico Press, 1954), in which Bentley, an accomplished pianist, married a Mexican señorita. Based on post records. 14 notes.   E. P. Stickney

1783.   Pfaller, Louis.   THE BRAVE BEAR MURDER CASE. *North Dakota Hist. 1969 36(2): 120-139.* Brave Bear was a member of the Cut Head band of Yanktonnais Sioux Indians who turned renegade and led a small gang of Indians in an 8-year reign of terror against Indian and white. Robbery and murder were the gang specialities and brutality was the usual trademark. Brave Bear was captured and escaped twice. The third time he was captured he was convicted for murder at a trial on 5 January 1882. Appeals were made as far as the President of the United States who refused clemency. On 16 November 1882 Brave Bear was hung at Yankton, North Dakota. Article presented originally on 11 February 1969 in a series of lectures on Western history by the author at Assumption Abbey, Richardton. Based on primary source materials; illus., photos, 30 notes.   E. P. Costello

1784.   Potter, Chester D.   REMINISCENCES OF THE SOCORRO VIGILANTES.   *New Mexico Hist. R. 1965 40(1): 23-54.* Reprinted from the Pittsburg *Dispatch,* commencing 25 May 1913. Led by Colonel E. W. Eaton, the vigilantes were organized in Socorro because the control of the machinery of law was in the hands of Mexicans native to the region who, under sheriff Garcia, refused to act when crimes were committed against other Americans. The vigilantes, whose membership was practically compulsory for Americans, lynched five, warned several other persons to leave town, and forewarned countless others not to come. Activities, key personnel, and what appears to be some folklore associated with the movement are presented.   D. F. Henderson

1785.   Rasch, Philip J.   OLD PROBLEM - NEW ANSWERS. *New Mexico Hist. R. 1965 40(1): 65-68.* Who was Billy the Kid? Sketches the theories of Louis Telfer, William H. Carson, and Philip J. Rasch.
                                                              D. F. Henderson

1786.   Rasch, Philip J.   THE RUSTLER WAR.   *New Mexico Hist. R. 1964 39(4): 257-273.* "The destruction in 1880 of the gang of cattle and horse thieves led by the notorious Lincoln County rustlers, Jessie J. Evans and Billy the Kid, did not automatically restore peace and quiet to the stockmen of New Mexico." Several large gangs, including the John Kinney band, operated in the territory from 1881 to 1885. The whole gambit of law enforcement officials, from local sheriffs to state militia, were utilized to pursue and eventually capture most of these banditti. The rustlers were tried, found guilty and sentenced. Cattle stealing did not cease, but "the day of the large band so powerful that they can [sic] be repressed only by mobilizing the military power of the state" became a thing of the past.   D. F. Henderson

1787.   Roberts, Gary L.   THE GUNFIGHT AT O.K. CORRAL: THE WELLS SPICER DECISION, 1881.   *Montana 1970 20(1): 62-74.* Summarizes a noted shoot-out and reprints the less well-known decision of Justice of the Peace Wells Spicer, in which he found the Earp brothers - Virgil, Wyatt, and Morgan - and their cohorts not guilty of any offense which would warrant binding them over for trail. Also included is Judge Spicer's open-letter reply to an unsigned threat against his life, received after his disposition of the case. Documented, biblio. note.
                                                              S. R. Davison

1788.   Roberts, Gary L.   IN PURSUIT OF DUTY: BEING THE ACCOUNT OF A HOMICIDAL AFFAIR AND ITS SUBSEQUENT TRIALS AND TRIBULATIONS.   *Am. West 1970 7(5): 26-33, 62-63.* Discusses an 1880-90 sequence of events that inspired parlor chatter and rocked the U.S. Supreme Court. Nevada's U.S. Senator William Sharon contrived a liaison with Sarah Althea Hill. He abruptly dismissed her and was sued for divorce on grounds of adultery. One of her lawyers, David Smith Terry, former chief judicial official of California, became her husband after Sharon's death. Court litigation and appeals kept the case alive for years. In presiding over a federal circuit court hearing in California, Stephen Johnson Field of the Federal Supreme Court found it necessary to prefer contempt charges against Terry and his wife. A courtroom altercation and jail sentences for the Terrys put Field's life in danger. When Field returned to California to hear other cases he was confronted by Terry. Field's bodyguard intervened and killed Terry and the murder charge against the bodyguard reached the U.S. Supreme Court. The high court's decision *In Re Neagle* (1890) had implications beyond the immediate case and chain of circumstances. It was declared to be "the broadest interpretation yet given to implied powers of the national government under the Constitution." 6 illus.   D. L. Smith

1789.   Roberts, Gary L.   THE WEST'S GUNMEN: I.   *Am. West 1971 8(1): 10-15, 64.* The cowtowns of Kansas spawned much of the folklore of the American West and provided the country with some of its most durable folk figures. Wyatt Earp, Bat Masterson, and Wild Bill Hickok have inspired generations of melodramatic writings and movies. The persistence of the gunfighter as a folk figure has inspired occasional analyses by literary critics, folklorists, historians, and sometimes psychologists. These run the gamut from "unabashed debunking" to "indiscriminate hero-worship." Suggesting lineal antecedents in American folklore, the historiography of the western gunfighter is traced from an 1867 article in *Harper's New Monthly Magazine.* It presented Wild Bill Hickok as the prototype hero, his claim never to kill a man "without good cause" as the code, and "fair and solitary combat" as the myth's basic ingredient. The blood and thunder writers of the late 19th century are succeeded by the romantic biographers of the 20th century as the legend makers of the gunfighters of the western cowtowns. 8 illus. Article to be continued.
                                                              D. L. Smith

1790.   Roberts, Gary L.   THE WEST'S GUNMEN: II.   *Am. West 1971 8(2): 18-23, 61-62.* Continued from previous article. The gunfighter, according to early writers, was a man of courage and honor. He had a keen sense of right and wrong, he played the role of civilizer on the frontier, and he was devoted to high ideals of personal conduct and public responsibility. As early as the 1920's, however, writers began to find the hero image difficult to accept. In their search for the true identity of the gunfighter, the legendary description began to suffer. By the 1950's a healthy skepticism and a closer attention to the sources began to create a different picture. As is frequently the case, the effects of scholarly revisionism were somewhat changed by pseudoscholarly debunking. Argues that "the sum of historical writing on the gunman is poor." The gunfighter will remain one of the favorites of American folklore and mass media entertainment, and the true picture will not soon emerge. The methodological and other reasons for this are formidable. 6 illus.

D. L. Smith

1791. Schlesinger, Andrew B. LAS GORRAS BLANCAS, 1889-1891 [The White Caps]. *J. of Mexican Am. Hist.* 1971 1(2): 87-143. An account of *Las Gorras Blancas* (The White Caps), a quasipopulist, Mexican-American night-riding group which flourished in northern New Mexico, particularly San Miguel County, in the late 19th century. The land grant problem was at the root of the discontent that this movement sprang from. As the new owners fenced in the old land grants the former users reacted in the only manner left - violence and terrorism. Delineates the relationship between *Las Gorras Blancas* and the Knights of Labor. Based mainly on primary sources; 170 notes.

G. L. Seligmann, Jr.

1792. Secrest, William B. THE LAW IN HAYS CITY. *Montana* 1969 19(2): 57-70. Hays City, Kansas, employed "Wild Bill" Hickok as sheriff in 1869 to quell a rowdy population of buffalo hunters, teamsters, and soldiers from nearby Fort Hays. The ensuing violent episodes enlarged Hickok's fame as a gunman devoted to protecting life and property. Within a few months he was able to withdraw, leaving the town relatively safe and orderly. Illus., 21 notes.

S. R. Davison

1793. Serven, James E. THE GUN - AN INSTRUMENT OF DESTINY IN ARIZONA. *Arizoniana* 1964 5(3): 14-27. Describes the crude forms of the arquebus (the wheel-lock and the match-lock) as used by the Spaniards in 1540, and traces the history and development of various types of firearms introduced to the Southwest, including the "Mississippi" and the Hawken rifles of 1841, the 1851 Model Sharps carbine, Smith and Wesson's .44 caliber cartridge revolver and Colt's .45 single action "Peacemaker," the Springfield .58 caliber Model of 1863 and .50-70 model of 1866. "It should perhaps be noted here that New Mexico, Arizona, and other western territories served as testing grounds for new military weapons. ...From one end of the Southwest to the other . . . the boom of the Colt and the bark of the Winchester echoed loudly in those final decades before Arizona statehood in 1912 . . . Out of all this powder burning has developed the orderly society of today's New Mexico and Arizona." 6 photos.

D. D. Cameron

1794. Smith, Helena Huntington. SAM BASS AND THE MYTH MACHINE. *Am. West* 1970 7(1): 31-35. Orphaned Indiana-farm-born Sam Bass left home for Denton, Texas, where he became "Honest Eph," a thrifty and conscientious teamster and hired hand. He bought a race horse and soon fell into bad company. After driving a herd of steers to the Black Hills, Bass and cronies began robbing stages. Because pickings were slim and suspicions were aroused, the gang headed south in 1877 to Nebraska and relieved a Union Pacific train of 60 thousand dollars in newly minted gold pieces. This and subsequent exploits put Texas Rangers on the trail in what the press called the "Bass War" of 1878. The difficulties of the terrain and the incompetence of his pursuers, not his own cleverness, accounted for his long success in eluding capture. The Bass War made Bass into a legend, the story of which involved long chases, narrow escapes, uninhibited spending, and betrayal by a friend. The myth machine has made Bass into one of the great American outlaws, as is exemplified by "The Ballad of Sam Bass." 2 illus.

D. L. Smith

1795. Theisen, Lee Scott. THE FIGHT IN LINCOLN, N.M., 1878: THE TESTIMONY OF TWO NEGRO PARTICIPANTS. *Arizona and the West* 1970 12(2): 173-198. Two rival groups, struggling for economic and political dominance of Lincoln County, New Mexico, plunged the area into lawlessness in 1878. Murders, embezzlement charges, and terror prevailed. A new sheriff, who was also made a deputy US marshal, enlisted the aid of Federal troops from nearby Fort Stanton to serve warrants for the arrests of several persons who had taken refuge in a fort-like home in Lincoln. The decisive week of 15-19 July 1878 in the Lincoln County War was brought to a climax when the sheriff set fire to the house. As its occupants fled the blaze, several of them were killed by the posse. The widow of the slain leader brought charges against the Army colonel who refused to intervene to save the men. Some 60 witnesses were heard in the subsequent court of inquiry at Fort Stanton in 1879. The author presents the testimony of two Negroes, who were em-

ployees of the captured party and had been present for most of the fight. Aside from the details of the affair which their statements contain, the documents are commentaries on frontier justice, western attitudes about race, and the prevalent mores of the day. Illus., map, 24 notes.

D. L. Smith

1796. Unrau, William E. INVESTIGATION OR PROBITY? INVESTIGATIONS INTO THE AFFAIRS OF THE KIOWA-COMANCHE INDIAN AGENCY, 1867. *Chronicles of Oklahoma* 1964 42(3): 300-319. It was charged in *Harper's New Monthly Magazine* and throughout the nation that there was an "Indian Ring" of Congressmen, commissioners, and Indian agents, formed especially to defraud the Indians. Indian agents were given jobs for party work and on 1,500 dollars a year could retire with fortunes in four years. The worst charges were directed against the son of General Henry Leavenworth, Kiowa-Comanche agent Jesse Henry Leavenworth, who had been dishonorably discharged from the army in 1863. In 1867 Leavenworth was charged with illegal sale of arms to the Indians. He protested that the Indians would starve unless they had guns for hunting. Corrupt traders and correspondents made false charges. The author indicates that Leavenworth was not guilty. 34 notes.

I. W. Van Noppen

1797. Walker, Henry P. RETIRE PEACEABLY TO YOUR HOMES: ARIZONA FACES MARTIAL LAW, 1882. *J. of Arizona Hist.* 1969 10(1): 1-18. In the early 1880's the Arizona Territory saw an unusually great outburst of violent crime. American and Mexican criminals took advantage of the presence of four jurisdictions where New Mexico and Arizona joined two Mexican States, Chihuahua and Sonora. Rustling of cattle and horses was widespread, as was violence in support of those activities. The local authorities seemed unwilling or unable to correct the situation. Laws hampered the action the Army could take in support of criminal justice. President Chester Alan Arthur (1830-86) on 3 May 1882 issued a proclamation which commanded the lawless to disperse peaceably or face Army enforcement of territorial laws. The decrease of crime in following months may have resulted from the better protective organization of the stockmen and from increasing internal feuds among the outlaws. Based primarily on contemporary newspapers and documents; 3 photos, 62 notes.

R. J. Roske

1798. Wharfield, H. B. APACHE KID AND THE RECORD. *J. of Arizona Hist.* 1965 6(1): 37-46. Includes an extract of the court-martial of the former sergeant of Apache Indian scouts, Apache Kid, in this biographical sketch. After that conviction in 1887, Apache Kid was retried and found guilty by an Arizona Territorial Court in 1889, but escaped. It is not known when he died, but the author reports that he may have lived in Mexico to as late as 1924.

J. D. Filipiak

1799. Witt, Grace. THE BAD MAN AS HIPSTER: NORMAN MAILER'S USE OF FRONTIER METAPHOR. *Western Am. Literature* 1969 4(3): 203-217. Traces the development of violence in Norman Mailer's major novels and links the heroes of each with the traditional hero of the Western frontier. Bravery and courage are the primary virtues of frontier heroes, and these attributes are evident in Mailer's heroes. Mailer sees himself as a "hipster" and his heroes reflect this image. He maintains that no frontier remains for 20th-century man, except violence. The bad man is a hero because he is an individualist in his rebellion against conformity and tradition. Mailer finally has open admiration for the killer. He contends that where danger does not exist, it must be created. Mailer must go back to the pioneer days of the West to find his ideals, yet he wants to forget past and future. His present is actually based on his interpretation of the past.

S. L. McNeel

1800. —. WILD BILL-MC CANLES TRAGEDY. *Nebraska Hist.* 1968 49(1): 1-50, 64-79.
Sheldon, Addison E. ROCK CREEK RANCH FIGHT: AN INTRODUCTION, *pp. 1-4.*
Hansen, George W. TRUE STORY OF WILD BILL-MC CANLES AFFRAY IN JEFFERSON COUNTY, NEBRASKA, JULY 12, 1861, *pp. 5-46.*
McCanles, William M. THE ONLY LIVING EYEWITNESS, *pp. 47-50.*
Nichols, George W. WILD BILL IN HARPER'S, *pp. 64-79.*
Reprinted articles from *Nebraska History* published in 1927 pertaining to the history of the "Wild Bill-McCanles Tragedy." On 12 July 1861 at

Rock Creek Ranch on the Oregon Trail in Nebraska occurred a controversial fight in which three men were killed. James B. "Wild Bill" Hickok in cold blood killed David C. McCanles and wounded James Woods and a man called Gordon who were then murdered, also in cold blood, by Horace Wellman and J. W. Brink respectively. Monroe McCanles, aged 12, a witness to his father's murder, escaped and related the tale of the three murders. His account differed from Hickok's original version that the three men were killed in self-defense. The details of the incident are carefully related and examined as is an embellished account by Hickok first printed in *Harper's New Monthly Magazine* in February 1867.

R. Lowitt

Culture

General

1801. Broadbent, Thomas L. THE SCHILLER CENTENNIAL IN COLUMBIA, CALIFORNIA: GERMANS IN A GOLD RUSH TOWN. *Am.-German R. 1963 29(6): 7-13.* An account of a festival commemorating Friedrich von Schiller's centennial, held in a California gold rush town in 1859. Pictures. G. H. Davis

1802. Carranco, Lynwood and Simmons, Wilma Rawles. THE BOONVILLE LANGUAGE OF NORTHERN CALIFORNIA. *Am. Speech 1964 39(4): 278-286.* An account and a glossary of a lingo invented by children in the 1880's in an isolated part of California. Older people adopted the language which is still used as a secondary language by some Boonville old-timers. A story in "Boont-link" begins: "There being a hob in Boont, Pete shied ottoing," which means "There being a dance in Boonville, Fred [not Pete] quit working." Based on the authors' experience, 14 notes. R. W. Shoemaker

1803. Davis, Ronald L. THEY PLAYED FOR GOLD: THEATER ON THE MINING FRONTIER. *Southwest R. 1966 51(2): 169-184.* Detailed account of the western theater including promoters, performers, and repertoires from the Eagle Theater in Sacramento "where the first professional dramatic performance in California was given in October, 1849," to Horace Tabor's Opera House in Leadville, Colorado opened in 1879. D. F. Henderson

1804. Eikel, Fred, Jr. NEW BRAUNFELS GERMAN. *Am. Speech 1966 41(1): 5-16 and (4): 254-260.* Part I. Gives a historical sketch of the Texas Germans and a description of this study's methodology. Although the German element in Texas has been Americanized, many of them still speak their own kind of German which, in part, is a fusion of dialects from various parts of Germany. Most of the immigrants came from Nassau, Hessen, Hessen-Nassau, Rhenish Prussia, Westfalen, and Hannover. 25 notes. Part II. Compares the phonology of New Braunfels German with that of standard German with six pages of comparisons of selected sounds and representative words written in phonetic symbols. Based on the author's knowledge of New Braunfels German; 2 diagrams, 15 notes. To be continued. R. W. Shoemaker

1805. Eikel, Fred, Jr. NEW BRAUNFELS GERMAN: PART III. *Am. Speech 1967 42(2): 83-104.* Deals with the morphology and the syntax of the type of German spoken in New Braunfels. The author compares the speech of three generations and finds that New Braunfels German stays quite close to standard German except in its syntax. Based on the author's personal knowledge of New Braunfels German; 26 notes. R. W. Shoemaker

1806. Ernst, Alice Henson. HOMER DAVENPORT ON STAGE. *Oregon Hist. Q. 1965 66(1): 39-50.* Biographical sketch of Homer Davenport, widely-known newspaper cartoonist, political observer, and lecturer, from boyhood in Silverton, Oregon, through a brief vaudeville career, especially as a lecturer in the great cities of the world. C. C. Gorchels

1807. González, Rafael Jesús. PACHUCO: THE BIRTH OF A CREOLE LANGUAGE. *Arizona Q. 1967 23(4): 343-356.* A discussion of the "Pachuco" subculture and language, both of which apparently originated in the El Paso-Juarez underworld. At first the argot of tightly-knit gangs in El Paso, the language has since spread throughout the Southwest and is no longer associated with organized gangs. The language is a combination of Spanish dialects, anglicized Spanish words, hispanicized English words, and some made-up words. 9 notes.

J. M. Hawes

1808. Gurian, Jay. THE UNWRITTEN WEST. *Am. West 1965 2(1): 59-63.* Asserts that the region west of the Mississippi-Missouri has been romanticized, made glamorous, and fantasied to the point where its history has been reduced to a cheap myth. Twentieth-century pulps, paperbacks, radio, television, and movies have perpetuated and perfected this parody. He suggests three contributing factors: the mind of the litterateur was reduced from metaphysical to merely physical capability by the overwhelming geography of the area; unremitting anti-intellectual vernacular roots nourished nearly all western art; and, during the post-Civil War western development, the weekly magazines and newspapers hoarded western materials to feed to hungry easterners who wanted to escape the social, political, and industrial disturbances of the era. His plea is for literature and history to portray the West as it really was and is, a considerable but not impossible assignment. D. L. Smith

1809. Hune, Charles V. FIRST OF THE GOLD RUSH THEATRES. *California Hist. Soc. Q. 1967 46(4): 337-344.* To meet the needs for entertainment of the miners far from home, the management of the Round Tent, the most popular saloon in the city of Sacramento, decided in 1849 to build a crude theater and import a troupe of actors. The plays produced are listed. The theater, closed for financial reasons early in November, reopened in December. Within a year three theaters opened in Sacramento, offering a different play every night. It was here that Edwin Booth's earliest years in the theater were spent, and here scores of other famous troupers contributed to the array of talent that crossed Sacramento's stages. Based in part on John Herbert McCabe, "Theatrical Journals and Diary, 1849-1882," unpublished, in the California State Library; 12 notes. E. P. Stickney

1810. Jensen, Joan M. AFTER SLAVERY: CAROLINE SEVERENCE IN LOS ANGELES. *Southern California Q. 1966 48(2): 175-186.* The later career of a New England abolitionist and woman suffrage advocate, who brought the kindergarten and the Unitarian Church to Los Angeles. 25 notes. H. Kelsey

1811. Kalisch, Philip A. HIGH CULTURE ON THE FRONTIER: THE OMAHA LIBRARY ASSOCIATION. *Nebraska Hist. 1971 52(4): 411-417.* Examines the brief history of the Omaha Library Association, established in 1857 when the community was less than three years old. The institution was incorporated under the laws of the Territory of Nebraska. It lasted a little more than three years, but was unable to survive hard times, unstable financial backing, and dissension among its members. R. Lowitt

1812. Koch, Robert. REDISCOVERY: THE POTTERY OF ARTUS VAN BRIGGLE. *Art in Am. 1964 52(3): 120-121.* Discusses the strange phenomenon of Van Briggle's production of *Art Nouveau* ceramics in *fin de siècle* Colorado Springs. Illus. W. K. Bottorff

1813. Lepley, John G. THE PRINCE AND THE ARTIST ON THE UPPER MISSOURI. *Montana 1970 20(3): 42-54.* The upper Missouri River was visited in 1833 by the science-minded German Prince Maximilian, who was accompanied by artist Karl Bodmer (1809-93). Indian hostility kept them from venturing further upstream than the site of later Fort Benton. The Prince described and the artist painted outstanding bits of the landscape, some of which still can be seen as it was then as it had been three decades earlier when explored by Lewis and Clark. Illustrated with Bodmer sketches and modern photos identifying some of the same locations. S. R. Davison

1814. Nolan, Paul T. THE BOOMERS: OKLAHOMA PLAYWRIGHTS OPENED THE TERRITORY. *Chronicles of Oklahoma 1963 41(3): 248-252.* A discussion of pioneer Oklahoma playwrights from 1896 to 1919, with emphasis on the neglect of this phase of Oklahoma's cultural heritage. Politicians, oilmen, cattlemen, and Indians have been memorialized but these playwrights have been neglected, probably because few of them had any stage success. Before World War I Oklahoma had 39 playwrights and at least 41 plays. The first play copyrighted in Oklahoma was in 1896. From 1900 to 1915 almost every Oklahoma town had one or more playwrights: Oklahoma City, five; Norman, three; five towns, two each; and over 20 towns, one each. Some of these 41 plays exist in manuscript copies in the Library of Congress, others in attic trunks. They are a monument to Oklahoma's forgotten pioneer playwrights.

I. W. Van Noppen

1815. Nolan, Paul T. TERRILL'S "PURGATORY": FIRST PLAY PRESENTED IN OKLAHOMA. *Chronicles of Oklahoma 1964 42(3): 246-252.* Ira N. Terrill's *A Purgatory Made of a Paradise* (1907), a heroic drama, was not the first play written in or copyrighted from Oklahoma, but it was the first play printed in the State. It is the earliest extant drama written by an Oklahoman dealing with the Oklahoma milieu. One copy exists in the Library of Congress. Terrill was a member of the first legislature of the territory, and was quite versatile: farmer, legislator, geologist, reformer, playwright. He was a controversial figure with strong friends and bitter enemies. The theme of the play is that the "Oklahoma Territory is being despoiled by dishonest men who are misusing the law to rob the honest settlers." The heroic couplets used in the play are artificial; as a result the play is of minor historical interest. 15 notes.

I. W. Van Noppen

1816. Nolan, Paul T. WHEN THE CURTAINS RISE, SCOUTS FALL OUT. *Southern Speech J. 1964 29(3): 175-186.* Examines the activities of some Indian fighter scouts who turned to the stage to capitalize on the public interest in the Indian wars in the West. The author analyzes some plays which some scouts wrote, the methods of staging Indian shows, and the professional jealousies among the scout-actor-playwrights. 17 notes.

H. G. Stelzner

1817. Richmond, Robert W. HUMOR ON TOUR: ARTEMUS WARD IN MID-AMERICA, 1864. *Kansas Hist. Q. 1967 33(4): 470-480.* Charles Farrar Browne (Artemus Ward), one of the most famous humorists in 19th-century America, made an extensive speaking tour in the West during 1863-64. His activities in California have been thoroughly covered. This is an account of the lesser known lectures "Robinson Crusoe" and "Babes in the Woods" that Ward used with great success on his trip back to the East. Ward's journey through Kansas and his speeches at Atchison, Leavenworth, Lawrence, Kansas City, and St. Joseph, Missouri are described in detail. Based on biographies, articles and local newspapers; illus., 15 notes.

W. F. Zornow

1818. Sutherland, Henry A. REQUIEM FOR THE LOS ANGELES PHILHARMONIC AUDITORIUM. *Southern California Q. 1965 47(3): 303-331.* Details the history of the building at Fifth and Olive Streets in downtown Los Angeles known as Philharmonic Auditorium, which was taken over by the Temple Baptist Church in November 1964. Hazard's Pavilion was built on the site in 1886-87 to satisfy the city's need for a large auditorium, and it housed all sorts of expositions, conventions, shows, and other events until 1904, when it was bought by a group of Baptists who planned a church there. The plans required more money than the congregation could raise by itself and an Auditorium Company was founded. It raised the money and built the building, which the church then rented. First known as Temple Auditorium, in 1920 it took the name of the recently founded Los Angeles Philharmonic Orchestra, which became a regular tenant until 1964 when the Music Center was completed.

A. K. Main

1819. Tanner, Jeri and McCullen, J. T., Jr. THE EYES OF TEXAS ON FLYING SAUCERS. *Kentucky Folklore Record 1967 13(1): 25-32.* Discusses the reaction to flying saucer reports in Texas in 1878, 1897, and, especially, during the past 20 years. The authors list the "descriptions" of the unidentified flying objects, the typical excitement, attempted explanations by spectators including frequent references to biblical passages, and scientific explanation of some of the phenomena. Based largely on newspaper accounts and editorial comments; 41 notes.

J. C. Crowe

1820. Weadock, Jack F. A DEDICATION TO THE MEMORY OF ROSS SANTEE, 1889-1965. *Arizona and the West 1965 7(3): 183-186.* Ross Santee spent much of his adult life in the American West of which he wrote. His short stories and 12 books, the subjects of which were usually cowboys, horses, and Indians, were illustrated by his own

sketches. His pen and brush have secured him a permanent place in the literature of the West. Appended with a selected list of his publications. Illus.

D. L. Smith

1821. Wood, Gordon R. DIALECT CONTOURS IN THE SOUTHERN STATES. *Am. Speech 1963 38(4): 243-256.* Deals with the presence of midland and southern words in those parts of the South settled after 1800. Its main purpose is to show the diversity of regional vocabulary found in Alabama, Arkansas, Florida, Georgia, Louisiana, Mississippi, Oklahoma, and Tennessee. The diversity of regional vocabulary results from three 19th-century phenomena: the advancing frontier, the growth of towns, and increase of regional communication, each of which can be associated with certain aspects of 20th-century regional vocabulary in the South. The study is based on written questionnaires dealing with such terms as "tow sack" (midland area) or "croker sack" (coastal area), both meaning "burlap bag," and is illustrated with eight maps showing the regions where the words are used and the boundaries of these regions; 4 notes.

R. W. Shoemaker

1822. Young, Mary. THE WEST AND AMERICAN CULTURAL IDENTITY: OLD THEMES AND NEW VARIATIONS. *Western Hist. Q. 1970 1(2): 137-160.* Traditional historiography was concerned with analysis of the frontier experience as a way of defining America's cultural identity, using the West as an image of American culture. After broadening the working definition of culture beyond simply trying to discover what was going on in the West, recent investigations have utilized the following areas of concern of American studies: meanings, values, and ideas the American attached to the pioneering experience and to the West; the meaning of the westward movement in terms of the American's concept of his culture and of himself; and the form and the role of the image of the western past and present. Brief commentary of traditionalist and revisionist approaches are followed by a closer examination of the analysis of three "myth-critics" - Henry Nash Smith, Alfred K. Moore, and Charles L. Sanford. Present studies stress both the persistent continuity of the frontier experience and its increasing rejection. Rejection is predicted on the assertion that the American westering past is "a source of false historical self-consciousness" which hinders the attempts of the American to reckon with his present problems. 65 notes.

D. L. Smith

Education

1823. Baird, W. David. SPENCER ACADEMY, CHOCTAW NATION, 1842-1900. *Chronicles of Oklahoma 1967 45(1): 25-43.* Spencer Academy stood as an important educational institution among the Choctaw. It educated many of the principal chiefs, leaders, and military officers from the tribe who served in the Civil War. The school was administered at various times by the Northern and Southern Presbyterians and by the tribe itself. Subject matter included geography, history, algebra, and music, as well as classical Greek and Latin at times. Based on the criteria of ability to teach English, the school was a failure, yet many felt it was the equal of New England schools. Illus., map, 43 notes.

K. P. Davis

1824. Barnds, William Joseph. NEBRASKA COLLEGE, THE EPISCOPAL SCHOOL AT NEBRASKA CITY 1868-1885. *Nebraska Hist. 52(2): 169-189.* Relates the history of Nebraska College, an Episcopalian school. The college failed because of financial problems, competition from state-supported colleges, internal difficulties, and the relatively small number of Episcopalians in the area.

R. Lowitt

1825. Brown, Richard D. THE AGRICULTURAL COLLEGE LAND GRANT IN KANSAS - SELECTION AND DISPOSAL. *Agric. Hist. 1963 37(2): 94-102.* Within six months after the passage of the Morrill Act, the Kansas Legislature passed a bill accepting the grant and obligating the state to the educational provisions of the Act. By July, 1863, 70 thousand of the 90 thousand acres allotted to Kansas had been carefully selected as good farm land by a commission appointed by the governor. The policy was adopted of selling only to actual settlers. Careful appraisals were made; consistent attempts to get the highest prices possible were made with appropriate sales promotion; expenses of administration were kept low; and during periods of depression, land was held from

the market. Most of the land was sold by 1888. Over 500 thousand dollars was realized for endowment of the Kansas agricultural college. Based on archives of Kansas State University.
W. D. Rasmussen

1826. Chapman, B. B. OLD CENTRAL OF OKLAHOMA STATE UNIVERSITY. *Chronicles of Oklahoma 1964 42(3): 273-290.* Commemorates Old Central, a building dedicated 15 June 1894 at Oklahoma State University (formerly Oklahoma Agricultural and Mechanical College). It was then the "pride of the people of the prairie. ...It is the only landmark known to all . . . who have graduated at the institution." The description of Old Central in the Stillwater *Gazette* of 25 August 1893 is included. In 1955 there was an attempt to raze Old Central, but dozens of prominent alumni wrote urging its preservation. 2 illus., 14 notes.
I. W. Van Noppen

1827. Corwin, Hugh D. THE FOLSOM TRAINING SCHOOL. *Chronicles of Oklahoma 1964 42(1): 46-52.* An account of Willis Folsom and the Folsom Training School at Smithville, Oklahoma. The school was founded by Methodist Episcopalians in 1920 to offer training to both Caucasians and Indians. With high scholastic and moral standards, it served the religious needs of the area. Tuition was low, and all students were required to work five hours a week for the school without pay. During the depression, the Methodist Board of Missions could not continue support and the institution closed. 6 notes, biblio.
I. W. Van Noppen

1828. Dale, Edward Everett. DAVID ROSS BOYD: PIONEER EDUCATOR. *Chronicles of Oklahoma 1964 42(2): 2-35.* David Ross Boyd was born near Coshocton, Ohio, in 1853. His father aided fugitive slaves. At 17, David began teaching for 40 dollars a month. In 1873 he entered Wooster University (now Wooster College), and in 1878 he became principal and then superintendent of the Van Wert schools. After holding that position for nine years, Boyd went west, became superintendent of the Arkansas City Schools and built a high school. He became president of the University of Oklahoma from 1892 to 1908. For the next four years he served as superintendent of education for the Presbyterian Home Missions, and from 1912 to 1919 he was president of the University of New Mexico. He retired in 1919 at the age of 66, and died in 1936. 6 illus.
I. W. Van Noppen

1829. Davis, William E. THE ENGINEERING EXPERIMENT AT COLORADO UNIVERSITY. *Colorado Mag. 1965 42(4): 330-343.* A short history of the College of Engineering at the University of Colorado. Founded in 1883 with one student, the college has grown into one of the outstanding schools in the nation. A rapidly advancing building program and the war relationship between deans, professors, and students are two factors which have brought about this success.
R. Sexauer

1830. Florer, John H. MAJOR ISSUES IN THE CONGRESSIONAL DEBATE OF THE MORRILL ACT OF 1862. *Hist. of Educ. Q. 1968 8(4): 459-478.* Lists and examines the arguments in Congress over the bill proposing to provide funds from the sale of public lands for agricultural and mechanical colleges. The bill, introduced by Justin Morrill of Vermont in 1856, was defeated by presidential veto, reintroduced in 1861 and passed in 1862. Morrill stressed the economic benefit to be reaped by the nation. Opposition came chiefly from Western congressmen and others who spoke of a "give-away," of federal intervention in state affairs, and who charged unconstitutionality and lack of precedence. Many Westerners feared that the bill would only aid Eastern land speculators and retard settlement of the West, and they were joined by others who rejected the costs involved and resented the "meddling" role of the Federal Government. References to the Civil War, to national pride, and to foreign competition were less frequently made in the Congressional debates than the author had expected. Based on the *Congressional Globe;* 74 notes.
J. Herbst

1831. Goda, Paul. THE HISTORICAL BACKGROUND OF CALIFORNIA'S CONSTITUTIONAL PROVISIONS PROHIBITING AID TO SECTARIAN SCHOOLS. *California Hist. Soc. Q. 1967 46(2): 149-171.* In 1852-53 a number of religious schools received State aid, but attempts to get State aid for Catholic schools increased and did not end with the 1855 legislation prohibiting it. Finally in 1875 President Grant in his national campaign came out strongly against State aid in the various States. In California the reaction to his message was uniformly favorable.

"In 1878 the long-pending revision of the California Constitution finally got under way." The California Teachers' Association commissioned the writing of a section on sectarian education which was adopted almost as written. Compromise between Catholics and those of other faiths on the school question in California was probably impossible. 86 notes.
E. P. Stickney

1832. Gower, Calvin W. LECTURES, LYCEUMS, AND LIBRARIES IN EARLY KANSAS, 1854-1864. *Kansas Hist. Q. 1970 36(2): 175-182.* Although preoccupied with their own problems that arose during the days of territorial strife and the later problems growing out of the war, the early settlers in Kansas had time to cultivate "The Three L's." An examination of the leading newspapers during the territorial period and early years of statehood reveals many references to recreational and intellectual activities centering around lectures, lyceums, and libraries. This spread beyond the major settlements at Lawrence, Leavenworth, and Topeka to some of the surrounding communities. These three elements were also important factors in the early educational development of Kansas. 23 notes.
W. F. Zornow

1833. Griffin, C. S. THE UNIVERSITY OF KANSAS AND THE YEARS OF FRUSTRATION, 1854-1864. *Kansas Hist. Q. 1966 32(1): 1-32.* The university that opened in Lawrence in 1866 was the product of many years of conflict. The factors that entered into the conflict included such things as rivalry between the advocates of public and private education, the efforts to make education an element in the struggle between Free Staters and Proslaveryites, the rivalry between towns to become the site of a school, coeducation versus all-male education, an attempt to identify the college with a religious denomination, and an effort to create an educational system that met the qualifications imposed by the State constitution. Based on local newspapers, State records, and manuscripts at the University of Kansas and Kansas State Historical Society.
W. F. Zornow

1834. Guenther, Richard L. THE SANTEE NORMAL TRAINING SCHOOL. *Nebraska Hist. 1970 51(3): 359-378.* Discusses the education of the Santee Sioux Indians at the training school in Nebraska. The school was founded along the Niobrara River in Nebraska. The school was founded in 1870, but economic exigencies forced it to close in 1936.
R. Lowitt

1835. Haselmayer, Louis A. GERMAN METHODIST COLLEGES IN THE WEST. *Methodist Hist. 1964 2(4): 35-43.* The heavy German immigration of the 1850's into the United States gave rise to five German Methodist colleges - German Wallace College, Berea, Ohio; Central Wesleyan College, Warrenton, Missouri; German College, Mt. Pleasant, Iowa; German College, Charles City, Iowa; and the Blinn Memorial College, Brenham, Texas. The author discusses the organization, faculty, courses of study, and student bodies of these colleges, as well as their decline and merger with other educational institutions. Based in part on archives of the Central Wesleyan College at Northwest Missouri State Teachers College, Kirksville, Missouri, and the Zwingli F. Meyer Collection of German-American Methodists at Mt. Pleasant, Iowa.
H. L. Calkin

1836. Hendrick, Irving G. ACADEMIC REVOLUTION IN CALIFORNIA: A HISTORY OF EVENTS TO THE PASSAGE AND IMPLEMENTATION OF THE 1961 FISHER BILL ON TEACHER CERTIFICATION, PART I AND PART II. *Southern California Q. 1967 49(2): 127-166 and (3): 253-295.* Part I. A description of social and political influences which contributed to the formation of new certification requirements in California in 1961. From 1850 to 1900 there was a tendency for the authority for the certification of teachers to become centralized in State hands and for normal schools to grow in number and influence. In 1901, the tendency was completed and the State entrusted the carrying out of the certification program to the colleges of education. From the beginning, however, there was opposition to this alignment. There was antipathy in the colleges and universities between subject matter departments and education departments and by the late 1950's there was societal disapproval of existing certification requirements and the control exerted by professional educators, not only in California but nationally. In particular, the quality of education courses and the number of such courses required for certification were attacked. The stage was set for reforms which would require prospective teachers to take more subject matter courses and less methodology work. Professional educators proposed changes, but these were hardly suited to appease those who objected to the control exercised by educationists since they still left control in the hands of educators. Instead, demand continued for a program of State testing, stricter public school curriculum requirements in basic subjects and foreign languages, and different teacher certification requirements. Based on public and organization documents, contemporary articles, and secondary sources; 92 notes. Part II. Prior to the legislative phase of the struggle for teacher certification reforms in California, the State Board of Education made recommendations. As early as 1958 the board became interested in the matter and it suggested that a single credential structure be created, that elementary teachers have five years of preparation, and that secondary teachers be permitted to teach only in their major and minor subject fields. The Fisher Bill which was introduced on 9 January 1961 by Senator Hugo Fisher of Mill Valley reduced the types of credentials from 40 to five, required all teachers to major in an academic subject, and to take five years of college training. Because of the emphasis on academic subject preparation, professional educators were joined in their opposition to the bill by those who taught practical arts rather than academic subjects. After several amendments and some opposition from pressure groups, the bill passed on 12 June 1961. It still required strong preparation in an academic subject although it also stressed the importance of student teaching as well. However, Senator Fisher was defeated for reelection in 1962 and the author believes it was largely due to his role in passing this revolutionary and controversial law. Based on public and organization documents, legislative proceedings, and the Hugo Fisher Papers; 80 notes.   W. L. Bowers

1837. Hendrick, Irving G. THE EARLY HISTORY OF CALIFORNIA STATE-PRINTED TEXTBOOKS. *Southern California Q. 1964 46(3): 223-238.* California is at present the only state printing its own elementary school textbooks. This policy, adopted as a result of the public's conviction that a "textbook ring" had corrupted school boards, has continued for 80 years despite criticism by California educators. Defenders argued it would be cheaper, more effective, and would simplify teaching; and all major parties in California supported the passage of an amendment to the State Constitution allowing the state to print textbooks. While the State Teacher's Association opposed the amendment, it passed in 1884 with little voter interest, thus establishing what was to become the largest and most successful venture in state textbook printing. Uses published sources.   J. Jensen

1838. Hodge, Patt. THE HISTORY OF HAMMON AND THE RED MOON SCHOOL. *Chronicles of Oklahoma 1966 44(2): 130-139.* In 1892 a post office was established in the home of James and Ida Hammon from whom the town took its name. The Red Moon Boarding School was established in 1897. It became the most modern school in western Oklahoma. The students planted trees, an orchard, built fences, and learned English. The girls learned to knit, sew, cook, and sing. The boys cared for poultry, hogs, cows, and cultivated the soil. All received an academic education. A laundry and a bake house, a chicken house, hog house, two cisterns, a windmill, and a pump were built. By 1912 the boarding aspect of the school was discontinued. Enrollment gradually declined but the school continued until 1925. In 1965 the building burned. 2 illus., an appendix, 12 notes.   I. W. Van Noppen

1839. House, R. Morton. WORKING OUR WAY THROUGH COLLEGE. *Chronicles of Oklahoma 1964 42(2): 36-54.* An account of an ambitious boy's determination to work his way through Oklahoma Agricultural and Mechanical College at Stillwater. The author tells of hoboing to the wheat fields and the grueling work in the harvest. 3 illus.   I. W. Van Noppen

1840. Hulse, James W. THE CENTENNIAL HISTORY OF THE UNIVERSITY OF NEVADA: A PROSPECTUS. *Nevada Hist. Soc. Q. 1970 13(1): 20-27.* The University of Nevada observes its centennial in 1974 and, if sufficient individual and institutional enthusiasm can be generated, a new history of the university will be published during the centennial year. Histories of higher education will be different in the future because some of the historians of the 1960's have suggested new ways to make individual institutional histories relate to the academic world as a whole. Revisionism is overdue in writing histories of universities. Several possible methods of writing the proposed history of the University of Nevada are suggested by the author. Individual contribu-

tions of some professors would outweigh the contributions of many of the university officers and should be so treated in the history. Both objective and subjective methods must be employed to provide any meaningful history of the University of Nevada. The older histories of the university suffer because of their insistence on objectivity alone. This type of history pays the price of not being relevant. Illus., 8 notes.
      E. P. Costello

1841. Jaeckel, Solomon P. EDWARD HYATT, 1858-1919: CALIFORNIA EDUCATOR. *Southern California Q. 1970 52(2): 122-154, and 52(3): 248-274.* Continued from previous article. Part II. Concerns Hyatt's entry into California school politics in 1894, his tenure as Riverside County Superintendent from 1895 to 1907, and his first two years as State Superintendent of Public Instruction (1907-09). After Hyatt's dismissal as teacher-principal at San Jacinto, he became a successful candidate for the office of Riverside County Superintendent of Schools. His "most important work" while serving in that was to make the periodic teacher institutes more inspiring and profitable through greater teacher participation. In 1906 Hyatt was the successful Republican candidate for State Superintendent of Public Instruction. Among his important activities during the first two years of his tenure were a campaign to give more statewide publicity to school affairs and efforts aimed at achieving more "internal communication in all divisions of the school enterprise." Based on the Hyatt Papers, public documents, and secondary sources; 85 notes. Part III. Focuses on the period 1908-19 and discusses Hyatt's views on politics and education, his support of a changed composition of the State board of education, and his efforts to obtain free textbooks for California schools. In his political and educational views, Hyatt stressed the necessity of keeping government and the schools close to the people. He therefore favored a State board of education composed of lay people rather than professional educators, as well as free textbooks for public schools. Both of these changes were realized in 1912. Hyatt was reelected State Superintendent of Public Instruction in 1910 and 1914. He ran again in 1918, despite a stroke in 1917 which "completely incapacitated him physically," and was defeated. He died on 7 December 1919. Based on public documents and secondary sources; 86 notes.   W. L. Bowers

1842. Jaeckel, Solomon P. EDWARD HYATT, 1858-1919: CALIFORNIA EDUCATOR, PART I. *Southern California Q. 1970 52(1): 33-35.* Discusses the career of California educator Edward Hyatt (1858-1919). The author deals with Hyatt's early life and his work as teacher-principal in the San Jacinto public grammar school between the years 1885-94. Hyatt was born in Ohio on 8 March 1858, but moved to California as a young man. While teacher-principal at San Jacinto he promoted a number of changes - an improved curriculum, new equipment, and good teacher-community rapport. Hyatt also taught high school courses which permitted San Jacinto graduates to enter the State university. When the San Jacinto school was included in a high school district in 1893, Hyatt and many parents refused to recognize the new situation. Litigation upheld them but Hyatt was dismissed by his superintendent in 1894. Based on the Hyatt Papers, public documents, and contemporary and secondary sources; 4 illus., 42 notes. Article to be continued.   W. L. Bowers

1843. Johnson, John L. ALBERT ANDREW EXENDINE: CARLISLE COACH AND TEACHER. *Chronicles of Oklahoma 1965 43(3): 319-331.* Exendine made football history as a player in 1907, on the second-team All-American. The Carlisle Indian School had been established in 1879 on the theory that Indians should continue many of the activities that they engaged in at home. They excelled in football under Coach "Pop" Warner. In 1908 Exendine became an assistant coach and developed the forward passing game, although it was not used widely until 1913. The Carlisle Indians had used it in 1907. Exendine coached Jim Thorpe and became his friend. In 1909 "Ex" became head coach at Otterbein. He coached at Georgetown from 1914 to 1922. He coached also at Washington State, Occidental, Northeastern, Oklahoma, and Oklahoma State. As a coach, educator, lawyer, and Indian agent he devoted a lifetime to the education of youth. 20 notes.
      I. W. Van Noppen

1844. Jorgenson, Lloyd P. MATERIALS ON THE HISTORY OF EDUCATION IN STATE HISTORICAL JOURNALS. *Hist. of Educ. Q. 1968 8(4): 510-527.* This bibliography contains material from *Minnesota History, Nebraska History Magazine, North Dakota History, Northwest Ohio Quarterly, Ohio Historical Quarterly, Chronicles of Oklahoma, Mid-America,* and *Wisconsin Magazine of History.*
      J. Herbst

1845. Kropp, Simon F. ALBERT J. FOUNTAIN AND THE FIGHT FOR PUBLIC EDUCATION IN NEW MEXICO. *Arizona and the West 1969 11(4): 341-358.* Albert Jennings Fountain served in New Mexico during the Civil War and married a local girl. After a brief venture into Texas politics, he moved to Mesilla in southern New Mexico to practice law, to promote local cultural projects, and to publish a newspaper. Involved too heavily in the anti-Jesuit issue in public education and, by implication, in other controversies because many of his Masonic and Republican friends were members of the Santa Fe Ring, Fountain wisely left the ring and his career in journalism to become a champion of law and order. The author details Fountain's attempts to establish public school education in Mesilla. By 1879 he was immersed in a lucrative law practice which eventually brought him leadership of local Republican politics and of the territorial legislature, and speakership of its lower house. 5 illus., 34 notes.   D. L. Smith

1846. Manley, Robert N. CHANCELLOR ALLEN R. BENTON COMES TO NEBRASKA. *Nebraska Hist. 1967 48(4): 305-329.* Surveys through text and letters Benton's years (1871-76) as first chancellor of the University of Nebraska. Family affairs, personal debts, politics, and Benton's growing disillusionment with Nebraska are discussed. The religious controversy which finally led to his resignation is examined and his tenure as chancellor is evaluated.   R. Lowitt

1847. McGowin, Kathleen Anne. TUCSON PUBLIC SCHOOLS, 1867-1874. *Arizoniana 1964 5(2): 38-43.* A prize-winning essay on the establishment and development of the public schools in Tucson. Emphasis is given to the struggle to obtain adequate financial support.   W. Unrau

1848. Nelson, David P. HIGHER EDUCATION: TO COMPETE OR TO COORDINATE. *Colorado Mag. 1972 49(2): 93-108.* The latest joint effort to coordinate publicly supported higher education in Colorado is a proposed higher education complex in Denver. The 1876 Colorado constitution, by creating four different governing boards for the various colleges and universities of Colorado, made coordination of State higher education difficult to achieve. Reviews efforts at coordination, particularly after 1937 when the presidents' association members voluntarily cooperated to get legislative approval for a 10-year building mill levy. The same legislature authorized public junior colleges under still different direction. While voluntary coordination, until 1964, frequently succeeded in getting financial aid for Colorado public higher education, it did not provide for other types of coordination. Dissatisfaction with voluntary coordination resulted, in 1965, in legislative creation of a Commission on Higher Education to coordinate activities at the colleges and universities. Based on government documents and on secondary sources; 7 illus., 37 notes.   O. H. Zabel

1849. Peffer, E. Louise. MEMORIAL TO CONGRESS ON AN AGRICULTURAL COLLEGE FOR CALIFORNIA, 1853. *Agric. Hist. 1966 40(1): 53-56.* John L. L. Warren prepared a memorial in 1853 asking for Federal assistance for an agricultural college in California. The text of the memorial is reproduced.   W. D. Rasmussen

1850. Polos, Nicholas C. SCHOOL LANDS IN CALIFORNIA. *Southern California Q. 1969 51(1): 63-70.* A persistent problem of California's early educational system was "the inadequacy of the State School Fund which resulted from poor management of the sales of school lands." Money from school land sales was frequently used to defray ordinary expenses of the State. In 1863 an act was passed which provided for the funding of the State's indebtedness to the School Fund. This act and the Revised School Law of 1866 furnished the beginning of a "well organized, legally supported program for state education" in California. In less than 20 years California accomplished what it took many States a hundred years to do. Based on State government documents and secondary works; 29 notes.   W. L. Bowers

1851. Polos, Nicholas C. SEGREGATION AND JOHN SWETT. *Southern California Q. 1964 46(1): 69-82.* From 1863 to 1867 John Swett was California's fourth superintendent of public instruction. Being a strong Union man, he argued that: 1) for self-preservation every representative government should provide for the education of every child and 2) the property of the state should be taxed to pay for that education. He was ahead of his time; not till 1886 did the NEA give attention to race

education. Based on newspapers, journals of the Senate and Assembly, and statutes of Swett's two administrations.   E. P. Stickney

1852. Polos, Nicholas C. A YANKEE PATRIOT: JOHN SWETT, THE HORACE MANN OF THE PACIFIC. *Hist. of Educ. Q. 1964 4(1): 17-32.* This appraisal of Swett, Civil War superintendent of public instruction in California, city administrator of the San Francisco schools, author, journalist, poet and educational statesman, stresses his New England heritage and his role as founder of California's public school system. A Union sympathizer, he proposed the "free school" bill of 1866 through which the public schools became the instrument of Americanization of all California settlers. Swett also helped build the Californian system of free education from kindergarten to the university.   J. Herbst

1853. Sawyer, R. McLaran. NO TEACHER FOR THE SCHOOL: THE NEBRASKA JUNIOR NORMAL SCHOOL MOVEMENT. *Nebraska Hist. 1971 52(2): 191-203.* Tells of the unique effort to improve rural teaching in Nebraska during 1903-14, when summer programs were conducted throughout the State to prepare new teachers for rural elementary schools and to improve the skills of those practitioners with little professional training. After 1914 other educational institutions in the State absorbed the program. The program resulted from the educational frontier that still existed in western Nebraska.   R. Lowitt

1854. Sawyer, R. McLaran. SAMUEL DE WITT BEALS, FRONTIER EDUCATOR. *Nebraska Hist. 1969 50(2): 173-183.* Delineates the educational career of Samuel DeWitt Beals (1826-1900) from his beginnings in New York State through his long experience in Nebraska as high school teacher, state superintendent, school principal, county school superintendent of Douglas County, superintendent of schools in Omaha, and finally as a high school teacher. All of his teaching in Nebraska was in the city of Omaha.   R. Lowitt

1855. Seaberg, Stanley and Mulhair, William. HIGH SCHOOL STUDENTS TEST THE FRONTIER THESIS. *Social Educ. 1965 29(5): 279-280.* A description of how Fremont High School students actually tested the Turner frontier thesis in their own communities. 11 notes.   F. Rotondaro

1856. Shatraw, Milton E. SCHOOL DAYS. *Am. West 1966 3(2): 68-71.* The one-room schoolhouse reminiscences of a Montana lad raised on a ranch. Despite the limitations and hardships of his frontier education, 1907-11, the author's solid scholastic foundation was confirmed when his family moved to the city of Helena and he had no difficulty keeping up with his own age group in the city's fifth grade. Illus.   D. L. Smith

1857. Spalding, Arminta Scott. FROM THE NATCHEZ TRACE TO OKLAHOMA: DEVELOPMENT OF CHRISTIAN CIVILIZATION AMONG THE CHOCTAWS, 1800-1860. *Chronicles of Oklahoma 1967 45(1): 2-24.* Legend among the Choctaw people tells of their ancient migration into the Mississippi area from a land far to the west. Relying on corn for food, the Choctaw lived a stoical existence, believing their creator had given them rules to live by and left them. Not until contact with Christian missionaries did the Indians conceive of worshipping a god. The first mission school was established in 1818 and became a major influencing factor in the history of the Choctaw civilization. This school, though disrupted, moved with the tribe when they migrated to present-day Oklahoma in 1831. The American Board for Foreign Missions continued to underwrite the tribal educational system with funds and missionaries. By 1860 the Indians were able to undertake the administering of the school system themselves. Maps, 81 notes.   K. P. Davis

1858. Squires, J. Duane. AN ADDRESS DEDICATING SQUIRES HALL. *North Dakota Q. 1964 32(2): 38-41.* Tribute to Vernon P. Squires, long-time professor at the University of North Dakota, by his son at the dedication of a building in his honor.   J. F. Mahoney

1859. Vandiver, Frank E. WALTER PRESCOTT WEBB: TEACHER. *Southwest R. 1963 48(4): 377-379.* Reflections on the teaching excellence of Walter Webb, late University of Texas historian.   D. F. Henderson

1860. Walsh, Thomas R. CHARLES E. BESSEY AND THE TRANSFORMATION OF THE INDUSTRIAL COLLEGE. *Nebraska Hist. 1971 52(4): 383-409.* Discusses the successful efforts of Bessey, Dean of the Industrial College of the University of Nebraska 1884-88, who transformed the college's approach from manual training to science education and research. Starting with no equipment, with an apathetic or opposed legislature and farm groups, and with a university torn by internal dissension, Bessey was able to lay the foundations of an educational complex that gained an international reputation. The Hatch Act (1887) provided funds for "investigation and experimentation" and the Morril Act (1862) provided funds for the teaching of "the great sciences which underlie agriculture and the mechanic arts."
R. Lowitt

1861. Watson, Elbert L. OKLAHOMA AND THE ANTI-EVOLUTION MOVEMENT OF THE 1920'S. *Chronicles of Oklahoma 1964 42(4): 396-407.* In 1923 the Oklahoma Legislature was the first to pass legislation against the teaching of evolution. House Bill 197 earmarking 750 thousand dollars for textbooks was passed, 87 to two, providing that none should teach the materialistic conception of history nor the Darwinian theory. In 1927 attempts were made to pass a bill to fine anyone teaching evolution. The campaign of Al Smith in 1928 diverted the efforts of the fundamentalists to attacking him as a wet and a Catholic. Subsequently agitation against evolution died down. 49 notes.
I. W. Van Noppen

1862. Watson, James E. ORIGINS OF POLITICAL SCIENCE AT THE UNIVERSITY OF CALIFORNIA. *J. of the West 1966 5(4): 441-453.* When Daniel Coit Gilman became president of the recently founded University of California at Berkeley in 1872, he called for an awareness of both internal issues and international relations. He sounded the keynote for a new emphasis in higher education upon the social and political sciences. How the study and teaching of political science got started at the university under Bernard Moses and his successor, David Prescott Barrows, is the subject of this article. Many of the outstanding members of the department and their contributions are mentioned. Based on published sources, 19 notes.
D. N. Brown

1863. Weber, Francis J. A MISSIONARY'S PLEA FOR GOVERNMENTAL ASSISTANCE. *Records of the Am. Catholic Hist. Soc. of Philadelphia 1966 77(4): 242-249.* Reproduces a 15-page letter of Eugene Casimir Chirouse, O.M.I., to James Willis Nesmith of Oregon, 28 August 1865. Father Chirouse documented the financial position of his mission among the Indians of Puget Sound and requested government support for a school.
J. M. McCarthy

1864. —. BETHEL COLLEGE: 75TH ANNIVERSARY. *Mennonite Life 1963 18(2): 51-96.* The entire issue is devoted to the past and present development of Bethel College, the first Mennonite college in the United States.
S

Literature and Folklore

1865. Amaral, Anthony. IDAH MEACHAM STROBRIDGE: FIRST WOMAN OF NEVADA LETTERS. *Nevada Hist. Soc. Q. 1967 10(3): 3-28.* The three books by Idah Meacham Strobridge, written between 1904 and 1909, have been forgotten. They were privately printed in limited editions and are seldom listed in catalogs of booksellers. She is, nevertheless, one of the few writers who has ever presented graphic and vivid impressions of the northern Nevada country. Her subject matter was reporting of what she had seen by living in the desert from the late 1860's to the end of the century. Appended is a facsimile reprint of "The Quail's Cañon," from *The Land of Purple Shadows* (1909). D. L. Smith

1866. Anderson, John Q. ANOTHER TEXAS VARIANT OF "COLE YOUNGER," BALLAD OF A BADMAN. *Western Folklore 1972 31(2): 103-115.* In 1962 the author collected in Texas a version of "Cole Younger," a traditional ballad about Thomas Coleman Younger (1844-1916), the notorious outlaw leader of the Younger Brothers Gang. Compares this version with 22 other known versions of the ballad. Such an analysis allows the identification of two different types of the same ballad. Discusses ballad material using the life of Cole Younger as a point

of reference. Composers were selective, choosing only those details that fit their purpose. In this case Cole Younger becomes more of a romantic folk hero than his actual life would indicate. 20 notes.
R. A. Trennert

1867. Anderson, John Q. THE LEGEND OF THE PHANTOM COACH OF EAST TEXAS. *Western Folklore 1963 22(4): 259-262.* Discussion of the legend of the phantom coach in east Texas. Relates this tale to others of English and Irish origin in an attempt to prove the vitality of the Anglo-Irish tradition in folklore in the Southern United States.
L. J. White

1868. Anderson, John Q. POPULAR BELIEFS IN TEXAS, LOUISIANA, AND ARKANSAS. *Southern Folklore Q. 1968 32(4): 304-319.* A sampling of popular beliefs about childhood, youth, and adulthood in Texas, Louisiana, and Arkansas shows that oral lore in the Southwest is in the mainstream of Anglo-American folk culture as represented in more extensive collections made elsewhere in the United States. Discusses findings and lists 174 specific examples of beliefs collected from several hundred informants. Concludes that a great body of oral lore persists among people who now live in an urban environment that has replaced the agrarian culture in which these popular beliefs were more vital. 9 notes.
P. McClure

1869. Arlt, Gustave O. BRET HARTE - THE ARGONAUT. *Southern California Q. 1962 44(1): 17-30.* Francis Bret Harte was the most typical and most strongly marked of all the literary figures of California. Gold seeking excited Harte and he compared the gold hunters of 1849 and the shipmates of Jason, who set out in search of the Golden Fleece. Harte settled down in San Francisco and helped found two famous periodicals - the *Californian* and the *Overland Monthly*. He left California in 1871 and for 30 years lived and worked in the Eastern United States and Europe. He was a keen and sympathetic observer of human nature, and an appreciative describer of inanimate nature. Thanks to the stories of Bret Harte, the early charm and romance of California will never be lost.
D. H. Swift

1870. Arrington, Leonard J. and Haupt, Jon. INTOLERABLE ZION: THE IMAGE OF MORMONISM IN NINETEENTH CENTURY AMERICAN LITERATURE. *Western Humanities R. 1968 22(3): 243-260.* Statements made in America about Mormons have tended in recent years to be favorable. Quite the contrary was true in the 19th century. Fifty novels and tales of adventure about Mormons published in the second half of that century (listed at the conclusion of this essay) advance seven stereotypes or images which contributed to the public opinion of Mormons: the drunken, abusive husband; the white slave procurer; the seducer; the sinister secret society; the sinful, fallen city; the lustful Turk; and the cruel, lustful Southern slaveholder. Four of the earliest novels, published by women authors in 1855 and 1856, are analyzed in detail. 28 notes.
A. Turner

1871. Ashliman, D. L. THE AMERICAN WEST IN TWENTIETH-CENTURY GERMANY. *J. of Popular Culture 1968 2(1): 81-92.* A discussion of the popularity of the American West as a motif in German popular literature and motion pictures. German *trivialroman* (pulp fiction) has since the 19th century used the American West as a physical and psychological setting. The motif has more recently appeared in motion pictures. The more artistic of German writers have also used the Western setting as a backdrop for various philosophical discussions of man and his place in nature and society. For both economic and political reasons, the motif has been less important in the popular culture of East Germany. 29 notes.
B. A. Lohof

1872. Atherton, Lewis. THE FARM NOVEL AND AGRICULTURAL HISTORY: A REVIEW. *Agric. Hist. 1966 40(2): 131-140.* Agricultural historians have tended to ignore farm novels in their research, but the monograph by Roy W. Meyer, *The Middle Western Farm Novel in the Twentieth Century* (Lincoln: U. of Nebraska Press, 1965), may help change this. The use of farm novels as sources should help the agricultural historian preserve humanistic traditions and values at a time when scientific methods are being stressed.
W. D. Rasmussen

1873. Barsness, John A. "A NEW LIFE": THE FRONTIER MYTH IN PERSPECTIVE. *Western Am. Literature 1969 3(4): 297-302.* Bernard Malamud's *A New Life* (New York: Farrar, Straus, and Giroux, 1961) is not a typical frontier myth. Malamud did present his character as an idealist, but the novel progressed to the point that the character was forced to recognize reality and, in so doing, he exhibited a strength which saved him from being destroyed by that recognition. A character in a typical frontier myth flees to the memory of the past when threatened by the present; Malamud's idealist realizes that escape is foolish and learns that he must get what he deserves as a result of his unrealistic thinking and actions. 2 notes.

S. L. McNeel

1874. Barsness, John A. THEODORE ROOSEVELT AS COWBOY: THE VIRGINIAN AS JACKSONIAN MAN. *Am. Q. 1969 21(3): 609-619.* Connects Theodore Roosevelt with the "archetypal western novel," *The Virginian* (New York: Paperback Library, Publishers' Distributing Corp., 1970), which was written in 1902 by Roosevelt's friend, Owen Wister. In addition to supplying his own variations to the cowboy tradition, Roosevelt contributed to the sentiment surrounding the exploits of Andrew Jackson. Both thus became assimilated into the larger figure of the cowboy as culture hero. Based on secondary sources; 48 notes.

R. S. Pickett

1875. Barsness, Larry. SUPERBEAST AND THE SUPERNATURAL: THE BUFFALO IN AMERICAN FOLKLORE. *Am. West 1972 9(4): 12-17, 62-63.* Folklore concerning the buffalo abounds even today. It is a continuation and embellishment on the fabricated lore of the early plainsmen. Tall tales and ingenious explanations are still created to serve a variety of purposes. Provides many examples of the persistent tales that fill the literature and quite often are accepted as fact, not fiction. From a forthcoming book. 7 illus.

D. L. Smith

1876. Boatright, Mody C. THE BEGINNINGS OF COWBOY FICTION. *Southwest R. 1966 51(1): 11-28.* The earliest novel in English with a cattle country setting was William Bushnell's *The Hermit of the Colorado Hills.* Boatright traces the cowboy in the literature of Joseph E. Badger, Edward S. Ellis, Prentiss Ingraham, and William G. Patten. The cowboy was not always a hero, although, if he were, certain taboos were observed. The good cowboy might enter a saloon, but would never take a drink in a home; he might smoke a pipe or a cigar, never a cigarette; he might kidnap a woman, never rape or seduce her.

D. F. Henderson

1877. Boatright, Mody C. THE FORMULA IN COWBOY FICTION AND DRAMA. *Western Folklore 1969 28(2): 136-145.* Discusses typical plots in cowboy fiction, from the popular magazine stories of the 1920's through motion pictures and television serials. A definite formula exists for Western fiction. After surveying more than 500 stories, reconstructs the seven basic plots. Almost every episode has a hero-heroine-villain theme, with the hero following a highly moralistic code of ethics that prevents him from acting for personal gain, wantonly killing, or committing a dishonorable act. Based on secondary sources; 12 notes.

R. A. Trennert

1878. Boatright, Mody C. J. FRANK DOBIE, 1888-1964. *Western Folklore 1965 24(3): 153-154.* Mainly a discussion about Dobie's contributions to scholarship.

J. M. Brady

1879. Brunvand, Jan Harold. "HONEY IN THE HORN" AND "ACRES OF CLAMS": THE REGIONAL FICTION OF H. L. DAVIS. *Western Am. Literature 1967 2(2): 135-145.* Describes the folklore quality of language and characterization in Harold Lenoir Davis' fiction. Davis saw the brutalizing effect of the Northwest frontier on its settlers, but he maintained an ironic sense of humor in style and viewpoint. What characterizes Davis' achievement is that he produced satisfying and individualized creative works about the Northwest which still managed to remain highly sympathetic to the style and spirit of traditional folk materials from the region. 11 notes.

R. N. Hudspeth

1880. Bullen, John S. ANNUAL BIBLIOGRAPHY OF STUDIES IN WESTERN AMERICAN LITERATURE. *Western Am. Literature 1970 4(4): 321-330.* Lists general studies, then authors followed by recent studies on those authors.

S. L. McNeel

1881. Burrows, Jack. RINGO. *Am. West 1970 7(1): 17-21.* The growing Ringo mythology puts its subject squarely in the literature of the romantic Old West. Southeastern Arizona gunman and rustler John (Johnny) Ringo (Ringgo, Ringgold) has become "the apotheosis of the western hero," an educated, solitary, and mysterious fast-draw artist who commanded intense loyalty of even the law and awesome fear of his victims. His deeds are recorded in print, on the screen, and in song. Contrary to the myth, there is no proof that he killed anyone. Even though the facts suggest that he died from "a drunken suicide with psychopathic tendencies," legend has proclaimed a much different explanation. Illus.

D. L. Smith

1882. Campa, Arthur L. PROTEST FOLK POETRY IN THE SPANISH SOUTHWEST. *Colorado Q. 1971 20(3): 355-363.* Hispano songs and poetry of protest in the Southwest lack the bitterness some authorities consider necessary to folk protest. Instead, traditional Hispano folk protest exhibits a picaresque tradition of wit and satire the origins of which extend back into the Middle Ages. Americans and their manners, the poor, work in the fields, World War II rationing, and the Tijerina affair are some of the themes which have been treated in a traditional manner in this literature of protest. More recently, bitterness has crept into some protests, and sometimes English words are used in them. Writers in this new vein often fail to write true poetry because they have lost their folk traditions through urbanization.

B. A. Storey

1883. Cawelti, John G. COWBOYS, INDIANS, OUTLAWS. *Am. West 1964 1(2): 28-35, 77-79.* The Western of today's movies, television, and novels elaborates the image of the West of the late 19th century dime novels and William F. (Buffalo Bill) Cody's Wild West shows. These, with little concern for accuracy, dealt with the 1850-70 cowboy-Indian-outlaw phase of the history of the Great Plains. Collectively they portrayed the mythology of the West. Primarily the creation of "dudes" rather than Westerners, they remain apart from accounts of travelers and settlers and 20th century serious historical novelists who present a more accurate and complete picture of the real West. This mythology evolves from earlier literature of the American frontier. The significance of the Western myth awaits the analysis of cultural historians.

D. L. Smith

1884. Clare, Warren L. "POSERS, PARASITES, AND PISMIRES": "STATUS RERUM," BY JAMES STEVENS AND H. L. DAVIS. *Pacific Northwest Q. 1970 61(1): 22-30.* Provides the text and circumstances of writing the "manifesto" entitled *Status Rerum* (1927), written by James Stevens and H. L. Davis as a scathing criticism of the "condition of literature in the Pacific Northwest in 1926." Davis had won the admiration of H. L. Mencken and Carl Sandburg, and Stevens was encouraged by Mencken.

C. C. Gorchels

1885. Cracroft, Richard H. THE AMERICAN WEST OF KARL MAY. *Am. Q. 1967 19(2 pt. 1): 249-258.* Discusses the American West as created in the nearly 40 volunes of the German adventure writer Karl May. May's Teutonic hero Old Shatterhand and the Indian chief Winnetou, the noble savage of Germanic imagination, held a powerful appeal for German readers. May's romanticism and his unvarnished nationalism shine through in the colorful adventures of Old Shatterhand, a sort of Christianized Siegfried. Old Shatterhand's overall superiority is contrasted against the vices and deficiencies of May's villains, the "half-breed, the Mormon and the Yankee." While May never really visited the Wild West, his thrilling narratives presented an image which peculiarly suited the views of his largely Germanic audience. Based on German literary criticism, extensive quotation from May's works, and some citations from American critics; 15 notes.

R. S. Pickett

1886. Curtin, L. S. M. SPANISH AND INDIAN WITCHCRAFT IN NEW MEXICO. *Masterkey 1971 45(3): 89-101.* Presents 12 short tales of witchcraft told to the author by Pueblo Indians of the Rio Grande and by Spanish-speaking informants of northern New Mexico. These stories indicate that witchcraft is still quite prevalent in New Mexico today. 2 photos, 5 notes, biblio.

D. Anness

1887. Davis, David Brion. VIOLENCE IN AMERICAN LITERATURE. *Ann. of the Am. Acad. of Pol. and Social Sci. 1966 364: 28-36.* "The frequency of fighting and killing in American literature is not necessarily proof of an unusually violent society, but literary treatments of violence have reflected certain historical conditions and circumstances. The growth of popular literacy created a mass audience whose attention could best be held by suspense, surprise, and startling contrast. The Revolution provided a model for later fiction in which the hero's triumph was not a blow against authority but rather a defeat of the Tory, who defied the sacred rules of the compact. This convention gave expression to a fear of factionalism and anarchy, and to a desire to identify one's own interests with a tradition of self-sacrificing unity. The ideal of social unity might conflict with the ideal of a self-sufficient and self-relying individual, but later writers projected the image of the individualistic hero into the vacant spaces of the West, where his violent acts were devoid of social consequence. Although both proslavery and antislavery writers tended to see the Negro as a pacific being, he has become a focal point of violence in twentieth-century literature. In the twentieth century, American writers have assimilated the older traditions of individualistic and racial violence to an antirationalistic philosophy which looks on violence as a regenerative or creative force, or as a symbol of reality."   J

1888. DePillis, Mario S. FOLKLORE AND THE AMERICAN WEST. *Arizona and the West 1963 5(4): 291-314.* Study of the American West has produced, according to the author, more hypotheses and interpretations than any other field in American history. He is concerned with folklore as one of the recent approaches. He rejects two types of folklorists as being unworthy of serious consideration for the contribution they make toward a better understanding of the American West: "fakelorists" who twist raw data into the romantic and folksy by selective, fabricative, and inventive processes; and "native son" folklorists who polish local color to make it meaningful to outsiders. The author is a proponent of the "scientific folklorist," one who studies folklore for its own research. Principally, scientific folklore can serve as a vehicle for values and attitudes and other abstractions which come from the masses of "inarticulate folk," and it can furnish indirect documentation of some ancient event or tradition. Even though American folklore studies began to come into their own as an adjunct to American history in the 1930's, folklore still has not won acceptance by professional historians. Except for the efforts of the folklore program at Indiana University, there is no other worthwhile attempt to bring respectability to the study of American folklore. The author concludes that, for the present, the folklorist needs the historian more than the reverse. Based on published folklore collections and studies; 46 notes.   D. L. Smith

1889. Dippie, Brian W. BARDS OF THE LITTLE BIG HORN. *Western Am. Literature 1966 1(3): 175-195.* Traces the persistence of versified accounts and tributes to the Little Big Horn battle. Using a variety of poetic quotations, the author reconstructs the progress of the battle. The habitually positive attitude toward Custer and the typical sentimental treatment of the event are described. The essay includes a discussion of the ballad and poetic treatment of the "Comanche" legend. The poets (all minor) created and sustained a myth about the man and the event. 63 notes, all published, but many from obscure sources.   R. N. Hudspeth

1890. Dippie, Brian W. JACK CRABB AND THE SOLE SURVIVORS OF CUSTER'S LAST STAND. *Western Am. Literature 1969 4(3): 189-202.* Gives "Jack Crabb," the main character in Thomas Berger's 1964 *Little Big Man* (New York: Dial Press), consideration among the historical and fictional "sole survivor" claimants of the Battle of the Little Big Horn (1876). A knowledge of Berger's sources would help illuminate the text, since the novel is thoroughly based on research. "Crabb's" literary antecedent is "John Clayton," and his historical antecedent is perhaps Jack Cleybourne. Berger's realization of the equal importance of myth and historical fact is crucial, enabling him to produce "a myth within a myth" that is based on history.   S. L. McNeel

1891. Dykes, Jeff. A DEDICATION TO THE MEMORY OF JAMES FRANK DOBIE, 1888-1964. *Arizona and the West 1966 8(3): 202-206.* A commentary on some of the principal works of author James Frank Dobie, and an evaluative tribute to his effectiveness in the classroom and his inspiration to young writers. Sometimes called "Mr. Southwest," he knew the area intimately and portrayed it in his books. The author subscribes to Dobie's own self-evaluation as being "too fond of facts for a fictionist and too fond of stories for a historian," yet he insists that many of Dobie's writings were both history and literature. Appended

with a selected list of Dobie's works related to the American Southwest. Illus.   D. L. Smith

1892. Fender, Stephen. THE WESTERN AND THE CONTEMPORARY. *J. of Am. Studies [Great Britain] 1972 6(1): 97-108.* Reexamines American fiction, mostly novels, on the American West. Discusses whether these writings are historically authentic, truthful in dealing with the history of the American West, and accurate in depicting their historical settings. Asks whether the fiction was realistic; concludes that it was essentially "romantic." Discusses the degree to which this literature reflects American values and contemporary issues in American life. Treats novels from James Fenimore Cooper's "Leatherstocking" stories to 20th-century novels about the American West. 7 notes.   H. T. Lovin

1893. Fierman, Floyd S. and West, James O. BILLY THE KID, THE COWBOY OUTLAW: AN INCIDENT RECALLED BY FLORA SPIEGELBERG. *Am. Jewish Hist. Q. 1965 65(1): 98-106.* An incident, recalled by Mrs. Flora Spiegelberg in her old age, involving Billy the Kid's ambush of a stagecoach and his duping by one of the women passengers. The story is analyzed as to the common folkloristic elements present which would lead one to wonder as to the veracity of the details remembered by the elderly woman. Both story and analysis are documented.   F. Rosenthal

1894. Fife, Austin. BALLADS OF THE LITTLE BIG HORN. *Am. West 1967 4(1): 46-49, 86-89.* An important legacy of those who wrestled with nature and the Indians to win the West is a folklore which preserves the past as it seemed to be in their hearts and minds, but not necessarily the way it was in reality. This lore is preserved in ballads and songs, anecdotes and stories, legends and tall stories, rhymes and riddles, place names and proverbs. The defeat of George Armstrong Custer at the Battle of Little Big Horn 25 June 1876 inspired several multiversed ballads. The music and lyrics of six and the ballads of two more are reproduced along with related commentaries. "Custer's Last Fierce Charge," "The Dying Scout," and "Custer's Last Stand" are typical titles. Biblio. note.   D. L. Smith

1895. Fife, Jim L. TWO VIEWS OF THE AMERICAN WEST. *Western Am. Literature 1966 1(1): 34-43.* Using Ralph Waldo Emerson and James Fenimore Cooper, the author defines two contradictory, traditional views of the West. Emerson saw the West as an affirmative possibility of American destiny; Cooper saw it as a pessimistic loss of possibility. The two views, both "romantic," are then seen to come down to our century in the work of Eugene Manlove Rhodes and Sinclair Lewis. Rhodes, affirming the West, tried to end the stereotypes of the cheap novel and film; Lewis attacked the stultifying dullness in the West. Both, the author concludes, call for a moral commitment.   R. N. Hudspeth

1896. Flanagan, John T. JOHN G. NEIHARDT, CHRONICLER OF THE WEST. *Arizona Q. 1965 21(1): 7-20.* After beginning with the comment: "The American West has never had a poet or a storyteller intellectually and imaginatively equal to its challenge," the author praises the poet laureate of Nebraska, John G. Neihardt, and comments on several of Neihardt's works, both prose and poetry.   J. D. Filipiak

1897. Folsom, James K. A DEDICATION TO THE MEMORY OF EUGENE MANLOVE RHODES, 1869-1934. *Arizona and the West 1969 11(4): 310-314.* The years 1881-1906 in which Eugene Manlove Rhodes lived in southwestern New Mexico working as a miner, teamster, road construction laborer, guide in an Indian war, and rancher, gave him the context for the prolific literary productivity of his later years. His fiction abounds with accurate and moving descriptions, with absolute fidelity to the facts of the Western life he had lived as a young man. The conflicts between justice and law and between right and legality are obsessive themes in his writings. Rhodes was caught in the dilemma of a Westerner who despised the East to which he moved and who longed for the West-that-was. He is at once an apologist for a sentimental past and a profound interpreter of the tragedy of change. Appended with a selected list of books concerning the Southwest. Illus.   D. L. Smith

1898. Frantz, Joe B. ADIOS TO A FREE MAN. *Am. West 1965 2(1): 34-38.* A tribute to J. Frank Dobie by a close personal friend. Dobie will be remembered as "the conscience of every Texas writer and many writers on western or nature subjects" and as "the preserver . . . of the wit and wisdom of another age." Dobie will ever be the starting point for anyone who again writes of "that triumvirate of the lonely West": the mustang, the longhorn, and the coyote. He was, above all, a champion of freedom, "a stray and a defender of strays." Illus.

D. L. Smith

1899. French, Carol Anne. WESTERN LITERATURE AND THE MYTH-MAKERS. *Montana 1972 22(2): 76-81.* Fiction about the West invariably utilizes plots which identify Good and Bad as antagonists. "Nothing in this formula requires a knowledge of western history. This lack of historical basis causes the western to be devoid of any literary merit whatever. . . . The western ignores historical complexities and bases itself on an extreme individualism in which the bulk of the people are nothing." Refers to several novels and television shows as examples of poor writing.

S. R. Davison

1900. French, Warren. WEST AS MYTH: STATUS REPORT AND CALL FOR ACTION. *Western Am. Literature 1966 1(1): 55-58.* Plea for organized, scholarly study of the vast "popular" fiction and film portrayals of the West. "Everyone admits that a myth of the Old West has developed and exercised great influence in this country and abroad, but little has been done to determine the exact nature of the contributions to this myth or their influence upon the audience's thought and action."

R. N. Hudspeth

1901. Gardner, Joseph H. BRET HARTE AND THE DICKENSIAN MODE IN AMERICA. *Can. R. of Am. Studies [Canada] 1971 2(2): 89-101.* Examines Francis Bret Harte's (1839-1902) contention that he "was the best imitator of Dickens in America." Most authorities of the late 19th century accepted this contention. Thus, "Harte presents the clearest test case for defining that Dickensian mode for which, as far as the critics were concerned, he set the norm." Surveys "a representative sample" of reviews and notices of Harte's work between 1870 and 1903. At first critics compared Harte to Dickens because of the similarities in their backgrounds. One of the most acute of the critics was Warren Cheyney, who wrote for the *Overland* in 1883. Cheyney "singled out the most characteristic feature of the Dickensian mode in late nineteenth-century America: the searching out of an exotic setting and the peopling of it with Dickensian eccentrics." Harte had discovered "the magic formula of presenting the same theatrical bill, only with new and original back-drops." 37 notes.

J. M. Hawes

1902. Gordon, Dudley C. CHARLES F. LUMMIS: PIONEER AMERICAN FOLKLORIST. *Western Folklore 1969 28(3): 175-181.* Charles Fletcher Lummis (1859-1928), founder of the Southwest Museum in Los Angeles, was not only an author and historian, but also a pioneer in recording American folklore. Between the mid-1880's and the early 1920's, Lummis recorded and published in magazines and journals numerous collections of folksongs from the Southwestern United States. His main interest was the folksongs of the Spanish- and Mexican-Americans in New Mexico. He was also responsible for collecting the songs of the men who built the Santa Fe Railroad and for photographing and describing a New Mexican passion play of the Penitentes, "wherein the leading player was crucified." 4 notes.

R. A. Trennert

1903. Gordon, Dudley C. CHARLES F. LUMMIS AND JACK LONDON: AN EVALUATION. *Southern California Q. 1964 46(1): 83-88.* Letters exchanged concerning an invitation by Lummis to London to join the Southwest Archaeological Society of Los Angeles. The author contrasts the two well-known authors in many respects. Letters reprinted in full.

E. P. Stickney

1904. Greenfield, Elizabeth. THE COWBOY ARTIST AS SEEN IN CHILDHOOD MEMORY. *Montana 1964 14(1): 38-47.* Recollections by one who knew Charles Marion Russell as a friend of children, exemplified by the animal tales he told to youngsters. Accompanying the article is Mrs. Anna P. Nelson's version of Russell's story, "The Medicine Arrow," which appeared in *Sports Afield,* January 1898.

L. G. Nelson

1905. Greiner, Francis J. VOICE OF THE WEST: HAROLD L. DAVIS. *Oregon Hist. Q. 1965 66(3): 240-248.* Bio-bibliographical sketch of Harold Lenoir Davis, author of novels, poetry, and short stories with western U.S. settings. Davis won the Harper Novel Prize, the Pulitzer Novel Prize, and other honors.

C. C. Gorchels

1906. Grenander, M. E. A LONDON LETTER OF JOAQUIN MILLER TO AMBROSE BIERCE. *Yale U. Lib. Gazette 1971 46(2): 109-116.* Though in retrospect he was a third-rate poet, westerner Cincinnatus Hiner, or Heine ("Joaquin"), Miller (1841-1913) was profusely acclaimed by English literati during the 1870's. He was the respected friend of other Californian writers, including Ambrose Gwinnett Bierce, Mark Twain, and Charles Warren Stoddard. Reprints an 1874 letter of Miller to Ambrose Bierce (from Yale's Bierce correspondence) which reveals the relationship of these Californian writers. 12 notes.

D. A. Yanchisin

1907. Gurian, Jay. LITERARY CONVENTION AND THE MINING ROMANCE. *J. of the West 1966 5(1): 106-114.* Argues that historians of the West have ignored the literary conventions of a century ago and have adopted many of the romantic excesses that their sources practiced. The author maintains that public tastes and level of education had an important effect on the images, details, and vocabulary of those contemporaries who chronicled the mining frontier; thus their style distorted the content. Modern historians have not understood this fact but have taken the descriptions literally. While the contemporary descriptions may be entertaining, they will not help the serious student to understand the pioneer West. Documented from published sources, 21 notes.

D. N. Brown

1908. Gurian, Jay. THE POSSIBILITY OF A WESTERN POETICS. *Colorado Q. 1966 15(1): 69-85.* Western American poetry has been merely a graphic response to landscape and to a noisy history. No distinctively Western poetics has developed; that is, Western authors have developed no literary theories and techniques to express the West imaginatively. However, in recent years there have been a few men who have taken a more creative approach to the West. Among these authors are John Neihardt, E. E. Cummings, Hart Crane, and Thomas Hornsby Ferril. There is no reason why an important poetic tradition cannot arise in Western writing.

B. A. Storey

1909. Gurian, Jay. STYLE IN THE LITERARY DESERT: "LITTLE BIG MAN." *Western Am. Literature 1969 3(4): 285-296.* Asserting that realism is a limited principle, especially for a Western novel, the author shows how Thomas L. Berger achieved a work of art in *Little Big Man* (New York: Dial, 1964) by using other methods. *Little Big Man* is first compared to Jack W. Schaefer's *Monte Walsh* (New York: Houghton Mifflin, 1963) to illustrate the limitations of realism. In language, for instance, Berger combined the coarse with the educated instead of continually relying on the "doggone it" phrases of *Monte Walsh*. Berger merged intuition and reason in language, characterization, and action, to such an extent that, for example, the Indians' superstition seemed sometimes credible. One of the most important facts about the novel is the point of view. Jack Crabb, the narrator, was white, but was brought up by the Indians, and thus he is able to speak from inside the Cheyenne culture. Berger said he read from 60 to 70 accounts of the West to give him a feel not only for facts about dates, places, and events, but also for the two world views expressed by whites and Indians. Berger's imagination was never sacrificed for realism, which is another key to the novel's literary success. And although Berger does not describe the West as traditional Western writers did, he does present it with genuine love and imagination.

S. L. McNeel

1910. Gyemant, Robert E. "JACK HAGGERTY" AND A CALIFORNIA LEGEND. *Western Folklore 1965 24(2): 105-108.* Explains how the legend of Jack Haggerty which is told in the Malibu area of southern California probably originated as a ballad in southern Michigan during the winter of 1872.

J. M. Brady

1911. Harrison, Lowell H. DAVY CROCKETT: THE MAKING OF A FOLK HERO. *Kentucky Folklore Record 1969 15(4): 87-90.* Compares the known achievements, personality, and attributes of Crockett (1786-1836), the folk hero, with the legendary feats, together with special reference to the factors responsible for the creation of the many legends. 9 notes.

J. C. Crowe

1912. Hartley, Margaret L. SOUTHWEST CHRONICLE. *Southwest R. 1964 49(4): vi-x, 397-398.* Review of J. Frank Dobie's *Cow People* (1964) a collection of stories about local history, plus reminiscences of his work with the *Southwest Review,* together comprising an obituary for Dobie who died in 1964.　　　　　　　　　　D. F. Henderson

1913. Helmick, Evelyn Thomas. MYTH IN THE WORKS OF WILLA CATHER. *MidContinent Am. Studies J. 1968 9(2): 63-69.* Analyzes the works of Willa Cather (1873-1947) in terms of her reliance on a classical literary approach to the American novel. Her adoption of the heroic epic to dramatize the Western frontier is shown by the prominence of Nature, as in the cycle of the seasons and the grandeur of the western landscape. Through the use of the myth, Willa Cather conveyed the enduring custom of human thought and feeling and thus enriched her writing with archetypal figures complemented by the universality of man's experience. Based on primary and secondary sources; 18 notes.　　　　　　　　　　B. M. Morrison

1914. Hendricks, George D. FOUR SOUTHWESTERN LEGENDS. *Western Folklore 1968 27(4): 255-262.* Four legends from Texas informants: "The Frenchman of Indianola Beach"; "Pancho Villa's Treasure"; "El Paso's Haunted House"; and "Ghost of the Drowned Girl," in three versions. 3 notes.　　　　　　　　　　D. L. Smith

1915. Higgins, John E. HAMLIN GARLAND'S DIARIES. *Wisconsin Mag. of Hist. 1963 46(4): 294-302.* From the diaries of Hamlin Garland comes little news of historical significance. Yet it is significant as the personal story of an interesting figure in an age just past.　　　　　　　　　　W. F. Peterson

1916. Hines, Donald M. HUMOR OF THE CITY HICK AND THE COUNTRY JAKE ON THE INLAND PACIFIC NORTHWEST FRONTIER. *Western R. 1971 8(1): 15-20.* Analyzes the contrasting forms of traditional folk humor in the Pacific Northwest. Mentions 34 anecdotal examples treating of the country boy in a disconcerting urban setting, or of the ignorance of the city man placed in a rural environment. Such humor served as a psychological safety valve which helped the pioneer to cope with the difficulties of pioneer life. Based on newspapers of the area, 1870-95; 6 notes.　　　　　　　　　　B. Newman

1917. Holsinger, M. Paul. HAMLIN GARLAND'S COLORADO. *Colorado Mag. 1967 44(1): 1-10.* Hamlin Garland, a member of "the big three" of Colorado fiction, wrote at the turn of the century using Colorado as a setting for his novels. It has been said that he caught the spirit of early Colorado in his fiction better than did nonfiction writers. In this monograph dealing with Garland in Colorado, the author quotes extensively from Garland's notebook, using his own words to describe the lure of the Rockies to a mid-Westerner. The author also cites Garland's novels which were written about Colorado, adding a very brief synopsis of each. Garland did not hesitate to show his dislike for the vulgar changes which civilization wrought in his beloved Colorado. Even after his return to the Midwest he remembered the Rockies as he had first seen them, not as he last saw them. Documented, illus., 24 notes.　　　　　　R. Sexauer

1918. Hoole, W. Stanley. JEREMIAH CLEMENS, NOVELIST. *Alabama R. 1965 18(1): 5-36.* Biographical sketch with emphasis on Clemens' career as a fiction writer. His significant novels are discussed: *Bernard Lile: an Historical Romance Embracing the Periods of the Texas Revolution and the Mexican War* (1856), *Mustang Gray: a Romance* (1857), *The Rivals: a Tale of the Times of Aaron Burr and Alexander Hamilton* (1860), and *Tobias Wilson: a Tale of the Great Rebellion* (1865). 36 notes.　　　　　　　　　　D. F. Henderson

1919. Houston, Neal B. A DEDICATION TO THE MEMORY OF HAMLIN GARLAND, 1860-1940. *Arizona and the West 1969 11(3): 208-212.* Garland's youth was spent on the Great Plains homestead frontier and his literary apprenticeship was served in the East. Subsequently he lived all over the country in a variety of environments and his experiences included participation in the Alaska gold rush. Garland wrote prodigiously. His output included dozens of books and scores of articles for American magazines and journals. His early works were concerned with the tragedy of the frontier and its people. Later his theme became the romantic West. He was probably best known, as the title of one of his semi-autobiographical books put it, as *A Son of the Middle*

Border (New York: MacMillan, 1962). His West was made up of individuals and families; Garland was not particularly concerned with the impersonal macrocosm of formal history. In a sense, his writings began where formal history stopped. Illus., appended with a selected list of his books.　　　　　　　　　　D. L. Smith

1920. Hutchinson, W. H. A CANDLE FOR THE SUN. *Am. West 1966 3(4): 62-64, 94.* Based on his experience of several years as a reviewer of Western Americana for a metropolitan newspaper, the author ruminates on some of the conclusions he has reached. Western Americana excludes writings on the contemporary West and fiction about the West of any period. Its temporal and spatial beginnings are at Fort Pitt in 1758 and extend to "existing, albeit diminishing, physical and psychological frontier pockets" such as those within his own youthful experiences. There are too few craftsmen today to make literary excellence a primary criterion. Instead, it is necessary to settle for content and what the reader can do with the content of these intellectual analyses that too often lack the immediacy of human experience. With few exceptions, eastern publishers, editors, critics, and reviewers are "incompetent" and are not ashamed of their ignorance. The author wonders why there are no saga tellers or poets of the West. Finally, it is his premise that "without the reviewer's candle to illuminate the sun of authorship" Western Americana would not reach the audience it deserves. Illus.　　　　　　　　　　D. L. Smith

1921. Hutchinson, W. H. I PAY FOR WHAT I BREAK. *Western Am. Literature 1966 1(2): 91-96.* Gives historical facts in support of incidents in the stories of Eugene Manlove Rhodes. Then offering examples from "The Trusty Knaves," "Beyond the Desert," "Aforesaid Bates," and "John Wesley Pringle," the author notes as the most significant element in Rhodes' writing the relation of man to open space. Although Rhodes occasionally covered reality with romanticism, his writing was of life as he had lived it when the West began and as it revealed his rugged individualism. His greedy villains were used to show the passing of traditional values as materialism emerged, while his heroes mirrored himself - a man conditioned by frontier experience. An environment of open space meant freedom of action and mobility. This heritage of ideal values comes alive in Rhodes's writing without idealizing the real. 3 notes.　　　　　　　　　　S. L. McNeel

1922. Hutchinson, W. H. THE WEST OF EUGENE MANLOVE RHODES. *Arizona and the West 1967 9(3): 211-218.* As a Western writer New Mexican Eugene Manlove Rhodes has been consistently overlooked. His portrayal of New Mexico and its people, their lives and values —he lived there from 1882 to 1906—are as authentic as any artifactual remains or any other evidence available. The most significant historical element in his writings, according to the author, is the relationship of man to open space. There were four freedoms of open space: freedom of action —not ended "until a man was too dead to skin"; freedom of mobility; limitless horizons, beyond the physical; infinite chances to pick oneself "off the floor of life" and try again. A small but impressive cluster of *aficionados* have perpetuated his cause. In this critical evaluation of his stories, the author makes a bid for a niche for Rhodes in the pantheon of those "who wrote truly about the West-That-Was." Illus.　　　　　　　　　　D. L. Smith

1923. Keleher, W. A. ERNA MARY FERGUSSON, 1888-1964. *New Mexico Hist. R. 1964 39(4): 345-350.* Address delivered 1 August 1964 at the memorial services for Miss Fergusson, author of *Dancing Gods* (1931), *Fiesta in Mexico* (1934), *New Mexico, A Pageant of Three Peoples* (1951), and several other books on the Southwest and Latin America.　　　　　　　　　　D. F. Henderson

1924. Kembel, John Haskell. THE WEST THROUGH SALT SPRAY: REBIRTH OF A CLASSIC. *Am. West 1964 1(4): 65-75.* Two Years before the Mast (1840) by Richard Henry Dana, Jr., best known as a pre-clipper ship era, life-at-sea classic, is also justly famous as an account of the California frontier a decade before it became a part of the United States. Dana wrote it primarily not to enhance his literary reputation or pocketbook, but because it might bring him some law practice related to maritime affairs and because it would help to publicize the real situation of the merchant seamen. The evolution and history of its text and publication are traced to a new edition that reinstates deleted words and passages to present the fullest text possible. Illustrated by a series of facsimile reproductions of Dana's manuscript notebook, his expanded manuscript journal, a page from the first published edition, and a page from the 1964 edition; other illustrations from the new edition. Bibliographical note.   D. L. Smith

1925. Kime, Wayne R. WASHINGTON IRVING AND FRONTIER SPEECH. *Am. Speech 1967 62(1): 5-18.* Contrary to H. L. Mencken's designation of Irving as "an Anglomaniac of great earnestness" in language, Irving, in fact, was a connoisseur of curious terms (English or foreign) and used them in his writings. Also, he defined or explained many unfamiliar terms which would otherwise be unknown. Irving's tour of the Far West resulted in three works, *A Tour of the Prairies* (1835), *Astoria* (1836), and *The Adventures of Captain Bonneville* (1837), in each of which he used and defined much frontier and trappers' language. The author presents a nine and a half-page glossary of such terms, indicating those that antedate dictionary definitions and are not ever included in dictionaries. Based on the author's perusal of the above works by Irving and of several American dictionaries; 6 notes.
                                                            R. W. Shoemaker

1926. King, James T. THE SWORD AND THE PEN: THE POETRY OF THE MILITARY FRONTIER. *Nebraska Hist. 1966 47(3): 229-245.* Surveys the poetry of the military frontier as a reflection of the life, attitudes, and ideas of the men who served during the period of its existence from 1815 to 1890.   R. Lowitt

1927. Krause, S. J. THE ART AND SATIRE OF TWAIN'S "JUMPING FROG" STORY. *Am. Q. 1964 16(4): 562-576.* Describes Twain as a master political satirist. Twain combined Down East and Old Southwestern humor in describing the contest between a Whiggish frog named Daniel Webster and a pugnacious frontier pup called Andrew Jackson.   R. S. Pickett

1928. Labor, Earle. A DEDICATION TO THE MEMORY OF JACK LONDON, 1876-1916. *Arizona and the West 1964 6(2): 93-96.* John Griffith London made his literary mark by exploiting the last American frontier. His fame still rests most securely on a series of northern sagas whose setting was Alaska. He perceived the symbolic possibilities of the American West and the value of conservation of its natural resources. He lived and practiced his ideas. His goal was to preserve as much as possible of the spirit and romance of the American West. He achieved this both in his works and in the legend that he inspired. London participated in the Klondike gold rush, pioneered in scientific farming and stockbreeding, and was a war correspondent. He was the first author to earn a million dollars for his writings, and packed into his short life a host of other activities. Appended with a bibliographical note, and a selected list of his works relating to the American West; illus.
                                                            D. L. Smith

1929. Lambert, Neal. A COWBOY WRITES TO OWEN WISTER. *Am. West 1965 2(4): 31-36.* Reading the installments of Owen Wister's *The Virginian* (1902) as they appeared in *The Saturday Evening Post,* an eastern youngster, Harry F. Bowen, was inspired. In 1931, a quarter of a century later, as a Colorado cowboy, he wrote a letter of appreciation to Wister. These chapters, wrote Bowen, "fetched me west." The letter, reproduced here, reflects the genuine enthusiasm with which *The Virginian* was received by those who participated in the kind of things of which it tells. Letter in the Wister Papers, Library of Congress.
                                                            D. L. Smith

1930. Lavender, David. THE PETRIFIED WEST AND THE WRITER. *Am. Scholar 1968 37(2): 293-306.* Literature must be freed from the stereotype of the West as exemplified in the television cowboy and the nomad Indian horseman. Historians and some novelists have already done this. There are fruitful sources to be mined in the newspapers of the Old West. The problem for the writer and the historian is that the editors in the Old West, having little of importance to write about, stressed the occurrence of violence. It is this exaggeration that secondary writers have accepted as normal. The author traces the failure to develop meaning and value out of the myth of the West through the work of a number of 19th- and 20th-century American fiction writers.
                                                            T. R. Cripps

1931. Lavender, David. RESPONSIBLE POPULARIZATION. *Pacific Northwest Q. 1966 57(3): 93-100.* Perceptive observations about the problems of writing "popular" history, with special reference to episodes of the early American West. The author analyzes pitfalls of some research methods, oversimplification, and colorless literary style, and makes a plea for professional historians to put enough literary art into their works to outdo amateurs.   C. C. Gorchels

1932. Leach, MacEdward. FOLKLORE IN AMERICAN REGIONAL LITERATURE. *J. of the Folklore Inst. 1966 3(3): 376-397.* "American" folklore has existed from the beginning of the nation and has been centered and developed in five regions: 1) New England and Boston, 2) New York and New York City, 3) Pennsylvania-Delaware and Philadelphia, 4) the Tidewater South (Baltimore and Charleston), and 5) Deep South and New Orleans. The cities have been the centers of the folklore regions, and later regions include the Midwest (Pittsburgh and St. Louis), the Southwest with no center, and the Far West and San Francisco. From these centers folklore and literature have radiated, and the history of American literature is the history of the adaptation of American folk materials. Other forces, however, such as politics and economics, also contribute to regionalism. Biblio.   J. C. Crowe

1933. Leithead, J. Edward. BUFFALO BILL: MULTI-STORIED SCOUT AND PLAINSHAW. *Am. Book Collector 1970 20(8): 20-26.* A narrative listing of all the dime novels and stories about Buffalo Bill from 23 December 1869 to 30 August 1919. Authors and plates are described, and the development of the various series of tales is discussed. Illus.   D. Brockway

1934. Leithead, J. Edward. THE DIAMOND DICKS: FRONTIER LAWMEN. *Am. Book Collector 1969 20(1): 19-25.* The dime novels about Richard and Bertrand Wade, the Diamond Dicks, first appeared in 1878 and ran until 1911. They were written by various authors. The author gives a listing of all the titles published along with a summary of the stories. The stories concern all parts of the West and its growth, including the final phases of its wildness as railroads, cattle, and mining towns appeared. Illus.   D. Brockway

1935. Leithead, J. Edward. THE OUTLAWS RODE HARD IN DIME NOVEL DAYS. *Am. Book Collector 1968 19(4): 13-19.* A list and description of dime novels about the James-Younger and Dalton gangs which appeared in the late 19th and early 20th centuries. Illus.
                                                            D. Brockway

1936. Leithead, J. Edward. THE SAGA OF YOUNG WILD WEST. *Am. Book Collector 1969 19(7): 17-22.* The *Wild West Weekly* began publication in 1902 and continued until 1927, publishing 644 original stories about Young Wild West and his companions. The dime adventure stories were set in all parts of the West. It was the most popular series of its time and was the only series to have a heroine in a constant prominent role. Two long quotes from a couple of tales are given. Illus.
                                                            D. Brockway

1937. Leithead, J. Edward. TANBARK AND SPANGLES IN DIME NOVELS. *Am. Book Collector 1970 20(6): 36-42.* A history and a list of all the circus and Wild West Show stories which appeared in the dime novel magazines in the late 1890's and early 1900's. Illus.
                                                            D. Brockway

1938. Long, E. Hudson. O. HENRY AS A REGIONAL ARTIST. *Essays on Am. Literature in Honor of Jay B. Hubbell* (Durham: Duke U. Pr., 1967): 229-240. "Though a journalist by trade, O. Henry was an artist who followed the school of regional writing." He successfully depicted New York, Texas, and, indeed, "every locality in which he ever lived." 12 notes.   C. L. Eichelberger

1939. Lyon, Thomas J. WASHINGTON IRVING'S WILDERNESS. *Western Am. Literature 1966 1(3): 167-174.* Discusses Irving's *The Adventures of Captain Bonneville* (1837) in which Irving wrote with a romantic view of the West; he generalized because he had little firsthand information, but he turned instead to the effect of the wilderness on the people. Irving "was aware of the dramatic and philosophical possibilities in mountain climbing." He succeeds in bringing the reader an "imaginative feeling for wild country." Published sources, 13 notes.
                                                            R. N. Hudspeth

1940. Malin, James C. EUGENE F. WARE, JOURNEYMAN POET - ACCEPTANCE BY FORT SCOTT. *Kansas Hist. Q. 1965 31(4): 396-441.* The subject of this article left Iowa for Kansas in 1867. His interests led him into the harness business, practice of law, journalism, and writing of poetry. His career was colorful enough to give rise to many accounts of why he chose to do what he did. The author separates fact from fancy in an effort to explain why Ware was attracted to poetry and the law. The author's subtitles give some indication of the nature of Ware's works. "Masculine Poetry for a Man's World" and "The Two Quests of Youth" serve to show that Ware sought to come to grips with frontier realities. If local newspapers mirrored the growth of frontier communities, Eugene Ware's poems, which appeared in the newspapers of Fort Scott, were an important factor in giving greater dimension to bare facts and statistics.　　　　　　　　　　W. F. Zornow

1941. Malin, James C. EUGENE F. WARE, MASTER POET - ACCEPTANCE BY FORT SCOTT AND THE STATE OF KANSAS - HISTORY AS BUSINESS (COMMERCE), AND AS WAR. *Kansas Hist. Q. 1966 32(4): 401-425.* Eugene Ware of Fort Scott was one of Kansas' most unusual poets. Among his extensive output were a number of occasional poems that were composed in response to an invitation or a particular inspiration. The author presents a number of his poems that were prepared for special holidays or for presentation before special groups. He has chosen the poems dealing with business and war. Ware's original concept of business centered around seaborne commerce, but he eventually wrote poems that reflected the spirit of industry and agriculture in the West. He drew on his five-year experience in the Civil War to provide the inspiration for a number of poems about the conflict. 3 notes.　　　　　　　　　　W. F. Zornow

1942. Malin, James C. EUGENE F. WARE'S LITERARY CHRONOLOGY. *Kansas Hist. Q. 1971 37(3): 314-332.* Eugene Fitch Ware (1841-1911), alias "Ironquill" or "Paint Creek" and other pen names, was a prolific Kansas author of the middle period. As a writer Ware was responsible for many legal opinions, but only a few of them have been included in this bibliography. Ware is best known as the author of a volume of verse, *The Rhymes of Ironquill,* which was issued in 15 editions. He also wrote several prose works of book length. Many of his verses were published in newspapers. This list represents the result of many years of research in newspapers to unearth the many poems that Ware wrote. Based on newspapers and manuscript collections in the Kansas State Historical Society.　　　　　　　　　　W. F. Zornow

1943. Manzo, Flournoy D. ALFRED HENRY LEWIS: WESTERN STORYTELLER. *Arizona and the West 1968 10(1): 5-24.* After a few years as a lawyer and prosecuting attorney in Ohio, Alfred Henry Lewis went west, probably early in 1883. He gained considerable experience as a cowpuncher, as a freighter, and as a sometime journalist in the Southwest before settling down to the law again, this time in Kansas City, Missouri. In 1889 Lewis told a humorous Western tale to a city editor who was so impressed that he encouraged Lewis to publish some of his stories in the newspaper. In a succession of stories, the famous Wolfville series, he drew upon his Southwest experiences to fashion humorous tongue-in-cheek tales in a stylized Western language. His grasp of detail of cowboy life and his Kansas, Colorado, Arizona, and New Mexico settings established him firmly. Later he became one of the leading Hearst journalists in the East, a close friend of President Theodore Roosevelt, an editor, and an author of note. His autobiographical Wolfville volumes brought him the most enduring fame: *Wolfville* (1897), *Sandburrs* (1898), *Wolfville Days* (1902), *Wolfville Nights* (1902), *Wolfville Folks* (1908), and *Faro Nell and Her Friends* (1913). 5 illus., 51 notes.
　　　　　　　　　　D. L. Smith

1944. Marshall, Margaret. ALKALI DUST IN YOUR EYES. *Am. Scholar 1968 37(4): 650-654.* A closely reasoned reappraisal of A. Conan Doyle's *A Study in Scarlet* (1887), part of which takes place in the Mormon world around Salt Lake City. The author, with some whimsy and humor, shows that Doyle grotesquely misplaced geographical points and erred in climatic conditions and other details.　　T. R. Cripps

1945. Maunder, Elwood R. AN INTERVIEW WITH JAMES STEVENS - THE MAKING OF A FOLKLORIST. *Forest Hist. 1964 7(4): 2-19.* Reared a "Hardshell" Baptist, James Stevens was steeped in Biblical folklore. Expelled from school at 15, he worked and told stories in the

construction and logging camps and sawmills of the Far West. His Paul Bunyan stories - *Paul Bunyan* and *The Saginaw Paul Bunyan* (New York: Alfred A. Knopf, Inc., 1925 and 1932) and "The Black Duck Dinner" *(American Mercury,* (February, 1924), and others - were inspired by the stories of woodsmen. Illus., 4 notes.　　B. A. Vatter

1946. Meier, A. Mabel. BESS STREETER ALDRICH: A LITERARY PORTRAIT. *Nebraska Hist. 1969 50(1): 67-100.* A careful examination of the literary career of a distinguished Nebraska novelist (1881-1954) whose seven novels and more than 160 short stories attracted attention by stressing the more positive aspects of small town life.
　　　　　　　　　　R. Lowitt

1947. Meyer, Roy W. HAMLIN GARLAND AND THE AMERICAN INDIAN. *Western Am. Literature 1967 2(2): 109-125.* Traces Garland's growing concern for the Indians and their fate. Garland, after several trips to the West, made a three-part literary portrayal of Indian life. *The Captain of the Gray-Horse Troop* (1902), a novel; *The Book of the American Indian* (1923), a collection of stories; and "The Silent Eaters," a prose poem, express Garland's fear that Indian culture was being changed by the coming of the white settlers. Although his attitude is touched by an unthinking paternalism, Garland sympathized with the complexities of Indian life. 29 notes.　　　　R. N. Hudspeth

1948. Meyer, Roy W. THE WESTERN FICTION OF MAYNE REID. *Western Am. Literature 1968 3(2): 115-132.* With references to over a dozen of Thomas Mayne Reid's nearly 60 novels, the author describes the Irishman's writings about the American Southwest as less than literary. His adventure stories all had similar plot structure. His three major character types were mountain men, Indians, and Mexicans, usually in Southwestern American or Mexican settings. He was obviously influenced by James Fenimore Cooper and many similarities are found to the works of Josiah Gregg. Even though Reid's wife insists in a biography of her husband that he was personally familiar with the areas about which he wrote, it is suggested that Reid at least borrowed from many others to supplement his own accounts, which sometimes lacked in geographic factuality. His three virtues lie in a vivid narration of action, lucid and direct language, and a fairly good view of the Southwest. Though not a literary giant, Reid did show a genuine enthusiasm for the Southwest in his writings. 32 notes.　　　　　　　　　　S. L. McNeel

1949. Miller, Robert Henry. THE PUBLICATION OF RAYMOND CHANDLER'S "THE LONG GOODBYE." *Papers of the Biblio. Soc. of Am. 1969 63(4): 279-290.* Collation of the existing typescript and three printings of *The Long Goodbye* (New York: Houghton Mifflin, 1954) reveal extensive textual changes, largely originating in an inability of English printers to render exactly for its reader audience the slang or parochialisms of California - the author's residence. Chandler's changes in the typescript clearly demonstrate his meticulousness and concern for craftsmanship. More than three pages of collation, 8 notes.
　　　　　　　　　　C. A. Newton

1950. Milton, John R. THE AMERICAN WEST: A CHALLENGE TO THE LITERARY IMAGINATION. *Western Am. Literature 1966 1(4): 267-284.* Discusses the problems facing the western writer. The land's history and topography are so vast and varied that the writer faces an unusually difficult problem: how to synthesize the images and themes without distortion. After describing this complexity, the author examines the work of A. B. Guthrie, Walter Clark, Frank Waters, Vardis Fisher, and Frederick Manfred to show the responses of the best western novelists to their culture. The conclusion finds "the far-flung materials need to be fused through the Coleridgean sense of the imagination."
　　　　　　　　　　R. N. Hudspeth

1951. Milton, John R. THE LAND AS FORM IN FRANK WATERS AND WILLIAM EASTLAKE. *Kansas Q. 1970 2(2): 104-109.* Feels that in Western novels land can be a significant force because of its spectacular characteristics, which stand out more because the land was so sparsely settled. Because of these qualities the land can be used symbolically and metaphorically as a means of extending man beyond himself through the use of devices such as intuition. William Derry Eastlake and Waters both try to find meaning for man in the environment and historical setting of which they write; but, unlike Waters, Eastlake has problems presenting believable characters. Neither author loses control of his nov-

els due to the lack of perspective which is often occasioned by land in many Western novels. Based largely on the works of William Eastlake and Frank Waters.
B. A. Storey

1952. Mobley, Lawrence E. MARK TWAIN AND THE "GOLDEN ERA." *Papers of the Biblio. Soc. of Am. 1964 58(1): 8-23.* A list of 60 Mark Twain items which appeared in the San Francisco *Golden Era* up to 17 April 1868.
C. A. Newton

1953. Molen, Dayle H. ANDY ADAMS: CLASSIC NOVELIST OF THE TRAIL. *Montana 1969 19(1): 24-35.* A biographical sketch of Andy Adams, best known as the author of *Log of a Cowboy,* published in 1903. He made little money on this or his few other books and spent his later years plainly and obscurely in Denver. Although fiction, his major book is described as "the finest volume written about the old cattle trail days." Illus., 12 notes.
S. R. Davison

1954. Murray, Robert A. THE JOHN "PORTUGEE" PHILLIPS LEGENDS, A STUDY IN WYOMING FOLKLORE. *Ann. of Wyoming 1968 40(1): 41-56.* A discussion of the evolution of the story of John Phillips' ride from Fort Philip Kearny to Fort Laramie during December 1866 from fact to myth. First the author presents a factual account of the ride, and then he traces the transformation of it into a regional myth. He shows how the uncritical use of pension claims, garbled newspaper accounts, and unreliable reminiscent accounts did this. Based on archival material in unit military records at the National Archives, published reminiscent accounts, newspapers, and secondary discussions of the event; 88 notes.
R. L. Nichols

1955. Nicoll, Bruce H. MARI SANDOZ: NEBRASKA LONER. *Am. West 1965 2(2): 32-36.* A biographical background essay of Mari Sandoz and the relationship to her father that nearly thwarted her literary career but led to the writing of *Old Jules* (1935) and fame as one of the leading writers of the trans-Missouri country. Illus.
D. L. Smith

1956. Olstad, Charles F. THE "WILD WEST" IN SPAIN. *Arizona and the West 1964 6(3): 191-202.* During the period of intellectual unrest in Spain in the late 1920's, the reading public discovered the western novels of Zane Grey. Thereafter it seemed that the appetite for pulp westerns was insatiable. Spanish writers, using American pseudonyms, published them by the hundreds. This pervading interest in the wild West became a significant determinant in the nature of the image of America abroad. The westerns seemed to provide adventure, romance, and escape for the depression ravaged Spaniards. The interest and demand has continued and has spread throughout Europe. The movement is analyzed and described.
D. L. Smith

1957. Peavy, Charles T. A LARRY MC MURTRY BIBLIOGRAPHY. *Western Am. Literature 1968 3(3): 235-248.* McMurtry, son and grandson of Texas cattlemen, had published three western novels by the time he was 30. He has since written and published much more material and has received several awards. Lists all of his writings to date, as well as a collection of manuscripts and typescripts housed at the University of Houston, which includes a series of letters discussing his early attempts at writing, and written to a friend, Mike Kunkel. His published writings are divided into fiction, poetry, nonfiction, *Houston Post* book reviews, and other book reviews. His manuscripts and letters are categorized as editorial correspondence. Based on the Kunkel Collection, unpublished and published material.
S. L. McNeel

1958. Perry, John. THE COVERED WAGON. *Film Heritage 1969 4(3): 17-22.* Argues that *The Covered Wagon* is a motion picture which revived America's flagging interest in western movie themes and which gave a dignity to the western that stimulated continuation of the western tradition for years after its release in 1924. The movie came from an adaptation by an Iowa newspaperman of Emerson Hough's novel. It was directed by James Cruze who never again reached the level of *Covered Wagon.* On the other hand, Colonel Tim McCoy, a scout on location with the movie company, went onto a long career in cowboy serials and pictures. With a pedestrian plot, sentimentalized folklore, and conventional editing, the strength of the movie rested heavily on beautiful photography and fine sense of history. Its success started a cycle of western films - *North of 36* (1924), *The Pony Express* (1925), *The Pioneer Scout* (1928) - which continued to the present.
T. R. Cripps

1959. Peterson, Clell T. CHARLES KING: SOLDIER AND NOVELIST. *Am. Book collector 1965 16(4): 8-12.* Charles King wrote fiction about Army life and Indian warfare on the plains in the years 1870-80. It was based on his experiences as a second lieutenant in the Army. Although his novels were subliterary, they were very popular and have been used as background material for numerous westerns. Documented, illus.
D. Brockway

1960. Peterson, Levi S. THE PRIMITIVE AND THE CIVILIZED IN WESTERN FICTION. *Western Am. Literature 1966 1(3): 197-207.* Outlines three views of the tension between civilization and the western wilderness: a complete acceptance of the life free from civilization, a rejection of the primitive as lawless and evil, an ambivalent attitude recognizing the valid appeal of freedom and the equally valid necessity for lawful order. The author sees the western novel as a "vehicle for debate" about frontier values in our culture. 9 notes, all from published sources.
R. N. Hudspeth

1961. Pickett, Calder M. EDGAR WATSON HOWE AND THE KANSAS SCENE. *Kansas Q. 1970 2(2): 39-45.* Discusses the "legend" that Howe's *The Story of a Country Town* (1882) was the first harsh literary attack on the Jeffersonian agrarian dream. The author argues that Howe was the son of a Methodist circuit-riding minister, and that as far as he was concerned life was naturally difficult. It was this difficult life which he described in *Country Town.* Howe was describing life as he saw it and as he felt it was everywhere. He was not attacking small town living because he in fact liked small town living, and he recognized that he was provincial and regional. Based partly on *The Globe,* Howe's newspaper.
B. A. Storey

1962. Polos, Nicholas C. EARLY CALIFORNIA POETRY. *California Hist. Soc. Q. 1969 48(3): 243-255.* John Swett, remembered largely for his contributions to California public education, was also a poet of some note. Though his poems have long been forgotten, contemporaries recognized his talent and his poems appeared in a number of magazines. Other poems by Swett can be found in his autobiography, his textbooks, and in his manuscript materials at the Bancroft Library. Swett's early poems fall into two periods: the period 1853-54 reflects his experiences in California as a participant in gold rush life; the period 1853-62 [sic] covers Swett's origins as a crusader for better schools and improved quality in education. Swett is described as a "poet of utilitarianism," whose poems were written for particular events and purposes. Not an intellectual, Swett believed that poetry served no purpose if it was not based in reality. A number of his poems are included. Based on Swett's poems and writings, and on documents and secondary sources; 30 notes.
A. Hoffman

1963. Powell, Lawrence C. A DEDICATION TO THE MEMORY OF MARY HUNTER AUSTIN, 1868-1934. *Arizona and the West 1968 10(1): 1-4.* Illinois-born Mary Hunter developed a passion for the early history and lore of California when her family homesteaded there after she had completed her college education. An unsuccessful marriage to a rancher, a career as a school teacher, and membership in an informal literary colony, along with her domineering personality and Bohemian proclivities, affected her writings which she had been producing since college days. From 1892 on, her stories, plays, novels, and essays earned her substantial sums from Western and national magazines. After a stay abroad and in the East where she was identified with feminist and Fabian movements she settled down in New Mexico where she became "a local sage and regional spokeswoman." Her 35 volumes and numerous other writings on the Southwest deal with history, travel, Indian lore, and related subjects. She could produce beautiful, lasting prose "when she forgot her own ego...and this happened all too rarely." Much of her later work was marred by egocentricity, mysticism and social zeal. Appended with a selected list of her works relating to the American Southwest and biographical studies of her life; illus.
D. L. Smith

1964. Purcell, Joanne B. TRADITIONAL BALLADS AMONG THE PORTUGUESE IN CALIFORNIA: PART I. *Western Folklore 1969 28(1): 1-19.* The informants who contributed to the author's collection of Portuguese traditional ballads came to California primarily from the Madeira Islands. They represent two generations who immigrated in two different periods: those above 60 who came in the 1920's; and those in their 30's and 40's who arrived within the last dozen years. There is an apparently considerable influence of written texts of the ballads upon oral transmission. Some are for instrumental accompaniment: other ballads are used with games and dances. Eight variants of 3 different ballad themes, with lyrics in Portuguese; musical scores; and commentary are presented here. 2 illus., 32 notes, biblio. To be continued.

D. L. Smith

1965. Purcell, Joanne B. TRADITIONAL BALLADS AMONG THE PORTUGUESE IN CALIFORNIA: PART II. *Western Folklore 1969 28(2): 77-90.* Continued from a previous article. Presents four Portuguese ballads and their texts, and discusses the variations the author has found in other versions from Portugal, Spain, Italy, Brazil, etc. The four ballads are "Casamento De Felha Do Galo," the story of a wedding between the louse and the flea, "Dom Varão," a ballad of a daughter who serves in war and the means she uses to keep from being discovered, "Noiva Arraiana," a narrative concerning the appearance of a long-absent husband who reclaims his wife as she is about to marry, and "Jesus Peregrino," the story of a farmer who gives charity to a poor man (Jesus) and is rewarded. All ballads show variants, yet the basic story is generally the same. 14 notes.

R. A. Trennert

1966. Putnam, Jackson K. DOWN TO EARTH: A. B. GUTHRIE'S QUEST FOR MORAL AND HISTORICAL TRUTH. *North Dakota Q. 1971 39(3): 47-57.* Historical novelists add an essential element of emotional understanding and empathy, as well as moral judgment, that is lacking in the works of historians. The author explains his thesis by analysis of Alfred Bertram Guthrie, Jr.'s, *Big Sky* (Boston, Mass.: Houghton Mifflin Co.), *Way West* (Boston, Mass.: Houghton Mifflin Co.), and *These Thousand Hills* (New York: New American Library, 1971) to illustrate both the description of emotional reaction to the western environment and the development of moral judgment. Guthrie's work is of enduring value for anyone seeking to understand the westward movement. 23 notes.

J. F. Mahoney

1967. Quimby, George I. HUMOR AMONG THE TREATY MAKERS AND FUR TRADERS OR "JOE MILLER'S JOKE BOOK" IN THE PACIFIC NORTHWEST. *Ethnohist. 1971 18(3): 267-271.* "English, Scotch, and Irish fur traders and others in the Pacific Northwest seemed to have relied heavily on material from *Joe Miller's Joke Book* for their early 19th century entertainment. A few excerpts from the [1839] edition are given to indicate the kind of humor these men appreciated."

J

1968. Rawles, Myrtle Read. "BOONTLING" - ESOTERIC SPEECH OF BOONVILLE, CALIFORNIA. *Western Folklore 1966 25(2): 93-103.* Contains a short history of the area and its language, with a list of words and expressions. Relies on interviews and secondary sources.

J. M. Brady

1969. Ringler, Donald P. MARY AUSTIN: KERN COUNTY DAYS, 1888-1892. *Southern California Q. 1963 45(1): 25-63.* Mary Austin (1868-1934) followed in the footsteps of several other famous American writers in writing about the California frontier. She lived in Kern County with her family from 1888 to 1892. Material drawn from her Kern County experience was used in about one-third of her published works. The author describes her life in the area, showing how much of it was used in her writing. 36 notes.

A. K. Main

1970. Ripley, Thomas Emerson. SHAKESPEARE IN THE LOGGING CAMP. *Forest Hist. 1964 8(3): 7-10.* Shakespeare-quoting George Moore was otherwise the prototype lumberjack of the novels and movies. He logged a Stillaguamish River tract in the 1890's for the Wheeler Osgood Company of nearby Tacoma, Washington, but made his own fortune as a British Columbian entrepreneur logging on the Tyee. Reprinted from *Green Timber,* a privately printed autobiographical memoir, now possessed by Mrs. Cornelia Ripley Sherman.

B. A. Vatter

1971. Roach, Joyce Gibson. THE LEGENDS OF EL TEJANO, THE TEXAN WHO NEVER WAS. *Western Folklore 1968 27(1): 33-43.* Legends about El Tejano are told in the Tucson area. Five are included in this study. Some of the details of El Tejano's life that appear in these stories are probably sheer fabrication. Others closely adhere to the real life events of William Brazelton, who may have inspired the

legends. Brazelton was a minor badman hero who flourished as a stage-robber in the Tucson area in the 1870's. Augmenting the regional subject matter in the legends are certain universal themes of folklore. Why the hero is called a Texan remains a mystery. Only one vague reference is made to Texas in the stories, and that is an improbable one. 26 notes.

D. L. Smith

1972. Robinson, Cecil. LEGEND OF DESTINY: THE AMERICAN SOUTHWEST IN THE NOVELS OF HARVEY FERGUSSON. *Am. West 1967 4(4): 16-18, 67-68.* After asserting that the American Southwest, with all the stimulation of a cross-cultural situation, has still to produce a literature of major consequence, the author submits the case of Harvey Fergusson. Fergusson's considerable number of novels and cultural histories are a significant step in the right direction. They have been too long neglected and should be reexamined. His prose is virile and clear. He "displays a shrewd understanding of the macrocosm of social change and the microcosm of individual human motivation." A central theme in his novels is his keen comprehension of the ambiguous relations between Mexicans and Anglo-Americans of the Southwest. Fergusson believes manifest destiny was an inexorable process. In portraying this he was probably at his best.

D. L. Smith

1973. Ross, Morton L. ALAN SWALLOW AND MODERN WESTERN AMERICAN POETRY. *Western Am. Literature 1966 1(2): 97-104.* Covering Swallow's 30-year study of poetry, describes his attempt to define regional Western poetry. In 1934 Swallow believed that the influence of environment was all-important to Western poets but, by 1937, he felt that geographic environment did not directly condition one's personal culture. He broadened his interest beyond regional verse in the 1940's. Swallow adopted the concept of a moral artist from Yvor Winters, involving himself in the relationship between aesthetic idea and practical technique. Swallow returned to the writing of specific Western poetry in the 1950's and found that Western writers commonly rejected the Eastern literary establishment. By the late 1950's he stated that a rationalistic spirit was imperative among Western writers. Although the author recognizes the limitations of Swallow's efforts, he considers them instructive for others who share Swallow's hope for a unique Western creativity. 17 notes.

S. L. McNeel

1974. Roucek, Joseph S. THE MYTHICAL ASPECTS OF THE "WILD WEST" IN AMERICAN MASS MEDIA OF COMMUNICATION. *Indian J. of Social Res. 1966 7(2): 137-144.* Surveys the use of the Western myth in literature, dime novels, movies, and TV from 1760 to the present, showing the West to have contributed a good deal to the element of violence in the American character. Discussing both what facts actually are and what the West has come to mean to Americans, the author points out the wide discrepancy between the two. 12 source citations.

B. A. Barbato

1975. Schneider, Lucy. "LAND" RELEVANCE IN "NEIGHBOUR ROSICKY." *Kansas Q. 1968 1(1): 105-110.* A discussion of Willa Cather's symbolic and specific use of "land" in her writings, with special emphasis on land symbolism in her story "Neighbour Rosicky." 4 notes.

B. A. Storey

1976. Slote, Bernice. WILLA CATHER AS A REGIONAL WRITER. *Kansas Q. 1970 2(2): 7-15.* Willa Cather obviously used regional materials in her writing, and these materials were heavily drawn from northwestern Nebraska to which her family had moved in the 1880's. However, while she used regional materials she treated universal themes. Because she had seen difficult times, she often described these and, as a result, some Nebraskans criticized her work. Other critics considered her work realistic because of this treatment of hard times. Based largely on Cather's works.

B. A. Storey

1977. Snell, Joseph W. THE WILD AND WOOLLY WEST OF THE POPULAR WRITER. *Nebraska Hist. 1967 48(2): 141-153.* Contends that most writing on the West is "an unsavory blend of legend, fiction, and invention with just a dash of fact thrown in for seasoning." Several examples from frontier Kansas history are cited to reveal how authors, chiefly because they neglect to do original research, repeat errors and distort information while writing under the guise of "historian."

R. Lowitt

1978. Sonnichsen, C. L.   BOOKS IN THE FIELD: FICTION AND HISTORY. *Wilson Lib. Bull. 1968 43(3): 249-255.* The author, a specialist in the fiction of the Southwest, presents the case for collecting regional novels and their value in the study of social history. Includes examples about the West, and traces the history of the "western." Discusses the current fictional treatment of the Mexican and Indian. Illus., biblio.   M. Kroeger

1979. Sonnichsen, C. L.   THE SHARECROPPER NOVEL IN THE SOUTHWEST. *Agric. Hist. 1969 43(2): 249-258.* Most novelists writing between 1920 and 1940 about sharecroppers in the Southwest agreed that cotton did "terrible things to the land and to the people on it." It took an exceptional person to defeat the "White Scourge." The novelists all hoped to bring about reforms. The leaders in the field of sharecropper fiction during the 1920's were Dorothy Scarborough and Ruth Cross. During the 1930's, writers included Charlie May Simon, Edwin Lanham, Sigman Byrd, and Edward Everett Davis. While these writers saw little but failure, the writers of the 1940's were more optimistic; they included George Sessions Perry, John W. Wilson, and John Watson. Based on the novels of the writers discussed.   W. D. Rasmussen

1980. Sonnichsen, C. L.   TOMBSTONE IN FICTION. *J. of Arizona Hist. 1968 9(2): 58-76.* Among the hundreds of western novels published in America, there have been several with the locale of the silver mining town of Tombstone. The first fictional treatment of Tombstone appeared in Alfred Henry Lewis' *Wolfville* (1897). This novel gave no space to the growing Wyatt Earp legend. However, with the publication of Walter Noble Burns's *Tombstone* (1927), the heroic treatment of Earp bloomed. Many novels followed over the years - works which generally saw the fight at the O.K. Corral in simplistically heroic terms. In 1958, when Oakley Hall wrote *Warlock*, the interpretation shifted. In this work the main characters, including Earp, were either cowardly, cynical, or depraved. This aberration did not continue. James Wyckoff, in his *John Slaughter's Way* (1963) returned to the earlier pattern of ignoring the Earp myth, while Robert Kreps's *The Hour of the Gun* (1947) carried the Earp legend to new heights of adulation. Concludes that the novelists have been influenced by the Earp legend but not overpowered by it; about half of them have shown discrimination in handling this theme.
                                                        R. J. Roske

1981. Sonnichsen, C. L.   THE WYATT EARP SYNDROME: A SOMEWHAT IRREVERENT INQUIRY INTO THE OLD WESTERN, THE NEW CRITICISM, AND THE PATHOLOGY OF THE AMERICAN PSYCHE. *Am. West 1970 7(3): 26-28, 60-62.* The once lowly western novel is the object of a revolution. Western stories were once considered as "myths in the making" and as something furnishing amusement, improvement, or escape. With Frank Waters' *The Colordao* (1946) and Henry Nash Smith's *Virgin Land* (1950), westerns came to be regarded as handy tools for psychoanalyzing the mind of the masses. These social documents reveal modern man and his society. Readers of these stories, according to this approach, are victims of the Wyatt Earp Syndrome. The "concurrent symptoms" of those who take satisfaction in the bloody-apocryphal deeds of Earp include loneliness, an inferiority complex, irrational fears, loss of moral values, and bloodlust. It is probably a safe guess that the western novel is here to stay. Whether it will look the same after the present revolution is another question.
                                                        D. L. Smith

1982. Steckmesser, Kent L.   CUSTER IN FICTION. *Am. West 1964 1(4): 47-52, 63-64.* An analysis of the novels concerned with George Armstrong Custer confirms that literary interpretation changes when historical interpretation changes. Frederick Whittaker's 1876 eulogistic biography and his 1882 Beadle's "dime biography" established the initial pattern. Juvenile and adult literature portrayed Custer with profound indifference to historical facts, as a truly romantic, heroic and legendary figure. This tradition came to an abrupt end with Frederick F. Van de Water's 1934 biography portraying Custer as an "impetuous and irresponsible egotist." This and Helen Hunt Jackson's 1881 plea for the Indians has changed the literary approach to a debunking effort. An "admirable" Custer has now been replaced by a "petulant and self-seeking neurotic" in Custerana. Illus.   D. L. Smith

1983. Steensma, Robert C.   THE DESERT SWEET: THE HOMESTEADER AND HIS LITERATURE. *Rendezvous 1968 3(2): 29-38.*

Pleads for a reevaluation of the historical and literary view of homesteading and homesteaders. Discusses the homesteader's fictional failures and accomplishments in order to call attention to this sizable part of Americana that was not all "hick" or "hayseed." Deals with promises and weaknesses of the Homestead Act (1862). Tolerable fiction from the western plains, as in Willa Cather and Hamlin Garland, is rare. Finds three tolerable novels (Ole Rølvaag's) among 60 bad, for South Dakota. Fiction stories of the West are photographic but do not show the realism necessary for an adequate reconstruction of individual lives. All of prairie literature has been victimized by the many bad novels and has not received the attention it deserves from historians or literary critics. Cather's *My Antonia* (1918) and Rolvaag's *Land of Giants* (1927) have especially suffered. Particularly perspicacious memorialist literature includes Elinore Pruitt Stewart's *Letters of a Woman Homesteader* (1961) and Martha L. Smith's *Going to God's Country*.   H. F. Malyon

1984. Steeves, Harrison R.   THE FIRST OF THE WESTERNS. *Southwest R. 1968 53(1): 74-83.* Claims that the writer of the first "Western"—a fictional account of the suppression of outlawry—was a German, Friedrich Gerstäcker, who spent about 10 months in Texas in 1838-39. On returning to Germany, Gerstäcker wrote two stories which can properly be labeled westerns, *The Regulators in Arkansas* (1845) and *The Moderators*.   D. F. Henderson

1985. Stegner, Wallace.   HISTORY, MYTH, AND THE WESTERN WRITER. *Am. West 1967 4(2): 61-62, 76-79.* It was predictable, and it happened that way, that a literature would emerge as a by-product when civilized people occupied "unrecorded, history-less, art-less new country" on the advancing American frontier. "Western writing" occurred as the last stage on successive frontiers such as New England and the Middle Atlantic states, but it did not happen this way in the West. Literary nativism began in the California gold rush country and in the cowboy Southwest, and it belatedly began in the Pacific Northwest and in the Mormon country, but not all over the West. This variety of plains, desert, lumber woods, California, Mexican border, and Mormon traditions, as well as the differences of climate, physiography, natural resources, characteristic occupations, and ethnic mixtures lacked enough in common to make for a western tradition. Further, "fiction factories" have "calcified" the most colorful western themes and characters into large and simple myth formulas. This combination of "mythic petrifaction" and "syncopated" change is not a circumstance conducive to the formation of a national character and its expression in the form of literature. Adapted from the introduction to a forthcoming book.
                                                        D. L. Smith

1986. Tamony, Peter.   HOODLUMS AND FOLK ETYMOLOGY. *Western Folklore 1969 28(1): 44-48.* "Hoodlum" was probably transmuted into the American language from the German in California in the 1860's but remained largely a localism in the San Francisco area until 1877. Folk etymologies had it otherwise, generally that the word was an offshoot of a proper name. The most likely folk explanation suggests that it was an enunciation of "huddle 'em," a figure of speech describing a group assault on one person. 12 notes.   D. L. Smith

1987. Taylor, Archer and Hand, Wayland D.   TWENTY-FIVE YEARS OF FOLKLORE STUDY IN THE WEST. *Western Folklore 1966 25(4): 229-245.* Describes folklore societies in the western half of the country and their activities since 1906, with emphasis on the last 25 years. Based on folklore journals, 29 notes.   J. M. Brady

1988. Taylor, J. Golden.   THE CELEBRATED JUMPING FROG OF CALAVERAS COUNTY BY MARK TWAIN. *Am. West 1965 2(4): 73-79.* On the centennial of its first appearance, Mark Twain's short story, "The Celebrated Jumping Frog of Calaveras County" is reprinted with an appraisal-introduction by J. Golden Taylor. Its literary significance is the artistry and authenticity with which this humorous incident in a western mining camp yields "fable-like insights into certain universal traits in human nature." As a piece of humorous writing it remains unexcelled in America. Its publication made Samuel Clemens into Mark Twain, a major writer in American literature. It is a piece of "superior humor." Illus.   D. L. Smith

1989. Taylor, Samuel W.   PECULIAR PEOPLE, POSITIVE THINKERS: AND THE PROSPECT OF MORMON LITERATURE.

Dialogue: A J. of Mormon Thought 1967 2(2): 17-31. Shows concern with "the unproductiveness of Mormon writing." Not that there is a lack of Mormon talent, but there is, among the Mormons, a literary tradition which has been oriented toward the building and maintenance of a certain public image. The author offers a three-point explanation of why a body of great Mormon literature has never materialized. First, Mormons began construction of a new public image after World War I, discarding embarrassing aspects of their heritage. Second, Mormons adopted an "S-2" mentality, saying nothing that was not forward-looking, progressive, and happy. Third, the "Mormon attitude toward literature remained unchanged from the persecution period" to the present. Either a writer was for the church or an enemy of it. There was no room for objective writing, and so with no external opposition and with internal discontent Mormon literature "gradually softened and decayed." Perhaps the intellectual climate is changing. *Dialogue: A Journal of Mormon Thought* is a "breath of cool air in the stifling atmosphere of our internal literature."

L. P. Hofeling

1990. Timpe, Eugene F.   BRET HARTE'S GERMAN PUBLIC. *Jahrbuch für Amerikastudien [West Germany] 1965 10: 215-220.* Due to the fact that Harte's writings have been published in Germany with no significant interruption for more than 90 years, he is depicted as a model of what the reception of an American author "would be expected to be but seldom is." Timpe's tracing of Harte's translators, reviewers, critics and audience in Germany from Ferdinand Freiligrath in 1872 to Karl Bleibtreu and Walther Fischer in the 1920's provides an insight into "the image of America as it had been created in the minds of the German people." Documented.   G. Bassler

1991. Turner, Justin G.   CONVERSATION WITH UPTON SINCLAIR. *Am. Book Collector 1970 20(8): 7-10.* The conversation concerned Upton Sinclair's marriages, his running for governor of California in 1934, his books, and his archives. The transcription of a note from him to Sol Lesser (1 October 1961) is included. Illus.   D. Brockway

1992. Walker, Don D.   THE GUN AND LASSO OF HENRY JAMES. *Western Humanities R. 1963 17(2): 178-180.* Discusses Henry James' style in his great novels of 1902-04, particularly his use of western language and imagery. Two of James' favorite authors, and, consequently, greatest influences were Bret Harte *(Tales of Trail and Town,* (1898) and Owen Wister *(Lin McLean,* (1898), and *The Virginian,* (1902). Although James (like Harte) lived in England, he had an excellent command of western colloquial speech, especially in speaking of weapons; in *Daisy Miller* (1879) and *The American* (1877) he used "gun" and "six-shooter" (words becoming common in the West) where his contemporaries still referred to the old-fashioned "pistol." The image of the lasso appears very extensively in his writing; examples are given from *The Ambassadors* and *The Golden Bowl* (1904). 15 notes.   A. K. Main

1993. Walker, Don D.   THE MOUNTAIN MAN AS A LITERARY HERO. *Western Am. Literature 1966 1(1): 15-25.* Describes the relationship between actual heroic mountain men and their literary counterparts. Beginning with the thesis that the mountain man was a truly indigenous heroic figure, the author discusses Hugh Glass, John Colter, John Johnson, and Jedediah Smith. He concludes that not only is the necessary literary control which creates art from history elusive but that the natural lack of introspection in these men discourages their literary use. Documentation from published sources.   R. N. Hudspeth

1994. Walker, Don D.   THE WESTERN HUMANISM OF WILLA CATHER. *Western Am. Literature 1966 1(2): 75-90.* Discusses humanism in Willa Cather's writing. Though unlike her naturalistic contemporaries, she was aware of and influenced by them. For example the biological determinism of Jack London and Frank Norris were in conflict with her view of the free human spirit. Miss Cather's focus was not on the natural world but on human passion. Her humanism was western because her novels were set in the Western American States where her characters humanized the landscape and found a happy relationship with the wild land. The author concludes with a discussion of Miss Cather's insight into human relationships. Although every human needs to relate to other humans, no relationship is ever totally satisfying, and so man finds himself seeking more humans while simultaneously pulling away from them. 68 notes.   S. L. McNeel

1995. Warner, Richard H.   A CONTEMPORARY SKETCH OF JACK LONDON. *Am. Literature 1966 38(3): 376-380.* Reproduces a description of Jack London written in 1916 by Marshall Bond, a Yale-educated mining engineer who met London in Dawson in the summer of 1897. Refers to London's keen interest in socialism, his affection for his dog, his experience in the Klondike, his home life in Oakland, California, and his visit to Bond's home in Santa Clara, California, which London refers to in the opening chapter of *The Call of the Wild.* 2 notes.

D. D. Cameron

1996. Wechsberg, Joseph.   WINNETOU OF DER WILD WEST. [With editorial introduction and translated passages by Richard H. Cracroft, "Siegfried in a Coonskin Cap."] *Am. West 1964 1(3): 32-39.* Through the fictional characters of Old Shatterhand, "a German Natty Bumppo . . . a mixture of Tom Mix, Hopalong Cassidy, Siegfried, and Christ," and Winnetou, a noble Apache chief, who is "a cultured blend of the finest traits of the Indian and German nations," Karl May conjured up, without seeing it, a novelized portrayal of the American West in dozens of volumes that have thrilled generations of German males, including Einstein, Hitler, and Albert Schweitzer. Illus.

D. L. Smith

1997. Westbrook, Max.   THE ARCHETYPAL ETHIC OF "THE OX-BOW INCIDENT." *Western Am. Literature 1966 1(2): 105-118.* Analyzes previous criticism of Walter Van Tilburg Clark's *The Ox-Bow Incident* (New York: The Press of the Readers Club, 1942), stating that it is much more than a cowboy story of literary value and that the critics have asked wrong questions and have thus praised the work for wrong reasons. Clark focused on internal emotions and meanings and implied that inner feelings must result in action. But, for the action to be healthy, a man must be a whole man, otherwise his action will emerge from a distorted projection of his inner self, perhaps in a horrible way. The values of such a whole man are comparable to Carl G. Jung's archetypal values. Clark believes that man's unconscious should be ethically responsible, although such a response is often attributed to the rational minds. The whole man is one in which the unconscious, or feeling, is his contact with reality, and reason is his conscious recorder of what the unconscious teaches. The subject of *The Ox-Bow Incident* then is man's mutilation of himself. The tragedy is that most modern men have already been alienated from archetypal reality. 3 notes.   S. L. McNeel

1998. Weston, James J.   SHARLOT HALL: ARIZONA'S PIONEER LADY OF LITERATURE. *J. of the West 1965 4(4): 539-552.* Sharlot Mabridth Hall was born in Kansas on 27 October 1870. When she was 11 her family moved to Arizona Territory where her father was to engage in ranching and mining. During the move she was thrown from a horse and suffered a spinal injury. The injury never fully healed and in 1890 she was confined to bed for an entire year. During her convalescence she began to write poems and articles. Some of these were published in western newspapers. Recovering her health she improved her 160-acre claim, but still found time to continue writing. In 1897 she wrote a historical article for *Land of Sunshine,* a California magazine edited by Charles F. Lummis. His interest brought her out of obscurity. In 1901 Lummis hired her for his staff of *Out West,* a position she held until 1909 when she resigned to accept a political appointment. Despite some ups and downs her influence as a writer and poet and her influence as a historian and politican continued until her death in 1943. Based on materials in the Sharlot Hall Museum; 53 notes.   D. N. Brown

1999. White, John I.   D. J. "KID" O'MALLEY . . . MONTANA'S COWBOY POET. *Montana 1967 17(3): 60-73.* Biographical sketch of a Montana cowboy whose primitive verse brought him some renown in his lifetime. He grew up on early Montana ranches and around the military posts in the area and had some of his poems published in local newspapers. He has some claim on authorship of the song "When the Work's All Done This Fall." In later years he produced a number of syndicated articles, based on his own experiences, which appeared in the weekly press of Montana. Based on O'Malley's writings and interviews with the author; illus.   S. R. Davison

2000. White, John I.   "GREAT GRANDMA." *Western Folklore 1968 27(1): 27-31.* The attention of the author was called to a 1962 article attributing a popular song, "Great Grandma," to the days of the California gold rush. "Actually the old gal is less than forty years old. I should know, because I happen to be her father." The author relates the circumstances of its composition and traces its growth to its present proportions. 8 notes.   D. L. Smith

2001. White, John I. A MONTANA COWBOY POET. *J. of Am. Folklore 1967 80(316): 113-129.* An account of the author's meeting in 1933 with a Montana cowboy poet, Dominick J. O'Malley (1867-1943), and of his subsequent correspondence with him. The text of several cowboy songs which were published in the *Stock Growers' Journal* in Miles City, Montana, in the early 1890's is reproduced. O'Malley asserts that he wrote "Sweet By-and-By Revised" in 1887. "Perhaps the most famous bit of verse to which Mr. O'Malley appears to have a clear title usually is known among ballad singers as 'When the Work Is Done Next Fall.' When it appeared in the *Stock Growers' Journal* on October 6, 1893, its writer called it 'After the Roundup' and modeled it on 'After the Ball,' the Charles K. Harris waltz-time song hit of 1892." Illus., photo, 8 notes.   D. D. Cameron

2002. White, John I. THE VIRGINIAN. *Montana 1966 16(4): 3-11.* Discusses the varied presentations and judgments concerning Owen Wister's famous character in his book, *The Virginian* (1902), about whom there has been controversy as to his authenticity as a Western hero. Among versions considered are the original novel, and adaptations for stage and screen.   S. R. Davison

2003. Whitford, Kathryn. CRUSADER WITHOUT A CAUSE: AN EXAMINATION OF HAMLIN GARLAND'S MIDDLE BORDER. *Midcontinent Am. Studies J. 1965 6(1): 61-71.* Attempts to explain why Hamlin Garland shifted the emphasis of his literary work from the Middle Border to the Far West. Garland's critics have pointed out that he was an opportunist, literary failure, and even guilty of evading moral responsibility. However, a close examination of the history of the Middle Border may provide the key to Garland's change of emphasis. The fact that the reforms he championed became passé at the height of his career may very well explain his abandonment of the Middle West as the scene of his literary endeavors.   B. M. Morrison

2004. Williams, Burton J. JOHN JAMES INGALLS: GEOGRAPHIC DETERMINISM AND KANSAS. *Midwest Q. 1965 6(3): 285-291.* Ingalls was most famous in his time for his three terms as U.S. Senator, beginning in 1873. Today he is better known as the author of such essays as "Catfish Aristocracy," published in the February 1872 issue of *Kansas Magazine,* and "Blue Grass," published in the September 1872 issue of the same magazine. He considered that frontier country developed democracy, low-lying lands bred an inferior race, and high lands a superior race. He wrote that beef eaters are superior to grain eaters and vegetarians, and that the people of blue grass areas are superior to those of coarse grass areas. The author concludes that we cannot be sure that much of Ingalls' exaggerated emphasis on geographical determinism was not facetious.   G. H. G. Jones

2005. Wylder, Delbert E. THOMAS BERGER'S "LITTLE BIG MAN" AS LITERATURE. *Western Am. Literature 1969 3(4): 273-284.* Refutes former critics' appraisals of Berger's *Little Big Man* (Greenwich, Conn.: Fawcett Crest Books, 1965) as not being literature, emphasizing the importance of placing the novel in the correct frame of reference. The author insists that Berger's successful control of tonal change in the novel's narrative perspective is what makes it literature. The novel is Barthian in approach but Western in its attitude concerning human values and humanity. Its framework is absurd because of the character Ralph Fielding Snell. But Crabb's story, although beginning comically, ends with enough seriousness to convince the reader of the fact that Old Lodge Skins is equivalent to Oedipus, the mythical tragic hero. The article maintains that the novel is not merely a satire on Westerns, but it is a commentary on mankind's weaknesses. Therefore, it is not totally Barthian, because serious comment is made. The article concludes by stating that the novel offers a general affirmation of what Max Westbrook terms "Western sacrality." 24 notes.   S. L. McNeel

2006. Wyman, Walker D. WESTERN FOLKLORE AND HISTORY. *Am. West 1964 1(1): 44-51.* Demonstrates with numerous examples that folk beliefs undergird and influence the western movement. The historian is obligated to collect folklore, to separate it from "fakelore," and to use it "to chink the cracks of history."
                                                                            D. L. Smith

Journalism and Publishing

2007. Alison, Elizabeth M. and Katz, William A. THORNTON FLEMING MC ELROY - PRINTER, POLITICIAN, BUSINESSMAN. *Pacific Northwest Q. 1963 54(2): 54-65.* Experiences and machinations of McElroy as a printer and seeker of profitable public printing contracts in the Pacific Northwest, 1852-85.   C. C. Gorchels

2008. Bass, Althea. THE CHEYENNE TRANSPORTER. *Chronicles of Oklahoma 1968 46(2): 127-140.* The newspaper *Cheyenne Transporter* was started in December 1879 in Darlington, Indian Territory. Its initial purpose was educational, but its coverage soon broadened to serve the interests of cattlemen and the military. As champion of the Indian point of view and a reflector of the society of this frontier outpost, its files, now in the archives of the Oklahoma Historical Society, furnish a valuable body of source material. Publication ceased sometime in 1886. 3 illus.
                                                                            D. L. Smith

2009. Belknap, George N. OREGON PRINTING BEFORE THE "SPECTATOR." *Papers of the Biblio. Soc. of Am. 1965 59(1): 50-55.* Discloses that the first printing in Oregon was not of the *Oregon Spectator* in February 1846, but a Champoeg County election ticket in the late spring of 1845. Medare G. Foisy was the printer.   C. A. Newton

2010. Blackorby, Edward C. GEORGE B. WINSHIP: PROGRESSIVE JOURNALIST OF THE MIDDLE BORDER. *North Dakota Q. 1971 39(3): 5-17.* Traces the career of Winship (1843-1931) as reforming editor-politician in North Dakota, 1879-1911. Editor-owner of the Grand Forks *Daily Herald,* he fought in the vanguard of political and agrarian reform movements. For a generation, his career in many respects paralleled that of LaFollette of Wisconsin. But because the milieu in North Dakota differed from that in Wisconsin, Winship's efforts were less successful and less personally rewarding than LaFollette's. Nonetheless he was a significant influence in shaping the character of North Dakota politics and legislation. Based on secondary sources; 56 notes.
                                                                          J. F. Mahoney

2011. Boeser, Linda. TWO COMSTOCK JOURNALISTS: SAMUEL L. CLEMENS AND WILLIAM L. WRIGHT AS REPORTERS AND AUTHORS. *Missouri Hist. R. 1965 59(4): 428-438.* The Virginia City *Territorial Enterprise* was an enterprising and unrestrained newspaper during the days of the Comstock Lode. Wright, who wrote under the pen name Dan De Quille, joined its staff in 1861 and remained for 31 years. The more famous Mark Twain joined the paper in 1862 and remained for two years. Wright had a greater respect for facts, which made him an excellent reporter but may have kept him from maturing into an audacious and popular writer like Twain. The attitudes of the two men toward such topics as Indians and outlaws are contrasted by referring to the treatment given such subjects in their literary efforts about the West, Wright's *The Big Bonanza* (1876) and Clemens' *Roughing It* (1871). 46 notes.   W. F. Zornow

2012. Bragg, Mary Jane. SOME SOUTHWEST IMPRINTS: PRESSES OF ARIZONA AND NEW MEXICO. *Southwest R. 1967 52(1): 26-42.* A survey of private and public printing in New Mexico and Arizona from its beginning in New Mexico in 1834 and Arizona in 1859 until the present. A number of titles and publishers are mentioned.
                                                                          D. F. Henderson

2013. Branch, Edgar M. MARK TWAIN REPORTS THE RACES IN SACRAMENTO. *Huntington Lib. Q. 1969 32(2): 179-186.* In September 1866, on his return from Hawaii and before his tour of lectures on the Sandwich Islands, Mark Twain reported the horse races at the State Fair for the *Sacramento Daily Union.* This was probably his last systematic work as a local reporter. Excerpts show some of the characteristic features of his writing. 9 notes.   H. D. Jordan

2014. Carranco, Lynwood. BRET HARTE IN UNION (1857-1860). *California Hist. Soc. Q. 1966 45(2): 99-112.* The three years (1857-60) Bret Harte spent in the town of Union (now Arcata, California) have been referred to as his lost years. He never cared to discuss these years in which he learned so much about writing and of frontier life because of the tragic massacre of 26 Feburary 1860 when a large number of peaceful Indians were brutally slain by a few whites who were never brought to trial. Harte, temporarily in charge of the local newspaper, bitterly attacked the perpetrators of the massacre, though not by name. Apparently the tide of opinion against Harte, as the author of the editorial, was strong enough to force him to leave Union. He profited by his experience there. Soon he was working on San Francisco newspapers, and in 1868 he became editor of *The Overland Monthly* in which his most famous stories appeared. 29 notes.   E. P. Stickney

2015. Dagenais, Julie. NEWSPAPER LANGUAGE AS AN ACTIVE AGENT IN THE BUILDING OF A FRONTIER TOWN. *Am. Speech 1967 42(2): 114-121.* The *Wichita Eagle* was a "booster" newspaper which had as its goal the growth and improvement of the town in all respects. The newspaper was founded in 1872, the same year as the town. From then until 1892 (the period covered in this study) the paper constantly - and often extravagantly and colorfully - had an optimistic spirit and was credited with contributing greatly to the growth of Wichita. The editor was "praised for his contribution to the building of Wichita, specifically for his refusal to recognize, in print, the faults and handicaps of his chosen city and for his determined emphasis on its achievements, potential and actual." Based on a sampling of the *Wichita Eagle* from 1872 to 1892; 22 notes.   R. W. Shoemaker

2016. Davis, O. L., Jr. E. H. CUSHING: TEXTBOOKS IN CONFEDERATE TEXAS. *Lib. Chronicle of the U. of Texas 1966 8(2): 46-50.* E. H. Cushing, editor of the Houston *Telegraph,* was responsible for the survival of Texas' schools through his printing of schoolbooks. They were the only schoolbooks available during the last two years of the Civil War. A history of the printing and a checklist of the schoolbooks are included.   D. Brockway

2017. Denny, Melcena Burns. CALIFORNIA'S FIRST NEWSPAPER. *Montana 1965 15(4): 28-41.* Using an antique press, with stale ink and unsuitable paper, Walter Colton and Robert Semple published California's first newspaper at Monterey in 1846, just as the region was passing into American hands. *The Californian* moved to San Francisco in 1847, where its merger with others led to the establishment of the *Alta California* in 1849. Quotations from the subject papers. Illus.
                                                                       S. R. Davison

2018. Drury, Clifford M. "THE OREGONIAN AND INDIAN'S ADVOCATE." *Pacific Northwest Q. 1965 56(4): 159-167.* The history of the two-year existence of *The Oregonian and Indian's Advocate* and the influence of this magazine in stimulating New England families to emigrate to Oregon. Sponsored by the Provisional Emigration Society and supported by the Methodist Church, the magazine failed because of lack of funds and criticism over an ambitious scheme to send a thousand Christian settlers to Oregon.   C. C. Gorchels

2019. Folkes, John. THREE NEVADA NEWSPAPERS: A CENTURY IN PRINT. *Nevada Hist. Soc. Q. 1970 13(3): 16-24.* Nevada was six years a State when the great period of American newspapers began. From 1860 until the present, Nevada has seen over 400 different newspapers. Currently a few more than 20 exist, three of which began in 1870. These three are the *Eureka Sentinel,* the *Nevada State Journal,* and the *Pioche Record.* The author details the history and problems of these three newspapers against the backdrop of Nevada history. Photo, 11 notes.   E. P. Costello

2020. Fraser, James H. INDIAN MISSION PRINTING IN ARIZONA: AN HISTORICAL SKETCH AND BIBLIOGRAPHY. *J. of Arizona Hist. 1969 10(2): 67-102.* From the 18th to the early 20th century, the spread of printing to areas outside of Eastern Asia and Europe was closely tied to the Roman Catholic and Protestant missionary effort. The arrival of the printing press in the American West was directly related to missionary activity. The process was delayed longer in Arizona because of a lack of dictionaries of the Indian languages. In 1910 the Franciscan Fathers at Saint Michaels published a Navajo catechism and the *Ethnological Dictionary of the Navajo Language.* After that, few of the missionary translators did their own printing and most of the translations were printed outside the State. Since World War II the major translator and printer has been Wycliffe Bible Translators, Inc. Lists all Indian mission printing in the Apache, Cocopa, Hopi, Navajo, Pai, and Pima languages. The Roman Catholic center at Saint Michaels now prints

in English. The demand for religious material in the Navajo language is strong. Indexes printers and presses, places of printing, and translators. Based on interviews and secondary sources; 6 illus., 39 notes, biblio.
                                                                       R. J. Roske

2021. Gibson, Arrell Morgan. A HISTORY OF THE UNIVERSITY OF OKLAHOMA PRESS. *J. of the West 1968 7(4): 553-561.* Traces the history of the press from its proposal by the University of Oklahoma's fifth president William Bennett Bizzell, in 1925, to the appointment of the press's third director Edward A. Shaw, in 1967. Between those dates it had published more than 750 books.   R. N. Alvis

2022. Goldblatt, Kenneth A. EDWIN BLISS HILL: PIONEER ARIZONA PRINTER. *J. of Arizona Hist. 1968 9(1): 18-29.* Discusses the career of Edwin Bliss Hill (1866-1949), a pioneer printer who operated a private press for many years. Born in 1866 in Ann Arbor, Michigan, he moved to Detroit while a child and there completed both his academic schooling and printing apprenticeship. Hill worked as a newspaperman and rose to the post of news editor of the *Detroit Journal* while pursuing his avocation as a printer-publisher of a private press. In 1901 he developed the symptoms of tuberculosis which caused him to move to rural southern Michigan. In 1908 Hill moved to Arizona where he worked for the U.S. Reclamation Service near Mesa. In 1918 he was transferred to Texas. In 1945, Hill returned to Arizona and resided in Tempe. From that time on, until his death on 6 April 1949, Hill continued to print pamphlets, leaflets, brochures, and broadsides. Although relatively obscure, the author believes that Hill made an enduring contribution to the development of printing in the Southwest. Based largely on newspapers and secondary accounts; 4 illus., 32 notes.   R. J. Roske

2023. Gower, Calvin W. KANSAS "BORDER TOWN" NEWSPAPERS AND THE PIKES PEAK GOLD RUSH. *Journalism Q. 1967 44(2): 281-288.* Denies the charge of several historians that Kansas newspapers in border-river towns were guilty of reckless journalism in connection with the 1859 "gold rush" into what is now Eastern Colorado. Editors of eight newspapers studied, after overcoming an early suspicion, greeted the news of the Cherry Creek gold discovery enthusiastically but, although they had "gold fever" themselves and hoped their communities would benefit from the rush, presented unfavorable reports as well as favorable ones. Optimistic reports got the greater space, but the editors viewed with alarm the procession of inadequately prepared gold seekers and asserted that even a well-equipped person might fail in the mining area. 45 notes.   S. E. Humphreys

2024. Grivas, Theodore. THE ARTHUR H. CLARK COMPANY, PUBLISHER OF THE WEST: A REVIEW OF SIXTY YEARS OF SERVICE, 1902-1962. *Arizona and the West 1963 5(1): 63-78.* England-born and apprenticed with a thorough training in all phases of publishing and bookselling, Arthur H. Clark refined his specialty in the cataloging of rare books in the employ of a Chicago dealer. After a short period in business for himself, he became the manager and a board member of a newly-formed Cleveland, Ohio, company. With the success met by *The Jesuit Relations,* 73 volumes of American source material, which he persuaded the firm to publish, Clark decided to establish the Arthur H. Clark Company in 1902. Here and in Glendale, California, where he relocated in 1930, under Clark, his principal assistant Paul W. Galleher, and his son Arthur H. Clark, Jr., the company has published hundreds of volumes of source material and monographs, widely acclaimed for their scholarship and format. Clark publications have won most of the principal book awards in the United States. The company has "an enviable reputation" as an old and rare book house. The Clarks and Galleher have maintained close and active professional ties with "founding father" status for prominent national organizations and journals. Photo. Bibliography of Clark publications.   D. L. Smith

2025. Gurian, Jay. SWEETWATER JOURNALISM AND WESTERN MYTH. *Ann. of Wyoming 1964 36(1): 78-88.* Disputes the interpretation of the frontier newspaper as a chronicle of violence, tall tales, and folk humor. Using the editorials and news content of *The Sweetwater Mines* and *The South Pass News,* (1868-69) he claims the newspapers of South Pass showed their community as orderly and law-abiding. Cites instances where they denounced other editors for exaggeration and stories of violence, and shows that they gave most space to advertising, local affairs, and mining news. Based on extant files of the two papers and published studies on frontier journalism.   R. L. Nichols

2026. Halaas, David F. FRONTIER JOURNALISM IN COLORADO. *Colorado Mag. 1967 44(3): 185-203.* Following the discovery of gold in the Pikes Peak region two presses came to the Cherry Creek country in 1859. Newspapers came but they had many tribulations, often moving to many localities. Obtaining subscribers and news items were problems. These early journals publicized the prosperity of the region to attract people and capital, seldom revealing the worst side of frontier life. The early newspapers did not actually reflect the towns and people they purported to represent. 6 illus., 79 notes.   I. W. Van Noppen

2027. Hall, Mark W. THE SAN FRANCISCO "CHRONICLE": ITS FIGHT FOR THE 1879 CONSTITUTION. *Journalism Q. 1969 46(3): 505-510.* The passage of the 1879 California constitution can be directly attributed to the campaign of the San Francisco *Chronicle.* Begun by the three de Young brothers as the *Daily Dramatic Chronicle* in January 1865, it tried to emulate a true newspaper. The *Chronicle's* concern for public welfare and its fight against monopolistic activities began early, as did anti-Chinese propaganda. The de Youngs saw themselves as protectors of the working class. By 1874, the *Chronicle* was America's 10th largest paper. With San Francisco's corrupt government exposed and corrected, the de Youngs turned their support to the reform policies of Denis Kearney and his fight for a new constitution. The *Chronicle* was the only major California newspaper to support the constitution. When Charles de Young died, M. H. de Young continued to battle corruption; but he modified the paper's sensational image. Based on primary and secondary sources; 44 notes.   K. J. Puffer

2028. Hensher, Alan. EARLE CLEMENS AND THE RHYOLITE "HERALD": TWENTIETH-CENTURY NEVADA PIONEERS. *Southern California Q. 1967 49(3): 311-325.* Concerns the Rhyolite *Herald* and Earle Clemens, its publisher and editor. Clemens started the *Herald* in the Bullfrog Mining District of southwestern Nevada in 1905 shortly after gold was discovered there. The fortunes of his venture followed those of the area: at the peak of the gold boom, Rhyolite had about seven thousand residents and Clemens had branch newspapers in a number of the surrounding communities, but by 1910 Rhyolite's population was only 675 and in the following year Clemens sold the *Herald* and moved to Terra Bella, California. The author also discusses the transition through which journalism was passing during the years at the turn of the century. These included changes from muscle power to electricity and from typesetting to linotypes, the impact of the telephone and automobile, and the trend toward centralized publishing. Based on newspaper files of the Rhyolite *Herald,* personal interviews, and secondary accounts; illus., 23 notes.   W. L. Bowers

2029. Holway, Hope. LUCIA LOOMIS FERGUSON (MRS. WALTER FERGUSON) 1886-1962. *Chronicles of Oklahoma 1963 41(4): 365-369.* A memorial tribute to Lucia Loomis Ferguson, editor of the weekly *Cherokee Republican* and author of the "Woman's View" and "Lucia Loomis" columns for the Scripps-Howard newspapers. Tribute is also paid to Mrs. Ferguson as a public-spirited citizen.
I. W. Van Noppen

2030. Hufford, Kenneth, ed. THE ARIZONA GAZETTE, A FORGOTTEN VOICE IN ARIZONA JOURNALISM. *J. of Arizona Hist. 1966 7(4): 182-187.* Concerns the *Arizona Gazette,* the second newspaper in the territory, first published in the summer of 1866 at La Paz, Yuma County. Vincent Ryan, the editor, moved it to Prescott in 1867, where its last issue appeared August 31 of that year. Illus., 5 notes, biblio.
J. D. Filipiak

2031. Hufford, Kenneth. P. W. DOONER: PIONEER EDITOR OF TUCSON. *Arizona and the West 1968 10(1): 25-42.* Canadian Pierson W. Dooner, a long-time resident of Tucson, Arizona, became associated with the *Arizonian* with its first issue in 1869. Late in January he became its editor and promptly changed its name to *Arizonan.* Theorizing that a frontier editor had to be "a fighting man—a first class bruiser"—to keep his paper from the control of dictatorial demagogues, he pledged to use the power of his press in an "absolutely fearless, impartial, and strictly truthful" manner. The *Arizonan* had a colorful career under his editorship. When he broke with the political interests of the territorial delegate to Congress, his press was confiscated. Furious, he conducted a frontal attack in the pages of the *Arizonan,* which he continued by using another press. His efforts were futile, however, and publication ceased a few

months after the election. Although Dooner was perceptive and articulate and sincerely interested in the development of Arizona, he exercised very little influence. 4 illus., 40 notes.   D. L. Smith

2032. Ippolito, Donna and Kopatz, Shirley. ALAN SWALLOW: PLATTEN PRESS PUBLISHER. *J. of the West 1969 8(3): 477-483.* Traces the life of Alan Swallow and his press in Denver. He published over 400 titles, divided almost evenly between literary works and Western Americana. After Swallow's death in 1966 the Swallow Press was bought by Morton Weisman who, with the help of Durrett Wagner, has kept it going in the spirit of Alan Swallow.   R. N. Alvis

2033. Johnson, Bobby H. BOOSTER ATTITUDES OF SOME NEWSPAPERS IN OKLAHOMA TERRITORY - "THE LAND OF THE FAIR GOD." *Chronicles of Oklahoma 1965 43(3): 242-264.* It was an editor's obligation to use his paper as an organ of public promotion. The author deals with five territorial newspapers and examines the extent to which they performed that function. The El Reno *Democrat,* the Kingfisher *Free Press,* the Watonga *Republican,* and the two successive papers in Arapaho, the *Arrow* and the *Bee,* all lived up to their obligation. The author concludes that while they were guilty of overstating the truth, it would be unfair to brand their editors as liars. And they were successful in publicizing their area, the western part of the territory. Census figures show that two of the counties, Canadian and Kingfisher, increased their population more than 120 percent from 1890 to 1900. Illus., 46 notes.   I. W. Van Noppen

2034. Kantor, J. R. K. FIFTY-TWO EARLY CALIFORNIA IMPRINTS IN THE BANCROFT LIBRARY: A SUPPLEMENTARY LIST TO GREENWOOD'S "CALIFORNIA IMPRINTS, 1833-1862." *Papers of the Biblio. Soc. of Am. 1964 58(2): 181-189.* Lists 52 additional items printed between 1850 and 1862 and located in the Bancroft Library.
C. A. Newton

2035. Katz, William A. THE COLUMBIAN: WASHINGTON TERRITORY'S FIRST NEWSPAPER. *Oregon Hist. Q. 1963 64(1): 33-40.* Birth and survival-struggles of a newspaper established in Washington Territory (northwestern United States), 1852-53.
C. C. Gorchels

2036. Katz, W. A. TRACING WESTERN TERRITORIAL IMPRINTS THROUGH THE NATIONAL ARCHIVES. *Papers of the Biblio. Soc. of Am. 1965 59(1): 1-11.* The U.S. Treasury Department Comptroller's correspondence, "now housed in the National Archives, afford one of the best single systematic approaches to the history of territorial printing and journalism available." Drawing on this correspondence, the author outlines varieties of information available on titles, costs, and the politics of printing in the territories, especially from 1842 to 1874.   C. A. Newton

2037. Keen, Elizabeth. WYOMING'S FRONTIER NEWSPAPER. *Ann. of Wyoming 1963 35(1): 88-101.* Discusses the Cheyenne, Laramie, and Douglas newspapers as sources for early Wyoming territorial history. Uses as examples news of opportunities for cattle and sheep raisers, tales of cattle roundups, notices of political meetings, and comments on the first women serving on a trial jury. Includes a checklist of territorial newspapers giving the place of publication, name of the paper, the dates of extant copies, and their depositories. Based primarily on newspapers and published state-local history.   R. L. Nichols

2038. King, C. Richard. COL. CAREY WENTWORTH STYLES. *Texana 1970 8(1): 1-29.* Discusses Styles's newspaper career. Styles was born in South Carolina, served in both the Mexican and Civil Wars, and later founded the *Atlanta Constitution.* He also served on the staffs of several Georgia newspapers. In 1881 Styles moved to Texas. During the next 10 years he edited and wrote for several Texas newspapers. A restless man, he was never able to stay long in any spot. Styles tirelessly pushed prohibition in his newspaper columns. After 1891 he retired in Stephensville, Texas, until his death from cancer in 1897. Based on contemporary newspapers and Texas-held manuscript collections; illus., 97 notes.
R. J. Roske

2039. King, C. Richard. NEWSPAPERS THAT REPUBLIC OF TEXAS READERS DIDN'T READ. *Texana 1967 5(2): 117-125.*

Study of the prospectuses of several Texas newspapers that were never published. These prospectuses preserve the flavor of the period. They illustrate the attitude of early Texans toward the press of the period and the aspirations of pioneer journalists. 4 notes.   W. A. Buckman

2040. Knight, Oliver. THE OWYHEE AVALANCHE; THE FRONTIER NEWSPAPER AS A CATALYST IN SOCIAL CHANGE. *Pacific Northwest Q. 58(2): 74-81.* Using *The Owyhee Avalanche* (Ruby City, Idaho Territory) as a model, the author discusses the role of the frontier newspaper (almost always issued weekly) in the embryonic towns of the trans-Mississippi West, 1863-72. Examples of newspaper articles on social topics are included.   C. C. Gorchels

2041. Lent, John A. THE PRESS ON WHEELS: A HISTORY OF THE FRONTIER INDEX OF NEBRASKA, COLORADO, WYOMING, ELSEWHERE? *Ann. of Wyoming 1971 43(2): 165-203.* Legh (Leigh) Richmond Freeman (1842-1915) and Frederick Kemper Freeman (1841-1928) published *The Frontier Index* between 1865 and 1884 under various titles in at least 14 towns. In the late 1860's they followed the construction of the Union Pacific Railroad westward from railhead to railhead in Nebraska, Colorado, and Wyoming. Mobility, financial stability, and an abundance of gossip and trivia distinguished *The Frontier Index* from other western newspapers. On the other hand, as they extolled the economic virtues of each successive location, carried on editorial feuds with other papers, supported law and order, and dabbled in local politics, the Freeman brothers typified the many western editors who promoted frontier towns and settlement. Based principally on *The Frontier Index,* other contemporary newspapers, and Freeman MSS.; illus., 157 notes.   G. R. Adams

2042. McKinney, Gary. OKLAHOMA GHOST TOWN JOURNALISM. *Chronicles of Oklahoma 1968 46(4): 387-408.* Because of fire, only a few pages remain of the newspapers published during the short life of Day County, 1893-1907. Gives a brief history of *The Day County Tribune,* and "a commentary, as complete as possible, on a journalistic donnybrook between *The Day County Progress* and *The Canadian Valley Echo.*" With the birth of the new State of Oklahoma in 1907 came the death of the old county of Day and its county seat, Grand. The *Progress* soon folded and the *Echo* under a changed name moved to nearby Cheyenne. Illus., 27 notes.   E. P. Stickney

2043. Nash, Lee M. SCOTT OF THE "OREGONIAN": THE EDITOR AS HISTORIAN. *Oregon Hist. Q. 1969 70(3): 196-232.* A biographical sketch of Harvey W. Scott as the preeminent contemporary historian of Oregon. Born in Illinois in 1838, Scott migrated to Oregon as a 14-year-old boy, and he actively lived through and described much Oregon history, especially in the years 1852-1910. His activities ranged from giving innumerable scholarly speeches about the Oregon country to participating in the writing and editing of vanity publications. He served as editor of Oregon's most distinguished newspaper and was the first president of the Oregon Historical Society.   C. C. Gorchels

2044. Newman, S. H., III. THE LAS VEGAS WEEKLY MAIL. *New Mexico Hist. R. 1969 44(2): 155-166.* Describes the efforts of M. A. "Ash" Upson to publish a democratic newspaper, the *Weekly Mail,* in Las Vegas, New Mexico. Upson managed just eight issues before turning the paper over to Simeon Harrison Newman. Newman was indicted under an omnibus bill in 1872 for having published a libel. From his cell, Newman attempted to edit the paper, but its demise was announced on 27 August 1872. Newman was eventually convicted and fined 100 dollars. 42 notes.   D. F. Henderson

2045. Ophus, John. CHAFFEE COUNTY EDITORS. *Colorado Mag. 1966 43(3): 225-236.* A discussion of the editors who guided the major newspapers of Chaffee County, Colorado, during the 1880's and 1890's. One of the most important papers, the *Salida Mail,* began in 1880 and is still published today as the *Mountain Mail.* Editors came from many different eastern states and many different occupations. Some were teachers, others were lawyers and merchants, and a few were newspapermen. Whatever their political philosophy, they were all outspoken and believed in the growth potential of their own areas. Documentation mainly from contemporary newspapers, correspondence, and interviews with relatives of the editors; illus., 58 notes.   R. Sexauer

2046. Pettit, Arthur G. MARK TWAIN'S ATTITUDE TOWARD THE NEGRO IN THE WEST, 1861-1867. *Western Hist. Q. 1970 1(1): 51-62.* The climax of Samuel Langhorne Clemens' personal race prejudice occurred during the years 1861-67 when he was in Nevada, California, and Hawaii. Also, in these years he assumed Mark Twain as his nom de plume as "white spokesman for the foolish, half-witted, slaphappy 'darky' of longstanding minstrel tradition." His racist views can be traced at least as far back as his boyhood apprenticeship to his hometown newspaper. When he went to Nevada in 1861 he found it expedient to become a "Unionized Southerner," but he did not feel compelled to change his convictions about blacks. Although a piece which he composed for a Virginia City paper while drunk showed his true feelings and forced him to flee from California, he continued to use the press as an outlet for his views. When he went to Hawaii as correspondent for a Sacramento paper, he referred to the natives as "niggers." Clemens' western experience reveals the distance he had yet to travel before he became basically liberal in his attitudes about blacks. Returning to the East in 1867, he began to evaluate his extreme feelings and soon launched a new career of liberal lip service to blacks. Most, but not all, of his violent prejudice was left behind in the West. 19 notes.   D. L. Smith

2047. Ryan, Pat M. TRAIL-BLAZER OF CIVILIZATION: JOHN P. CLUM'S TUCSON AND TOMBSTONE YEARS. *J. of Arizona Hist. 1965 6(2): 53-70.* An excerpt from a forthcoming book by Yale University Press. The author treats the experiences of John P. Clum in Tucson and Tombstone, Arizona after he resigned as Indian agent at the San Carlos Agency in 1877. Clum published the *Arizona Citizen* at Tucson and Florence, in 1880 started the *Tombstone Epitaph,* and later held various municipal offices. Included is an account of the Clanton-Earp street fight (the gunfight at the O. K. Corral), and six pictures, one being a reproduction of Clum's oath of office as mayor of Tombstone. Many primary sources are cited, the most valuable being the Clum materials in the Division of Special Collections, University of Arizona Library, 63 notes.   J. D. Filipiak

2048. Sageser, A. Bower. JOSEPH L. BRISTOW: THE EDITOR'S ROAD TO POLITICS. *Kansas Hist. Q. 1964 30(2): 153-162.* Bristow (1861-1944) was born in Kentucky but came to Kansas as a boy. He planned to become a pastor, but his interests in journalism were aroused when he edited his college paper. He began to operate a local paper and returned to this profession after some effort to study law. As a publisher in Salina, Kansas he became interested in the problem of irrigation, joined many organizations to sponsor this movement; and tried to use the irrigation issue as a means of winning national office. He increased his reputation during the McKinley-Roosevelt era by uncovering a series of postal frauds. His newspaper in Salina became identified with the Progressive cause during the early days of this century; by 1908 the way was open for his election to the US Senate. Based largely on Bristow's personal papers and local Kansas newspapers.   W. F. Zornow

2049. Schmidt, Paul C. THE PRESS IN NORTH DAKOTA. *North Dakota Hist. 1964 31(4): 216-222.* County newspapers were essential in Dakota Territory because homesteaders were required to run proof notices for five consecutive weeks to prove up their claims. This cost each homesteader from five to 15 dollars and kept many newspapers going. After the number of homesteaders declined, about 1919, the number of newspapers dwindled. During the period of 1880 to 1919 newspapers gave publicity to townsites, promoted immigration, praised their communities' weather, civic achievements, and economic prospects. By 1919 the Nonpartisan League's program successfully reduced the legal advertising for the weekly press and set up a newspaper in each county and its own press association. The result was survival of only the best and most competently managed newspapers. 13 notes.   I. W. Van Noppen

2050. Smith, Dwight L. THE NIMS AND CZAR INCIDENTS IN THE DENVER PRESS. *Colorado Mag. 1971 48(1): 49-58.* Analyzes the coverage by the Denver newspapers in 1889-90 of the survey of the Colorado River by Robert Brewster Stanton as a possible route for a low-grade railroad, the Denver, Colorado Cañon and Pacific. The *Denver Times* apparently printed fabricated material about the fate of the survey party when the party's photographer, Frederick A. Nims, was injured. The *Rocky Mountain News* attempted, unsuccessfully, to smear Stanton as incompetent and dictatorial in outlook. Yet from those newspapers and the *Denver Republican,* "the history of the entire expedition might well be reconstructed." 3 photos, 22 notes.   O. H. Zabel

2051. Splitter, Henry Winfred. NEWSPAPERS OF LOS ANGELES: THE FIRST FIFTY YEARS, 1851-1900. *J. of the West 1963 2(4): 435-458.* Outlines the history of typical papers of the Los Angeles area and describes their development, purposes, contents, and makeup, as well as the editor and his impact. The first paper, the *STAR,* began publishing in 1851 and had a Spanish language supplement. The *Daily Express* (now merged with the *Herald-Examiner)* is the oldest paper in Los Angeles. Papers of this time had monetary difficulties and changed hands frequently. But they served a definite cultural and scholarly need and involved such personalities as Colonel Harrison Gray Otis and reporter Charles F. Lummis. Makeup was different, with ads on the front page and no headlines. During this period columnists appeared, pictures were used for the first time, modern comics began, and advertising became the major source of newspaper revenue. The editor himself was a kindly-regarded jack-of-all-trades, and his office was a public gathering place. Based mostly on newspapers; 32 notes. K. P. Davis

2052. Vorpahl, Ben Merchant. A SPLENDID LITTLE WAR: FREDERIC REMINGTON'S REACTIONS TO THE 1898 CUBAN CRISIS AS REVEALED THROUGH HIS LETTERS TO OWEN WISTER. *Am. West 1972 9(2): 28-35.* Frederic Remington (1861-1909) was a correspondent in Cuba during the Spanish-American War. He was attracted to the war by a love for physical action and adventure. His accounts were concerned with excitement and action, with no attempt at analysis or interpretation. He saw in the war the same kind of excitement that had conquered the West. Increasingly, however, he changed his mind on this point and came to view the war as a historian. Excerpted from a forthcoming book. 6 illus. D. L. Smith

2053. Weber, Francis J. A CALIFORNIA MINIOGRAPHY. *California Hist. Q. 1972 51(1): 85-89.* An annotated listing of 30 miniature books on California. The books exemplify the craftsmanship involved in creating miniature letters, illustrations, and binding. Issued in limited editions, the books cover such topics as the 1879 constitutional convention, pioneer printers, and the California missions. Photos. A. Hoffman

2054. Weber, Francis J. CATHOLIC JOURNALISM IN CALIFORNIA. *Southern California Q. 1964 46(2): 169-177.* Gives names of newspapers and their editors. Includes some of the many periodicals such as the *Serra Bulletin* and the *Western Jesuit.* An appendix lists a preliminary checklist 1853-1963 with titles, years, founders, and places. Documented. E. P. Stickney

2055. West, William Lemore. THE MOSES HARMAN STORY. *Kansas Hist. Q. 1971 37(1): 41-63.* After his arrival in Kansas in 1879, Moses Harman (1830-1910) became involved with the Valley Falls Liberal League. Between 1880 and 1896 he served in Valley Falls, Lawrence, and Topeka as an editor of such journals as *The Kansas Liberal,* Valley Falls *Liberal,* and *Lucifer the Light Bearer.* In 1896 he moved to Chicago and continued his journal under the title, *The American Journal of Eugenics.* He made one final move (to Los Angeles) in 1908. The strong stand Harman took against existing governments, political parties, organized religions, and existing customs made him the target of much criticism and the defendant in many legal actions. Traces his journalistic career and his many bouts with the law. Based mainly on material from Harman's various newspapers; illus., 159 notes. W. F. Zornow

2056. —. [EDWIN B. HILL]. *Am. Book Collector 1967 18(2): 19-27.*
Goldstone, Adrian. THE SEARCH FOR EDWIN B. HILL, *p. 19.*
Muir, Gertrude Hill. EDWIN BLISS HILL: PIONEER PRIVATE PRINTER OF THE SOUTHWEST, *pp. 20-21.*
Myers, John Myers. A CHECK-LIST OF ITEMS PUBLISHED BY THE PRIVATE PRESS OF EDWIN B. HILL, *pp. 22-27.*
Edwin B. Hill began printing in 1882. From then until he died he printed small editions of poems, literary magazines, and books while living in Arizona. He published several of Thoreau's works as Thoreau wrote them. The check list contains 206 items and five sources of biographical information. D. Brockway

Photography

2057. Andrews, Ralph W. HE KNEW THE RED MAN. *Montana 1964 14(2): 2-12.* Between 1900 and 1920 Edward S. Curtis induced many tribes to reenact traditional and ancient ceremonies which he described and photographed for his 20-volume work, *The North American Indian,* extensively quoted here. S. R. Davison

2058. Booth, Larry; Olmsted, Roger; and Pourade, Richard F. PORTRAIT OF A BOOM TOWN: SAN DIEGO IN THE 1880S. *California Hist. Q. 1971 50(4): 363-394.* A pictorial essay of San Diego in the boom of the 1880's. The photographs reflect the excitement, growth, and sense of speculation experienced by San Diegans as thousands of people came to the city through means of drastically reduced passenger rates to invest and speculate in San Diego's future. The photographs illustrate the real estate barbeques, the budding streetcar lines, the Coronado hotel, and an assortment of incipient restaurants, merchandise stores, factories, and saloons. Even though the bubble burst, the boom years enhanced San Diego's potential. 34 photos. A. Hoffman

2059. Branda, Eldon S. PORTRAIT OF A COWBOY AS A YOUNG ARTIST. *Southwestern Hist. Q. 1967 71(1): 69-77.* Erwin Evans Smith (1886-1947) played cowboy as a lad in Texas and was consumed with the ambition of documenting the life and work of the cattlemen who were fast disappearing from the American scene. In a methodical fashion he worked as a cowboy to achieve authenticity, trained himself as a photographer to collect pictorial documentation, and was trained under artists and sculptors. That any of his clay models were ever cast in bronze or marble is doubtful. His some ten thousand photographic negatives, however, are works of art in themselves. They are regarded as the most sensitive and authentic pictorial record of cowboy life ever made. 34 notes. D. L. Smith

2060. Brinckerhoff, Sidney B. GRAPHIC ARTS ON THE ARIZONA FRONTIER: FRONTIER SOLDIERS IN ARIZONA. *J. of Arizona Hist. 1971 12(3): 167-182.* A picture essay of frontier soldiering in Arizona in the 1870's, 1880's, and 1890's. 19 photos. D. L. Smith

2061. Castles, Jean I. "BOXPOTAPESH" OF CROW AGENCY. *Montana 1971 21(3): 84-93.* During the first third of this century, Fred E. Miller (1868-1936) lived in the region of the Crow Reservation in southern Montana, recording anecdotes of the people and making photographs of them and their land. After his death, his 500 glass-plate negatives drifted into unsympathetic hands and were thrown onto the city dump; only a few, which had been made into prints, are preserved. His nickname, "High Kicker" (Boxpotapesh), he earned through his skill with a football while he was working with his Indian friends to interest them in sports. 13 photos. S. R. Davison

2062. Daniels, David. PHOTOGRAPHY'S WET-PLATE INTERLUDE IN ARIZONA TERRITORY: 1864-1880. *J. of Arizona Hist. 1968 9(4): 171-194.* In 1860 there were no photographers in the region called Arizona; yet, 10 years later there were many photographers in the territory who took tens of thousands of photographs. One reason for the spread of photography to Arizona was the replacement of the more primitive daguerreotype process by the wet-plate system. Almost all of the photographers in Arizona in the late 1860's and throughout the 1870's were nonresident, transient professionals who were drawn there by the chance to take unusual pictures. The Federal Government also authorized official photographers to accompany survey parties within Arizona. By 1880 photography changed in character with the introduction of the dry plate and films. Based largely on census returns and contemporary newspapers; illus., 9 photos, 37 notes. R. J. Roske

2063. Fuermann, George M. HOUSTON, 1880-1910. *Southwestern Hist. Q. 1967 71(2): 226-246.* The 16 pictures of this photographic essay concern the period of "municipal adolescence" of Houston. The first two decades of the 1880-1910 coverage of the pictures might be subtitled "the recuperative years," or the era in which the municipal government recovered from Reconstruction. A commentary locates and describes each of the scenes. 8 notes. D. L. Smith

2064. Hatch, Heather S. GRAPHIC ARTS ON THE ARIZONA FRONTIER: RAILROAD STATIONS AND ROUNDHOUSES. *J. of Arizona Hist. 1971 12(2): 101-111.* Thirteen photographs from the Henry and Albert Buehman Memorial Collection, Arizona Pioneers' Historical Society, depict railroad depots, roundhouses, and locomotives in Arizona and New Mexico in the 1880's. D. L. Smith

2065. Martinson, Arthur D. THE STORY OF A MOUNTAIN: A PICTORIAL HISTORY OF MOUNT RAINIER NATIONAL PARK. *Am. West 1971 8(2): 34-41.* George Vancouver made the first recorded discovery of Mount Rainier in May 1792 while exploring Puget Sound. He named it in honor of a friend and fellow officer in the British Royal Navy, Rear Admiral Peter Rainier. It was 40 years, however, before a white ventured into the area which now comprises the national park; he was a Hudson's Bay Company employee on a search for medicinal herbs. As the Pacific Northwest figured increasingly in the American frontier movement, scientific curiosity and political considerations made Mount Rainier more than a scenic wonder. The summit was conquered for the first time in 1870. With the advent of the transcontinental railroad, Mount Rainier shortly became a tourist mecca. Mount Rainier and the surrounding forest area became the Nation's fifth national park in 1899. 11 illus., 2 maps. D. L. Smith

2066. Miller, Alan Clark. LORENZO LORAIN: PIONEER PHOTOGRAPHER OF THE NORTHWEST. *Am. West 1972 9(2): 20-26.* While Lieutenant Lorenzo Lorain (1831-82) was stationed in the Pacific Northwest, 1856-61, he experimented with outdoor photography. His surviving photographs are rare historical documents of Army life, Indians, and Pacific Northwest scenes. 9 photos, biblio. D. L. Smith

2067. Olmsted, Roger; Weinstein, Robert A.; and Holliday, J. S. IN SAN FRANCISCO & THE MINES, 1851-1856. *Am. West 1967 4(3): 40-49.* A photographic essay of buildings, the waterfront, gold rush scenes, portraits, and other subjects of gold rush California, particularly of San Francisco and its environs, with explanatory captions. Map. D. L. Smith

2068. Olsen, Robert W., Jr. CLEM POWELL AND KANAB CREEK. *Kiva 1968 34(1): 41-50.* "Twice in 1872 Walter Clement Powell was in the canyon cut by Kanab Creek. Both times he was there in connection with the work of the Powell Survey. His job both times was to photograph this part of Arizona. The first trip was unsuccessful. The second trip was crowned with success." J

2069. Paher, Stanley W. TAKEN BY THE WIND: THE PHOTOGRAPHIC PORTRAIT OF SOME FORMERLY PROSPEROUS BOOMTOWNS - REMNANTS OF THE AGE OF BONANZA AND BORRASCA. *Am. West 1970 7(3): 9-17.* A 19-photograph essay, with captions and brief comments, of Nevada ghost towns of the 1860's-1910's era: Candelaria, Belmont, Goldfield, Fairview, and Rawhide. Excerpted from *Nevada Ghost Towns and Mining Camps* (Berkeley: Howell-North Books, 1970), by Stanley W. Paher. D. L. Smith

2070. Pattison, William D. COLLECTOR'S CHOICE: THE PHOTOGRAPHS OF A. J. RUSSELL. *Am. West 1969 6(3): 20-23.* In 1868 Andrew J. Russell became the official photographer for the Union Pacific Railroad. His pictorial record covers the route from Omaha to Sacramento. The author describes his discovery in 1960 of the Russell glass plate collection in the American Geographical Society library and his identification of Russell as the photographer. The pictures had been credited to Steven Sedgewick, a lyceum lecturer who had used them to illustrate his talks, and in whose estate they were found. Illus. D. L. Smith

2071. Peterson, Thomas H., Jr. GRAPHIC ARTS ON THE ARIZONA FRONTIER: A TOUR OF TUCSON - 1874. *J. of Arizona Hist. 1970 11(3): 179-201.* Selects 20 glass plate pictures from the thousands in the Henry and Albert Buehman Memorial Collection at the Arizona Pioneers' Historical Society. They were taken in Tucson, probably in November 1874. Presents the pictures as a tour of the territorial capital, identifies buildings, persons, and occasions, and keys their location to an accompanying map. D. L. Smith

2072. Richmond, Robert W. KANSAS THROUGH A CAMERA IN 1867: STEREOGRAPHS FROM ALEXANDER GARDNER'S PHOTOGRAPHIC ART GALLERY. *Am. West 1965 2(3): 51-57.* Alexander Gardner was a Mathew Brady-trained, wet-plate photographer. After seven years' experience with Brady in the Civil War period, Gardner headed west with his darkroom on wheels on a transcontinental journey. From mid-September through mid-October in 1867, his camera focused on scores of Kansas subjects. Illus. from a collection in the Kansas State Historical Society, biblio. note. D. L. Smith

2073. Row, A. Tracy. GRAPHIC ARTS ON THE ARIZONA FRONTIER: THE FACE OF EARLY PHOENIX. *J. of Arizona Hist. 1972 13(2): 109-122.* Presents some of the familiar landmarks of Phoenix, 1879-1907. From the collections of the Arizona Historical Society; 20 photos. D. L. Smith

2074. Sargent, Shirley. PICTURES FROM YOSEMITE'S PAST: GALEN CLARK'S PHOTOGRAPH ALBUM. *California Hist. Soc. Q. 1966 45(1): 31-40.* Discussion of a leather photograph album in the Yosemite Museum vault, presented to Galen Clark, Yosemite pioneer, by a party of travelers on 20 April 1866. Its pages are filled with pictures of the party and people of note, among them many well-known Californians and many members of Clark's family. Galen Clark was a member of the original board of Yosemite commissioners appointed in 1864. Illus., 19 notes. E. P. Stickney

2075. Ulph, Owen. NO TRADE FOR HEROES: ANDREW ALEXANDER FORBES AND THE LIFE OF THE WORKING COWBOY. *Am. West 1968 5(4): 13-23.* Seldom do historians challenge the generally accepted truism that cattle ranching and cowpunching were among the most glamorous activities of the old West. That it was hard and hazardous work is indicated by a few, but reality is not sufficiently stressed. Realistically, cow business was "tough, tedious, monotonous drudgery." For the cattleman it meant "unending risks and uncertain returns." The cowhand could be sure of long hours, poor pay, bad food, unsatisfactory living conditions, and little diversion. Grubby descriptions of the cowboy's plight are hard to come by simply because he refused to be pitied or to permit his name to be associated with human exploitation and misery. Indeed he developed "a sardonic respect for the malevolent and the perverse that bordered on masochistic affection for all forms of affliction." From 1890 to 1910, Andrew Alexander Forbes, an itinerant photographer, traveled over the Southwest. His unembellished photographs reflect the characteristics of ranch life more accurately than can any garnished prose. The author's text is illustrated by 13 Forbes photographs and a Forbes self-portrait. D. L. Smith

2076. Webb, Tedd. TEXAS VICTORIAN. *Art in Am. 1969 57(4): 96-99.* A photographic essay documenting the happy alliance of two seemingly incompatible life-styles, those of Texas and Victorianism. The Texas Architectural Survey, sponsored by the Amon Carter Museum and the School of Architecture of the University of Texas, recently generated an interest in architecture as a visual history of Texas. Among the results of this effort was an exhibit of Tedd Webb's photographs, from which these photographs come. 7 photos. W. D. Chauvin

2077. Weinstein, Robert and Olmsted, Roger. EPIC ON GLASS. *Am. West 1967 4(1): 10-23.* Andrew Joseph Russell had served as official photographer for the U.S. Military Roads Construction Corps during the Civil War. In 1868 he left his private photographic studio in the East to become official photographer for the Union Pacific Railroad then building westward across the Great Plains. From hundreds of wetplate collodion negatives that he made, 13 views are here reproduced. The plates are in the archives of the American Geographical Society. D. L. Smith

2078. Weinstein, Robert A. GOLD RUSH DAGUERREOTYPES. *Am. West 1967 4(3): 33-39, 71-72.* In 1839 the first workable solution for fixing a permanent photochemical image on metal was discovered by Louis Jacques Daguerre. Almost at once daguerreotypy spread throughout Western Europe and America. Surviving daguerrean views of all early American cities of importance abound. As the technical aspects were perfected the daguerreotypes improved. San Francisco and the gold rush of 1849 are more thoroughly documented through this medium than any other city or activity. Biographical information is given about some of the photographers and their pictures are examined for the detailed documentary contributions which they make. The bibliographical note locates the principal daguerreotype collections. 23 illus., biblio. note.

D. L. Smith

2079. Weinstein, Robert A.   GOLD WAS FOR THE YOUNG. *California Hist. Soc. Q. 1970 49(4): 352-interleaves.* Commentary and 16-page picture portfolio on gold rush history. The illustrations include 49ers, various types of mining, San Francisco buildings, and the expansion of the Wells, Fargo and Company in express and banking. 13 illus., 21 photos.

A. Hoffman

2080. Weinstein, Robert A. and Olsted, Roger.   IMAGE MAKERS OF THE COLORADO CANYONS. *Am. West 1967 4(2): 28-39.* Photographers have been associated with expeditions into and through the Grand Canyon of the Colorado River in Arizona since 1871. Their efforts have given the world, except for those who have visited the rims and the fewer who have climbed down into its depths, its impressions of this spectacle of nature. This picture essay illustrates the text which lists some of the photographers and describes methods used as well as the difficulties of working in the area.

D. L. Smith

2081. Weinstein, Robert A. and Belous, Russell E.   INDIAN PORTRAITS: FORT SILL, 1869. *Am. West 1966 3(1): 50-63.* Solely for his personal satisfaction, William S. Soule left home in Boston in 1869 to photograph the Indians of the western Plains. With few photographic or daguerreotype records of Plains Indians made before Soule, he must be regarded as a pioneer in this form of documentation. The 14 photographs in this picture essay were made from the wet-plate collodion negatives taken at Fort Sill, Oklahoma Territory, in 1869, now in the collection of the Los Angeles County Museum.

D. L. Smith

2082. Weinstein, Robert A.   LUMBER SHIPS AT PUGET SOUND. *Am. West 1965 2(4): 50-63.* Photographic material is coming into its own as documentary evidence for the historian. Important and heretofore neglected collections are being recognized for their worth, finding their way into archives and libraries. The William Hester collection documents the men and the sailing ships involved in the considerable lumber export trade of the Pacific Northwest at the close of the 19th century. A representative sampling from the collection of some four thousand glass negatives at the San Francisco Maritime Museum are used as illustrations.

D. L. Smith

2083. Weinstein, Robert A.   THIS ISLAND SANTA CATALINA WAS A JEWEL IN THE SEA . . . *California Hist. Q. 1972 51(3): 244-252.* A photographic essay showing Avalon and its environs on Santa Catalina Island. Since the late 19th century, Santa Catalina, off Los Angeles, has served as a resort area. The photographs trace the island's evolution from rustic hideaway to famous tourist attraction. No source for the photographs was given. 9 photos.

A. Hoffman

2084. —.   ANSEL ADAMS AND THE NATIONAL PARKS. *Am. West 1969 6(5): 17-24, 41-48, 65-72.* Presents three portfolios of the photographic artistry of Ansel Adams (b. 1902), which portray the sweep and wonder, the power and the glory, of America's wilderness landscapes. The 17 illustrations presented herein are "a tribute and a counterpoint to the beauty of our national parks."

D. L. Smith

2085. —.   DESCENT INTO THE SAVAGE: 1867. *Am. West R. 1967 1(1): 20-21.* Discusses one aspect of the life of Timothy O'Sullivan, photographer. He was the official photographer for Clarence King's geological exploration of the 40th parallel. Having learned his trade from Matthew Brady, his training was put to good use in the Civil War and then in the West. The King expedition left San Francisco late in the spring of 1867 and headed east. A stopover was made at Virginia City to look at its mines and mineral production. One of the most successful mines was the Savage. Gathering up his voluminous equipment he "descended to the mine's bottom most depths" to take the first underground mining photographs in history. Illus.

O. L. Miller

2086. —.   GRAPHIC ARTS ON THE ARIZONA FRONTIER: MINING IN ARIZONA. *J. of Arizona Hist. 1970 11(1): 23-31, (2): 115-125.* Part I. Presents 13 captioned photos from the Henry and Albert Buehman Memorial Collection at the Arizona Pioneers' Historical Society. They were taken in 1879 and the 1880's and concern various aspects of mining on the Arizona frontier. Part II. Albert Buehman, pioneer photographer, traveled with mule, photographic wagon, and primitive equipment to mining operations throughout Arizona. Shows 15 captioned photographs taken in the last three decades of the 19th century.

D. L. Smith

2087. —.   JOHN ALVIN ANDERSON, FRONTIER PHOTOGRAPHER. *Nebraska Hist. 1970 51(4): 469-480.* A selection of the photographic work of Anderson (1869-1948) pertaining to the history of Nebraska in the late 19th century.

R. Lowitt

Art and Architecture

2088. Adams, Ansel.   FREE MAN IN A FREE COUNTRY: THE WEST OF MAYNARD DIXON, WITH A SELECTION OF HIS PAINTINGS AND POEMS, AND AN ESSAY ON UNDERSTANDING. *Am. West 1969 6(6): 40-47.* In middle age, self-taught book and magazine illustrator Maynard Dixon (1875-1946) tired of city life and sought the comparative peace of life in Utah and Arizona. In his paintings, drawings, and murals, he caught the spirit of the land and its people, particularly that of the Indian, the pioneer, and the Spanish American. His style developed as "a sparse, acrid, but compassionate statement" of the arid beauty of the Southwest. 9 illus.

D. L. Smith

2089. Amaral, Anthony.   A DEDICATION TO THE MEMORY OF WILL JAMES, 1892-1942. *Arizona and the West 1968 10(3): 206-210.* Will James (born Ernest Dufault in French Canada) left home as a young boy to become a western cowboy. After about a decade of drifting among western ranches and cow camps, serving a prison term for rustling cattle, and stunting in movies, he married and settled down to a career of writing and illustrating. He produced prodigious quantities of illustrated articles on cowboys for numerous books and leading national magazines. *Lone Cowboy,* a fabricated autobiography, gained him tremendous popularity. He became a legendary figure to his fans, principally in the East, in the 1920's and 1930's. As indebtedness, family difficulties, and alcohol became personal problems, they affected his writings and career. James's earlier writings and art were his best. Illus., appended with a selected list of his books.

D. L. Smith

2090. Barrows, Wray.   THE COHN MANSION - FOLSOM, CALIFORNIA. *Western States Jewish Hist. Q. 1968 1(1): 14-19.* Deals with the bizarre architectural tastes of the builder and longtime occupant of a large house in Folsom, Phillip C. Cohn, a California State senator 1913-16. Treats the Jewish community of Folsom, which was founded in 1860. Mentions Cohn's father-in-law, Simon Cohn, a general merchant in Folsom, and Jacob Hyman, also of Folsom. 2 photos, 4 notes, biblio.

R. E. Levinson

2091. Beeler, Joe.   AN ARTIST LOOKS AT THE AMERICAN INDIAN. *Montana 1964 14(2): 83-90.* Compares various western tribes in regard to facial features, physique, and personal characteristics.

S. R. Davison

2092. Boileau, Thornton I. and Boileau, Margot.   JOE SCHEUERLE: MODEST MAN WITH FRIENDLY PALETTE. *Montana 1971 21(4): 39-58.* Presents 33 portraits of western Indians, painted by Scheuerle (1873-1948) between 1896 and 1938. Scheuerle was brought to America as a child and received early art training. He was a skilled commercial artist, and the Indian portraits reflect a personal hobby. He was a close friend and frequent companion of Charles M. Russell, Louis Hill (president of the Great Northern Railway), Buffalo Bill Cody, and many Indian notables including Red Cloud. Only genuine modesty and dislike of publicity kept him from greater fame during his lifetime.

S. R. Davison

2093. Burkhalter, Lois.   "MY REAL FRIEND, JOE." *Am. Heritage 1965 16(3): 44-45.* A George Catlin portrait highlights this account of Catlin's "real friend," Joe Chadwick, who had nursed the artist during a cholera attack on the plains. When they met over a year later Catlin painted the portrait of Chadwick. The latter went to fight for the Texans in their revolt against Mexico and was killed in the Goliad massacre 27 March 1836.　　　　　J. D. Filipiak

2094. Coke, Van Deren. THE WORLD OF ART: A SAINT-CARVER IN NEW MEXICO. *Art in Am. 1965 53(1): 124-127.* Reviews the revival of the ancient art form, the santo, by José Mondragon. Illus.　　　　　W. K. Bottorff

2095. Connally, Ernest Allen. TEXAS ARCHITECTURE. *Historic Preservation 1964 16(6): 220-228.* The French found ruins in Texas of two buildings from a Spanish lost colony, one dated 1588. With the French establishment founded by La Salle in 1685, the continuous European architectural tradition began. The author surveys the 18th-century buildings, and then carries the Anglo-American "overlay" on this Spanish and Mexican province from 1812 to 1890. Illus.　　　　　E. P. Stickney

2096. Cutright, Paul R. LEWIS AND CLARK PORTRAITS AND PORTRAITISTS. *Montana 1969 19(2): 37-53.* Attempts to account for all the known portraits of Meriwether Lewis and William Clark and to identify the artists who created these pictures of the explorers. Those named are Joseph Bush, George Catlin, Chester Harding, John W. Jarvis, Charles Willson Peale, and Charles B. J. F. de Saint-Mémin. In addition to comments on the work produced by these artists, mention is made of pictures whose creators are not known, including some that appear to be spurious. Illus., 28 notes.　　　　　S. R. Davison

2097. Demos, John. GEORGE CALEB BINGHAM: THE ARTIST AS SOCIAL HISTORIAN. *Am. Q. 1965 17(2, Part 1): 219-228.* Two major categories, "town society" and "river society," serve to divide Bingham's perceptions of frontier society along the Missouri River. Bingham generally depicted town dwellers engaged in intense political democracy and rivermen frolicking or relaxing on their boats. For Bingham, the two groups illustrated the "social apartheid of river towns." Squatters, fur-traders and others whom Bingham portrayed typified divergent groups intent on expressing their own brand of integrity in frontier America. 6 illus., 13 notes.　　　　　R. S. Pickett

2098. Dieterich, Herbert R., Jr. THE ARCHITECTURE OF H. H. RICHARDSON IN WYOMING: A NEW LOOK AT THE AMES MONUMENT. *Ann. of Wyoming 1966 38(1): 49-53.* Discusses the monument erected to the memory of Oakes Ames and Oliver Ames, Jr. by the Union Pacific Railroad near the old town of Sherman, Wyoming. Designed by Henry Hobson Richardson, the granite monument has plaques of the Ames brothers done by the sculptor Augustus Saint-Gaudens. This monument is the only work done by Richardson west of St. Louis. It is considered as representative of his work and helped to establish him as the leading American architect of the day. Based on published secondary material; illus., 13 notes.　　　　　R. L. Nichols

2099. DuPlessix, Francine and Gray, Cleve. MUSEUMS: THOMAS GILCREASE AND TULSA. *Art in America 1964 52(3): 64-73.* Reviews the career of Thomas Gilcrease, the founder of Tulsa's Gilcrease Museum. Its five thousand paintings and statues are represented in the article by pictures of works by Remington, C. W. Peale, West, Whistler, Inness, Eakins, and others. Illus.　　　　　W. K. Bottorff

2100. Dykes, Jeff C. TENTATIVE BIBLIOGRAPHICAL CHECK LISTS OF WESTERN ILLUSTRATORS. LORENCE F. BJORKLUND. *Am. Book Collector 1970 20(3): 19-23.* A list of 11 books illustrated by Bjorklund and of two books about him, together with tips on collecting him. Illus.　　　　　D. Brockway

2101. Dykes, Jeff C. TENTATIVE BIBLIOGRAPHIC CHECK LISTS OF WESTERN ILLUSTRATORS. RUFUS FAIRCHILD ZOGBAUM. *Am. Book Collector 1968 19(2): 25-28.* A check list of 47 books illustrated by Rufus Fairchild Zogbaum (1849-1925) and 10 biographical sources together with tips about collecting his work. Illus.　　　　　D. Brockway

2102. Dykes, Jeff. TENTATIVE BIBLIOGRAPHIC CHECK LISTS OF WESTERN ILLUSTRATORS. *Am. Book Collector 1966-67 17(1): 24-25, (2): 15-19, (4): 18-21, 1967 17(5): 15-19, (6): 11-13, (7): 17-19, and (8): 17-20.* Lists books by E. M. (Buck) Schiwetz, Frank

E. Schoonover, Charles Schreyvogel, Elmer Boyd Smith, Herbert Morton Stoops, Edward Howard Suydam, and John William Thomason, Jr., with sources and tips on collecting them.　　　　　D. Brockway

2103. Dykes, Jeff C. TENTATIVE BIBLIOGRAPHIC CHECK LISTS OF WESTERN ILLUSTRATORS. *Am. Book Collector 1963-66 13(8): 21-27, (9/10): 40-45, 14(1): 40-42, (2): 29-31, (3): 25-29, (4): 19-23, 1964 14(5): 9-12, (6): 25-28, (7): 25-28, (8): 27-29, (9): 25-27, (10): 58-61, 15(1): 19-21, (2): 22-26, (3): 27-29, (4): 22-27, 1965 15(5): 10-13, (6): 28-32, (7): 26-28, (8): 25-32, (9): 17-21, (10): 34-36, 16(1): 8-11, (2): 7-10, (3): 20-31, (4): 22-31, 1966 16(5): 26-31, (6): 34-39, (7): 21-28, (8): 23-25, (9): 12-13, (10): 23-28.* A series of lists of books which contain illustrations by the following artists: Ernest L. Blumenschein (1874-1960), Edward Borein (1872-1947), Harold D. Bugbee (1900-63), Will Crawford (b. 1869), Harold Cue, Edward Willard Deming (b. 1860), Mayard Dixon (1875-1946), Harvey T. Dunn (b. 1884), W. Herbert (Buck) Dunton (1878-1936), Nick Eggenhofer, Robert Farrington Elwell (1874-1962), Anton Otto Fischer (1882-1962), Thomas Fogarty (1873-1938), Philip R. Goodwin (b. 1882), Peter Hurd (b. 1904), D. C. Hutchinson, Will James (1892-1942), Frank Tenney Johnson (1874-1939), Arthur Ignatius Keller (1867-1924), William Henry Dethlep Koerner (d. 1938), Tom Lea (b. 1907), William Robinson Leigh (1866-1955), Fernand Harvey Lungren (1859-1932), John N. Marchand (1875-1921), Don Luis Perceval (fl. 19c.), Frederic Remington (1861-1909), Clarence Rowe (b. 1878), Ross Santee (1888-1965).　　　　　D. Brockway

2104. Dykes, Jeff C. TENTATIVE BIBLIOGRAPHIC CHECK LISTS OF WESTERN ILLUSTRATORS: THREE TEXAS ILLUSTRATORS. *Am. Book Collector 1967 17(10): 17-22.* A check list of 10 books illustrated or written by Jerry Bywaters, 4 biographical sources; of 53 books illustrated by Jose Cisneros, 3 biographical sources; and of 18 books illustrated by Ben Carlton Mead, 1 biographical source. There are tips about collecting the works of each. Illus.　　　　　D. Brockway

2105. Dykes, Jeff C. TENTATIVE BIBLIOGRAPHIC CHECK LISTS OF WESTERN ILLUSTRATORS. *Am. Book Collector 1967 18(4): 26-27.* One of a series of checklists of books and their illustrators. There are four illustrated by Dan Muller with one biographical source and 13 books illustrated by Walter Shelley Phillips with three biographical sources and tips about collecting each. Illus.　　　　　D. Brockway

2106. Edwards, Malcolm. "SUBSTANTIAL, FIRE-PROOF EDIFICES..." MADE SO BY THE MARVELOUS INVENTION OF IRON DOOR AND WINDOW SHUTTERS. *California Hist. Q. 1971 50(4): 431-437.* The major danger experienced by California gold rush towns came from the threat of fire. Built of wood and populated by cigar-smoking men who used lanterns and open hearths, towns were destroyed and rebuilt several times over. To combat the spread of fire from one building to another, structures were built of more permanent materials such as brick and masonry. To safeguard the wooden portions of these buildings, the owners installed iron shutters on doors and windows. In addition to their service in preventing the spread of fire, the shutters also provided protection from intruders. Door latches of varying sophistication were attached to the shutters. San Francisco and Sacramento were centers of shutter manufacture, but local blacksmiths also made them. The shutters proved so durable that many were rescued from ghost towns and used on buildings in subsequent mining settlements. Despite the protection afforded by iron shutters, people in their haste frequently forgot to close them when fire threatened. Photos.　　　　　A. Hoffman

2107. Ellsberg, William. CHARLES, THOU ART A RARE BLADE. *Am. West 1969 6(2): 4-9; (3): 40-43, 62.* Part I. Working in Great Falls, Montana, to replenish his depleted funds to continue his studies at the university, the author met cowboy Charles M. Russell, painter of the Indian and cowboy West. From this chance encounter in 1915 when the author was 18, there developed an intimate friendship. In this reminiscence are recounted impressions of the man and his artistry, his character, and his humaneness. 8 illus. Part II. Refutes the estimate of art critics that Russell lacked versatility by indicating the great variety of objects, animate and inanimate, that were subjects of his efforts and the endless mediums he used for his creations. He employed almost any materials available for his sculptures. Also refuted is the assertion that Russell could not draw the female figure. 6 illus.　　　　　D. L. Smith

2108. Ewers, John C. "CHIEFS FROM THE MISSOURI AND MISSISSIPPI" AND PEALE'S SILHOUETTES OF 1806. *Smithsonian J. of Hist. 1966 1(1): 1-26.* In response to an invitation to visit the United States issued by President Thomas Jefferson in 1803 with the intention of cementing relations with the Indians of the territory of the Louisiana Purchase, numerous tribes sent delegates eastward in the years immediately following. The second large contingent visited Washington and other centers in the winter of 1805-06. While in Philadelphia, the profiles of many of the members of the party were drawn by the renowned artist Charles Willson Peale. Ten of these silhouettes survive in the collections of the Smithsonian Institution and the author here identifies some of them while telling the story of their journey and of Peale's work. Among the more prominent of the men identified are Sagessaga, or the Wind, head chief of the Little Osage, and two interpreters, Paul Chouteau and Joseph Barron. Based on contemporary manuscript sources and newspaper accounts as well as on the 10 surviving profiles which form a part of the 15 illustrations. 89 notes.   J. J. McCusker

2109. Ewers, John C. CYRUS E. DALLIN, MASTER SCULPTOR OF THE PLAINS INDIAN. *Montana 1968 18(1): 35-43.* Biography of a versatile sculptor whose work ranged from notable figures of Western Indians to the angel Maroni atop the Mormon Temple in Salt Lake City. Coming from the Utah village of Springville, he met difficulty in finding acceptance in the East, but in his lifetime was recognized abroad as well as in America. Much of his work was done in Europe and New England on a variety of historical subjects; he is best known for his statues of Indians.   S. R. Davison

2110. Ewers, John C. A UNIQUE PICTORIAL INTERPRETATION OF BLACKFOOT INDIAN RELIGION IN 1846-1847. *Ethnohist. 1971 18(3): 231-238.* "Sometime in 1846 or 1847 a Blackfoot Indian artist painted for Father Nicolas Point, S.J., an unsigned watercolor depicting various aspects of Blackfoot Indian religious beliefs. The details of this painting are interpreted here for the first time."   J

2111. Ewers, John C. WINOLD REISS: HIS PORTRAITS AND PROTEGES. *Montana 1971 21(3): 44-55.* Describes the work of Reiss (1888-1953), a leading painter of Blackfoot Indian portraits between 1919 and 1953, emphasizing his dedication to accuracy and his humane interest in the Blackfeet. Reiss' help and encouragement to young Indians led several into careers in art. Illus.   S. R. Davison

2112. Forrest, James Taylor. ROBERT OTTOKAR LINDNEUX: LAST OF COWBOY ARTISTS. *Great Plains J. 1966 6(1): 32-35.* Biography of Lindneux who was born in New York in 1871, studied art in Europe and returned to the United States at the turn of the century. He went West, worked as a cowboy, and painted the western scene - Rocky Mountains, Indians, whites, and animals - with great technical ability and a strong sense of the dramatic. His paintings are found in many major museums and private collections. At 96 he now lives in Denver.   O. H. Zabel

2113. Freed, Eleanor. TEXAS ROUNDUP. *Art in America 1968 56(5): 102-105.* An expanding interest in art, showing a "new urbanity," is apparent in such Texas galleries as Meredith Long and Co. (Houston) with a large collection of 19th- and 20th-century American paintings, Kiko Galleries (Houston) with a new international collection, Louisiana Gallery (Houston) with pre-Columbian art, Valley House (Dallas) with an outdoor gallery of sculpture, and other galleries in these cities and in Fort Worth. Illus.   W. K. Bottorff

2114. Freed, Eleanor. A WINDFALL FOR TEXAS. *Art in Am. 1969 57(6): 78-85.* The celebrated collection of 20th-century American paintings owned by the novelist James Albert Michener has been given to the University of Texas at Austin. The benefaction, unusual in that it was made to a university instead of a museum, has no limiting stipulations. Instead, the university is to make the widest possible use of it. The collection is made up of virtually unknown artists as well as celebrated ones such as John Marin, Thomas Hart Benton, Arthur Dove, Morris Louis, Max Weber, Larry Rivers, and Richard Anuszkiewicz. Illus.   W. D. Chauvin

2115. Goeldner, Paul. THE ARCHITECTURE OF EQUAL COMFORTS: POLYGAMISTS IN UTAH. *Historic Preservation 1972 24(1): 14-17.* Discusses the architecture adopted by polygamous Mormon families in Utah. Examples are few and usually unpretentious. In Midway are two houses built by John Watkins, an English convert and builder who had three wives. The first house contained three apartments, and his first wife continued to live there after the second house was finished. Built about 1868 of soft brick and symmetrical in design, the second house was so admired that Watkins and Moroni Blood, the carpenter who helped him, were commissioned to build several similar houses in Midway. Another example is the house built by Samuel Pierce Hoyt in Hoytsville in 1863. Mentions two of the houses used by Brigham Young and his many wives. They are the Beehive House (1853-55) and the adjoining Lion House (1856). Some houses contained "polygamy pits" - hiding places used to escape US marshals. Photos.   J. M. Hawes

2116. Goosman, Mildred. OLD GABE OF HER MAJESTY'S ENGLISH LIFE GUARDS. *Am. West 1969 6(6): 14-15.* When William Drummond Stewart traveled with the American Fur Company's cavalcade out of St. Louis in 1837 for the annual rendezvous in the Rocky Mountains, he took with him a cuirass and helmet of the English Life Guards. It was a gift to James Bridger, famed mountain man who was nicknamed "Old Gabe." Artist Alfred Jacob Miller, who was commissioned by Stewart to sketch and later make oil paintings of scenes and highlights of the rendezvous, sketched "Old Gabe" in the cuirass and helmet and mounted on a horse. Illus.   D. L. Smith

2117. Hamilton, Henry W. and Hamilton, Jean Tyree. REMINGTON SCHUYLER, ARTIST AND WRITER. *Missouri Hist. Soc. Bull. 1969 25(2): 118-122.* Remington Schuyler was a Western writer and artist. His poems, short stories, serials, and columns were widely read. Greater fame was achieved through his hundreds of magazine covers and illustrations, camouflage designs for ships, murals, book dust jacket sketches, and a variety of other illustrative materials. His favorite subjects for both his art and writing were Indians and the cattle country of the American West. Remington Schuyler employed about a dozen pen names, by-lines, and signatures. 8 illus.   D. L. Smith

2118. Hammer, Kenneth. THE PRAIRIE SOD SHANTY. *North Dakota Hist. 1968 35(1): 57-61.* Describes the construction and utilization of the sod shanty, sod house, dugout, and sod stables by the early homesteaders on the northern Great Plains. The "soddies," as these settlers were called, opened the plains in the 1870's and 1880's. 3 illus.   D. L. Smith

2119. Harkins, Michael J. GEORGE WASHINGTON LININGER: PIONEER MERCHANT AND ART PATRON. *Nebraska Hist. 1971 52(4): 347-357.* Examines the career of Lininger (1834-1907), who was a merchant, philanthropist, art patron, and politician. Lininger was partially responsible for fostering the development of art in Omaha in the late 19th century. His private gallery, constructed in 1888, became a center of the arts in the city for almost two decades. Some of the items he collected are now in the Joslyn Art Museum.   R. Lowitt

2120. Haverstock, Mary Sayre. HUDSON RIVER PAINTERS IN THE WEST. *Montana 1966 16(3): 65-73.* In 1870 three noted landscape painters spent the summer in the western mountains already made famous by Albert Bierstadt's work. These artists, Sanford R. Gifford, Worthington Whittredge and John Kensett, were impressed by the Rockies but used them only as backgrounds, leaving to Bierstadt and Thomas Moran the more sensational views of peaks and canyons. Illustrated with the subjects' paintings and their portraits.   S. R. Davison

2121. Heald, Weldon F. THOMAS MORAN: PAINTER OF GRANDEUR. *Montana 1965 15(4): 42-54.* An Irish immigrant boy became the most noted painter of western landscapes. Thomas Moran's dramatic pictures helped persuade Congress to establish Yellowstone National Park. Association with western explorers and surveyors led to his painting of Grand Canyon, Teton and Colorado scenes. Illustrated by portraits and his own art.   S. R. Davison

2122. Hogarth, Paul. OFF TO THE PLAINS! *Am. West 1968 5(6): 4-17.* Victorian Englishmen were given glimpses of the rest of the world from elaborately drawn illustrations which appeared in London's weekly picture papers supplied by their traveling staff artists. The *London Graphic* was one of the outstanding examples. Its reputation for the superior quality, faithfulness to reality, and value as works of art of its illustrations was worldwide. They were reprinted extensively throughout Europe and the United States. Pre-eminent as a "Special Artist," as these artist-reporters were called, was Arthur Boyd Houghton. An 1869-70 assignment in the United States resulted in 72 published illustrations, 34 of which are Western subjects—mainly confined to a visit to the Mormons in Utah, a buffalo hunt in Nebraska, and a Nebraska Pawnee agency. Usually they were accompanied by articles or short texts edited from Houghton's own descriptive notes. Their fidelity and realism are in contrast to the usual through-Victorian-eyes approach. 8 illus., biblio. note.　　　　　D. L. Smith

2123. Holzhuber, Franz. SKETCHES FROM NORTHWESTERN AMERICA AND CANADA. *Am. Heritage 1965 16(4): 49-64.* Holzhuber was an Austrian who came to America in 1856, bound for a job as a musical conductor in Milwaukee. He spent four years traveling up and down the Mississippi River area, sketching and making notes. His sketchbooks became the source for water colors and oils, many of which are reproduced here from those owned by the Glenbow Foundation of Calgary, Alberta.　　　　　J. D. Filipiak

2124. Howard, Brett. CHARLES RUSSELL, COWBOY ARTIST. *Mankind 1968 1(6): 24-31.* Charles Marion Russell became one of America's greatest artistic chroniclers of the westward movement, and ultimately he earned for himself the honorific, the "cowboy artist." Going west at the age of 16, Russell became part of the rapidly changing frontier. Developing his own painting techniques, he portrayed the transformation of western society and illustrated the passing of a great period in American history. Illus.　　　　　P. D. Thomas

2125. Hutchinson, W. H. THE MYTHIC WEST OF W. H. D. KOERNER. *Am. West 1967 4(2): 54-60.* William Henry David Koerner was a versatile artist-illustrator who gained considerable experience, skill, versatility, and notoriety by working on newspapers, designing packaging, and illustrating for some of the best popular periodicals of the day. He gravitated toward the *Saturday Evening Post* as that prestigious magazine increasingly used western stories. His cover paintings and illustrations for the *Post,* other magazines, and books, soon earned for Koerner, according to the author, status as "a great iconographer of the West." The authors he illustrated include all of the greats of the 1920's and 1930's. Koerner is credited with a significant role in creating the popular concepts of the period of the "West-That-Was." 6 Koerner illus.　　　　　D. L. Smith

2126. Jordan, Philip D. THE PEOPLE PAINT THE PLAINS. *Pacific Northwest Q. 1970 61(2): 94-100.* With special reference to the Joslyn Art Museum of Omaha, Nebraska, the author discusses the evolution of art forms in the United States and describes the work of some artists who sketched and painted the details of the landscape and people found in the trans-Missouri country during the year's 1833-1900. Included are illustrations of paintings by W. H. D. Koerner and Thomas Hart Benton.　　　　　C. C. Gorchels

2127. Kennedy, Michael S. W. H. D. KOERNER: PORTRAYER OF PIONEERS. *Montana 1965 15(1): 52-65.* Artist Koerner is receiving belated notice as an illustrator of western books and short stories. His oils and water colors preserve the more prosaic but important aspects of westward travel and settlement, in contrast to the abundance of pictures dealing with violence and excitement.　　　　　S. R. Davidson

2128. Kovinick, Phil. SOUTH DAKOTA'S "OTHER" BORGLUM. *South Dakota Hist. 1971 1(3): 207-230.* Describes Solon Hannibal Borglum (1868-1922), who visited South Dakota, lived and studied among its people, and created sculptures that won him recognition in the United States and Europe. Solon was referred to as "probably the most original sculptor of the American West that this country has produced." 2 illus., 46 notes.　　　　　D. H. Swift

2129. Krakel, Dean. MR. LEIGH AND HIS STUDIO. *Montana 1967 17(3): 40-59.* Recounts the circumstances of the removal of William R. Leigh's studio from New York City to the Thomas Gilcrease Institute of American History and Art in Tulsa, Oklahoma, after negotiations with the artist's heirs. Leigh spent much of his time in the southwestern United States, finding there the models for his favorite subjects - range horses and wild animals. Illus., photos.　　　　　S. R. Davison

2130. LeRoy, Bruce. MOSQUITOES, MULES, AND MEN. *Am. Heritage 1965 16(3): 102-107.* A dozen reproductions from the sketchbook of Alfred Downing are shown. He was a government topographer on several surveys of the Northwest from 1873 to 1883, and, though his sketches may not rate as good art, they illustrate a grasp of detail and a sense of humor. The sketchbook is now in the collection of the Washington State Historical Society in Tacoma.　　　　　J. D. Filipiak

2131. Miller, Nancy. THE EQUESTRIAN STATUE OF GEORGE WASHINGTON. *Idaho Yesterdays 1966 10(3): 16-19.* "The story of the statue of General Washington, carved by Charles Leopold Ostner (1828-1913), which has been on display for almost a century at the Idaho Statehouse." The statue was carved from Ponderosa pine over a 4-year period; only ordinary carpenter's saws and chisels were used. It was presented to the Idaho Territory on 8 January 1869. After surviving dry rot and vandalism for nearly 100 years on top of the capitol building, the statue was placed in a plate glass case for exhibition. 3 illus., 10 notes.　　　　　D. H. Swift

2132. Miller, Nancy. PIONEER PORTRAITS: CHARLES LEOPOLD OSTNER. *Idaho Yesterdays 1966 10(3): 12-15.* Features several paintings by the early Idaho artist, Charles Leopold Ostner (1828-1913). Examines Ostner's life, including his paintings of mining scenes and animals, particularly horses. The last 25 years of his life were spent traveling in Canada and Alaska. 4 illus.　　　　　D. H. Swift

2133. Monaghan, Jay. THE HUNTER AND THE ARTIST: A UNIQUE PARTNERSHIP IN THE DOCUMENTATION OF THE MOUNTAIN MAN'S WEST. *Am. West 1969 6(6): 4-13.* Alfred Jacob Miller was a young European-trained artist employed by a Scottish sportsman and big-game hunter, William Drummond Stewart, to accompany him on a fur brigade out of St. Louis. Stewart was known to most of the prominent mountain men and had already made a few trips to the fur-trading rendezvous in the Rocky Mountains. He took Miller along on the 1837 fur traders' caravan to record the scenery, the Indians, and the whites who traded and lived with them. Miller sketched well over one hundred scenes from which he made large oil paintings. On some of the sketches he made invaluable marginal notes of observations on the rendezvous and of his employer. When Stewart inherited a baronetcy, a castle, and considerable acreage, he called Miller to Scotland to finish the paintings. Stewart endeavoured to remake his piece of Scotland into the American West by such efforts as importing buffalo and Indians. Scottish rills, highland fens, and flora and fauna began to appear in modified form in Miller's portrayal of the West. Stewart's eccentric career and Miller's second-rate talents were an improbable combination, but they are inseparable. Without the other, each man's reputation would have been "a historical nonentity." 10 illus., biblio. note.　　　　　D. L. Smith

2134. Peterson, Charles. PREFABS IN THE CALIFORNIA GOLD RUSH, 1849. *J. of the Soc. of Architectural Historians 1965 24(4): 318-324.* During the rapid growth of San Francisco, induced by the gold rush, prefabricated buildings were imported from many sources: wooden frame houses came from Monterey, California, New York, Philadelphia, Hong Kong, New Zealand, and Tasmania; galvanized iron buildings were brought from New York, Manchester and Liverpool but soon proved unsuitable in the California climate. Based on memoirs and building trade journals. 11 illus.　　　　　D. McIntyre

2135. Richey, Elinor. WITH NEVER A ROVING EYE. *Mankind 1969 2(3): 43-49.* Alameda, California, has the largest concentration of Victorian houses in the West. The various forms of Victorian architecture in the city are examined, and attempts to maintain the pattern of 19th-century architecture in the area are reviewed. Illus.

P. D. Thomas

2136. Robinson, Willard B. HELENA'S FABULOUS BUSINESS BLOCKS. *Montana 1968 18(1): 44-59.* A study of the business blocks erected in Montana's capital city after a series of fires had proved the need for stone and mortar to replace flimsy original structures. By the mid-1880's, increased affluence permitted some attempt at magnificence. Local bricks and granite and homemade ornamental iron components were combined by Eastern architects to create an impressive if somewhat mongrel style. " . . . to avoid any appearance of the provincial, they had sought a derivative architecture that would create a metropolitan atmosphere."

Illustrations are original drawings of buildings which are still standing.
S. R. Davison

2137. Rogers, Fred B. A PAINTER IN MENDOCINO: SOME EARLY VIEWS OF CALIFORNIA'S REDWOOD COAST. *Am. West 1968 5(5): 36-40.* Artist Alexander Edouart was invited to join "a recreational excursion" of lawyers and government employees into the redwood country of northern California. On this jaunt and on a trip the following year (1858) Edouart visited and sketched an Indian reservation, the group he traveled with, and other scenes. Five of his sketches and an illustrated map are reproduced.
D. L. Smith

2138. Russell, Don. THOSE LONG-LOST CUSTER PANELS. *Pacific Historian 1967 11(4): 28-35.* An account of the tracking down of two side panels that had been painted as part of a work done by Cassily Adams (probably in 1885) of the Custer disaster at the Little Big Horn. A later reworking by a lithographer had omitted the side panels. Upon reading of the missing panels, two staff members of the Arizona Pioneers' Historical Society set about trying to find them and did so in their own museum. The author traces the route of the original painting through various cellars and warehouses until it burned with the Fort Bliss Officers' Club in 1946. Perhaps the painting is best known as a lithograph used as an advertisement by a beer company. Illus.
T. R. Cripps

2139. Scherger, R. H. E. W. (BILL) GOLLINGS: UNSUNG SAGEBRUSH ARTIST. *Montana 1965 15(2): 68-85.* This once obscure western artist is becoming recognized for his oils and etchings. Living quietly in Sheridan, Wyoming, after years of drifting, Gollings started painting with supplies obtained by mail order, and discovered that his work was commercially salable. From 1912 until his death in 1932 he devoted himself to art. Based largely on his autobiography in *Annals of Wyoming*, October 1932.
S. R. Davison

2140. Spaulding, Edward Selden, ed. and Parshall, Douglas. [CALIFORNIA ETCHINGS]. *Noticias 1967 Occasional Papers (9): [1-19].* A collection of etchings of Santa Barbara and California by artists who have lived in Santa Barbara. Acknowledges the influence and encouragement of Edward Borein (1872-1947) in the field, and provides an impression of him. 18 illus.
T. M. Condon

2141. Stehle, Raymond L. FIVE SKETCHBOOKS OF EMANUEL LEUTZE. *Q. J. of the Lib. of Congress 1964 21(2): 81-93.* Before painting the mural *Westward the Course of Empire Takes Its Way* above the west staircase of the Capitol, 1861-63, Emanuel Leutze made trips to the Rockies and Pacific Coast 1859-61. Letters written to the artist by Captain Montgomery C. Meigs (in charge of the Capitol Extension) and sketches preserved in five notebooks recently acquired by the Library shed light on the muralist's reputation, training, travels, techniques and associations, 1841-63. Letters bearing on other commissions - prospective or executed - are also published. Illus.
H. J. Graham

2142. Stenzel, Franz R. E. S. PAXSON, MONTANA ARTIST. *Montana 1963 13(4): 50-76.* Appreciation has recently increased for the paintings of Edgar S. Paxson, who worked in Montana some four decades preceding his death in 1919. Starting as a teamster and ranch hand, Paxson moved first to signpainting and card-lettering, later acquiring skill in water color and oil. His first studio was in Deer Lodge, his later ones in Butte and Missoula. Because of the belated recognition of his work, it is probable that many of his pictures remain unidentified and will yet be "discovered" in the hands of dealers, Montana families, and various individuals. Some of his best work is seen as murals at the State Capitol in Helena and in the Missoula County Courthouse, and in framed pictures at the Whitney Gallery in Cody, Wyoming. Based on information from the Paxson family and on material in Dr. Stenzel's collection of the artist's papers.
S. R. Davison

2143. Stone, Lois C. ANDREW JACKSON GRAYSON, ARTIST-NATURALIST OF THE PACIFIC SLOPE. *Am. West 1965 2(3): 19-31.* In 1846 Andrew Jackson Grayson and his family moved to California, where he became proprietor of a general store and bookshop, participated in civic affairs, panned gold, and painted birds. His first exposure to John James Audubon's *Birds of America* in 1853, turned him singlemindedly to pursue what until then was only "an amiable hobby." His paintings and ornithology became well-known through exhibitions and publications in California and Mexico. The collapse of Maximilian's Mexican empire ended his sponsorship of a magnum opus publication in folio, with hand-colored plates and texts in three languages. The untimely death of Grayson a few years later further removed fulfillment of the project. Based on manuscript materials and newspapers principally in the Bancroft Library, including colored illustrations. Excerpted from a forthcoming book. Biblio.
D. L. Smith

2144. Sully, Langdon. GENERAL SULLY REPORTS. *Am. Heritage 1964 16(1): 52-63.* Biographical sketch of Alfred Sully, a graduate of West Point who saw his first important service in the Mexican War. Sully later served in frontier California and in the Great Plains after the Civil War. A talented artist, Sully sketched as he soldiered, and the article is illustrated with his drawings and paintings.
H. F. Bedford

2145. Turner, Justin G. EMANUEL LEUTZE'S MURAL "WESTWARD THE COURSE OF EMPIRE TAKES ITS WAY." *Manuscripts 1966 18(2): 4-16.* Emanuel Leutze, German-born artist, was commissioned by the U.S. Government to paint a mural on the western wall of the Capitol. Leutze, painter of *Washington Crossing the Delaware, Washington Rallying the Troops at Monmouth,* and some 60 others, painted the mural entitled *Westward the Course of Empire Takes Its Way.* He wanted to present "the grand peaceful conquest of the great west" and in doing so he reflected his "love of adventure, hero worship, and fondness of wild lethal fun." Included are Leutze's notes on the Capitol mural. Illus., 31 notes.
C. J. Allard

2146. Viola, Herman J. INVITATION TO WASHINGTON - A BID FOR PEACE: AND, AS PART OF THE ARTFUL MANEUVER, CHARLES BIRD KING IS COMMISSIONED TO PAINT THE GUESTS' PORTRAITS. *Am. West 1972 9(1): 18-31.* Aroused by the activities of American traders and trappers in their midst and emboldened by the obvious inadequacy of the American military presence in the Upper Missouri River region, several roving tribes of restive Indians were posing a real threat in 1821. At his own suggestion, their agent led a delegation of chiefs and warriors from the more militant tribes to the national capital to obviate the risk of war through the use of diplomacy. They arrived in Washington in late November 1821. A tour of eastern cities, forts, arsenals, and navy yards, as well as audiences with the President, impressed both the delegation and their hosts. Prominent artists requested the Indians to sit for portraits. Charles Bird King was commissioned by the Federal government to make 25 portraits. The tribes represented in the delegation did remain relatively peaceful as white settlement reached the Upper Missouri. 10 illus., biblio.

D. L. Smith

2147. Welsch, Roger L. NEBRASKA'S ROUND BARNS. *Nebraska Hist. 1970 51(5): 49-92.* A survey and catalog of 36 round barns which the author has found in Nebraska. Terminology and the advantages and disadvantages of round barns are discussed by the author, who views them within the orbit of American folklore.
R. Lowitt

2148. Wilder, Mitchell A. A MUSEUM IN SEARCH OF THE WEST. *Am. West 1965 2(1): 54-58.* The Amon Carter Museum of Western Art was established in Fort Worth, Texas in 1961 "for the study and documentation of westering North America." The museum program includes exhibitions, publications, and permanent collections, principally of painting, sculpture, and photography. Illus.
D. L. Smith

2149. Wilkins, Thurman. MAJOR POWELL AND THOMAS MORAN IN CANYON COUNTRY. *Montana 1969 19(4): 16-31.* The artist Moran associated himself with John Wesley Powell in examining and describing the Grand Canyon area in the mid-1870's. Since they collaborated on magazine articles as well as on Powell's official report, the work of the painter and the explorer-photographer was mutually helpful. Usually Moran was able to make only photographs or preliminary sketches in the field, and he later produced his monumental oils in his studio. Based on correspondence, Powell's reports, and newspaper items; illus., 37 notes.
S. R. Davison

2150. Wood, Thomas and Hill, Douglas. THE COALVILLE TABERNACLE. *Dialogue: A J. of Mormon Thought 1967 2(2): 61-74.* The authors traveled several areas of Utah becoming immersed in the culture, history, and aesthetic value of various examples of Mormon

Church architecture. Hill photographed the structures and Wood attempted to classify, capture, and fix those buildings which seemed to be a unique mixture of history, geography, and art. Their most exciting discovery was the Coalville Tabernacle, almost a hundred years old, a "somewhat Victorian-Gothic structure with stained glass windows replete with Mormon motifs, a lavishly painted ceiling chased with ornamental designs, and scrollwork featuring commanding portraits of Hyrum Smith, Brigham Young, Wilford Woodruff, and John Taylor." Photos.   L. P. Hofeling

2151. —. BATTLE OF THE ARICKAREE (OR BEECHER ISLAND), SEPTEMBER 17-25, 1868. *Kansas Hist. Q. 1968 34(1): Frontispiece.* Four pages describe the battle between Brevet Colonel George A. Forsyth's 50 civilian scouts from Kansas and hundreds of Cheyenne and Sioux warriors on the Arickaree branch of the Republican River in what is now Yuma County, Colorado. It provides background material for the cover illustration "The Battle of the Arickaree (or Beecher Island)" by Robert Lindneux, a painting now owned by the State Historical Society of Colorado. Forsyth's six-page dispatch on 19 September is reproduced. 3 photos.   W. F. Zornow

2152. —. [BOREIN DRAWINGS AND VERSE]. *Noticias 1967 Occasional Papers (7): [1-29].* Drawings and verse by Edward (1872-1947) and Lucile Borein, mostly from Christmas cards the couple sent. The subjects are the West and California and include cowboys, burros, the De La Guerra *Casa Grande* in Santa Barbara, California, cattle drives, and wagon trains. Includes an etching made for the Rough Riders' reunion on Long Island in July 1910. 26 illus.   T. M. Condon

2153. —. BRINTON MEMORIAL BUILDS NEW GALLERY. *Hist. News 1965 20(10): 224.* Reports construction of a reception gallery at the Bradford Brinton Memorial ranch museum in Big Horn, Wyoming. The museum buildings, located on a former cattle ranch, house the Western art and Americana collections of the estate. Illus.
                                              D. L. Smith

2154. —. THE BUFFALO BILL MUSEUM IN CODY. *Art in Am. 1969 57(4): 100-103.* Discusses displays and the physical plant at the Buffalo Bill Historical Center at Cody, Wyoming, on the border of Yellowstone National Park. The new multimillion-dollar Buffalo Bill Museum adjoins the Whitney Gallery of Western Art. Among the artists represented are Remington, Russell, and Catlin. Summarizes Cody's life. Illus.   W. D. Chauvin

2155. —. A GALLERY OF HORSES: WITH SKETCHES AND CAPTIONS. *Am. West 1972 9(3): 32-35.* Presents 10 sketches selected from Frederick Remington's illustrated essay on the evolution of the American bronco, "Horses of the Plains," *Century,* January 1889. The captions are excerpted from his text.   D. L. Smith

2156. —. REDISCOVERY: AN INDIAN SKETCHBOOK. *Art in Am. 1969 57(5): 82-87.* Reproductions of the sketchbook of Zo-tom, a 19-year-old Kiowa in 1869. The 16-page sketchbook begins with Zo-tom's raids from Oklahoma into Texas in 1869-70 and includes his surrender in 1875 and exile to Fort Marion in St. Augustine, Florida. The sketches were probably the result of the encouragement of the prison commander, Captain Richard Henry Pratt, to produce curios to be sold at the fort. Zo-tom called his book "A History of Indian Prison Life." Illus.   W. D. Chauvin

2157. —. [ROBERT FARRINGTON ELWELL]. *Am. Book Collector 1964 14(8): 21-26.*
Mark, Frederick A. LAST OF THE OLD WEST ARTISTS, *pp. 21-22.*
Avery, George M. BOB ELWELL - PROFESSIONAL, *pp. 23-24.*
Elwell, Kathryn K. MY YEARS WITH BOB ELWELL, *pp. 25-26.*
Personal recollections of Robert Farrington Elwell, an artist who portrayed the Western United States.   D. Brockway

2158. —. [TERRITORIAL RANCH HOUSES]. *J. of Arizona Hist. 1970 11(4): 229-254.*

Stewart, Janet Ann. TERRITORIAL RANCH HOUSES OF SOUTHERN ARIZONA, 1863-1912, *pp. 229-245.* Studies selected 19th-century southern Arizona ranch houses to document them and to identify patterns of building development during the territorial years, 1863-1912. Defines southern Arizona as Cochise, Pima, and Santa Cruz counties. Cattlemen fused their own architectural ideas with those already established in the Spanish-Mexican tradition. Ultimately they built houses in the most sophisticated and latest Eastern fashion. The coming of the railroad in 1880 removed their dependence on indigenous building materials. The massive mud-brick wall and beam construction, the Spanish colonial town plan, and the urban courtyard design and its rural hacienda house style were Mediterranean transplants. The 19th-century American tradition began fusion into the Spanish-Mexican in the 1880's. By the end of the century specifically American structures were being built. 4 illus., 29 notes.

—. GRAPHIC ARTS ON THE ARIZONA FRONTIER: TERRITORIAL RANCH HOUSES OF SOUTHERN ARIZONA, *pp. 246-254.* A map and 15 photographs of ranch houses discussed in the preceding article.   D. L. Smith

Music

2159. Anderson, John Q. THE BALLAD OF GRAHAM BARNETT, BADMAN OF THE BIG BEND IN TEXAS. *Western Folklore 1965 24(2): 77-85.* Traces the life of Graham Barnett and shows how the ballad was written. It also contains a copy of the ballad and tells how it fits the pattern of ballads about western badmen. Based primarily on interviews.   J. M. Brady

2160. Barsness, John. THE DYING COWBOY SONG. *Western Am. Literature 1967 2(1): 50-57.* The author disputes the authenticity of most cowboy songs by showing that a majority were written by sophisticated musicians for popular entertainment. The songs glamorize the cowboy in the familiar romantic vein; the versification and metrics are generally beyond the capacity of unsophisticated cowboys. 12 notes.
                                              R. N. Hudspeth

2161. Bauer, Harry C. LET'S TAKE KATHLEEN HOME ONCE MORE. *Pacific Northwest Q. 1969 60(1): 25-28.* A report of efforts of historical research undertaken by the author to refute a legendary account of the origin in the Pacific Northwest of the ballad "I'll Take You Home Again, Kathleen," followed by information about work of other researchers in revealing the history of the song.   C. C. Gorchels

2162. Davis, Ronald L. SOPRANOS AND SIX-GUNS: THE FRONTIER OPERA HOUSE AS A CULTURAL SYMBOL. *Am. West 1970 7(6): 10-17, 63.* Civic conscience and a cultural inferiority complex developed as western boom communities passed from the raw frontier stage of rowdiness and immorality. Growth in population and wealth brought a yearning for the obvious and pretentious symbols of culture. Overt signs of gentility and respectability would benefit merchants, land speculators, the parvenu rich, and the image these communities sought to project. The most coveted symbol of instant culture became the frontier opera house. The theater gave the urban frontiersman a visible tie with the best of European civilization. Opera houses flourished in the western cowtowns and mining regions in the post-Civil War 19th-century. The pseudo-sophistication of the frontier opera house was an expression of the better way of life which the frontiersmen were trying to emulate. 8 illus.   D. L. Smith

2163. Denisoff, R. Serge. THE RELIGIOUS ROOTS OF THE AMERICAN SONG OF PERSUASION. *Western Folklore 1970 29(3): 175-184.* Many songs of propaganda and protest in America came originally from religious songs. Looks at the growth of early religious music as a means of communicating a message. Methodism and the frontier camp meeting created many of the methods later used by protesters. From these roots came Abolitionists, Grangers, and Populists. Eventually the labor movement adopted and rewrote familiar religious songs to make them a vehicle of protest. In such ways the Industrial Workers of the World (IWW) and the Communist Party of the early 20th century came to adopt protest songs as a key element in their fight to organize unskilled labor. The civil rights movement has used religious song extensively. Compares the original hymns and the revised songs of persuasion. Based primarily on printed sources; 42 notes.   R. A. Trennert

2164. Durham, Lowell M.   ON MORMON MUSIC AND MUSICIANS.   *Dialogue: A J. of Mormon Thought 1968 3(2): 19-40.* Discusses Mormon music and musicians. A survey of Mormon musicians revealed little belief in the existence of "a Mormon music." Discusses Mormon hymns, composers, and performers, from 1835 on. The Mormon Tabernacle Choir leads all other forms of Mormon music in audience, range, and "'good' accruing to the Church," but "is frequently caught in a pincer-movement - proselyting vs. musicality." Church music's principal problem is the lack of competent conductors and organists. 9 photos, 16 notes, 4 appendixes.   J. L. Rasmussen

2165. Fife, Alta and Fife, Austin, eds.   THE TEMPO OF THE RANGE.   *Western Folklore 1967 26(3): 177-181.* In this 1959 interview the late J. Frank Dobie, chronicler of the West, discussed the role and the effect of music in the work of the cowboys with the cattle. It was used to soothe and to excite. Sometimes there were lyrics; frequently only "la-la-la-la" types of extemporaneous improvisations were made on the familiar tunes. Lyrics and tunes of gospel hymns were favorites with the cowboys. Accordions, guitars, and fiddles were occasional accompaniments. Six musical scores are given.   D. L. Smith

2166. Fife, Austin and Fife, Alta.   PUG-NOSED LIL AND THE GIRL WITH THE BLUE VELVET BAND: A BRIEF MEDLEY OF WOMEN IN WESTERN SONGS.   *Am. West 1970 7(2): 32-37.* Camp followers and other women of easy virtue made dramatic early appearances in cow towns, army posts, mining towns, and railroad junctions. They were celebrated in ballads and songs such as: "No Use for the Women," "Belle Starr: Queen of the Desperadoes," "Pug-Nosed Lil," and "The Girl with the Blue Velvet Band." Included is the score for one song and the lyrics for all four. Derived from a forthcoming book. 4 illus.   D. L. Smith

2167. Giannone, Richard.   THE SOUTHWEST'S ETERNAL ECHO: MUSIC IN "DEATH COMES FOR THE ARCHBISHOP."   *Arizona Q. 1966 22(1): 5-18.* An interpretation of the symbolic use of music "for the spontaneous, direct, and universal expression of feeling which blends ethnic variety into spiritual unity" in Willa Cather's *Death Comes for the Archbishop* (New York: Alfred A. Knopf, 1927). Documented.   J. D. Filipiak

2168. Greenway, John.   WOODY GUTHRIE: THE MAN, THE LAND, THE UNDERSTANDING.   *Am. West 1966 3(4): 24-30, 74-78.* Woody Guthrie, dying of an incurable brain crippling disease, was a sometime indigent tramp, seaman, sign painter, busboy, and spittoon cleaner. He also composed at least 1,400 songs. In this biographical and literary analysis of Guthrie, the author calls him "the greatest figure in American folksong" and favorably compares various aspects of his works, clothed in the immediacy and simplicity of the best Negro spirituals, with those of other literary giants. The best of his songs are those which came out of his Dust Bowl experiences in the 1930's. While he composed love ballads, labor songs, and songs about the beauty and promise of America, the most typical were songs of protest which were, in a sense, autobiographical. Text interlaced with numerous excerpts of Guthrie ballads, 7 illus.   D. L. Smith

2169. Gunn, Elizabeth and Greenfield, Elizabeth.   THE GOOSE THAT SANG.   *Montana 1967 17(1): 20-35.* Biography of Frederick William Kuphal, who came to Montana in 1882 as an infant in a German immigrant family. The title stems from his childish fancy that a violin, hanging on the wall, resembled a roast goose which would sing when storked with a "stick." Learning to play the instrument, he became a professional violinist in Helena and advanced to a long career in important posts with the Los Angeles Philharmonic Orchestra. Based on interviews with Kuphal, who supplied many anecdotes concerning the orchestra and its numerous distinguished conductors. Illus.   S. R. Davison

2170. Hatch, Heather S., ed.   MUSIC IN ARIZONA TERRITORY. *J. of Arizona Hist. 1971 12(4): 263-280.* From a diverse background, the music of Arizona Territory developed in sophistication to include marching bands, orchestral concerts, and operettas. Pictures soloists, ensembles, and formal organizations of Indians, Mexicans, miners, soldiers, and others. The instruments range from an "Apache Fiddle" and a Pima cane flute to the harp of a Tucson pioneer mother. Some of the pictures were taken at social and formal occasions in the 1880's-1900's, and some at military formations or patriotic celebrations. Based on the collections of the Arizona Historical Society; 22 photos.   D. L. Smith

2171. Howard, James H.   JOHN F. LENGER: MUSIC MAN AMONG THE SANTEE.   *Nebraska Hist. 1972 53(2): 195-215.* Discusses the band organized by Lenger, a Bohemian immigrant, among the Santee Sioux on the Niobrara Reservation in 1884, and details Lenger's Indian Costume.   R. Lowitt

2172. Linscome, Sanford A.   HENRY HOUSELEY, VERSATILE MUSICIAN OF EARLY DENVER.   *Colorado Mag. 1972 49(1): 1-18.* Frontier Denver was far from the western stereotype of musical provincialism. Actually, a magnificent opera house built in 1881 attracted superior musical entertainment; a series of English organists served St. John's Episcopal Cathedral; a fine orchestral tradition was established; Trinity Methodist Church in 1888 installed one of the largest pipe organs in the Nation; and Frank Damrosch, son of Leopold, developed an outstanding choral organization. One of the dynamos in the amazing developments in Denver from his arrival in 1888 until his death in 1925 was the English musician, Henry Houseley, who came as deputy organist for St. John's. He was not only an accomplished organist, but also an orchestral conductor, church musician, choral director, composer, and director of music at Denver University. Houseley left Denver "a memorable legacy of fine musical culture." Illus., 61 notes.   O. H. Zabel

2173. Ryan, Pat M.   HALLO'S OPERA HOUSE: PIONEER THEATER OF LINCOLN, NEBRASKA.   *Nebraska Hist. 1964 45(4): 323-330.* Recounts the brief history of this opera house, constructed in 1873 and burned to the ground in 1875. Reconstructed under different auspices in 1876, it had a checkered career until 1902 when the building was converted into office space.   R. Lowitt

2174. Smith, Elizabeth H.   THE STORY OF EMMA WIXOM, THE GREAT OPERATIC DIVA FROM THE MOTHER LODE.   *California Historian 1967 13(3): 85-88.* Discusses the life of Emma Wixom who took the stage name of Emma Nevada and became an outstanding concert and opera singer. Emma's early life was spent in the mining towns of California and Nevada. Emma "began to sing as soon as she could talk." After training in San Francisco and Paris, she was showered with acclaim in concerts and opera in Europe and the United States. Following her marriage to Raymond Palmer, her career continued as a teacher. She died in 1940.   O. L. Miller

2175. White, John I.   THE STRANGE CAREER OF "THE STRAWBERRY ROAN."   *Arizona and the West 1969 11(4): 359-366.* Curley W. Fletcher (1892-1954) was a California cowpuncher and song writer. His song "The Outlaw Broncho" was probably first published in 1914, was polished up a bit, and soon achieved fame under a new title, "The Strawberry Roan." It is one of the most popular and best known Western ballads. It appears on a score of records and in dozens of books. It is the story of a braggart bronco buster who finally met his match and admitted there might be a few more "matches" around, very few. Fletcher's authorship was often not credited and sometimes disputed. His colorful career of varied activities from catching wild horses to writing poetry brought him wealth and renown.   D. L. Smith

2176. Winfrey, Dorman H.   DEVELOPMENT OF MUSIC ON THE AMERICAN FRONTIER.   *Texana 1967 5(2): 141-165.* Observes the heritage of American music from England and Germany. Considers six areas of American music: Indian, Negro, Southern Religious, Lumbering, Great Plains, and Gold Rush. Analyzes the influence of America on European composers through the works of Dvorák, Debussy, and Puccini. Little if any American music developed on the American frontier. European composers did more with American frontier aspects in music than did Americans, perhaps because the nature of the frontier has not given Americans the time or the opportunity to develop their own music. 88 notes.   W. A. Buckman

Science and Medicine

2177. Anderson, John Q. MAGICAL TRANSFERENCE OF DISEASE IN TEXAS FOLK MEDICINE. *Western Folklore 1968 27(3): 191-199.* The universal theme that disease and ailments may be transferred from one person to another or to a plant or an animal is significant in Texas folk medicine. Sympathetic magic by set ritual is the means by which the disease is transmitted. The examples here presented are put into three categories: person-to-person transference, transfer from people to animals, transmission to plants. 21 notes.　　　D. L. Smith

2178. Baird, Violet M. AUGUSTE SAVARDAN AND THE "GREAT SOCIETY" ON THE TRINITY, 1855-1858. *Texana 1967 5(1): 53-67.* Auguste Savardan (1792-1867) was a French physician who spent three years at the Fourierist colony of La Réunion, in Dallas County. Emphasizes Savardan's accounts of medical practice in the colony, his interest in natural history, and his relationship with Victor Prosper Considérant, the colony's leader. Includes information on Savardan's life before and after his Texas experience. Based principally on Savardan's memoirs, *Un Naufrage au Texas* (Paris, 1858); 35 notes.
　　　J. E. Findling

2179. Behle, William H. THE UTAH ACADEMY OF SCIENCES, ARTS AND LETTERS. *Utah Hist. Q. 1968 36(3): 239-262.* Describes the beginnings of the academy and reviews its activities in several areas, including the programs presented at various meetings (this includes a discussion of the academy's association with the Pacific Division of the American Association for the Advancement of Science), the discussion of resolutions relating to public affairs (primarily conservation), the expansion in the 1920's of the academy's interest into the humanities and social sciences, the establishment of a junior academy in the 1950's, and the publications program (primarily the *Proceedings of the Utah Academy of Sciences, Arts and Letters*). The author was president of the academy in 1959-60.　　　S. L. Jones

2180. Brodhead, Michael J. A DEDICATION TO THE MEMORY OF ELLIOTT COUES, 1842-1899. *Arizona and the West 1971 13(1): 1-4.* Elliott Coues was probably the greatest ornithologist of his day. He presented polished manuscripts to the prominent scientific societies of the country before he was 20. On the Arizona frontier as a Union Army surgeon he had plenty of time to collect and study birds and to publish monographs in the foremost American and British scientific journals. At Southern posts during Reconstruction he took up herpetology and mammalogy. Other assignments took him over much of the West. After 1881, Coues, now a civilian, worked for the Hayden Survey and its successor, the U.S. Geological Survey. Early in the 1890's Coues prepared a new edition of the Lewis and Clark journals, especially to supply geographical and biological annotations from his own experiences and scientific observations. He developed a passion for the history of Western exploration and travel and reedited several accounts of other travelers. The strain from these added interests was too much; Coues collapsed and soon died at the age of 57. Coues preferred to be called a "curator of historical materials." Even though he bowdlerized shamelessly and much of his historical effort has been superseded, his contribution was considerable. His incredible energy produced perhaps one thousand articles and books. Illus., biblio.　　　D. L. Smith

2181. Camp, Charles L. OLD DOCTOR YATES. *J. of the West 1963 2(4): 377-400.* Lorenzo Gordin Yates was a dentist who became known for his amateur naturalist activities in California during the latter part of the 19th century. Yates was born in England and studied in Wisconsin. In 1864 he moved to Centerville, California, in Alameda County. The dentist's activities were extensive in anthropology, conchology, invertebrate and vertebrate paleontology, geology, botany, paleobotany, horticulture and floriculture. He was well-known for his scientific expeditions and his vast collections of shells, fossils and other artifacts. Although he had limited formal schooling, Yates published some 300 short articles in newspapers and magazines and did considerable lecturing in the California area. He was a member of a number of scientific societies and corresponded with several noted scholars on his various interests. One of his collections of fossils is now in the Chicago Museum of Natural History. He served as president of the Santa Barbara Natural History Society and as Horticulture Commissioner of Santa Bar-

bara County. The author includes numerous details and Latin names of the various natural finds and studies by Yates. Illus., maps, 11 notes.
　　　K. P. Davis

2182. Clary, David A. THE ROLE OF THE ARMY SURGEON IN THE WEST: DANIEL WEISEL AT FORT DAVIS, TEXAS, 1868-1872. *Western Hist. Q. 1972 3(1): 53-66.* Weisel served as post surgeon at Fort Davis in west Texas, 1868-72. From his medical records and the other garrison reports, it is determined that he was a typically competent and conscientious medical officer. Incessantly he worked to improve the sanitary conditions of the fort and the physical facilities of the hospital. He tested new medicines for army use, condemned bad food stores, supervised the operation of the bakery, sent unusual autopsy remains to an army museum, collected mammal skeletons for Washington, and carried out other tasks routinely assigned to all garrison officers. 36 notes.
　　　D. L. Smith

2183. Collins, Dean T. CHILDREN OF SORROW: A HISTORY OF THE MENTALLY RETARDED IN KANSAS. *Bull. of the Hist. of Medicine 1965 39(1): 53-78.* In 1848 Massachusetts became the first state to provide training facilities for the mentally retarded. Kansas, 33 years later, became the 12th state to establish a school for the retarded which underwent numerous changes of administration and in concepts of treatment during the ensuing 80 years. The author treats the subject under such headings as "The School at Winfield," "The First Revolution," "The Period of Lay Administration," "The Second Revolution," and "Postscript."　　　W. L. Fox

2184. Connolly, James B. AUDUBON AT HIS BEST. *North Dakota Hist. 1964 31(4): 223-229.* At 58 Audubon had reached his peak in knowledge when he spent almost five months on an expedition to the mouth of the Yellowstone River. Traveling by woodburning steamboat he had ample time while the boat loaded wood to take trips to the prairies for specimens. He cataloged several species of wildlife new to science. Ornithology continued as his first and lasting love. Audubon's *Missouri River Journals* were not published until 1891, after biographers had made his earlier nature excursions celebrated. Illus., 16 notes based chiefly on secondary sources, biblio.　　　I. W. Van Noppen

2185. Cutright, Paul Russell. "I GAVE HIM BARKS AND SALT-PETER . . ." *Am. Heritage 1963 15(1): 58-61, 94-101.* A medical history of the Lewis and Clark expedition, as practiced and recorded by both Lewis and Clark, which also surveys American medical knowledge at the start of the 19th century. Considering the state of medicine at the time, the medical record of the expedition was extraordinary, even without the presence of a qualified doctor, thanks to the medical interests of President Jefferson, who prevailed upon Dr. Benjamin Rush to advise Lewis and Clark prior to the expedition. Illus.　　　C. R. Allen, Jr.

2186. Cutright, Paul Russell. JEFFERSON'S INSTRUCTIONS TO LEWIS AND CLARK. *Bull. of the Missouri Hist. Soc. 1966 22(3): 302-320.* Quotes extensively from and comments on the instructions which Thomas Jefferson (1743-1826), while President, issued to Captains Meriwether Lewis (1774-1809) and William Clark (1770-1838) before the Lewis and Clark Expedition of 1804-06. Not wishing to be solely responsible for the contents of the instructions, Jefferson consulted members of his Cabinet and various scientific friends. "From this collective effort emerged a final paper, unique, distinguished. It was a blueprint for discovery, the product of a powerfully original and disciplined mind. No exploring party before or since has been provided with a set of instructions so inclusive, so technically knowledgeable, so electric with ideas, so charged with foresight. The instructions which Jefferson put into the hands of Lewis and Clark clearly reflected his appetites, his thinking, and his persistent preoccupation with scientific matters. That Lewis and Clark regarded them as law and made observations on temperature and rainfall, minerals, mountains and interlocking streams, animals, plants, and warbonneted Indians, which they committed to writing, is now a matter of record." 75 notes.　　　D. D. Cameron

2187. Cutright, Paul Russell. MERIWETHER LEWIS PREPARES FOR A TRIP WEST. *Bull. of the Missouri Hist. Soc. 1966 23(1): 3-20.* An account of how Captain Meriwether Lewis (1774-1809), co-leader of the Lewis-Clark Expedition, prepared for his trip West at the request of President Thomas Jefferson (1743-1826) early in 1803. Jefferson, who was then President of the American Philosophical Society, wrote almost identical letters to five fellow members of the A.P.S. in Philadelphia - Andrew Ellicott (1754-1820), Dr. Robert Patterson (1743-1824), Dr. Benjamin Rush (1745-1813), Dr. Benjamin Smith Barton (1766-1815), and Dr. Caspar Wistar (1761-1818) - asking them to assist and instruct Lewis in preparation for his expedition (along with William Clark). During May and June of 1803, Lewis received abundant advice from each of these five men, together with Jefferson's own suggestions. "He received counsel on what instruments, reference books, and medical supplies would serve his needs. Above and beyond all this, he lived daily in the company of the most distinguished scientists of his day. Within a fortnight he would set out for uncharted parts of the continent where he would need a full measure of such attributes." 51 notes.

D. D. Cameron

2188. Cutright, Paul Russell. MERIWETHER LEWIS: BOTANIST. *Oregon Hist. Q. 1968 69(2): 148-170.* Discussion of observations and botanical collections made by Meriwether Lewis on the Lewis and Clark Expedition to the Pacific Ocean from St. Louis, Missouri, and other western travels in the first decade of the 19th century, with supplemental information on the history of botanical specimens up to modern times. Herbariums containing specimens are identified. Illustrated with copies of mounted specimens collected by Lewis in 1804 and 1806.

C. C. Gorchels

2189. Divett, Robert T. UTAH'S FIRST MEDICAL COLLEGE. *Utah Hist. Q. 1963 31(1): 51-59.* Provides detailed information on the history of the Medical College of Utah, which was founded at Morgan, Utah, in 1880, graduated a class in 1882, and closed in 1883. The central figure in the history of the college was Dr. Frederick S. Kohler, a native of Pennsylvania. A woman of considerable importance in Utah's history, Emeline Grover Rich was a member of the graduating class of 1882. An attack on the college by the Salt Lake *Daily Herald* and hostile community sentiment forced the college to close.

S. L. Jones

2190. Elsner, John. REMINISCENCES OF EARLY DENVER. *Am. Jewish Arch. 1972 24(1): 27-38.* This memoir was offered as a toast at the 1908 annual banquet of the National Jewish Hospital for Consumptives. Dr. Elsner arrived in Denver from New York in 1866, was appointed Denver county physician in 1870, organized the first medical society in the State in 1871, and helped establish the NJHC. Photo.

E. S. Shapiro

2191. Fowler, Don D. and Fowler, Catherine S. JOHN WESLEY POWELL, ANTHROPOLOGIST. *Utah Hist. Q. 1969 37(2): 152-172.* Review of Powell's activities in research on the origins, tribal organization, and culture of the American Indians of the West, concluding that he is a transitional figure in American anthropological studies, noteworthy mostly for the organization of investigations and contributing little to the literature or the theoretical conceptualizations of the field.

S. L. Jones

2192. Gibson, Arrell M. MEDICINE SHOW. *Am. West 1967 4(1): 34-39, 74-79.* Because of the competition of the emerging medical profession and of the resourceful pioneer family remedies, itinerant drug peddlers found business exceedingly slow. To push sales of their products they revived the medieval practice of attracting crowds by melodrama, song and dance teams, and other forms of entertainment. The medicine show came into its own between 1865 and 1900, "the bonanza age of public exploitation." By 1900 there were hundreds of such traveling shows, varying from single-wagon affairs to huge tent operations. When it came to "pure unabashed misrepresentation" the medicine-show hawkers made pikers of con men, speculators, stock promoters, and other such agents. The pattern that usually developed consisted of ballyhoo such as newspaper advertising or a brass band parade to attract an audience; entertainment to further whet the recreation-hungry frontier crowd's appetite for more; the medicine pitch or spiel, often so morbidly colorful and appealing as to be as entertaining as it was commercial; and closing entertainment, the anticipation of which usually held the crowd through the commercial part of the show. Liniments, tonics, bitters, and all sorts of nostrums, many of which were all-purpose, contained liberal amounts of alcohol, or were said to contain exotic ingredients, were the stock-in-trade of the quacks. Medicine shows went into decline after 1900 because of increased sophistication which lessened susceptibility to the pitchman's blarney, competition of magic-lantern shows and primitive motion pic-

tures, and State and Federal regulation. Today's radio and television pitchmen, however, still use spiels "cut from the same old cloth of purest hokum." Illus., biblio. note.

D. L. Smith

2193. Green, John R. NEUROSURGERY ON THE FRONTIER: AN INCIDENT IN 1883. *Montana 1967 17(3): 18-29.* Episodes in the life of Dr. George McCrerry, who in 1883 performed probably the first surgical opening of the skull in Arizona, then a frontier area. The patient was a young soldier at Fort Whipple, who had suffered a concussion when a horse kicked him in the head. Based on archival materials (including the damaged skull) in Washington, D.C., and on published works on territorial Arizona. Illus.

S. R. Davison

2194. Groh, George. DOCTORS OF THE FRONTIER. *Am. Heritage 1963 14(3): 10-11, 87-91.* American doctors and medical profession on the Western frontier.

S

2195. Hagemann, E. R., ed. ARIZONA TERRITORY - 1878: THE DIARY OF GEORGE H. R. MORAN, CONTRACT SURGEON, UNITED STATES ARMY. *Arizona and the West 1963 5(3): 249-267.* With a few months of hospital service for the Union Army in 1865, a few years of private practice, and a stint (1874-77) as a civilian physician attached to Army posts (contract surgeon) in the Carolinas, George Henry Roberts Moran became contract surgeon in Arizona Territory for the years 1878-81. The anonymous manuscripts diary in the Duke University Library, with entries for 1 February to 21 September 1878, by an Army surgeon stationed at Camp Bowie and Camp Thomas, Arizona Territory, is established by the editor as Moran's. Moran traveled from Baltimore, Maryland, to San Francisco, California, and on to Yuman, Arizona, by rail. From Yuma he marched to eastern Arizona and settled down to the routine of garrison life. His brief entries reflect the dull routine of isolation punctuated only by patrols into the surrounding Chiricahua stronghold. 110 notes.

D. L. Smith

2196. Hall, Edith Thompson. THE BIOGRAPHY OF A PIONEER NEBRASKA DOCTOR: JOHN WESLEY THOMPSON. *Nebraska Hist. 1963 44(4): 277-295.* Born in Ohio in 1860, Dr. Thompson went to Nebraska to practice in 1886. He died in 1926 after almost 40 years of practice in the state.

R. Lowitt

2197. Hampton, H. D., ed. WITH GRINNELL IN NORTH PARK. *Colorado Mag. 1971 48(4): 273-298.* Hampton provides an introduction which introduces George Bird Grinnell and indicates that, by 1879, North Park in Colorado had seen some mining activity and was seeing the beginning of the cattle industry. Eight articles Grinnell published in *Forest and Stream* in late 1879 after a trip into the area are reproduced in abbreviated form. The article describes, in some detail, the flora and fauna as well as the terrain of the North Park area. It also anticipates the displacement of the Utes by white men and forecasts pollution and destruction of wildlife and timber. Map, illus., 8 notes.

O. H. Zabel

2198. Ketner, Kenneth L. A STUDY OF THE USE OF MADSTONES IN OKLAHOMA. *Chronicles of Oklahoma 1968 46(4): 433-449.* The madstone treatment for hydrophobia (rabies) was widespread in early Oklahoma. The stone, generally from a deer, supposedly "sucked" the "poison." Mentions several accounts of its use. Traces the belief in the bezoar or snake stone to ancient Persia. Arabs used it in the Middle Ages. 43 notes, biblio.

E. P. Stickney

2199. Lange, Erwin F. JOHN JEFFREY AND THE OREGON BOTANICAL EXPEDITION. *Oregon Hist. Q. 1967 58(2): 111-124.* A report of the travels and botanical work of John Jeffrey from 1849 to 1854. Reproduced are summaries of bulletins issued by the British-financed Oregon Botanical Association concerning Jeffrey's work and other related activities.

C. C. Gorchels

2200. Lange, Erwin F. MAJOR CHARLES E. BENDIRE AND THE BIRDS OF OREGON. *Oregon Hist. Q. 1965 66(3): 233-239.* Sketch of Major Charles E. Bendire as a part-time ornithologist while he served in army camps mostly in Oregon and Idaho during the years of 1868 to 1883. He was so successful in his avocation that upon retirement from the army in 1886 he was named honorary curator of oology (the study of bird eggs) at the U.S. National Museum. Excerpts from his writings are included.

C. C. Gorchels

2201. Nash, Gerald D. **THE CONFLICT BETWEEN PURE AND APPLIED SCIENCE IN NINETEENTH-CENTURY PUBLIC POLICY: THE CALIFORNIA STATE GEOLOGICAL SURVEY, 1860-1874.** *Isis 1963 54(176): 217-228.* The California Survey, one of many such 19th-century state projects but better financed and organized than most, made many important scientific contributions, but it foundered from "the lack of a clear conception of its tasks by its various supporters." Josiah Whitney, its leader and later professor of geology at Harvard, was an advocate of pure research and "had scant appreciation of the necessity to produce practical results and to cultivate a friendly public. The lawmakers [in the Assembly, responsible to mining and agricultural interest,] had neither patience, sympathy, nor understanding for achievements of long-range scientific value. For them, research was a means to an end only, a method to promote the more rapid exploitation of resources." Based on publications of the California Legislature and Survey.
W. P. Moore

2202. Osgood, Ernest S. **A PRAIRIE DOG FOR MR. JEFFERSON.** *Montana 1969 19(2): 54-56.* When Lewis and Clark sent back to President Jefferson a consignment of hides, skeletons and other specimens, they included a live prairie dog, along with four magpies and a prairie chicken. The rodent and one magpie survived the boat trip from the Mandan villages to St. Louis and a longer voyage to New Orleans and on to the capital. Jefferson welcomed the pets, kept them briefly at the White House, and found a home for them in the private zoo of Charles Willson Peale, the artist.
S. R. Davison

2203. Pike, Donald G. **FOUR SURVEYORS CHALLENGE THE ROCKY MOUNTAIN WEST: FIGHTING BUREAUCRACY AND INDIANS IN A WILD LAND.** *Am. West 1972 9(3): 4-13.* Most who worked in the Rocky Mountains in the 1870's were bent on exploiting natural resources. Outstanding exceptions were expeditions and surveys for scientific examination of the land to provide the first systematic information on the West. The four principal surveys were largely products of individual initiative with the reluctant cooperation of an indifferent government. Ferdinand Vandeveer Hayden (1829-87) had a passion for topography and made notable contributions on the Yellowstone region and Colorado. Geologist Clarence King (1842-1901) mapped and evaluated a 100-mile strip along the 40th parallel from the eastern slope of the Sierra to the western edge of the Great Plains. The various expeditions under then-Lieutenant George Montague Wheeler (1842-1905) endeavored to produce systematic maps of the West beyond the 100th meridian. John Wesley Powell (1834-1902) achieved fame from his surveys of the Grand Canyon of the Colorado area. The reports of these men and their expeditions furnished much data and lobbying leverage for public and governmental concern. 8 illus., biblio.
D. L. Smith

2204. Riley, Paul D. **DR. DAVID FRANKLIN POWELL AND FORT MC PHERSON.** *Nebraska Hist. 1970 51(2): 153-170.* A brief account of Powell's interesting frontier experiences in 1873 in the vicinity of Fort McPherson, Nebraska, one of the most noted military posts on the Great Plains. Powell was a contract surgeon at Fort McPherson and extensive quotes are included from the diary and letters written by him about travels and Indian warfare.
R. Lowitt

2205. Rogers, Frank B. **THE RISE AND DECLINE OF THE ALTITUDE THERAPY OF TUBERCULOSIS.** *Bull. of the Hist. of Medicine 1969 43(1): 1-16.* Altitude climatotherapy for tuberculosis became very popular in the second half of the 19th century. Accounts of exploration in the Rocky Mountains frequently commented on the salutary effects of the climate in this area. The end of the Civil War and the gold strikes of the 1860's stimulated large scale immigration to Colorado; by 1880 one third of the population was comprised of consumptives who had come there for their health. By 1908 the apex of high altitude therapy had been reached, and by World War II climatotherapy was no longer popular. Based on primary and secondary sources; 67 notes.
P. D. Thomas

2206. Saunders, J. B. **THE FIELDING H. GARRISON LECTURE: GEOGRAPHY AND GEOPOLITICS IN CALIFORNIA MEDICINE.** *Bull. of the Hist. of Medicine 1967 41(4): 293-324.* Examines the growth of the medical profession in California in relationship to the State's particular geography and geopolitical patterns. Scurvy helped to establish the demographic patterns of settlement. In the 19th century,

California became famous for its sanatoriums and number of physicians. Down to World War II, California had more physicians per unit of population than any other State, and at present it still ranks near the top in this respect. Based on primary and secondary sources, newspapers, monographs, and periodicals; illus., 95 notes.
P. D. Thomas

2207. Sedell, Ellen C. **THE LOST PORT ORFORD METEORITE.** *Oregon Hist. Q. 1968 69(1): 29-49.* A meteorite found by John Evans, geologist, in 1856 near Port Orford, Oregon, has been sought by other scientists and pseudoscientists in the decades since, in the Rogue River Mountains of Oregon. The author gives details of clues found in diaries and other papers from 1861 to 1964. 41 notes.
C. C. Gorchels

2208. Skabelund, Donald. **COSMOLOGY ON THE AMERICAN FRONTIER: ORSON PRATT'S KEY TO THE UNIVERSE.** *Centaurus [Denmark] 1965 11(3): 190-204.* Examines an unusual book, *Salt Lake City, 1879,* by Orson Pratt (1811-81), one of the original apostles of the Mormon Church. With no formal training beyond grammar school, Pratt undertook to explain a wide range of celestial and terrestrial phenomena by blending Newtonian physics with his own mathematical theories. It is shown that the results of some of his explanations are theoretically unsound, yet others show an imaginative foresight of relativistic physics. Pratt's importance as the first Mormon scientist is stressed as is his influence on shaping Mormon theology. Documented.
J. Stanndard

2209. Snoddy, Donald D., ed. **MEDICAL ASPECTS OF THE LEWIS AND CLARK EXPEDITION.** *Nebraska Hist. 1970 51(2): 115-151.* A compilation of all references from the journals (chiefly the Thwaites edition) of Meriwether Lewis and William Clark relating to sickness, accident, and medical practice during their famous expedition covering the years 1804-06.
R. Lowitt

2210. Splitter, Henry Winfred. **HEALTH IN SOUTHERN CALIFORNIA, 1850-1900.** *J. of the West 1969 8(4): 526-558.* Discusses health as an impetus for settlement in southern California, particularly in the Los Angeles area. Beginning with the early tales of extreme longevity due to the climate, the author deals with sanitation, the founding of hospitals, and the influx of health faddists.
R. N. Alvis

2211. Thompson, Kenneth. **THE AUSTRALIAN FEVER TREE IN CALIFORNIA: EUCALYPTS AND MALARIA PROPHYLAXIS.** *Ann. of the Assoc. of Am. Geographers 1970 60(2): 230-244.* "Trees of the genus *Eucalyptus* from Australia were spread widely and numerously through California after the 1850's. Several factors favored their spread, notably the production of timber and fuel, often with unrealistic hopes of financial gain. Planting for windbreaks and decorative purposes was also commonplace. An important and overlooked additional reason for the rapid dissemination of Eucalypts in California, especially in the 1870's and 1880's, was the belief that trees of this genus, particularly *Eucalyptus globulus* or blue gum, could prevent or diminish the serious malaria problem that beset portions of the state. That certain forms of vegetation, especially trees, represented sanitary influences was an ancient notion and it survived even the germ theory of disease. The supposed method whereby eucalypts achieved their healthful influence was through the trees' imagined capacity to absorb or neutralize the noxious gases that were believed to cause malaria. This erroneous and antique miasmatic etiology of malaria, together with belief in eucalypt prophylaxis, was demolished in the late nineteenth century when it was revealed that the disease was caused by blood parasites transmitted by the bites of anopheline mosquitoes."
J

2212. Thompson, Kenneth. **CLIMATOTHERAPY IN CALIFORNIA.** *California Hist. Q. 1971 50(2): 111-130.* The view that climate and geography were major factors in determining health or sickness enjoyed great popularity in the latter half of the 19th century. A salubrious climate was thought to be of great importance in the treatment and cure of a number of illnesses and diseases, while certain regions were believed to contribute to the causes of those diseases. With the germ theory yet to gain acceptance and licensing of medical practitioners a thing of the future, many people believed climatotherapy would work. Boosters publicized California as a locale where climatotherapy had produced miraculous cures; because people accepted climatotherapy as a valid medical practice, health-seekers migrated to California in significant numbers. Despite California's reputation for cures, however, there is little proof that beyond the modest benefit of a mild, sunny climate, climatotherapy could work miracles. Illus., 69 notes.

A. Hoffman

2213. Thompson, Kenneth. IRRIGATION AS A MENACE TO HEALTH IN CALIFORNIA: A NINETEENTH CENTURY VIEW. *Geographical R. 1969 59(2): 195-214.* "In accordance with the theory prevailing in the nineteenth century, malaria and other diseases were believed to be caused by the inhalation of some type of gaseous poison, or miasma, created from the decomposition of organic matter, most abundantly generated in moist places such as marshes. The spread of irrigation in California was said to exacerbate the formidable health problems with miasmatic disease, which included not only malaria but also typhoid fever and other diseases. Thus during the early years of American settlement in California there was vigorous debate over the possible conflicts between irrigation agriculture and public health. Some persons, including most doctors, were implacably opposed to irrigation on the grounds that it led to production of disease-causing miasma. Others maintained that judicious water use and crop selection could minimize the health problems. Still others saw no health hazards involved. Resolution of the controversy came after the scientific discoveries that produced the germ theory of disease, and eventually malaria control became a matter of mosquito abatement rather than of reduction of miasma." J

2214. Tye, Dorothy A. A LODESTONE IN TIME. *Pacific Historian 1969 13(1): 42-53.* An account of two episodes in the life of George Madeira, mining engineer, geologist, historian, philosopher, and amateur astronomer, who built the first amateur astronomical observatory in California and discovered the Great Comet of 1861 with a three-inch refractor telescope. The first episode recounts his difficult journey to California with his father and others in 1862 and discusses his intense interest in astronomy. The second, set in 1887, tells of his return to the observatory he had built in 1860 near the town of Volcano, and of his association with James Lick, who bequeathed money for a great observatory and telescope on Mt. Hamilton. Mentions the rise and decline of the town of Volcano, which flourished in gold rush days, was ravaged by hydraulic mining, and finally was destroyed by fire. Relates the unveiling of a monument to Madeira on the site of his old observatory in 1969. 5 illus.

F. I. Murphy

2215. Will, Drake W. LEWIS AND CLARK: WESTERING PHYSICIANS. *Montana 1971 21(4): 2-17.* Examines the medical and health aspects of the Lewis and Clark Expedition, 1804-06, stressing the role of Dr. Benjamin Rush (1745-1813), who briefed the leaders, suggested questions to be answered regarding native populations (more ethnological than clinical), and outlined health precautions for the exploring party. Rush also recommended a list of medical supplies, including "30 gallons of spirits of wine." Excepting the unavoidable death of Sergeant Charles Floyd, there were no fatalities and few minor illnesses and injuries. Credits the foresight and wisdom of the captains who were able not only to bring their men through but also to minister to numerous Indians who sought their help. Includes tentative diagnoses in modern terms of ailments identified in the journals as "Biliose Chorlick" and "inward fevers." Based on official correspondence and journals; 54 notes.

S. R. Davison

2216. Yochelson, Ellis L. MONUMENTS AND MARKERS TO THE TERRITORIAL SURVEYS. *Ann. of Wyoming 1971 43(1): 113-124.* A compilation of historical monuments and markers and geographic place-names which commemorate the scientific explorations of Ferdinand Vandeveer Hayden (1829-87), Clarence King (1842-1901), George Montague Wheeler (1842-1905), and John Wesley Powell (1834-1902). Between 1867 and 1879 each headed territorial surveys which provided invaluable geological, geographical, zoological, botanical, and ethnological knowledge of the Western United States. Monuments and signs adequately mark only the routes of Powell's explorations of the Green and Colorado Rivers, however, and few geographic features bear the names of any of the four men. Moreover, except for Powell's gravesite, even their burial places remain obscure. Although Powell was truly a national figure, Hayden, King, and Wheeler deserve equal recognition for their efforts, and the routes and noteworthy points of their expeditions should be properly marked. Illus.

G. R. Adams

Religion

General

2217. Adams, Robert H. MARKERS CUT BY HAND. *Am. West 1967 4(3): 59-64.* Before the adoption of simple crosses or machine-lettered and machine-polished marble stones from the Anglo communities for their graves, the Spanish Americans used monuments fashioned by carpenters and stonecutters in their extra time. Their craft, among the richest of the once common folk arts, is almost gone in the area from Santa Fe to Taos, New Mexico, where it was once most prominent. The ravages of the weather, souvenir hunters, and more modern replacements will remove the remaining ones in a few years unless some concerned effort to save them is made. 12 illus.

D. L. Smith

2218. Brunn, Stanley D. and Wheeler, James O. NOTES ON THE GEOGRAPHY OF RELIGIOUS TOWN NAMES IN THE U.S. *Names 1966 14(4): 197-202.* An examination of religious town names in the United States. A religious place name is defined here as the name of a town or individual mentioned in the Bible or a saint's name. Heaviest concentrations of religious town names appear in the east central area extending from Pennsylvania to Missouri and in California and along the gulf coast from Texas to Florida. Salem, Lebanon, and Athens occur most frequently. California, Ohio, Pennsylvania, Illinois, and Missouri, in that order, show the largest number of religious town names. Based on 1960 U.S. Census and Biblical concordances and dictionaries; 9 notes.

D. Lindsey

2219. Jennings, Warren A. ISAAC MC COY AND THE MORMONS. *Missouri Hist. R. 1966 61(1): 62-82.* Isaac McCoy was a Baptist missionary accused by the Mormons of organizing and leading an armed band seeking to drive them from Jackson County, Missouri, in 1833. Excerpts from McCoy's papers in the Kansas State Historical Society are presented to show that he accompanied the band entering Mormon territory as a peacemaker rather than as a man fostering violence. Some references in McCoy's papers to the value of Mormon property suggest that he was interested in speculation, but the author concludes that all of McCoy's motives were of the highest type.

W. F. Zornow

2220. Nelson, Ronald R. THE LEGAL RELATIONSHIP OF CHURCH AND STATE IN CALIFORNIA. *Southern California Q. 1964 46(1): 11-53, and (2): 125-160.* Chapter I, "Areas of Rights and Privileges," shows that the California Supreme Court has upheld religious liberty but that civil government in the state has not been completely divorced from religion. Chapter II, "Religion in the Public Schools," discusses the development of a released-time program. The Zorach decision called attention to the support the public schools thus give to church groups by recruiting pupils. Other problems discussed are devotional Bible reading and prayers, as well as the flag-saluting problem. Chapter III, "Parochial Schools and the State," discusses the most lively of present church-state questions. Supreme Court decisions have cast doubt on the right of parochial schools to exist. Indirect assistance has been given in California, ranging from tax exemption to free transportation of parochial pupils in public schools buses. Chapter IV, "Incorporation and Tax Exemption for Religious Societies," shows that state supervision involves the state in the internal affairs of the churches. Chapter V, "Sunday Laws," shows these were a political issue in the 1880's, but were repealed on a state-wide basis. In conclusion the author predicts that the demand for aid to parochial schools will continue and that the privilege of tax exemption will be challenged in coming years. Based on debates of California's two constitutional conventions, and upon legislative acts, but primarily on judicial decisions and legal opinions. Carefully documented.

E. P. Stickney

2221. Weber, Francis J., ed. FATHER LAWRENCE SCANLAN'S REPORT OF CATHOLICISM IN UTAH, 1880. *Utah Hist. Q. 1966 34(4): 283-289.* Presents, with an introduction, the text of a report by a missionary priest in Salt Lake City to the Société de la Propagation de la Foi, Paris, which provided subsidies for the parish. Dated 8 November 1880, it reports on activities of the preceding decade, commenting on Protestant missionary activities in the area. He recommended emphasis upon education among the Mormon youth, having concluded that "there is no use in reasoning with" the adults. The original report is now in the archives of the Archdiocese of Los Angeles. 13 notes.

S. L. Jones

The Mormon Experience

2222. Alexander, Thomas G. FEDERAL AUTHORITY VERSUS POLYGAMIC THEOCRACY: JAMES B. MC KEAN AND THE MORMONS, 1870-1875. *Dialogue: A J. of Mormon Thought 1966 1(3): 85-100.* In 1870 President Ulysses Simpson Grant appointed James McKean chief justice of Utah, and thus began one of the most brief yet controversial encounters between the Federal Government and the Mormon theocratic state. "As the conflict evolved, a considerable amount of violence took place between Mormons and Gentiles in which McKean and his court were directly involved." Orson F. Whitney claimed that McKean was a part of a "ring" of Federal officers who had come to Utah for personal profit. However, McKean saw his duty consisting of a drive to halt crime and to punish criminals, and to undermine the power of a theocratic state which he believed to be engaged in illegitimate conflict with Federal authority.

L. P. Hofeling

2223. Alexander, Thomas G. and Allen, James B., eds. THE MORMONS IN THE MOUNTAIN WEST: A SELECTED BIBLIOGRAPHY. *Arizona and the West 1967 9(4): 365-384.* Mormon historiography has progressed through three rather clearly defined phases: noted travelers of the 1850's and 1860's described Mormon society and presented the first general image of the kingdom of the Saints; the literature of the 1870-1920 period was generally divided between muckraking attempts to discredit Mormon society and apologia designed to defend it; and writers since then have been more detached and scholarly than before. Significant contributions have appeared in increasing numbers since 1950. The 77 volumes and articles of the bibliography concern the Great Basin Mormons. Doctoral dissertations are excluded. The selections are representative examples of different authors and of the three phases of Mormon historiography. The annotations are concerned with content, sources utilized, circumstances of writing, other contextual information, and critical evaluation.

D. L. Smith

2224. Allen, James B. THE COMPANY TOWN: A PASSING PHASE OF UTAH'S INDUSTRIAL DEVELOPMENT. *Utah Hist. Q. 1966 34(2): 138-160.* Reviews and analyzes the establishment and development of company towns in Utah. Most company towns were established to provide facilities for men working at remote mining and processing facilities. New developments, particularly modern transportation, have made most of them obsolete. The author discusses the economics of company towns, the reactions of recent immigrants to them, and the political and economic pressures exerted by owners upon the workers and tenants.

S. L. Jones

2225. Amann, Peter. PROPHET IN ZION: THE SAGA OF GEORGE J. ADAMS. *New England Q. 1964 37(4): 477-500.* Born about 1811 in New Jersey, George Washington Joshua Adams began his evangelistic career as a lay Methodist minister, converting to Mormonism in 1840. During the next 10 years, he rose to prominence successively in at least three competing branches of the Mormon Church, falling into disfavor in each after charges of drunkenness, immorality, and embezzlement, followed by expulsion and excommunication. By 1851, his credit exhausted among sectarians, Adams become star and manager of a touring theatrical company, while continuing to preach at various churches on Sundays. His Church of the Messiah, of which he was president, flourished in Maine, where a monthly church newspaper proved successful also. Announcing in early 1864 a great mission to make Palestine a fit place of the Jews' return, so as to hasten the Second Coming of Christ, Adams launched a great fund-raising drive. A year later, he sailed to Jaffa and arranged the purchase of six acres of land, and in August 1866 156 colonists left for Jaffa. Misrepresentation, mismanagement, drunkenness, and fraud on the part of Adams, added to violent quarreling between him and his wife, doomed the American colony. American consular personnel were relieved over the departure of the Adamses for England in 1868. Unsuccessful in England, Adams returned to the United States to preach for a decade before his death. Terms such as crook, psychopath, and fanatic perhaps do scant justice to the complexities of such a man. Based partly on unpublished letters and documents; 52 notes.

R. V. Calvert

2226. Anderson, Richard L. JACKSON COUNTY IN EARLY MORMON DESCRIPTIONS. *Missouri Hist. R. 1971 65(3): 270-293.* Missouri was one of 10 States in which the Latter-Day Saints played an important role. Many travelers going to the West wrote about Missouri and the other States through which they passed. The Latter-Day Saints had a special interest in Missouri, since their leaders regarded it for some time as their ultimate destination. Those who wrote about Missouri did so with great perception and deep feeling. These descriptions of life in Jackson County reveal the blend of vision and pragmatism that characterized the Rocky Mountain Zion after the first planned colony in Missouri was abandoned. Based on a wide sampling from the Mormon archives in Utah of newspapers, pamphlets, correspondence, and private journals that were written during the stay in Missouri; illus., 48 notes.

W. F. Zornow

2227. Arrington, Leonard J. CHARLES MACKAY AND HIS "TRUE AND IMPARTIAL HISTORY" OF THE MORMONS. *Utah Hist. Q. 1968 36(1): 24-40.* Shows that the influences which led to the compilation of Mackay's, *The Mormons: Or Latter-Day Saints. With Memoirs of the Life and Death of Joseph Smith, the "American Mahomet"* in 1851 were chiefly the Mormon missionary efforts in Great Britain as directed by Orson Pratt beginning in 1840 and Mackay's participation in the studies of the life of the English industrial workers directed by Henry Mayhew. The sources of Mackay's information, the character of the work as a compilation, the superiority of its illustrations, and subsequent works of a similar nature are discussed.

S. L. Jones

2228. Arrington, Leonard J. THE INTELLECTUAL TRADITION OF THE LATTER-DAY SAINTS. *Dialogue: A J. of Mormon Thought 1969 4(1): 13-26.* A frontier environment and the attitude of American opinion has hindered the development of Mormon intellectualism, which has gone through four stages: 1) 1830-44, basic writings of Joseph Smith, 2) 1844-67, the elaboration of Joseph Smith's teaching, evidenced mainly by the writings of Brigham Young's advisers, the writers in Mormon magazines, newspapers, and pamphlets, and Utah educators, 3) 1867-96, a defining, refining, and organizing period to meet the increasing challenges, especially the coming of the railroad to Utah in 1869, and 4) 1896-1969, a period of creative adaptability in which Mormon thought faces the ideas of evolution, the Higher Criticism, behaviorism, communism, and other cross-currents of modernism. Based on secondary sources; 33 notes.

W. J. McNiff

2229. Arrington, Leonard J. SCHOLARLY STUDIES OF MORMONISM IN THE TWENTIETH CENTURY. *Dialogue: A J. of Mormon Thought 1966 1(1): 15-32.* Scholarly treatises on Mormon culture began in this century as the result of graduate research in the social sciences. The first treatise was presented by Edgar Wilson in 1906 at the University of Berlin. Since then more than a hundred dissertations have been written on aspects of Mormon life. However, there is still no satisfactory general history of the Mormons, there are few acceptable biographies of Mormon leaders, and there is a lack of interpretive accounts of Mormons in the 20th century. *Dialogue: A Journal of Mormon Thought* and the newly formed Mormon Historical Association seek to overcome these deficiencies through the examination, clarification, and promotion of Mormon studies. A chronological list of Ph.D. dissertations on Mormon culture and history is included.

L. P. Hofeling

2230. Arrington, Leonard J. THE SEARCH FOR TRUTH AND MEANING IN MORMON HISTORY. *Dialogue: A J. of Mormon Thought 1968 3(2): 56-65.* Discusses the history of historical recordkeeping within the Mormon Church. Most histories of the Church have been "unduly respectful of certain authority, placing credence in accounts that should have been subjected to critical analysis." Historians must get "outside" of events, read contemporary sources, and write interpretative history. Certain built-in bias has influenced impressions of Church history: theological marionette bias, male bias, solid achievement bias, centrifugal bias, and the unanimity bias. To be authentic, Mormons depend on the historian telling the truth. Truth will strengthen the testimony.

J. L. Rasmussen

2231. Ashliman, D. L. THE IMAGE OF UTAH AND THE MORMONS IN NINETEENTH-CENTURY GERMANY. *Utah Hist. Q. 1967 35(3): 209-227.* Surveys 19th-century German writing about Utah, both imaginative and scientific, and concludes that though generally it lacked objectivity, it was less malicious than that being published in other countries where Mormon missionaries were achieving greater success.

S. L. Jones

2232. Barrett, Gwynn W. DR. JOHN M. BERNHISEL: MORMON ELDER IN CONGRESS. *Utah Hist. Q. 968 36(2): 143-167.* A biographical sketch of Bernhisel, graduate of the Medical Department of the University of Pennsylvania (1827), medical practitioner in Pennsylvania and New York, and a convert to Mormonism in the first decade of its existence. He purchased land in Nauvoo and moved to that colony, where he became a close associate of Joseph Smith. Henceforth he was closely associated with all the activities of the Mormons, joining the others in the movement to Utah. He was Utah's first territorial delegate to Congress, serving from 1851 to 1859, and again from 1861 to 1863. He spent the rest of his life in Salt Lake City, practicing medicine and in other ways taking a leading part in the development of Utah. Based on the Bernhisel Letter File in the Latter-Day Saints Church Historian's Library, miscellaneous Bernhisel letters in the Huntington Library, letters possessed by H. F. Bernhisel, Lewiston, Utah, and letters in the Brigham Young University Library and the Utah State Historical Society Library.

S. L. Jones

2233. Billington, Ray A. THE ORIGINS OF HARVARD'S MORMON COLLECTION. *Arizona and the West 1968 10(3): 211-224.* In 1910, when Frederick Jackson Turner left the University of Wisconsin to become a professor at Harvard University, Mrs. Alice Forbes Perkins Hooper eagerly awaited his arrival. Mrs. Hooper wanted to memorialize her late father, Charles Elliott Perkins, who had built the Burlington Railroad system. She was persuaded to make a gift toward the establishment of a Western collection of books and manuscripts for Turner to use in his teaching and research. The Harvard Commission on Western History was appointed, prominent alumni were enlisted, and a 3,000 book and pamphlet collection on Mormon history became the principal object. The Utah-based collection, the reluctance of Mrs. Hooper to part with nearly 7,000 dollars, and the provenance of the now famous Western collection at Harvard University are the ingredients of the story of Mrs. Hooper's efforts, which almost met with success. 4 illus., 30 notes.

D. L. Smith

2234. Bitton, Davis and Allen, James B. ANTI-INTELLECTUALISM IN MORMON HISTORY. *Dialogue: A J. of Mormon Thought 1966 1(3): 111-140.* During the 19th century there was a surprising degree of compatibility between Mormonism and current intellectual thought. But a transformation took place in the church between 1880 and 1914 when the leaders of the church moved away from social planning and reform impulses toward republicanism and a conservative economic and political orientation. Because of this shift in Mormon thought and the critical nature of the intellectual, the church and its membership today evidence an open aversion to intellectualism. L. P. Hofeling

2235. Bitton, Davis. B. H. ROBERTS AS HISTORIAN. *Dialogue: A J. of Mormon Thought 1968 3(4): 25-44.* Examines Brigham Henry Roberts' (1857-1933) historical writings, and their quality and his place in Mormon historiography. His writing was highly personal, had a tendency of special pleading, was moralistic, and had a number of limitations: it lacked advanced historical training, lacked the resource of the modern increase in scholarship, had little interpretative sophistication, and held the past century's conception of historian as moral judge. His works, however, should still be read for his "zest, his empathy, and his sweep of vision." J. L. Rasmussen

2236. Bitton, Davis. MORMONS IN TEXAS: THE ILL-FATED LYMAN WIGHT COLONY, 1844-1858. *Arizona and the West 1969 11(1): 5-26.* When Brigham Young became leader of the Mormons after the 1844 assassination of Joseph Smith, Lyman Wight refused to recognize Young's authority over him. Wight led a band of dissidents to Texas from their temporary location in Wisconsin. There he founded a colony near Austin and managed to keep the settlement intact until his death in 1858. Wight's ability and dedication were reflected in his membership on the Council of Twelve Apostles. Stripped of this title and excommunicated, he still upheld what he believed was his role and that of the church. His efforts were beset with a multitude of problems - Indians, the vagaries of nature, economic stringency, apparent inability to plant firm roots in any one community, and internal disunity. The story of Wight's

colony illustrates the fitful existence of many of Smith's followers in the troubled times after his death. 3 illus., map, 39 notes.

D. L. Smith

2237. Bitton, Davis. A RE-EVALUATION OF THE "TURNER THESIS AND MORMON BEGINNINGS...." *Utah Hist. Q. 1966 34(4): 326-333.* Challenges the conclusions and the methodology of an article by Alexander Evanoff. The author questions Evanoff's conclusions that Mormonism originated among frontiersmen in a frontier setting and that it was democratic in its early career in Utah. He suggests that Evanoff has not worked with an adequate definition of terms such as frontier, democracy, and individualism, and that his application of the Turner hypothesis was too simple. S. L. Jones

2238. Brooks, Juanita. JEST A COPYING - WORD FOR WORD. *Utah Hist. Q. 1969 37(4): 375-395.* The author relates her activities in locating, copying, and finding permanent library depositories accessible to the public for the records of the Mormon pioneers. The author includes information on the ways in which the search for sources aided her and others in her writing about the Mormon frontiersmen, particularly with regard to her book *Mountain Meadows Massacre* (Oklahoma: U. of Oklahoma Press, 1966) and to the career of John Doyle Lee.

S. L. Jones

2239. Brooks, Juanita. THE MORMONS IN CARSON COUNTY, UTAH TERRITORY. *Nevada Hist. Soc. Q. 1965 8(1): 3-23.* A narrative account of the colonization attempts of the Church of Jesus Christ of Latter-Day Saints (Mormons) in Carson County, Nevada while it was still a part of Utah Territory, 1846-57. Documented with 45 notes, 7 from MSS sources. J. D. Filipiak

2240. Brooks, Juanita. A PLACE OF REFUGE. *Nevada Hist. Soc. Q. 1971 14(1): 13-24.* Soon after arriving in Utah the Mormons began to seek an alternate home for settlement. In 1858, the year following the Mormon War, the Mormon leadership was deeply concerned about possible persecution by the U.S. Government. To prepare for such an eventuality, the Mormons sent a party to locate a possible site for relocation of the Mormon community. The area chosen for the "Place of Refuge" was in Meadow Valley near the site of present day Panaca, Nevada. The Mormons never needed the site, but the exploring party was the first to cultivate land in the region, a full six years before the first permanent settlement was founded in Meadow Valley. Based mainly on primary sources; 18 notes. E. P. Costello

2241. Buchanan, Frederick S. SCOTS AMONG THE MORMONS. *Utah Hist. Q. 1968 36(4): 328-352.* Traces the story of Mormon missionary activities among the Scots and the consequent migration to the United States of some five thousand of them. Scottish contributions to Mormon society are described. Most of the immigrants came from Scotland's industrial cities, where unemployment was at high levels. They settled predominantly in northern Utah, where they were quickly assimilated into the general population. Based in part on manuscript journals in the Latter-Day Saints Church Historians Library, Salt Lake City, and newspaper accounts. S. L. Jones

2242. Bufkin, Donald. THE LOST COUNTY OF PAH-UTE. *Arizoniana 1964 5(2): 1-11.* Traces the evolution of Pah-Ute County boundaries with particular emphasis given to the role played by territorial politicians and the Church of Jesus Christ of Latter-Day Saints in retarding settlement of southern Nevada and northwestern Arizona.

W. Unrau

2243. Cable, Mary. SHE WHO SHALL BE NAMELESS. *Am. Heritage 1965 16(2): 50-55.* Relates the discovery that the author's great, great grandmother was the fifth wife of Brigham Young. Augusta Adams left her husband in Boston to marry Young after she heard him give a lecture. She lived until 1886 and was credited with being "the first woman in New England" to become a Latter-Day Saint. Some explanation of the Mormon beliefs regarding plural marriage is given.

J. D. Filipiak

2244. Cannon, M. Hamlin. THE MORRISITE WAR: INSURRECTION BY A SELF-STYLED PROPHET. *Am. West 1970 7(6): 4-9, 62.* As early as 1857 Joseph Morris claimed he received revelations from

Christ. His numerous revelations, prophetic sermons, and charismatic effect caused him and his followers to be excommunicated. In 1861 Morris established a new church and settlement to the north of Salt Lake City and prepared for the imminent second advent of Christ. His followers were generally Mormon converts from Europe who became increasingly militant and well-disciplined. Morris prepared to assume Brigham Young's mantle and to depose all dissident elements. When his prophecies were not fulfilled, the disillusioned left and the hard core became more fanatical. In early 1862 three dissidents who attempted to leave with their property were jailed. The Morrisite War began when a territorial writ of habeas corpus was burned and a militia posse moved in, killing Morris and a few others. The Morrisites were brought to trial and their case complicated Mormon-Gentile problems. Splinter successor groups flourished briefly, but failed. Court litigation continued until 1879. 5 illus., biblio. note.   D. L. Smith

2245. Cardon, A. F. SENATOR REED SMOOT AND THE MEXICAN REVOLUTIONS. *Utah Hist. Q. 1963 31(2): 151-163.* Reveals how Senator Reed Smoot attempted during the Taft and Wilson administrations to influence American and Mexican policies in order to protect the interests and lives of Mormon settlers in northern Mexico. Some of the material is drawn from Senator Smoot's diaries, now in the possession of the author's wife. There are several quotations from the diaries, which are to be published by the University of Utah Press.   S. L. Jones

2246. Carmer, Carl. "HERE IS MY HOME AT LAST!" *Am. Heritage 1963 14(2): 26-33, and 98-102.* The last part (III) of a series on the Mormons. Traces Brigham Young's leadership of the Mormons from 1844 when they left Illinois to their entry into Salt Lake Valley in 1847. Illus.   C. R. Allen, Jr.

2247. Carter, Paul A. RECENT HISTORIOGRAPHY OF THE PROTESTANT CHURCHES IN AMERICA. *Church Hist. 1968 37(1): 95-107.* Summarizes shifts in Protestant church history over the past 35 years and offers suggestions for future work in the area. The dominant position of neo-orthodox or liberal theology, the narrow definition of a Protestant "mainstream," and the virtual exclusion of groups such as Lutherans and Mormons from consideration have been challenged. The distinction between secular and religious histories of religion is no longer significant. Nonetheless the cleavage between religious history and church history or between the study of religion as prophetic movement and religion as a series of institutions continues. While recognizing the values of a church history even of "religions of the Christian perimeter" the author cautions that some aspects of American religion such as Negro religion, New Thought, or "peace of mind" do not lend themselves to such treatment and that the tendency to speak of church rather than churches may mask a failure to appreciate the positive aspects of religious pluralism. Based on recently published literature in the field; 55 notes.   S. C. Pearson, Jr.

2248. Chastenet, Jacques. L'EPOPEE DES MORMONS [The Mormon Epic]. *R. de Paris [France] 1966 73(10): 1-9.* Describes the origin of the Church of Jesus Christ of Latter-Day Saints, its persecution, and the famous trek to the state of Deseret, now Utah. The emphasis is on the personalities of the leading Mormon prophets, Joseph Smith and Brigham Young.   J. Clarke

2249. Cheville, Roy A. THE ONE HUNDRED AND FORTY-FIVE YEARS OF THE LATTER DAY SAINT MOVEMENT. *Encounter 1965 26(1): 19-38.* An abridged survey of the Latter Day Saint movement. The nature and self-identification of the movement are discussed to get the "feel and the outlook." A complex of factors provided the occasion for its appearance in 1820 and helped to determine the form it took. The first 24 years of the movement and its fragmentation after the death of Joseph Smith in 1844 is documented up to the year 1965. 3 notes, biblio.   D. H. Swift

2250. Christmas, R. A. THE AUTOBIOGRAPHY OF PARLEY P. PRATT: SOME LITERARY, HISTORICAL, AND CRITICAL REFLECTIONS. *Dialogue: A J. of Mormon Thought 1966 1(1): 33-43.* Pratt's autobiography, edited and published posthumously by his son in 1874, offers a "different perspective on Mormon history in which the exodus to the Rockies seems more like a tragedy than an epic in view of the great failures of community relations and democratic process during

the Missouri and Illinois periods. Although primarily published to provide church-members with interesting sketches of Church history and to promote faith, Pratt's autobiography has additional value as a general reflection of frontier manners." Equally important is the literary value of the work which may be considered the best of Mormon letters in the 19th century. The author suggests that it may wait until the next persecution before Mormon letters will again attain some significant literary height.   L. P. Hofeling

2251. Clayton, James L. FROM PIONEER TO PROVINCIALS: MORMONISM AS SEEN BY WALLACE STEGNER. *Dialogue: A J. of Mormon Thought 1966 1(4): 105-114.* Evaluates the attitudes of Wallace Stegner regarding the Mormons, whom Stegner found so often to be suitable subjects for his writing. The author claims that Stegner wrote much in praise of Mormons during their pioneer period but, after settlement was completed, Stegner described Mormons as being drab and colorless. He also claims that Stegner displays an ambivalence regarding the authoritarianism of Mormon society which was praiseworthy. However, once the wilderness was subdued that same authoritarianism became a liability. It is claimed that Stegner's lack of sympathy or respect for Mormon doctrine caused him to misplace his emphasis.   L. P. Hofeling

2252. Cumming, John. THE DESERET PRIMER. *Am. Book Collector 1965 15(8): 8-10.* The Mormons invented a phonetic alphabet, called the Deseret Alphabet, in 1853. In it symbols represented individual sounds. A primer was printed in 1868. The effort to establish this alphabet met with failure. Illus.   D. Brockway

2253. Davis, David B. SOME IDEOLOGICAL FUNCTIONS OF PREJUDICE IN ANTE-BELLUM AMERICA. *Am. Q. 1963 15(2): 115-125.* Establishes a connection between the presence of nativist thought and conflicts of interest in liberal thought. Attackers of the Masons, Mormons and Catholics revealed an inherited preoccupation with the conflict between individual freedom and popular will. "Ideological tensions" manifested themselves in attacks on minority groups who seemed to provide convenient images of coercion and secrecy. Apparently yearning for loyalties of their own and puzzled as to what to do about tradition, many of the nativists vilified minorities while extolling the virtues of the nation. In this manner, they managed to resolve their own tensions concerning American ideals.   R. S. Pickett

2254. DePillis, Mario S. HOSEA STOUT'S DIARY AND THE HIDDEN RHETORIC OF MORMON HISTORY. *Southern California Q. 1966 48(2): 195-201.* Attempts to show that Mormon history has a unique personnel, structure, and perspective, largely because scholars in the field have usually had an ideological involvement with their subject. The author uses the two-volume edition of Hosea Stout's diaries to show the need to "read between the lines" for a full appreciation of Mormon history.   H. Kelsey

2255. DePillis, Mario S. THE QUEST FOR RELIGIOUS AUTHORITY AND THE RISE OF MORMONISM. *Dialogue: A J. of Mormon Thought 1966 1(1): 68-88.* In treating the subject of the rise of Mormonism, historians have neglected the interpretations of standard Mormon historians such as B. H. Roberts, Orson F. Whitney, and Joseph Fielding Smith. Non-Mormon historiography has failed in three ways in its approach to the origins and rise of Mormonism. First, it has been dominated by the Utah period. Secondly, it has contrasted the first two leaders as the impractical visionary versus the pragmatic and frontierwise master colonizer. Thirdly, serious studies have rarely considered early Mormonism as a religion whose study was governed by the same canons of modern scientific methodology as, say, Congregationalism. Thus the author suggests a serious reevaluation of the early period of Mormon development, which he characterizes, under the leadership of Joseph Smith, as a "pragmatically successful quest for religious authority."   L. P. Hofeling

2256. Dyer, Alvin R. BUREAU OF INFORMATION ERECTED ON THE SITE OF THE LIBERTY JAIL AT LIBERTY, MISSOURI. *Missouri Hist. R. 1963 57(4): 379-388.* Prophet Joseph Smith and five companions were placed in jail in Liberty, Missouri in 1838. During his incarceration, Prophet Smith had revelations from the Lord of the principles of "righteous dominion" and "unrighteous dominion" in the state.

The jail was used until 1856. It was later demolished and the stones used to construct a private dwelling. The Church of Jesus Christ of Latter-Day Saints has commemorated the historic imprisonment of its founder by erecting an information bureau on the site of the old jail and using most of the reclaimed stones in its construction. W. F. Zornow

2257. Edwards, Elbert B. EARLY MORMON SETTLEMENTS IN EARLY NEVADA. *Nevada Hist. Soc. Q. 1965 8(1): 25-43*. Briefly describes the colonization experiments of the Mormons in the southern portion of present-day Nevada. It covers the period when that area was a part of Utah Territory, then Nevada Territory, and then a state (in 1864). 32 notes. J. D. Filipiak

2258. Evanoff, Alexander. THE TURNER THESIS AND MORMON BEGINNINGS IN NEW YORK AND UTAH. *Utah Hist. Q. 1965 33(2): 157-173*. Challenges Whitney R. Cross's contentions in *The Burned-Over District* (New York: Russell & Russell, 1950) that Western New York at the time of the rise of Mormonism was not a frontier region and that Mormonism had a greater appeal for Easterners than for frontiersmen. The author concludes that, excepting for a brief period of theocratic control between 1847 and 1849, the Mormons conformed with historian Frederick Jackson Turner's expectations in their reactions to the frontier environment of Utah. S. L. Jones

2259. Fife, Austin E. MYTH FORMATION IN THE CREATIVE PROCESS. *Western Folklore 1964 23(4): 229-239*. Proposes the thesis that an author in writing anything, no matter how objective it is supposed to be, is engaged in the process of myth formation. The thesis is illustrated "by using the discipline of folklore as a point of departure" as well as Austin and Alta Fife's published study of Mormon folklore *Saints of Sage and Saddle: Folklore Among the Mormons* (Peter Smith, 1956) as an example. L. J. White

2260. Flanders, Robert. SOME REFLECTIONS ON THE KINGDOM AND THE GATHERING IN EARLY MORMON HISTORY. *Dialogue: A J. of Mormon Thought 1968 3(2): 156-160*. An analysis of Mormon origins of the idea of a communitarian "Kingdom of God" and the unique social movement of the "Gathering." The author also implies that Mormons have been more interested in plans than purposes, probably because of a heavy reliance on the "overawing charisma of the Prophet," and their scripture literalism. What happens when divinely ordained plans fail? A reaction against Young by Reorganites. The major task is, however, reconciling freedom and collectivism, in reconciling the Kingdom and the Gathering. J. L. Rasmussen

2261. Flanders, Robert B. WRITING ON THE MORMON PAST. *Dialogue: A J. of Mormon Thought 1966 1(3): 49-61*. Feels that the fears and tensions which have heretofore prevented the writing of a competent Mormon history are gone. "The time is ripe for the study of Mormon history to emerge on a new plane of maturity." However, the lamentable fact is that there is no satisfactory biography of Joseph Smith or Brigham Young, nor have there been published satisfactory histories of the Utah Mormons or the Reorganized Church. As of now the Latter-Day Saints have not demanded that these and other vital histories be written. L. P. Hofeling

2262. Fleming, L. A. THE SETTLEMENTS ON THE MUDDY, 1865 to 1871: "A GODFORSAKEN PLACE." *Utah Hist. Q. 1967 35(2): 147-172*. Analyzes the reasons for the establishment of and relates the major events in a Mormon settlement in what is now known as the Moapa Valley in Southeastern Nevada. In establishing the settlement the Mormon Church was motivated by the desire to open a sea route for the delivery of supplies via the Colorado River, the hope of establishing the cultivation of cotton in the area, and the intent to forestall the possibility of non-Mormon settlement. The settlement did not prosper, and a series of disasters culminating in the locating of the community in the new state of Nevada in 1866 led to the decision to abandon the community in 1871. S. L. Jones

2263. Fox, Feramorz Y. and Arrington, Leonard J., ed. EXPERIMENT IN UTOPIA: THE UNITED ORDER OF RICHFIELD, 1874-1877. *Utah Hist. Q. 1964 32(4): 355-380*. An excerpt from an unpublished study "Experiments in Cooperation and Social Security Among the Mormons: A Study of Joseph Smith's Order of Stewardships,

Cooperation, and Brigham Young's United Order." The Richfield community was only one of more than a hundred cooperative communities established by Brigham Young and his associates in Utah in the 1870's. Leader of the Richfield community was Joseph A. Young, son of Brigham. The organization and activities of the community are described, largely on the basis of the records of the governing board which had charge of the community. The materials from which the author derived his information are in the Latter Day Saints Church Historian's Library, Salt Lake City; illus., 4 notes. S. L. Jones

2264. Francaviglia, Richard V. MORMON CENTRAL-HALL HOUSES IN THE AMERICAN WEST. *Ann. of the Assoc. of Am. Geographers 1971 61(1): 65-71*. "The Central-hall house was brought into the American West by Mormons, members of the Church of Jesus Christ of Latter-Day Saints. This house type has two basic floor plans, the narrow 'I' and the wider 'Four over Four' types. The central-hall plan has a rich folklore in Mormon Country. Although some 'Gentiles' built this type, it was generally outmoded by the time the West was opening up. Gentile settlements were dominated by Victorian and other stylistic influences which the Mormons rejected for religious and cultural reasons. The Central-hall house, along with other cultural elements, is helpful in detecting areas of the West settled by the Mormons." J

2265. Gayler, George R. ATTEMPTS BY THE STATE OF MISSOURI TO EXTRADITE JOSEPH SMITH, 1841-1843. *Missouri Hist. R. 1963 58(1): 21-36*. Joseph Smith's difficulties did not end after moving his Mormon headquarters from Missouri to Nauvoo, Illinois. Missouri authorities tried to extradite him to stand trial for alleged crimes against the people of Missouri. Smith was arrested in Quincy, Illinois on 4 June 1841. A few days later he was tried in Monmouth before Judge Stephen A. Douglas, but he was quickly dismissed. In 1842 a second attempt was made to extradite Smith. An attempt had been made to shoot Lilburn Boggs, the Governor of Missouri, which was blamed on the Mormons. Missouri tried to extradite Smith, but in a trial in Springfield early in 1843, the writ was again denied. After failing in a third attempt to extradite Smith in 1843, Missouri gave up. Based on local and national newspapers and various histories of the Church of Latter-Day Saints. W. F. Zornow

2266. Hansen, Klaus J. JOSEPH SMITH & THE POLITICAL KINGDOM OF GOD. *Am. West 1968 5(5): 20-24, 63*. The efforts of Joseph Smith through Mormonism are viewed by the author as being in the tradition of those who interpret the words of the prophet Daniel (Daniel 2:44) to mean that God's kingdom is literal and political. By 1844 Smith had completely fused his religious and political aspirations. With Manifest Destiny in full bloom, it seemed to the Mormons that the United States was the logical instrument for their divinely inspired political mission. If Smith could be elected as its president, this might be a springboard for world dominion. An alternative was the establishment of a monarchy within territory under the jurisdiction of Texas. This and the suppression of an attempted apostate newspaper which threatened to reveal some of the inner secrets of his Council of Fifty were prime factors in the martyrdom of Smith and his brother. From the author's *Quest for Empire* (East Lansing: Michigan State U. Press, 1967). 4 illus., biblio. note. D. L. Smith

2267. Hansen, Klaus J. THE METAMORPHOSIS OF THE KINGDOM OF GOD: TOWARD A REINTERPRETATION OF MORMON HISTORY. *Dialogue: A J. of Mormon Thought 1966 1(3): 63-83*. Historians for generations have believed that the key to the "Mormon question" was the understanding of the theory and practice of polygamy. The author suggests that though the doctrine of polygamy is important, he would direct attention to the concept of a political kingdom of God as "promulgated by a secret Council of Fifty." Further, he suggests that Mormon leaders may have "subtly invited assaults" on the institution of polygamy" in order to shield an institution of greater significance for Mormon history, the political Kingdom of God." The metamorphosis of this concept from a purely political to an ecclesiastical concept and the "cessation of the centralized control over Mormon politics" can be attributed to two points: the decline in the expectancy of the Second Coming and loyalty to the Constitution of the United States as a "point of doctrine." L. P. Hofeling

2268. Hansen, Ralph W. AMONG THE MORMONS: A SURVEY OF CURRENT LITERATURE. *Dialogue: A J. of Mormon Thought 1966 1(1): 152-155.* The first of a series of bibliographical columns to be presented in each issue. Each column will be devoted to "books, pamphlets, and articles published during the past year. The winter issue will deal with dissertations on Mormon subjects and each summer issue will include reviews of articles appearing in various journals."

L. P. Hofeling

2269. Hardy, B. Carmon. THE AMERICAN SIBERIA: MORMON PRISONERS IN DETROIT IN THE 1880'S. *Michigan Hist. 1966 50(3): 197-210.* Deals with the imprisonment of four Arizona Mormons in the Detroit House of Correction from December 1884 until October 1886. They had been found guilty of violating the Edmunds Law (1882) which prohibited polygamy in the territories, and their experiences, as reported in the church-owned *Desert News,* hastened the exodus of Mormons into Mexico to avoid arrest. Utilizes many primary and secondary sources, including manuscript collections at Brigham Young University and the Church Historian's Office, Salt Lake City, Utah.

J. K. Flack

2270. Hardy, B. Carmon. "THE TREK SOUTH: HOW THE MORMONS WENT TO MEXICO." *Southwestern Hist. Q. 1969 73(1): 1-16.* One of the longest and most difficult of all Mormon colonization projects occurred in the last quarter of the 19th century as a direct response to the crusade in the United States against the unpopular doctrine of polygamy. In 1884 the Church of Jesus Christ of Latter-Day Saints officially began to advise heads of families to prepare to flee the unfriendly environment. Land was purchased and the faithful who wished began to make the long journey over tremendous physical obstacles to Mexico, to the area of Casas Grandes and the valley of Chihuahua. Many had to sell their lands and belongings at considerable loss but, with great spirit, they organized themselves and went by railroad or by wagon trains to their new colony. A set of directions was finally published in 1888, but most of these Mormons arrived at their destination after suffering from lack of water, abundance of mud and gumbo, hostile Indians, danger from rattlesnakes, shortage of grazing for the animals, and the intransigence of Mexican border officials.

R. W. Delaney

2271. Haseltine, James L. MORMONS AND THE VISUAL ARTS. *Dialogue: A J. of Mormon Thought 1966 1(2): 17-29.* Art forms were apparently encouraged by Brigham Young. Usually the performing arts received more support from church authorities because of group involvement. Because of this preference, throughout Utah's history visual art forms have never been strongly cultivated. There are three significant obstacles to full cultivation of interest and talent in the visual arts. First, Mormon attitudes toward the use of nude models have precluded the instructional and constructional importance of the human form in art. Second, art instructors face the problem of telling their students that art and architecture commissioned by the church are often not of significant quality. Third, art appreciation in Utah has been hindered by the lack of adequate exhibition space. It is to be hoped that these difficulties will be overcome. There is an alphabetic list of Utah artists.

L. P. Hofeling

2272. Holsinger, M. Paul. HENRY M. TELLER AND THE EDMUNDS-TUCKER ACT. *Colorado Mag. 1971 48(1): 1-14.* Anti-Mormonism came to a climax in the Edmunds-Tucker Act (1887). Polygamy was the most important of the many causes of opposition to the Mormons. In 1885 Republican Senator George Franklin Edmunds of Vermont introduced a severe bill into the Senate which provided for dissolution of plural marriages, the forced testimony of wives against their husbands, abrogation of woman suffrage in Utah Territory, and abolition of the corporate structure of the Church of Jesus Christ of Latter-Day Saints. One of the few Senators to openly oppose the bill was Henry Moore Teller of Colorado. He did not support polygamy, but felt the Edmunds bill was illegal and unconstitutional. As Teller feared, the Act was followed by persecution and anger. Eventually the Mormons bowed to Federal law and in 1890 "the doctrinal sanction of polygamy officially ended." There is no evidence that Teller ever regretted his stand on the Edmunds-Tucker Act. His stand did not hurt his career because he was returned repeatedly to the Senate. Illus., 47 notes.

O. H. Zabel

2273. Holsinger, M. Paul. SENATOR GEORGE GRAHAM VEST AND THE 'MENACE' OF MORMONISM, 1882-1887. *Missouri Hist. R. 1970 65(1): 23-36.* Vest was a constitutionalist who was very interested in personal liberties. Vest was one of the few members of Congress to speak in defense of the Mormons when their practice of polygamy made them the subject of particularly repressive legislation in 1882 and 1887. Based on books, articles, theses, and the *Congressional Record;* illus., 49 notes.

W. F. Zornow

2274. Hubbard, George U. ABRAHAM LINCOLN AS SEEN BY THE MORMONS. *Utah Hist. Q. 1963 31(2): 92-108.* Lincoln was involved with the Mormons in all the stages of his political career. In the 1840's, as a candidate for various offices, Lincoln attempted to woo Mormon votes; but, because of the political opportunism of the Mormons, he did not always succeed. In his debates with Douglas in the 1850's, Lincoln tried to embarrass his opponent by showing the inconsistency between Douglas' attempts to restrict the Mormons and the principles of popular sovereignty. But the Republican Party had demanded the extinction of polygamy, and the Mormons supported the Democrats in the election of 1860. In the early period of the Civil War the Mormons had mixed feelings about Lincoln's administration; but in 1863, in an interview with Mormon leader, T. B. H. Stenhouse, Lincoln pledged that he would leave the Mormons alone if they would leave him alone. Lincoln kept his word, and at his death was highly regarded by the Mormons.

S. L. Jones

2275. Ivins, Stanley S. NOTES ON MORMON POLYGAMY. *Utah Hist. Q. 1967 35(4): 309-321.* Concludes that while certain leaders such as Joseph Smith and Brigham Young were enthusiastic protagonists of and participants in plural marriage, the great majority of Mormon men were not and that the experiment was not a satisfactory test of plurality of wives as a social system.

S. L. Jones

2276. Jennings, Warren A. THE ARMY OF ISRAEL MARCHES INTO MISSOURI. *Missouri Hist. R. 1968 62(2): 107-135.* A few months after the Mormon residents of Jackson County, Missouri, were prevented from creating a religious community called Zion, an expeditionary force marched from Kirtland, Ohio, to aid them in regaining their lands. "Zion's Camp" became a controversial topic in Mormon history. This is an account of the expedition. Although the expedition aided the Mormons in Missouri, convinced them that the church was interested in their welfare, healed a breach between the elders in Zion and the leaders in Kirtland, and brought forward a number of men who were to be active in Utah, it antagonized a number of Missourians who had been friendly to the Mormons and strengthened the case of those who argued that the Mormons planned to use military force to build a community in Missouri. Based on articles, newspapers, biographies and autobiographies; illus., 96 notes.

W. F. Zornow

2277. Jennings, Warren A. THE EXPULSION OF THE MORMONS FROM JACKSON COUNTY, MISSOURI. *Missouri Hist. R. 1969 64(1): 41-63.* Approximately 1,200 Mormons settled in Jackson County. The original settlers forced them to sign an agreement that one-half would move from the County by 1 January 1834, and that the rest would vacate before 1 April. When the Mormons tried to assert their rights by appealing to the State government, the settlers responded by resorting to force to carry out the agreement. This is an account of the armed struggles between the settlers and Mormons in October and November 1833. Based on newspapers, books, articles, and local histories; illus., photos, 84 notes.

W. F. Zornow

2278. Jennings, Warren A. FACTORS IN THE DESTRUCTION OF THE MORMON PRESS IN MISSOURI, 1833. *Utah Hist. Q. 1967 35(1): 56-76.* Introduced into Jackson County, Missouri, in 1832 as an instrument for the propagation of the Mormon faith, the *Evening and Morning Star,* edited by William Wines Phelps, soon became a focal point of gentile opposition to Mormon settlement in the area. A major factor in gentile hostility was belief that the Mormons were agitating slaves and free Negroes. It was the publication in July 1833 of an article headed "Free People of Color" which precipitated the agitation which led to destruction of the newspaper's press by a gentile mob on 20 July 1833, a preliminary action in a series of events which led to the expulsion of the Mormons from the county in November 1833. Based in part on manuscript materials in the Office of the Historian of the Reorganized Church

of Jesus Christ of Latter-Day Saints and contemporary newspaper accounts.
S. L. Jones

2279. Jennings, Warren A. THE FIRST MORMON MISSION TO THE INDIANS. *Kansas Hist. Q. 1971 37(3): 288-299*. The Mormons succeeded in establishing missions among the Indians in Kansas during the winter of 1838-39, but their first effort in 1830-31 - the principal subject of this article - ended in failure. Probably the first effort failed because of the prejudice that existed against missionaries on the part of Indian agents and others along the frontier, and because of the Indian intercourse laws which forbade the settlement or residence by whites on Indian lands except by those specially licensed by the Superintendent of Indian Affairs. Based on primary and secondary sources in the Kansas State Historical Society and the University of Missouri at Kansas City; illus., map, 49 notes.
W. F. Zornow

2280. Jennings, Warren. IMPORTUNING FOR REDRESS. *Bull. of the Missouri Hist. Soc. 1970 27(1): 15-29*. Details the efforts of 1,200 Mormons - expelled from their homes and deprived of their property rights in Jackson County in 1833 - to obtain redress. They enlisted support from Governor Daniel Dunklin. An irate citizenry nevertheless ensured safety to the perpetrators of the offenses against the Mormons and made it impossible for the Mormons to secure redress through the Missouri courts. An armed confrontation of Mormon forces (in Zion's Camp) and their opponents in Missouri was averted. The Mormons appealed unsuccessfully to President Andrew Jackson for Federal intervention to ensure Mormon rights in Missouri. Between 1836 and 1844 Joseph Smith, the Mormon leader, sought redress from Congress. Smith tried unsuccessfully to enlist the support of John C. Calhoun and other prominent Americans. Based primarily on newspaper accounts and on manuscripts in the Western Historical Manuscripts Collection at the University of Missouri; 53 notes.
H. T. Lovin

2281. Jones, Gerald E. AN EARLY MORMON SETTLEMENT IN SOUTH DAKOTA. *South Dakota Hist. 1971 1(2): 119-131*. A survey of the settlement at Vermillion that the Mormons sought as a refuge from persecution. Personal accounts of Mormon settlers describe the settling and temporary life of Fort Vermillion. The settlement ended in the spring of 1846 when the Mormons left to join the main body of Saints traveling toward the Rocky Mountains. Illus., 39 notes.
D. H. Swift

2282. Judex. QUE SON LOS MORMONES? [What are the Mormons?] *Estudios Centro Americanos [El Salvador] 1965 20(210): 295-298*. A discussion of the rise, spread, and teachings of Mormonism. The aim is to explain to Latin Americans the basic facts concerning this sect which is making such strides among the Spanish-speaking peoples. Mention is made of the youth of Joseph Smith and of the "gold plates" on which he professed to have found a revelation written in hieroglyphics. The difficulties Smith encountered and the opposition to his doctrines are set forth in a sketch that traces the Mormons to their arrival in the Salt Lake area. Points of doctrine are summarized and the author's objections to them set forth. The final section is a warning to Latin Americans against this religious group. "If every Protestant sect presents to sane criticism many vulnerable points, that of the Mormons offers an exceedingly great number of such points." Based on P. J. M. Ganuza, S.J., "Porvenir del Ecumenismo en Nuestras Tierras," *Estudios Centro Americanos* 1965 20(203): 83-87; P. Prudencio Damboriena, S.J., *Fe Catolico e Iglesias y Sectas de la Reforma* (Madrid, 1961); Francis X. Curran, S.J., *Major Trends in American History* (New York, 1946).
D. C. Corbitt

2283. Lythgoe, Dennis L. NEGRO SLAVERY AND MORMON DOCTRINE. *Western Humanities R. 1967 21(4): 327-338*. A survey of pronouncements on the subjects including some by Joseph Smith and Brigham Young. In spite of ambivalence or vagueness in some of the statements, Mormon doctrine has been close to the Southern position on the Negro as bearer of the curse of Ham, slavery as a divine institution, intermarriage, abolition, and segregation, with States' rights called in to support the position. Records show that at least two Negroes were admitted to the priesthood of the early Mormon church, but the policy has since been firm that Negroes might become members but must be excluded from the priesthood. The church stressed the necessity for humane treatment of slaves. Besides published works, use has been made of files in the Church Historian's Office, Salt Lake City. 40 notes.
A. Turner

2284. Mauss, Armand L. MORMON SEMITISM AND ANTI-SEMITISM. *Sociol. Analysis 1968 29(1): 11-27*. Refers to Charles Y. Glock and Rodney Stark's *Christian Beliefs and Anti-Semitism* (New York: Harper and Row Publishers, 1966) as an overview to his more specialized subject. Theological beliefs indicate that Mormons as well as Jews are Semites. Mormon theology is more concerned with "future redemption" than with "past misdeeds." In a simple sense anti-Semitism (for the Mormons) is opposed to the will of God. Despite a relative high rate of negative religious ideas about Jews, Mormons exhibit a low degree of secular anti-Semitism. Findings indicate that orthodoxy, ritual involvement, and particularism are not linked directly to secular anti-Semitism, but are linked to each other. The author believes that one of his hypotheses is verified in that the Mormon faith, in upholding a generic Semitic origin, neutralizes modern inclinations toward anti-Semitism. Thus, a purely theological indoctrination such as demonstrated by the Mormon faith can act to reduce hostility toward minority groups. Based on questionnaires returned by 249 (52 percent) respondents; 11 tables, fig., 34 notes.
A. S. Freedman

2285. McLaws, Monte. THE ATTEMPTED ASSASSINATION OF MISSOURI'S EX-GOVERNOR, LILBURN W. BOGGS. *Missouri Hist. R. 1965 60(1): 50-62*. On 6 May 1842, an unidentified person wounded the ex-governor of Missouri, Lilburn W. Boggs, as he sat in his home in Independence. Boggs had had trouble with the Mormons during his administration. One of them, Orrin P. Rockwell, was tried and acquitted. An examination of the local newspapers and Mormon literature indicates that the ends of justice were served by the acquittal of Rockwell. No evidence has been found to implicate the Mormon leaders Rockwell served. The riddle of who fired the shot has not been solved.
W. F. Zornow

2286. Meinig, D. W. THE MORMON CULTURE REGION: STRATEGIES AND PATTERNS IN THE GEOGRAPHY OF THE AMERICAN WEST, 1847-1964. *Ann. of the Assoc. of Am. Geographers 1965 55(2): 191-220*. Analysis of the expansions, contractions, and reexpansions of an American subculture to provide a refined definition of the culture region. The region is defined as consisting of three parts, the core in the Wasatch Oasis, a domain covering much of Utah and southeastern Idaho, and a sphere extending from eastern Oregon to Mexico. Illus., maps, 71 notes.
W. R. Boedecker

2287. Mitchell, Robert C. DESERT TORTOISE: THE MORMON TABERNACLE ON TEMPLE SQUARE. *Utah Hist. Q. 1967 35(4): 279-291*. Surveys the history of the construction of the Salt Lake Tabernacle and reviews briefly the major cultural, religious, and political events which have occurred in it.
S. L. Jones

2288. Morgan, Dale L. LITERATURE IN THE HISTORY OF THE CHURCH: THE IMPORTANCE OF INVOLVEMENT. *Dialogue: A J. of Mormon Thought 1969 4(3): 26-32*. There is a Mormon literature, starting with the Book of Mormon. Involvement has been the life-blood of Mormon writing, as seen in their hymns, in the autobiographies of Parley P. Pratt, Hosea Stout, Pridley Meeks, Abner Blackburn, and Anne Clark Turner, and in the works of Eliza R. Snow. The future of Mormon literature lies in becoming involved in the cross-currents of contemporary life - racial equality, sexual equality, and the bomb. Note.
W. J. McNiff

2289. Morgan, Dale L. A WESTERN DIARY. *Am. West 1965 2(2): 46-47, 93*. A review essay of Juanita Brooks, ed., *On the Mormon Frontier: The Diary of Hosea Stout, 1844-1861*, two volumes (Salt Lake City: U. of Utah Press and Utah State Historical Society, 1965). The Stout diary is "one of the most magnificent windows upon Mormon history" that has ever been opened. Stout joined the Saints in Missouri in 1837. The diary begins with his ordination as an elder in the Quorum of Seventies. Stout chronicles daily life in Nauvoo, passage across Iowa, life at winter quarters on the Missouri River from late 1846 to the spring of 1848, his overland journey in 1848, and his considerable role in the maturation of the Utah settlement. An 1852-53 missionary stint to China and the 1854 establishment of a Mormon colony in Wyoming are a part of Stout's career. The Stout diary is regarded as "must" source material for anyone concerned not only with the history of Mormons but also that of the West. Illus.
D. L. Smith

2290. Mortensen, A. R. MORMONS, NEBRASKA AND THE WAY WEST. *Nebraska Hist. 1965 46(4): 259-271.* Survey of early Mormon history, stressing the significance of the sojourn on Indian lands in Nebraska in 1847-48. R. Lowitt

2291. Olson, John Alden. PROSELYTISM, IMMIGRATION AND SETTLEMENT OF FOREIGN CONVERTS TO THE MORMON CULTURE IN ZION. *J. of the West 1967 6(2): 189-204.* In order to build a last Mormon community in Utah and maintain the church doctrine of self-sufficiency, artisans, mechanics, and farmers were needed. Church leaders sought these by making converts among the poor of Great Britain and Scandinavia. Prior to 1900 the act of conversion was synonymous with emigration to help build the new Zion. The various missions sent to Western Europe, their nature, and degree of success are stressed. In Britain most converts and emigrants came from urban artisans and mechanics while the Scandinavian migrants can be characterized by their agrarian orientation. The story of the emigrants in Zion and the reasons why emigration virtually ended by the end of the 19th century are traced. They lent, by sheer numbers, a consolidating force in Zion. Documented from published sources, 71 notes. D. N. Brown

2292. Paul, Rodman W. THE MORMONS AS A THEME IN WESTERN HISTORICAL WRITING. *J. of Am. Hist. 1967 54(3): 511-523.* The Mormons have not been the subject of the serious historical research their importance deserves. Few adequate biographies exist, even of Brigham Young, and virtually no scholarship has been devoted to their history since 1877. This dearth can be attributed partly to the fact that archives have not been made available to scholars, and that provincial attitudes and a highly-charged emotional atmosphere denigrate objective study. There has, however, been much social science research done, nearly all of it concluding that Mormons developed a unique, self-contained state with many of the features of nationalism but built out of American materials. This social heritage can be helpful, but also restrictive and conservative. At any rate, this theme might be the central one around which historical studies may be oriented. K. B. West

2293. Petersen, William J. MORMON TRAILS IN IOWA. *Palimpsest 1966 47(9): 353-384.* Treats the experiences of the Mormons while crossing Iowa in their migrations from Nauvoo in 1846 and in 1856 during the handcart expeditions. The rigors overcome by the second group, largely English immigrants, are detailed through quotations from a diary kept by Archer Walters, one of the migrants. Illus., maps. D. W. Curl

2294. Peterson, Charles S. "A MIGHTY MAN WAS BROTHER LOT": A PORTRAIT OF LOT SMITH - MORMON FRONTIERSMAN. *Western Hist. Q. 1970 1(4): 393-414.* Smith's (1830-92) experience included service in the Mormon Battalion, gold mining in California, cavalry assignments from President Abraham Lincoln, a term as a county sheriff, a preaching mission to England, and management of cooperative sheep and cattle herds. He was revered as the leader of the Nauvoo Legion in the Utah War (1857) in a raid against the Federal Army's supply trains and livestock as they approached Utah. Smith's efforts during 1876-92 as a colonizer and leader in northern Arizona are most significant. Administrative and policy decisions and the church's failure to define roles and obligations complicated his assignments. He handled a jurisdictional dispute involving an Indian mission and Navajo animosity. Circumstances necessitated fort-like communal living in close confinement and a life of unremitting toil. Smith's Spartan character allowed little concern for the comforts or welfare of his associates. His efforts to establish a social and spiritual union were a failure, but his business endeavors were a notable success against overwhelming odds. 51 notes. D. L. Smith

2295. Sears, Hal D. THE SEX RADICALS IN HIGH VICTORIAN AMERICA. *Virginia Q. R. 1972 48(3): 377-392.* Describes the varying attitudes of 19th-century groups - Mormons, Shakers, Oneidans, Spiritualists, anarchists, and others - toward marriage and sex. The year 1871 saw the end of "serious and widespread discussion of sexual alternatives in nineteenth-century America." Some "sex radicals" nevertheless continued the discussion. Thus, they raised "questions of government censorship and individual self-ownership." Numerous publications appeared, such as *Lucifer the Light Bearer* which was edited and published 1883-1907 by Moses Harman (1830-1910). Their advocacy of free love and their use of blunt language resulted in suppression in Comstockian America. O. H. Zabel

2296. Smiley, Winn Whiting. AMMON M. TENNEY: MORMON MISSIONARY TO THE INDIANS. *J. of Arizona Hist. 1972 13(2): 82-108.* Tenney (1844-1925) learned Spanish from an orphaned Mexican boy adopted by his mother. At the age of 14, Tenney, a Mormon, served as an interpreter on an official proselytizing and exploring expedition into the Hopi country. After similar assignments, militia duty, work with the US Geological Survey, plural marriage, and building up a substantial ranching and cattle business in the Southwest, Tenney was asked in 1875 by church officials to become a missionary in southern Arizona and northern Mexico. For the balance of his life Tenney was an active and zealous Mormon missionary and colonizer in the Southwest and Mexico. Frequently he salvaged potentially explosive situations from disaster because of his ability to get along with the Indians and the Mexicans. 3 illus., map, 48 notes. D. L. Smith

2297. Sorenson, John L. ANCIENT AMERICA AND THE BOOK OF MORMON REVISITED. *Dialogue: A J. of Mormon Thought 1969 4(2): 80-94.* Lists 136 items of similarities between Near East and Mesoamerican cultures in pre-Columbian period. The accuracy of the Book of Mormon is more and more attested to by recent scholarship. Table. W. J. McNiff

2298. Taylor, Phillip A. M. THE LIFE OF BRIGHAM YOUNG: A BIOGRAPHY WHICH WILL NOT BE WRITTEN. *Dialogue: A J. of Mormon Thought 1966 1(3): 101-110.* Very little is known about Brigham Young. The easily accessible evidences of his life and career portray him only as the leader, colonizer, and public figure. Knowledge is scant about how he formulated and directed policy, and from extant documents little can be gleaned about his private life and personality. The author feels that the attitude of the Mormon Church regarding full access to sources which could lead to a better understanding of Young is crippling. He hopes for a more relaxed policy toward the private resources of the church but does not foresee any such move in the future. L. P. Hofeling

2299. Thompson, Dennis L. RELIGION AND THE IDAHO CONSTITUTION. *Pacific Northwest Q. 1967 58(4): 169-178.* Analysis of topics pertaining to religious rights while the constitution of the new State of Idaho was being written. With examples of early drafts and influences of some politicians, the author shows rationale leading to disfranchisement of members of the Church of Latter-Day Saints (Mormons). The constitution, with its undemocratic provisions, was adopted without opposition among the delegates (51 to 0) in 1889, but shortly after statehood (1894) the Mormons were given voting privileges. C. C. Gorchels

2300. Williams, J. D. THE SEPARATION OF CHURCH AND STATE IN MORMON THEORY AND PRACTICE. *Dialogue: A J. of Mormon Thought 1966 1(2): 30-54.* Asks "how far may a church and its leaders invade the political arena without seriously breaching the separation of church and state?" Regarding his own faith as one which is involved in politics, the author evaluates the "major constructs of Mormonism which bear on politics, the struggle-for-statehood period which shaped latter-day political thinking, the forms of LDS Church involvement in politics, and the issues and dilemmas which are posed by such involvement." L. P. Hofeling

2301. Williams, J. D. THE SEPARATION OF CHURCH AND STATE IN MORMON THEORY AND PRACTICE. *J. of Church and State 1967 9(2): 238-262.* "How far may a church and its leaders invade the political arena without seriously breaching the separation of church and state?" The *Documents and Covenants* of the Mormon Church (1835) clearly reject religious interference in political matters, but *The Book of Mormon* (1830) and Mormon experience sustain a tradition of political involvement by the church collectively and by individual church officers. Churches should have the right of self-defense when governments threaten basic doctrines and principles. Church officers should not be automatically excluded from political involvement as individuals, but church members should not allow their political views to be shared by religious leaders. An alternative to this approach is a policy of noninvolvement in political matters by religious leaders which would have the virtue of avoiding schisms in the church over political issues. Based on Mormon Church documents and histories, and newspapers and periodicals; 63 notes. G. W. Hull

2302. Young, Karl. BRIEF SANCTUARY: THE MORMON COLONIES OF NORTHERN MEXICO. *Am. West 1967 4(2): 4-11, 66-67.* In 1852 Mormon leader Brigham Young publicly proclaimed the doctrine of plural marriage. Effective Federal antipolygamy legislation was not written until 1874 and 1882. After losing the legal battles some went underground, but many looked for sanctuary elsewhere. As early as 1875 new sites for settlement were scouted in northern Chihuahua. In 1885, even before the church had purchased lands there, Mormon families crossed the border and encamped along Mexican streams. Arrangements made with the Mexican officials, they set out in systematic Mormon fashion to adapt themselves to the physical circumstances of their new homeland. Their towns, all named in honor of prominent men in their adopted land, became the breadbasket of Chihuahua and were pointed to as models for Mexicans to follow. Prospering under a favorable national regime, they were placed in a precarious position when nevolutionist Francisco I. Madero headquartered his operations in northern Chihuahua on the doorstep of the Mormon colonies. Madero was compelled to live off the country when pressed by federal forces. For self-protection the Mormons soon smuggled in high-powered rifles. The appearance of still another revolutionary group, incidents which approached the brink of disaster, and confiscation of Mormon supplies and arms forced the evacuation of the Mormons to Texas in 1912. Within a short time, however, many of the refugees filtered back to their Mexican homes and succeeded in riding out the storms of the revolution because it was their conviction that, in the long run, there was more opportunity for them there than in the United States. To them, Mexico was now more than just a haven for those with more than one wife. Map, 6 illus., biblio. note.

D. L. Smith

2303. —. TRIBUTE TO STANLEY S. IVINS. *Utah Hist. Q. 1967 35(4): 307-309.* Biographical sketch and a review of Ivins' studies in Mormon history. "Perhaps Stanley's greatest service to history has been the generous assistance he has given to other scholars." At his death in 1967, it was found that he had willed his library of more than a thousand books and pamphlets, his notebooks and index, and private family records to the library of the Utah State Historical Society.

S. L. Jones

Other Sects and Groups

2304. Antrei, Albert. FATHER PIERRE DE SMET. *Montana 1963 13(2): 24-43.* A summarized biography of the first Jesuit missionary in the northern Rocky Mountains. De Smet, born in Belgium in 1801, spent 10 years among Indians of the lower Missouri Valley before his establishment of a mission for the Salish of western Montana in 1841. His vigor and ability led to further assignments in founding missions to other tribes, including a temporarily unsuccessful attempt among the Blackfeet. Particular emphasis is placed on De Smet's later service in winning Indian support of projected treaties, especially the noted Fort Rice Treaty of 1868.

S. R. Davison

2305. Barnds, William Joseph. A CHRONOLOGICAL ACCOUNT OF EFFORTS MADE TO SECURE A BISHOP FOR THE TERRITORIES OF NEBRASKA AND KANSAS IN 1856. *Hist. Mag. of the Protestant Episcopal Church 1963 32(1): 27-36.* Analyzes the action of General Convention. Faulty communication between the two houses and the fear of getting a bishop entangled in a nasty political situation contributed to the Deputies' defeat of the Bishops' proposal to create a new missionary district.

E. Oberholzer, Jr.

2306. Barnds, William Joseph. THE EPISCOPAL CHURCH IN NEBRASKA SINCE 1875. *Hist. Mag. of the Protestant Episcopal Church 1964 33(3): 185-223.* Continuation of an earlier article, "The Episcopal Church in Nebraska to 1875," (which appeared in the issue of 1962 31(1): 21-35). Both articles are designed to furnish background information for a contemplated centennial history of the diocese. The life of the Episcopal Church in Nebraska has been a spotty one since 1856. Scarcity of money and clergy have yet to be entirely erased. After more than one hundred years of missionary endeavor there are more churches and educational institutions defunct than in operation. The article is chronological in treatment and is sketchy after 1945. Documented.

E. G. Roddy

2307. Barnds, William Joseph. THE MINISTRY OF THE REVEREND SAMUEL DUTTON HINMAN, AMONG THE SIOUX. *Hist. Mag. of the Protestant Episcopal Church 1969 38(4): 393-401.* The Reverend Samuel Dutton Hinman served as a missionary to the Sioux Indians in the Dakota and Nebraska Territories and Minnesota for almost three decades after the beginning of the Civil War. Most of this time was spent in Dakota, and his success owed much to his willingness to live among the Indians and speak and minister in their language. He organized schools, ordained native ministers, and taught them practical skills in a "trade school." After his wife died, he became involved in a nasty dispute with Bishop William Hobart Hare over some supposed improprieties. Nevertheless, the author declares him to be the "Godfather" of Episcopal work among the Sioux. Based primarily on research in Episcopal periodicals; 23 notes.

J. B. Boles

2308. Barnes, Lela, ed. LETTERS OF ALLEN T. WARD, 1842-1851, FROM THE SHAWNEE AND KAW (METHODIST) MISSIONS. *Kansas Hist. Q. 1967 33(3): 321-376.* Eighteen letters written by Ward to his parents, brother, and sister between 25 June 1842 and 23 February 1851. They are now in the possession of his descendants in Topeka, Kansas, and Urbana, Illinois. The most important letters are the dozen that Ward wrote while teaching at the mission's Indian manual labor school. The letters provide information about the many problems associated with missionary activities on the frontier and the day-by-day operation of a school dedicated to providing Indian children with instruction in English, manual arts, and agriculture. Illus., 26 notes.

W. F. Zornow

2309. Barrows, June. A VERMONTER'S DESCRIPTION OF A SUNDAY IN LOS ANGELES, CALIFORNIA, IN 1852. *Vermont Hist. 1970 38(3): 192-194.* Hiland Hall (1795-1885), U.S. Land Commissioner, wrote his home pastor in North Bennington, Vermont, on 26 September 1852, about the festival of the Virgin that day. The feast was celebrated with Masses, illumination, bells, cannon, carousing and bullfighting - not a New England Sunday.

T. D. S. Bassett

2310. Beless, James W., Jr. THE EPISCOPAL CHURCH IN UTAH: SEVEN BISHOPS AND ONE HUNDRED YEARS. *Utah Hist. Q. 1958 36(1): 77-96.* Organized in seven sections on the basis of the careers of the bishops who headed the Episcopal Church in Utah to 1967. The author's major concern is with the building of churches, hospitals, schools, the establishment of cemeteries, and similar activities. Some attention is directed to attitudes toward and relationships with the Mormon Church. Based on reminiscences, the annual reports of the bishops (in the Office of Episcopal Bishop of Utah, Salt Lake City), and newspaper accounts.

S. L. Jones

2311. Belgum, Gerhard L. LUTHERANS AND RIGHTISTS IN CALIFORNIA. *Lutheran Q. 1966 18(3): 227-234.* A discussion of the effect of the right-wing movement on the Lutheran Church in California, concluding that the church was "touched . . . but by no means knocked off balance by the rightist cause."

R. B. Lange

2312. Bender, Norman J. CRUSADE OF THE BLUE BANNER IN COLORADO. *Colorado Mag. 1970 47(2): 91-118.* Describes the extension of Presbyterianism into Colorado and the Rocky Mountains, and suggests that, contrary to the fears of eastern church leaders, the western churches tried to follow traditional patterns. The leading Presbyterian missionary was the Reverend Sheldon Jackson who, from 1869 to 1884, promoted extension of Presbyterianism in the West. The "Blue Banner," symbol of Presbyterianism, was promoted by continuous use of military terminology in Jackson's *Rocky Mountain Presbyterian* and other Presbyterian statements. Roman Catholics and Mormons were looked upon as important antagonists. The author finds evidence of the western desire to follow eastern church patterns in standardized record keeping, church architecture, disciplinary practices, and emphasis upon education. Illus., 120 notes.

O. H. Zabel

2313. Berkhofer, Robert F., Jr. PROTESTANTS, PAGANS, AND SEQUENCES AMONG THE NORTH AMERICAN INDIANS, 1760-1860. *Ethnohistory 1963 10(3): 201-232.* Of all acculturative agents, Protestant missionaries who sought establishment of a "scriptural, self-propagating Christianity," were most aggressive and demanded greatest change on the Indians' part. Efforts of six denominations (Quaker,

Moravian, Baptist, Methodist, Presbyterian, Episcopalian) among six tribes (Oneida, Seneca, Cherokee, Choctaw, Ojibwa-Sioux, Nez Perce), all of which had lost substantial autonomy, are reviewed: four patterns of response are noted, and the degrees of cultural fragmentation discussed and analytically diagrammed.   H. J. Graham

2314. Blanchet, F. N. and Vaughan, Elizabeth, trans. OREGON GRAPESHOT. *Oregon Hist. Q. 1968 69(3): 269-271.* A letter written by the vicar general of the missions in the Oregon Territory to the bishop of Quebec in 1844, describing the arrival of nuns and Father Pierre de Smet in the settlement of Saint Paul on the Willamette River and subsequent activities in establishing a mission and a school. Plans are outlined for the establishment of other missions, and an appeal is made to the bishop for financial assistance.   C. C. Gorchels

2315. Bliss, Helen. BIBLIOGRAPHY OF THE WORKS OF CLIFFORD MERRILL DRURY, 1934-1969. *J. of Presbyterian Hist. 1970 48(2): 143-157.* An annotated bibliography of the works of Drury (b. 1897), a historian of religion specializing in the area west of the Mississippi River. Drury served pastorates in China and Idaho and from 1938 to 1963 taught church history at San Francisco Theological Seminary. From 1943 to 1956 he was the official historian of the U.S. Navy Chaplain Corps. Lists Drury's works in chronological order from 1934 to 1969.
                                    S. C. Pearson, Jr.

2316. Brackenridge, R. Douglas. SUMNER BACON: "THE APOSTLE OF TEXAS." *J. of Presbyterian Hist. 1967 45(3): 163-179 and (4): 247-255.* Part I. Sketches the career of this first Cumberland Presbyterian minister in Texas. Having been reared in New England where he received little formal education, Bacon was converted during a Cumberland Presbyterian revival at Fayetteville, Arkansas, and sought a license to preach in Texas. Denied this because of inadequate education, he entered Texas in 1829 and carried on an itinerant lay ministry in spite of the hostility of Mexican Government officials and the indifference of many settlers. In 1832 he was again refused ministerial status in Arkansas, but he received ordination from a new presbytery in Louisiana in 1835. Bacon distributed Bibles for the American Bible Society and organized Sunday schools in connection with his itinerant ministry. He participated in the Texas struggle for independence from Mexico under orders of General Sam Houston and after the war established his headquarters at San Augustine. 60 notes. Part II. With permission of the Synod of Mississippi Bacon organized a Texas Presbytery in 1837 and became its first moderator. However, suffering from ill health and from false charges against him of drunkenness and misappropriation of missionary funds - charges of which he was eventually cleared - Bacon devoted less time to church affairs after 1837. He made his last extensive missionary tour in 1842 and was chosen moderator of the Texas Synod at its first meeting in 1843. He died in 1844. Bacon's influence on Texas Cumberland Presbyterianism was great. He was charitable and broadminded in dealing with other denominations, but his lack of education, part-time ministry, and lack of interest in Christian nurture or stewardship shaped his denomination long after his death. Based on published materials and manuscripts in the library of Trinity University; 30 notes.   S. C. Pearson, Jr.

2317. Brown, Lawrence L., ed. BISHOP FREEMAN AND THE NEBRASKA-KANSAS ELECTION OF 1856. *Hist. Mag. of the Protestant Episcopal Church 1963 32(2): 157-170.* A report by Bishop Freeman of the Southwest to the Board of Missions (1853) and a statement by him to the House of Bishops (1856), edited, with an introduction, by Professor Brown. The statements suggest that Bishop Freeman opposed the creation of a missionary district of Nebraska and Kansas because it would further diminish funds which might otherwise be applied to the salaries of missionary clergymen.   E. Oberholzer

2318. Canfield, Francis X. A DIOCESE SO VAST: BISHOP RESE IN DETROIT. *Michigan Hist. 1967 51(3): 202-212.* Describes the activities of Frederic Rese, first Catholic Bishop of the Michigan Diocese, between 1833 and 1840. Until 1837, when Michigan became a State, Bishop Rese's jurisdiction extended over what is now Michigan, Wisconsin, Iowa, Minnesota, and portions of North and South Dakota. From the few extant primary sources it is clear that Rese devoted most of his attention to Michigan alone, where he conducted missionary activities, established parishes, and founded educational institutions in Detroit.
                                    J. K. Flack

2319. Chitty, Arthur Ben. LEONIDAS POLK: A MEDIOCRE GENERAL BUT A GREAT BISHOP. *Civil War Times Illus. 1963 2(6): 16-20.* Leonidas Polk was the first North American bishop to enter the military. Polk's religious contributions can be divided into three periods: his ministry in Tennessee, his missionary episcopate in the Southwest, and his bishopric in Louisiana. As Episcopal Bishop of Louisiana he saw perhaps his greatest achievement completed in 1860 when the University of the South was built. After war broke out, Polk was urged to enter the Army. He came from a well-known family of military leaders and had attended military school. In June 1861 he joined the Confederate Army as General Polk. He was shot and killed on 14 June 1864. "In war he was a very good soldier. But he was also wrong. In the Church he was magnificent - and right." 4 illus.   M. J. McBaine

2320. Corwin, Hugh D. PROTESTANT MISSIONARY WORK AMONG THE COMANCHES AND KIOWAS. *Chronicles of Oklahoma 1968 46(1): 41-57.* Protestant missionary work among the Comanche and Kiowa of southwestern Oklahoma began as early as 1869 with Quakers appointed by the government to serve as agents. Subsequent efforts have been conducted under the aegis of the Baptist, Mennonite, Methodist, Presbyterian, and Reformed denominations. 25 notes.
                                    D. L. Smith

2321. Denton, Charles Richard. THE UNITARIAN CHURCH AND 'KANSAS TERRITORY,' 1854-1861. *Kansas Hist. Q. 1964 30(3): 307-338.* The long-run history of Unitarianism in Kansas has been one of unrealized ambitions. The American Unitarian Association saw the territorial strife of the 1850's as a means of building a liberal Christian community on the frontier. Reverend Ephraim Nute was sent to Lawrence, Kansas in 1854 to establish the first congregation. His career in Lawrence, the efforts to gain support for the Kansas mission, and the cooperation between the A.U.A. and various immigrant aid schemes are the major themes of the article. Based largely on material in the *Quarterly Journal of the American Unitarian Association* and the *Christian Register.*   W. F. Zornow

2322. Denton, Charles R. THE UNITARIAN CHURCH AND "KANSAS TERRITORY," 1854-1861 - CONCLUDED. PART 2, 1856-1861. *Kansas Hist. Q. 1964 30(4): 455-491.* An account of the Unitarian mission in Lawrence, its principal leaders, and the relationships between the missionary efforts, political and economic conditions in Kansas, and the American Unitarian Association. The activities of Reverend Ephraim Nute (1819-1897), the missionary, and those of Edmund Whitman (1812-83), the builder of the church, are described in detail. Major attention is also given to Daniel Foster (1816-64) and John S. Brown (1806-1902); the latter took over the mission when Foster and Nute became chaplains during the war. Based on archival material in the Kansas State Historical Society.   W. F. Zornow

2323. Drury, Clifford M. HANGED TWICE IN EFFIGY. *J. of Presbyterian Hist. 1963 41(2): 89-102 and (4): 237-242.* Dr. William Anderson Scott (1813-85), founder and first pastor of Calvary Presbyterian Church in San Francisco (1854-61), editor of the *Pacific Expositor,* founder and first acting president of San Francisco Theological Seminary (1871-85), was the only clergyman in California's history hanged twice in effigy. The first instance was on 5 October 1856, the result of his opposition to the organization and activity of the local Vigilance Committee. An ardent Southern sympathizer, he was again hanged in effigy on Sunday, 22 September 1861. The author provides full description of both incidents and discusses related events both in San Francisco and in the denomination on the local and national levels. Based on church records, newspapers, and periodicals.   W. D. Metz

2324. Etulain, Richard. ST. JOSEPH'S CHURCH IN IDAHO CITY. *Idaho Yesterdays 1967 11(1): 32-36.* Roman Catholic missionaries established St. Joseph's Church in November 1863. It was strongly supported until the middle 1870's when the mining boom faded. The church has served as a mission church since 1877 and has continued to hold services on East Hill, overlooking the old mining city. 2 illus., 18 notes.   D. H. Swift

2325. Feldhause, Mary Grace. FATHER PETER MASTEN DUNNE, S.J.: A BIO-BIBLIOGRAPHY. *Records of the Am. Catholic Hist. Soc. of Philadelphia 1963 74(1): 24-61.* Covers the family background, early religious education, and priestly and teaching career of one of the finest historians of the Church in America. His historical fairness caused him to be criticized in his early years as too Protestant, but the same magazine which criticized him later published these articles. His opposition to narrow and uncritical history made his contributions more valuable to his church as well as to historians. His work on early Catholic missionaries of the West led him to active leadership in many historical societies. His work included nine such volumes, several others, and hundreds of articles and reviews, as well as years of editorial service on *America*. With 17 pages of bibliography.

C. G. Hamilton

2326. Fogde, Myron Jean. THE PROTESTANT MINISTER FACES FRONTIER MONTANA. *Montana 1965 15(1): 26-36.* The first Protestant effort in the territory followed the gold rush of the early 1860's and was largely directed at finding and reclaiming people who had been church members in the "states." The most successful preachers among the miners and ranchers used a rugged and simple approach, while the more scholarly or fastidious ministers failed and went home in despair. Based on contemporary newspapers and church records.

S. R. Davison

2327. Franklin, William E. THE RELIGIOUS ARDOR OF PETER H. BURNETT, CALIFORNIA'S FIRST AMERICAN GOVERNOR. *California Hist. Soc. Q. 1966 45(2): 125-131.* Traces the religious development of Peter Hardeman Burnett from his youth when he was a deist, through his 30's when he joined the Disciples of Christ Church, to the time he became a Catholic convert. After the massacre of 14 inhabitants of the Waiilatpu Mission in 1847, he defended his faith in answer to a scathing denunciation from the pulpit accusing certain Catholics of having incited the Indians to the barbarous massacre. Later he published *The Path Which Led a Protestant Lawyer to the Catholic Church* (1859), here characterized as a "verbose polemic arguing the truth of Catholicism." Its popularity among Catholics is witnessed by a fourth edition in 1872 and an abridged version in 1909. The author, whose doctoral thesis was on Burnett's political career, found no evidence that religion played a part in Burnett's political activities or his brief career on the Supreme Court of California. 27 notes.

E. P. Stickney

2328. Fraser, James H. INDIAN MISSION PRINTING IN NEW MEXICO: A BIBLIOGRAPHY. *New Mexico Hist. R. 1968 43(4): 311-318.* Although the first missionary activity in New Mexico can be dated from approximately 1539, not until 1877 was mission printing produced. John Menaul, a Presbyterian missionary, "must be given credit for being the first missionary-linguist-printer" in New Mexico. The bibliography, containing 17 entries, is divided into three language groups. 13 notes.

D. F. Henderson

2329. Gooch, John O. WILLIAM KEIL, A STRANGE COMMUNAL LEADER. *Methodist Hist. 1967 5(4): 36-41.* William Keil was devoted to mysticism and magic before becoming a Methodist local preacher in 1839. He soon left the Methodist Church and adopted communal principles. In 1844 he founded a communal religious settlement at Bethel, Missouri, and later at Aurora, Oregon. Activities of Keil and his two settlements are described by the author. Documented, 25 notes.

H. L. Calkin

2330. Gould, Richard A. and Furukawa, Theodore Paul. ASPECTS OF CEREMONIAL LIFE AMONG THE INDIAN SHAKERS OF SMITH RIVER, CALIFORNIA. *Kroeber Anthrop. Soc. Papers 1964 31: 51-67.* Describes in detail Indian Shaker ceremonies among the Indians of Smith River, California, showing the gestures used in the curing ceremony. The Indian Shaker Church was founded in 1881 and the community at Smith River in the 1930's. Commonly-held beliefs among the Shakers on curing, Bible usage, and language usage are examined. The Indian Shaker Church may be a focus for Indian identity, despite and perhaps because no one tribe is represented in any numbers, and because of the common Indian elements which form such a large part of the services. Based on primary and secondary sources, and field investigation; 5 illus., biblio.

C. N. Warren

2331. Green, Frank L. H. K. W. PERKINS, MISSIONARY TO THE DALLES. *Methodist Hist. 1971 9(3): 34-44.* Henry Kirk White Perkins (1814-84) served as a Methodist missionary to the Indians at The Dalles, Oregon, 1837-44. Relates the story of Perkins' personal life, his

relations with others of the missionary mission, and his ministry to and experiences with the Indians. 10 notes.

H. L. Calkin

2332. Green, Norma Kidd. THE PRESBYTERIAN MISSION TO THE OMAHA INDIAN TRIBE. *Nebraska Hist. 1967 48(3): 267-288.* Discusses the work of various Presbyterian missionaries to the Omaha tribe from 1856 to the 1930's, when the last mission church succumbed to the depression.

R. Lowitt

2333. Harrell, David Edwin. PARDEE BUTLER: KANSAS CRUSADER. *Kansas Hist. Q. 1968 34(4): 386-408.* Pardee Butler is shown to have been one of the most prominent reformers in Kansas and a highly-respected preacher and organizer in the Disciples of Christ church. Butler was a strong man who found himself drawn into every religious and reform issue that arose in Kansas during his 33-year association with the region. Abolitionism during the territorial period and prohibition during the years immediately after the Civil War were the dominant issues. Butler was attracted to both of them. Since it was in connection with these two reform movements that Butler left his greatest impression on the history of Kansas, the author limits his study to them. Based on local newspaper reports, religious periodicals, articles, recollections and other published writings by Butler; illus., 103 notes.

W. F. Zornow

2334. Harrington, Marie. A RANCHO CELEBRATED LA FIESTA DE LA SANTA CRUZ. *Masterkey 1968 42(2): 75-78.* In the old days of California the widely scattered ranchos were so far from the pueblo church in Los Angeles that the rancheros and their families usually celebrated their important religious feast days at their ranchos, inviting friends and neighbors from far and near to join them for the lavish fiesta which sometimes lasted several days. This article is a detailed account of the feast day of 4 May at the Reye y Marquez rancho in Santa Monica Canyon. Photo.

C. N. Warren

2335. Harrod, Howard L. THE BLACKFEET AND THE DIVINE "ESTABLISHMENT." *Montana 1972 22(1): 42-51.* Examines the conflict between Methodist and Roman Catholic clergy on Montana's Blackfeet Reservation when President Grant's Peace Policy was implemented by assigning this area to Protestants after it had long been a field of Jesuit work. Friction was especially strong in 1876-83, when the Methodist John Young served as Blackfeet Agent and quarreled with Fathers John Imoda and Peter Prando over their respective jurisdiction in school matters. Based on archival materials in the Museum of the Plains Indian, Browning, Montana; illus., 40 notes.

S. R. Davison

2336. Harrod, Howard L. EARLY PROTESTANT MISSIONS AMONG THE BLACKFEET INDIANS: 1850-1900. *Methodist Hist. 1967 5(4): 15-24.* During the period from 1850 to 1900 Protestant missions to the Blackfeet Indians evolved from abortive efforts of the Presbyterians to a well established Methodist ministry. An institutional foundation was firmly established, but the missionaries were not well trained and often supported government policies which involved coercion of the Blackfeet. The author discusses the early Presbyterian attempts, Methodist evangelism in the 1870's and 1880's, the permanent Methodist mission, and the reasons for failures and successes. 33 notes.

H. L. Calkin

2337. Howell, Erle. JAMES HARVEY WILBUR, INDIAN MISSIONARY - FOUNDER OF METHODISM IN THE INLAND EMPIRE. *Methodist Hist. 1969 7(2): 17-27.* Gives a biographical account of James Harvey Wilbur, founder of Methodism in Washington and northern Idaho and one of Methodism's topflight Indian missionaries. The author discusses his relations with the Indians and his position in the Methodist Church from 1859 to 1887. In addition there are earlier biographical data and a summary of developments on the Yakima Reservation. Based on a diary of Wilbur at Willamette University and records of the Pacific Northwest, Oregon, and Columbia River Annual Conferences of the Methodist Church; 16 notes.

H. L. Calkin

2338. Howell, Erle. JOHN P. RICHMOND, M.D., FIRST METHODIST MINISTER ASSIGNED TO THE PRESENT STATE OF WASHINGTON. *Methodist Hist. 1970 9(1): 26-35.* Biographical account of John P. Richmond (1811-95), who became the first Methodist minister in Washington when he was assigned to the Indian Mission at

Nisqually on Puget Sound in 1840. He served there for two years. In addition to being a Methodist preacher, Richmond was a physician, politician, and superintendent of schools. 32 notes.   H. L. Calkin

2339.   James, Eleanor.   THE SANCTIFICATIONISTS OF BELTON. *Am. West 1965 2(3): 65-73.* In 1866, Martha White McWhirter, a devout Methodist, had a religious experience out of which she considered herself "sanctified" for a special purpose. Her weekly afternoon prayer meetings gained other sanctified female converts and strained relations with the churches of Belton, Texas. The enforced celibacy and other preachments of this self-styled prophetess brought troubles with the unsanctified husbands of her followers. By taking in washings, nursing, and other activities the Sanctified Sisters built up an independent income. The dream of financial security led to a smoothly-run hotel venture. Inheritance netted the sisters real estate and other property. For no apparent reason the flourishing female communistic enterprise disposed of its community properties in Texas in 1899 and moved to Washington, D.C. The accumulated funds were sufficient to keep the founding sisters reasonably comfortable in their declining years. Men were not barred but the few who joined the group stayed for only a short time. Biblio. note, illus.
D. L. Smith

2340.   Jenkins, Myra Ellen.   NEW MEXICO - 1863. *Hist. Mag. of the Protestant Episcopal Church 1963 32(3): 221-223.* Tells of Bishop Joseph Cruickshank Talbot's visit to New Mexico and of his relations with Antonio José Martinez, a political figure recently excommunicated from the Roman Catholic Church.   E. Oberholzer

2341.   Jessett, Thomas E.   ANGLICANISM IN WASHINGTON TERRITORY. *Hist. Mag. of the Protestant Episcopal Church 1963 32(2): 131-138.* A brief survey of the work of the Church of England and the Episcopal Church in the area, 1836-89.   E. Oberholzer

2342.   Jessett, Thomas E.   A CONCISE HISTORY OF THE CHURCH IN THE PACIFIC NORTHWEST. *Hist. Mag. of the Protestant Episcopal Church 1967 36(2): 109-126.* Chronological sketch of the Anglican (later Episcopal) church in Oregon, Washington, and Idaho from the pioneer years of the 19th century to 1967.   E. G. Roddy

2343.   Jessett, Thomas E.   THE EPISCOPAL CHURCH IN TACOMA, WASHINGTON. *Hist. Mag. of the Protestant Episcopal Church 1965 34(4): 377-383.* An address delivered at the 75th anniversary celebration of Christ Church, Tacoma, Washington, on 2 June 1964, which sketches the history of Episcopalianism in Tacoma from the early 1870's to the opening of the century. The selection of the town in 1875 as the western terminus for the Northern Pacific Railroad changed the sleepy mill community of one hundred persons into a bustling city of 36 thousand within less than 20 years. By 1890 there were five Episcopal churches in addition to the residence of the first bishop of Washington Territory, the Right Reverend John Adams Paddock. Documented.
E. G. Roddy

2344.   Jessett, Thomas E.   ORIGIN OF THE TERM "BLACK ROBE." *Oregon Hist. Q. 1968 69(1): 50-59.* Traces the evolution of the use of the term "Black Robe" from the original descriptive phrase for Church of England clergymen in the Winnipeg, Canada, area in 1821 to the widely accepted name used for Roman Catholic Jesuit missionaries in Eastern Washington Territory and Idaho Territory to 1847.
C. C. Gorchels

2345.   Jessett, Thomas E.   THE REVEREND PETER EDWARD HYLAND: FOUNDER OF THE CHURCH ON PUGET SOUND. *Hist. Mag. of the Protestant Episcopal Church 1968 37(3): 245-274.* Outlines the life of the Reverend Hyland (1829-1909), traces each period of the minister's life until his retirement in 1907. Illus., 117 notes, drawing often from the Hyland family papers and local newspapers.
E. G. Roddy

2346.   Jore, Léonce.   THE FATHERS OF THE CONGREGATION OF THE SACRED HEARTS (CALLED PICPUS) IN CALIFORNIA. *Southern California Q. 1964 46(4): 293-313.* Originally published in *French American Review* (1950 3: 34-62). The first two Picpus Fathers came to California in 1832 after being driven out of Hawaii, but they left in 1837 in the hope of being allowed to re-settle in the Islands. A second group came from Chile between 1848 and 1856 and attempted to establish an educational system in California, but either died or returned to Chile. The author discredits the theory that the Jesuits worked to eliminate the Picpus Fathers from education in northern California in the 1850's, concluding that the suggestion by the Jesuits that the Picpus Fathers concentrate their activities in southern California had merit because they were too dispersed over the entire state and their educational projects were already a failure. The new bishop of California evidenced no interest in retaining them in his diocese. Between 1909 and 1935 five more Picpus Fathers came, but they too either died or left California. Uses published sources. Some notes do not cite source of information.   J. Jensen

2347.   Juhnke, James C.   J. G. EWERT—A MENNONITE SOCIALIST. *Mennonite Life 1968 23(1): 12-15.* Describes the career of Jacob Gerhard Ewert, Mennonite pamphleteer, journalist, and professor at Tabor College. Born in Poland in 1874, Ewert migrated to Hillsboro, Kansas, with his family at the age of eight. He is remembered for his advocacy of Christian Socialism, pacifism, and temperance. Although he did not carry the Mennonites with him into the Socialist camp, Ewert was accepted and loved by his brethren. During World War I he "was among the most active Mennonite leaders in counseling young draftees, providing news about the war and the draft through the newspapers, and in defending the Mennonite position to government and to the public." For several years before his death in 1923 he was general secretary of the Kansas prohibition movement. Based on Ewert's published writings and other primary sources.   D. J. Abramoske

2348.   Kent, H. R., ed.   BISHOP LAY'S PROPOSED MISSIONARY JOURNEY TO NEW MEXICO. *Hist. Mag. of the Protestant Episcopal Church 1966 35(1): 99-103.* Bishop Henry Champlin Lay (1823-85) was consecrated Missionary Bishop of the Southwest in 1859. His territory included Arkansas, Indian Territory and "parts adjacent." Keenly interested in the New Mexican portion of his vast district, Lay sought the assistance of fellow Episcopal clergymen in planning an 1861 exploration of New Mexico and Arizona "all Romanist or heathen." The Civil War put an end to his proposed journey. Documented.   E. G. Roddy

2349.   Krahn, Cornelius.   RESEARCH ON URBAN MENNONITES. *Mennonite Life 1968 23(4): 189-192.* Presents a list of 50 books, articles, and dissertations written since 1894 on the urban origin of Anabaptism in Europe and on various aspects of modern urban Mennonite life in Canada and the United States. An introductory essay suggests opportunities for further research. "The Dutch Mennonites," for example, "furnish an unusual opportunity to study the various aspects of secularization and urbanization from the earliest days to the present." The archival records of Amsterdam, which are available in the United States on microfilm, have not been fully utilized. Much research remains to be done on rural and urban Mennonites in Canada.

D. J. Abramoske

2350.   Luebke, Frederick C.   GERMAN IMMIGRANTS AND THE CHURCHES IN NEBRASKA, 1889-1915. *Mid-America 1968 50(2): 116-130.* An immigration study designed to provide a statistical basis for an interpretation of the assimilation of German immigrants into American society. Based on data drawn from the biographies of 653 first and second generation Germans living in four selected regions of latter 19th-century Nebraska, the study indicates that a positive relationship existed among Lutheran and Catholic church membership, European birth, rural residence, and identification with the Democratic party; conversely, memberships in non-Lutheran Protestant churches or in no church tended to be found among those of American birth, urban residence, lodge membership, and identification with the Republican Party. Based primarily on Government and State documents as well as periodical literature; 20 notes.   J. F. Scaccia

2351.   Lyon, T. Edgar.   RELIGIOUS ACTIVITIES AND DEVELOPMENT IN UTAH, 1847-1910. *Utah Hist. Q. 1967 35(4): 292-306.* Describes the activities and motives of non-Mormon religious groups in Utah in this period. Included in the account are the Jews, the Unitarians, Roman Catholics, the Protestant Episcopal Church, and the Evangelical Christian Churches (Presbyterians, Methodists, Congregationalists, Baptists, Lutherans, and Church of Christ). Of these only the Evangelical Christian group attempted any major missionary or reform activities. This paper was presented at a meeting of the Utah State Historical Society in September 1964.   S. L. Jones

2352. McGloin, John Bernard. ANTHONY LANGLOIS, PIO-NEER PRIEST IN GOLD RUSH SAN FRANCISCO. *Southern California Q. 1967 49(4): 407-424.* Concerns the life of Father Anthony Langlois, pioneer priest of the San Francisco gold rush. Born in 1812 in Quebec Province, Canada, he was ordained a priest in 1838. He served as a missionary to the Indians in the Oregon Country from 1842 to 1849. While on his way back to Quebec in 1849, he stopped in San Francisco where he was prevailed upon to stay and become founder of Saint Francis parish. In 1850 he became vicar of the San Francisco Bay area and shortly thereafter vicar of the northern half of the Monterey diocese. His activities until his death in 1892 are detailed. Based on archival materials, contemporary articles, and secondary sources; 43 notes.

W. L. Bowers

2353. McGloin, John Bernard. PATRICK MANOGUE, GOLD MINER AND BISHOP AND HIS "CATHEDRAL ON THE COM-STOCK." *Nevada Hist. Soc. Q. 1971 14(2): 24-31.* Patrick Manogue (1831-95), who was a gold miner before his ordination as a Catholic priest, was assigned to Virginia City to minister to Catholic miners working the Comstock Lode. During his long and often hazardous tenure in the area, first as a priest, then as a bishop, Manogue became a legend, even in his own time. The church that he built and called St. Mary in the Mountains is still referred to as the Cathedral on the Comstock in memory of the long and unselfish service of Father Manogue. St. Mary in the Mountains celebrated its 75th anniversary on 8 September 1935. Photo, 12 notes.

E. P. Costello

2354. McGloin, John Bernard. "PHILOS" - (GREGORY J. PHE-LAN, M.D., 1822-1902): COMMENTATOR ON CATHOLICISM IN CALIFORNIA'S GOLD RUSH DECADE. *Records of the Am. Catholic Hist. Soc. of Philadelphia 1966 77(2): 108-116.* Outlines the career of Phelan and cites a selection of his letters to eastern newspapers to demonstrate that we are indebted to him for literate, interesting, and accurate accounts of the Catholic Church in California. 31 notes.

J. M. McCarthy

2355. McLoughlin, Virginia Ward Duffy, ed. ESTABLISHING A CHURCH ON THE KANSAS FRONTIER: THE LETTERS OF THE REV. O. L. WOODFORD AND HIS SISTER HENRIETTA, 1857-1859. *Kansas Hist. Q. 1971 37(2): 153-191.* After a brief career as principal of the Cherokee Male Seminary, the Reverend Oswald Langdon Woodford (1827-70) returned to the East to get married. He and his bride set out for Kansas in March 1857. After failing to receive a call in Lawrence, the young pastor made his way to the new community of Grasshopper Falls where he achieved a modest success. Eventually he gave up the ministry, returned east, and became a farmer. The letters to his parents, the Hartford *Daily Courant,* and the American Home Missionary Society, and two letters from his sister Henrietta, who joined him in Kansas after the death of his wife, are filled with information about the political, economic, and religious development in Kansas during the violent territorial period. Illus., 21 notes.

W. F. Zornow

2356. Mehlhoff, Carole. HARMONY GROVE: A LITTLE EPIC OF AMERICA. *Pacific Historian 1966 10(2): 28-33.* An account of David Staples and Dean Jewett Locke of the Boston and Newton Joint Stock Company, both of whom came to California in 1849 and later in 1853 founded the Harmony Grove Church 60 miles inland from San Francisco. In 1965 it was purchased, after years of disuse, as a San Joaquin Valley landmark. Based on local sources; illus., photos.

T. R. Cripps

2357. Meschter, Daniel Y. HISTORY OF THE PRESBYTERIAN CHURCH IN RAWLINS, WYOMING. *Ann. of Wyoming 1966 38(2): 173-212.* Discusses the founding and first 16 years of the history of the France Memorial Presbyterian Church in Rawlins, Wyoming. This group was organized in 1869, only a year after Rawlins had been settled. Included is material on the problems of personnel, finances, and erection of a church building. The role of individual leaders such as the Reverend Sheldon Jackson in establishing and maintaining a small congregation in a frontier community is shown. Based on church session records and correspondence in the archives of the Presbyterian Historical Society, Philadelphia; illus., 92 notes. To be continued.

R. L. Nichols

2358. Meschter, Daniel Y. HISTORY OF THE PRESBYTERIAN CHURCH IN RAWLINS, WYOMING. *Ann. of Wyoming 1967*

39(1): 69-103. Continued from previous article. Discusses the personalities and actions of Margaret and James France, for whom the church was named. The problems of establishing a church with less than half a dozen members, of obtaining a minister, and of financial support are considered. The careers of several ministers receive attention. Based on church session records and archival material of the Presbyterian Historical Society, Philadelphia; illus., 65 notes.

R. L. Nichols

2359. Miller, Clifford R. THE RELIGIOUS EXPOSITOR: ORE-GON PIONEER JOURNAL. *Oregon Hist. Q. 1963 64(2): 123-136.* Efforts to establish a religious journal in frontier territory, 1846-55; some editorial policies are noted.

C. C. Gorchels

2360. Nash, John D. SALMON RIVER MISSION OF 1855: A REAPPRAISAL. *Idaho Yesterdays 1967 11(1): 22-31.* "The Pacific Northwest's earliest Mormon colony brought several hundred missionaries to central Idaho between 1855 and 1858." Explains the reasons for establishing a Mormon mission among the Bannock and Shoshoni Indians on the Salmon River. The mission was built and manned as a fort in an isolated valley. Outlines the relationships between the Mormons and the mountaineers and illustrates the collision of three frontier cultures, which resulted in an Indian raid that closed the mission in 1858. 2 illus., 52 notes.

D. H. Swift

2361. Owen, J. Thomas. WHAT HAPPENED TO THE PLAZA CHURCH? *Masterkey 1965 39(4): 141-149.* Reviews the building and rebuilding history of the Los Angeles Plaza Church. First built in 1822, the church was still in use in 1965. Based on primary and secondary sources; 2 illus.

C. N. Warren

2362. Palmer, Everett W. METHODIST PIONEERS, FOUNDING FATHERS OF SEATTLE. *Methodist Hist. 1964 2(4): 1-9.* Concludes that perhaps no major city in the United States owes quite as much to Methodist pioneers as Seattle, Washington. Discussed is the role of preachers and laymen in establishing and building churches, establishing schools, starting businesses, and bringing people to the area to populate it and fill many types of jobs.

H. L. Calkin

2363. Peeke, Carroll. THE FORGOTTEN MAN. *Hist. Mag. of the Protestant Episcopal Church 1966 35(2): 173-181.* Biographical sketch of the Reverend Dr. John Leonard Ver Mehr (1809-86), founder of Grace Church (now Grace Cathedral), San Francisco, California. After building his 20 by 60 foot chapel, in 1849, he turned his hand to part-time school-mastering and, after his dismissal from the staff of Grace Church, to journalism and farming. At his death he was the oldest priest, by residence, in California. Notes.

E. G. Roddy

2364. Peeke, Carroll. ONE HUNDRED YEARS BEFORE SOUTH BEND. *Hist. Mag. of the Protestant Episcopal Church 1970 39(3): 245-249.* Lengthy excerpts from the address of the Right Reverend William Ingraham Kip, first bishop of the Episcopal Diocese of California, to his diocesan convention on 6 May 1869. Three problems the Episcopal Church faced in 1869 - "Ritualism, Radicalism and Divorce" - were the same faced by the Special General Convention almost a century later.

A. J. Stifflear

2365. Pfaller, Louis. THE FORGING OF AN INDIAN AGENT. *North Dakota Hist. 1967 34(1): 62-76.* Beginning his service at the Indian Agency of Devil's Lake (near Fort Totten) in Dakota Territory as a blacksmith in 1871, James McLaughlin won the respect of Major Forbes, the agent, and of the soldiers at Fort Totten, the Indians, and his fellow employees. Forbes paid McLaughlin a tribute and won for him an increase in salary. When Forbes died in 1875, McLaughlin applied to the vicariate apostolic of northern Minnesota for the position of agent. The Indian agencies had been assigned to the denominations as a means of civilizing the natives. Although all who knew McLaughlin supported his application, Paul Beckwith was appointed by the Commissioner of Indian Affairs at the suggestion of Father J. B. A. Brouillet, head of the Commission of Catholic Indian Missions. Beckwith was soon jealous of McLaughlin's prestige with the Indians and soldiers. A lack of harmony led Beckwith to dismiss McLaughlin, but Beckwith was inexperienced and unsuccessful. He resigned 1 July 1877, and McLaughlin was then appointed to the post, serving until his death in 1923. Illus., 33 notes.

I. W. Van Noppen

2366. Point, Nicolas. RELIGION AND SUPERSTITION: VIGNETTES OF A WILDERNESS MISSION. *Am. West 1967 4(4): 34-43, 70-73.* Father Nicolas Point was a missionary to the Blackfeet, Coeur d'Alene, and Flathead Indians from 1840 to 1847. Later he organized his rough journals into six volumes which he titled "Recollections of the Rocky Mountains." A painter of considerable ability, he included in the "Recollections" many of the illustrations he had executed in the field to communicate the tenets of Christianity to the Indians and to record his day-to-day life in the mission. Point's journals were translated and edited by Joseph P. Donnelly and published in 1967 as *Wilderness Kingdom - Indian Life in the Rocky Mountains: 1840-1847* (New York: Holt, Rinehart and Winston). Anecdotal selections from the journal, with 14 illustrations, are presented here bearing out Father Point's conviction that Indian "medicine" was the principal obstacle in the way of their conversion and civilization.   D. L. Smith

2367. Rainsford, George N. DEAN HENRY MARTYN HART AND PUBLIC ISSUES. *Colorado Mag. 1971 48(3): 204-220.* Henry Martyn Hart, dean of St. John's Cathedral (Episcopalian) in Denver, was "the most famous clergyman ever to minister in Colorado." Deals with Dean Hart as a clergyman trying to make the church relevant, rather than as a builder or preacher. Dean Hart made particularly good use of the press to influence social issues. Of particular concern to him were charity, supervision of saloons and brothels, recreation, political integrity, Sabbath observance, crime, and the failure of public education to provide moral education. He also advocated the social responsibility of wealth and proposed an amazing plan for sharing the wealth which became known as "The Dean's Divine Income Tax." During his 41 years (1879-1920) in Denver, Dean Hart was a constructive genius who helped shape the spiritual and moral development of the pioneer community. "His effectiveness was sometimes questionable, his reasons likewise, but his Christian goodwill and concern never." Illus., 33 notes.   O. H. Zabel

2368. Ruby, Robert H. A HEALING SERVICE IN THE SHAKER CHURCH. *Oregon Hist. Q. 1966 67(4): 347-355.* Report of observations by the author of vocal and energetic religious activities in the Shaker Church in the Northwest originated by John Slocum, a Puget Sound Indian who claimed that God gave him spiritual inspiration in a dream in 1882.   C. C. Gorchels

2369. Salmans, Mary Blake. MRS. BLAKE'S SUNDAY SCHOOL. *New Mexico Hist. R. 1963 38(4): 312-322.* Reflections on the establishment of a Sunday school in Deming, New Mexico, in 1882, including a visit from the toughest cowboy in town.   D. F. Henderson

2370. Schaeffer, Claude E. EARLY CHRISTIAN MISSION OF THE KUTENAI INDIANS. *Oregon Hist. Q. 1970 71(4): 325-348.* Probes the background of Christian forms of worship among Indians of the Columbia plateau, with special reference to Kutenai Indians among the Flathead region in Montana. Treats the period 1824-39. Describes the school life of the Indians as directed by Anglican missionaries. Depicts disappointing results of attempts by white missionaries to train Indian neophytes to assume a missionary role.   C. C. Gorchels

2371. Schaeffer, Lyle. UNTO THESE HILLS: A GOLDEN ANNIVERSARY SKETCH OF THE ORIGINS OF THE COLORADO DISTRICT. *Concordia Hist. Inst. Q. 1972 45(4): 247-268.* The history of the Colorado District of the Lutheran Church-Missouri Synod. The Colorado District, covering Colorado and parts of Kansas, New Mexico, Arizona, Texas, and Utah, had its origins in Carl Wulsten's "Colfax Agricultural and Industrial Colonization of Fremont County" in 1870. The colony failed, but its members reorganized as the Hope Lutheran Church of Westcliffe, the first permanent Lutheran congregation in Colorado. Reverend Johann Gottlieb Michael Hilgendorf was instrumental in the creation of this congregation. Later, many other pastors organized congregations in the region. Outstanding among them was Carl F. Schmid, the "Desert Missionary" of New Mexico. In 1921 the congregations established the original Colorado District, which took its present form in 1947. Based on primary and secondary sources; 107 notes.   B. W. Henry

2372. Seiber, Richard A. DAVID E. BLAIN: THE METHODIST CHURCH IN WASHINGTON, 1853-1861. *Methodist Hist. 1963 1(3): 1-17.* David E. Blain was the founder of Methodism in Seattle, Territory of Washington, in 1853. The author discusses the organizing of the Methodist Episcopal Church by Blain, his subsequent pastorates in Washington and Oregon until 1861, the difficulties of travel in a frontier area, society during territorial days, and his relationships with the Flathead Indians. Some details of his earlier and later activities are included. Based on unpublished letters and letters printed in the *Christian Advocate* of that period.   H. L. Calkin

2373. Shade, Rose Marian. VIRGINIA CITY'S ILL-FATED METHODIST CHURCH. *J. of the West 1969 8(3): 447-453.* The unfortunate Methodist Church in Virginia City, built in 1861, was blown down, burned down, and even involved in scandal. Four buildings were erected on the church's lot between 1861 and 1876. The final church was finally torn down in 1957.   R. N. Alvis

2374. Steckler, Gerard G. THE FOUNDING OF MOUNT ANGEL ABBEY. *Oregon Hist. Q. 1969 70(4): 312-332.* A detailed account of the factors, happenstances, and human considerations which led to the founding of the Mount Angel Abbey under the Roman Catholic Benedictine religious order, 1879-83. Includes incidents which led to the borrowing of money at seven-and-a-half percent interest in order to purchase the hilltop land for the Abbey in 1882. Photo, notes.   C. C. Gorchels

2375. Steinmetz, Paul B. THE RELATIONSHIP BETWEEN PLAINS INDIAN RELIGION AND CHRISTIANITY: A PRIEST'S VIEWPOINT. *Plains Anthropologist 1970 15(48): 83-86.* "The American Indian who is dedicated to his own religious tradition and to Christianity has the same identity crisis that the Jewish convert did in the early church. The Jews discovered that their religious tradition was the foreshadowing of Christianity, containing the types of Christ, and that Christ fulfilled and did not destroy their Jewish tradition. The Christian Indian today can do the same by discovering that his Sacred Pipe and the tradition for which it stands is also a foreshadowing of Christ in his office of mediator, and the type of the whole plan of salvation. The Christian Indian can understand that Christ is the Living and Eternal Pipe who fulfills and does not destroy their sacred pipe. Without this fundamental insight all blending of the two traditions will be superficial."   J

2376. Stoddard, Robert H. CHANGING PATTERNS OF SOME RURAL CHURCHES. *Rocky Mountain Social Sci. J. 1970 7(1): 61-68.* Explores some dynamic characteristics of rural churches by examining their spatial manifestations. Specifically, this concerns the spatial distribution of open-country churches in a Nebraska county for the years 1894-1968. The author presents the distribution changes and some associations which help to explain those changes. 3 tables, 3 figs., 6 notes.   R. F. Allen

2377. Stoffel, Jerome. THE HESITANT BEGINNINGS OF THE CATHOLIC CHURCH IN UTAH. *Utah Hist. Q. 1968 36(1): 41-62.* Shows the peripheral nature of Utah in Catholic activities under Spanish-Mexican, French-Canadian, and US territorial auspices until the Diocese of Salt Lake was established in 1891. The major emphasis is given to the activities which followed establishment of US jurisdiction over the region, when the first Catholic priest came to the Territory as a chaplain assigned by the US Army to the Utah Expeditionary Force. Based on Church and Army records, the diary and scrapbook of John Wolcott Phelps (on microfilm at the Utah State Historical Society), and contemporary newspaper accounts.   S. L. Jones

2378. Thompson, Erwin N. NARCISSA WHITMAN. *Montana 1963 13(4): 15-27.* As the recent bride of Dr. Marcus Whitman, missionary and physician, Narcissa was one of the first two white women to cross the plains and mountains to the Oregon country. She lived at the Waiilatpu Mission to the Cayuse Indians from 1836 to 1847, gradually losing both health and hope as mission efforts showed little result in improving the natives. The tragedy culminated in a general massacre of whites at the mission in 1847. Undocumented.   S. R. Davison

2379. Uplegger, Francis J. A BRIEF REVIEW OF NEARLY NINETY YEARS OF LIFE BY THE GRACE OF GOD. *Concordia Hist. Inst. Q. 1965 38(3): 146-150.* Focuses on the author's training at Concordia Seminary in St. Louis and his ministry in the Midwest. In 1919 he began his long career as a missionary with an Apache Indian Mission in Arizona.   D. J. Abramoske

2380. Vernon, Walter N. MC MAHAN'S CHAPEL. *Methodist Hist. 1970 9(1): 46-52.* An account of McMahan's Chapel, designated a National Historic United Methodist Landmark. The chapel, in Sabine County, Texas, was established in 1833. It apparently is the oldest Protestant church with a continuous history in Texas. Discusses the problems confronting Methodists in Texas from 1824 to 1832, as well as activities at the chapel from 1833 to 1956. 11 notes.   H. L. Calkin

2381. Vollmar, Edward R. THE ARCHIVES OF THE MISSOURI PROVINCE OF THE SOCIETY OF JESUS. *Manuscripta 1968 12(3): 179-189.* Discusses the history of the Jesuit archives now deposited in the Pius XII Memorial Library of St. Louis University. The boundaries of the Missouri Province of the Society of Jesus have changed often, although the offices always have been in St. Louis. The province now includes Missouri, Kansas, Colorado, Wyoming, Oklahoma, and some of southwest Illinois. Describes sources of material currently received, the 11 classes of organization in the collection, important individual documents, and details of an ongoing microfilming project. 4 notes.
                                                              P. McClure

2382. Wagner, Oswald F. LUTHERAN ZEALOTS AMONG THE CROWS. *Montana 1972 22(2): 2-19.* Two German clergymen, Moritz Braeuninger and Johann Jacob Schmidt, attempted to establish a Lutheran mission among the Crow Indians of Montana and Wyoming in 1858-60. The missionaries made a brief contact with the Crow, but hostility of the neighboring Sioux led to abandonment of the project and to Braeuninger's death in 1860. Although befriended by individual Army officers and fur traders, the two believed that these groups treated the Indians unfairly. Based on the missionaries' reports, recently found in church archives; 14 illus., 30 notes.   S. R. Davison

2383. Wallace, Jerry. HOW THE EPISCOPAL CHURCH CAME TO ARIZONA. *J. of Arizona Hist. 1965 6(3): 101-115.* The early years of the Episcopal Church in Arizona are treated with emphasis on the various appointed bishops. From published and unpublished church records with some other published works. Illus., 39 notes.
                                                              J. D. Filipiak

2384. Weber, Francis J. ARIZONA CATHOLICISM IN 1878: A REPORT BY JOHN BAPTISTE SALPOINTE. *J. of Arizona Hist. 1968 9(3): 119-139.* Salpointe was a French-born missionary who came to the West eight years after his ordination as a priest. He was sent in September 1868 to the newly established Vicariate Apostolic of Arizona (which then included a small portion of southern New Mexico and west Texas). After 10 years of service, Salpointe, then a titular bishop, prepared a report on the state of Arizona Catholicism. In his survey of the Church in Arizona, Salpointe reported that missionary activity by the Jesuits had begun in the latter years of the 17th century. This promising beginning was swept away by a great Indian rebellion which occurred in the mid-18th century. Before the Jesuit missionaries could rebuild their missions, as was done in other Spanish colonies at that time, they were banished by order of the crown. Their successors, the Franciscans, made a great deal of progress until the 1820's. At that time, when Mexico won its independence from Spain, the missionaries had to take an oath of allegiance to the new state or leave. All the missionaries in Arizona elected to go. As a result, they could not be replaced and the missions decayed. When the United States took possession of Arizona, there was a period when Church activities were greatly neglected. By 1864 only San Xavier del Bac remained open for religious services. Consequently, Pope Pius IX created the Vicariate Apostolic of Arizona. There then followed a period of rapid growth in both Catholic population and church construction. Based largely on Salpointe's report in the archives of the Archdiocese of Los Angeles; 51 notes.   R. J. Roske

2385. Weber, Francis J. THE CHAPEL IN THE SEA. *Records of the Am. Catholic Hist. Soc. of Philadelphia 1968 79(3): 141-146.* Although the earliest association of Catholicism with Santa Cruz Island (off the California coast at Santa Barbara) dates to 1542, no permanent mission was established there. Thus there was some confusion when in 1936 the Archdiocese of Los Angeles discovered a chapel on the island. The circumstances of the building of the chapel by the Caire family are detailed in a lengthy memorandum from the daughter of the long-time owner of the island. 6 notes.   J. M. McCarthy

2386. Weber, Francis J., ed. GRANT'S PEACE POLICY: A CATHOLIC DISSENTER. *Montana 1969 19(1): 56-63.* A letter from missionary John Baptist Camillus Imoda, S.J., to his superior Father J. B. A. Brouillet concerning the replacement of Catholic clergy by Methodist agents on the Blackfeet Reservation early in the 1870's. The letter is dated 30 January 1874. His complaint is based on the arbitrary breaking of the long Catholic contact with the Indians, and the relatively little previous Protestant activity. The editor provides background facts and a sketch of Father Imoda's life. Illus.   S. R. Davison

2387. Weber, Francis J. AN HISTORICAL SKETCH OF SAINT VIBIANA'S CATHEDRAL, LOS ANGELES. *Southern California Q. 1962 44(1): 43-56.* The erection of a cathedral where episcopal functions could be performed properly and worthily was planned by the Catholic bishops of California as early as 1856. Bishop Thaddeus Amat designated the church of Our Lady of Sorrows in Santa Barbara as his procathedral from 1856 to 1876. The Asistencia of Our Lady of the Angels in Los Angeles was dedicated as Saint Vibiana's Cathedral in 1869. The remains of Saint Vibiana were enshrined in a crystal and gilt casket in a special ceremony on completion of the cathedral in 1876. For 90 years the noble Cathedral of Saint Vibiana has been a silent witness to the great events and ceremonies of the Diocese of Los Angeles. 33 notes.
                                                              D. H. Swift

2388. Weber, Francis J. IN SEARCH OF A BISHOP. *Southern California Q. 1963 45(3): 235-243.* A report of efforts to research details of the life of Francisco Mora y Borrell, bishop of Monterey-Los Angeles from 1878 to 1896. Mora was born in a village in northeastern Spain in 1827. He excelled in religious studies, and in the 1850's he came to America with Thaddeus Amat, bishop of Monterey, who had been in Spain seeking vocations for California. After studying in Missouri, he came to California in 1856 and was ordained in Santa Barbara. In 1866 he was made vicar general of the Diocese of Monterey-Los Angeles, in 1873 he became Amat's assistant, and after Amat's death in 1878 he became bishop. In 1896 a serious carriage accident necessitated his resignation, and he returned to Spain where he died nine years later. The author undertook a lengthy and successful search for Mora's burial place and, after learning from an obituary that Mora had wished to be interred in his former diocese, made arrangements to have his remains moved to Los Angeles in 1962. 21 notes.   A. K. Main

2389. Weber, Francis J. THE LOS ANGELES CHANCERY ARCHIVES. *Americas 1965 21(4): 410-420.* Guide to "those files pertaining directly to the historical development of California Catholicism" (not, e.g., "matrimonial and departmental archives").   D. Bushnell

2390. Weber, Francis J. THE SAN FRANCISCO CHANCERY ARCHIVES. *The Americas 1964 20(3): 313-321.* Guide to materials in the Chancery Archives of the Roman Catholic Archdiocese of San Francisco, covering "only those files pertaining directly to the historical development of California Catholicism" and omitting, e.g., "the vast collection of matrimonial and departmental archives." Preceded by a short historical sketch of the archdiocese and of diocesan archival procedures in the Roman Catholic Church.   D. Bushnell

2391. Weisenburger, Francis P. GOD AND MAN IN A SECULAR CITY, THE CHURCH IN VIRGINIA CITY, NEVADA. *Nevada Hist. Soc. Q. 1971 14(2): 2-23.* Virginia City in its wild boom days was more masculine and less inhibited by the restraining influences of cultured women than any of the many other mining towns of the American West. Liquor, gambling, prostitution, fighting, and lawlessness were uninhibited. Nearly all religions established or tried to establish ministries in Virginia City; even some patently bogus "ministers of the Word" tried their hand. Father Patrick Manogue, of the Catholic faith, was one of the most successful ministers in terms of tenure and accomplishment during the rougher days. For all their exterior roughness, the miners were generous to churches and charities. Organized religion prospered and fell along with the population as the Comstock Lode decreased in yield. Organized religion and church-sponsored activities were influential in bringing civilization to Virginia City. Photo, 134 notes.   E. P. Costello

2392. West, Roberta. HOW METHODISM CAME TO NORTH MONTANA. *Methodist Hist. 1967 5(3): 18-34.* The first Methodist sermon was preached in Montana in 1864 with the first church being built the same year. The author recounts the growth of Methodism in Montana from that date until 1939. The assignment and activities of preachers, the organization of the church structure, financial problems, the growth of the church and the establishment of Methodist institutions throughout the northern part of the State are presented. Based largely on Montana Methodist publications and Methodist conference minutes; 27 notes.

H. L. Calkin

2393.　Will, Clark Moor.　AURORA COLONY CHURCH BELLS. *Oregon Hist. Q. 1966 67(3): 273-276.* Tells the story of how church bells, allegedly the first brought to the Pacific coast of the United States, made in Germany, were transported to the Old Colony Church in Aurora, Oregon, in 1867. Illus.

C. C. Gorchels

2394.　Willging, Eugene P. and Hatzfeld, Herta.　CATHOLIC SERIALS OF THE NINETEENTH CENTURY: OKLAHOMA - NEW MEXICO.　*Records of the Am. Catholic Hist. Soc. of Philadelphia 1963 74(3): 174-184 and (4): 233-250.* Continuation of a definitive list of serials, by states.

C. G. Hamilton

2395.　Young, Gertrude.　THE CORRESPONDENCE OF A NIOBRARA ARCHDEACON.　*Hist. Mag. of the Protestant Episcopal Church 1963 32(1): 3-15.* Based on the letters of Edward Ashley (d. 1931), a missionary in South Dakota from 1874 to 1931. The letters tell of the work of the Episcopal Church in the area.

E. Oberholzer

2396.　—.　MINUTES OF TEXAS PRESBYTERY 1839-1843. *J. of Presbyterian Hist. 1967 45(4): 256-272.* From its formation in 1837 until the creation in 1843 of a Texas Synod the Texas Presbytery of the Cumberland Presbyterian Church was the only Presbyterian judicatory in Texas. The minutes of the fourth through the 10th stated sessions of the Presbytery are reproduced except for part of the records of the eighth session in November 1841 which are lost. The minutes not only detail the admission and dismissal of ministers and pastoral assignments but also make reference to the state of religion in the Republic of Texas. Generally deplorable conditions are reported though evidence of a revival is suggested after 1841. The manuscript minutes are at the Presbyterian Historical Society.

S. C. Pearson, Jr.

3. THE AMERICAN WEST: REGIONS

General

2397. Axes, Ruth Frey. MORE PUBLISHED WRITINGS OF HENRY R. WAGNER, INCLUDING TRIBUTES AND BIBLIOGRAPHIES. *California Hist. Soc. Q. 1968 47(3): 273-284.* Lists three bibliographies of publications of Henry Raup Wagner (1862-1957). The author adds 10 new items, indicates some yet unpublished works, lists the recipients of the Henry R. Wagner Memorial Award established in 1959 by the California Historical Society to honor its founder, and mentions some publications about Wagner under the heading "Outcroppings."
E. P. Stickney

2398. Bannon, John Francis. HERBERT EUGENE BOLTON: HIS "GUIDE" IN THE MAKING. *Southwestern Hist. Q. 1969 73(1): 35-55.* The *Guide* referred to is Bolton's *Guide to Materials for the History of the United States in the Principal Archives of Mexico* (1913). This monumental piece of research, used by graduate students in Latin-American history since 1913, was done under the auspices of the Department of Historical Research of the Carnegie Institution of Washington. Generally, the article details the trials and tribulations of preparing the *Guide* - even Mexican archivists didn't know what they had in their archives - from letters which Bolton wrote to his brother Frederick, President Houston, and others at the University of Texas, and to J. Franklin Jameson of the Carnegie Institution. Professor Bolton's correspondence with numerous people is housed in the Bancroft Library, University of California, Berkeley.
R. W. Delaney

2399. Baritz, Loren. THE IDEA OF THE WEST. *Am. Hist. Rev. 1961 66(3): 618-640.* Surveys the thoughts and dreams of man, from Ancient Egypt to the present, pertaining to "the West." For example, to the Greeks the Elysian fields lay to the west and were the abode of heroes and gods. The "New World" of the Western Hemisphere was explored partly in search of El Dorado, the Seven Cities of Cíbola, or Quivira. These and many other fabled lands in the West are examined. 89 notes.
W. A. Buckman

2400. Barker, Nancy Nichols. IN QUEST OF THE GOLDEN FLEECE: DUBOIS DE SALIGNY AND FRENCH INTERVENTION IN THE NEW WORLD. *Western Hist. Q. 1972 3(3): 153-168.* The French foreign ministry lacked substantive information on the American West and Mexico in the mid-19th century. While France was interested in circumscribing manifestation of American manifest destiny, it was also determined to forestall British intervention in Central America. Unfortunately the foreign ministry had to rely upon inexperienced junior members of the diplomatic corps for collection and evaluation of needed intelligence information. Alphonse Dubois de Saligny was such a person. While working his way upward to the position of secretary to the French legation in Washington he developed an interest in the trans-Mississippi West and began to promote renewed French expansion in the New World. Also ambitious for himself, Dubois de Saligny was largely responsible for France's activities in the Republic of Texas. Later he played a strategic part in French intervention in Mexico during the American Civil War. 39 notes.
D. L. Smith

2401. Baum, Willa Klug. ORAL HISTORY: A REVIVED TRADITION AT THE BANCROFT LIBRARY. *Pacific Northwest Q. 1967 58(2): 57-64.* In the context of expressing appreciation of the convenience in the use of modern tape recorders in collecting oral history, the author gives an account of the efforts of Hubert Howe Bancroft in accumulating oral history via dictation in the 1870's and 1880's. Details of Bancroft's methods are given, and comments are made on the validity of oral memoirs. The author makes an appeal to historians for greater use of oral history materials.
C. C. Gorchels

2402. Bloom, John Porter. CONFERENCE ON THE HISTORY OF THE TERRITORIES OF THE UNITED STATES, NOVEMBER 3-4, 1969. *Prologue: J. of the Nat. Archives 1969 1(3): 43-50.* Held at the National Archives building under the direction of the author, present editor of *The Territorial Papers of the United States,* this meeting was the fifth in a series of conferences on various subjects being sponsored by the National Archives and Records Service. At the opening session, Clarence Edwin Carter, late editor of the *Territorial Papers,* was honored through the presentation of reminiscences of him by Philip D. Jordan and Harold W. Ryan. The four sessions of scholarly papers centered on the 1787 Northwest Ordinance, relations between the US Congress and the territories, territorial courts of the Far West, and the territories in the 20th century. Authors and titles are mentioned and brief summaries of papers presented at sessions and at luncheon and dinner meetings are given. The author concludes with the full text of the Jordan and Ryan tributes to Carter. 4 illus.
W. R. Griffin

2403. Eblen, Jack Ericson. STATUS, MOBILITY, AND EMPIRE: THE TERRITORIAL GOVERNORS, 1869-90. *Pacific Northwest Q. 1969 60(3): 145-153.* Studies the political activities of the Territorial Governors immediately before the Territories achieved statehood, 1869-90. Appointment by Presidents of the United States was but one factor which caused uneven performances by the Governors. The Territorial Governors nevertheless "appear to have been at least as conscientious as any other group of politicians in United States history." Shows the career profiles of the Governors, including college degrees, previous occupations, military experience, and other political offices.
C. C. Gorchels

2404. Frykman, George A. THOUGHTS TOWARD A PHILOSOPHY OF NORTHWEST HISTORY. *Idaho Yesterdays 1964 8(3): 26-32.* A plea for reconstruction of the philosophy of history to include the relations of nation with region and locality. The dilemma of the western regional and local historian is that he has a set of ideas and methods which describe a society which has passed out of existence. He must contend with the Romantic Enlightenment notion of the noble savage, as well as the Puritan view that the frontier is a land of violent struggle between the forces of good and evil. F. J. Turner's valuable insights into the Mississippi Valley have been perpetuated as a standard for judging all parts of the West. National historians have tended to ignore sections in the wake of rampant industrialization of the nation. The author views favorably such "exciting departures" as Walter Webb's *The Great Frontier* and H. Stuart Hughes' *History as Art and as Science.* He suggests a reappraisal of Manifest Destiny as a starting point for relating national purpose to Northwest settlement. A further study of the "myths" of the Far West must lead the historian to a fresh understanding of the relations of locality to nation.
M. Small

2405. Garnsey, Morris. ARIDITY AND POLITICS IN THE WEST. *Colorado Q. 1965 14(2): 151-160.* Environment to some degree determines human economic behavior and to some degree human behavior influences environment. This is illustrated by studying the relationship of Western aridity to Western politics. Biblio.
A. Zilversmit

2406. Goldwater, Barry M. THE WEST THAT WAS. *J. of the West 1968 7(5): 445-455.* An address delivered at the Eighth Annual Conference of the Western History Association, Tucson, Arizona, 18 October 1968. After relating anecdotes about his Uncle Morris, the speaker points out the shortcomings of the "synthesis" approach to Western history and attempts to show the value of local history and local biography to the understanding of the settling of the West.
R. N. Alvis

2407. Hill, Gertrude. SOUTHWESTERN DOZEN. *New Mexico Hist. R. 1967 42(3): 229-231.* A bibliography pertaining to the Southwest.
D. F. Henderson

2408. Hine, Robert V. AN ARTIST DRAWS THE LINE. *Am. Heritage 1968 19(2): 28-35, 102-103.* Comments on the role of John Russell Bartlett (1805-86) as a U.S. Commissioner charged with drawing a two thousand-mile boundary line between the United States and Mexico under terms of the Treaty of Guadalupe Hidalgo. Appointed to his post in June 1850, Bartlett took his party to the "initial point" at Dona Ana on the Rio Grande and worked in a westerly direction during spring 1851.

The survey team, however, was plagued with internal dissension. Southern members felt the line should be further south - eight miles north of El Paso. Hunger, bickering, bad weather, and an inhospitable terrain combined with scurvy and typhoid fever to slow the work. During these intervals Bartlett studied the aboriginal inhabitants, sketched their villages, and examined "extensive ruins." The resulting Bartlett-Garcia Conde boundary line was denounced by Democratic Senators who believed the line would impede construction of a transcontinental railroad. Bartlett, A Whig appointee, lost his position when Franklin Pierce assumed office in 1853. Illus., maps.   J. D. Born, Jr.

2409. Holmes, Oliver W. MANAGING OUR SPANISH AND MEXICAN SOUTHWESTERN ARCHIVAL LEGACY. *Southwestern Hist. Q. 1968 71(4): 517-541.* Gives archival histories of the Southwestern States and describes microfilm projects to make them more readily available for use. Mentioned are records at the University of Texas and the New Mexico State Records Center and Archives. 16 notes.
                    D. L. Smith

2410. Hunt, William R. NORTHWEST BIBLIOGRAPHY FROM DALL TO LADA-MOCARSKI. *Pacific Northwest Q. 1971 62(3): 117-120.* Mentions principal published volumes cataloging and describing books written about Alaska, British Columbia, western America, and North Pacific lands. Includes full bibliographic citations of 11 important titles.   C. C. Gorchels

2411. Jordan, Philip D. A DEDICATION TO THE MEMORY OF CLARENCE EDWIN CARTER, 1881-1961. *Arizona and the West 1968 10(4): 308-312.* While Wisconsin- and Illinois-educated Clarence Edwin Carter was a professor of history at Miami University in Ohio (1910-31), he established a reputation as a skilled editor, particularly in several volumes of *Collections* of the Illinois State Historical Society and of the correspondence of General Thomas Gage. In 1931, he was appointed editor of *The Territorial Papers of the United States.* In this capacity he produced 26 volumes in the next 30 years, sponsored at first by the Department of State and later by the National Archives, despite the fact that about one-fourth of his time was occupied in budget making and related activities necessary to keep the project alive. He was a meticulous editor with rigid standards, a master craftsman who demanded as much from others. Appended with a selected bibliography of his works. Illus.   D. L. Smith

2412. Lovelace, Lisabeth. THE SOUTHWEST COLLECTION OF THE EL PASO PUBLIC LIBRARY. *Great Plains J. 1972 11(2): 161-166.* The Southwest Collection of the El Paso Public Library was largely the work of Maud Durlin Sullivan, director of the library from 1908 to 1943. It includes material about the Spanish Borderlands - Texas, New Mexico, Arizona, and northern Mexico. Books are the foundation of the collection. Reference materials on Indians of the Southwest are particularly strong. A picture collection, an index of local newspapers, and some archival materials make the Southwest Collection both a reference source for the serious scholar and an interesting source for the casual reader. Note.   O. H. Zabel

2413. Mattes, Merrill J. FUR TRADE SITES: THE PLAINS AND THE ROCKIES. *Minnesota Hist. 1966 40(4): 192-197.* A condensed portion of a larger paper by the author entitled "Landmarks, Posts and Rendezvous: The Plains and the Rockies." It is a pictorial guide to the western fur trade sites of the United States.   P. L. Simon

2414. Neil, William A. THE AMERICAN TERRITORIAL SYSTEM SINCE THE CIVIL WAR: A SUMMARY ANALYSIS. *Indiana Mag. of Hist. 1964 60(3): 219-240.* Analyzes the historiography of writings on the American territories and their administration over the last one hundred years. Three broad categories of materials are discussed: the writings of people living at the time in Western territories or states; the observations of people influenced by the rise of imperialism at the turn of the century; the work of academicians seeking to relate the study of the territorial system as an institution to the larger perspectives of American history. Westerners were generally critical (unfairly, thinks the author) of the territorial system for seemingly slowing down the move toward statehood; those influenced by the new Manifest Destiny reflected in their study of the territories the debate between Imperialists and anti-Imperialists; academicians offered a variety of interpretations, ranging

from assertions that our system resembled the English colonial system to statements that the haphazard, *ad hoc* development of the territories made the phrase "territorial system" an oversimplified, near-denial of historical facts.   J. F. Findlay

2415. Owens, Kenneth N. PATTERN AND STRUCTURE IN WESTERN TERRITORIAL POLITICS. *Western Hist. Q. 1970 1(4): 373-392.* "Chaotic factionalism" is an apt label for the earliest type of frontier politics which was usually disruptive, confused, intensely combative, and highly personal. Eventually, a more stable and lasting organizational pattern replaced this style of politics, usually manifested in a no-party, one-party, or two-party system. Each of these systems had its peculiar characteristics and deeply affected the later development of territorial and State political institutions. The one-party system, best suited to the professional politicians, prevailed in Minnesota, Oregon, Kansas, Washington, Dakota, and Oklahoma. Only in Nebraska and Colorado did the two-party system develop, and then only on a provisional and temporary basis. The no-party pattern, in which the institutions of party government were managed by coalitions of local interests cutting across party lines, emerged in Utah, Montana, Wyoming, and New Mexico. Statehood was achieved in Nevada while chaotic factionalism still gripped the underpopulated area. In Idaho and Arizona a two-party distorted pattern evolved into a no-party system. As the wide-open factional turmoil of territorial politics was overcome, western governments assumed a distinct elitist character. Such interpretation damages the image of the frontier as a realm of natural democracy, and supports the claim that territorial government was a successful agent of American expansion.
                    D. L. Smith

2416. Owens, Kenneth N. RESEARCH OPPORTUNITIES IN WESTERN TERRITORIAL HISTORY. *Arizona and the West 1966 8(1): 7-18.* Asserts that historians have too long neglected the political history of the States beyond the first tier of those west of the Mississippi in their territorial periods. Long after statehood the form of political leadership, the style of government, and the structure of politics continued to reflect the territorial heritage. In this respect, the western experience was probably more influential and significant than the initial experiment in the Old Northwest. Fresh pioneering studies are forcing reappraisal of many traditional views. Urgently needed are detailed histories of individual territories. Basic research materials are abundant: government documents in the National Archives, manuscripts in the Library of Congress, local territorial archives, personal papers of territorial politicians, territorial newspapers, and public documents originating in both territorial and Federal agencies. Frontier historians pursuing pioneer political life will shed new light and understanding on pioneer social and economic conditions. Considering that the territorial period ranged from three and a half to 62 years, with the average over 25 years, and that it extended from 1848 to 1912, the neglect of this subject by historians seems even more unfortunate. 18 notes.   D. L. Smith

2417. Reilly, P. T. HOW DEADLY IS BIG RED? *Utah Hist. Q. 1969 37(2): 244-260.* Lists all the deaths occurring in the Colorado River between 1869 and 1967 and describes the circumstances attending them to demonstrate that the deaths have usually occurred because of carelessness, inadequate information, faulty equipment, or other conditions which put the fault on the victim rather than the river.
                    S. L. Jones

2418. Saum, Lewis O. PAT DONAN'S WEST AND THE END OF THE AGE OF HATE. *Pacific Northwest Q. 1969 60(2): 66-76.* Pat Donan (1839-1902), journalist, traveler, and promoter, was a Mississippi-born son of a preacher, raised in Florida and Missouri. He was an acerbic and hate-ridden defender of the South after the end of the Civil War. Donan is said to have emerged from his 15 years of "soul-sickness" in 1880 after spending some months on the western frontier. Later he wrote "boomer tracts" in which the Dakotas and sections of the Pacific Northwest were rhapsodized. The author concludes with philosophic comments on "the West as a safety valve." Documented.   C. C. Gorchels

2419. Strickland, Rex W. A DEDICATION TO THE MEMORY OF EUGENE CAMPBELL BARKER, 1874-1956. *Arizona and the West 1966 8(4): 301-304.* Texas born and Texas and eastern educated Eugene Campbell Barker spent his professional career at the University of Texas. His principal research interest was the history of his State, as biographer and editor of the papers of the leaders of the Republic of Texas. He was managing editor of the *Southwestern Historical Quarterly* for 27 years, president of the Mississippi Valley Historical Association, author of several textbooks for intermediate and secondary schools, and a stern but judicious taskmaster to his students. In his writings he destroyed the Southern slave conspiracy hypothesis as an explanation for the acquisition of Texas and the Mexican Cession; he assessed the role of Texas in westward expansion and national development; and he pointed out that Mexican intransigency and oppression only partially explain the Texan Revolution and the Mexican War. Includes a selected list of Barker's publications relating to the Southwest. Illus., appendix.

D. L. Smith

2420. Taber, Ronald W. SACAGAWEA AND THE SUFFRAGETTES. *Pacific Northwest Q. 1967 58(1): 7-13.* Sacagawea, the Indian woman who accompanied her husband as guide and interpreter on the Lewis and Clark expedition, was hailed as a heroine by the women's suffrage movement, especially in Oregon and Wyoming from 1902 to 1921. Activities of some of the women who led the struggle for equal suffrage are related, including their efforts in fund raising and political campaigns. C. C. Gorchels

2421. Tutorow, Norman E. and Abel, Arthur R. WESTERN AND TERRITORIAL RESEARCH OPPORTUNITIES IN TRANS-MISSISSIPPI FEDERAL RECORDS CENTERS. *Pacific Hist. R. 1971 40(4): 501-518.* Six Federal Records Centers house the western Territorial and State archives, including Alaska, Hawaii, and the Pacific Territories. The authors summarize the holdings of major importance at each of the centers, and detail uses of the material by writers, researchers, lawyers, etc. The authors list the titles of inventories published so far for these centers, which are still largely untapped as a source for local history. Based on primary and secondary sources; 47 notes.

E. C. Hyslop

2422. Wells, Merle W. WALLA WALLA'S VISION OF A GREATER WASHINGTON. *Idaho Yesterdays 1966 10(3): 20-31.* "An account of the dispute over the location of the North Idaho-East Washington boundary." Discusses the various geographical boundaries of the Pacific Northwest during the territorial period (1860-89). North Idaho and the adjacent territory of Washington were separated by a political boundary which had little or no geographic justification. Citizens of Walla Walla (Washington) and Lewiston (Idaho) were engaged in a see-saw battle to convince Congress to enact boundaries favorable to each community. The territorial system demanded hasty admission of States, regardless of whether they had suitable boundaries or not. Geographic lines were the main factor in determining the present boundary. 8 illus., 40 notes. D. H. Swift

2423. Wilson, Major L. OF TIME AND THE UNION: KANSAS-NEBRASKA AND THE APPEAL FROM PRESCRIPTION TO PRINCIPLE. *Midwest Q. 1968 10(1): 73-87.* Studies the Kansas-Nebraska Act (1854) and the debates over it in Congress. A key provision of the measure repealed the Missouri Compromise, which had for 34 years banned slavery in the North. By undoing an arrangment made by an earlier generation and sanctioned by the passing years, the repeal invited the protagonists in debate to seek some timeless principle by which to regulate slavery. It represented a movement from prescription to principle. In larger terms it was a movement from the laws of history to the laws of nature. The principle on which the nation had been founded was freedom, but the free soil advocates favored freedom nationally and slavery locally. G. H. G. Jones

2424. —. STATE HISTORIES AND BIBLIOGRAPHIES. *Western Hist. Q. 1971 2(2): 171-194.* From lists submitted by historians in the 50 States and the District of Columbia, the editors have compiled this list, by States, of the best general State histories and bibliographies. Includes an occasional brief editorial evaluation or description. Excludes periodical literature and series sets of State historical societies, libraries, and archives. D. L. Smith

The Great Plains States

General

2425. Aeschbacher, W. D. HISTORICAL ORGANIZATION ON THE GREAT PLAINS. *North Dakota Hist. 1967 34(1): 93-104.* Traces the organization of state historical societies from the Massachusetts Historical Society in 1790, a private association of well-to-do individuals with sufficient leisure, interest, and resources for the society to prosper. Similar organizations were formed in the cities and in state capitals. Membership was small, exclusive, and selective. The Middle West, in contrast, utilized the genius of the frontiersmen for voluntary association, obtained state or even territorial support, and their historical societies were tax-supported. The Wisconsin Historical Society, with Lyman Draper to support it, is an excellent example. The Minnesota Historical Society was outstanding and others followed, marking historic sites and preserving their history. I. W. Van Noppen

2426. Alford, Terry L. THE WEST AS A DESERT IN AMERICAN THOUGHT PRIOR TO LONG'S 1819-1820 EXPEDITION. *J. of the West 1969 8(4): 515-525.* Brings into focus some of the nebulous body of American belief in a trans-Mississippi desert and the appearance of that belief before the Long expedition of 1819-20. The writings of Pike, Lewis and Clark, Brackenridge, and the widely used map of John Melish are among the items examined. R. N. Alvis

2427. Allen, John L. GEOGRAPHICAL KNOWLEDGE AND AMERICAN IMAGES OF THE LOUISIANA TERRITORY. *Western Hist. Q. 1971 2(2): 151-170.* Although Americans were uncertain as to the extent, contents, and value of the Louisiana Territory when its acquisition was announced in the public press on 4 July 1803, a considerable accumulation of geographical lore was generally accessible to the interested and curious. American geographical thought about Louisiana was conditioned by travel accounts of European and American explorers in the area before the purchase, published spirited public debates that followed the news of the cession on its worth and value, correspondence to the eastern newspapers from Americans on the western frontier, and the works of the geographers and cartographers. From this literature or geographical lore, Americans in 1804 could derive a composite idea that Louisiana was outsized, stretched to the Pacific, and was laced with wide rivers navigable to their sources. Its soil was the world's best, its climate was easy, and its natives fit classical Homeric descriptions. Here was the land of opportunity with sufficient room for expansion of the ideal agrarian republic. Louisiana's vast rivers, with short portages, opened the way to the Pacific, the Orient, and beyond. With it America could achieve her destiny. 2 maps, 48 notes.

D. L. Smith

2428. Andrew, Bunyan Hadley. OKLAHOMA'S RED RIVER BOUNDARY: UNDER U.S. SUPREME COURT DECISION IN 1927. *Chronicles of Oklahoma 1966 44(3): 246-253.* Texas became a State 29 December 1845. In 1859 a joint U.S.-Texas commission surveyed the Texas boundary. The U.S. commissioners maintained that the South Fork was the main stream. Texas claimed the North Fork as the boundary and passed an act naming the territory between the forks Greer County. The United States never conceded this. In 1882 there was another joint survey - still disagreement. In 1896 the Supreme Court held the South Fork to be the main branch and stated that Greer County was not a part of Texas, that the south bank was the Texas boundary. Oklahoma on becoming a state acquired a boundary coterminous with Texas. In 1918-19 oil was discovered along the Red River. Oklahoma sued to have the south bank made the boundary. Texas argued for the middle of the river. The Supreme Court held that the south bank was the boundary. The line was marked to take care of avulsion. The Court held that title to the bed of the river did not go to Oklahoma but belonged to the United States. 36 notes. I. W. Van Noppen

2429. Barker, Watson. WADING TO CALIFORNIA: THE INFLUENCE OF THE FORTY-NINERS ON THE NOTION OF A GREAT AMERICAN DESERT. *Great Plains J. 1964 3(2): 35-43.* Briefly reviews the origins of the widely-accepted "Great American Desert" legend. It asserts that, while the Forty-niners found desert areas such as the Humboldt Sink where lack of water was a serious problem, 1849 was an exceptionally wet year. The gold rush, therefore, added to the old notion of the American Desert by: 1) showing deserts were limited to a few specific areas; 2) over-emphasizing the terrors of the desert; 3) portraying the Plains as wetter than they normally were; and 4) publicizing the West as a land of opportunity. Based on comments by travelers.

O. H. Zabel

2430.   Barksdale, E. C.   INTRODUCTION.   Essays on the Am. Civil War (Austin: U. of Texas Press, 1968), pp. 19-27. Describes the genesis and purpose of the Walter Prescott Webb Memorial Lecture series, presented each year beginning in 1966 at the University of Texas at Arlington. The author also analyzes Webb the man, Webb the historian, and his views on the role of history and the history teacher in higher education.

E. C. Murdock

2431.   Bell, Robert Galen.   JAMES C. MALIN AND THE GRASS-LANDS OF NORTH AMERICA.   Agric. Hist. 1972 46(3): 414-424. Discusses Malin's approach (post 1936) to the history of the plains and attempts to put his work into a historiographical framework. Handicapped by a heavy writing style and poor organization, Malin nevertheless opened a whole new area to scholars by applying the findings of several sciences to the history of the Trans-Mississippi West. 41 notes.

D. E. Brewster

2432.   Bennett, James D.   OASIS CIVILIZATION IN THE GREAT PLAINS.   Great Plains J. 1967 7(1): 26-32. A discussion of the adaptation of man to the Great Plains - the area stretching from Canada into Mexico between the Rocky Mountains on the west and essentially the 98th meridian on the east. While numerous excesses of climate occur in the area, the most serious is a shortage of water and uneven distribution of rainfall throughout the year. Two techniques developed to meet the peculiar conditions, dry farming and irrigation, have had limited success. The result was a "leap-frog type of settlement" leading to an oasis type of arrangement rather than the steady expansion characteristic of other sections of the United States. While man has largely taken over the Great Plains, "he has not yet learned fully how to meet the caprices of nature." 14 notes.

O. H. Zabel

2433.   Bierbaum, Milton E.   FREDERICK STARR. A MISSOURI BORDER ABOLITIONIST: THE MAKING OF A MARTYR.   Missouri Hist. R. 1964 58(3): 309-325. Starr, a Presbyterian minister, was a prominent abolitionist in western Missouri during the first year of the Kansas-Missouri conflict in 1854-55. He came to Weston in 1850 to serve as a pastor, but he soon became interested in the slavery issue and began to conduct a school for slaves. This project was soon abandoned, but after the passage of the Kansas-Nebraska Bill, Starr became active in a squatters' association to found Leavenworth. As the proslavery forces gained additional strength in western Missouri, Starr continued to assert that slavery was a moral and political evil. He left Weston early in 1855, after being warned or compelled to leave. A meeting at the Weston court house denounced ministers who opposed slavery, but the sentiments that were echoed from Starr's small pulpit were rapidly being repeated throughout the East. Based on local newspapers, histories, and the Starr papers in the State Historical Society of Missouri.

W. F. Zornow

2434.   Chester, Edward W.   THE GREAT PLAINS STATE CONSTITUTIONS AND THE WEBB THESIS.   Great Plains J. 1971 10(2): 71-82. Analyzes Great Plains State constitutions to test Walter Prescott Webb's hypothesis that the West was politically radical. Examines the political composition of State constitutional conventions, liberal provisions in constitutions (such as woman suffrage and water rights), the influence of business interests on constitutions, the Anglo-Saxon predominance in framing constitutions, and the patterning (but later revision) of constitutions of Great Plains States on eastern models. Concludes that "the Webb thesis stands validated, with some important reservations." 71 notes.

O. H. Zabel

2435.   Deutsch, Eberhard P.   THE CONSTITUTIONAL CONTROVERSY OVER THE LOUISIANA PURCHASE.   Am. Bar Assoc. J. 1967 53(1): 50-57. Recounts the familiar circumstances and constitutional issues of the Louisiana Purchase. Senator Wilson Cary Nicholas of Virginia is regarded as the primary influence in convincing Jefferson to exercise a broad construction of the treaty-making powers under the Constitution. John Taylor, States' rightist, and Senator Uriah Tracy of Connecticut, a Federalist, were the leading opponents to the article of the treaty calling for immediate annexation. Those fighting the treaty soon revealed ulterior political motives which undermined their arguments. 48 notes.

H. M. Ward

2436.   Dillon, Richard H.   STEPHEN LONG'S GREAT AMERICAN DESERT.   Pro. of the Am. Phil. Soc. 1967 111(2): 93-108. Discusses the origin, acceptance, and ultimate rejection of the myth of the Great American Desert. Although Meriwether Lewis and William Clark made an early visit to the plains region of mid-America, it remained for their successors, notably Zebulon Pike and particularly Stephen H. Long, to promulgate the desert myth. In fact, the fruits of Long's exploratory trek to the plains in 1819-20 proved to be largely negative: the most significant result was the growth of the idea that an inhospitable desert existed in what was then the western part of the United States, serving as a formidable barrier to expansion. The author describes the journey and notes those of Long's associates who were instrumental in contributing to the desert myth, specifically such men as Edwin James, who wrote an account of the journey, and William Henry Swift, the topographer and cartographer for the mission. The myth prevailed for 30 years, after which the area was for awhile regarded as a pastoral region, until the opposite myth - the Garden of the World - emerged to complete the pendulum's swing. Developing agricultural prosperity followed by the ravages of the 1930's proved that the plains are neither desert nor natural garden but somewhere between the two extremes. Based largely on Edwin James' diary and published account of the expedition as well as on other printed sources and secondary materials, illus., map, 80 notes.

W. G. Morgan

2437.   Dillon, Richard H.   STEPHEN LONG'S GREAT AMERICAN DESERT.   Montana 1968 18(3): 58-74. Traces the rise of conflicting myths regarding the Great Plains. The concept of a Great American Desert is attributed largely but not exclusively to Major Stephen Long and his associate Edwin James. The second idea, a belief in the area as a garden, resulted from some success and much propaganda connected with new techniques in irrigation and dry-farming. The drought of the 1930's and the subsequent recovery suggest that the Great Plains are neither desert nor garden, but something "in between." Based on official reports and writings of early Western explorers and recent published appraisals by historians and geographers. Illustrations are portraits of the men involved.

S. R. Davison

2438.   Dobie, J. Frank.   ON MY FRIEND, WALTER PRESCOTT WEBB.   Great Plains J. 1963 2(2): 37-41. Personal experiences reprinted from the Houston Post, 17 March 1963.

S

2439.   Donan, Phineus.   A SCREAM FROM THE AMERICAN EAGLE IN DAKOTA, 1885.   Am. West 1968 5(4): 45-47. The 1885 Fourth of July oration by Colonel Phineus Donan portrays Dakota Territory as playing the preeminent role as "the cradle of liberty and progress" in the trans-Mississippi West. It was published by a railroad as a propaganda piece. 3 illus., facsimile of the Donan oration, and marginalia sketches.

D. L. Smith

2440.   Dunn, Roy Sylvan.   THE SOUTHWEST COLLECTION AT "TEXAS TECH."   Am. Archivist 1965 28(3): 413-419. As a separate department of Texas Technological College, the Southwest Collection was established in 1955. Occupying 16,000 cubic feet, the collection includes maps, newspapers, periodicals, microfilm, tape recordings, photographs, books, manuscripts, and some college records. Non-Texas material includes the papers of Elijah Parish Lovejoy, 1804-91, abolitionist, and Daniel I. J. Thornton, 1924-56, governor of Colorado. Other significant collections are listed, primarily as Texan and recent acquisitions. Notes describe other types of materials.

D. C. Duniway

2441.   Egan, Gail N. and Agogino, George A.   MAN'S USE OF BISON AND CATTLE ON THE HIGH PLAINS.   Great Plains J. 1965 5(1): 35-43. The Great Plains with its large herbivora, including bison and cattle, has supported man's existence for over 11 thousand years. The author describes the bison as a human food source and then explains their replacement on the Great Plains in the 19th century by cattle. Based on secondary sources; map.

O. H. Zabel

2442. Farnham, Thomas J. THE FEDERAL-STATE ISSUE AND THE LOUISIANA PURCHASE. *Louisiana Hist. 1965 6(1): 5-25.* Timothy Pickering hoped to prevent the inclusion of Louisiana by an appeal to strict interpretation of the Constitution. But his real objection and that of the New England Federalists generally was that New England would be a permanent minority; the balance of the Union would be destroyed. When the Federalists failed in the Senate, they organized a project of disunion, which, however, met with little support. Finally, a proposed amendment to the U.S. Constitution was introduced and adopted in the Massachusetts State House, limiting representation in the national legislature to free persons. When Pickering presented this amendment to the Senate, it was speedily tabled and forgotten. 58 notes.
E. P. Stickney

2443. Fielder, Mildred. AT DEADWOOD. *Am. West 1968 5(4): 44,48.* Chinese participation in the Fourth of July festivities in 1888 are taken from the local newspapers of this Dakota Territory town.
D. L. Smith

2444. Fite, Gilbert C. HISTORY AND HISTORIANS OF THE GREAT PLAINS. *North Dakota Q. 1966 34(4): 89-95.* Reviews the story of white settlement of the Great Plains area and argues that little work has been done in the study of the area as a region. Randall Parrish ends too soon; Walter Prescott Webb did not attempt a broad history. The author calls for a multivolume study of the area and suggests a chronological division breaking in the late 1890's, 1930, and 1941. Based on primary and secondary sources; 8 notes.
J. F. Mahoney

2445. Frantz, Joe B. WALTER PRESCOTT WEBB. *Am. West 1964 1(1): 40-43.* According to the author, who was a student and colleague, Webb thought of himself as "a universally minded writer whose universe just happened to come home to the American West with some frequency." He was a writer-artist who tackled a historical problem as a lawyer would prepare a brief. Like a politician he ignored contrary evidence. Most historians are generally obsessed with "demonstrable activity"; but Walter Prescott Webb's career is proof that "we must still make room along the road for the slower man who takes time to view the scenery and think on what he sees."
D. L. Smith

2446. Gibson, A. M. MUSEUM OF THE GREAT PLAINS: PURPOSE AND PROSPECTS. *Great Plains J. 1963 3(1): 25-31.* Views the Great Plains as neither a forbidding proto-desert nor a Garden of Eden, but as the least understood of the nation's sections. The prospects for the region can be discovered by examining its instructive past. The author briefly describes certain characteristics of the area, including the noble qualities of its citizens - tenacity, energy, imagination, inventiveness, and humor. The article concludes with praise for what the University of Oklahoma, the O. U. Press, the Museum of the Great Plains, and the *Great Plains Journal* are doing to explain and interpret the area.
O. H. Zabel

2447. Harrison, Benjamin. PROCLAMATION OF ADMISSION. *North Dakota Hist. 1964 31(3): 165-166.* President Benjamin Harrison reviewed the following procedure: Congress on 22 February 1889 provided for the adoption of statehood, division into two States, and holding a constitutional convention at Bismarck, which would adopt the Constitution of the United States and form a State constitution and State government in conformity with the provisions of the U.S. Constitution. North and South Dakota were to reach an agreement concerning the division of all property belonging to the Territory of Dakota and each should assume its share of the debts and liabilities of the same. Whereas the people had voted to accept the constitution so drawn up and the Governor had so certified, the President proclaimed North Dakota admitted to statehood.
I. W. Van Noppen

2448. Harrison, Lowell H. PLANTED FORESTS - WILL THEY SUCCEED ON THE PLAINS? *Great Plains J. 1969 8(2): 75-78.* Discusses the analysis of various theories used to explain the lack of trees on the plains as presented by John Strong Newberry, one of the leading geologists and paleontologists of the time. It concludes cautiously, suggesting "we fear that the chances for forests on open prairies - just where they are most needed - are but very dubious." Quoted from the 27 September 1873 issue of the *Army and Navy Journal.* 4 notes.
O. H. Zabel

2449. Hart, Charles Desmond. THE NATURAL LIMITS OF SLAVERY EXPANSION: KANSAS-NEBRASKA, 1854. *Kansas Hist. Q. 1968 34(1): 32-50.* A study of the congressional debate on the Kansas-Nebraska bill of 1854 to sample public opinion on the limits of slavery expansion. The words of the 152 congressmen who debated on this issue during the winter and spring of 1854 are offered to show the various shades of opinion that developed during the discussion. The debate shows that there was a difference of opinion among congressmen from free States as to whether slavery would expand into this territory. The debate over slavery in the territories had concerned an area far removed from the States, but in 1854 the struggle for power in the territories assumed a new meaning when slavery was introduced in Kansas, a territory contiguous to the States. Based on the *Congressional Globe;* 67 notes.
W. F. Zornow

2450. Hollon, W. Eugene. ADVENTURES OF A WESTERN HISTORIAN. *Western Hist. Q. 1971 2(3): 244-259.* After a decade of attending Texan schools sandwiched between stints of teaching and coaching in the public schools and odd jobs, the author obtained his Ph.D. under Walter Prescott Webb at the University of Texas in 1942. The author taught at the University of Oklahoma, 1945-67, and has since been at the University of Toledo in Ohio. His teaching and research interests concern the American West. He considers *The Great American Desert* (New York: Oxford U. Press, 1966) his most significant work. Illus., biblio.
D. L. Smith

2451. Jones, Douglas C. MEDICINE LODGE REVISITED. *Kansas Hist. Q. 1969 35(2): 130-142.* In 1867 an Indian peace commission concluded a treaty at Medicine Lodge, Kansas, with the Comanche, Kiowa, Cheyenne, Arapaho, and Plains Apache, the wild tribes south of the Arkansas River. Since 1926 the residents of the area have often reenacted the incident. The ceremony in 1967 marking the centennial of the original event was conducted on such a grand scale that it may well be the last time that the incident will be commemorated. This account is both a description of the reenactment in 1967 and an effort to add supporting detail and to correct some factual errors appearing in the reports of the original participants and the 9 jounalists who accompanied them to the site. Based on newspaper reports, Government records and monographs; illus., photo, 18 notes.
W. F. Zornow

2452. Knudson, Jerry W. NEWSPAPER REACTION TO THE LOUISIANA PURCHASE: "THIS NEW, IMMENSE, UNBOUNDED WORLD." *Missouri Hist. R. 1969 63(2): 182-215.* Extensive quotations from the Washington *National Intelligencer,* Philadelphia *Aurora,* New York *Evening Post,* Boston *Columbian Sentinel,* Boston *Independent Chronicle,* Richmond *Enquirer,* and Richmond *Recorder* show the range of public opinion in the United States on Spain's transfer of the territory to France, America's negotiations to acquire Louisiana, the sale and transfer to the United States, and early exploration of the territory. The quotations are tied together with paragraphs summarizing the general history of the purchase (1802-03). Based on articles, monographs on Franco-American relations, and biographies; illus., 90 notes.
W. F. Zornow

2453. Kroeker, Marvin. DECEIT ABOUT THE GARDEN: HAZEN, CUSTER AND THE ARID LANDS CONTROVERSY. *North Dakota Q. 1970 38(3): 5-21.* Describes the opposition of Colonel William B. Hazen to false advertising of the Northern Pacific grant, George Armstrong Custer's "booster" rebuttal, and the controversy between them. Hazen argued that the area between the 98th meridian and the Rockies generally lacked sufficient rainfall to be agriculturally productive and asserted that bond-selling campaigns misled the public and the government. Custer, on the contrary, pictured a verdant land in which, even in the depth of winter, "I have never had occasion to wear an overcoat," and challenged Hazen's credentials while exaggerating his own. Hazen was essentially correct concerning the difficulty of settlement at the time, but too pessimistic when he declared the entire High Plains area incapable of supporting substantial settlement. Based on primary and secondary sources; map, 2 photos, 38 notes.
J. F. Mahoney

2454. Lewis, G. Malcolm. EARLY AMERICAN EXPLORATION AND THE CIS-ROCKY MOUNTAIN DESERT, 1803-1823. *Great Plains J. 1965 5(1): 1-11.* Examines the origin of the "Great American Desert" concept as applied to the area between the Missouri River and the Rocky Mountains. It asserts that explorers between 1803 and 1823, especially Zebulon M. Pike, James Long and Edwin James, were responsible for originating it. After 1825 the "Great American Desert" concept was widely publicized by travel books, atlases, etc. Only during the 1840's with acquisition of territory, further exploration and westward movement did the concept of the Great Plains develop. 38 notes.

O. H. Zabel

2455. Lewis, G. Malcolm. THE GREAT PLAINS AND ITS IMAGE OF FLATNESS. *J. of the West 1967 6(1): 11-26.* Notes that the tendency to apply the word "plain," with its connotation of flatness or smoothness, to the plateau-like region east of the Rocky Mountains has persisted from the days of the earliest explorers to the present. The development of that description is traced and some reasons offered for the persistence of the flat image. The author shows that the description is incorrect and concludes that this image has been disadvantageous to the people trying to develop the region. A clearer understanding of the plateau nature of the Great Plains would have resulted in more appropriate legislation for the region. Based on published sources, map, tables, 75 notes.

D. N. Brown

2456. Lewis, G. Malcolm. THREE CENTURIES OF DESERT CONCEPTS IN THE CIS-ROCKY MOUNTAIN WEST. *J. of the West 1965 4(3): 457-468.* Detailed study of the origin and development of the concept of the Great American Desert according to the Spanish, French, English, and American explorers who crossed the Great Plains. The author concludes that Americans used the word desert in a different connotation from others and that Zebulon Pike and Stephen H. Long strengthened the idea that the area was useless for an agrarian society. In 1857 William Gilpin began his successful attempt to destroy the desert concept, and thus ended three centuries of misappraisal of the region. Based on published sources, map, 58 notes.

D. N. Brown

2457. Lewis, G. Malcolm. WILLIAM GILPIN AND THE CONCEPT OF THE GREAT PLAINS REGION. *Ann. of the Assoc. of Am. Geographers 1966 56(1): 33-51.* Considers the development of Gilpin's concept. It was a powerful motivating factor influencing settlement of the region but was too generalized and incomplete as a basis for predicting economic development. Illus., 10 maps, 71 notes.

W. R. Boedecker

2458. Mardock, Robert W. THE PLAINS FRONTIER AND THE INDIAN POLICY, 1865-1880. *Nebraska Hist. 1968 49(2): 187-201.* Surveys the gradual shift in public opinion on the plains, evident by the late 1870's, from favoring a policy of exterminating the Indians to one of educating and civilizing them by breaking up tribal relations and making them self-sustaining. Federal policies with regard to the Indians are examined within this context.

R. Lowitt

2459. McCown, Robert A. A COMPARISON OF THE HOLDINGS OF FOUR LIBRARIES ON GREAT PLAINS HISTORY. *Great Plains J. 1970 9(2): 91-99.* Describes and compares the holdings of four libraries which have outstanding collections on the Great Plains. The Yale University Library has the Beinecke and Coe Collections. The DeGolyer Foundation Library at Southern Methodist University has comprehensive holdings in the cattle trade, the Dakotas, frontier and pioneer life, Indians, Kansas, Nebraska, railroads, Western travel, and exploration. The Newberry Library of Chicago has a "good deal of material on statemaking," the Edward E. Ayer Collection on American Indians, and the Edward D. Graff Collection of Western Americana. The Minnesota Historical Society Library is not limited to Minnesota history and has important manuscript collections including the Pond and Neill Papers. 19 notes.

O. H. Zabel

2460. McDermott, John Francis. SOME RECENT BOOKS ABOUT FRENCH LOUISIANA AND SOME BOOKS TO COME. *Louisiana Hist. 1967 8(1): 53-65.* Surveys recent works on French Louisiana and research in progress. The article is especially concerned with the publication of manuscript collections, travel accounts, and other primary sources.

R. L. Woodward

2461. Moore, Dorothy L. WILLIAM A. HOWARD AND THE NOMINATION OF RUTHERFORD B. HAYES FOR THE PRESIDENCY. *Vermont Hist. 1970 38(4): 316-319.* Chairman of the Michigan delegation to the Republican National Convention at Cincinnati in 1876, William Alanson Howard announced on the fifth ballot that Michigan's 21 votes, previously scattered, were united on Hayes, and started Hayes' rise to nomination on the seventh ballot. Hayes appointed Howard the Governor of Dakota Territory, 1876-80. Howard was born in Hinesburgh, Vermont, in 1813, graduated from Middlebury College in 1839, rose in Whig and Republican politics as a Detroit lawyer and orator, 1840-61, became a Congressman, 1854-60, chairman of the Kansas Investigating Committee, 1856, president of the Grand Rapids and Indiana Railroad, and unsuccessful candidate for the U.S. Senate. Summarizes Martha M. Bigelow's political sketch in *Michigan History* (March 1958).

T. D. S. Bassett

2462. Moore, John Preston. ANTONIO DE ULLOA: A PROFILE OF THE FIRST SPANISH GOVERNOR OF LOUISIANA. *Louisiana Hist. 1967 8(3): 189-218.* Discusses transfer of Louisiana from France to Spain and details Spanish policy in acquiring Louisiana. Traces the career and policies of Governor Antonio de Ulloa from his arrival in Havana in 1765 to his departure from New Orleans in 1768. Based on secondary and archival sources in Spain and Louisiana; 72 notes.

R. L. Woodward

2463. Morris, Artemisia Suman. CAPTAIN DAVID L. PAYNE: THE CIMARRON SCOUT. *Chronicles of Oklahoma 1964 42(1): 7-25.* This sketch of the life of Captain David L. Payne appears on the 75th anniversary of the famous "run" of 22 April 1889. Payne, a native of Indiana, moved to Kansas in 1858, became a scout, and served with distinction throughout the Civil War. He was four times a member of the Kansas Legislature, was active in politics, and owned a ranch east of Wichita. In 1879 he sought to settle a district in the Indian Territory known as Oklahoma. He organized and led "boomers" to the border of the territory, but these settlers were restrained by U.S. troops. Payne was arrested and tried. Later he led four other expeditions of attempted settlement. He was preparing to lead another expedition when he died in 1884. Payne's agitation speeded up the settlement of Oklahoma. Editorial introduction and note, illus.

I. W. Van Noppen

2464. Morrison, Frank B. AMERICA WILL TURN TO THE HEART OF AMERICA. *J. of the West 1967 6(1): 9-19.* Describes how residents of the area of the Great Plains adapted to the hostile and unfamiliar environment and predicts that this area will be the spring from which all America will draw its life for it offers untapped resources and vast potential.

D. N. Brown

2465. Morton, W. L. A CENTURY OF PLAIN AND PARKLAND. *Alberta Hist. R. 1969 17(2): 1-10.* Discusses the role of the plains in the life of the Indian, the fur trader, and the early farmer, considering the impact of the East upon the settlement of the West and of the significant differences that existed.

H. M. Burns

2466. Parker, Watson. MOODS, MEMORIES, AND MIRAGES: THE DESERT IN AMERICAN MAGAZINES. *Am. West 1964 1(4): 58-63.* The Great American Desert, like the American frontier, changed its locale with the march of man across the continent. This desert, like the mythology it created, varied with the passing of the years. Whatever its shape or form or location, its mystique - curiosity, romanticism, and fanatical zeal - filled all who touched it. This desert-bred mysticism is more clearly shown in periodical literature of the past hundred years than anywhere else. Those who have written about the desert are divided into three distinct groups: explorers, geologists, botanists, boosters, and speculators who loved it for the sake of knowledge, wealth, or wonder; planners and designers who wanted power and prestige; and desert dwellers. The last group accepted the desert for what it was and attempted to deal with it on its own terms. Illus., bibliographical citations from the literature.

D. L. Smith

2467. Plummer, Mark A. LINCOLN'S FIRST DIRECT REPLY TO DOUGLAS ON SQUATTER SOVEREIGNTY RECALLED. *Lincoln Herald 1969 71(1): 27-32.* Contains the text and an introductory analysis of a reminiscence by Brinton Webb Woodward of an exchange of speeches by Stephen A. Douglas and Abraham Lincoln in Bloomington, Illinois, on 26 September 1854. The subject was the Kansas-Nebraska Act. Brinton's reminiscences are found to be at variance on several points with reports of the events and speeches of that day in Bloomington published in Illinois newspapers shortly after the exchange occurred.

S. L. Jones

2468. Prucha, Francis Paul. INDIAN REMOVAL AND THE GREAT AMERICAN DESERT. *Indiana Mag. of Hist. 1963 59(4): 299-322.* Effectively disputes a widely accepted statement in American history textbooks that in the early 19th century the US government sought to solve the Indian problem by removing Indians west of the Mississippi River into the area known as the "Great American Desert." None of the official plans for Indian removal in the 1820's and 1830's contemplated use of lands designated in maps of that time as part of this "Desert," nor did even the critics of the government's plans mention such an idea. The author concedes some Indians might have been settled there, but only "by chance"; given present historical evidence, "the idea that the Indians were deliberately disposed of in the desert loses all credibility."
J. F. Findlay

2469. Rose, Margaret. THE ARCHIVES OF DAKOTA TERRITORY. *Am. Archivist 1963 26(3): 307-313.* The problem of dividing the records of the Territory of Dakota between the proposed new states of North and South Dakota was finally solved only by drawing lots. Details are given of all the commission meetings and decisions. 10 notes.
E. P. Stickney

2470. Rundell, Walter, Jr. A DEDICATION TO THE MEMORY OF WALTER PRESCOTT WEBB, 1888-1963. *Arizona and the West 1963 5(1): 1-3.* Walter Prescott Webb (1888-1963) made a fundamental impact on American historiography. His *The Great Plains* (New York: Blaisdell, 1959) demonstrated the effect of the Plains environment on the institutions that had matured in the eastern woodlands. His *The Great Frontier* (Austin: U. of Texas Press, 1964) applied Frederick Jackson Turner's frontier hypothesis on a global basis. Photo, biblio.
D. L. Smith

2471. Rundell, Walter, Jr. WALTER PRESCOTT WEBB: PRODUCT OF ENVIRONMENT. *Arizona and the West 1963 5(1): 4-28.* The principal works of Walter Prescott Webb are examined as to what inspired and prompted the writing of each, what the purpose and message of each seems to be, and Webb's emergent philosophy of history. The professional reception of these studies is also considered. The message of *The Great Plains* (New York: Blaisdell, 1959) is contained in its subtitle, "A Study in Institutions and Environment." Its primary purpose was to present representative ideas about the region rather than to write its history. Webb utilized the same approach in *The Great Frontier* (Austin: U. of Texas Press, 1964) by attempting to put his subject in the context of Western civilization, calling the settled area of Europe "the Metropolis" and the rest of the world "the Great Frontier." *The Texas Rangers* (Austin: U. of Texas Press, 1965) was a pungent and learned treatment of a frontier institution. The economic domination of the North, through the tariff, Civil War pensions, and patent monopolies, (over the South and West, which contained the largest share of natural resources) was the theme of *Divided We Stand*. Another volume, *More Water for Texas* (Austin: U. of Texas Press, 1954), popularized and vitalized a Federal study of what he regarded as the most serious problem of his state. Environment and his experiences within that environment explain Webb's analyses. He was interested in broad outlines rather than with the weight of documentation. Notes.
D. L. Smith

2472. Russell, Robert Royal. THE ISSUES IN THE CONGRESSIONAL STRUGGLE OVER THE KANSAS-NEBRASKA BILL, 1854. *J. of Southern Hist. 1963 29(2): 187-210.* Although public lands policy, Indian policy, and railroad routes were involved in the struggle over the Kansas-Nebraska Bill, not more than five votes in the two houses of Congress combined were turned on the final vote by anything but the slavery issue. The slavery provisions were a compromise hammered out with great difficulty between a majority of Northern Democrats and nearly all Southern members, Democratic and Whig. The Northern Democrats made great sacrifices of interests and principles, and personal political advantage for the sake of party unity and sectional accommodation. The bill nevertheless fell far short of meeting what the great majority of Southern congressmen thought were the South's just demands. Based chiefly on Congressional debates.
S. E. Humphreys

2473. Scanlon, James E. A SUDDEN CONCEIT: JEFFERSON AND THE LOUISIANA GOVERNMENT BILL OF 1804. *Louisiana Hist. 1968 9(2): 139-162.* The acquisition of Louisiana by the United States brought many problems, not the least of which was provision of a government for the territory, largely inhabited by people alien to Anglo-American traditions and laws. President Thomas Jefferson's idea was to provide rule under existing Spanish and French laws and customs by an oligarchy which would gradually introduce U.S. customs and laws. This is revealed through Jefferson's correspondence and his drafts of a government bill and two proposed constitutional amendments regarding Louisiana, all of which are reprinted here. Jefferson's ideas were finally achieved through passage, with certain modifications imposed by the Congress, of the Louisiana Government Bill (1804). Based on the Jefferson Papers, *Annals* of the 8th Congress, and other contemporary materials; 54 notes.
R. L. Woodward

2474. Schellenberg, James A. COUNTY SEAT WARS: A PRELIMINARY ANALYSIS. *J. of Conflict Resolution 1970 14(3): 345-352.* "Violence in the selection of US county seats is discussed as a means of studying conditions of violent conflict. The incidence of violence in county seat controversies of twelve midwestern states is analyzed, and the frequency of violence is found to be highest in the Great Plains states during the 1880s. Possible explanations for the observed patterns are briefly explored. Land speculation, involving intense hopes and uncertainties about land values during that period in that area, is salient among the possible factors, but others need to be examined. The extremes of behavior of individuals in the more severe controversies over country seat location also require more study. The discreteness of this kind of issue, the fact that many similar decisions have been made without violence, and the fact that this kind of issue now seems 'extinct' in the US are all advantageous to the student of conflict."
J

2475. Schnell, J. Christopher. WILLIAM GILPIN AND THE DESTRUCTION OF THE DESERT MYTH. *Colorado Mag. 1969 46(2): 131-144.* Explorers, from the 16th-century Spanish to those of the early 19th century, described the area between the Missouri and the Rockies as a desert. By 1830 the notion of the "Great American Desert" was firmly entrenched and hindered development. William Gilpin (1813-94) did as much as anyone to promote a new and attractive image for the area. As a military officer he crossed the trans-Missouri West from 1843 to 1848. For years, in reports, articles, emigrant guides, and speeches (always with an eye to personal profit), he praised the West, using all the skills of a promoter. Initially, he promoted the Kansas City area, but later he shifted his abode and attention to Colorado where he was the first territorial governor. Illus., 25 notes.
O. H. Zabel

2476. Shoemaker, Arthur. ALEXIS PIERRE BEATTE. *Chronicles of Oklahoma 1967 45(2): 207-210.* Biographical information on Beatte is vague and scarce. Little is known beyond that he was a hunter and guide for an occasional traveling party or Army expedition on the Great Plains, that he married an Osage Indian, and that his latter days were spent in Missouri. 5 notes.
D. L. Smith

2477. Smith, Ronald D. NAPOLEON AND LOUISIANA: FAILURE OF THE PROPOSED EXPEDITION TO OCCUPY AND DEFEND LOUISIANA, 1801-1803. *Louisiana Hist. 1971 12(1): 21-40.* Beginning in 1801 Napoleon planned and ordered vast preparations for the occupation and administration of Louisiana to implement his determination to rebuild French power in America. Preparations took place on the Dutch coast in 1802 while French diplomats negotiated with Spain for transfer of ownership of Louisiana to France. The severe winter of 1802-03 delayed the departure of the expedition. The delay, combined with three other factors, caused Napoleon to abandon his extensive preparations and to sell Louisiana to the United States: 1) a growing and aggressive U.S. interest in Louisiana opposing French reoccupation of the Mississippi Valley, 2) seeming inevitability of worsening relations with Britain and a renewal of the war as the British began to blockade the Dutch coast, and 3) serious setbacks suffered by French forces in Santo Domingo. Based principally on French archival records; 51 notes.
R. L. Woodward

2478. Sterling, Everett W. THE INDIAN RESERVATION SYSTEM ON THE NORTH CENTRAL PLAINS. *Montana 1964 14(2): 92-100.* Traces the establishment of early reservations in Minnesota and the Dakotas, 1851-58, and discusses the philosophy of this approach to Indian problems.
S. R. Davison

2479. Welsch, Roger L. THE MYTH OF THE GREAT AMERICAN DESERT. *Nebraska Hist. 1971 52(3): 255-265.* "... I am using the term 'myth' here not in its common sense, that is, that there never was such a desert, but rather to describe the current opinion that there was no desert at all. ...Is Nebraska a desert? Of course not. But that is not the question. Instead we must ask, *'Was* Nebraska a desert?' and the answer to that question is yes. ...Because the conditions then fit the contemporary concept of 'desert,' it was one; modern concepts and conditions are not even relevant to the question." 2 photos, 5 notes.   S

2480. White, E. M. and Lewis, J. K. RECENT GULLY FORMATION IN PRAIRIE AREAS OF THE NORTHERN GREAT PLAINS. *Plains Anthropologist 1967 12(37): 318-322.* "Modern gully formation in the Great Plains and Southwestern United States has been attributed variously to over-grazing, farming, and climatic change. Pre-settlement prairie fires in the Northern Great Plains burned the protective vegetation so that gradients of drainageways were adjusted to more sediment than they receive today when wild fires are uncommon. Gully cutting may be an adjustment of the gradient to new conditions. Erosion caused by overgrazing today may not be different from that caused by wild grazing animals in the pre-settlement period." Biblio.   J

2481. Wishart, David J.; Warren, Andrew; and Stoddard, Robert H. AN ATTEMPTED DEFINITION OF A FRONTIER USING A WAVE ANALOGY. *Rocky Mountain Social Sci. J. 1969 6(1): 73-81.* Definitions of a frontier have varied and the authors attempt to develop an index to define "frontier" that utilizes more than population density and recognizes spatial and temporal variation in land potential. Using data on the Great Plains (1860-90), the authors test their theoretical wave definition. 2 fig., 10 notes.   R. F. Allen

North Dakota

2482. Brudvig, Glenn. THE DEVELOPMENT OF PUBLIC LIBRARY SERVICE IN NORTH DAKOTA. *North Dakota Q. 1963 31(3): 61-66.* Traces the development of public library service in North Dakota from early privately-sponsored efforts through the period of Carnegie grants to the implementation of the federal Library Services Act of 1956. Most development is found in the towns, as the traditional public library was not equipped to serve rural folk until the advent of all-weather roads and the bookmobile.   J. F. Mahoney

2483. Christopher, Henrietta Conmy. THE PEMBINA STATE MUSEUM. *North Dakota Hist. 1967 34(1): 101-104.* Built on the site of Fort Daer, refuge of the Selkirk settlers, this museum has a site occupied since 1797. In 1960 Pembina citizens through their Community Club asked for a museum. An appropriation by the legislature of five thousand dollars was to be matched locally. Volunteer labor built the structure, dedicated in 1962, when an additional five thousand dollars was voted for a heritage center. The Barry Collection, valued at thirty thousand dollars, has been displayed there since 1965. It contains equipment from Fort Pembina, 1870-97, and clothing, furniture, and household equipment used by pioneer families and Indians. Illus.   I. W. Van Noppen

2484. Cory, Robert. RUSSELL REID: A FRIEND'S RECOLLECTION. *North Dakota Hist. 1967 34(4): 283-294.* Russell Reid became a permanent member of the staff of the State Historical Society of North Dakota in 1923. His specialties were ornithology and photography. In 1930 he became superintendent, serving in that capacity until 1965. For 20 years he was editor of *North Dakota History.* Reid's best writing concerned subjects of popular lore and the history of the State. His most valuable contributions were edited editions of documentary source materials. 5 illus.   D. L. Smith

2485. Halvorson, Elmer H. THE BUFFALO TRAILS MUSEUM. *North Dakota Hist. 1968 35(1): 68-72.* The Buffalo Trails Museum was established in a three-village area in Williams County, North Dakota, when funds were alloted in 1966 by the Federal Office of Economic Opportunity. Professional help was enlisted, and the museum was opened in 1967 as a vehicle for the preservation of the cultural heritage and history of the region. 2 illus.   D. L. Smith

2486. Hunter, William C. JOHN MILLER, FIRST GOVERNOR OF NORTH DAKOTA. *North Dakota Hist. 1967 34(1): 31-45.* John Miller, born in New York of Scottish ancestry, came to North Dakota during the bonanza farm period, 1878-89. A Republican, he entered politics and was elected North Dakota's first Governor, serving two years, after which he devoted his time to farm management. The greatest victory he won as governor was the defeat of a charter for a State lottery. Later he became associated with various land companies. He was interested in civic and social improvement until his death in 1908. Illus., 50 notes.   I. W. Van Noppen

2487. Mattison, Ray H. THE FLOOD OF 1881. *North Dakota Hist. 1967 34(3): 225-241.* The winter of 1880-81 was one of the most severe in the history of North Dakota. The first blizzard struck in October. By January many railroads were snowed in. Ice on the Missouri was 38 inches thick. The snow and cold continued through February. Fuel and food were short. Warnings of floods came early, but the great break-up of ice did not begin until 30 March. On 1 April the Missouri River rose six feet. The floods created havoc, with direct losses totaling a million dollars. Some of the towns never recovered. 11 illus., 65 notes.   I. W. Van Noppen

2488. Mattison, Ray H. THE STATE HISTORICAL SOCIETY OF NORTH DAKOTA: A BRIEF HISTORY. *North Dakota Hist. 1967 34(4): 295-319.* Antecedents of the State Historical Society of North Dakota date from 1889. Lacking public support, however, continuity in its history was broken in 1897. Rejuvenated in 1903, with a change to its present name, the society has survived legislative and economic difficulties, growing and expanding its programs significantly. 14 illus., 49 notes.   D. L. Smith

2489. Miller, John. FIRST MESSAGE OF THE GOVERNOR OF NORTH DAKOTA TO THE LEGISLATIVE ASSEMBLY DELIVERED AT BISMARCK, NOVEMBER 20, 1889. *North Dakota Hist. 1964 31(3): 167-187.* The first Governor of North Dakota, John Miller, advised the legislature concerning the bonded indebtedness of Dakota Territory assumed by North Dakota and the amount of money received from the territory, and he followed by a prediction of tax receipts and estimated expenses. He proposed the prohibition of alcoholic beverages, the guarding of the purity of elections, and the taxing of railroad property as well as the gross earnings of railroads. He surveyed the institutions, including the penitentiary, the hospital for the insane, and the university, all of which already existed. He held the existing railroad and warehouse rates detrimental to business interests, and maintained that high interest rates were retarding immigration. Recommendations included establishment of an insurance commission, a library, a board of health, a militia and ordnance, irrigation, a commissioner of agriculture and statistics, support of public schools by use of public lands, and the building of necessary buildings in Capitol Park.   I. W. Van Noppen

2490. Petty, Warren James. HISTORY OF THEODORE ROOSEVELT NATIONAL MEMORIAL PARK. *North Dakota Hist. 1968 35(2): 384-441.* The park is in the Badlands area along the Little Missouri River in western North Dakota. It was created in 1947. Roosevelt had frequented the area in the 1880's and 1890's on hunting expeditions and in cattle ranching. 21 illus., 167 notes.   D. L. Smith

2491. Pfaller, Louis. NORTH DAKOTA WEATHER: AN ANALYTIC SUMMARY OF CONDITIONS OVER THE LAST CENTURY. *North Dakota Hist. 1967 34(3): 258-271.* By compiling data about a century of North Dakota weather through analysis of official weather records, Brother Philip Kress, O.S.B., detected certain important trends. Five tables show these trends with annual mean temperature and other statistics. 23 notes.   I. W. Van Noppen

2492. Purdon, Florence. THE RICHLAND COUNTY HISTORICAL SOCIETY. *North Dakota Hist. 1966 33(4): 420-426.* The Highland County Historical Museum opened on 1 July 1966. It was made possible by a gift to the historical society of 70 shares of stock in the Rosemeade Potteries by Robert J. Hughes, after the death of Mrs. Hughes whose dream of such an institution had persisted for 13 years. Volunteer work and almost daily donations of old things contributed to building and operating the dignified modern 100 thousand-dollar structure which records the history of the area. It includes room settings, a small claim shack (furnished), farm machinery, horse drawn vehicles, and Indian artifacts. A small one-room schoolhouse will be placed on the museum grounds. Illus.   I. W. Van Noppen

2493. Reid, Russell. VERENDRYE'S JOURNEY TO NORTH DAKOTA IN 1738. *North Dakota Hist. 1965 32(2): 117-129.* Sieur de la Vérendrye was the first white man to leave a record of his travels through North Dakota. La Vérendrye's journal consists of letters written to his superiors. One such letter covering the period 20 July 1738 to May 1739 is discussed. Some of the historical and archaeological interpretations of the journal are analyzed. One important clue concerning the actual areas La Vérendrye visited is his mention of Indian tribes. Illus., map, 39 notes to primary and secondary sources.   M. J. McBaine

2494. Rose, Margaret. MANUSCRIPTS OF STATE HISTORICAL SOCIETY. *North Dakota Hist. 1963 30(1): 17-61.* Lists all collections which have been cataloged and to which numbers have been assigned. A code indicates the location and size of collections, and the contents of each collection are described briefly.   I. W. Van Noppen

2495. Sherman, William E. THE BOODLERS. *North Dakota Hist. 1967 34(3): 208-223.* North Dakota was a poor State. It needed a source of revenue to relieve the tax burden. The Louisiana State Lottery Company proposed to liquidate the debt and support the schools. Many people argued that the State needed the revenue from the lottery. Most of the newspapers were in favor of the lottery bill in the 1889-90 legislature. Under the bill eight men would control the lottery and the State would be powerless for 50 years to restrict and regulate the corporation. Protests arose, opposition was aroused. Ten Pinkerton agents were hired to investigate bribery. When one of these agents uncovered evidence of widespread bribery, the bill was defeated. 9 illus., 55 notes.
I. W. Van Noppen

2496. Smith, Marjorie. STUTSMAN COUNTY MUSEUM. *North Dakota Hist. 1966 33(3): 319-321.* The formal opening of the Stutsman County Memorial Museum in Jamestown, North Dakota, attracted 500 visitors, 2 June 1965. Members of the Fort Seward Historical Society of Jamestown were hosts. Housed in the former George Lutz residence, its memorabilia represented the pioneer history of Stutsman County and Dakota Territory. It contains Indian curios, a gun collection, many types of dishes, antique fans, a period piano and organ, handmade drums, and a banjo. On the third floor is a scale model of Fort Seward and a medical exhibit of instruments used by early-day doctors. The museum will preserve and exhibit the wealth of Americana formerly stored in attics. Photo.   I. W. Van Noppen

2497. Spalding, Burleigh F. CONSTITUTIONAL CONVENTION, 1889. *North Dakota Hist. 1964 31(3): 151-164.* Judge Spalding was a member of the North Dakota Constitutional Convention. The history of Dakota Territory is traced from its organization in 1861. In 1889 an act was passed for dividing the area if the people approved. The constitutional convention in Bismarck, on the Fourth of July 1889, began with a parade of U.S. troops and Indians. Committees were appointed to locate the capital and the State institutions. A single tax and a unicameral legislature were considered, and a disagreement occurred over the method of taxing railroads. Limited indebtedness of the State and protection of school funds were adopted. Appendix.   I. W. Van Noppen

2498. Vantible, J. Liess. HISTORICAL WRITINGS OF RAY H. MATTISON: A SELECT BIBLIOGRAPHY 1946-1969. *North Dakota Hist. 1969 36(3): 279-285.* A selected bibliography of the writings of Ray H. Mattison, retired former superintendant of the State Historical Society of North Dakota.   J. M. Bumsted

2499. Wilson, Wesley C. DOCTOR WALTER A. BURLEIGH: DAKOTA TERRITORIAL DELEGATE TO 39TH AND 40TH CONGRESS: POLITICIAN EXTRAORDINARY. *North Dakota Hist. 1966 33(2): 93-103.* One of the early pioneers of North Dakota, Walter A. Burleigh served the territory as an Indian agent and as a Republican delegate to the U.S. Congress. While agent, he employed the Sioux as adjuncts for the U.S. Army and also began encouraging them to adopt an agrarian way of life. Congressman from 1864-69, Burleigh was a strong force in politics and engaged in enterprises connected with the Dakota Territory and the Missouri River areas. Back in Dakota after his congres-

sional defeat in 1869, he became an active influence in steamboat business, his boats plying the waters of the Missouri with needed freight. However, his business was wiped out by the great flood of 1881 and he then moved on to Montana Territory where he entered public service in several capacities. There he died on 8 March 1896. Documented from contemporary newspapers and related works, illus., 33 notes.   R. Sexauer

2500. Wilson, Wesley C. GENERAL JOHN B. S. TODD, FIRST DELEGATE, DAKOTA TERRITORY. *North Dakota Hist. 1964 31(3): 189-194.* A cousin of Mrs. Abraham Lincoln, a cultured gentleman born in Kentucky, General Todd was a Democrat, a veteran of the Mexican War, and a former Indian agent. In the first election held in Dakota Territory he won the office of Delegate to Congress. His service ended in 1864. Todd also served as vice president of the Historical Society of Dakota in 1865, and in 1866 he was elected speaker of the territorial legislature. He continued to be a leader until his death in 1871. 19 notes.
I. W. Van Noppen

2501. —. LIBRARY NOTES. *North Dakota Hist. 1964 31(2): 135-139.* A bibliography of theses which can be found in the library of the State Historical Society of North Dakota. Arranged in alphabetical order, the theses relate to all aspects of North Dakota history from such specific studies as the history of Fort Union to more general analyses. 102 entries.
M. J. McBaine

2502. —. RESUME OF ANNUAL MEMBERSHIP MEETING OF THE STATE HISTORICAL SOCIETY, DECEMBER 7, 1963. *North Dakota Hist. 1964 31(1): 5-24.*
Ewald, Paul A. OPEN LETTER TO THE MEMBERSHIP OF THE STATE HISTORICAL SOCIETY, *pp. 5-7.* Explains the legal background and objectives of the historical society.
Baker, Howard W. ADDRESS, *pp. 11-17.* Outlines proposed Federal legislation to assist states in establishing and maintaining recreational programs.
Fridley, Russell. THE CHANGING HISTORICAL SOCIETY, *pp. 19-24.* Compares privately established and controlled societies of Eastern States with state-supported Middle Western ones. The society is challenged to help individuals of our time of specialization to understand and perpetuate the ties that hold us together - the common heritage of traditions, customs, and values.
I. W. Van Noppen

2503. —. THE TRAILL COUNTY HISTORICAL SOCIETY. *North Dakota Hist. 1966 33(2): 220-222.* The first in a series on the county and local historical societies of North Dakota. Formed out of an effort to save the residence of Amos L. Plummer, a pioneer banker in Hillsboro, North Dakota, the historical society was incorporated on 19 October 1965. The Plummer house has since become the official Traill County Museum, displaying articles which belonged to Traill County pioneers. Illus.   R. Sexauer

South Dakota

2504. Bates, J. Leonard. WALSH OF MONTANA IN DAKOTA TERRITORY. *Pacific Northwest Q. 1965 56(3): 114-124.* Personal and political activities of Thomas J. Walsh (later U.S. Senator from Montana, 1913-33) while he resided in Dakota Territory, especially in the town of Redfield, 1884-90.   C. C. Gorchels

2505. Conrad, Jane. CHARLES COLLINS: THE SIOUX CITY PROMOTION OF THE BLACK HILLS. *South Dakota Hist. 1972 2(2): 131-171.* Charles Collins, a newspaperman and promoter from Sioux City, Iowa, campaigned to open the Black Hills gold fields to development. There were numerous attempts to organize settlers' parties to the Black Hills and to promote Sioux City as the best route to the gold fields. The Gordon expedition and Jenny party were organized and financed by Sioux City businessmen and resulted in a national clamor to open the Black Hills to mining development. Collins' promotion of the Black Hills brought population, trade, and wealth to the Northwest, but little fame to himself. 8 illus., 98 notes.   D. H. Swift

Nebraska

2506. Bakken, Douglas. CHRONOLOGY OF NEBRASKA STATEHOOD. *Nebraska Hist. 1967 48(1): 81-90.* A chronological listing, with a brief explanatory account, of the steps to Nebraska statehood from 1859 to 1867 when the territory entered the Union.
R. Lowitt

2507. Bright, Thomas R. THE ANTI-NEBRASKA COALITION AND THE EMERGENCE OF THE REPUBLICAN PARTY IN NEW HAMPSHIRE: 1853-1857. *Hist. New Hampshire 1972 27(2): 57-88.* In the second American party system, 1828-44, Jacksonian Democrats opposed banks, corporations, government-financed internal improvements, and Federal interference with slavery, at least in New Hampshire, which they controlled. Neither party was strong for social reforms, but more Whigs were for temperance. Democrat John P. Hale's bolt in 1845 over the annexation of Texas led to victories for the 1847 Whig-Free Soil coalition. The Compromise of 1850 detached more Democrats who could not support the Fugitive Slave Act. The Nebraska territorial bill further eroded the Democrats, who could not elect either US Senator for New Hampshire in the summer of 1854. A State prohibition bill further fractured the Democrats, one-quarter of whom supported it. Banks and corporations were dead issues to Democrats. Late in 1854 the nativist Americans began to draw from all three parties. These "Know Nothings" emerged in the March 1855 election with governorship and a large majority under their label. Soon calling themselves "Anti-Nebraska Americans," they elected US Senators, removed Democrats from offices, and adopted the Free Soil and prohibition platforms. Their antiforeign actions were moderate. The "American Republicans," including all but a few die-hard Whigs, won State and presidential elections in 1856 and dominated New Hampshire politics for a century. They were, in platform and leadership, the old Whig Party writ large, with infusion of former Democrats for whom free soil, prohibition, or nativism were the most important issues. Based on analysis of House roll calls, 1853-57; 4 illus., 81 notes.
T. D. S. Bassett

2508. Hronek, Sharon. THE BATTLE OF OMAHA. *Am. West 1969 6(4): 10-11.* In 1856 Omaha was established as the capital of the Nebraska Territory. Despite all efforts to relocate it, including legislative maneuvering, fist fights, bombastic threats, journalistic controversy, and even a period of two legislatures, Omaha managed to hold on to the coveted honor until 1867. With statehood that year, the capital city was changed to Lincoln. 4 illus.
D. L. Smith

2509. Kivett, Marvin F. THE NEBRASKA STATE HISTORICAL SOCIETY. *Hist. News 1967 22(8): 177-179.* Absorbing a previous society which existed only on the statute books, the Nebraska State Historical Society was established in 1878. Over the years the society has expanded its activities and program concerned with all phases of Nebraska and Middle Western history. Among its notable accomplishments: it provoked the meeting of Middle West historical societies and university departments of history that formed the Mississippi Valley Historical Association (presently the Organization of American Historians) and it pioneered Plains archaeological research. 6 illus.
D. L. Smith

2510. Lowitt, Richard, ed. BLACKLEDGE ON NORRIS: REFLECTIONS ON NEBRASKA JUSTICE IN THE 1890'S. *Nebraska Hist. 1965 46(1): 67-76.* A 1936 memorandum by Judge Louis H. Blackledge recalling his youth as a Nebraska lawyer when George W. Norris was the judge of the district in which he practiced.
A

2511. Parsons, Stanley B. WHO WERE THE NEBRASKA POPULISTS? *Nebraska Hist. 1963 44(2): 83-99.* Based in large part on a careful analysis of seven Nebraska counties and employing various methodological techniques, observations, conclusions are offered about the constituency of Nebraska Populism. The core group was wheat farmers who were "particularly vulnerable to economic crisis."
R. Lowitt

2512. Plumb, J. H. A FRESH DIMENSION OF INTELLECTUAL DELIGHT. *Nebraska Hist. 1969 50(1): 101-105.* A reprinting of a column for *The Saturday Review* of 31 August 1968 calling attention to the delights of dipping into local history with some reference to that of the State of Nebraska.
R. Lowitt

2513. Sellers, James L. FAIRVIEW DEDICATION. *Nebraska Hist. 1964 45(4): 343-346.* Brief interpretative remarks about William Jennings Bryan made at the dedication of his home as a state and national landmark on 26 September 1965.
R. Lowitt

2514. Socolofsky, Homer E. WHY SETTLE IN NEBRASKA-THE CASE OF JOHN ROGERS MALTBY. *Nebraska Hist. 1963 44(2): 123-132.* Delineates the career of John Rogers Maltby, who left Maine at the age of 23, spent 15 years moving from place to place on frontiers all over the world, and then in 1868 came to Nebraska, where in 1871 he settled down in Clay County, achieving a modicum of success - economic and otherwise.
R. Lowitt

2515. Stanley, Ruth Moore. N. K. GRIGGS AND THE CONSTITUTIONAL CONVENTION OF 1871. *Nebraska Hist. 1965 46(1): 39-65.* Records the observations and remarks of N. K. Griggs, one of 52 delegates, meeting in Lincoln for two months in 1871, who adopted a constitution, not accepted by the electorate. In the main it followed the Illinois Constitution of 1870.
R. Lowitt

2516. Thavenet, Dennis. THE TERRITORIAL GOVERNORSHIP: NEBRASKA TERRITORY AS EXAMPLE. *Nebraska Hist. 1970 51(4): 387-409.* Examines the role of the territorial governor, focusing on Nebraska Territory. Discusses methods of appointment and details responsibilities to various groups in the territory and in Washington. Discusses the five territorial governors of Nebraska from 1854 to 1876.
R. Lowitt

2517. Thurman, Melburn D. A CASE OF HISTORICAL MYTHOLOGY: THE SKIDI PAWNEE MORNING STAR SACRIFICE OF 1833. *Plains Anthropologist 1970 15(50, part 1): 309-311.* "Repetition as a substitute for analysis has often resulted in the perpetuation of error. Here the literature of one such myth is traced, and the myth (that there was an attempted Morning Star Sacrifice in 1833) exposed."
J

2518. Warner, Mildred. [INDIANS AND THE NEBRASKA TERRITORIAL GOVERNMENT]. *Great Plains J. 1970 9(2): 53-66.* INDIANS CHALLENGE THE NEBRASKA TERRITORIAL GOVERNMENT: I, *pp. 53-58.* Reviews the problems between the Indians and the Nebraska Territory between 1854 and 1859. Early governors not only asked the Federal Government for assistance when the Indians failed to stay in designated areas or attacked emigrants along the Oregon Trail, but several times sent territorial militia into the field. The policy of peaceful coexistence of whites and Indians slowly strangled the Indians. The reservation system and the destitution of the Indians disrupted coexistence. Hostilities along the western border increased as the 1850's ended. 9 notes. THE ATTITUDE OF THE NEBRASKA TERRITORIAL GOVERNMENT TOWARDS THE INDIANS: II, *pp. 59-66.* In the latter part of Nebraska's territorial period the clash of Indians and whites was precipitated by the Colorado gold rush and the Civil War. By the Treaty of Fort Wise (1861) the Cheyenne and Arapahoe ceded most of their lands between the Platte and the Arkansas rivers. With the 1862 Sioux uprising in Minnesota, the Second Nebraska Cavalry was organized as Nebraskans demanded severe measures against the Indians. Indians took the warpath in the summer of 1864 and attacks were made in the valley of the Little Blue in eastern Nebraska. Late in the fall of 1864 the Chivington Massacre occurred at Sand Creek in Colorado. Three widely-held frontier concepts help explain it: the Indians could be controlled by severe measures, the Confederates were inciting the Indians, and the Indians should be exterminated. In 1865 peace was made with the Cheyenne and Arapahoe, but a Sioux war began. In 1867 Congress appointed a Peace Commission to study the Indian problem. In the 1870's most Indians were removed from Nebraska. 30 notes.
O. H. Zabel

2519. Welliver, Mrs. Andy, ed. LETTER - ORION CLEMENS TO WILLIAM HEMPHILL JONES, ACTING COMPTROLLER OF TREASURY, WASHINGTON D.C. APRIL 29, 1863. *Nevada Hist. Soc. Q. 1963 6(1): unpaged.* Orion Clemens was secretary of the Nevada Territory. He defends in this facsimile manuscript his expenditures for the fiscal year 1862, some of which had been questioned by the Treasury Department. A picture is thus presented of economic conditions in the territory. The letter is published without editorial apparatus.
G. B. Dodds

2520. Wesser, Robert F. GEORGE W. NORRIS: THE UNICAM-ERAL LEGISLATURE AND THE PROGRESSIVE IDEAL. *Nebraska Hist. 1964 45(4): 309-321.* Surveys the role of George W. Norris in establishing the unicameral system in Nebraska in 1934 and relates Norris' ideas about it to earlier Progressive thought.

R. Lowitt

Kansas

2521. Anderson, George L. ATCHISON, 1865-1886, DIVIDED AND UNCERTAIN. *Kansas Hist. Q. 1969 35(1): 30-45.* An attempt to determine why Atchison failed to realize its goal of becoming the great railroad center of Kansas. People rather than geography are shown to have been more important in accounting for Atchison's failure to keep pace with Kansas City, Leavenworth, and other cities as a railroad center. Atchison's leading citizens made a mistake in trying to give their town eastern connections through St. Louis rather than through the more important Chicago. The same leaders also missed their chances in the West. Instead of concentrating on the Southwest, the West, or the North-west, the leaders of Atchison scattered their efforts and lost all three areas. Controversies surrounding the building of bridges, stockyards, elevators, warehouses and railroad yards, and other enterprises also demonstrated the disharmony that plagued Atchison. Based on newspapers, articles, and books; illus., 41 notes.

W. F. Zornow

2522. Argersinger, Peter H. ROAD TO A REPUBLICAN WATER-LOO: THE FARMERS' ALLIANCE AND THE ELECTION OF 1890 IN KANSAS. *Kansas Hist. Q. 1967 33(4): 443-469.* Kansas was com-pletely committed to the Republican Party in 1888. Two years later that party lost the legislature, the Senate seat it controlled for 18 years, five of seven seats in the House of Representatives, and came close to losing the governorship. This is an account of how dissident farm groups, un-happy over poor economic conditions during the late 1880's, joined forces with the Democrats to unseat the entrenched Republicans. Only in three-ticket districts did the Republicans save their positions. The Democrats and Populists saw the advantage in offering fusion tickets, and they put this lesson to good use in subsequent elections in Kansas and other States. Based on newspapers, monographs, magazine articles; 98 notes.

W. F. Zornow

2523. Baltimore, Lester B. BENJAMIN F. STRINGFELLOW: THE FIGHT FOR SLAVERY ON THE MISSOURI BORDER. *Missouri Hist. R. 1967 62(1): 14-29.* As an outspoken member of the proslavery Platte County Self-Defensive Association, Stringfellow helped to define for many people the terms involved in the struggle over slavery in Kansas Territory. All his words and actions served to make others take an ex-treme stand in opposition to or in support of slavery. He knew that only the most vigorous support of slavery would insure its perpetuation. Based on newspapers, articles, monographs, and manuscripts in the State His-torical Society of Missouri and the Kansas State Historical Society; illus., 68 notes.

W. F. Zornow

2524. Barry, Louise. AN ADDENDUM TO "KANSAS BEFORE 1854: A REVISED ANNALS." *Kansas Hist. Q. 1967 33(3): 377-405.* A series of notes correcting errors in and adding pertinent information to the *Revised Annals* that were published in the 23 issues of the Quarterly between spring 1961 and summer 1967.

W. F. Zornow

2525. Barry, Louise, comp. KANSAS BEFORE 1854: A REVISED ANNALS; PART EIGHTEEN, 1849. PART NINETEEN, 1850. *Kansas Hist. Q. 1965 31(3): 256-339, 1966 32(1): 33-112.* A summary of the key events which took place in the Kansas region during these years. The California gold rush is the major topic. Many Forty-niners traveling along the Oregon-California trail kept extensive diaries. There were also many military expeditions moving across Kansas toward Santa Fe, Oregon and California. The traffic along the western trade routes was unusually heavy. The author attempts to catalog most of these move-ments and to supplement this narrative with additional information about the activities of local settlers. The compiler has drawn on diaries to provide innumerable observations on the daily experiences of the immi-grants.

W. F. Zornow

2526. Barry, Louise. KANSAS BEFORE 1854: A REVISED AN-NALS. *Kansas Hist. Q. 1963 29(1): 41-81; (2): 143-189, and (3): 324-359.* First article ("Part 9, 1836-1837"), second article ("Part 10, 1838-1839"), and third article ("Part 11, 1840-1841"): a brief summary of some of the key events which took place in the Kansas area, by two-year periods. Major attention is given to events concerning military affairs, Indian relations, missionary activities, the movement of settlers through the area, land surveys, federal laws pertaining to the area, and vital statistics.

W. F. Zornow

2527. Barry, Louise. KANSAS BEFORE 1854: A REVISED AN-NALS. *Kansas Hist. Q. 1963 29(4): 429-486; 1964 30(1): 62-91; (2): 209-244; (3): 339-412.* Continued from parts 12-15, 1842-46. A brief summary of the key events which took place in the Kansas region during each single year. Major attention is given to events concerning military affairs, Indian relations, missionary activities, floods, vital statistics, trade caravans, the movement of settlers and traders over the Santa Fe and Oregon Trails, land surveys, federal laws pertaining to the area, opera-tions against the Pawnee. The years 1844-45 were marked by the expedi-tions of Colonel Stephen W. Kearney to the Rockies, and Lieutenant John C. Fremont to California.

W. F. Zornow

2528. Barry, Louise. KANSAS BEFORE 1854: A REVISED AN-NALS, PART SIXTEEN, 1847; PART SEVENTEEN, 1848. *Kansas Hist. Q. 1964 30(4): 492-559 and 1965 31(2): 138-199.* Continued from Parts 9-11 and Parts 12-15. A summary of the key events which took place in the Kansas region during these years. The major topics include: the construction of Fort Mannes, an investigation of irregularities at the agency of the Mississippi Sacs and Foxes, and the arrest of Colonel John C. Frémont (1813-90), the discovery of gold in California, traffic on the trails to Oregon and Santa Fe, the return march of the soldiers from Mexico, and the fourth exploration trip led by John C. Frémont.

W. F. Zornow

2529. Barry, Louise. KANSAS BEFORE 1854: A REVISED AN-NALS. PART 20, 1851. *Kansas Hist. Q. 1966 32(2): 210-282.* Contin-ued from previous article. A chronological summary of the key events which took place in the Kansas region during the year. Steamboats on the Missouri, the movement of immigrants and goods along the trails to Santa Fe, California, and Oregon, the activities of the U.S. Army, the govern-ment's dealings with the Indians, and a cholera epidemic were topics of particular interest during the year. To be continued.

W. F. Zornow

2530. Barry, Louise. KANSAS BEFORE 1854: A REVISED AN-NALS. PART 21, 1852; PART 22, 1853 AND PART 23, 1854. *Kansas Hist. Q. 1966 32(4): 426-503, 1967 33(1): 13-64, and (2): 172-213.* Concludes a chronological summary of the key events which took place in the Kansas region during the years 1540 to 1854. Steamboats on the Missouri, the movement of immigrants and merchandise along the trails to Santa Fe, California, and Oregon, the activities of the U.S. Army, the government's dealings with the Indians, birth notices, and obituaries are the topics of particular interest. Based largely on newspapers, government publications, and microfilms of papers in the National Archives; illus., map, tables.

W. F. Zornow

2531. Barry, Louise, ed. A KANSAS CATTLE RANCH. THE AMERICAN CATTLE COMPANY'S 23,000 ACRES IN CLARK COUNTY-A VALUABLE TRACT. *Kansas Hist. Q. 1969 35(1): 46-49.* An article appeared in the 1 July 1890 issue of the Manhattan *Daily Republican* describing the editor's visit to the most extensive cattle ranch in Kansas and to the adjacent 13,000-acre Perry ranch on which the owner was experimenting with irrigation techniques. Illus., 9 notes.

W. F. Zornow

2532. Brodhead, Michael J. A POPULIST SURVIVAL: JUDGE FRANK DOSTER IN THE 1920's. *Kansas Hist. Q. 1968 34(4): 443-456.* Frank Doster (1847-1933) is shown to have been one of a small group of Kansans who kept the spirit of liberalism alive during the so-called Age of Normalcy. Doster moved easily from the Republican Party to the Greenback, Union Labor, People's, and the liberal wing of the Democratic Party. He was identified with almost every radical idea that caught public attention during his half century in Kansas. He was often accused of being a Socialist or a Communist, but he is shown to have been anything but a Communist in the Marx-Lenin mold. His speeches and addresses, which are described at length, reveal him to be a reformer more interested in abstract concepts than in the specific pieces of legislation that constitute a reform program. He performed a valuable service in keeping the spirit of liberalism alive in a conservative era. Based on the Doster Papers in the University of Kansas library and some local newspaper reports; photo, 21 notes.   W. F. Zornow

2533. Brown, Al Theodore. BUSINESS "NEUTRALISM" ON THE KANSAS BORDER: KANSAS CITY, 1854-1857. *J. of Southern Hist. 1963 29(2): 229-240.* Kansas City, Missouri, was incorporated in 1853 near two older communities it was soon to eclipse, Westport and Independence. With the opening of Kansas to settlement, it followed a different policy from the other two. Although the slave population of its county was about 17 percent and its population was proslavery, its business leaders nevertheless saw that their economic interests were linked to the development of Kansas, whether by pro-Northern or pro-Southern settlers. During the Kansas crisis they strove to maintain stable conditions in their community which were favorable to trade and immigration. Community leadership tried not to lose any opportunity of making money, though this meant exciting the hostility of Missourians around them.   S. E. Humphreys

2534. Davis, Kenneth S. ELI THAYER AND THE KANSAS CRUSADE. *New England Galaxy 1963 5(2): 23-33.* Eli Thayer (1819-99) did not organize the New England Emigrant Aid Company of Massachusetts as a benevolent institution but as a money making business. He was, however, attacking slavery in the process. He sought by colonization to make Kansas a laboratory demonstration of the inferiority of slave labor to free labor, a demonstration so convincing that the South's faith in slavery would be shaken.   T. J. Farnham

2535. Dirks, Martha. TEEN-AGE FOLKLORE FROM KANSAS. *Western Folklore 1963 22(2): 89-102.* A list of one of the divisions of teenage folklore - jokes, compiled from a survey taken among 226 high school students in a small western Kansas town. The list is divided into four groups: sick jokes, historical character jokes, little moron jokes, and knock-knock jokes.   L. J. White

2536. Emmons, David M. RICHARD SMITH ELLIOTT, KANSAS PROMOTER. *Kansas Hist. Q. 1970 36(4): 390-401.* Kansas has been a fertile field for promoters since territorial days. Of the many promoters employed by the Kansas Pacific Railroad, none was more important than Richard Smith Elliott. This farmer, inventor, printer, Indian subagent, newspaper editor, and real estate dealer worked for the railroad when many believed it possible to increase rainfall on the plains by unusual means. Elliott thought planting trees would work. The railroad financed three such projects (at Wilson's Creek, Ellis, and Pond Creek). The projects did not increase rainfall, but indirectly might have inspired the Timber Culture Act of 1873. They did have much to do with raising the value of railroad-held property. Based on manuscripts in the Kansas State Historical Society and Missouri Historical Society, St. Louis, and on secondary sources; 2 photos, 55 notes.   W. F. Zornow

2537. Gambone, Joseph G., ed. KANSAS - A VEGETARIAN UTOPIA: THE LETTERS OF JOHN MILTON HADLEY, 1855-1856. *Kansas Hist. Q. 1972 38(1): 65-87.* Hadley (1835-1902) became a vegetarian when he was a student at Earlham College in Richmond, Indiana. He came to Kansas when his father was appointed superintendent of the Friends' Shawnee Mission. At the same time, Henry S. Clubb, the leading advocate of vegetarianism in the United States, was proposing to establish a vegetable colony in Kansas. Reprints the text of seven letters written by Hadley between April 1855 and May 1856 to his friend George Allen. Because most of the letters were written at the Friends' Mission, they contained valuable information about the early religious history of Kansas as well as information about the vegetable colony on the Neosho River. Based on primary and secondary sources; 3 illus., 35 notes.
                                                              ·W. F. Zornow

2538. Gambone, Joseph G. SAMUEL C. POMEROY AND THE SENATORIAL ELECTION OF 1861, RECONSIDERED. *Kansas Hist. Q. 1971 37(1): 15-32.* The fraud and corruption which ended Samuel Clarke Pomeroy's senatorial career in 1873 have always been accepted as the hallmarks of his entire career after he came to Kansas in 1854. A

reconsideration of the earlier career reveals that Pomeroy performed valuable services as a leader in the Free State movement, a founder of the State Republican Party, and as the director of an important relief program during the famine days of territorial Kansas. He required no dishonesty to win the senatorial election of 1861 from a people who regarded him with respect and gratitude for his many services and accepted him as a man isolated from the political intrigues that attended the birth of Kansas. Based on manuscripts in the Kansas State Historical Society, Massachusetts Historical Society, and the Library of Congress, and on secondary sources; illus., 60 notes.   W. F. Zornow

2539. Gambone, Joseph G. STARVING KANSAS: THE GREAT DROUGHT AND FAMINE OF 1859-60. *Am. West 1971 8(4): 30-35.* The bumper crop year of 1859 lulled the settlers of Kansas Territory into believing that the economic distress of the Panic of 1857 was gone forever. This belief was shattered by the drought of 1859-60, which brought an unprecedented period of hardship to the Territory. Crop failures, economic stagnation, and starvation changed "Bleeding Kansas" into "Starving Kansas." As the situation deteriorated, thousands of settlers left to return to their former homes in the East. When local politicians and speculators who sought to protect their own interests ignored or discredited pleas for help, a relief movement had to be organized by outsiders. Relief from the East was not forthcoming, however, until the Republican Party espoused the cause as a part of its campaign in the presidential election of 1860. Statehood in 1861 gave the relief movement added impetus. Relief, the return of adequate rainfall in 1861, and the outbreak of the Civil War soon made Kansas a breadbasket for the Union Army. Map, 6 illus.   D. L. Smith

2540. Gleason, Ruth, comp. RECENT ADDITIONS TO THE LIBRARY. *Kansas Hist. Q. 1968 34(2): 201-228.* A partial list of books received by the Kansas State Historical Society from 1 October 1966 to 30 September 1967. These additions, by purchase, gift or exchange, are grouped under the following general headings: books by Kansans and about Kansas, books on American Indians and the West, genealogy and local history, and books on United States history, biography, and allied subjects.   W. F. Zornow

2541. Gower, Calvin W. KANSAS TERRITORY AND ITS BOUNDARY QUESTION: "BIG KANSAS" OR "LITTLE KANSAS." *Kansas Hist. Q. 1967 33(1): 1-12.* A discussion of the conflict in Kansas Territory during 1858 and 1859 between those who hoped to bring Kansas into the Union with a western boundary that included the goldfields of Colorado and a northern boundary that included Nebraska Territory south of the Platte River and those who hoped to bring Kansas into the Union with less extensive boundaries. The "Little Kansas" group which won the argument is judged to have a more realistic position, since it supported boundaries that were reasonable and recognized that the inhabitants of the goldfields and the land south of the Platte did not want to be part of Kansas. Based on newspapers; 2 maps, 42 notes.
                                                              W. F. Zornow

2542. Griffin, C. S. THE UNIVERSITY OF KANSAS AND THE SACK OF LAWRENCE: A PROBLEM OF UNSUCCESSFUL HONESTY. *Kansas Hist. Q. 1968 34(4): 409-426.* The Free-State Hotel, the property of the New England Emigrant Aid Company, was one of several buildings destroyed in the sack of Lawrence, Kansas, on 21 May 1856. After many unsuccessful efforts to get damages from the US Government, the company turned its interests over to the university in 1897. This is an account of the university's 32-year battle to win a claim that was based on a gross misreading of the facts in the case. After summarizing the alleged facts and the numerous efforts made by both the company and school to collect, the author reaffirms the conclusion that no claim really existed since it was impossible to prove that the building had been destroyed by a Federal official acting in the line of duty. Based on University of Kansas archives, the New England Emigrant Aid Company Papers in the Kansas State Historical Society, articles, newspapers, Federal and State published records; illus., 55 notes.   W. F. Zornow

2543. Haven, R., ed. JOHN BROWN AND HEMAN HUMPHREY: AN UNPUBLISHED LETTER. *J. of Negro Hist. 1967 52(3): 220-224.* Gives the background and text of a letter of 18 April 1857 from John Brown to the Reverend Heman Humphrey, retired president of Amherst College, in which Brown optimistically reported on his plans to organize resistance to the proslavery government in Kansas and to raise the funds necessary for such a project.   L. Gara

2544. Hickman, Russell E.   THE REEDER ADMINISTRATION INAUGURATED. PART 1.   *Kansas Hist. Q. 1970 36(3): 305-341.* Andrew Horatio Reeder (1807-64) was a competent attorney from Pennsylvania, but he had no national reputation; therefore, it was a mistake to appoint the unknown provincial attorney to the office of territorial governor, largely because it was felt such action would strengthen the Democratic Party in Kansas. Moreover, difficulties in Kansas in 1854 required the presence of a man with a national reputation. Reeder regarded the election of a delegate to Congress on 29 November to be more urgent than the taking of a census or the election of a legislative assembly. The author describes in some detail the course of the voting for a congressional delegate in each of the 16 districts of Kansas. The presence of strangers at the polls in most districts made the question of residence the most vital point in the whole election. Based on articles, books, newspapers, the *Statutes at Large,* the *Report of the Special Committee Appointed to Investigate the Troubles in Kansas,* and other government publications; map, 123 notes. Article to be continued.
W. F. Zornow

2545. Hoffhaus, Charles E.   FORT DE CAVAGNIAL: IMPERIAL FRANCE IN KANSAS, 1744-1764.   *Kansas Hist. Q. 1964 30(4): 425-454.* This small base marked the western end of a series of French forts stretching westward from Fort Duquesne to Kansas. It was built mainly to foster trade among the Kansa Indians. The article centers around the commanders and their small detachments of men at this outpost, and the role played by this fort in French imperial history is traced. Later explorers passing through this region commented on the remnants of the fort that were still standing. In a sense, the fort was the "first city" of Kansas. Based on French archival material, unpublished theses, and western historical literature.   W. F. Zornow

2546. Jones, Dorothy V.   A PREFACE TO THE SETTLEMENT OF KANSAS.   *Kansas Hist. Q. 1963 29(2): 122-136.* Before Kansas was opened for white settlement, it had already become a haven for many Indian tribes of the eastern states. During 1832, while Chief Black Hawk led some Sac and Fox in a war against the United States and a cholera epidemic swept through the tribes of the middle west, Colonel James B. Gardiner was assigned the job of moving several groups of Indians in Ohio to Kansas. This article, which is based largely on the five-volume collection of correspondence on the subject of Indian emigration compiled by the Twenty-third Congress, recounts the grim journey from Ohio to Kansas. The Shawnees and Ottawa found much to admire in the white man's culture. There was not total harmony between both races, but they were closer in Kansas than in many other states. The author regards this incident as the first step toward the settlement of Kansas and mutual tolerance between the races.   W. F. Zornow

2547. Kantor, Alvin R.   PRESIDENT FOR A DAY.   *Manuscripts 1969 21(1): 11-16.* On 4 March 1849, the Honorable David R. Atchison (1807-86), President of the U.S. Senate, began to act as the temporary chief executive of the United States. According to the stipulations of the Succession Law, he served in this capacity until Zachary Taylor assumed the office on Monday, 5 March 1849. In later years, Atchison became one of the most powerful men in the Democratic Party. Defeated in his attempt to win reelection to the Senate in 1855, he became one of the leaders of the Missouri "border ruffians" who raided the Kansas Territory (1855-56). The text of a letter from Atchison to Captain J. W. Denver is reproduced. Illus., photo.   P. D. Thomas

2548. Koppes, Clayton R.   THE WILDEST OF COW TOWNS: NEWTON.   *Mennonite Life 1968 23(3): 115-118.* Describes the violence and vice that characterized Newton, Kansas, in 1871-72, when it served as a cow town for the Atchison, Topeka, and Santa Fe. "Kansas' contribution to the Wild West tradition has been its cow towns. Dodge City has become a national synonym for frontier savagery; Abilene and Wichita have achieved a lesser renown. Probably even less famous is Newton. Yet Newton, for a season, was the roughest of the cow towns. More men died violent deaths in Newton during its period of seamy glory than in a comparable span of time in any other cow town." By 1874, however, when central Kansas was beginning to feel the impact of the great Mennonite immigration, Newton was already taking on the appearance of civilization.   D. J. Abramoske

2549. Larson, Bruce L.   KANSAS AND THE NONPARTISAN LEAGUE: THE RESPONSE TO THE AFFAIR AT GREAT BEND, 1921.   *Kansas Hist. Q. 1968 34(1): 51-71.* The farmers' Nonpartisan League was established in North Dakota in 1915 and came to Kansas in 1917. On 12 March 1921 some leaders of the movement were chased out of Great Bend by antileaguers and others were tarred later in the day. The newspaper coverage of the incident is analyzed at great length. Opposing views on the league were very strong in Kansas. Since the league did not organize in Kansas until after America entered World War I and its leaders were very critical of "special interests," it was easy to accuse the movement of being radical or even pro-German. The incident at Great Bend is described as an example of the spirit of intolerance that endured even after the war. Based on newspapers, unpublished theses, and papers in the Kansas State Historical Society; illus., 87 notes.
W. F. Zornow

2550. Linkugel, Wilmer A.   LINCOLN, KANSAS, AND COOPER UNION.   *Speech Monographs 1970 37(3): 172-179.* Deals with Abraham Lincoln's speaking tour in Kansas in December 1859. It is thought by some that Lincoln's Kansas tour was simply a "dry run" for his Cooper Union address. Existing data provide grounds to discount the statement that Lincoln's Atchison speech was the same one he was to give at Cooper Union. The New York speech was developed directly from the material Lincoln used in Kansas. Apparently, Lincoln realized the singular importance of his New York appearance to his political career; for this reason it would seem plausible that he wanted to try out some of his ideas in remote Kansas with the belief that speeches given there would not receive the attention of the eastern newspapers. The same speech given in Illinois, Ohio, or Indiana would have gotten into the newspapers, thereby spoiling Lincoln's plans for the New York speech. Based on newspaper accounts; 33 notes.   D. R. Richardson

2551. Madden, John L.   THE FINANCING OF A NEW TERRITORY: THE KANSAS TERRITORIAL TAX STRUCTURE, 1854-1861.   *Kansas Hist. Q. 1969 35(2): 155-164.* The agrarian nature of the Kansas economy, with its emphasis on land as the main source of wealth coupled with the prevailing attitude toward taxation, led the territorial legislature to direct its tax structure toward the property tax. The tax structure established by the territorial legislature laid the foundation for the tax structure of the State of Kansas after 1861. Included are tables showing population composition, labor force composition, and manufacturing and agriculture (1860), and showing territorial indebtedness and the warrants issued by the Territory of Kansas (1855-61). Based on the author's unpublished dissertation, State histories, State laws and territorial statutes; 13 notes.   W. F. Zornow

2552. Malin, James C.   AT WHAT AGE DID MEN BECOME REFORMERS?   *Kansas Hist. Q. 1963 29(3): 250-266.* Editor E. W. Hoch's comment that the members of the 1891 Kansas legislature looked ten years older than the members of the preceding legislature provided the author with inspiration to compare the ages of both houses of the legislature and the congressional delegation from 1866 to 1900. It is demonstrated that reform movements were not the exclusive handiwork of younger men. In fact, the younger men tended to gravitate toward the more conservative Republican Party. The wearing of beards and mustaches was a custom that changed greatly during the period. Photographs of the legislatures show that the younger members gradually adopted the practice of appearing with well-trimmed mustaches or clean-shaven faces. The latter trend was accelerated by the Spanish-American war. Based on local newspapers, and bluebooks of the legislature.   W. F. Zornow

2553. Malin, James C.   THE MONEY QUESTION: THE EDUCATION OF SENATOR H. B. KELLY.   *Mid-America 1966 48(4): 234-257.* State Senator and newspaper owner H. B. Kelly of McPherson, Kansas, came to realize that the explanations of causes and the formulation of solutions of the economic and social ills of Kansas required a perspective broader than Kansas. His development on the money question provides an opportunity to study the local and national ramifications of the question.   L. D. Silveri

2554. Marple, Robert P.   THE CORN-WHEAT RATION IN KANSAS, 1879-1959; A STUDY IN HISTORICAL GEOGRAPHY. *Great Plains J. 1969 8(2): 79-86.* Tests, statistically, the implication of historians that the agricultural pattern of early Kansas, in terms of corn-wheat ratio, was determined by the source of immigration. In 1879 the corn-wheat ratio was 183 to 100 acres; in 1959 it was 19 to 100 acres. After a county-by-county study, the author concludes that, as historians have implied, farmers from humid areas originally "tended to plant corn rather than wheat." Charts, maps, 8 notes.   O. H. Zabel

2555. Miller, Nyle H. THE ANNUAL REPORT. *Kansas Hist. Q. 1970 36(1): 74-100.* The report submitted at the 94th Annual Meeting of the Kansas State Historical Society on 21 October 1969, dealing with the following general subjects: appropriations and budget requests, special projects, archaeology, archives and manuscripts, the library, microfilm division, the museum, newspaper and census division, historic sites, and subjects for research. As of 30 September 1969 the Society had 118,286 bound volumes of clippings, periodicals, State publications, general books, and specialized material on Kansas, local history, genealogy, Indians, and the West.   W. F. Zornow

2556. Miller, Nyle H. THE KANSAS STATE HISTORICAL SOCIETY. *Hist. News 1966 21(4): 77-79.* After three abortive attempts to institutionalize the preservation of the historical records of the state, the Kansas State Historical Society was successfully launched in 1875. The society is concerned with Kansas, Western, and Indian history, and has expanded its services and facilities to include archives, displays, historic sites, and publications. Illus.   D. L. Smith

2557. Nathan, Meyer. THE ELECTION OF 1916 IN KANSAS. *Kansas Hist. Q. 1969 35(1): 50-63.* Examines the factors that led to the defeat of Charles Evans Hughes in Kansas in the presidential election of 1916. This was only one of four occasions that Kansas has failed to support the Republican nominee since 1861. Conservative Republicans claimed that the State administration scuttled the national ticket by campaigning only lukewarmly for Hughes. The Progressive Republicans-whose position seems more justifiable on the basis of the evidence presented-claimed that the State administration campaigned vigorously for Hughes who lost the State because of the weak campaign he conducted. Based on newspapers and manuscripts in the Kansas State Historical Society; illus., 27 notes.   W. F. Zornow

2558. Nugent, Walter T. K. SOME PARAMETERS OF POPULISM. *Agric. Hist. 1966 40(4): 255-270.* Populism was primarily a political response to economic trouble. A study of groups of Republicans and Populists in Kansas in 1889-92 indicates that the sociological differences were not great, but a much larger percentage of the Populists were farmers and their economic situations were more precarious. Based on quantitative analysis of data collected from census records, newspapers, and county records.   W. D. Rasmussen

2559. Oates, Stephen B. TO WASH THIS LAND IN BLOOD . . . JOHN BROWN IN KANSAS. *Am. West 1969 6(4): 36-41.* Connecticut-born John Brown (1800-59) was raised in Ohio's Western Reserve to fear the Calvinist God and to hate slavery and its defenders. He memorized the entire Bible and aspired to become a minister, but an eye inflammation and a shortage of funds forced him to abandon this plan. Tragedy and failure were his lot: his first wife and two of their seven children died of emotional problems; seven of 13 children of his second marriage died in childhood; his tannery business was wiped out in the Panic of 1837, the first of a succession of failures of his business ventures. His life was a series of obsessions, not confined to slavery, which he pursued with single-minded determination. Increasingly Brown became involved in the antislavery movement. He worked in the Underground Railroad, opposed "black laws," attempted integration of a church he attended, and grew violent in his denunciations. He chided Negroes for passive submission to white oppression, exhorted others to kill anyone trying to enforce the Fugitive Slave Law, and even enlisted over 40 Massachusetts blacks in a mutual-defense organization. Until five of his sons who had moved to Kansas informed him that the territory was in danger of becoming a slave state, Brown had planned to migrate there to try land speculation. Believing in predestination, he felt that he was foreordained to come to grips with his destiny in Kansas. He moved there in 1855 and soon became a prominent figure in the momentous controversy to determine whether Kansas was to become a slave or a free state. 5 illus. Article to be continued.   D. L. Smith

2560. Oates, Stephen B. TO WASH THIS LAND IN BLOOD . . . JOHN BROWN IN KANSAS. *Am. West 1969 6(6): 24-27, 61-62.* Continued from previous article. When a Georgia contingent camped on Indian lands near Pottawatomie, Kansas Territory, John Brown was more than ever convinced that the slavery issue would soon erupt into full-scale war on the prairie. With the sacking of Lawrence by proslavers in May 1856, Brown became outraged at the seeming passive reaction of the free-staters and the newly arrived Federal troops. He led his small party into proslave territory and murdered five people. Reciprocal reprisals and guerrilla war soon raged in southeastern Kansas. Brown evaded arrest and continued to lead others in what he regarded a holy war against slavery. As a new governor backed by Federal troops embarked on a program of pacification and the dispensing of evenhanded justice, Brown, his family, and close associates left Kansas. Convinced that his arrest had been ordered, sick with dysentery and fever, and filled with visions of a greater mission still to be accomplished, Brown planned extensive fund- and men-raising campaigns in the East. Adapted from a forthcoming biography. Illus., biblio. note.   D. L. Smith

2561. Parrish, William E. THE GREAT KANSAS LEGISLATIVE IMBROGLIO OF 1893. *J. of the West 1968 7(4): 471-490.* Gives a detailed account of the events leading up to and culminating in the confrontation between Republicans and Populists in the Kansas Legislature of 1893. Sweeping virtually all State offices in the election of 1892, the Populists found, to their dismay, that they did not have control of the House. They refused to accept this situation and for 35 days rival Houses sat and no State business was able to proceed. Neither side was willing to compromise. The State Supreme Court, on 25 February 1893, ruled that the Republican House was a legal body and few days later the Populist members joined the session. Their role as obstructionists cost them much popularity and the Populists were swept from power in 1894.   R. N. Alvis

2562. Petersen, Albert J., Jr. THE GERMAN-RUSSIAN SETTLEMENT PATTERN IN ELLIS COUNTY, KANSAS. *Rocky Mountain Social Sci. J. 1968 5(1): 52-62.* A discussion of the impact of settlement patterns of German-Russian immigrants. German Catholics who had settled in Russia in 1876 began to move to America. The author outlines factors which contributed to the settlement pattern and analyzes political participation and voting trends. 4 tables of voting data, photo, map, and 30 notes.   R. F. Allen

2563. Powers, Ramen and Younger, Gene. CHOLERA ON THE PLAINS: THE EPIDEMIC OF 1867 IN KANSAS. *Kansas Hist. Q. 1971 37(4): 351-393.* The authors describe the background to the appearance of cholera on the plains, the spread of the disease through Kansas, and its impact on the communities and Army posts it visited, and offer an explanation for the epidemic. The epidemic usually has been attributed to three companies of the 38th Infantry which were moving across Kansas from Jefferson Barracks, Missouri, to Fort Union, New Mexico. The evidence shows that the cholera probably wintered in the civilian population after the epidemic of 1866. The civilians moving along the same trail followed by the 38th Infantry always provided the first clinical cases of the disease at the various Kansas towns and forts. Based on reports of the U.S. Surgeon General's Office and on secondary sources; map, 3 tables, 166 notes.   W. F. Zornow

2564. Riley, Paul D., ed. A WINTER ON THE PLAINS, 1870-1871 - THE MEMOIRS OF LAWSON COOKE. *Kansas Hist. Q. 1971 37(1): 33-40.* The region between the Smoky Hill River in Kansas and the Platte River in Nebraska was a major buffalo range in the 1870's, the home of the "Republican herd." Many memoirs of hunters who worked other ranges exist, but few accounts by hunters of the "Republican herd" remain. Cooke's brief memoir is one. Little is known about him before or after the hunt. He apparently decided to hunt buffalo upon leaving the employ of the Kansas Pacific Railroad after August 1870. Reproduces the account which appeared in the Hebron (Nebraska) *Journal* on 13 November 1879 and described the hunt along Prairie Dog and Sappa creeks in Norton and Decatur counties. Buffalo hunting was both tiring and exciting work. Based on secondary sources; 11 notes.   W. F. Zornow

2565. Schwartzeoff, Calvin F. THE RUSH COUNTY-SEAT WAR. *Kansas Hist. Q. 1970 36(1): 40-61.* The struggle between Walnut City and La Crosse to become the county seat of Rush County is divided into two key periods. The first period (1877-78) was climaxed by an election of doubtful honesty that ended with victory for Walnut City. The second period (1886-88) was climaxed by a second election to determine the county seat and by a sharp struggle in the State courts to determine whether the first election was valid. During the interval from 1879 through 1885 the two cities fought to establish Eastern Railroad connections by way of the Santa Fe and Missouri Pacific. Although the Supreme Court finally upheld the 1878 election, La Crosse finally won out in its struggle to validate the second election in 1887. Based on local newspapers and State publications; illus., 93 notes.   W. F. Zornow

2566. Schwendemann, Glenn. NICODEMUS: NEGRO HAVEN ON THE SOLOMON. *Kansas Hist. Q. 34(1): 10-31.* An account of a community in Kansas from the time it was founded by some former slaves from Kentucky then living in Topeka to the closing of the United States Post Office in 1953. Most attention is paid to the growth years through the 1880's when Nicodemus showed signs of developing into a commercial community of some importance. Biographies of some of the more prominent of the early settlers are sketched and evidence is offered in support of a contemporary appraisal that Nicodemus was "the bravest attempt ever made by people of any color to establish homes in the high plains of Western Kansas." Based on articles, local newspapers and manuscripts in the Kansas State Historical Society; illus., 83 notes.
W. F. Zornow

2567. Seiler, William H. MAGAZINE WRITERS LOOK AT KANSAS, 1854-1904. *Kansas Hist. Q. 1972 38(1): 1-42.* Examines 80 articles on Kansas that appeared in more than 35 journals during the first 50 years of Kansas history. Topics included slavery, local politics, territorial strife, Populism, geography, geology, social life, natural resources, flora, fauna, and prohibition. The average reader undoubtedly could pick up about as much information about Kansas from magazine articles as he could from the newspapers, pamphlets, and books of the period. The presidential address delivered at the annual meeting of the Kansas State Historical Society, 19 October 1971. Illus., 85 notes, biblio.   W. F. Zornow

2568. Socolofsky, Homer E. WYANDOT FLOATS. *Kansas Hist. Q. 1970 36(3): 241-304.* By treaty in 1842 the Wyandots ceded land in Ohio and Michigan for 148 thousand acres west of the Mississippi. Article 14 granted, by patent in fee simple, a section of land to each of 35 named persons. These were "floating" grants, not tied to a particular piece of land; their location on unclaimed land provided an almost unlimited region from which the choice could be made. A new treaty in 1855 made the floats easily assignable. The author shows that, by the time the last float was filed in 1858, all 35 had become important factors in the land history of Kansas. While some floats provided important sites for such towns as Lecompton, Topeka, Lawrence, Manhattan, Emporia, Burlington, Kansas City, and Doniphan, others covered valuable farm and business sites in the Blue and Neosho river valleys, and in Atchison, Johnson, Douglas, and Shawnee counties. Based on books, articles, government publications, and manuscripts in the Kansas State Historical Society, National Archives, and Bureau of Land Management in Washington; illus., maps, 173 notes.   W. F. Zornow

2569. Souders, Floyd R. THE SMALL TOWN AND ITS FUTURE. *Kansas Hist. Q. 1969 35(1): 1-16.* Describes four Kansas communities: Spivey and Zenda in Kingman County and Marshall and Cheney in Sedgwick County. The first two on the Englewood branch of the Atchison, Topeka and Santa Fe Railroad flourished briefly during the 19th century before declining to mere villages. Marshall flourished between 1872 and 1883. When the Wichita and Western branch of the Santa Fe by-passed Marshall, Cheney began to grow. It continued to develop during a period in which many rural communities in Kansas passed into oblivion. The author suggests a number of ways in which the residents of declining rural communities might evaluate their plight and take steps to halt further decay. Based on newspapers; illus., map, 5 notes.
W. F. Zornow

2570. Sutherland, Keith. CONGRESS AND THE KANSAS ISSUE IN 1860. *Kansas Hist. Q. 1969 35(1): 17-29.* The question of whether Kansas would be a free or slave state had been settled on the local level before 1860, but the issue remained alive on the national level. The argument centered around whether Kansas would be admitted to the Union in 1860, and whether admission would be granted before or after

the presidential election. Each presidential candidate was forced to take a position on Kansas. The debate on the fourth enabling bill is shown to have had political implications in spite of the time devoted to boundary lines, Indian lands, and population requirements for admission to the Union. Both the Democrats and Republicans in Congress apparently were willing to use Kansas as a tool in the presidential election. Based on the *Congressional Globe,* newspapers, and manuscripts in the Library of Congress, the Kansas State Historical Society, the Massachusetts Historical Society, the University of Rochester, and the Indiana Historical Society; 28 notes.   W. F. Zornow

2571. Templar, George. THE FEDERAL JUDICIARY OF KANSAS. *Kansas Hist. Q. 1971 37(1): 1-14.* The U.S. district judge for Kansas describes the career of the nine Federal district judges appointed by the President and confirmed by the Senate from 1861 to 1945 (all judges appointed since 1945 remain on the bench). Sketches the life of each man, circumstances of each appointment, and interesting episodes during each man's tenure. A revised version of the presidential address before the Kansas State Historical Society, 20 October 1970. Based on secondary sources; illus., 17 notes.   W. F. Zornow

2572. Trombold, Elizabeth. KANSAS HERITAGE THROUGH TRAVEL. *Daughters of the Am. Revolution Mag. 1971 105(3): 256-262.* Appeals for an understanding of the heritage of Kansas. Supplies a compendium of facts relating to Kansas history, including Indian tribes once inhabiting the area, Indian-white relations, the attainment of territorial status and of statehood, the position of Kansas in the Westward Movement, the development of railroads, and population increase. Details the development of the aircraft industry in Kansas. There is much to be proud of in being a Kansan. Illus.   D. A. Sloan

2573. White, Lonnie J. WHITE WOMEN CAPTIVES OF THE SOUTHERN PLAINS INDIANS, 1866-1875. *J. of the West 1969 8(3): 327-354.* Tells of the experiences of several women captured by the Indians during raids in Kansas. The stories are related in detail and transcripts and newspaper stories are included. All of the experiences are similar. Men in the party were killed immediately and the younger women were carried off. If the Indian camp was attacked, the prisoners were killed. When the women were returned, they told of cruel treatment and were often pregnant.   R. N. Alvis

2574. Williams, Burton J. JOHN JAMES INGALLS: THE SUMNER YEARS. *Kansas Hist. Q. 1967 33(4): 409-442.* An account of the New England boyhood and early manhood of John J. Ingalls and of the many experiences he had in Sumner, a now-forgotten town that once had great expectations of becoming a Western metropolis during the Kansas territorial period. In Sumner, Ingalls met most of the people who were to influence him during a long career that led from local politics to the United States Senate. "Catfish Aristocracy" and "Blue Grass," two essays that Ingalls wrote on the basis of his experiences in Sumner, are said to have given him a reputation that he never would have acquired as an attorney or politician. Based on the Ingalls Papers in the Kansas State Historical Society, the James A. Garfield Papers in The Library of Congress, and newspapers; illus., 103 notes.   W. F. Zornow

2575. Wyatt, P. J. SO-CALLED TALL TALES ABOUT KANSAS. *Western Folklore 1963 22(2): 107-111.* Collection of tall tales about Kansas weather.   L. J. White

2576. Zakrzewska, Barbara. VALLEY GROOVES IN NORTHWESTERN KANSAS. *Great Plains J. 1965 5(1): 12-25.* Draws attention to widely distributed unique valley grooves in the high plains of northwestern Kansas. The author analyzes possible explanations of the origin of the grooves, discounting old wagon trails, former animal trails and flood channels. In the author's opinion, the grooves are best explained as rather recent settling lines over joints or fault lines in the earth's crust. Based on observation and printed sources. Illus., maps, tables, 12 notes.
O. H. Zabel

2577. —. BYPATHS OF KANSAS HISTORY. AN EXCURSION TO THE UNION PACIFIC END-OF-TRACK. *Kansas Hist. Q. 1968 34(1): 97-99.* An account from the 16 July 1868 issue of the *Kansas Weekly Tribune* of Lawrence recounting how 250 residents of Manhattan, Kansas, spent the Fourth of July holiday on a picnic excursion from

Manhattan via such towns as Junction City, Abilene, Salina, Ellsworth, Hays City and several smaller communities to Monument in Logan County, the end of the track of the Union Pacific Railway, Eastern Division. The trip was enlivened by the appearance of a band of Cheyenne near Oakley and the United States 7th Cavalry encamped near Hays City.

W. F. Zornow

2578. —. [POPULISM]. *Kansas Q. 1969 1(4): 24-112.*
Argersinger, Peter H. PENTECOSTAL POLITICS IN KANSAS: RELIGION, THE FARMERS' ALLIANCE, AND THE GOSPEL OF POPULISM, *pp. 24-35.*
Williams, Burton J. THE KANSAS ALLIANCE VS. "MR. REPUBLICAN": THE CASE FOR THE ACCUSED, *pp. 40-48.*
Clanton, O. Gene A ROSE BY ANY OTHER NAME: KANSAS POPULISM AND PROGRESSIVISM, *pp. 105-112.*
Kansas Populism in the 1880's and 1890's.

B. A. Storey

Oklahoma

2579. Ballenger, T. L. THE ILLINOIS RIVER. *Chronicles of Oklahoma 1968 46(4): 450-459.* Gives the history and geography of the Illinois River in Oklahoma. Numerous Indian villages from prehistoric times have left evidence of their existence. When Sam Houston left Tennessee, he came to the Cherokee village on Deep Creek a mile from where it flows into the Illinois River. This historic and scenic territory has furnished a "means of livelihood for prehistoric as well as historic man - sportsman, farmer, cowman, industrialist, and recreationist." 9 notes.

E. P. Stickney

2580. Boles, David C. THE PRAIRIE OIL & GAS COMPANY 1901-1911. *Chronicles of Oklahoma 1968 46(2): 189-200.* Major discoveries of oil deposits were made in the midcontinent area (Texas, Oklahoma, and Kansas) about 1900. Despite the efforts of oil companies, production exceeded transportation and refining facilities. The Prairie Oil & Gas Company, chartered in 1901, was created to own and operate producing properties and to buy, sell, and transport oil through pipelines. Because of legal limitations and policy, the company produced a small proportion of the area's petroleum. However, by 1911 it had developed the world's largest piping and storage facilities. 59 notes.

D. L. Smith

2581. Bryant, Keith L., Jr. THE JUVENILE COURT MOVEMENT: OKLAHOMA AS A CASE STUDY. *Social Sci. Q. 1968 49(2): 368-376.* Studies the effort of Benjamin B. Lindsey, working with Kate Bernard, a social worker in Oklahoma, to provide a juvenile court system for that State. The Oklahoma Juvenile Court Law was enacted in 1909. 40 notes.

D. F. Henderson

2582. Bryant, Keith L., Jr. KATE BARNARD, ORGANIZED LABOR, AND SOCIAL JUSTICE IN OKLAHOMA DURING THE PROGRESSIVE ERA. *J. of Southern Hist. 1969 35(2): 145-164.* Anger over "low prices of farm commodities, the high railroad and interest rates, the presence of territorial officials appointed by the federal government, and the unregulated growth of business" made Oklahoma "ripe for reform" in the early 1900's. The potential "became effective through the unique ability and energy of Kate Barnard," who spearheaded a coalition of humanitarians and representatives of organized labor. These Oklahoma progressives, who do "not fit the stereotyped pattern" espoused reforms advocated by social workers, unionists, and the lower classes, and transmitted them into legislative enactments. 83 notes.

I. M. Leonard

2583. Bryant, Keith L., Jr. LABOR IN POLITICS: THE OKLAHOMA STATE FEDERATION OF LABOR DURING THE AGE OF REFORM. *Labor Hist. 1970 11(3): 259-276.* Between 1904 and 1910 organized labor in Oklahoma enthusiastically entered the political arena. Working with allies such as the Farmers' Union, the social Progressives, and upper middle-class Progressives, the unions helped write the State's first constitution and were instrumental in obtaining passage of Progressive labor and welfare legislation. Union political activity was a major contributor to the Progressive movement in Oklahoma. Based on Oklahoma newspapers, *Proceedings of the State Federation of Labor,* and public documents; 64 notes.

L. L. Athey

2584. Chapman, Berlin B. THE ENID "RAILROAD WAR": AN ARCHIVAL STUDY. *Chronicles of Oklahoma 1965 43(2): 126-197.* An account of a town and railroad contest. When the Chicago, Rock Island and Pacific Railway and its subsidiary the Chicago, Kansas and Nebraska Railway built a road through the Indian Territory a controversy ensued over the locations of townsites and county seats. Sites were chosen, and the railroad company "induced some Cherokee Indians to take their allotments at these stations and bought them out in the same deal." White speculators resented this fact. Secretary of the Interior Hoke Smith had the sites changed to less desirable locations with bogs and quicksands. Violence erupted in the "railroad war." There was an extended congressional debate over whether the people should be allowed to vote as to their choice of county seats. People of South Enid harassed the railroad, shot at or over trains, and tore up the track. They sought a mandamus to compel the railroad to built a station but the Supreme Court of Oklahoma Territory would take no action. Bridges were blown up and a freight train was wrecked because trestle supports had been sawed in two. Congress passed a bill requiring the railroad to built depots at South Enid and Round Pond. Thus a town won in a fight with a railroad. Appendix and 96 notes.

I. W. Van Noppen

2585. Chapman, B. B. THE LAND RUN OF 1893, AS SEEN AT KIOWA. *Kansas Hist. Q. 1965 31(1): 67-75.* Cordelia Rumsey was at Kiowa on 16 September 1893 and witnessed the land run into the Cherokee Outlet. On 18 September she wrote a letter to her son in which she described the events from 10 September, when men began to assemble along the line until the rush began. She insisted the signal for the rush was premature and suggested that her husband was prepared to give testimony to that effect, if action were taken against the soldiers.

W. F. Zornow

2586. Chilcott, Winona Hunter. SYLVESTER WITH MARSTON. *Chronicles of Oklahoma 1967 45(1): 68-72.* Briefly describes Dr. Marston and his tenure as Indian agent of the Union Mission in Muscogee, Indian Territory. Born in Maine, he received his D.D. degree in 1852 and later became president of Burlington University in Iowa. After some additional religious work, Dr. Marston accepted the Indian agency appointment from President Grant. He stayed at the agency until it was closed in 1878. The author believes Marston could have accomplished more in some other capacity, for he was a talented man. Appendix describing the agency's physical assets and an invoice of property.

K. P. Davis

2587. Clark, J. Stanley. CAROLYN THOMAS FOREMAN. *Chronicles of Oklahoma 1968 45(4): 368-375.* Carolyn Thomas Foreman (1872-1967) was a historian of Oklahoma as well as an assistant to the career of her husband Grant as a historian. Author and coauthor of numerous books and articles, her principal contributions were a history of prestatehood printing and a study of Indians abroad. Mrs. Foreman also inspired the Indian-Pioneer History project that resulted in the compilation of some 90 bound volumes. Illus., biblio., note.

D. L. Smith

2588. Dale, Edward E. A DEDICATION TO THE MEMORY OF GRANT FOREMAN, 1869-1953. *Arizona and the West 1964 6(4): 271-274.* Ill health and an employment opportunity motivated Ulysses Grant Foreman to quit his position in a midwestern law firm for legal fieldwork with the Commission to the Five Civilized Tribes (the Dawes Commission) in Indian Territory. Foreman gradually withdrew from the practice of law to devote his time to research and writing in Southwest history, particularly as it concerned the Indians of Oklahoma. His articles and books, largely a labor of love, compose a sizable bibliography. Appended with a selected list of his works relating to the American West, illus.

D. L. Smith

2589. Ellinger, Charles Wayne. THE DRIVE FOR STATEHOOD IN OKLAHOMA, 1889-1906. *Chronicles of Oklahoma 1963 41(1): 15-38.* Between 1889, when the government opened for settlement Oklahoma Territory, an area purchased from the Indians of Indian Territory, and 1906, the question of statehood for either territory was debated by Congress and urged by residents. Four possible plans were considered: a single state, combining the two territories; separate states; admission of Oklahoma with the Indian nations' being admitted piecemeal; and no statehood for Indian Territory. As single statehood would result in a Democratic majority, Republican leaders favored two states. To support a single state, conventions were held, committees were formed, and commercial clubs of the cities of both territories cooperated. Religious, social, and economic inter-territorial organizations impressed Congress, and when finally the Republican Party of Oklahoma Territory favored union, single statehood was assured. Newspapers, Congressional Record, and other documents were used.   I. W. Van Noppen

2590. Ellinger, Charles Wayne. POLITICAL OBSTACLES BARRING OKLAHOMA'S ADMISSION TO STATEHOOD 1890-1906. *Great Plains J. 1964 3(2): 60-83.* Shows that in 1906 both Oklahoma Territory and Indian Territory were qualified by area and population for statehood. He traces in detail the history of relative strength of political parties in Indian Territory, which was heavily influenced by Southern views and the Democratic Party, and in Oklahoma Territory which was influenced more by Northern views and the Republican Party. He insists that Republic influence, in spite of claims by Oklahoma Territory Republic leaders, was waning and that national Republican leaders, therefore, approved single rather than separate statehood in 1907.
O. H. Zabel

2591. Everett, Mark R. IN MEMORY OF ANNA LEE BROSIUS KORN. *Chronicles of Oklahoma 1966 44(2): 144-146.* Anna B. Korn died 12 October 1965 at the age of 96 and was buried in Hamilton, Missouri, where she was born. She wrote the state song for Missouri. She published a number of poems and wrote a state song for Oklahoma. An active clubwoman, she authored legislation establishing 16 November as Oklahoma Day. She was a director of the Oklahoma Historical Society and established the Oklahoma Memorial Association and Hall of Fame. Photo.   I. W. Van Noppen

2592. Farrar, Harold R. NELSON FRANKLIN CARR. *Chronicles of Oklahoma 1965 43(3): 332-339.* Nelson Franklin Carr, known as the "Pioneer of the Big Caney," first white resident of the area, was born in 1844 in New York State, died in 1925 in Bartlesville. In 1859 Nelson and his mother filed homestead claims near Fort Scott, Kansas. He served in the Civil War. In 1866 he and his brother-in-law opened a trading post near present Oswego, Kansas. In 1867 he opened a trading post in present Washington County, Oklahoma, near land purchased by the Delaware and Osage Indians. In 1881 he built an eight-room house. When his store was burned by Indians in 1868 he went into the timber business. He was the first white man to raise corn on a large scale in the area, and he built a gristmill. He sold the mill in 1875 and devoted time to farming and cattle raising. At one time he had five thousand acres under fence and a thousand under cultivation. After 1905 he devoted his time to his oil holdings. Over a hundred producing oil wells were drilled on his land. 20 notes.   I. W. Van Noppen

2593. Foreman, Carolyn Thomas, ed. AN OPEN LETTER FROM TOO-QUA-STEE TO CONGRESSMAN CHARLES CURTIS, 1898. *Chronicles of Oklahoma 1969 47(3): 298-311.* Presents a letter written by DeWitt Clinton Duncan to protest the Curtis Act before Congress which would have ended the tribal governments in Indian Territory and would have allotted the lands to the individual Indians. Duncan was a powerful writer of the Cherokee, who was born in Dahlonega in the eastern Cherokee nation and moved west along the Trail of Tears. He graduated from Dartmouth College in 1861, taught school in Indian Territory, served as a lawyer, and wrote poetry under his Cherokee name – "Too-qua-stee." Additional material provides biographical information on Duncan and a booklet he wrote entitled *Story of the Cherokees.* 2 notes.
K. P. Davis

2594. Franklin, J. L. THE FIGHT FOR PROHIBITION IN OKLAHOMA TERRITORY. *Social Sci. Q. 1969 49(4): 876-885.* Through the efforts of the Women's Christian Temperance Union and the Anti-Saloon League, the well-entrenched liquor interests were defeated in 1907 when prohibition was included in the first Oklahoma constitution. The struggle began in 1888. Local opinion grew to the point that, by 1906, statewide prohibition seemed possible. By the Oklahoma Enabling Act (1907), Congress linked the Indian Territory and Oklahoma Territory and required continuation of prohibition in the Indian portion as a condition of statehood for the whole. Based chiefly on newspapers and public documents; 45 notes.   M. Hough

2595. Franklin, Jimmie L. THAT NOBLE EXPERIMENT: A NOTE ON PROHIBITION IN OKLAHOMA. *Chronicles of Oklahoma 1965 43(1): 19-34.* The Enabling Act which provided for statehood for Oklahoma prohibited the sale of alcoholic beverages in Indian Territory. The constitutional convention faced the necessity of deciding whether such sale would be legal in the western part of the State. The Anti-Saloon League and the Women's Christian Temperance Union campaigned for complete prohibition and these forces won. The first legislature enacted a law providing for State dispensaries in which liquors would be sold upon doctors' prescriptions, such sales to be registered with the names of the purchasers. Such sales were to be located only in towns of over two thousand population. As some counties had no such towns, an effort was made to amend the law in the next session of the legislature to allow every county to have at least one such dispensary. This amendment failed to pass. After much agitation, in 1911 a new law was passed abolishing the dispensaries. Thus prohbiiton continued for more than half a century more in Oklahoma. 65 notes.
I. W. Van Noppen

2596. Gilles, Albert S., Sr. UNCLE SIM'S TRADING STORE. *Southwest R. 1964 49(4): 342-351.* Folksy reminiscences of six years spent by Albert S. Gilles, Sr. in his father's trading store at Faxon, Oklahoma, serving settlers and Indians alike. Relates type of products sold, problems of bill collection, and freighting.
D. F. Henderson

2597. Gilstrap, Harry B., Jr., ed. COLONEL SAMUEL LEE PATRICK. *Chronicles of Oklahoma 1968 46(1): 58-63.* Samuel Lee Patrick served as an Indian agent to the Sac and Fox near Stroud, Oklahoma, from 1889 to 1895. His "Notes" contain miscellaneous information including comments on some of the leaders. 2 illus.   D. L. Smith

2598. James, Parthena Louise. THE WHITE THREAT IN THE CHICKASAW NATION. *Chronicles of Oklahoma 1968 46(1): 73-85.* After 1871, the influx of whites into the Chickasaw Nation in Oklahoma posed a threat. Civil War veterans leased land from the Chickasaw or hired themselves out to the Indians as laborers. As with the emancipated Negroes in their midst, the whites as citizens were not subject to the jurisdiction of the Indians. The Chickasaw were fearful of the time when they might be outnumbered. Their one hope, they believed, was allotment of their lands to individuals. Legal technicalities prevented this in the 1870's. 70 notes.   D. L. Smith

2599. Johnson, B. H. REPORTS OF THE GOVERNORS OF OKLAHOMA TERRITORY, 1891 TO 1899. *Chronicles of Oklahoma 1966 44(4): 365-379.* Investigates the promotional activities of Oklahoma governors as reflected in their reports to the Secretary of the Interior for the years 1891 to 1899. Governors were appointed by the President. Their reports dealt with population, schools, taxable property, railroad freight, agriculture, and laws. Masterful propaganda was included, such as mention of the "soft Italian climate" and "pure" American inhabitants. In 1890 the population was 61,834. By 1900 it was 398,331. The people were "God-fearing," and religion, schools, and the press were praised. It was reported that there were few criminals and a high percentage of school children. Oklahoma weather and climate were eulogized, as were agriculture, stock raising, and the fiscal condition. The governors advocated statehood. The author concludes that the historian should evaluate these reports with care. 4 illus., 24 notes.   I. W. Van Noppen

2600. Johnson, Bobby H. SINGING OKLAHOMA'S PRAISES: BOOSTERISM IN THE SOONERLAND. *Great Plains J. 1971 11(1): 57-65.* Summarizes promotional sentiment and techniques in Oklahoma Territory, 1890-1907. Exaggerated advertising of the Territory occurred in railroad brochures, in the press, and in Governors' reports to the Secretary of the Interior, and at international expositions. Land companies, local commercial clubs, and professional promoters added their support to Oklahoma as a place to settle and invest. 31 notes.
O. H. Zabel

2601. Jones, Stephen. CAPTAIN FRANK FRANTZ, THE ROUGH RIDER GOVERNOR OF OKLAHOMA TERRITORY. *Chronicles of Oklahoma 1965 43(4): 374-393.* Praises Frantz as governor of the Oklahoma Territory in 1906 and 1907. He was entrusted with appropriating public money to finance the government. Congress had provided that certain sections of each township be leased to finance schools and public buildings. In 1906 the school lands were 3,100,875 acres, with an income of two thousand dollars daily. An oil operator named Millikan started to drill on school lands. The Warren amendment was pending in Congress to eliminate the state's right to the mineral title. Frantz went to Washington to lead the defeat of the Warren amendment. His decisive leadership in these instances has realized two hundred million dollars for Oklahoma schools. Because of several controversial sections in the State's proposed constitution, he was defeated in the election for its first governor. 33 notes.   I. W. Van Noppen

2602. Loomis, Augustus W. SCENES IN THE INDIAN TERRI-TORY: KOWETAH MISSION. *Chronicles of Oklahoma 1968 46(1): 64-72.* In 1851, Augustus W. (Gustavus) Loomis published *Scenes in the Indian Territory* from his observations as an army commander in the area in the 1840's. Reprinted here is the portion dealing with a visit he made to the Kowetah Mission, near present Coweta, Oklahoma. Education, Negro interpreters, recreation, as well as a history of the mission are briefly described. 8 notes.   D. L. Smith

2603. Luttrell, John E. RICHARD HENRY CLOYD. *Chronicles of Oklahoma 1965 43(2): 122-125.* Born in Tennessee in 1891, he came with his parents to Oklahoma in the early 1900's. Before World War I he was a teacher, principal, and superintendent. From 1926 to 1932 he was secretary of the University of Oklahoma Alumni Association. In 1928 he received his law degree. He then became president of Phi Delta Phi. He served as mayor of Norman, a representative in the State legislature, and clerk of the House. During World War II he was a colonel and later served as general attorney for the Veterans Administration. His final position was as judge of the city court of Norman.
                    I. W. Van Noppen

2604. McRill, Leslie A. FERDINANDINA: FIRST WHITE SET-TLEMENT IN OKLAHOMA (1719). *Chronicles of Oklahoma 1963 41(2): 126-159.* Established more than 200 years ago by Lieutenant Claude du Tisné, under auspices of Sieur de Bienville of New Orleans among the Caddoan Indians along the Middle Arkansas River, above the mouth of the Canadian River, this settlement was a fur trading establishment. The study has two parts: 1) discoveries made by Claude du Tisné and Bérnard de la Harpe; 2) discoveries of the sites made by residents of more recent times. Lengthy quotations are made from an unpublished manuscript by Dr. Joseph B. Thoburn, describing the culture of the Caddoan tribes as revealed by the sites of their villages. Illustrations include artifacts, photographs of panoramic views, and a map showing the location of Ferdinandina. An appendix relates the founding of the settlement to the history of Europe at the time. Based on translations of contemporary French accounts and the Thoburn manuscript, 1930.
                    I. W. Van Noppen

2605. Meredith, H. L. AGRARIAN SOCIALISM AND THE NE-GRO IN OKLAHOMA, 1900-1918. *Labor Hist. 1970 11(3): 277-284.* Surveys the relationship between the Negro and the Socialist Party in Oklahoma. The party split on the question of Negro suffrage, although the official position was to encourage Negroes to vote Socialist. The passage of the Grandfather Clause (1910) reduced the Negro vote, and the Green Corn Rebellion (1917) destroyed the Socialist Party. Based on census reports, newspapers, and the files of the Socialist Party of America; 32 notes.   L. L. Athey

2606. Meredith, H. L. OSCAR AMERINGER AND THE CON-CEPT OF AGRARIAN SOCIALISM. *Chronicles of Oklahoma 1967 45(1): 77-83.* Ameringer has been recognized as among the most influential of those who infused a strong "native populistic" strain into the socialism of early 20th-century America. When Ameringer arrived in Oklahoma in early 1907, the Socialist movement had little identity as a result of oscillating between revolutionary and legal action. By using gradualism, the land question, class struggle, and Christian elements in the Socialist ideology, he helped to give meaning to the structure of socialism in Oklahoma and the Southwest. The Socialist movement gave the farm population an outlet for their grievances. In seeking answers to their problems, Ameringer gave a new outlook to American socialism and agrarianism. 23 notes.   K. P. Davis

2607. Miner, H. Craig. THE CHEROKEE OIL AND GAS CO., 1889-1902: INDIAN SOVEREIGNTY AND ECONOMIC CHANGE. *Business Hist. R. 1972 46(1): 45-66.* Provides "a case study of industrial pressure on American Indian policy." The Cherokee company was probably the first to begin developing the mid-continent oil field with wells on Indian lands in Oklahoma. While the Indians involved came to oppose the operations of the company on their tribal lands, even to the extent of bringing a suit against the Secretary of the Interior, they were unsuccessful in the face of a prevailing economic philosophy that held that no small minority can be allowed to stand in the way of progress. The white value structure was assumed to be the appropriate one for the interpretation and solution of the problem of whether these valuable oil lands ought to be developed. Based mainly on government records and documents; 66 notes.   C. J. Pusateri

2608. Monahan, Forrest D., Jr. THE KIOWA-COMANCHE RES-ERVATION IN THE 1890's. *Chronicles of Oklahoma 1968 45(4): 451-463.* The Kiowa-Comanche Indian Reservation in southwestern Oklahoma Territory became an island in a sea of white settlement in the late 19th century. The three million acres of rich grasslands and timber were coveted by the whites. Encroaching settlers generated considerable friction. With the passage of the Dawes Act (1887) ending the reservation system, a commission was appointed to handle the allotment of lands in the Kiowa-Comanche Reservation. By coercion, the commission forced an agreement on the Indians and obtained their signatures. Such negative notoriety attended the contract, however, that Congress waited until 1901 to ratify it and open the reservation for settlement. 78 notes.
                    D. L. Smith

2609. Montgomery, Ed. PAUL ATLEE WALKER. *Chronicles of Oklahoma 1966 44(2): 140-143.* Born in Pennsylvania in 1881, Walker came to Oklahoma in 1905 as principal of Shawnee High School, received his Ph.D. degree in 1908, his law degree in 1910, became attorney for the Corporate Commission, and won a legal battle that saved state shippers a million dollars a year. He helped stop wasteful practices in the oil fields. As a member of the Federal Communications Commission, he investigated the American Telephone and Telegraph Company and radio broadcasting. He became chairman of the FCC in 1952. He died in 1965.
                    I. W. Van Noppen

2610. Pickens, Donald K. A NOTE IN OKLAHOMA HISTORY: HENRY C. BROKMEYER AMONG THE CREEK INDIANS. *Chronicles of Oklahoma 1967 45(1): 73-76.* Henry C. Brokmeyer (1828-1906) was a German who migrated to the United States and worked his way to St. Louis. After attending Georgetown University (Kentucky) and Brown University, he began to seriously study German literature and philosophy. His first interest was the work of Hegel. After the Civil War, Brokmeyer served as lieutenant governor of Missouri and continued his philosophic activities. He developed an interest in the Creek Indians while acting as lawyer for a railroad in Oklahoma. His activities among the Creeks are little known. "The detailed story of this missionary of Hegelian speculation among the Creeks must remain a curio of Oklahoma history." 6 notes.   K. P. Davis

2611. Rulon, Philip R. ANGELO CYRUS SCOTT: LEADER IN HIGHER EDUCATION, OKLAHOMA TERRITORY. *Chronicles of Oklahoma 1969 47(1): 494-514.* Scott earned his bachelor's degree and M.A. from the University of Kansas, and his LL.B. and LL.M. from the Columbia School of Law in Washington, D.C. He taught public school in Iola, Kansas, worked as a legal clerk, and was executive secretary to an ex-governor of Kansas. Scott went to Oklahoma in the 1889 land rush, opened a law office, published the first newspaper in Oklahoma City, became a Federal commissioner, sat in the legislature, and chaired the Oklahoma World Columbian Exposition Committee. In 1892, he barely missed being appointed the second Governor of the Territory. After serving as chairman of the Department of English at Oklahoma State University at Stillwater in 1898-99, Scott became its fifth president. He held that position until 1908. Today, Scott is noted for the gifted faculty he assembled (from Stanford, Harvard, Chicago, Maryland, Wisconsin, and Johns Hopkins), for his rapport with the students, and for his progressive educational philosophy. Besides working to offer a broad and enlightened curriculum, Scott spent considerable time in speaking to gain public support for higher education and in lobbying within the Territory and in Washington for additional financial support. The superior administrative ability of this last territorial president of Oklahoma State University developed a school for the people that was ahead of its time. Illus., 57 notes.   K. P. Davis

2612.   Schruben, Francis W.   THE RETURN OF ALFALFA BILL MURRAY.   *Chronicles of Oklahoma 1963 41(1): 38-65.* "Alfalfa Bill" Murray, the first "landowner to grow alfalfer" married Alice Hearrell, one-eighth Chickasaw and one-eighth Choctaw. He became a citizen of the Chickasaw Nation. Elected to Congress in 1912, he opposed Wilson's candidacy in 1916 and was defeated. In 1924 he sought to colonize Bolivia but failed. In 1930, with almost no money, he ran for Governor of Oklahoma, became the people's candidate, waged a very astute campaign, and won. He had hitchhiked over the State and lived on cheese and crackers. In 1934 he became anti-New Deal and in 1936 he backed Landon. As a result he was defeated in the 1938 primaries. 132 notes.
                                                    I. W. Van Noppen

2613.   Wahrhaftig, Albert L. and Thomas, Robert K.   RENAISSANCE AND REPRESSION: THE OKLAHOMA CHEROKEE. *Trans-action 1969 6(4): 42-48.* Examines the historical and sociological factors that have created the present relationship of the Cherokee people with the dominant white society of Oklahoma. Due to their differences toward assimilation in the 19th century, the Cherokee divided into two parties. One has tried to retain the status and ways of an autonomous group, while the other has seen full assimilation into white society as the way to survival. White society has called those Cherokee who have assimilated good, successful, and acceptable, and called those who have maintained autonomy and separateness, shiftless and failures. The myth of assimilation has suited the ends of those who created it. This in turn has led to the disguise of the social system of the entire State. Even many contemporary sociologists have been wedded to these myths in their description of Cherokee society. That is another type of racism. Illus., biblio.   A. Erlebacher

2614.   Whitlow, Mary Spencer.   AUGUSTINE NEWTON SPENCER, FOUNDER OF YUKON.   *Chronicles of Oklahoma 1964 42(4): 379-384.* A. N. Spencer, originally a rancher, rode the old Chisholm Trail, became a railroad conductor in the Oklahoma Territory and moved to Oklahoma City about 1890. Fifteen miles west of there he founded Yukon, organized a bank, and became its president; he sold real estate and established schools. He continued to build railroads and operated an experimental farm. Spencer died in 1901.   I. W. Van Noppen

2615.   Wilkerson, John C., Jr.   THOMAS JEFFERSON HARRISON. *Chronicles of Oklahoma 1963 41(2): 122-125.* Thomas Jefferson Harrison, a member of the Board of Directors of the Oklahoma Historical Society, was born 7 March 1885 in Fayetteville, Arkansas, and lived in Pryor, Oklahoma, until his death on 18 March 1963. He was a Mason, a member of the Knights Templar, a Rotarian, mayor for 16 years, and was widely known for his interest in Oklahoma history, which he helped to preserve. He helped to make possible the new Pryor Library. He was public-spirited, a wise counselor, and a dedicated Christian.
                                                    I. W. Van Noppen

2616.   Wilson, Terry Paul.   THE DEMISE OF POPULISM IN OKLAHOMA TERRITORY.   *Chronicles of Oklahoma 1965 43(3): 265-274.* The Populist Party was formed just as the Territory of Oklahoma was being created, and, as this was an agricultural area, the objectives of the Populists won followers. The only important race in Oklahoma was that for territorial delegate in Congress. Dennis T. Flynn, Republican, won the position in both 1892 and 1894, but in 1896 Oklahoma Democrats fused with Populists in support of one candidate, James Yancy Callahan, a Methodist minister. Callahan ran on a platform of free silver, while his opponent, Flynn, emphasized "free homes," which should have been of far greater importance to Oklahomans because their homestead payments were soon to fall due. Although William Jennings Bryan, the candidate of Democrats and Populists for president, lost the election, Callahan won and spent two ineffective years in Congress as an unvoting delegate, accomplishing nothing. In 1896 Flynn was returned as the delegate, and the Populist Party collapsed for want of enthusiasm. 45 notes, chiefly from newspaper accounts.   I. W. Van Noppen

2617.   Wright, Muriel H.   NOTES ON COLONEL ELIAS C. BOUDINOT.   *Chronicles of Oklahoma 1964 41(4): 382-407.* Elias C.

Boudinot was a Cherokee leader, soldier, statesman, and Confederate Congressman. Boudinot believed that the Indians should be U.S. citizens, that they should own their lands individually with deeds to their property, and that the Indian Territory should be an organized territory of the United States. He established a tobacco factory because the Treaty of 1866 "provided for no regular taxation of any property or enterprise in the Cherokee Nation." His factory was seized by U.S. revenue collectors for his nonpayment of excise taxes. He took his case to the courts, but the Supreme Court decided against him in 1871. He continued to practice law and to operate his farm. He opened a new townsite on the M.K. and T. Railway, and furthered the sale of the Cherokee Outlet by his Nation. He died 27 September 1890. This article contains 20 pages of tributes to Boudinot by distinguished fellow citizens.   I. W. Van Noppen

Texas

2618.   Anderson, John Q.   FOR THE UGLIEST MAN: AN EXAMPLE OF FOLK HUMOR.   *Southern Folklore Q. 1964 28(3): 199-209.* From the colonial period and faintly surviving in somewhat modified form into the present, the folk custom of rewarding the ugliest man in any group or community is traced. The custom existed in England and appears to have been strongest in frontier regions of the United States; remnants are noted today in Texas.   H. Aptheker

2619.   Barker, Nancy N.   DEVIOUS DIPLOMAT: DUBOIS DE SALIGNY AND THE REPUBLIC OF TEXAS.   *Southwestern Hist. Q. 1969 72(3): 324-334.* When the unfenced pigs of a neighbor invaded the property of Alphonse Isidoré Dubois de Saligny, the repercussions were international. The Count de Saligny happened to be the French chargé d'affaires to the Republic of Texas. Because of the "Pig War" and because the Texas congress would not accept his elaborate colonization scheme, the frustrated diplomat pulled strings with the French minister of finances, his brother-in-law, to sabotage negotiations for a sizable French loan to Texas. Access to significant French manuscripts reveals that Dubois was something of a fraud, that his entire career is replete with misrepresentations, and that the comic opera Pig War was not all that it seemed to Texans at the time. Dubois' role in Texas history will have to be rewritten. 24 notes.   D. L. Smith

2620.   Barker, Nancy N.   THE REPUBLIC OF TEXAS: A FRENCH VIEW.   *Southwestern Hist. Q. 1967 71(2): 181-193.* Heretofore, most of the information accessible to scholars concerning Franco-Texan relations from 1838 to 1846 has of necessity been confined to what could be derived from Texas sources. The French Foreign Ministry has consistently refused to permit reproduction of any entire section of its archives. The author was instrumental in obtaining copies on microfilm of the entire French diplomatic and commercial correspondence pertaining to the Republic of Texas. This cache of manuscripts is exceedingly rich in detail. 15 notes.   D. L. Smith

2621.   Bauer, K. Jack.   THE UNITED STATES NAVY AND TEXAS INDEPENDENCE: A STUDY IN JACKSONIAN INTEGRITY.   *Military Affairs 1970 34(2): 44-48.* The activities of the American naval force in the Gulf of Mexico during the period 1835-38 demonstrated the desire of Andrew Jackson's administration to maintain its international obligations and neutrality during the Texas Revolution. Based on naval and diplomatic records; 9 notes.   A

2622.   Boney, F. N., ed.   THE RAVEN TAMED. AN 1845 SAM HOUSTON LETTER.   *Southwestern Hist. Q. 1964 65(1): 90-92.* On Houston's second marriage.   S

2623.   Brack, Gene.   MEXICAN OPINION AND THE TEXAS REVOLUTION.   *Southwestern Hist. Q. 1968 72(2): 170-182.* Prior to the Texas Revolution, Mexico tended to admire the United States for its institutions, its virile economy, its stable government, and the determined energy of its people. Many of its citizens felt their country could profit from American methods in dealing with the problems of nationhood. At the same time, however, American expansionism as it moved in Mexico's direction was a cause for apprehension. Texas was tremendously important to Mexico as a valuable province. It was also looked upon as the place where American expansion had to be checked. The Texas Revolution was so traumatic a defeat that Mexicans could not comprehend its conclusiveness for years. It confirmed their fears that intrigue and force would become standard American procedure. They sensed that Americans regarded Mexicans as inferior. Probably more than any other single factor, the Texas Revolution shaped the Mexican attitude toward its northern neighbor. Taken in part from the author's doctoral dissertation; 42 notes.

D. L. Smith

2624. Brauer, Kinley J. THE MASSACHUSETTS STATE TEXAS COMMITTEE: A LAST STAND AGAINST THE ANNEXATION OF TEXAS. *J. of Am. Hist. 1964 51(2): 214-231.* Describes the attempts of a group of anti-annexationists in Massachusetts, who organized the Massachusetts State Texas Committee, to prevent acceptance by the House of Representatives of the proslavery Texas constitution and to defeat the bill to admit Texas into the Union. The committee united various antislavery forces in Massachusetts into one unit, and the experience gained by its leaders, such as Charles Sumner, Charles Francis Adams, Henry Wilson, John Gorham Palfrey, helped to forge a more permanent union of antislavery forces in the North.

H. J. Silverman

2625. Bryan, J. Y. TEXAS BY A NOSE. *Southwest R. 1970 55(2): 165-174.* Discusses the acceptance by the U.S. Senate in 1845 of a Joint Resolution admitting Texas as a State. The Senate had rejected a treaty of annexation in June 1844 by a vote of 35 to 16, but approved the joint resolution by a 27 to 25 vote in February 1845. The author contends that the contest had followed party considerations rather than sectional bias.

D. F. Henderson

2626. Campbell, Randolph. THE WHIG PARTY OF TEXAS IN THE ELECTIONS OF 1848 AND 1852. *Southwestern Hist. Q. 1969 73(1): 17-34.* It has been generally thought that the Whig Party died out in Texas immediately after 1845 because of Whig opposition to annexation in 1844 and 1845 and the fact that Texas was not represented in the Whig national convention of 1844. This view is not historically correct since the Whig Party in Texas organized for the national elections of 1848 and 1852, campaigned very diligently, and received a significant minority of the vote. In those elections, they challenged the Democrats on such issues as a national bank, protective tariff, preservation of the Union, and federally supported internal improvements. The author shows that the Whig membership included a high incident of professional men and received healthy support from commercial interests and from people where Federal projects were likely to occur. Based on primary sources.

R. W. Delaney

2627. Casdorph, Paul Douglas. NORRIS WRIGHT CUNEY AND TEXAS REPUBLICAN POLITICS, 1883-1896. *Southwestern Hist. Q. 1965 68(4): 455-464.* From 1883 to 1896, Texan-born Negro Norris Wright Cuney was the Republican Party leader in his State. From his appointment in 1871 as sergeant-at-arms of the State legislature, lawyer Cuney's professional political career was in the ascendancy. His control of the Negro element in the State party gave him control of the entire party. National Republican success in the election of 1888 gave Cuney the position of collector of customs in Galveston, one of the most important Federal positions in the South. The growing white-colored breach in the State party, his relationships with leaders of the national party, and Republican defeat in national elections had much to do with the downfall of Cuney. 62 notes.

D. L. Smith

2628. Conger, Roger N. E. M. PEASE LETTERS 1836-1841. *Texana 1964 2(4): 289-310.* Elisha Marshall Pease was a Governor of Texas in the middle 1850's. The author gives a brief account of Pease's life up to the time the letters were written. The eight letters reflect the days of the Texas revolution and the early struggles for recognition by foreign powers. With these letters is a brief handwritten account by Pease of his early days in Texas. 4 notes.

W. A. Buckman

2629. Connor, Seymour V. A DEDICATION TO THE MEMORY OF HORACE BAILEY CARROLL, 1903-1966. *Arizona and the West 1970 12(1): 1-4.* Texas-born and educated, Carroll became a professor at the University of Texas and the director of the State historical society. Here his major effort was as the editor of the *Southwestern Historical Quarterly* and of the pioneering publication *The Junior Historian.* Carroll was endowed with unusual organizational ability as reflected in the revi-

talization he accomplished in the State historical society. His contributions to Texas bibliography and research aids were monumental. He applied his drive, energy, and talents to others' projects with the same devotion he gave his own. More important than all of these qualities, however, was the profound effect he had on undergraduates in his Texas history classes. Here he was at his best. Appended with a selected list of his writings related to the American Southwest. Illus.

D. L. Smith

2630. Davis, William C. REMEMBER THE ALAMO! *Am. Hist. Illus. 1967 2(6): 4-11, 53-57.* The myth-shrouded event of the siege and capture of the Alamo in San Antonio is treated at some length. Spain had used Texas primarily as a buffer between her more valuable colony, Mexico, and first France and later the United States. In 1821 Mexico's declaration of independence led to difficulty as the Mexicans then attempted to exercise authority over the area. The climax came with the lengthy siege of the fortress that finally fell 6 March 1836 under the 10-to-1 odds in favor of President Santa Anna's force. There is mention of the subsequent battle of San Jacinto where the rallying cry of Sam Houston's victorious forces was "Remember the Alamo."

J. D. Filipiak

2631. Day, James M. JAMES KERR: FRONTIER TEXIAN. *Texana 1964 2(1): 24-43.* James Kerr was one of the earliest settlers of southwest Texas. He came to Texas from Missouri in 1825 as Surveyor General for Green De Witt's colony. He became an associate of many prominent Texans and served Texas in several capacities. His main occupation was as a land agent, but he also worked as a lawyer, a surveyor, and, in his later years, a doctor. He served Texas as a soldier and public servant in both elective and appointive offices. 85 notes.

W. A. Buckman

2632. Day, James M. RECOLLECTIONS OF ALEXANDER HORTON. *Texana 1964 2(4): 253-288.* An introduction gives a brief account of the life of Alexander Horton. He served Texas as a soldier, lawman, and public servant. He was a close friend to Sam Houston, being his aide-de-camp during the revolution. Presents four selections from Horton's reminiscences. The first two describe the land and people of San Augustine County. The third is an account of the Battle of Nacogdoches in which loyalists to Santa Anna defeated Mexican insurrectionists. The last selection relates a bloody family feud. Biblio., appendix.

W. A. Buckman

2633. Dixon, Ford. TEXAS HISTORY IN MAPS. *Texana 1967 5(2): 99-116, (3): 238-267.* Part I. History of the making of maps of the area of Texas. The author covers from the first map of the gulf coast, probably made in 1507, through those of the conquistadors and the French, to Stephen Fuller Austin's map and the end of the frontier period in Texas about 1885. Part II. Archival and historical examination of the James Perry Bryan Map Collection. Bryan is a successful Texas lawyer whose ancestors helped to found the State of Texas. The collection includes over 120 original maps including more than 30 hand-drawn copies of maps housed in the Archives of the Indies in Spain. 54 notes.

W. A. Buckman

2634. Dobie, J. Frank. JAMES BOWIE. *Am. West 1965 2(2): 4-13, 90-91.* James Bowie was "a gaudy legend of gaudy violence" who was rescued from defeat in life and a tarnished reputation by the Alamo in the Texan Revolution. An ingenious and opportunistic frontiersman, he speculated in lands, filibustered, fought Indians, tamed wild horses, rode alligators, smuggled slaves, married into wealth and high society, became a respectable linguist, and generally involved himself in anything of adventure and hoped-for-profit that could be found in Louisiana, Arkansas, Texas, and sometimes Mexico. Convenience even dictated that he assume Mexican citizenship. Bowie is principally remembered for three things, each inextricably garnished by legend: 1) he popularized a knife that became part of the standard equipment of frontiersmen and was regarded as its greatest and best wielder in the old Southwest; 2) he searched for but never found the fabled Lost San Saba Mine, now known as the Lost Bowie Mine, which still lures men on; and 3) he achieved immortality as one of the martyrs at the Alamo. Dobie's last publication, excerpted from a biographical chapter which he contributed to the *Heroes of Texas.* Illus., biblio., note.

D. L. Smith

2635.   Edwards, Olga.   AN 1849 LOOK AT TEXAS.   *Stirpes 1971 11(2): 48-50.* Reprints a letter from M. C. Rogers of Huntsville to John Mullendore, 22 May 1849. It reports family news, discusses Huntsville's potential as State capital, and describes agricultural activities in Texas.
                                                                    L. R. Murphy

2636.   Ericson, J. E.   THE DELEGATES TO THE CONVENTION OF 1875: A REAPPRAISAL.   *Southwestern Hist. Q. 1963 67(1): 22-27.* A statistical description of the delegates to the Texas Constitutional Convention of 1875.
                                                                    J. A. Hudson

2637.   Field, William T.   FORT COLORADO: A TEXAS RANGER FRONTIER OUTPOST IN TRAVIS COUNTY, TEXAS.   *Southwestern Hist. Q. 1968 72(2): 183-199.* Fort Colorado, also known as Fort Coleman and Coleman's Fort, was a Texas Ranger fort from 1836 to 1838. In 1965, the author supervised an archaeological-historical investigation and excavation to determine the precise location and description of the fort. 44 notes.
                                                                    D. L. Smith

2638.   Fleischer, Mary Beth, ed.   DUDLEY G. WOOTEN'S COMMENT ON TEXAS HISTORIES AND HISTORIANS OF THE NINETEENTH CENTURY.   *Southwestern Hist. Q. 1969 73(2): 235-242.* Dudley G. Wooten (1860-1929) was president of the Texas State Historical Association, lawyer, editor, Congressman, and columnist for the *Baptist Standard.* Reprints his 1898 article in the *Standard,* "Perversions of History." Wooten, who edited *A Comprehensive History of Texas, 1685-1897,* was outraged that most Texas historians, biographers, and narrative writers magnified and romanticized the adventurous aspects of the great men who had built a nation in the wilderness, while the same writers dwarfed the essentials of their heroic labor and wisdom. He lamented the historical fabrication of the facts about the first European discoveries, the mission enterprises, the triumph of Anglo-American colonization, and the Texas Republic, and maintained that such licensed romance should be suppressed by the State Historical Association.
                                                                    R. W. Delaney

2639.   Frantz, Joe B.   LONE STAR MYSTIQUE.   *Am. West 1968 5(3): 6-9.* Texas is "an international stereotype" characterized by "empire-size" activities, wealth, and egos. Texans are regarded as wheeler-dealers, violent, and holders of extravagant wealth. The author essays the singular background of Texas from Spanish days to the present to explain the basis for what he terms the "mystique." At the same time, however, he protests that true Texans are properly modest and self-critical.
                                                                    D. L. Smith

2640.   Gard, Wayne.   LIFE IN THE LAND OF BEGINNING AGAIN: IT IS THE MOST PERFECT PURGATORY. . . .   *Am. West 1968 5(3): 42-49.* During the years of the Republic of Texas, life was not easy in the "land of beginning again." The author catalogs the social, cultural, religious, and political aspects of the rough pioneer conditions that prevailed. Except for the danger posed by the possible reappearance of Mexican armies, the special circumstances of a struggling young nation that sustained its independence in the hope of being annexed into the United States, and the tribes of marauding Indians with which the settlers had to reckon, Texas was another rather typical American frontier. The evolution from the primitive to a more comfortable situation with the necessary social, political, and economic amenities to form the base for a future American State was steady and motivated by "sheer exuberance." 5 illus.
                                                                    D. L. Smith

2641.   Garrett, Jenkins.   A 1971 LOOK AT SAN JACINTO.   *Stirpes 1971 11(2): 43-47.* Describes the Battle of San Jacinto, 21 April 1836, "a memorable and sacred date." Factors such as population, military strength, and economic wealth favored Mexico. Attributes the victory of the Texans to the able leadership of Samuel Houston and the people's dedication to their cause.
                                                                    L. R. Murphy

2642.   Greene, A. C.   MESQUITE AND MOUNTAIN CEDAR.   *Southwest R. 1969 54(3): 314-320.* Brief reflections on the history, use, and value of two trees native to West Texas—the mesquite, and the Mountain Cedar.
                                                                    D. F. Henderson

2643.   Hartwell, Joan M.   MARGARET LEA OF ALABAMA, MRS. SAM HOUSTON.   *Alabama R. 1964 17(4): 271-279.* Brief biographical sketch of Margaret Moffette Lea (1819-67), daughter of Temple and Nancy Lea of Marion, Alabama, wife of Sam Houston, president of the Republic and governor of the State of Texas.
                                                                    D. F. Henderson

2644.   Holmes, Jack D. L.   MAPS, PLANS AND CHARTS OF LOUISIANA IN PARIS ARCHIVES: A CHECKLIST.   *Louisiana Studies 1965 4(3): 200-221.* Locates 120 maps of early Louisiana available in the three most important archives (Bibliothèque Nationale, Bibliothèque du Dépôt de la Marine, and Archives Nationales) of Paris. The maps deal with the Gulf Coast, Mississippi River, Louisiana, Louisiana Posts, New Orleans, Alabama, Florida and Texas.
                                                                    G. W. McGinty

2645.   Horton, Louise, ed.   SAMUEL BELL MAXEY ON THE COKE-DAVIS CONTROVERSY.   *Southwestern Hist. Q. 1969 72(4): 519-525.* Two previously unpublished letters from Maxey to his wife, which discuss the 1874 controversy over the governorship of Texas between Richard Coke and Edmund Jackson Davis, and which demonstrate an excellent insight into Texas and U.S. problems of the time.
                                                                    R. W. Delaney

2646.   Jones, Robert L. and Jones, Pauline H.   MEMUCAN HUNT: HIS PRIVATE LIFE.   *Texana 1966 4(3): 213-232.* A study of the private life of one of Texas' founders treats the years following 1842 when Memucan Hunt had essentially finished his office-holding, but not office-seeking, career. Born in North Carolina in 1807 he lived for a time in Mississippi, coming to Texas at the time of the Texan Revolution. He transported and equipped volunteers from the United States to help Texas. He himself served for a time as Texan Minister to the United States and then as the Texan Secretary of the Navy. In the 1840's Hunt clashed continually with Sam Houston and so lessened considerably his hopes for further political advancement. While Texas was still an independent republic he unsuccessfully sought the vice presidency, and after annexation to the United States, he futilely aspired to a senatorship. After statehood, Hunt successfully pushed a claim to be recompensed for sums spent helping the revolution. Settling in Galveston, he tried to promote a railroad which would link that city to the Red River. His health failed and he died while on a trip to Tennessee at age 48. Based on the Hunt Papers in the Texas State Archives, contemporary newspapers, and printed documents; 61 notes.
                                                                    R. J. Roske

2647.   Jones, Robert L. and Jones, Pauline H.   ROBERT HAMILTON, SIGNER OF THE TEXAS DECLARATION OF INDEPENDENCE.   *Texana 1967 5(3): 215-233.* Hamilton was born in Scotland in 1780 and came to America in 1807. In 1835 he bought land which later proved to be partly in Texas and partly in Arkansas. When the Texas revolution came he was chosen as a delegate to the constitutional convention. Exact records of his activities at the convention were not kept; but he participated in several major committees, played a prime role in the wording of the constitution, and was a signer of the declaration of independence for Texas. Then he was appointed as a special agent to the United States to obtain financial aid for the new republic. Due to an official blunder, not on his part, his negotiations with the United States were unsuccessfully cut short. He then returned to his land and developed it into a successful plantation. His public service lasted only about six months, but in that time he earned the reputation of a gentleman and a patriot among his fellow Texans. 58 notes.
                                                                    W. A. Buckman

2648.   Jordan, Terry G.   THE IMPRINT OF THE UPPER AND LOWER SOUTH ON MID-NINETEENTH CENTURY TEXAS.   *Ann. of the Assoc. of Am. Geographers 1967 57(4): 667-690.* Establishes a dichotomy in the economic and social development of the American South. Using census data, the author determines that the settlement of Texas reflects this dichotomy. Distinct patterns based on differences of population origin and correlations with other cultural phenomena are identified. These included: 1) the occurrence and distribution of Negro slavery, 2) the cultivation of cotton, 3) the cultivation of wheat, 4) the cultivation of corn, 5) the cultivation of rice, 6) the cultivation of tobacco and hemp, 7) the use of draft animals, 8) the occurrence of food surpluses and deficiences, 9) voting behavior on the issue of secession. 3 tables, 12 maps, 61 notes.
                                                                    W. R. Boedecker

2649.   Jordan, Terry G.   THE ORIGIN OF ANGLO-AMERICAN CATTLE RANCHING IN TEXAS: A DOCUMENTATION OF DIFFUSION FROM THE LOWER SOUTH.   *Econ. Geography 1969*

45(1): 63-87. This is a study of the antebellum beginnings of cattle ranching within Texas. Although Frederick Jackson Turner was aware of the continuing westward trend of the cattle industry from the Atlantic coast, later writers have tended to follow Walter Prescott Webb in assuming a Mexican origin for cattle ranching. The author demonstrates that the Austin colonists and squatters coming from the lower South migrated west with cattle, some of the longhorns bought in Louisiana. These settled in the stretch of coastal prairie between the Sabine and the Guadalupe rivers, and drove trail herds to market in New Orleans. Only after 1850 did settlers from the coastal prairie move into the semiarid diamond between the Guadalupe and the Rio Grande rivers in which Webb postulated the origin of the industry. They brought with them some Spanish-American cattle handling methods which had already been assimilated. 2 tables, 8 figs., 99 notes, many to MS census records in the Texas Archives.   J. E. Caswell

2650. Jordan, Terry G.   THE TEXAN APPALACHIA. *Ann. of the Assoc. of Am. Geographers 1970 60(3): 409-427.* "A distinctive culture developed in the Appalachian South by the early 1800's, typified mainly by a preservation of archaic traits, including the persistence of a frontier way of life. The bearers of this culture spread to the Ozark-Ouachita area of Missouri and Arkansas in the first half of the nineteenth century. The present paper is a documentation of a second major transplantation of the southern mountaineer - to the hills of central Texas. Evidence of a migration from Appalachia and Ozarkia to the Texas hills in the 1845-1880 period is presented. This movement of people was guided at least in part by environmental perception, for the southern mountaineers sought lands in Texas similar to those they left behind and applied to the physical features of their new home the same descriptive place-names used in the Ozarks and Appalachians. Various characteristics of the economy, standard of living, folkways, cultural landscape, and educational levels in the Texas hill area are reminiscent of the highland South. The best interpretation of these similarities is to regard the hillsmen of Texas as hitherto ignored southwestern representatives of the southern mountaineer culture."   J

2651. Labadie, Nicholas Descompo and Oates, Stephen B., ed. "LET US ATTACK THE ENEMY AND GIVE THEM HELL!" THE BATTLE OF SAN JACINTO: AN EYEWITNESS ACCOUNT. *Am. West 1968 5(3): 26-34.* Nicholas Descompo Labadie, a Canadian, practiced medicine and surgery in Galveston and Anahuac, Texas. When Santa Anna moved into Texas in early 1836, Labadie joined the "Beaumont and Liberty boys" to repel the invader. Too late for the Alamo, the Liberty Company joined Sam Houston's retreating army on the Colorado River. Labadie describes the hasty exodus of American colonists from the path of Santa Anna's armies, known as the "Runaway Scrape," and the Battle of San Jacinto where the fortunes of Santa Anna and Texas were reversed. Labadie introduced a prisoner to Houston. The prisoner was Santa Anna. This account, which was based on Labadie's campaign journal, was published in the 1859 issue of the *Texas Almanac.* 5 illus.
D. L. Smith

2652. Lombardi, John V.   SOBRE UNA "CASA BOLIVAR" EN TEXAS [About a Bolivar House in Texas]. *Rev. de la Soc. Bolivariana de Venezuela 1966 25(87): 389-392.* Henry Austin, cousin of Stephen F. Austin, named his home on the Brazos River in Texas "Bolívar" in honor of the great liberator of northern South America. Mention of this is found in the recently published diaries of Henry Austin's sister Mary Austin Holley, who visited there in 1831 and 1835.   R. O. Hudson

2653. Lowden, Lucy.   "BLACK AS INK - BITTER AS HELL": JOHN P. HALE'S MUTINY IN NEW HAMPSHIRE. *Hist. New Hampshire 1972 27(1): 27-50.* Led by Isaac Hill and Franklin Pierce, the Democrats controlled the New Hampshire legislature and congressional delegation from March 1829 to March 1845. They differed on local issues and avoided controversy over slavery. The Democratic Nashua *Gazette* on 16 November 1843 called proposals to annex Texas "black as ink - bitter as hell." But the Democrats gradually swung to Polk's view in 1843-44; after his nomination they were influenced by patronage prospects. John Parker Hale, a regular Democrat from Dover during his first term in Congress, 1843-45, opposed the gag rule against abolitionist petitions. With annexation imminent, his attempt to insure free soil in Texas failed, and he bolted on this central party plank. Thereupon the regulars called a special convention which revoked his renomination, but

he ran as an Independent and prevented the election of the regular. A coalition of Whigs, abolitionists, and free soilers won the September 1845 elections to the legislature, which elected a Whig Governor and Hale as Speaker and subsequently US Senator. The seeds of the Republican Party had been sown in New Hampshire. 4 illus., 88 notes.
T. D. S. Bassett

2654. Maxwell, Robert S.   MANUSCRIPT COLLECTIONS AT STEPHEN F. AUSTIN STATE COLLEGE. *Am. Archivist 1965 28(3): 421-426.* Describes the collections held in the East Texas Room of the Stephen F. Austin State College Library, consisting of papers, diaries, and a few rare books, and the holdings of the Bureau of East Texas Research, an official Forest History Repository. The bureau, established in 1952, documents lumbering in the woods of East Texas, 1880-1930, railroading, and a few other industries. Included is an oral history program.   D. C. Duniway

2655. Miller, Thomas Lloyd.   MEXICAN-TEXANS AT THE ALAMO. *J. of Mexican Am. Hist. 1971 2(1): 33-44.* Investigates, by studying the Texas land office records, the number and identity of the Mexican-Texans who died defending the Alamo. Previous study on the personnel who defended the Alamo inaccurately placed two Mexican-Texans inside the walls. There were a minimum of six Mexican-Texans in the battle. Says "that not all the heirs of the Alamo patriots, Anglo-Texans and Mexican-Texans, received their just rewards in land." 52 notes.   G. L. Seligmann, Jr.

2656. Moore, Walter B.   HAMILTON STUART. *Texana 1966 4(1): 23-32.* Biographical sketch of Hamilton Stuart, influential Galveston newspaper editor, politician, and adviser to Sam Houston. Documented.
W. Elkins

2657. Moorman, Evelyn Buzzo.   A RED ROVER'S LAST LETTER. *Texana 1966 4(1): 14-22.* Abishai Mercer Dickson, one of the volunteer "Alabama Red Rovers" killed by the Mexicans at the massacre at Goliad, wrote his wife a last letter which is reproduced here. Selected phrases from the letter relate to his past and to events leading up to his death.
W. Elkins

2658. Oates, Stephen B.   THE HARD LUCK STORY OF THE SNIVELY EXPEDITION. *Am. West 1967 4(3): 52-58, 77-79.* Beset with internal troubles the young Republic of Texas looked toward the west for solutions to her national difficulties. Ambitious expansionist talk pictured a continental empire that would rival the United States. Greater Texas was envisioned as extending west to the Pacific, including several Mexican provinces south of the present international border. Jacob Snively, a veteran of the Texas Revolution, was commissioned to intercept Mexican caravans operating in "Texas" territory over the Sante Fe Trail for booty to bolster the republic's depleted treasury and reputation. It might well open the way for the advance of Texas to the Pacific. Captain Philip St. George Cooke's Federal force disarmed Colonel Snively's Santa Fe expedition of 1843. Cooke was exonerated of charges of insult to Texas when a court of inquiry proved the incident had taken place within American territory. Illus., map, biblio. note.   D. L. Smith

2659. Overbeck, Ruth Ann.   ALEXANDER PENN WOOLDRIDGE. *Southwestern Hist. Q. 1964 67(3): 317-349.* Presents a sketch of the life and public career of Alexander Penn Wooldridge during the years 1847 to 1892. Emphasis is given to Wooldridge's role in securing the establishment of the main branch of the University of Texas at Austin. Article to be continued.   R. L. Williamson

2660. Overbeck, Ruth Ann.   ALEXANDER PENN WOOLDRIDGE. *Southwestern Hist. Q. 1964 67(4): 524-558.* Continued from a previous article. Wooldridge served on the boards of both the University of Texas at Austin and the Girl's Industrial College in Denton. He served as a delegate to the 1899 national bankers' convention and helped bring the Missouri, Kansas and Texas Railroad to Austin. In 1903, his first wife died from typhoid. In 1905, he allowed his bank to merge with another. In 1909, he began the first of several terms as mayor of Austin. He remarried in 1917 and continued in State and local offices until his death on 8 September 1930. Before his death he was presented with Austin's first annual "Most Worthy Citizen" award. His bust was placed in the public library which opened in 1933. Based mainly on primary sources; 138 notes.   W. A. Buckman

2661. Parsons, Edmund Morris. THE FREDONIAN REBELLION. *Texana 1967 5(1): 11-52.* A history of the separatist rebellion centered at Nacogdoches in 1826-27. Haden Edwards received a large land grant in East Texas in April 1825. An impatient man, Edwards factionalized the local residents by demanding proof of their title to land holdings. In response to Edwards' demands, a vigilante group led by Martin Parmer initiated the first stage of the rebellion. Within weeks, Haden Edwards, with his brother Benjamin, assumed control of the movement with the expanded goal of independence for Texas. A third and final phase of the rebellion occurred after a skirmish between the rebels and some Mexican settlers, when moderate elements were excluded from leadership positions. This caused defection in the ranks and the rapid dissolution of the movement. Traces the role of Stephen F. Austin, whose colony lay between Nacogdoches and the Mexican provincial capital of San Antonio. Based on manuscript sources; 160 notes. J. E. Findling

2662. Patterson, Gerard A. SAM HOUSTON. *Am. Hist. Illus. 1967 2(5): 20-27.* A biographical sketch of Sam Houston, President of the Republic of Texas, from his birth in Virginia in 1793 to his death in 1863. The struggle for Texan independence from Mexico receives the greatest emphasis. J. D. Filipiak

2663. Presley, James. SANTA ANNA'S INVASION OF TEXAS: A LESSON IN COMMAND. *Arizona and the West 1968 10(3): 241-252.* In February 1836 General Antonio López de Santa Anna marched northward to put down the rebellion in the Mexican state of Texas. He relied on traditional methods to organize and equip his army: forcing loans and mortgages; recruiting whomever and wherever he could, including convicts and non-Spanish-speaking Indians; and permitting an equal number of non-soldier camp followers to come along. His army, ill-equipped and accustomed to a tropical climate, moved into the Texas winter, suffering from a multitude of troubles - shortage of food and supplies, inadequate transportation, wretched medical facilities, weakened morale from lack of chaplains to administer last rites to those dying, harassment by hostile Indians, insufficient feed for draft animals and beef cattle, lack of adequate water supplies, and desertions. Despite these difficulties, Santa Anna marched toward San Antonio, hoping to prove that his generalship was invincible. Although he won the Battle of the Alamo, it was a near-Pyrrhic victory. It was, nevertheless, a new war and he moved on to other victories and toward ultimate success. Suddenly, ingloriously, and unexpectedly, however, Santa Anna was defeated at San Jacinto in 1836 and was captured by the Texans. The 1836 campaign demonstrated that Santa Anna's army, more effective at stamping out political revolts in the interior, was not adequate to cope with logistic, supply, and strategy problems on the northern frontier. 2 illus., map, 25 notes. D. L. Smith

2664. Richmond, Robert W., ed. LETTER FROM WISE COUNTY, TEXAS: BEING A DESCRIPTION OF THE LONE STAR STATE A CENTURY AGO. *Am. West 1972 9(2): 42-47.* Moses Wiley, unidentified, wrote a detailed letter to the *Salina County Journal.* Written from Wise County, Texas, the letter was published 21 September 1871. It described cattlemen, Indians, the Army, society, and flora and fauna, and was liberally sprinkled with comments and opinions. 6 illus., note. D. L. Smith

2665. Robinson, Cecil. FLAG OF ILLUSION: THE TEXAS REVOLUTION VIEWED AS A CONFLICT OF CULTURES. *Am. West 1968 5(3): 10-17.* One of the principal forces at work which helps to explain the Texan Revolution was the considerable intransigence and general unwillingness of American colonists there to make any concessions to the culture and customs of their adopted homeland. The deeply-felt incompatibility was manifested when they professed lip-service allegiance to Roman Catholicism to obtain land grants from the government and then openly professed their Protestantism and their disdain for the Catholic Church. The general feeling of racial superiority of the Anglo-American immigrants was the source of much misunderstanding. The democratic political assumptions of the Texans clashed with the viceregal rule and political practices of the Mexicans. Slavery, the place and role of the military, and the administration of justice were other areas of trouble. The author concludes, given this situation, that the revolution was inevitable. 2 illus., 2 maps. D. L. Smith

2666. Shively, Charles. AN OPTION FOR FREEDOM IN TEXAS, 1840-1844. *J. of Negro Hist. 1965 50(2): 77-96.* In 1839 Stephen Pearl

Andrews moved from Louisiana to Texas where he became involved in a plan to attract free settlers and to abolish slavery. Andrews believed that cooperation with the British government could help to accomplish his objectives. Although he found some Texans sympathetic to his program, others were strongly opposed, and twice he was expelled from Texas for his views. Andrews visited England to obtain support for Texas emancipation but a combination of circumstances led to a perpetuation of slavery in Texas rather than a decision in favor of human freedom. L. Gara

2667. Simmons, Marc S., ed. SAMUEL T. ALLEN AND THE TEXAS REVOLUTION. *Southwestern Hist. Q. 1965 68(4): 481-488.* Connecticut-born Samuel T. Allen was attracted to Texas by the prospect of cheap land and the opportunity to make his fortune. Two of his letters (1830, 1836) to brothers still in Connecticut are reproduced and edited. They reveal the vigorous faith of frontiersmen in the economic possibilities of Texas and a hearsay account of some of the highlights of the revolution. 12 notes. D. L. Smith

2668. Sneed, Edgar P. A HISTORIOGRAPHY OF RECONSTRUCTION IN TEXAS: SOME MYTHS AND PROBLEMS. *Southwestern Hist. Q. 1969 72(4): 435-448.* Counters the traditional view of historians that the Ku Klux Klan in Texas during Reconstruction appeared and functioned only in response to physical and political dangers, that it seldom resorted to illegal methods, and that it largely disbanded in the late 1860's; that the administration of the Radicals in Texas didn't change, or try to change, things very much; that the Freedman's Bureau has not rightly been blamed for many things; that Radical rule in Texas did not result in economic poverty and chaos. These and other myths have greatly reduced the reliability and permanent value of the history of Reconstruction Texas. R. W. Delaney

2669. Somers, Dale A. JAMES P. NEWCOMB: THE MAKING OF A RADICAL. *Southwestern Hist. Q. 1969 72(4): 449-469.* Radical Republicans in Texas have customarily been pictured as a group of vindictive, avaricious, and corrupt politicians. Many, however, were deeply committed to loyalty to the Union and to equal political and civil rights, and they considered the Republican Party as the only party capable of preserving the fruits of victory after the Civil War. James P. Newcomb of San Antonio, like other "scalawags," has been treated harshly by students of Reconstruction in Texas. However, his career was a logical extension of his training and experience. He was a newspaperman, strong supporter of the American or Know-Nothing Party, and active supporter of the Union at the time of the secession crisis in Texas. He left Texas rather than indulge in secession and went to California. It appeared to him that Congressional Reconstruction alone could preserve the fruits of victory. He evolved from a southern Unionist to a Radical Republican and rose rapidly in those ranks. Richard Coke's inauguration in 1874 brought Radical Reconstruction to an end in Texas; reaction set in and the stereotype of the Radical politician emerged. Reputations were besmirched but there were more reasons for becoming a Radical Republican than graft and patronage. R. W. Delaney

2670. Stern, Madeleine B. STEPHEN PEARL ANDREWS, ABOLITION, AND THE ANNEXATION OF TEXAS. *Southwestern Hist. Q. 1964 67(4): 491-523.* An account of the role of a young lawyer in the preliminaries to the annexation of Texas by the United States. Andrews, a northerner, an abolitionist, and a successful lawyer, moved from New Orleans to Houston in 1839. He set up a prosperous law practice and began to express his abolitionist feelings. At first he was met with favorable reactions, but in March 1843 he was driven out of Galveston. The next month he was driven out of Texas. The young antislavery lawyer then went to Britain, where his activities followed much the same pattern of initial success and then failure. He tried to gain official British backing for the abolition of slavery from Texas and for the prevention of annexation of Texas by the United States. His plans were thwarted by the official Texas representative in Britain, and procedures were put into action which quickly brought about the annexation of Texas and the continuation of slavery in Texas. 15 notes. W. A. Buckman

2671. Stewart, Sheila. DR. CHARLES BELLINGER STEWART. *Texana 1966 4(4): 323-340.* Stewart came to Texas from South Carolina in 1830 at the age of 24, settling in Brazoria as the proprietor of a drugstore. He became active in colonial politics and became secretary of several early Texas conventions. In 1835, he moved to the political center of Texas, San Felipe de Austin, and received a license to practice medicine. He was chosen a delegate to the Constitutional Convention in March 1836, and designed the first official seal of Texas. A signer of the Texas Declaration of Independence, he was appointed a member of the committee to draft the Constitution of the Republic of Texas, after which he retired from politics and moved to a farm near Montgomery, Texas. He favored annexation to the United States and became an outspoken States-rightist in the secession crisis of 1860-61. Reprints a copy of Stewart's obituary, published in the Willis (Texas) *Index,* 30 July 1885. Based on manuscript and secondary sources; 43 notes.   J. E. Findling

2672. Tade, George T. THE ANTI-TEXAS ADDRESS: JOHN QUINCY ADAMS' PERSONAL FILIBUSTER. *Southern Speech J. 1965 30(3): 185-198.* Provides an account of an address-turned-filibuster. The article provides a clear statement of Adams' views on the annexation of Texas, slavery, and freedom of petition and debate. The author estimates the effectiveness of the address. 53 notes.   H. G. Stelzner

2673. Turner, Martha Anne. FOUR LETTERS FROM J. PINCKNEY HENDERSON. *Texana 1967 5(4): 359-365.* During the time these letters were written, J. Pinckney Henderson was foreign minister of the Republic of Texas to England and France. The letters illustrate his loyalty to the new republic and his efforts to gain political recognition and commercial rights for it abroad. The first three letters presented were written to Dr. Robert Anderson Irion, Secretary of State for President Houston. The last letter went to Houston himself. Henderson's efforts were even more successful than these letters indicate. 14 notes.
                    W. A. Buckman

2674. Tutorow, Norman E. THE WHIGS OF OHIO AND TEXAS ANNEXATION. *Northwest Ohio Q. 1971 43(1): 23-33.* Investigates whether the Ohio Whigs kept a united front or pursued consistent policies on annexation of Texas when that became an issue after 1836. An analysis of the *Congressional Globe,* newspapers, and other media in which the Whigs had an opportunity to express oral or written sentiments on annexation of Texas reveals that they were consistently opposed to it, because it meant the extension of slave territory. The same evidence suggests that the Ohio Democrats were equally united in their support for annexation of Texas. 56 notes.   W. F. Zornow

2675. Tutorow, Norman E. WHIGS OF THE OLD NORTHWEST AND TEXAS ANNEXATION, 1836-APRIL, 1844. *Indiana Mag. of Hist. 1970 66(1): 56-69.* Deals with the question of Texas annexation in Indiana, Ohio, Michigan, and Illinois, as debated in Congress, the State legislatures, and the newspapers of the four States. Screens Whig and Democratic journals in these States for partisan positions and examines votes on the issue to determine whether the question was political or based on one's view of slavery. Objection to the acquisition of Texas in the Old Northwest prior to 1842 was bipartisan and was based primarily on antislavery principles. Ohio led the region in opposing annexation as well as in antislavery sentiment. Partisan division emerged in 1838 on the vote on the Preston annexation resolution, but was not clear-cut into the early 1840's. Whigs generally opposed annexation, as did many northern Democrats, out of fear that the measure would extend the area of slavery and thereby the influence of the South. Whigs realized that if Texas joined the Union it would be as a Democratic State. The Old Northwest, in its divisions on slavery, its pro- and anti- Texas elements, and its political divisions, showed itself to be the Nation in microcosm. 85 notes.   A

2676. Tyler, Ronnie C. FUGITIVE SLAVES IN MEXICO. *J. of Negro Hist. 1972 57(1): 1-12.* During the 40 years prior to the Civil War, thousands of American slaves escaped to Mexico. The trip across the border seemed easy to most who were uninformed, yet the semidesert conditions between the United States and Mexico made the exercise difficult and hazardous. Enough slaves escaped, however, to cause Texans to plead with the Federal Government for intervention with Mexico. The State Department was not able to obtain an extradition treaty because of the precarious balance between northern and southern political forces and the strong humanitarian position of the Mexican Government. The Confederacy did not meet with any success in this matter, either. 38 notes.
                    R. S. Melamed

2677. Ulph, Owen. THE MAVERICK: REFLECTIONS ON FACT, FICTION, FANTASY, AND THE IDEOLOGY OF THE FREE MAN. *Am. West 1969 6(3): 44-48, 61.* Although semantics give a negative connotation to the term maverick as something withdrawn or excluded from society, the opposite is nearer the truth. The maverick is not a psychoneurotic recluse, but is the rebel against the gods of the multitude. It is not the maverick who is out of step with society; society is out of step with him. The term was inspired by Texas pioneer Samuel A. Maverick (1803-70) who was transformed into a mythical superman through the embellishment of a meager fragment of reality. The true character of the man, however, was much the opposite. Those who rescue him from his reputation pay homage to decency and render service to fact, but also undermine a passionate legend. There is room and need for both in our heritage. 5 illus.   D. L. Smith

2678. Wiederaenders, Roland P. THE IMMIGRATION AND SETTLEMENT OF THE WIEDERAENDERS FAMILY. *Concordia Hist. Inst. Q. 1969 42(3): 113-118.* The Wiederaenders family stems from Annaberg, Saxony. Carl Gottlob Wiederaenders, born in 1790, was a master cooper. In 1854 he migrated with his family to Round Top, Texas. His eldest son, also named Carl Gottlob (1825-90) and also a cooper, worked for two plantation owners and then bought a small farm for 50 cents an acre in the Rabbs Creek Community near Serbin, Texas, in 1856. Carl Gottlob's young family had much work to do on the new farm: "land to clear, a crop to plant, and fences to build; in fact little thought was given to providing even the simplest of comforts." Not till the winter of 1857 was a log cabin built. Life was nonetheless easier than it had been in Germany. This one branch of the Wiederaenders family was destined to serve the Lutheran churches in America with 21 ministers and 19 parochial school teachers.   D. J. Abramoske

2679. Winden, Carl T. SWEDISH PIONEER MUTUAL AID SOCIETIES IN TEXAS. *Swedish Pioneer Hist. Q. 1965 16(2): 100-103.* This study of various mutual aid societies in Texas attempts to reflect the integrity and high standards of the Swedish pioneers. Settlers were lured to Texas by S. M. Swenson (1816-96) and had to work for him one year to pay for their passage. Meager material resources and the cost of horses were responsible for the establishment of the first mutual aid society in the 1870's. Prosperity resulted in better homes and barns which were protected by newly formed mutual insurance associations. These mutual aid societies, which limited membership to people of Scandinavian origin, prided themselves on their prompt settlements. The successful operation of these pioneer aid associations was evidence of the inherent integrity of the membership and it is impressive that none of the societies was ever involved in a lawsuit.   P. O. Clifton

2680. Winfrey, Dorman. "GONE TO TEXAS": SOURCES FOR GENEALOGICAL RESEARCH IN THE LONE STAR STATE. *Stirpes 1969 9(3): 87-95.* An annotated listing of sources for Texas family history including bibliographies, finding guides, printed census returns, archives, and libraries. Special attention is devoted to the extensive genealogical resources of the Texas State Library, Austin.
                    L. R. Murphy

2681. Winfrey, Dorman. THE MIRABEAU BUONAPARTE LAMAR PAPERS. *Stirpes 1970 10(4): 160, 1971 11(1): 33-35.* Continued from previous article. Part V. Discusses the opposition of President Lamar (1798-1859) to the annexation of Texas to the United States. He also "laid the foundation on which Texas public education still rests" by providing for the sale of public lands and the use of the proceeds to support schools. Part VI. The last years of Lamar's Presidency of the Texas Republic ended with his defeat by Sam Houston in the 1844 election. Lamar subsequently traveled throughout the South, accompanied General Zachary Taylor to Mexico, and served as American Minister in Nicaragua. He died 18 December 1859.   L. R. Murphy

2682. Winfrey, Dorman. THE MIRABEAU BUONAPARTE LAMAR PAPERS. *Stirpes 1969 9(4): 123-125, and 1970 10(1): 36-38, 10(2): 72-73.* Part I. A brief discussion of the acquisition by the Texas State Library of the personal papers of Mirabeau B. Lamar and of their subsequent publication. The author then traces Lamar's early life in Georgia and briefly evaluates his role in Texas politics. Illus. Part II. Traces Lamar's activities from the time he left Georgia (1828) through his arrival in Texas (1835). The author discusses Lamar's participation in the Texas War for Independence, his writings on early Texas history, and his emergence as a Texas political leader. Part III. Describes Lamar's activities and policies as president of the Republic of Texas (1838-41). The author focuses on his efforts to establish a national identity for Texas through economic stability, the establishment of the capitol at Austin, and expansion into New Mexico. Article to be continued.

L. R. Murphy

2683. Winfrey, Dorman. THE MIRABEAU BUONAPARTE LAMAR PAPERS. *Stirpes 1970 10(3): 107-108.* Continued from a previous article. Describes the activities of President Lamar during the years 1839-41, concentrating on his role in planning and carrying out an invasion against Santa Fe, New Mexico. Although many Texans blamed Lamar for the failure of the expedition, none had objected before its departure. Article to be continued. L. R. Murphy

2684. Winfrey, Dorman H. THE TEXAS STATE LIBRARY. *Hist. News 1965 20(9): 199-201.* Traces the growth of the Texas State Library, Austin, including the founding of its precursor as the National Library of the Republic of Texas in 1839, its several costly fires and a period of neglect through Reconstruction; its creation as the Texas State Library and Historical Commission in 1909; its more creative archivists such as Caldwell W. Raines; its holdings, including a large collection of manuscripts, newspapers, census materials (much of which is on microfilm), books concerning Texas, and the project which has facilitated the publication of 35 volumes of "manuscript archives" since 1912. Illus.

J. H. Keiser

2685. Wodehouse, Lawrence. THE CUSTOM HOUSE, GALVESTON, TEXAS, 1857-1861, BY AMMI BURNHAM YOUNG. *J. of the Soc. of Architectural Historians 1966 25(1): 64-67.* An account of the building of the Galveston Custom House, including the relations of the Treasury Department with the contractors. Documented, illus.

D. McIntyre

2686. Wooster, Ralph A. EARLY TEXAS POLITICS: THE HENDERSON ADMINISTRATION. *Southwestern Hist. Q. 1969 73(2): 176-192.* The year 1845 witnessed both the completion of the annexation of Texas and the first administration in the political history of the new State. After filling the available offices, the new government turned to the problems at hand: the need for a Democratic party organization in opposition to the Whigs, the outbreak of war between Mexico and the United States with the concomitant controversy over the Rio Grande, the New Mexican border dispute, and the State's public debt. By 1847, with a new State administration, a number of these problems had been solved. Still outstanding, however, was the solution to the public debt and the New Mexican boundary dispute. Although it had been recognized that the sale of public lands to the national government would reduce the debt considerably, many legislators had not favored the sale until the approximate amount of the debt had been calculated. Thus, although the new State was early on the road toward political maturity, not until the Compromise of 1850 were the thorniest of Texas' problems solved.

R. W. Delaney

2687. Wooster, Ralph. TEXANS CHOOSE A CAPITAL SITE, 1850. *Texana 1966 4(4): 351-357.* Deals with the popular election held in 1850 to determine the permanent site for the capital of Texas. Contemporary newspaper accounts indicate that the election attracted much citizen attention and much spirited campaigning among the various municipalities vying for the honor of serving as the capital location. These localities included Austin (the temporary capital), Washington-on-the-Brazos (the historic site of Texas independence), Huntsville (whose citizens pledged an ornate capital building), Tawakanah (centrally located), and Palestine (the favorite of East Texas). In the election, Austin emerged the easy winner, with Tawakanah second and Palestine third. A voting analysis shows that Austin's overwhelming support from the counties of central and west Texas, including distant El Paso County, provided the margin of victory. Based on secondary sources; 30 notes.

J. E. Findling

2688. Wooster, Ralph A. TEXAS MILITARY OPERATIONS AGAINST MEXICO, 1842-43. *Southwestern Hist. Q. 1964 67(4): 465-484.* Samuel (Sam) Houston tried to follow a policy of peace with Mexico during his second administration as president of Texas. However, the

Mexican Government forced him to be aggressive. In several invasions of South Texas, Mexican troops captured towns and took captives. Retaliatory expeditions were most unsuccessful, with many casualties and many Texans taken prisoner. Most of the prisoners were marched to Mexico City and held for a winter and spring in Perote prison. Eventually all the prisoners were released through the efforts of the US minister to Mexico. The annexation of Texas by the United States only added to the difficulties, and eventually led to full-scale war. 62 notes.

W. A. Buckman

The Rocky Mountain and Intermontane Province States

General

2689. Aguirre, Yjinio F. THE LAST OF THE DONS. *J. of Arizona Hist. 1969 10(4): 241-255.* The descendants of a wealthy Spanish miner and landowner (Don Juan Antonio Aguirre, who lived in the 18th century in Nueva Vizcayce Province, New Spain) moved into the American Territory of New Mexico in the 1850's. One of them, Don Pedro Aguirre, became prominent as a rancher and flour miller. He established his sons as wagon freighters in a business which stretched across the New Mexico Territory and lasted the remainder of the century. The Aguirres then turned exclusively to ranching, and continue as prominent ranchers in Arizona. In 1960, however, an era ended when the last Aguirre to be addressed as "don," Higinio Aguirre, died. 11 photos.

R. J. Roske

2690. Albright, Horace Marden. THE GREAT AND NEAR-GREAT IN YELLOWSTONE. *Montana 1972 22(3): 80-89.* Memoirs of the author, Superintendent of Yellowstone Park 1919-29 and Director of the National Park Service until 1933. Recollections of noted visitors and of problems involved in setting up civilian administration, opening park roads to autos, and fighting off attacks on the park's integrity by irrigation interests. 8 illus.

S. R. Davison

2691. Altshuler, Constance Wynn. AT NOON, IN MESILLA. *J. of Arizona Hist. 1968 9(4): 219-221.* The United States took formal possession of the Gadsden Purchase at ceremonies in Mesilla, New Mexico Territory, on 15 November 1854. Mesilla was a town of two thousand Mexicans who had originally moved there to escape American rule in New Mexico after the Treaty of Guadalupe Hidalgo (1848). These Mexicans, however, accepted without incident the transfer of control to the United States in the ceremony staged by Lieutenant Colonel Dixon S. Miles and his troops. Based largely on an order found in the National Archives; 3 notes.

R. J. Roske

2692. Bakken, Gordon M. THE ENGLISH COMMON LAW IN THE ROCKY MOUNTAIN WEST. *Arizona and the West 1969 11(2): 109-128.* Legal history, especially the role of English common law, has been grossly neglected and dismissed as one of the most corrupt and weak parts of the territorial American West. The two assumptions that territorial justice was dispensed by political hacks and that territorial law was negated by the later State constitutions are misleading generalities which are discredited by closer scrutiny. Territorial legislatures and courts constantly sought to implement Eastern doctrines and American-modified English law to suit the local conditions of the arid West. Aside from the New Mexico and Utah areas which had been governed under Spanish civil law, English common law was adopted by the first territorial legislatures. Almost immediately, expeditious alterations were begun in a constructive and creative process. Substantial but simplified legal procedures were introduced to assure that technicalities would not defeat the ends of justice. Remolding of the water law was the most dramatic area of change made by territorial courts in English common law. The context for the writing of Western State constitutions and law was the territorial experience. 53 notes.

D. L. Smith

2693. Braeman, John. ALBERT J. BEVERIDGE AND STATEHOOD FOR THE SOUTHWEST, 1902-1912. *Arizona and the West 1968 10(4): 313-342.* When Albert J. Beveridge acceded to the chairmanship of the Senate Committee on Territories in late 1901, Oklahoma, New Mexico, and Arizona Territories, as well as the unorganized Indian Territory, were the only exceptions to statehood in the contiguous span of the continental United States. With free silver a dead issue, the statehood movement took on new life. In 1910, before the statehood bill for New Mexico and Arizona was passed, Beveridge was prejudiced against the Southwest because he feared that admission of States from this area would upset the balance of power in the Senate on matters of business and government, foreign policy, and the tariff. He feared that the three States would be Democratic. However, Arizona and New Mexico were admitted in 1912. The long struggle was a principal turning point in Beveridge's shift from stand-pattism to progressivism, from a battle to make his country safe for his party, to a larger struggle against entrenched "interests." 9 illus., 65 notes.   D. L. Smith

2694. Burnett, Philip M. THE DEVELOPMENT OF STATE LIBRARIES AND LIBRARY EXTENSION SERVICE IN ARIZONA AND NEW MEXICO. *Lib. Q. 1965 35(1): 31-51.* Presents a comparative explanation of the two statewide library programs, in states similar in basic geographic and financial conditions, and indicates different lines of development toward nearly equivalent present-day services. Prior to the federal Library Services Act (1956) development often depended upon the forcefulness of interested persons and associations. The Arizona State Library Association and the state library director, Mulford Winsor, accelerated growth in the Department of Library and Archives at the expense of an effective extension service and a library coordinating body. In New Mexico, Julia Asplund led the movement to provide adequate extension service and to create in 1941 a State Library Commission. There was no single state library in New Mexico, however, until 1961.
C. A. Newton

2695. Crampton, C. Gregory. STANDING UP COUNTRY: THE CANYON LANDS OF UTAH AND ARIZONA. *Am. West 1964 1(4): 12-25.* Picture essay concerned with the sandstone masterpieces of erosion - the plateaus, mesas, buttes, and canyons that have been sculptured by the Colorado River system in the Southwest. The text sketches the history of the Colorado River from the Indians to the Glen Canyon Dam. Illustrations are taken from the recently published volume of the same title.   D. L. Smith

2696. Forbes, Jack D. THE ETHNOHISTORIAN IN THE SOUTHWEST. *J. of the West 1964 3(4): 430-436.* Defines ethnohistory as "national history," or the history of nations or of ethnic groups. Supposedly many historians have been doing such history for years, but the author suggests that historians of the Southwest have not used it in a literal sense. He traces the nature and scope of the concept and argues that, to write a true ethnohistory, historians, anthropologists, and sociologists must become familiar with and utilize the material available outside of their own disciplines. For example, the student of Southwestern history must understand not only the culture of the Anglo-American but also of the Indian. Only then can he handle the challenge posed by different viewpoints. The author maintains that the history of the Southwest and of the United States demands an all-inclusive ethnohistory. Documented from published sources, 8 notes.   D. N. Brown

2697. Frantz, Joe B. THE MEANING OF YELLOWSTONE: A COMMENTARY. *Montana 1972 22(3): 5-11.* Summarizes the history of the area now incorporated in Yellowstone National Park. Sketches exploration and traces extension of the park concept to more recent reservations. Considers new problems of crowding and of damage from roads and other installations.   S. R. Davison

2698. Gray, John S. TRAILS OF A TRAILBLAZER: P. W. NORRIS AND YELLOWSTONE. *Montana 1972 22(3): 54-63.* Biographical sketch of Philetus W. Norris, Superintendent of Yellowstone Park 1877-82. Attention centers on his unsuccessful attempt to enter and explore the park region in 1870. Based on the Norris Papers and secondary sources; 4 illus., 6 notes.   S. R. Davison

2699. Hampton, H. Duane. THE ARMY AND THE NATIONAL PARKS. *Montana 1972 22(3): 64-79.* Traces early park history, presenting evidence that Yellowstone was in danger of abandonment when the Army accepted responsibility for local administration in 1886. Credits the military with saving Yellowstone and the later parks from destruction

by vandals and poachers. When the National Park Service was created in 1916, civilian management was on a firmer basis than before the Army interlude. Based on official correspondence and records; 8 illus., 53 notes.
S. R. Davison

2700. Hill, James E., Jr. EL HORCON: A UNITED STATES-MEXICAN BOUNDARY ANOMALY. *Rocky Mountain Social Sci. J. 1967 4(1): 49-61.* Describes treaty arrangements establishing the U.S.-Mexican border from 1848 and then focuses upon one section to show how the shifting Rio Grande has affected the definition of boundaries. The section studied is on the southern boundary of Hidalgo County, Texas, and the problem was initiated with the illegal diversion of the river by a Texas irrigation company in 1906. After relating the impact of this 1906 change throughout this century, the author outlines the legal inconsistencies of the border delineation. Maps, 33 notes.   R. F. Allen

2701. Knight, Oliver. ROBERT E. STRAHORN, PROPAGANDIST FOR THE WEST. *Pacific Northwest Q. 1968 59(1): 33-45.* Biographical sketch of Robert E. Strahorn, with emphasis on his role as a writer who publicized the Rocky Mountain regions of the United States in the pioneering days of 1877 to 1883. Strahorn was employed by the Union Pacific Railroad as head of the "literary bureau" (an antecedent of the modern publicity department) during those years. In his books, such as *To the Rockies and Beyond, Resources of Montana,* and *Resources of Idaho,* he wrote "slanted propaganda," regularly using "favorable symbols for the West (luscious fruits, thriving cities, low death rate) and unfavorable symbols for the East (rocky and barren soil, overcrowded, enervating, marshy)."   C. C. Gorchels

2702. Krutch, Joseph Wood. THE EYE OF THE BEHOLDER. *Am. West 1967 4(2): 18-21.* Since Europeans first saw the Grand Canyon of the Colorado River in Arizona some four centuries ago it has changed imperceptibly. Attitudes toward it have changed, however, as a result of the social, economic, scientific, and aesthetic concerns which affected their attitudes toward almost every aspect of the world in which they lived. To the Spanish explorers in 1540 the area was a defacement of the earth and an obstacle to their explorations. Later visitors thought it might be useful because of the river which flowed through it. Soon conservationists came to regard it as a priceless treasure of wonder and beauty that was threatened by the ravages of exploitation. Today it is once again coveted for purposes of exploitation. Illus.   D. L. Smith

2703. Larson, Robert W. TAFT, ROOSEVELT AND NEW MEXICO STATEHOOD. *Mid-America 1963 45(2): 99-114.* Although Theodore Roosevelt had shown little initial enthusiasm for New Mexico statehood, by 1908 he had become thoroughly committed to statehood for Arizona as well as New Mexico. President Taft conscientiously pushed the Roosevelt program. But when the constitutions of the two territories were formulated, differing political philosophies of the two men came into conflict, thus helping to widen the breach between them.
L. D. Silveri

2704. Larson, T. A. WOMAN SUFFRAGE IN WESTERN AMERICA. *Utah Hist. Q. 1970 38(1): 7-19.* Suggests that, although the spirit of the frontier may have been a significant factor in producing woman suffrage in Western states and territories in some instances, and particularly in Wyoming and Utah, mere chance turned the trick.
S. L. Jones

2705. Marcella, Gabriel. SPANISH-MEXICAN CONTRIBUTIONS TO THE SOUTHWEST. *J. of Mexican Am. Hist. 1970 1(1): 1-15.* Discusses the various influences (cultural, linguistic, and legal) of the Spanish and Mexican heritage in the Southwest. 30 notes, biblio.
G. L. Seligmann, Jr.

2706. Murray, Genevieve. THE "LOST" DAKOTA TERRITORY. *North Dakota Hist. 1968 35(1): 62-67.* In the evolution of boundaries through the creation and redefinition of territories and the establishment of states, a triangle-shaped tract of land at the confluence of Montana, Wyoming, and Idaho was overlooked. Once a part of Dakota Territory, it became lost because of faulty maps and inaccurate surveys. It was assigned to the Territory of Montana in 1873. Of indeterminate size, post-World War I surveys defined it precisely as a timbered mountainside area of slightly over four by two miles. 2 maps.   D. L. Smith

2707. Osborn, Earl B.   I REMEMBER POPPING THE SILK IN YELLOWSTONE.   *Montana 1972 22(3): 102-105.* Recollections of a stage-driver who handled a four-horse team in Yellowstone, 1906. 5 illus.
S. R. Davison

2708. Paladin, Vivian A. and Shaw, S. Rose.   YELLOWSTONE PARK BY CAMP: SHAW AND POWELL CAMPING COMPANY. *Montana 1972 22(3): 94-101.* A photo-essay describing the facilities of the Shaw and Powell Camps during the company's operation between 1898 and 1917, before its merger into the Yellowstone Park Camping Company. 14 illus.
S. R. Davison

2709. Powell, Donald M.   MATERIALS RELATING TO NEW MEXICO AND ARIZONA IN THE SERIAL SET 1846-1861. *New Mexico Hist. R. 1970 45(1): 47-77.* Continued from a previous article. An annotated checklist of 140 documents. "References are arranged serially by the volume of the Serial Set."
D. F. Henderson

2710. Powell, Donald M.   MATERIALS RELATING TO NEW MEXICO AND ARIZONA IN THE SERIAL SET 1846-1861. *New Mexico Hist. R. 1969 44(4): 315-342.* An annotated checklist of 121 documents. The checklist "is intended to provide a key to the information on New Mexico and Arizona in the 'Serial Set' (the serially numbered set of documents published for the use of Congress) for the period between the War with Mexico and the Civil War. . . . It is not a detailed index, but a clue to the primary subject matter of documents dealing in whole or considerable part with the area." To be continued.
D. F. Henderson

2711. Robinson, Cecil.   SPRING WATER WITH A TASTE OF THE LAND: THE MEXICAN PRESENCE IN THE AMERICAN SOUTHWEST.   *Am. West 1966 3(3): 6-15, 95.* With the industrialization of agriculture and the rise of urbanized suburbs, the author suggests that American standardization is a blight on the land. A notable exception to this is resisting this encroachment. With examples drawn from American literature, the Mexican influence on the Southwest is demonstrated as it results in a Mexican-American culture and set of values. The question is pondered as to whether the resolution of conflicts between Mexican-American and Anglo-American ways will resolve with the triumph of American standardization. The author is hopeful that "the Southwest may yet retain its savor." Illus.
D. L. Smith

2712. Selmeier, Lewis W.   FIRST CAMERA ON THE YELLOWSTONE A CENTURY AGO.   *Montana 1972 22(3): 42-53.* Photographs taken by William Henry Jackson during the Hayden Expedition's tour of the Yellowstone in 1871 were among materials circulated in Congress to enlist votes for the park's establishment. Concludes that, "it was his stunning, on-the-spot photographs . . . which played a major role in designating the area as the nation's first national park." 9 illus.
S. R. Davison

2713. Spring, Agnes Wright.   SAMUEL MALLORY: HAT KING IN THE WEST.   *Montana 1965 15(2): 24-37.* This member of the hat-making family of Danbury, Connecticut, took part in the gold rushes to Colorado in 1860 and Montana in 1864. He served in the legislative bodies of both territories as well as that of Connecticut. His diary of the trip to Montana appears as an appendix here.
S. R. Davison

2714. Taylor, Morris F.   PLAINS INDIANS ON THE NEW MEXICO-COLORADO BORDER: THE LAST PHASE, 1870-1876. *New Mexico Hist. Rev. 1971 46(4): 315-336.* Describes Indian attacks in the New Mexico-Colorado border area in the early 1870's. Cheyenne, Kiowa, and Arapaho committed incursions into the Canadian River region during the first half of the 1870's. The bands were generally composed of "young bucks" desiring to perpetuate the old way of life. Recurrent factors which prompted such activity were "(1) the growing impact of the buffalo slaughter by white hunters south of the Arkansas; (2) the spread of the liquor traffic; (3) the militant urgings by some of the Kiowa and Comanche to resistance and revenge;" and (4) "organized horse thievery by white men, ranging from Kansas to the Texas Panhandle and hitting Indian herds as well as ranchers' stock." Although various military units were ranged against the Indians, no single concerted campaign was undertaken. The raids during the summer of 1874 turned out to be the last real flourish of the Plains Indians. 99 notes.
D. F. Henderson

Montana

2715. Bodkin, Mathias.   THOMAS FRANCIS MEAGHER, 1823-1867.   *Studies [Ireland] 1968 57(225): 49-53.* Biographical sketch of Thomas Francis Meagher discussing his boyhood in Waterford, Ireland; his association with Daniel O'Connell, the Irish nationalist leader; his banishment to Tasmania; and his eventual escape in 1852 to the United States, where he achieved the rank of brigadier general in the Union Army and was instrumental in establishing the State of Montana.
A. J. Hamilton

2716. Brown, Margery H.   METAMORPHOSIS AND REVISION: A SKETCH OF CONSTITUTION WRITING IN MONTANA. *Montana 1970 20(4): 2-17.* Summarizes events leading to Montana's Constitutional Convention (1889), including premature efforts in 1866 and 1884. Shows that the 1889 session had to do little more than retrace the steps of the 1884 group, adopting an estimated 90 percent of the earlier document. Based on primary sources; illus., 25 notes.
S. R. Davison

2717. Cheney, Roberta Carkeek.   MONTANA PLACE NAMES. *Montana 1970 20(1): 48-61.* Origins have been found for 1,694 place-names; typical examples are cited, such as Indian words, local geography, and names of early postmasters and ranchers. Montana has had some 1,900 post offices, but now has fewer than 400. Based on a forthcoming book. 5 notes.
S. R. Davison

2718. Cheney, Roberta C.   WHITE BEAR'S RENUNCIATION. *Montana 1964 14(2): 72-73.* White Bear, whose family were the last Indian residents of Montana's Madison Valley, resisted white intrusions stoutly, even putting to death his newborn grandson because the father was a white man.
S. R. Davison

2719. Cockhill, Brian, ed.   THE QUEST OF WARREN GILLETTE. *Montana 1972 22(3): 12-30.* Diary of Warren C. Gillette, Helena merchant with the Washburn-Doane Expedition, 1870. Describes the unsuccessful first search for Truman C. Everts who strayed from the party and was rescued five weeks later. 10 illus., map.
S. R. Davison

2720. Cutright, Paul Russell.   LEWIS ON THE MARIAS 1806. *Montana 1968 18(3): 30-43.* Recounts the adventures of Meriwether Lewis in his reconnaissance of the Marias River as a side trip on the return journey in 1806. A skirmish with the Blackfeet Indians was the most prominent single incident. The author, a biologist, points out Lewis' interest in collecting plant specimens even while fleeing the country after this dangerous encounter. Based on the Lewis and Clark journals, and on guided visits to the area; illus.
S. R. Davidson

2721. Dahl, Victor C.   GRANVILLE STUART IN LATIN AMERICA.   *Montana 1971 21(3): 18-33.* Noted as a Montana pioneer, Granville Stuart (1834-1918) is less known for his service as U.S. Minister to Uruguay and Paraguay, 1894-98. He found his frontier background no handicap in meeting the requirements of the diplomatic position. His correspondence from South America reflects his continuing interest in chances to acquire a fortune in mining, cattle, and land, a goal which had eluded him in Montana. Unable to persuade his American friends to finance any speculative ventures, he returned to live out his life in circumstances close to poverty. Based mostly on Stuart papers; illus., 45 notes.
S. R. Davison

2722. Davison, Stanley R.   1871: MONTANA'S YEAR OF POLITICAL FUSION.   *Montana 1971 21(2): 44-55.* The only Republican to serve as Montana's delegate to Congress in the first 12 terms of the territorial period was William Horace Clagett (1838-1901), elected in 1871. His victory came from a skillfully planned and vigorously executed campaign that capitalized on a factional fight in the majority Democratic ranks. A coalition ticket in key counties was a major tactic in winning the votes of disgruntled Democrats, angered at their party's nomination of Edwin Warren Toole (1839-1905) in place of the incumbent, James Michael Cavanaugh (1823-79). Based on territorial newspapers and fragmentary records of the Republican Central Committee; illus., 28 notes.
A

2723. Graham, John Talbot. THE LAST OF THE HOMESTEADERS. *Montana 1968 18(2): 62-75.* Recollections of a Kansan who attempted to raise grain on dry land in northern Montana during the years of the World War I boom and the drought which followed. Failure came in spite of a good background, determination, financial reserves, and supplemental income from teaching school, drilling wells, and raising horses. Large-scale, mechanized farming now has replaced the inadequate techniques of the original homesteaders. Illus.   S. R. Davison

2724. Hill, Burton S. BOZEMAN AND THE BOZEMAN TRAIL. *Ann. of Wyoming 1964 36(2): 204-233.* Discusses John M. Bozeman's efforts to find a shorter route from the Oregon Trail to Virginia City, Montana in 1863 and 1864. The author includes some biographical information about Bozeman and numerous incidents which occurred on the Bozeman Trail. Based on manuscript materials in Montana Historical Society, and published diaries and reminiscences. Illus., 63 notes.   R. L. Nichols

2725. Johnson, Olga W. EARLY LIBBY AND TROY. *Montana 1966 16(3): 44-55.* Anecdotes of pioneer life in Montana's northwest corner from fur trade times to the present. Successive booms in railroading, mining, and lumber have featured the area's economic life. Illus.   S. R. Davison

2726. Karlin, Jules A., ed. YOUNG JOE DIXON IN THE FLATHEAD COUNTRY. *Montana 1967 17(1): 12-19.* In 1891 the youthful Joseph M. Dixon, recently arrived in Montana from North Carolina, spent a week on a business errand in the still primitive region around Flathead Lake. Impressed by the picturesque country, reached by stagecoach and steamboat, he wrote an account of it for his college magazine, the Guilford *Collegian.* His article, incorporated herein, not only describes the area but also reveals something of the personality of the future senator and governor. Illus., 6 notes in editor's introduction.   S. R. Davison

2727. Lottich, Kenneth V. MID-CONTINENT MONTANA. *Indian Sociological Bull. [India] 1965 2(3): 161-166.* Sketches the geography, resources, and history of Montana. The author describes that State as the last frontier of the original 48 and as an area where one can find the primeval allure and beauty of America that once was everywhere. He concludes that the traveler can find intimate contact there with an early American heritage of forest, stream, and mountain together with the opportunities for relaxation and the outdoor sports that go with them.   M. J. Horacek

2728. Mitchell, Jessie Lincoln. PORTAL TO THE PAST: THE BLACKFEET. *Montana 1964 14(2): 75-81.* In 1932 General Hugh L. Scott visited the Blackfeet Reservation for a reunion with old friends and a session of ceremony and sign-talking.   S. R. Davison

2729. Paladin, Vivian A., ed. PROPER BOSTONIAN, PURPOSEFUL PIONEER. *Montana 1964 14(4): 31-56.* Henry N. Blake's career included service in the Union Army, editorship of early Montana newspapers, law practice in Virginia City, and terms in political offices such as US attorney and justice of the Territorial Supreme Court. When 78 years old, Blake wrote these memoirs, stressing the period of his life in Montana and recounting anecdotes of his experiences there.   S. R. Davison

2730. Roeder, Richard B. MONTANA PROGRESSIVISM. *Montana 1970 20(4): 18-27.* Contends that Montana legislation during the period 1900-15 was more in tune with Progressivism than is generally acknowledged. Examples cited concern provisions for direct legislation, child welfare, food and drug standards, and restraints on vice. Based on newspapers and official reports; 33 notes.   S. R. Davison

2731. Smith, George M. MONTANA MEMOIRS OF AN UNCOMMON MAN: MINER, ENGINEER, INVENTOR, ENTERTAINER, ARTIST. *Montana 1967 17(3): 74-83.* Originally a letter filled with reminiscences and anecdotes, written to the publishers and here presented as an article. His recollections over a broad field of interests and activities add up to a substantial sketch of life in the mountains of the West in the first quarter of this century. Illus.   S. R. Davison

2732. Spence, Clark C. SPOILSMAN IN MONTANA. *Montana 1968 18(2): 24-35.* An unfavorable portrayal of Montana's third territorial governor, who brought to the office only mediocre ability at a time when superior qualities were called for to heal wounds left by Civil War turmoil. James Ashley enlarged his problems by needlessly challenging the strongly Democratic legislature with issues that were sure to arouse hostility. He was dismissed by President Grant after only a few months on the job. Based on contemporary newspaper accounts, congressional documents, and correspondence of the principals; portraits of Ashley and political associates.   S. R. Davison

2733. Spence, Clark C. THE TERRITORIAL BENCH IN MONTANA: 1864-1889. *Montana 1963 13(1): 25-32, and 57-65.* As a western region undergoing 25 years of political apprenticeship, Montana Territory displayed many attitudes common to the territories in general. The people believed themselves to be held in "colonial bondage," and complained of the evils of territorial government: meager appropriations and a generally unappreciative Congress. Most of the complaints centered around the judicial system, with politically appointed judges coming from out of state and knowing little of mining law. Combined original and appellate jurisdiction was another evil. Although there were only three judgeships, turnover was frequent and a total of 19 judges served. A few had distinct ability, most notably Chief Justice Decius Wade, in office from 1871 to 1887. Dissatisfaction with the courts was a big factor in the successful drive for statehood in 1889. Based largely on Territorial Reports printed as congressional documents, and statutes of Congress and the territorial legislature.   L. G. Nelson

2734. White, Carl J. FINANCIAL FRUSTRATIONS IN TERRITORIAL MONTANA. *Montana 1967 17(2): 34-45.* In 1868 the New York banking firm of J. & W. Seligman & Co. was swindled out of some 200 thousand dollars by the manager of their Helena branch, one S. H. Bohm. Despite frequent letters and the sending of personal emissaries the Seligmans never received an accounting of their funds, and only belatedly recouped a portion of the money. Based on the Seligmans' outgoing correspondence; illus.   S. R. Davison

2735. Whiteside, Fred. WILD AND WOOLLY POLITICS: CIRCA 1878. *Montana 1963 13(3): 34-39.* The author, later prominent in state politics, witnessed some weird irregularities at the polls in the little town of Wilder's Landing on the Missouri River in territorial Montana. His account is edited and supplied with substantial comment by Dorothy Johnson.   L. G. Nelson

2736. Wilson, William E. BLIZZARDS AND BUFFALO - 1880. *Montana 1969 19(1): 36-49.* The author and three other young men set out impulsively from the Black Hills late in 1880 to hunt buffalo in Montana. They killed a few of the rapidly dwindling herd before a blizzard and starvation drove them back to the settlements. These reminiscences were recorded late in Wilson's life, shortly before his death in 1938.   S. R. Davison

Idaho

2737. Bird, Annie Laurie. IDAHO'S FIRST TERRITORIAL GOVERNOR. *Idaho Yesterdays 1966 10(2): 8-15.* "An evaluation of the career of William [Henson] Wallace [1811-79], one of the leading founders of Idaho." The author lists nine of the main criticisms of Wallace made by early writers of Idaho history and then briefly discusses the circumstances relating to each point. "Frontier Politician" probably best describes Wallace's character. Wallace was not a great man, but he had executive ability, and was friendly, likeable, honest, and patriotic. It is unfortunate that circumstances prevented him from serving Idaho as a residential governor. Illus., 16 notes.   B. B. Swift

2738. Boone, Lalia Phipps. NAMES OF IDAHO COUNTIES. *Names 1968 16(1): 19-26.* From 1805 to 1919, British-American influence dominated Idaho place-naming. New names were given to the original Indian names, or the Indian names were translated into English. Between 1805 and 1855, French trappers and traders added French names. Spanish influence ended in 1819 but some indirect Spanish influence continued until 1900. Of 44 Idaho counties, 29 have English names, nine Indian, five French, and one Spanish. Discusses patterns of place-naming: 60 percent of names commemorate individuals or Indian tribes, 33 percent derive from descriptive features, and the remaining names are divided in origin between toponyms and local incidents. 10 notes.

P. McClure

2739. Cooper, John Milton, Jr. WILLIAM E. BORAH, POLITICAL THESPIAN. *Pacific Northwest Q. 1965 56(4): 145-158.* A sketch of Idaho's Senator Borah, characterizing him primarily as an oratorical role-player somewhat lacking in genuine statesmanship. Claudius O. Johnson's comments indicate considerable disagreement with this thesis, citing specific achievements of Borah's. Commentator Merle W. Wells indicates that he feels Cooper has made misleading statements, and shows why he thinks Cooper's conclusions are open to doubt.
C. C. Gorchels Gaboury, William J. FROM STATEHOUSE TO BULL PEN; IDAHO POPULISM AND THE COEUR D'ALENE TROUBLES OF THE 1890's. *Pacific Northwest Q. 1967 58(1): 14-22.* Only three years after Idaho was admitted to the Union as a State, the nation-wide economic depression of 1893 wrought havoc in this new State so dependent on mining, cattle raising, and agriculture. The author tells about the activities in the mining industries of labor unions and the Populist Party, with particular attention to the period of hard times in Idaho, 1892-99.

C. C. Gorchels

2740. Limbaugh, Ronald H. THE CARPETBAG IMAGE; IDAHO GOVERNORS IN MYTH AND REALITY. *Pacific Northwest Q. 1969 60(2): 77-83.* Taking the governors of the Territory of Idaho as examples, the author discusses the contention that political patronage in the hands of the Presidents of the United States after the Civil War gave nonresidents a much-criticized advantage over local office seekers in "the postwar contest for political spoils" from 1863 to 1890. The author concludes that low salaries and other factors minimized the potential bad effects of carpetbagging in Idaho.

C. C. Gorchels

2741. Todd, A. C. COUSIN JACK IN IDAHO. *Idaho Yesterdays 1964 8(4): 2-11.* A discussion of "mining in Idaho as seen by a Cornish miner who wrote letters home to his family in Cornwall." The author describes the history of mining and the poor working conditions in Cornwall. From 1830 to 1900 probably a third of Cornwall's population left for "the promised land of the American West." Parts of letters written home to Cornwall by Richard Thomas, who came to America in 1902 and to Idaho in 1904, are reprinted. The letters, covering the period Thomas spent in Idaho (September 1904 to February 1906), describe his early hardships in finding work and then more favorable conditions when working for three dollars a day. Thomas was never very happy away from his native Cornwall and after almost 20 years in the United States he made plans to return. On the morning of departure he had a heart attack and died. Illus., 12 notes.

B. B. Swift

2742. Wells, Merle W. CALEB LYON'S INDIAN POLICY. *Pacific Northwest Q. 1970 61(4): 193-200.* Working during the Civil War and the disruptive aftermath, a time of great difficulty for any territorial official, Caleb Lyon (1821-75), the Governor of Idaho Territory, 1864-66, was a leader in trying to establish judicious Indian policies. Frustrated in his efforts to grant acceptable areas of land to the Indians for their reservations, Lyon also failed to gain government confirmation of his treaties with the Indians. The treaties, as proposed by Lyon, were considered benchmarks in attempts to treat the Indians with consideration and dignity.

C. C. Gorchels

2743. Wells, Merle. IDAHO'S CENTENNIAL: HOW IDAHO WAS CREATED IN 1863. *Idaho Yesterdays 1963 7(1): 44-58.* Reviews the procedures by which Congress set up the territories of Oregon, Washington, Montana, and Idaho. The author analyzes the emerging problems which led to numerous boundary changes and the political manipulations which accompanied the changes. The Northwest quarrel was finally settled when, on 4 March 1863, President Lincoln signed the Idaho Organic Act creating an Idaho Territory, with boundaries satisfactory to the leaders of the already-created Washington Territory. Final boundary adjustments did not come until the creation of Wyoming Territory in 1868, but for all practical purposes Idaho assumed its present shape and pattern of development in 1864, when much of the original Idaho Territory was made a part of the Montana and Dakota territories. Numerous maps show the several proposed and accepted boundary changes. Research based on Northwest newspapers, territorial records, and records of Congress.

M. Small

2744. —. FOOTNOTES TO HISTORY. *Idaho Yesterdays 1964 8(1): 33-36.* Examines the various suggestions as to the origin and meaning of the word "Idaho." Apparently the naming of Idaho was directly connected to rejection of the name "Idaho" for the state of Colorado. There is strong evidence that "Idaho" is a synthetic word, not of Indian origin as traditionally held. In fact, it is reasonably certain that no known Indian dialect contains the word "Idaho" - nor any similar word suggesting "Gem of the Mountains" or "sunrise," the two most widely accepted meanings.

M. Small

2745. —. FOOTNOTES TO HISTORY. *Idaho Yesterdays 1963 7(3): 20-21.* Reproduction from the Idaho State Archives of a report submitted to Governor E. A. Stevenson in September 1888, by William Budge, on the history of Bear Lake County, Idaho, 1863-88.

M. Small

Wyoming

2746. Bakken, Gordon M. VOTING PATTERNS IN THE WYOMING CONSTITUTIONAL CONVENTION OF 1889. *Ann. of Wyoming 1970 42(2): 225-235.* Examines the delegate voting during the Wyoming Constitutional Convention (1889) using the quantitative techniques of cluster bloc analysis and the Guttman scaleogram. Notes limitations in these techniques, but suggests that using both of them reduces their weaknesses to an acceptable level. Six general blocs existed, and the voting patterns depended more upon sectional quarrels, local economic interest, and personality than upon ideological grounds. Concludes that the territorial experience was significant in determining delegate voting, and that quantitative devices offer an additional means for studying legislative behavior. Based on legislative journals and published secondary material; 5 tables, 14 notes.

R. L. Nichols

2747. Burkes, Glenn R. HISTORY OF TETON COUNTY. *Ann. of Wyoming 1972 44(1): 73-106.* Teton County officially was created in 1921. Recounts the expeditions which mountain men, soldiers, missionaries, and miners made to the region during the 19th century. The mountain valley known as Jackson Hole was the scene of intense fur trading operations before 1840, but few whites visited the area during 1840-60. Several prospecting expeditions entered the valley in the 1860's but failed to find significant quantities of precious minerals. Four major government-sponsored scientific expeditions passed through the valley between 1860 and 1876 and brought more national attention but no changes. Only in the 1880's did permanent settlers begin coming into the valley. They established ranches and worked as guides for nonresident hunters. In fact, wildlife, particularly elk, remains one of the area's chief natural resources and means of economic support. Based mainly on secondary sources and on interviews; 134 notes. Article to be continued.

G. R. Adams

2748. Clough, Wilson O. WYOMING'S EARLIEST PLACE NAMES? *Ann. of Wyoming 1965 37(2): 211-220.* Suggests that although explorers mentioned the area within present Wyoming as early as 1521, little was known about it until after 1800. The naming of geographic features of Wyoming by explorers and fur traders from Lewis and Clark to Jim Bridger is discussed, concentrating on the period 1800 to 1847. Based on Carl I. Wheat, *Mapping the Trans-Mississippi West, 1540-1861* (4 vols., San Francisco, 1957-60), and published travel accounts. 7 notes.

R. L. Nichols

2749. Gould, Lewis L. JOSEPH M. CAREY AND WYOMING STATEHOOD. *Ann. of Wyoming 1965 37(2): 157-169.* Contends that securing the passage of the act admitting Wyoming as a state in 1890 was the most important achievement of Carey's political career, and that this has not been placed in its proper context in either state or national politics. Includes a series of letters from Carey to Willis Van Devanter while the statehood bill passed through Congress to support the thesis. Letters are part of the Van Devanter Papers in the Library of Congress. Illus., 36 notes.

R. L. Nichols

2750. Gould, Lewis L.   A. S. MERCER AND THE JOHNSON COUNTY WAR: A REAPPRAISAL.   *Arizona and the West 1965 7(1): 5-20.* Asa Shinn Mercer, a press agent, promoter, and journalist, achieved fame as author of *The Banditti of the Plains,* regarded as a classic of Americana. (A recent edition of the book was published in 1954 by the University of Oklahoma Press). It was a stinging indictment of the cattle barons of Wyoming for their supposed role in the 1892 Johnson County war. Because of the supposed coercion and harassment which he suffered and the repression of his book, Mercer has been pictured as a "cow-country Zola." When examined in the context of Wyoming politics, however, a different picture emerges. Mercer's *Northwestern Live Stock Journal* (Cheyenne, Wyoming) was established in 1883. It served the cause of the Wyoming State Growers Association, and received the association's advertising and its blessings of Mercer's frequent efforts to secure government employment. The overly confident Wyoming Republicans suffered defeat in the 1892 elections primarily because they had become identified with the procattle interest and their involvement in the unpopular Johnson County war. His ebbing financial resources and his sense of opportunism catapulted Mercer and his *Journal* into the Democratic-Populist camp. His rewards were a minor position and considerable notoriety. Still financially embarrassed he spent the winter of 1893 writing *Banditti* in hopes it would enhance his position and pocketbook. The issue was no longer in the election of 1894 and the Democrats in Wyoming were crushed. As a politician, Mercer was a dismal failure. Based on manuscripts in University of Wyoming Library, the National Archives, Wyoming State Historical Society, newspaper files, and secondary accounts; 3 illus., 51 notes.   D. L. Smith

2751. Grey, Don.   NOTES ON WYOMING HISTORY, A FLINTLOCK PISTOL IN THE FRED HESSE COLLECTION.   *Ann. of Wyoming 1963 35(2): 210-212.* Discusses the possible origins of a flintlock pistol found on the Hesse 28 Ranch and includes a sketch. The author concludes that the pistol dated from the period 1790-1830, and was probably of French manufacture.   R. L. Nichols

2752. Griffiths, David B.   POPULISM IN WYOMING.   *Ann. of Wyoming 1968 40(1): 57-71.* Claims that because the cattle barons dominated the politics and economy of Wyoming, populism in that State differed from that in other Far Western States. He supports this thesis by showing that the basic drives of populism resulted from the invasion of hired gunmen in the Johnson County War. The obvious connection between State Republican leaders and the Wyoming Stockgrowers' Association led to populism. The party failed to make a lasting impact on State politics because its members could not agree on independent action or fusion with the Democrats. Based on published primary or secondary material; 55 notes.   R. L. Nichols

2753. Haines, Aubrey L.   LOST IN THE YELLOWSTONE: AN EPIC OF SURVIVAL IN THE WILDERNESS.   *Montana 1972 22(3): 31-41.* Reviews the details of Truman C. Everts' experience while lost from the Washburn-Doane party, 1870. Based on reports of searchers and Everts' own account; 12 illus., 13 notes.   S. R. Davison

2754. Henderson, Paul.   NOTES ON WYOMING HISTORY. THE GRAVE OF JOEL J. HEMBREE, 1843.   *Ann. of Wyoming 1963 35(2): 201-207.* Discusses the finding of the grave in December 1961 and the attempts to learn the identity and story of its occupant, a nine-year-old member of the Applegate Company who died enroute to Oregon. Contains lengthy quotations from contemporary journals describing the boy and his death and burial.   R. L. Nichols

2755. Holsinger, M. Paul.   WILLIS VAN DEVANTER: WYOMING LEADER, 1884-1897.   *Ann. of Wyoming 1965 37(2): 170-206.* Argues that historians have concentrated on Van Devanter's career as a justice of the U.S. Supreme Court, and have ignored his earlier political and judicial activities in Wyoming between 1884 and 1897. This article discusses Van Devanter's early alliance with corporate livestock producers, and traces his role as a leading Republican in territorial and early state politics, as well as his legal activities in Wyoming. Based on extensive use of the Van Devanter Papers in possession of the family, court decisions, newspapers, and published secondary material. Illus., 171 notes.   R. L. Nichols

2756. Keyes, Verna K.   THE ORIGIN OF THE WYOMING STATE FLAG.   *Ann. of Wyoming 1967 39(1): 65-68.* A reminiscent account of the 1916 contest to design a State flag for Wyoming. The author describes how she drew the winning entry after waking during the night with a clear mental picture of it. She describes the flag and explains the symbolism used in the design. Illus.   R. L. Nichols

2757. Larson, T. A.   WYOMING STATEHOOD.   *Ann. of Wyoming 1965 37(1): 4-29.* Discusses the movement for statehood in Wyoming, particularly during the 1880's, and shows that the Republican territorial governor and territorial delegate led their party in this movement. Wyoming Democrats either opposed statehood or wanted to wait until they controlled the territorial government. Describes the state constitutional convention and lists the major disputes as: size of counties, organization of the state judiciary system, woman suffrage, legislative apportionment, taxes on mining corporations, and the location of permanent state institutions. Illus., 10 notes.   R. L. Nichols

2758. McDermott, John D.   THE SEARCH FOR JACQUES LARAMEE: A STUDY IN FRUSTRATION.   *Ann. of Wyoming 1964 36(2): 169-174.* Discusses the attempt to determine whether or not there was a Jacques LaRamee from whom the name Laramie, Wyoming was later derived. Suggests that LaRamee's first name was Joseph, not Jacques, but is unwilling to posit this as the final answer. Concludes that whatever his first name, LaRamee was a French Canadian. Based on genealogical research and published materials.   R. L. Nichols

2759. Olson, Frederick I.   THE SELF-MADE MAN IN WYOMING: AN AUTOBIOGRAPHICAL FRAGMENT FROM GOVERNOR DEFOREST RICHARDS.   *Ann. of Wyoming 1965 37(2): 207-209.* Includes a biographical discussion of DeForest Richards, Wyoming governor from 1898 until 1903. In a letter, printed with the article, Richards states that his election as governor was the result of hard work and honesty, a self-made man. Based on secondary material and the letter owned by the author. Illus., 6 notes.   R. L. Nichols

2760. Paulson, George W.   THE CONGRESSIONAL CAREER OF JOSEPH MAULL CAREY.   *Ann. of Wyoming 1963 35(1): 21-81.* Graduate thesis examines Carey's three terms as territorial delegate beginning in 1885, during which he demanded increased survey funds, defended the cattlemen, and worked for statehood. Shows that Carey as a US Senator from 1891-95 voted against the silver interests of his constituents, but reaches no decision about Carey and the Johnson County War. Discusses Carey's role in the passage of the Desert Land Act. Based primarily on published sources including *Congressional Record,* Senate and House Documents, and state and local materials.   R. L. Nichols

2761. —.   EXCERPTS FROM THE "CHEYENNE DAILY SUN."   *Ann. of Wyoming 1965 37(1): 32-73.* Contains excerpts which discuss the Wyoming reactions to statehood at five separate celebrations. Includes descriptive material, political speeches, poetry, and patriotic statements.   R. L. Nichols

Colorado

2762. Bakken, Gordon M.   THE IMPACT OF THE COLORADO STATE CONSTITUTION ON ROCKY MOUNTAIN CONSTITUTION MAKING.   *Colorado Mag. 1970 47(2): 152-175.* Uses quantitative analysis to evaluate roll-call votes in the Colorado Constitutional Convention of 1875-76. Discusses the influence of three key issues - eminent domain, taxation of mining industries, and water rights - on later constitutional conventions in other mining States such as Idaho, Montana, Utah, and Wyoming. Concludes that "although later conventions considered their own particular territorial experience as the most relevant factor in drawing up provisions in their conventions, all paid close attention to the work of the Centennial State delegates of 1876." Illus., 64 notes.   O. H. Zabel

2763. Banard, Charles J.   THEODORE ROOSEVELT AND COLORADO POLITICS: THE ROOSEVELT-STEWART ALLIANCE. *Colorado Mag. 1965 42(4): 311-326.* An analysis of the politics of Colorado after the campaign of 1896, with special emphasis on the Roosevelt-Philip B. Stewart alliance and the nationwide ramifications of this friendship. The author outlines the factors that contributed to the splits within the Democratic and Republican Parties in Colorado until 1912.

R. Sexauer

2764. Black, Robert C. JOHN GILLIS MILLS-"BAD GUY" FROM VERMONT. *Vermont Hist. 1968 36(4): 236-239.* A Dartmouth dropout (1872), a suspect in two murders in Mississippi (1875), Mills triggered a brawl (1883) between Republican cliques near a silver camp in Grand County, Colorado, that killed five. Documented from MSS and newspapers.

T. D. S. Bassett

2765. Burg, B. Richard. ADMINISTRATION OF JUSTICE IN THE DENVER PEOPLE'S COURTS: 1859-1861. *J. of the West 1968 7(4): 510-521.* Seeks to demonstrate that the English and American traditions carried by the majority of the settlers to the West were often a more important influence on the institutions they established than on the frontier environment. The author details the criminal prosecutions which took place in Denver between 1859 and the creation of the Colorado Territory early in 1861. In the absence of any effective form of regulation from Kansas Territory, of which the pioneers were nominally a part, they created a system of people's courts. Ad hoc in nature, these courts operated in an open and public manner. Except for a short interlude when a vigilance committee operated in Denver, these courts succeeded remarkably well. They made a conspicuous effort to imitate the legal traditions firmly established in the more settled parts of the nation and bore no resemblance to the image of cursory and brutal justice often associated with the frontier.

R. N. Alvis

2766. Cannon, Helen. FIRST LADIES OF COLORADO: EMMA FLETCHER THOMAS. *Colorado Mag. 1972 49(2): 163-170.* A brief biography of Mrs. Thomas (1853-1940), wife of Charles S. Thomas, Governor of Colorado (1899-1901) and US Senator from Colorado (1913-21). Based on documents in the State Historical Society of Colorado Library, and on secondary sources; 3 illus., 23 notes.

O. H. Zabel

2767. Cannon, Helen. FIRST LADIES OF COLORADO: CELIA O. CRANE WAITE. *Colorado Mag. 1969 46(2): 120-130.* Widowed Celia O. Crane (1845-1937) was the second wife of Davis Hanson Waite, Colorado's Populist governor (1893-95). She was not a conventional First Lady. Instead of tending to "women's interests," sharing her husband's reform ideas, she gave her time and energy to aiding and protecting him. After her husband's defeat for a second term, she spoke out bitterly against women who, voting for the first time in Colorado, opposed the party which enfranchised them. The Waites retired to Aspen where he died in 1901. She lived until 1937. Illus., 27 notes.

O. H. Zabel

2768. Cannon, Helen. FIRST LADIES OF COLORADO. REBECCA HILL EATON. *Colorado Mag. 1965 42(1): 37-45.* Biographical sketch of Mrs. Benjamin Harrison Eaton whose husband was governor of Colorado, 1885-87.

I. W. Van Noppen

2769. Cannon, Helen. FIRST LADIES OF COLORADO: ELLA NYE ADAMS. *Colorado Mag. 1966 43(2): 121-131.* Of English ancestry, born in Bangor, Maine, Ella Charlotte Nye married Alva Adams, governor of Colorado for three terms during the period 1887-1905. Ella continued to be socially active until her death in 1931.

I. W. Van Noppen

2770. Cannon, Helen. FIRST LADIES OF COLORADO: JANE OLIVIA BARNES COOPER. *Colorado Mag. 1967 44(2): 129-138.* One of a series of biographical sketches of Colorado's first ladies, this one deals with the wife of the sixth Governor, 1889-1891. Of New England parentage (her father was a Congregational minister and an abolitionist), Jane Olivia was born in Ohio, graduated from Rockford seminary, and married a lawyer, Job Adams Cooper. The family moved to Colorado and prospered. Mrs. Cooper was active in charitable and philanthropic organizations all of her life, an energetic and tireless woman. Mr. Cooper gave the land for the campus of Colorado Woman's College. The Craig Rehabilitation Hospital, a sanitarium for the treatment of tuberculosis, was Mrs. Cooper's crowning achievement. 4 illus., 37 notes.

I. W. Van Noppen

2771. Collins, George W. COLORADO'S TERRITORIAL SECRETARIES. *Colorado Mag. 1966 43(3): 185-208.* Traces the history of Colorado's Territorial secretaries from 1861 to 1876, relating the events occurring during the terms of the five secretaries who held office between these years. The author does not claim to reach a value judgment on the record of the secretaries, stating that much research is yet to be done. Many new documents will be found in the future which will shed new light on this public official who functioned as secretary, sometimes acting governor, and always as the voice of the people. Based on contemporary newspapers; the official publication of the Colorado Territory laws after each session of the territorial assembly; and significant books; illus., 108 notes.

R. Sexauer

2772. DeLorme, Roland L. COLORADO'S MUGWUMP INTERLUDE: THE STATE VOTERS' LEAGUE, 1905-1906. *J. of the West 1968 7(4): 522-530.* Chronicles the formation, activity, and demise of Colorado's State Voters' League. Established at the urging of Judge Ben B. Lindsey (1869-1943), the league was to be nonpartisan and devoted to progressive legislation, including a primary law and State protection of bank deposits. The league failed to get statewide support and ended being largely a Denver-based organization. When the elections of 1906 in Denver brought victories to the entrenched party machines, the league dissolved itself.

R. N. Alvis

2773. Draper, Benjamin. HUBERT HOWE BANCROFT IN COLORADO. *Colorado Mag. 1971 48(2): 92-107.* Deals with Bancroft's materials on the history of Colorado, collected between 1883 and 1889. Colorado history was included in volume 25 of Bancroft's *Works.* Argues that Bancroft and his agents, as they interviewed Coloradoans, had "two inseparable functions: selling books and gathering notes on local history." Bancroft's publishing house, the History Company, in San Francisco, using materials gathered by interview and from other sources, published his 39-volume *Works* and, later, seven volumes of biographical accounts, *The Chronicles of the Builders.* While the books were written to sell, notes on the interview sheets often give Bancroft's real opinions. In the Bancroft materials there is a great deal of valuable local history, for "Bancroft appears to have anticipated, whatever his reasons, the present-day emphasis on the importance of gathering oral history." Based on materials in the Bancroft Library at the University of California, Berkeley; illus., 28 notes.

O. H. Zabel

2774. Gower, Calvin W. GOLD RUSH GOVERNMENTS. *Colorado Mag. 1965 42(2): 114-132.* Efforts to form a government in the new gold rush territory began as early as 1858 when delegates were sent to Congress and to the Kansas legislature to press for the organization of the territory. Several methods were proposed, such as a provisional government or statehood, but there was no government other than local until the organization of the Territory of Colorado in 1861.

R. Sexauer

2775. Gower, Calvin. KANSAS TERRITORY AND THE PIKE'S PEAK GOLD RUSH: GOVERNING THE GOLD REGION. *Kansas Hist. Q. 1966 32(3): 289-313.* Beginning with the creation of Arapahoe County in 1855, the territorial legislature of Kansas tried to organize a form of government in the territory west of a line running due north from the northeast corner of New Mexico to the boundary between Kansas and Nebraska. By the time Kansas entered the union in 1861 the efforts were neither successful nor popular. Control over the region was minimal because of the great distance and because the inhabitants on both sides of the line did not really wish to cooperate. Based on local newspaper accounts and various official records of the Kansas territorial government.

W. F. Zornow

2776. Guice, John D. COLORADO'S TERRITORIAL COURTS. *Colorado Mag. 1968 45(3): 204-224.* Discusses the judiciary of the first four years in Colorado Territory. The author praises the work of Chief Justice Benjamin F. Hall and indicates the weaknesses of the other early justices, calling them "judicial derelicts" and "carpetbaggers." In view of the handicaps - the territorial system, politics, inadequate facilities, and the Civil War - the judiciary's "contribution was significant" for it provided "an orderly transition of jurisdiction." In 1866 "a new era in the history of the territorial Supreme Court began." Illus., 83 notes.

O. H. Zabel

2777. Guice, John D. MOSES HALLETT, CHIEF JUSTICE. *Colorado Mag. 1970 47(2): 136-151.* A brief biography of Hallett (1834-1923), who served as Chief Justice of Colorado Territory from 1866 to 1876 and then as U.S. District Judge of Colorado until 1906. His opinions on mining and water law made him internationally famous, and railroad litigation was also a special concern. While he did not seek political office, he was an adroit politician. Hallett was also a successful businessman and his wealth was derived from promotional activities. From 1892 until 1902 Hallett served as the first dean and professor of the new University of Colorado Law School. His career stands "as a compelling argument against the image of the judiciary as always the weakest branch of territorial administration." Illus., 66 notes. O. H. Zabel

2778. Hafen, LeRoy R. MY FIRST MONTHS AS COLORADO'S STATE HISTORIAN. *Colorado Mag. 1969 46(3): 209-219.* After completion of his history training in 1924 at the University of California under Herbert E. Bolton, the author accepted the position as Colorado State Historian. He describes settling his family in Denver, meeting people of the community and State associated with the Historical Society, and trips he made in July and August to historical sites in the State. Illus., 4 photos. O. H. Zabel

2779. Loeffler, M. John. THE POPULATION SYNDROMES ON THE COLORADO PIEDMONT. *Ann. of the Assoc. of Am. Geographers 1965 55(1): 26-66.* As the metropolitan, urban, rural, and "new" population syndromes of the Piedmont region place ever-increasing demands on the limited resources of the region, particularly water, previously established balances have been upset. "The people of the Piedmont must strive for a balance in their cultural landscape that prescribes the highest resource-use values in a spectrum of rapid change. . . . A wise and achievable balance in irrigation agriculture, industry, and sprawl dwelling can be attained by reducing the less effective irrigated acreage and allocating its water to residential use and to industries which have integrated the recycling and reuse of water into their operations. . . . It is within this framework of water values, its innumerable and complex applications, and the inventory of recoverable and sanitized water that the landscape balance of the Piedmont will have to be resolved." Illus., maps, tables, 46 notes. W. R. Boedecker

2780. Marshall, William E. THE STATE HISTORICAL SOCIETY OF COLORADO. *Hist. News 1966 21(10): 204-207.* From its beginning in 1879, the history and development of the State Historical Society of Colorado is traced to its present multifaceted program and services. These include prehistoric as well as historic archaeology, maintenance of historic sites, the loan of artifacts to schools, conducted tours, the collection of manuscripts and printed materials, and many other related activities. 5 illus. D. L. Smith

2781. McClellan, Barbara. A COLORADO SHORT LINE RAILROAD: THE FLORENCE AND CRIPPLE CREEK, 1894-1915. *Arizona and the West 1971 13(2): 129-142.* The Cripple Creek gold rush began in 1891. Freighting and shipping the ore out by stagecoach and wagon was slow and expensive. The nearest reduction mills were located at Florence, about 40 miles to the south. Planning for a railroad to connect the Cripple Creek district and Florence began in 1892. Construction commenced two years later and moved northward from Florence through tunnels and over wooden and iron bridges, with 30-degree curves, and requiring blasting of sheer mountain walls. The three-foot narrow gauge even went over the Wilbur loop, a lariat-like configuration, to better enable the cars to ascend a steep grade. It took about six months to construct the 40.3-mile line over the rugged terrain, an amazing engineering feat that cost an estimated 800 thousand dollars. It was in operation in mid-1894. After 1900 Colorado Springs began milling Cripple Creek's gold ore. It was a 10-mile shorter haul by a new railroad to Colorado Springs than to Florence. The demise of the Florence and Cripple Creek was foreshadowed by a flood in mid-1912 which wiped out 12 of its bridges and five miles of its tracks. These and other circumstances brought dissolution of the line in 1915. 7 illus., map, 37 notes. D. L. Smith

2782. McConnell, Virginia. CAPTAIN BAKER AND THE SAN JUAN HUMBUG. *Colorado Mag. 1971 48(1): 59-75.* Describes the operations of Captain Charles Baker as he promoted expeditions into the San Juan, Colorado, region with reports of gold and good agricultural lands. Various parties entered the wilderness of the San Juan in the fall and winter of 1860-61, only to be disappointed. Feelings rose against Baker. In the fall of 1861 he joined the Confederate Army. After the war, in 1867, Baker reportedly was killed by Indians (or perhaps by a member of one of his former expeditions) along the Colorado River. In the 1870's rich ores were found in the San Juan region. Baker, however, had not discovered them, "he was merely a promoter." 4 photos, map, 70 notes. O. H. Zabel

2783. McConnell, Virginia. "FOR THESE HIGH PURPOSES." *Colorado Mag. 1967 44(3): 204-223.* The architect of the Colorado State Capitol Building Elijah E. Myers stated that the capitol should be built for the high purposes of the government of the State. In the beginning the territorial, state, county, and city governments had to use temporary buildings. The State, constituted in 1876, did not have a capitol until 1908 because of territorial rivalries and litigation between land donors and the State. In 1868 Henry Cordes (or Cordis) Brown deeded land in Denver, but in 1879 he revoked the deed. In 1881 Denver became the permanent capitol. In 1885 an act was passed for the construction of the capitol. In 1889 two million dollars was authorized. The capitol was completed in 1908 at a cost of 2,729,389.63 dollars, with much granite, marble, stained glass, and a gilded dome. A civic center was planned, with city and county buildings, many statues, monuments, art works, and landscaping. By 1960 the last building was completed and master planning was arranged for future construction. This civic center and capitol represent the aspirations of a people. 9 illus., 98 notes. I. W. Van Noppen

2784. Morris, John R. THE WOMEN AND GOVERNOR WAITE. *Colorado Mag. 1967 44(1): 11-19.* It was during the term of Davis Waite as governor of Colorado that women gained voting rights in that state. Such an act was his greatest legislative accomplishment; but, strangely enough, the next year Waite turned against suffrage and toured the country speaking in opposition. In this monograph the most dramatic episode in the story of equal rights in Colorado is outlined. Because of the approval of Colorado males, their female counterparts were given the right to vote in 1893. After this success Waite commented that women should be allowed to vote because there should be no taxation without representation, and the right to vote should be based on intelligence, not sex. If women paid taxes and possessed enough intelligence to protest unfair laws they should vote. However, after Waite was defeated in 1894, he changed his mind and came to believe that the majority of the women had voted against him. Despite this change of heart, he gave Colorado women the vote. Illus. R. Sexauer

2785. Murray, Robert B. THE SUPREME COURT OF COLORADO TERRITORY. *Colorado Mag. 1967 44(1): 20-34.* Concerns a topic pertinent to an understanding of the Colorado Territorial Court and ultimately the development of law in the Western States. Just how did the Colorado judges apply English common law in the Western territory? The author believes that it was not applied blindly, rather it was modified and sometimes changed to fit the prevailing circumstances. He outlines the conditions in Colorado at this time and the judicial system which had been created. To give weight to his argument he examines several milestone cases in which the Supreme Court of the territory did not hesitate to create new law as the diverse conditions dictated. Based on Colorado court records; illus., 24 notes. R. Sexauer

2786. Thompson, Gregory C. and O'Neil, Floyd A. FORT LEWIS MILITARY RECORDS. *Colorado Mag. 1969 46(2): 166-168.* Summarizes the history of the southwestern Colorado post Fort Lewis. It was established in 1878 at Pagosa Springs, moved to Hesperus in 1879, abandoned in 1891, used as an Indian school until 1910 and then, until 1956, as Fort Lewis A and M College. In 1968 a joint project of Fort Lewis College and the University of Utah extracted the records of Fort Lewis from the National Archives. Copies of the documents, providing a case study of a western military post, are available at both institutions. Illus. O. H. Zabel

2787. Suggs, George G., Jr. CATALYST FOR INDUSTRIAL CHANGE: THE W.F.M., 1893-1903. *Colorado Mag. 1968 45(4): 322-339.* In its first decade, ending in 1903, the Western Federation of Miners became a powerful force in Colorado politics. Violence associated with strikes, particularly over wages and hours, gave the federation the popular image of ruthlessness. Moreover, in 1897 president Edward Boyce of the federation took the union out of the American Federation of Labor and from then on publicly advocated socialism as the solution of the miners' problems. While the delegates to the annual conventions gave some support, it is doubtful that the rank and file miners supported socialism. In any case, political influence, willingness to use force, and increasing socialist orientation prepared the way for two years of industrial warfare (1903-05) which broke the power of the federation in Colorado. Illus., 36 notes.　　　　O. H. Zabel

2788. Taylor, Morris F. FORT STEVENS, FORT REYNOLDS, AND THE DEFENSE OF SOUTHERN COLORADO. *Colorado Mag. 1972 49(2): 143-162.* Details the history of two forts in southeastern Colorado. Fort Stevens, near the base of the Spanish Peaks, was authorized in the summer of 1866 and ordered discontinued the following September. Fort Reynolds was established on the upper Arkansas River near Pueblo in 1867 and abandoned in 1872. The military reservation was opened to settlement in 1874. While it was scheduled to be one of the largest posts on the plains, it achieved neither size nor importance. Based on government documents and secondary sources; illus., 2 maps, 100 notes.　　　　O. H. Zabel

2789. Taylor, Morris F. TRINIDAD LEGENDS. *Colorado Mag. 1964 41(2): 155-157.* Traces the history of the name of Trinidad, Colorado.　　　　I. W. Van Noppen

2790. West, Elliott. JEROME B. CHAFFEE AND THE MC COOK-ELBERT FIGHT. *Colorado Mag. 1969 145-165.* Discusses a Republican feud involving the Colorado Territorial delegate to Congress Jerome B. Chaffee and President Ulysses S. Grant. Early in 1874 Grant nominated his friend and former military subordinate Edward M. McCook as governor of Colorado, replacing the ally of Chaffee, Sam Elbert. Chaffee opposed confirmation and considerable scandal was publicized. McCook was confirmed by one vote, but Chaffee permitted a Democrat to be elected as delegate to Congress in the fall. To unite the Colorado Republican Party, pressure was brought upon McCook to resign. A few months later Chaffee became one of the senators of the new State of Colorado. Illus., 61 notes.　　　　O. H. Zabel

2791. Williams, Burton J. THE PLATTE, THE PLAINS AND THE PEAK: GRAND THEORY AND LOCAL HISTORY. *Great Plains J. 1968 8(1): 1-15.* Summarizes the social and political conditions of the Plains and, particularly, of the Pikes Peak gold regions of western Kansas (now Colorado), as depicted in four contemporary accounts. Albert Deane Richardson, Henry Villard, Horace Greeley, and John J. Ingalls all visited the area between 1859 and 1861. All of these observers noted the shiftlessness, laziness, untruthfulness, lawlessness, selfishness, drunkenness, and violence they saw as characteristic. The author contrasts these contemporary accounts with the rather idealized human characteristics attributed to the frontier by Frederick Jackson Turner and asserts that Turner's frontier hypothesis and several of his subsequent essays are, in essence, no more than sophisticated Populist rhetoric. He concludes that broad theory needs to be tempered by careful comparison with State and local history. Biblio.　　　　O. H. Zabel

2792. —. A BULL MOOSE IN THE ROCKIES. A PICTORIAL RECORD OF T. R. IN COLORADO. *Colorado Mag. 1965 42(4): 327-329.* A series of photographs taken of Theodore Roosevelt on one of his Colorado visits.　　　　R. Sexauer

2793. —. TALES TOLD WITH MARKERS. *Colorado Mag. 1970 47(3): 183-268.* The State Historical Society of Colorado devotes this entire issue to presenting a listing of historic landmarkers erected for 40 years through 1969. A map of each region with numbered sites of historical markers precedes the corresponding text of each marker. In all, 144 numbered existing markers and six missing markers are included. The marker presentation is followed by an alphabetical list of those included. Illus., photos.　　　　O. H. Zabel

Utah

2794. Alexander, Thomas G. CHARLES S. ZANE, APOSTLE OF THE NEW ERA. *Utah Hist. Q. 1966 34(4): 290-314.* Reviews the decisions of Zane as chief justice of the Utah Supreme Court between 1884 and 1893 in the context of conflicting historical interpretations of the relationship in that period between the United States Government and the Mormon settlers. Zane is portrayed as liberal toward the Mormons in conflicts between settlers and outside corporations in cases involving employees' claims for compensation for injuries suffered at work, in conflicts between property rights and public rights, and in educational controversies between Mormons and gentiles; but on religious questions, such as the enforcement of legislation barring polygamy, his views on morality and his insistence on strict conformity with the law made him appear illiberal. Based on the "Journal History" in the Church of Latter-Day Saints Historian's Library, Salt Lake City, court records, and contemporary newspaper accounts.　　　　S. L. Jones

2795. Alexander, Thomas G. FROM DEARTH TO DELUGE: UTAH'S COAL INDUSTRY. *Utah Hist. Q. 1963 31(3): 235-247.* Traces the historical development of Utah's coal mining industry, which is viewed in six distinct stages: 1849-68, 1869-81, 1882-1919, 1920-41, 1942-50, and 1951-63. Coal mining in Utah has gone from scarcity and underdevelopment to overproduction and limitation of output. Based in part on materials in the Utah State Archives and contemporary newspaper accounts. Illus., 29 notes.　　　　S. L. Jones

2796. Alexander, Thomas G. JOHN WESLEY POWELL, THE IRRIGATION SURVEY, AND THE INAUGURATION OF THE SECOND PHASE OF IRRIGATION DEVELOPMENT IN UTAH. *Utah Hist. Q. 1969 37(2): 190-206.* Looks at the water problems faced by Utah in the decade after 1888 against the background of the findings of the national irrigation survey completed by John Wesley Powell between 1888 and 1893. In Utah and elsewhere in the West the questions of private versus public interests and of local versus national control were raised, questions to be debated for a generation before the United States would arrive at definite answers.　　　　S. L. Jones

2797. Allen, James B. THE COMPANY TOWN: A PASSING PHASE OF UTAH'S INDUSTRIAL DEVELOPMENT. *Utah Hist. Q. 1966 34(2): 138-160.* Reviews and analyzes the establishment and development of company towns in Utah. Most company towns were established to provide facilities for men working at remote mining and processing facilities. New developments, particularly modern transportation, have made most of them obsolete. The author discusses the economics of company towns, the reactions of recent immigrants to them, and the political and economic pressures exerted by owners upon the workers and tenants.　　　　S. L. Jones

2798. Allen, James B. ECCLESIASTICAL INFLUENCE ON LOCAL GOVERNMENT IN THE TERRITORY OF UTAH. *Arizona and the West 1966 8(1): 35-48.* Direct responsibility for Utah's colonization, economic development, and early political structure was assumed by the Mormon Church. The church had brought the early settlers there and it was only natural that it should assume direction of affairs concerning the expansion and development of the area. With no professional ministry all the laymen were expected to be active in the local church government. Moreover, it was believed that God's kingdom was political as well as spiritual and that, therefore, church authorities were directly responsible for the effective operation of the civil government, too. Given that most settlers were there because they were Mormons, it was only right that the local government and the church should work together to achieve common objectives. Until local counties were organized the local church officials exercised all the civil functions. After civil authority was established the dual role of the church was much evident. By the same token, county governments were sometimes involved in ecclesiastical affairs. The influence of the church also extended into the territorial government itself. Considered in historical perspective, this phenomenon was a necessary and desirable condition because of the unique political and religious situation in Utah. Derived in part from county court minutes and other manuscript sources; 38 notes.　　　　D. L. Smith

2799. Allen, James B. THE UNUSUAL JURISDICTION OF COUNTY PROBATE COURTS IN THE TERRITORY OF UTAH. *Utah Hist. Q. 1968 36(2): 132-142.* Given original jurisdiction in both civil and criminal actions by the territorial legislature in 1852, the county probate courts in Utah became focal points for controversy between Mormons and gentiles and between local Territorial and Federal judges. The jurisdiction of the probate courts was reduced by the Poland Bill passed by Congress in 1874, but the courts were not entirely abolished until Utah entered the Union. S. L. Jones

2800. Arrington, Leonard J. ABUNDANCE FROM THE EARTH: THE BEGINNINGS OF COMMERCIAL MINING IN UTAH. *Utah Hist. Q. 1963 31(3): 192-219.* Describes the early development of commercial mining in Utah. The first stimulus was provided by US Army troops sent by Lincoln in 1862 under the command of Colonel Patrick E. Connor, but serious commercial exploitation came only after the completion of the transcontinental railroad in 1869. By the early 1870's the rich ores at the surface were exhausted, and now massive amounts of capital and new technologies were needed to extract lower grades of ore. The general economic impact of these mining developments is discussed. Documented from printed sources, illus., 63 notes. S. L. Jones

2801. Arrington, Leonard J. and Alexander, Thomas G. CAMP IN THE SAGEBRUSH: CAMP FLOYD, UTAH, 1858-1861. *Utah Hist. Q. 1966 34(1): 3-21.* Analyzes the impact economically and socially upon Utah of the brief existence of Camp Floyd, established in 1858 when Federal troops under the command of Colonel Albert Sidney Johnston were dispatched to Utah to suppress a reported insurrection against United States authority by the Mormon settlers. The history of the camp following its abandonment in 1861 down to the present when it is under development as a state historic park is told. Based in part on the diaries of soldiers who engaged in the expedition; illus., 34 notes. S. L. Jones

2802. Arrington, Leonard J. COOPERATIVE COMMUNITY IN THE NORTH: BRIGHAM CITY, UTAH. *Utah Hist. Q. 1965 33(3): 198-217.* Narrates the establishment and growth of a cooperative community enterprise at Brigham City, Utah, under the direction of Lorenzo Snow. Beginning in 1864 with a general store the cooperative, with Snow utilizing strict religious sanctions which gave the enterprise a virtual monopoly of all commercial activity in the community, expanded into a number of thriving agricultural and manufacturing activities. Important factors in the project were the exploitation of the special skills of European converts, reinvestment of a very large proportion of the profits in the further growth of the enterprise, and the use of local scrip as currency. A series of misfortunes beginning with the burning of a large woolen factory in 1877 exposed the weaknesses of the project. The decline which followed resulted in liquidation completed in 1896. Based mainly on published letters of Snow and materials in the Church of Latter Day Saints Historian's Library at Salt Lake City; illus., 41 notes. S. L. Jones

2803. Arrington, Leonard J. and Alexander, Thomas G. SUPPLY HUB OF THE WEST: DEFENSE DEPOT OGDEN, 1941-1964. *Utah Hist. Q. 1964 32(2): 99-121.* Details the history of the Defense Depot Ogden. Its purpose until January 1964 was as a "general store" for the US Army, supplying almost anything on short notice. The depot was of great strategic importance during World War II and the Korean War. The installation assumed its present name on 1 January 1964 when it ceased to be exclusively an army supply base and became a Department of Defense supply agency for all the military services in the western part of the United States, Alaska, Hawaii, and overseas in the Pacific and the Far East. Based in large part on special historical studies and other materials in the Depot Public Information Office at Defense Depot Ogden; illus., 15 notes. S. L. Jones

2804. Arrington, Leonard J. and Alexander, Thomas G. THE U.S. ARMY OVERLOOKS SALT LAKE VALLEY: FORT DOUGLAS, 1862-1965. *Utah Hist. Q. 1965 33(4): 326-350.* Relates the history of the US Army installation at Fort Douglas, just east of Salt Lake City, from its establishment during the Civil War to its deactivation, announced on 19 November 1964. The author emphasizes the economic impact of the fort upon Salt Lake City and Utah. Illus., 85 notes. S. L. Jones

2805. Arrington, Leonard J.; Alexander, Thomas G.; and Erb, Eugene A., Jr. UTAH'S BIGGEST BUSINESS: OGDEN AIR MATERIEL AREA AT HILL AIR FORCE BASE, 1938-1965. *Utah Hist. Q. 1965 33(1): 9-33.* Starts off with a statistical demonstration that the supply and maintenance operations of the Ogden Air Materiel Area (OOAMA) at Hill Air Force Base are larger in every respect than those of any other business in Utah and then provides an account of the major stages in the growth of OOAMA since 1938. This growth is shown as paralleling US military involvement such as in the Korean War and technological changes such as the development of intercontinental ballistic missiles. Based on three volumes prepared by OOAMA's historian, Miss Helen Rice, and a master's thesis ("The Economic Impact of Hill Air Force Base on the Ogden Area," Utah State U., 1955) written by Colonel John D. McConahay; illus., 20 notes. S. L. Jones

2806. Arrington, Leonard J. and Alexander, Thomas G. UTAH'S FIRST LINE OF DEFENSE: THE UTAH NATIONAL GUARD AND CAMP W. G. WILLIAMS, 1926-1965. *Utah Hist. Q. 1965 33(2): 141-156.* An account of military reserve units organized by the Mormons and the Territory and State of Utah, beginning with the Nauvoo Legion, organized in the 1840's in Illinois. The National Guard was established in Utah in 1894, but no provision for permanent facilities was made prior to World War I. These facilities, located at Jordan Narrows near Lehi, were designated Camp Williams in 1928. Based on materials in the Utah State Historical Society, newspaper accounts, and published materials; illus., 17 notes. S. L. Jones

2807. Bowers, Donald W. and Hastings, Donald W. CHILDSPACING AND WIFE'S EMPLOYMENT STATUS AMONG 1940-41 UNIVERSITY OF UTAH GRADUATES. *Rocky Mountain Social Sci. J. 1970 7(2): 125-136.* Examines the factors of religion and wife's employment status as related to fertility and childspacing for a contrived population of University of Utah family units. A survey of 890 Utah alumni focused on 1) the differences in family size according to wife's employment status for Mormon and non-Mormon couples, and 2) intervals between marriage and first birth and between successive children according to couples' religious preference and wife's employment status. Fertility and childspacing patterns among working wives differed from their nonworking counterparts. Mormon couples, whether the wife worked or not, had higher fertility and shorter intervals between marriage and first birth than non-Mormons. The sequential relationship between the period wives worked and childspacing was not established. 10 tables, 13 notes. A. P. Young

2808. Brooks, Juanita. THE MOUNTAIN MEADOWS: HISTORIC STOPPING PLACE ON THE SPANISH TRAIL. *Utah Hist. Q. 1967 35(2): 137-143.* Urges the restoration and preservation of a monument erected in 1932 at Mountain Meadows in Utah to commemorate the massacre of about 140 immigrants in September 1857. The massacre and other major incidents in the history of Mountain Meadows are described. S. L. Jones

2809. Buchanan, Dorothy J. LIFE "ON THE ROAD": REMINISCENCES OF A DRUMMER IN UTAH. *Utah Hist. Q. 1966 34(1): 22-29.* Reminiscences of Henry C. Jacobs (1876-) of his life as a traveling salesman in Utah between 1894 and 1902 as told by his daughter. Illus. S. L. Jones

2810. Cardon, A. F. MOUNTAIN MEADOWS BURIAL DETACHMENT, 1859: TOMMY GORDON'S DIARY. *Utah Hist. Q. 1967 35(2): 143-146.* Contains the text of Gordon's diary from 21 April to 30 May 1859 when, as a laborer employed by the United States Army unit operating in Utah Territory under the command of Albert Sidney Johnston, he was a member of a party which buried the remains of the victims of the Mountain Meadows Massacre of 1857. S. L. Jones

2811. Clyde, George D. UTAH AFTER STATEHOOD. *Utah Hist. Q. 1964 32(1): 3-8.* The text of Governor George D. Clyde's speech presented at the Statehood Day observance on 6 January 1964. He sketches Utah's economic and social growth. Illus. S. L. Jones

2812. Cooley, Everett L. THE UTAH STATE HISTORICAL SOCIETY. *Hist. News 1967 22(1): 20-22.* The Utah State Historical Society was founded in 1897 to perpetuate the memory and accomplishments of the Mormon pioneers. Its activities continued to be severely restricted because of a lack of funds even after it became an agency of the State government in 1917. From World War II, however, with newly assigned responsibilities, the addition of professional personnel, the former governor's mansion as its home with other space in the State capital, a widely acclaimed publications program, a growing membership, and a network of local chapters throughout the State, the society has matured into one of the most progressive and forward-looking in the nation. Illus.

D. L. Smith

2813. Crampton, C. Gregory, ed. MILITARY RECONNAISSANCE IN SOUTHERN UTAH, 1866. *Utah Hist. Q. 1964 32(2): 145-161.* Provides the text of the reconnoitering report written by Franklin B. Woolley, adjutant to Captain James Andrus' military expedition from Saint George, Utah Territory, to the mouth of the Green River and back in 1866. A chart of the country traversed and the official muster roll, are included. The editor has also provided introductory comments and explanatory notes to the text. The original copy of the report is in the Military Records Section of the Utah State Archives, Salt Lake City. Illus., 18 notes.

S. L. Jones

2814. Culmsee, Carlton F. FLIMFLAM FRONTIER: SUBMARGINAL LAND DEVELOPMENT IN UTAH. *Utah Hist. Q. 1964 32(2): 91-98.* Relates the experiences of the author's family with promotional schemes for the development of submarginal land in the Escalante Valley in southern Utah. Land promoters, frequently exploiting the attractiveness of the desert for homesites and recreation, are still active, though the shortage of water remains a problem. Illus.

S. L. Jones

2815. Ekker, Barbara Baldwin. FREIGHTING ON THE COLORADO RIVER: REMINISCENCES OF VIRGIL FAY BALDWIN. *Utah Hist. Q. 1964 32(2): 122-129.* Relates how Baldwin helped the Mid-West Exploration Company search for oil on the Colorado River downstream from Moab, Utah, between 1924 and 1929. Based on Baldwin's reminiscences as dictated to the author and a brief diary maintained by Baldwin. Illus.

S. L. Jones

2816. Ellsworth, S. George. UTAH'S STRUGGLE FOR STATEHOOD. *Utah Hist. Q. 1963 31(3): 60-69.* In this address, delivered at the statehood celebration, 4 January 1963, at Salt Lake City, Utah, the author reviewed "the trials and persecutions and troublous times" of the half century antecedent to Utah's attainment of statehood. Chief subjects of the address were the struggles between the Mormons and settlers of other religious beliefs, the acts of Congress intended to suppress polygamy, and the capitulation by the Mormons beginning in 1890 to the demands that they end polygamy, with the result that Utah was admitted to statehood in 1896. The address concluded that "Accommodation by the people of Utah to the norms of American society yielded enormous dividends. . . ."

S. L. Jones

2817. Frazier, Russell G. BINGHAM CANYON THROUGH THE EYES OF A COMPANY DOCTOR. *Utah Hist. Q. 1965 33(4): 283-288.* Reminiscences, mostly about friends in Bingham. Frazier was the resident physician of the Utah Copper Company for 40 years, beginning in 1918. Illus.

S. L. Jones

2818. Gunn, Wilhelmina J. THE ELSINORE HOUSE: A DRUMMER'S HOME AWAY FROM HOME. *Utah Hist. Q. 1966 34(1): 30-37.* Reminiscences of how the author's family established and managed a hotel at Elsinore, Utah, a settlement of Danish converts to the Mormon Church. The account centers on activities and relationships of the family. Illus.

S. L. Jones

2819. Hansen, Gary B. INDUSTRY OF DESTINY: COPPER IN UTAH. *Utah Hist. Q. 1963 31(3): 262-279.* Details the copper industry's history in Utah, tracing the changes in production techniques, capitalization, and ownership which led to the large-scale production of the present day. Illus., 48 notes.

S. L. Jones

2820. Harline, Osmond L. UTAH'S BLACK GOLD: THE PETROLEUM INDUSTRY. *Utah Hist. Q. 1963 31(3): 291-311.* Traces the exploration for oil, the development of the wells, the building of pipelines, the exploitation of natural gas, and the establishment of oil refineries in Utah. Though oil seepage was observed in Utah in 1847, it was 1948 before the first commercially profitable well was sunk. Illus., 64 notes.

S. L. Jones

2821. Jacobson, Pearl F. UTAH'S FIRST RADIO STATION. *Utah Hist. Q. 1964 32(2): 130-144.* Chronicles the difficulties and final success of Utah's first commercial radio station, KZN (Salt Lake City), which began operations on 6 May 1922. Photographs, including one of those participating in the first broadcast, are included. Information for the article was obtained mainly from the personal files and memoirs of Nathan O. Fullmer, one of the founders of the station. 29 notes.

S. L. Jones

2822. Jennings, Jesse D. and Sharrock, Floyd W. THE GLEN CANYON: A MULTI-DISCIPLINE PROJECT. *Utah Hist. Q. 1965 33(1): 34-50.* Provides a survey of the studies undertaken in 1957 by the University of Utah Department of Anthropology under contract with the National Park Service in the area primarily in Utah to be flooded by Lake Powell. The area will lie behind Glen Canyon Dam. Study has concentrated on but has not been exclusively restricted to the areas which will be covered by water. The author discusses some of the interpretations and controversies which have resulted from the findings and emphasizes the necessity for an interdisciplinary approach to the solution of many of the problems encountered. The project has been financed mainly through funds provided by the National Park Service under the terms of the Historic Sites Act of 1935. Illus., 16 notes.

S. L. Jones

2823. Johnson, Rue C. THEATRE IN ZION: THE BRIGHAM CITY DRAMATIC ASSOCIATION. *Utah Hist. Q. 1965 33(3): 187-197.* Tells how Brigham City pioneer Lorenzo Snow and others established a theater, first in Snow's home in 1855 and the following year in the basement of the courthouse, which was still under construction. The author discusses the personalities involved, the plays which were produced, and various aspects of physical problems arising in the productions. Based on biographies and memoirs of the pioneer settlers, interviews by the author, and contemporary newspaper accounts; illus., 31 notes.

S. L. Jones

2824. Larson, Gustive O. BULWARK OF THE KINGDOM: UTAH'S IRON AND STEEL INDUSTRY. *Utah Hist. Q. 1963 31(3): 248-261.* Discusses the history of the iron and steel industry in Utah from the frustrated efforts of the 19th century to the construction by the US Defense Department of the Geneva Steel Plant near Provo in 1942-44. After the war, this plant was sold to the United States Steel Corporation and is now an important factor in the economy of the western United States. Illus., 36 notes.

S. L. Jones

2825. Mackinnon, William P. THE BUCHANAN SPOILS SYSTEM AND THE UTAH EXPEDITION: CAREERS OF W. M. F. MAGRAW AND JOHN M. HOCKADAY. *Utah Hist. Q. 1963 31(2): 127-150.* In 1857 the Buchanan administration sent federal troops into Utah Territory. Subsequently it appeared that there was no threat of disorder in Utah sufficient to justify the use of federal troops. This article agrees with earlier accounts which have ascribed the intervention to bias against the Mormons, politics, spoils, and patronage; but it differs from the earlier analyses in placing stronger emphasis on economic motives, mainly the desire for patronage and lucrative government contracts. The demonstration of this argument is found in the author's analysis of the activities of two men, W. M. F. Magraw and John M. Hockaday, both of whom were closely associated with the Buchanan administration. Based on government documents, particularly reports of special congressional investigations, and on the Buchanan Collection of the Historical Society of Pennsylvania.

S. L. Jones

2826. Miller, David E., ed. A GREAT ADVENTURE ON GREAT SALT LAKE: A TRUE STORY OF KATE Y. NOBLE. *Utah Hist. Q. 1965 33(3): 218-236.* An account written by Mrs. Noble of how she with her first husband Uriah J. Wenner and their three children lived on Frémont Island in Great Salt Lake in the years 1886-91. The editor has provided additional information about the island, its history, and the Wenners in an introduction and footnotes. The text of a statement written by John E. Jones after a visit to the island in 1942 and letters to him from Mrs. Noble and her daughter, Blanche H. Wenner, concerning the burial ground on the island are provided also. Illus., 36 notes.

S. L. Jones

2827. Morgan, Dale L. UTAH BEFORE THE MORMONS. *Utah Hist. Q. 1968 36(1): 3-23.* Reviews the presently known sources of information about Utah left by men who visited the region before 1847. The record of exploration and development prior to 1819 is slight and yields little useful information. Also there appears little likelihood that it will be extended. After 1819 the records of fur trappers, travelers, explorers, and members of military expeditions provide a wealth of information which continues to expand as scholars discover new sources.
S. L. Jones

2828. Nelson, Elroy. THE MINERAL INDUSTRY: A FOUNDATION OF UTAH'S ECONOMY. *Utah Hist. Q. 1963 31(3): 178-191.* Discusses the historical development of Utah's mining and milling industry since 1847 and its economic impact in the State. The annual value of mineral production before 1860 was less than 10,000 dollars. By 1960, production had increased to 400 million dollars annually. The major growth came after 1940, in response to the needs created by World War II and the technological development of the last two decades. Illus., 4 notes.
S. L. Jones

2829. Noall, Claire. SERBIAN-AUSTRIAN CHRISTMAS AT HIGHLAND BOY. *Utah Hist. Q. 1965 33(4): 316-325.* Describes how Serbian and Austrian customs of celebrating Christmas were observed by Paul Richards, company physician and surgeon for the United States Mining, Smelting, and Refining Company at the Highland Boy Mine in Bingham Canyon, Utah. Based in part on the Richards' typescript memoirs.
S. L. Jones

2830. Papanikolas, Helen Zeese. LIFE AND LABOR AMONG THE IMMIGRANTS OF BINGHAM CANYON. *Utah Hist. Q. 1965 33(4): 289-315.* Surveys the changing patterns of immigration into the mines in Bingham Canyon, dealing with the Greek immigrants who came in large numbers in the first decade of the 20th century. About half of the article is devoted to describing the part played by Greek workers and strike breakers in the 1912 strike of the Western Federation of Labor against the Utah Copper Company at Bingham. Based on contemporary newspaper accounts and interviews; illus., 92 notes.
S. L. Jones

2831. Poll, Richard D. A STATE IS BORN. *Utah Hist. Q. 1964 32(1): 9-31.* Describes the preparations for statehood and the reactions of Utah's citizens to presidential approval of the enabling legislation. Economic and social life in Utah at the time are also covered. Illus., 49 notes.
S. L. Jones

2832. Richardson, Elmo R. FEDERAL PARK POLICY IN UTAH: THE ESCALANTE NATIONAL MONUMENT CONTROVERSY OF 1935-1940. *Utah Hist. Q. 1965 33(2): 109-133.* Provides a detailed description of the negotiations between representatives of the Department of the Interior and members of the State Government of Utah regarding a proposed scenic and recreational area in southeastern Utah. Misunderstandings developed primarily over the question of the possibilities of economic exploitation of the region and the desire of State officials to retain access for commercial use of any areas so suited which might be placed within the monument. The author concludes that men on both sides were responsible for the misunderstandings which led to the abandonment of the project in 1940. Based primarily on the Governors' Papers of the State of Utah and the Franklin D. Roosevelt Papers at Hyde Park; illus., 33 notes.
S. L. Jones

2833. Romney, Miles P. UTAH'S CINDERELLA MINERALS: THE NONMETALLICS. *Utah Hist. Q. 1963 31(3): 220-234.* Describes, in the main statistically, the development of industrial nonmetallic minerals (specifically slat, clay, stone, limestone, phosphate, gypsum, sand, sulphur, Gilsonite, Bentonite, potash) in Utah. Three distinct periods of growth are discerned: 1848 to 1869, when the transcontinental railroad was completed; between 1869 and 1940, when growth was steady but not spectacular; and since 1940, when production increased tenfold. Illus., 36 notes.
S. L. Jones

2834. Sorensen, Don. WONDER MINERAL: UTAH'S URANIUM. *Utah Hist. Q. 1963 31(3): 280-290.* Summarizes the interest in radium, vanadium, and uranium which has developed in different historical epochs and the consequent impact on the mining of uranium ore in Utah. The author concentrates on the developments resulting from the

heavy demand for radium during the period between 1898 and 1923. Illus., 22 notes.
S. L. Jones

2835. Wood, David L. EMPEROR DOM PEDRO'S VISIT TO SALT LAKE CITY. *Utah Hist. Q. 1969 37(3): 337-352.* Describes the 1876 visit of Emperor Dom Pedro II of Brazil and the reactions of the citizens of Utah. Dom Pedro's visit to Salt Lake City "had been prompted by Brazil's participation in the impending Philadelphia Exhibition," and his visit to the United States was the "first stop on an extended two-year world tour, during which he intended...to 'see the chief centers of industry to learn something that may be of use'" to his country when he returned. Based mainly on newspaper accounts; 53 notes.
S. L. Jones

2836. —. [UTAH'S CATTLE INDUSTRY]. *Utah Hist. Q. 1964 32(3): 179-320.*
Cooley, Everett L. AN OVERVIEW OF UTAH'S CATTLE INDUSTRY, *pp. 179-182.* This survey of the history of the cattle industry in Utah serves as an introduction to an issue of the *Utah Historical Quarterly* devoted entirely to various phases of the historical development of the cattle industry in that State. Illus.
Walker, Don D. THE CATTLE INDUSTRY OF UTAH, *pp. 182-197.* Narrates the history of the steady growth of the beef cattle industry in Utah during the last half of the 19th century. Sources of cattle importation, the opening of new range areas, improvements in stock raising, and adjustment to climatic conditions figure prominently in the account. Two census tables, one giving totals for the entire State, the other giving the numbers of cattle in the various counties during this period, are provided. Based mainly on newspaper sources and reports of the US Census Bureau; illus., 55 notes.
Peterson, Levi S. THE DEVELOPMENT OF UTAH LIVESTOCK LAW, *pp. 198-216.* Describes how the interaction between the territorial legislature, county governments, and livestock men shaped the development of livestock law in Utah during the territorial period. Three areas of livestock regulation are discussed: grazing on the public lands, settlement of disputes over the ownership of range animals, and fencing. Use of the public lands tended to come under the control of the territorial legislatures and the county governments, often resulting in local regulations which were in conflict with Federal policy. Based in part on materials in the Utah State Archives, including records of some of the county courts; illus., 58 notes.
Cracroft, Richard H. THE HERALDRY OF THE RANGE: UTAH CATTLE BRANDS, *pp. 217-231.* Gives specific examples of how brand marks were chosen, how they were applied to cattle, how they were occasionally illegally altered, and how an official register of brands has been maintained by Utah territorial and State Governments since 1849. Illus., 19 notes.
Price, Virginia N. and Darby, John T. PRESTON NUTTER: UTAH CATTLEMAN, 1886-1936, *pp. 232-251.* The major stages in the career of a Utah cattle baron are portrayed and his methods of acquiring land and cattle and the management of his herds are described. Nutter began his cattle operations in Colorado, where he had been prospecting for gold. New York associates provided financial support. Based on materials in the possession of his daughter, Virginia N. Price; illus., 12 notes.
Young, Karl. WILD COWS OF THE SAN JUAN, *pp. 252-267.* Reminiscences collected by the author of wild cattle chases in a 1962 trip into the wild canyon country of southeastern Utah in the company of seven old-time cowboys. Illus.
Walker, Don D. THE CARLISLES: CATTLE BARONS OF THE UPPER BASIN, *pp. 268-284.* Information about the founding and operations of a large-scale cattle grazing company, The Kansas and New Mexico Land and Cattle Company, Limited, financed by British capital. The account focuses upon the activities in Utah from 1870 to 1900 of the company's two agents, the brothers Harold and Edmund Septimus Carlisle. Much attention is devoted to hostile encounters with cattle rustlers, horse thieves, sheep herders, and Indians. Based chiefly on published materials and the typescript of Frank Silvey, "History and Settlement of Northern San Juan County . . .," in the Utah State Historical Society; illus., 64 notes.
Roberts, N. Keith and Gardner, B. Delworth. LIVESTOCK AND THE PUBLIC LANDS, *pp. 285-300.* Surveys the influence exer-

cised by Federal land policy, particularly as defined by the Forest Service and the Bureau of Land Management, upon cattle grazing operations in Utah. Illus., 24 notes.

Lambert, Neal. AL SCORUP: CATTLEMAN OF THE CANYONS, pp. 301-320. Narrates the life story of John Albert Scorup, cowboy and cattle rancher. Particular attention is given to Scorup's cattle herding operations in White Canyon, Utah. Based primarily on interviews with cattlemen, reminiscences of Scorup recorded by one of his daughters, and a privately printed (1944) account, *J. A. Scorup, A Utah Cattleman* by Stena Scorup; illus., 71 notes.

S. L. Jones

Nevada

2837. Brodhead, Michael J. ACCEPTING THE VERDICT: NATIONAL SUPREMACY AS EXPRESSED IN STATE CONSTITUTIONS, 1861-1912. *Nev. Hist. Soc. Q. 1970 13(2): 2-16.* Studies the various State constitutional expressions of the doctrine of national supremacy from the beginning of the American Civil War to the eve of World War I. Before the Civil War no State constitution touched on the question directly, but after 1865 nearly all of the Southern States and the new Western States incorporated some acknowledgement of Federal supremacy in their constitutions. The apparent acceptance of Federal supremacy by Southern States just after the Civil War is seen by the author as evidence that the South had accepted the verdict of the war and was more interested in taking up more vital matters, such as the status of the Negro. The Nevada Constitution of 1863 incorporated the Federal supremacy principle, but this constitution failed ratification. The 1864 constitution of Nevada was accepted by the voters. The 1864 version contained and still contains what is the most all-encompassing statement of subordination to Federal power to be found in any of the State constitutions. Illus., photo, 37 notes. E. P. Costello

2838. Egan, Ferol. WARREN WASSON, MODEL INDIAN AGENT. *Nevada Hist. Soc. Q. 1969 12(3): 3-26.* Warren Wasson, a native New Yorker raised in Illinois, emigrated to the Far West in 1849. In 1851 he went back to the East but returned the following year. Wasson became friendly with the Washo and Paiute Indian tribes and, by 1858, had become an intermediary between the appointed Indian Agent and his Indian charges. In September 1860, Wasson was made Acting Indian Agent for Nevada. Although he was appointed U.S. Marshal for the Territory of Nevada in March 1862, he continued settling disputes between various Indian tribes. Wasson was a rarity in Indian-white relations and was respected by both ethnic groups. Based mostly on primary sources, Government reports, memoirs, and letters; illus., photos, 20 notes. E. P. Costello

2839. Goodwin, Victor. LEWIS RICE BRADLEY: PIONEER NEVADA CATTLEMAN AND NEVADA'S FIRST COWBOY GOVERNOR. *Nevada Hist. Soc. Q. 1971 14(4): 10-22.* Bradley (1805-79) and his son were the first to operate with livestock on a large scale in Nevada and the first to bring Texas longhorn cattle into Nevada in large numbers. The elder Bradley served two terms as Governor of Nevada (1871-78) and was the second Governor of the State. While Governor, Bradley was commonly known as "Old Broadhorns" and "His Oxcellency." Bradley, although born in Virginia, wandered ever westward until he finally settled in the area around Elko, Nevada. He and his son were first engaged in driving Texas steers from Missouri to the California gold fields but found it more profitable to establish ranching operations in Nevada using Texas longhorns as the mainstay of the herd. The drives to California could then be made at a fraction of the risk and in a much shorter time. As Governor, Bradley left his mark by insisting that Nevada have a first-class school system and that all business interests, including the Comstock mines, pay their share of State revenue needs. This latter principle brought him in sharp conflict with the mining interests and led to a narrow defeat for a third term as Governor. Based on primary and secondary sources; illus., 49 notes. E. P. Costello

2840. Mack, Effie Mona. WILLIAM MORRIS STEWART, 1827-1909. *Nevada Hist. Soc. Q. 1964 7(1/2): 3-121.* A partial biography of the first U.S. senator from Nevada. Stewart, an ardent silverite, is credited with coining the term "Crime of 1873," as being the "Father of the

Mining Laws of the U.S.," and as the author of the 15th Amendment. He served for 28 years in the Senate, 1865-75 and 1887-1905; once hired Mark Twain as his Washington secretary for three months; and was the son-in-law of Henry Stuart Foote, senator, governor and Confederate congressman from Mississippi. 58 notes, bibliographic essay and a special nine-page index are included. J. D. Filipiak

2841. Richards, Kent D. THE AMERICAN COLONIAL SYSTEM IN NEVADA. *Nevada Hist. Soc. Q. 1970 13(1): 28-38.* A critique of the system used by the Federal Government to govern territories while they were preparing for statehood. Territorial Nevada is examined in some detail. Nevada became a territory in 1861 along with Colorado and Dakota. Secretary of State William Henry Seward secured the governorship of Nevada for a political friend, James Warren Nye. The remainder of the important territorial officials were also political appointees; therefore, fealty was owed Washington by the territorial officials. Entrepreneurs moved in and made profitable contacts with the territorial officials, particularly the judicial appointees whose salaries were so low that such expedients were necessary for economic solvency. Nye limited his ambitions to extending his power and wealth, others were simply unfit to even hold office let alone profit from it. By 1864 Nevada was in sad economic, political, and moral straits because of the miserable performance of the political appointees. Illus., photo, 39 notes.

E. P. Costello

2842. Richards, Kent D. WASHOE TERRITORY: RUDIMENTARY GOVERNMENT IN NEVADA. *Arizona and the West 1969 11(3): 213-232.* Although American mountain men were traversing Washoe (the early name for Nevada) as early as 1827, permanent settlement was not established until 1851 when the Mormons located a way station en route to the California gold fields. In the absence of any governmental authority, some 50 Mormons and Gentile prospectors and cattle ranchers drew up a Washoe code concerned with land claims. In time, its coverage was enlarged. Mormon-Gentile relations deteriorated and letters and petitions were soon reaching Washington. Gentiles even asked to be annexed to California. Utah Territory countered this by incorporating the area as a county. When Federal troops were sent to Utah in 1857, the Mormons left Washoe. The Gentiles took over and launched a move for separate territorial status. The end of an Indian war in 1860, new problems occasioned by the mining boom of 1859 and the national North-South cleavage, and the failure of a newly formed provisional territorial government led to the creation of Nevada Territory by Congress in 1861. The pragmatic attempts to establish workable frontier institutions had failed and the paternalistic territorial system was welcomed. According to the author, Nevada's experience was similar to the evolution of government struggle on many other western frontiers. 4 illus., 4 maps, 40 notes. D. L. Smith

2843. Shepperson, Wilbur. THE IMMIGRANT IN NEVADA'S SHORT STORIES AND BIOGRAPHICAL ESSAYS. *Nevada Hist. Soc. Q. 1970 13(3): 2-15.* In 1870, six years after being admitted to the Union, Nevada had the largest percentage of foreign-born population of any State in the United States. In the 19th century, Irish, Cornish, Germans, Italians, Swiss, Chinese, Mexicans, and French Canadians predominated. In the early 20th century, Greeks, Slavs, Danes, Japanese, Italians, and Basques poured in. The infusion of cultural diversity made the immigrant historically significant in Nevada. The literature about Nevada and the people gives a good idea of the impact of the immigrant on early Nevada. Many of the legends and tales of pioneer Nevada survive only in the many short stories with a Nevada locale. Almost two thousand biographical essays survive from the period of heavy immigration. The Canadians and North Europeans received the most historical and biographical attention. The Basques, Chinese, and Mexicans appear only infrequently in biographical essays but frequently as characters in short stories. Italians, Greeks, Slavs, and Japanese appear to have been ignored by both biographers and short story authors. Photo, 8 notes.

E. P. Costello

2844. Townley, John M. THE DELAMAR BOOM. *Nevada Hist. Soc. Q. 1972 15(1): 2-19.* The story of the development and short existence of a small, one-company-owned mining district in the late 19th and early 20th centuries in southeastern Nevada. After the discovery of low-grade high-volume gold ore, the entire productive operation was bought by Captain J. R. De La Mar of New York City, who had made a fortune in the western mining industry. Two towns, Pioche and Delamar, feuded throughout the period, primarily over which town would be sufficiently strong to dominate the county and hence the county revenues. By 1895, the dust from mining operations was causing an unhealthy situation in which all exposed underwent fibrosis of the lungs, internal bleeding, and a miserable death. The fame of the Delamar Mining District rests more on the tragedy of the sickness than it does on gold. The peak years for gold production were 1896 to 1900. During this period, mining operations earned more than eight million dollars. By 1900 the honeymoon was over. A fire consumed most of the town and things were never the same again despite the discovery of some additional pockets of high-grade ore. Delamar quietly gave up the ghost when high-grade ore petered out. Based on primary sources; photo, 31 notes.   E. P. Costello

New Mexico

2845. Carson, Wm. G. B. WILLIAM CARR LANE, DIARY. *New Mexico Hist. R. 1964 39(3): 181-234, and (4): 274-332.* William Carr Lane, M.D. (1789-1862), former mayor of St. Louis, and representative in the Missouri legislature, was appointed by President Fillmore as territorial governor of New Mexico, July 1852. He served as governor for 11 months. The first part of the diary reproduced here was kept during the period 28 February to 19 April 1853, while as governor he was on a tour of inspection of the lower Rio Grande Valley. Lane was particularly observant of wild life and farm crops, frequently mentioning the yield per acre of wheat and corn. The final section of the diary contains entries from 20 April to 25 December 1853. Lane had completed his tour of inspection on 28 April, having travelled 1,123 miles. Lane was opposed in an election for territorial delgate by Padre José Manuel Gallegos. On election day, Lane philosophically recorded: "This day is to decide the question, whether my vanity is to (be) fed, by being election Delegate, or my substantial interests are to be promoted." His interests were promoted; Lane was decisively defeated. Lane closed out his affairs in New Mexico, and departed for St. Louis 1 October. His informative comments on the territory between New Mexico and Missouri during a 28 day journey occupy most of the remainder of the diary. Annotated.
                                                                              D. F. Henderson

2846. Coke, Van Deren. TAOS AND SANTA FE. *Art in America 1963 51(5): 44-47.* Discussion of art and environment in New Mexico, 1882-1942, emphasizing the work of Marsden Hartley, Georgia O'Keeffe, and others.
                                                                              W. K. Bottorff

2847. Farrar, Harold R., ed. TALES OF NEW MEXICO TERRITORY 1868-1876. *New Mexico Hist. R. 1968 43(2): 137-152.* Autobiographical reflections of New Mexico from 1868 to 1876 by Horatio Russ Farrar, freight wagon driver, bridge construction worker, Army scout, and railroad worker. Included is the "Death of Three Comanches," "My First Bear," "An Indian Joke," and a "Letter from New Mexico." 6 notes.
                                                                              D. F. Henderson

2848. Heaston, Michael D. THE GOVERNOR AND THE INDIAN AGENT: 1855-1857. *New Mexico Hist. R. 1970 45(2): 137-146.* Analyzes the conflict between territorial governor David Meriwether and one of three Indian agents for the territory, Abraham G. Mayers. Strife developed over expenses, territorial politics, and supplies for the Indians. Mayers eventually took his complaints to Washington, D.C., without success. Based primarily on Letters Received by the Office of Indian Affairs, 1849-80, in the National Archives; 34 notes.   D. F. Henderson

2849. Jenkins, Myra Ellen. A DEDICATION TO THE MEMORY OF RALPH EMERSON TWITCHELL, 1859-1925. *Arizona and the West 1966 8(2): 103-106.* Ralph Emerson Twitchell was an attorney or special counsel for the Santa Fe Railroad for all of his adult life. He was prominent in Mew Mexico legal circles and politics, held State and local offices, and was an articulate spokesman for civic, patriotic, and historical causes and organizations. He was active in the Historical Society of New Mexico and frequently donated manuscripts, books, and artifacts to it. Twitchell was the founder and first editor of *Old Sante Fe,* a historical quarterly. His descriptive catalog of the Spanish archives of the State (two volumes edited from the documents) and the publicity he gave them preserved them from looting and loss. Also he literally saved them from

an 1892 fire at the territorial capitol building. Although not a professional historian, his nine volumes and many pamphlets and articles entitle him to paternal status for the writing of New Mexico history. Illus., appendix.
                                                                              D. L. Smith

2850. Laron, Robert W. THE PROFILE OF A NEW MEXICO PROGRESSIVE. *New Mexico Hist. R. 1970 45(3): 233-244.* Brief sketches of four New Mexican Progressives - Miguel Antonio Otero, governor and first Republican politician to openly challenge the power of the Old Guard; Herbert James Hagerman, governor; George Curry, governor and conservation leader; and Bronson Cutting, newspaper owner and chairman of the State Progressive Party. 32 notes.
                                                                              D. F. Henderson

2851. Larson, Robert W. BALLINGER VS. ROUGH RIDER GEORGE CURRY: THE OTHER FEUD. *New Mexico Hist. R. 1968 43(4): 271-290.* The Gifford Pinchot-Richard A. Ballinger feud, involving the Forest Service of the Department of Agriculture with the Department of the Interior, is well known. Another lesser known feud between Ballinger and George Curry may also have affected the Taft-Roosevelt relationship. On 25 October 1909, George Curry, a Roosevelt appointee as Governor of New Mexico, offered his resignation to President Taft who accepted it. "The prime factor which motivated both the resignation and its acceptance was Ballinger's uncompromising hostility toward Curry." Curry later became the first Congressman to follow Roosevelt to the Bull Moose side. Based on Roosevelt and Taft papers; 62 notes.
                                                                              D. F. Henderson

2852. Lecompte, Janet. THE MANCO CURRO PASS MASSACRE. *New Mexico Hist. R. 1966 41(4): 305-318.* In Manco Curro Pass Jicarilla Apache attacked a party of 14 men and two children on 19 June 1848 killing four men and capturing the children. The annotated account of one of the survivors is reproduced. Based on manuscripts and newspapers, 33 notes.   D. F. Henderson

2853. Mason, George. NEW MEXICO HALL OF FAME. *New Mexico Hist. R. 1964 39(3): 251-252.* New Mexico's Hall of Fame, "which immortalizes those who have made towering contribution to the state's rich history," was increased to an honor roll of eight in October 1964, with the addition of Don Juan de Oñate, Christopher (Kit) Carson, and William A. Keleher.   D. F. Henderson

2854. Moore, Mary Lu. A DEDICATION TO THE MEMORY OF MAURICE GARLAND FULTON, 1877-1955. *Arizona and the West 1967 9(4): 313-316.* In 1920, with an educational and teaching background east of the Mississippi River, Maurice Garland Fulton joined the faculty of New Mexico Military Institute in Roswell as a specialist in English literature. He was soon captivated by the history and lore of New Mexico. He bacame the foremost authority on the Lincoln County War and performed a distinct service in his crusade to separate history and folklore. His perspective broadened to include the entire State. He also became an authority on the Santa Fe trade. He did much to interest others in the cause of State and local history. Unfortunately Fulton failed to record much of the information which he had collected and it vanished with him. Appended with a list of his works relating to the Southwest; illus.
                                                                              D. L. Smith

2855. Moore, Mary Lucille. NEW MEXICO THESES AND DISSERTATIONS IN HISTORY: A PRELIMINARY CHECKLIST. *Arizona and the West 1970 12(4): 355-386.* This list of some 350 theses and 70 dissertations on New Mexico topics was compiled principally in response to a 1967 questionnaire. Some beyond that date have been added. The list starts with an 1889 dissertation and a 1903 thesis. It excludes all items dealing with the history of New Mexico in an Arizona checklist of 1965. Interdisciplinary contributions and items of a historical nature that are normally listed under other subject classifications as economics, education, and sociology are included. Except for a list of those that belong in a general category, these graduate essays are classified under Spanish, Mexican, Territorial, and Since Statehood labels. The greatest number fall under the Territorial category with the history of education, military affairs, and regional studies in the forefront. The list reveals certain virtually untouched areas.
                                                                              D. L. Smith

2856. Murphy, Lawrence R. RECONSTRUCTION IN NEW MEXICO. *New Mexico Hist. R. 1968 43(2): 99-115.* Analyzes and evaluates Reconstruction activities in New Mexico "as they affected the abolition of Indian slavery and debt peonage." Although various attempts were made to end slavery—the Civil Rights Bill of 1866, the 13th amendment, and special acts concerning New Mexico—they encountered determined and effective opposition. After Reconstruction, "with economic and social change, involuntary servitude in New Mexico disappeared." Based chiefly on newspapers and Territorial Papers of the United States Senate, New Mexico, NA-RG 46; 63 notes. D. F. Henderson

2857. Murphy, Lawrence R. WILLIAM F. M. ARNY, SECRETARY OF NEW MEXICO TERRITORY, 1862-1867. *Arizona and the West 1966 8(4): 323-338.* A devout member of the Disciples of Christ who was inspired with reforming zeal and an ardent Republican Party worker who had political training and experience, William Frederick Millon Arny was awarded an Indian agency in New Mexico in 1861. Pursued with characteristic enthusiasm and determination, this earned him appointment as Secretary for the Territory of New Mexico the following year. Due to the Governor's illness and absence, Arny became acting governor and moved to punish those who had aided recent Confederate invaders. Abolitionist Arny took steps to liberate hundreds of Indians held as slaves and to erase a peon law which had resulted in involuntary servitude. He took steps to promote education under the Federal Morrill Act. His influence gained the removal of the corrupt Democratic Superintendent of Indian Affairs and a presidential appointment of a Republican in his place. By the return of the Governor, Arny had successfully formed a strong Republican nucleus which was grappling with the Democratic organization for control of New Mexico. Throughout the remaining years, Arny used the powers of his office and his personal influence to firmly establish his party in the territory and to assure its dominance for many successive decades. Based in part on manuscripts in the National Archives; illus., 43 notes.

D. L. Smith

2858. Naegle, Conrad K. THE REBELLION OF GRANT COUNTY, NEW MEXICO IN 1876. *Arizona and the West 1968 10(3): 225-240.* The Santa Fe ring, a political and economic clique, maintained a strangle-hold on New Mexico politics in the 1870's. Gerrymandering and the use of Federal troops in the legislative halls were among the steps the ring took to keep control. Grant County, with Silver City as its seat, in southwestern New Mexico was much victimized by the ring's actions. Both a Grant County man elected as speaker of the House and the House were deprived of power when the ring organized and empowered its own House. Silver City was denied incorporation, and the county was refused legislation necessary to establish an effective school system. The county representation was reduced by proclamation of the governor. The situation deteriorated to the point that Grant County adopted a "Declaration of Independence" from the Territory of New Mexico and clamored for annexation to Arizona. Arizona believed it would benefit by the annexation of Grant County, the most flourishing county in all of New Mexico during the 1870's. Arizona's delegate to Congress introduced an annexation resolution, but it died while in committee. With Congress considering the matter, the Santa Fe ring viewed the desires and needs of Grant County more favorably. The county and its seat were granted unusual powers of local self-government and autonomy in education. 10 illus., 40 notes. D. L. Smith

2859. Rasch, Philip J. FEUDING AT FARMINGTON. *New Mexico Hist. R. 1965 40(3): 215-232.* Attempts to unravel the story of the feud between the partisans of Lawrence G. Murphy, James J. Dolan and John H. Riley on the one side and those of Alexander A. McSween and John S. Chisum on the other. The feud commenced in 1878 at Lincoln County, New Mexico, and did not completely subside until the early 1880's. Contemporary newspaper material in the New Mexico State Records Center and Archives and statements by the descendants of various individuals involved are used. 54 notes. D. F. Henderson

2860. Rouss, G. Martin. THE ARCHIVES IN THE SPECIAL COLLECTION OF THE ZIMMERMAN LIBRARY. *Great Plains J. 1972 11(2): 116-124.* Traces the growing awareness from 1927 to 1940 of the need to preserve archival materials concerning New Mexico history. After the legislature designated the New Mexico Historical Society official custodian of the State's archives, materials began to be deposited at the

University of New Mexico in Albuquerque. Stimulation came from the 400th anniversary of the Coronado Expedition (1940) and the Works Progress Administration's activities. Newspaper collections and literary, business, and oral history were added between 1940 and 1959. The legislature again stimulated growth of the collection in 1959 when it created a State Commission of Public Records. Today the collection, housed in the university's Zimmerman Library, spans seven centuries and includes 284 collections. Mentions the most notable, by title. Lists the major divisions of the indexes. Based on primary and secondary sources; 25 notes.

O. H. Zabel

2861. Sanchez, Jane C. "AGITATED, PERSONAL, AND UNSOUND. . . ." *New Mexico Hist. R. 1966 41(3): 217-230.* Detailed account of the conflict between ex-General Robert Byington Mitchell, governor of the New Mexico Territory, and the territorial legislature. On 14 January 1868, the legislature passed a joint resolution requesting Congress to remove the governor, and two weeks later passed another resolution requesting congressional approval of all laws not approved by the governor before the final adjournment of the legislative assembly. The difficulties were resolved by the departure of Governor Mitchell in February 1869. Based on Assembly Papers, State Records Center and Archives, Santa Fe; 21 notes. D. F. Henderson

2862. Shishkin, J. L. "THE NEW MUSEUM IS A WONDER. . . ." *Palacio 1967 74(3): 5-16.* Traces the early history of the Fine Arts building of the Museum of New Mexico from its inception in 1912 to its completion in 1917. A need for another structure to house the growing collections of the museum had been predicted in 1912 by Dr. Edgar L. Hewitt, the founder of the museum. The design of the building was inspired by the Spanish Mission churches at Acoma, San Felipe, and Cochiti Pueblos. Illus. S. A. Eger

2863. Theisen, Gerald, ed. A BRIEF MEMOIR. *New Mexico Hist. Rev. 1971 46(4): 351-355.* Reproduces the memoir of Julian Aragon y Perea from his birth in 1830 to approximately 1895. Aragon witnessed as a youth the American takeover of New Mexico, traveled with an ox-train returning to the United States from Santa Fe in 1848, organized a company of Union volunteers at the outbreak of the Civil War but resigned in 1862 when most of his company deserted, and after the war applied himself to commerce, planting, freighting, and breeding cattle. 5 notes. D. F. Henderson

2864. Warner, Michael J. PROTESTANT MISSIONARY ACTIVITY AMONG THE NAVAJO, 1890-1912. *New Mexico Hist. R. 1970 45(3): 209-232.* Commencing with the so-called Quaker Peace Policy formulated by President Ulysses S. Grant, the increase in missionary activities was dramatic. The Peace Policy was terminated in 1882. Although the Government continued to allot reservation lands to those missionary societies which expressed a desire to begin or expand their efforts with the Indians, activity declined. The author discusses general missionary activity during the years 1890-1901 and 1901-12, and Presbyterian Activity during the years 1901-12. 60 notes.

D. F. Henderson

2865. Weber, David J., ed. SAMUEL ELLISON ON THE ELECTION OF 1857. *New Mexico Hist. R. 1969 44(3): 215-221.* Reprints two letters from the territorial secretary of New Mexico, Samuel James Josiah Webb relating to the 1857 election for delegate to the U.S. Congress between Miguel Antonio Otero and Spruce M. Baird. 16 notes. D. F. Henderson

2866. Westphall, Victor. THE PRESIDENT'S REPORT, DECEMBER 14, 1963. *New Mexico Hist. R. 1964 39(2): 157-159.* Traces briefly the history of the Historical Society of New Mexico, founded in 1859 at Santa Fe. D. F. Henderson

Arizona

2867. Ball, Larry D., ed. NO CURE, NO PAY, A TOM HORN LETTER. *J. of Arizona Hist. 1967 8(3): 200-202.* An edited letter which Tom Horn, sometime army scout, lawman, and Pinkerton operative, wrote to US Marshal William K. Meade on 7 November 1896. In

it Horn offered, if well rewarded for success and allowed to go out alone, to kill or drive out the "Black Jack Band" which was then terrorizing southeastern Arizona. Apparently his offer was not accepted by Marshal Meade. The document is in the correspondence of the US Marshal's Office, Arizona Territory, Arizona Pioneers' Historical Society. Illus., 5 notes.
　　　　　　　　　　　　　　　　　　　　　　　　R. J. Roske

2868.　Blair, Bob D.　FOOTNOTES TO HISTORY: THE MURDER OF WILLIAM JOE GILES, 1905.　J. of Arizona Hist. 1966 7(1): 27-34. An account of the shooting of William Joe Giles in Winslow, Arizona, in October 1905 by J. N. "Pete" Pemberton, who was sentenced to 25 years in the territorial penitentiary in Yuma but who did not serve the complete term. Illus., biblio.　　　　　　　J. D. Filipiak

2869.　Bowe, Patricia.　VIGNETTES OF ARIZONA PIONEERS: JAMES MITCHELL BARNEY: HISTORIAN OF HISTORIANS. Arizoniana 1963 4(2): 28-34. Barney's family became prominent at Yuma around 1864, largely owing to his uncle, Colonel J. M. Barney. Colonel Barney owned the Silver King Mine, laid a road across the desert and was elected first mayor of Arizona City. James Barney, whose mother was a Papago Indian, worked as surveyor, county recorder and engineer in the US Grazing Service in Arizona. He became the historian of Arizona and his writings represent personal experience and careful research into records.　　　　　　　　　　　　　　　M. Petrie

2870.　Brandes, Ray and Wallace, Andrew.　A CENTENNIAL CHECKLIST OF READINGS FOR THE STUDY AND TEACHING OF ARIZONA HISTORY.　Arizoniana 1963 4(1): 14-22; (2): 19-27; (3): 9-18; and (4): 39-48. Bibliography on Arizona history. Topical arrangement.

2871.　Dailey, Elsie M.　JOHN BAPTISTE SALPOINTE: FIRST RO-MAN CATHOLIC BISHOP OF ARIZONA.　Arizoniana 1963 4(1): 23-30.

2872.　Doan, May Cargill.　I WOULDN'T TRADE THESE YES-TERDAYS: THE REMINISCENCE OF MAY CARGILL DOAN. J. of Arizona Hist. 1965 6(3): 116-131. The first part of the memoirs of a daughter of Andrew Hays Cargill, an Arizona pioneer, regarding her father and providing a description of life in Yuma, Arizona, after she arrived there in 1902. Editorial and corrective notes have been added. Illus. To be continued.　　　　　　　　J. D. Filipiak

2873.　Doan, May Cargill.　I WOULDN'T TRADE THESE YES-TERDAYS: THE REMINISCENCES OF MAY CARGILL DOAN. J. of Arizona Hist. 1965 6(4): 188-203. Conclusion of the author's reminiscences of early 20th-century life in the Arizona Territory, particularly the communities of Yuma and Silverbell. Illus., map, notes.
　　　　　　　　　　　　　　　　　　　　　　　　J. D. Filipiak

2874.　Fazio, Steven A.　MARCUS AURELIUS SMITH: ARIZONA DELEGATE AND SENATOR.　Arizona and the West 1970 12(1): 23-62. After training and practice in law in his native Kentucky and a few years in California, Marcus Aurelius Smith (1852-1924) moved to Tombstone, Arizona Territory, in 1880. In this booming mining community he soon became well-known and respected. His interests centered on Democratic politics and the local law-and-order theme. After a term as a district attorney, Smith was elected in 1886 as the Territorial delegate to Congress. This was the first of eight elections he was to win to that position; and he further served two terms as a US Senator from Arizona. Smith was an old-line conservative who based his career on wide popular appeal and solid economic backing. He worked hard, but his impact was not great. He repeatedly championed statehood for Arizona but did not get it. Failure rewarded most of his efforts to get reclamation legislation. He was a significant and successful political figure in Arizona for some 40 years, faithfully echoing his constituents' hopes and dreams and satisfying the needs of various Arizona corporate interests. 4 illus., 98 notes.
　　　　　　　　　　　　　　　　　　　　　　　　D. L. Smith

2875.　Feather, Adlai.　ORIGIN OF THE NAME ARIZONA. New Mexico Hist. R. 1964 39(2): 89-100. Three men were instrumental in getting the name "Arizona" applied, first, to the territory and, later, the state which bears that appellation. José Francisco Velasco revived the name in Noticias Estadisticas del Estado de Sonora, etc. (Mexico, 1850).

Charles D. Poston, an adventurer and promoter of mines and land grants, drawing upon Velasco's account, suggested the name to James A. Lucas, a man interested in the territorial status of the area, who accepted it. The name was adopted in 1856 and no other was suggested thereafter.
　　　　　　　　　　　　　　　　　　　　　　　　D. F. Henderson

2876.　Feather, Adlai.　THE TERRITORIES OF ARIZONA. New Mexico Hist. R. 1964 39(1): 16-31. In February 1863 when President Lincoln signed the document separating the territory of Arizona from New Mexico, there were two territories of Arizona. One was formed by the Confederacy, which included Doña Ana County of New Mexico, and one was formed by the United States. Which would survive depended upon the outcome of the war. 16 notes.　　　D. F. Henderson

2877.　Fireman, Bert M.　FREMONT'S ARIZONA ADVENTURE. Am. West 1964 1(1): 8-19. The collection of political debts by John C. Fremont secured for him appointment to the governorship of Arizona Territory in 1878. During his three years in office, "Fremont's promotion of mining, and incidentally his own welfare, was consistent with activities of his predecessor and his successor. He reached farther than they because of his prominence. He was less successful, possibly because he was unskilled and unlucky in business." Whether his "aberrations and follies" can be attributed to a lack of principle or whether he was unable to appraise men and situations remains an unanswered question.
　　　　　　　　　　　　　　　　　　　　　　　　D. L. Smith

2878.　Fontana, Bernard L.　PRESIDENT PIPES FROM ARIZONA. Chesopiean 1968 6(6): 160-161. "Glazed clay pipes with the label and molded likeness of 3 different U.S. Presidents, Washington, Fillmore, and Pierce, have been unearthed on sites in southern Arizona. The author is trying to obtain information concerning their origin and date of manufacture."　　　　　　　　　　　　　　　　　　AIA(1:3:15)

2879.　Goff, John S.　THE APPOINTMENT, TENURE AND RE-MOVAL OF TERRITORIAL JUDGES: ARIZONA - A CASE STUDY.　Am. J. of Legal Hist. 1968 12(3): 211-231. A history of the appointment and removal of Arizona territorial judges during 1863-1912. Emphasizes the political influence exercised upon appointments and removals. Details the type of man appointed. 100 notes.
　　　　　　　　　　　　　　　　　　　　　　　　L. A. Knafla

2880.　Goff, John S.　THE ARIZONA CAREER OF COLES BASH-FORD.　J. of Arizona Hist. 1969 10(1): 19-36. Bashford (1816-78), a native of New York, became a lawyer and moved in 1850 to Wisconsin. A power in the new Republican Party, he lost a disputed election for the governorship in 1855; the State Supreme Court seated him in 1856. Shortly after he left office, there appeared some evidence that a railroad had bribed him. Although never convicted of any wrongdoing, Bashford left Wisconsin permanently in 1863. At the organization of the Arizona Territory he moved there, settling in what became the town of Prescott. He became territorial attorney general, as well as the first attorney admitted to practice in the territory. He served in the territorial upper house in the first and second legislatures. In 1866, despite circulation of the old Wisconsin charges, he won election as a congressional delegate for a two-year term. Because he found the delegate position expensive, he did not run for reelection in 1868. Instead he served as territorial secretary from April 1869 until his health began to fail in July 1876. He died in April 1878. Based on contemporary documents, correspondence, and newspapers; photo, 62 notes.　　　　　　R. J. Roske

2881.　Goff, John S.　CHARLES D. POSTON FOR GOVERNOR! J. of Arizona Hist. 1967 8(1): 45-53. Describes the series of unsuccessful attempts by Charles D. Poston, the "Father of Arizona Territory," to be named territorial governor. With each change of administration for most of the period 1863 to 1902, Poston tried to get the appointment without success.　　　　　　　　　　　　　　　　　J. D. Filipiak

2882.　Goff, John S.　JOHN TITUS, CHIEF JUSTICE OF ARIZONA, 1870-1874.　Arizona and the West 1972 14(1): 25-44. After an eastern law career and five years as chief justice of Utah Territory, Titus was appointed to a similar position in Arizona Territory. During his tenure (1870-74) he presided over the Federal and Territorial courts within his jurisdiction. The Federal court was comparable to present district courts, and the Territorial court resembled present State superior courts. Titus was regarded as one of the ablest and most respected of the 40 territorial justices in Arizona. He maintained good relations with Washington, D.C., and generally avoided antagonizing local interest groups. He remained nonpolitical and independent, and reflected a practical interpretation of frontier attitudes and needs. He defended the settlers against the Indians, and territorial rights against the Federal Government. 2 illus., 43 notes.   D. L. Smith

2883. Goff, John S. MICHIGAN JUSTICE IN ARIZONA: HENRY T. BACKUS. *Michigan Hist. 1968 52(2): 110-122.* Discusses the legal career of Henry Titus Backus as one of Arizona's three territorial judges between 1865 and 1869. From the legislative records of Arizona it is conluded that "the governmental and legal systems of frontier areas were largely reproductions of those of the settled and established states." Based on documents in the National Archives; 5 illus., 60 notes.
J. K. Flack

2884. Goff, John. THE ORGANIZATION OF THE FEDERAL DISTRICT COURT IN ARIZONA, 1912-1913. *Am. J. of Legal Hist. 1964 8(2): 172-179.* The establishment of a federal district court in Arizona, when that state entered the Union in 1912, was deeply embroiled in the national politics of the period. Democrats successfully delayed a permanent appointment until President Wilson had come into office in March, 1913. Arizona's willingness to experiment with judicial recall and advisory preference elections for federal judges constituted the main factor in President Taft's opposition to the views of Democratic leaders.
N. C. Brockman

2885. Goff, John S. WILLIAM T. HOWELL AND THE HOWELL CODE OF ARIZONA. *Am. J. of Legal Hist. 1967 11(3): 221-233.* A biographical outline of the life of William T. Howell, Federal judge in the Arizona Territory (1863-65), and some notes on the enactment and revision of a legal code written for the territory by the jurist. The author traces Howell's life from his birth in Michigan, through his various public and private occupations in the Midwest and in the Arizona Territory, to his death after returning to Michigan late in life. Based on the Howell File, *Appointment Papers,* Department of Justice, National Archives, the *Newaygo Republican,* and Journals of the Territorial Legislature; 67 notes.   G. P. Smith

2886. Harte, John Bret. FRANK C. LOCKWOOD: HISTORIAN OF THE SOUTHWEST. *Arizona and the West 1967 9(2): 109-130.* Frank Cummins Lockwood, trained in literature and philosophy, had a varied career as a minister, college professor, Chautauqua lecturer, temperance worker, politician, and author. In 1916 he joined the faculty of the University of Arizona where he served in many capacities including a stint as "interim President." Following World War I service with the YMCA and as an Army lecturer abroad, he was able to pursue an avocational interest in history more diligently, particularly the pioneer history of Arizona. From published materials and government documents, Lockwood went to manuscript diaries, journals and reminiscences, and the newspapers. He sought out first-hand accounts in the vernacular, being more interested in the characters who played upon this stage than in the forces which motivated them. He was rarely profound or philosophical. Six of his 10 historical books, substantial portions of the other four, and 17 of his articles were biographical. 4 illus., 46 notes.
D. L. Smith

2887. Herner, Charles H. ARIZONA'S COWBOY CAVALRY. *Arizoniana 1964 5(4): 10-26.* "No other state or territory matched the speed and efficiency with which Arizona gathered her first quota of volunteers for the Spanish-American War." Alexander O. Brodie, a graduate of West Point (1870) with experience in Arizona, was chosen to head the volunteers, with William Owen "Buckey" O'Neill and James H. McClintock as other members of the triumvirate. Brodie was supported by the governor, the newspapers, and the citizens in general. O'Neill died a spectacular death at the head of his troop. In 1901 Roosevelt appointed Brodie governor of Arizona. Illus., 75 notes.   E. P. Stickney

2888. Hinton, Harwood. ARIZONA THESES & DISSERTATIONS: A PRELIMINARY CHECKLIST. *Arizona and the West 1965 7(3): 239-264.* The checklist of graduate degree research papers was compiled primarily from a 1963 questionnaire submitted to graduate schools throughout the country. It is emphasized that the list is not

exhaustive because of the incomplete response to the questionnaire and because other sources of information still need to be explored, including topics in other fields related to history. The list is subdivided under six headings: general, Spanish, Mexican, territorial, since statehood, and addenda. The last is an unclassified list compiled since the questionnaire. It includes 275 masters' theses and 46 doctoral dissertations. The list reveals that popular areas of research for graduate students are the territorial period with Indian affairs leading, and since statehood with politics in the forefront. Neglected areas include biography.   D. L. Smith

2889. Hogan, F. William. VIGNETTES OF ARIZONA PIONEERS: JOHN MILLER: PIONEER LAWMAN. *Arizoniana 1963 4(2): 41-45.* John Miller, a colorful personality, acted as constable, US marshal, restaurant keeper, poundmaster, jailor and later as judge, postmaster and chairman of the Board of Supervisors. He killed a man in self-defense and had several fights with Apaches.   M. Petrie

2890. Hunter, George S. THE BULL MOOSE MOVEMENT IN ARIZONA. *Arizona and the West 1968 10(4): 343-362.* When President William Howard Taft, in a 1910 speech in Phoenix, belittled the initiative, referendum, and recall reforms which Arizona hoped to incorporate into its constitution, he hurt the already sagging fortunes of the territory's Republican Party. In 1911 when he vetoed the new Arizona constitution, popular support shifted to the Democrats. These factors enabled personal friends of Theodore Roosevelt to launch the progressive movement in Arizona under the Bull Moose banner. Roosevelt spoke in Arizona and the Progressives bought a newspaper and campaigned diligently. The results in Arizona mirrored the national outcome. The Republicans were not reunified until after the national convention of 1916. The State's Democratic Party remained entrenched in county and State politics. 4 illus., 50 notes.   D. L. Smith

2891. Johnston, Bernice. FIFTY YEARS OF THE ARIZONA ARCHAEOLOGICAL AND HISTORICAL SOCIETY. *Kiva 1966 32(2): 41-56.* Traces the history of the society founded 14 April 1916. Photographs of charter members, and students in Indian costume, and excursions such as one to Lee's Ferry via Tuba City in 1923 highlight the text. The society was lots of fun, but members managed to get in serious digging between parties, papers, and publications. A program card, reproduced from the 16 October 1916 meeting, indicates the depth of early society endeavors. 13 photos.   M. W. Machan

2892. Lamar, Howard R. CARPETBAGGERS FULL OF DREAMS: A FUNCTIONAL VIEW OF THE ARIZONA PIONEER POLITICIAN. *Arizona and the West 1965 7(3): 187-206.* The pioneer Federal appointees of Arizona are usually described as a group of parasitic carpetbaggers who, like the industrial and railroad robber barons, made negative rather than positive contributions. Revisionist studies of the robber barons reclothe them as creative amoral geniuses who made intelligent contributions to the development of the industrial revolution. The author examines Arizona's political pioneers in a functional way instead of using the usual moralistic approach to determine their positive contributions to the maturation process of the territorial period. In reviewing the political evolution in Arizona through the careers of some of its prominent political practitioners, particularly Richard C. McCormick, Anson P. K. Safford, and John C. Frémont, the author discerns a similarity to the overall process in other territories. They were the propagandists, brokers, and the entrepreneurs that were necessary for the transition of the territory through the pioneering process. 3 illus., 44 notes.
D. L. Smith

2893. Mattison, Ray H. THE CONTROVERSY OVER THE TUMACACORI AND BACA LAND GRANTS. *J. of Arizona Hist. 1967 8(2): 71-90.* The lengthy legal controversy regarding the two land grants in southern Arizona is covered, from their time of assignment through various court cases extending into the 20th century. 70 notes, mostly from government sources.   J. D. Filipiak

2894. Meredith, H. L. RECLAMATION IN THE SALT RIVER VALLEY, 1902-1917. *J. of the West 1968 7(1): 76-83.* Describes the irrigation project in the Salt River Valley of Arizona. This was the first successful major attempt to reclaim a portion of the arid West and "examples in construction, contracting, dealing with large numbers of private land owners and decisions on water rights made the valley the prototype followed throughout the region." Based largely on government documents; map, 28 notes.   E. A. Erickson

2895. Morey, Roy D. THE EXECUTIVE VETO IN ARIZONA: ITS USE AND LIMITATIONS. *Western Pol. Q. 1966 19(3): 504-515.* The veto is an overrated tool of executive power, and this is true in Arizona, rated a "strong" veto State, because its Governor has an extended period of time in which to exercise his veto and because to override it requires a two-thirds vote of the entire membership in each House. From 1912 to 1963, almost 17 thousand bills were introduced in the legislature, and 4,634 became law; of these but 182 were vetoed, or four percent of all those presented to Governors, while 12 percent of these were passed over the veto. The vote has permitted the Governor to participate in the legislative process but certainly not to lead it; it is rather a negative device occasionally used by rather harassed Governors against harassed legislatures. Fig., 3 tables, 30 notes.   H. Aptheker

2896. Morey, Roy D. THE SPECIAL SESSION: ASSET OR LIABILITY? *Southwestern Social Sci. Q. 1966 46(4): 437-444.* Analysis of the special session in Arizona from 1912 to 1963, including the reasons for calling sessions, the effect of the threat of a special session, and success of the special session. 3 tables.   D. F. Henderson

2897. Olsen, Robert W., Jr. PIPE SPRING, ARIZONA, AND THEREABOUTS. *J. of Arizona Hist. 1965 6(1): 11-20.* Provides a summary of the history of the vicinity of Pipe Spring, Arizona, a national monument since 1923, and notes early expeditions that passed the point, the origin of its name, and its acquisition by the Mormons. Based on primary and secondary sources; illus., biblio. note.
                                                         J. D. Filipiak

2898. Olsen, Robert W., Jr. WINSOR CASTLE: MORMON FRONTIER FORT AT PIPE SPRING. *Utah Hist. Q. 1966 34(3): 218-226.* Describes how pressure on the Church of the Latter-Day Saints to populate the remote frontier regions led to the establishment of a stock-raising company and the building of a fort for protection against the Indians at Pipe Spring, near the Arizona-Utah border. Since 1923 the restored fort has been a part of the National Park System. Based on manuscript records in the Church of Latter-Day Saints Historian's Library, Salt Lake City, and contemporary newspaper accounts; photos.   S. L. Jones

2899. Parker, Marjorie Clum. JOHN P. CLUM: THE INSIDE STORY OF AN INIMITABLE WESTERNER. *Am. West 1972 9(1): 32-37.* Young John Philip Clum (1851-1932) of New York was nominated by his Dutch Reformed Church as agent to the San Carlos Apache in Arizona Territory. He ordered the US cavalry off the reservation and rebuilt a concept of self-government akin to tribal law. After three years thousands of other Apache had joined them and lived at peace on the reservation. Clum and the Apache militia made the only forcible capture of Geronimo. Arizona merchants and political pressure forced the Indian Bureau to return the Army and thereby undo all Clum's accomplishments. He then established and became the courageous and irascible reporter of the *Tombstone Epitaph*. He was elected mayor of Tombstone. After his defense (in the *Epitaph*) of the Earp brothers' role in the OK Corral incident put a price on his own head, and after the premature death of his wife, Clum sold the paper to spend the rest of his life writing and wandering. Among his other colorful adventures, he was dispatched during the gold rush as a special commissioner to establish the first American post office in Alaska. 4 illus.   D. L. Smith

2900. Patzman, Stephen N. LOUIS JOHN FREDERICK JAEGER: ENTREPRENEUR OF THE COLORADO RIVER. *Arizoniana 1963 4(1): 31-36.*

2901. Pedersen, Gilbert J. THE FOUNDING FIRST. *J. of Arizona Hist. 1966 7(2): 45-58.* A revision of a paper given at the 6th Annual Arizona Historical Convention in May 1965 on the First Territorial Legislature of Arizona which convened in Prescott in 1864. The major work of the legislature is described, particularly their enactment of a new legal code drawn up by William T. Howell.   J. D. Filipiak

2902. Peterson, Thomas H., Jr. THE BUCKLEY HOUSE: TUCSON STATION FOR THE BUTTERFIELD OVERLAND MAIL. *J. of Arizona Hist. 1966 7(4): 153-167.* Early in October 1858 the Butter-

field Overland made its first stop in Tucson, its station being the Buckley House located in present downtown Tucson. The successive changes of ownership of the building are mentioned. Illus., 45 notes.
                                                         J. D. Filipiak

2903. Powell, Donald M. CURRENT ARIZONA BIBLIOGRAPHY. *Arizona Q. 1969 25(3): 229-233.* A bibliography which "attempts to be a complete list of all separately issued works of nonfiction about Arizona except those from official state and federal sources. From the latter selected items are included." The present list of 52 titles covers the first half of 1969 and includes doctoral dissertations, articles in university bulletins, publications of small regional presses, private (company-sponsored) works, as well as standard articles and books. "Current Arizona Bibliography" appears twice a year in *Arizona Quarterly*.
                                                          J. M. Hawes

2904. Rusho, W. L. LIVING HISTORY AT LEE'S FERRY. *J. of the West 1968 7(1): 64-75.* A glimpse at the history of the West through the people (missionary, cowboy, Indian, outlaw, lawman, trader, settler, and government scientist) who have used Lee's Ferry, Arizona, to cross the Colorado River. Based on narratives of Western expeditions and secondary sources; illus., map, 33 notes.   E. A. Erickson

2905. Sacks, Benjamin. ARIZONA'S ANGRY MAN: UNITED STATES MARSHAL MILTON B. DUFFIELD. *J. of Arizona Hist. 1967 8(1): 1-29; (2): 91-119.* Part I. Born in Virginia in 1810, Duffield was the first US Marshal in Arizona Territory, appointed 6 March 1863. His life is detailed to his resignation in November 1865. 97 notes. Part II. Concerns Duffield's life from 1865 to his murder on 5 June 1874. The author considers him "one of the truly unique characters of the west." 88 notes, primarily from unpublished sources.   J. D. Filipiak

2906. Sacks, Benjamin. THE CREATION OF THE TERRITORY OF ARIZONA. *Arizona and the West 1963 5(1): 29-62, and (2): 109-148.* Part I. The acquisition of land (of which Arizona was a part) by the United States in 1848 as a result of the Mexican War complicated the prevailing sectional strife which was fast becoming the central problem of the country. This controversy was a greater obstacle to territorial organization for Arizona than the woeful public ignorance of the region and its potential for development. The territory of New Mexico, including the area of Arizona, was created by the Compromise of 1850. The Gadsden Purchase (1853), increasing population, opening of mines, disposition of public lands, Indian depredations, a potential transcontinental railroad, and the establishment of overland mail routes were pressing considerations for territorial organization apart from New Mexico. Prominent among the champions of such organization were Sylvester Mowry and Charles Debrill Poston. Continued frustration prompted the establishment in 1860 of a short-lived extralegal provisional government for the territory of Arizona which comprised the southern one-third of the present states of Arizona and New Mexico. Part II. Secession of Southern states in 1860 seemingly halted the movement to create Arizona as a Federal territory; but it brought increased importance to Arizona in the minds of the leaders of the seceded states. Central to this thinking was the possibility of a transcontinental wagon road or railway across the area to link the Confederacy with the California gold fields, new-found mineral wealth in Arizona, and the renewed hope of Texans to regain land they had lost in the Compromise of 1850. Territorial organization of Arizona under the Confederacy was granted in February 1862. Northern military forces soon brought the collapse of this government, which was replaced in June 1862 by a provisional territorial arrangement under a Union officer. Poston's efforts in the territory and in the national capital earned for him the sobriquet of "Father of Arizona." Insufficient credit has been given to Samuel Peter Heintzelman, whose military and mining efforts were notable labors for the cause. The article, with additional appendixes and illustrations, is to be published in book form. Based on newspapers, government documents, published and manuscript source materials, and other monographic studies of the author in preparation; illus., maps, 145 notes.   D. L. Smith

2907. Sacks, Benjamin. PROCLAMATION IN THE WILDERNESS: THE SALARY CLAUSE IN THE TERRITORIAL ACT, WITH A NOTE ON ILLEGAL PAYMENTS TO GOV. GOODWIN. *Arizoniana 1964 5(3): 1-13.* Describes the circumstances under which John Noble Goodwin (1824-87) issued the proclamation establishing the territorial government of Arizona on 27 December 1863 at Navajo Springs. "The reason usually given for raising the flag at Navajo Springs is that the officials - because they were late in arriving - desired to be entered on the payroll as soon as possible after crossing into Arizona, presumably in consideration of a clause in the Organic Act which stipulated that 'no salary shall be due or paid the officers created by this act until they shall have entered upon the duties of their respective offices *within the Territory'*. . . . The Act of Congress provided that in order to receive their salaries for the year 1863 the new officials must arrive within the limits of the new territory on or before the last day of December 1863. . . . Although [Goodwin] received two different salaries concurrently from March 4, 1865, to March 31, 1866, one as Governor and the other as Delegate to the 39th Congress, he did not report these dual payments to the proper authorities in Congress. . . . Whether or not the overpayments were ultimately returned has not been ascertained, but the debt was on record as late as 1884." 48 notes.   D. D. Cameron

2908. Sacks, Benjamin. SYLVESTER MOWRY: ARTILLERY-MAN, LIBERTINE, ENTREPRENUER. *Am. West 1964 1(3): 14-24, 79.* Sylvester Mowry, an 1852 West Point graduate, was commissioned and assigned to duty in Utah. He soon became involved with a married daughter-in-law of Brigham Young. Thus began the spectacular career of "this lusty, hot-tempered officer." By 1855 he was stationed at Fort Yuma and shortly became interested in the Spanish history of the area, its Indians, and its mines. While he is described as a "flamboyant voluptuary" and a "sensual artilleryman" he nevertheless played prominent roles in mining and politics. His facile pen publicized the resources of the Gadsden Purchase. Mowry was thrice elected as delegate to Congress from the Territory of Arizona. "More than any other man prior to the Civil War," he "labored indefatigably" for the political maturation of Arizona. Based on an unpublished comprehensive biographical study. Illus., bibliographical note.   D. L. Smith

2909. Smalley, Flora. "WE SLEPT IN THE WAGON": AN ARIZONA CAMPING TRIP, 1902. *J. of Arizona Hist. 1971 12(3): 183-212.* The author joined her sister and brother-in-law on a wagon trip in Arizona in 1902. The brother-in-law was inspecting a proposed route for an extension of the Santa Fe Railroad. They traveled from Tucson to Oracle, Mammoth, Dudleyville, Riverside, Troy, Florence, Red Rock, and back to Tucson. Includes the author's seven letters back home, describing the overland trip. 17 photos.   D. L. Smith

2910. Thrapp, Dan L. THE "MARRIAGE" OF AL SIEBER. *J. of Arizona Hist. 1970 11(3): 175-178.* In his biography of Al Sieber, a famous Indian scout of Arizona, the author asserted that Sieber succeeded so well with the Indians because "he left their women alone." In the 1960's, progeny of Al Sieber by Apache women began to cast doubt on the author's assertion. To his satisfaction, however, he has now established that the Sieber children were offspring of a Yavapai Al Sieber. The Indian was probably an orphan raised by the famous bachelor scout, and probably took the scout's name as his own. 6 notes.   D. L. Smith

2911. Trockur, Emanuel. NAVAJOLAND'S FIRST PRINTING ESTABLISHMENT. *Palacio 1968 75(3): 36-41.* A major problem facing all missionaries working with the Navajo Indians has been the linguistic barrier. When the Franciscans began their mission at St. Michaels, Arizona, in October 1898, they quickly learned that few Navajos spoke English. None of the missionaries knew Navajo. To surmount the problem, they began intensive study of the Navajo language and also devised ways to transcribe it. In 1909 the Franciscans set up the first printing establishment on the Navajo Reservation, and in 1910, along with a Navajo-English catechism, they published the *Ethnological Dictionary of the Navajo Language.* Since then, the Franciscans have produced many Navajo-English books, both religious and secular. Illus.
          S. A. Eger

2912. Walker, Dale L. ARIZONA'S BUCKY O'NEILL AND THE ROUGH RIDERS. *Montana 1971 21(1): 60-71.* William Owen O'Neill was in turn a newspaperman, law officer, candidate for Congress, mayor of Prescott (Arizona), and a captain in Theodore Roosevelt's Rough Riders in the Spanish-American War. O'Neill was killed early in the action at the battle of San Juan Hill. His life was marked by a blend of scholarly intelligence, bravery to the point of recklessness, and considerable ambition. 3 illus., 6 photos.   S. R. Davison

2913. Walker, Henry Pickering. TEACHER TO THE MOJAVES: THE EXPERIENCES OF GEORGE W. NOCK, 1887-1889. *Arizona and the West 1967 9(2): 143-166; (3): 259-280.* Part I. Nock and his family lived on the Colorado River Indian Reservation from 1887 to 1890. The 300,800-acre reserve was located on the Colorado River between Yuma, Arizona, and Needles, California, largely within the present State of Arizona. Nock served as superintendent and principal teacher at the Colorado Indian Agency school on the reservation and his wife as matron and teacher. A seamstress, a cook, and a laundress completed the personnel roster of the school. Enrollment during the Nock period varied from 55 to 70, about 60 percent of the eligible Mojave children on the reservation. The fundamentals of reading, writing, arithmetic, and the vocational arts were the concerns of the school. Within a year or so after the Nocks left the reservation he prepared his recollections of the experience among the Mojave as part of a book-length manuscript which he probably hoped to publish. Edited and annotated here are five chapters which describe their stay of several weeks in Yuma and the steamboat trip up the river en route to the reservation, the climate and the country, the agency, and the routine of the school. 4 illus., map, 60 notes. Part II. Contains nine chapters of the Nock manuscript concerning his experiences. They are, essentially, an ethnohistorical account of Mojave life and culture—dress, homes, customs, religion. Included is an eyewitness account of the death rites of the second-in-authority among the local Mojave. The narrative closes with the return of the Nocks to Yuma, en route back to their home in Virginia. 4 illus., 29 notes.   D. L. Smith

2914. Woodin, James Edward. THOMAS FITCH: THE RESTLESS ORATOR. *Arizoniana 1963 4(1): 37-41.*

2915. —. THE ATTEMPT TO STEAL THE CAPITAL IN 1885. *Arizoniana 1963 4(4): 66-69.* Reproduces a letter from R. N. Leatherwood, a Pima County legislator, written from the Council Chamber at Prescott during a meeting of the 13th Territorial Legislature. It reveals plans with Tucson businessmen to obtain funds with which to tempt other legislators to help move the capital from Prescott to Tucson. "Examination of the document against its background of territorial politics reveals the value a single letter may have if critically approached." Facsimile as well as transcription of the letter.   E. P. Stickney

2916. —. DOCUMENTS OF ARIZONA HISTORY: A CONVERSATION BETWEEN GENERAL JAMES H. CARLETON AND SAM HUGHES IN 1862. *Arizoniana 1963 4(3): 26-32.* The importance of reminiscences of pioneers should not be underestimated, but this type of material must be carefully evaluated. The document from the archives of the Arizona Pioneers' Historical Society selected for reprinting here was reproduced with modern spelling in Frank Lockwood's *Life in Old Tucson, 1854-1864, as remembered by the Little Maid, Atanacia Santa Cruz* (1943). The notes and conclusion of the editors in this article show the document's defects. The route, the date, and the people are wrongly remembered, yet the document has been "relied upon by previous writers without any qualifications." Documented.   E. P. Stickney

2917. —. DOCUMENTS OF ARIZONA HISTORY: THE FIRST ARIZONA HISTORICAL SOCIETY - A LETTER FROM RICHARD C. MC CORMICK. *J. of Arizona Hist. 1965 6(2): 90-91.* A page introduction to a letter from McCormick, the first secretary of the Territory and first president of the Arizona Historical Society, to H. R. Stiles, librarian of the Long Island Historical Society, dated 20 December 1864, indicating that the Arizona Society had recently been established.
          J. D. Filipiak

The Pacific Coast States

General

2918. Bolkhovitinov, N. N. RUSSIA AND THE DECLARATION OF THE NON-COLONIZATION PRINCIPLE: NEW ARCHIVAL EVIDENCE. *Oregon Hist. Q. 1971 72(2): 101-126.* In the early 1820's, the Monroe Doctrine, and specifically the noncolonization principle, brought vigorous opposition from British envoys, and at least one diplomatic minister tried to provoke the Russians also to defy the principle. However, evidence indicates that the declaration of the Monroe Doctrine did not inflict harm on the relations between the United States and Russia. In actuality Czarist Russia "did not take seriously all sorts of general declarations of a far-away republican government and did not seek, without serious cause, to endanger its relations with the US." Based on primary and secondary sources; 67 notes.   C. C. Gorchels

2919. Bromberg, Erik. A BIBLIOGRAPHY OF THESES AND DISSERTATIONS CONCERNING THE PACIFIC NORTHWEST AND ALASKA: SUPPLEMENT, 1958-1963. *Oregon Hist. Q. 1964 65(4): 362-391.* Latest supplement to the foundation bibliography published in *Pacific Northwest Quarterly,* of July 1949, which was followed by an extended bibliography in the April 1951 issue of the same periodical. Another supplement appeared in the March 1958 issue of *Oregon Historical Quarterly.* This supplement lists 478 theses and dissertations, followed by a good index.   C. C. Gorchels

2920. Bromberg, Erik. BIBLIOGRAPHY OF THESES AND DISSERTATIONS, PACIFIC NORTHWEST AND ALASKA: SUPPLEMENT, 1964-1970. *Oregon Hist. Q. 1971 72(3): 225-279.* Extensive supplemental bibliography to bring together all the M.A. and Ph.D. theses "written in the Pacific Northwest in the field of social sciences which pertain to Alaska or to the Northwest or any part thereof." This list, covering the production of 1964-70, shows a wide range of topics, including military history, economic history, husband-wife decisionmaking, geography, recreation, newspapers, and conservation, among many others.   C. C. Gorchels

2921. Brown, D. Alexander. BRIDES BY THE BOATLOAD FOR THE NORTHWEST. *Am. Hist. Illus. 1966 1(1): 40-46.* During the first half of the 19th century there was a tremendous shortage of women in Oregon, Washington, and California. Numerous unsuccessful attempts were made to induce women to travel west, but possibly the most successful promoter was Asa Shinn Mercer. His first attempt to bring eligible young women from the east coast failed when he was able to get only 11 girls to accompany him on the journey in 1864. His second attempt in 1865-66 was far more succesful. After many discouraging experiences he was finally able to obtain financial backing and a vessel for the adventure. Although the local newspapers and journals were uncomplimentary of the trip, Mercer was able to get 100 young women to risk the long trip around South America. The cargo of 100 females safely docked in Seattle on 29 May 1866 under the watchful eyes of hundreds of waiting bachelors. Mercer's later life is reviewed. 3 illus.   M. J. McBaine

2922. Clark, Andrew Hill. THE STRATEGY AND ECOLOGY OF MAN'S OCCUPATION OF THE INTERMONTANE NORTHWEST. *Pacific Northwest Q. 1969 60(2): 98-102.* Reviews the book *The Great Columbia Plain: A Historical Geography, 1805-1910* by D. W. Meinig (Seattle: U. of Washington Press, 1968) and discusses such topics in the Pacific Northwest as the unimportance of political boundaries, the importance of places over persons, the role of religious missions, and the reasons why pioneer travelers considered the area unattractive.

C. C. Gorchels

2923. Conrat, Maisie and Conrat, Richard. EXECUTIVE ORDER 9066: ALL ENEMIES LOOK THE SAME. *California Hist. Q. 1971 50(3): 313-320.* A pictorial essay showing anti-Japanese hostility and the evacuation of Japanese Americans and Japanese aliens from the Pacific coast. The photographs are from the National Archives.

A. Hoffman

2924. Edland, Roy E. THE "INDIAN PROBLEM": PACIFIC NORTHWEST, 1879. *Oregon Hist. Q. 1969 70(2): 101-137.* While white settlers were steadily moving into the territory of the northwest corner of the United States in the latter quarter of the 19th century, the native Indians frequently reacted violently as they resisted losing their lands. The objectives and policies at that time of the US Office of Indian Affairs and the US War Department (sometimes in conflict) are reviewed. Such influences as the passing of the Homestead Act and the general economic collapse in the Mississippi valley, 1837 to 1842, are considered. Compromises with the Indian tribes of the Northwest, and special consideration for Chief Moses and his followers, finally brought peace in 1879, as Chief Moses was granted his choice of a separate Indian reservation in northeastern Washington Territory.   C. C. Gorchels

2925. Gough, Barry M. BRITISH POLICY IN THE SAN JUAN BOUNDARY DISPUTE, 1854-72. *Pacific Northwest Q. 1971 62(2): 59-68.* In the boundary dispute between the United States and Great Britain over the San Juan Islands, 1854-72, the British Government acted with restraint characterized by the mid-Victorian era despite strong commercial and military pressures. Studies the background of the controversy and the incidents and negotiations which led to the Treaty of Washington of 1871.   C. C. Gorchels

2926. Gough, Barry M. H.M.S. "AMERICA" ON THE NORTH PACIFIC COAST. *Oregon Hist. Q. 1969 70(4): 292-311.* Gives the background of naval activities on the Pacific coast of North America during the nonviolent struggle between the United States and Great Britain for the Oregon country (1844-48), with special reference to the role of the British warship *America.* John Gordon, captain of the *America,* disobeyed naval instructions and chose instead to participate in a profitable project of delivering specie from Mexico to England. Based on primary sources including official naval correspondence, diaries, and journals.   C. C. Gorchels

2927. Hansen, William A. THOMAS HART BENTON AND THE OREGON QUESTION. *Missouri Hist. R. 1969 63(4): 489-497.* The interest of Thomas Hart Benton (1782-1858) in Oregon developed as a result of his acquaintance with explorers and trappers who made their way to the West by way of St. Louis, and as result of his extensive study and research on the potential of the West during the period August 1818 to September 1820 when he was editor of the St. Louis *Enquirer.* Election to the U.S. Senate in 1820 gave Benton an opportunity to bring his arguments in support of American expansion before a national audience. Hundreds of other voices were raised in support of American interests in Oregon, but the voice of Senator Benton seems to have been unwavering in its support of America's destiny in the Northwest. Based on biographies, articles, memoirs, and the *Congressional Globe;* illus., map, photos, 39 notes.   W. F. Zornow

2928. Johannsen, Robert W. A DEDICATION TO THE MEMORY OF CHARLES M. GATES, 1904-1963. *Arizona and the West 1965 7(4): 283-286.* Charles M. Gates was a specialist in the history of the Old Northwest and the Pacific Northwest. As a regionalist he studied the growth of the West, especially as it related to national development on the broader scale. It was his conviction that an understanding of the economic development of the West through urbanization of the frontier furnished an important key to a better understanding of national growth. The West recognized that Eastern capital and enterprise were necessary for maturation of the frontier but resented that the region would thereby lose its economic and cultural autonomy. Gates served the profession in several capacities: as manuscripts curator at the Minnesota Historical Society, as a regional historian for the National Park Service, as editor of the *Pacific Northwest Quarterly,* and as a professor at the University of Washington. Appended with a selected list of his publications relating to the American West; illus.   D. L. Smith

2929. Nasatir, Abraham P. A DEDICATION TO THE MEMORY OF JOHN CARL PARISH, 1881-1939. *Arizona and the West 1971 13(2): 108-112.* Parish lived and taught in and wrote about his native Iowa for most of his first 40 years. He also served in various editorial capacities with the State historical society. Moving to the University of California at Los Angeles in 1922, Parish became active in professional circles in the Far West. Among other contributions, he launched the *Pacific Historical Review.* Illus., biblio.   D. L. Smith

2930. Oliphant, J. Orin. SOME NEGLECTED ASPECTS OF THE HISTORY OF THE PACIFIC NORTHWEST. *Pacific Northwest Q. 1970 61(1): 1-9.* Summarizes some aspects of the history of the region of the United States known as the Pacific Northwest during the period 1783-1889. The author discusses topics which have not had penetrating study: stockraising, fences, economic dependence, cultural dependence, subregional development, and especially religious influences.

C. C. Gorchels

2931. Rischin, Moses. BEYOND THE GREAT DIVIDE: IMMIGRATION AND THE LAST FRONTIER. *J. of Am. Hist. 1968 55(1): 42-53.* The history of the Far Western region has never become integrated within a framework of either American or world history. To historians east of the Rockies it has seemed a backwater unworthy of serious scholarly attention, and its communities have not been studied by sociologists (except for some studies on Indian villages, utopian colonies, and Japanese relocation centers). Scholars in the area have too often been distracted by the quixotic mystique of a unique identity with Spain and the hemisphere. A more fruitful approach to the history of the region would be a discussion of immigrant groups and the development of communities, institutions, and social groups in a plural community. Documented principally from secondary sources.

K. B. West

2932. Schaeffer, Claude E. WILLIAM BROOKS, CHINOOK PUBLICIST. *Oregon Hist. Q. 1963 64(1): 41-54.* William Brooks's association with Indians in the Pacific Northwest and his efforts to publicize problems of the Indians, 1835-39.

C. C. Gorchels

2933. Steckler, Gerard G. THE CASE OF FRANK FULLER: THE KILLER OF ALASKA MISSIONARY CHARLES SEGHERS. *Pacific Northwest Q. 1968 59(4): 190-202.* A detailed account of the activities of Frank Fuller, an apparently demented man, who was convicted of the murder of Charles John Seghers, the Roman Catholic bishop of Vancouver Island, in 1886. With a background of missionary activities in the region of the Pacific Northwest and Alaska, this article shows the human conflicts among Jesuits, Protestant missionaries, and others who were anxious to bring the Christian faith to the Indians.

C. C. Gorchels

2934. Swan, James G. AT SHOALWATER BAY. *Am. West 1968 5(4): 39.* Swan's own 1853 narrative of a Fourth of July celebration is taken from his *The Northwest Coast* which was republished in 1966.

D. L. Smith

2935. Teiser, Sidney. OBADIAH B. MC FADDEN, OREGON AND WASHINGTON TERRITORIAL JUDGE. *Oregon Hist. Q. 1965 66(1): 25-37.* Sketch of political activities in Oregon and Washington territory, 1853-1875, with Obadiah McFadden in the role of territorial judge.

C. C. Gorchels

2936. Warner, Jonathan T. CALIFORNIA AND OREGON: A SPEECH. *Southern California Q. 1963 45(4): 337-353.* A speech delivered at Rochester, New York, in August 1840, by Jonathan Trumbull Warner, also known as Juan José Warner of Southern California, stressing the importance of California and Oregon as fertile and strategic parts of the North American continent. The speaker felt that the impending settlement and occupation of these territories by large numbers of white settlers would be an important historical event in the process of securing the entire continent. It is an early example of the growing spirit of Manifest Destiny in America.

A. K. Main

Washington

2937. Berner, Richard C. THE PORT BLAKELY MILL COMPANY, 1876-89. *Pacific Northwest Q. 1966 57(4): 158-171.* Discusses the reasons and methods leading to the development of the lumber industry in Washington Territory from 1879 to 1889 to the extent that production increased from 160 million feet in 1879 to over a billion feet in 1889. The progress of Port Blakely Mill Company is described against a background of economic forces, labor supply, and other factors.

C. C. Gorchels

2938. Blackford, Mansel G. REFORM POLITICS IN SEATTLE DURING THE PROGRESSIVE ERA, 1902-1916. *Pacific Northwest Q. 1968 59(4): 177-185.* Depicts the currents and countercurrents in the unusually exciting elections in Seattle from 1900 to 1920. Analyzes such factors as attempts to eliminate an area of gambling houses and brothels, measures for municipal ownership, female suffrage, and labor unionism.

C. C. Gorchels

2939. Boylan, Bernard L. CAMP LEWIS: PROMOTION AND CONSTRUCTION. *Pacific Northwest Q. 1967 58(4): 188-195.* An account of the efforts of residents of Tacoma, Washington, and vicinity to transform 70,000 acres of beautiful countryside into the largest military cantonment in the United States (1916-17) allegedly to lift the city out of its economic doldrums. Details of the promotional campaign and subsequent construction are given.

C. C. Gorchels

2940. Burnham, Howard J. LOCAL HISTORY IN THE PACIFIC NORTHWEST: THE FORT VANCOUVER HISTORICAL SOCIETY. *Hist. News 1965 20(6): 131-133.* Traces the growth and achievements of the historical society of Vancouver, Washington, including the establishment of a 19th-century fort as a national historic site, publication of a journal, founding of a museum, preservation of a grist mill and mansion, and the providing of programs for members and visitors. Illus.

J. H. Keiser

2941. Champlin, Ardath I. ARTHUR L. MARSH AND THE WASHINGTON EDUCATION ASSOCIATION, 1921-40. *Pacific Northwest Q. 1969 60(3): 127-134.* Sketches the activities of Arthur L. Marsh, especially as executive secretary (1921-40) of the Washington Education Association and editor (1921-48) of *Washington Education,* against a backdrop of events and progress in educational development in Washington, 1919-51.

C. C. Gorchels

2942. Cramer, Richard S. BRITISH MAGAZINES AND THE OREGON QUESTION. *Pacific Hist. R. 1963 32(4): 369-382.* Contends that British magazines, regardless of political persuasion, from 1820 to 1846 consistently rejected the American demand for territory north of the Columbia River because they believed it to be a British possession by right. In this they reflected the then current political instability in Great Britain.

J. McCutcheon

2943. Doig, Ivan. PUGET SOUND'S WAR WITHIN A WAR: A FIGHT FOR POLITICAL POWER IN THE MID-NINETEENTH CENTURY. *Am. West 1971 8(3): 22-27.* When Victor Smith was appointed U.S. collector of customs for Puget Sound in 1861, Port Townsend was the port of entry for Washington Territory. Smith, "a lodestone for calamity," soon set his schemes in motion. He wangled a job as lighthouse keeper for his otherwise unsuccessful father, tried to take over the local Republican newspaper with patronage "plums," and advocated moving the customs house to another town where he was buying real estate. Smith, a champion of Salmon P. Chase, was soon embroiled with territorial officials who were predominantly champions of President Abraham Lincoln. While Smith was in the national capital the man left in charge uncovered substantial evidence of fraud and official misconduct. Smith returned with congressional authority to transfer the port of entry to Port Angeles. He threatened to shell the customs house and the town with the cannon of a revenue cutter before the records were surrendered to him. Smith weathered grand jury charges of embezzlement and other efforts to remove him. Port Townsend was unable to get the customs house back until Smith's career ended in a shipwreck. 5 illus., map, biblio.

D. L. Smith

2944. Finger, John R. HENRY YESLER'S "GRAND LOTTERY OF WASHINGTON TERRITORY." *Pacific Northwest Q. 1969 60(3): 121-126.* Following the passage of permissive legislation by the territorial legislature in 1875, a number of lotteries were organized in Washington Territory in the mid-1870's. Yesler's lottery was the most elaborate. Yesler, a prominent Seattle businessman, is believed to have promoted the lottery to get out of debt, while supposedly raising money for a public wagon road. Sales of lottery tickets did not reach the volume needed to cover the costs of the prizes, and the scheme failed. Discusses legal complications and political influences of antigambling forces.

C. C. Gorchels

2945. Foster, David William and Hoffman, Robert J. SOME OBSERVATIONS ON THE VOWELS OF PACIFIC NORTHWEST ENGLISH (SEATTLE AREA). *Am. Speech 1966 41(2): 119-122.* A disagreement with 12 aspects of Charles Kenneth Thomas' *Introduction to the Phonics of American English* (2d ed., 1958) in regard to pronunciation in the Pacific Northwest. This concerns vowel sounds in such words as "hurry, worry," "fog, frog," "ask, aunt," and "not, nod." The authors believe that "Thomas's analysis is accurate on many counts but differs widely from our own observations" in various vowel sounds. The article is based mostly on the authors' knowledge of linguistics and the speech of the Seattle area; 8 notes.   R. W. Shoemaker

2946. Hanson, Minnie Harris. SEATTLE MUSEUM OF HISTORY AND INDUSTRY. *Hist. News 1968 23(9): 171-173.* The Seattle Museum of History and Industry is a private museum owned and operated by the Seattle Historical Society. Except for city-supplied custodial help, it is entirely self-supporting. Its principal concerns are the history of Seattle, the State of Washington, and the Pacific Northwest area. Its specialties are seasonal and topical exhibits that draw capacity crowds and guided tours for school children and other groups. 3 illus.
D. L. Smith

2947. Hynding, Alan A. EUGENE SEMPLE'S SEATTLE CANAL SCHEME. *Pacific Northwest Q. 1968 59(2): 77-87.* Under the leadership of Eugene Semple, former territorial governor of Washington, much effort and money was expended in changing the waterfront of Seattle from 1889 to 1918. The principal projects of digging canals and reclaiming tide- and shorelands are described, with details about overcoming legal obstacles, raising money for construction, and eliminating objectors. Personal and business letters, official reports, and newspapers are cited as sources.
C. C. Gorchels

2948. Inkster, Tom H. INTERNATIONAL STORM OVER THE SAN JUANS. *Montana 1967 17(1): 36-43.* Friction between the United States and Great Britain developed over the disputed boundary in the San Juan Island group in the Puget Sound area from 1846 to 1872. It is suggested that one crisis, in 1861, resulted from attempts by American military leaders in the region to start a war with England in hopes of averting the threat of civil war in the United States. Illus.
S. R. Davison

2949. Jarvis, Reed. SAN JUAN ISLAND'S PIG WAR. *J. of the West 1968 7(2): 236-245.* Tells of an incident involving the killing of a farmer's pig which grew to international proportions. Both American and British troops occupied San Juan Island in Puget Sound. Although long delayed by the Civil War, a settlement was finally reached in which the United States' claim to the island was upheld. Described is the long effort to have the sites of the American and English camps made into a national park. Success finally came in 1966, and the first superintendent was appointed in 1967.   R. N. Alvis

2950. Kizer, Benjamin H. COLONEL PATRICK HENRY WINSTON. *Pacific Northwest Q. 1970 61(2): 72-76.* Presents humorous biographical highlights of the life of Patrick Henry Winston (1847-1903), with particular attention to his experiences in the State of Washington during the years 1886-1903, as a target of real estate sharks and as a politician.   C. C. Gorchels

2951. Kizer, Benjamin H. MAY ARKWRIGHT HUTTON. *Pacific Northwest Q. 1966 57(2): 49-56.* Biographical sketch of orphan May Arkwright Hutton through early years of privation in mining towns of Idaho, the successful investment of her small wages in a mine which became a bonanza; then middle-aged years in Spokane as a philanthropist, establishing and supporting homes for orphans. Included are incidents of her roles in union labor activities and politics.   C. C. Gorchels

2952. Mays, Milton A. HENRY JAMES IN SEATTLE. *Pacific Northwest Q. 1968 59(4): 186-189.* In his visit to Seattle in 1905, James spent three days as the guest of his nephew, and left with fewer criticisms of that city than of other cities and regions of the United States. It was believed that James was gathering material for a "Western" volume of *The American Scene.* Criticizes James' inability "to respond more fully to the West."   C. C. Gorchels

2953. McInnis, Raymond G. OPPORTUNITIES FOR HISTORICAL RESEARCH IN WASHINGTON STATE. *Studies in Hist. and Soc. 1969 1(2): 7-16.* Much historical material is located in Washington State but, unfortunately, scholars make little use of it. Five key centers for research exist in the Puget Sound region: The Federal Records Center in Seattle, the Washington State Historical Society in Tacoma, the Washington State Library, the Washington State Law Library, and the Washington State Archives. The Federal Records Center contains a wealth of historical materials such as the records of government agencies in the Northwest, the records of the Bureau of Indian Affairs, and the records of the five U.S. district courts in the Northwest. The major drawback for researchers using the Federal Records Center is that most materials must be used in the building. The Washington State Historical Society contains the personal papers of many important persons and the records of businesses located in the Pacific Northwest. The Washington State Law Library has a complete collection of the legislative records of Washington. The Washington State Library has a large collection of documentary materials on microfilm. As for the Washington State Archives, it contains government materials, but for the moment this center is in the process of being reorganized to facilitate the use of sources. Documentation based on articles dealing with source materials in Washington State; 7 notes.
S. R. Sherter

2954. Ripley, Thomas E. SHAKESPEARE IN THE LOGGING CAMP. *Am. West 1967 4(2): 12-16.* George Moore, trained and experienced in lumbering in Wisconsin, moved into the big tree forests of the Puget Sound country in Washington. The rough and ready prototype of the lumberjack of the movies and novels, he was hired on as the big boss of a logging operation for a company of which the author was the president. When a copy of the works of William Shakespeare found its way into camp and into Moore's hands, he soon became an addict. Moore found his thoughts transmuted into words and soon his logger's talk was interlarded with quotations from Shakespeare. This account is a chapter from *Green Tree*, a memoir of the author's life in the Tacoma area. 5 illus., note, biblio.   D. L. Smith

2955. Simmons, Robert. THE TRANSITION OF THE WASHINGTON EXECUTIVE FROM TERRITORY TO STATEHOOD. *Pacific Northwest Q. 1964 55(2): 76-86.* A study of the evolution of the powers of the governor in Washington during territorial days 1853-89. Includes a close analysis of powers allowed and changed over the years. Tables summarize specific powers of the state's executive officers.
C. C. Gorchels

2956. Taber, Ronald W. WRITERS ON RELIEF: THE MAKING OF THE WASHINGTON GUIDE, 1935-1941. *Pacific Northwest Q. 1970 61(4): 185-192.* Personality clashes and policy difficulties stand out in this account of the writing of the book, *Washington: a Guide to the Evergreen State,* a volume in the *American Guide Series,* "compiled" by workers of the Federal Writers' Program of the Work Projects Administration (originally the Works Progress Administration), 1935-41. Amid charges that Communists had prominent roles in the project, the book was finally completed and appraised as a "disappointment," reading "like the dull flat prose of a bad textbook."   C. C. Gorchels

2957. Thompson, Albert W. THE EARLY HISTORY OF THE PALOUSE RIVER AND ITS NAMES. *Pacific Northwest Q. 1971 62(2): 69-76.* Comprehensive account of historical events associated with a small river in eastern Washington, the "Palouse River," with special reference to the origin of the name. The "false ascription of French origin to what is in reality an Indian name is a widespread phenomenon."
C. C. Gorchels

2958. Wright, Martha R. "HOOTENANNY": MORE OF ITS PAST. *Am. Speech 1966 41(1): 56-58.* Early meanings of "hootenanny" were such different things as "hillbilly" or "thingumajig." Apparently in the summer of 1940 in Seattle it acquired the meaning of "a combination of any and all types of group entertainment" and this meaning spread eastward. How it acquired this meaning is uncertain, but the meaning may have been used earlier by hillbilly musicians. 8 notes.
R. W. Shoemaker

Oregon

2959. Belknap, George N. MCMURTRIES OREGON IMPRINTS: A FOURTH SUPPLEMENT. *Oregon Hist. Q. 1963 64(2): 137-182.* A few words about sources of information followed by detailed title page lists of 144 books, pamphlets, and broadsides published in Oregon before 1871.
C. C. Gorchels

2960. Belknap, George N. MORE ADDENDA TO BELKNAP, OREGON IMPRINTS. *Papers of the Biblio. Soc. of Am. 1972 66(2): 178-210.* Provides new information, primarily from contemporary newspapers, concerning 137 titles recorded in the author's *Oregon Imprints 1845-1870* (Eugene: U. of Oregon Books, 1968). Extensive annotation of changes, with numerous excerpts from newspapers, of each title change. 12 notes.
C. A. Newton

2961. Belknap, George N. AN OREGON MISCELLANY. *Papers of the Biblio. Soc. of Am. 1963 57(2): 191-200.* Annotations of seven major Oregon imprints.
C. A. Newton

2962. Chadwick, Stephen James. THE RECOLLECTIONS OF STEPHEN JAMES CHADWICK. *Pacific Northwest Q. 1964 55(3): 111-118.* Chadwick, son of an Oregon pioneer of 1851 who later became governor of the state, was intimately associated with early political and social history of Oregon. This is a rambling account of education, amusements, and domestic activities, as well as politics, especially in Roseburg, Oregon, 1855-83.
C. C. Gorchels

2963. Davis, Hugh H., ed. THREE LETTERS OF WILLIAM GIRD, "VETERAN OF TURF, FIELD, AND FARM." *Oregon Hist. Q. 1967 68(2): 141-152.* Three letters written by Oregon pioneer William Gird between 1852 and 1864. They describe general conditions (especially political events and economic development) in Oregon, as well as personal experiences.
C. C. Gorchels

2964. Dieppre, Harold C. CORRUPTION AND THE DISPUTED ELECTION VOTE OF OREGON IN THE 1876 ELECTION. *Oregon Hist. Q. 1966 67(3): 257-372.* Analysis of legalistic and other factors involved in deciding how Oregon's electoral votes should be counted in the dramatic contest for the Presidency of the United States between Rutherford B. Hayes and Samuel J. Tilden, 1876.
C. C. Gorchels

2965. G., C. M. ARTHUR E. THROCKMORTON, 1913-1962. *Pacific Northwest Q. 1963 54(1): 33-35.* Necrology of a supporter of the Oregon Historical Society.
S

2966. Hendrickson, James E. THE RUPTURE OF THE DEMOCRATIC PARTY IN OREGON, 1858. *Pacific Northwest Q. 1967 58(2): 65-73.* Analyzes the dissention in the Democratic Party in Oregon, 1857-59, as manifested by the development of opposing cliques - one under the leadership of Joseph Lane and the other headed by Asahel Bush. The author concludes that the controversy over slavery in the nation at that time was not an important factor in the party split. Based on new primary source materials located in the Lilly Library, Indiana University.
C. C. Gorchels

2967. Husband, Michael B. SENATOR LEWIS F. LINN AND THE OREGON QUESTION. *Missouri Hist. R. 1971 66(1): 1-19.* Entering the US Senate in 1833 after a successful career as a physician, Lewis Fields Linn (1795-1843) soon became interested in the Far West. His work culminated with the introduction of five resolutions in 1839. He asserted that America's claim to Oregon was indisputable, that the President should tell Great Britain that the joint treaty for the occupation of Oregon would be terminated, that American laws should be extended to Oregon, that American troops should be sent to Oregon, and that 640 acres of land should be given to any white man who would cultivate them for five years. These resolutions became a major cause of the great migration to Oregon in 1843. Based on books, articles, the *Congressional Globe*, Senate documents, and manuscripts in the Bancroft Library, Berkeley; illus., 37 notes.
W. F. Zornow

2968. Johannessen, Carl L.; Davenport, William A.; Millet, Artimus; and McWilliams, Steven. THE VEGETATION OF THE WILLAMETTE VALLEY. *Ann. of the Assoc. of Am. Geographers 1971 61(2): 286-302.* "The vegetation of the Willamette Valley, Oregon, has been modified by man for centuries. The earliest white men described the vegetation as extensive prairies maintained by annual fires set by Indians. The cessation of burning in the 1850s allowed expansion of forest lands on the margins of the former prairies. Today some of these forest lands have completed a cycle of growth, logging, and regrowth. Much of the former prairie is now in large-scale grain and grass seed production and is still burned annually. The pasture lands of the Valley are still maintained as open lands with widely scattered oaks."
J

2969. Kennedy, Philip W. OREGON AND THE DISPUTED ELECTION OF 1876. *Pacific Northwest Q. 1969 60(3): 135-144.* Details local political conflicts and disputes in Oregon which were magnified in importance because of the close contest in the national presidential election in 1876. Potentially only one electoral vote for the Democratic candidate from Oregon could have changed the presidential election, and Samuel Jones Tilden rather than Rutherford Birchard Hayes might have become President. A national Electoral Commission finally settled the issues by ruling in favor of the Oregon Republican electors.
C. C. Gorchels

2970. McClintock, Thomas C. SETH LEWELLING, WILLIAM S. U'REN AND THE BIRTH OF THE OREGON PROGRESSIVE MOVEMENT. *Oregon Hist. Q. 1967 68(3): 197-220.* An account of the early development and gradual decline of one phase of progressive political activities under the leadership of Lewelling and U'Ren in Oregon, 1892-98. Financial problems, personalities, and adoption of progressive planks by major political parties eroded potential success. Illus.
C. C. Gorchels

2971. McDonald, Lucile Saunders. ALL AROUND THE TOWN. *Oregon Hist. Q. 1963 64(3): 259-266.* Brief account of David Wittenberg and family, early settlers in Portland, Oregon, 1859-1911.
C. C. Gorchels

2972. Reinhardt, Richard. THE SHORT, HAPPY HISTORY OF THE STATE OF JEFFERSON. *Am. West 1972 9(3): 36-41, 63.* Gilbert E. Gable, mayor of Port Orford on the southern Oregon coast, was unhappy because Oregon had not developed the timber and mineral resources of his Curry County. To draw attention to this negligence he asked for legal sanction to transfer the county from Oregon to California. The publicity was instant and widespread, the reaction was a display of hostility and ridicule and indifference, and his manifesto soon blossomed into a full-fledged independence movement. This 1941 cry of liberation was reminiscent of the provincial chauvinism that had surfaced several times before in the area even before Oregon and California had been admitted to the Union. As recently as 1935, a facetious secession movement in northern California had dramatized the lack of good highways along the coast. Gable's bid for attention brought forth several proposals. What emerged was the secession state of Jefferson, with ensign and regalia, border patrols, militia, and a shadow government. As one reporter characterized it, the movement was "partly mad, partly in fun, partly earnest." With the sudden death of Gable, a publicity carnival, and the Japanese attack on Pearl Harbor, the secessionist state of Jefferson ceased to exist. 5 illus., map.
D. L. Smith

2973. Richards, Kent D. THE METHODISTS AND THE FORMATION OF THE OREGON PROVISIONAL GOVERNMENT. *Pacific Northwest Q. 1970 61(2): 87-93.* Examines the role of Methodist missionary leaders in establishing provisional government in Oregon from the time Jason Lee and Ewing Young arrived in 1834 to the diminution of missionary authority in 1845. The author discusses the reasons for the establishment of the Champoeg meetings, "whereby the Methodists attempted to establish a government which would serve missionary ends and ideals but would also command support from a majority of settlers." 34 notes.
C. C. Gorchels

2974. Schroeder, John H. REP. JOHN FLOYD, 1817-1829: HARBINGER OF OREGON TERRITORY. *Oregon Hist. Q. 1969 70(4): 333-346.* Called a "passionate prophet of the Oregon Country" while he served as a member of the US House of Representatives (1817-29), John

Floyd (1783-1837) urged vigorous Government activities to gain control of the Pacific coastal territories. His frequent speeches and remarks delivered in the US Congress, especially between 1821 and 1829, emphasized the high potential commercial value which would come with controlling the natural resources and trade from the Oregon Country.

C. C. Gorchels

2975. Smith, Thomas H. AN OHIOAN'S ROLE IN OREGON HISTORY. *Oregon Hist. Q. 1965 66(3): 218-232.* Letters written in primitive form by a pioneer in eastern and southern Oregon to his brother in Ohio. Details in the letters include descriptions of Rogue River Indian skirmishes, the dispositions of cross-country travelers, the cost of food and the wages received by unskilled laborers.

C. C. Gorchels

2976. Snoddy, Oliver. A CLAN NA GAEL CONSTITUTION AND RITUAL FROM PORTLAND, 1916. *Irish Sword [Ireland] 1970 9(36): 216-235.* The constitution and a part of the initiation ritual of the Portland circle of the Clan Na Gael, reprinted from copies in the National Museum of Ireland. Discusses the clan and identifies members of the Portland clan. 4 notes.

H. L. Calkin

2977. Teiser, Sidney. CYRUS OLNEY, ASSOCIATE JUSTICE OF OREGON TERRITORY SUPREME COURT. *Oregon Hist. Q. 1963 64(4): 309-322.* Member of a pioneering family (moving from Pennsylvania to Ohio to Iowa to Oregon), Cyrus Olney served as early judge in Oregon Territory, 1853-57, and was a businessman and legislator in Oregon until his death in 1870.

C. C. Gorchels

2978. Teiser, Sidney. REUBEN P. BOISE, LAST ASSOCIATE JUSTICE OF THE OREGON TERRITORY SUPREME COURT. *Oregon Hist. Q. 1965 66(1): 5-24.* Highlights of the life of Reuben Boise in Oregon, with emphasis on his career as jurist, legislator, lawyer, farmer, and businessman, 1850-1907.

C. C. Gorchels

2979. Teiser, Sidney. WILLIAM STRONG, ASSOCIATE JUSTICE OF THE TERRITORIAL COURTS. *Oregon Hist. Q. 1963 64(4): 293-307.* Experiences of a Cleveland, Ohio, lawyer who accepted an appointment in 1849 by President Zachary Taylor to be Associate Justice of the Supreme Court in the territory of Oregon. Without law books or serene judicial atmosphere, Strong made an admirable record as jurist, legislator, and soldier, 1850-87.

C. C. Gorchels

2980. Vaughan, Thomas and Winch, Martin. JOSEPH GERVAIS, A FAMILIAR MYSTERY MAN. *Oregon Hist. Q. 1965 66(4): 331-362.* A biography of Joseph Gervais and a description of his role in the early history of the upper Willamette Valley. This documented account shows, mostly for the period 1811-61, the development of farms and minor industries and tells about the growth of population, governmental problems, and the influence of the churches.

C. C. Gorchels

2981. Wells, W. W. [LETTER TO GOVERNOR A. C. GIBBS]. *Oregon Hist. Q. 1964 65(3): 296.* One-page letter describing a near-violent election incident at Canyon City, Oregon in 1864.

C. C. Gorchels

California

2982. Acker, Elizabeth S. LOS ANGELES. *Special Lib. 1968 59(3): 153-157.* An introductory description and history of Los Angeles for the benefit of the Special Libraries Association. An 18-item bibliography is appended.

D. Brockway

2983. Alba, Jose C. FILIPINOS IN CALIFORNIA. *Pacific Historian 1967 11(3): 39-41.* Explores Filipino migration to the United States. After the Spanish-American War of 1898 Filipino nationals, during the long tutelege period, were allowed into the United States with little objection. But after the establishment of the Commonwealth in 1934 Filipinos immigrated only under the quota system which allowed them a hundred migrants a year. During the 20th century Filipinos entered all of the strata of American life from rural pickers to skilled technicians and university graduates. They settled chiefly in the coastal cities, mainly in California. Photo.

T. R. Cripps

2984. Anderson, Walt. JOAQUIN MURIETA. *Am. Hist. Illus. 1967 2(1): 49-53.* It is not always possible to determine the line of distinction between truth and folklore in an account of Murieta's life. Much of the confusion stems from the "biography" of Murieta written about 1853 by John Rollin Ridge, which reads like a novel and presents the subject as a hero. From there the legend grew, like that of Robin Hood, until Ridge's Murieta was incorporated into historical works and was perpetuated through Walter Noble Burns's *The Robin Hood of El Dorado* (1932) and its 1936 film version. Today the majority of historians are convinced that most of the Murieta story is based on imagination.

J. D. Filipiak

2985. Andrews, Thomas F. THE AMBITIONS OF LANSFORD W. HASTINGS: A STUDY IN WESTERN MYTH-MAKING. *Pacific Hist. R. 1970 39(4): 473-491.* Calls for reappraisal of the historical importance of Hastings. Attacks the still-prevalent impression that he plotted to become president of California and visited Sam Houston in Texas to gain support for a California revolt against Mexico. Although Hastings did make a trip to California by way of Mexico, and did publish a guidebook praising California that was responsible for associating his name with the ill-fated Donner party, his main objective was probably only the active promotion of overland migration to California - as research into contemporary letters and memoirs, including those of John Sutter, seems to prove. 66 notes.

E. C. Hyslop

2986. Baird, Joseph Armstrong, Jr. THE MANSION OF THE CALIFORNIA HISTORICAL SOCIETY, 2090 JACKSON STREET, SAN FRANCISCO. *California Hist. Soc. Q. 1969 48(4): 309-324.* Describes the history of the building which houses the California Historical Society headquarters. Built as a home for William Franklin Whittier, a prominent San Francisco businessman, the building was constructed between 1894 and 1896. The cost of construction has been estimated between 90 thousand dollars and 152 thousand dollars. After the house passed out of the possession of Whittier's descendants it served as residence for a series of occupants, including the consul for Nazi Germany and Mortimer Adler's Institute of Philosophical Research. In 1956 the California Historical Society purchased the property; in recent years the society has also acquired several adjacent lots which were originally owned by Whittier. The author also describes the architectural features and interior decorations of the building that has come to be called The Mansion. Like others of the genre, The Mansion was constructed originally as a private residence and now serves an institutional purpose. Illus., photo, 24 notes.

A. Hoffman

2987. Batman, Richard Dale. THE CALIFORNIA POLITICAL FRONTIER: DEMOCRATIC OR BUREAUCRATIC? *J. of the West 1968 7(4): 461-470.* Examines California politics in the light of Frederick Jackson Turner's thesis that American democracy is fundamentally the outcome of the experiences of the American people in dealing with the West. The California experience seems to belie that thesis. The men prominent in the early formative days of California political institutions seem to have been men of considerable political experience in the East who came to California with the express purpose of forming those institutions. By and large they dominated the national political offices from California. A number of young lawyers similarly dominated the State offices. The author concludes that further study of Western politics might show that the American West was a politician's frontier where the opportunities were more bureaucratic than democratic in nature.

R. N. Alvis

2988. Batman, Richard Dale. GLENN MARTIN BUILDS AIRPLANES... AND PEOPLE BUILD THEIR CHURCHES. *J. of the West 4(3): 425-447.* Tells the progress of Orange County in the development of transportation and in the social and cultural growth of the county. Until the late 1870's road and river transportation was all that was available, but then railroads were built. Highways were not an important factor until the first highway commission approved a program to build 117 miles of paved roads. The population boom after World War II intensified the need for highways and the Santa Ana and San Diego Freeways were built. Although the county has no significant airport, it was once the home of Glenn Martin, a leading pioneer in aviation. Social and cultural advances include the establishment and expansion of numerous churches and fraternal organizations, the operation of the Grand Opera House, the beginning of a library and a historical society, and, not least, the opening of Disneyland in 1955. Tourists are also attracted by the fine beaches, the Laguna Beach Art Festival, the San Juan Capistrano Mission, and Knott's Berry Farm. Based on published sources, 171 notes.

D. N. Brown

2989. Batman, Richard Dale. "GOSPEL SWAMP . . . THE LAND OF HOG AND HOMINY." *J. of the West 1965 4(2): 231-257.* Deals with the development of agriculture in the county. In 1850 Orange County had few farms, but Jean Louis Vignes, who came to Los Angeles in 1831, had pioneered the wine industry. Vineyards were soon planted near Anaheim and other communities in Orange County. As the grape industry blossomed, farmers began to move into the valley on both sides of the Santa Ana River. All types of grain, pumpkins, potatoes, and livestock were raised in the valley. In the 1880's a blight struck the grape industry and destroyed almost all the vines. As the grape industry died most of the land was converted into citrus groves and by 1910 a solid agricultural basis had been established. Until World War II Orange County depended on agriculture and the processing industry for a living, but since then more land has been withdrawn from production. Labor supply and adequate moisture have always been a problem. Irrigation and flood control projects have helped solve the latter. Documented from newspapers and other published sources, illus., 191 notes.

D. N. Brown

2990. Batman, Richard Dale. GREAT CITIES GROW ON CITRUS LANDS. *J. of the West 4(4): 553-576.* Traces the development of education from the very small elementary schools with limited resources through the establishment of a modern school system which provides services from kindergarten through college. Just as the educational system has undergone vast changes in the last century, so has the way of life in the county. Originally Orange County was primarily rural, but since 1940 it has become an urban center. The county is becoming more industrialized and agriculture is of declining importance. Among the problems demanding solution are the development of mass transportation, an adequate water supply, recreational facilities for an expanding population, and a school system that can keep pace with the ever-increasing number of students. Based on published material, illus., 128 notes.

D. N. Brown

2991. Baur, John E. CALIFORNIA'S NINETEENTH-CENTURY FUTURISTS. *Southern California Q. 1971 53(1): 1-40.* Discusses 19th-century "prophets" and their prophecies of California's future. Forecasting the area's future began with the Spanish in the 17th century, but became a popular fad only among Anglo-Saxons in the 19th century. Prophecies, although some were pessimistic, tended to emphasize a bright industrial future for California. Prophets included such famous individuals as Hinton Rowan Helper (1829-1909), Henry David Thoreau (1817-62), Richard Henry Dana, Jr. (1815-82), and Daniel Webster (1782-1852). The prophecies tell us more about the people who made them and their times than about the future. Based mainly on 19th-century sources; 139 notes.

W. L. Bowers

2992. Bayless, June E., ed. MY STORY AT MOLINO VIEJO. *California Hist. Soc. Q. 1969 48(2): 171-175.* The manuscript of Rebecca Humphreys Turner's *My Story: a Pioneer* and a letter to her from her fiancé William F. Turner have been deposited with the San Marino Public Library. Mrs. Turner's family lived at El Molino Viejo, now the southern California quarters of the California Historical Society. Bayless relates the circumstances by which the letter came to be written. A series of misunderstandings in 1871 caused the engaged couple to be estranged for a time. The problem was solved after Turner's letter made a tardy arrival.

A. Hoffman

2993. Beach, Frank L. THE EFFECTS OF THE WESTERN MOVEMENT ON CALIFORNIA'S GROWTH AND DEVELOPMENT, 1900-1920. *Internat. Migration Rev. 1969 3(3): 20-35.* Summarizes the impact of the migration of over one million Americans to California, 1900-20. This propaganda-inspired migration effected changes in every aspect of the State's life, and, of greatest importance, established a pattern of growth which has become a permanent characteristic of California culture and institutions. Abstract in Spanish, French, and German. Based on secondary sources; 8 tables, 42 notes.

G. O. Gagnon

2994. Bean, Walton. IDEAS OF REFORM IN CALIFORNIA. *California Hist. Q. 1972 51(3): 213-226.* The definition of reform in California history since statehood has encompassed a wide variety of ideologies. Crusades against local corruption, for prohibition, and against railroad domination marked the 19th century, while in the early years of the 20th century the progressive movement, the Industrial Workers of the World (I.W.W.), and the socialists made their impression. Warns against oversimplification in assessing these reform movements. As for more recent reform efforts, a pattern has emerged wherein the electorate has repudiated extremes from the political left and right, following the promises of politicians who used the term reform as a means of rejecting reform efforts that went beyond the tolerance of most voters. In the balance, left-wing extremism has proved more costly to liberal reformers than right-wing extremism has harmed conservatives. Reform in California today suggests a history that is cyclical rather than evolutionary; the ideology of Governor Ronald Reagan toward reform bears a remarkable resemblance to the cries for reform uttered in the 1850's. Based on secondary sources; 46 notes.

A. Hoffman

2995. Bergman, G. M. THE NEGRO WHO RODE WITH FREMONT IN 1847. *Negro Hist. Bull. 1964 28(2): 31-32.* Reviews the contribution of Jacob Dodson, a Negro youth, who was with John C. Frémont on his famous ride from Los Angeles to Monterey, California in 1847 to confer with General Stephen Kearney on the capture of Los Angeles.

L. Gara

2996. Beyer, John. A NEW MUSEUM FOR THE WEST. *Am. West 1969 6(6): 34-39.* The Oakland (California) Museum, acclaimed to be one of the most important new regional museums in the country, opened in September 1969. Its collections are devoted primarily to California ecology, history, and art. Its goal is to become a "major force for the shaping of community values, for altering in some degree man's approach to the past, his present, and his future." Through an educational program, including traveling exhibits, it hopes to extend its influence far beyond Oakland. 30 illus.

D. L. Smith

2997. Biddick, William, Jr. THE CELEBRATED EMMA LE DOUX CASE. *Pacific Historian 1967 11(4): 37-54.* An account of a trunk murder discovered on 24 March 1906 in Stockton, California, in the baggage room of the Southern Pacific Railway. Soon after, the police apprehended Emma LeDoux for the murder of A. N. McVicar. Newspapers made a carnival of gore from the impending trial. The author follows the details of the relationship between the two principals in the days before the murder, establishing her reputation as an "oddity." Then in great detail the narrative exposes the story of the trial and its subsequent conclusion of a verdict of guilty in the first degree. After a number of appeal procedures, Emma LeDoux was paroled in the custody of her sister in 1920, but a year later was returned to custody when her sister complained that she had been running a house of prostitution. Paroled again in 1925, she broke parole with a conviction for theft and returned to prison at Tehachapi where she died in 1941. The article is offered as a look into legal and judicial practices in Stockton in the early 1900's. Documented from court records, interviews, and newspapers; illus., 56 notes.

T. R. Cripps

2998. Brown, Norman D. EDWARD STANLY: FIRST REPUBLICAN CANDIDATE FOR GOVERNOR OF CALIFORNIA. *California Hist. Soc. Q. 1968 47(3): 251-272.* After a political career in his native North Carolina, which he represented as a Whig in Congress for several terms, Stanly retired from public life in 1853 and moved to California to practice law. To defeat the Know-Nothing ticket in San Francisco County he agreed to run for the State senate on the Whig ticket. The Republican Party was organized in California in 1856, and the following year Stanly, though a proslavery man, was nominated for governor. He repudiated all platforms and "went simply for a reformation of government affairs." In the campaign he denounced the Nebraska bill, argued against the Dred Scott decision, and upheld the power of Congress to legislate on territorial matters. Though he differed from the Republicans in his refusal to endorse the Wilmot Proviso or to disavow the admission of any future slave States, these differences did not commend him to his former friends of the American (Know-Nothing) Party; the result was that the Democrats won. In 1861 he favored Lincoln and the Union and in 1862 accepted Lincoln's appointment as Union Military Governor in North Carolina with the duty of promoting Unionist sentiment, a position which he held until the signing of the Emancipation Proclamation. After the war he supported Andrew Johnson. 82 notes.   E. P. Stickney

2999. Brudnoy, David. RACE AND THE SAN FRANCISCO SCHOOL BOARD INCIDENT: CONTEMPORARY EVALUATIONS. *California Hist. Q. 1971 50(3): 295-312.* The attempt by the San Francisco School Board to segregate 93 Japanese pupils from white students provoked widespread comment (1905-07). While labor leaders, California representatives, and San Francisco politicians favored segregation, President Theodore Roosevelt and many legal scholars opposed the move. However, Roosevelt's position was less in terms of humanitarian concern than of recognition that the Empire of Japan commanded considerable political and military influence in world affairs. His arguments therefore reflected a diplomatic viewpoint; pointedly excluded from discussion was the issue of other minority races, such as the Chinese and Koreans, who were already segregated. Ironically, the Japanese themselves did not oppose the exclusion of other minority races. Based on secondary sources; 68 notes.   A. Hoffman

3000. Burchell, Robert A. BRITISH IMMIGRANTS IN SOUTHERN CALIFORNIA, 1850-1870. *Southern California Q. 1971 53(4): 283-302.* A statistical analysis of British and Irish immigration to southern California, 1850-70. Many British immigrants came to southern California seeking social and economic opportunity rather than political rights, and they achieved more success there than in the eastern United States. Moreover, there was definite trend during the 20-year period for British-born immigrants to move from other occupations to agricultural pursuits. This development was especially significant as it concerned the Irish, because it contradicts the generalization that Irish immigrants shunned the land when they came to America. Among British immigrants to southern California, the males outnumbered the females about two to one. Most of the immigrants were in their economically most productive years, with few of them very young or very old. With the exception of the Irish, they readily intermarried with other groups. Many came to California from other parts of the United States where they had not been as successful as they were in California. Because they arrived during the first 20 years of California's statehood, they took a prominent part in the political life of the State. Based on manuscript schedules of the 1850, 1860, and 1870 census reports, and on secondary sources; 13 tables, 58 notes.   W. L. Bowers

3001. Burns, Robert E. TWENTY YEARS AT WORK ON A FOUNDATION. *Pacific Historian 1967 11(2): 3-9.* An address given at the 20th California History Institute announcing the foundation's new role as a Pacific center for studies in Western history. The author sees history as a means of preserving the "westering" pioneer spirit and supports his contention with evidence from John Steinbeck and Leland Case. The project began with the Bancroft and Huntington Libraries and added the California Historical Association. With the creation of a California History Foundation in 1947 and the appointment of Rockwell Hunt as director, the idea enlarged further. In 1953 the local historical societies were federated and in 1957 the Jedediah Smith Society was founded, at the same time as the ęPacific Historian. Recently a Rockwell Hunt Chair in Western history has been endowed by the foundation. 2 photos.
                    T. R. Cripps

3002. Carranco, Lynwood and Genzoli, Andrew. CALIFORNIA REDWOOD EMPIRE PLACE NAMES. *J. of the West 1968 7(3): 363-380.* Gives historical backgrounds of place names in the Humboldt Bay area, more than 90 percent of which are of English or American origin.   R. N. Alvis

3003. Carranco, Lynwood. THREE LEGENDS OF NORTHWESTERN CALIFORNIA. *Western Folklore 1963 22(3): 179-185.* Discusses three popular legends that originated in northwestern California: the King's Peak Legend, the Lost Cabin Legend, and the Bigfoot Legend. Relates these legends to known historical facts in an attempt to ascertain their validity: No definite conclusions reached.   L. J. White

3004. Caughey, John Walton. THE CALIFORNIAN AND HIS ENVIRONMENT. *California Hist. Q. 1972 51(3): 195-204.* A survey of the effect of man on the California environment from prehistoric times to the present. Describes seven stages: the period of the Indians, who lived in harmony with the environment; the period of Spanish settlement and the beginnings of irrigation; the Mexican period, when Anglo-American and Russian fur traders decimated the sea otter and the beaver; the gold rush period, with the first devastating effects upon the landscape through lumbering and hydraulic mining; the railroad age; the era of prosperity, growth, economic depression, and expansion; and the modern era. Within the last two eras, the environment has begun to protest man's abuses. Smog, oil seepages, destruction of animal life, and loss of agricultural land through freeway sprawl and suburban developments have proved costly to the environment. From prehistoric times to the recent past, Californians have been optimistic about their future, but the ever-increasing pollution of the State requires a new orientation by Californians toward a value system which will recognize that people are also a part of the ecological chain of life.   A. Hoffman

3005. Caughey, John W. YOUNG CALIFORNIANS AND THEIR HISTORY. *Southern California Q. 1964 46(1): 1-10.* The fourth grader for whom California history is a required course is entitled to know something of the rough side of California's past. The study should build awareness of how modern California came to be what it is - a story of tensions and conflicts, and of remarkable achievement. Historians have concerned themselves too little about the content of this most crucial level of instruction, although the method is admittedly outside their expertness.
                    E. P. Stickney

3006. Chernykh, E. L. AGRICULTURE OF UPPER CALIFORNIA: A LONG LOST ACCOUNT OF FARMING IN CALIFORNIA AS RECORDED BY A RUSSIAN OBSERVER AT FORT ROSS IN 1841. *Pacific Historian 1967 11(1): 10-28.* A reprint of a first-hand observation of California farming practices first published in 1841 in Russia. The account describes in great detail climate, rainfall, prevailing winds, temperatures, barometric pressures, and terrain in Northern California around Fort Ross. Also described are the "archaic" and "primitive" plows and harrows used to produce cereals and vegetables. The observer then relates the predilection of Californians for meat and corn and concludes with a detailed analysis of crops unique to California and some examination of the agricultural economy of the region. Illus., map, tables.   T. R. Cripps

3007. Chicester, Lola A. and Kersten, Earl W., Jr., eds. VISION OF LONG AGO . . . A RECOLLECTION. *Nevada Hist. Soc. Q. 1963 6(2): 29-42.* An annotated, previously unpublished poem of the experiences of Victor Hugo Larson (1872-1955) in the Antelope Valley on the California-Nevada border. 18 notes.   J. D. Filipiak

3008. Choy, Philip P. GOLDEN MOUNTAIN OF LEAD: THE CHINESE EXPERIENCE IN CALIFORNIA. *California Hist. Q. 1971 50(3): 267-276.* Surveys the presence of the Chinese in California. Compelled to emigrate by internal disorders in their homeland, the Chinese who came to California found hostility and opposition to their presence. The enmity was based on an asserted economic threat and an overt racism. Isolated from the general society by discrimination and the control of the Chinese merchant elite, most Chinese remained in the seclusion of their Chinatowns. New immigration was cut off by the 1882 exclusion act. Chinese Americans found their duality a puzzle, as they seemed bisected culturally - Chinese by race, Americans by birth. The Chinese image improved during World War II; the exclusion acts were repealed, and Chinese Americans took an increasing part in American society. Many found opportunities in private industry and public agencies. The Chinatowns, especially San Francisco's, remained ghettos, however, and in the recent past Chinese American youths have begun to take an active role in the civil rights movement. Based on secondary sources; 25 notes.   A. Hoffman

3009. Choy, Wilbur W. Y. THE CHINESE IN CALIFORNIA. *Pacific Historian 1967 11(2): 16-22.* A chronicle of the coming of the Chinese from Kwantung and its capital, Canton, from 1850 through the 19th century. The first Chinese came in the wake of the deterioration of Ching Dynasty power and the unpopularity of the Manchus. They were pulled by the need for railroad labor and attendant services created by the California gold rush. The first waves of immigrants came to San Francisco which remained the "Main City" even though others migrated to Stockton and Sacramento. Once here they preserved a sense of community by imposing their rural extended kinship system on the new urban environment. The author closes the narrative with an account of Chinese contributions to American life ranging from labor to politics to the art of Dong Kingman and the rarified technology of the screen cameraman, James Wong Howe. 5 photos.   T. R. Cripps

3010. Clark, Thomas D. EDWIN BRYANT AND THE OPENING OF THE ROAD TO CALIFORNIA. *U. of Wyoming Pub.* 1971 37: 29-43. Bryant (1805-69), a journalist, published the first account of California immediately after it gained independence. *What I Saw in California* appeared in bookstores just as gold fever swept the United States, and the book consequently reached a wide audience. Bryant published an anti-Jackson newspaper in Massachusetts and Kentucky before going to the Pacific coast. Bryant held a civil post under the newly created government. He made several trips across the country and gained national attention as an authority on California. Bryant's book was not the earliest account of a western trip nor the best written, but it was detailed and reliable. 95 notes.   H. B. Powell

3011. Daniels, Roger and Peterson, Eric F. CALIFORNIA'S GRANDFATHER CLAUSE: THE "LITERACY IN ENGLISH" AMENDMENT OF 1894. *Southern California Q.* 1968 50(1): 51-58. The nativist, elitist, Anglo-Saxon climate in the United States of the 1890's touched California in the form of an amendment to the State constitution which disenfranchised anyone who could not read English. While there was initially some opposition to the amendment among legislators, it evaporated in the face of petitions from the electorate and both the legislative vote and the popular referendum were overwhelmingly in favor of the change. Although support of the amendment was couched in high moral terms and pragmatic justification based on alleged improvement of the electorate and politics, the authors contend that it was clear that the antiforeign attitudes of the period were chiefly responsible for the amendment's endorsement. Based on contemporary newspaper and periodical materials and public documents; 25 notes.   W. L. Bowers

3012. Davis, Donald G., Jr. THE IONACO OF GAYLORD WILSHIRE. *Southern California Q.* 1967 49(4): 425-453. Concerns the ionized belt venture of Henry Gaylord Wilshire, wealthy and colorful California social crusader and real estate developer. The belt consisted of coils of wire and an electrical current and supposedly gave relief to a variety of ailments. It was manufactured between 1925 and 1927 as the "Ionaco" from the words "ionization" and "company." Most doctors and local historians have considered it medical quackery developed for commercial gain. The author thinks that money was only part of Wilshire's concern. He states that Wilshire invented the belt in 1924 while searching for a cure for his own severe headaches and that he began manufacturing it because he thought he would be helping people. The writer bases this conclusion on evidence found in Wilshire's correspondence. He also disputes the charges that Wilshire profited handsomely from the venture, for when labor, sales, and advertising costs are considered, the return was about 26 percent, which he does not consider excessive. He does agree that the medical principles of the belt were unsound and that it had no physiological value. He also agrees that Wilshire's advertising was fraudulent for he claimed medical knowledge he did not possess and he gave endorsements from fictional doctors and medical schools. Wilshire died in 1927 and the Iona Company collapsed shortly thereafter. Based on the Gaylord Wilshire Papers, University of California, Los Angeles, and secondary sources; 95 notes.   W. L. Bowers

3013. Davis, W. N., Jr. CALIFORNIA LOCAL HISTORY IN THE STATE ARCHIVES. *California Historian* 1967 13(3): 89-93. Reviews the holdings of the California State Archives on the subject of State and local history. Selected are a few samples of the vast holdings. Examples include county election returns, incorporation files, material on education and Indian problems, the reports of the State Railroad Commissions, and public utilities records. The author concludes by adding "that to him who is alert and perceptive, nearly every word in these archival documents tells an instructive and fascinating story."   O. L. Miller

3014. Day, Clarence Burton. THE THOMAS DAY HERESY CASE IN THE SYNOD OF CALIFORNIA. *J. of Presbyterian Hist.* 1968 46(2): 79-106. Reviews the major events in what is described as "The Greatest Heresy Trial in the History of Presbyterianism on the Pacific Coast." Thomas Franklin Day, an Old Testament scholar who studied under Charles A. Briggs and William R. Harper, assumed a professorship of Old Testament at San Francisco Theological Seminary in 1890. Objec-

tions to his teaching resulted in an investigation by a committee of the seminary's board of directors in 1906, but the investigation found the objections without foundation. Thereupon the opposition introduced resolutions in the Synod of California requiring Day to answer specific questions on his beliefs and teachings regarding such issues as the historicity of the Genesis account of creation and the Mosaic authorship of the Pentateuch. Day finally presented his answers to the Synod of 1910. Of his 25 answers, the Synod disapproved 14. The board of the seminary sought to conciliate all groups in the church and retain Day, but in the Synod of 1911 conservatives elected several of their party to the seminary's board and secured a resolution requesting Day's resignation. Day resigned, effective at the end of the spring term in 1912. Based on minutes of the Synod of California and other published materials and an unpublished biography of Day; 39 notes.   S. C. Pearson, Jr.

3015. Derby, George H. SQUIBOB'S VISIT TO BENICIA IN 1850: THE P-H SCRAPBOOK: NO. 1. *Pacific Historian* 1966 10(1): 42-48. A reprinting of a comic essay written in 1850 by Derby who wrote under the pseudonym of "Squibob." The author's chief concern is the satirizing of the inadequacies of frontier hotels in the community of Benicia. Documented from published sources; illus.   T. R. Cripps

3016. Dickison, Roland. ONOMASTIC AMELIORATION IN CALIFORNIA PLACE NAMES. *Names* 1968 16(1): 13-18. Examines improvements or changes in original place names, with examples mostly from the region around the American River, east of Sacramento. The original motivation in attributing names to places was an attempt to convey a sense of geographical features, the dominant activity of the area, or perpetuation of the memory of a person or place. Clarity of understanding is interrupted when the original, and often colorful, names are altered or "improved." Current names such as Sierra Oaks Vista contrast with names such as Jackass Gulch and Poor Man's Creek. 9 notes.
                                                            P. McClure

3017. Dillon, Richard H. GRIZZLY ADAMS: A MAN TO MATCH OUR MOUNTAINS. *Pacific Historian* 1967 11(2): 23-34. A moderate chastisement of white Anglo-Saxon Protestant pioneers who both mistreated minorities such as Indians and then ignored their contributions to the history of California. In effect, it is an introduction to a problem faced by the author in composing a volume of colorful contributors to California life. He chooses as a narrow focus on the California Yankee a man called Grizzly Adams, a pioneer of the 1850's who cut a trail to the West, as a Yankee who cannot be omitted. He deals with Adams as a legendary figure. Illus.   T. R. Cripps

3018. Doughty, Robin W. SAN FRANCISCO'S NINETEENTH-CENTURY EGG BASKET: THE FARALLONS. *Geographical R.* 1971 61(4): 554-572. "The effects of man on island fauna are proverbial. During the past 150 years different groups have occupied the Farallon Islands, off San Francisco, and have seriously disrupted their abundant and varied marine life. Boston and Russian sealers hunted sea mammals to the point of extinction; fishermen plundered seafowl of their eggs for commercial gain; others reduced seabird populations through their presence and through oil pollution. These barren rocks were among the few places along the Pacific coast of the United States where murre eggs were harvested commercially for several decades. This essay describes egging on the Farallons and the decline of the murre population, which led to the prohibition of egging. At present moves are under way to establish the Farallons as a Wilderness Area free from human disturbance. The islands' birds will be studied systematically to aid in rehabilitating their depleted numbers."   J

3019. Dowty, John B. THE KERN COUNTY HISTORICAL SOCIETY. *Hist. News* 1967 22(5): 113-115. The Kern County (California) Historical Society was formed in 1931 to collect, preserve, and disseminate information relating to the history of the county. The society has an active publications program, a museum and library, a 35 building pioneer village, a historical markers program, and other historical programs. 6 illus.   D. L. Smith

3020. Dudley, Norman. RECENT CALIFORNIANA. *Southern California Q.* 1965 47(1): 103-110. This account of recent acquisitions in California history includes a description of the Robert B. Honeyman, Jr. Collection at the Bancroft Library (U. of California, Berkeley), consisting

mainly of pictorial art. Other new collections at the University of California, Los Angeles, Huntington Library, Honnold Library, California Historical Society Library, and San Francisco Public Library are also listed, along with collecting and indexing being done by other California institutions.
                                                                    J. Jensen

3021. Eiselen, Malcolm R.   THE DAY THAT CALIFORNIA CHANGED WORLD HISTORY.   *Pacific Historian 1966 10(1): 49-57.* A detailed account of election day 7 November 1916 when Woodrow Wilson went to bed prepared for defeat in the presidential race, only to find that California's late returns enabled him to defeat Charles Evans Hughes. Beginning with a conventional treatment of the differences between the two candidates, the author then shows that Hughes unwittingly became the victim of a California factional fight when he visited the State. The recently victorious Progressives under Hiram Johnson were opposed by the remnants of an Old Guard machine led by William H. Crocker. Johnson's Senate fight was more important to both factions than was Hughes's election. Hughes allowed himself to be used by the conservatives when he appeared at a meeting presided over by Crocker. His innocent prefatory remarks alienated the Progressives. A day later Hughes allowed himself to be served a luncheon by strikebreaking waiters. Finally, he inadvertently failed to pay his respects to Johnson when both men coincidentally turned up at the same hotel. The election returns showed the fruits of the Progressives' decision not to work for Hughes's victory. There is further speculation on the possibly changed course of history of American foreign policy toward Germany had Hughes won. Germany, the author points out, believed that Wilson would not enter a major war but that Hughes would do so readily. Illus.
                                                                    T. R. Cripps

3022. Elliott, Mary Joan, ed.   THE 1851 CALIFORNIA JOURNAL OF M.V.B. FOWLER.   *Southern California Q. 1968 50(2): 113-160.* Concerns the journal of Matthew Van Benschoten Fowler of New York who was one of the thousands who flocked to California after 1848. Fowler possessed an observant eye and his journal is "a literate, cool appraisal of California life in 1851 as viewed by an educated Easterner." As a customs inspector in San Francisco, he saw and reported much about people and events. Later, while in search of land suitable for farming, he gave detailed views of ranchos and missions which he saw in the Santa Clara Valley. He also described a session of the State legislature which he attended in San Jose. Frustrated and discouraged with his prospects in California, Fowler impulsively boarded a steamer for Panama and the last 21 pages of his 62-page journal describe his trip and the isthmian crossing. Reproduced are entries only for the period 21 February to 5 April 1851 when Fowler was a customs official. In an introduction, the editor discloses other details about Fowler's career, both prior and subsequent to his California odyssey. Based on a document held by the University of California, Los Angeles; 74 notes.
                                                                    W. L. Bowers

3023. Evans, Peter A.   THE FIRST HUNDRED YEARS: A DESCRIPTIVE BIBLIOGRAPHY OF CALIFORNIA HISTORICAL SOCIETY PUBLICATIONS, 1871-1971.   *California Hist. Q. 1971 50(2): 163-194.* Founded in 1871, the California Historical Society has published many "special" publications apart from its *Quarterly,* which began in 1922. These publications have included translations of documents, speeches and addresses, scholarly papers, contemporary diaries, studies in local history, the monthly *Notes,* art catalogs, and a miscellaneous assortment of brochures, broadsides, keepsakes, reprints from the *Quarterly,* and other ephemera. Only seven publications were printed between 1871 and 1922; the strength of the society's publication program dates from 1922, with the efforts of scholars such as Henry R. Wagner, Charles L. Camp, Robert E. Cowan, and other organizers and sponsors who devoted time, money, and energy to put the society on a firm foundation.
                                                                    A. Hoffman

3024. Evans, William Edward.   THE GARRA UPRISING: CONFLICT BETWEEN SAN DIEGO INDIANS AND SETTLERS IN 1851.   *California Hist. Soc. Q. 1966 45(4): 339-349.* Sees the Garra uprising near San Diego in 1851 as an example of a fight for survival by the Indians in a primitive, highly competitive environment. The Anglo-American migration into California after 1849 was interpreted by the Indian as a threat to his culture. He responded accordingly. Antonio Garra chose to lead an uprising rather than pay a property tax to which all Southern California was opposed. This decision was unwise because there was a movement on foot to obtain the franchise for Christianized

Indians. Had Garra acted otherwise "he might have prevented many deaths, and perhaps led the way to Indian suffrage in California." Based on material in the National Archives and newspapers, 33 notes.
                                                                    E. P. Stickney

3025. Fisher, James A.   THE POLITICAL DEVELOPMENT OF THE BLACK COMMUNITY IN CALIFORNIA, 1850-1950.   *California Hist. Q. 1971 50(3): 256-266.* Blacks have actively participated in the political process in California since the days of the Gold Rush. Although a comparatively small minority numerically until World War II, California's black community has asserted its right to migrate to California, to testify in court, to vote, and to serve on juries. Many of these rights were won through campaigns waged in the 19th century. Blacks also resisted attempts to channel their children into vocational or industrial schools. More recently, the black community has been able through elected representatives to take a more active voice in political affairs. The accomplishments of the black community must be weighed against its struggle to achieve equality in the face of intolerance and racial injustice. Based on secondary sources; 35 notes.
                                                                    A. Hoffman

3026. Fisher, James A.   THE STRUGGLE FOR NEGRO TESTIMONY IN CALIFORNIA, 1851-1863.   *Southern California Q. 1969 51(4): 313-324.* A discussion of the 12-year struggle (1851-63) of California Negroes to gain the right to testify "for or against white persons in state courts." During these years, Negroes unavailingly petitioned the legislature to repeal anti-Negro testimony laws which had been passed in 1850 and 1851. They also made speeches, held conventions, and published editorials in the short-lived newspaper *The Mirror of the Times* (San Francisco). Repeal of the laws finally came in 1863, probably due in large part to the humanitarian impulses toward Negroes generated by the Civil War, although the author suggests that the 12 years of Negro agitation also had some impact on legislative sentiment. Based on contemporary newspaper accounts, public documents, and secondary sources; 52 notes.
                                                                    W. L. Bowers

3027. Forbes, Jack D.   THE NATIVE AMERICAN EXPERIENCE IN CALIFORNIA HISTORY.   *California Hist. Q. 1971 50(3): 234-242.* California Indians represent in microcosm the Indian experience in North America. Nonmaterialistic and inner-directed, for 15 thousand years the Indians of California thrived in at least 500 groups, living generally in peace with each other. They built no monuments and kept no slaves, but instead discouraged the garnering of material wealth and looked on hospitality and sharing as important virtues. When the materialistic and technologically oriented Europeans confronted the Indians, physical conquest was accomplished without much difficulty. The conquest by the Spaniards and the genocidal campaigns of the Anglo-Americans reduced the Indian population of California by some 90 percent. In the past 100 years the Indians have slowly been recovering from these shocks to their physical existence, stubbornly maintaining their spiritual identities through passive and nonviolent resistance to the white man's religion, exploitation, and bureaucracy. Note.
                                                                    A. Hoffman

3028. Franklin, William E.   THE ARCHY CASE: THE CALIFORNIA SUPREME COURT REFUSES TO FREE A SLAVE.   *Pacific Hist. R. 1963 32(2): 137-154.* Examines the legal arguments for and against freeing a slave brought to California by a citizen of Mississippi. Believes the decision was consistent with the views of Justice Burnett who disliked Negroes, slave or free, and wanted them barred from the community in which he lived.
                                                                    J. McCutcheon

3029. Furlong, Martha Rice.   BY LAND AND SEA: THE STORY OF SOME EARLY SANTA BARBARANS.   *Noticias 1967 13(2): 1-15.* The schooner "Eustace" was launched at Newburyport, Massachusetts, in 1864 under the command of Captain Matthew W. Furlong. "Motives for selecting Santa Barbara as the goal for the Furlongs varied from the founding of the first Episcopal Church to carrying cargo between Santa Cruz Island and the Mainland." Furlong was the skipper until 1869, when the ship was sold; he decided to stay in Santa Barbara, marry, and engage in business. Reprints a letter from his sister, Mary Elizabeth Furlong, who told of her trip around the Horn in 1864-65. Reproduces several of the voluminous letters to her brothers in the East, in which she gave pictures of her life in Santa Barbara. Discusses the Reverend Thomas George Williams, the first rector of Trinity Church (Episcopal) in Santa Barbara. The Furlongs spent their later years in San Francisco. Illus.
                                                                    E. P. Stickney

3030. Gibson, James R. RUSSIA IN CALIFORNIA, 1833. *Pacific Northwest Q. 1969 60(4): 205-215.* Sketches the activities of Russians in the early settlement in California, with particular reference to the observations of Ferdinand Petrovich Wrangel as reported following his inspection of the colony in 1833. Wrangel's report describes the settlement of Fort Ross, pointing out the economic considerations of grain-raising, stockbreeding, and other efforts. Charts show the number of inhabitants in the settlement by sex, age, and race. Based largely on Russian records and papers; notes.
C. C. Gorchels

3031. Gibson, Patricia. CALIFORNIA AND THE COMPROMISE OF 1850. *J. of the West 1969 8(4): 578-591.* Reviews the situation in the United States leading to the Compromise of 1850. Discusses the place of California in the bargaining. With slavery the paramount issue in Congress, the requests for recognition by the settlers of the California territory were bypassed. In California this created a local situation which resulted in the first resolution of Henry Clay's Compromise and brought about the formation of the State of California.
R. N. Alvis

3032. Gordon, Dudley. CALIFORNIA'S FIRST HALF-CENTURY OF STATEHOOD, 1850-1900. *Southern California Q. 1971 53(2): 133-146.* A description, including excerpts, of Charles Fletcher Lummis' *The Right Hand of the Continent,* a "socio-economic-cultural analysis of California and its achievements during the first fifty years of statehood." The work was copyrighted by Harper's in 1899 but because of a disagreement which arose with Lummis it was not published by them. In 1902-03, Lummis, a Los Angeles journalist-historian, published 13 chapters of the book in his magazine, *Out West.* Quoted excerpts from the series emphasize California's early population growth, its contributions to the Nation in terms of natural resource wealth and prominent political and literary figures, and its relationship to specific aspects of national development, e.g., the need for steamboats, railroads, and a pony express to tie California to the East coast.
W. L. Bowers

3033. Gould, Richard A. INDIAN AND WHITE VERSIONS OF "THE BURNT RANCH MASSACRE": A STUDY IN COMPARATIVE ETHNOHISTORY. *J. of the Folklore Inst. 1966 3(1): 30-42.* A comparison of a white account of an Indian massacre in northwestern California with several accounts gathered from Tolowa Indians who had heard of the "massacre" when very young reveals little "objective" history but is evidence that historians select "the happenings and impressions which had meaning in the light of the values and attitudes of their respective cultures." 11 notes.
J. C. Crowe

3034. Gregg, James E. NEWSPAPER EDITORIAL ENDORSEMENTS AND CALIFORNIA ELECTIONS, 1948-62. *Journalism Q. 1965 42(4): 532-538.* Study of eleven California daily newspapers, accounting for 40 percent of the total newspaper circulation in the state, in biennial elections from 1948 through 1962 shows that newspaper editorial endorsements are significantly influential in election outcomes; have a greater influence upon the outcome of local elections than on state and national elections; have a greater influence on measures than on candidates; are less influential when voters have other sources of information upon which to reach decisions, such as incumbency or radio-television "exposure." Endorsements of candidates of a party opposite to that which the newspaper usually supports are more influential, as voters apparently pay more attention to them. But all endorsements are so influential that it behooves publishers to keep in mind the obligations they undertake when they make endorsements. Notes on theory and methodology.
S. E. Humphreys

3035. Griffiths, David B. ANTI-MONOPOLY MOVEMENT IN CALIFORNIA, 1873-1898. *Southern California Q. 1970 52(2): 93-121.* Discusses antimonopoly reform movements in California between 1873 and 1898. Reform parties and associations mentioned include the People's Independent Party (1873-79), the International Workingmen's Association (Socialist, 1881-86), the San Francisco Nationalist Club (Bellamy Socialists, 1889-90), and the Populist Party (1891-98). All of these groups were antimonopolistic and were opposed to the Southern Pacific Railroad which was the most powerful political and economic force in California during these years. All of them also suffered from factionalism, which was one of the chief causes for their decline. Despite failure to gain their goals at the time, many of their ideas were later promoted by California Progressives. Based on primary and secondary sources; 111 notes.
W. L. Bowers

3036. Guice, C. Norman, ed. THE "CONTENTIOUS COMMODORE" AND SAN FRANCISCO: TWO 1850 LETTERS FROM THOMAS AP CATESBY JONES. *Pacific Hist. R. 1965 34(3): 337-342.* Two letters pointing out the defenseless position of San Francisco, California in case of blockade.
J. McCutcheon

3037. Guzman, Ralph. THE FUNCTION OF ANGLO-AMERICAN RACISM IN THE POLITICAL DEVELOPMENT OF CHICANOS. *California Hist. Q. 1971 50(3): 321-337.* A survey of Anglo-American attitudes toward Chicanos in California, from the viewpoint of how Anglos have looked upon the political development of Chicanos with presupposed ideologies. These include the stereotypes accorded to Chicanos in this century, from arguments alleging their racial inferiority, praising their docility, and holding them responsible for their own poverty, to asserting their propensity toward violence. Despite efforts of Chicanos to assert their identity in the face of such racist views, Anglos still labor under numerous misapprehensions about Chicano participation in political activity and socioeconomic advancement. Even now the question of who legitimately represents the Chicano community, though asked by Anglos, requires an answer fitting Anglo definitions and preconceptions. Based on secondary sources; 39 notes.
A. Hoffman

3038. Hawgood, John A., ed. A LETTER OF JOHN AUGUSTUS SUTTER. *U. of Birmingham Hist. J. [Great Britain] 1965 10(1): 90-94.* Gives the text of a letter from John Augustus Sutter, whose enterprises in Northern California helped to open up the area to settlement. The letter, dated 1 May 1852, to boyhood friend Jacob Hess in his native German town of Kandern, reveals both something of the development of California and the flamboyant character of Sutter himself. The German language original is in the town museum of Massillon, Ohio. 7 notes.
D. H. Murdoch

3039. Hayes, Hugh E. CAPTAIN WILLIAM S. MOSS: CALIFORNIA CHARACTER EXTRAORDINARY. *Pacific Historian 1967 11(4): 3-16.* Moss made a fortune in New Orleans and at the beginning of the Civil War he freed 96 slaves and migrated to California. At the death of Abraham Lincoln, Moss ran a headline in his paper, a Democratic sheet reflecting his Virginia heritage: "Sic Semper Tyrannis!" The resultant mob outside his San Francisco shop created a destructive riot for which Moss sued the city. His residence was a stylish house in San Leandro outside Oakland, and he also had a ranch near Stockton where he died in 1883. Documented from interviews, published accounts, manuscript collections, and newspapers; 2 photos.
T. R. Cripps

3040. Heizer, Robert F. CIVIL RIGHTS IN CALIFORNIA IN THE 1850'S - A CASE HISTORY. *Kroeber Anthropological Soc. Papers 1964 31: 129-137.* Presents the report of the case of *The People vs. Hall,* 1 October 1854, as determined by the Supreme Court of the State of California. The defendant, who had been previously convicted of murder on the testimony of Chinese witnesses, was cleared under extended interpretation of Sections 394 and 14 of the California Criminal Act. These sections state that the testimony of "Black, Mulatto or Indian" witnesses is not permissible in trying cases involving "White" defendants. The extension was made to include "Chinese" due to a suggested common origin of the Indian and Chinese "Races." The author includes some comments on racial discrimination and Indian indentureship in California. Based on primary and secondary sources; biblio.
C. N. Warren

3041. Holland, Francis, Jr. and Walker, Theodore. NINETEENTH CENTURY SHORE WHALING IN SAN DIEGO. *Western Explorer 1964 3(2): 13-19.* Shore whaling involved waiting along the coastline for California gray whales which migrated every summer from their feeding grounds in the Bering Sea to the lagoons of Baja California. It began in San Diego shortly after 1855 and continued until the late 1880's. During that time nearly 2,000 whales were slaughtered by the San Diego whaling industry as its "contribution to the decline in numbers of the California Gray Whale." The authors argue that the intense whaling activity reflected typical 19th-century attitudes concerning conservation: "the resource exists in abundance, there is no reason to believe it won't last forever." There is virtually no secondary information on shore whaling in San Diego. Newspapers are the most profitable primary source; illus., notes.
W. L. Bowers

3042. Holton, Charlotte P. THE WHITNEY GEOLOGICAL SURVEY: ITS CONFLICT WITH THE CALIFORNIA LEGISLATURE. *J. of the West 1969 8(2): 200-208.* Describes the career of Josiah Dwight Whitney (1819-96) as the first incumbent of the office of California State Geologist. His job was "to make an accurate and complete geological survey of the state, and to furnish in his report of the same, proper maps, and diagrams . . . with a full and scientific description of its rocks, fossils, soils, and minerals, etc. . . ." The State hoped to find new mineral deposits, and it reduced the amount of money to support the office when new deposits were not found. Whitney finally gave up in disgust in 1875 and returned to Harvard University. 2 appendixes.   J

3043. Hoopes, Chad L. REDICK MC KEE AND THE HUMBOLDT BAY REGION, 1851-1852. *California Hist. Soc. Q. 1970 49(3): 195-219.* McKee was one of the three Indian agents authorized to negotiate treaties with the California Indians. A niggardly Congress, white settlers, and ambiguous authorizations and instructions plagued McKee and his associates. McKee assumed the responsibility of negotiating with Indian tribes in northern California. He traveled to Humboldt Bay and sought to establish a reservation for the Eel River Indians, to protect the Indians from the settlers' demands. McKee found himself jammed between the needs of the Indians and the claims of the white settlers. A series of 18 treaties concluded by the three agents in 1851 established reservations. The U.S. Senate rejected these treaties on the grounds that the agents had granted immense areas, including choice lands, to the Indians. Meanwhile, California launched a policy of extermination against the Indians. Finally a system of military posts in conjunction with Indian reservations was adopted. McKee's humanitarian efforts contrast with the attitudes of Governor John Bigler and several California legislators. Based on Congressional and State documents and published sources; 62 notes.   A. Hoffman

3044. Hutchinson, W. H. BEAR FLAG AND LONE STAR: TWO IMPERIAL POWERS AND THEIR STEREOTYPES. *Southwestern Hist. Q. 1968 72(2): 141-151.* A humorous address reviewing the histories and chamber-of-commerce aspects of Texas and California, with Texas running second.   D. L. Smith

3045. Huxley, Aldous. I. OZYMANDIAS, THE UTOPIA THAT FAILED. *California Hist. Q. 1972 51(2): 117-130.* Llano del Rio was a cooperative Socialist colony which existed 1914-18 in the Antelope Valley. Founded by Job Harriman, the Llano colony was intended as a self-sufficient, cooperative society that would provide for its members in employment, recreation, education, and welfare. Memberships were sold through the capitalistic device of stock certificates. Although over a thousand people were attracted to the colony, lack of water, internal dissension, and financial difficulties caused the abandonment of the California site and a move to a new location in Louisiana in 1918. Discusses philosophical and psychological aspects of the Llano experiment, and the lessons learned by Harriman and the colonists from the experience. Illus.   A. Hoffman

3046. Johnson, Kenneth M. CALIFORNIA'S CONSTITUTION OF 1879: AN UNPAID DEBT. *California Hist. Soc. Q. 1970 49(2): 135-141.* The delegates who met in 1878 to create a new constitution for the State of California were allotted 150 thousand dollars for expenses, with no funds provided for expenses incurred after the hundredth day of the convention. The convention lasted 157 days and, to meet the added expenses, scrip was issued to delegates, clerks, janitors, etc., to the approximate amount of 75 thousand dollars. A section in the new constitution provided for payment of this debt by the legislature. However, unhappiness over the new constitution, which failed as a panacea for the State's problems, resulted in the legislature's refusal to pay for the warrants. A second reason lay in speculation, as a few persons purchased the scrip at a discount in hopes of realizing a profit when payment was authorized. Such schemes were unsuccessful; to this day the State of California has never paid. Illus., photo, 8 notes.   A. Hoffman

3047. Johnson, Kenneth M. A LITTLE BIT MORE ON PARKER H. FRENCH. *Southern California Q. 1967 49(3): 305-310.* Concerns a little-known court case involving Parker H. French, California pioneer lawyer, and James Lick, early day millionaire and philanthropist. The case concerned a lot in San Francisco which both men bought independently of each other, one from the original Mexican owner who had

purchased it in 1846, and the other from a man who had a power of attorney. The court was to decide whether the rightful purchaser was French who had bought the lot from the owner or Lick who had obtained it from the possessor of the power of attorney. The case was heard three times between 1856 and 1859. Twice the District Court ruled in Lick's favor and was reversed by the California Supreme Court when French appealed the decision. The third time the lower court ruled in French's favor and the Supreme Court upheld the decision when Lick appealed it. Based on California State Supreme Court records.   W. L. Bowers

3048. Kagan, Paul. II. PORTRAIT OF A CALIFORNIA UTOPIA. *California Hist. Q. 1972 51(2): 131-154.* A pictorial essay which traces Llano del Rio's history in California. Illus., 15 notes.   A. Hoffman

3049. Kahn, Edgar M. JUDAH PHILIP BENJAMIN IN CALIFORNIA. *California Hist. Soc. Q. 1968 47(2): 157-173.* Judah Benjamin was born of Jewish parents 6 August 1811 on the island of Saint Croix. The family moved to the United States about 1813 and by 1822 were settled in Charleston, South Carolina. At 14 Benjamin entered Yale but left without a degree and went to New Orleans, where in 1832 he was elected to the Louisiana House of Representatives. In 1849 he was admitted to practice before the US Supreme Court and three years later was elected a Senator. In 1860 he arrived in California on a mineral and land law case but left to join the Confederate Cabinet. After the Civil War he escaped to England where he won distinction as a barrister. In 1883 he moved to Paris, where he died in 1884. His several biographers have not adequately covered the California years, being mistaken as to the date of his arrival in that State. The question of this date is fully investigated here, with documentation.   E. P. Stickney

3050. Leadingham, Grace. JULIET WELLS BRIER: HEROINE OF DEATH VALLEY. *Pacific Historian 1964 8(1): 13-20.* Attempts to depict the early life of Juliet W. Brier, "a member of the most unfortunate overland emigrant party of 1849." She was born in 1814 in Bennington, Vermont. As depressed conditions worsened in the 1820's the family moved to Michigan. Their early life was influenced by revivalism and Horace Greeley's temperance speeches. While still poverty-stricken in Michigan, she married a Pennsylvania circuit rider, James Brier, and in 1841 began a life of "wayfaring." No sources cited save for one letter: Julia Brier to "My dear brother", 25 February 1849 and a brief reference to the St. Joseph Company, Michigan "vital statistics."   T. R. Cripps

3051. Leiby, James. STATE WELFARE ADMINISTRATION IN CALIFORNIA, 1879-1929. *Pacific Hist. R. 1972 41(2): 169-187.* Describes the development of the theory and administration of social welfare in California from the concept of "public charity" to the establishment of the State Department of Social Welfare in 1927. The notable progress which had taken place within a generation recognized the role of the State government but was still concerned primarily with those outside the labor market. The depression to follow, which led to demands for economic security of labor and a new Federal role, had not yet been foreseen. 57 notes.   E. C. Hyslop

3052. Lloyd, C. L. SANTA BARBARA. *Noticias 1963 Occasional Papers (2): [3-36].* An 1893 description of Santa Barbara. Answers supposed questions of would-be immigrants to the area. Pictures the country and its agrarian attributes, population, and climate. Describes the Santa Ynez Valley, Los Alamos, Santa Maria, Lompoc, and Santa Barbara itself, its valley, floral carnival, and hotel accommodations. 3 illus., note.   T. M. Condon

3053. Lowman, Matt P., II and Johnson, Richard Colles. THE CALIFORNIA "CONSTITUTION" OF 1849. *Papers of the Biblio. Soc. of Am. 1969 63(1): 25-29.* The first edition of the *Constitution* was printed in 1849 in two settings. Notes errors and differences in the two settings; haste in printing probably caused them. 11 notes.   C. A. Newton

3054. Lowney, Barbara. LADY BOUNTIFUL: MARGARET CROCKER OF SACRAMENTO. *California Hist. Soc. Q. 1968 47(2): 99-112.* Mrs. Crocker (1821-1901) was born Margaret Ellen Rhodes, the 13th child in the family. Her youth was that of a pioneer woman in northern Ohio. At the age of 26 she met Edwin Bryant Crocker, a lawyer and widower, in South Bend, Indiana. After marriage they moved to

Sacramento, where he set up a successful law practice and was later appointed to the Supreme Court of California. The Crockers were noted for their hospitality and charity, and for founding an outstanding art gallery. On 6 May 1885 Sacramento held a floral festival in her honor. Illus., 38 notes.   W. A. Buckman

3055. Mawn, Geoffrey P. FRAMEWORK FOR DESTINY: SAN FRANCISCO, 1847. *California Hist. Q. 1972 51(2): 165-178.* Yerba Buena, the town that become San Francisco in 1847, required a survey plan for the properties and lots. The work involved in conducting the survey was done by Jasper O'Farrell, a civil engineer and surveyor. Opposition from some property owners, earlier inaccurate surveys, and arguments over the pattern to be followed were some of the problems that confronted O'Farrell. The project took over four months. The survey provided clear title for existing properties, mapped out streets, and opened up beach and water lots for sale. The survey stimulated the fledgling city's development, protected land titles, and provided a source of revenue for civic improvements. Based on primary and secondary sources; 2 illus., 2 maps, 36 notes.   A. Hoffman

3056. McDow, Roberta M. STATE SEPARATION SCHEMES, 1907-1921. *California Hist. Soc. Q. 1970 49(1): 39-46.* An account of the schemes proposed between 1907 and 1921 for separating California into two States. Motivation for separation arose out of alleged inequities in political representation, assessed valuation of counties, and passage of legislation. Movements for separation can be detected in 1907, 1909, 1914, and 1921. A leading spokesman for separation during this period was State Senator Robert Nelson Bulla. The proposals for separation all failed, inevitably because of a lack of popular support and recognition that many of the grievances were more apparent than real. Los Angeles feared that separation would result in a loss of Owens Valley water. There was also an overriding loyalty by people to the State as a whole rather than to a particular section of it. Based chiefly on contemporary newspaper accounts; 38 notes.   A. Hoffman

3057. McDow, Roberta M. TO DIVIDE OR NOT TO DIVIDE?: CALIFORNIA'S HUNDRED YEAR DEBATE! *Pacific Historian 1966 10(4): 22-33.* Discusses the numerous attempts to divide California into two states, from the first constitutional debates in 1849 to the 1965 Dolwig Bill. Not all attempts were serious, but some, like the Pico Act of 1859, passed both houses of the legislature. After the Civil War placed a stigma on separatist movements the newspapers resurrected the idea in the 1870's. Southern enthusiasm reached a peak with plans for "the Constitutional Convention for the State of Southern California" in 1881, but waned afterward. Increasing tax assessments on land kept interest alive, especially in the growing Los Angeles area. After the turn of the century, natural phenomena intruded in the argument, including such issues as water resources and earthquakes. Other debates centered on the rivalry between Los Angeles and San Francisco and on apportionment in the legislature. As late as 1965, when polls revealed that majorities of both Northerners and Southerners opposed division, the idea has been taken less seriously than in the past. Documented chiefly from newspapers, local histories, scholarly journals, and local witnesses; illus.
                                          T. R. Cripps

3058. Melendy, H. Brett. KLAMATH COUNTY, A STRUGGLE FOR POLITICAL EXISTENCE. *California Historian 1964 10(3): 65-70.* Inadequate financial resources, isolation, and lack of industry or any basic agricultural commodity prevented elected officials in Klamath County from putting into operation the normal governmental services expected. When neighboring counties grew, and after trying out three county seats, Klamath County was divided between Humboldt and Siskiyou counties. Residents of Siskiyou voted against accepting part of Klamath but lost their appeal to the California State Supreme Court. Assets were divided by a four-man commission appointed by the legislature in 1876. 21 notes.   E. P. Stickney

3059. Modell, John. CLASS OR ETHNIC SOLIDARITY: THE JAPANESE AMERICAN COMPANY UNION. *Pacific Hist. Rev. 1969 38(2): 193-206.* By the 1930's the fruitstand was the symbol of economic strength to the older Japanese Americans but of frustration to the younger ones. Describes the threat which unionization posed in this situation to the ethnic and family solidarity of the Nisei. The Retail Food Clerks' Union of the American Federation of Labor (AFL) made a con-

certed effort to organize the food industry in Los Angeles in 1937. Traces the conflict between this union and the subsequent Nisei-organized union and the effect of both on racial cohesion and interracial labor problems. 34 notes.   E. C. Hyslop

3060. Moore, Helen L. A DEDICATION TO THE MEMORY OF ROCKWELL DENNIS HUNT, 1868-1966. *Arizona and the West 1967 9(3): 207-210.* Californian Rockwell Dennis Hunt's 1895 doctoral dissertation (Johns Hopkins University) concerned the genesis of the State's first constitution. His academic career in various institutions of the State culminated in the graduate deanship of the University of Southern California. His postretirement activities included the directorship of the California History Foundation and formation of the Conference of California Historical Societies. His articles and 19 books were primarily concerned with the history of the State and the history of some of its educational institutions. He had participated in and witnessed much of the history he wrote about. Appended with a selected list of his writings; illus.   D. L. Smith

3061. Moriarty, James Robert, III and Weyland, William Robert. EXCAVATIONS AT SAN DIEGO MISSION. *Masterkey 1971 45(4): 124-137.* This report follows up an earlier "proposed project" account in *Masterkey 1969 43(3): 100-108* on the Historic Site Archaeological Project still in progress at San Diego Mission by students at the University of San Diego. The authors present a general, preliminary report on the excavations during 1969-71. Over 50 thousand artifacts have been collected from the site. The stratigraphic sequence is complex and continuous from 2,000 B.C. to the present. Because of the unexpected finding of a military graveyard, the project is stressing early occupation of the Mission by American troops. Illus., 15 photos, chart.   D. Anness

3062. Nihart, Brook. A NEW YORK REGIMENT IN CALIFORNIA, 1846-1848. *Military Collector and Historian 1969 21(2): 1-11.* Stevenson's Regiment of New York Volunteers (variously known as the California Guard or Regiment, the N. Y. Legion, and the 7th or 1st N. Y.) was raised for service in California during the conflict with Mexico. The unit was remarkable in two respects: it was composed of artisan volunteers who planned to colonize California after their service; and it was a force of combined arms with one mounted company and its own six-gun battery. The uniforms and services of the regiment are detailed. 8 plates, 34 notes.   D. C. Oliver

3063. Nostrand, Richard L. THE SANTA YNEZ VALLEY: HINTERLAND OF COASTAL CALIFORNIA. *Southern California Q. 1966 48(1): 37-56.* Isolated and remote, this small interior valley has, throughout the period of white settlement, been dependent on markets and trading centers outside the local environment. Maps, 67 notes.
                                          H. Kelsey

3064. Nuttall, Donald A. GASPAR DE PORTOLA: DISENCHANTED CONQUISTADOR OF SPANISH UPPER CALIFORNIA. *Southern California Q. 1971 53(3): 185-198.* Portolá led the expedition in 1769 which established Spanish control of Upper California and discovered San Francisco Bay. Portolá, respected by historians and honored by having his name given to a city, numerous streets, and a State park, was a "disenchanted conquistador" because he left his distasteful job as Governor of Lower California only to find the expectations in his new undertaking even more disappointing. Based on primary sources in the Mexican National Archives and on secondary sources; 68 notes.
                                          W. L. Bowers

3065. Olmsted, Roger R. "THE CHINESE MUST GO!" *California Hist. Q. 1971 50(3): 285-294.* A pictorial essay depicting contemporary views of anti-Chinese agitation. Labor leader Denis Kearney urged the exclusion of Chinese from the United States, a view that gained widespread approval in California during the depression period of the 1870's. Cartoons showed the Chinese as an incessant horde seeking to overwhelm the United States by sheer numbers and to monopolize labor and trade. Based on illustrations from collections in the Bancroft Library, the Oakland Museum, and John Howell Books.   A. Hoffman

3066. Olmsted, Roger. THE SENSE OF THE SEVENTIES - CALIFORNIA 100 YEARS AGO. *California Hist. Q. 1971 50(2): 131-162.* More than just the interval between the "gold-grabbing" and the "land-grabbing" years, the decade of the 1870's was a time of transition when the old was still mixed with the new. San Francisco and Los Angeles were erecting new buildings and experimenting with public transportation, new industries were growing rapidly, and the people were a fascinating mixture of *Californios,* "49ers" who had grown with the State, and entrepreneurs with new ideas. 42 photos.   A. Hoffman

3067. Olmsted, Roger R.   THE SQUARE-TOED PACKETS OF SAN FRANCISCO BAY. *California Hist. Q. 1972 51(1): 35-58.* Describes the scow schooners which plied the bay region with cargoes of hay, shingles, lumber, grain, and other bulk products. Box-like in appearance, the scow schooner was an unusual type of sailing ship, but it filled an important utilitarian function in bringing cargoes to cities in the bay region and up the tributaries of the bay. With the development of the internal combustion engine, the schooners became motor scows, and as such lingered on through the 1930's. 20 photos.   A. Hoffman

3068. Pauly, Thomas H.   J. ROSS BROWNE: WINE LOBBYIST AND FRONTIER OPPORTUNIST. *California Hist. Q. 1972 51(2): 99-116.* The possibility of increased Federal taxes on domestic wines prompted California wine growers to send a lobbyist to Washington, D.C., in 1866. The person sent was J[ohn] Ross Browne (1821-75), author, sometime Federal agent, and expert on western mining. The choice of Browne as lobbyist stemmed from his friendship with Benjamin D. Wilson, a major grower of grapes in southern California. Browne also had the support of Colonel Agoston Haraszthy, a northern California grape grower, although several years earlier Browne had figured in an investigation of Haraszthy's handling of the San Francisco mint, an issue that may have caused Haraszthy's resignation. Browne's lobbying activities succeeded in removing the tax on domestic wine entirely and in increasing the tax on imported wines. In addition, Browne won a position as Federal commissioner of western mineral reserves; while conscientious in his representation of the wine growers' interests, he did not hesitate to take advantage of bettering his personal position. The author reproduces a letter from Browne to Wilson. Based on secondary sources; 6 illus., 51 notes.   A. Hoffman

3069. Phoenix, John.   AT SAN DIEGO. *Am. West 1968 5(4): 43-44.* Taken from an 1855 publication. This Fourth of July celebration occurred probably in 1853.   D. L. Smith

3070. Pohlmann, John O.   ALPHONZ E. BELL: A BIOGRAPHY. *Southern California Q. 1964 46(3): 197-217 and (4): 315-343.* Part I. Traces Bell's life from his birth in East Los Angeles, through his student days, theological interests, and tennis championships, to ventures in land development and the discovery of oil on his Santa Fe Springs ranch in 1921. Part II. Covers his development of Bel-Air, the building of his estate "Capo di Monte," the controversy over his attempts to start a cement industry, and his role as benefactor of Occidental College and UCLA. The author emphasizes the large number of accomplishments and the consistent interest in developing Southern California by a man who was one of the wealthiest men in California and one of the largest landowners in Southern California. Uses interviews as well as manuscript and published sources.   J. Jensen

3071. Pomfret, John E.   THE HUNTINGTON LIBRARY: FIFTEEN YEARS' GROWTH, 1951-1966. *California Hist. Soc. Q. 1966 45(3): 241-257.* In the past decade, substantial material has been added in the Civil War field under the direction of Allan Nevins, chairman of the Centennial Commission appointed by President John F. Kennedy. "Efforts have been made to collect in nearly all facets of California's history in the period 1850-1900." Special funds have made possible awards of grants-in-aid to assist scholars working on California and southwestern history; of 30 such scholars, 17 eventually published books. The "art collections are well-known throughout the English-speaking world." Horticulturists from many countries are attracted by the botanical gardens. About 360 thousand visitors come to the Art Gallery, the library exhibitions, and the Botanical Gardens each year.
                                                E. P. Stickney

3072. Posner, Russell M.   THE LORD AND THE DRAYMAN: JAMES BRYCE VS. DENIS KEARNEY. *California Hist. Q. 1971 50(3): 277-284.* After Bryce published his study *The American Commonwealth* in 1888, he received a letter from Kearney protesting the chapter

"Kearneyism in California." Kearney complained that the account was overcritical, distorted, and inaccurate. As a fairminded person, and possibly because of the chance that Kearney might sue, Bryce invited Kearney to present his version of the anti-Chinese agitation of the late 1870's. Kearney responded with a 20-page letter. According to Kearney, his role in bringing attention to the Chinese economic threat was a major one; he had attended as many as five meetings a night, given 130 speeches, and had made the Workingmen's Party into an influential force at the 1879 state constitutional convention. As a result of Kearney's letter, Bryce modified a number of his statements in the book's next edition and included portions of the letter in an appendix. In later editions Bryce added a paragraph that placed Kearney and the Workingmen's Party in a broader and more sympathetic perspective. Based on the correspondence between Bryce and Kearney at the Bodleian Library, Oxford; note.
                                                A. Hoffman

3073. Potter, Hugh O.   OWENSBORO'S ORIGINAL PROPRIETOR. *Register of the Kentucky Hist. Soc. 1971 69(1): 1-16.* Richard Barnes Mason (1797-1850) inherited large tracts of land in Kentucky from the estate of his grandfather, George Mason of Gunston Hall. The acreage included a large part of Owensboro which Richard Mason sold in 1822 for five dollars per acre. Mason (for whom San Francisco's Mason Street and Fort Mason were named) has remained an obscure figure because he did not attempt to gain personal acclaim. Entering the Army in 1817, Richard Mason quickly gained importance. Mason served in California under Stephen Kearney and replaced Kearney as military governor in 1847. Highlights of Mason's military governorship in California included the discovery of gold and attendant problems, and his personal conflict with John C. Frémont which led to a challenge to a duel which was never consummated. Based on county records and secondary sources; 52 notes.   J. F. Paul

3074. Putnam, Jackson K.   POLITICAL CHANGE IN CALIFORNIA, A REVIEW ESSAY. *Southern California Q. 1971 53(4): 345-355.* Discusses political changes in recent California history in terms of the book, *Political Change in California; Critical Elections and Social Movements, 1890-1966* by Michael P. Rogin and John L. Shover (Westport, Conn.: Greenwood, 1970). Party realignment in 1896 forced the Democrats into minority status for the next 40 years. Early in the century, support for reform shifted from rural, Anglo-Saxon, Protestant, middle-class, antilabor elements centered in the south to urban, northern-based, prolabor forces supported by Catholics, the foreign-born, and Bay Area middle-class elements. From this last development emerged the liberal New Deal coalition of the 1930's and the identification of southern California with conservatism. The Democrats found new unity in 1936 and delivered presidential majorities for the next 20 years but were never strong within the State. Rogin and Shover believe that the conservative character of southern California politics is important in the explanation of this paradox. They theorize that right-wing political behavior in that region stems from rapid population growth and a technologically created "synthetic landscape" which have produced a suppressed disappointment phenomenon. Because the American dream has been frustrated, southern Californians look for scapegoats, i.e., minorities, Communists, etc. The reviewer disagrees and argues that conservatism in southern California is due more to the fact that many have achieved material success and now resent any threat to it, real or imagined. The book is important, despite certain shortcomings. 7 notes.   W. L. Bowers

3075. Reinhardt, Richard, ed.   AT SANTA CRUZ. *Am. West 1968 5(4): 40-41.* These observations of Frank H. Gassaway of a Fourth of July celebration first appeared in a San Francisco, California, newspaper in 1882.   D. L. Smith

3076. Reinhardt, Richard.   TAPEWORM TICKETS AND SHOULDER STRIKERS. *Am. West 1966 3(4): 34-41, 85-88.* In the 1850's-70's, while California was still "a bandit-infested wilderness," its infant towns were subjected to all of the infamous practices of election fraud and boss rule known to the similar machines that controlled big city politics in the East. Other ingenious devices and methods were also employed. "Shoulder strikers" were sometimes hired by bosses to patrol polling places to keep the opposition from tampering with their false-bottomed ballot boxes or whatever else close scrutiny might reveal. Each party and nearly every candidate printed a ballot in any desired shape and color. A voter could scratch out a name and write in a substitute or even paste over part of the ticket with a sticker which a rival candidate supplied. Extraordinary pains were taken to design ballots under the strictest secrecy and so intricately as to make them harder to paste over or scratch out. One of these, the "Vallejo Tapeworm," an "ineluctable, unexpungable, irrefrangible" ballot was 5 1/4 inches by 1/2 inch and contained 26 candidates and two constitutional amendments in "diamond" type barely legible to the naked eye. Ballot corruption lessened with reform legislation, especially with the adoption of the Australian ballot system in 1891. Illus.

D. L. Smith

3077. Righter, Robert W. THEODORE H. HITTELL AND HUBERT H. BANCROFT: TWO WESTERN HISTORIANS. *California Hist. Q. 1971 50(2): 101-110.* Theodore Henry Hittell and Hubert Howe Bancroft brought out their multivolume histories of California at almost the same time, yet Hittell never requested permission, and was never invited, to use the resources of Bancroft's collection. The two men were never friends; although neither writer ever abused the other publicly by name, each disagreed with the methods the other had used. Bancroft saw in his "factory" approach to writing history the merit of amassing and digesting materials far in excess of what any single researcher could plow through. On the other hand Hittell, in the tradition of the romantic historians of the 19th century, believed that literary excellence practiced upon a manageable body of source materials yielded better history than Bancroft's "scientific" approach which sacrificed style for production. More than seven decades after the publication of the histories by Hittell and Bancroft, students and scholars still find much of value in both works - Hittell's for its narrative and literary qualities, Bancroft's for its encyclopedic amounts of information. Based on correspondence at the Bancroft and Huntington Libraries, the writings of the two historians, and other published works; photo, 38 notes.

A. Hoffman

3078. Righter, Robert W. THEODORE HENRY HITTELL: CALIFORNIA HISTORIAN. *Southern California Q. 1966 48(3): 289-306.* A brief biography of a California attorney, editor, and legislator, whose historical work was contemporary with that of Hubert Howe Bancroft. Although he was less prominent than Bancroft, Hittell's four-volume *History of California* (San Francisco, 1885-97) is still a standard reference. His treatment of legal questions is considered to be particularly sound, but Hittell is open to criticism for his unsympathetic view of Catholic missions.

H. Kelsey

3079. Righter, Robert W. WASHINGTON BARTLETT: MAYOR OF SAN FRANCISCO, 1883-1887. *J. of the West 1964 3(1): 102-114.* Washington Bartlett was born in 1824 but did not come to California until 1849. During the 1850's he was actively engaged as a journalist and publisher. Turning to politics he was elected county clerk of San Francisco County for three terms. In the 1870's he was elected to the California State Senate and twice during the 1880's was elected Mayor of San Francisco. In 1887 he was elected Governor of California but he died the same year. Despite the fact that San Francisco operated under the weak-mayor system of government, Bartlett was able to make his influence felt in that office. His major fight was over city water rates, but, due largely to the opposition of Chris Buckley, the powerful Democratic boss, he was unable to secure a reduction. He was more successful in preventing private companies from securing monopolies in the field of public transportation. Bartlett proved to be a capable and honest public executive. That San Francisco did not have a more efficient and honest government during the 1880's was due to the venality of other city officials and the system of government under which the city operated. Based on published sources, 69 notes.

D. N. Brown

3080. Robinson, W. W. MYTHMAKING IN THE LOS ANGELES AREA. *Southern California Q. 1963 45(1): 83-94.* Various myths about California and particularly Los Angeles which have prevailed in the past and present are described. Some examples: before California had been seen by white men, it was thought to be an island inhabited by passionate black Amazons; the widely-believed myth that ranchos and other land grants were made in the early period by the king of Spain (they were actually made by the local governor or his representative, only one by the viceroy in Mexico City); California's legendary Robin Hood bandit, Joaquin Murrieta; and the myth that Los Angeles was originally founded with formal ceremony, pomp, and circumstance (it began very quietly as a pueblo in 1781).

A. K. Main

3081. Robinson, W. W. SOUTHERN CALIFORNIA IN FIFTY VOLUMES. *Southern California Q 1968 50(1): 1-4.* Comments on the occasion of the publication of the 50th volume of the *Southern California Quarterly.* Among the impressive contributions of the journal are: the story of the founding of Los Angeles which appeared in 1931; the 1836 census of Los Angeles which was published in 1936; the Mojave Indian studies which were seen in 1965-66 issues; biographies of Pío Pico, J. J. Warner, and Antonio María Lugo which appeared between 1894 and 1896; and account of old highways of the Los Angeles area which was published in 1905; and the story of Henry Dalton of Azusa which was in the 1917 volume. In 1958-59, a cumulative index for the preceding years was compiled, and since then annual indexes have been provided.

W. L. Bowers

3082. Ruiz, Russell A. THE SANTA BARBARA PRESIDIO. *Noticias 1967 13(1): 1-13.* The Presidio, founded in 1782, remained the center of Santa Barbara even after Mexican independence. The arrival of Fremont in 1847, however, found the Presidio abandoned. "The Indian, Mexican, and Spanish soldiers were the real pioneers who first came to this country." Concludes with a preliminary report by Timothy S. Hillebrand on archaeological excavations on the Presidio Chapel site. Illus., map.

E. P. Stickney

3083. Schuyler, Robert L. THE EXHUMATION OF PETER LEBEC: ONE OF THE EARLIEST EXAMPLES OF HISTORIC SITES ARCHAEOLOGY IN CALIFORNIA. *Masterkey 1968 42(4): 142-147.* One of the new areas of interest to American archaeologists and historians is that referred to as "Historic Sites Archaeology." Historic sites archaeology can be defined as simply an interest in remains dating from the historic period in America. The minimum requirement for excavating a historic site to qualify as legitimate archaeology is that the project be motivated by the desire to gain or check specific historical data. Excavation of the grave of Peter Lebeck (d. 1837) by the Foxtail Rangers in 1890 was probably the first example in California of historic site archaeology since it was not only carefully planned and carried out but also was motivated by a legitimate goal - the scholarly search for knowledge. Photo, 7 notes.

C. N. Warren

3084. Shelp, Willard B., Jr. PROHIBITION IN THE MOJAVE DESERT. *Bull. of the Missouri Hist. Soc. 1972 28(4): 267-272.* The author reminisces about his experiences in 1918 on the Mojave Desert. In 1918, he went to California to help his company's resident agent sell Bevo, a weak beer that was legal then. The author was unable to overcome customer resistance to the product in Imperial Valley towns. In desperation for sales, he traveled by automobile to Blythe, a distant desert community. Details perils of Mojave Desert travel in 1918.

H. T. Lovin

3085. Shover, John L. THE CALIFORNIA PROGRESSIVES AND THE 1924 CAMPAIGN. *California Hist. Q. 1972 51(1): 59-74.* For California Progressives, four critical issues highlighted the 1924 electoral campaign. These were the efforts to win control of the legislature from the supporters of economy-minded Governor Richardson; the plan to place a State-financed water plan on the ballot as an initiative; the decision whether to support Hiram Johnson in his bid for the Republican presidential nomination; and in the face of Johnson's failure to get the nomination, the decision whether to support LaFollette against Coolidge. Although California Progressives worked for these goals, the movement was fragmented, and no unifying group supported all four issues. Some Progressives supported part of the program but opposed others. Of the four issues, the Progressives succeeded only in winning control of the legislature. Johnson lost the bid for the nomination and sat out the election; LaFollette supporters were handicapped by their inability to vote for LaFollette directly as a Progressive, because his electors were listed as Socialists on the ballot. The water bonds campaign was also defeated. Nevertheless, despite the defeats and lack of coordination, there was considerable overlap in the public declarations of support by prominent Progressive leaders on these four issues. Progressives thus provided alternatives in an election year that otherwise gave voters little opportunity for choice. Based on primary and secondary sources; 63 notes.

A. Hoffman

3086. Spearman, Walter. THE BARON AND THE SEÑORITA. *Am. Hist. Illus. 1966 1(4): 40-46.* The Russian Baron Nikolai Rezanov dreamed of making the entire areas of Alaska, California, and Hawaii part of the Russian Empire. In 1805 he sailed to Alaska and found the Sitka colony suffering from starvation. He continued on to the Spanish settlement of San Francisco hoping to sell his cargo for food to take back to the Alaskan colony. He was welcomed by the Spanish commandant José Arguello. It is only speculation as to whether Rezanov actually fell in love with Arguello's 15-year-old daughter Concepción or whether he merely pretended in order to gain his needed supplies. Whatever his reasons, it is certain that he did view this marriage alliance as a beginning link toward his goal of a Russian colony in California. While returning to gain the czar's permission for the marriage he died. Concepción joined a convent at the news of his death. Even though the dream was never realized, a small colony (Fort Ross) was established. However, the Russian American Company did not prosper there, and in 1841 John Augustus Sutter purchased Fort Ross from the Russians. 5 illus.

M. J. McBaine

3087. Stanley, Gerald. SENATOR WILLIAM GWIN: MODERATE OR RACIST? *California Hist. Q. 1971 50(3): 243-255.* Recent authors, revising earlier estimates of Gwin's political allegiances, have considered him a moderate in political and social issues surrounding slavery and the Civil War. Actually, Gwin was a political opportunist who brought his Mississippi sympathies with him to California. Gwin opposed the migration of free Negroes to California; his vote against a slavery provision for the 1849 State constitution was based less on principle than on political considerations. In the 1860 election, Gwin supported Breckinridge rather than Douglas, the regular Democratic candidate. His intrigues on behalf of the Confederacy and the institution of slavery during and after the Civil War belie the moderate image Gwin sought for himself in later life. Based on primary and secondary sources; 61 notes.

A. Hoffman

3088. Stone, Lois C. ANDREW JACKSON GRAYSON, ARTIST-NATURALIST OF THE PACIFIC SLOPE. *Am. West 1965 2(3): 19-31.* In 1846 Andrew Jackson Grayson and his family moved to California, where he became proprietor of a general store and bookshop, participated in civic affairs, panned gold, and painted birds. His first exposure to John James Audubon's *Birds of America* in 1853, turned him singlemindedly to pursue what until then was only "an amiable hobby." His paintings and ornithology became well-known through exhibitions and publications in California and Mexico. The collapse of Maximilian's Mexican empire ended his sponsorship of a magnum opus publication in folio, with hand-colored plates and texts in three languages. The untimely death of Grayson a few years later further removed fulfillment of the project. Based on manuscript materials and newspapers principally in the Bancroft Library, including colored illustrations. Excerpted from a forthcoming book. Biblio.

D. L. Smith

3089. Taper, Bernard. MARK TWAIN'S SAN FRANCISCO. *Am. Heritage 1963 14(5): 50-53, 93-94.* Recounts Samuel Clemens' (Mark Twain) sojourn of two years in San Francisco, beginning in 1865, by the end of which time he was on his way to becoming a national figure. Illus.

C. R. Allen, Jr.

3090. Tennis, George. CALIFORNIA'S FIRST STATE ELECTION, NOVEMBER 13, 1849. *Southern California Q. 1968 50(4): 357-394.* On 13 November 1849 Californians voted to ratify their State's new constitution and elected officers for their new State government. Ratification of the constitution was never in doubt and the focus of this article is on the candidates, the campaign, and the election results. The campaign "was essentially not one of issues but of personalities" and data on all candidates for major offices are accordingly given. Problems associated with conducting an election in such a vast area possessing only primitive means of communication and transportation are discussed. Successful candidates are indicated and an assessment of the reasons for their victories is presented. The author concludes that the election's chief significance lies in the fact that by holding it Californians endorsed a State constitution and organized a State government without going through the transitional stage of territorial development. Based on letters, public documents, contemporary sources, and secondary accounts; 172 notes.

W. L. Bowers

3091. Thompson, Kenneth. INSALUBRIOUS CALIFORNIA. *Ann. of the Assoc. of Am. Geographers 1969 59(1): 50-64.* Considers sections of the earliest reports of the State which identified certain portions of the area as being inherently unhealthy and unsuited for settlement. These accounts were based on reports of the occurrence of malaria and other miasmatically derived diseases. Consequently regions characterized by the existence of marshes or bodies of stagnant water were considered to be unhealthy and to be avoided. The Central Valley in particular was identified as undesirable for habitation. It was not until the development of the germ theory of disease that a new perception of these environments emerged. Map, 73 notes.

W. R. Boedecker

3092. Van Winden, Kathe. THE ASSASSINATION OF ABRAHAM LINCOLN: ITS EFFECT IN CALIFORNIA. *J. of the West 1965 4(2): 211-230.* News of the assassination of Lincoln reached San Francisco on 16 April 1865 but Los Angeles did not hear of the crime until two days later. In both cities there was a manifestation of great respect for the martyred President. In both cities an obsequy was held on 19 April. For several days prior to the services San Francisco was in a virtual state of anarchy. Major General Irvin McDowell issued the famous General Orders No. 27 on 17 April which said that any newspaper expressing any sympathy with the assassination would be seized and suppressed. Before and after this order mobs destroyed several newspapers thought to have been sympathetic to the Confederate cause. The city was finally placed under martial law and all was quiet when the memorial services were held. Illus., 20 notes.

D. N. Brown

3093. Wagner, Carol Daily. PALEONTOLOGY AT THE UNIVERSITY OF CALIFORNIA: THE HISTORY OF BACON HALL. *J. of the West 1969 8(2): 169-182.* Traces the history of Bacon Hall from its origin as a home for the collections, art, sculpture, and books of Henry Douglas Bacon, to its demolition in 1961. Includes photographs taken in 1890 and 1893. Originally an art and library building, it housed the departments of Geology, Paleontology, and Mineralogy in 1912 when it no longer proved adequate for the University's library. Gives biographical sketches of those who taught in Bacon Hall, including John Campbell Merriam, Andrew Cowper Lawson, Bruce Lawrence Clark, Charles Lewis Camp, William Diller Matthew, and Ralph Works Chaney.   J

3094. Watkins, T. H. CONQUEST OF THE COLORADO: EARTH-MOVERS, DAM-BUILDERS, AND THE END OF A FREE RIVER. *Am. West 1969 6(4): 4-9, 48, 60.* When the California Development Company cut into the Colorado River in 1901 to divert water into the Imperial Valley which triggered a chain of events that created the Salton Sea, it launched modern man's first major effort to turn the river to his own ends. Power use, flood control, irrigation, recreation, conservation, and other purposes have been served by dams, canals, aqueducts, and other engineering marvels. Tracing these developments in their political and economic contexts, it is concluded that the West's "wildest, freest river" has been made into "one of the greatest plumbing systems in the history of the world." At the expense of much the river has to offer, it is further destined to become "an enormous pipeline . . . one of the most admirably expansive engineering marvels of the century." Illus., note, biblio.

D. L. Smith

3095. Weber, Francis J. A BIBLIOGRAPHY OF CALIFORNIA BIBLIOGRAPHIES. *Southern California Q. 1968 50(1): 5-32.* Discusses bibliographies of California history from Alexander S. Taylor's *Bibliografa Californica* published in 1863 to several collections of references on California development which were published in 1967. An annotated checklist containing 121 bibliographies of California history is included. 42 notes.

W. L. Bowers

3096. Weger, M. Anita. JOSEPH SCOTT: A LIFE OF SERVICE. *Southern California Q. 1966 48(3): 241-264.* The life and career of a noted California attorney, Los Angeles civic leader, and prominent Catholic layman. Illus., 113 notes.

H. Kelsey

3097. Wolf, John Quincy. WHO WROTE "JOE BOWERS"? *Western Folklore 1970 29(2): 77-89.* "Joe Bowers" is a famous folksong that dates back to the California gold rush and tells the story of a forty-niner who is jilted by his girl back in Missouri. Eliminates the many supposed authors as well as the possibility of authorship by a real Joe Bowers. The most probable author is John Woodward, an entertainer in California during the early gold rush. A member of the same group of entertainers composed the music. Points out some of the value the poem has in frontier culture. Based on secondary sources; 21 notes.

R. A. Trennert

3098. Wollenberg, Charles. ETHNIC EXPERIENCES IN CALIFORNIA HISTORY: AN IMPRESSIONISTIC SURVEY. *California Hist. Q. 1971 50(3): 221-233.* Except for Hawaii, California's multiethnic heritage may be the most varied of the continental United States. Surveys the experiences of Indians, Chinese, Japanese, Mexicans, and blacks in California. These minority groups hold a common denominator of discrimination, prejudice, and exploitation in California history. These themes, however, do not comprise the total experience of these ethnic groups. Their involvement in politics, economic development, and foreign policy issues, as well as the contributions stemming from their cultural and social backgrounds, requires intensive study by historians. Offers a bibliographic essay and a chronology of events relating to California's ethnic monorities, 1834-1971. A. Hoffman

3099. Wood, Raymund F. JUAN CRESPI, THE MAN WHO NAMED LOS ANGELES. *Southern California Q. 1971 53(3): 199-234.* An account of four early Spanish expeditions based on Fray Juan Crespi's diaries: the Portolá expedition from Loreto in Lower California to the Monterey-San Francisco Bay area in Upper California (6 March 1769-24 May 1770), the Pedro Fages expeditions to explore the San Francisco Bay area (March-April 1772) and to resupply the Spanish garrison at San Diego (April-September 1772), and the Juan Perez sea expedition up the coast to British Columbia and Alaska (June-August 1774). Much of the account concerns the Portolá expedition's march through present-day Orange County and Los Angeles, when Crespi gave the name "Los Angeles" to the valley where the city is now located. Discusses Crespi and his importance as a missionary-explorer. The 20th-century admiration of Fray Junípero Serra has detracted from the accomplishments of Crespi and other Franciscans in Upper California. Based chiefly on Crespi's diaries; 23 illus., 25 notes. W. L. Bowers

3100. Woodlett, William. LOS ANGELES LANDMARKS. *Historic Preservation 1966 18(4): 161-163.* Describes the survey of historic structures in Los Angeles made by the Historic Buildings Committee of the Southern California Chapter of the American Institute of Architects. Also described is the work of the Los Angeles Cultural Heritage Board in historic preservation. Illus. J. M. Hawes

3101. Woodruff, Janice A. SACRAMENTO LOCAL MUSEUM OPENS. *Hist. News 1967 22(6): 136-138.* The Sacramento (California) City and County Museum was opened on 19 April 1967, with 16 exhibits which depict the history of the area from its earliest times. Plans for the expansion of exhibits and activities depend to a considerable extent on whether or not the museum will be able to relocate in the Old Sacramento Historic Area now in the process of development. 5 illus. D. L. Smith

3102. Wright, Austin T. AN ISLANDIAN ON THE ISLANDS. *Southern California Q. 1963 45(1): 65-82.* A letter written by the author of the utopian novel *Islandia* (New York: New American Library, 1942) regarding a trip made to the Santa Barbara Channel islands in 1931. An introduction by Lawrence Clark Powell outlines the history of the little-known islands and states that Wright's letter "constitutes the fullest description yet made of Santa Rosa and Santa Cruz [islands]. It also beautifully conveys the spirit and feeling of the islands and their relation to the mainland." A. K. Main

3103. —. [CHARLES FLETCHER LUMMIS, CALIFORNIA HISTORIAN].
Gordon, Dudley. JUNIPERO SERRA: CALIFORNIA'S FIRST CITIZEN. *Masterkey 1969 43(1): 22-29.* Deals primarily with the tireless efforts of Charles F. Lummis in promoting California and working for the beatification of Junípero Serra. Gives many interesting similarities between Lummis and Serra and discusses their contributions to California. Serra was "a builder of missions" and Lummis was "a preserver of these missions." A non-Catholic, Lummis was instrumental in incorporating the Landmarks Club of California in 1895. He was the first historian to translate Serra's *Diary* which he published in his *Out West* magazine in 1902. If and when Serra is canonized, it will be mainly due to the efforts of Lummis. Photo.
James, H. C. RECOLLECTIONS OF LUMMIS. *Masterkey 1969 43(2): 67-71.* Lummis, Californian historian, author, editor, publisher, conservationist, and avid crusader for the beatification of Junípero Serra, was one of California's most colorful personalities. Recounts several personal encounters with the fiery Lummis while James was a director for the Trailfinders' School in the early 1900's. Photo. C. N. Warren

3104. —. FLORAL FESTIVAL, SANTA BARBARA, CALIFORNIA. *Noticias 1967 Occasional Papers (8): [1-32].* Contains copies of 1895 "photo-gravures" (by N. H. Reed) of the Santa Barbara Flower Festival. Includes a description by Annie Laurie, "A Merry Battle Waged With Flowers." 31 photos. T. M. Condon

3105. —. LA FAVORITA, RESIDENCE OF WM. P. GOULD, EL MONTECITO, CALIFORNIA. *Noticias 1968 Occasional Papers (11): [1-28].* Contains pictures of William P. Gould's gardens at La Favorita, his Montecito residence. The gardens were the subject of a book published in 1905. Includes a poem, "The Santa Ynez." Illus., 24 photos. T. M. Condon

3106. —. [ROCKWELL DENNIS HUNT]. *Pacific Historian 1966 10(1): 4-14; (2): 10-13.*
Burns, Robert E. A CALIFORNIA HISTORIAN CLOSES A LONG CHAPTER: MEMORIAL TRIBUTE TO DR. ROCKWELL HUNT BY PRESIDENT ROBERT E. BURNS AT UNIVERSITY OF THE PACIFIC CHAPEL, *pp. 4-6.* A tribute to Hunt, a Johns Hopkins Ph.D. and director of the California History Foundation, as "Mr. California," closing with Sam Walter Foss's poem "Bring Me Men to Match My Mountains." Illus.
Hunt, Rockwell D. FREEPORT: MY BOYHOOD HOMETOWN: REMINISCENCES BY ROCKWELL HUNT FROM HIS "BOYHOOD DAYS OF 'MR. CALIFORNIA,'" *pp. 7-14.* A nostalgic account of life in Freeport, a small town on the Sacramento River, in the 1860's. Included is a description of the buildings and commercial institutions with humorous comments on the local characters. Illus.
Short, Alan. CALIFORNIA LEGISLATURE, 1966 REGULAR SESSION, SENATE RESOLUTION RELATIVE TO THE PASSING OF ROCKWELL DENNIS HUNT, *pp. 10-13.* A facsimile of a California Senate resolution testifying to the worth of the historian and teacher Rockwell Hunt. It traces his career from Napa College to Johns Hopkins, then back to Napa as a professor of history. Note is made of his books and his directorship of the California History Foundation and finally the Senate expresses its sorrow at his passing. T. R. Cripps

4. THE CANADIAN WEST

General

3107. Arnold, Abraham J. THE CONTRIBUTION OF THE JEWS TO THE OPENING AND DEVELOPMENT OF THE WEST. *Tr. of the Hist. and Sci. Soc. of Manitoba [Canada] 1968/69 (25): 23-37.* In 1882 the first group of Jewish refugees from Russian pogroms arrived in western Canada. They came on the advice of the Russo-Jewish Committee in London, but it was two years before land was allocated to them, southwest of Moosomin. The settlement was not successful and it was assumed by the government that Jews were unsuited for farming, and hence not to be encouraged as immigrants. Many did make their living as peddlers but the success of half a dozen later farm colonies, which flourished for more than 50 years, proves their agricultural abilities. By 1911 there were 10,741 Jews on the prairies. 62 notes.
L. F. S. Upton

3108. Baptie, Sue. EDGAR DEWDNEY. *Alberta Hist. R. 1968 16(4): 1-10.* An assessment of the role of Edgar Dewdney - trail blazer, Indian commissioner, lieutenant governor of the Northwest Territories, minister of the interior, and lieutenant governor of British Columbia - in the political affairs of western Canada. Emphasis is on his role in Indian affairs and in particular on his involvement with the Riel Rebellion of 1885.
H. M. Burns

3109. Betts, William J. FROM RED RIVER TO THE COLUMBIA. *Beaver [Canada] 1971 301(1): 50-55.* John Flett (1815-92) joined the expedition that brought 23 families from Red River to the Hudson's Bay Company's farm at Fort Nisqually, in 1841. Reprints Flett's "Sketch of the Emigration from Selkirk's Settlement to Puget Sound in 1841" from the Tacoma *Daily Ledger* of 1885. Illus.
L. F. S. Upton

3110. Birrell, Andrew. FORTUNES OF A MISFIT; CHARLES HORETZKY. *Alberta Hist. R. [Canada] 1971 19(1): 9-25.* Describes the career of Horetzky as explorer and photographer in conjunction with surveys of Canadian Pacific Railroad routes through the Rocky Mountains in the late 19th century. Controversy developed as a result of his recommendations.
H. M. Burns

3111. Bocking, D. H. EXPERIENCES OF A DEPRESSION HOBO. *Saskatchewan Hist. [Canada] 1969 22(2): 60-65.* Excerpts from letters written by an [unnamed] young English immigrant during 1930-33. Describes the experiences of a hobo traveling in train boxcars and working in relief camps from Toronto to Vancouver.
C. A. Bishop

3112. Brouillette, Benoit. LES COURANTS COMMERCIAU ENTRE LES PROVINCES DE LA PRAIRIE ET L'EXTERIEUR [The flow of trade between the Prairie Provinces and the outer prairies]. *Mémoires de la Soc. Royale du Can. [Canada] 1968 6(4): 125-141.* Transportation has been essential to economic success for this region which, although in the middle of the continent, has access to all parts of the world. Rail, road, and sea routes are specified, along with the commodities carried. Tables.
L. F. S. Upton

3113. Burpee, Lawrence J. LA VERENDRYE - PATHFINDER OF THE WEST. *Can. Geographical J. [Canada] 1963 66(2): 44-49.* Inspired by an Indian report, La Vérendrye searched for a route from Lake Superior to the Pacific, in the 1730's-40's. He failed in that object but he did discover Western Canada - the Winnipeg River, Lake Winnipeg, and the Rivers Red, Assiniboine and Saskatchewan, and was the first to cross the great plains to the Missouri. Illus., maps.
A. H. Lawrance

3114. Camsell, Charles. MY HOME TOWN. *Can. Geographical J. [Canada] 1964 68(2): 46-51.* The author's early life at Fort Simpson, in the Mackenzie River district. Describes a journey with a fur brigade from Fort Simpson to Prince Albert. Illus., map.
A. H. Lawrance

3115. Carrière, Gaston. LA PÈRE ALBERT LECOMBE, O.M.I., ET LE PACIFIQUE CANADIEN [Father Albert Lacombe, O.M.I.,

and the Canadian Pacific Railroad]. *R. de l'U. d'Ottawa [Canada] 1968 38(1): 97-131 and 38(2): 316-350.* Continued from a previous article. Outlines Father Lacombe's relations with the third president of the Canadian Pacific Railroad, Sir Thomas Shaughnessy, and with other railroad leaders. He continued throughout his later life to cooperate with the CPR. In 1892 he directed an excursion of priests and bishops from Montreal to Vancouver, and in 1895 he organized an excursion of clerics to Manitoba for the consecration of a bishop. The same year he served as an envoy of the mayor of Edmonton to Ottawa and Montreal. Lacombe died in 1916. In 1967, the CPR named its new Edmonton hotel "Le Château Lacombe" after the Oblate missionary.
J. M. Bumsted

3116. Carrière, Gaston. LA PERE ALBERT LECOMBE, O.M.I., ET LE PACIFIQUE CANADIEN [Father Albert Lacombe, O.M.I., and the Canadian Pacific Railroad]. *R. de l'U. d'Ottawa [Canada] 1967 37(2): 287-321, (3): 510-539.* It has been said that the two greatest influences on the making of the Canadian West were the Oblates of Mary Immaculate and the Canadian Pacific Railroad. These two organizations combined in the person of Father Albert Lacombe, who was appointed in 1880 as missionary on the Canadian Pacific Railroad line on behalf of the spiritual welfare of the Indians and the workingmen on the road. In recognition of his assistance in pacifying the Indians, he was feted by the officials of the Canadian Pacific Railroad in Calgary in 1883, and was made "president" of the railroad for the luncheon hour. He thereafter kept the title of honorary president. His assistance to the railroad continued in many ways. Based on unpublished papers of Lacombe, including lengthy selections from his journal. To be continued.
J. M. Bumsted

3117. Carrière, Gaston. LE PERE ALBERT LACOMBE, O.M.I., ET LE PACIFIQUE CANADIEN [Father Albert Lacombe, O.M.I., and the Canadian Pacific Railroad]. *R. de l'U. d'Ottawa [Canada] 1967 37(4): 611-638.* Continued from a previous article. Among Father Lacombe's other services to the Canadian Pacific Railroad was the provision of information on the western prairies and mountain passes which greatly assisted the road's engineers in planning the route. He also played an important role in the second Riel Rebellion, when in response to a request from Prime Minister John A. MacDonald, he successfully used his influence to keep the Blackfoot Indians pacified during the uprising. Throughout his life, Lacombe was honored and beloved by such leaders of the Canadian Pacific Railroad as George Stephen (Baron Mount Stephen) and Sir William Van Horne. To be continued.
J. M. Bumsted

3118. Carrière, Gaston L'HONORABLE COMPAGNIE DE LA BAIE-D'HUDSON ET LES MISSIONS DANS L'OUEST CANADIEN [The Hudson's Bay Company and missions in western Canada]. *R. de l'U. d'Ottawa [Canada] 1966 36(1): 15-39 and 36(2): 232-257.* Both complimentary and derogatory comments were made by missionaries regarding the Hudson's Bay Company's attitude toward them. The author presents the viewpoint of those in authority - their attitude toward the missionaries' impact on Indian culture and their attempt to avoid favoritism among the various Christian denominations despite a natural preference for the Church of England. Company officials refused to get involved in religious matters and wanted to be on good terms with all the missions. The successful mission was welcome, especially if temperance followed conversion. The company had to approve the establishment of missions, however, and its first consideration was always whether they would hurt trade. Relations on the whole were good. Numerous quotations from documents in the archives of the Hudson's Bay Company.
L. F. S. Upton

3119. Carrière, Gaston. L'HONORABLE COMPAGNIE DE LA BAIE D'HUDSON ET LES MISSIONS DANS L'OUEST CANADIEN [The honorable Hudson's Bay Company and the missions of the Canadian West]. *Can. Catholic Hist. Assoc. Annual Report [Canada] 1965 32: 63-80.* In spite of many specific complaints, the Roman Catholic missions received many proofs of generosity and comprehension from the Hudson's Bay Company. The first purpose of the company was trade, and it attempted to stay aloof from any religious affairs, wishing only to maintain good relations with all denominations. The missionaries and their superiors were gratified by the attitude of the company. 73 notes.

C. Thibault

3120. Carrothers, Edward H. THREE TRIPS TO PEACE RIVER COUNTRY. *Alberta Hist. R. [Canada] 1965 13(4): 24-29.* A description of trips made to seek ranch land in the Peace River country.

H. M. Burns

3121. Carter, David J. THE ARCHBISHOPS' WESTERN CANADA FUND AND THE RAILWAY MISSION. *Saskatchewan Hist. [Canada] 1969 22(1): 13-28.* When it became apparent that Anglican missionary activities, in western Canada since 1820, were being withdrawn, a special appeal in 1909 brought results. Upon the recommendations of a chaplain with similar experience in South Africa, funds and volunteers were solicited for the establishment of missions and railway missions for a 10-year period. The Archbishops' (of Canterbury and York) Western Canada Fund was launched in 1910. Also, from the Australian bush, the mission effort borrowed the Brotherhood concept. The Brotherhood was a monastic-like order of single men who provided a roving ministry supplemented by laymen. Under a district missionary, laymen were located at strategic centers along railway lines. The purpose of the plan was to provide church services for developing settlements until they could establish their own churches. In all, the AWCF attracted 138 workers. One hundred sixty-eight sites were obtained; 70 churches and 25 parsonages were built. 5 illus., 17 notes.

D. L. Smith

3122. Carter, David J. ARCHBISHOPS' WESTERN CANADA FUND. *Alberta Hist. R. [Canada] 1968 16(1): 10-17.* An account of the response by the Anglican Archbishops of Canterbury and York to an appeal from western Canada for men and money to meet the challenge of providing for the religious needs of the growing population. Details the fund's launching, impact, and problems.

H. M. Burns

3123. Chalmers, John W. MYSELF THE WANDERER: CANADA'S LITERATE ARTIST, PAUL KANE. *Montana 1970 20(4): 36-49.* Analyzes the art of Paul Kane (1810-71), who painted the people and scenery of the land between the Great Lakes and the Rockies, and on to the coast, during a trip in 1845-48. His pictures have enough realism to give them documentary value, and they display elements of romanticism which reflect his European training. Concludes by comparing Kane's work with that of his contemporary, George Catlin (1796-1872). Based mostly on Kane's writings; illus., 18 notes.

S. R. Davison

3124. Chalmers, J. W. STRANGERS IN OUR MIDST. *Alberta Hist. R. [Canada] 1968 16(1): 18-23.* Discusses Ukrainian settlers in western Canada and their attitude toward education, considering efforts to stress English language instruction for the adult immigrants and children.

H. M. Burns

3125. Cousins, William James. THE EARLY HISTORY OF CROW'S NEST PASS. *Alberta Hist. R. [Canada] 1965 13(4): 1-8.* History of various explorations of Crow's Nest Pass describing trails and terrain with firsthand accounts.

H. M. Burns

3126. Craig, G. M. LETTERS IN CANADA: 1965. SOCIAL STUDIES, LOCAL AND REGIONAL. *U. of Toronto Q. [Canada] 1966 35(4): 472-477.* Survey of works published in 1965 which concern particular sections of Canada and some which do not fit into local or regional classifications. Topics discussed in the local and regional books include: a visitor's impressions of Newfoundland; a history of the maritime provinces, 1712-1857; a biography of Frontenac; descriptions of Montreal; events in Quebec during the 1960's; Toronto under French rule; a diary of the wife of Upper Canada's first lieutenant governor for the years 1791-96; a biography of a pioneering figure in the settlement of southwestern Ontario; a study of Scottish "Loyalists" from New York who came to Ontario during the American Revolution; the 1837 rebellion in Upper Canada; a social history and pictorial record of Toronto in the 19th century; public welfare administration in Ontario, 1791-1893; a history of Manitoba; accounts of homesteading in Saskatchewan and Alberta; the credit union movement in Saskatchewan; scenic descriptions of the British Columbia coast, six major Canadian mountain peaks and two rivers. Subjects covered by the nonlocal and nonregional books include: a history

of Canada's flag; the history of Canada prior to federation; a history of the Jews in Canada to 1900; Canadian-American boundary disputes; Canada's role in the race to build the atom bomb during the Second World War; and biographies of certain Canadian political, literary, artistic, and scientific figures.

W. L. Bowers

3127. Craig, Joan. THREE HUNDRED YEARS OF RECORDS. *Beaver [Canada] 1970 301(Autumn): 65-70.* Describes the accumulation and preservation of the Hudson's Bay Company's records, from their first lodging in London in 1671 to the completion of the microfilming process in 1966 in cooperation with the Public Archives of Canada. Three thousand two hundred linear feet of records are held at the company's archives in Beaver House, London.

L. F. S. Upton

3128. Crofton, George J. A POET IN SCARLET. *Alberta Hist. R. [Canada] 1967 15(3): 17-23.* A collection of poems written by the author, who was a member of the Northwest Mounted Police group making the great trek into Western Canada in 1874.

H. M. Burns

3129. Dales, John R. SOME HISTORICAL AND THEORETICAL COMMENTS ON CANADA'S NATIONAL POLICIES. *Queen's Q. [Canada] 1964 71(3): 297-316.* National policy under Sir John A. Macdonald consisted of three pillars: government support for railroad building, Western settlement, and manufacturing development. The traditional view was that the role of the tariff was to inhibit Canadian-American trade in order to promote East-West trade in Canada, and thus to provide revenue for the Canadian transcontinental railways. In the last decade of the 19th century the Canadian economy reacted favorably to the "closing" of the American frontier, rising world prices, falling shipping rates, and the development of the technique of making paper from wood pulp. Thus economic forces triumphed over the national policies of Macdonald and his successors. 6 notes.

E. P. Stickney

3130. Dashew, Doris W. THE STORY OF AN ILLUSION: THE PLAN TO TRADE "ALABAMA" CLAIMS FOR CANADA. *Civil War Hist. 1969 15(4): 332-348.* An account of the abortive American efforts to annex certain Canadian provinces, particularly British Columbia, Red River (Manitoba), and Nova Scotia, in exchange for the dropping of the *Alabama* claims against Great Britain for Civil War damages. The campaign reached a peak in the spring and summer of 1870, with American expansionists, Canadian separatists, and British anti-imperialists seemingly combining forces. The plan was dropped late in 1870 because, on the one hand, the British authorities continued to postpone a decision on the matter while, on the other, American "commercial and financial groups" pressed the U.S. Government for a quick settlement of the dispute on the merchant marine *Alabama* on a cash basis.

E. C. Murdock

3131. Davies, K. G. FROM COMPETITION TO UNION. *Minnesota Hist. 1966 40(4): 166-177.* Studies what the author calls the "clash of styles" in the struggle between the North West and the Hudson's Bay Company between 1800 and 1821. As he sees it, the Hudson's Bay Company tended to be more formal, sober, and persistent - more British, while the North West Company was dashing, flamboyant, and extravagant - more Canadian. A further important feature was the position of moral righteousness assumed by the 5th Earl of Selkirk and his colleagues of the Hudson's Bay Company. Material from the Hudson's Bay Company Archives.

P. L. Simon

3132. Dempsey, Hugh A. DAVID THOMPSON OF THE PEACE RIVER. *Alberta Hist. R. [Canada] 1966 14(1): 1-10, (2): 14-21.* Excerpts from the original journal of David Thompson, explorer and cartographer, written during a survey trip to the Peace River. The second installment describes journeys made to explore the Peace and the Notikewin Rivers, and trading post life.

H. M. Burns

3133. Dempsey, Hugh A. DAVID THOMPSON UNDER SCRUTINY. *Alberta Hist. R. [Canada] 1964 12(1): 22-28.* A review of Dr. Richard Glover's introduction to the new edition of *David Thompson's Narratives, 1784-1812* (Champlain Society Publication), which portrays Thompson not as a hardy explorer and patient cartographer but as a deserter, a bad leader, a distorter of facts through omission, a possible coward, and the man who made mistakes which contributed to Britain's loss of Oregon. The value of Glover's introduction is admitted but the

wisdom of such a blanket criticism being attached to the *Narratives,* a standard reference work, is questioned. Glover's criticisms have not undergone close scrutiny and may be doing Thompson a disservice. Illus.
G. Emery

3134. Dempsey, Hugh. THE "THIN RED LINE" IN THE CANADIAN WEST. *Am. West 1970 7(1): 24-30.* When, in 1870, the Canadian West was transferred from the Hudson's Bay Company to the newly-formed Dominion of Canada, no provision was made for legal jurisdiction. Montana-based traders, with whiskey as their main stock in trade, moved across the border. Prosperous and reasonably peaceful Indians were impoverished and victimized, and were even killed by the whiskey traders. American manifest destiny proponents proclaimed the traders as advance agents of northern expansion. In the summer of 1873, a troop of former British soldiers and young Canadians was raised, dubbed the North-West Mounted Police, and sent to Winnipeg, Manitoba, the gateway to the western prairies. A 900-mile trek (the Great March) to the Blackfoot country in southern Alberta had near disastrous consequences for the Mounties. By early 1875 intertribal warfare had been subdued, the whiskey trade was ended, and the area was safe for travelers. Unlike the American West, where settlement usually preceded law and where violence was a way of life, the Mounted Police arrived before large-scale settlement. By the time of the Klondike gold rush of 1897-98, the Mounted Police had not only a history but also a considerable body of legend. The fictional, stereotyped "Mountie" legend began with the poetic eulogies that members wrote to departed members of the force, and it was further romanticized in numerous novels written by ex-Mounties. Today the romantic image is firmly fixed. 9 illus.
D. L. Smith

3135. DenOtter, Andy A. IRRIGATION AND THE LETHBRIDGE NEWS. *Alberta Hist. R. [Canada] 1970 18(4): 17-25.* Discusses the campaign waged by E. T. Saunders, editor of the *Lethbridge News* in Alberta, during 1888-1900 on behalf of irrigation in the Palliser Triangle of western Canada.
H. M. Burns

3136. Driedger, Leo. A PERSPECTIVE ON CANADIAN MENNONITE URBANIZATION. *Mennonite Life 1968 23(4): 147-152.* Outlines some Canadian urban trends, describes the concentrations of Mennonites in Canadian cities, and explores some possible types of urban Mennonite communities which may be emerging in Canada. Since 1861 the proportion of urban population increased roughly by 5 percent each decade. From 1786, when the first Mennonites came to Canada, until well into the 20th century, most Mennonites lived in rural areas. Three types of Mennonite urban communities now appear to be developing: "rurban satellites," small cities surrounded by large rural Mennonite hinterlands; "ethnic urbanism," metropolitan areas like Winnipeg with large rural Mennonite hinterlands; and "urban accommodation," large metropolitan areas like Ottawa where Mennonites are present but form no identifiable Mennonite community. Based mostly on census reports and other published sources; 6 tables, 19 notes.
D. J. Abramoske

3137. Eccles, W. J. NEW FRANCE AND THE WESTERN FRONTIER. *Alberta Hist. R. [Canada] 1969 17(2): 23-31.* Considers the development of the Canadian West during the French regime in Canada, discussing the factors involved in expansion and the difference from the English expansion to the south. The impact of the effect of the peculiarities of Canadian conditions on central colony social mobility is described.
H. M. Burns

3138. Finlay, John L. CLUES TO SOCIAL CREDIT: ORAGE AND THE NEW AGE. *J. of Can. Studies [Canada] 1969 4(1): 46-54.* A review article prompted by Wallace Martin's *The New Age Under Orage* (Manchester U. Press, 1967). The background of Social Credit in Canada and England was much richer than suggested, and the anarchism found there was not Fascist in implication. The 19th-century doctrine of evolutionary continuity was overthrown by the new doctrine of change and mutation by sudden leaps. This touched the apocalyptic note in the anarchism of A. R. Orage, the editor of *The New Age,* a London weekly newspaper, despite his animus against progress - another element in anarchism. Based on secondary sources; 29 notes.
G. E. Panting

3139. Gibson, James R. FOOD FOR THE FUR TRADERS: THE FIRST FARMERS IN THE PACIFIC NORTHWEST, 1805-1846.

J. of the West 1968 7(1): 18-30. Contrasts the fortunes of agriculture in the Russian Far East and North American Pacific Northwest. In both areas the chief reason for expansion was a lucrative trade in furs—Russia's expansion eastward across Siberia in the 16th and 17th centuries and French and English expansion across Rupert's Land in the 17th and 18th centuries. Both encountered difficulties in supplying foodstuffs to remote outposts and consequently turned to locally grown provisions. In the Russian Far East the severe climate and unenthusiastic serfs defeated attempts at agricultural self-sufficiency. In the Pacific Northwest, on the other hand, the temperate climate and freehold farmers not only satisfied local needs (of the Hudson's Bay Company) but even provided surpluses for export to the Russian-American Company. Based on published private papers and journals and secondary sources; 2 maps, 60 notes.
E. A. Erickson

3140. Gingras, Larry. MEDALS AND TOKENS OF THE HBC. *Beaver [Canada] 1968 299(Summer): 36-43.* The Hudson's Bay Company has issued medals to commemorate important events in its history, the earliest in 1791. The company also made use of tokens as counters from the earliest time, using "One Made Beaver" as the measure of value. After the establishment of the Red River settlers, promissory notes were issued and remained in circulation until 1870. The author to date has found 26 different medals, 86 different tokens, and 46 different paper moneys. Illus.
L. F. S. Upton

3141. Goertz, Adalbert. STATISTICS OF MENNONITES IN CANADA. *Mennonite Life 1968 23(4): 192.* Lists the number of Mennonites in Alberta, British Columbia, Manitoba, Ontario, and Saskatchewan as recorded by the Canadian census reports from 1911 to 1961.
D. J. Abramoske

3142. Grahl-Madsen, Atle IDENTITY AND EQUALITY: LEGAL PROBLEMS OF NATIONAL MINORITIES. *Cooperation and Conflict [Norway] 1970 5(4): 275-281.* A critical review of Tore Modeen's *The International Protection of National Minorities in Europe* (Åbo Akademi: Åbo, 1969) and L. C. Green's *Canada's Indians - Federal Policy, International and Constitutional Law* (The Government of Alberta: Edmonton, 1970). Modeen, who has limited his study to national minorities in Europe, observes that actual equality will only be achieved when a minority enjoys special rights safeguarding it against assimilation. Tells of the treaty system up to World War II, notably the system created in the wake of World War I. "The text is all too often interspersed with irrelevancies; matters of principal interest are scattered throughout the book without any attempt being made to view them coherently; [but] he has definitely made the point that this problem is as worthy of serious legal study today as it has ever been." Green's book is a critique of the policy position paper which the Canadian Government issued in 1969 on the status of the country's Indians. "Prof. Green concedes that the 'Indian Treaties' may not be treaties in the sense of international law, but he makes a very strong case for their being agreements having created legal obligations of a permanent character, which neither side can evade unilaterally.... Prof. Green deserves commendation for placing the issue in a greater context, which in turn means that the problem of Canada's Indians also becomes meaningful for lawyers on distant shores."
D. D. Cameron

3143. Janzen, Waldemar. THE MENNONITES AND THE CITY. *Mennonite Life 1968 23(4): 186-188.* Although the old rural patterns continue to be highly valued as Mennonites migrate to urban centers, the question is whether Mennonites can also view positively the style of life of the large city. The city has the "potentialities of sustaining life and of offering freedom.... It is quite possible to cultivate genuine human community in the city.... For the Christian it opens up a wide area for the exercise of Christian love.... To be a good Samaritan in the city demands attentiveness and sensitivity, for the man by the road is easily missed in the crowd."
D. J. Abramoske

3144. Kaye, V. J., ed. THE RUTHENIANS. *Can. Slavonic Papers [Canada] 1968 10(1): 96-99.* A reprint of a 1909 newspaper article (Winnipeg *Free Press* describing the Ukrainian (then called Ruthenian) immigrants to Canada and praising their adaptability, capacity for work, and intelligence. They are called a "valuable factor in building up the West."
R. V. Layton

3145. Keenleyside, Hugh L. COLUMBIA RIVER POWER DEVELOPMENT. *Can. Geographical J. [Canada] 1965 71(5): 148-161.* In 1964 the Columbia River Treaty between Canada and the United States was ratified. It provides for the construction of dams which will stop flood damage and provide cheap electricity. Map, illus.

A. H. Lawrance

3146. Kravchuk, Petro. IVAN FRANKO TA UKRAINS'KA TRUDOVA EMIHRATSIIA V KANADI [Ivan Franko and the Ukrainian labor emigration to Canada]. *Ukrains'kyi Istorychnyi Zhurnal [USSR] 1966 (8): 70-80.* Ivan Franko's friend Joseph Oles'kiv went to Canada in 1895 in order to be able to advise Ukrainians on how to settle there. Another of Franko's friends, Kyrylo Genyk, emigrated from Galicia to Canada in 1896. In Frnako's house in Winnipeg, Ukrainian activists met. The published works of Franko as well as celebrations and publications in his memory are noted.

N. Andrusiak

3147. Lee, Lawrence B. THE MORMONS COME TO CANADA, 1887-1902. *Pacific Northwest Q. 1968 59(1): 11-22.* Efforts of the Church of the Latter-day Saints to establish colonies in western Canada, 1887-1902, were successful despite opposition from many residents and the press. Paternalism of the government of the Dominion of Canada played an important part in this success. Elder Card, a leader in the movement, chose Canada because "he thought it strange that grandchildren of Americans who had revolted against the English monarch should now be forced to seek refuge on British soil from legalized persecution by the United States government."

C. C. Gorchels

3148. Lower, Arthur R. M. CANADA AT THE TURN OF THE CENTURY, 1900. *Canadian Geographical J. [Canada] 1965 71(1): 3-13.* None of the Canadian universities of the period aimed at more than good undergraduate teaching. In 1901 a vast population shift was beginning. The number of persons of British and French origin decreased from 87 percent of the total population to 74.1 percent in 1961. When the Boer War came, French Canada could not view it with English eyes. The Boer War marked for Canada a coming of age as a nation. But the Alaska Boundary Award (1903) was regarded by nearly everyone in Canada as a bitter defeat of British by Americans; few could face the realization that to Britian her own interests far transcended Canada's. Illus.

E. P. Stickney

3149. MacMillan, Hugh. ON THE TRAILS OF THE NOR'WESTERS. *Alberta Hist. R. [Canada] 1969 17(2): 11-15.* Reviews the author's experiences in tracking down and acquiring archival material pertaining to the North West Company and its activities in the Canadian West during the early part of the 19th century.

H. M. Burns

3150. Mary Eileen, Sister. MOTHER MARY ANN, FOUNDRESS OF THE SISTERS OF SAINT ANN: HER CONTRIBUTION TO THE CHURCH IN BRITISH COLUMBIA, ALASKA AND THE YUKON. *Can. Catholic Hist. Assoc. Annual Report [Canada] 1965 32: 47-62.* Marie Esther Sureau (1809-90) founded the Daughters of Saint Ann in 1848 to educate children of both sexes in Quebec. The community, after several struggling decades, has spread across Canada and into the United States, devoting its efforts to teaching, nursing, and social service. This work in the Provinces of British Columbia, the Yukon, and Alaska is studied in detail. 66 notes.

C. Thibault

3151. McCook, James. SOME OLD FORTS OF THE CANADIAN WEST. *Canadian Geographical J. [Canada] 1968 76(5): 166-173.* Red River carts loaded with fur-trade supplies traveled once between the forts and posts of the Canadian West. Two round trips of 1,800 miles each, from Fort Garry (Winnipeg) to Fort Edmonton, employed a cart driver from May to September. The harsh journey took hardy men of great endurance through Indian lands, difficult terrain, and unpredictable weather. The first stop out of Fort Garry was Fort Ellice built in 1831 and one of the most elaborate places on the trail. The modest post at Touchwood Hills, 50 miles from a major river, was the next post after Ellice. The last leg of the journey led to Edmonton, the end of the line for the Red River carts. Illus., map.

C. J. Allard

3152. McLaughlin, Charles E. THE CATENHEAD PARTY. *Alberta Hist. R. [Canada] 1963 11(4): 1-6.* First-person account of a journey under pioneering conditions from Wolf Creek down the McLeod River, the Lesser Slave River, through various difficulties to the final destination, Halfway River Flats on the Peace River in British Columbia.

E. W. Hathaway

3153. McMicking, Thomas. THE OVERLANDERS IN ALBERTA, 1862. *Alberta Hist. R. [Canada] 1966 14(3): 1-11.* Account of the journey from Fort Pitt to Yellowhead Pass by the leader of the St. Catherine, Ontario party which became known as the Overlanders of 1862. Their attempt to reach the Cariboo Gold Fields in British Columbia by direct route across the prairies and the Rockies is described.

H. M. Burns

3154. McNaughton, A. G. L. THE PROPOSED COLUMBIA RIVER TREATY. *Int. J. [Canada] 1963 18(2): 148-165.* McNaughton argues that the treaty should not be approved by the Canadian Parliament because, as it stands, the treaty surrenders valuable Canadian rights. The International Joint Commission in its joint *Report* of 1959 agreed that the exercise of cooperative effort and dual control was the best means of developing the resources of the Columbia. The principles agreed to by the I.J.C. have been "down graded" in the negotiations since 1959. The control of Canadian storages have been "vested in the U.S. Entity, both in regard to power and flood control."

A. Orr

3155. Morton, W. L. A CENTENNIAL OF NORTHERN DEVELOPMENT. *Polar Record [Great Britain] 1970 15(95): 145-150.* Summarizes the administrative history of northwestern Canada, from the creation of the judicial division of Algoma in 1858 through the establishment of Manitoba and the Northwest Territories in 1870, the separation of Alberta and Saskatchewan in 1905, and the northern extension of Manitoba, Ontario, and Quebec in 1912. Illus.

L. L. Hubbard

3156. Northrup, Minnie. BORDEN'S WESTERN TOUR, A PERSONAL GLIMPSE. *Alberta Hist. R. [Canada] 1966 14(2): 22-26.* Diary of the wife of Member of Parliament Will Northrup recounting a 1902 tour of western Canada made as a member of the party accompanying Conservative Party leader, and later Prime Minister, Robert L. Borden.

H. M. Burns

3157. Nute, Grace Lee. KNIGHTS OF THE WATERWAYS. *Beaver [Canada] 1967 298(Summer): 11-17.* Describes the life of the voyageurs as seen in the diaries of three contemporaries. Major Joseph Delafield was the U.S. representative appointed in 1823 to survey the border between the United States and British North America. Frances Ramsey Simpson was the wife of Canadian Governor Sir George Simpson, and accompanied her husband on a honeymoon trip by canoe across the continent in 1830. Captain John Henry Lefroy was a soldier-surveyor of the early 1840's whose diary has recently been edited and published. Illus.

L. F. S. Upton

3158. Olson, Sigurd STREAM OF THE PAST: EXPLORATIONS INTO THE LIVES OF THE VOYAGEURS, AND MEMORIES OF GOOD MEN AND GOOD TIMES LONG VANISHED. *Am. West 1969 6(2): 28-33.* Serving as a guide in the voyageur country of the upper Great Lakes and Canada, the author absorbed and relived much that he had read about. He here recounts, as a reminiscence, his subsequent retracing of the routes of early explorers over much of Canada and the United States. He is convinced this is the way to make history come to life. He is also convinced that the wilderness areas in which this can be done need to be guarded against the inroads of modern highways and too much accessibility, to preserve them for future generations. Adapted from a forthcoming book; illus., map.

D. L. Smith

3159. Painting, G. E. THE FISHERMEN'S PROTECTIVE UNION OF NEWFOUNDLAND AND THE FARMERS' ORGANIZATIONS IN WESTERN CANADA. *Can. Hist. Assoc., Annual Report [Canada] 1963: 141-151.* (Report of the annual meeting held at Quebec 5-8 June 1963). A comparative study of the farmers' and fishermen's organizations which supported the development of Canada's political and economic empire. The Fishermen's Protective Union and the Grain Growers' Grain Company, succeeded respectively by the Union Trading Company and the United Grain Growers, began as vehicles for education and indoctrination but later launched commercial ventures and undertook political activities.

R. E. Wilson

3160. Peel, Bruce. ENGLISH WRITERS IN THE EARLY WEST. *Alberta Hist. R. [Canada] 1968 16(2): 1-4.* Review of works by English writers who depicted frontier life in Western Canada, some of whom were R. M. Ballantyne, John Mackie, and Mrs. Jessie M. Saxby.
H. M. Burns

3161. Regehr, T. D. THE CANADIAN NORTHERN RAILWAY: THE WEST'S OWN PRODUCT. *Can. Hist. R. [Canada] 1970 51(2): 177-187.* Examines the policies of the Canadian Northern Railway as a response to prairie transportation needs and complaints in the early 1900's. The early successes and later failures of this railway have generally been ascribed to financial opportunism and political corruption. Evidence is presented indicating that the success of the Canadian Northern was based on a willingness to meet and alleviate specific western railway grievances. Based on unpublished papers and company and government records, most of which are now in the custody of the Public Archives of Canada.
A

3162. Regenstreif, S. Peter. A THREAT TO LEADERSHIP: C. A. DUNNING AND MACKENZIE KING. *Dalhousie R. [Canada] 1964 44(3): 272-289.* Describes the unsuccessful political maneuvers designed to weaken Mackenzie King's hold on the Liberal Party, with particular attention paid to the activities of the western Progressives in advancing the cause of Charles A. Dunning, premier of Saskatchewan. Material based on personal interviews and unpublished papers of political leaders of the time, especially the papers of A. K. Cameron in the Public Archives of Canada. 50 notes.
M. B. Rex

3163. Rehwinkel, Alfred M. LAYING THE FOUNDATION OF A NEW CHURCH IN WESTERN CANADA. *Concordia Hist. Inst. Q. 1965 38(1): 3-15.* An autobiographical article printed in recognition of the 55th anniversary of the author's graduation from Concordia Seminary. The author focuses on his experience as a young Lutheran minister in western Canada from 1910 to about 1922. He emphasizes the hardship of the frontier life, the religious apathy of European immigrants, and the conflicts caused by the widely divergent backgrounds of the Lutheran immigrants. Missionary activity was further hampered by the "ungodly" rivalry between opposing Lutheran synods. Nonetheless, the Lutheran Church did succeed as "a socializing and integrating force for a transplanted population."
D. J. Abramoske

3164. Rolland, Walpole. MY ALBERTA NOTEBOOK. *Alberta Hist. R. [Canada] 1970 18(1): 21-30.* A contemporary comment on pioneer conditions in western Canada by a civil engineer employed by the Land Department of the Canadian Pacific Railway in the 1880's. These observations appeared in *The Emigrant*, a Winnipeg magazine.
H. M. Burns

3165. Roy, R. H. WEST OF THE MOUNTAINS - AND EAST. *Alberta Hist. R. [Canada] 1969 17(2): 16-22.* Compares the settlement of British Columbia with that of the Prairie and Atlantic Provinces. The impact of the fur trade and the influence of Americans on the development of the Province are emphasized.
H. M. Burns

3166. Rutherford, P. F. W. THE WESTERN PRESS AND REGIONALISM, 1870-96. *Can. Hist. R. [Canada] 1971 52(3): 287-305.* Newspapers reflect stereotypes common in their community. Examines the development of regional attitudes toward culture, economics, politics, and nation. The West was very much an offshoot of Ontario society. Growth of a strong Canadianism and regional alienation coincided. Based on an analysis of newspaper editorials in Manitoba and the Northwest Territories.
A

3167. Sargent, George H. STARVATION IN THE MOUNTAINS. *Alberta Hist. R. [Canada] 1969 17(4): 26-28.* A contemporary account of the hardships encountered by a Canadian Pacific Railway surveying party when traveling from a supply station on the Columbia River to Kicking Horse Cache. Extracts from the diary of F. E. Sheldon, a member of the party, describes near-starvation conditions reached during the journey through the mountains.
H. M. Burns

3168. Savoie, Donat. BIBLIOGRAPHIE D'EMILE PETITOT, MISSIONNAIRE DANS LE NORD-OUEST CANADIEN [Bibliography of Emile Petitot, missionary of the Canadian Northwest]. *Anthropologica 1971 13(1/2): 159-168.* "Emile Petitot (1838-1916) was an Oblate missionary. He wrote extensively about the life he led in the Canadian Northwest and of the history, languages and customs of the native population. After introducing Father Petitot's theories of history, development and anthropology, the author presents a bibliography of eighty-one items."
AIA(3:1:196) J

3169. Sawka, Patricia. THE HUTTERIAN WAY OF LIFE. *Can. Geographical J. [Canada] 1968 77(4): 126-131.* The Hutterites of Canada are among the least-known of Canada's minorities, and the pressure of contemporary society threatens their communal existence. The Hutterite Brotherhood began in Moravia in 1525 as a branch of the Anabaptist Movement. After centuries of oppression, the first Hutterites reached Manitoba in the 1870's. A larger group came from the United States to Western Canada in 1918. Canadian prejudice against the Hutterites stems from the group's pacifism and self-sufficiency. Discusses Hutterite society in Canada. 6 illus.
R. D. Tallman

3170. Serven, James E. GUNS OF THE CANADIAN WEST. *Am. West 1967 4(1): 30-33, 71-74.* Citing the bow and arrow as an example, the author maintains that survival tools often became war weapons, and that the weapons of the past often become the toys of the future. The theme of this study is that the story of the guns that helped to conquer the Canadian West - Manitoba, Saskatchewan, Alberta, and British Columbia - is inseparable from the story of the development of that territory. Within this framework the evolution of the gun can be traced from tool to weapon to collector's item. The first firearms were items of trade, usually flintlocks from the Hudson's Bay Company for furs from the Indians. While the guns enabled the Indians and half-breeds to harvest greater fur crops, their complete dependence on the trading posts for guns and powder held abusive use in check. The 1858 British Columbia Fraser and Thompson Rivers gold rushers brought American caplock and breech-loading rifles, muskets, and pistols. In the mid-19th century, the Canadian Army carried back-East muskets, but soon replaced them with more up-to-date American rifles. Still other makes and types came with the Métis troubles, clashes with the Indians, creation of the Northwest Mounted Police, homesteaders, the rebellion, construction of the transcontinental railroad, and other developments that changed the role of the gun primarily from tool to weapon. The final stage has been reached and the author asserts that for the collector "a rich array of guns" is still to be found in Canada. Illus., biblio. note.
D. L. Smith

3171. Sloan, Roberta W. THE CANADIAN WEST, AMERICANIZATION OR CANADIANIZATION. *Alberta Hist. R. [Canada] 1968 16(1): 1-7.* Discusses immigration promotion and the fears of Canadians that settlers from the United States would Americanize western Canada.
H. M. Burns

3172. Smith, S. H. ENGLISH CHARLIE. *Alberta Hist. R. [Canada] 1964 12(3): 26-27.* A biographical account of "English Charlie" whom the author knew around 1900. A veteran of the California (1849) and Cariboo (1860's) gold rushes, "English Charlie" tried homesteading around Edmonton after being drawn east in the 1870's by rumors of gold along the Saskatchewan River. Illus.
G. Emery

3173. Spry, Irene M. ROUTES THROUGH THE ROCKIES. *Beaver [Canada] 1963 294(Autumn): 26-39.* Describes the known crossings of the Canadian Rockies by white men before Palliser's expedition surveyed the passes in 1857-60. Many of the actual routes used are difficult to identify from contemporary descriptions. Many Indians and halfbreeds undoubtedly knew the routes, which were used, for example, in the war of the Blackfoot Confederacy and the Kootenays. Illus.
L. F. S. Upton

3174. Spry, Irene M. THE TRANSITION FROM A NOMADIC TO A SETTLED ECONOMY IN WESTERN CANADA, 1856-1896. *Mémoires de la Soc. Royale du Can. [Canada] 1968 6(4): 187-201.* The Hudson's Bay Company had maintained peace in Rupert's Land for the benefit of the fur trade; the Plains Indians had achieved a rough balance of power between themselves; the organization of the Métis provided internal security and a degree of external protection. This stable order broke down in the 1860's with the decline of the Hudson's Bay Company, the arrival of smallpox and trade-whiskey, and the disappearance of the buffalo. Anarchy was prevented by the creation of the North West

Mounted Police. But the basic need was for capital to convert to a farming economy and this did not come until the railway opened the area to settlers.

L. F. S. Upton

3175. Stamp, Robert M. J. D. EDGAR AND THE PACIFIC JUNCTION RAILWAY: THE PROBLEMS OF A NINETEENTH CENTURY RAILWAY PROMOTER. *Ontario Hist. [Canada] 1963 55(3): 119-130.* James Edgar, interested in diverting the trade of the Canadian West to Toronto, determined to build a branch line from the transcontinental railway to Toronto. In spite of a wide business and political experience as well as influential support for his scheme in the early stages of his struggle, the railroad was never constructed, due to changes in government policy, alteration in the route of the transcontinental, and the ability of a rival company to gain the support of the conservative government. Based on unpublished Edgar papers and contemporary newspaper accounts. 50 notes.

J. M. E. Usher

3176. Tessendorf, K. C. GEORGE SIMPSON: CANOE EXECUTIVE. *Beaver [Canada] 1970 301(Summer): 39-41.* Comments on the extensive travels and business efficiency of Sir George Simpson (ca. 1787-1860), Governor-in-Chief for the Hudson's Bay Company in Rupert's Land from 1826 to 1860. Included are quotes from contemporaries who shared in one or more of Simpson's travels. Illus.

L. F. S. Upton

3177. Thielman, George G. THE HUTTERITES IN CONTEMPORARY SOCIETY. *Mennonite Life 1970 25(1): 42-46.* Describes the Hutterites, a small group of Christians now living in western Canada and the Dakotas of the United States. The Hutterites originated in Moravia in 1553 when they separated from the Mennonites because they wanted to practice the Apostolic "principle of community of goods." They also insisted on a stricter application of the principle of nonresistance. Persecuted, they eventually settled in southern Russia. It was in the late 19th century that they came to Canada and the United States. During World War I the Hutterites in the United States suffered more persecution than any other pacifist group. The Canadians subjected them to considerable harassment during World War II. In spite of widespread hostility, the Hutterites continue to maintain their unique communal life. Based on published sources; 23 notes.

D. J. Abramoske

3178. Thomas, L. G. HISTORIOGRAPHY OF THE FUR TRADE. *Alberta Hist. R. [Canada] 1969 17(1): 21-26.* Reviews the historiography of the period of the Canadian West when the fur trade was the dominant activity, mentioning writers on this period and their works.

H. M. Burns

3179. Thomas, Lewis H. DOCUMENTARY SOURCES FOR TEACHING WESTERN CANADIAN HISTORY. *Alberta Hist. R. [Canada] 1969 17(4): 23-25.* Discusses the documentary sources available with respect to the history of Western Canada, and considers particular types of collections and their strengths and weaknesses. Emphasis is placed on the impact of microfilm on newspaper collections.

H. M. Burns

3180. Thomson, D. W. THE 49TH PARALLEL. *Geographical J. [Great Britain] 1968 134(2): 209-215.* A lecture given to the Royal Geographical Society in October 1967 outlining the origins of the 49th Parallel as the boundary between the United States and Canada, and giving details of the Anglo-American Boundary Commission's survey of 1872.

D. H. Murdoch

3181. Vanderhill, Burke G. CHANGING PATTERNS IN THE PEACE RIVER COUNTRY. *Can. Geographical J. [Canada] 1968 77(1): 2-13.* The Peace River region has become an island of economic development in northern Alberta, British Columbia, and can no longer be considered a true frontier. Transportation - roads, railways, pipelines - lift the region out of cultural and economic isolation. While the region is still characterized by the "mystique of the north," Peace River joins the mainstream of Canadian economic and social life. Peace River country emerged from its pioneer stage of development during the 1950's; now the trend is toward urban living and there is a marked transition in agriculture. While the country has come of age, a development plateau has not been reached. Illus., map.

R. D. Tallman

3182. Whitelock, E. C. OFFICERS OF THE NORTH WEST MOUNTED POLICE, 1878. *Military Collector and Historian 1963 15(3): 84-85.* "Almost any incident could have caused a flare up which would have involved the Army of the United States and the Indian tribes, and it is to the credit of the [Canadian] North West Mounted Police that they handled themselves with the necessary restraint" in 1878. Illus.

C. L. Boyd

3183. Williams, Glyndwr. HIGHLIGHTS OF THE FIRST 200 YEARS OF THE HUDSON'S BAY COMPANY. *Beaver [Canada] 1970 300(Autumn): 4-64.* Reviews 10 topics: the granting of the charter; the Anglo-French war in Hudson Bay; the [Arthur] Dobbs crisis; the exploration of the prairies; the move inland to the Cumberland House (1744); rivalry with the Nor'Westers; George Simpson and John McLoughlin; and the end of company monopoly and rule (1857-70). Illus., 9 maps, biblio.

L. F. S. Upton

3184. Williams, Glyndwr. THE HUDSON'S BAY COMPANY AND ITS CRITICS IN THE EIGHTEENTH CENTURY. *Tr. of the Royal Hist. Soc. [Great Britain] 1970 20: 149-171.* Examines the position of the Hudson's Bay Company in the 18th century. From its foundation in 1670 until the mid-18th century the company preserved secrecy over its operations. This secrecy stemmed originally from a desire to prevent competitors from exploiting its weaknesses but developed into an almost unbreakable custom. Apart from the trading aspects secrecy protected the company from the attacks which were leveled against the other chartered companies in the early 18th century. However, the quest for the North-West Passage drew the government's and the public's attention to northwest America and so to the company. The official inquiry which followed the failure of the 1741 expedition occasioned great interest in the idea and a desire to break the company's monopoly on trade in that region; thus attacks on the company increased in scope and intensity. A change in the attitude over secrecy in the company resulted partly from cooperation with the scientific interests of the Royal Society but mainly from the Governorship of Samuel Wegg, 1780-99. He helped to distinguish between information which because of its commercial significance was confidential and the rest. He built up goodwill instead of antagonism, and the resultant improved standing of the company was a major factor in its survival. Based on the records of the Hudson's Bay Company and on other primary and secondary sources; 76 notes.

L. Brown

3185. Winther, Oscar O. A DEDICATION TO THE MEMORY OF ROBERT CARLTON CLARK, 1877-1939. *Arizona and the West 1969 11(1): 1-4.* Robert Carlton Clark was "crossfertilized" in the Turner and Bolton interpretations of Western American history. Texas and Wisconsin trained, he spent his academic career at the University of Oregon where he also served for many years as editor of the *Oregon Historical Quarterly.* His fortes were in directing graduate students and in his own research and writing. Clark was one of the earliest scholars to gain access to the Hudson's Bay Company Archives in England. His studies replaced the heavily missionary-oriented accounts of the Pacific Northwest. Illus., appended with a selected list of his publications.

D. L. Smith

3186. Yuzyk, Paul. 75TH ANNIVERSARY OF UKRAINIAN SETTLEMENT IN CANADA. *Ukrainian Q. 1967 23(3): 247-254.* Discusses the Ukrainian contribution to the development of Canada since the arrival of the first Ukrainian immigrants in 1891. Tremendous contributions to agriculture, achievements in industry, business, and Canadian politics are elaborated and service to the country stressed. "Ukrainian culture is being woven gradually into the multi-coloured fabric of the composite Canadian culture."

Y. Slavutych

3187. —. THE COLD BARREN WEST. *Alberta Hist. R. [Canada] 1964 12(4): 25-26.* An editorial of the London *Truth,* 1 September 1881. It warned British investors against Canadian Pacific Railway bonds which were up for sale at the time. The Canadian West was cold and barren and could not support a railway. Always Canada, Britain's most overrated colony, has been willing to spend, if Britain provided the money. Canada, a debt-ridden country, has made money out of loyalty.

G. Emery

3188. —. COLUMBIA RIVER TREATY RATIFIED. *External Affairs [Canada] 1964 16(11): 546-547.* Agreement between Canada and the United States to provide hydroelectric power and flood control benefits.

R. D. Fiala

3189. —. THE COLUMBIA RIVER TREATY AND PROTOCOL. *External Affairs [Canada] 1964 16(3): 98-110.* An analysis of the Treaty and clarifying protocol between the United States and Canada, signed 17 January 1961, approved by the US Senate 16 March 1961, but not yet ratified by Canada. This includes an agreement for the sale of downstream power benefits to the United States for part of the treaty period, as well as the advantages to Canada. The article further provides an analysis of the British Columbia-Canada Agreements. 3 tables, illus., maps.   S

3190. —. COLUMBIA RIVER DEVELOPMENT. *External Affairs [Canada] 1964 16(2): 38-39.* Agreements reached between Canada and the United States on flood control, hydroelectric power and water use on the Columbia River.   S

3191. —. [THE CONFEDERATION OF CANADA]. *R. de Hist. de Am. 1968 (65/66): 7-51.*
Stacey, C. P. THE DEFENSE PROBLEM AND THE CANADIAN CONFEDERATION, *pp. 7-14.*
Smith, Wilfred I. CONFEDERATION AND THE BRITISH CONNECTION, *pp. 15-24.*
Bonenfant, Jean-Charles LE QUEBEC ET LA NAISSANCE DE LA CONFEDERATION CANADIENNE [Quebec and the birth of the Canadian Confederation], *pp. 25-32.*
Thomas, Lewis H. CONFEDERATION AND THE WEST, *pp. 33-40.*
Glazebrook, G. de T. CONFEDERATION AND TRANSPORTATION, *pp. 41-51.*
A series of articles published in commemoration of the formation of the Canadian Confederation, relating to several problems that faced the new political entity. "The longest undefended frontier in the world" was not planned that way, but developed as a result of fortuitous circumstances, primarily the Treaty of Washington (1871). The new political union maintained contact with Great Britain and the Empire through a Governor General, and then a High Commissioner whose office subsequently acquired a quasi-ambassadorial status and function. The French-speaking Canadians, who exercised no great weight in political matters, originated none of the various projects for restructuring Canadian administration. They reluctantly accepted the Confederation idea as the best way to preserve their cultural and religious entity and to keep the goodwill of the English-speaking majority. The Confederation idea proved to be the essential principle for successful governance of the vast territories of western Canada in a pluralistic society. The key to Canadian economic life lay in the formation of a better transportation system than had been provided by the canoe and the inland waterways. Curiously, there was frank opposition to railroad construction from those who opposed selected routes, from those who thought the project too expensive, or from those of the maritime provinces who felt no need for long-distance transportation facilities. With adequate government subsidy the railroad won over all opposition.   T. B. Davis

3192. —. GLEASON: PRESENTING A RARE COLLECTION OF EARLY WILDERNESS PHOTOGRAPHY. *Am. West 1971 8(4): 16-27.* Herbert Wendell Gleason (1855-1937) made some 30 trips to the Rocky Mountain West of Canada and the United States to make photographs for his illustrated lectures on natural history and horticulture. Presents 18 views from Gleason's glass plate negatives collection. Includes descriptive passages from LeRoy Jeffers, *The Call of the Mountains* (1922).   D. L. Smith

3193. —. LETTERS FROM THE WEST. *Alberta Hist. R. [Canada] 1967 25(3): 8-16.* A collection of letters published in the *Manitoba Free Press* and written to counteract incorrect information concerning the Northwest Mounted Police.   H. M. Burns

3194. —. NORTHWEST MOUNTED POLICE: A BRIEF HISTORY. *Alberta Hist. R. [Canada] 1967 15(3): 1-7.* An account of the origin and development of the Northwest Mounted Police. Based on "An Historical Outline of the Force," a report prepared by the Royal Canadian Mounted Police in Ottawa.   H. M. Burns

3195. —. REPORTS ON ARCHIVES. *Bull. of the United Church of Can. [Canada] 1965 18: 34-42.* Brief reports of the United Church Archives Committees: those of the Central Archives at Victoria University (Toronto), the Alberta Conference, the British Columbia Conference,

the Hamilton Conference, the London Conference, the Maritime Conference, and the Montreal and Ottawa Conference. The reports include brief statements of acquisitions in the past year, which have been "about normal." Most material is in the form of church records, although the Central Archives are building substantial holdings of church newspapers and private papers.   B. D. Tennyson

The Prairie Provinces

General

3196. Alcock, F. J. SCOW BRIGADE ON THE ATHABASKA. *Canadian Geographical J. [Canada] 1967 74(3): 92-99.* Describes "a journey down the Athabaska during the last year [1914] in which the scow brigades carried northward to Lake Athabaska the season's freight of Chipewyan and the Slave and Mackenzie river posts." The Athabaska scow is a flat-bottomed boat 50 feet long and with a width of eight feet at the bottom and 12 feet at the top. It is steered by means of a 35-foot sweep and four 22-foot oars which are used when it is necessary to make headway. The scows rarely made the return trip, the majority being broken up for lumber at Lake Athabaska. Illus., map.
      C. J. Allard

3197. Allan, Iris, ed. A RIEL REBELLION DIARY. *Alberta Hist. R. [Canada] 1964 12(3): 15-25.* The diary of Robert K. Allan, recording his experiences while serving in the campaigns against Louis Riel and against the Indians of Chief Big Bear. Born in Ontario, Allan had been with the Winnipeg civil service prior to the outbreak of the rebellion. He died in Edmonton in 1942. Illus.   G. Emery

3198. Ballantine, Archie. RECOLLECTIONS AND REMINISCENCES: STEAMBOATING ON THE SASKATCHEWAN. *Saskatchewan Hist. [Canada] 1965 18(3): 99-114.* The author (1858-1942) worked as a watchman on the steamboat *North West* in the summer of 1885, and tells of his experiences on the route up and down the Saskatchewan River between Edmonton and Cumberland Lake. Included is material relevant to the Métis rebellion and the fight at Duck Lake.   A. H. Lawrance

3199. Bartlett, Fred E. THE ORDEAL OF WILLIAM MACTAVISH. *Beaver [Canada] 1964 295(Autumn): 42-47.* William Mactavish (1815-70) was governor of Assiniboia and Rupert's Land from 1858-70. As such, he might have been expected to play a decisive part in the crises surrounding Riel's resistance of Canadian authority. The governor had considerable influence with the Métis, but showed little disposition to use it. He was critically ill in the winter of 1869-70 and could do nothing to stop Riel's usurpation of authority. He resigned, and died two days after arriving in England in July 1870. Illus.   L. F. S. Upton

3200. Bellan, R. C. RAILS ACROSS THE RED - SELKIRK OR WINNIPEG. *Hist. and Sci. Soc. of Manitoba Papers, [Canada] 1961-62 1964 Series 3(18): 69-77.* The first trading posts were built at Winnipeg because of the confluence of the Red and Assiniboine rivers. Outside interest came only after the introduction of the steamboat on the Red River in 1859. When discharged, troops sent in 1870 to deal with Louis Riel settled in the colony. In 1872 rail connection through Fargo was available to the Atlantic seaboard. The decision to build the transcontinental railway through Selkirk was hotly contested. "The Hudson's Bay Company played a key role in the struggle to draw the railway through Winnipeg." Winnipeg's economic and political strength proved superior to Selkirk's natural advantages. 21 notes.   E. P. Stickney

3201. Bicha, Karel Denis. THE AMERICAN FARMER AND THE CANADIAN WEST, 1896-1914: A REVISED VIEW. *Agric. Hist. 1964 38(1): 43-46.* Relying on meager evidence earlier writers have exaggerated the movement of American farmers to the Canadian West. Probably there were not more than 200 thousand permanent settlers in the Prairie Provinces from the United States. The importance of the Dominion's promotional activities has been underestimated, and there is evidence that the performance of American settlers did not measure up to expectations of Canadian authorities.   W. D. Rasmussen

3202. Bicha, Karel Denis. THE PLAINS FARMER AND THE PRAIRIE PROVINCE FRONTIER, 1897-1914. *Pro. of the Am. Phil. Soc. 1965 109(6): 398-440.* See previous abstract.   W. G. Morgan

3203. Bicha, Karel Denis. THE PLAINS FARMER AND THE PRAIRIE PROVINCE FRONTIER, 1897-1914. *J. of Econ. Hist. 1965 25(2): 263-270.* Discusses the reasons that drove nearly 600 thousand immigrants from the United States into the Canadian provinces of Saskatchewan and Alberta between 1897 and 1914. Factors that brought about the decline of this immigration as well as its permanent economic impact upon the region are also evaluated. Uses printed sources, both contemporary and secondary.   E. Feldman

3204. Boon, T. C. B. THE CENTENARY OF THE SYLLABIC CREE BIBLE 1862-1962. *Bull. United Church of Can. [Canada] 1964 17: 27-33.* A Bible easily read by the Indians of the Northwest was an achievement, the climax of many years of work by Anglican and Wesleyan Methodist missionaries. The title page of the Syllabic Cree Bible bears the single name William Mason, but the records of the British and Foreign Bible Society which published it indicate it was the work of William Mason assisted by his wife Sophia Mason, Henry B. Steinhauer (a native Methodist pastor), John Sinclair (a half-breed), and other natives. This Bible went through 10 editions between 1862 and 1909, and was reset for a new edition in 1961. 28 notes.   E. P. Stickney

3205. Boon, T. C. B. THE INSTITUTE OF RUPERT'S LAND AND BISHOP DAVID ANDERSON. *Hist. and Sci. Soc. of Manitoba Papers, [Canada] 1961-62 1964 Series 3(18): 92-111.* Commemorates the centenary of the Institute of Rupert's Land, a short-lived organization founded 12 February 1862 and a milestone in the history of culture in western Canada, and gives an account of the life of its first president, Bishop David Anderson (1814-85), consecrated first bishop of Rupert's Land 19 May 1848. When Bishop Anderson left the diocese in 1864 the number of clergy had increased from five to 22. During his episcopate 10 new churches were built. 70 notes.   E. P. Stickney

3206. Boudreau, Joseph A. WESTERN CANADA'S "ENEMY ALIENS" IN WORLD WAR ONE. *Alberta Hist. R. [Canada] 1964 12(1): 1-9.* Immigrants from Germany and Austria-Hungary formed 7.8 percent of the prairie population in 1916. Of these, 87 percent were from the Austrian Ukraine. All of them had to register as "enemy aliens" on the outbreak of war and 8,579 males were interned. Many of these people lost their jobs in 1914 because of their national origins. Many remained unemployed until a labor shortage was felt in 1916. In an unnecessary affront, all of these people were disenfranchised in the 1917 elections. Illus.   G. Emery

3207. Bowsfield, Hartwell. LOUIS RIEL'S LETTER TO PRESIDENT GRANT, 1875. *Saskatchewan Hist. [Canada] 1968 21(2): 67-75.* Following his meeting with Ulysses S. Grant, Louis Riel (1844-85), drew up a list of proposals he wished to place before the U.S. Government. (This document was discovered in Winnipeg in 1966.) Riel wished to force Canada to abide by its treaty with his government of 1869, claiming he had 68 thousand supporters in the West and Canada less than ten thousand, while "the Mounted police can hardly take care of their horses." He proposed to retain allegiance to England, encourage a large immigration of French Canadians and Irish Americans, issue bonds, and enlist the support of Quebec. He hoped the U.S. Government would deny passage to any armed forces sent to attack him. 15 notes.   L. F. S. Upton

3208. Buck, Ruth Matheso, ed. DOCUMENTS OF WESTERN HISTORY: THE JOURNAL OF ELEANOR SHEPPHIRD MATHESON, 1920. *Saskatchewan Hist. [Canada] 1969 22(2): 66-72, (3): 109-117.* Part I. A daily journal of a canoe trip from The Pas to Lac La Ronge, a distance of 700 miles, in the summer of 1920. Eleanor Matheson was accompanied by her husband, the Reverend Canon Matheson, Archdeacon John Alexander Mackay, and Miss K. Halson. Indian missions were the destination of the canoe journey. 14 notes. Part II. More daily details of events on the trip by canoe with missionaries from the Pas to Lac La Ronge and back in 1920. Photos, 13 notes.   C. A. Bishop

3209. Carrière, Gaston. NOS ARCHIVES ET LA SOCIETE CANADIENNE D'HISTOIRE DE L'EGLISE CATHOLIQUE [Our archives and the Canadian Society for the History of the Catholic Church]. *R. de l'U. d'Ottawa [Canada] 1964 34(1): 73-96.* An introduction to the holdings of some 30 Canadian diocesan archives. Particularly rich are those of the archdioceses of Quebec, Montreal, Rimouski, Ottawa, Saint-Boniface, and Edmonton. The author notes the contributions made since 1934 by the Canadian Society for the History of the Catholic Church and outlines additional work necessary for a satisfactory ecclesiastical history of Canada. He appends a list of 18 doctoral and 33 masters' theses presented to the Université d'Ottawa which are related to this subject.   J. H. Smart

3210. Champagne, Antoine. THE VERENDRYES AND THEIR SUCCESSORS, 1727-1760. *Tr. of the Hist. and Sci. Soc. of Manitoba [Canada] 1968/69 (25): 5-22.* Pierre Gaultier de Varennes LaVerendrye, sieur de la Verendrye (1685-1749), and his sons and nephew played by far the most prominent part in the discovery of the Canadian West. Gives a brief biography and character sketch of this fur trader and explorer. In 1743 he claimed the West for France by burying a lead tablet on a hilltop near the present Pierre, South Dakota. 29 notes, biblio.   L. F. S. Upton

3211. Champagne, Antonio. GRAND RAPIDS: AN OLD HISTORICAL SPOT, 1727-1760. *Hist. and Sci. Soc. of Manitoba Papers [Canada] 1962 111(19): 6-23.* The importance of Grand Rapids as the center of efforts, begun by La Vérendrye in 1727, to attain the Western Sea. Considers the lesser known history of the area up to the end of the French regime in 1760. Maps: Ochaga Map of 1727-29, p. 12; Section of the 1740 map, p. 16; Lower Saskatchewan, p. 20.   R. J. C. Ford

3212. Cherwinski, W. J. C. "HONORE JOSEPH JAXON, AGITATOR, DISTURBER, PRODUCER OF PLANS TO MAKE MEN THINK, AND CHRONIC OBJECTOR. . . ." *Can. Hist. R. [Canada] 1965 46(2): 122-133.* Using previously undiscovered documents as a lead to further material, the author has attempted to fill in three previously undocumented decades in the life of Honore Joseph Jaxon, an individual who is of interest not so much because of his connection with Louis Riel during the North West Rebellion but rather because he exemplified the unselfish, idealistic agitators and organizers who are so much a part of the radical tradition of western Canada and the western United States.   A

3213. Church, G. C. DOMINION GOVERNMENT AID TO THE DAIRY INDUSTRY IN WESTERN CANADA, 1890-1906. *Saskatchewan Hist. [Canada] 1963 16(2): 41-58.* The creameries operated by the Dominion Government in the region now known as Saskatchewan were not as successful as those in Alberta. By 1905 there remained only four government operated creameries in Saskatchewan. Farmers were turning to beef cattle and wheat. In Alberta many regions were less suited for wheat growing and more suited for dairying, and the Dominion Government appeared to take a more active interest in dairying in Alberta. Based on the author's unpublished master's thesis (U. of Saskatchewan, 1960).   A. H. Lawrance

3214. Clinskill, James. MEMBER OF THE TERRITORIAL ASSEMBLY FOR BATTLEFORD, 1888. *Saskatchewan Hist. [Canada] 1969 22(1): 29-33.* Recollections of James Clinskill of his first election campaign in 1888 for the Territorial Assembly of the Northwest Territories and of his first impressions as a member of the legislature. His election was vigorously contested. In the assembly he witnessed the genesis of a struggle with the lieutenant governor for control of finances. Taken from his reminiscences in the Saskatoon Public Library and the Saskatchewan Archives; illus.   D. L. Smith

3215. Dempsey, Hugh A., ed. THE LAST LETTERS OF REV. GEORGE MC DOUGALL. *Alberta Hist. R. [Canada] 1967 15(2): 20-30.* Collection of letters written by George McDougall, Wesleyan Methodist Church Superintendent of Missionary work in western Canada. The letters describe activities among the Cree, Stony, and other Indian tribes in the area.   H. M. Burns

3216. Doty, James. A VISIT TO THE BLACKFOOT CAMP. *Alberta Hist. R. [Canada] 1966 14(3): 17-23.* Report of a journey from Fort Benton, Montana north into Alberta by U.S. Representative Doty to secure attendance of the tribes and bands of the Blackfoot Nation at a treaty conference arranged by the American Government to be held on the upper Missouri River. Reproduced from a manuscript copy in the U.S. National Archives.   H. M. Burns

3217.   Fisher, A. D.   CULTURAL CONFLICTS ON THE PRAIRIES, INDIAN AND WHITE.   *Alberta Hist. R. [Canada] 1968 16(3): 22-29.* Describes the unique features of the prairie culture of Indians and the impact of European culture upon this established form. There is a discussion of geographic considerations in the evolution of Indian culture and the development of tribal life.   H. M. Burns

3218.   Fraser, W. B.   BIG BEAR, INDIAN PATRIOT.   *Alberta Hist. R. [Canada] 1966 14(2): 1-13.* Account of the career of the Cree Indian Chief, Big Bear, appraising his role in the Frog Lake Massacre, and indicating that, contrary to popular belief, this was not an attack planned in league with Louis Riel who also led uprisings in western Canada during this period.   H. M. Burns

3219.   Graig, G. M.   LETTERS IN CANADA: 1964, SOCIAL STUDIES, LOCAL AND REGIONAL.   *U. of Toronto Q. [Canada] 1965 34(4): 443-450.* Reviews works with Canadian local and regional themes and works by or about Canadians and published during 1964. Among the subjects covered by the books are the life and career of Sir Arthur Hamilton Gordon (1829-1912), who was lieutenant-governor of New Brunswick from 1861 to 1866; the history of Prince Edward Island from early times to 1873; Joseph Howe of Nova Scotia; Quebec and French Canada; Ontario history; exploration of Canada's western Provinces; immigrant settlement in the Prairie Provinces; fur-traders and trading in northern Canada; and biographies of two Canadian doctors.   W. L. Bowers

3220.   Green, Alan G.   REGIONAL ASPECTS OF CANADA'S ECONOMIC GROWTH, 1890-1929.   *Can. J. of Econ. and Pol. Sci. [Canada] 1967 33(2): 232-245.* Asserts that Canadian economic growth featured a large regional redistribution of economic activity, caused primarily by the settlement of the Prairie Provinces and the exploitation of staples, especially wheat. 5 tables, 9 notes.   R. V. Kubicek

3221.   Hafter, Ruth.   THE RIEL REBELLION AND MANIFEST DESTINY.   *Dalhousie R. [Canada] 1965 45(4): 447-456.* Explains why the Métis under Louis Riel did not join the United States while they controlled Rupert's Land. Riel was a strong Catholic and Catholic clergy supported Britain. The Métis felt they would get no recognition of their special status in religion and language from the United States. The American annexationist movement was limited to residents of Minnesota, merchants of Detroit and a few railroad men. The British made a show of force with Garnet Joseph Wolseley's expedition. The Canadian government was caught up in the idea of Manifest Destiny at a time when the United States was more interested in Tariff protection than in territorial expansion.   L. F. S. Upton

3222.   Holmes, Mrs. Robert.   EXPERIENCES OF A MISSIONARY'S WIFE.   *Alberta Hist. R. [Canada] 1964 12(2): 18-25.* With her husband, an Anglican missionary, the author arrived in Edmonton from Liverpool in 1902. Their life in the Athabaska country, where he served 1902-04, and in the Peace River country, where he served until 1915, is described. Her husband died in 1916 in Saskatchewan.   G. Emery

3223.   Irvine, A. G.   A PARLEY WITH BIG BEAR.   *Alberta Hist. R. [Canada] 1963 11(4): 19.* Describes the incident that persuaded the Indian chief Big Bear to stop molesting the government surveyors.   E. W. Hathaway

3224.   Jaenen, C. J.   RUTHENIAN SCHOOLS IN WESTERN CANADA 1897-1919.   *Paedagogica Hist. [Belgium] 1970 10(3): 517-541.* Surveys the experiments in bilingual education which led to the creation of a mosaic rather than a melting pot. Official policy was to reconcile minority rights with majority rules while it was believed that unity could be achieved in diversity. Local officials did not observe this policy. Details the separate developments of Ukrainian language teaching in Manitoba, Saskatchewan, and Alberta. In Manitoba the precedent of bilingual schools for French citizens was used to accommodate the various minorities. It was thought that such schools were merely transitional, and bilingualism was abandoned out of fear of Balkanization of the Province. In the two other Provinces conditions were not as favorable; in Saskatche-

wan the authorities treated the Ukrainians with hostility. Based on primary sources.   D. Visser

3225.   Jamison, Sheilogh S.   ERA OF THE BIG RANCHES.   *Alberta Hist. R. [Canada] 1970 18(1): 1-9.* Discusses the development of particular big cattle ranches in the southern prairie section of Western Canada, and corrects misconceptions regarding the subject. The author discusses the relationship of ranching in Canada to that of the American Northwest, with emphasis on the dissimilarities.   H. M. Burns

3226.   Kennedy, Howard Angus.   MEMORIES OF '85.   *Canadian Geographical J. [Canada] 1965 70(5): 154-161.* An article written 50 years after the action recorded by this war correspondent in the North West Rebellion, first appeared in the *Canadian Geographical Journal* in August 1935. The author describes the march to the relief of Battleford, taking five days for a distance of 150 miles, crossing the Saskatchewan River 30 miles north of Swift Current, and the march to Batoche, the Métis' headquarters, under General Middleton. The capture of Louis Riel's headquarters came in time to halt the Métis' march. The surrender of the chiefs is described. Illus., map.   E. P. Stickney

3227.   Kinnaird, George J.   AN EPISODE OF THE NORTH-WEST REBELLION, 1885.   *Saskatchewan Hist. [Canada] 1967 20(2): 71-75.* This account, written probably 30 years after the events described, is a personal recollection by the man who was in charge of Fort Ellice at the time of the rebellion. He outfitted the corps known as Boulton's Scouts organized by Major Charles Boulton.   A. H. Lawrance

3228.   Knill, William D.   THE HUTTERITES, CULTURAL TRANSMISSION IN A CLOSED SOCIETY.   *Alberta Hist. R. [Canada] 1968 16(3): 1-10.* Describes the communal society of the Hutterian Brethren, brought from the Austrian Tyrol and established on the prairies of western Canada. The historical background of the sect and a discussion of methods utilized in transmission of their cultural heritage and of their system of education are given.   H. M. Burns

3229.   Koester, C. B.   "MR. DAVIN'S PAMPHLET ON THE NORTH WEST": A BUREAUCRATIC COMEDY OF ERRORS.   *Saskatchewan Hist. [Canada] 1963 16(1): 27-32.* Relates the circumstances of the publication in 1891-92 of a paperbound work of one hundred pages entitled *Homes for Millions,* edited by Nicholas Flood Davin, one of four M.P.'s for the North West Territories and founding editor of the Regina *Leader.* The lieutenant governor's office pressed for major revision which would omit entirely the name of Davin. The subsequent correspondence is related. The outcome was that the pamphlets were issued as originally printed.   A. H. Lawrance

3230.   Lawrence, H. Frank.   EARLY DAYS IN THE CHINOOK BELT.   *Alberta Hist. R. [Canada] 1965 13(1): 9-19.* The author, a Liverpool native, arrived in Winnipeg in 1882 and moved west with the construction crews who were laying the Canadian Pacific Railway track west at the rate of 2.5 miles per day. Near Calgary he left the railway crews and went to the southern Alberta ranch country. He describes the cattle drives there and the personalities he encountered. Illus.
                                                          G. Emery

3231.   Lee, Lawrence B.   THE CANADIAN-AMERICAN IRRIGATION FRONTIER, 1884-1914.   *Agric. Hist. 1966 40(4): 271-283.* Canadian irrigation undertakings in the Prairie Provinces date from 1879. Thereafter, Canadian irrigation was an activity consciously promoted by the government. Residents of southern Alberta began to agitate for reclamation projects about 1884 and welcomed Mormon immigrants as people who knew how to irrigate. The campaign to gain support for reclamation resulted in the Northwest Irrigation Act of 1894. This carefully drawn act provided for government licensing of water rights, a provision which was efficiently administered. The first large-scale project, that of the Alberta Railway and Irrigation Company, was a success primarily because of Mormon cooperation. Based on published Canadian source material.
                                                          W. D. Rasmussen

3232.   Lester, Carl.   DOMINION LAND SURVEY.   *Alberta Hist. R. [Canada] 1963 11(3): 20-28.* The story of the surveying of the territory of Rupert's Land from the establishment by Lt. Col. Dennis of the Winnipeg, or Principal, Meridian, the Red River Rebellion, the establishment of a Board of Examiners for the licensing of surveyors and various revisions thereof, and the adoption of the photo-topographical method for accurate lowcost mapping of mountainous and inaccessible areas.

E. W. Hathaway

3233. Lupul, Manoly R. THE CAMPAIGN FOR A FRENCH CATHOLIC SCHOOL INSPECTOR IN THE NORTH-WEST TERRITORIES, 1898-1903. *Canadian Hist. R. [Canada] 1967 48(4): 332-352.* Examines the Catholic Church as a political pressure group in Regina and Ottawa and the reactions of the Territorial and Federal Governments to the pressure. From the evidence it is clear that the church and state were both to blame for the Territorial Government's failure to grant the French Catholic minority a school inspector. Based mainly on unpublished documents in the Roman Catholic archives in western Canada and in the public archives in Regina and Ottawa.   A

3234. Lyle, Guy R. THE REV. ISAAC M. BARR: APOSTLE OF THE CANADIAN NORTHWEST. *Am. Book Collector 1966 17(2): 10-14.* The Reverend Isaac M. Barr proposed "to settle an 'all-British' colony on the prairie of the Canadian Northwest." In pamphlets published in 1902-03 he described the settlement and recruited persons to go there. It was well-organized on paper, but the colonists found few of his promises fulfilled when they arrived. Documented, illus.

D. Brockway

3235. MacGregor, James. LORD LORNE IN ALBERTA. *Alberta Hist. R. [Canada] 1964 12(2): 1-15.* Lord Lorne's three-month trip through the Canadian prairies made him the first governor-general to visit this region. Representatives of the British press and a reporter for the Toronto *Globe* covered the journey and the result was the first extensive first-hand information on the Canadian West available to the world. The image of a West unsuited to settlement was largely discredited. The account of the journey was written by the Reverend James MacGregor, an Edinburgh friend of Lord Lorne.   G. Emery

3236. Malouin, Reine. MONSEIGNEUR JEAN GAIRE, P.D. GRAND MISSIONAIRE-COLONISATEUR DE L'OUEST CANADIEN [Monseigneur Jean Gaire, P.D. grand missionary-colonizer of West Canada]. *Rapport: Soc. Canadian d'Hist. de l'Eglise Catholique [Canada] 1964 31: 85-97.* Born in French Lorraine, Abbé Gaire was a 30-year old priest when he was inspired to become a missionary-colonizer. In 1888 he came to Canada where he went first to Manitoba and founded there Grande-Clairière. In western Canada he founded a number of other churches and schools. His recruiting trips to France were successful, though he was wrongfully accused by some slanderers of making a profit from them. His 37 years of self-denying service were recognized by the Pope.   E. P. Stickney

3237. Marwick, Ernest W. CHIEF FACTOR JAMES SUTHERLAND AND HIS ORKNEY CORRESPONDENCE. *Beaver [Canada] 1966 297(Winter): 44-51.* Letters by James Sutherland (1778-1844) recently come to light, cover, with some notable gaps, 1814-44. Sutherland, chief factor of the Hudson's Bay Company and a member of the Council of Assiniboia, retired at Red River. These letters and some by his sons and son-in-law were written to their relatives in the Orkney Islands. Includes quotations from the letters and a facsimile of part of one of them; illus.   L. F. S. Upton

3238. Meyer, Roy W. THE CANADIAN SIOUX: REFUGEES FROM MINNESOTA. *Minnesota Hist. 1968 41(1): 13-28.* Following the end of the Sioux uprising of 1862, several thousand of the defeated Indians fled to Canada seeking a refuge. At first they were treated as refugees and given temporary aid. Later, as the years passed, they were accepted as permanent residents and reservations were established for them at such places as Standing Buffalo and Wood Mountain in Saskatchewan and Turtle Mountain, Oak Lake, Long Plant and others in Manitoba. The author feels that the Canadian approach to its Indian problem, while similar to that of the United States, was more humane and, in the long run, more successful. The Parliamentary Sessional Papers provided the bulk of the source material.   P. L. Simon

3239. Morgan, E. C. SOLDIER SETTLEMENT IN THE PRAIRIE PROVINCES. *Saskatchewan Hist. [Canada] 1968 21(2): 42-55.* In 1917 the Canadian Government passed the Soldier Settlement Act setting up a board authorized to lend veterans up to 2,500 dollars to set up farms on Dominion lands. However, since most of the best land was gone, a further act in 1919 increased the amounts to be lent and provided for the purchase of lands held for speculation, school lands, and uncultivated portions of Indian reserves. By the end of 1924, 24,148 veterans had been established, but the rate of abandonment was 21 percent. In 1942 the Minister of Immigration reported that in all 109,034,331 dollars had been advanced to establish 25,017 soldier settlers, of whom 8,118 remained on the land, 884 had sold out, and 13,041 had abandoned their holdings or been forced out by foreclosure. The author studies one such settlement, Prairie River, Saskatchewan. 99 notes.   L. F. S. Upton

3240. Morton, W. L. THE NORTH WEST COMPANY, PEDLARS EXTRAORDINARY. *Minnesota Hist. 1966 40(4): 157-165.* An interpretive article on the operations of the North West Company during its history. The author's thesis is that prior to 1821 the company was an extraordinarily successful union of European capital and business enterprise combined with Indian skills. He holds further that the merger in 1821 with the Hudson's Bay Company was really more a victory than a defeat because it forced on the victorious competitor "the mode of operation and labor force" which the North West Company had developed and by which it had flourished in the past.   P. L. Simon

3241. Pearce, William. CAUSES OF THE RIEL REBELLION, A PERSONAL VIEW. *Alberta Hist. R. [Canada] 1968 16(4): 19-25.* An analysis of troubles with Indian half-breeds in western Canada which resulted in the rebellion led by Louis Riel in 1885. Included is an account of the capture, trial, and execution of Riel.   H. M. Burns

3242. Peel, Bruce. THE COAL FLEET. *Alberta Hist. R. [Canada] 1964 12(4): 8-14.* In 1882 coal mines were opened up at Coal Banks (now Lethbridge), and in 1883 a river fleet was established to haul the coal to the railway at Medicine Hat on the South Saskatchewan River. However, because of the short navigation season, which was partly caused by the river route's fluctuating water levels, the coal fleet proved an uneconomical means of transportation. In 1885 the railway was extended to Coal Banks, and the steamer fleet, after performing badly as troop transports during the Louis Riel rebellion, was obsolete. Illus.   G. Emery

3243. Peel, Bruce. FIRST STEAMBOATS ON THE SASKATCHEWAN. *Beaver [Canada] 1964 295(Autumn): 16-21.* The first steamboat to try to connect the Red and Saskatchewan Rivers was the *Chief Commissioner,* built at Lower Fort Garry and launched in June 1872. Unable to get through the Dauphin River, she was used exclusively on Lake Winnipeg. An unnamed ship launched in August 1873 was sunk after steaming only 14 miles. Its successor was the *Northcote,* launched in the following year, whose maiden voyage of 490 miles from Grand Rapids to Carlton House was made in 12 days. Illus.   L. F. S. Upton

3244. Regehr, T. D. SERVING THE CANADIAN WEST: POLICIES AND PROBLEMS OF THE CANADIAN NORTHERN RAILWAY. *Western Hist. Q. 1972 3(3): 283-298.* An inexpensive and extensive railway system was a prerequisite of occupation and settlement of the Canadian prairies. The Canadian Northern Railway provided this kind of service during the great settlement boom in the early part of the 20th century. Its promoters epitomized the prevailing frontier optimism and led the prairie farmers in a successful assault on the eastern-controlled national railway policy. Research does not confirm assertions that unscrupulous and opportunistic C.N.R. promoters built the railway with the aid of corrupt politicians and dubious financial transactions. Map, 49 notes.   D. L. Smith

3245. Roy, R. H., ed. RIFLEMAN FORIN IN THE RIEL REBELLION. *Saskatchewan Hist. [Canada] 1968 21(3): 100-111.* The diary of John Andrew Forin, 26 March - 27 July 1885, is his account of the Riel Rebellion as a member of the Queen's Own Rifles of Canada. From its entries emerge the fairly common Liberal and Presbyterian opinions of the rebellion, the unreliability of intelligence about the rebels' moves, the increase of supply difficulties as the Queen's Own moved beyond the railhead, and the high morale of the men. Illus.   D. L. Smith

3246. Scott, Walter H. THE BEAVER RIVER ROUTE. *Alberta Hist. R. [Canada] 1963 11(2): 20-22.* Describes and includes a sketch map of the Beaver River Route, part of the fur trade route to the west; the first

mention of it in journals and letters, and its final abandonment except for local use in favor of a trail constructed from Edmonton to Fort Assiniboine.
E. W. Hathaway

3247. Shlepakov, A. M. BILIA DZHEREL UKRAINS'KOI TRUDOVOI IMMIHRATSII V KANADI [Beginnings of the Ukrainian labor immigration in Canada]. *Ukrains'kyi Istorychnyi Zhurnal [USSR] 1966 (6): 50-58.* Ukrainian emigration to Canada began in 1891. Mainly, the Ukrainian immigrants became farmers but soon occupied various positions in the new country.
N. Andrusiak

3248. Silver, A. I. FRENCH CANADA AND THE PRAIRIE FRONTIER, 1870-1890. *Can. Hist. R. [Canada] 1969 50(1): 11-36.* Looks for attitudes preventing French Canadians from participating in settlement of the prairie, despite constitutional guarantees of school and language rights. Fear of sterility of the land, fear of persecution by Anglo-Canadians, and conviction that only Quebec and not all of Canada was the real homeland of French Canadians contributed to their trepidation. The author concludes that French-Canadian society did not produce the type of personality that could become a "frontiersman." Based on newspapers, pamphlets, letters of colonizers.
A

3249. Smith, David E. A COMPARISON OF PRAIRIE POLITICAL DEVELOPMENTS IN SASKATCHEWAN AND ALBERTA. *J. of Can. Studies [Canada] 1969 4(1): 17-26.* A study of the contribution of the Canadian federal system to the rise of the Co-operative Commonwealth Federation in Saskatchewan and of the Social Credit Party in Alberta. Political tradition rather than economic and social structure accounts for the differing developments in the two Provinces. When the existing party system was threatened after 1911, the Saskatchewan Liberals preserved themselves by repudiating the National Liberals; while the United Farmers of Alberta entered politics to overthrow a corrupt party system. After 1921, there was no alternative party in Alberta such as the Liberal Party of Saskatchewan. Based on secondary sources; 2 tables, 30 notes.
G. E. Panting

3250. Smith, T. R. THE STEAMBOAT LILY. *Saskatchewan Hist. [Canada] 1964 17(2): 55-59.* An account of the river steamer which provided a service on the North Saskatchewan river system in 1878-83, and which pioneered a service on the South Saskatchewan River as far as Medicine Hat. The chief hazard, rocks at low water, caused the wrecking of the *Lily* in 1883. Photograph.
A. H. Lawrance

3251. Spafford, D. S. THE ORIGIN OF THE FARMERS' UNION OF CANADA. *Saskatchewan Hist. [Canada] 1965 18(3): 89-98.* The depression following the First World War was the occasion for the setting up at Ituna, Saskatchewan, of the Farmers' Union, which within two years had a membership estimated at ten thousand. Although Socialist ideas figured distinctly in the preamble to the constitution, the union did not propose to take an active part in politics. The Appendix reproduces the draft constitution of the Farmers' Union of Canada, 25 July 1922.
A. H. Lawrance

3252. Stanley, George F. G. LOUIS RIEL. *R. d'Hist. de l'Amérique Française [Canada] 1964 18(1): 14-26.* Describes the career of Louis Riel (1844-85) and his organization of two resistance movements to the federal government. As the leader of the Métis nation he won special rights written into the Manitoba Act of 1870, but he went into exile. Returning in 1884 to defend his people on the Saskatchewan, he was captured and executed. He became the symbol of the struggle between French and English Canada for the West, which in turn involved the issue of whether Canada was a dualistic federation or an English-dominated unitary state. Riel, French-speaking and Roman Catholic, came to stand for the maintenance of ethnic and cultural diversity with the Dominion.
L. F. S. Upton

3253. Thomas, L. H. DOCUMENTS OF WESTERN HISTORY: LOUIS RIEL'S PETITION OF RIGHTS, 1884. *Saskatchewan Hist. [Canada] 1970 23(1): 16-26.* Discusses the petition of rights by Louis Riel in 1884. Andrew Spence as Chairman of the Committee and William Henry Jackson as Secretary supported the petition, but when the government made no reply, Riel formed his Provisional Government in 1885. Before the rebellion, William Pierce was chosen to investigate the matter and presented a report. Riel's petition was presented by Jackson and

involved a list of grievances, while Pierce's report exonerated the government's action. Included in the correspondence is a letter from the editor of the Regina *Leader,* Nicholas Flood Davin, who supported a claim for parliamentary representation and provincial status for the Northwest. Based on primary and secondary sources, including the petition and letters in the Public Archives of Canada; 7 notes.
C. A. Bishop

3254. Warkentin, John. DAVID THOMPSON'S GEOLOGY: A DOCUMENT. *J. of the West 1967 6(3): 468-490.* Thompson, a fur trader, surveyor, and geographer in western America from 1784 to 1812, wrote a narrative in the 1840's detailing his experiences. In the narrative he made no attempt to arrange the geological information into a systematic portrayal of the geology of the interior of North America. Bound into one of the many volumes of his journals held by the Public Archives of Ontario is a 12-page description of the geology of the area extending from the Rocky Mountains to the eastern end of Lake Superior. It is this document which is printed and analyzed by the author. Primary sources, 85 notes.
D. N. Brown

3255. Winks, Robin W. CONTROLLING FACTORS IN CANADIAN-AMERICAN RELATIONS. *Australian J. of Pol. and Hist. [Australia] 1968 14(2): 193-203.* Although U.S.-Canadian relations are harmonious, they were not always so. Stresses the "negatives" of Canadian history - that the nation was not British or French or American. An evolutionary rather than a revolutionary movement to independence took place. Even in the Prairie Provinces (which might be expected to closely resemble the northern plains States) there are notable differences between the United States and Canada that stem from the role in settlement of Hudson's Bay Company and the good order provided by the Mounted Police north of the border. Detects a shift from the old Canadian dream - of conquering the land and peopling the plains - to a new dream of Canada fulfilling a world role as a middle power.
D. McIntyre

3256. —. SMALLPOX EPIDEMIC OF 1869-70. *Alberta Hist. R. [Canada] 1963 11(2): 13-19.* Three documents from *The Manitoban,* published at Red River (now Winnipeg) telling the story of the epidemic, its effects on the prairies, and attempts at precautions.
E. W. Hathaway

Manitoba

3257. Allison, Carlyle. W. J. PHILLIPS, ARTIST AND TEACHER. *Beaver [Canada] 1969 300(Winter): 4-13.* An account of the life of Walter J. Phillips (1884-1963), an artist who spent most of his active career in Winnipeg. Between 1914 and 1924 he painted mostly at or near the Lake of the Woods; from then until 1936 he painted mostly prairie scenes; and after 1936 he painted the west coast and the Rockies. Illus.
L. F. S. Upton

3258. Alvey, John. THE NELSON: MANITOBA'S OWN RIVER. *Can. Geographical J. [Canada] 1969 78(1): 2-11.* The Nelson River, which is entirely within Manitoba, was discovered in 1612 by Captain Thomas Button. Its basin is one of North America's main drainage areas, encompassing 414 thousand square miles. Between Lake Winnipeg and Hudson Bay the Nelson drops 712 feet, making the river one of the great hydroelectric power resources of the continent. The colorful history of the Hudson Bay Railway is closely tied to that of the Nelson River. Hydroelectric development of the river began in 1957 with construction of the Kelsey Generating Station to supply power to the mining and smelting operations of the International Nickel Company of Canada at Thompson, Manitoba. Power from the new Kettle Generating Station will be exported. 10 illus., map.
R. D. Tallman

3259. Barry, James P. THE WOLSELEY EXPEDITION CROSSES THE GREAT LAKES. *Inland Seas 1968 24(2): 91-107.* In 1870 the Canadian Government dispatched a military expedition under Colonel Garnet J. Wolseley to put down the insurrection of Louis Riel in the Red River valley. Despite the threat of Fenian attacks and American limitations on the use of the Sault Sainte Marie Canal, the expedition moved by water to Thunder Bay on Lake Superior. From there it marched overland to Fort Garry (Winnipeg) and put down the insurrection without fighting. Based on Wolseley's reports, other contemporary accounts, and monographic studies; illus., 72 notes.
K. J. Bauer

3260. Bartlett, Fred E. THE FALL OF FORT GARRY. *Beaver* [Canada] 1966 296(Spring): 48-52. Describes the occupation of Fort Garry, Red River, by the Métis under Louis Riel in November 1869, the culmination of 12 years of political agitation. The fort could not have been defended, for the Hudson's Bay Company had no support in the community; advocates of annexation to Canada had denied the company's rights in the territory, and the Scots settlers and English half-breeds were neutral. The author disputes the testimony of James Mulligan, who claimed he had warned the company in advance, and blamed it for not defending the post. Illus.
L. F. S. Upton

3261. Bercuson, David J. THE WINNIPEG GENERAL STRIKE: COLLECTIVE BARGAINING AND THE ONE BIG UNION ISSUE. *Can. Hist. R.* [Canada] 1970 51(2): 164-176. Examines Cabinet reaction to the One Big Union and demonstrates how fear prompted the Borden government to ignore the root cause of the general strike of May 1919. The author points specifically to the Minister of Labour Gideon Robertson's intervention in mediation proceedings and shows how he played on the anxieties of conservative railway unionists. The mediators allowed themselves to be swept up in the Government's anti-O.B.U. crusade and provided essential ammunition for a rapid defeat of the strike. Based mainly on the Borden Papers and on newspaper sources. A

3262. Bessason, Haraldur A FEW SPECIMENS OF NORTH AMERICAN-ICELANDIC. *Scandinavian Studies* 1967 39(2): 115-146. Cites numerous examples of North American-Icelandic, that is, Icelandic spoken or written in immigrant communities in Canada and the United States. The author gathered his information about American-Icelandic linguistic usage from interviews (recorded on tapes) with 30 Canadian Icelanders, 10 of whom were residents of Arborg, a rural community in Manitoba, and 20 of whom were from the urban area of Winnipeg, Manitoba. Five of the informants were born in Iceland and came to Manitoba at an early age; 15 were second-generation Canadians; ten were of the third generation. Among the English "loans," or linguistic borrowings, "nouns by far the most common and constitute a much larger group than the verbs which form the second largest category." After discussing and illustrating the changes that have occurred in Icelandic family surnames, Christian names, and place-names, the author points out that his study "does not imply a value judgment on the North American-Icelandic language; neither does it state anything about the linguistic skills or the functional vocabulary of the average AI speaker." 3 maps, 110 notes.
D. D. Cameron

3263. Boissenault, Charles-Marie. L'EXPEDITION DU NORD-OUEST: LE RAPPORT WOLSELEY [The Northwest expedition: the Wolseley Report]. *Tr. of the Royal Soc. of Can.* [Canada] 1970 8: 123-131. An account of the Riel resistance at Red River and of the expedition sent out from Ontario to suppress it in 1870. If he had chosen, Riel could have put up a stiff fight, but Colonel Garnet Joseph Wolseley (later first Viscount Wolseley), in command of the expedition, never seemed to realize this. 17 notes.
L. F. S. Upton

3264. Bonenfant, Jean-Charles. LA DUALITE LINGUISTIQUE AU MANITOBA [Linguistic duality in Manitoba]. *Tr. of the Royal Soc. of Can.* [Canada] 1970 8: 133-140. The Manitoba Act (1870), the "Constitution" of the province, provided for the use of English and French both in the legislature and in the schools. At that time about half the resident population spoke French; by 1891 only 11 thousand of 152 thousand did so. Discusses the events of 1889-90 that led to the abolition of French as an official language. This step violated the understanding on which Manitoba had joined Canada. 12 notes.
L. F. S. Upton

3265. Boon, Thomas C. B. THE ARCHDEACON AND THE GOVERNOR. *Beaver* [Canada] 1968 298(Spring): 41-48. The life of William Cockran (d. 1865), missionary for the Anglican Church, who arrived at the Red River Settlement in 1825 as a teacher. There are excerpts from his diary, which all Church Missionary Society ministers were required to keep, although Cockran gave his up in 1841. Several meetings with Governor in Chief Sir George Simpson are related. Illus.
L. F. S. Upton

3266. Bowles, Richard S. ADAMS GEORGE ARCHIBALD, FIRST LIEUTENANT GOVERNOR OF MANITOBA. *Tr. of the Hist. and Sci. Soc. of Manitoba* [Canada] 1968/69 (25): 75-88. Archibald

was a Nova Scotia lawyer and politician and a father of Confederation. He was Lieutenant Governor of Manitoba, 1870-72, and held the same office in Nova Scotia, 1872-83. In Manitoba he had to create a government for an isolated community of 10 thousand settlers with no telegraphic or other regular means of contact with the outside world. Further, the settlement was bitterly divided in the wake of the Riel resistance. Archibald had to contend with the first census, the demarcation of the boundary line, smallpox, and a Fenian invasion. His action in shaking (albeit unknowingly) the hand of Louis Riel caused such an uproar in Ontario that Archibald decided to resign.
L. F. S. Upton

3267. Brown, Alice E. THE FUR TRADE POSTS OF THE SOURIS-MOUTH AREA. *Hist. and Sci. Soc. of Manitoba Papers,* [Canada] 1961-62 1964 Series 3(18): 78-91. Two kinds of evidence are examined: the physical evidence of the sites themselves and the written evidence from letters and journals of fur traders, 1793-1821. One journal not previously studied, that of William Yorstone, the man in charge of Brandon House from 1810 to 1821, provides important materials. Archeological investigation should be fruitful, for the whole area was an important point-of-pause in the Indians' yearly migrations and was certainly one of the original centers of fur trade activity in the plains area of Manitoba. 2 maps, 16 notes.
E. P. Stickney

3268. Brown, Mrs. E. J. EARLY DAYS OF MINNEDOSA. *Tr. of the Hist. and Sci. Soc. of Manitoba* [Canada] 1964/65 3(21): 7-11. Gives a description of the events and personalities involved in the settlement of the Minnedosa area of western Manitoba.
W. D. Smith

3269. Burghardt, A. F. A HYPOTHESIS ABOUT GATEWAY CITIES. *Ann. of the Assoc. of Am. Geographers* 1971 61(2): 269-285. "Gateway cities develop between areas of differing intensities or types of production; they are located towards one end of their tributary areas; and they are heavily committed to transportation and wholesaling. It is hypothesized that if the tributary area of a gateway city is large enough and productive enough to support the rise of large central places, then the gateway will be shorn of much of its previous hinterland and will itself come to function as a central place. The pattern of growth of Winnipeg fits the sequence set out in the hypothesis. Briefer case studies of Cincinnati, St. Louis, Minneapolis-St. Paul, and Cluj [Rumania] also support the hypothesis. The rise of gateways is dependent upon the presence of threshold values for distance, and levels of productivity. The gateway concept may help explain the existence of twin cities, but is in opposition to the basic spatial postulate of the von Thünen model."
J

3270. Careless, J. M. S. THE DEVELOPMENT OF THE WINNIPEG BUSINESS COMMUNITY, 1870-1890. *Tr. of the Royal Soc. of Can.* [Canada] 1970 8: 240-254. Discusses the effect the economic leaders had in shaping the growth of Winnipeg from river-bank hamlet to metropolis in 20 years. The first businessmen were individual free traders who had set up shop outside the Hudson's Bay Company's Fort Garry. Business conditions in the city improved rapidly after 1878 with the rise of grain marketing and milling and the building of the first rail outlet to Pembina. The building of the Canadian Pacific Railroad brought real boom conditions between 1880 and 1883. Even though the settlers did not arrive in vast numbers, the business community continued to grow as Winnipeg's agricultural hinterland advanced. 78 notes.
L. F. S. Upton

3271. Carter, George E. LORD SELKIRK AND THE RED RIVER COLONY. *Montana* 1968 18(1): 60-69. Defends Lord Selkirk's action in establishing a refuge in what is now Manitoba for poor migrants from Scotland and Ireland early in the 19th century. His decision to work with the Hudson's Bay Company led to reprisals from the rival North West Company, whose partisans have charged Selkirk with seeking profits rather than the welfare of his colonists. 62 notes to published works, illus.
S. R. Davison

3272. Chism, James V. EXCAVATIONS AT LOWER FORT GARRY, 1965-1967; A GENERAL DESCRIPTION OF EXCAVATIONS AND PRELIMINARY DISCUSSIONS. *Can. Historic Sites* [Canada] 1972 (5): 9-96. "In 1965, 1966, and 1967 the National Historic Sites Service contracted the University of Manitoba to excavate at the site of Lower Fort Garry National Historic Park, Manitoba. This Hudson's

Bay Company post was occupied by the Company from 1830 to 1911 after which it was used as a country club until the federal government opened it to the public in 1961. Twenty-two major excavations, four minor excavations and numerous tests were conducted during the three-year period. This report is a summary of that field work with correlation where possible with the documentary data bearing on each excavation. The site demonstrated the inaccuracy of the commonly accepted theory that cut nails had replaced wrought nails for general construction purposes by 1800 and a new but as yet vague chronology for this section of the continent has been suggested."　　　　　J

3273. Fisher, Murray. LOCAL GOVERNMENT REORGANIZATION. *Hist. and Sci. Soc. of Manitoba Papers, [Canada] 1960-61 1964 Series 3(17): 15-23.* Local government in Manitoba logically falls into four periods: 1) prior to 1870, 2) 1870-86, 3) 1886 to the present, and 4) the future. Local government in Manitoba has not yet adapted itself to cope adequately with changed economic and social conditions. Yet local government, with the exceptions of the creation of metropolitan Winnipeg and the establishment of school divisions for secondary education, remains about the same as it was 75 years ago. The main topics to be investigated by the Municipal Enquiry Commission are: 1) reorganization of local government outside Winnipeg, provincial-municipal relations, 3) municipal finance, and 4) coordination of the decentralized provincial and federal administrative units with the proposed units of local government.　　　　　E. P. Stickney

3274. Fowke, Edith. THE RED RIVER VALLEY. *Alberta Hist. R. [Canada] 1965 13(1): 20-25.* Rejects the theory, formerly accepted, that the song "The Red River Valley" was an offshoot of the song "The Bright Mohawk Valley," published in 1896. Further research had indicated that "The Red River Valley" was a soldier's song, originating in Manitoba's Red River Valley during the first North West Rebellion, in 1869. Illus.　　　　　G. Emery

3275. Fridley, Russell W. WHEN MINNESOTA COVETED CANADA. *Minnesota Hist. 1968 41(2): 76-79.* Pinpoints one of those many instances - this one by the Minnesota State Legislature in 1868 - when Americans tried to achieve the annexation to the United States of a part of Canada. The attempt was the unsuccessful culmination of a scheme begun by Alexander Ramsey as part of his many political schemes with the aid of James Wickes Taylor and was tied to the ultimate purchase of Alaska so as to achieve territorial contiguity with the rest of the States.　　　　　P. L. Simon

3276. Friesen, John. MANITOBA MENNONITES IN THE RURAL-URBAN SHIFT. *Mennonite Life 1968 23(4): 152-159.* Describes the growth of the Mennonite urban population, particularly in Winnipeg, and discusses the causes of the rural-urban shift. Among rural Mennonites of Manitoba the influx to the city began after 1945. Technological and economic changes are among the major causes for the migration to the cities. Based on recent published sources; illus., 2 charts, table, 8 notes.　　　　　D. J. Abramoske

3277. Friesen, William. A MENNONITE COMMUNITY IN THE EAST RESERVE: ITS ORIGIN AND GROWTH. *Hist. and Sci. Soc. of Manitoba Papers [Canada] 1962 111(19): 24-42.* Examines the origins of the Mennonites who live in Manitoba, the origin and growth of the town of Steinbach, and the development of education for Mennonite children. Quotation: Hamilton, J. C. "The Prairie Province" (1875). Maps: The East Reserve, p. 30; Village and Field Plan of Steinbach from original by John C. Reimer, p. 33.　　　　　R. J. C. Ford

3278. Goldring, Philip. LOWER FORT GARRY. *Beaver [Canada] 1970 301(Summer): 26-38.* The stone fort on the Red River was begun by the Hudson's Bay Company in 1831. The author describes the changes in the functions of the fort and famous incidents connected with it up to its present status as a National Historic Park and tourist attraction. Illus.　　　　　L. F. S. Upton

3279. Herstein, H. H. THE GROWTH OF THE WINNIPEG JEWISH COMMUNITY AND THE EVOLUTION OF ITS EDUCATIONAL INSTITUTIONS. *Tr. of the Hist. and Sci. Soc. of Manitoba [Canada] 1965/66 3(22): 27-66.* A history of the Jews and their schools in Winnipeg. Biblio.　　　　　W. D. Smith

3280. Hildebrand, Menno. THE SOMMERFELD MENNONITES OF MANITOBA. *Mennonite Life 1970 25(3): 99-107.* Describes the religious and social life of the Sommerfeld Mennonite Church, Manitoba, which was founded in 1890. Worship and communion services, church membership and baptism, holidays, the use of Low and High German, and courtship and wedding customs are among the topics discussed. No matter how hard the Sommerfeld Mennonites have tried to keep the status quo, things have changed. In 1935, for example, a group broke away over the issues of evening services, music in the church, Sunday school, and a mission outreach. In 1958 another split occurred over the question of the use of electricity in the church. In 1948 many of the more conservative members migrated to South America. Based on the author's personal observations and secondary sources; illus.　　　　　D. J. Abramoske

3281. Jaenen, C. J. FOUNDATIONS OF DUAL EDUCATION AT RED RIVER, 1811-34. *Tr. of the Hist. and Sci. Soc. of Manitoba [Canada] 1964/65 3(21): 35-68.* Attempts to shed new light on the question of a single versus a dual system of education in Manitoba by examining education during the first years of organized settlement there.　　　　　W. D. Smith

3282. Jaenen, C. J. FRENCH PUBLIC EDUCATION IN MANITOBA. *R. de l'U. d'Ottawa [Canada] 1968 38(1): 19-34.* At the time of Confederation there were three kinds of separate schools in Canada: for special linguistic groups, special racial groups, and special denomination groups (really a dual-confession Protestant-Catholic division). Despite a long tradition of French education in Manitoba, the province received no special protection from the British North America Act when it entered Confederation in 1870 because it had no statutory provision for public schools. There is, indeed, little evidence that French was officially a language of instruction in Manitoba with any constitutional guarantees. Nevertheless, there was a legal vacuum which was filled by French Catholic Schools. Legal uncertainties and national crises have permitted this situation to continue, and recently (1967) the Province in Bill 59 has made French a language of instruction in certain public schools. 24 notes.　　　　　J. M. Bumsted

3283. Kuch, Peter. ARCH DALE: THE PICTORIAL SPOKESMAN OF THE WEST. *Hist. and Sci. Soc. of Manitoba Papers [Canada] 1962 111(19): 44-49.* A brief résumé of the life and work of Archie Dale, the cartoonist, who worked for the *Winnipeg Free Press* in 1910 and from 1927 to 1954. Reproduction of cartoons, pp. 46, 49.　　　　　R. J. C. Ford

3284. LeFoc, D., ed. THE PIONEERS - LETTERS FROM THE EMIGRANTS 1845-54. *Contemporary R. [Great Britain] 1967 210(1212): 12-18.* The texts of three letters from Abraham Cowley, dated July 1845, July 1847, and December 1854, to the Reverend Rice, Fairford, Gloucestershire. Reveals insight into the lives of the early settlers of Red River Settlement [now in Manitoba], Prince Rupert's Land, in the mid-19th century.　　　　　D. H. Murdoch

3285. MacInnis, Grace. J. S. WOODSWORTH - PERSONAL RECOLLECTIONS. *Tr. of the Hist. and Sci. Soc. of Manitoba [Canada] 1967/68 (24): 17-26.* Recollections by the daughter of James Shaver Woodsworth (1874-1942). Emphasizes his speedy and firm decision in the light of principle. He was pitchforked into politics by the Winnipeg General Strike of 1919 when he spent a brief period in jail. From 1921 to 1942 he was an M.P. from Winnipeg. One of his proudest achievements was to force Mackenzie King into instituting the Old Age pension in 1926. A lifelong pacifist, Woodsworth voted against Canada's entry into World War II.　　　　　L. F. S. Upton

3286. Mallory, Enid Swerdfeger. THE LIFE OF LOWER FORT GARRY. *Can. Geographical J. [Canada] 1963 66(4): 116-123.* Surveys the history of the fort founded in 1831 on the west bank of the Red River below St. Andrew's Rapids. Also tells of the relics which are today on display there. Photographs.　　　　　A. H. Lawrance

3287. Martin, J. E. THE 150TH ANNIVERSARY OF SEVEN OAKS. *Tr. of the Hist. and Sci. Soc. of Manitoba [Canada] 1965/66 3(22): 99-111.* On 19 June 1816, a party of some 60 Métis under the leadership of Cuthbert Grant appeared before Fort Douglas in the Red

River Settlement. The governor of the colony, Robert Semple, instead of keeping his men within the fort, decided to go out to parlay with the Métis. A shot was fired for an unknown reason by a person who has never been determined. When the smoke cleared, after what has become known as the massacre of Seven Oaks, Governor Semple and 20 of his men had been killed; one Métis was also killed.   W. D. Smith

3288. Martin, Joe. BLOODSHED AT SEVEN OAKS. *Beaver* *[Canada] 1966 297(Winter): 36-40.* This year marks the 150th anniversary of the Battle of Seven Oaks at a site now in the north end of Winnipeg. The fight was the end result of a conflict between the North West Company of Montreal and Lord Selkirk, who had received a 116 thousand square mile grant of land from the Hudson's Bay Company. Selkirk wished to move settlers to the forks of the Red and Assiniboine Rivers; the Nor'Westers feared this would cut their fur trade and provisioning routes. The first group of settlers was persuaded to move to Upper Canada at the Nor'Westers' expense, but a second group under Robert Semple arrived and destroyed the Nor'Westers' post. A few days later the skirmish occurred. Semple and 20 of his men were killed by some of the Métis in the employ of the North West Company. Illus.
                                                L. F. S. Upton

3289. McCook, James. FRONTIERSMEN OF FORT ELLICE. *Beaver [Canada] 1968 299(Autumn): 34-39.* Describes life at Fort Ellice, two hundred miles west of Winnipeg, between 1831 and 1891, and concentrates on three men: Henry Millar, farmer; Jacob Beads, carpenter; and the Reverend Thomas Cook, missionary and schoolteacher. The fort was established in 1831 to counter American competitors. The last building was sold to settlers for its timber in 1891. Illus.
                                                L. F. S. Upton

3290. McCormack, A. R. ARTHUR PUTTEE AND THE LIBERAL PARTY: 1899-1904. *Can. Hist. R. [Canada] 1970 51(2): 141-163.* Examines the electoral career of Arthur Puttee, first Independent Labor M.P. in Canada. The author develops the thesis that Puttee's election was not the result of a class movement but rather of a split in the Liberal Party caused by a revolt against Clifford Sifton's leadership. The conclusion is that class consciousness was not sufficiently strong among Winnipeg workers to allow them to abandon the old parties. Based on the Sifton and Laurier manuscripts and on contemporary newspapers.   A

3291. McCutcheon, B. R. THE PATRONS OF INDUSTRY IN MANITOBA, 1890-1898. *Tr. of the Hist. and Sci. Soc. of Manitoba [Canada] 1965/66 3(22): 7-25.* A detailed account of the Patrons of Industry and their activites in Manitoba. Their place in the history of Canadian agricultural movements is also established.
                                                W. D. Smith

3292. Metcalfe, William H. PORTAGE LA PRAIRIE. *Canadian Geographical J. [Canada] 1968 76(2): 64-71.* The town of Portage La Prairie, Manitoba, is the only place in Canada that was once a republic. The town was originally headquarters for French explorers. By the 19th century English-speaking settlers established local government. In 1868, under the leadership of Englishman Thomas Spence, the town became a short-lived republic which lasted until it failed to collect taxes and held a farcical trial of a nontaxpaying citizen. The author describes the growth and present-day condition of this beautiful country town. Illus.
                                                C. J. Allard

3293. Morton, W. L. MANITOBA'S HISTORIC ROLE. *Hist. and Sci. Soc. of Manitoba Papers [Canada] 1962 111(19): 50-57.* Argues that the Historical and Scientific Society of Manitoba should join with the Historical Society of St. Boniface to investigate and report upon the possibilities of restoring in Manitoba the duality and equality of French and English, from which the Province sprang. Believes the University of Manitoba and St. Boniface College should also live out the history of the Province, and lead Canada by example to a solution of the crisis of sentiment between French- and English-speaking Canadians.
                                                R. J. C. Ford

3294. Morton, W. L. THE 1870 OUTFIT AT RED RIVER. *Beaver [Canada] 1970 300(Spring): 4-11.* Reviews the development of a settled community at the forks of the Red and Assiniboine rivers, and the increasing interest of Canadians in extending their influence to the area.

The fur trade created the Red River settlement, but it took the impetuosity of Louis Riel to make it into the Province of Manitoba in 1870. A new agricultural society emerged, but did not end the fur trade overnight; rather, the two ways of life blended. For example, pemmican was repalced by flour, bacon, and butter, which was the produce of the farmer and not the hunter. Except for those *Métis* (French half-breeds) who moved west to the Saskatchewan River, there was no break between the old and new life. The Hudson's Bay Company continued its fur operations in the north while vastly expanding its retail outlets for the settlers. Illus.
                                                L. F. S. Upton

3295. Muir, G. A. A HISTORY OF THE TELEPHONE IN MANITOBA. *Tr. of the Hist. and Sci. Soc. of Manitoba [Canada] 1964/65 3(21): 69-82.* Description of the development of the Manitoba Telephone System including its venture into radio broadcasting. The author discusses why the Provincial government bought out the Bell Telephone Company in 1907.
                                                W. D. Smith

3296. Perkins, Mekkim S. THE SAGE OF "NEW ENGLAND." *Am.-Scandinavian R. 1964 52(3): 277-284.* Tells of the emigration from Iceland during the last three decades of the 19th century and the establishment of Icelandic settlements in Manitoba.
                                                J. G. Smoot

3297. Peters, Victor. THE HUTTERIANS - HISTORY AND COMMUNAL ORGANIZATION OF A RURAL GROUP IN MANITOBA. *Hist. and Sci. Soc. of Manitoba Papers, [Canada] 1960-61 1964 Series 3(17): 6-14.* This group of descendants of the Anabaptists, whose cardinal article of faith is the common ownership of all their property, left the Ukraine in 1874 to settle in Manitoba, South Dakota, Alberta, Saskatchewan, and Montana. Most of the American colonies transferred to Canada in 1918 on the same terms as had been extended to the Mennonites: exemption from military service. Since World War II the Hutterian colonies have become targets for public criticism. Alberta and Manitoba restrict Hutterian expansion. An account follows of life in their cluster-type villages, with their democratic government, highly diversified agriculture, and emphasis on religion and family life. Illus., 11 notes.
                                                E. P. Stickney

3298. Rogge, J. R. SOME RECENT ECONOMIC DEVELOPMENTS IN NORTHERN MANITOBA. *Geography [Great Britain] 1972 57(3): 207-216.* "Northern Manitoba is currently experiencing a rapid phase of economic development. Although the mining industry has been present since the 1930's, the contribution of the industry to the provincial economy and national mining productivity was until recently essentially insignificant. Since the late 1950's, the expansion of mining generally, and of the nickel industry specifically, has not only helped to restructure the provincial economy, but also contributes very significantly to the national metallic mineral product. In the wake of the developing mining industry, other northern resources are also being increasingly exploited. The hydroelectric developments are geared to the mining industry as well as to the southern markets. Likewise, the roads constructed in response to the demand of the mining industry are also facilitating the expansion of the forestry and tourist industries."   J

3299. Stanley, G. F. G. L'INVASION FENIENNE AU MANITOBA [The Fenian invasion of Manitoba]. *R. d'Hist. de l'Amérique Française [Canada] 1963 17(2): 258-268.* Prints a diary kept by Abbé J. -B. Proulx at St. Boniface, Manitoba, 1-20 October 1870. W. B. O'Donohue (d. 1877), formerly treasurer of Riel's provisional government, hoped for a Fenian invasion of Manitoba to link up with the discontented Métis. Riel himself denounced such a plan and the invasion was a farce. With Métis support, however, such an attempt could have provoked a serious civil war.
                                                L. F. S. Upton

3300. Stevenson, Alex. APPRENTICE VOYAGE 1867. *Beaver [Canada] 1967 297(Spring): 50-55.* Describes the voyage of Isaac Cowie, Hudson's Bay Company apprentice, from Stromness Harbour to Fort Qu'Appelle. He sailed in the *Prince Rupert* 1 July 1867, arrived at York Factory on 12 August, and at Fort Qu'Appelle on 26 October.
                                                L. F. S. Upton

3301. Stevenson, Hugh A. THE PRIME MINISTER'S SON GOES WEST. *Beaver [Canada] 1963 294(Winter): 32-43.* An account of Hugh John Macdonald (1850-1929), with special reference to his part in the Red

River Expedition of 1870. Hugh John was appointed ensign and related his travels in letters to his school friend James H. Coyne. He settled in Winnipeg in 1882 and saw action in the Saskatchewan Rebellion. After a spell in federal politics he led the Manitoba Conservatives to victory in 1899. He was premier for less than a year, retiring after an unsuccessful bid to reenter federal politics. Illus.   L. F. S. Upton

3302. Stobie, Margaret. BACKGROUNDS OF THE DIALECT CALLED BUNGI. *Tr. of the Hist. and Sci. Soc. of Manitoba [Canada] 1967/68 (24): 65-75.* Bungi is a form of speech still heard along the old fur trade routes and in the area from Lower Fort Garry to the mouth of the Red River in Manitoba. It is an English dialect deriving from the mainly Gaelic-speaking employees of the Hudson's Bay Company (English was their second language) and the English they taught the Cree Indians. Its most distinctive characteristic today is its "lilting cadence." 23 notes.   L. F. S. Upton

3303. Stormon, John A. A HISTORY OF THE INTERNATIONAL PEACE GARDEN. *North Dakota Hist. 1964 31(4): 205-215.* The 2,339.3 acre tract of the International Peace Garden was located near the geographical center of the American continent in 1932. The land was given by the Province of Manitoba and the State of North Dakota, after four years of planning by a group of distinguished gardeners. A cairn of native stone bears the inscription, "To God in His Glory, we two nations dedicate this garden and pledge ourselves that as long as men shall live, we will not take up arms against one another." Articles of incorporation were filed in Manitoba and North Dakota. A 100 percent Federal grant was received from the Federal Emergency Administration of Public Works. A Civilian Conservation Corps camp was installed in 1934 and aided in the garden's development until 1941. Other organizations contributed. The garden houses an International Music camp, weekly encampments of the Royal Canadian Legion, the North Dakota Farm Bureau, the North Dakota Farmers' Union, Boy Scouts, church groups, and other youth activities. Illus.   I. W. Van Noppen

3304. Stubbs, Roy St. George. LAW AND AUTHORITY IN RED RIVER. *Beaver [Canada] 1968 299(Summer): 17-21.* The rather uncertain nature of law in Assiniboia was shown in the case of Hugh Matheson vs. Adam Thom in 1850. Thom, the recorder (or judge) of Rupert's Land was the only qualified lawyer in the area and was sued for a 25 pound debt. While admitting the debt, his behavior so antagonized the other magistrates, the jury, and the spectators that violence was expected. Thom was notorious for his suspicions of all French-speaking Roman Catholics. Illus.   L. F. S. Upton

3305. Stubbs, Roy Saint George. THE WEST'S FIRST NOVEL. *Beaver [Canada] 1969 300(Winter): 14-17.* Alexander Begg (1839-97) published a novel entitled *Dot it Down, A Story of Life in the North-West* (Toronto: Hunter Rose and Co., 1871). He wrote it while running a general store at Red River, and it suffers from an over melodramatic style. The plot and excerpts from the text are given. Several of the characters are drawn from life; the villain, Cool, was John Christian Schultz, eventually Lieutenant Governor of Manitoba, and "Dot-it-Down" was Charles Mair, the poet. Illus.   L. F. S. Upton

3306. Studness, Charles M. ECONOMIC OPPORTUNITY AND THE WESTWARD MIGRATION OF CANADIANS DURING THE LATE NINETEENTH CENTURY. *Can. J. of Econ. and Pol. Sci. [Canada] 1964 30(4): 571-584.* Concerned mainly with North Dakota and Manitoba, this study notes the large proportion of Canadian settlers emigrating to North Dakota in the 1870's and the increasing popularity of Manitoba in the 1880's and 1890's. The economic attractions of both areas are discussed, as are the land policies of the Canadian government. The author finds that while farming profits were higher on the Canadian prairies, the lack of railroads and of readily available land led many to choose the American rather than the Canadian prairies. 4 tables, 25 notes.   J. Usher

3307. Syrnick, J. H. EARLY UKRAINIAN TEACHERS. *Tr. of the Hist. and Sci. Soc. of Manitoba [Canada] 1964/65 3(21): 25-34.* A tribute to the Ukrainian teachers in early Manitoba whose work made possible the transition of the Ukrainians from European rural to North American urban society.   W. D. Smith

3308. Vogt, Reinhard and Friesen, Jim. THE MENNONITE COMMUNITY IN WINNIPEG. *Mennonite Life 1964 19(1): 13-15.* Comments on the religious life of Winnipeg's Mennonites and touches on the difficulties involved in the move from a rural to an urban environment. Only 5,500 of an estimated 20 thousand persons of Mennonite background are presently members of Winnipeg's Mennonite churches. The authors characterize the Mennonite community as pietistic, neglectful of theology, clannish, and unaware of social and cultural questions.
                                                  D. J. Abramoske

3309. Weir, T. R. SETTLEMENT IN SOUTHWEST MANITOBA, 1870-1891. *Hist. and Sci. Soc. of Manitoba Papers, [Canada] 1960-61 1964 Series 3(17): 54-64.* The progress of settlement was subject to three controls: time of the survey, quality of the land, and accessibility and technological changes. Minor controls were land speculation and the advice of land agents. Until 1886 settlement was largely contained by those lands lying east of the Souris and Pipestone rivers. Settlement in the late 1880's did much to fill in the empty lands to the west of these rivers. Only a few sections remained after 1891 without at least one quarter being preempted or sold, and by 1913 southwest rural Manitoba was completely settled. Map, 17 notes.   E. P. Stickney

3310. —. [FORT GARRY]. *Can. Historic Sites [Canada] 1970 4: 10-188.*
Miquelon, Dale. A BRIEF HISTORY OF LOWER GARRY, *pp. 10-43.* "In 1831-32, construction began on Lower Fort Garry, the Hudson's Bay Company post near Selkirk, Manitoba. One of the Company's major posts in the provisioning of the fur trade, this fort was involved also in the economic development of the West. In 1965, the Department of Indian Affairs and Northern Development undertook the restoration of the Stone Fort to the height of its existence, the 1850s. The author traces the history of Lower Fort Garry from its beginnings to its establishment as a National Historic Site."
Ingram, George. INDUSTRIAL AND AGRICULTURAL ACTIVITIES AT LOWER FORT GARRY, *pp. 44-93.* "Industrial and agricultural activities which developed at Lower Fort Garry between the 1850s and the 1870s included experimental farming, boat building, brewing and distilling, and other activities involving the construction of additional buildings in and near the fort. The activities at the fort relating to provisioning and transportation are discussed in detail during the height of their development."
Ingram, George. THE BIG HOUSE, LOWER FORT GARRY, *pp. 94-165.* "At all major trading posts of the Hudson's Bay Company, a large house was built to accommodate officers of the Company. The Big House at Lower Fort Garry, an imposing stone structure, served in this and other capacities. Many important visitors shared the warm hospitality within its walls during the fort's ownership by the Company. In 1913, when the fort was leased by the Motor Country Club of Winnipeg, the Big House became a centre of social activity, a role which it played until the early 1960s when Lower Fort Garry was given to Canada by the Hudson's Bay Company."
Morrison, William R. THE SIXTH REGIMENT OF FOOT AT LOWER FORT GARRY, *pp. 166-175.* "The Sixth, or Royal First Warwickshire Regiment of Foot was sent to Lower Fort Garry during 1846-48 to protect British interests in the threat of war between Britain and the United States. The danger proved to be illusory, and the attack against which the regiment stood guard never came."
Morrison, William R. THE SECOND BATTALION, QUEBEC RIFLES, AT LOWER FORT GARRY, *pp. 176-188.* "The Second Battalion, Quebec Rifles, was part of the expeditionary force sent to Red River in 1870 to suppress the Red River Rebellion. The force arrived after Riel and his followers had fled, and after less than a year at Lower Fort Garry, the battalion was disbanded, some returning to their homes in the East and others settling in the Red River area."   J

Saskatchewan

3311. Bailey, Mrs. A. W. THE YEAR WE MOVED. *Saskatchewan Hist. [Canada] 1967 20(1): 19-31.* The story of one family that was forced by drought conditions in southern Saskatchewan in the 1930's to establish a new home in the north. Illus.   A. H. Lawrance

3312. Becker, A. ST. JOSEPH'S COLONY, BALGONIE. *Saskatchewan Hist. [Canada] 1967 20(1): 1-18.* The story of the small colony of German Catholics from the Ukraine who settled in Saskatchewan in the 1880's. Illus., 35 notes.   A. H. Lawrance

3313. Bennett, J. W. RECIPROCAL ECONOMIC EXCHANGES AMONG NORTH AMERICAN AGRICULTURAL OPERATORS. *Southwestern J. of Anthrop. 1968 24(3): 276-309.* Deals with the reciprocal exchange systems of two groups - ranchers and farmers - in the western portion of the Province of Saskatchewan. Three major categories of exchange relationships were studied: dyadic exchange partnerships which involved only two men and could be exchanges with or without monetary calculations; group exchange rings which consisted of three or more men who cooperated on specific tasks or exchanged particular kinds of information or commodities; and formal cooperative task performance composed of instrumental groups who assembled at regular intervals to perform predictable large-scale tasks. While not all the exchange values are monetary, the rules of social exchange can be equally predictable; however, while there exist some calculated exchanges involving money payments and values, they are disguised by an aura of voluntarism and openhandedness expressed in the values of an egalitarian frontier society. The exchange groups formed the basis of a good portion of the social life in the area and to put a monetary value on the exchanges would be viewed as crass and unfriendly. It is suggested that similar socioeconomic reciprocities among tribal and peasant peoples are equally susceptible of "market" rules of analysis - although, once again, one must recognize differences in magnitude and impersonality. It is, in fact, local character of these exchanges, wherever one may find them, that introduces the sociosymbolic dimension, not any basic difference in the economics. Based on a Saskatchewan Cultural Ecology Research Project; 13 notes, biblio.   C. N. Warren

3314. Bennett, John W. and Kohl, Seena. TWO MEMORANDA ON SOCIAL ORGANIZATION AND ADAPTIVE SELECTION IN A NORTHERN PLAINS REGION. *Plains Anthropologist 1963 8(22): 238-248.* "The two brief pieces to follow are preliminary reports on social anthropological aspects of a study of cultural ecology in the southwestern portion of the Province of Saskatchewan. A synopsis of the study was published in a previous issue of this journal [May, 1963]."   J

3315. Bocking, D. H. POLITICAL AMBITIONS AND TERRITORIAL AFFAIRS, 1900-04. *Saskatchewan Hist. [Canada] 1965 18(2): 63-75.* Traces the dissension which developed between F. W. G. Haultain, Premier of the Northwest Territories, and Walter Scott, who became Member of Parliament for West Assiniboia in 1900 with Haultain's support. As the leader of a nonpartisan territorial government, Haultain was in a unique position. At the same time his political commitments were to the Conservative Party. In the end it was the conflict of party interests which caused the break between the two men.   A. H. Lawrance

3316. Bocking, D. H. SASKATCHEWAN'S FIRST PROVINCIAL ELECTION. *Saskatchewan Hist. [Canada] 1964 17(2): 41-54.* In this election in December 1905 the leader of the provincial Liberal Party, Walter Scott, who had recently been chosen by the lieutenant governor to form the first government was challenged by F. W. G. Haultain, the former territorial premier. Haultain and the Conservatives tried to retain the nonpartisan vote in the face of the Liberal decision to precipitate party division in the new province. The reasons for Scott's victory are examined in detail. Map.   A. H. Lawrance

3317. Brennan, J. William. C. A. DUNNING AND THE CHALLENGE OF THE PROGRESSIVES: 1922-1925. *Saskatchewan Hist. [Canada] 1969 22(1): 1-12.* After World War I disenchanted Canadian farmers organized the Progressive Party to establish Provincial and Federal Governments that would be responsive to the demands of western wheat growers. Prairie agriculture was depressed and the farmers were

deserting the Liberal and Conservative Parties. More than any other person Liberal Premier Charles Avery Dunning saved Saskatchewan from falling to the Progressives. Dunning's considerable role in the 1925 national success of the Liberals earned him a cabinet position in the Federal Government. Four years later the Conservatives gained control in Saskatchewan. Based in part on the author's master's thesis; 52 notes; illus.   D. L. Smith

3318. Brock, Peter. VASYA POZDNYAKOV'S DUKHOBOR NARRATIVE. PARTS ONE AND TWO. *Slavonic and East European Rev. [Great Britain] 1964 43(100): 152-176; 1965 43(101): 400-414.* Describes life in the Dukhobor settlements in Saskatchewan during the first decade of the 20th century, showing how Petr V. Veregin maintained his leadership over the sect but lost most of the new arrivals from Russia after 1905. These independents broke with the prevailing pattern of unconditional community and submission to authority.   R. E. Weltsch

3319. Brown, Lorne. A HINTERLAND REBELS: THE STORY OF THE SASKATCHEWAN FARMERS' MOVEMENT. *Can. Dimension [Canada] 1972 8(8): 32-41.* Prairie settlement designedly was a captive hinterland for metropolitan interests. The one-crop economy of Saskatchewan is evidence for this change. There is an outflow of population from the province today due to insufficient industrial and farming employment. U.S. industrial dominance is a factor in this situation. This sort of situation is not new, and in the past the reaction has been local organizations which moved into provincial politics. Usually such organizations began as radical, then became more conservative as they gained influence or power. This experience stimulated new radical groups. The most significant of such groups comprised wide ranges of political views and were not monolithic, doctrinaire parties. Attacks the present provincial government and argues that a new grass-roots radical movement is forming as a result of the present more conservative stance of the government.   W. B. Whitham

3320. Buck, Ruth M. LITTLE PINE: AN INDIAN DAY SCHOOL. *Saskatchewan Hist. [Canada] 1965 18(2): 55-62.* An account of the school on the Little Pine Reserve which was opened in 1923. Based on notes and an unfinished manuscript written by the late Reverend Canon Edward Ahenakew, 1885-1961.   A. H. Lawrance

3321. Calderwood, William. THE DECLINE OF THE PROGRESSIVE PARTY IN SASKATCHEWAN, 1925-1930. *Saskatchewan Hist. [Canada] 1968 21(3): 81-99.* The Progressive Party in Saskatchewan started as a farmers' attempt in 1919 to achieve results by direct political action. In the federal elections of 1921 the party emerged as an important political force, with especially impressive results in Saskatchewan. The tide was turned, however, in the 1925 federal elections both at the national and provincial levels. The electorate's disillusionment with the farmers' movement was registered more emphatically in the federal elections of the next year. Hostility toward the Liberals and the advent of the Ku Klux Klan catalyzed a Progressive-Conservative alliance during the election of 1929 which survived the 1930 demise of the Progressive Party in the province for four years. 2 illus., 78 notes.   D. L. Smith

3322. Clinkskill, James. EXPERIENCES OF STARTING AND CONDUCTING A STORE IN SASKATCHEWAN IN THE EARLY '80S. *Saskatchewan Hist. [Canada] 1964 17(1): 24-30.* These recollections of the author's early storekeeping experiences at Battleford are taken from his extensive unpublished reminiscences, copies of which are in the Saskatchewan Archives and the Saskatoon Public Library. Photograph.   A. H. Lawrance

3323. Fergusson, Charles B. A GLIMPSE OF 1885. *Saskatchewan Hist. [Canada] 1968 21(1): 24-29.* A letter from Harold E. Ross (1859-1935) to his parents describing his experiences in the Saskatchewan River resistance during the North West Rebellion of 1885. Ross retired from the Mounted Police in 1884 and became deputy sheriff of Prince Albert. He was captured by Gabriel Dumont when the insurrection broke out, and held for seven weeks until freed at the Battle of Batoche. 4 notes.   L. F. S. Upton

3324. Forsyth, Robert and Morrison, Alva. HOMESTEADING ON THE CARROT RIVER. *Beaver [Canada] 1971 302(1): 53-57.* Reminiscences of Forsyth, a pioneer who came out as a young boy from Ontario in 1903 to Carrot River two days (by wagon) north of Prince Albert. At age 18 he owned an entire quarter section of land.

L. F. S. Upton

3325. Hamilton, Z. M. PRAIRIE PEOPLE. THE HONOURABLE G. W. BROWN, 1860-1919. *Saskatchewan Hist. [Canada] 1965 18(1): 32-37.* Reprint of an article published in *The Morning Leader* of 18 February 1919 on the occasion of the death of Brown who was lieutenant-governor of Saskatchewan, 1910-15. The title has been changed and certain sections have been omitted.

A. H. Lawrance

3326. Hanson, Stan D. POLICING THE INTERNATIONAL BOUNDARY AREA IN SASKATCHEWAN, 1890-1910. *Saskatchewan Hist. [Canada] 1966 19(2): 61-73.* Describes the problems faced by the North West Mounted Police in an area where lawlessness was encouraged by the proximity of the international line. Horse and cattle stealing was prevalent. Archival materials, 2 illus., map, 42 notes.

A. H. Lawrance

3327. Harrington, Lyn. PRAIRIE BATTLEFIELD. *Can. Geographical J. [Canada] 1963 66(1): 28-37.* The story of the Louis Riel Rebellion and its suppression at Batoche, Saskatchewan. Photographs of the site on the occasion of the visit in 1962 of the Royal Regiment of Canada. Map.

A. H. Lawrance

3328. Huel, Ray. THE FRENCH CANADIANS AND THE LANGUAGE QUESTION, 1918. *Saskatchewan Hist. [Canada] 1970 23(1): 1-15.* In 1912, representatives of Saskatchewan's French-Canadian community assembled to form an association to defend and promote the ethnic and religious rights of French Canadians. Out of the controversy over separate schools versus public schools emerged the question of bilingualism. At the School Trustees Convention of 1917, the Anglo-Saxon population opposed the teaching of French in schools, while the French supported their right for bilingualism. When the matter reached the provincial legislature in 1918, an amendment was passed making English the sole language to be used during regular school hours with the exception that French could be taught in grade one and in other grades as a subject of study for one hour a day. Premier William Martin justified the concession at the Assembly in December 1918 and the French element reluctantly but optimistically accepted the compromise. Based on primary and secondary sources in the Archives of Saskatchewan; 82 notes.

C. A. Bishop

3329. Jackmen, Sydney W. THE ROWBOTTOM DIARIES. *Saskatchewan Hist. [Canada] 1968 21(2): 56-66.* Two short diaries by F. E. K. Rowbottom (1869-1955) who emigrated from Huddersfield, England, for the health of one of his children. Rowbottom was part owner of a woolen mill and had the money to finance an exploratory journey by himself in 1906-07; he returned with his family in April 1907 to a homestead seven miles out of Marshall, Saskatchewan. The diaries show the difficulties faced by settlers from the Old World.

L. F. S. Upton

3330. Johnson, Gilbert. THE PATAGONIA WELSH. *Saskatchewan Hist. [Canada] 1963 16(3): 90-94.* Tells the story of the Welsh settlers who in 1865 set up a colony in Patagonia and then, after 37 years, reestablished themselves in Saskatchewan near to what is now Bangor. In Canada the way of life of these settlers did not differ greatly from that of other immigrants.

A. H. Lawrance

3331. Kennedy, Allan. REMINISCENCES OF A LUMBERJACK. *Saskatchewan Hist. [Canada] 1966 19(1): 24-34.* Based on a series of tape-recorded interviews with the editor of *Saskatchewan History.* Described is the life and work of Kennedy, a lumberjack in the Prince Albert district between 1910 and 1930. Photographs.

A. H. Lawrance

3332. Klaus, J. F. THE EARLY MISSIONS OF THE SWAN RIVER DISTRICT, 1821-69. *Saskatchewan Hist. [Canada] 1964 17(2): 60-76.* The story of the missionary activity in the Swan River District, which extended from Lakes Winnipegosis and Manitoba west to the 105th meridian, and from the International Boundary north to the Red Deer River. Map.

A. H. Lawrance

3333. Koester, C. B. THE CLERKSHIP IN SASKATCHEWAN. *Saskatchewan Hist. [Canada] 1963 16(2): 59-70.* Begins with a brief survey of the role of the clerk in the English parliament. Relates the present-day functions of the clerk, in which Canadian practice corresponds closely to that of Westminster, and lists the men who have held the position in Saskatchewan. In a young legislature where the speakership is regarded as temporary, the clerk has a particularly important job as the guardian of the legislature and its traditions against any attempts at tyranny by the executive. Photographs.

A. H. Lawrance

3334. Koester, C. B. NICHOLAS FLOOD DAVIN: POLITICAL POET OF THE PRAIRIES. *Dalhousie R. [Canada] 1964 44(1): 64-74.* Discussion of the poetical works and philosophical ideas of a 19th century Saskatchewan editor and political leader. The fact that under frontier conditions a native literature was emerging is taken by the author as indication that the cultural level of the prairie settlements was not so low as sometimes believed.

M. B. Fox

3335. Lawton, Alma. RELIEF ADMINISTRATION IN SASKATOON DURING THE DEPRESSION. *Saskatchewan Hist. [Canada] 1969 12(2): 41-59.* During the 1930's, Saskatchewan was hit by a serious drought and the Depression, which created major unemployment and relief problems. Unemployment relief was considered a local responsibility rather than a Federal or Provincial one. Although some assistance came from these latter sources, it was always temporary, a situation which led to much confusion over responsibilities. The city of Saskatoon was chosen to illustrate relief problems. In 1932, a Civic Relief Board was established to superintend the administration of relief. Since the object was to keep relief costs low, local relief officers were generally unpopular with recipients. After 1934, cash relief replaced commodity allowances obtainable at the municipal relief store, alleviating some of the hardships associated with obtaining sufficient relief. Following World War II, the unemployment problems decreased and the Federal and Provincial governments took measures to ensure adequate social welfare facilities. Study of urban communities during the Depression indicates that hardships were severe but often produced a community spirit of charity and cooperation. 90 notes.

C. A. Bishop

3336. MacDonald, R. H. FORT BATTLEFORD, SASKATCHEWAN. *Can. Geographical J. [Canada] 1963 67(2): 54-61.* Surveys the history of the fort and the settlement which was once the seat of government and the police headquarters at the junction of three Indian nations. The fort was significant at the time of the Riel Rebellion. Map, photographs.

A. H. Lawrance

3337. MacKay, J. A. THE JOURNAL OF THE REVEREND J. A. MACKAY, STANLEY MISSION, 1870-72. *Saskatchewan Hist. [Canada] 1963 16(3): 95-113.* This distinguished Anglican missionary and Cree scholar was in charge of the Stanley mission on the Churchill River from 1864 to 1867. These extracts from his journal, covering part of the period at the mission, give an insight into the character of the man and his work as a pioneer missionary. Photographs.

A. H. Lawrance

3338. McDougald, Mrs. James. RECOLLECTIONS AND REMINISCENCES: CYPRESS HILLS REMINISCENCES. *Saskatchewan Hist. [Canada] 1970 23(1): 27-30.* In 1882 the Canadian Pacific Railway reached Maple Creek, a small community composed of settlers from Quebec, freighters, railway employees, and store owners. The North West Mounted Police Barracks was built near the town in 1883. There were also Anglican, Presbyterian, and Methodist churches, and a Catholic priest visited the community. The first school was opened nearby in 1897 and an Agricultural Society was established in 1894. The author's father and uncle settled near Maple Creek in 1890. By the late 1890's two doctors were in residence, and in 1904 a hospital was opened. The population included persons from a variety of ethnic backgrounds, and in 1906-07 many homesteaders arrived.

C. A. Bishop

3339. Megill, William J. POTASH IN CANADA'S PAST AND SASKATCHEWAN'S PRESENT. *Can. Geographical J. [Canada] 1964 68(6): 178-187.* Survey of Canada's potash industry with historical sketch.

E. W. Hathaway

3340. Miller, Carman, ed. LORD MELGUND AND THE NORTHWEST CAMPAIGN OF 1885. *Saskatchewan Hist. [Canada] 1969*

22(3): 81-108. Reproduces the diary of Lord Melgund (Gilbert John Elliot-Murray-Kynynmond, Fourth Earl of Minto, 1845-1914) that describes the "North West Campaign" of 1885. After serving in campaigns in the Middle East and Africa, Melgund became viceregal military secretary in Canada. In 1885, he was engaged as Chief of Staff by Major General Frederick Dobson Middleton in the campaign against Louis Riel's Métis and Indian rebels. The journal describes Melgund's trip from Ottawa to the Saskatchewan Plains and subsequent encounters with Indians at Fish Creek and Batoche. On the first day of the Batoche battle against Poundmaker's forces, Middleton sent Melgund to Ottawa "for private and personal reasons." Based on materials in the Public Archives of Canada; photos, 40 notes. C. A. Bishop

3341. Moon, Robert. DAVIN - BALD EAGLE OF THE PRAIRIES. *Beaver [Canada] 1965 296(Summer): 36-41.* Nicholas Flood Davin (1843-1901), Irish lawyer and journalist, migrated to Canada and arrived in Regina in 1882 to found a newspaper, the *Leader,* forerunner of the present Regina *Leader-Post.* In 1887 he was chosen MP for the federal riding of Assiniboia West. Famous for his wit and drinking ability, he now became the champion of western interests at Ottawa. He was Canada's representative at the Boston celebrations of Queen Victoria's jubilee. Defeated in the general election of 1900 he lost heart and committed suicide in Winnipeg the following year. Illus.

L. F. S. Upton

3342. Morgan, E. C. THE BELL FARM. *Saskatchewan Hist. [Canada] 1966 19(2): 41-60.* The story of the large farming enterprise at Indian Head promoted in 1882 by Major William R. Bell. It failed financially and was sold to meet the creditors' demands in 1896. As an experiment in large-scale dry farming technique it was illustrative. Based on archival materials in the Saskatchewan Archives Office, illus., map, 91 notes.

A. H. Lawrance

3343. Morgan, E. C. PIONEER RECREATION AND SOCIAL LIFE. *Saskatchewan Hist. [Canada] 1965 18(2): 41-54.* Based on replies to questionnaires distributed by the Saskatchewan Archives to people who settled in the area just before and after the formation of the province. Photographs. A. H. Lawrance

3344. Parley, Kay. MOFFAT, ASSINIBOIA, NORTH-WEST TERRITORIES. *Saskatchewan Hist. [Canada] 1967 20(1): 32-36.* The story of Moffat, a community founded in 1882, its development and its decline.

A. H. Lawrance

3345. Peters, Herbert. MARTENSVILLE: HALF-WAY HOUSE TO URBANISM. *Mennonite Life 1968 23(4): 164-168.* Martensville is a recently founded village located 11 miles north of Saskatoon, Saskatchewan. Ninety percent of the town's population are descendants of Dutch-German Mennonites who migrated from Prussia to Russia after the 1790's and from Russia to Canada in the 1870's. The founding of the town, its population, housing and planning, economy, power, water, and telephone facilities, and schools are discussed. The prevailing conservative values of Martensville are typical of the pioneer or near-pioneer existence from which many of its inhabitants are only one step removed. Most of the residents are unskilled workers and have little appreciation of formal education. Religious values tend to be rather static, beliefs very concrete, and the Bible is interpreted literally. Villages like Martensville serve a useful purpose in lessening the effects of cultural shock on displaced rural people who are still unprepared to be urbanites. Based on school records and interviews with residents of Martensville; illus., 3 notes. D. J. Abramoske

3346. Rendell, Alice. LETTERS FROM A BARR COLONIST. *Alberta Hist. R. [Canada] 1963 11(1): 12-27.* Letters described in detail the arrival and first months in Canada of the settlers who established Lloydminster, Saskatchewan. Photographs: Barr colonists purchasing supplies, Saskatoon, April 1903, p. 13; Ready to leave Saskatoon, May 1st, 1903, p. 15; Lloydminster, late 1903, p. 17; Lloydminster, 1904, p. 20; Lloydminster, August 1904, p. 23; Log church, 1906, p. 25.

R. J. C. Ford

3347. Rendell, Lloyd. LAND CLAIMS IN THE PRINCE ALBERT SETTLEMENT. *Saskatchewan Hist. [Canada] 1966 19(1): 1-23.* Describes the early delays and difficulties in dealing with land claims in

the district around Prince Albert, Saskatchewan. An earlier settlement would have eliminated one of the many factors which prevented the Prince Albert settlement from achieving the great promise of the early years. Based on archival materials, 2 maps. A. H. Lawrance

3348. Rodwell, Lloyd. THE SASKATCHEWAN ASSOCIATION OF MUSIC FESTIVALS. *Saskatchewan Hist. [Canada] 1963 16(1): 1-21.* Tells the story of the first 50 years of the association which has organized annual music festivals. Many eminent British musicians have acted as adjudicators; possibly the most famous and the most popular was Sir Hugh Robertson, founder of the Glasgow Orpheus Choir. The University of Saskatchewan has been closely linked with the association and has given financial support. A. H. Lawrance

3349. Rodwell, Lloyd. SASKATCHEWAN HOMESTEAD RECORDS. *Saskatchewan Hist. [Canada] 1965 18(1): 10-29.* Comments on the value of the Homestead Records of the former Department of the Interior which were deposited in the Saskatchewan Archives in 1956, and gives examples of the type of information available. A name index has been created by means of which files for any one homesteader can be located. A. H. Lawrance

3350. Smith, D. E. THE MEMBERSHIP OF THE SASKATCHEWAN LEGISLATIVE ASSEMBLY, 1905-66. *Saskatchewan Hist. [Canada] 1967 20(2): 41-63.* Examines the members of the Legislative Assembly, to consider the effects upon them of the disappearance of the Conservative Party and the rise of the Cooperative Commonwealth Federation, and to contrast their socioeconomic characteristics with those of the population as a whole. 27 notes. A. H. Lawrance

3351. Spafford, D. S. 'INDEPENDENT' POLITICS IN SASKATCHEWAN BEFORE THE NONPARTISAN LEAGUE. *Saskatchewan Hist. [Canada] 1965 18(1): 1-9.* Many farmers, exasperated with the main political parties, hoped to promote their interests through nonparty political organizations. Two expressions of this demand, direct legislation and the nomination of independent farmer candidates, had by 1914 proved impracticable and the building of a third party became increasingly attractive. A. H. Lawrance

3352. Spry, Irene M. DID PALLISER VISIT SASKATCHEWAN IN 1848? *Saskatchewan Hist. [Canada] 1963 16(1): 22-26.* Was John Palliser correct in thinking that his travels by the "White-earth River" had taken him into British territory? One difficulty is the indiscriminate use of the names White-earth River and White River. Another is that the maps of the time showed a White Earth River running from north of the US-Canadian line to the Mississippi. In fact this river, the modern White Earth, rises south of the border. However, it is likely that in his hunting trips in that region, Palliser did cross over into what is now the southeast corner of Saskatchewan. Map. A. H. Lawrance

3353. Thompson, W. P. A UNIVERSITY IN TROUBLE. *Saskatchewan Hist. [Canada] 1964 17(3): 81-104.* In 1919 the board of governors of the University of Saskatchewan dismissed four members of the faculty, two of whom were popular speakers known throughout the province. The board did not give adequate reasons for its action. Consequently numerous demands were made for an investigation. A formal inquiry by three judges of the Court of King's Bench "found the dismissals not merely justified but necessary for the good of the university." The "big mistake" of the governors was made through an excess of kindness; the offer of a leave of absence with an agreement to resign was interpreted as weakness. Based on documents. 18 notes. E. P. Stickney

3354. Tollefson, Edwin A. THE AFTERMATH OF THE MEDICARE DISPUTE IN SASKATCHEWAN. *Queen's Q. [Canada] 1965 72(3): 452-465.* Three years after the Saskatchewan doctors' strike, Medicare has been fully accepted by the general public and political parties; the medical profession remains officially opposed, although neither the quality of care nor patient loads have suffered. Problems have developed over policing the plan, revising the fee schedule, and hospital privileges for doctors supporting Medicare, but general prosperity and ingenious postponements of a major confrontation make immediate prospects for the plan bright, although the medical profession will remain antagonistic.

M. Abrash

3355. Toombs, M. P. A SASKATCHEWAN EXPERIMENT IN TEACHER EDUCATION 1907-1917. *Saskatchewan Hist. [Canada] 1964 17(1): 1-11.* Describes the attempt to establish a training school for teachers for the non-English-speaking communities, especially the Ruthenians (a term interpreted loosely to include Ukrainians and other Slavic groups). In 1917 there was a change in policy whereby all young people regardless of ethnic origin attended a common high school and normal school. A. H. Lawrance

3356. Turner, A. R. SASKATCHEWAN PLACE NAMES. *Saskatchewan Hist. [Canada] 1965 18(3): 81-88.* Considers the origins of many of the place names in the province. Indians, missionaries, fur traders, pioneer settlers, and railway officials are among those responsible for choosing names, which often reflect phases or incidents in Canadian history. A. H. Lawrance

3357. Turner, A. R. SURVEYING THE INTERNATIONAL BOUNDARY, THE JOURNAL OF GEORGE M. DAWSON. *Saskatchewan Hist. [Canada] 1968 21(1): 1-23.* In 1872 a joint British and American commission began to survey the 49th parallel from the Great Lakes to the Rocky Mountains. George Mercer Dawson (1849-1901) was appointed naturalist and geologist and kept a journal now deposited at McGill University. This excerpt relates to the Saskatchewan area and runs from 13 September to 23 October 1873. 46 notes. L. F. S. Upton

3358. Wiebe, Rudy. TOMBSTONE COMMUNITY. *Mennonite Life 1964 19(4): 150-153.* Discusses the rise and decline of the author's boyhood "home town," the sparsely settled Speedwell-Jackpine community of Mennonites in Saskatchewan. The experience of these Mennonite pioneers, who had migrated from the Dakotas, Minnesota, Kansas, and Russia, proved again that homesteading "broke down completely when a quarter section of thin rocky soil in the short growing season of northern latitudes was counted on to support a family." D. J. Abramoske

3359. —. [CARLTON HOUSE.] *Beaver [Canada] 1966 297(Autumn): 32-41.*
Klaus, J. F. EARLY TRAILS TO CARLTON HOUSE, pp. 32-39. Carlton House was established by the Hudson's Bay Company in 1795 just below the forks of the Saskatchewan River. The first trail southeast to Red River ran via Fort Pelly on the Assiniboine River. In 1825 Governor George Simpson established the shorter but more dangerous route through the Touchwood Hills. When the General Winter Express was authorized by the Hudson's Bay Company in 1832 it started from Carlton House. The post attained its greatest importance in the 1860's when the freighting of goods from Fort Garry began on a large scale. With the coming of the railway, Carlton House was abandoned.
Clarke, Russ. CARLTON HOUSE RECONSTRUCTION, pp. 40-41. The reconstruction of Carlton House began in the summer of 1966 as a Saskatchewan jubilee and centennial project to be used as a museum. The buildings had been destroyed during the Northwest Rebellion of 1885. Preliminary excavations made in 1964 established the position of the bastions and palisade. Illus. L. F. S. Upton

3360. —. THE GRENFELL MECHANIC'S AND LITERARY INSTITUTE MINUTE BOOK, 1892-95. *Saskatchewan Hist. [Canada] 1964 17(3): 105-110.* The institute, founded in 1892, received a small grant in each of the three successive years. Early in 1896 indebtedness caused it to close, the main reason being a sharp drop in membership. Only selected portions of the minutes are here reproduced. 7 notes. E. P. Stickney

3361. —. POLITICS AND PATRONAGE, 1894. *Saskatchewan Hist. [Canada] 1965 18(1): 30-31.* Reprints and comments on a political broadside published in 1894 in the North Qu'Appelle electoral district. William Sutherland, the sitting member, won the 1894 election. There were complaints that he misused his control of expenditure on public works. A. H. Lawrance

3362. —. RAILWAY BRANCH LINES. *Saskatchewan Hist. [Canada] 1967 20(2): 64-70.* Examples of the type of letters received by members of the government of Saskatchewan requesting that influence be used to have a branch rail line built, 1919-20. A. H. Lawrance

Alberta

3363. Ahern, H. G. IN SEARCH OF A HOMESTEAD. *Alberta Hist. R. [Canada] 1965 13(2): 16-18.* The author's experiences in acquiring a homestead in the Red Deer country, his impressions of Calgary and his trip are described. Illus. G. Emery

3364. Bailey, Mary C. THE BEGINNING OF LESLIEVILLE. *Alberta Hist. R. [Canada] 1965 13(4): 21-23.* A description of the settlement of Leslieville, Alberta by one of the original settlers. H. M. Burns

3365. Bailey, Mary C. REMINISCENCES OF A PIONEER. *Alberta Hist. R. [Canada] 1967 15(4): 17-25.* An account of pioneer life in the Red Deer area of Alberta by an original settler. H. M. Burns

3366. Barnes, J. A. HOME ON A CANADIAN ROCKPILE. *Can. Geographical J. [Canada] 1964 68(1): 18-21.* Describes how the author's grandfather left South Dakota in September 1912 and took up farming in Alberta, built a sod house (unique in the area), survived the winter, found in spring that only 10 of his 640 homesteaded acres were economically farmable, and persevered through rains, hail, and fires. E. W. Hathaway

3367. Cantlon, F. M. BREAKING THE PRAIRIE SOD. *Alberta Hist. R. [Canada] 1965 13(3): 22-24.* Relates the event of the first plowing of prairie lands near Chinook, Alberta. H. M. Burns

3368. Chalmers, John W. FORT DUNVEGAN: FUR POST AND MISSION ON CANADA'S PEACE RIVER. *Montana 1969 19(1): 50-55.* In 1913, Fort Dunvegan, ancient fur trading post on Canada's Peace River, seemed on the verge of a dazzling new future. The occasion was an attempt to sell farmlands and town lots, in the familiar style of land promotions. Occupied as early as 1805 by fur traders, the post had been important in the business of the North West and Hudson's Bay Companies, and it had the headquarters for both Catholic and Protestant missionaries. The 20th-century attempt to colonize and revive the old site was not successful, and the owners abandoned it in 1918. Illus., map. S. R. Davison

3369. Chalmers, John W. SOCIAL STRATIFICATION OF THE FUR TRADE. *Alberta Hist. R. [Canada] 17(1): 10-20.* Examines the development of social classes in the area of Fort Chipewyan, Alberta, among explorers and fur traders. H. M. Burns

3370. Cochrane, H. G. IRRIGATION IN ALBERTA. *Alberta Hist. R. [Canada] 1968 16(2): 14-16.* History of irrigation projects in the "Palliser Triangle" area of western Canada. Discussion of the activities of the Alberta Irrigation Company and the Canadian Pacific Irrigation Department. H. M. Burns

3371. Côté, M. M. ST. ALBERT, CRADLE OF THE CATHOLIC CHURCH IN ALBERTA. *Can. Catholic Hist. Assoc. Annual Report [Canada] 1965 32: 29-35.* Relates the settlement of St. Albert, its selection as the administrative center of the Roman Catholic establishment in Alberta, and the evolution of religious institutions. 32 notes. C. Thibault

3372. Creighton, Oswin. MISSION TO LAC LA NONNE. *Alberta Hist. R. [Canada] 1965 13(3): 1-6.* Description of the author's journey as an Anglican Church missionary with comments upon pioneer conditions in Alberta. H. M. Burns

3373. Cross, Alfred E. THE ROUNDUP OF 1887. *Alberta Hist. R. [Canada] 1965 13(2): 23-37.* The roundup of 1887 in southern Alberta, which gathered up two thousand cattle, followed the worst winter in the cattle ranching history of North America. Many ranchers lost 75 percent of their stock, some lost 100 percent, and most lost at least 40 percent of their stock. Personalities and memories of the roundup are described. Illus.

G. Emery

3374. Dempsey, Hugh A. DAVID THOMPSON ON THE PEACE RIVER. PART III. *Alberta Hist. R. [Canada] 1966 14(4): 14-24*. Continued from a previous article. Excerpts from the original journal of David Thompson, explorer and cartographer, written during a survey trip to the Peace River.

H. M. Burns

3375. Dempsey, Hugh A. JERRY POTTS: PLAINSMAN. *Montana 1967 17(4): 2-17*. Sketch of a heretofore obscure half-breed who assisted the Northwest Mounted Police in establishing themselves in Alberta in 1874. His service continued for the next 25 years as a scout, interpreter, and consultant on Indian matters. Heavy drinking marred an otherwise heroic career and led to his premature death. Based on interviews with Potts' acquaintances and on published sources, illus.

S. R. Davison

3376. Dempsey, Hugh A., ed. THOMPSON'S JOURNEY TO THE RED DEER RIVER. *Alberta Hist. R. [Canada] 1965 13(1): 1-8 and (2): 7-15*. The portion of David Thompson's journals covering his trip to the Red Deer River in October 1800. At this time, the Hudson's Bay Company and the North West Company had both established their first posts in the Rocky Mountains. Thompson, representing the latter company, made this trip to intercept the Kootenais Indians before they reached the Hudson's Bay post with their furs. The second part covers Thompson's trip of November 1800, his second trip of the year. Travelling with Duncan McGillivray, he went south to the Bow River country from Rocky Mountain House to learn the country and to look for mountain passes. Illus.

G. Emery

3377. Denny, Cecil. TRAIL TO THE YUKON. *Alberta Hist. R. [Canada] 1967 15(3): 24-28*. An account of the opening of the Peace River Yukon Trail from Edmonton, Alberta, to Teslin in the Yukon Territory by a member of the original party.

H. M. Burns

3378. DenOtter, Andy A. IRRIGATION IN SOUTHERN ALBERTA, 1882-1901. *Great Plains J. 1972 11(2): 125-137*. Describes the first major irrigation project on the Canadian prairies, in the western part of the Palliser Triangle in southern Alberta near Lethbridge. In spite of the building of the Canadian Pacific Railway, settlement in southern Alberta was disappointing in the 1880's. The first large-scale irrigation project began there in 1893 under the auspices of Elliot Galt and C. A. Magrath who headed the Alberta Irrigation Company. Their purpose was to develop lands for sale. Little success was achieved until after 1896 when favorable government action, English financial backing, and a feasibility study gave support. An arrangement with the Mormons to dig the irrigation canal in return for payment in cash and land, and a subsidy from the Canadian Pacific Railway, resulted in finishing the 115-mile canal in 1900. Oddly, work on the canal was hampered in 1898-99 by "torrential rains and floods." Settlement was also hampered in the early 20th century by intermittent wet years in a usually semiarid territory. The persistence of Galt and Magrath through many years transformed the "dry, short-grass plains to attractive, fertile farm lands." Based on primary and secondary sources; map, 36 notes.

O. H. Zabel

3379. denOtter, Andy A. SOCIAL LIFE OF A MINING COMMUNITY: THE COAL BRANCH. *Alberta Hist. R.[Canada] 1969 17(4): 1-11*. Describes life along the Alberta Coal Branch, a cluster of small mining settlements along a railway branch-line, 120 miles from Edmonton. The author considers institutions that broke through the insularity of such communities.

H. M. Burns

3380. Drouin, Emeric O. ST. PAUL DES METIS. *Alberta Hist. R. [Canada] 1963 11(4): 12-14*. The story of an attempt to found a farming colony for the Métis people and persuade them to abandon nomadic life and adopt sedentary ways.

E. W. Hathaway

3381. Dyke, F. S. LIFE IN A SURVEY CAMP. *Alberta Hist. R. [Canada] 1966 14(3): 12-16*. Relates the experiences of the author, chief of a plane table party conducting survey work in connection with the Canadian Pacific Railroad project to irrigate three million acres of land in southern Alberta.

H. M. Burns

3382. Emery, G. N. METHODIST MISSION AMONG THE UKRAINIANS. *Alberta Hist. R. [Canada] 1971 19(2): 8-19*. Discusses the Methodist Church's extensive missionary activity among the Ukrainian immigrants of east central Alberta as a result of the arrival of 12 thousand Ukrainians in western Canada in 1898. Mentions the work of Reverend Charles H. Lawford, first Methodist missionary in the area.

H. M. Burns

3383. Fisher, C. B. MY FATHER THE SPEAKER. *Alberta Hist. R. [Canada] 1968 16(1): 24-28*. Recollections of Charles Wellington Fisher, Speaker of the House of the Alberta Provincial Legislature (1906-21) written by his son, who discusses the political life and activities of the era.

H. M. Burns

3384. Gladstone, James. INDIAN SCHOOL DAYS. *Alberta Hist. R. [Canada] 1967 15(1): 18-24*. Recollections of school days spent at St. Paul's Mission schools on the Blood Reservation and at Calgary Industrial School.

H. M. Burns

3385. Godsal, F. W. OLD TIMES. *Alberta Hist. R. [Canada] 1964 12(4): 19-24*. The author became a cattle rancher in the Pincher Creek area on the advice of Lord Lorne, whom he knew in Ottawa. The country, the roundups, travels, and the improvement of stock are described. In 1885 the railway brought settlers to invade his lease, so, after reserving some water holes for future use, he arranged with the government to surrender nine-tenths of his lease. Illus.

G. Emery

3386. Griffiths, Thomas M. BELATED FRONTIER. *Am. West 1968 5(1): 4-10, 73-75*. Until the present century, the Peace River country was in an isolated backwater in northwestern Canada. Its once rich fur resources had been tapped by the Hudson's Bay Company and the area contained a few meager settlements, trading posts, and missionary stations. This Peace River country is bounded approximately by the 55th and 60th parallels of north latitude and the 114th and 122nd meridians of west longitude in northwestern Alberta spilling over somewhat into British Columbia. The region did not experience the orderly succession which characterized many other frontiers but "in one dizzying leap" made the transition from a fur-trading to a farming frontier. These 75 million acres of prime agricultural land lie far beyond the climatic limit of grain culture which ends just a bit north of Edmonton in central Alberta. Natural conditions which mitigate the otherwise inhospitable climate include a lower evaporation rate and a longer frost-free period than is usual for such latitudes. A homestead system and other governmental considerations encouraged development. Modern technology deprived the region of many of the uncertainties that normally plague other frontiers. Quick-maturing spring wheat, rust-resistant strains of wheat, the crawler-type tractor and clearing blade, deep well-drilling rigs, and modern transportation facilities play significant roles. Map, 5 illus., biblio. note.

D. L. Smith

3387. Hallett, Mary. THE SOCIAL CREDIT PARTY AND THE NEW DEMOCRACY MOVEMENT, 1939-1940. *Can. Hist. R. [Canada] 1966 47(4): 301-325*. A study of the alliance between the Social Credit Party and W. D. Herridge's New Democracy movement before and during the 1940 federal election campaign. Anxious to advance in the federal field, William Aberhart associated Social Credit with W. D. Herridge's New Democracy, a vague protest movement seeking to unite all reformers. Alarmed by Herridge's campaign for conscription, Aberhart repudiated Herridge but for a short time retained the name "New Democracy." Based on the private papers of W. D. Herridge, interviews with and letters from Social Crediters and others associated with Herridge, and newspaper reports.

A

3388. Hosie, Inez B. LITTLE WHITE SCHOOL HOUSE. *Alberta Hist. R. [Canada] 1967 15(4): 26-28*. Describes school life in the Potter Creek district of Alberta, with discussion of the teaching community and the central role of the school in the social life of the area.

H. M. Burns

3389. Hughes, Katherine. THE LAST GREAT ROUNDUP. *Alberta Hist. R. [Canada] 1963 11(2): 1-7*. This reprint of an article from the *Edmonton Bulletin*, 22 June 1907, (reprinted in the *Southern Alberta News* five days later) tells the story of "what is probably the last great roundup of cattle in the history of southern Alberta." Many ranches participated in a communal effort to collect some 130 thousand head of range cattle dispersed during the disastrous winter of 1906-07.

E. W. Hathaway

3390. Inderwick, Mary E.   A LADY AND HER RANCH.   *Alberta Hist. R. [Canada] 1967 15(4): 1-9.* Extracts from letters written by a cattle rancher's bride describing life in the Pincher Creek area of Alberta. Details are given of visits to the Indian reservations and to Fort McLeod.

H. M. Burns

3391. Jameson, Sheilagh S.   GIVE YOUR OTHER VOTE TO THE SISTER.   *Alberta Hist. R. [Canada] 1967 15(4): 10-16.* Account of a campaign on behalf of Roberta Catherine MacAdams, a nursing sister and one of the first two women representatives to serve in the Alberta Legislature. Details regarding her background, her decision to stand for election as an armed services representative in 1917, and of her later life are given.

H. M. Burns

3392. Jameson, Sheilagh S.   A VISIT TO CALGARY'S NEW MUSEUM.   *Alberta Hist. R. [Canada] 1965 13(2): 19-22.* Views Calgary's new museum as a sign of Alberta's maturity, when it preserves its records of the past as well as concerning itself with present action. Gives a brief history of the Glenbow Foundation which provides the exhibits for the museum, and the museum is described. Illus.

G. Emery

3393. Kerr, John R.   ALHAMBRA.   *Alberta Hist. R. [Canada] 1968 16(2): 19-24.* Portrayal of frontier life in the Alhambra District of Alberta, Canada.

H. M. Burns

3394. MacDonell, R. A.   BRITISH IMMIGRATION SCHEMES IN ALBERTA.   *Alberta Hist. R. [Canada] 1968 16(2): 5-13.* Discussion of activities by a religious organization directed toward the promotion of immigration to and settlement of Alberta.

H. M. Burns

3395. MacGregor, James G.   GREENWICH HOUSE.   *Alberta Hist. R. [Canada] 1963 11(4): 7-11.* Examines records of various early travelers with a view to establishing that the location of Greenwich House built by Peter Fidler on the shore of Lac la Biche [Red Deer Lake] was not, as has generally been assumed, at the northeast corner of the modern town of Lac la Biche, but rather to the northwest of the modern town at a location shown approximately in two sketch maps. These maps also show Fidler's approach route together with the other route through Beaver Lake he has hitherto been supposed to have followed.

E. W. Hathaway

3396. Marshall, W. R.   ON THE TRAIL TO BANFF, 1912.   *Alberta Hist. R. [Canada] 1966 14(4): 25-28.* An account of an automobile trip made in 1912 from Calgary to Banff. Descriptions are given of the travel hardships encountered.

H. M. Burns

3397. Maze, Lillian Armstrong.   COLUMBIA HOUSE.   *Alberta Hist. R. [Canada] 1964 12(2): 15-17.* A description of the activities at Columbia House, a hotel and popular gathering spot within the site of present day Edmonton.

G. Emery

3398. McDougall, Mrs. John.   INCIDENTS OF MISSION LIFE, 1874.   *Alberta Hist. R. [Canada] 1966 14(1): 26-29.* Comments on the hardships experienced by a settler in the Bow River Valley.

H. M. Burns

3399. McGuinness, Robert.   MISSIONARY JOURNEY OF FATHER DE SMET.   *Alberta Hist. R. [Canada] 1967 15(2): 12-19.* An account of a journey made by a Jesuit priest, Pierre Jean De Smet, for the purpose of arranging a peace treaty between the Blackfoot and Plateau tribes. The portions reproduced refer to experiences in the Province of Alberta.

H. M. Burns

3400. McGusty, H. A.   AN ENGLISHMAN IN ALBERTA.   *Alberta Hist. R. [Canada] 1966 14(1): 11-21.* Excerpts from a diary giving observations on life in Northwest Canada.

H. M. Burns

3401. McQuarrie, A. H.   BUILDING THE EDSON TRAIL.   *Alberta Hist. R. [Canada] 1966 14(4): 1-6.* Recollections concerning incidents connected with the building of the Edson Trail in Alberta, Canada, as remembered by an early pioneer of Alberta.

H. M. Burns

3402. Moodie, D. W.   ALBERTA SETTLEMENT SURVEYS.   *Alberta Hist. R. [Canada] 1964 12(4): 1-7.* An account of the settlement or river lot surveys carried out in Alberta. Because the patterns of the regular township surveys cover most of the prairies, settlement survey patterns might be overlooked. With origins in Quebec, this survey system provided for long narrow lots on river, lake, or road frontage. It was mostly used in northern Alberta and offered certain advantages. Whereas the township surveys predetermined the location of roads, the settlement surveys provided road routes which could take into account pre-existing settlement and the lay of the country. Illus.

G. Emery

3403. Morrow, John.   THE DEVILLE STORY.   *Alberta Hist. R. [Canada] 1964 12(4): 15-18.* The author's experiences as a squatter on land east of Edmonton along the rumored route for the Winnipeg-Edmonton railway. Railway construction moved through the area in 1908, creating needed jobs for the settlers. In 1909 the railway was completed and the community which grew up in the area, Deville, had a school and a store by 1912. Illus.

G. Emery

3404. Nelson, J. G. and Byrne, A. R.   MAN AS AN INSTRUMENT OF LANDSCAPE CHANGE - FIRES, FLOODS AND NATIONAL PARKS IN THE BOW VALLEY, ALBERTA.   *Geographical R. 1966 56(2): 226-238.* Traces the destruction of the original forest cover in the Bow Valley with the routing of the Canadian Pacific Railway in 1881 and subsequent forest fires and floods. Lack of early records make it difficult to establish a relationship between fires and floods, but evidence is sufficient to determine that reestablishment of vegetation has reduced floods, but to an undetermined degree. Comparative photographs, maps.

R. L. McBane

3405. Niddrie, John G.   THE EDMONTON BOOM OF 1911-1912.   *Alberta Hist. R. [Canada] 1965 13(2): 1-6.* The author's experiences during the land boom. In March 1912 he left his job with the Department of Agriculture to take employment in a real estate office, one of 400 real estate offices which he estimated were in the city of 31 thousand. He describes the height of the boom which was reached when the Hudson's Bay Company sold off their lots. The boom broke when these lots glutted the market. Illus.

G. Emery

3406. Niddrie, J. G.   SUNDRE SETTLERS.   *Alberta Hist. R. [Canada] 1970 18(1): 14-20.* Describes the early settlement and stories about pioneer life in Sundre, Alberta, during the 1890's.   H. M. Burns

3407. Parrott, Michael.   TURNER VALLEY.   *Can. Geographical J. [Canada] 1964 69(4): 141-151.* The story of the finding of gas and oil in the Turner Valley and its exploitation. Discusses types of equipment used, speculation, modern discoveries, and includes some statistics. Photographs.

E. W. Hathaway

3408. Peel, Bruce.   STEAMBOATS ON THE SASKATCHEWAN.   *Alberta Hist. R. [Canada] 1968 16(3): 11-21.* Tells of the sternwheel riverboats which plied the Saskatchewan River from Grand Rapids to Edmonton. Described are the physical obstacles encountered and the reasons for cessation of operations on this waterway.

H. M. Burns

3409. Pennie, A. M.   A CYCLE AT SUFFIELD.   *Alberta Hist. R. [Canada] 1963 11(1): 7-11.* The chief superintendent of the Suffield Experimental Station describes the blossoming in the early 1900's, the decay in the 1920's, and the reawakening in the 1940's of Suffield, which is in southeastern Alberta. The early rise is shown to be related to the largest commercial grain farming enterprise in Canada, and the fall to the lack of adequate irrigation. The later rise is considered to be quite typical of cycles elsewhere in Canada, in that it was due to circumstances quite unrelated to the original growth; it was the result of the coming of the Defence Research Board's Experimental Station. The station occupies more than one thousand square miles of otherwise useless prairie.

R. J. C. Ford

3410. Roe, Frank Gilbert.   EDMONTON A CENTURY AGO.   *Alberta Hist. R. [Canada] 1964 12(1): 10-16.* Discusses the origins of the name "Edmonton" and the locational factors which established Edmonton on its present site. Foods of the day, the fur economy, the transportation systems, and the character of the chief factor of the post are all described. Illus.

G. Emery

3411. Rowand, John. A LETTER FROM FORT EDMONTON. *Alberta Hist. R. [Canada] 1963 11(1): 1-6.* The New Year's letter of 10 January 1840 from John Rowand, chief factor at Fort Edmonton to Governor George Simpson and the chief factors and traders in the Northern Department of the Hudson's Bay Company. Gives news and gossip about his district, freely attacks his superiors, and is candid about problems in trading with the Blackfoot Indians. Photographs: Rowand, p. 3; Paul Kane's painting of Fort Edmonton c. 1847, p. 4.

R. J. C. Ford

3412. Royick, Alexander. UKRAINIAN SETTLEMENTS IN ALBERTA. *Can. Slavonic Papers [Canada] 1968 10(3): 278-297.* Gives genealogical information on early Ukrainian settlers in Alberta, their place of origin in the Ukraine (most were from Galicia and Bukovina), and their settlement sites in Alberta. There is some discussion of the preservation of dialects and customs. Based mostly on periodicals and interviews; 7 tables, map, 112 notes.

R. V. Layton

3413. Schultz, Harold J. PORTRAIT OF A PREMIER: WILLIAM ABERHART. *Can. Hist. R. [Canada] 1964 45(3): 185-211.* Draws on interviews, private files, reprints of radio broadcasts, mimeographed booklets, as well as more conventional materials, for an interpretation of Canada's first Social Credit premier. William Aberhart's fundamentalist cast of mind revealed itself equally well in all three fields that he entered - teaching, preaching, and politics. He was authoritarian, but hardly dictatorial, in his political leadership for his interest in the spiritual and physical well-being of the province was intense and sincere. Never understanding the radical economic and political implications of Social Credit, Aberhart preferred to promote reform and good government in office. His championing of provincial rights and his superb organizing abilities were the practical reasons for his success as a politican.

A

3414. Sibbald, Andrew. WEST WITH THE MC DOUGALLS. *Alberta Hist. R. [Canada] 1971 19(1): 1-4.* Account of a journey to Alberta taken together with Reverend George McDougall and David McDougall in 1887. Describes life at Stoney Indian Mission, which was founded by Reverend John M. McDougall.

H. M. Burns

3415. Strom, Theodore. WITH THE EAU CLAIRE IN CALGARY. *Alberta Hist. R. [Canada] 1964 12(3): 1-11.* The author's experiences while working for the Eau Claire Company in Calgary. He arrived in 1886 to help build the company's lumber mills. In 1889 the company built its first light plant and its competition with a rival light company is reviewed. The author describes his experiences with prohibition, Indians, the Salvation Army, and with the company's debtors while trying to collect overdue bills. Illus.

G. Emery

3416. Thomas, L. G. THE RANCHER AND THE CITY: CALGARY AND THE CATTLEMEN, 1883-1914. *Mémoires de la Soc. Royale du Can. [Canada] 1968 6(4): 203-215.* The arrival of the Canadian Pacific Railway in Calgary in 1883 gave the tiny hamlet the chance to become the market center for ranching in the area. Although the pioneers of Calgary thought in terms of mining, farming, and industry as well, the cattlemen used the town and imposed their own characteristics on it. Ranchers were a minority after settlers began to come in, but they lasted as a social unit until the First World War destroyed them.

L. F. S. Upton

3417. Tims, John W. ANGLICAN BEGINNINGS IN SOUTHERN ALBERTA. *Alberta Hist. R. [Canada] 1967 15(2): 1-11.* An account of the early history of the Anglican church in Alberta. Work with various Blood and Blackfoot Indian tribes is described.

H. M. Burns

3418. VanTighem, Frank. FATHER LEONARD VAN TIGHEM, O.M.I. *Alberta Hist. R. [Canada] 1964 12(1): 17-21.* Belgian born, Father VanTighem went to Lachine in 1874 as a lay brother of the Order of Mary Immaculate. By 1875 he was working as a carpenter in Edmonton, and in 1881 he became a priest in his order. This led to extensive missionary work in southern Alberta where he served, with the exception of two brief periods, for the rest of his life. He was one of the three great Roman Catholic pioneers of southern Alberta. Illus.

G. Emery

3419. Weadick, Guy. ORIGIN OF THE CALGARY STAMPEDE. *Alberta Hist. R. [Canada] 1966 14(4): 20-28.* History of the origin of the Calgary Stampede and of its role in re-creating an atmosphere of western frontier days. Subsequent revivals of the stampede are discussed.

H. M. Burns

3420. West, Karen. CARDSTON: THE TEMPLE CITY OF CANADA. *Can. Geographical J. [Canada] 1965 71(5): 162-169.* This town was founded by Mormon pioneers from Utah in 1887, and after initial difficulties which were overcome by irrigation, has progressed steadily. Illus.

A. H. Lawrance

3421. Williams, J. Earl. ORIGIN AND DEVELOPMENT OF PUBLIC TELEPHONES IN ALBERTA. *Alberta Hist. R. [Canada] 1963 11(2): 8-12.* Traces the course of the gradual replacement of the Bell Telephone Company in Canada by publicly owned and operated companies, with attention to relevant factors in the climate of public opinion (strong farmers' cooperatives, widespread reading of Henry George), with special attention to Alberta; and finally, since 1933, the development of farmer-owned mutual companies in unprofitable rural areas.

E. W. Hathaway

3422. Williams, Milton. TWICE DISAPPOINTED. *Alberta Hist. R. [Canada] 1963 11(4): 15-18.* Personal recollections of two incidents involving the results, first, of a misunderstood order and, secondly, misinformation from a fleeing civilian during the march from Calgary northward to the Saskatchewan to suppress the North West Rebellion of 1885.

E. W. Hathaway

3423. Young, Harrison S. IMPRESSIONS OF FORT EDMONTON. *Alberta Hist. R. [Canada] 1966 14(1): 22-25.* A description of life at the chief post of the Hudson's Bay Company.

H. M. Burns

3424. Young, Morley A. R. THE BUFFALO AT ELK ISLAND PARK. *Alberta Hist. R. [Canada] 1965 13(1): 26-28.* In 1907 Elk Island Park was built as temporary accommodation for 250 buffalo which had been purchased by the Canadian government. In 1909 these buffalo were to have been moved to Wainwright Park, built in that year. However, 46 of the buffalo eluded capture and became the basis of an Elk Island Park herd which today totals 750. Illus.

G. Emery

3425. —. ALONG THE C AND E LINE. *Alberta Hist. R. [Canada] 1964 12(3): 12-14.* A description of the people and the country along the Calgary and Edmonton Railway which was written by a reporter for the Edmonton *Bulletin* in 1893. Previous to the completion of the line in 1891, Red Deer had been the only settlement between Calgary and Edmonton. The changes which had taken place are described.

G. Emery

3426. —. LETTERS FROM A SKINNER. *Alberta Hist. R. [Canada] 1965 13(4): 9-20.* A series of letters written by a young British ex-army officer describing his experiences as a skinner for the Sunderland Canadian Lands Company Ltd. in 1925.

H. M. Burns

British Columbia

3427. Clemson, Donovan. KAMLOOPS: CITY IN THE SAGE. *Can. Geographical J. [Canada] 1967 74(1): 18-27.* Story of the thriving town of Kamloops, which was called Cumeloups by the Shuswap Indians who still own land nearby. The area, now noted for its cattle and sheep ranches, was once a mining area. In the early days it was also a center of the fur trade. The town is known for its beautiful gardens in a near-desert area. The past decade has seen a tremendous growth in population, industry, and recreational facilities in Kamloops. Photos.

W. A. Buckman

3428. Cousine, W. J. NO LOYALIST IN BRITISH COLUMBIA. *Alberta Hist. R. [Canada] 1969 17(3): 20-27.* An account of friction between rival groups during the settlement of what is now British Columbia during the 1830's and 1840's.

H. M. Burns

3429. Currie, A. W. THE VANCOUVER COAL MINING COMPANY. *Queen's Q. [Canada] 1963 70(1): 50-63.* The history of one of the largest Canadian mining concerns, in existence from 1862 to 1902.

The company - in which John Galsworthy's father played a preeminent role - was the background for the play *Strife*.   M. Abrash

3430. DeRosier, Arthur H., Jr. THE SETTLEMENT OF THE SAN JUAN CONTROVERSY. *Southern Q. 1965 4(1): 74-88.* The Oregon Treaty of 1846 left open to argument the location of the U.S.-Canadian boundary in the Strait of Juan de Fuca. The resulting dispute dragged on until 1871 when Britain and the United States agreed to abide by the decision of the Emperor of Germany. The resulting award supported the claims of the United States.   D. A. Stokes

3431. Evans, Howard R. CARIBOO GOLD. *Mankind 1967 1(2): 66-71.* Review of the discovery of gold in British Columbia in February of 1858 and the subsequent rush of California miners to the region. The California mines were in a period of decline, and the area around the Fraser River in British Columbia became the center for mining activities. By 1865 the shallow claims were exhausted, the mines were beginning to flood, and expenses skyrocketed. Illus., biblio.   P. D. Thomas

3432. Fidler, Vera. SPIRAL TUNNELS—ENGINEERING MARVEL AND TOURIST DRAW. *Can. Geographical J. [Canada] 1967 74(2): 52-57.* One of the most popular sights in British Columbia's Yoho National Park is Spiral Tunnel Viewpoint. Tourists stop there to see a Canadian Pacific Railway train winding its way in and out of the famous spiral tunnels. The tunnels were driven out of solid rock in 1908-09 to create one of the most interesting examples of grade reduction in the world. Originally (1884) the tracks were laid in a break-neck descent from the top of Kicking Horse Pass to the village of Field, dropping 237 1/2 feet to the mile. This adventuresome "Big Hill" was avoided when the tunnels were open to traffic in August 1909. The tunnels reduced the gradient of the track from as steep as 5.5 percent to 2.2 percent maximum. Illus.   C. J. Allard

3433. Fry, Jack. FORT DEFIANCE. *Beaver [Canada] 1967 298(Summer): 18-21.* Captain Robert Gray (1755-1806) was the first American to circumnavigate the globe; he also discovered and gave his ship's name to the Columbia River, and built a log fort on an island off the west coast of Vancouver Island in the fall of 1791, where he and his men stayed until March 1792. The recent identification of Fort Defiance (as Gray called his camp) about two-thirds of the way up on the eastern shore of Lemmens Inlet, on Meares Island, near Tofino, British Columbia, is described. Digging and diving at this point in 1966 recovered bricks thought to be used in the building of Fort Defiance. Illus.   L. F. S. Upton

3434. Gibson, William Carleton. FRANK FAIRCHILD WESBROOK (1868-1918): A PIONEER MEDICAL EDUCATOR IN MINNESOTA AND BRITISH COLUMBIA. *J. of the Hist. of Medicine and Allied Sci. 1967 22(4): 357-379.* Born in 1868 in Canada, Wesbrook received his M.D. from the University of Manitoba. He then spent three years at Cambridge in England, where he worked with Sir Charles Sherrington. At the age of 38 he was made dean of the faculty of the medical school at the University of Minnesota. He held this post until 1913 when he returned to Canada as the first president of the University of British Columbia. Wesbrook was interested in the problem of bacterial infections and during his younger career did much work on that subject. Later he became concerned with the issues in medical education. The author is concerned largely with his ideas on medical education and explores Wesbrooks' strictures against compartmentalism, his interest in the role of alumni in university government, the problem of standards and specialization, and others. 13 notes.   G. N. Grob

3435. Gough, Barry M. "TURBULENT FRONTIERS" AND BRITISH EXPANSION: GOVERNOR JAMES DOUGLAS, THE ROYAL NAVY, AND THE BRITISH COLUMBIA GOLD RUSHES. *Pacific Hist. R. 1972 41(1): 15-32.* John S. Galbraith's theory of the "turbulent frontier" as an explanatory factor in British expansion during the Victorian era is applied by the author to events in British Columbia 1850-63. Governor Douglas of Vancouver Island felt it necessary to request naval support from England to prevent and inhibit the undermining of authority by the influx of Americans during the gold rush, especially to the Fraser River area. The presence of the British vessels provided the support needed to consolidate the authority of the Governor. This, with other measures taken by Douglas and the British Government, led finally to the establishment of British Columbia as a Crown Colony even though its addition to the Empire was not consciously sought. 70 notes.   E. C. Hyslop

3436. Hanbury, Michael. ABBOT AELRED CARLYLE: MISSIONARY IN VANCOUVER. *Am. Benedictine R. 1969 20(3): 352-367.* Traces the missionary work of the Benedictine Abbot Carlyle who settled in remote British Columbia at four different locations, the last of which was in Vancouver from 1937 to 1951. There he was assigned responsibilities as chaplain and director of Saint Vincent's Home and Shelter, editor of the weekly *British Columbia Catholic,* promoter of the *Apostolatus Maris* among the seamen in the port, and chaplain of the city prison of Oakalla just outside Vancouver. These latter two positions, especially the prison chaplaincy, occupied most of his energies and established him as "the best-loved priest in British Columbia." Upon his retirement, Abbot Carlyle returned to Prinknash Abbey, Gloucester, England, from which he had come in 1921 and where he died in 1956. Based on the diary and letters of Abbot Aelred Carlyle in the Archives of Prinknash Abbey; 4 notes.   E. J. O'Brien

3437. Hardwick, Walter G. ROLL-ON-ROLL-OFF FERRIES: A REVOLUTION IN MARINE TRANSPORTATION IN BRITISH COLUMBIA. *Can. Geographical J. [Canada] 1964 69(5): 152-161.* The development of steamship communication in British Columbia, from the first coal transports and paddlewheeled steamers to the roll-on-roll-off ferries of the present day, is described. Illus.   M. Petrie

3438. Harrington, Lyn. THE FRASER - GREAT RIVER OF THE WEST. *Can. Geographical J. [Canada] 1963 67(4): 110-117.* This description of the course of the river includes a brief historical survey from 1793, when Alexander Mackenzie canoed on the upper waters, to the present. Map, photographs.   A. H. Lawrance

3439. Harrington, Robert F. EULACHON AND THE GREASE TRAILS OF BRITISH COLUMBIA. *Can. Geographical J. [Canada] 1967 74(1): 28-31.* Account of a passing phenomenon in British Columbia. Eulachon, spelled in many ways, are a fish of the smelt family. Many were eaten fresh in the early days by the Indians, but the main reason for the annual catch was to extract the oil from these fish. Describes the capture, extraction of the oil, and the manual transportation of the grease. This product was a basic item of diet, eaten with other foods and by itself. The native Indians were mainly involved in this work. The hauling of this grease into the back country over many years formed two major trails into the interior. Modernization has almost brought an end to this way of life, because there is no longer a great demand for product, and the "grease trails" are disappearing.   W. A. Buckman

3440. Harrington, Robert F. PADDLEWHEEL STEAMERS OF THE ARROW LAKES. *Can. Geographical J. [Canada] 1966 72(2): 58-65.* The story of the early steamboats on the upper Columbia River and the Arrow Lakes. Photographs.   A. H. Lawrance

3441. Harrington, Robert F. PRINCE GEORGE: WESTERN WHITE SPRUCE CAPITAL OF THE WORLD. *Can. Geographical J. [Canada] 1968 77(3): 72-83.* Prince George, near the geographic center of British Columbia, is Canada's fastest-growing city because of its position as a transportation hub and because of the importance of its forest-based industries which account for 70 percent of the city's payroll. The region was first explored by Sir Alexander Mackenzie in 1793, and Simon Fraser visited the area in 1806. Arrival in 1914 of the Grand Trunk Pacific (later part of the Canadian National Railways) started the city's period of modern growth. Illus., map.   R. D. Tallman

3442. Hart, William S. 18TH CENTURY NAVAL ARTISTS ON THE NORTHWEST COAST. *Alberta Hist. R. [Canada] 1969 11(3): 1-9.* Discusses late 18th-century naval exploration of the coast of western Canada and paintings and drawings made on a voyage to Nootka Island by British naval officers.   H. M. Burns

3443. Hayes, Edmund. GRAY'S ADVENTURE COVE. *Oregon Hist. Q. 1967 68(2): 100-110.* Describes the voyages of the ship *Columbia,* 1787-92, which was the first American vessel to circumnavigate the globe; also, the ship is credited with the discovery of the mouth of the Columbia River in 1792. The author relates his recent experiences in determining from old logs and maps the exact location of Adventure Cove, a port-base for the *Columbia* in 1792 on the coast of Vancouver Island. Illus.

C. C. Gorchels

3444. Haynes, Bessie Doak. GOLD ON QUEEN CHARLOTTE'S ISLAND [SIC]. *Beaver [Canada] 1966 297(Winter): 4-11.* In August 1850 came the first news of a gold discovery at Englefield Bay, Queen Charlotte Islands. Little gold was found, and what there was had been an offshoot or "blow," a freak often found in mining areas. Nevertheless, prospectors were attracted to the islands, and there was considerable concern at the presence of Americans. Royal Navy ships were sent, and in September 1852 James Douglas, governor of Vancouver Island, was commissioned lieutenant governor of Queen Charlotte Islands in order to establish his authority to deal with the situation. There were numerous incidents between hostile Indians and gold seekers. Included are excerpts from the log of the *Georgianna* giving an account of its wreck and the capture of its passengers by Haida Indians. Illus.

L. F. S. Upton

3445. Howard, Irene. VANCOUVER SWEDES AND THE LOGGERS. *Swedish Pioneer Hist. Q. 1970 21(3): 163-182.* Two excerpts from the longer work, *Vancouver's Svenskar: A History of the Swedish Community in Vancouver.* The first part gives biographical sketches of individuals prominent in the early Swedish community in Vancouver. By the 1890's there was a tightly-knit community. The second part deals with the labor movement among Vancouver loggers. Scandinavians were a prominent element in the logging camps, and played a large part in the union movement. On 26 January 1934, the crew at Bloedel's Menzies Bay logging camp voted to strike. The strike spread and halted logging operations for three months. It was a prime factor in bringing about minimum wage legislation in the logging industry and in helping to establish labor's right to engage in collective bargaining. Based on primary and secondary sources; 33 notes.

K. J. Puffer

3446. Ironsides, R. G. and Tomasky, E. DEVELOPMENT OF VICTORIA SETTLEMENT. *Alberta Hist. R. [Canada] 1971 19(2): 20-29.* History of Victoria, from settlement as an Indian mission to present farming community status. Consideration of Indian land claims, establishment of Hudson's Bay Company trading post, and character of population.

H. M. Burns

3447. Jackson, C. Ian. "A TERRITORY OF LITTLE VALUE": THE WIND OF CHANGE ON THE NORTHWEST COAST 1861-1867. *Beaver [Canada] 1967 298(Summer): 40-45.* Between 1838 and 1867 the Hudson's Bay Company leased the mainland of southeast Russian America, as far as Cape Spencer. In 1863 the company decided against renewing the lease, largely because the Russians could no longer enforce a monopoly; but the company changed its mind as reports of favorable trade came in. The lease was renewed in 1865 for two years at an advanced rate. Chief Factor William Tolmie in Victoria wrote a survey of the future of the west coast: the proposed Overland Telegraph would be hostile to the fur trader unless the company gained the right to provision the contractors, posts should be established on the Stikine and Skeena Rivers, and the company might consider buying the coastal territory from the Russians.

L. F. S. Upton

3448. Johnson, F. Henry. THE DOUKHOBORS OF BRITISH COLUMBIA. *Queen's Q. [Canada] 1964 70(4): 528-541.* Forty years of resistence by Doukhobor extremists (Sons of Freedom) to public education was finally broken by separating the parents from their children for six years. The children have accepted and benefited from regular education, but the episode raises difficult questions of minority rights and government toleration.

M. Abrash

3449. Johnson, F. Henry. THE UNIVERSITIES OF BRITISH COLUMBIA. *Can. Geographical J. 1966 73(6): 182-193.* Surveys the institutions of higher learning in British Columbia, giving the history of their development and their present standing and contributions. The major institutions are the University of British Columbia in Vancouver and the University of Victoria. The Macdonald Report of 1962 called for decentralization with the establishment of junior and regional colleges, as well as provincial supervisory boards over academic standards and grants. This report basically has been carried out with the founding of Simon Fraser University, Vancouver City College, and Selkirk College. Notre Dame University of Nelson is becoming a major private institution. Canada sends only half as many 18- to 21-year-olds to college as the United States, but British Columbia has the highest percentage in Canada. Illus., table.

W. A. Buckman

3450. Johnson, Patricia. MC LEOD LAKE POST. *Beaver [Canada] 1965 296(Autumn): 22-29.* This trading post, now located on the John Hart Highway north of Prince George, British Columbia, was the first permanent post erected in British territory west of the Rocky Mountains. Founded by Simon Fraser on behalf of the North West Company in 1805, it was taken over by the Hudson's Bay Company in 1821. The visits of numerous travelers are noted, including that of Governor George Simpson, who thought "McLeod Lake is the most wretched place in the Indian Country," (1828). Quotes from the McLeod Lake Journal (1845 to 1848) in the Glenbow Foundation, Calgary. Illus.

L. F. S. Upton

3451. Jones, J. Michael. THE RAILROAD HEALED THE BREACH. *Can. Geographical J. [Canada] 1966 73(3): 98-101.* Residents of Victoria on Vancouver Island expected the terminus of the Canadian Pacific Railroad to be in their town. When the news came from Ottawa that Vancouver on the mainland would be the terminus, Victoria threatened secession. Relates the healing of the breach by the construction of the Esquimalt and Nanaimo Railway on Vancouver Island. Gives a brief history of that line. Illus.

W. A. Buckman

3452. Jost, T. P. REV. A. G. MORICE, DISCOVERER AND SURVEYOR, AND THE PROBLEMS OF THE PROPER GEOGRAPHICAL NAMES IN NORTH CENTRAL BRITISH COLUMBIA. *R. de l'U. d'Ottawa [Canada] 1967 37(3): 463-476.* Father A. G. Morice of the Order of Oblates of Mary Immaculate is one of the unsung heroes of discovery and surveying in British Columbia. Born in France, he came to Canada in 1880 and, after his ordination as a priest, he served as a missionary in the interior of British Columbia from 1882 to 1908. While performing his spiritual duties, Father Morice always carried with him a compass, a barometer, a sounding line, and a notebook. He collected enormous quantities of scientific data on areas into which he was the first white man to penetrate, and he published more than 50 scientific works on north central British Columbia. He named many points which still remain unnamed on Provincial maps. An appendix lists some of the geographical features named by Father Morice.

J. M. Bumsted

3453. Kogler, Rudolf K. DEMOGRAPHIC PROFILE OF THE POLISH COMMUNITY IN CANADA. *Polish Am. Studies 1968 25(1): 51-62.* Deals with the growth and distribution of the Polish ethnic group in Canada, 1900-60. The numbers grew from 6,300 to 323,517. The move was from the Prairie Provinces to Montreal, Toronto, and Vancouver. Deals with sex and age distribution, marital status, fertility, and language.

S. R. Pliska

3454. Laxdal, Jon K. THE OKANAGAN VALLEY. *Can. Geographical J. [Canada] 1967 75(5): 150-161.* The Okanagan Valley is, in addition to being the second ranking fruit growing area in Canada, a four-season playground for holidayers. The valley is a sheltered north-south trench (a part of the Fraser Plateau), lying in the southern interior of British Columbia between the Cascade Mountains on the west and the Monashee Mountains on the east. The valley has been an area of fur trade, gold mines, sheep and cattle ranches, and with the development of irrigation it has become an important fruit growing center. The valley has its own lake monster called Ogopogo, whose presence in Lake Okanagan is attested to by reliable residents and visitors. Illus., maps.

C. J. Allard

3455. Lee, Lawrence B. DOMINION DITCHES AND BRITISH COLUMBIA CANALS: A HISTORY OF THE WESTERN CANADA IRRIGATION ASSOCIATION. *J. of the West 1968 7(1): 31-40.* Surveys the origins and activities of the Western Canada Irrigation Association (1907-26). The author concluded that although it was not as large and did not have the wealth and reputation of its model and sister institution in the United States (the National Irrigation Congress formed in Salt Lake City in 1891), it did play a significant role in obtaining legislative aid for irrigation and improvement of irrigation practices. Based largely on newspaper articles, reports of the Western Canada Irrigation Association, and the association's official journal; 65 notes.

E. A. Erickson

3456. Letkemann, Peter. MENNONITES IN VANCOUVER: A SURVEY. *Mennonite Life 1968 23(4): 160-164.* Reports on the responses to questionnaires sent to 98 married men in two Vancouver Mennonite churches. The questions dealt with residential patterns, cultural aspects, social interaction, social participation, and occupational dimensions. The respondents are categorized into two groups - those who are descendants of immigrants from Russia prior to World War II and those who came directly from Russia and Germany after World War II. It is concluded that, first, the contrast between Group I and Group II indicates significant differentiation within an ethnic group; second, some cultural patterns tend to persist, while others rapidly disappear; third, Mennonites are not actively involved in occupational organizations, voluntary organizations, or in social services not connected with the church; and, last, Mennonite visiting patterns suggest that frequent interaction with relatives and other Mennonites does not exclude interaction with non-Mennonites. 2 maps, 4 notes.   D. J. Abramoske

3457. Lewis, Palmer G. BABINE LAKE. *Beaver [Canada] 1968 299(Summer): 26-35.* Babine Lake in British Columbia was first visited by white traders Daniel Harmon and James McDougall in 1812. The Hudson's Bay Company opened a post, Fort Kilmaurs, there in 1822, and this was later replaced by Fort Babine located at the northern end of the west arm of the lake. An Indian village on the site of Fort Kilmaurs, known as Old Fort, remains to this day. The lake still yields fine sockeye salmon, the mountains are well-timbered, and extensive copper deposits are now being exploited in the area. Illus.   L. F. S. Upton

3458. Ley, Ronald. BRIEF HISTORY OF THE FRASER VALLEY REGIONAL LIBRARY. *Can. Lib. [Canada] 1967 24(2): 127-130.* Rural library service began in British Columbia in 1927, based somewhat along the line of county service in the United States. Since there are no counties, it was based on a geographical area, Fraser Valley. Actual library service began in August 1930 in Chilliwack. The service grew rapidly. Headquarters were moved to Abbotsford. The system has 25 branches and 2 bookmobiles. It has been a training ground for many good librarians.   D. Brockway

3459. Little, C. H. OFF-SHORE EXPLORATION FOR GAS AND OIL. *Can. Geographical J. [Canada] 1968 77(4): 108-115.* With the growing demand for oil in the world, major companies have begun probing coastal waters of Canada, in British Columbia, the Maritimes, and the Arctic. The Supreme Court of Canada in 1967 gave the Canadian Government jurisdiction over offshore mineral rights. Discusses, in the Canadian context, details of drilling from offshore platforms, and the hazards involved. No major discoveries have been reported, but drilling continues. 13 illus., 2 maps.   R. D. Tallman

3460. Lomax, Alfred L. DR. MC LOUGHLIN'S TROPICAL TRADE ROUTE. *Beaver [Canada] 1964 295(Spring): 10-15.* From 1829 to 1859 the Hudson's Bay Company used Honolulu as a transshipment point between London and the Columbia River post of Fort Vancouver. Consumer goods were brought to Hawaii from London via Cape Horn; the vessels then loaded with sugar, molasses, salt, rice and coffee for the mainland. On the return trip they brought beaver furs, salmon, lumber, flour, wool. As the Oregon Country became Americanized, the Hudson's Bay Company gave up Fort Vancouver and closed its Hawaiian agency in 1859. Illus.   L. F. S. Upton

3461. Lyman, S. M.; Willmott, W. E.; and Ho, Berching. RULES OF A CHINESE SECRET SOCIETY IN BRITISH COLUMBIA. *Bull. of the School of Oriental and African Studies [Great Britain] 1964 530-539.* Seven photographs of the original text and a translation of a body of rules of a British Columbia branch of the *Chih-kung T'ang* (part of the Triad or Hung Society of China) dating from about 1882, which was found in a gold-mining town. Brief introductory comments about Chinese secret societies in North America.   D. McIntyre

3462. McKay, W. A. THE STORY OF THE CANADIAN FUR TRADE. *Beaver [Canada] 1965 296(Autumn): 36-41 and (Winter): 12-16.* This continuing survey of the fur trade is concerned with the Pacific coast operations of the Russians, British and Spanish, and in particular with the Nootka Sound controversy of 1790, expansion to the Pacific Northwest, the establishment of British Columbia, and the decline of the trade in face of settlement. Furs, however, remain an important

trade item, and the Winter Fur Auction at Beaver Hall in London is still held. Furs exported to London in 1963 were worth 48 million pounds, and of that 41 million pounds were re-exported. Illus.   L. F. S. Upton

3463. McKechnie, N. D. THE MINERAL INDUSTRY IN BRITISH COLUMBIA. *Can. Geographical J. [Canada] 1969 78(3): 76-89.* The development of British Columbia rests on mining the mineral wealth of the Province. Lists six major events in the mining history of British Columbia: the discovery of coal in 1835 on Vancouver Island, the discovery of placer gold in the Cariboo in 1858, the discovery of silver-copper ores on Toad Mountain in 1886, the use of the oil-flotation process of ore concentration in 1912, the completion of the Alaska Highway through the province during World War II, and the open-pit mining of the Bethlehem copper deposit in Highland Valley in the 1960's. These advances in exploration and mining technology in turn led to further development of British Columbia's natural resources. Predicts further growth of the Province, tied to its mining industry. 13 illus., map, table.   R. D. Tallman

3464. Meyers, Leonard W. VIA THE FRASER CANYON. *Beaver [Canada] 1965 296(Winter): 26-31.* The Cariboo Wagon Road from Yale to Soda Creek, just above Williams Lake, British Columbia, was built over its 400-mile length between 1861 and 1864 by a force of Royal Engineers. The next major construction in the Fraser Canyon was the Canadian Pacific Railway, despite an original decision to run the railway north to Prince George. Between 1880 and 1887 a route was blasted along the banks of the Fraser at a cost of up to 300 thousand dollars a mile. The Canadian Northern Railway was later built along the opposite bank. Within the last decade came the Trans-Canada Highway: one mile of that, through the China Bar bluffs, cost over two million dollars. Illus.   L. F. S. Upton

3465. Moeller, Beverley B. CAPTAIN JAMES COLNETT AND THE TSIMSHIAN INDIANS, 1787. *Pacific Northwest Q. 1966 57(1): 13-17.* Documented account of conflict between the crew of an English fur-trading ship and Tsimshian Indians near [Queen] Charlotte Isles, British Columbia, based on the "Journal of the 'Prince of Wales'" by sailor James Colnett.   C. C. Gorchels

3466. Osing, Olga. CANADA'S VOLCANIC CITY-ROSSLAND, B.C. *Can. Geographical J. [Canada] 1966 73(5): 166-171.* Rossland is a mountain mining town just a few miles north of the US border. In the past it has produced six million tons of gold and copper ore worth 125 million dollars. These deposits are the result of volcanic activity in times past. The town basically lies within an old volcanic rim. Recent developments in the area include skiing facilities and molybdenum mining. Illus.   W. A. Buckman

3467. Patterson, E. Palmer, II. ARTHUR E. O'MEARA, FRIEND OF THE INDIANS. *Pacific Northwest Q. 1967 58(2): 90-99.* Indians in British Columbia were in danger of losing most of their land as a consequence of the efforts of the Provincial Government to limit the land holdings of Indian families to no more than 20 acres, while the Province was being settled by whites in the latter half of the 19th century. From 1909 to 1927 Arthur E. O'Meara devoted his energies to the fight on behalf of the Indians to gain more favorable terms. The author concludes that O'Meara's ultimate contribution was little more than acting as a catalyst in encouraging the Indians to voice their grievances and organize for action. 26 notes.   C. C. Gorchels

3468. Peake, F. A. THE MYSTERY OF JOHN POSTLETHWAITE. *Pacific Northwest Q. 1969 60(4): 199-204.* An account of schemes leading to the naming of Postlethwaite as bishop-designate of the Diocese of New Westminster in British Columbia and the hint of scandal which led to his withdrawal.   C. C. Gorchels

3469. Reid, Patricia H. SEGREGATION IN BRITISH COLUMBIA. *Bulletin. United Church of Can. 1963 16: 1-15.* The issue of segregation arose in 1859-60 in a mission in British Columbia begun by the Congregational Unions in Canada and England. The first missionary, Rev. William F. Clarke, would have nothing to do with the "Negro corner" requested by some of his white parishioners. When his British colleague, Rev. Matthew Macfie, arrived shortly after Clarke, he began to hold separate services involving segregation of Negroes. Clarke's work for a time prospered, and a small church was erected. When the Colonial Missionary Society finally awakened to the situation, they upheld Clarke's position and recalled Macfie. Copiously documented from *The Canadian Independent Magazine.*   E. P. Stickney

3470. Robin, Martin. THE SOCIAL BASIS OF PARTY POLITICS IN BRITISH COLUMBIA. *Queen's Q. [Canada] 1966 72(4): 675-690.* The two major British Columbian provincial parties reflect a sharp social cleavage. Militant industrial unionism (fostered by extractive industries) supports the New Democratic Party, while conservative farmers support Social Credit. In power since 1952, Social Credit is more conservative than the Alberta variety and distinctly antisocialist and antilabor, but gets workers' votes because of gains in prosperity and employment. Despite Social Credit's many successes, the NDP is sufficiently well organized and strong (30 percent of the popular vote) to serve as a real opposition, and at the same time its socialist ideology keeps farmers, big business and small business together behind Social Credit.   M. Abrash

3471. Robinson, J. Lewis. NANAIMO, B. C. *Can. Geographical J. [Canada] 1965 70(5): 162-169.* Describes the economic development of a city on Vancouver Island. Coal mining, initially the main industry, was started by the Hudson's Bay Company in 1852. In 1886 a railway connected Nanaimo with Victoria, and the Canadian Pacific Railway reached Vancouver. The improved transportation facilities stimulated coal, but after 1925 coal production declined steadily. After World War II Nanaimo improved and developed supply-service-transport functions to become the leading commercial center of the east coast of Vancouver Island. Its strategic geographic position directly west of Vancouver made it an important distribution center. Thus, "a town which might have died with the decline of coal mining found a new reason for existence in its significant geographical position." Illus., map, 5 notes.
                    E. P. Stickney

3472. Robinson, J. Lewis. THE ROCKY MOUNTAIN TRENCH IN EASTERN BRITISH COLUMBIA. *Can. Geographical J. [Canada] 1968 77(4): 132-141.* The Rocky Mountain Trench is the longest gash in the surface of North America, extending 1,100 miles from western Montana through eastern British Columbia to the Yukon Territory. Discusses the geological origins and geographic characteristics of the trench. Most settlements in the trench are small. Ranching and mining are the main economic pursuits. The construction of dams on trench rivers for hydroelectric power will attract some industry to the region, although Vancouver will receive most of the power. 6 illus., 4 maps, 2 notes.
                    R. D. Tallman

3473. Roy, R. H. THE EARLY DEFENSE AND MILITIA OF THE OKANAGAN VALLEY, 1871-1914. *Pacific Northwest Q. 1966 57(1): 28-35.* Discusses problems of obtaining satisfactory quarters, officers, and men for military preparedness in Okanagan Valley, British Columbia, Canada. Men looked on the militia as a social club and as a means of providing immediate protection in the frontier area if needed.
                    C. C. Gorchels

3474. Scargill, M. H. CANADIANISMS FROM WESTERN CANADA, WITH SPECIAL REFERENCE TO BRITISH COLUMBIA. *Mémoires de la Soc. Royale du Can. [Canada] 1968 6(4): 181-185.* The English language has undergone a "sea change" in adapting itself to Canadian conditions. Many distinctive British Columbian words (potlatch, chuck, skookum) come from the Chinook jargon, the trade language of the Pacific coast which is a mixture of Chinook, Nootka, Salish, French, and English. Mining also contributed new words. "Crummy" comes from the boxcar used to carry men to and from work in the lumber camps.   L. F. S. Upton

3475. Schieder, Rupert. MARTIN ALLERDALE GRAINGER. *Forest Hist. 1967 11(3): 6-13.* Grainger was born in London (1874), reared in Australia, and educated at Blundell's and King's College, Cambridge. He was an adventurer in mining and logging in British Columbia and published a novel *Woodsmen of the West* in England. He was a prolific writer throughout his lifetime. As a secretary to the minister of lands in British Columbia, he was influential in passage of the Forest Act of 1912 and the creation of the provincial Forest Service. As Chief Forester, he promoted protection, a timber-testing laboratory, creation of the University of British Columbia Department of Forestry, and reforesta-

tion. After his death in 1941, the Forest Service appropriately named after him Grainger Creek in the Cascade Mountains. Illus.
                    B. A. Vatter

3476. Silverman, Peter Guy. MILITARY AID TO CIVIL POWER IN BRITISH COLUMBIA; THE LABOR STRIKES AT WELLINGTON AND STEVESTON, 1890, 1900. *Pacific Northwest Q. 1970 61(3): 156-164.* Relates the uncommon use of national military force to maintain local law and order on two occasions in British Columbia (1890 and 1900). Labor strife involving coal miners and fishermen provided the impetus for calling out the militia in both instances, but there was little or no justification for military involvement.   C. C. Gorchels

3477. Stainsby, Donald. VANCOUVER ISLAND'S WEST COAST. *Can. Geographical J. [Canada] 1965 70(2): 50-57.* Describes a winter voyage of the *Tahsis Prince,* the only vessel to maintain a scheduled service linking the communities on the west coast of Vancouver Island. Illus., map.   A. H. Lawrance

3478. Stemo, L. Johanne. ESTATE AT ASHCROFT. *Beaver [Canada] 1963 294(Autumn): 50-54.* Clement Francis Cornwall (1835-1910) and Henry Tennant Cornwall (1837-1892) established a pioneer farm on the Thompson River in 1859 that soon became an important ranch, sawmilling, and staging town. Aspects of life there are described from Henry's diary. Clement was elected a member of the first legislative assembly of British Columbia, appointed to the Senate at Confederation, and became lieutenant governor of the province in 1881. Illus.
                    L. F. S. Upton

3479. Stubbs, Roy St. G. SIR MATTHEW BAILLIE BEGBIE. *Tr. of the Hist. and Sci. Soc. of Manitoba [Canada] 1968/69 (25): 49-74.* An account of the life of Begbie (1819-94) who went to British Columbia in 1858 as its first judge, and later became its first Chief Justice. Many stories of his conduct on the bench testify to his success in imposing British order. Gives accounts of several actions tried before him between 1858 and 1891; Begbie never lost the habit of getting himself into hot water. Although he fell short of greatness as a judge he was the right man in the right place at the right time. 66 notes.   L. F. S. Upton

3480. Thomson, Don W. DEVILLE AND THE SURVEY CAMERA IN CANADA. *Can. Geographical J. [Canada] 1966 72(2): 52-57.* Discusses the use of the camera in surveying and mapping British Columbia. The system was developed under Edouard Gaston Deville, surveyor general of Canada from 1885 to 1924. Photographs, diagram.
                    A. H. Lawrance

3481. Weber, Ralph E. RIOT IN VICTORIA, 1860. *J. of Negro Hist. 1971 56(2): 141-148.* Much anti-Negro feeling existed on Vancouver Island after 1850. Most of the differences concerned the extension of voting privileges to the Negro immigrants of the region. Reproduces three newspaper selections from the *Colonist* of Victoria which illustrate the expectations and frustrations of Negroes on the island. 4 notes.
                    R. S. Melamed

3482. Wells, Oliver N. RETURN OF THE SALISH LOOM. *Beaver [Canada] 1966 297(Spring): 40-45.* Blankets were one of the principal trade items of the Salish and an index of wealth before the Hudson's Bay Company introduced fur and salmon trading with the opening of the Fort Langley post in 1827. Gold seekers and missionaries ended the blanket economy. The recent revival of blanket weaving and one of the looms now in use are described. Illus.   L. F. S. Upton

3483. Wynne, Robert E. AMERICAN LABOR LEADERS AND THE VANCOUVER ANTI-ORIENTAL RIOT. *Pacific Northwest Q. 1966 57(4): 172-179.* Immigration of Orientals to British Columbia from 1887 to 1907 (with as many as 8,125 Japanese arriving in 1907 alone) caused friction and ultimately violence. The author shows the influence of Americans from the State of Washington in stimulating unrest. A description of mob rioting of 6 September 1907 gives details of the factors leading to violence and reasons for the moderate aftermath.
                    C. C. Gorchels

3484. Young, Peggy. NOOTKA SOUND. *Beaver [Canada] 1966 297(Summer): 28-34.* The first Europeans in these waters off the west coast of Vancouver Island were a Spanish expedition in 1774. Captain James Cook named the sound King George's Sound in March 1778. After the publication of Cook's journals, fur traders took an interest in the area, and the Spanish decided to assert their claim. The result was the "Spanish Armament Crisis" of 1790. In 1795 the Nootka Convention was ratified by Britain and Spain after Captain Vancouver and the Spaniard, Quadra, had failed to reach agreement on the spot. By 1825 the fur trade passed beyond Nootka. The area is currently little developed, although iron ore is mined and a large sawmill is under construction. Illus.

L. F. S. Upton

Yukon Territory and Northwest Territories

3485.　Baxter, Dow V.　THE CHILKOOT TRAIL THEN AND NOW.　*Beaver [Canada] 1964 295(Summer): 10-17.* Reminiscences by Ben Card, son of the proprietor of the Seattle Hotel, Sheep Camp, in 1898, compared with observations made on the spot in 1963. Illus.

L. F. S. Upton

3486.　Berton, Pierre.　FORTYMILE: AMERICAN OUTPOST IN THE CANADIAN NORTH.　*U. of Toronto Q. [Canada] 1958 27(4): 413-423.* A description of the Yukon mining town of Fortymile which was located on Canadian soil near the present Dawson City, but which was American in every other respect. Established by Americans in 1887, it was much like the roaring Wild West communities of the United States in its social characteristics. During the mid-1890's Canadian officials imposed Canadian law-and-order and most of the Americans moved across the border to Alaska leaving Fortymile a ghost town.

W. L. Bowers

3487.　Bond, Marshall, Jr., ed.　TO THE KLONDIKE: WITH A BIG DOG WHO MET JACK LONDON.　*Am. West 1969 6(1): 44-48.* Marshall Bond, Sr., and his brother witnessed the 1897 arrival in Seattle of the first gold cargo from the Klondike gold area of Canada and Alaska. Inspired, they were grubstaked by their father and departed within a week for Skagway by ship, arriving ahead of the main rush. From there they traveled by packtrain down the Yukon to Dawson City. At Dawson the brothers became friends with Jack London. Jack, one of the dogs they brought with them from Seattle, became the hero of London's *Call of the Wild* (1903). This is a selection from Bond's journal entries and letters edited by his son; from a forthcoming book. 6 illus.　D. L. Smith

3488.　Bronson, William.　RUSH TO THE YUKON.　*Am. West 1965 2(2): 66-80, 93.* A 22 photograph essay of the Klondike gold rush of the 1890's. Its primary concern is the difficult journey over Chilkoot and White Passes to Dawson. Photographs principally from Bancroft Library, map.　D. L. Smith

3489.　Ferrel, Ed.　DOWN THE RIVER TRAIL OF '98 IN A MODERN CANOE.　*Beaver [Canada] 1964 295(Autumn): 48-54.* Describes a trip from Lake Bennett to Dawson and then to Circle City, Alaska, following the water route taken by gold seekers. Illus.

L. F. S. Upton

3490.　Judd, David.　SEVENTY-FIVE YEARS OF RESOURCE ADMINISTRATION IN NORTHERN CANADA.　*Polar Record [Great Britain] 1969 14(93): 791-806.* During the Klondike Gold Rush the Dominion government maintained law and order but most social services were left to private organizations. Government interest in the North declined from 1905 to 1920, when the discovery of oil led to further field activity. Attempts were made to preserve native economies by protecting furbearing animals and introducing reindeer. Except for geologic mapping there was little government activity during the Depression. From 1958 to 1965 the government invested 86 million dollars to build a railroad into a new mining district; another 100 million dollars was spent to build roads. Petroleum exploration in the Arctic Islands stimulated government resource controls and research. Probably future official activity will concentrate on improving transportation, participating financially in

industries offering employment to northern natives, and ensuring that private investment includes Canadian participation. Based on government reports; notes, biblio.　L. L. Hubbard

3491.　Leithead, J. Edward.　THE KLONDIKE STAMPEDE IN DIME NOVELS.　*Am. Book Collector 1971 21(4): 23-29.* Before the Klondike stampede in the last decade of the 19th century, the gold rush was not an unfamiliar setting to dime novels in the United States; however, the romance of the gold rush made its greatest impression in the serial tales set in the Klondike gold fields in Canada's Yukon Territory. Reviews the Klondike dime novels as collectors' items, discussing their authors and publishers and providing authoritative checklists. 8 illus.

D. A. Yanchisin

3492.　Lotz, J. R.　THE SQUATTERS OF WHITEHORSE: A STUDY OF THE PROBLEMS OF NEW NORTHERN SETTLEMENTS.　*Arctic [Canada] 1965 18(3): 173-188.* Many Whitehorse residents have built shacks on government or company land, without authorization or proper public utilities. In summer, many of the men work on construction projects, returning home to live on unemployment benefits during the winter. Formerly a refuge for the nonconformist, government regulations now prevent further squatting. "The squatters of Whitehorse illustrate the social and economic dilemma of those who wish to live in the old northern way in a region with a tenuous economic base." Data from the author's survey, Dominion statistics, and a Central Mortgage and Housing Corporation study.　J. E. Caswell

3493.　Lotz, Jim and Innes-Taylor, Alan.　THE YUKON DITCH. *Can. Geographical J. [Canada] 1967 74(4): 124-131.* In the fall of 1966, the last of the great gold dredges closed down in the Dawson area. In all the years of gold production, the Klondike produced a quarter of a billion dollar's worth of the yellow stuff. A.N.C. Treadgold was the one man most responsible for the large amounts of gold taken out of the gravel of the Klondike. Treadgold formed the Yukon Gold Company in 1906 and with large numbers of laborers, vast amounts of material, and hard work he constructed the Yukon Ditch consisting of 38 miles of ditch, 19.6 miles of flume, and 12.6 miles of pipe. It dropped the water from Ogilvie Mountains a total of 1,112.8 feet in 70.2 miles. Between 1908 and 1919 the enterprise paid 11 million dollars in dividends. Illus., map.

C. J. Allard

3494.　McLeod, D. M.　LIQUOR CONTROL IN THE NORTHWEST TERRITORIES: THE PERMIT SYSTEM, 1870-91.　*Saskatchewan Hist. [Canada] 1963 16(3): 81-89.* The system by which liquor could be obtained only by permission of the Lieutenant-Governor was intended, in 1873, to protect the Indians. It developed into a regular means of supplying the settlers but was fraught with administrative difficulties. Meanwhile the prohibitionists fought to restrict the issue of permits. In 1891 the system came to an end when the people of the Territories were given the power to determine their own liquor policy.

A. H. Lawrance

3495.　Peake, F. A.　CHURCH AND SOCIETY DURING THE KLONDIKE GOLD RUSH.　*Hist. Mag. of the Protestant Episcopal Church 1969 38(3): 219-235.* Sketches the pioneer society of Dawson and the surrounding territory at the turn of the 19th century, together with statistical details of religious affiliations, sex, population and ethnic origins of the more than 25 thousand prospectors who poured into the Klondike in search of gold. Based on primary and secondary sources; 23 notes.　E. G. Roddy

3496.　Thomson, Don W.　THE YUKON AND WILLIAM OGILVIE.　*Can. Geographical J. [Canada] 1966 73(6): 194-197.* William Ogilvie was an explorer, surveyor, administrator, and natural diplomat. In 1887 he surveyed the 141st meridian, the Alaska-Yukon boundary, to determine the point at which it intersected the Yukon River. Later, during the Klondike gold rush days, he became famous for his honesty as a settler of claim disputes. In 1898 he accepted the position of Commissioner of the Yukon Territory. He gradually restored law and order and set up new mining regulations. He left the office in 1901 with high commendation. At the age of 66 he contracted pneumonia near James Bay and died in a Winnipeg hospital in November 1912. Today a mountain, a range, a glacier, a valley, and a town bear his name. Illus., map.

W. A. Buckman

5. THE ALASKAN SCENE

General

3497. Eels, Francis R. THE FAIRBANKS ECONOMIC COMMUNITY. *Arctic [Canada] 1967 20(2): 134-137.* Fairbanks, located in the Tanana River valley, is the second largest city in Alaska and a trade and transportation center for communities scattered over 227 thousand square miles. Founded in 1901, its population in 1967 was 19 thousand, with 11 thousand in the suburbs. Gold mining was of importance until 1942. Government employment is now the mainstay of the community. Fairbanks is of major significance as a transportation center, freight being transferred from train and truck to aircraft for delivery throughout central, western, and northern Alaska. If mining increases in that area, Fairbanks will profit. Agriculture is developing at a slow rate. Much timber is imported. The University of Alaska with its Geophysical Institute and nearby space science facilities constitute important economic forces. Almost half the 70,854 tourists who came to Alaska in 1964 reached Fairbanks. Pan American World Airways has proposed to make Fairbanks a stop on a great circle route from New York to Japan.
J. E. Caswell

3498. Hickel, Walter J. THE WEALTH OF THE LAND AND THE GROWTH OF ALASKA. *J. of the West 1967 6(3): 357-361.* In the hundred years since the United States acquired Alaska the mainspring of its growth has been the development of natural resources. The author contends that this pattern will continue and notes that individuals and companies are being attracted by the oil, timber, fish, and minerals that abound in the State. Illus.
D. N. Brown

3499. Hinckley, Ted C. ICE FROM "SEWARD'S ICEBOX." *Pacific Historian 1967 11(3): 28-38.* Over the story of exploitation of new mineral wealth in California and Alaska from 1850 to 1870 the author superimposes the story of shipping ice from Alaska to warmer climates. Alaska depended more on the San Francisco trade than did the Californians on Alaska. The trade had begun in the days of Russian America when ships from Fort Ross, later Sutter's Fort, traded with the Mexicans and the Americans. But as trade slumped the Russians sold Fort Ross to Sutter and eventually Alaska to America. Gradually, gold and whaling increased the American commitment to the West Coast and even before the sale of Alaska an ice company began trading in the commodity. In exchange wheat went to Sitka. The American Russian Commercial Company's contract for ice simply ran over into a new American period and was included in the Alaska purchase price. From the ice trade the author traces the growth of new industries: fishing, canning, the seal trade, and the vigor with which San Francisco merchants sought to dominate or monopolize them. Documented from newspapers, manuscripts, and published sources; illus.
T. R. Cripps

3500. Hinckley, Ted C. SHELDON JACKSON AS PRESERVER OF ALASKA'S NATIVE CULTURE. *Pacific Hist. R. 1964 33(4): 411-424.* Recounts the work of a Presbyterian missionary in collecting artifacts and information on Alaskan culture. Jackson helped to found the Alaska Natural History and Ethnology Society and the Sheldon Jackson Museum.
J. McCutcheon

3501. Hunt, William R. TO BRIDGE THE GAP. *Beaver [Canada] 1969 300(Summer): 50-53.* Traces the idea of establishing a route from Europe to North America via the Bering Strait. John Ledyard was turned back 4,000 miles from his starting place at Saint Petersburg in 1788. Captain John Dundas Cochrane of the Royal Navy crossed Russia to Kamchatka in 1820. Individual hopes were replaced by those of the Western Union Telegraph Company in 1865 and a variety of railway promoters. Harry De Windt traveled vast distances at the turn of the present century to assess the feasibility of a rail link across the strait. Illus.
L. F. S. Upton

3502. Jensen, Billie Barnes. ALASKA'S PRE-KLONDIKE MINING: THE MEN, THE METHODS, AND THE MINERALS. *J. of the West 1967 6(3): 417-432.* The American miner who went to Alaska after the United States purchased that territory did not work a virgin field, for the Russians were not without some knowledge of the available mineral resources. Some Russians were very active in mining, but it was Americans who exposed much of Alaska's mineral wealth even before the great Klondike strike. Individuals and companies both played an important part in the development of this frontier. The author discusses the various minerals which were mined, the employment and exploitation of Indians and Chinese in an effort to cope with the serious lack of labor, and the development of mining law. Concludes that mining in Alaska followed the same patterns as in other areas and that this frontier paved the way for later permanent settlers. Based largely on newspapers and other published sources; 67 notes.
D. N. Brown

3503. Kleber, Louis C. ALASKA . . . RUSSIA'S FOLLY. *Hist. Today [Great Britain] 1967 17(4): 229-235.* Describes the competition between Russia, Spain, Britain, and the United States for the exploitation of Alaska. The author states that only through Russia's involvement in the Crimean War was Secretary of State William Henry Seward able to purchase Alaska for two cents an acre on 30 March 1867. The development of Alaska since that time is discussed. Based on secondary sources.
L. A. Knafla

3504. Lindsey, David. ALASKA: FROM RUSSIA WITH LOVE. *Mankind 1967 1(3): 75-84.* A survey of American interest and disinterest in Alaska and the circumstances behind the purchase of that territory by the United States in 1867. American reaction to the new acquisition was immediate, and the greatest real estate bargain in history was said to have been the purchase of a "daft" Secretary of State, William Henry Seward. Illus.
P. D. Thomas

3505. Long, John Sherman. WEBB'S FRONTIER AND ALASKA. *Southwest R. 1971 56(4): 301-309.* Analyzes the Alaskan frontier with the approach that Walter Prescott Webb used to study the Great Plains. Comparisons are made with the Great Plains in the following areas: the impact and influence of geography, the effect on Indian cultures, and the problems of agriculture (including ranching and farming). The analysis suggests "that the region is a laboratory for a review of the opinions of historians on the role and significance of the frontier in the saga of the American people. Alaska is a culmination of frontier patterns."
D. F. Henderson

3506. Lotz, J. R. A NEW WAY TO ALASKA. *Can. Geographical J. [Canada] 1964 68(2): 52-55.* Describes the new ferry route to Alaska, linking Prince Rupert with Skagway, and makes reference to the history of places on the route. Photographs.
A. H. Lawrance

3507. Moore, Terris. ALASKA'S FIRST AMERICAN CENTURY: THE VIEW AHEAD. *Polar Record [Great Britain] 14(88): 3-13.* Summarizes the history of Alaska from the establishment of the Russian-American Company (1799). The author points out that Alaska is larger than all four Scandinavian countries together, but growth projections based on that comparison fail to take into account the centuries Scandinavia has had to develop a population and its "proximity to the European markets, and intellectual and cultural centres." Also discussed is the failure of present population growth to justify the controversial Ramparts Dam. However, Alaska remains in the top five of the fastest growing States of the Union, while certain other States have been losing population. 12 notes.
J. E. Caswell

3508. Pierce, Richard A. NEW LIGHT ON IVAN PETROFF, HISTORIAN OF ALASKA. *Pacific Northwest Q. 1968 59(1): 1-10.* Concludes that Petroff was an able historian despite his lapses as a "composing-room Munchausen" and a "falsifier of public documents." As an expert on Alaskan history, Petroff wrote much for Hubert Howe Bancroft. Details about Petroff's writing here are spiced with accounts of his misadventures as a three-time army deserter and enigmatic qualities to which "only psychiatry would have the key."
C. C. Gorchels

3509. Rasche, Herbert H. ALASKA PURCHASE CENTENNIAL: 1867-1967. *Arctic [Canada] 1967 20(2): 63-76.* A survey of Alaska's history. Vitus Bering and Alexei Chirikov first sighted and surveyed the Alaskan coast in 1741. The first permanent Russian post was established in 1784. Russian desire to withdraw to a more readily defended boundary led her to seek a friendly power as purchaser. After purchase by the United States in 1867, sealing rights were leased to a commercial firm, surveys were begun by the Coast Survey and in 1895 by the Geological Survey. Gold strikes caused a momentary boom, and were followed by the entry of large corporations into mining, fish canning, and lumbering. Not until 1912 did Congress grant Alaska territorial status. After World War II had started, military bases were rapidly developed, and the Alcan Highway built. The Cold War demanded continued development of defenses. Statehood was achieved in 1959, permitting more effective economic development. Illus., 2 maps, biblio. J. E. Caswell

3510. Ray, Dorothy Jean. KAUWERAK, LOST VILLAGE OF ALASKA. *Beaver [Canada] 1964 295(Autumn): 4-13.* Investigates the legend of a lost village in the heart of the Seward Peninsula reputedly founded by Cossacks from Siberia in the mid-17th century. The reason for the story lies in the fact that Kauwerak differed from coastal villages in having dwellings of turf and logs entirely above ground. The settlement dwindled until the Gold Rush of 1898, when the boom-town of Mary's Igloo appeared briefly on its site. Illus. L. F. S. Upton

Russian America

3511. Allen, Robert V. ALASKA BEFORE 1867 IN SOVIET LITERATURE. *Q. J. of the Lib. of Congress 1966 23(3): 243-257.* Covers mainly Russian-language articles and monographs of the Soviet period in the Library of Congress relating to the discovery, exploration, and administration of Alaska before its acquisition by the United States. "Russian rule in Alaska and the economic activities of the Russian American Company [have] been neglected by Soviet writers," as has Alaskan ethnography. Hence "Americans interested in the history of Alaska still must rely heavily on H. H. Bancroft and on the works listed in Wickersham's bibliography, as other publications are useful chiefly for correcting detail without adding a large amount of new information." Documented, illus. H. J. Graham

3512. Belov, Mikhail. THE SALE OF ALASKA. *Mankind 1967 1(3): 74, 85-88.* Examines the domestic and foreign problems which led to Russia's sale of Alaska. The Russian-American Company was unable to effectively utilize the resources of Alaska because of Russia's internal problems. Just prior to the sale of Alaska in 1866, there were only about 600 Russians in the area. The czarist government, feeling that it could not defend the area, sold it instead to the United States. Illus. P. D. Thomas

3513. Boon, Thomas C. B. WILLIAM WEST KIRKBY: FIRST ANGLICAN MISSIONARY TO THE LOUCHEUX. *Beaver [Canada] 1965 295(Spring): 36-43.* William W. Kirkby (1828-1907) went to the northwest from England for the Church Missionary Society as a missionary school master. He was ordained a priest in 1856. He journeyed to Fort Yukon, at the junction of the Porcupine and Yukon rivers in what is now Alaska, in 1861 and 1862. Lengthy excerpts from the account Kirkby wrote for *The Nor'Wester* of Red River, 5 March 1862, are used to describe the trip and the customs of the Kutchin or Loucheux Indians. This people lived in the area from the Mackenzie River to Bering Strait, north of latitude 65. Illus. L. F. S. Upton

3514. Gilbert, Benjamin Franklin. THE ALASKA PURCHASE. *J. of the West 1964 3(2): 163-174.* United States interest in Alaska dates back to 1845, when Senator Robert J. Walker proposed to President-elect Polk that Russia might be persuaded to cede the territory. Not until the Crimean War in 1853 did it seem likely that Russia might dispose of the territory. Despite British and French intervention in the war, Alaska remained Russian, but the conflict did cause a reexamination of Russian interests and, after the war, the effort was revived. In 1857 Baron de Stoeckl urged the sale, but, despite increasing contacts between official and unofficial representatives of the two governments, nothing resulted until after the Civil War. Russian imperialism in the Far East, inability

to defend her overseas possessions, her lack of reason for additional territory, and the financial decline of the Russian-American Company were all reasons why Russia agreed to sell the territory to the United States in 1867. Stoeckl and Secretary of State Seward agreed to the terms of a treaty, including a purchase price of 7,200,000 dollars, on 30 March, and on 9 April the Senate, despite the jeers of the press, ratified the agreement. On 18 October 1867 the formal transfer occurred and the United States had acquired its first noncontiguous territory. Published sources, 61 notes. D. N. Brown

3515. Nichols, Robert, ed. and Croskey, Robert, ed. THE CONDITION OF THE ORTHODOX CHURCH IN RUSSIAN AMERICA; INNOKENTII VENIAMINOV'S HISTORY OF THE RUSSIAN CHURCH IN ALASKA. *Pacific Northwest Q. 1972 63(2): 41-54.* Translation of a short history of the Russian Orthodox Church in Alaska [by Innokentii (Ioann Evsieevich Popov-Veniaminov), a Russian Orthodox priest, and originally published in Russian in 1840] which describes activities of the church and its followers in Alaska and vicinity in 1839. The narrative identifies location of church buildings, gives statistics on members, and has observations on the deplorable living conditions among natives. Also includes the earlier history of the growth of Russian religious efforts, 1759-1839. Mentions the "Aleuty" and delineates their characteristics. 41 notes. C. C. Gorchels

3516. Pierce, Richard A. ALASKA IN 1867 AS VIEWED FROM VICTORIA. *Queen's Q. [Canada] 1967 74(4): 666-673.* Excerpts from newspapers of the time tell how Canadians reacted against the U.S. acquisition of Alaska out of a fear of U.S. expansionism. U.S. possession of Alaska failed, however, to become a great barrier to Canadian interests. Further described are the conditions and events in Sitka during the transition from Russian to U.S. control. M. Abrash

3517. Pierce, Richard A. IVAN PETROFF AND THE FAR NORTHWEST. *J. of the West 1964 3(4): 436-439.* The Russian-born translator Ivan Petroff aided Hubert Bancroft in writing the histories of Alaska, the northwest coast, and California. The primary biographical source of Petroff is Bancroft's *Literary Industries* published in San Francisco in 1890. The author suggests that there are numerous inaccuracies if not outright fabrications in this sketch. He presents new information on this minor figure and suggests that his post-Bancroft career casts doubt on the accuracy of some of his translations. Therefore, a reexamination of the Russian era of Alaskan and northwest coast history is necessary. Documented from published sources, 6 notes. D. N. Brown

3518. Pierce, Richard A. PRINCE D. P. MAKSUTOV: LAST GOVERNOR OF RUSSIAN AMERICA. *J. of the West 1967 6(3): 395-416.* On 18 October 1867 Alaska was formally transferred to the United States. Presiding over the liquidation of the affairs of the Russian Government and of the Russian-American Company was Prince Dmitrii P. Maksutov, the chief manager of the company establishments, a position tantamount to that of governor. The title of prince was granted to the family in the 17th century. Dmitrii, born in 1832, was educated by tutors and at the Naval Academy at Saint Petersburg. He served in the Russian Navy and in 1858 was appointed assistant chief manager of the Russian-American colonies. In 1863, by order of the Emperor, he was appointed acting chief manager. The author details the life of Maksutov and his family in Alaska and the part he played in the sale of the company's assets in that territory. The prince died in 1889. Based largely on newspaper and other published sources; illus., 66 notes. D. N. Brown

3519. Schulte, Nordholt, J. W. DE AANKOOP VAN ALASKA DOOR AMERIKA [The acquisition of Alaska by America]. *Spiegel Historiael [Netherlands] 1968 3(5): 259-264.* Discusses the events leading up to the U.S. acquisition of Alaska 100 years ago. William Henry Seward, U.S. Secretary of State, headed the negotiations for the American side. He had a vision of America as a great power, and it was with this in mind that he pressured for the acquisition of Alaska. From his countrymen he received little support for his ideal; they settled the matter with a smiling shrug, because they wanted to thank the Russians for their sympathy during the Civil War. G. van Roon

3520. Sherwood, Morgan B. A NOTE ON THE PETROFF NOTE. *J. of the West 1964 3(4): 440.* Comments on the note by Richard A. Pierce which appear in *Journal of the West* 1964 3(4): 436-439. The author maintains that most histories of Alaska are overly dependent upon Bancroft's *History of Alaska 1730-1885,* and suggests that the main pillar of Bancroft's volume, the labors of Ivan Petroff, is beginning to weaken. Agreement is reached with Pierce that a scholarly reexamination of the Russian era of Alaskan history is necessary.   D. N. Brown

3521. Sherwood, Morgan B. SCIENCE IN RUSSIAN AMERICA, 1741 TO 1865. *Pacific Northwest Q. 1967 58(1): 33-39.* Scientific observations were a by-product of the pursuit of furs in Alaska by Russians almost from the time of Bering's expedition in 1741 to 1865 when the Russians were trading as far up the Yukon River as Tanana. Achievements in natural history, geology, geography, botany, ethnology, and meteorology are cited; and the names of men who made scientific reports are listed. Also mentioned are some cogent activities by Englishmen and Americans in Alaska in the middle of the 19th century.
                                                                    C. C. Gorchels

3522. Shipley, Nan. ANNE AND ALEXANDER MURRAY. *Beaver [Canada] 1967 298(Winter): 22-26.* Anne Campbell (1831-1907) met Alexander Hunter Murray (1819-74) in 1846 as she was returning home from Miss Davis' school at Lockport. They were married and sent to the Hudson Bay Company's isolated new post of Fort Yukon in what is now Alaska. Murray kept a notebook with sketches of life in the wilderness. By 1856 he had won promotion to chief trader and in 1862 was in charge of Lower Fort Garry. He retired in 1865. Illus.
                                                                    L. F. S. Upton

3523. Wheeler, Mary E. EMPIRES IN CONFLICT AND COOPERATION: THE "BOSTONIANS" AND THE RUSSIAN AMERICAN COMPANY. *Pacific Hist. R. 1971 40(4): 419-441.* Analyzes Russo-American competition and cooperation as viewed in St. Petersburg and the Alaskan colonies. By 1795, America was the main threat to Russian domination of the Pacific fur trade and rival to the newly chartered Russian-American Company under the direction of Alexsandr Andreevich Baranov (1746-1819). Hampered by constant lack of cooperation from St. Petersburg in sending essential supplies, ships, and leadership to the colonies, Baranov found it expedient to cooperate with the "Bostonians" in joint fur hunting expeditions. Meanwhile, negotiations continued regarding trade and territorial rights between the two countries, culminating in the Russo-American Convention of 1824 which marked the end of Russian expansion. That conclusion was as much related, however, to the policies of the Russian Government which had resulted in the establishment of only eight permanent settlements during the previous 40 years. Based on primary and secondary Russian and American sources; 74 notes.
                                                                    E. C. Hyslop

3524. White, John I. THE PURCHASE OF "RUSSIAN AMERICA." *Am. Hist. Illus. 1967 2(3): 12-21.* The acquisition of Alaska—from the original offer of 5 million dollars by the United States in the spring of 1867 through the flag-raising ceremonies in October of that year—is described. Emphasis is given to Edouard de Stoeckl, Russian minister to the United States, and the conclusion indicates he may have spent as much as 65 thousand dollars for lobbyists to get the purchase approved by the US Senate.
                                                                    J. D. Filipiak

Pre-Statehood Alaska, 1867-1959

3525. Benoit, Raymond. JACK LONDON'S "THE CALL OF THE WILD." *Am. Q. 1968 20(2, pt. 1): 246-248.* Examines London's novel (1903) in the light of its pastoral characteristics. Buck, the dog who leaves "civilization" for the wilds of Alaska, is depicted as escaping from the demands of a corrupt society. London contrasts the trio of Charles, Hal, and Mercedes, examples of an "artificial and complex civilization," with the noble John Thornton and his cohorts. Even the language of the novel presents contrasting moods and styles. 2 notes.   R. S. Pickett

3526. Bloom, Jessie S. THE JEWS OF ALASKA. *Am. Jewish Arch. 1963 15(2): 97-116.* Wide-reaching recollections of Alaskan life, 1898 through 1959, by an Irish-Jewish pioneer, who with her husband Robert was a leader in educational and community life in Fairbanks for over 50 years.
                                                                    A. B. Rollins

3527. Bronson, William. NOME. *Am. West 1969 6(4): 20-31.* When placer gold was first panned from the Snake River in the summer of 1898, a new gold rush was triggered. Most of those who flocked to Alaska's Seward Peninsula that summer were disappointed stampeders from the Klondike. When summer arrived in 1899 thousands more had helped create a new boomtown, called Nome, and were prepared to get rich. What really ended the Klondike rush was the news from Nome that its beaches and tidewater contained the richest diggings of that sort ever known. By the height of the 1900 season some 18 thousand men and women were participating in the exciting venture. The beach sands were soon worked out. Newcomers fanned out further into the interior and occasionally met with success, but generally did not. This last great American gold rush reached its peak in 1900 and then the area declined in importance. Today Nome is cold and remote, still clinging to its harborless location on a stretch of the Bering Sea that is frozen solid for seven months of the year. Map, 23 photos.   D. L. Smith

3528. Bucksar, Richard G. THE ALASKA HIGHWAY: BACKGROUND TO DECISION. *Arctic [Canada] 1968 21(4): 215-222.* The first serious consideration given to constructing the Alaska Highway dates from the founding of two associations in Fairbanks and Dawson City to stimulate public interest. In 1930 the US Congress authorized 10,000 dollars for a feasibility and economics study. The report was made in 1933, but bills to implement it failed. At that time the cost was estimated at 2 million dollars for the Alaska section and 12 million dollars for the Canada section. Only after the Japanese attack on Pearl Harbor was the project and appropriation approved by the US President. On 14 February 1942 the Chief of Engineers issued a directive. Nine months and six days later the road was completed at a cost of 139,794,507 dollars, 10 times the peacetime estimate and 14 years after the initial planning began. Table, 8 notes.   J. E. Caswell

3529. Buzanski, Peter M. ALASKA AND NINETEENTH CENTURY AMERICAN DIPLOMACY. *J. of the West 1967 6(3): 451-467.* Discusses some of the diplomatic problems which arose after the U.S. purchased Alaska in 1867. Briefly covered are the diplomacy of the purchase, the pelagic sealing controversy, the North Pacific Sealing Convention, and the boundary dispute between the United States and Canada. The author concludes that the acquisition of Alaska complicated American foreign affairs, but that the bargain made in 1867 was well worth the trouble. Based on published sources and government reports, 37 notes.
                                                                    D. N. Brown

3530. Campbell, Charles S., Jr. THE BERING SEA SETTLEMENTS OF 1892. *Pacific Hist. R. 1963 32(4): 347-367.* Traces the involved diplomatic negotiations of the United States, Canada, and Great Britain, 1890-92, which led to arbitration in 1893.
                                                                    J. McCutcheon

3531. Gilbert, Benjamin Franklin. ECONOMIC DEVELOPMENTS IN ALASKA, 1867-1910. *J. of the West 1965 4(4): 504-521.* Presents the highlights of the economic development of Alaska from the date of its acquisition by the United States until 1910. The author traces the fur industry which during the early American period was the most vital economic factor in the territory's development, and devotes some attention to Russian mining activity and its later development under American control. While gold attracted the most interest, copper and coal were also mined to some degree. Prior to 1910 agricultural pursuits were confined to small areas and were largely experimental, but the fishing industry was of real importance to the economy of Alaska by 1910. Based on published sources; map, 104 notes.   D. N. Brown

3532. Hinckley, Ted C. THE EARLY ALASKAN MINISTRY OF S. HALL YOUNG, 1878-1888. *J. of Presbyterian Hist. 1968 46(3): 175-196.* Sketches the work of the Reverend and Mrs. Samuel Hall Young as Presbyterian missionaries in Alaska. Young, the son of a Presbyterian minister, was educated at Wooster College and Western Seminary where he heard Sheldon Jackson speak on behalf of Alaskan mission needs and volunteered for service there. Young was commissioned by the Presbyterian Board of Home Missions in 1878 and assigned to a mission station at Wrangell. He married Fannie Kellogg, a missionary teacher already in Alaska, and they engaged in educational work from 1878 to 1888. They first established a day school and then in 1884 began a residential agricultural school, the Tlingit Training Academy. The academy duplicated existing facilities, became a source of considerable contention, and finally failed in the absence of sufficient support. It was closed in 1888, and the Youngs returned to the United States. Based on published materials and manuscript collections of the Presbyterian Historical Society; 76 notes.

S. C. Pearson, Jr.

3533. Hinckley, Ted C. EXCERPTS FROM THE LETTERS OF DR. CLARENCE THWING, PRESBYTERIAN MISSIONARY TO WRANGELL, ALASKA, DURING THE MID-1890'S. *J. of Presbyterian Hist. 1963 41(1): 37-55.* Thwing, a doctor of medicine, following ordination and an internship at the Presbyterians' main mission center at Sitka, went to Wrangell as pastor of the church there. The 25 letters quoted are drawn from his *Letter Book, 1892-1895,* deposited at the San Francisco Theological Seminary, San Anselmo, California, and provide a realistic and detailed picture of the life of an Alaskan missionary and of the community in which he worked.

W. D. Metz

3534. Hinckley, Ted C. THE INSIDE PASSAGE: A POPULAR GILDED AGE TOUR. *Pacific Northwest Q. 1965 56(2): 67-74.* Alaska as a magnet for tourists, 1867-1900, including methods of traveling, attractions, the role of residents, and the names of distinguished visitors, with special attention to Sitka and Indians. Documented.

C. C. Gorchels

3535. Hinckley, Theodore C. and Hinckley, Caryl. IVAN PETROFF'S JOURNAL OF A TRIP TO ALASKA IN 1878. *J. of the West 1966 5(1): 25-70.* The first publication of an original journal located in the Bancroft Library, Berkeley, California. The editors have included much information on Petroff, who aided Hubert Howe Bancroft in writing his history of Alaska. Petroff had much firsthand knowledge of Alaska and he continued to research and write about the territory after his employment with Bancroft ended. Some historians believe that Petroff was an imposter, that he was not a Russian, and that he forged some of the historical materials he delivered to Bancroft. The editors pass no judgment on that question, but they do conclude that he not only collected much valuable data but also played a significant role in the pioneer history of Alaska. The journal itself records a trip he made to Alaska in 1878 in search of materials for the Bancroft Library in San Francisco. It provides a picture of the land, the people, and the problems of that territory only a few years after it became an American possession. 116 notes.

D. N. Brown

3536. Hinckley, Ted C. THE PRESBYTERIAN LEADERSHIP IN PIONEER ALASKA. *J. of Am. Hist. 1966 52(4): 742-756.* Describes late 19th-century Presbyterian missionary activity in Alaska. The author concludes that Presbyterian leadership in Alaska was a reflection of such contemporary currents as the social gospel movement, civil service and temperance reform, women's rights, improved public education, and compassion for the "vanishing American."

H. J. Silverman

3537. Hinckley, Ted C. PROSPECTORS, PROFITS AND PREJUDICE. *Am. West 1965 2(2): 58-65.* Even though Juneau prospered for a while on its placer gold diggings they soon played out. On nearby Douglas Island the Alaska Mill and Mining Company introduced modern machinery to exploit the lode. Chinese labor was all that could be obtained because of the low wages the company had to pay of necessity. In 1886 the discontented unemployed miners of Juneau crossed to the island, took the Chinese by force, and shipped them off to Wrangell. Illus., biblio. note.

D. L. Smith

3538. Hinckley, Ted C. SHELDON JACKSON COLLEGE: HISTORIC NUCLEUS OF THE PRESBYTERIAN ENTERPRISE IN ALASKA. *J. of Presbyterian Hist. 1971 49(1): 59-79.* Dr. Sheldon Jackson, prominent Presbyterian clergyman, organized Protestant missionary and educational efforts for Alaskan native children at Sitka after the Army closed its temporary school there in 1877. Jackson persuaded a young Yale graduate, Reverend John Green Brady, to establish a ministry at Sitka, at that time a rough, isolated trading and mining boom-town. Jackson was rivaled in his efforts by Dr. Aaron Lindsley, a Presbyterian leader from Portland, Oregon. Lindsley sent his niece, Fannie Kellogg, to Sitka where she established a school for the Indians in 1878. With the help of the Navy from 1879 to 1881, compulsory education legislation was enforced. Jackson was successful in 1884 in obtaining a grant from Congress for training Alaskan native children. The school at Sitka, later

known as Sheldon Jackson Institute, taught practical trade skills and Christian moral values. Jackson insisted that Alaskan Indians could be assimilated into western society. The school became the largest in the Territory and was later expanded to junior college status. In 1945, Caucasians were admitted for the first time. Recently Sitka and Sheldon Jackson College have been overshadowed by Anchorage and the new Alaskan Methodist University. The continuing prestige of Jackson's school among Alaskans is in doubt. Based on primary and secondary sources; 78 notes.

S. C. Pearson, Jr.

3539. Hinckley, Ted C. SHELDON JACKSON AND BENJAMIN HARRISON. *Pacific Northwest Q. 1963 54(2): 66-74.* The work of Sheldon Jackson, Presbyterian missionary in Alaska, in promoting legislation in the Congress of the United States for the welfare of Alaskans, 1800-92.

C. C. Gorchels

3540. Hinckley, Ted C. THE UNITED STATES FRONTIER AT SITKA, 1867-1873. *Pacific Northwest Q. 1969 60(2): 57-65.* The first American-type governmental body was created in Alaska in the hamlet of Sitka in 1867 shortly after the United States purchased Alaska from Russia. The author examines the history of the Sitka City Council (1867-73), showing the influences of official acts in the far-off mainland of the United States, the hopes for economic development, and the vagaries of human beings. The unexpected failure of the city to thrive economically brought collapse of the council in 1873.

C. C. Gorchels

3541. Hinckley, Ted C. WILLIAM H. SEWARD VISITS HIS PURCHASE. *Oregon Hist. Q. 1971 72(2): 127-147.* Details the journey in 1869 by William Henry Seward and his entourage on the newly-completed cross-country railroad, followed by a cruise to Alaska to inspect territory which Seward had been influential in persuading the US Government to purchase from Russia. Seward was a flowery orator much admired by settlers in the Pacific Northwest. Seward was pleased with the territory he inspected on the tour, but he was overly optimistic in thinking that major development would take place in Alaska within a generation. Based on primary and secondary sources; illus., map, 55 notes.

C. C. Gorchels

3542. Hunt, William R. "I CHOPPED WOOD"; GEORGE M. PILCHER ON THE YUKON. *Pacific Northwest Q. 1972 63(2): 63-68.* Pilcher was a woodcutter, homesteader, trapper, trader, engineer, miner, journalist, artist, and inventor. The author has condensed Pilcher's 21 diaries covering 1898-1933. Concentrates on Pilcher's activities in frontier settlements along the lower Yukon River, his experiences during the long, confining winters and the active summers, and his relations with natives, pioneer settlers, and transients. 27 notes.

C. C. Gorchels

3543. Koeniger, Neil R. ALASKA: THE FORGOTTEN LAND—1867-84. *Pacific Historian 1967 11(1): 37-41.* An account of the first years of official apathy toward Alaska after its transfer from Russian to American hegemony. Yet with the establishment of a customs post, the Alaska Commercial Company seal monopoly, and the stationing of an Army unit, prosperity and optimism grew. But Congress soon retrenched, canceled the jobs of civil servants, and closed the region to private purchases and squatters. The military became the sole administrator of the territory. Optimism declined with the economy, incidents with the Indians increased, and Sitkans even had to petition the British Navy for protection against the tribes. Not until 1884 did increasing commercial activity in fishing, canning, and gold stimulate the passage of a civil government bill. Based on published secondary accounts; illus., map, 19 notes.

T. R. Cripps

3544. McQueen, Verden. ALASKAN COMMUNICATIONS 1867-1914. *Airpower Historian 1964 11(1): 16-23.* Continued from 1961 8(4). This part discusses the 1901-03 technical pioneering. Included are accounts of Safety Harbor-St. Michael wireless system and the construction of the Washington-Alaska Cable and Telegraph System.

K. J. Bauer

3545. Mecutchen, Valerie Stubbs. ALASKA'S FIRST STAR-SPANGLED FOURTH. *J. of the West 1967 6(3): 433-439.* Describes how the citizens of Sitka, Alaska, celebrated the Fourth of July in the year 1868, the first celebration of this day in the newly-acquired territory. The day was marked by sporting events, music, a parade, and patriotic speeches.

Particularly emphasized is the oration delivered by William Sumner Dodge depicting events at Sitka during its first year under the flag of the United States and giving expression to Alaskan hopes for the future.

D. N. Brown

3546. Mecutchen, Valerie Stubbs. STARS AND STRIPES OVER ALASKA. *Smithsonian J. of Hist. 1967 2(3): 1-16.* In 1867 the transference of Russian America to the United States took place in the town of Sitka, Alaska. The author reveals new details concerning the negotiations and their aftermath. One vexing problem, the distinction between government and private property, persisted after the commissioners completed their work. The Russians sold valuable property owned by the Russian-American Company at Sitka, Kodiak, and elsewhere to American speculators, thus defrauding the US Government. Based on archival material in the Department of the Army; 15 illus., 12 notes.

W. L. Willigan

3547. Patty, Stanton H. ALASKA SPROUTS WINGS. *Aerospace Historian 1967 14(1): 15-21.* A summary of military aviation in Alaska beginning with the arrival of four DeHavilland Liberty airplanes on a New York to Nome flight ending 24 August 1920. Reviews stories of Colonel Ben Eielson, Pacific Alaska Airways, Ladd AFB and Elmendorf AFB, the Japanese raid at Dutch Harbor, the retaking of Attu and Kiska, and the Alaskan Air Command. 4 illus.   R. J. Parkinson

3548. Schmandt, Raymond H. ALASKA MISSIONARY LETTERS, 1888-1890. *Records of the Am. Catholic Hist. Soc. of Philadelphia 1968 79(3): 147-180.* The Society of Jesus has since the 1880's provided the majority of Catholic clergy in Alaska. Presents 13 letters composed by seven of the early Jesuit missionaries in Alaska. Biographies of the seven precede the text of the letters. 10 notes.

J. M. McCarthy

3549. Sherwood, Morgan B. ARDENT SPIRITS: HOOCH AND THE OSPREY AFFAIR AT SITKA. *J. of the West 1965 4(3): 301-344.* An account of the illegal liquor traffic in Alaska during the latter part of the 19th century. Alaskan natives had learned to use alcohol during the Russian period of control, but in 1870 authorities of the United States flatly prohibited the importation of distilled spirits. The Army was responsible for enforcing prohibition but received little assistance from the citizenry. As importation was limited, the Indians and whites began to manufacture their own. Stills were established and bootlegging flourished. One concoction manufactured by the Hoochinoo Indians carried their name forward to the 1920's when the whole nation went dry under the Volstead Act and the popular name for bootleg liquor became "hooch." The author details the effort of military and civil authorities to control the illicit traffic in Alaska during the late 19th century. They were about as successful as were their counterparts in the 1920's. Based on archival material in the Bancroft Library, newspapers, and Congressional Reports; illus., 213 notes.   D. N. Brown

3550. Sloss, Frank H. and Pierce, Richard A. THE HUTCHINSON, KOHL STORY. *Pacific Northwest Q. 1971 62(1): 1-6.* Discusses the circumstances and motivations among the seven men who became associates in a partnership developed 1867-68 to buy out Russian commercial interests in Alaska after the United States purchased the territory. Contrary to formerly held ideas, a complex chain of events brought the partners together after the end of Russian rule.   C. C. Gorchels

3551. Smith, Glenn. EDUCATION FOR THE NATIVES OF ALASKA: THE WORK OF THE UNITED STATES BUREAU OF EDUCATION, 1884-1931. *J. of the West 1967 6(3): 440-450.* During the Russian period of Alaskan history the Eastern Orthodox Church and Russian trading companies provided some schools, but these were closed as the Russians withdrew and the Americans did little to replace them. The U.S. Commissioner of Education John Eaton became interested in Alaska after he took office in 1870 but his requests for money to launch a school system were ignored by Congress until his causes was joined by a Presbyterian minister named Sheldon Jackson. Their lobbying succeeded when Congress in 1884 instructed the Secretary of the Interior to provide for a system of schools. Jackson was appointed General Agent for Education in Alaska. The author traces the pioneering educational efforts of Jackson. He discusses the problems which arose during his tenure and those of his successors. In 1933 the work of the Bureau of Education in

Alaska was assumed by the Bureau of Indian Affairs. Based largely on government reports; 37 notes.   D. N. Brown

3552. Sunder, John E., ed. THE REVEREND OCTAVIUS PARKER'S "JOURNEY FROM SAN FRANCISCO ... TO ANVIK, ALASKA, TAKEN AT A TIME WHEN A DIRECT JOURNEY WAS IMPRACTICABLE" (1888). *Hist. Mag. of the Protestant Episcopal Church 1965 34(4): 333-348.* Journal entries of Octavius Parker (6 August to 24 October 1888), describing an 80-day sea and land journey from San Francisco to Anvik, Alaska, via the Bering Sea and the Kuskokwin and Yukon rivers. Interesting comments on geography, climate, Indian life, the dangers of travel by skin canoe and the missionary outposts of Moravians, Roman Catholics, Episcopalians and Russians. Lack of good food, illness, natural hazards and trouble with Indians made the journey a struggle for survival. The 27-page narrative is a part of the Alaska MSS collection of the Church Historical Society, Austin, Texas. Map, notes.

E. G. Roddy

3553. Van Nostrand, Jeanne. "THE SEALS ARE ABOUT GONE...." *Am. Heritage 1963 14(4): 10-17, and 78-80.* Traces the efforts of conservationist Henry Wood Elliott (1846-1930), from 1872 to 1926 to prevent the extinction of the Alaskan fur seal herd in the Pribilof Islands. Undocumented. Illus. by his paintings.

C. R. Allen, Jr.

3554. Watkins, T. H. THE AMERICANIZATION OF SITKA. *Am. West 1965 2(2): 50-57.* Founded in 1804 as New Archangel, Sitka became the center of Russian enterprise in Alaska, including the Russian-American Fur Company. By 1867 its population consisted of some nine hundred Russians, half-breeds, and civilized Aleutians. Frantic activity greeted its transfer to the United States, but it soon became apparent that the town offered little to sustain its hoped-for promise. Furs were hard to come by and brought low prices. Hostile natives and short seasons discouraged gold hunting. The social structure of the town which the Russian government and church tenously maintained disintegrated under American occupation with cheerful debauchery of soldiers and demoralized civilians. When the troops were withdrawn in 1877 for duty in the Indian wars in continental United States, Sitka became a sleepy town which simply drifted until the establishment of full civil government in 1884. Photographs from Eadweard Muybridge Collection, Bancroft Library. Contemporary watercolor by Frederick Whymper. Biblio., note.

D. L. Smith

3555. Wharton, David. STAMPEDE TOWNS OF THE UPPER YUKON. *Am. West 1967 4(4): 44-52, 73-75.* In 1964 the author, photographer Philip Hyde, and five others boated down the Yukon River from Eagle, near the Canadian border, to Tanana, at the junction of the Yukon and Tanana Rivers in the center of Alaska. The journey of two weeks searched out the relics of the Klondike gold rush days. The towns of Eagle, Circle, Fort Yukon, Beaver, Rampart, and Tanana, their history and their present occupants and economies are described. A conservationist plea is made against a proposed multi-billion-dollar dam that would flood the entire upper Yukon Valley. Illus., map.   D. L. Smith

3556. Wilson, Clifford. THE SURRENDER OF FORT YUKON ONE HUNDRED YEARS AGO. *Beaver [Canada] 1969 300(Autumn): 47-51.* Fort Yukon was built in 1847 by the Hudson's Bay Company near the forks of the Yukon and Porcupine rivers, 115 miles inside Russian America. The fort was described by two Western Union Telegraph Company men, W. H. Dall and Frederick Whymper, who visited it in 1867, the year that the territory of Russian America was purchased by the United States. American efforts, governmental and private, to close down Fort Yukon succeeded in August 1868 after a U.S. Army team on the spot verified that the fort was within Alaska. Based on private and official correspondence; illus.   L. F. S. Upton

3557. Wilson, William H. THE ALASKAN ENGINEERING COMMISSION AND A NEW AGRICULTURAL FRONTIER. *Agric. Hist. 1968 42(4): 339-350.* Commercial agriculture is a marginal undertaking in Alaska. Costs of clearing land of trees and moss are high and farming is highly competitive with a restricted local market. Limited capital, relatively infertile soil, long, severe winters, a short growing season, and the impracticability of exporting products because of high production costs hinder farming. These problems had been recognized by the

Alaskan Engineering Commission by about 1915, when it began a campaign to develop agriculture in Matanuska River Valley to provide traffic and food supplies for the Alaska Railroad, then under construction. Many of those taking up homesteads were part-time farmers, so land clearing went slowly. The commission undertook a major program to aid agriculture between 1915 and 1920, but early successes gave way to failures. The lack of markets was even more of a problem than the erratic growing seasons. Based upon Alaska Railroad Archives.

W. D. Rasmussen

3558. Wilson, William H. THE FOUNDING OF ANCHORAGE. *Pacific Northwest Q. 1967 58(3): 130-141.* An account of the pioneer days of Alaska's largest city, showing fast development from first construction in 1915 to an early peak population of 3,928 in 1917, through the influenza epidemic of 1918, and the decline of population to 1,858 by 1920. Topics such as land speculation, the first telephone system, establishment of schools, and recreational activities of people (gambling, prostitution, and bootlegging of liquor) are included.

C. C. Gorchels

6. THE POST FRONTIER WEST, 1890-1945

General

3559. Abbey, Edward. HALLELUJAH, ON THE BUM: A YOUNG MAN'S PILGRIMAGE ACROSS THE GREAT WEST FROM THE WARM, GREEN HILLS OF PENNSYLVANIA INTO A LAND OF PROMISE. *Am. West 1970 7(4): 11-14.* In the summer of 1944, when he was a boy of 17, the author bummed his way around the country. He hitchhiked, rode boxcars and buses from his home in Pennsylvania to the Pacific Northwest, went down into California and through the Southwest, and came back home again. The author reminisces of his adventures. Illus.   D. L. Smith

3560. Amaral, Anthony. THREAT TO THE FREE SPIRIT: THE QUESTION OF THE MUSTANG'S FUTURE. *Am. West 1971 8(5): 13-17, 62-63.* Nevada's first antimustang bill was passed in 1897 when the wild horses outnumbered people. These gypsy horses are regarded by ranchers as worthless predators of grass and water. There are now eight to 10 thousand horses and there is concern that any further increase in their number will jeopardize livestock and wildlife and ruin an already depleted range. More than 80 percent of Nevada is public land and therefore under the direct supervision of the U.S. Bureau of Land Management. B.L.M. officials agree with the ranchers to whom they lease grazing lands for their cattle and sheep. Since the livestock have to compete against the wild horses for grass they are forced to range farther and farther. The horses have caught the sympathetic eye of the public as a symbol of the Old West. Commercial mustangers who slaughter the horses for fertilizer and pet food, sportsmen who decimate the herds with automatic weapons from aircraft, and ranchers who are concerned with the future of the grazing lands have inspired (in reaction) a wild horse preservation movement. This will undoubtedly result in legislation affording some measure of protection to the horses. 8 illus.
D. L. Smith

3561. Baccus, James C. YOUR GIFT IS THEIR TOMORROW. *North Dakota Hist. 1965 32(3): 139-175.* A history of the North Dakota Children's Home Society (now Children's Village) in Fargo, North Dakota, traces the development of the idea that a children's home should be a temporary custodian and that children should be placed in foster homes unless they need therapy first. The Children's Village opened in September 1956. It has always been independent of the State government but has served children for whom the State was responsible. Gifts and endowments and wise leadership have kept the enterprise alive through many difficulties. Having always been progressive in its practices, very little had changed in child welfare in North Dakota. Illus., 31 notes.
I. W. Van Noppen

3562. Baker, Robert A. HOLD-UP OF THE GOLDEN STATE LIMITED. *Pacific Historian 1964 8(1): 53-55.* Firsthand account of the holdup on 16 September 1916 of a crack train as seen by a clerk on the train. A brief statement on the trial and sentencing of the thieves is included.   T. R. Cripps

3563. Beebe, Lucius. SANTA FE'S INEFFABLE DE LUXE. *Am. West 1965 2(3): 13-18.* A description of the 1911-17 Atchison, Topeka and Santa Fe's deluxe weekly train between Chicago and Los Angeles which tempted passengers with a luxurious ride on "this perfumed pleasure barge" for a surcharge. Excerpted from a forthcoming book. Illus.   D. L. Smith

3564. Bollinger, Edward T. and Bollinger, Alice. BIG SNOW ON ROLLINS PASS. *Colorado Mag. 1967 44(1): 53-63.* Describes the efforts of the trainmen of the Denver, Northwestern and Pacific Railroad to get through Rollins Pass, west of Denver, after a particularly bad snow in February of 1905. The snow in the pass had drifted to 24 feet, completely covering the track and cuts. Construction crews, working on railroad tunnels, and sawmill workers on the west side of the pass needed and expected new supplies, so it was mandatory that a train break through the snow walls to relieve the men on the other side. To expedite matters,

it was decided to combine the plow train with the passenger train heading west from Denver. Pushing this combination up the pass with three engines and a plow, the drifts were so bad that at one point it took the train an hour and a half to blow one mile of track clear. Finally, unable to clear the snow all the way to the top because of the increasing winds, several of the party hiked to the nearest telegraph shack, four miles back, for relief. The passenger train finally rolled into its destination 15 hours late. Based on interviews with the principles involved; illus., 9 notes.
R. Sexauer

3565. Borough, Reuben W. THE LITTLE JUDGE. *Colorado Q. 1968 16(4): 371-382.* Discusses Benjamin Barr Lindsey (1869-1943), a late friend of the author. Lindsey was a pioneer in the development of juvenile courts and in espousing "Companionate Marriage." He entered the Colorado bar in 1894 after learning law in a Denver office. As a judge in Denver from 1901 until the 1920's he was a noted reformer who made many enemies. As a result he was shunted into Denver's juvenile court, where he could do little damage to business interests. In 1929 his enemies managed to have him disbarred in Colorado, but he moved to California to practice law. In 1934 he became a judge in Los Angeles. In 1935 the Colorado Supreme Court, at its own initiative, reinstated Lindsey to the Colorado bar.   B. A. Storey

3566. Brewer, Helene Hooker. A MAN AND TWO BOOKS. *Pacific Hist. R. 1963 32(3): 221-234.* Explores the influence of J. Allen Smith's *Spirit of American Government* (1907) and Frederic Howe's *Privilege and Democracy* (1910) on the thinking of Francis J. Heney, a "radical" Progressive who fought for judicial recall in California in 1911 and for conservation.   J. McCutcheon

3567. Bridges, Lamar W. ZIMMERMANN TELEGRAM: REACTION OF SOUTHERN, SOUTHWESTERN NEWSPAPERS. *Journalism Q. 1969 46(1): 81-86.* On 1 March 1917, American newspapers reported a German proposal to Mexico urging that Mexico and Japan join Germany in an alliance against the United States if America entered the European War. In order to learn the reaction in the South and Southwest, the area most directly affected, the author read 13 daily newspapers from 1 March 1917 until America's decision to enter the war, 8 April 1917. The reaction to the news of the Zimmermann telegram was mostly anger; danger of a Mexican attack was considered remote. The exposure was considered important for its unifying effect on the American people, and it showed the great need for military preparedness. It proved to the newspapers the need for stamping out German autocracy if democracy were to survive. They considered the Zimmermann proposal an act of war, but a blunder rather than a threat. Based on primary sources; 47 notes.   K. J. Puffer

3568. Brunvand, Jan Harold. FOLK SONG STUDIES IN IDAHO. *Western Folklore 1965 24(4): 231-248.* The article is in three parts: the career of George Morey Miller, 1917-37, and his work at the University of Idaho; 1937-62, a time of little activity; since 1962, when the pace was quickened. A folklore class at the University of Idaho has done much work, particularly with two newspapers. Lists of songs and some texts are included.   J. M. Brady

3569. Burdick, Charles B. A HOUSE ON NAVIDAD STREET: THE CELEBRATED ZIMMERMANN NOTE ON THE TEXAS BORDER? *Arizona and the West 1966 8(1): 19-34.* An anonymous tip to American immigration authorities on 7 February 1917 led them to a morals case involving a 14-year-old girl and a Mexican actor in a San Antonio, Texas, house. Questioning revealed that the girl, a brother and a sister, and another man, all Austrian aliens who had been living in Mexico, were residents of the house on Navidad Street. An alleged uncle was an official in the Austro-Hungarian enbassy in Mexico. Olga Visser, 20, sister of the minor, volunteered information and documents to negotiate for her and her family's release. They concerned Austrian and German plans to use Mexico as a base of operations against the United States if war came between the United States and those countries. Details of the documents and the investigation reached Washington the same day as the publication of the Zimmermann Note, a German proposal to entice Mexico into war with the United States. Convinced of a genuine plot which perhaps was related to the Zimmermann Note, American authorities were surprised when Miss Visser's principal accomplice later confessed that the entire affair was a product of his imagination, spurious notes and all. Subsequent activities of the group only confused the situation further. The author offers subjective observations to support the affair as fraudulent and arguments to support it as a genuine plot. He concludes that even though the mystery may never be solved it influenced the fears of the American government of German intrusions in the Western hemisphere. 3 illus., 35 notes.   D. L. Smith

3570. Casey, Ralph D. A BOOK REVIEW-ESSAY: 50 YEARS OF OREGON JOURNALISM SCHOOL HISTORY. *Journalism Q. 1965 42(4): 668-672.* George S. Turnbull's *Journalists in the Making* (Eugene, Oregon: U. of Oregon School of Journalism, 1965) is a descriptive and documentary account of the University of Oregon School of Journalism, in its first half-century (ending in 1962), written by a man whose life was intimately bound up with it over many years, as professor and dean. The school was established as a result of the coming together of a university president, Prince Lucien Campbell, who had been a reporter, and Eric W. Allen, who gave up a newspaper career to guide the journalism school for almost 32 years, "grouping the program around the cultural as well as the professional."   S. E. Humphreys

3571. Cash, McKinley. ON THE TRACK OF THE POWER BOYS. *J. of Arizona Hist. 1967 8(4): 248-255.* As a soldier stationed in Arizona, McKinley Cash participated in the successful search for the "Power Boys" who had refused to register for the draft during World War I. In February 1918, four lawmen attempted to arrest Jeff Power, a miner, and his business associate Tom Sisson for questioning in connection with the mysterious death of Power's daughter. Jeff Power, Tom Sisson, and Power's two sons, Tom and John, resisted arrest and killed three of the four lawmen. Jeff Power was also killed in the fighting, but his two sons, although injured, successfully escaped with Tom Sisson. The three fugitives fled into New Mexico and from there across the border to Mexico. Another patrol, not Cash's, captured the Powers Boys in Mexico and returned them to Arizona where they were tried, convicted, and imprisoned for life.   R. J. Roske

3572. Chernik, V. P. THE RODILLA TOWERS: AN ARCHITECTURAL PHENOMENON. *Am. West 1972 9(1): 10-11, 63.* From 1921 to 1954, Italian immigrant Sam Rodilla (d. 1966), a tile setter by trade, erected 15 towers in the Watts district of southern California. Up to 104 feet tall, they are constructed of steel, cement, seashells, and soft-drink bottles. Self-trained from an encyclopedia, Rodilla built the towers unaided by anyone else and completely by hand. The total effort consumed seven thousand sacks of cement, 75 thousand seashells, and truckloads of bottles. In addition to his regular employment, Rodilla spent eight hours a day on his towers. Each spire is unique, and each is unexplainable as to purpose, design, or significance. Together they constitute his avant-garde rendition of pop art. Rodilla has been acclaimed and ridiculed. At one time the city of Los Angeles ordered the structures razed. Art critics over the world forced the city to back down after a cable which exerted 10 thousand pounds of pull on the tallest tower snapped rather than pulling down the tower. Today the towers are a part of a city beautification program and will become the focal point in a new park. 2 illus.   D. L. Smith

3573. Clark, Edith K. O. THE DIARY OF EDITH K. O. CLARK. *Ann. of Wyoming 1967 39(2): 217-244.* Presents a verbatim printing of the diary kept by Miss Edith K. O. Clark during the summers of 1933 and 1934. A former teacher and Wyoming State Superintendant of Public Instruction, she recorded her impressions while building a log cabin near Buffalo, Wyoming. Her diary includes descriptions of logging, scenery, weather, wildlife, and forest fire. Illus.   R. L. Nichols

3574. Clark, Norman. THE "HELL-SOAKED INSTITUTION" AND THE WASHINGTON PROHIBITION INITIATIVE OF 1914. *Pacific Northwest Q. 1965 56(1): 1-16.* Comprehensive analysis of factors influencing the outcome of an election to ban liquor and saloons in the State of Washington in 1914. It shows detailed voting results in city and rural area election wards. Includes description of the activities of prominent men, newspapers, and churches in supporting or opposing the legislation.   C. C. Gorchels

3575. Clark, Norman H. ROY OLMSTEAD, A RUM-RUNNING KING ON PUGET SOUND. *Pacific Northwest Q. 1963 54(3): 89-103.* Misadventures of a Seattle policeman in unlawfully distributing liquor during the prohibition years. Legal action and court trials (up to the decision by the US Supreme Court) against Olmstead are rich in detail.   C. C. Gorchels

3576. Colley, Charles C. GOOD ADVICE TO AN ARIZONA GAMBLER: THE GANS-NELSON FIGHT, GOLDFIELD, NEVADA, 1906. *J. of Arizona Hist. 1968 9(2): 96-98.* The author tells of the Joe Gans-"Battling" Nelson prizefight staged in Goldfield in September 1906. Almost all other States still banned the sport. The fight was an early promotion of George Lewis "Tex" Rickard, who achieved worldwide acclaim in the 1920's as a boxing promoter. In this fight, Nelson was a heavy favorite with fans and newspapermen alike. However, as a result of inside information, one of the local gamblers, Jack D. Moore, wired a former Tucson associate, Joseph L. Wiley, to bet on Gans. If Wiley did, he won a great deal of money, since Gans was declared the winner on a foul in round 42. Based on the Joseph Lee Wiley Papers, the Arizona Pioneers' Historical Society, and on contemporary newspapers; photos, 7 notes.   R. J. Roske

3577. Cook, Philip L. RED SCARE IN DENVER. *Colorado Mag. 1966 43(4): 308-326.* Discusses the causes of the "Red Scare" in Denver. It is suggested that it was a result of the exploitation of a threat of a Bolshevik revolution by newspapers, postwar frustrations, and the constant reminders of the threat of communism from such eminent public officials as President Woodrow Wilson and Attorney General Alexander Palmer. The fear of communism reached its height in Denver when the Amalgamated Association of Street and Electric Railway Employees of America went on strike on 1 August 1920. This strike resulted in a number of deaths, but after its culmination the fear of a Bolshevik revolution faded out of existence. The most lasting effect of the "Red Scare" was that it placed an increasing amount of emphasis on Americanism. Illus., 80 notes.   I. W. Van Noppen

3578. Cooper, Harold. THE GREAT NEBRASKA NAVY: ITS ORIGIN AND GROWTH. *Nebraska Hist. 1967 48(4): 331-334.* Discussion of the founding for public relations purposes of the Nebraska Navy by Lieutenant Governor Theodore W. Metcalfe, (1930-32) and of its subsequent rapid growth to about 20 thousand appointees all with the rank of admiral.   R. Lowitt

3579. Cotroneo, Ross R. SNAKE RIVER RAILROAD. *Pacific Northwest Q. 1965 56(3): 106-113.* Detailed account of an ill-fated campaign to augment the railroad service in the Snake River Valley and to obtain a major bridge across the river between Lewiston, Idaho, and Clarkston, Washington, 1925-30.   C. C. Gorchels

3580. Culmsee, Carlton. THE FRONTIER: HARDY PERENNIAL. *Utah Hist. Q. 1967 35(3): 228-235.* Asserts that the frontier experience and its influences did not end with 1890 and that the experience of solitude in the frontier wilderness continues to be important to the American in the 20th century.   S. L. Jones

3581. Culp, Edwin D. OREGON POSTCARDS. *Oregon Hist. Q. 1965 66(4): 303-330.* An illustrated account of postcards, showing scenes in Oregon particularly during the years of 1898 to 1918, with special reference to deltiology (postcard collecting). Included are biographical sketches of nine men prominent for their work in producing Oregon postcards.   C. C. Gorchels

3582. Daniels, Roger. WORKERS' EDUCATION AND THE UNIVERSITY OF CALIFORNIA, 1921-1941. *Labor Hist. 1963 4(1): 32-50.* A survey of the workers' education program sponsored by the University of California. Establishment of the program was largely due to the interest of Paul Sharrenberg, secretary-treasurer of the California State Federation of Labor, 1909-36. The program was administered from its establishment in 1921 until his retirement in 1941 by John L. Kerchen, who for ten years prior to his appointment was a teacher of vocational education at Oakland Technical High School.   J. H. Krenkel

3583. Darst, W. Maury, ed. SEPTEMBER 8, 1900: AN ACCOUNT BY A MOTHER TO HER DAUGHTERS. *Southwestern Hist. Q.*

1969 73(1): 56-82. Reprints two letters which give an account of the confusion in Galveston after the destructive hurricane and 14-foot tidal wave of 8 September 1900. The two letters give news of the friends and acquaintances of the John Focke family. The hurricane was a major disaster in which about six thousand people lost their lives and most of Galveston was wrecked, with property damage estimated at more than 25 million dollars. Following the two letters are some photos of the destruction and of members of the John Focke family of Galveston.

R. W. Delaney

3584. Davies, Richard O. ARIZONA'S RECENT PAST: OPPORTUNITIES FOR RESEARCH. *Arizona and the West 1967 9(3): 243-258.* The recent past of Arizona's history lends itself to chronological divisions: the progressive era from which statehood emerged in 1912, the twenties, the age of the Great Depression, and the last quarter-century of rapid growth. The one central theme that unifies 20th-century Arizona history is the interaction of the State with external political and economic forces. Its small population, arid climate, and lack of capital has forced the State to depend heavily on outside support for its economic development. Before 1930, land companies, railroads, and mining corporations accounted for most of its economic growth. Since then, Federal Government sources have played increasingly important roles. By the agreement of this and previous bibliographical surveys, the 20th century is the most neglected area of historical investigation and the period of greatest potential. The older historiography needs to be recast in light of regional and national dependence. Specific opportunities for research are indicated in this survey of recent Arizona history. 27 notes.   D. L. Smith

3585. Davis, Jackson. DRAMATIC STOCK IN DALLAS, 1920-1925. *Southern Speech J. 1963 29(1): 34-46.* This critical look at the course of stock theater in Dallas provides insights into the vicissitudes of a dramatic form which clung to techniques of an older day and which offered plays that did not reflect the cultural revolution then sweeping New York and other large theater centers. 54 notes.

H. G. Stelzner

3586. Deahl, William E., Jr. THE CHADRON-CHICAGO 1,000-MILE COWBOY RACE. *Nebraska Hist. 1972 53(2): 167-193.* Details the 13-day horse race from Chadron, Nebraska, to Chicago, Illinois, in 1893. The race coincided with the World's Columbian Exposition and was a contribution to America's celebration of its past. The finish line was at the grounds of Buffalo Bill's Wild West, adjacent to the exposition grounds. Buffalo Bill (Colonel William Frederick Cody) greeted the riders as they finished the race. Joe B. (Old Joe) Gillespie of Coxville, Nebraska, was credited with the victory, although John Berry, who had helped to lay out the route, finished first. Map, 3 photos, 69 notes.

R. Lowitt and S

3587. Doerr, Arthur H. and Sutherland, Stephen M. HUMID AND DRY CYCLES IN OKLAHOMA IN THE PERIOD 1930-1960. *Great Plains J. 1966 5(2): 84-94.* A study of weather records of Oklahoma shows dry decades in the 1930's and 1950's and a humid period in the 1940's. Although individual years within each decade show considerable fluctuation, there is also an alternating recurrent pattern of humid and subhumid decades. Mean climatic conditions show that most of the state is "humid sub-tropical . . . and only the panhandle and northwest are semiarid." Maps, tables.   O. H. Zabel

3588. Edmonds, D. H. "FRANKIE AND JOHNNY." *Am. West 1966 3(1): 20-29, 79.* In 1906, the author, then a young man, went by train to a small cow town in northern Montana to take his first job in a trading post. With fictionalized names of his associates, he reminisces about his four-year stay, "as seen and remembered by me." One of the favorite recollections was of a particular rendition of "that immortal western saloon classic, 'Frankie and Johnny.'" When Edmonds saved enough money he left town to study medicine.   D. L. Smith

3589. Ericson, J. E. and McCrocklin, James H. FROM RELIGION TO COMMERCE: THE EVOLUTION AND ENFORCEMENT OF BLUE LAWS IN TEXAS. *Southwestern Social Sci. Q. 1964 45(1): 50-58.* The Texas legislature in 1961 enacted a "sweeping new regulation of Sunday business activity designed primarily for the protection of local merchants from what was alleged to be unfair competitive practices of out-of-state business interests." Texas "blue laws" date from 1871. The

new law suffers from the "same inherent weakness of all blue laws and related legislation, the almost countless difficulties of enforcement."

D. F. Henderson

3590. Fowler, Gene. THE AMOROUS SENATOR: THE SCANDALOUS LIFE OF A LOP-EARED BURRO. *Am. West 1970 7(2): 28-31.* Senator was a burro that the author called his own as a 9-year-old boy and later recalled in the present account. He is variously ascribed such qualities as: libelous, clairvoyant, loquacious as any chanticleer, a gentleman. The 6-year-old critter had served in a Rocky Mountain packtrain. The Senator was the boy's playmate until he was banished for eating dishcloths that were hanging out to dry. Later the Senator was discovered in a herd of wild burros, giving much attention to "the most dissipated, flea-bitten Jenny I ever had seen." The boy was crushed when Senator rejected his calls and returned to the jenny. Excerpted from the author's *Timber Line.* 5 illus., biblio. note.   D. L. Smith

3591. Gebhard, David. THE SPANISH COLONIAL REVIVAL IN SOUTHERN CALIFORNIA (1895-1930). *J. of the Soc. of Architectural Historians 1967 26(2): 131-147.* An analysis of Spanish Colonial architecture in Southern California which illustrates its remoteness from Californian colonial precedents and its connection with the avant-garde architecture of the United States. The revival had three phases: "Mission Revival" beginning in the 1880's, which was based on Spanish Colonial models in Santa Fe; the "Mediterranean" phase, which lasted from about 1910 to the 1930's, when the models were Spanish, Mexican, or North African; and the revival from the 1920's merged with the pre-Columbian revivals of Frank Lloyd Wright's major west coast buildings. The author suggests that to design houses, hotels, or auto salesrooms in a Spanish style was not different from basing 19th-century railway stations on Roman Baths or 20th-century factories on Assyrian or Babylonian architecture. Often "style" was suggested by a few details only (arcades, scalloped gables, tiled roofs, bell towers, broad unbroken stucco surfaces). Where ornament was sought it was often found in Islamic or Sullivanesque designs thus linking the revival with an indigenous American development. Documented from architectural periodicals, 23 photos.

D. McIntyre

3592. Gerlach, Allen. CONDITIONS ALONG THE BORDER - 1915, THE PLAN DE SAN DIEGO. *New Mexico Hist. R. 1968 43(3): 195-212.* "From 1910 to 1916 the Mexican Republic suffered from acute political instability as one Plan after another was issued against claimants to the presidency." The Plan de San Diego, ostensibly written in San Diego, Texas, called for an armed uprising on 20 February 1915 of Mexican nationals and American citizens of Mexican extraction. Its aim was to capture, and eventually annex to Mexico, Texas, New Mexico, Arizona, Colorado, and Upper California. The plan, formulated by Huertistas with significant German involvement, was most probably "merely a diversionary element in the larger Huerta-Orozco revolution." Based on *Records of the Department of State Relating to the Internal Affairs of Mexico, 1910-1929,* National Archives Microfilm Publication; 2 appendixes, 82 notes.   D. F. Henderson

3593. Goldman, Harry L. NIKOLA TESLA'S BOLD ADVENTURE: STRANGE EXPERIMENTS CONDUCTED BY AN ELECTRONIC WIZARD AT THE TURN OF THE CENTURY. *Am. West 1971 8(2): 4-9.* Pioneer electrical inventor Nikola Tesla (1856-1943) went to Colorado Springs in 1899 to conduct a wide variety of experiments. This immigrant from Yugoslavia was a prodigious inventor whose scientific achievements established much of the groundwork for radio communications, including the science of radio-guided missiles. His contributions include the system of alternating-current power transmission and motors, ideas and apparatus for industrial induction heating and welding, diathermy with its medical applications, and many others. Tesla's so-called "World System" of communications would embody an interconnection of telegraph, telephone, and stock ticker services, provide safe navigation without the aid of compasses, synchronize clocks throughout the world from a radio-controlled master station, provide worldwide personal telephone communications by use of a device to be carried in the pocket, and transmit electric power without using wires. Tesla's experiments on the east coast were subject to the physical limitations of his laboratory, so he decided to move to the wide open spaces of the West. He erected an experimental station in a pasture near Colorado Springs. The dry and rarefied atmosphere seemed particularly suited to his laboratory efforts. Here he concluded that the earth was charged with electricity which might be tapped to supply power to energy-starved places anywhere on the globe. These efforts and an attempt to establish a world radio broadcasting station in New York came to naught because he was unable to get sufficient backing from potential but skeptical promoters. 4 illus.   D. L. Smith

3594. Goodman, Jack. MID-CENTURY CROSSING BY RAIL. *Utah Hist. Q. 1969 37(1): 135-143.* Reminiscences of a boyhood journey westward in 1928 from Chicago on the Union Pacific Railroad's "Overland Limited."   S. L. Jones

3595. Grant, H. Roger. INSURANCE REFORM: THE CASE OF WEBB MC NALL IN KANSAS. *Kansas Hist. Q. 1970 36(1): 62-73.* McNall was one of the new breed of State insurance commissioners seeking to reform a business that was under heavy attack during the 1890's. By enforcing existing statutes, initiating new reform legislation, and encouraging the mutual and fraternal movements, McNall checked some abuses by insurance companies in Kansas. Even after he was forced from office by a powerful insurance lobby in Topeka, McNall battled for insurance reform. As consultant for the life insurance division of his lodge, the Ancient Order of United Workmen (AOUW), he sought to provide its members with dependable low-cost life insurance. Based on Kansas Insurance Department records in the Kansas State Historical Society; illus., 31 notes.   W. F. Zornow

3596. Greenfield, Elizabeth. SHAKESPEARIAN "CULTURE" IN MONTANA, 1902. *Montana 1972 22(2): 48-55.* The Great Falls Shakespeare Club presented "A Midsummer Night's Dream" in 1902. The site was the H. H. Nelson ranch near Cascade, and participants were society ladies of Great Falls, including Mrs. Charles M. Russell, whose artist husband contributed a comic sketch of the affair as it broke up in a rainstorm. The author, a daughter of the hostess, recalls the episode from early childhood.   S. R. Davison

3597. Grenier, Judson A. UPTON SINCLAIR: A REMEMBRANCE. *California Hist. Soc. Q. 1969 48(2): 165-169.* Presents personal impressions of Sinclair (1878-1968) based on correspondence and a series of oral interviews. After the muckraking era had passed, Sinclair continued to live in southern California for half a century. For many years he was difficult to reach for interviews, but eventually he made himself available to serious scholars and journalists. Sinclair had a subtle sense of humor, a mild personality, and a willingness to sympathize with human frailty. To meet Sinclair personally was to find that the controversial author did not match accurately the descriptions given by his critics. During the interviews, Sinclair displayed a tendency toward repetition of anecdotes already told and a concentration upon events that occurred in the first third of his life. Note.   A. Hoffman

3598. Groesbeck, Kathryn D. A SOUTHWEST PHOTOGRAPHIC EXPEDITION, 1898-99. *Utah Hist. Q. 1966 34(3): 191-201.* Traces the travels of two men and a boy on a commercial photographic tour of parts of Utah, Colorado, New Mexico and Arizona between 27 July 1898 and 10 July 1899. The journal maintained by one of the adult members of the tour is published here. One of the members of the party, David Huish, who was 10 at the time (presently living at Roosevelt, Utah) still possesses 64 of the stereographic views made during the trip. Four of the views are reproduced here.   S. L. Jones

3599. Groman, George L. W. A. WHITE'S POLITICAL FICTION: A STUDY IN EMERGING PROGRESSIVISM. *Midwest Q. 1966 8(1): 79-93.* William Allen White, editor of the *Emporia* (Kansas) *Gazette,* was one of the foremost advocates of progressivism, the middle-class reform movement of the first 15 years of the 20th century. In editorials, short stories, and novels White advertised progressivism in alerting the public to the dangers of corporate influence and demonstrating ways to strengthen government in legislation and administration. Here each of his short stories and novels is described and related to progressive reform rooted in rural conservatism. The pervading theme of White's work seems to be the conflicting propensities in man for good and evil, and for selfishness and selflessness. Biblio. of books and articles by and about White.   G. H. G. Jones

3600. Gunns, Albert F. THE MOONEY-BILLINGS CASE; AN ESSAY REVIEW. *Pacific Northwest Q. 1969 60(4): 216-220.* Reviews two books concerning the infamous trial and legal outrages associated with the series of industrial dynamitings in the San Francisco Bay area in 1916, which led to the conviction of supposedly innocent men - Thomas J. Mooney and Warren K. Billings. The books are *The Mooney Case* by Richard H. Frost (Stanford: Stanford U. Press, 1968), and *Frame-Up: The Incredible Case of Tom Mooney and Warren Billings* by Curt Gentry (New York: W. W. Norton and Co., 1967).   C. C. Gorchels

3601. Hagan, John P. FREDERICK H. KOCH AND NORTH DAKOTA: THEATER IN THE WILDERNESS. *North Dakota Q. 1970 38(1): 75-87.* Recounts the career of Frederick Henry Koch (1877-1944), professor of drama and a theatrical innovator at the University of North Dakota, 1905-18. In 1910 he founded the Sock and Buskin Society as an adjunct of university life. The organization, consisting of faculty, students, and others, produced plays and drama criticism, stimulated new playwrights, including Maxwell Anderson, and was instrumental in developing folk drama in North Dakota. Based on primary and secondary sources; 4 illus., 60 notes.   J. F. Mahoney

3602. Hager, William M. THE PLAN OF SAN DIEGO: UNREST ON THE TEXAS BORDER IN 1915. *Arizona and the West 1963 5(4): 327-336.* A 1915 irredentist plot, the "Plan of San Diego," so dubbed because the border town of San Diego, Texas, seemed to be the center of much of what transpired, is still an enigma as to its conspirators and precisely how it fitted into the troubled times along the Mexican-American border. The ambitious plan envisioned conquering California, Arizona, New Mexico, Colorado, and Texas, and creating an "independent Mexican republic" which would later ask for annexation by Mexico. After that the revolutionaries would seize Utah, Wyoming, South Dakota, Nebraska, Kansas, and Oklahoma, from which an independent republic would be created to serve as a buffer between Mexico and "the damned big-footed creatures of the north." Apparently the latter was to become a Negro republic. The plan was discovered before it could hatch. Rather than "a grand design" as it was regarded at the time, the author concludes that it was a stratagem to camouflage border raids with constitutionality and to earn American recognition for Mexican revolutionist Venustiano Carranza. Based on government documents, newspaper reports, and monographic studies; 39 notes.   D. L. Smith

3603. Harley, R. Bruce. THE BEGINNINGS OF MARCH FIELD, 1917-1918. *Southern California Q. 1971 53(2): 147-158.* Describes the efforts made in 1917-18 by Riverside businessmen to get the Federal Government to locate an Army aviation training camp, March Field, near their city. Summarizes the landholding history of the site. 4 illus., map, 28 notes.   W. L. Bowers

3604. Hicks, John D. MY NINE YEARS AT THE UNIVERSITY OF NEBRASKA. *Nebraska Hist. 1965 46(1): 1-27.* A delightful account of the author's nine years (1923-32) at the University of Nebraska as a professor, department chairman, and dean.   R. Lowitt

3605. Hines, Donald M. SUPERSTITIONS FROM OREGON. *Western Folklore 1965 24(1): 7-20.* Collection of folk beliefs compiled by the author and various informants during the years 1890-1962. Introductory paragraph asserts that Oregonians "possess a body of local lore that has been enlarged and enriched with beliefs from elsewhere." The folk beliefs listed range from "superstitions about the body" to "superstitions about the weather or astronomy."   L. J. White

3606. Hinkle, Stacy C. WINGS AND SADDLES: THE AIR AND CAVALRY PUNITIVE EXPEDITION OF 1919. *Aerospace Historian 1968 15(3): 12-15, 34-39, (4): 30-36, 44-45, 1969 16(4): 28-33.* Part I. An account of the American intervention into Mexico in the summer of 1919. Francisco (Pancho) Villa had attacked Juarez, Mexico, during the weekend of 14-16 June. American troops from Fort Bliss crossed the border to assist the federal troops, and to prevent shooting across the Rio Grande into El Paso. After describing the establishment of the Border Aerial Patrol, of which the author was a member, relates incidents during patrols. Details the experiences of Lieutenants H. G. Peterson and P. H. Davis. These officers became lost due to the poor available maps, and crash-landed in Mexico. They were captured by *villista* bandits and held for 15 thousand dollars in ransom. The money was raised and contact was effected with the bandit leader. Map, 4 photos. Part II. Recounts the recovery of Lieutenants Davis and Peterson from their Mexican *villista* captors and reconstructs the events of their forced landing and captivity. After the recovery of the pilots, a punitive expedition into Mexico was ordered to capture the bandits responsible. Details the first two days of the expedition. 5 photos. Part III. Describes the final air and cavalry patrol efforts to capture the *villista* bandit-kidnapers. The mission was halted on 23 August 1919, with successes in several areas: the bandit chief had been killed; 17 bandits were captured; relations between Mexico and the United States were improved, especially by the prompt withdrawal of US troops after the mission; and the cooperation of air and ground units initiated tactical operations which were of much value. The problems thus revealed challenged the fledgling Air Service to improve airplanes and aeronautical knowledge. Photo.   C. W. Ohrvall

3607. Hoffman, Abraham. ANGELES CREST: THE CREATION OF A FOREST HIGHWAY SYSTEM IN THE SAN GABRIEL MOUNTAINS. *Southern California Q. 1968 50(3): 309-345*. Discusses the building of a highway system in the San Gabriel Mountains of southern California. Although some interest in a road system in the mountains arose as early as the 1890's, the first serious concern came at the end of World War I when the Automobile Club of Southern California conducted a survey and stirred up public sentiment for such a project. Major forest fires in 1919 and 1924 also made clear to many people the necessity of such a road system for fire fighting as well as for scenic and recreation purposes. From 1919 to 1961, advocates of the system struggled to get local, State, and Federal funds appropriated to carry on the work. Because the roadway system traversed a part of the Angeles National Forest, it received considerable Federal subsidization. However, disagreements over routes to be taken, the source of funds, the kind of construction to be used, the width of roads, a depression and a war delayed the final completion of the Angeles Crest Highway System until 1961. Based on letters, interviews, contemporary accounts, and secondary sources; map, 145 notes.   W. L. Bowers

3608. Hogin, James E. THE LIFE AND EDUCATIONAL CONTRIBUTIONS OF JAMES WILLIAM HARRIS. *Paedagogica Historica [Belgium] 1968 8(1): 42-62*. The long professional career of James William Harris (1878-1957), from principal of a small high school in North Dakota to dean emeritus of the College of the Pacific's School of Education, is traced. Harris' role in California teacher education and his contributions to the child development movement are chronicled. Although not widely known, Harris was highly respected by many as a great teacher. Harris was an American "Mr. Chips" and a number of opinions from contemporaries are quoted to support this view. Based on Harris' papers and diary, published sources, and personal interviews; 23 notes.
E. R. Beauchamp

3609. Hogue, Alexandre. A PORTRAIT OF PANCHO DOBIE. *Southwest R. 1965 50(2): 101-113*. Relates experiences during two weeks of 1931 when the author was painting a portrait of J. Frank Dobie, Texas historian and folklorist.   D. F. Henderson

3610. Holsinger, M. Paul. THE OREGON SCHOOL BILL CONTROVERSY, 1922-1925. *Pacific Hist. R. 1968 37(3): 327-341*. The nativism of the 1920's was manifested in many ways. Uniquely in Oregon religious and political groups secured an abridgement of educational freedom in response to what they were convinced was the threat of foreign domination. Inspired through agitation by the Scottish Rite Masons and the Ku Klux Klan, in November 1922, the voters of the State approved an initiative proposal which required nearly all youngsters between eight and 16 to be educated only by the State. National attention and opinion were focused on this Oregon measure which would close all religious and secular private schools. The law passed by the legislature in response made Americanism and patriotism mandatory subject matter in the public schools. Before it could go into effect, however, test cases progressed through the courts. In 1925, in a landmark decision, Pierce vs. Society of Sisters, the United States Supreme Court declared the law unconstitutional. 57 notes.   D. L. Smith

3611. Hope, Clifford R. KANSAS IN THE 1930'S. *Kansas Hist. Q. 1970 36(1): 1-12*. Presents a few general observations and personal recollections about the Great Depression's impact on Kansas. The author concludes that, even in hard times, life in Kansas went on very much as

it had during prosperity. Major attention is given to such topics as the great dust storms of 1934 and 1935, population shifts as a result of the Depression, and the gubernatorial election of 1930. Revised from the author's presidential address before the Kansas State Historical Society in Topeka on 21 October 1969. Based on reports of the State Department of Agriculture, books, articles, and local newspapers; 21 notes.
W. F. Zornow

3612. Horn, C. Lester. OREGON'S COLUMBIA RIVER HIGHWAY. *Oregon Hist. Q. 1965 66(3): 249-271*. In the era when paved highways were rare in the United States, men like Sam Hill, Sam Lancaster, John B. Yeon, and Simon Benson took the leadership in planning and constructing a remarkable highway along the Columbia River in Oregon. This article, with many illustrations, relates activities of men in overcoming difficulties and in completing the highway through a singularly scenic route.   C. C. Gorchels

3613. Howell, Edgar M. HARVEY DUNN: SEARCHING ARTIST OF THE WEST. *Montana 1966 16(1): 41-56*. After a successful career as a magazine illustrator, combat artist in World War I, and teacher of painting, Harvey Dunn devoted his later years to a series of pictures based on memories of his youth in South Dakota. Illus.
S. R. Davison

3614. Hubbell, Jay B. SOUTHWEST REVIEW, 1924-1927. *Southwest R. 1965 50(1): 1-17*. Published as the *Texas Review* by the University of Texas 1915-24, the periodical's name was changed to *Southwest Review* and sponsorship transferred to Southern Methodist University in 1924. The author sketches the history of the *Review*, 1924-27, when he was co-editor with George Bond and Herbert Gambrell.
D. F. Henderson

3615. Huckleberry, E. R. IN THOSE DAYS . . . TILLAMOOK COUNTY. *Oregon Hist. Q. 1970 71(2): 116-140*. Reminiscences by a physician who lived in Tillamook County, covering medical experiences, anecdotes about people of the region, and activities in commercial and social development, 1923-45. Special attention is given to World War II activities, since the county was thought to be vulnerable to Japanese invasion.   C. C. Gorchels

3616. Huntley, Chet. I CATCH THE BANK ROBBER. *Am. West 1968 5(5): 16-19*. Excerpted from his book *The Generous Years: Remembrances of a Frontier Boyhood* (New York: Random House, 1968) the author tells of one of "the more scarifying episodes" of his boyhood in the railroad town of Whitehall, Montana. In his third year of high school, Huntley worked after school and Saturdays doing odd jobs at the local bank. He discovered the painstaking efforts of a would-be robber to break into the bank safe from the roof and was one of the principals in the capture of the culprit. Illus.   D. L. Smith

3617. Jensen, Vernon H. THE "LEGEND" AND THE "CASE" OF JOE HILL. *Dialogue: A J. of Mormon Thought 1967 2(1): 97-109*. Joe Hill, a member of the Industrial Workers of the World and a radical labor organizer, was convicted of murdering John G. Morrison and his son in Salt Lake City 10 January 1914. The author, in reviewing Philip Foner's book entitled "The Case of Joe Hill," (New York: International Publishers, 1965) accuses Foner of attempting to prove the "frame-up" of Joe Hill and the legend which has grown around the case. Foner is especially faulted for claiming that Joe Hill was a victim of the Mormon Church and the business interests. His interpretation of the Hill trial is attacked. Foner apparently could find "only prejudice and sinister machinations" in the trial.   L. P. Hofeling

3618. Jessett, Thomas E. THE EPISCOPATE OF WILLIAM MORRIS BARKER, SECOND MISSIONARY BISHOP OF OLYMPIA. *Hist. Mag. of the Protestant Episcopal Church 1970 39(3): 251-263*. Traces the history of the Episcopal diocese of Olympia during the episcopate of William Morris Barker (1894-1901). Based primarily on diocesan records and church periodicals of the period; 37 notes.
A. J. Stifflear

3619. Johnson, J. R. COLONEL JOHN MILLER STOTSENBURG: A MAN OF VALOR. *Nebraska Hist. 1969 50(4): 339-357*. Recounts Stotsenburg's military career, focusing on his service in the West and as

Professor of Military Science and Tactics at the University of Nebraska. The author emphasizes his career with the First Nebraska Regiment in the Philippines during and immediately after the Spanish-American War. Stotsenburg was killed in action in April 1899, serving as colonel in command of the First Nebraska Regiment during the Philippine campaign.   R. Lowitt

3620. Jorgenson, Lloyd P. THE OREGON COMPULSORY SCHOOL ATTENDANCE LAW OF 1922. *Catholic Hist. R. 1968 54(3): 455-466.* In 1922 the voters of Oregon approved an initiative petition requiring all children between the ages of eight and 16, with certain exceptions, to attend public school. The admitted intent of the law was to destroy nonpublic schools. Similar legislation was under consideration in several other States. Masonic bodies were the chief proponents of the measure, which was supported also by the Ku Klux Klan and other organizations. From the time of its enactment, the law was under attack by Roman Catholic bodies, many Protestant groups, and the secular press. A Roman Catholic school and a private military academy secured an injunction against the law from a United States District Court. Upon appeal to the United States Supreme Court, the law was invalidated in 1925, on the grounds that it was a violation of both human and property rights as well as of religious freedom.   A

3621. Juhnke, James C. JOHN SCHRAG ESPIONAGE CASE. *Mennonite Life 1967 22(3): 121-122.* Describes the ordeal of John Schrag, a Mennonite farmer who lived near Burton, Kansas, during World War I. Remaining loyal to the Mennonite doctrine of nonresistance, Schrag refused to buy war bonds. A patriotic mob, enraged by Schrag's failure to support the war effort, almost lynched him on 11 November 1918. He was accused of desecrating the flag, brought to trial for violating the Espionage Act, and found not guilty. Based on interviews and newspapers.   D. J. Abramoske

3622. Kitt, Edith Stratton. MOTORING IN ARIZONA IN 1914. *J. of Arizona Hist. 1970 11(1): 32-65.* The author (1878-1968) made a motor trip to northern Arizona and the Grand Canyon in 1914. Presents her diary of the 28 May-2 July journey. Details the camping trip from Tucson, via Phoenix and Prescott, to the Grand Canyon, returning by way of Flagstaff, Winslow, Springerville, Globe, and Phoenix. Her observations reflect her many and varied interests and the adventures of motoring in 1914. 7 illus., map, 15 notes.   D. L. Smith

3623. Kropp, Simon F. HIRAM HADLEY AND THE FOUNDING OF NEW MEXICO STATE UNIVERSITY. *Arizona and the West 1967 9(1): 21-40.* Quaker educated Hiram Hadley was a pioneer in educational development. He founded teacher training institutions in Indiana and Nebraska and promoted them in other states. He authored a textbook in teaching English. Publishing experience and recognition as a minister of the Society of Friends were added to his qualifications. Ill health of a son caused the Hadleys to move to Las Cruces, New Mexico, in 1887. Soon he was well-established in the real estate business. Almost immediately he set out to improve the educational facilities of the community. A local group was instrumental in establishing Las Cruces College in 1888, and Hadley, a member of its board of trustees, was named president. It opened in September with Hadley, his daughter, and another lady who were the faculty. By mid-year enrollment reached 64. In reality it was an elementary, college preparatory, and business school combined into one. It also became a focus of cultural activity. In 1889 the territorial legislature authorized a land grant agricultural college and experiment station to be located in Las Cruces. The New Mexico Agricultural College replaced Las Cruces College and Hadley was appointed president of the faculty. Democrats labeled the growing new school as a Republican enterprise with a Masonic hierarchy. Indeed most of the officials were of both affiliations. Albert B. Fall, a local Democrat, was determined to build a party machine at the expense of destroying Republican rule in the area. Control of the college became a battle ground and Hadley a victim in 1894. Hadley subsequently served as vice president (de facto head) of the State university in Albuquerque, as professor in the Las Cruces school, as territorial superintendent of public instruction, and as a regent of the Las Cruces school. Hadley had placed New Mexico Agricultural College on the road to success. It later became the present New Mexico State University. 4 illus., 48 notes.   D. L. Smith

3624. Larson, A. Karl. ZION NATIONAL PARK WITH SOME REMINISCENCES FIFTY YEARS LATER. *Utah Hist. Q. 1969 37(4): 408-425.* Outlines the history of man's known contacts with the gorges comprising Zion National Park and contains, in somewhat greater detail, a reminiscence of the author's experiences in the region, including his participation in the events associated with President Harding's visit in 1923.   S. L. Jones

3625. Leab, Daniel J. PARE LORENTZ AND AMERICAN GOVERNMENT FILM PRODUCTION. *Midcontinent Am. Studies J. 1965 6(1): 41-49.* A historical survey of the pioneering efforts of Pare Lorentz in the production of documentary films contracted by the government to acquaint the population with the economic and social issues confronting the New Deal. *The Plow That Broke the Plains* and *The River* are cited as two outstanding examples of Lorentz' skill and innovation. His films set a standard by which even contemporary documentary film makers may be judged.   B. M. Morrison

3626. Lee, Ellen K. HELENA MODJESKA AND THE FRANCISCO TORRES AFFAIR, SUMMER, 1892. *Southern California Q. 1969 51(1): 35-56.* Polish Actress Helena Modjeska spent part of her life on an Orange County ranch which she acquired in 1888. This is primarily an account of the murder of her ranch foreman William McKelvey during the summer of 1892 and the subsequent lynching of Francisco Torres, a Modjeska ranch hand who was accused of the crime. Near the end of July 1892, McKelvey deducted two-and-a-half dollars from Torres' weekly earnings to pay his road poll tax and Torres, who spoke little English, apparently did not understand but thought he was being cheated. He claimed later that he killed McKelvey in self-defense, but before he could be given a trial a mob of armed and masked men took him out of the Santa Ana jail where he was being held and hanged him from a telephone pole. What impact these events had on Madame Modjeska is not known, but the author suggests that she probably never forgot the horror of the summer of 1892. Based on personal letters, newspaper articles, and secondary works; 51 notes.   W. L. Bowers

3627. Leyerzapf, James W. "NEAREST BY AIR TO EVERYWHERE" - AVIATION PROMOTION IN KANSAS CITY: 1925-1931. *Missouri Hist. R. 1972 66(2): 246-267.* The year 1925 was crucial in Kansas City's development as an aircraft center. First, Louis E. Holland, an enthusiastic supporter of aviation, acquired an influential role in the Chamber of Commerce. Second, commercial aviation was stimulated by the Kelly Air Mail Act, which transferred the air mail from public to private operation. Holland played an important role in the work of pioneer air companies such as National Aircraft Transport (NAT), Western Air Express (WAE), Transcontinental Air Transport (TAT), and Transcontinental and Western Air (T and WA), the predecessor of today's Trans-World Airlines (TWA). Other businessmen joined Holland in his efforts to develop Kansas City's aircraft and aviation industries, but the city's political leaders were equally helpful. At several points they provided improvements that were necessary to the Chamber of Commerce's promotional efforts. Based on secondary sources; 8 illus., 54 notes.   W. F. Zornow

3628. Liston, Sally Macready. WHEN SIGHTSEEING MEANT SITE-SEEKING. *Aerospace Historian 1968 15(1): 39-43.* The story of the 1924 pioneer photo-mapping project. Lieutenant John A. Macready and Captain A. W. Stevens conceived the idea of using airplanes to photograph inaccessible areas for mapmaking. Unfortunately, the Army Air Service did not have funds for this project. Stephen Mather, Director of the Public Park Service, underwrote the project for six dollars a day. The flight took the airmen from Dayton, Ohio, to the Pacific Northwest and then down the Pacific coast. The mission ended at Holbrook, Arizona, when they cracked up their DH-4 on landing. Covering 20 thousand miles, they took 3,600 pictures of national parks, prospective dam sites, and emergency landing fields. 5 photos.   C. W. Ohrvall

3629. Littlefield, Henry M. THE WIZARD OF OZ: PARABLE ON POPULISM. *Am. Q. 1964 16(1): 47-71.* The initial Oz story is a Midwesterner's "symbolic allegory" describing America's entry into the 20th century. Not a political activist himself, Lyman Frank Baum expressed his Democratic Populism through a child's fantasy. He lifts Everyman Dorothy out of barren Kansas and sets her down upon a wicked Eastern witch. Dorothy thus frees the proletarian Munchkins and begins her odyssey to the nation's capitol. There, she is to gain an audience from the Wizard of Oz himself. Trekking along a treacherous golden road, Dorothy acquires a self-doubting agrarian, a dehumanized laborer, and a Bryanesque lion as allies. Dorothy's forces manage to overcome the hostile Western environment, but the vaunted Wizard offers little assistance for he turns out to be a bumbling fraud. On the strength of her own integrity and the power of her magic *silver* shoes, Dorothy spirits herself back home.   R. S. Pickett

3630. Loeblin, John M. THE KELLY FIELD JAZ-WAGON. *Aerospace Historian 1967 14(1): 34-35.* A personal reminiscence of the unintentional contribution of Kelly Field to the Armistice parade in downtown San Antonio, 11 November 1918. A truck rigged with a Liberty engine, the propeller facing rear and downward, sprayed horse manure from the pavement onto bystanders and reviewing stands.
                                                       R. J. Parkinson

3631. Lottinville, Savoie. FELLOWSHIPS AT OKLAHOMA. *Scholarly Publishing 1970 2(1): 33-39.* Discusses the University of Oklahoma's program of fellowships in publishing. For 22 years the program has given young people aspiring to careers in scholarly publishing practical experience by introducing them to the actual processes involved in the operation of a university press and the production of scholarly books.
                                                       J. A. Casada

3632. Lowitt, Robert. A NEGLECTED ASPECT OF THE PROGRESSIVE MOVEMENT: GEORGE W. NORRIS AND PUBLIC CONTROL OF HYDRO-ELECTRIC POWER, 1913-1919. *Historian 1965 27(3): 350-365.* Attempts to show that George W. Norris, as a result of his decisive role in breaking the power of the Speaker of the House, quickly came to adopt managerial views as contrasted with regulating the economy when he began his term as U.S. senator. In espousing these views, Norris was reiterating in the field of hydroelectric power what several public figures were already suggesting in other areas. Based on published sources and on the Francis G. Newlands Papers, Yale University Library, and on the George W. Norris Papers, Library of Congress.
                                                       M. McAuley

3633. Lucht, Gary. SCOBEY'S TOURING PROS: WHEAT, BASEBALL AND ILLICIT BOOZE. *Montana 1970 20(3): 88-93.* Rivalry between Scobey and Plentywood, Montana, led to fierce baseball competition in the mid-1920's. Professionals were hired, notably by Scobey, where ex-Chicago White Sox stars played in 1925 and 1926. In a boom area and during the disorderly times of Prohibition, players lived in a rough style and did no training; however, a high level of play was maintained.
                                                       S. R. Davison

3634. Luebke, Frederick C. SUPERPATRIOTISM IN WORLD WAR I: THE EXPERIENCE OF A LUTHERAN PASTOR. *Concordia Hist. Inst. Q. 1968 41(1): 3-11.* Comments on and reproduces portions of an unpublished typescript, "Some Reminiscences of My Life," written in 1931 by the Reverend Herman E. Studier (1859-1947), a pastor of a rural German Lutheran congregation near Barneston in Gage County, Nebraska. During World War I an extraordinary number of incidents occurred "which involved the loss of free speech, guilt by association, accusation by secret informers, terrorism, and violence." Not unusual were the experiences of Herman Studier, who, because of his pro-German views, was harassed by militantly patriotic individuals and organizations. The interrogations of Studier by both the Nebraska State Council of Defense, which was investigating "all manifestations of 'kaiserism,'" and the Gage County Council of Defense are described in detail. Studier's "Reminiscences" are part of the William H. Werkmeister Collection, Nebraska State Historical Society.   D. J. Abramoske

3635. Lund, Herbert Z., Jr. THE SKELETON IN GRANDPA'S BARN. *Utah Hist. Q. 1967 35(1): 31-36.* Traces the moving and final disposal of the skeleton of a man executed for murder at Salt Lake City in 1912. The condemned man had willed his skeleton to the author's grandfather to be used for medical research.   S. L. Jones

3636. Lunde, Richard M. THE RELIGIOUS POPULATIONS OF NORTH DAKOTA. *North Dakota Q. 1963 31(1/2): 38-42.* North Dakota has the highest percentage of any state of rural church members

and the lowest percentage of urban church members. The state's religious population has apparently increased more since 1916 than the religious population of any other state. The state has not been able to afford being over-churched; accordingly there has been a decline of 20 percent in the number of church buildings since 1916, while the average membership per church has increased threefold. The Catholics have been declining while the Lutherans have been increasing rapidly. Based on official sources. Biblio.   E. P. Stickney

3637. MacPhee, Donald A. THE CENTRALIA INCIDENT AND THE PAMPHLETEERS. *Pacific Northwest Q. 1971 62(3): 110-116.* Reviews selected writings published 1920-67 about the so-called Centralia Massacre, in which members of the American Legion and Industrial Workers of the World (IWW) had a murderous confrontation in the small city of Centralia on 11 November 1919. Background material shows qualifications and reasons for involvement of the various pamphleteers. Based on primary and secondary sources; 38 notes.
                                                       C. C. Gorchels

3638. Manley, Robert N. LANGUAGE, LOYALTY AND LIBERTY: THE NEBRASKA STATE COUNCIL OF DEFENSE AND THE LUTHERAN CHURCHES, 1917-1918. *Concordia Hist. Inst. Q. 1964 37(1): 1-16.* Envisioned principally as a wartime agency to mobilize the state's economic resources, it soon became apparent that the council's "real impact would be felt in the field of loyalty investigations." It "deliberately sought to focus public indignation" against the Missouri Synod. It banned the teaching or use of foreign languages in the schools, placed restrictions on foreign language religious services, and required the licensing of "alien teachers and preachers." The author also discusses the reactions of the Lutherans to these measures and relates the work of the council to pre- and post-World War I nativism in Nebraska. Based on manuscripts and published primary sources.   D. J. Abramoske

3639. Martin, Douglas D., ed. AN APACHE'S EPITAPH: THE LAST LEGAL HANGING IN ARIZONA - 1936. *Arizona and the West 1963 5(4): 352-360.* Earl Gardner, an Arizona Apache Indian, was a three-time killer. He was condemned by a Federal court to die on the gallows, as provided for by a 1790 law of Congress. Rumor of a planned Apache armed protest brought Federal agents to the San Carlos Reservation and precipitated the secret execution of Gardner. The grisly details of the bungled hanging on 13 July 1936, as reported later by the press, brought a change in the Federal statute. Henceforth, Federal executions were to be done in the manner prescribed by the legislation of the state wherein the crime was committed. Two articles from the *Phoenix Gazette,* excerpts from correspondence between the Attorney General and the Secretary of the Interior, and the House Committee on the Judiciary report, which became the basis for the new Federal statute, are reprinted here. 5 notes.   D. L. Smith

3640. Mathes, Michael. THE TWO CALIFORNIAS DURING WORLD WAR II. *California Hist. Soc. Q. 1965 44(4): 323-331.* In December 1941, despite Mexico's neutrality, the Mexican government acted cooperatively with the United States for protection of the west coast. In January 1942 by executive agreement Presidents Manuel Avila Camacho and Franklin Delano Roosevelt set up the Mexico-U.S. Defense Board which resulted in intensive patrol of Baja California and the arrest of 18 Japanese. On 1 June 1942 Mexico declared war on Germany, Italy, and Japan. On 4 August the so-called braceros program was instituted; under this unique agreement calling for the contracting of 75 thousand agricultural workers the first group arrived in California 29 September 1942. The continuing influx of these braceros brought needed aid to California although the increasing Mexican population gave rise to some social and political controversy. A long conflict over the Colorado River ended with a treaty of 3 February 1944 which allowed an adequate amount of water to Baja California. The postwar years have seen continued cooperation between the two Californias. 45 notes.
                                                       E. P. Stickney

3641. Megaw, R. PRICKLY PEAR AND THE PANAMA-PACIFIC EXPOSITION. AN INCIDENT IN COMMONWEALTH-STATE RELATIONS. *J. of the Royal Australian Hist. Soc. [Australia] 1969 55(2): 159-170.* An Australian pavilion was included in the Panama-Pacific Exposition held in San Francisco in 1915 to celebrate the opening of the Panama Canal in 1914. The author reconstructs Australian preparations and the many wranglings which went on concerning the exhibit, which subjected ex-Prime Minister Alfred Deakin, one of Australia's representatives, to considerable abuse. Documented from Commonwealth archives.   D. McIntyre

3642. Meyer, Michael C. THE MEXICAN-GERMAN CONSPIRACY OF 1915. *Americas 1966 23(1): 76-89.* Partisans of ousted Mexican dictator Victoriano Huerta engaged in plotting against his revolutionary successors from exile in the United States, while also proclaiming the objective of regaining territories lost by Mexico to the United States. They established contact with Huerta, with whom German agents were also in contact, in Spain and, in the spring of 1915, the German Government provided money and the promise of further assistance for restoring him to power. However, Huertist efforts were ultimately defeated by the action of U.S. authorities after Huerta himself had entered the United States to take part. Based on U.S., German, and Mexican archival and published sources; 54 notes.   D. Bushnell

3643. Morrell, James F. and French, Giles. BUBBLE SKINNER. *Oregon Hist. Q. 1968 59(4): 293-305.* An episode delineates the shortcomings of an early automobile (a pre-1909 model) in use during a period of competition between two railroad companies in the Deschutes Canyon in Oregon in 1909. Problems of travel in the area are emphasized. Illus.   C. C. Gorchels

3644. Mulligan, Raymond A. NEW YORK FOUNDLINGS AT CLIFTON-MORENCI: SOCIAL JUSTICE IN ARIZONA TERRITORY, 1904-1905. *Arizona and the West 1964 6(2): 104-118.* In 1904, a parish priest in the mining area of Clifton and Morenci, Arizona, informed the New York Foundling Hospital that 40 children could be placed in homes within his congregation. When the children, from 18 months to five years of age, and the hospital representatives arrived they were placed in Mexican-Indian homes in less than suitable circumstances. Enraged Anglo families formed a vigilante group who took the children and redistributed them. Several days later the hospital representatives boarded the train for the East with 21 of the children, barely escaping the wrath of mobs and threats. The remainder became the subject of lawsuits being appealed to the U.S. Supreme Court. The Anglo families won final custody. In the litigation mob action was called "committee meetings" and the surrender of the children to the armed vigilante groups as "voluntary" action. Thus abstract justice played a lesser role in the court decision than the spirit of the frontier. Based on manuscripts in the University of Arizona library, court records, and secondary accounts; 37 notes.   D. L. Smith

3645. Munch, Francis J. VILLA'S COLUMBUS RAID: PRACTICAL POLITICS OR GERMAN DESIGN? *New Mexico Hist. R. 1969 44(3): 189-214.* Analyzes the precipitating causes of Francisco Villa's raid on Columbus, New Mexico, on 9 March 1916. Following a detailed study of Mexican-American provocations and Mexican-German provocations, the author concludes that "Villa's raid on Columbus, New Mexico, combined Mexican-American provocations with a Mexican-German conspiracy." Based primarily on the records of the Department of State Relating to the Internal Affairs of Mexico, 1910-1929, in the National Archives; 90 notes.   D. F. Henderson

3646. Myatt, William L. THE DENVER COMMUNITY PLAYERS. *Colorado Mag. 1964 41(2): 135-146.* From 1924 until 1934 the 'little theater" functioned in Denver.   I. W. Van Noppen

3647. Myers, Samuel I. DICK WICK HALL: HUMORIST WITH A SERIOUS PURPOSE. *J. of Arizona Hist. 1970 11(4): 255-278.* DeForest Hall (1877-1926) adopted his boyhood name of Dick, studied ornithology and engineering at the University of Nebraska for one year, and went to Arizona Territory. He lived with the Hopi Indians and was adopted into the tribe. Eventually he left them to become heavily involved in the white mainstream. Hall led a varied career in newspaper publishing, real estate, promoting, mining, and writing. He became a serious and aggressive fighter for improvement of his adopted western Arizona. In the 1920's Hall was catapulted to fame as a humorist, a cross between Mark Twain and Will Rogers, when the *Saturday Evening Post* badgered him into submitting copies of the *Salome Sun,* his mimeographed handout, which he wrote for customers at his gasoline station. An early death deprived him not only of the pleasure of seeing his dreams of improve-

ments for his area realized, but probably also of his chances of making a significantly more serious contribution to American literature. 8 illus., 62 notes.   D. L. Smith

3648. Myrick, Donald. GRAPHIC ARTS ON THE ARIZONA FRONTIER: RECOLLECTIONS OF AN ARIZONA RANCH SCHOOL IN 1911. *J. of Arizona Hist. 1971 12(1): 51-63.* In 1911 the author spent his last half-year before college in attending the Evans School for boys at Mesa. The school emphasized common sense, self-reliance, independence, initiative, classical preparatory studies, exploratory horseback camping trips, and other outdoor activities. 21 photos.   D. L. Smith

3649. Newton, Craig A., ed. VERMONTERS IN TEXAS: A REASSESSMENT OF NATIONAL GUARD DUTY IN THE MEXICAN BORDER IN 1916. *Vermont Hist. 1969 37(1): 30-38.* A son's analysis of the diary of Harold D. Newton, who served as quartermaster and mess sergeant for Company K in Texas. The diary shows good morale resulting from State pride, but the soldiers liked little of their guard duties and were glad to get home after three months' service.   T. D. S. Bassett

3650. Niemeyer, Vic. FRUSTRATED INVASION: THE REVOLUTIONARY ATTEMPT OF GENERAL BERNARDO REYES FROM SAN ANTONIO IN 1911. *Southwestern Hist. Q. 1963/1964 67(2): 213-225.* Recounts an unsuccessful attempt of Bernardo Reyes, retired General de División of the Mexican army, to organize a force of Texans and Mexicans to invade Mexico and overthrow the regime of President Francisco Madero.   J. A. Hudson

3651. Oliver, William E. PILGRIMAGE ON WHEELS. *Utah Hist. Q. 1964 32(1): 57-79.* Uses a diary kept by William Oliver to describe a motor trip taken in 1921 from Salt Lake City to San Francisco. He compares that trip with one taken in 1962. Illus.   S. L. Jones

3652. Patterson, James T. THE NEW DEAL IN THE WEST. *Pacific Hist. R. 1969 38(3): 317-327.* Compares the impact of the New Deal in the West and other regions of the Nation. Discusses why differences existed. Emphasizes the tradition of independence and resistance to Federal interference. Distinctive political traditions and factors in the Western States contributed to vitiation of the effectiveness of the programs. Evaluation of the New Deal period should include special consideration for sectional problems. Based on secondary sources; 29 notes.   E. C. Hyslop

3653. Powell, Lawrence Clark. STRICTLY LOCAL. *Southern California Q. 1965 47(4): 347-355.* A plea for a literature rooted in southern California, which might communicate the essence of the area to people elsewhere. The author asserts that southern California has had only one writer, Raymond Chandler, who knew and loved the area well, and made it the background and root of several novels of universal appeal. The wish is expressed that some author could do for the southern California of the 1960's what Chandler did for the area of the 1930's.   A. K. Main

3654. Pratt, Lowell Clark. THEODORE ROOSEVELT "DISCOVERS" CALIFORNIA. *J. of the West 1964 3(1): 40-46.* For two weeks in May 1903 President Theodore Roosevelt journeyed by special train throughout California. His major traveling companions included Secretary of the Navy William H. Moody, his private secretary, William Loeb, and, for part of the trip, Governor George C. Pardee of California. During his stay Roosevelt made some 50 speeches, mostly from the rear platform of his train. Most of his remarks were mere pleasantries, but in some instances he spoke on the issues of the day. He advocated conservation, good forestry practices, the development of water resources, and the promotion of agriculture. At Los Angeles he spoke of the necessity of having a Navy capable of maintaining the American position in the Pacific as well as the Atlantic, and at Watsonville he said that the Pacific must pass under American influence. His speeches impressed the people of California and indicated to the world that the United States intended to maintain its position in the Orient.   D. N. Brown

3655. Pritchard, Robert L. ORANGE COUNTY DURING THE DEPRESSED THIRTIES: A STUDY IN TWENTIETH-CENTURY LOCAL HISTORY. *Southern California Q. 1968 50(2): 191-207.* The traumatic experience of the Great Depression of the 1930's shook the traditionally conservative faith of the people of Orange County, California, but failed to alter it fundamentally. The emphasis on self-reliance and individualism waned somewhat but was not abandoned as Orange County citizens sought to interpret the Depression and the New Deal program in terms of their conservative philosophy. Many concluded that the changes wrought by the Depression required the temporary expansion of the Federal Government's role and they therefore supported the New Deal and the Democratic Party. But when the New Deal shifted leftward after 1936 and as economic conditions improved, they ceased to support the Democrats and the traditional conservatism which had characterized the people of the county reasserted itself stronger than ever. Based on Orange County histories, public documents, and newspaper files: 41 notes.

W. L. Bowers

3656. Reader, Benjamin G. THE MONTANA LUMBER STRIKE OF 1917. *Pacific Hist. R. 1967 36(2): 189-207.* Describes how the I.W.W. (Industrial Workers of the World) strike was broken through a combination of local suppression, Federal troops, Federal and State prosecutions, plus newspaper attacks and calls for patriotism during the war. The result was the destruction of the I.W.W. among lumber workers. From McLeod Papers plus newspapers and periodicals, 52 notes.

J. McCutcheon

3657. Reimnitz, Charles A. TOGETHERNESS IN NEBRASKA. *Concordia Hist. Inst. Q. 1971 44(2): 69-78.* Discusses the founding and rapid growth of the Nebraska District of the Missouri Synod, indicating the many pastors who labored in the late 19th and early 20th century to create a strong Lutheran faith in Nebraska. So successful were their efforts that in 1922 two districts, Northern and Southern Nebraska, were created. Since then consolidation efforts within both districts have allowed a reunification of the Northern and Southern Districts in July 1970. Mentions the position of the Nebraska Lutheran Church, with its strong German background and tradition, during World Wars I and II. Based on secondary sources; photo, 34 notes.

A. M. Brescia

3658. Reynolds, Clark G. ATTACK OF THE PAPER BALLOONS. *Airpower Historian 1965 12(2): 51-55.* Describes the 1944-45 attempt by Japan to attack the U.S. west coast with bombs carried by unmanned balloons launched into the trans-Pacific jet stream.

K. J. Bauer

3659. Riehl, Stella. RESCUE OF A BEAUTIFUL AND HISTORIC CHURCH: ST. MARK'S AND ST. LUKE'S, TACOMA, WASHINGTON. *Hist. Mag. of the Protestant Episcopal Church 1968 37(3): 215-243.* Sketches the rescue from destruction of a West Coast church. The "rescuers" consisted of a small group of families who saw the need for an Episcopal Sunday School in their area of the city; they expanded to form Saint Paul's Guild, purchased lots, and in 1920 opened an old gymnasium as their first church. Saint Luke's, consecrated in 1883, had fallen into near hopeless disrepair by the 1920's. Eventually the Sunday school gathering now known as Saint Mark's, contracted to buy and move it to the north end, piece by piece. The new St. Luke's was dedicated in June 1947. Illus.

E. G. Roddy

3660. Ripley, John W. ANOTHER LOOK AT THE REV. MR. CHARLES M. SHELDON'S CHRISTIAN DAILY NEWSPAPER. *Kansas Hist. Q. 1965 31(1): 1-40.* The Congregationalist minister Charles Sheldon wrote a highly successful book, *In His Steps* (1896), in which he described how the residents of a town decided to live for one year as Jesus would and how the local editor agreed to publish his paper with no news of crime, entertainment, liquor, tobacco or other things of which Jesus might not approve. In 1899 the owner of the Topeka *Daily Capital* offered Sheldon his own paper to conduct a one-week experiment in publishing a Christian daily; the special issues of Sheldon's paper appeared from 13 to 17 March 1900. The steps leading to this journalistic experiment, the experiment itself, and the aftermath are described in detail. The reactions of other Kansas newspapers and representative papers in major cities are traced.

W. F. Zornow

3661. Rosenberg, Arnold S. THE RISE OF JOHN ADAMS KINGSBURY. *Pacific Northwest Q. 1972 63(2): 55-62.* Kingsbury was an outstanding social work leader, 1911-35. In early years he lived in poor circumstances in the West (mostly in Kansas and Washington), 1876-92. He was a successful student (1892-1908) in Yakima, Tacoma, Seattle, and New York on the way toward becoming a distinguished social worker. 41 notes.

C. C. Gorchels

3662. Rosenstone, Robert A. MANCHESTER BODDY AND THE L.A. DAILY NEWS. *California Hist. Soc. Q. 1970 49(4): 291-307.* E. Manchester Boddy (1891-1967) became editor of the *Los Angeles Daily News* in 1926 and promptly boosted circulation through crusades against vice and corruption. From 1932 on Boddy supported a number of liberal and reform movements and enthusiastically backed the New Deal. As the only Democratic paper in Los Angeles, the *Daily News,* under Boddy's supervision, enjoyed a successful run during the 1930's and 1940's. Boddy's newspaper was open to groups that otherwise found difficulty in obtaining fair-minded press coverage. At a time when other newspapers found the going difficult, the *Daily News* thrived. After World War II however, decline set in. Tiring of the hard work involved in running a newspaper, Boddy turned to politics, but lost the Democratic senatorial nomination to Helen Gahagan Douglas in 1950. Boddy sold his stock and severed his connection with the newspaper in 1952. Two-and-one-half years later the paper went bankrupt. While Boddy may not have remained a liberal to the end, his work with the *Daily News* typified an era of personal journalism, crusades, and Democratic allegiance, all of which produced a lively newspaper. Based on personal interviews, newspaper and periodical articles; 52 notes.

A. Hoffman

3663. Ross, Hugh. UNIVERSITY INFLUENCE IN THE GENESIS AND GROWTH OF JUNIOR COLLEGES IN CALIFORNIA. *Hist. of Educ. Q. 1963 3(3): 143-152.* Junior colleges were first proposed to relieve universities from giving undergraduate instruction on the freshman-sophomore level. In 1907 California enacted legislation for such instruction to be offered in high schools. By 1915 the University of California at Berkeley granted credits for one year's work done at a junior college, and in 1927 Stanford University began to reduce its lower division. As more junior colleges appeared a movement for their affiliation with the University began in 1921, but was terminated in 1926, as it proved too cumbersome and as it prevented the junior colleges from serving as community colleges. In 1959 the *Master Plan for Higher Education in California* provided for a distribution of the state's students to junior and state colleges and the University of California.

J. Herbst

3664. Ross, R. Controneo. THE GREAT NORTHERN PACIFIC PLAN OF 1927. *Pacific Northwest Q. 1963 54(3): 104-112.* Efforts of major railroads in the Northern and Western United States to combine operations, following national railroad legislation of 1920, and reasons for lack of progress.

C. C. Gorchels

3665. Roth, Barbara Williams. THE 101 RANCH WILD WEST SHOW, 1904-1932. *Chronicles of Oklahoma 1966 43(4): 416-431.* The rodeo developed in the 1890's; it was supplemented by 1900 with wild west shows. The Miller Brothers 101 Ranch Show fascinated Americans. They had thundering hooves, daring rescues, lots of gunfire, the pony express, stage holdups, and, of course, lots of Indians. After the show was originated in Oklahoma, the Miller Brothers took it all over the world. After World War I, the expense of maintaining the show increased until, plagued by depression and the movies, it broke up in 1932. 4 illus., 41 notes.

I. W. Van Noppen

3666. Rowley, William D. THE LOUP CITY RIOT OF 1934: MAIN STREET VS. THE "FAR-OUT" LEFT. *Nebraska Hist. 1966 47(3): 295-327.* Careful and detailed examination of the Loup City riot in the summer of 1934 wherein a group of radical agitators sought to arouse farmers against the capitalist system. Background conditions, radical activities in Nebraska, and the results and significance of the riot are all fully discussed.

R. Lowitt

3667. Rundell, Walter, Jr. STEINBECK'S IMAGE OF THE WEST. *Am. West 1964 1(2): 4-17, 79.* Discusses the novels of John Steinbeck as "particularly significant" records of social history in western American settings. Steinbeck focuses on the impact of the Great Depression, race and class prejudices, religion, the automobile, whorehouses, and the influence of ideas on social philosophies and actions. Earlier an advocate of collective action to cure social ills, changing circumstances and times have led him to discard this approach because it imposes limitations on the individual mind and spirit of man.

D. L. Smith

3668. Sandos, James A. GERMAN INVOLVEMENT IN NORTHERN MEXICO, 1915-1916: A NEW LOOK AT THE COLUMBUS

RAID. *Hispanic Am. Hist. R. 1970 50(1): 70-88.* On 10 January 1916, Francisco (Pancho) Villa's men captured a train near Santa Isabel, Mexico, and massacred 16 of the 17 Americans aboard. On 9 March his men raided the American town of Columbus, New Mexico, just across the border. Theorizes that the train massacre was a matter of revenge for US support of Carranza, but that the raid on Columbus was for another purpose, as only 17 Americans were killed in the entire town. The Germans were interested in fomenting a war between the United States and Mexico, and Villa's close advisor, personal physician, and bookkeeper was Dr. Lyman B. Rauschbaum, an Austrian-German. Rauschbaum's compatriot, Felix A. Sommerfeld, became Villa's representative and purchasing agent in New York but also served as a German agent. The author believes that Rauschbaum talked Villa into attacking Columbus in an effort to provoke a war. Rauschbaum convinced Villa that the bank in Columbus was withholding Villa's money, and that the men from whom he had bought supplies in Columbus had been cheating him. Villa was also interested in the possibility of confiscating the munitions and horses at the garrison at Columbus. The raid was successful for Villa but failed to provoke a war. More work should be done to examine German activities in Mexico during the pre-World War I period. 111 notes.

B. D. Johnson

3669. Sandos, James A. THE PLAN OF SAN DIEGO: WAR AND DIPLOMACY ON THE TEXAS BORDER, 1915-1916. *Arizona and the West 1972 14(1): 5-24.* In 1915 Venustiano Carranza and Francisco (Pancho) Villa were the chief political-military contenders for control of Mexico. The presence of their forces and followers of the deposed military dictator Victoriano Huerta in the Texas-Mexico border areas, the economic disparity of the two dissimilar cultures along the international border, the strained Mexican-American diplomatic relations, and the uncertainties of New World involvement in World War I all made the Rio Grande border a tinderbox. On 6 January 1915, nine jailed partisans in Monterrey, Mexico, pledged themselves to the "Plan of San Diego, Texas." They proposed to liberate American racial minority groups, to regain Mexico's lost territory from the United States, and to establish Negro and Indian nations. The entry of German propaganda and apparently other efforts complicated the picture. The plan collapsed in 1916 because of stepped-up Mexican and American military vigilance and because of the disparity of the motives of its supporters. At least 27 raids accounted for property losses and casualties on both sides of the border. None of the goals of the plan were realized. 5 illus., map, 43 notes.

D. L. Smith

3670. Saum, Lewis O. THE WESTERN VOLUNTEER AND "THE NEW EMPIRE." *Pacific Northwest Q. 1966 57(1): 18-27.* From a study of attitudes of Western volunteer units in the U.S. Army of 1898 and 1899 the author concludes that most soldiers had moral and patriotic motives rather than economic objectives in being willing to fight in Cuba and the Philippines. Some emphasis is placed on the contention that citizen-soldiers had few thoughts of substance on the role of the United States in historic expansion and destiny. The author also shows the deep-seated antagonism of Americans toward native Filipinos despite the role of defending them against the Spanish.

C. C. Gorchels

3671. Schaefer, Lyle L. THE LUTHERAN SANITARIUM AT WHEAT RIDGE. *Concordia Hist. Inst. Q. 1971 44(2): 57-68.* Examines the history and development of what is today the Lutheran Hospital and Medical Center at Denver. From its beginning in 1904 as a tuberculosis sanitarium, the Wheat Ridge facility has served many of the Lutheran faith (and non-Lutherans as well) afflicted with the disease. When the number of tuberculosis patients declined in the 1950's, the facility was converted to a general hospital. Discusses the growth of the Wheat Ridge sanitarium from tent colony origins, the prominent Lutherans who aided that growth, and the several trust funds which helped the facility to succeed over the years. Based on primary and secondary sources; 4 photos, 54 notes.

A. M. Brescia

3672. Schaffer, Ronald. THE MONTANA WOMAN SUFFRAGE CAMPAIGN; 1911-14. *Pacific Northwest Q. 1964 55(1): 9-15.* Describes the role of Jeannette Rankin and others in gaining equal voting rights for women in Montana. Contemporary arguments for and against suffrage are given. Colorful campaign methods, including fund-raising methods, are described.

C. C. Gorchels

3673. Schippers, Donald J. WALKER AND EISEN: TWENTY YEARS OF LOS ANGELES ARCHITECTURE, 1920-1940. *Southern California Q. 1964 46(4): 371-394.* During the 1920's, when Los Angeles reached a peak of building unequaled again until the 1950's, the Walker and Eisen firm obtained the bulk of contracts for large buildings. Eisen acted primarily as contact man and organizer while Walker supervised most of the designing. Together they planned a large number of apartment houses, hotels and commercial buildings designed in the Beaux-Arts tradition which emphasized Romanesque and Gothic trim. With the depression came a movement to simplify, a greater use of concrete, steel and plywood, and the elimination of ornamentation. Architects for "tough-headed businessmen," they were not pace-setters, but as one friend said, they were "not behind anybody either." Uses interviews, Albert R. Walker Collection at UCLA, and published sources.

J. Jensen

3674. Schwartz, Jerome L. EARLY HISTORY OF PREPAID MEDICAL CARE PLANS. *Bull. of the Hist. of Medicine 1965 39(5): 450-475.* Describes and traces the development of the forms of prepaid medical care insurance from 1787 to 1929. "The first prepaid medical care plans were organized by fraternal societies and mutual benefit associations, which began to appear in the United States as early as 1787 with the formation of the Free African Society in Philadelphia. Initial health benefits provided by these associations were cash disability payments, aiming to replace a portion of the income lost during sickness. Later these employee groups, which had formed independent of employers, expanded the limited cash benefits into medical service programs. . . . Around 1900, employee and industrial medical care plans were organized and later came to be known as 'contract practice.' The Workingmen's Compensation Laws, passed before World War I, stimulated the further development of prepaid plans. Remote areas in Washington, Oregon, Minnesota, and Pennsylvania, associated with lumbering, mining, and railroading industries, saw the founding of contract plans sponsored by industry, employees, physicians, hospitals, and medical societies. The early history of group insurance, private physician clinics, and hospital service plans laid the basis for the present day health insurance coverage under prepayment." 84 notes.

D. D. Cameron

3675. Shatraw, Milton. CHRISTMAS AND THE COMET: THE REMEMBRANCE OF A SEASON ON THE HIGH PLAINS. *Am. West 1969 6(6): 28-33, 62-63.* As a boy in Montana, the author saw Halley's comet one summer evening in 1910. A newspaper reported that the tail of the comet contained poisonous gas and that, if the earth should pass through it, all life on the planet would end. Although there was only one chance in a million that this would occur, the boy became obsessed with the idea that it would happen. Eventually he was convinced that the catastrophe would occur on Christmas morning. The author reminisces about his experiences and apprehension of catastrophe. Taken from a forthcoming book. 2 illus.

D. L. Smith

3676. Shepperson, Wilbur S. SOCIALIST PACIFISM IN THE AMERICAN WEST DURING WORLD WAR I. A CASE STUDY. *Historian 1967 29(4): 619-633.* In 1916 a group of Socialists established the community of Nevada City in the Lahonton Valley area of Nevada, thus reviving a 19th-century plan to win the West for the Socialist Party and concurrently providing a retreat for pacifists. Job Harriman and C. V. Eggleston founded the colony at Nevada City and, as a massive reclamation project, made the land cultivable. Immigrants flocked in. Socialism became a political reality in Nevada and neighboring States, with pacifism one of its principal tenets. The war and the draft, in addition to some unsuccessful financial ventures, brought about the failure of the colony in 1918. 36 notes.

F. J. Rossi

3677. Shochat, Fern Dawson. THE VOLUNTARY COOPERATIVE ASSOCIATION OF LOS ANGELES, 1913-1922. *Southern California Q. 1963 45(2): 169-180.* Tells of one of the many "improvement societies" which flourished in southern California in the early part of the century. George Thomas Millar, born in Ireland in 1868, came to Los Angeles in 1912 after involvement in a utopian experiment in Mexico and there met Ernest Dawson, proprietor of Dawson's Book Shop. Millar had become convinced that the politically-oriented socialism of his day did not offer a solution and was interested in embarking on a new experiment in *Constructive Socialism,* the title of a pamphlet setting forth his basic ideas. He interested Dawson and James Watson, an employee of

Dawson's, and the three of them founded the Voluntary Cooperative Association in 1913. Their hope was to establish a free, cooperative society which would provide for all its members without forcing any of them to accept anybody's ideas or direction. By 1915 the organization was doing well, but Dawson's bookstore was failing, and he felt obliged to withdraw from the V.C.A. and go back to his store. This blow as well as the wage boom of World War I which drew off a good deal of manpower prevented the V.C.A. from growing, though it managed to continue its activities until 1922.   A. K. Main

3678. Simms, L. Moody, Jr., ed.   A HORROR OF HOOPS. *Southwestern Hist. Q. 1968 72(1): 88-92.* Rebelling against hoopskirt fashions, the ladies of Brenham, Texas, organized the Anti-Crinoline League in 1893. The members of the short-lived organization condemned the contemporary fashions and published the "Chaldean Manuscript," a satire on women's dress, in the local newspaper; but they continued to wear hoopskirts and crinolines. 8 notes.   D. L. Smith

3679. Slater, Peter G.   BEN LINDSEY AND THE DENVER JUVENILE COURT: A PROGRESSIVE LOOKS AT HUMAN NATURE. *Am. Q. 1968 20(2, pt. 1): 211-223.* Benjamin Barr Lindsey's experience as Judge of the Denver Juvenile Court caused him to reflect on human nature and the proper treatment to be accorded to social deviants. In his efforts to carry out his work as a reform-minded judge, Lindsey adopted a theory of human behavior based on three principles - the inherent goodness of mankind, environmental causation, and the impulsive character of individuals. The inconsistencies represented by the three views were reflected in Lindsey's daily activity. Lindsey derived his understandings from "Reform Darwinism," but the theoretical extremes of environmentalism and individual moralism, on which Lindsey and most Progressives acted, revealed a contradictory, yet productive, approach to youth crime. Based on Lindsey MSS; 42 notes.   R. S. Pickett

3680. Smith, Florence A.   [COOS RIVER SCHOOL DAYS]. *Oregon Hist. Q. 1965 66(1): 52-57.* A letter to the editor giving a brief account of personal experiences of a teacher in the isolated area of Coos River Valley, Oregon, especially during the years 1910-17.
                                                        C. C. Gorchels

3681. Sonderling, Jacob.   FIVE GATES - CASUAL NOTES FOR AN AUTOBIOGRAPHY. *Am. Jewish Arch. 1964 16(2): 107-123.* Memoirs of a rabbi from a Hungarian Hasidic family, who, after German university training, came to the United States, and has been rabbi of Fairfax Temple in Los Angeles for nearly 30 years. These memoirs provide observations of life in the new world, and also give insights to the cultural shock such a man would undergo in this situation.
                                                        A. B. Rollins

3682. Standing, Arnold R.   A FRIENDLY HOUSE BY A HISTORIC ROAD: THE HAMPTON-BIGLER HOME. *Utah Hist. Q. 1968 36(3): 233-238.* Tells of the changes in ownership and function of a stone house built near a ford in the Bear River between Collinston and Fielding in Box Elder County, Utah. The house was operated as a hotel into the second decade of the 20th century. In the 1960's the house was threatened with destruction by plans for a highway and by the reservoir of a dam to be constructed on the Bear River. In 1967 a team from the Historic American Building Survey measured, sketched, and photographed the house. The records of their work are on file in the Library of Congress and the Utah State Historical Society.   S. L. Jones

3683. Starnes, Gary B.   JOSEPH SIDNEY FLETCHER: TEXAS LAWMAN. *Texana 1970 8(1): 30-37.* A native Texan, Fletcher (1906-66) devoted his life to law enforcement work within his State. His formal education ended with grade school, but he served for four years in the Navy and he learned the trade of a welder. After his discharge he took various welding jobs until the Depression. In 1931 Fletcher joined the highway patrol. An ambitious man, he took a wide variety of scientific detection courses in his spare time. In the mid-1930's he was a highway patrolman on special assignment to the Bureau of Identification and Records in Austin. There he soon won a reputation as a scientific crime fighter. As a result of his successes, he was appointed assistant director of the Texas Department of Public Safety in January 1945, and after a reorganization of that agency he was named deputy director in 1957. Five years later he left State service to take the more lucrative post of secretary-

general manager of the Texas and Southwestern Cattle Raisers' Association. From this post he successfully combatted cattle theives until he died of cancer in December 1966. Based on contemporary newspapers, manuscripts, and personal interviews; 43 notes.   R. J. Roske

3684. Steckmesser, Kent L.   THE OKLAHOMA ROBIN HOOD. *Am. West 1970 7(1): 38-41.* Georgia-born Charles Arthur (Pretty Boy) Floyd was raised in the oak-studded foothills of the Ozarks in Eastern Oklahoma. In these primitive circumstances the sixth-grade dropout soon earned a local reputation as a "heller." Temperamentally disinclined to farm the red claybank to support his wife and infant son, he launched a career in crime with a 1925 holdup of a Saint Louis payroll. During his stretch in the penitentiary, he acquired an education in crime from his fellow inmates. Bootlegging and bank robbery became his specialties, and he spread fear from Ohio to Oklahoma. Bank insurance rates went up and five-hundred-man posses were in pursuit. A legend of invincibility grew as his spectacular escapes and exploits multiplied. A Robin Hood image built up as he became generous with the loot and distributed much of it to the penniless tenant farmers of his hill country environs. He was a hero of ballads and movies, and a cycle of Oklahoma folk tales portrayed him as an American Robin Hood. 2 illus.   D. L. Smith

3685. Sterkx, H. E.   UNLIKELY CONQUISTADORS: ALABAMIANS AND THE MEXICAN BORDER CRISIS OF 1916. *Alabama R. 1971 24(3): 163-181.* Brief survey of the attitudes and opinions of Alabamians to the Mexican border crisis of 1916. Probably only two people had personal contact with either the revolutionary leaders or Mexican civilians - Captain Hamilton Bowie and Maude Hawk Wright. Newspapermen, persons writing letters to editors, and many politicians, took a rather dim view of the Mexicans, although there were defenders, such as Mrs. Samuel Hodgson and Congressman George Huddleston. In June 1916 thousands of young men volunteered for active duty when President Wilson mobilized the entire National Guard into Federal service. Eventually four thousand Alabamians were sent to Nogales, El Paso, or San Antonio. Early hopes of glory soon faded into the dreariness of garrison duty. In February 1917 the units were finally returned to Alabama. Based primarily on newspapers; 73 notes.
                                                        D. F. Henderson

3686. Studebaker, Marvin F.   CUBBERLEY VS. SAN DIEGO: THE TRIALS OF A SCHOOLMASTER. *Southern California Q. 1965 47(3): 269-289.* The story of the confrontation of Ellwood Patterson Cubberley, a well-known expert on educational administration, with the fledgling public education system in San Diego, California, from 1896 to 1898. San Diego was in a bust period following the boom of the 1880's, and the entire situation was chaotic. The public education system had fallen victim to lengthy battles of politically-oriented members of the Board of Education. Upon request from some members of the board, David Starr Jordan, first president of Stanford University, suggested Cubberley for the post of superintendent. His term was four years, but he served only two, finally leaving in 1898 because of continual efforts by members of the board and various local citizenry to thwart his plans for putting the school system into proper shape. 46 notes.
                                                        A. K. Main

3687. Sultz, Philip W.   CONVERSATION WITH JOE PFEIFFER. *Am. West 1965 2(4): 18-21.* Joe Pfeiffer homesteaded and lived in the Jackson Hole, Wyoming, country for over a half century. In 1962, at age 84, he granted an interview to the author, the questions and answers of which are the content of the article. The remarks are biographical, descriptive of pioneer life, and couched in colorful speech. Illus.
                                                        D. L. Smith

3688. Taber, Ronald W.   VARDIS FISHER AND THE "IDAHO GUIDE": PRESERVING CULTURE FOR THE NEW DEAL. *Pacific Northwest Q. 1968 59(2): 68-76.* An account of the creation and prospering of an emergency relief program for unemployed writers, 1935-40, under the Federal Writers' Project of the Works Progress Administration, with details on the success of one of the guide books subsequently written under the leadership of Vardis Fisher, *Idaho: A Guide in Word and Picture* (1937). "The real goals of accomplishment were established by Fisher himself and not by the Federal Government." Included are excerpts from many favorable book reviews published in leading newspapers.   C. C. Gorchels

3689. Tamony, Peter. GURNEY: A SAN FRANCISCO WORD GOES NATIONAL. *Pacific Historian 1966 10(1): 15-20.* Traces the local usage of the term "gurney" from San Francisco to its acceptance into *Webster's Third International Dictionary* (1961). During the 1890's low budgets prevented San Francisco police from using a closed vehicle for transporting prisoners. After a newspaper campaign the daughters of James Fair donated such a wagon to the Police Department. Earlier Theodore Gurney had patented a running gear for horse-drawn vehicles. The resulting appearance was markedly similar to that of the new San Francisco police wagons by virtue of the forward seating of the drivers. Gradually, San Franciscans, especially Berkeley medical students who took cabs to cross county lines in order to drink, came to refer to any cab as a "gurney," and finally the word was applied to hospital vehicles used to wheel patients throught the corridors. The usage soon grew into a national generic term for wheeled hospital vehicles. Documented from newspapers, San Francisco Municipal Reports, Patent Office Reports, published accounts, and the resources of the Oakland Public Library: illus.   T. R. Cripps

3690. Thayer, Harriet and Thayer, Ruth, ed. ONE-ROOM SCHOOL, 1900. *Oregon Hist. Q. 1971 72(3): 197-208.* Recounts the experiences of a fledgling teacher in a pioneer Oregon community on the Columbia River, as reflected in letters written in 1900. Describes her lodgings, the schoolroom, Swiss-German immigrants, and the environment.
                                                        C. C. Gorchels

3691. Toelken, Barre. TRADITIONAL FIDDLING IN IDAHO. *Western Folklore 1965 24(4): 259-262.* Tells the story of the "National Oldtime Fiddlers' Contest and Folk Music Festival" held each June in Weiser, Idaho. Also describes the rules and the contest's support among the local people.   J. M. Brady

3692. Towne, Charles W. PREACHER'S SON ON THE LOOSE WITH BUFFALO BILL CODY. *Montana 1968 18(4): 40-55.* Reminiscences of a journalist who, as a young man, worked briefly in 1902 for "Buffalo Bill" Cody on his ranch near Yellowstone Park and at his hotel and newspaper in Cody, Wyoming. Illus.   S. R. Davison

3693. Tucker, Frank H. EAST MEETS WEST: WOODROW WILSON IN 1894. *Colorado Mag. 1972 49(2): 109-115.* Describes Wilson's lectureship entitled "Value of Constitutional Government" at Colorado College Summer School of Science, Philosophy and Languages in 1894. The journey impressed Wilson with the vastness of America and stimulated his political ambitions. Based on secondary sources; 3 illus., 21 notes.   O. H. Zabel

3694. Tuttle, William M., ed. WILLIAM ALLEN WHITE AND VERNE MARSHALL: TWO MIDWESTERN EDITORS DEBATE AID TO THE ALLIES VERSUS ISOLATIONISM. *Kansas Hist. Q. 1966 32(2): 201-209.* White, the editor of the *Emporia Gazette,* and Marshall, the editor of the *Cedar Rapids Gazette,* were chairmen of national organizations in 1940 trying to influence America's policy toward the war in Europe. White's Committee to Defend America by Aiding the Allies differed from Marshall's isolationist and pacifist No Foreign War Committee. Between 14 June and 15 July 1940 the two men exchanged nine statements in which they explained their respective positions. The statements from the White Papers in the Library of Congress are reproduced in the article.   W. F. Zornow

3695. Tweney, George H. AIR TRANSPORTATION AND THE AMERICAN WEST. *Montana 1969 19(4): 68-77.* Traces the establishment and growth of commercial flying in the Western United States, with emphasis on scheduled passenger and mail service. Starting in 1920, the business has developed from a matter of experiments and stunts to an established mode of transportation. The contribution of the Boeing firm is stressed. Based on published sources; illus., 7 notes.
                                                        S. R. Davison

3696. Tyack, David B. THE PERILS OF PLURALISM: THE BACKGROUND OF THE PIERCE CASE. *Am. Hist. R. 1968 74(1): 74-98.* In 1922 the citizens of Oregon passed an initiative requiring all children between eight and 16 years to attend public schools. This action led to the famous United States Supreme Court case of *Society of Sisters of the Holy Name vs. Pierce et al* in 1925 which reaffirmed the right of

private schools to exist. The author explores the background of the initiative measure, the political alignments for and against it, and the legal argument as a case study of the purposes and limits of American public education. Although national educational leaders spoke out against the law and lawyers predicted that it would be ruled unconstitutional, Oregon public school teachers largely approved the measure. In vain, minority groups, parochial school leaders, and civil rights spokesmen protested; the bill passed by a comfortable majority. The briefs in the district and Supreme Federal courts pointed out the violation of property rights, the privileges of parents, and the dangers of a public monopoly of schooling. In the *Pierce* case the Supreme Court ruled the measure unconstitutional, thus strengthening pluralism in American society.   A

3697. Tyler, Ronnie C. THE GREATEST SHOW IN MEXICO: A WILD WEST SPECTACULAR IN THE BULL RING. *Am. West 1972 9(3): 42-47.* To recoup recent losses on an eastern tour, the 101 Ranch Wild West Show toured Mexico. The climax of the 1908 tour came in Mexico City when William (Bill) Pickett, the most famous of the American cowpunchers, a Negro, attempted to throw a Mexican bull. His bravery was unquestioned, but the *aficionados* were displeased with his performance. Thereafter police protection was openly evident to protect the show from further riot. 10 illus., biblio.   D. L. Smith

3698. Ulloa, Berta. LAS RELACIONES MEXICO-NOR-TEAMERICANAS, 1910-1911 [Mexican-North American relations, 1910-11]. *Hist. Mexicana [Mexico] 1965 15(57): 25-46.* An account of events between the United States and Mexico in the troubled immediate post-Díaz period. The discussion includes the brief presidency of Francisco León de la Barra, the activities of Henry Lane Wilson, the neutrality laws of the United States and their violations, the possible intervention by the United States, permission for troops of the United States to chase rebels into Mexico, and permission for Mexican troops to cross the territory of the United States. Based primarily on documents and archival materials, 59 notes.   C. E. Frazier

3699. Urbanek, Mac. LEW BARLOW OF GILLETTE. *Ann. of Wyoming 1964 36(2): 234-238.* Includes a discussion of Lew Barlow's life as a rambler and collector of artifacts and fossils at Gillette, Wyoming from 1898 until 1964. Illus.   R. L. Nichols

3700. Viseltear, Arthur J. COMPULSORY HEALTH INSURANCE IN CALIFORNIA, 1915-18. *J. of the Hist. of Medicine and Allied Sci. 1969 24(2): 151-182.* Describes the movement for health insurance in California. Focuses on the State's official investigatory body, the Social Insurance Commission, which was created to promote health insurance legislation during 1915-18. The efforts of this body were destroyed through the propaganda tactics of commercial insurance companies, certain employers' associations, organized labor, physicians, and Christian Scientists. 105 notes.   J. L. Susskind

3701. Warne, Clinton. THE MUNICIPAL CAMPGROUNDS OF KANSAS. *Kansas Hist. Q. 1963 29(2): 137-142.* During the 1920's, many towns throughout the United States established municipal campgrounds to provide accommodations for the increasing number of persons who enjoyed travel by automobile. Many such camps were established in Kansas. They were usually located close to the center of town, where motorists were able to purchase their supplies. Such camps provided economic advantages for the town in which they were located, but there was strong opposition from hotel owners and operators of commercial tourist ventures. The main charges were that such camps created bad sanitary conditions and catered to less desirable elements. Kansas organized a Tourist Camp Bureau to combat their problems, but the municipal camps deteriorated, and even the "hobo" campers eventually avoided them. By 1928 the movement was drawing to a close in Kansas. Based on newspaper reports and contemporary articles on the subject.
                                                        W. F. Zornow

3702. Waters, Alvin W. THE LAST OF THE GLIDDEN TOURS, MINNEAPOLIS TO GLACIER PARK, 1913. *Minnesota Hist. 1963 38(1): 205-215.* Describes the last of one of the famous annual automobile reliability runs.   S

3703. Watne, Joel Andrew. PUBLIC OPINION TOWARD NON-CONFORMISTS AND ALIENS DURING 1917, AS SHOWN BY

THE FARGO "FORUM." *North Dakota Hist. 1967 34(1): 5-29.* The *Forum* was sympathetic to royalty and seemed to condemn the Serbs during the summer of 1914, but with the declaration of war a pro-Ally sentiment developed. Possible waves of immigrants to North Dakota were anticipated. Moving first to the defense of pacifists, then to extreme patriotism, the paper promoted Americanism and condemned Socialists, draft dodgers, and the IWW (Industrial Workers of the World). It welcomed extralegal mob action as long as no blood was shed and encouraged a search for subversives. The Fargo *Forum* illustrates what happens when the masses get carried away by the conspiracy theory of history and trample on individual liberties. Illus., 50 notes.

I. W. Van Noppen

3704. Weber, Francis J. CANDIDATE OF LAST RESORT? *Am. Benedictine R. 1968 19(2): 193-202.* Shows that John J. Cantwell's appointment as bishop of the diocese of Monterey-Los Angeles, which post was vacant for two years, was not a matter of choosing a desperation candidate since Cantwell's name was among the first considered for this important post in 1915 even though his selection did not occur until 1917. 43 notes.

E. J. O'Brien

3705. Wharfield, H. B. A FIGHT WITH THE YAQUIS AT BEAR VALLEY, 1918. *Arizoniana 1963 4(3): 1-8.* Escaping notice because of World War I struggles at the time, the skirmish of 9 January 1918, west of Nogales, Arizona, involved Troop "E" of the Negro 10th US Cavalry under Captain Frederick H. L. Ryder and a band of some 30 Yaquis. Text of a letter of reminiscence by Ryder is included. Documented, illus.

E. P. Stickney

3706. Whisenhunt, Donald W. THE BARD IN THE DEPRESSION: TEXAS STYLE. *J. of Popular Culture 1968 2(3): 370-386.* Discusses popular opinion during the Depression as seen in the popular verse which emanated from Texas during the 1930's. The opinions of "plain folks" are often ignored by historians, but such opinions are reflected in letters to the editor, letters to public officials, etc. Concentrating on those communications which took the form of verse, the author assesses the mood of "plain folks" in Texas during the Depression. These materials reflect a general unhappiness during the 1930's, a disgust with Herbert Hoover and the Republican Party, and a general faith in Franklin Delano Roosevelt as a savior. Based on the author's doctoral dissertation; 25 notes.

B. A. Lohof

3707. White, John I. A BALLAD IN SEARCH OF ITS AUTHOR. *Western Am. Literature 1967 2(1): 58-61.* Identifies Joseph Mills Hanson as the author of the poem which became the supposedly authentic "Cowboy Song." Hanson published the poem in *Leslie's Monthly Magazine* in October 1904. The poem was set to music and later was included by John Lomax in his 1910 edition of *Cowboy Songs.* Following this republication (which omitted the author's name) the words became accepted as authentic.

R. N. Hudspeth

3708. Wickens, James F. THE NEW DEAL IN COLORADO. *Pacific Hist. R. 1969 38(3): 275-291.* Analyzes the impact of the New Deal programs on Colorado and the conflict over control of the programs. With both rural and urban crises resulting from the Depression, Colorado provides a typical study of the effect of the New Deal on a Western State. Describes the political situation within the State Democratic party and the consequences of reform effectiveness. The social history of the State rather than political or economic thinking was revolutionized by the New Deal measures. Based on secondary sources; 60 notes.

E. C. Hyslop

3709. Wickens, James F. TIGHTENING THE COLORADO PURSE STRINGS. *Colorado Mag. 1969 46(4): 271-286.* Discusses attempts by the Colorado State government between the two world wars to reform administration procedures for handling fiscal matters. The author concludes that little was accomplished. In a period of expanded Federal power, Colorado "resisted assuming greater responsibility for its citizens' need" and continued to accept the 19th-century belief "that small government automatically meant good government." Illus., 43 notes.

O. H. Zabel

3710. Wilder, Judith C. THE YEARS OF A DESERT LABORA-TORY. *J. of Arizona Hist. 1967 8(3): 179-199.* Describes a laboratory built on a hill in southern Arizona near Tucson. In September 1903 the laboratory was founded by two desert botanists Daniel T. MacDougal and Frederick V. Coville. At first only one scientist was stationed there, but the staff soon grew. The depression and shifting research interests caused the laboratory to close in 1937. In August 1940, the Forest Service of the US Department of Agriculture took over the site. The Forest Service refurbished the buildings and enlarged the facility. Important work in forest research was pressed for the remainder of the Federal agency's control of the laboratory complex. In 1960 the University of Arizona acquired the facilities, except for one building and greenhouse which were indefinitely leased to the Forest Service. Since that time the University of Arizona has devoted the site to geochronology (earth-time study).

R. J. Roske

3711. Wilkins, Robert P. THE NON-ETHNIC ROOTS OF NORTH DAKOTA ISOLATIONISM. *Nebraska Hist. 1963 44(3): 205-221.* Rejects the notion that pro-German sentiment was responsible for North Dakota isolationism from 1914 to the present. It can best be explained in terms of a rural people with a prejudice against Eastern business classes and interests, and also against wars which allowed the wealthy to profit and the poor to suffer. The importance of liberalism in the pattern of opposition to foreign involvement is also asserted and documented.

R. Lowitt

3712. Wilkins, Robert P. THE NONPARTISAN LEAGUE AND UPPER MIDWEST ISOLATIONISM. *Agric. Hist. 1965 39(2): 102-109.* A review of Nonpartisan League history, from 1916 to 1960, suggests that the isolationist sentiment of North Dakota people was not due to pro-German sentiment. A belief that federal spending for war benefited the East more than the Middle West and that it reduced expenditures for internal improvements and for agriculture was probably more important. Based on newspapers and manuscript collections.

W. D. Rasmussen

3713. Wilkins, Robert P. NORTH DAKOTA AND THE FORD PEACE SHIP. *North Dakota Hist. 1966 33(4): 379-398.* The only State governor who accepted Henry Ford's invitation to join his mission to Copenhagen and Stockholm (1915-16) in an effort to arrange for a peace conference in Europe was L. B. Hanna of North Dakota. Other famous members known as pacifists were Madame Rosika Schwimmer, a Hungarian intellectual, Jane Addams, and David Starr Jordan. The American press ridiculed the venture and Hanna's critics accused him of political motives, although he avowed at the end of the trip that if he had never been an advocate of peace before he was after his experiences in Europe. In retrospect Hanna seems to have been in agreement with North Dakota isolationists in Congress at the time and far ahead of his time as viewed by an ever-growing number of scholars at mid-century.

I. W. Van Noppen

3714. Wilson, Howard Lee. "TOP OF THE WORLD" BROAD-CASTS: WYOMING'S EARLY RADIO. *Ann. of Wyoming 1971 43(1): 5-52.* Details the founding and operation of Wyoming's first radio station, KFBU. Organized by Episcopal Bishop Nathaniel Seymour Thomas (1867-1937) and located in the basement of St. Matthew's Cathedral in Laramie, the noncommercial station functioned intermittently from 1922 to 1929 and broadcast religious and educational programs and sporting events. Despite continuing contributions from Mary Averell Harriman (1851-1932), philanthropic widow of Edward Henry Harriman (1848-1909), the former president of the Union Pacific Railroad, and a 1927 arrangement with the University of Wyoming to share operating expenses, the station suffered incessant financial difficulties. Thomas' inefficient implementation of plans and frequent absences from the State further hindered operations. In 1928, church officials finally initiated efforts (unsuccessful) to transfer the station to the university. In 1929, they closed the installation after the Federal Radio Commission declined to renew the license. Illus., 55 notes, appendixes.

G. R. Adams

3715. Woolley, Ivan M. THE 1918 'SPANISH INFLUENZA' PANDEMIC IN OREGON. *Oregon Hist. Q. 1963 64(3): 246-258.* Effect in Oregon of the worldwide influenza epidemic of 1918. The article includes description of efforts of officials and doctors to alleviate tragedies, the measures taken to reduce infection, and statistics of deaths.

C. C. Gorchels

3716. Worley, Lynda F. WILLIAM ALLEN WHITE: KANSAN EXTRAORDINARY. *Social Sci. 1966 41(2): 91-98.* A study of the origins and nature of the progressivism of William Allen White (1868-1944). White's parents brought to him a heritage of New England puritanism (father) and Midwestern abolitionism (mother), both of which prepared his mind for the progressivism of Theodore Roosevelt. White saw progressivism as a manifestation of abolitionist principles in an industrial age. By 1901 he had shed his conservatism of Populist days and launched into a crusade against the "bond-holding aristocracy" and "Jim Crow" legislation, at the same time that he supported prohibition, direct legislation, and suffrage for women. Drawn largely from White's publications.   M. Small

3717. Young, Karl. A FIGHT THAT COULD HAVE MEANT WAR. *Am. West 1966 3(2): 16-23, 90.* The raid of the bandit leader, Pancho Villa, on Columbus, New Mexico, on the night of 9 March 1916, reflected his anger at American recognition of his political enemy, Venustiano Carranza, and his hope for a Mexican-American war that would work to his benefit. American forces under John J. Pershing crossed into Mexico to capture Villa. Diplomatic relations were nearly strained to the breaking point. Carranza sent an ultimatum to Pershing ordering him to retreat northward and to attempt no further penetration of Mexican soil. An American cavalry troop was dispatched toward a town some 100 miles further to test the Mexican will to carry out the threat of trouble for violation of the ultimatum. The encounter was disastrous for the Americans. The narration of this incident at Carrizal, Chihuahua, is based principally on interviews with the Mormon scout survivor, Lemuel Spilsbury. Illus., map, biblio.   D. L. Smith

Politics

3718. Alexander, Charles C. THE KLU KLUX KLAN IN TEXAS POLITICS IN THE 1920'S. *Mid-America 1964 46(1): 3-28.* A survey of the Klan's political career in Texas, its techniques and difficulties, successes and failures, throws light into a hitherto hidden corner of the history of the state. It clarifies the whole problem of the Klan as a political force in the twenties, and also is an interesting case study of how secret nativist and vigilante societies get into politics and the methods they employ.   L. D. Silveri

3719. Argersinger, Peter H. THE MOST PICTURESQUE DRAMA: THE KANSAS SENATORIAL ELECTION OF 1891. *Kansas Hist. Q. 1972 38(1): 43-64.* Every Kansas senatorial election since 1871 had been marked with some kind of trouble, but the most excitement came in 1891 when the People's Party (later called the Populist Party) succeeded in electing William Alfred Peffer (1831-1912). The election showed that the People's Party was dominated by recent Republicans such as Peffer, that the People's Party was seriously hampered by persistent factionalism that almost even kept it from selecting its own candidate for the Senate, that the Democrats had little influence in the People's Party although they continually made every effort to influence its decisions, and that the Republican Party was willing to resort to the worst kind of sectional and partisan appeals to save its position in Kansas. Based on primary and secondary sources in the Library of Congress, Kansas State Historical Society, and Minnesota Historical Society; 2 illus., 4 photos, 72 notes.   W. F. Zornow

3720. Arrington, Leonard. THE NEW DEAL IN THE WEST: A PRELIMINARY STATISTICAL INQUIRY. *Pacific Hist. R. 1969 38(3): 311-316.* Reports prepared for President Franklin D. Roosevelt during the presidential campaign of 1940 analyzed the amount of assistance given to each of the 48 States by New Deal agencies during 1933-38. The reports are available in the library of the Bureau of the Budget but have not been used systematically by historians. On a per capita basis, the highest economic benefits went to 14 Western States. Based on primary sources; 3 tables.   E. C. Hyslop

3721. Ashby, Darrell Leroy. PROGRESSIVISM AGAINST ITSELF: THE SENATE WESTERN BLOC OF THE 1920'S. *Mid-America 1968 50(4): 291-304.* Examines the western bloc's attempt to create a powerful voice within the easterly-oriented Republican Party. To achieve this end a group of western Senators came together in 1927 in what they hoped would be a united and growing bloc of agrarian interest. Ironically, the group's leader, Senator William E. Borah of Idaho, seems to have been the major cause of its discord. The author details the confusion and then total disruption which resulted from this group's attempt to establish a united front on such issues as the McNary-Haugen form relief bill, prohibition, and their choice for Republican presidential nominee. Based on primary and secondary sources; 56 notes.   R. J. Eilerman

3722. Avery, Ruth Sigler. CYRUS STEVENS AVERY. *Chronicles of Oklahoma 1967 45(1): 84-91.* Oklahoma pioneer Cyrus S. Avery (1871-1963) moved to the State in 1907. He first sold life insurance after receiving his B.A. degree in 1897 from William Jewel College, Missouri. He soon became a farmer, organized the Avery Realty Company, was vice-president of the Leavell Coal Company and secretary-treasurer of the Togo Oil Company in Tulsa. He served as county commissioner, as president of the Eastern Oklahoma Agricultural Association, and as the State's first highway commissioner. Avery was the unsuccessful Democratic candidate for governor in the 1934 primary election. Many felt he exemplified "The Tulsa Spirit." illus.   K. P. Davis

3723. Bandza, Alfred. THE REFERENDUM IN NORTH DAKOTA: 1918-1960. *North Dakota Q. 1963 31(1/2): 1-4.* Concerns the use by North Dakotans of the referendum procedure in their constitution. The referendum has been used by educators and harassed taxpayers. It seems to have been an instrument of articulate minorities of either the left or the right, rather than exclusively an instrument of liberalism or of conservatism. Review article based on a recent master's thesis at the University of North Dakota.   E. P. Stickney

3724. Bates, J. Leonard. T. J. WALSH: HIS GENIUS FOR CONTROVERSY. *Montana 1969 19(4): 3-15.* Traces the career of Thomas J. Walsh in Montana, from his arrival as a young lawyer in 1890 through his rise to prominence in Democratic circles and into his years as a senator after 1912. Instances are cited showing his ability and zeal in courtroom cases involving deeply controversial issues. Based chiefly on Walsh's speeches and correspondence, 34 notes.   S. R. Davison

3725. Bayard, Charles J. THE COLORADO PROGRESSIVE REPUBLICAN SPLIT OF 1912. *Colorado Mag. 1968 45(1): 61-78.* Gives a detailed analysis of the failure of the two wings of the progressive Republicans to unite in Colorado in 1912. The Denver progressives, led by Edward P. Costigan, supported Theodore Roosevelt and favored forming a third party. The out-state progressives, led by Philip Stewart, who ran for the gubernatorial nomination and lost, preferred to stay within the Republican Party and reform it. "The results were almost preordained; the Democrats swept into office and Colorado politics slipped back into old familiar patterns." Illus., 48 notes.   O. H. Zabel

3726. Bergman, H. J. THE IMPEACHMENT TRIAL OF JOHN H. SCHIVELY. *Pacific Northwest Q. 1968 59(3): 128-136.* Gives a detailed account of the impeachment proceedings against the first elected insurance commissioner of the State of Washington in 1909, which were initiated by reform Governor Marion E. Hay. The Washington State Senate refused to support the impeachment, and both Schively and Hay lost political power at the end of their terms in 1912. Based on newspapers and other sources; notes.   C. C. Gorchels

3727. Bicha, Karel Denis. JERRY SIMPSON: POPULIST WITHOUT PRINCIPLE. *J. of Am. Hist. 1967 54(2): 291-306.* The key to Simpson's character is not easy to find. He has been portrayed as a boorish, illiterate demagogue or as an astute, self-educated political leader who "assumed a crudity to which he was a stanger." Neither is essentially correct. "Sockless Jerry's" political behavior was a result of two personality traits: a profound fatalism which led him to expect the failure of his Populist cause, and an inability to concentrate systematic efforts on specific reform measures. Together they rendered him a very unreliable servant of the Populist movement. A member of Congress from 1890 to 1894 and 1896 to 1898, he was ineffective and unreliable in his activities on behalf of reform measures. In truth, he was sincere only in his advocacy of low tariffs and antimilitarism, neither of which was central to the Populist program. In matters of free silver, grain grading, railroad regulation, and labor legislation he rendered lip service that was often betrayed by his actions in Congress. In 1900 the Populist convention in

Kansas humiliated him by refusing to endorse his nomination for Senator. Based principally on local newspapers and the *Congressional Record*.

K. B. West

3728.   Bowles, B. Dean.   LOCAL GOVERNMENT PARTICIPATION AS A ROUTE OF RECRUITMENT TO THE STATE LEGISLATURE IN CALIFORNIA AND PENNSYLVANIA, 1900-1962. *Western Pol. Q. 1966 19(3): 491-503.* A common assumption in the literature of political science is the "training-ground thesis" - i.e., the idea that in the American system local officeholding is the way to State and then to national political officeholding, and that this is a way of testing and weeding. But this idea requires empirical testing and logically need not hold, for the Federal system is far from a monolithic one. On the basis of a study of 1,840 biographies of members of both houses in California and Pennsylvania, from 1900 to 1962 inclusive, it is clear that local government participation does not serve as the route of recruitment to the State legislature. It is one of the routes but there are several others and statistically local apprenticeship is not the most important among these. 4 tables.

H. Aptheker

3729.   Branan, Herbert L.   PORTRAIT OF GOVERNOR LEON C. PHILLIPS.   *Chronicles of Oklahoma 1968 46(2): 122-126.* Biographical remarks made at the presentation of a portrait of Leon C. Phillips, governor of Oklahoma, 1939-43, to the Oklahoma Historical Society. Phillips' principal contributions were in the areas of higher education and in budget balancing provisions in the state constitution. Illus.

D. L. Smith

3730.   Budig, Gene A. and Walton, Donald B.   THE DAY GEORGE NORRIS DIED.   *Nebraska Hist. 1969 50(1): 55-61.* An account of the last days of former Senator George Norris in McCook from late August until his death on 2 September 1944.

R. Lowitt

3731.   Burbank, Garin.   AGRARIAN RADICALS AND THEIR OPPONENTS: POLITICAL CONFLICT IN SOUTHERN OKLAHOMA, 1910-1924.   *J. of Am. Hist. 1971 58(1): 5-23.* A study of voting patterns in precincts of Marshall County shows strong support for the Socialist Party among the predominantly native, white tenant farmers of the area, 1910-16. During World War I the support for Socialism nearly disappeared, but by 1922 a radical Farmer-Labor Reconstruction League had emerged as a political force. When, in 1923-25, the Ku Klux Klan dominated Oklahoma, the League and Marshall County farmers opposed Klan candidates, supported John Walton, "the Klan fighter," and fought William Pine, Klan-supported gubernatorial candidate in 1924. The case study provides evidence to show that radical farm-labor politics was not narrowly bigoted and ethnocentric as implied by Richard Hofstadter and others. 5 tables, 69 notes.

K. B. West

3732.   Cadenhead, Ivie E., Jr.   WILL ROGERS: FORGOTTEN MAN.   *Midcontinent Am. Studies J. 1963 4(2): 49-57.* Sees Will Rogers as one of a long line of cracker-barrel humorists who "came as close to being a national spokesman during the latter part of his career as any one writer has ever become." Like many Americans he was "a product of the frontier, of the rural scene and of small town life." He was an Oklahoma cowboy who was part Indian. His attacks on the follies of Congressmen showed his anti-democratic leanings. He was largely responsible for the last minute avalanche of telegrams that resulted in the defeat of a resolution to make the United States a member of the World Court. 26 notes.

E. P. Stickney

3733.   Caldwell, Dorothy J.   CARRY NATION, A MISSOURI WOMAN, WON FAME IN KANSAS.   *Missouri Hist. R. 1969 63(4): 461-488.* A brief biographical sketch of the famous prohibition leader Carry Nation (1846-1911) who won national prominence by smashing Kansas saloons in Medicine Lodge, Kiowa, Wichita, and Topeka. Her family background and youth are described briefly. The author gives a detailed description of her visit to Saint Louis, Kansas City, and other Missouri towns in 1901. Based on local newspapers, biographies, articles, local histories, and biographical directories; illus., 105 notes.

W. F. Zornow

3734.   Clanton, O. Gene.   INTOLERANT POPULIST? THE DISAFFECTION OF MARY ELIZABETH LEASE.   *Kansas Hist. Q. 1968 34(2): 189-200.* A biographical sketch of a distinguished Populist orator

with a major emphasis on the period from 1890 to 1894. She became estranged from the Populists when they began to think of fusing with the Democrats. She accused the Populist administration of being allied with gambling interests. Efforts to remove her as a member of the Board of Charities sparked a lively court battle over the governor's removal power. The keys to Mrs. Lease's actions during this period are to be found in her exaggerated sense of self-importance, her hatred for any thought of fusing with the Democrats, and her failure to understand the problems of her times. Based on articles, newspapers, and a manuscript biography in the Kansas State Historical Society; illus., 35 notes.

W. F. Zornow

3735.   Coletta, Paolo E.   THE NEBRASKA DEMOCRATIC CAMPAIGN OF 1910.   *Nebraska Hist. 1971 52(4): 359-382.* Discusses the divisive campaign of 1910 as it affected the fortunes of the Nebraska Democratic Party. Prohibition was the divisive issue, and William Jennings Bryan raised it by not supporting the party's candidate for Governor, James C. Dahlman, who was an avowed "wet." Dahlman lost the election, and Bryan lost the support of the Democratic Party in his home State.

R. Lowitt

3736.   Coletta, Paolo.   THE PATRONAGE BATTLE BETWEEN BRYAN AND HITCHCOCK.   *Nebraska Hist. 1968 49(2): 121-137.* An account of the break between William Jennings Bryan and Gilbert M. Hitchcock which began over their differing views on prohibition and split the Nebraska Democratic Party at the end of the 19th century. It culminated in a bitter battle over patronage in Nebraska during the first administration of Woodrow Wilson when Bryan was secretary of state and Hitchcock a U.S. Senator. The result was capitulation for Bryan when, in May 1916 after he had left the cabinet, Wilson acceded to Hitchcock's patronage requests.

R. Lowitt

3737.   Cook, R. G.   PIONEER PORTRAITS: WELDON B. HEYBURN.   *Idaho Yesterdays 1966 10(1): 22-26.* "This biographical sketch of a prominent Idaho United States Senator is based upon a thesis prepared at the University of Idaho." A lawyer-politician, Weldon Brinton Heyburn (1852-1912) helped to write the fundamental law of Idaho and served in the Senate from 1903 to 1912. The author traces the political history and issues of the 1890's in northern Idaho. Heyburn was an extreme conservative, and a firm believer in the US Constitution, opposing any attempts to change it by amendments. Foremost among his legislative contributions was his successful campaign to get a pure food and drug law passed by the Senate. 62 notes.

D. H. Swift

3738.   Cook, Rufus G.   THE POLITICAL SUICIDE OF SENATOR FRED T. DUBOIS OF IDAHO.   *Pacific Northwest Q. 1969 60(4): 193-204.* A summary of the political maneuvers and controversy over anti-Mormonism (1903-07) which led to the political decline of U.S. Senator Fred Thomas Dubois of Idaho.

C. C. Gorchels

3739.   Crouch, Barry A.   DENNIS CHAVEZ AND ROOSEVELT'S "COURT-PACKING" PLAN.   *New Mexico Hist. R. 1967 42(4): 261-280.* Assesses the various factors which influenced and perhaps determined New Mexican Senator Dennis Chavez' eventual support of the attempt by FDR to increase the size of the Supreme Court. Although letters from constituents ran strongly against the proposal, and New Mexican law associations and the press were opposed, Chavez voted in favor of the bill. In part he wished to see Sam G. Bratton, a Federal circuit judge and former Senator from New Mexico, considered as a replacement for Willis VanDevanter on the Supreme Court. A negative vote from either Carl Hatch or Chavez would have ended Bratton's chances. Chavez also was indebted to the administration for "all the backing it had given him in past years." Based on newspapers and letters from the Dennis Chavez Papers, University of Albuquerque; 43 notes.

D. F. Henderson

3740.   Dalstrom, Harl A.   "REMOTE BIGNESS" AS A THEME IN NEBRASKA POLITICS: THE CASE OF KENNETH S. WHERRY. *North Dakota Q. 1970 38(3): 23-32.* Republican Senator Wherry (1892-1951) was in the tradition of William Jennings Bryan (1860-1925) and George William Norris (1861-1944) in that all three opposed "Remote bigness" - Bryan "Big Money," Norris "Big Business," and Wherry "Big Government" and "Big Bureaucracy." Wherry attacked the Federal Reserve and New Deal agencies but was careful to support parity administration. Wherry's view that farmers and small businessmen were the backbone of the Nation motivated his actions and reflected the sentiments of his constituency. Though Wherry's career spanned years of dynamic change in the American economy, he tried to maintain the economic patterns in which he had grown to manhood and prospered. Based on secondary sources; illus., 41 notes.　　　　J. F. Mahoney

3741. DeLorme, Roland L. EDWARD COSTIGAN AND THE COLORADO BAR: A CASE STUDY OF THE STATUS REVOLUTION. *Mid-Am. 1967 49(3): 200-213.* The early career of Edward Costigan, who began his law practice in Denver in 1900, illustrates the status revolution that undermined the American lawyer's professional independence and political power and made him a potential champion of reform. Costigan ostensibly found and made the adjustments necessary to a fruitful law practice. He met the criteria for prestige: admission to his calling, education, acceptance by his colleagues in professional organizations, class position, and public recognition. But he sought a greater public role. In the emerging business civilization, however, independent professionals like Costigan did not find an open door to political preferment readily available. Based largely on the Costigan Papers at the University of Colorado; 84 notes.　　　　L. D. Silveri

3742. DeWitt, Howard A. CHARLES L. MC NARY AND THE 1918 CONGRESSIONAL ELECTION. *Oregon Hist. Q. 1967 68(2): 125-140.* An account of the political campaign in Oregon in 1918 which led to the nomination and election of Charles L. McNary to the U.S. Senate, reflecting influences of World War I and local conditions.
　　　　C. C. Gorchels

3743. Donovan, Ruth G. THE NEBRASKA LEAGUE OF WOMEN VOTERS. *Nebraska Hist. 1971 52(3): 311-328.* Surveys the history of the Nebraska League from its creation in June 1920 to the present, stressing its concern with issues pertaining to the welfare of women and children.　　　　R. Lowitt

3744. Durden, Robert F. THE "COW-BIRD" GROUNDED: THE POPULIST NOMINATION OF BRYAN AND TOM WATSON IN 1896. *Mississippi Valley Hist. R. 1963 50(3): 397-423.* The Populists were not tricked into nominating Bryan but did so for the survival of the People's Party. Watson's choice was necessary to harmonize the factions within the party. The Populists were deeply committed to the free silver doctrine. "Free silver, far from being a 'cow-bird,' had swept the Populists into an important role in the epochal campaign of 1896." To most Populists socialism was the real, late-coming "cow-bird" that tried to capture the nest. The author quotes Chester M. Destler *(American Radicalism, 1865-1901,* p. 254; 1946) that events at Chicago foreshadowed the fate of the attempt to graft an alien collectivism into the traditional pattern of American democratic radicalism. 67 notes.　　　　E. P. Stickney

3745. Dyson, Lowell K. THE RED PEASANT INTERNATIONAL IN AMERICA. *J. of Am. Hist. 1972 58(4): 958-973.* In the mid-1920's the Third International under the direction of Nikolai Ivanovich Bukharin (1888-1938) moved toward the idea of building support among peasants and proletariat for revolutions that then appeared quite distant. To that end, the Krestintern, or Red Peasant International (called the Farmers International in the United States), set up the United Farmers Educational League in Bismarck, North Dakota, under the direction of Alfred Knutson, former organizer for the Nonpartisan League and the Farmer Labor Party. Knutson published the *United Farmer* and tried to make alliances with Farm-Labor Union of the Southwest, the Western Progressive Farmers, and other farmer-labor parties. However, internal dissension, the failure of political action, and a new Stalinist line that encouraged a hard immediate revolutionary line, doomed the movement. 92 notes.　　　　K. B. West

3746. Finger, John R. THE POST-GUBERNATORIAL CAREER OF JONATHAN M. DAVIS. *Kansas Hist. Q. 1967 33(2): 158-171.* Between his defeat for reelection as Governor of Kansas in 1924 and his death in 1943, Jonathan Davis sought office in 10 elections. He was victorious in two of them. The author offers a brief account of each campaign and concludes that the 1926 and 1936 elections were the most significant, since they provide good examples of intraparty factionalism. Davis' views consisted of paradoxical elements, including, at various times, a demand for increased government services but with less government expenditure. Based on newspapers, the Governor's papers, State publications, and secondary books; illus., 86 notes.
　　　　W. F. Zornow

3747. Finney, Ruth. HIRAM JOHNSON OF CALIFORNIA. *Am. Hist. Illus. 1966 1(7): 20-28.* Gives a personality profile of a leading political figure and discusses the 30-odd years he influenced American politics. The author feels that Johnson is remembered mainly for his isolationist policies, notably his crusade against corruption, his years as California governor, his campaign for open primaries, and his activities as "Bull Moose" Party organizer. Johnson's political career is traced from 1911, with particular emphasis on his achievements in the Senate. One of his greatest accomplishments was his fight for the first Colorado River project. 6 illus.　　　　M. J. McBaine

3748. Flynn, G. Q. THE NEW DEAL AND LOCAL ARCHIVES: THE PACIFIC NORTHWEST. *Am. Archivist 1970 33(1): 41-52.* Describes materials in Federal Records Centers pertaining to the 1930's and the New Deal. Examines the present state of New Deal historiography, pointing out that most studies have been on a national scale and from a presidential viewpoint. Many disputes about the origins of the New Deal can be resolved only by consulting regional and local materials. Surveys different kinds of research materials available in the Pacific Northwest: public records in major historical depositories; local newspapers; personal papers in manuscript form; and university theses. Suggests several ways of using these sources, including the study of local history. 25 notes.
　　　　D. E. Horn

3749. Fry, Amelia. ALONG THE SUFFRAGE TRAIL: FROM WEST TO EAST FOR FREEDOM NOW! *Am. West 1969 6(1): 16-25.* A half century of agitation enfranchised women in a dozen western states. The activist suffragist Congressional Union was impatient for this reform to be written into the Federal Constitution. A freedom booth at the Panama Pacific International Exposition in San Francisco in 1915 resulted in a petition on an 18-thousand-foot roll of paper that boasted a half-million signatures. A five-day Women Voters' Convention whipped up enthusiasm for a cross-country mission to add names to the petition, garner public statements of support from local congressmen, and to stage parades and rallies. Although transcontinental automobile travel was still a rigorous pioneering venture, grass widow Sara Bard Field accepted the challenge to take the cause and the suffrage petition to President Woodrow Wilson himself and to the Congress for its opening of the 1915-16 session. Two ladies had just bought an Overland and wanted to drive it to Rhode Island. They offered to take Sara Field on the jaunt from San Francisco to Washington by way of New England. No detail was overlooked; a female press agent preceded her, by train, to round up autocades, bands, mayors, congressmen, and governors, thus assuring fitting receptions in each city on the way. Not without considerable hardship and opposition, the mission was completed. The 19th amendment was not proposed and ratified into the Constitution, however, until after the war, in 1920. Based partly on Sara Bard Field's oral history manuscript; 11 illus., biblio. note.　　　　D. L. Smith

3750. Fuller, John F. THE PRESS AND THE 1938 NORTH DAKOTA ELECTION. *North Dakota Hist. 1968 35(1): 28-56.* North Dakota Republican Governor William Langer was a candidate for the United States Senate in the election of 1938. The major newspapers in the State, from which the smaller and local papers generally got their political news and editorial inclinations, were anti-Langer. They disapproved of his socialistic ventures and progressionism, and employed such key words as "purge," "machine government," "payroller," and "rape" to conjure up an instant mental image to the reader. Langer was too late in his effort to undo this damage. More than any other single factor, the press was responsible for his defeat. 13 illus., 93 notes.　　　　D. L. Smith

3751. Gothberg, John A. THE LOCAL INFLUENCE OF J. R. KNOWLAND'S OAKLAND "TRIBUNE." *Journalism Q. 1968 45(3): 487-495.* The career of Congressman Joseph Russell Knowland (1873-1966) as a holder of public office ended in 1914 with his defeat for the U.S. Senate. He retained his position of influence, however, in East Bay and California politics. On 3 November 1915 he became publisher of the Oakland *Tribune.* Knowland and the "Kelly Machine" inevitably clashed, first in 1923, over the selection of a new district attorney. The Knowland victory, which launched the career of Earl Warren, hurt the Kelly forces, and the machine came to an end in a crucial 1930 election. In the mid-1920's Knowland and the Oakland *Tribune* were powerful forces in the East Bay, and successfully influenced the outcome of bond issues and governmental changes. Knowland's activity in the organiza-

tional life of the community, his experience as a politician, and his behind-the-scenes political activity all made the *Tribune* effective. Based on primary sources; 32 notes.
                                                                    K. J. Puffer

3752. Greenbaum, Fred. THE COLORADO PROGRESSIVES IN 1906. *Arizona and the West 1965 7(1): 21-32.* In the early history of the Progressive movement in Colorado, 1906 stands out as a milestone year. Reformers had to reckon with an apathetic mayor and an uninterested district attorney when they went after saloons, gambling, commercial prostitution, and other vice in Denver. They were also faced with the organized political resistance inspired by public utilities against their efforts in the municipal elections of that year. The Progressives forged alliances to pressure for State reform legislation and to nominate Progressive leaders for statewide offices. Although their efforts netted them little in 1906, they had lain the groundwork that would oust the Denver machine and institute an experiment in commission government, see much of the Progressive program enacted by the State, and lead to the formation of a vigorous Progressive Party within the next decade. Based on the Lincoln Steffens Papers at Columbia University, the Benjamin B. Lindsey Papers at the Library of Congress, the Edward P. Costigan Papers at the University of Colorado, and newspaper accounts; 40 notes.
                                                                    D. L. Smith

3753. Griffiths, David B. FAR WESTERN POPULISM: THE CASE OF UTAH, 1893-1900. *Utah Hist. Q. 1969 37(4): 396-407.* Concludes that Populism in Utah drew its support primarily from urban and labor sources and built its program around labor reform legislation and political reform. Two Salt Lake City leaders appear as central figures in the Populist movement in Utah - Henry W. Lawrence, the party's candidate for governor in 1895, and Warren Foster, editor of the *Inter-Mountain Advocate.* Based mainly on contemporary newspapers and the William Jennings Bryan Papers (Library of Congress), Davis H. Waite Papers (Colorado State Archives, Denver), and the J. R. Rogers Papers (Washington State Archives, Olympia).
                                                                    S. L. Jones

3754. Griffiths, David B. FAR-WESTERN POPULIST THOUGHT: A COMPARATIVE STUDY OF JOHN R. ROGERS AND DAVIS H. WAITE. *Pacific Northwest Q. 1969 60(4): 183-192.* Analysis of the somewhat conflicting ideological beliefs of two politicians who were elected governors as members of the Populist Party - one, Davis Hanson Waite, governor of Colorado in 1892, and the other, John Rankin Rogers, governor of Washington in 1896. Such concepts as the single tax, the natural right to free land, imperialism, and the farmer-labor alliance are discussed against the backdrop of brief biographical sketches covering the years 1838-1901.
                                                                    C. C. Gorchels

3755. Grow, Stewart L. THE UTAH LEGISLATURE AND THE INCOME TAX AMENDMENT. *Utah Hist. Q. 1968 36(3): 222-232.* Relates how Utah's Republican legislature and governor acted to defeat Utah's ratification of the 16th amendment to the Constitution, although Utah Republicans had formally endorsed it. Based principally on newspaper accounts and the published journals of both houses of the Utah Legislature.
                                                                    S. L. Jones

3756. Hall, Tom G. CALIFORNIA POPULISM AT THE GRASSROOTS: THE CASE OF TULARE COUNTY, 1892. *Southern California Q. 1967 49(2): 193-204.* Populists in Tulare County, California, were a diverse lot in 1892. They included established fruit growers and those newly involved in fruit cultivation; people who advocated the single tax idea and those who opposed it; individuals who promoted irrigation, cooperatives, and improved farming techniques and those who did not; and men who believed free silver was the solution to the money problem and those who thought a socialist state was a better remedy. However, all shared the belief that something was wrong with the existing system and all wanted something done to improve it. Specifically, all were opposed to the large, corporate farmer, the land speculator, and the alien land company, and all advocated public ownership of the railroads. The author's conclusion that Tulare County Populists were small farmers led by rural editors and other professional men, many of whom had already been members of third parties prior to becoming Populists, gives support to the same findings in other studies of Populism. Based largely on contemporary newspaper accounts and county histories. 39 notes.
                                                                    W. L. Bowers

3757. Hanson, Bertil L. COUNTY COMMISSIONERS OF OKLAHOMA. *Midwest J. of Pol. Sci. 1965 9(4): 388-400.* Examines the Oklahoma county commissioner and the role played by him in local and state politics. The commissioners surveyed usually had a modest education, served for long periods of time, and had as their major concern the care of county roads. "Their influence [in state politics] is considerable, but it is not obvious," and they only "try to be influential when they themselves stand to gain or lose." The author concludes that although the commissioners lack high office and outstanding talents, "they do display an opportunism, a practical sense, and an indirect influence on state politics that is worthy of attention." 11 notes.
                                                                    J. W. Thacker, Jr.

3758. Hanson, Bertil L. OKLAHOMA'S EXPERIENCE WITH DIRECT LEGISLATION. *Southwestern Social Sci. Q. 1966 47(3): 263-273.* Assessment of the impact of direct legislation on politics during the last 58 years. Included is a detailed analysis of who initiated petitions, i.e., special interest groups, legislature, or governor; voter participation in elections; and the effect on the party system. The author concludes that direct legislation appears "to impair good executive-legislative relations and to discourage the growth of responsible, issue-oriented parties." 18 notes.
                                                                    D. F. Henderson

3759. Harvey, Richard B. GOVERNOR EARL WARREN OF CALIFORNIA: A STUDY IN "NON-PARTISAN" REPUBLICAN POLITICS. *California Hist. Soc. Q. 1967 46(1): 33-51.* Analyzes the nature and techniques of Governor Warren's nonpartisan political approach from 1943 to 1953. His views on social legislation diverged from those held by many of his fellow Republicans. He tried not to mix his two roles, part leader and public servant. By deemphasizing Republican ties and promising nonpartisanship in managing State affairs, he won many Democratic votes. The elimination of crossfiling in 1954 requiring candidates on every primary ballot to designate their party preference caused an "upsurge in Democratic fortunes at the polls in California in the late fifties." 41 notes.
                                                                    E. P. Stickney

3760. Hendrickson, Kenneth E., Jr. SOME POLITICAL ASPECTS OF THE POPULIST MOVEMENT IN SOUTH DAKOTA. *North Dakota Hist. 1967 34(1): 77-92.* A Farmers' Club was founded in Deuel County, Dakota, in 1884 by Henry Langford Loucks, an immigrant from Canada. Its members affiliated with the National Farmers' Alliance. Dakota farmers entered the protest against railroad practices and got a limited railroad commission established. Failing to elect the two U.S. Senators when South Dakota became a State, the Alliance formed an Independent Party, then allied with the Democrats and elected James Henderson Kyle to the Senate. Independents joined the Populist Party and in 1892 elected 17 members to the South Dakota legislature. In 1896 Andrew E. Lee, a fusionist, was elected governor. Under him South Dakota adopted several reform measures. Fusion was not accomplished at the county level. The Populists never gained control of the State government. Their greatest success came through coalition with the Silver Republicans and Democrats. Illus., 97 notes.   I. W. Van Noppen

3761. Hill, C. Warren. COLORADO PROGRESSIVES AND THE BULL MOOSE CAMPAIGN. *Colorado Mag. 1966 43(2): 93-113.* Traces the Progressive Party in Colorado from 16 June 1910 until the 1916 election. Roosevelt's speaking engagements in Colorado and attitudes of newspapers are cited. The author accounts for the defeat of the ticket in 1912, 1914, and 1916 when the leaders supported Charles E. Hughes.
                                                                    I. W. Van Noppen

3762. Hoffman, George. POLITICAL ARITHMETIC: CHARLES L. MC NARY AND THE 1914 PRIMARY ELECTION. *Oregon Hist. Q. 1965 66(4): 363-378.* Details of the closely contested election for the Oregon Republican nomination for Oregon Supreme Court justice between future U.S. Senator Charles Linza McNary and Henry L. Benson, in which Benson won by one vote. Documented from Oregon newspapers.
                                                                    C. C. Gorchels

3763. Holsinger, M. Paul. FOR GOD AND THE AMERICAN HOME: THE ATTEMPT TO UNSEAT SENATOR REED SMOOT, 1903-1907. *Pacific Northwest Q. 1969 60(3): 154-160.* Even though physical violence toward members of the Church of Jesus Christ of Latter-day Saints was largely a thing of the past, when Reed Smoot was elected to the U.S. Senate by the Utah Legislature in 1903, much opposition arose across the Nation. The election of Smoot, a successful banker, manufacturer, and political organizer, was opposed almost exclusively because he was an "apostle" in the Mormon Church. Relates the details of the opposition and describes the four-year verbal battle which ultimately brought Senate acceptance of Smoot's qualifications.

C. C. Gorchels

3764. Holsinger, M. Paul. J. C. BURROWS AND THE FIGHT AGAINST MORMONISM: 1903-1907. *Michigan Hist. 1968 52(3): 181-195.* Traces the abortive four-year effort of Michigan Senator Julius Caesar Burrows to expel from Congress his fellow Republican Reed Smoot of Utah. Smoot was an apostle of the Mormon Church and one of the denomination's most conspicuous officials. Burrows had been a persistent critic of Mormonism in Congress for over two decades and the "Smoot Case" provided him with ammunition for a major assault against Mormon hierarchy and doctrine. Directing the fight from his position as chairman of the Senate Committee on Privileges and Elections, Burrows conducted lengthy hearings designed to enrage passions against polygamy - even though Smoot neither believed in nor practiced plural marriage. In 1904 as the issue reached a climax, the Michigan Legislature affirmed its support of Burrow's crusade by reelecting him unanimously. He did not fare as well in the Senate, however, when his motion to bar Smoot was finally defeated in 1907. Three years later, in Michigan's first direct senatorial election, he was retired from office, having served nearly 40 years in Congress. Based on manuscript sources, newspapers, the *Congressional Record,* and other public documents; 5 illus., 55 notes.

J. K. Flack

3765. Hornbein, Marjorie. THREE GOVERNORS IN A DAY. *Colorado Mag. 1968 45(3): 243-260.* A discussion of the disputed Colorado gubernatorial election of 1904 in which fraud was evident both in behalf of Democrat and former governor Alva Adams who won a majority of the votes counted, and incumbent Republican James Peabody. A deal between Democratic and Republican leaders concerning appointment of the new supreme court justices resulted in the inauguration of Adams on 10 January 1905. Peabody protested and a joint legislative committee investigated and submitted a majority report supporting Peabody and two minority reports, one supporting Adams and the other Republican Lieutenant Governor Jesse McDonald. A strange scheme was worked out by which Peabody was declared the legally elected governor in return for his resignation in 24 hours and his replacement by McDonald. "The Republicans had won the long and bitter contest." Illus., 61 notes.

O. H. Zabel

3766. Hutchinson, W. H. PROLOGUE TO REFORM: THE CALIFORNIA ANTI-RAILROAD REPUBLICANS, 1899-1905. *Southern California Q. 1962 44(3): 175-218.* A brief study of California political history during the Progressive movement. There was a coalition of reform-minded Republicans with a strong southern California flavor. Its visible leader was Thomas Robert Bard of Hueneme of Ventura County. The author hypothesizes that Bard's election as U.S. Senator enabled the antimachine Republicans to sustain a continuing opposition to the Southern Pacific Railway's political power. The antirailroad Republicans were instrumental in the nomination of George C. Pardee for governor in 1902. In 1910 Hiram W. Johnson won the campaign for governor under the slogan "Kick the Southern Pacific out of politics." After Johnson's election the shift in emphasis by the Lincoln-Roosevelt league was from simple political reform to Progressive politics. Illus., 139 notes.

D. H. Swift

3767. Israel, Fred L. KEY PITTMAN AND NEW DEAL POLITICS. *Nevada Hist. Soc. Q. 1971 14(3): 19-25.* Sketches the political career of Key Pittman (1872-1940), the colorful senior Senator from Nevada. His credo would permit no interest other than Nevada, unless support of other interests would benefit Nevada. "Nevada first, last, and all the time" was his motto. Pittman was first elected to the Senate at age 41, and retained his seat for 27 years, until his death. He was an alcoholic and was given to very undignified actions when drunk, which was nearly always. To do something for the silver interests became a ruling passion with him. During the early New Deal days he was the prime mover of the silver subsidy which President Franklin Delano Roosevelt accepted after much pressure from both sides to the issue. Pittman was a Roosevelt man, and Roosevelt rewarded him by funneling Nevada patronage

through him. Pittman feuded with most of Roosevelt's cabinet and was constantly at war with the intellectual elements of the New Deal administration. Based on primary sources; 10 notes. E. P. Costello

3768. Jensen, Joan M. ANNETTE ABBOTT ADAMS, POLITICIAN. *Pacific Hist. R. 1966 35(2): 185-201.* Re-creates Mrs. Adams' career in California law and politics, her campaign for the vice-presidential Democratic nomination in 1920 and her work as assistant attorney general. The author concludes that, despite gaining suffrage in California in 1911, women in California found it difficult to get elected to political office.

J. McCutcheon

3769. Johnson, Warren B. MUCKRAKING IN THE NORTHWEST: JOE SMITH AND SEATTLE REFORM. *Pacific Hist. R. 1971 40(4): 478-500.* The causes which Smith promoted as a political reporter and publisher for Seattle newspapers provide a study of urban Progressivism during the first two decades of the 20th century. Smith championed the "straphanger" or underdog, fought for direct democracy and municipal reform, attacked public service monopolies, and with his paper led the movement for the recall campaign against Mayor Hiram C. Gill in 1911. Along with other Progressives and crusading journalists of the prewar years, Smith knew the value of the use of publicity and exposure in achieving urban reform. Based primarily on the Joseph E. Smith Papers, University of Washington; 68 notes.

E. C. Hyslop

3770. Kane, Ralph J. THE PARADOX OF CALIFORNIA POPULISM. *North Dakota Q. 39(3): 34-46.* Finds California Populism split between urban, socialist-oriented, and rural, capitalist-oriented groups. Generally prosperous through the period (1890's) and largely entrepreneurial in outlook, the California farmer was not attracted to the monetary or conspiratorial theories of Plains-State Populism. Urban Populists, leaning toward socialism, worked at best uneasily with their rural counterparts. California Populism was torn by internal strife and more resembled Progressivism than other varieties of Populism. Based on secondary sources; 81 notes.

J. F. Mahoney

3771. Kerr, William T., Jr. THE PROGRESSIVES OF WASHINGTON, 1910-12. *Pacific Northwest Q. 1964 55(1): 16-27.* Primarily an analysis of the groups of citizens forming the backbone of the Progressive Party in the State of Washington. The Progressive movement under the leadership of Miles Poindexter (and of Theodore Roosevelt on the national level) enjoyed political success and power especially in 1910 through 1912. The author concludes that Progressive leadership in the state came in large part from "the native born, the moderately prosperous, and the better educated elements of the state."

C. C. Gorchels

3772. Kneeshaw, Stephen J. and Linngren, John M. REPUBLICAN COMEBACK, 1902. *Colorado Mag. 1971 48(1): 15-29.* Analyzes the political fortunes of the various parties in Colorado from 1892 to 1902, when the Populists upset the Democratic-Republican balance. In 1892 the Populists and their silver plank carried Colorado but Populist Governor Davis H. Waite's record won back the governorship in 1894 for the Republicans. However, the national Republican Party's adoption of a gold plank, the bolting of Senator Henry Moore Teller (although Republican Senator Edward O. Wolcott remained loyal), and the fusion of Silver Republicans, Democrats, and Populists nearly annihilated the Republican Party in Colorado in 1896. The victory of the Republicans again in 1902 was due less to the traditional explanation - return of Silver Republicans and patronage - than to the conservative voting patterns of rural areas and to the return of prosperity. 3 photos, 23 notes.

O. H. Zabel

3773. LaForte, Robert S. THEODORE ROOSEVELT'S OSAWATOMIE SPEECH. *Kansas Hist. Q. 1966 32(2): 187-200.* Gifford Pinchot and William Allen White were responsible for ex-President Roosevelt's speech on 31 August 1910. White was responsible for raising the speech above the level of mere generalization about reform by incorporating in it a list of specific reforms that the Kansas Republicans had approved on 30 August. The speech produced mixed emotions. Some feared "big government." Some agreed that the reforms were needed. Many reacted according to the degree of political advantage or disadvantage that the ideas expressed in the speech offered them. The speech became the basis of the Progressive Party platform in 1912. Based on the manuscripts of the persons involved which are in the Library of Congress and Kansas State Historical Society.   W. F. Zornow

3774. Larson, T. A. THE NEW DEAL IN WYOMING. *Pacific Hist. R. 1969 38(3): 249-273.* Describes the difficulties with which the programs of the New Deal slowly penetrated Wyoming, a State noted for its frontier spirit. The influence of stockmen and mining and oil developers, who were committed to independence from Federal control, caused only reluctant acceptance of Federal relief measures. Although welfare reform caused permanent changes, the shift from a land economy to the exploitation of natural resources, rather than the influence of the New Deal, caused much of the change in the State's economy during this period. Based on secondary sources; 71 notes.   E. C. Hyslop

3775. Loewy, Jean. KATHERINE PHILIPS EDSON AND THE CALIFORNIA SUFFRAGETTE MOVEMENT, 1919-1920. *California Hist. Soc. Q. 1968 47(4): 343-350.* In one decade (1911-21) Katherine Philips Edson moved from a suffragette to a Presidential appointee as a member of an international conference (Washington Conference on the Limitations of Armaments, 1921). The author details her political career in California including her membership in and chairmanship of the State Industrial Welfare Commission from 1913 to 1931. She played an important part in the passage of the State's equal suffrage referendum in 1911. When woman suffrage again became important to California, she was a delegate to the 50th Anniversary Jubilee Convention of the National American Woman Suffrage Association in March 1919 which led to the passage of the 19th amendment and the formation of the League of Women Voters. The California Legislature did not meet in special session for the exclusive purpose of ratifying the amendment until 1 November 1919. This paper was presented at the regional meeting of the Southern California branch of the national history honorary society Phi Alpha Theta in 1963. 35 notes.   E. P. Stickney

3776. Lowitt, Richard. A CASE STUDY IN BIOGRAPHICAL RESEARCH: GEORGE W. NORRIS. *J. of Lib. Hist. 1969 4(2): 123-132.* Discusses the appropiate methodological approach to the study of the career of Senator George William Norris (1861-1944) of Nebraska. The author has worked with the Norris papers in the Library of Congress (one of the largest collections there), the *Congressional Record,* and various newspapers. Comments on the drawbacks of personal interviews. 6 notes.   V. S. Ekrut

3777. Lowitt, Richard. SENATOR NORRIS AND HIS 1918 CAMPAIGN. *Pacific Northwest Q. 1966 57(3): 113-119.* In 1917 Senator George W. Norris, Nebraska Republican, voted against the U.S. congressional resolution which declared war on Germany. Despite this unpopular deed which was expected to make his reelection almost impossible, Norris was reelected to the U.S. Senate in 1918 due to effective support from powerful political friends and lack of unity within the ranks of the opposing Democratic Party.   C. C. Gorchels

3778. Luebke, Frederick C. MAIN STREET AND THE COUNTRYSIDE: PATTERNS OF VOTING IN NEBRASKA DURING THE POPULIST ERA. *Nebraska Hist. 1969 50(3): 257-275.* Challenges David F. Trask's theory (presented in the June 1965 issue of *Nebraska History)* that the Panic of 1893 caused the small businessmen of the towns to identify "the large business concerns of the North and East as the sources of their economic distress," or to place "'Main Street' in the same camp with the countryside." Based on the election records of 186 precincts in 15 Nebraska counties, the author probes the conflicts between the towns and countryside, during both the pre-Populist and Populist period. He finds that there was not a significant town and country conflict in the pre-Populist election of 1888; that "distinctive qualities of rural and small town voting, apparently precipitated by the Populist movement, continued almost as strongly after the waning of the Populist party"; and that "town precincts were remarkably persistent in their attachment to the Republican party throughout the Populist era." 26 notes.   G. Baldelli

3779. Malone, Michael J. C. BEN ROSS: IDAHO'S COWBOY GOVERNOR. *Idaho Yesterdays 1966 10(4): 2-9.* "A study of the political career of the first native Idahoan to be elected governor." Ross's political career is traced from 1923 to 1930, when he was mayor of Pocatello, through the years of his governorship in Idaho (1931-37). Ross

was one of the last of a colorful breed of agrarian politicians who left an impression of rugged individualism and independence on State politics. The fundamental source of his political strength was his ability to capture the sentiments and votes of the farming populace. Illus., 38 notes.   D. H. Swift

3780. Malone, Michael P. MONTANA POLITICS AND THE NEW DEAL. *Montana 1971 21(1): 2-11.* Examines the impact of the New Deal on politics in Montana. Early Democratic success bound that party together. After 1936, factionalism and the defection of Burton K. Wheeler brought an end to this unity. "Viewed in retrospect, the New Deal worked no apparent revolution in Montana politics."   S. R. Davison

3781. Malone, Michael P. THE NEW DEAL IN IDAHO. *Pacific Hist. R. 1969 38(3): 293-310.* Describes the effectiveness of the urban and liberal reform movement of the New Deal on Idaho, a rural and conservative State. The Depression came late but devastatingly to Idaho. In the administration of relief measures Charles Ben Ross, the Democratic governor, was a key figure, often at odds with the national administration as well as with his State party. This political infighting in turn affected the success of many of the New Deal programs. Some reforms in agriculture and social security remained after most of the programs ended in 1938 with the downfall of Ross and the end of an interlude of Democratic supremacy in Idaho. Based on secondary sources; 45 notes.   E. C. Hyslop

3782. Martinson, Henry R. "COMES THE REVOLUTION . . .": A PERSONAL MEMOIR. *North Dakota Hist. 1969 36(1): 40-109.* The author was at one time the secretary of the Socialist Party in North Dakota and editor of its paper, the *Iconoclast.* It is his contention that in its some 15 years of existence in the 1910's and the 1920's the party initiated demands for reform in such areas as agriculture, and social and labor legislation. Further, the party sparked the movements resulting in establishment of the Bank of North Dakota, and the State Mill and Elevator. Socialist ideals "will live on forever," even though there may never be another socialist party in the State. 15 illus.   D. L. Smith

3783. May, Irvin M., Jr. PETER MOLYNEAUX AND THE NEW DEAL. *Southwestern Hist. Q. 1970 73(3): 309-325.* Discusses the years of the New Deal's economic policies as seen by Peter Molyneaux, influential editor of a leading politically oriented publication, the *Texas Weekly.* As a Texas Democrat, Molyneaux not without reservations supported President Franklin D. Roosevelt's first year emergency measures to attack the Depression. Following a general disillusionment with acts such as the NIRA, PWA, and CWA, Molyneaux, responsive to Texas business and cotton interests, vehemently protested the passage of the Social Security Act, the Townsend Plan, and most important, Roosevelt's agricultural and tariff policies, which he believed would not only lead the Democratic Party and the Nation down the road to radicalism and socialism, but would also prolong the Depression by restricting foreign trade. Molyneaux thus articulated the growing fear on the part of Southern conservatives of the basic divergence in social philosophies between those who advocated a paternalistic government control and those to whom such interference was anathema to individual initiative and free enterprise. Although powerless to change the course of the New Deal, Molyneaux emerges as representative of the dilemma of conservatives who could neither support the Republicans nor the Democratic New Deal.   R. W. Delaney

3784. McCarran, Margaret Patricia. PATRICK ANTHONY MC CARRAN, 1876-1954. *Nevada Hist. Soc. Q. 1968 11(3-4): 3-66; 1969 12(1): 5-75.* Part I. This biography by his daughter tells of McCarran's birth at Reno, Nevada, in 1876, his boyhood on a nearby ranch, and his education in the public schools. After working his way through the University of Nevada, McCarran raised sheep and read law. Successful as a lawyer he became a county district attorney, a member of the State legislature, and a justice of the Nevada supreme court. From 1922 to 1932 he practiced law in a private firm and was prominent in the State bar association. He was elected to the United States Senate on the Democratic ticket in 1932. There McCarran supported reform and worked diligently for his State, but he was by no means a rubber stamp for the New Deal. 6 illus., 71 notes. Part II. After reelection to his second term in the United States Senate in 1938, he continued in that capacity until his death in

1954. His considerable influence was felt beyond his work on the important judiciary and appropriations committees. His last years were marked by his strong anti-Communist stand. 7 illus., 190 notes.

D. L. Smith

3785. McCarthy, G. Michael. COLORADO'S POPULIST LEADERSHIP. *Colorado Mag. 1971 48(1): 30-42.* Using Populist leaders in Colorado, explores two common theses concerning Populist leaders. The first thesis holds that Populist leadership came neither from the ranks of farmers nor from silver interests but from "professional men, rural editors, third-party veterans, and professional reformers." The author finds only one Colorado Populist leader with silver interests, few farmers, no third-party veterans, and no professional reformers. He does find editors, but the most important professions represented in Colorado Populist leadership were "real estate, retail marketing, law and education." The second thesis holds that when the Populist movement collapsed, its leaders joined the Progressive movement. The later activities of Colorado Populist leaders do not support this thesis. 5 photos, 72 notes.

O. H. Zabel

3786. McCoy, Donald R. ALFRED M. LANDON, WESTERN GOVERNOR. *Pacific Northwest Q. 1966 57(3): 120-126.* Summary of the role of Landon in his efforts to help Kansas avoid some economic difficulties during early depression years, 1932-36, with emphasis on his help to petroleum interests and his success in obtaining Federal relief funds for his state. Biblio. of original sources.

C. C. Gorchels

3787. McEdwards, Mary. UPTON SINCLAIR, CALIFORNIA'S EPIC PROPHET. *U. of Wyoming Publications 1968 34(10): 181-203.* In 1934 Sinclair ran for governor of California on the Democratic ticket. Focuses on Sinclair's Socialist oriented EPIC platform (End Poverty in California), discussing his philosophy and the opposition's reaction to it. Sinclair lost the election to Frank Merriam by a margin of 181 thousand votes of the nearly two million votes cast, while 25 EPIC candidates were elected to the assembly. Sinclair's ideas had a limited impact on Merriam's administration. 96 notes.

H. B. Powell

3788. Melendy, H. Brett. CALIFORNIA'S CROSS-FILING NIGHTMARE: THE 1918 GUBERNATORIAL ELECTION. *Pacific Hist. R. 1964 33(3): 317-330.* Details the failure of the Direct Primary Law of 1913 to serve the democratic ends the California Progressives intended. In 1918 the Democrats were denied a candidate for governor because James Rolph, a Republican, who cross-filed on both the the Democratic and Republican tickets, won the Democratic nomination but lost the Republican. The election law, however, would not permit him to run on the Democratic ticket.

J. McCutcheon

3789. Meredith, Howard L. CHARLES W. MACUNE'S "FARMERS' ALLIANCE." *Lib. Chronicle of the U. of Texas 1966 8(2): 42-45.* One base of the People's Party was the agrarian base contributed by the Farmers' Alliance of the 1890's. The University of Texas Archive Collection holds Charles W. Macune's own manuscript account of the Farmers' Alliance, giving its meaning, purpose, and history.

D. Brockway

3790. Metz, Leon C. PAT GARRETT: EL PASO CUSTOMS COLLECTOR. *Arizona and the West 1969 11(4): 327-340.* Although he achieved fame of sorts in 1881 for killing a notorious New Mexican outlaw, failure plagued Pat Garrett's subsequent ventures in ranching, water resources development, law enforcement, and horse racing. He turned to politics and, in 1901, received presidential appointment as Collector of Internal Revenue Customs at El Paso, Texas. In that capacity he worked conscientiously. Although never accused of dishonesty, he was sometimes declared incompetent. His principal difficulty, as in the past, was his personality. Although he was satisfactory to the President himself, Garrett caused considerable controversy by not playing favorites in the execution of his office. Not reappointed as collector in 1905, he retired to his ranch in New Mexico where, three years later, he was shot to death. 3 illus., 26 notes.

D. L. Smith

3791. Moore, Carl M. JOSEPH CHRISTOPHER O'MAHONEY: A BRIEF BIOGRAPHY. *Ann. of Wyoming 1969 41(2): 159-186.* Traces the life of Joe O'Mahoney, who was born on 5 November 1884 at Chelsea, Massachusetts, and died in the U.S. Naval Hospital at Bethesda, Maryland, on 2 December 1962. After working as a newspaperman and a lawyer, O'Mahoney entered politics as an aide and campaigner for John B. Kendrick (1857-1933), the first Democratic Senator from Wyoming; he served briefly as first assistant postmaster general in 1933; and, when Senator Kendrick died in late 1933, he was appointed to complete his unexpired term. For 27 of the next 29 years he represented Wyoming in the U.S. Senate, opposing Franklin Roosevelt's plan to pack the Supreme Court, chairing the Temporary National Economic Committee, and in 1948 being considered as a possible vice presidential candidate. The author portrays O'Mahoney as thinking of himself as a guardian of the little man, although not necessarily of being anti-business. Based on the *Congressional Record,* personal interviews, archival material, and secondary sources; illus., photos, 99 notes.

R. L. Nichols

3792. Neuringer, Sheldon. GOVERNOR WALTON'S WAR ON THE KU KLUX KLAN: AN EPISODE IN OKLAHOMA HISTORY, 1923 TO 1924. *Chronicles of Oklahoma 1967 45(2): 153-179.* By late 1922 the Ku Klux Klan had become such a menace that several States began to make efforts to restrict it. John Calloway Walton, elected Governor of Oklahoma in 1922, at first seemed to curry the favor of the Klan. Walton's unprecedented popularity as Governor declined rapidly because of ineptitude and blundering. A Tulsa abduction incident triggered Walton's war on the Klan, partly, at least, to shore up his political fortunes. The Klan was so deeply entrenched and politically powerful that a showdown eventuated between the Governor and the legislature resulting in the impeachment of the Governor. Walton's bids to regain political power and advantages on the anti-Klan issue were not successful. 81 notes.

D. L. Smith

3793. Nugent, Walter T. K. HOW THE POPULISTS LOST IN 1894. *Kansas Hist. Q. 1965 31(3): 245-255.* During the two years that followed their successes in the 1892 election, the Populists in Kansas were weakened by a series of national and local misfortunes. The depression of 1893 and the Pullman strike of 1894 were events that cast a long shadow. The inexperienced Populists of Kansas were further hurt by their inability to carry out a local reform program in 1893. Republican leader Cyrus Leland may have played an astute game by using his own influence and that of dissident Populists to get the Populist Party to take a position on prohibition and woman's suffrage totally unacceptable to the Democrats. Failing to get Democratic support and arguing among themselves, the Populists were easy targets in 1894. Based on local newspapers.

W. F. Zornow

3794. O'Brien, Patrick G. VALIDITY OF HISTORICAL CHARACTERIZATIONS: CAPPER AND CURTIS. *Southwestern Social Sci. Q. 1968 48(4): 624-631.* Contests the accepted interpretation of insurgency and progressivism during the 1920's through a study of two Kansas Senators - Arthur Capper, traditionally presented as an insurgent and progressive, and Charles Curtis, commonly described as a regular and conservative. On four issues regarded as having a progressive character, the Senators agreed on three. The author contends that although the Senators did differ, they also had important similarities. 38 notes.

D. F. Henderson

3795. Oden, William E. TENURE AND TURNOVER IN RECENT TEXAS LEGISLATURES. *Southwestern Social Sci. Q. 1965 45(4): 371-374.* Study of 14 sessions of the House of Representatives from 1935 to 1961. Of 2,121 men studied: 39.5 percent had no previous legislative experience, 28.6 percent had one previous legislative experience, 13.8 percent had two, seven percent had three, 11 percent had four or more. The study raises numerous questions, but supplies few answers.

D. F. Henderson

3796. Olin, Spencer C., Jr. HIRAM JOHNSON, THE LINCOLN-ROOSEVELT LEAGUE, AND THE ELECTION OF 1910. *California Hist. Soc. Q. 1966 45(3): 225-240.* The purpose of the Lincoln-Roosevelt Republican League was to destroy the power of the Southern Pacific Railroad Company in California politics. Its candidate for governor in 1910, Hiram Johnson, invested the cause of political reform with a kind of "dynamic righteousness" similar to that of Theodore Roosevelt in the East. Poor handling of the league's campaign caused Johnson to set up his own independent organization. Johnson staked his campaign on the railroad issue, displaying shrewd insight into the farm economy by showing the large farmers that they could make even more profits by forcing the railroad to charge equitable rates. The election was primarily a conflict between two groups of capitalists: large farmers and ranchers, and the railroad interests. Johnson's victory in the primary was followed by his election as governor. Based largely on the Rowell and the Johnson Papers, Bancroft Library; 46 notes.   E. P. Stickney

3797. O'Rourke, Paul A. SOUTH DAKOTA POLITICS DURING THE NEW DEAL YEARS. *South Dakota Hist. 1971 1(3): 231-271.* Discusses why South Dakota Democrats did not bring substantial reform and why they ultimately failed at the polls while the national New Deal succeeded. Governor Thomas Berry's proposals did not satisfy the large farm organizations. Concludes that "continuity rather than change characterized the state's response to the economic crisis of the decade." The Depression in South Dakota "did not permanently shake its citizens' loyalty to the Republican party and caused no real change in their individualistic values." 2 illus., table, 113 notes.   D. H. Swift

3798. Paterson, Thomas G. CALIFORNIA PROGRESSIVES AND FOREIGN POLICY. *California Hist. Soc. Q. 1968 47(4): 329-342.* A discussion of William E. Leuchtenburg's article "Progressivism and Imperialism: The Progressive Movement and American Foreign Policy 1898-1916" in the *Mississippi Valley Historical Review* of December 1952. Paterson argues that there was no unified Progressive attitude toward foreign policy and, in the case of California, finds that Progressives "were decidedly split on questions of foreign relations." Specifically, American-Mexican relations during the Mexican Revolution and the preparedness controversy before American entry into World War I illustrate the interrelationship of domestic reform and international affairs. Only a few Progressives championed intervention in the Mexican Revolution. The preparedness issue contributed to the disruption of national progressivism. Based on the Hiram Johnson Papers, Chester Rowell Papers, Franklin K. Lane Papers, and John D. Works Papers, all in the Bancroft Library, University of California, Berkeley, several unpublished Ph.D. dissertations at the University of California, Berkeley, and numerous published works; 62 notes.   E. P. Stickney

3799. Patterson, Samuel C. THE ROLE OF THE LOBBYIST: THE CASE OF OKLAHOMA. *J. of Pol. 1963 25(1): 72-92.* A study of the social and political background of lobbyists in the 1961 Oklahoma state legislature, the interests they represented, and the roles they played. Two-thirds of the 62 registered lobbyists returned the mailed questionnaires. The author found that the typical lobbyist is a middle-aged, relatively well-educated, professional staff member who resides in the capital city. He more generally represents a business group. He plays the differentiated role as either contact man, informant, or watchdog.
B. E. Swanson

3800. Paul, Justus F. THE KU KLUX KLAN IN THE MIDWEST: A NOTE ON THE 1936 NEBRASKA ELECTIONS. *North Dakota Q. 1971 39(4): 64-70.* Via the few letters extant, traces the aid of the Nebraska Protective Association (the local Klan) to the Republican campaign in Nebraska in 1936. Apparently national committeeman Hugh Butler secretly financed a Klan campaign in support of Robert G. Simmons for US Senator, in opposition to George William Norris who was running as an independent and supporter of President Franklin Delano Roosevelt. Based on manuscript and secondary sources; illus., 18 notes.
J. F. Mahoney

3801. Paul, Justus F. THE MAKING OF A SENATOR: THE EARLY LIFE OF HUGH BUTLER. *Nebraska Hist. 1968 49(3): 247-267.* Surveys the first 60 years of the life of Hugh Butler, born in 1878. His career as a prominent grain merchant and farmer in Nebraska is examined, as is his decision to seek a Senate seat in 1940. He won the first of three successful contests for the Senate in 1940.   R. Lowitt

3802. Petersen, Eric Falk. THE END OF AN ERA: CALIFORNIA'S GUBERNATORIAL ELECTION OF 1894. *Pacific Hist. R. 1969 38(2): 141-156.* The election of 1894 took place against a background of labor strife, agrarian unrest, and unemployment. The candidates of the Populist, Republican, and Democratic parties addressed themselves to the four basic issues of the day: the depression, State expenditures, currency, and railroad regulation. Discussion of the issues on which the candidates generally agreed gave way in the last weeks of the campaign to abuse and mudslinging. Although a general Republican landslide occurred, James Herbert Budd (1853-1908) won the governor-

ship. He was the last Democratic Governor of the State until 1938. Based on Los Angeles and San Francisco newspapers; 52 notes.
E. C. Hyslop

3803. Petersen, Erik F. THE STRUGGLE FOR THE AUSTRALIAN BALLOT IN CALIFORNIA. *California Hist. Q. 1972 51(3): 227-243.* In the late 19th century, voting procedure in the United States was marred by corrupt practices. The idea of inaugurating the Australian ballot - a system of voting that would insure a minimum of corruption at most, and the right to a private vote - aroused considerable controversy. California experienced a difficult campaign for the Australian ballot, because reformers tangled with stand-pat politicians and with those who had a vested interest in keeping the old system. The Australian ballot entailed more than a private vote; it also meant that ballots, hitherto printed and distributed by political parties, would thereafter be printed by the State. It also proposed to do away with such abuses as piece clubs (groups of political opportunists), harassment by opponents' followers, and dishonest tabulations. After an extended campaign which saw heated debate, the Australian ballot was legislated into being in 1891. While the Australian ballot did not solve all of the abuses that could be detected in the electoral process, its adoption in California suggests that reformers there were not as helpless in the face of Southern Pacific machine domination as they have been pictured. Based on legislative records, and on other primary and secondary sources; illus., 49 notes.
A. Hoffman

3804. Peterson, Paul V. WILLIAM JENNINGS BRYAN, "WORLD-HERALD" EDITOR. *Nebraska Hist. 1968 49(4): 349-371.* An account, including correspondence, pertaining to Bryan's becoming editor (in 1894) of the *World-Herald* in Omaha, a position he held for 13 months and which he used as a vehicle for his political career.
R. Lowitt

3805. Phillips, William W. GROWING UP WITH THE COUNTRY: ASLE J. GRONNA'S APPRENTICESHIP. *North Dakota Q. 1971 39(3): 18-28.* Traces the career of Gronna until his first election to Congress in 1904. Son of Norwegian immigrants, he early manifested business skills which he parlayed into a fortune based on diversified interests in land, banking, publishing, and retailing. As a member of the North Dakota Territorial Legislature he was allied with the Republican machine, but revealed notable traces of reformist sentiment. Dropped for a time by the machine, he bounced back to win election as a regular Republican in 1904. Based on interviews and secondary sources; 45 notes.
J. F. Mahoney

3806. Pickens, William H. BRONSON CUTTING VS. DENNIS CHAVEZ: BATTLE OF THE PATRONES IN NEW MEXICO, 1934. *New Mexico Hist. R. 1971 46(1): 5-36.* Analysis of the Senate campaign between Bronson Murray Cutting (Republican incumbent, Harvard graduate, and displaced New Yorker), and Dennis Chavez (native New Mexican and the State's Congressman). Cutting defeated Chavez by 2,284 votes out of 152,172. The Democrats had hoped that the same forces that swept them to victory in 1932 would prevail in 1934. Cutting, however, stole key issues, carried the larger counties with over 70 percent Spanish-speaking population, and forced Chavez to a draw in the three counties with most of the mining labor vote, thus electrifying the Republican Party. 76 notes.
D. F. Henderson

3807. Richardson, Elmo R. WESTERN POLITICS AND NEW DEAL POLICIES. *Pacific Northwest Q. 1963 54(1): 9-18.* A study of the political and bureaucratic life of Theodore A. Walters of Idaho, who served for four years (1933-37) as assistant secretary of interior. Appointed by F. D. Roosevelt as a sop for Westerners who were disgruntled over the appointment of Secretary Harold Ickes, Walters was more interested in patronage and in resource interests of his own state than in the overall responsibilities of his job, and was distrusted by Ickes as a petty politician. Although he declined to run for political office, preferring his departmental job, he played an active role in Democratic politics in Idaho during the early New Deal years.   R. E. Wilson

3808. Rogin, Michael. PROGRESSIVISM AND THE ELECTORATE. *J. of Am. Hist. 1968 55(2): 297-314.* An intensive analysis of the electorate supporting the Progressive Hiram Johnson in 1910 and 1916 and Woodrow Wilson in the latter year indicates that Southern California was never a stronghold of Progressive sentiment. That area did give Johnson support in 1910 partially because of antirailroad sentiment among the farmers but largely because it was a heavily Republican area. By 1916, however, Progressives had become identified with labor legislation, and this brought them the support of the Bay Area working class and some immigrant groups in Northern California. At the same time this support alienated the native-stock Protestant, middle-class voters in the South who voted heavily against Johnson and Wilson in 1916. The alignment continued in the 1920's when Johnson and Robert LaFollette both won support from workers and small farmers, while incurring the opposition of an increasingly conservative South.   K. B. West

3809. Rothlisberger, Orland A.   THE POPULIST NATIONAL CONVENTION IN SIOUX FALLS.   *South Dakota Hist. 1971 1(2): 155-165.* Discusses the background and political development of the Populist Party in South Dakota. The successful securing of the National Convention in Sioux Falls in 1900 was the climax to the party's influence in the State. The small attendance was the result of internal tensions within the party. The fall elections of 1900 completed the disintegration. Illus., 30 notes.   D. H. Swift

3810. Ruetten, Richard T.   SENATOR BURTON K. WHEELER AND THE INSURGENCY IN THE 1920's.   *U. of Wyoming Pub. 1966 32: 111-131, 164-172.* Western reformers in the United States Senate in the 1920's have been badly maligned or otherwise ignored. This is due to the inordinate reliance on one-sided sources, the lack of formal organization and official program of the Western insurgents, and the inadequate definition of progressivism which puts all reformers in one "typical" mass. Turn-of-the-century progressivism disintegrated in the experience of World War I except with a group of Western reformers who thus formed "a viable link between prewar progressivism and the New Deal." The West continued to work for relief and reform, principally because the deterioration of economic conditions was greater there than elsewhere in the country. This contingent of Senators perceived many of the real problems of the age and proposed numerous viable solutions in the face of hostility and opposition from nearly every other section. Burton K. Wheeler from Montana and others won election to the Senate in 1922 on a wave of agrarian discontent. Although there was no well-knit organization, they all had much in common—humble origins, belief in agrarian ideology, distrust of the urban East and political opportunists. They were passionate pacifists but not isolationists, independent, iconoclastic, and inspired by economic protest. Wheeler's senatorial career is traced. His foremost contribution to the cause of progressivism and to the nation in the 1920's, according to the author, was his investigation of the Department of Justice and the attorney general. 110 notes.   D. L. Smith

3811. Ruetten, Richard T.   SHOWDOWN IN MONTANA, 1938. *Pacific Northwest Q. 1963 54(1): 19-29.* Describes the role played by Senator Burton Wheeler in contributing to the defeat of Representative Jerry O'Connell in the election of 1938. Wheeler had fallen out of the good graces of President F. D. Roosevelt because of his opposition to the Supreme Court reorganization plan, and because he opposed the president's foreign policies. Young Congressman O'Connell, an enthusiastic New Dealer, challenged Wheeler's leadership in Montana Democratic circles, with Roosevelt's tacit support. So Wheeler threw his support to the Republican candidate, Dr. Jacob Thorkelson, who also had the endorsement of the AFL-CIO, and Dr. Francis L. Townsend. Thorkelson's victory brought O'Connell's political career to an end and eliminated a troublesome rival for Wheeler.   R. E. Wilson

3812. Rumble, Walker.   GUTZON BORGLUM, MOUNT RUSHMORE AND THE AMERICAN TRADITION.   *Pacific Northwest Q. 1968 59(3): 121-127.* Borglum (1871-1941) is famous as the sculptor who carved the faces of four presidents of the United States on the rocky side of Mount Rushmore in South Dakota, but he is also known as an activist in agrarian politics. His political and social beliefs, as expressed primarily from 1890 to 1932, reflect his convictions that agrarianism and the inherent superiority of Anglo-Saxon civilization inspired men from the western part of the United States to greatness for the benefit of the entire nation.   C. C. Gorchels

3813. Rylance, Daniel.   A CONTROVERSIAL CAREER: GERALD P. NYE, 1925-1946.   *North Dakota Q. 1968 36(1): 5-19.* Surveys the career of Senator Nye, especially in relation to North Dakota politics,

to determine the reasons for his eventual defeat. Contrary to general views, Nye's isolationism had only a minor influence on his defeat in 1944 and on his unsuccessful comeback effort in 1946. The significant reasons for Nye's loss were a widespread feeling that Nye neglected North Dakota's interests; his divorce and remarriage which, though discreet, alienated many constituents; unusually acute and effective campaigning by the Democrats; and William Langer's long-time personal and political opposition. Illus, 85 notes.   J. F. Mahoney

3814. Schruben, Francis W.   THE RETURN OF "ALFALFA BILL" MURRAY.   *Chronicles of Oklahoma 1963 41(1): 38-65.* William H. (Alfalfa Bill) Murray, self-educated lawyer politician of Oklahoma, claimed to have been the "father of the Oklahoma Constitution." He served as US Representative from 1912 to 1916. After a series of political defeats he spent five years, 1924-29, trying to found a colony in Bolivia. He then returned penniless to Oklahoma and in 1930 entered the contest for governor. His campaign was financed by small gifts. To his supporters, the poor of rural districts, in his *Blue Valley Farmer* and in his speeches he promised little, but protested against wealth and special privilege. His chief opponent was self-made millionaire Frank Buttram. A run-off primary between Murray and Buttram was necessary and Murray won, against the opposition of the press. Conservative newspapers then backed Republican Ira Hill in the general election. Murray's victory was remarkable. He faced "entrenched and powerful orthodox opposition" and won with his own publication and his self-organized machine.

I. W. Van Noppen

3815. Shaffer, Ralph E.   FORMATION OF THE CALIFORNIA COMMUNIST LABOR PARTY.   *Pacific Hist. R. 1967 36(1): 59-78.* Relates the struggle within the California Socialist Party especially during the crucial 1917-19 period which led to the establishment of the Communist Labor Party and then the California Communist Party. 47 notes, based mostly on the *Oakland World.*   J. McCutcheon

3816. Shipps, Jan.   UTAH COMES OF AGE POLITICALLY: A STUDY OF THE STATE'S POLITICS IN THE EARLY YEARS OF THE TWENTIETH CENTURY.   *Utah Hist. Q. 1967 35(2): 91-111.* Views Utah's political maturity as arriving with a Democratic victory in the State election of 1916. This established a two-party system in Utah and destroyed the control held by Senator Reed Smoot over Republican and State politics. The author concentrates on the factional struggles which occurred in the Republican Party in this period, particularly over the Prohibition issue. Contention over the latter issue is seen as being central in the destruction of Republican supremacy. Based in part on the papers of Governor William Spry in the Utah State Archives.

S. L. Jones

3817. Shover, John L.   THE PROGRESSIVES AND THE WORKING CLASS VOTE IN CALIFORNIA.   *Labor Hist. 10(4): 584-601.* Examines the hypothesis that leaders of organized labor in California strongly endorsed Progressivism and that, after 1914, the major political support for Progressives came from the working class districts of the State's two principal cities. Using election data from Los Angeles and San Francisco, the voting patterns for Hiram W. Johnson are studied. The hypothesis is upheld by the data. The author calls for a further examination of the thesis in other urban areas which, if sustained, could lead to a major reevaluation of progressivism. Seven tables of voting data, 60 notes.   L. L. Athey

3818. Shover, John L.   WAS 1928 A CRITICAL ELECTION IN CALIFORNIA?   *Pacific Northwest Q. 1967 58(4): 196-204.* Analyzes the presidential election in California in 1928 to determine the significance of the vote for the Democratic candidate Alfred E. Smith. With graphs and correlation coefficients, the results of other elections are compared with the returns for 1928, and the author concludes that the 1928 election in California was not a forward step in the process that led to the emergence of a strong Democratic constituency in 1932.

C. C. Gorchels

3819. Smith, Duane.   COLORADO AND JUDICIAL RECALL. *Am. J. of Legal Hist. 1963 7(3): 198-209.* Using contemporary newspapers and articles, the author discusses the adoption of recall of judicial decisions in Colorado, the only state that adopted this feature. Also recounts the two major cases affecting the question in Colorado jurisprudence, concluding that the power of recall of judicial decisions never amounted to much in practice.   N. C. Brockman

3820.   Smith, Robert Earl.   COLORADO'S PROGRESSIVE SENATORS AND REPRESENTATIVES. *Colorado Mag. 1968 45(1): 27-41.* Discusses the extent to which the Colorado Congressmen took the lead in national Progressive legislation and supported it with their votes from 1900 to 1920. The author analyzes support of 19 specific Congressmen for such legislation as the Hepburn Act, Mann-Elkins Act, Clayton Act, Federal Trade Commission Act, LaFollette's Hours of Service Act, and the Adamson Act. He concludes that "individually Colorado congressmen ranged from radical to conservative, but collectively they were sympathetic to the major goals of progressivism." He suggests that the West and the South were more important as "the backbone of national reform legislation during the Progressive era" than the East. Illus., chart, 54 notes.   O. H. Zabel

3821.   Snyder, J. Richard.   THE ELECTION OF 1904: AN ATTEMPT AT REFORM. *Colorado Mag. 1968 45(1): 16-26.* The elections of 1904 saw an early Progressive reform battle in Colorado. Although the Progressives, working within the traditional parties, were defeated, the election was a turning point in Colorado politics. Denver's city election in March approved a new charter, but it had been stripped of limitations on the privileges of public service utilities. In May a Progressive Republican was defeated for mayor. In the State elections of November 1904 the corporate interests, supporting Governor James H. Peabody, were able, by political maneuvering, to continue their control. Although Peabody did not continue as governor, they succeeded in having the election of Alva Adams declared void, in keeping control of the senate by having the supreme court declare fraud in certain precincts that had gone Democratic, and in packing the supreme court. While the procedure used was unusual, the practice of evading the will of the people was not. "It was the kind of practice which produced political progressivism." Illus., 52 notes.   O. H. Zabel

3822.   Soderbergh, Peter A.   UPTON SINCLAIR AND HOLLYWOOD. *Midwest Q. 1970 11(2): 173-191.* An account of Sinclair's war with Hollywood. Sinclair and the motion picture industry both took residence in the Los Angeles area in 1915. Sinclair published a Socialist magazine beginning in 1918, ran for Congress in 1920 and 1922, and for Governor in 1926. In 1927 he aimed his guns on the movies with two books, *Money Writes* and *Oil!*, with scathing surveys of American literature and cinema. He vituperated the weaknesses of Hollywood with merciless prose until 1935. The studios returned fire in the form of rejecting all his movie production efforts and Sinclair responded with *Upton Sinclair Presents William Fox*, which exposed the brutal milieu in which William Fox lost control of his company. When Sinclair ran for Governor in 1934 on a platform advocating State income tax and higher taxes on corporations, the movie industry unleashed a campaign in which all theaters joined in a concerted action to defeat him, and they did.
                                    G. H. G. Jones

3823.   Stanley, Ruth Moore.   ALICE M. ROBERTSON, OKLAHOMA'S FIRST CONGRESSWOMAN. *Chronicles of Oklahoma 1967 45(3): 259-289.* Miss Robertson, a Republican, was elected Oklahoma's first congresswoman in 1921 over a veteran Indian-Democrat in a Democratic State. Her widely known efforts, going back to the Spanish-American War, to supply soldiers with canteen-type comforts and her unique classified advertising newspaper campaign were prominent factors in the success. Ironically, her opposition to a World War I bonus bill was a principal reason for defeat in her bid for reelection in 1923. 6 illus., 75 notes.   D. L. Smith

3824.   Stephens, Oren.   "COIN" HARVEY: THE FREE SILVER MOVEMENT'S FRUSTRATED PROMOTER. *Am. West 1971 8(5): 4-9.* In the midst of the panic of 1893 William Hope Harvey wrote *Coin's Financial School* (1894) which became an immediate bestseller. Coin analyzed the crash and offered a solution. He contended that the repeal of the Sherman Silver Purchase Act was responsible for the debacle. Free coinage of silver, therefore, was the obvious panacea. So effective was his prose and logic that Harvey converted the academic theory of free silver into a household patent remedy. Harvey's efforts figured prominently in the campaign of propaganda for free silver and the 1896 nomination of William Jennings Bryan by the Democratic, Populist, and National Sil-

verite parties. With the return of prosperity he became disillusioned that the Democrats no longer gave credence to his ideas, that they no longer believed that free silver was a valid political theory. He "dropped into oblivion to keep company with his theories." He grieved that he had somehow failed the common man who was now beguiled by the current but transitory prosperity. Harvey wrote other books and promoted various ideas, including an analysis of the 1929 crash. He even managed to get 53,425 votes as the Liberal Party presidential candidate in 1932. He died in poverty, destitution, and peace in 1936. 8 illus.
                                    D. L. Smith

3825.   Trask, David F.   A NOTE ON THE POLITICS OF POPULISM. *Nebraska Hist. 1965 46(2): 157-161.* Suggests as a hypothesis that Populism in politics was an alliance of farmers and small-town businessmen affected by the Panic of 1893 and critical of big business. The author also suggests that these businessmen Populists later became Progressives and provide continuity between the two movements. The author calls for a testing of this hypothesis.   R. Lowitt

3826.   Trask, David Stephens.   FORMATION AND FAILURE: THE POPULIST PARTY IN SEWARD COUNTY 1890-1892. *Nebraska Hist. 1970 51(3): 281-301.* Analyzes the Populist Party in Seward County, 1890-92, focusing on the inhabitants and conditions to understand why the farmer forsook agriculture for politics.   R. Lowitt

3827.   Venn, George W.   THE WOBBLIES AND MONTANA'S GARDEN CITY. *Montana 1971 21(4): 18-30.* Traces the struggle by leaders of the Industrial Workers of the World to disrupt civic life in Missoula briefly in 1909. The immediate object was to organize support for the IWW and to attack local employment agencies accused of defrauding clients. The indirect goal seems to have been the testing and perfecting of tactics such as street speaking and clogging of courts and jails with agitators assembled from other towns. The episode marked the rise to prominence of Elizabeth Gurley Flynn (1890-1964), who went on to a lifetime career in radical politics. Flynn became chairman of the Communist Party U.S.A. in 1961.   S. R. Davison

3828.   Vindex, Charles.   RADICAL RULE IN MONTANA. *Montana 1968 18(1): 3-18.* Sheridan County and the town of Plentywood, Montana, began their political life by endorsing Bull Moose Republicans in 1912 but later became "the only American community actually governed by practicing 'reds' who, far from concealing their radicalism, proclaimed it through the columns of a uniquely militant newspaper, the *Producers News.*" The editor and leading local Communist was Charles E. Taylor, a native of rural Minnesota. Files of this paper provide the documentation of this instance of Communist rule in a Montana county. Illustrated with a portrait of Taylor, and photos of scenes depicting the time and place.   S. R. Davison

3829.   Walker, Don D.   THE TAFT VICTORY IN UTAH IN 1912. *Utah Hist. Q. 1964 32(1): 44-56.* Describes the activities of the Republican, Democratic, and Progressive Republican Parties in Utah during the State conventions in May and the national conventions of 1912. Documented from contemporary Utah newspapers.   S. L. Jones

3830.   Walsh, James P.   ABE RUEF WAS NO BOSS: MACHINE POLITICS, REFORM, AND SAN FRANCISCO. *California Hist. Q. 1972 51(1): 3-16.* Contrasts the career and methods of Abraham Ruef with the bossism practiced in other large cities, and concludes that Ruef was not a boss at all. Unlike such bosses as Curley, Hague, and Tweed, Ruef lacked the organization essential for a political machine. He had no working-class connections and no political organization intimate with the needs and problems of city residents down to the block level, and made no effort to control votes. Instead, Ruef was an opportunist. He analyzed San Francisco's ethnic composition, decided that a labor candidate with ethnic ties could win in a three-cornered race for mayor, and secured the nomination of Eugene E. Schmitz on the newly formed Union Labor Party ticket. In the short run Ruef was extremely successful; lacking a political machine, however, he failed to establish an ongoing basis of support. The candidates he presented for office had little loyalty to him and actually were more amenable to the prosecutors who promised them immunity during the graft trials. Likewise, the graft prosecutors operated without a broad base of public support; the public identification with Schmitz resulted in his reelection to public office after the trials. Based on secondary sources; illus.   A. Hoffman

3831. Wells, Merle W. FRED T. DUBOIS AND THE NONPARTISAN LEAGUE IN THE IDAHO ELECTION OF 1918. *Pacific Northwest Q. 1965 56(1): 17-29.* With shrewd leadership and a variety of political maneuvers, a pressure group called the Nonpartisan League, under the leadership of Dubois, influenced an upset victory in the election of 1918 in Idaho. Legal, technical, and personal problems are analyzed. Documented.   C. C. Gorchels

3832. Wenger, Robert E. THE ANTI-SALOON LEAGUE IN NEBRASKA POLITICS, 1898-1910. *Nebraska Hist. 1971 52(3): 267-292.* Views the Nebraska league as part of the Progressive impulse wherein middle-class citizens envisioned themselves as leading the way to a more moral, stable, efficient, prosperous, and equitable society.   R. Lowitt

3833. Werner, Jane. THE PRESS AND THE POPULISTS. *Colorado Mag. 1970 47(1): 44-61.* Discusses the part played by newspapers in the 1892 election in Colorado. Thomas Patterson's *Rocky Mountain News* strongly supported the Populist ticket and was emulated by local weeklies in smaller communities. However, the author concludes that the advocation of free and unlimited coinage of silver in the national platform was the real reason for the Populist victory in the mining State of Colorado. The newspapers were following the popular trend rather than leading it. Illus., 38 notes.   O. H. Zabel

3834. Wilkins, Robert P. THE PEACE ISSUE IN THE GENERAL ELECTION OF 1914. *North Dakota Hist. 1963 30(2/3): 97-100.* Evidence reduces the belief that North Dakota isolationism was prompted by pro-German sentiment. Peace was the issue in 1914 in North Dakota, and President Wilson's handling of foreign affairs seemed destined to lead the United States into the war.   I. W. Van Noppen

3835. Wilkins, Robert P. REFERENDUM ON WAR? THE GENERAL ELECTION OF 1916 IN NORTH DAKOTA. *North Dakota Hist. 1969 36(4): 296-335.* Discusses the peoples' role in determining US foreign policy. The mechanism used by the people in North Dakota in 1916 was the presidential election of that year. The Democratic Party relied mainly on the fact that America had been kept out of the European war; however, the Democratic Party of North Dakota was split over President Wilson's call for a larger military machine and the submarine policy. The Republican national platform pledged full support and protection to Americans abroad and on the high seas. Republican candidate Charles Evans Hughes spoke in favor of an honorable peace and settlement of differences with Germany. This met with approval in the *Bismarck Tribune.* The Democratic national platform reiterated the theme "He kept us out of war." Hughes made three major speeches in North Dakota, hammering away at the themes of preparedness, firmness, and prosperity. President Wilson's foreign policy was attacked as weak or dangerously provocative, depending on the views of the attacker. The Republican Party in North Dakota could not unite behind Hughes because of rampant factionalism. Speaker activity on the part of the North Dakota Democratic Party was crucial in saving the day for Wilson. Most of their arguments were calculated to appeal to the voters' economic interpretation of politics. Wilson won the State with 51 percent of the vote, a new high for a Democratic candidate. North Dakota's vote can be interpreted as a vote against involvement in the European war. Based primarily on newspaper sources; illus., photos, 141 notes.   E. P. Costello

3836. Wilson, Charles M. A CROSS OF GOLD. *Am. Hist. Illus. 1970 5(8): 4-9, 43-48.* On the eve of the Democratic convention of 1896, William Jennings Bryan was a 36-year-old ex-Congressman from Lincoln, Nebraska, and a pro-silver Chautauqua lecturer who had lately been battered down by the Nebraska legislature (165-16) in his quest of a US Senate seat. On the fifth ballot at the convention he became the unanimous choice. He became a national political figure and was renominated for President in 1900 and 1908. The reason for the 1896 nomination was his "Cross of Gold" speech. Identifying "we, the common people," and "they, the rich," his final lines are classic: "We shall answer their demands by saying to them. You shall not press down upon the brow of labor the crown of thorns. You shall not crucify mankind on a cross of gold!" Based on primary sources; 10 illus.   D. Dodd

3837. Wilson, James Q. A GUIDE TO REAGAN COUNTRY. THE POLITICAL CULTURE OF SOUTHERN CALIFORNIA. *Commentary 1967 43(5): 37-45.* The political culture of Southern California is a particular consequence of its historical development through the 1930's and 1940's. During that period large numbers of people migrated from the midwest and the near south to Southern California, and there became involved in a new style of life. Unlike other immigrants to large urban areas, they settled not in apartments or flats but in individual houses, tens of thousands of them, that were built in and around the suburban communities of Los Angeles. They brought with them stubbornly individualistic fundamental protestantism and added to it a definite feeling of the sanctity of private property and the virtue of individualistic effort. The polity of Southern California is largely made up of the children of these immigrants, who grew up in a fairly fluid environment with very little group identification and a strong sense of property, as well as highly individualistic mobility both resulting from the prevalence and necessity of private automobiles for transport. Unlike the people of eastern urban societies, the people of Southern California found their identification not in groups but as families and individuals. Southern California politics has reflected this, with little party organization or solidarity, and an emphasis instead on populism, in which issues easily became extreme and colored with questions of morality. The Southern Californian experience seems to have been the vanguard of similar developments all over the growing American West, and the growing importance of this kind of politics can be seen in the capture of the Republican Party by Goldwater in 1964. In the past, American democracy has wisely refrained from entanglement in issues of morality; and the author fears for the time when politics is taken over by them. "Our system of government cannot handle matters of that sort (can any democratic system?) and it may be torn apart by the effort."   A. K. Main

3838. Zanger, Martin. POLITICS OF CONFRONTATION: UPTON SINCLAIR AND THE LAUNCHING OF THE ACLU IN SOUTHERN CALIFORNIA. *Pacific Hist. R. 1969 38(4): 383-406.* The waterfront strike at San Pedro in 1923 brought Sinclair into the headlines as a crusader in support of the radical labor unionists and the Industrial Workers of the World (IWW), although he himself remained faithful to the idea of peaceful revolution. The strike turned into a free speech fight for which Sinclair and others were arrested. The Los Angeles police and press attacked him, while the national and left-wing labor press praised his stand. The most enduring result of the San Pedro affair was Sinclair's use of the situation to publicize the launching of one of the most important constituent affiliates of the American Civil Liberties Union (ACLU). He took an active part in its formation by writing and by helping to raise money. Based on primary and secondary sources; 91 notes.   E. C. Hyslop

3839. —. DENVER'S DEMOCRATIC INVASION. *Colorado Mag. 1964 41(3): 185-197.* In 1908 the Democratic Party, recognizing the significance of the West in national politics, held its national convention in Denver's new auditorium. This was the first of numerous regional and national meetings for Denver. Opinion was divided as to the city's ability to handle the huge influx of visitors. The city provided many entertainment features. Based on newspaper accounts.   I. W. Van Noppen

3840. —. [THE KU KLUX KLAN IN COLORADO]. *Colorado Mag. 1965 42(2): 93-113.*
Davis, James H. COLORADO UNDER THE KLAN, *pp. 83-108.* During the 1920's, the Ku Klux Klan was an important power faction in Colorado politics. Through the influence of Grand Dragon John Galen Locke, it hoped to obtain passage of measures which would discriminate against Catholics and minority groups. Several courageous legislators succeeded in stopping Governor Clarence J. Morley's Klan-oriented program. Only through the efforts of these legislators was Colorado saved from the near disaster which Klan dominance meant.
Mazzulla, Fred and Mazzulla, Jo. A KLAN ALBUM, *pp. 109-113.* Photographs of both the Ku Klux Klan and the ladies auxiliary, a unique Colorado group.   R. Sexauer

Economic Activity

3841. Alexander, Thomas G. and Arrington, Leonard J. UTAH'S SMALL ARMS AMMUNITION PLANT DURING WORLD WAR II. *Pacific Hist. R. 1965 34(2): 185-196.* Describes the economic effects during and after the war of a 19 million dollar plant constructed by the Federal government and eventually sold at a fraction of cost.

J. McCutcheon

3842. Anderson, Bryce W. THE BOMB AT THE GOVERNOR'S GATE. *Am. West 1965 2(1): 12-21, 75-76.* Frank Steunenberg, elected governor of Idaho in 1896 and 1898 with union labor support, suppressed violent efforts of the Western Federation of Miners to unionize Coeur d'Alene mines in 1899. He was killed by a bomb on 30 December 1905, by Albert E. Horsely (aliases Harry Orchard, Thomas Hogan, Goglan) and others. The trial of William Dudley ("Big Bill") Haywood, general secretary of the Western Federation of Miners, and others who were charged by Horsley with making him their tool, gained wide attention with Clarence Darrow for the defense and William E. Borah for the prosecution. Horsley was convicted and the others were acquitted or their charges dismissed. Illus., biblio. note.   D. L. Smith

3843. Anderson, Walt. THE "TIMES" DYNAMITING CASE. *Am. Hist. Illus. 1968 2(10): 47-51.* When the Los Angeles Times Building was bombed on 1 October 1910, and 21 employees of the Los Angeles *Times* were killed, the paper immediately blamed the labor unions. The *Times* knew its enemies, for the paper's owner, H. G. Otis, "was one of the country's strongest opponents of the drive toward closed union shops, and no man was more bitterly hated by Labor than . . . Otis." In April 1911, "John J. McNamara, 28, the secretary of the International Association of Bridge and Structural Iron Workers; his brother James B. McNamara, 27; and . . . Ortie McManigal were apprehended as suspects." Everyone in America who was sympathetic to management was sure of their guilt, and everyone who was sympathetic to labor was sure of their innocence. Clarence Darrow, a strong friend of the union movement, consented to conduct the defense. During the course of the trial the McNamara brothers confessed to having planted the bomb. Their confession "dealt a crippling blow to organized labor in southern California." Moreover, by the conclusion of the case, Darrow had been indicted for attempting to bribe a juror. Darrow was never found guilty, but when he left Los Angeles two years later, "he was nearly bankrupt, and his wife had suffered a nervous breakdown." 4 illus.   R. V. McBaine

3844. Andreano, Ralph. THE STRUCTURE OF THE CALIFORNIA PETROLEUM INDUSTRY, 1895-1911. *Pacific Hist. R. 1970 39(2): 171-192.* Concentrates on the competitive dynamics which shaped the structure of the California oil industry during the first decade of the 20th century. Analyzes the production and consumption of crude and fuel oil and asphalt, and summarizes the power structure of the three major firms involved: Standard Oil, Union Oil, and the Southern Pacific Railroad, which in turn was a majority stockholder in the Associated Oil Company, the major association of independent producers. As opposed to the national situation, no single firm had a monopoly position, permitting earlier entry into the field by new competitive firms. 8 tables, 30 notes.   E. C. Hyslop

3845. Arrington, Leonard. LAUNCHING IDAHO'S BEET SUGAR INDUSTRY. *Idaho Yesterdays 1965 9(3): 16-28.* Discusses the agricultural history of Idaho, suggesting that a region should specialize in the production of commodities which it can produce at the lowest relative cost. The history of the Utah-Idaho Sugar Company is traced from 1891 to 1950. Primary officials of the Mormon Church sought to build additional sugar factories in areas settled by Mormons. Many plants were developed with the financial assistance of the American Sugar Refining Company of New York City. New technology after 1939 increased the efficiency and profits of the larger and centrally located plants. 3 illus., 29 notes.   D. H. Swift

3846. Atherton, Lewis. STRUCTURE AND BALANCE IN WESTERN MINING HISTORY. *Huntington Lib. Q. 1966 30(1): 55-84.* Examination of the long-continued activities of a relatively unsuccessful mining promoter brings out the economic realities of discovery and development in far western nonferrous mining. The papers of Theodore J. Lamoreaux in the Huntington Library make possible a clear picture of the difficulties of this industry in balancing the factors of land, labor, and capital. The unrelenting efforts of the promoter to obtain capital - always in short supply - for development of insecurely controlled resources of largely speculative value show in some detail the reasons for the aura of sharp practice, tension between the western and eastern investors, and the violence of labor relations which characterized mining history.

H. D. Jordan

3847. Ballard, Shreve. BEFORE THE FREEWAY CAME. *Noticias 1966 12(4): 4-7.* Describes the means of travel in the Santa Barbara area around 1910. The Southern Pacific Railroad, with a local family providing two presidents by 1930, had small stations at the Hotel Miramar and the Montecito (now the Biltmore). The author remembers tying his horse to a hitching rail on his way to see a Western. He describes the journey to school (by train and stagecoach) near Ojai; and also a boardwalk connecting the dirt road between Ventura and Carpinteria. The dirt road over Casitas Pass was considered one of the most dangerous pieces of road between Los Angeles and San Francisco. Photos.

T. M. Condon

3848. Barnes, Donald M. THE EVERETT MASSACRE: A TURNING POINT IN I.W.W. HISTORY. *Organon 1969 1(1): 35-42.* The International Workers of the World free speech fight at Everett, Washington, on 15 November 1916 was one of the last open, revolutionary activities of that organization. Although a large number of Wobblies were involved in the altercation at Everett, where a deputy sheriff was killed, only one Wobbly was put on trial, and he was acquitted. During the trial, the prosecuting attorney introduced I.W.W. publications as evidence of the subversive and dangerous character of the organization. Because of the implications of this evidence, the I.W.W. under William Dudley Haywood took the initiative in altering the radical tone of the literature which the organization had previously circulated. I.W.W. publications became less radical and more defensive in tone. Recruiting techniques were also altered. On a broader scale, I.W.W. evidenced a declining devotion to revolution. This occurred as the I.W.W. entered a period of decline and passed from the effective sphere of action in American labor history. Based on primary and secondary sources; 34 notes.

P. W. Kennedy

3849. Bayard, Charles J. THE 1927-1928 COLORADO COAL STRIKE. *Pacific Hist. R. 1963 32(3): 235-250.* Examination of the role of the IWW and the events of the coal strike. Relates it to the cyclical pattern of strikes in the mining industry of the region.

J. McCutcheon

3850. Bayne, Nedra. THE BROADWATER: RELIC OF ELEGANCE. *Montana 1969 19(3): 58-66.* Charles A. Broadwater opened a resort hotel and natatorium on the outskirts of Helena, Montana, in 1889. Too large and costly for the limited patronage of a small city in a cold-weather environment, it was never profitable. A succession of owners operated the place after its builder's death in 1892, until the severe earthquakes of 1935 wrecked the pool. The hotel served as a night club briefly, but now remains only as an architectural relic. Illus.

S. R. Davison

3851. Belknap, Michael R. THE ERA OF THE LEMON: A HISTORY OF SANTA PAULA, CALIFORNIA. *California Hist. Soc. Q. 1968 47(2): 113-140.* By the time citrus growing began to be profitable (1890's), Santa Paula had become the recognized center of the California oil industry, but new strikes in other parts of the State caused many oilmen to move elsewhere. Much as oilmen would have welcomed a boom, Santa Paula never had one because landowners did not wish to sell their land. Another reason for the absence of industry lay in the fact that the mainline of the Southern Pacific Railroad bypassed Santa Paula. After 1940 the lemon industry began to die and during World War II Santa Paula became a "bedroom community" for Navy workers at Port Hueneme and Point Magu. Based partly on interviews; illus., 103 notes.

E. P. Stickney

3852. Blackford, Mansel G. BUSINESSMEN AND THE REGULATION OF RAILROADS AND PUBLIC UTILITIES IN CALIFORNIA DURING THE PROGRESSIVE ERA. *Business Hist. R. 1970 44(3): 307-319.* In 1911-15, "the Progressive-controlled California legislature enacted bills embodying a wide range of economic reforms. Among the most important were those which created a new railroad commission with vastly enlarged powers and which brought public utilities under state supervision. Groups of businessmen were in the vanguard of both reforms. The driving force for railroad regulation came less from an outraged public seeking lower rates than from shippers and merchants who wanted to stabilize their businesses. Public utility officers spearheaded campaigns for the passage, and, later, the enlargement of the Public Utilities Act. They hoped state regulation would end competition between their companies, improve the value of their utilities' securities, and allow them to escape continual wrangling with county and municipal authorities." Although the businessmen "were influential in obtaining the passage of bills incorporating many of their desires, no group of businessmen achieved hegemony over the California legislature or the railroad commission in the Progressive Era. Laws desired by some businessmen were opposed by others. . . . It is probably wrong to see too sharp a dichotomy between the best interests of business groups and the general public." Based on governmental records of California and on contemporary periodicals; 63 notes.

C. J. Pusateri

3853. Borne, Lawrence R. TRIUMPH TO DISASTER: COLONEL JAMES A. OWNBEY. *Colorado Mag. 1971 48(4): 319-336.* By 1910 Ownbey had established the basis for a thriving coal industry in the Wootton Land and Fuel Company near Trinidad. His major financial backer and partner was J. P. Morgan, a long-time friend. However, two events of 1913 caused trouble for Ownbey: labor difficulties and the death of Morgan. Labor troubles contributed to a substantial financial loss in 1914 and litigation with the Morgan estate in the next several years was disastrous for Ownbey before his death in 1927. Illus., 83 notes.

O. H. Zabel

3854. Borne, Lawrence R. THE WOOTTON LAND AND FUEL COMPANY, 1905-1910. *Colorado Mag. 1969 46(3): 189-208.* Describes the rapid and successful development of the Wootton Land and Fuel Company under the direction of "Colonel" James A. Ownbey. Between 1905 and 1910 Ownbey acquired and developed huge holdings of coal lands near Trinidad, Colorado, with the support of eastern capitalists such as J. P. Morgan and B. P. Cheney. Eastern capital, western resources, convenient location of the Santa Fe Railroad, and Ownbey's ability are credited with the success. 10 photos, 59 notes.

O. H. Zabel

3855. Brazier, Richard. THE MASS I.W.W. TRIAL OF 1918: A RETROSPECT. *Labor Hist. 1966 7(2): 178-192.* A memoir of the famous "Wobbly" trial of 1918 by the only surviving member of the General Executive Board of the I.W.W. (Industrial Workers of the World) at the time. Impressions and reflections upon the criminal charges, jails, prisoner activities, fellow defendants, counsel for prosecution and defense, the jury, and Judge K. M. Landis are given.

L. L. Athey

3856. Brewer, Thomas B. STATE ANTI-LABOR LEGISLATION: TEXAS - A CASE STUDY. *Labor Hist. 1970 11(1): 58-76.* Surveys the struggle over antilabor legislation in Texas for 50 years. Although antilabor forces were finally successful in 1947, the statutes have not resulted either in substantial protection of workers not desiring unionization or the retardation of unions. The enactment of the laws came more from the permeating influence of business than traditional rural hostility. Based on Texas legislative records, the *Proceedings* of the Texas State Federation of Labor, and newspapers; 81 notes.

L. L. Athey

3857. Brown, Mrs. Hugh. RAILROAD DAYS: A MEMOIR OF TONOPAH, 1904. *Am. West 1968 5(6): 24-28.* In an excerpt from her book *Lady in Boomtown* (Palo Alto: American West Publishing Co., 1968), the author recalls the three-day celebration in July 1904 of the completion of a shortline railroad linking Tonopah to the outside world. This marked the end of the days of the stagecoach and twenty-mule teams. The affair included such treats as fireworks, dancing, free refreshments, literary exercises, music, games, and drilling. 7 illus.

D. L. Smith

3858. Bryant, Frank B. HAPPY DAYS AND HAPPY MEN. *Idaho Yesterdays 1965 9(3): 8-15.* A former superintendent of the Italian Mine, the author describes his adventures in the Salmon River Mountains

from 1909 to 1911. Included are character sketches of freight drivers and stage handlers who drove long distances between Leesburg and points in western Montana. Describes the early railroads and prominent gold mines which were the economic base of east central Idaho. 2 illus.

D. H. Swift

3859. Caldwell, Edwin L. HIGHLIGHTS OF THE DEVELOPMENT OF MANUFACTURING IN TEXAS, 1900-1960. *Southwestern Hist. Q. 1965 68(4): 405-431.* Cotton, cattle, corn, and lumber were the main supports of the Texas economy in 1900. All but corn were produced primarily for external markets. Manufacturing was small scale and tailored primarily for local needs. The turning point in 1900 marked the first significant development in the oil industry. Texas has progressed to industrialization "on the coat-tails of the oil and gas industry." Despite rapid growth, however, the status of the economy must be described as one of "continued industrial immaturity," in 1960. Table, 7 notes.

D. L. Smith

3860. Carlson, Alvar W. LIGNITE COAL AS AN ENABLING FACTOR IN THE SETTLEMENT OF WESTERN NORTH DAKOTA. *Great Plains J. 1972 11(2): 145-153.* Lignite was widespread and accessible for easy exploitation. "Homesteaders began arriving in southwestern North Dakota in the late 1890's, but the major influx came during the first two decades of the 1900's." Lignite was used as a selling point by homestead locators. Considerable lignite was mined and used locally or shipped to eastern North Dakota, but "little lignite left North Dakota." Because of its low heating power, special larger stoves were needed. "The use of lignite in rural homes started to decline with the introduction of the Peerless kerosene kitchen stove and the oil burner in the 1920's." Some farmers still use lignite; otherwise it "is used mainly for generating electricity at local utility plants." The scars of abandoned strip and open pit mines are still visible on the rural landscape. Based mainly on secondary sources; 5 photos, 13 notes.

O. H. Zabel

3861. Clark, Dwight L. THE GIANNINIS - MEN OF THE RENAISSANCE. *California Hist. Soc. Q. 1970 49(3): 251-269 and (4): 337-351.* Part I. Amadeo Peter Giannini founded the Bank of America and built it into a financial empire. In many ways he ill-fitted the banker's stereotype. Fond of opera, affable, and possessing an amazing memory, Giannini was also shrewd and meticulous in his business dealings. He detested yes-men, committees that evolved into bureaucracies, and conformity. The author recalls these characteristics in a series of anecdotes dealing with the court fight between Giannini's Transamerica Corporation and the Securities and Exchange Commission, Giannini's methods of work, his operations during the Depression, his endorsement of and later opposition to the Roosevelt administration, and his colorful personality. Photos, 3 notes. Part II. Reminiscences of Attilio Henry Giannini, A. P. Giannini's younger brother. A physician by training, Attilio served as senior executive of the Bank of America in Southern California from 1931 to 1943. Known as having a positive personality and reputed to be difficult to work with, Attilio was a friend to those who were honest with him. Attilio and the author became strong friends. Relates anecdotes about Attilio during the Depression. Mentions Attilio's boldness in advancing money to the businessmen erecting the Santa Anita Racetrack, his battles with bureaucracy, and his concern and assessment of individual worth. Unlike Amadeo, Attilio enjoyed reading and platform speaking. He died of a heart attack at a Loyola University Regents meeting in 1943.

A. Hoffman

3862. Clark, Norman H. EVERETT, 1916, AND AFTER. *Pacific Northwest Q. 1966 57(2): 57-64.* Detailed account of dramatic labor strife in Everett, Washington, 1916-17, leading to "Bloody Sunday," showing the role of Industrial Workers of the World and other participants. Biblio. notes and comments on sources and conflicting historical evidence.

C. C. Gorchels

3863. Clinch, Thomas A. COXEY'S ARMY IN MONTANA. *Montana 1965 15(4): 2-11.* Although failing to overtake the original expedition, several western sections of Coxey's Army were organized in 1894. One formed in Butte by a William Hogan seized railroad trains for transportation east, only to be stopped in the Billings area by U.S. marshals and army troops, after gunfire and some casualties. Another attempt was made by flatboat down the Missouri River. Montana participants were largely miners and solidly Populists, a variation from the usual agrarian nature of that group. Largely based on contemporary accounts in the Montana press.

S. R. Davison

3864. Clough, Wilson O. PORTRAIT IN OIL. THE BELGO-AMERICAN COMPANY IN WYOMING. *Ann. of Wyoming 1969 41(1): 5-31.* Discusses the discovery of oil in Wyoming and the organization and activities of the Belgo-American Company between 1900 and 1904. The author examines the company statements to European investors and notes the discrepancies between its claims and performance. Charges were leveled by Louis Magné in his *Histoire de la Société Belgo-Américaine des Pétroles du Wyoming* (Brussels, 1904) that the company had no facilities to produce oil in Wyoming, and that inadequate transportation, a lack of working capital, and competition from American firms would inhibit future exploitation of the oil. Illus., 10 notes, biblio.

R. L. Nichols

3865. Colley, Charles C. ARIZONA, CRADLE OF THE AMERICAN DATE GROWING INDUSTRY, 1890-1916. *Southern California Q. 1971 53(1): 55-66.* The present center of the American date-growing industry is in the Coachella Valley of California, but the enterprise began in Arizona between 1890 and 1916. Discusses the early attempts to grow palms from seed, the difficulties in acquiring good offshoots from the Middle East, the haphazard and often unsuccessful planting of the offshoots obtained, and the struggle to eradicate insect pests such as the *Parlatoria*. Most of the early experimentation with date palms took place in Arizona, but the leadership in scientific and commercial production of dates in the United States shifted to California by 1916. Based mainly on Department of Agriculture (USDA) sources; 2 illus., 38 notes.

W. L. Bowers

3866. Conlin, Joseph R. THE HAYWOOD CASE: AN ENDURING RIDDLE. *Pacific Northwest Q. 1968 59(1): 23-32.* Recounts the events related to the historical murder trial of labor leader William Dudley "Big Bill" Haywood at Boise, Idaho, in 1907, with background information leading to the trial. Haywood was tried for allegedly participating in the murder of Frank Streusenberg, Idaho newspaper publisher, governor, and sheep rancher. The trial is said to have been the culmination of bitter labor-management disputes in the metal mining industry during the late 1890's and early 1900's. Calling in a variety of sources, the author examines the factors and roles of the principal participants in the murder case and presents theories on the motivations of the antagonists.

C. C. Gorchels

3867. Cotroneo, Ross R. COLONIZATION OF THE NORTHERN PACIFIC LAND GRANT, 1900-1920. *North Dakota Q. 1970 38(3): 33-48.* Until the reorganization of the company after the Panic of 1893, the Northern Pacific Railroad endured repeated failures. After 1896, however, traffic increased and land sales were up. The road adopted a policy of depending on land companies to recruit immigrants to the territory it served, these having previously obtained railroad lands at low cost on this understanding. Generally the railroad eschewed the more blatant efforts to gain settlers, though its emigration department at various times sponsored traveling shows and public meetings. Generally it held to the policy that regular recruitment of satisfied settlers, rather than a sudden surge of misled migrants, would bring long-term growth and stability. Based on primary and secondary sources; 67 notes.

J. F. Mahoney

3868. Cotroneo, Ross R. WESTERN LAND MARKETING BY THE NORTHERN PACIFIC RAILWAY. *Pacific Hist. R. 1968 37(3): 299-320.* The land grant holdings of the Northern Pacific Railway which were located west of Montana were supervised and managed separately as "the western district." Although by 1900 most of the food agricultural land had been disposed of, there were still vast tracts of grazing land and enormous amounts of timber holdings. After that date, farming areas were usually sold in small tracts to settlers. Grazing acreage was generally so poor that disposing of it was a serious problem. The timber lands were of high quality and value and were sold to various large lumber companies. Much of the prime timber was bought by Frederick Weyerhaeuser at extremely low rates. As the demand for timber increased over the years and the supply dwindled rapidly, firmer control was exercised over prices and sales. There was constant concern as to whether prices were high enough to insure the company a fair return. The author concludes that the policies of the Northern Pacific in the 1900-20 years were generally

similar to the activities of other land-owning railroads. They attempted to accomplish two specific goals: to sell land and resources to provide funds for building, maintenance, and paying off mortgages; and to populate the region to provide the markets and business necessary to sustain the railroad. 72 notes.

D. L. Smith

3869. Coulter, C. Brewster. THE BIG Y COUNTRY: MARKETING PROBLEMS AND ORGANIZATION, 1900-1920. *Agric. Hist. 1972 46(4): 471-488.* Deals with efforts by fruit growers in the Yakima Valley to improve their marketing position through cooperatives, most notably via the Yakima Valley Fruit Growers' Association (YVFGA). Attempts to establish a co-op encompassing the entire Northwest ultimately failed, but smaller, regional co-ops such as the YVFGA survived and provided badly needed protection against the hazards of the open market. Based on the records of the Yakima Valley Fruit Growers' Association, and on interviews and newspapers; 41 notes.

D. E. Brewster

3870. Dubofsky, Melvyn. JAMES H. HAWLEY AND THE ORIGINS OF THE HAYWOOD CASE. *Pacific Northwest Q. 1967 58(1): 23-32.* Contends that conscious efforts were made in Idaho by lawyers and industrialists as well as the State government in the 1890's to eradicate an entire labor organization, the Western Federation of Miners. Given considerable emphasis in this account is the chameleon role of attorney James H. Hawley who participated in the court trials and maneuvers related to the labor-management strife of the day.

C. C. Gorchels

3871. Dubofsky, Melvyn. THE LEADVILLE STRIKE OF 1896-1897: AN APPRAISAL. *Mid-America 1966 48(2): 99-118.* Utilizing the official papers of Governor Albert A. MacIntyre (1895-97) and Governor Alva Adams (1897-99) the Leadville, Colorado strike is examined. The larger significance of the strike for the history of the American labor movement is established.

L. D. Silveri

3872. Dubofsky, Melvyn. THE ORIGINS OF WESTERN WORKING CLASS RADICALISM, 1890-1905. *Labor Hist. 1966 7(2): 131-154.* Asserts that the origins of radical unionism in America must be sought in the process of capitalist growth and the larger trends transforming the industrial world rather than in Turnerian terms of frontier uniqueness. Rapid economic and social change in the American West resulted in a "social polarization" and the development of a class ideology which followed the Marxian pattern of development. The shift from unionism to radicalism by the Western Federation of Miners is traced, and the shift is related to the historical trends of Populism, trade unionism, the growth of modern technology and corporate capitalism, and the alliance between corporate capitalism and government. 73 notes.

L. L. Athey

3873. Due, John F. THE CITY OF PRINEVILLE RAILWAY AND THE ECONOMIC DEVELOPMENT OF CROOK COUNTY. *Econ. Geography 1967 43(2): 170-181.* After railroads had bypassed Prineville, her citizens voted in 1916 to build a connection to the nearest line. The city was unable to sell its railway on its completion in 1918 and had to operate it. The principal outbound traffic at first was cattle; inbound merchandise was soon lost to rising motor transport. From 1925 through 1937 the line operated at a loss. Then lumber mills began to move into the area. After years of high output during World War II, production declined to nearly a sustained yield basis. The 1965 traffic was 4.7 million ton miles. The railway has been completely modernized and produces sufficient revenue that the city property tax has been eliminated. The railway has been of utmost importance for the development of the lumber industry. Economic trends in Crook County, 1890-1960, are summarized. Prineville's experience demonstrates the ability of a government to undertake and sustain a long-range investment project significant for its economic development, when prospective returns are too uncertain and remote for private enterprise to undertake it. Map, 2 tables.

J. E. Caswell

3874. Dyche, William K. TONGUE RIVER EXPERIENCE. *Forest Hist. 1964 8(1/2): 2-16.* A memoir of William K. Dyche, manager of a banker-owned logging and lumbering operation on the Tongue River watershed in Big Horn National Forest, Wyoming. Dyche provided efficient working conditions for his crews, readily adopted and devised improved operations and business technology, and maintained contact with all branches of the firm despite unfriendly climate and terrain. Dyche left the firm when the market declined. 5 photos.　　　　　　　B. A. Vatter

3875. Epley, Malcolm. BLACK GOLD HARBOR. *California Historian 1967 13(4): 113-116.* Presents a survey of the history "of legislation and litigation relating to the Long Beach Harbor, the oil found in the earth structure beneath it, and the disposition of the immense cash returns from this source." The author reviews the tidelands relationship with the State of California. Long Beach had developed its tidelands, which included oil reserves, based on a court decision of 1930. The city proceeded with extensive harbor development and made highly favorable contracts with oil companies. Large amounts of revenue soon filled the city treasury. In 1952 Long Beach promoted a law in which 50 percent of the "excess" revenues could be used for projects other than the tidelands or shoreline development; however, a Long Beach citizen, Felix Mallon, filed a suit challenging this law. The State Supreme Court held that, since Long Beach did not own the tidelands but held them in "trust," and if the money was not needed for trust purposes, the "excess" revenues reverted to the trustor, the State. In 1956 the city compromised with the State, giving 120 million dollars to Sacramento and promising 85 percent of new oil revenues. The author claims "Long Beach rightly feels that it deserves some measure of recognition for this contribution." In closing, the author points to the improvements to Long Beach due to the oil revenues and the "fabulous windfall for all California citizens." Based on a speech delivered to the southern California Symposium of the Conference of California Historical Societies.　　　　　　　O. L. Miller

3876. Escolas, Edmond L. WYOMING'S PIONEER LIFE INSURANCE COMPANY. *Ann. of Wyoming 1969 41(2): 187-192.* A brief history of the Wyoming Life Insurance Company from its organization in March 1911 to its demise in July 1926. The author stresses the difficulties encountered in a State with a small population and without a large amount of capital. Incorporated by a group including politicians, cattlemen, attorneys, and business leaders, the company never achieved the anticipated capital or profits. The company underwent several name changes, and for a while was controlled by the Western Holding Company. It expanded with the Colorado Life Insurance Company in 1921; however, without ever paying a dividend it went out of business in 1926. Based on newspapers, *Index to Corporations,* and various life insurance fact books; illus., photos, 31 notes.　　　　　　　R. L. Nichols

3877. Escolas, Edmund L. THE RISE OF WORKMEN'S COMPENSATION IN WYOMING. *Ann. of Wyoming 1963 35(2): 174-200.* Discusses the Wyoming socioeconomic structure between 1900 and 1915, showing that 70 percent of the population lived in rural areas and most of the rest were urban workers employed by coal mining, oil drilling, and manufacturing concerns. Claims that both labor and business agreed on the need for a workmen's compensation law. When passed in 1915, union leaders claimed the law lacked adequate compensation. Based on published United Mine Workers records, legislative and court records, and state histories.　　　　　　　R. L. Nichols

3878. Evans, William B. and Peterson, Robert L. DECISION AT COLSTRIP. *Pacific Northwest Q. 1970 61(3): 129-136.* Open-pit coal mining was nurtured by the Northern Pacific Railroad in Colstrip, 1919-24, for economic reasons and allegedly to "break the expected coal strike" of laborers in other mines of the region. Discusses legalistic considerations and methods of making the enterprise profitable.

　　　　　　　C. C. Gorchels

3879. Fahey, John. COEUR D'ALENE CONFEDERACY. *Idaho Yesterdays 1968 12(1): 2-7.* The Mine Owners' Association of the Coeur d'Alene district in northern Idaho was a confederacy of managers that lasted from 1891 to about 1916. This organization fought the railroads, smelter trusts, and the local farmers on occasion. Money was spent for detectives, strike-breakers, and political support. Workmen's blacklists were circulated in code to mine owners in Colorado and British Columbia. The association was started to stabilize the costs of production, and by united action uncertainty was replaced by predictability.

　　　　　　　G. Barrett

3880. Fischer, Duane D. THE SHORT, UNHAPPY STORY OF THE DEL NORTE COMPANY. *Forest Hist. 1967 11(1): 12-25.* The Del Norte Company of California was organized in 1902 with the expec-

tation that redwood would replace white pine in the market. The company's fortunes varied, and it closed its books in 1950. 13 illus.

　　　　　　　B. A. Vatter

3881. Friedheim, Robert L. PROLOGUE TO A GENERAL STRIKE: THE SEATTLE SHIPYARD STRIKE OF 1919. *Labor Hist. 1965 6(2): 121-142.* A three-cornered struggle involving employers, employees, and the Emergency Fleet Corporation precipitated a shipworkers' strike which evolved into a city-wide sympathy strike. This strike almost presents "a case study of how a government wartime production agency should *not* deal with workers in the industry it sought to regulate." Based on contemporary newspaper articles and memoranda of government, management, and labor leaders.　　　　　　　J. H. Krenkel

3882. Friedheim, Robert L. and Friedheim, Robin. THE SEATTLE LABOR MOVEMENT, 1919-20. *Pacific Northwest Q. 1964 55(4): 146-156.* Unique in radicalism, cohesiveness, and ideology, organized labor in Seattle has an especially interesting history. Activities of special groups and talents of leaders (with portraits) during 1919-20 are recounted here. Contrary to national policies of the American Federation of Labor at that time, Seattle unionists favored labor in politics, industrial unionism, and nationalization of key industries, and the Seattle representative cast the sole vote in opposition to the reelection of Samuel Gompers as president of the American Federation of Labor in 1919 and 1920.

　　　　　　　C. C. Gorchels

3883. Gadd, John D. C. SALTAIR, GREAT SALT LAKE'S MOST FAMOUS RESORT. *Utah Hist. Q. 1968 36(3): 198-221.* Provides the story of the construction, management, and financing of a summer resort built on the south shore of Great Salt Lake, primarily to serve the citizens of Salt Lake City, Ogden, and nearby communities. The receding of the lake waters from the site and storm damage created problems almost from the beginning. Later the automobile opened competing diversions to Saltair's patrons. The resort never fully recovered from a disastrous fire which occurred in 1925 and it was closed in 1958. Subsequent attempts to make public or private use of the site and its decaying facilities have failed. Based mainly on newspaper accounts and personal interviews; illus.　　　　　　　S. L. Jones

3884. Gallaway, B. P. POPULATION TRENDS IN THE WESTERN CROSS TIMBERS OF TEXAS, 1890-1960: ECONOMIC CHANGE AND SOCIAL BALANCE. *Southwestern Hist. Q. 1964 67(3): 376-396.* Studies the culture of the Cross Timbers region of Texas, as exemplified by 11 counties central to the region. The conclusion is reached that the area is primarily agricultural in its economy, has a population of low density and exhibits a high degree of ethnic homogeneity and social balance.　　　　　　　R. L. Williamson

3885. Gilmore, N. Ray and Gilmore, Gladys W. THE BRACERO IN CALIFORNIA. *Pacific Hist. R. 1963 32(3): 265-282.* Describes the bracero (temporary Mexican agricultural worker) system in California from World War I to the end of 1963 in terms of how it works, what political and economic issues have been involved, which groups favor and oppose it and what U.S. policy has been.　　　　　　　J. McCutcheon

3886. Giovinco, Joseph. DEMOCRACY IN BANKING: THE BANK OF ITALY AND CALIFORNIA'S ITALIANS. *California Hist. Soc. Q. 1968 47(3): 195-218.* The Bank of Italy was established in 1904 in San Francisco by A. P. Giannini on a democratic basis to serve the little fellow. The author focuses on its relationship with California's Italians. Soon after its incorporation, the Bank of Italy opened a branch in the Mission district of San Francisco and in 1910 one in San Jose. The solicitors of the bank embarked on a "crusade for new accounts." Their principal function was to maintain the good will of the local Italian population in the various communities throughout the State. By 1930 the bank had outgrown its immigrant status and had become the Bank of America National Trust and Savings Association. Based on Bank of America archives; illus., 73 notes.　　　　　　　E. P. Stickney

3887. Glaser, David. MIGRATION IN IDAHO'S HISTORY. *Idaho Yesterdays 1967 11(3): 22-31.* Migratory elements have traditionally tamed the wilderness, built the cities, and cleared the frontier. The Gem State's early migrants were miners. By 1900 many were engaged in agriculture because many workers were needed for the irrigated land.

World War I brought a general labor shortage in Idaho, but teen-agers took up the slack. The economic conditions of the 1930's caused the Federal Government, under the bureau of Farm Security Administration, to construct labor camps for farm workers. The governor's Migratory Labor Committee, established in 1955, was primarily interested in improving living conditions. The lot of migratory workers was gradually improved with the growth of the State. The present wages and living conditions of seasonal workers in Idaho are as good as those in any State. Illus., 44 notes.   B. B. Swift

3888. Graham, John. UPTON SINCLAIR AND THE LUDLOW MASSACRE. *Colorado Q. 1972 21(1): 55-67.* After coal miners struck in southern Colorado in 1913, a climax was reached in the struggle between miners and operators in the "Ludlow Massacre" of 20 April 1914, when the Colorado National Guard attacked and burned the strikers' tent colony. Upton Sinclair was outraged by the miners' reports of what happened at Ludlow, and he decided to agitate for them. He knew that the workers were striking for unionization, personal liberty, better conditions, and higher wages. Sinclair picketed the Rockefeller offices in New York City because the Rockefellers controlled the largest of the Colorado coal companies, Colorado Fuel and Iron. He was jailed for three days for disturbing the peace, "investigated" the situation in Colorado, and eventually wrote *King Coal* on the basis of the information he had gathered.   B. A. Storey

3889. Groth, Clarence W. SOWING AND REAPING: MONTANA BANKING - 1910-1925. *Montana 1970 20(4): 28-35.* Examines the era of bank failures in agricultural counties of Montana between 1921 and 1925, when half of the State's 428 banks closed. Concludes that the cause was an excessive number of small, weak banks in the grain-growing areas where the postwar slump wiped out land values and related loans. Refutes earlier views that the new Federal Reserve System managed its policies purposely to destroy small rural banks. Based on published sources; illus., 14 notes.   S. R. Davison

3890. Gutfeld, Arnon. THE MURDER OF FRANK LITTLE: RADICAL LABOR AGITATION IN BUTTE, MONTANA, 1917. *Labor Hist. 1969 10(2): 177-192.* The murder of Frank Little, an Industrial Workers of the World organizer, culminated a five-year struggle between miners' unions and the Anaconda Copper Co., and it greatly influenced events in Montana. A hysterical antiunion campaign followed; Federal troops were ordered into Butte; anti-sedition bills were supported on the State and national levels of government. Based on local newspapers, material from the National Archives, and manuscripts from the Montana Historical Society.   L. L. Athey

3891. Gutfeld, Arnon. THE SPECULATOR DISASTER IN 1917: LABOR RESURGENCE AT BUTTE, MONTANA. *Arizona and the West 1969 11(1): 27-38.* The Anaconda Copper Mining Company dominated politics and economics in Montana and controlled the press. The 8 June 1917 holocaust in its Speculator Mine in Butte was Montana's worst single mine disaster. The disaster triggered a turbulent strike by the already restive labor force in this, the Nation's most productive mining district. Various labor organizations, including the Industrial Workers of the World and the American Federation of Labor, and the leading politicians of the State became intimately involved. Anaconda paralyzed the State's economy with a complete shutdown, the press characterized the strikers as traitors, and the tensions of World War I complicated the picture. Before the end of the year enough strikers had returned to work so that the strike was called off. Anaconda had successfully exploited labor's weakness in the mines. 5 illus., 27 notes.   D. L. Smith

3892. Halverson, Guy and Ames, William E. THE BUTTE "BULLETIN": BEGINNINGS OF A LABOR DAILY. *Journalism Q. 1969 46(2): 260-266.* The Butte *Daily Bulletin* existed from 1917 to 1924. It participated in the political and social issues of the period and could claim significant accomplishments. Its history began with the mine fire of 8 June 1917 which took 164 lives. The authors trace events preceding the strike which began 13 June, and the strike itself. The press was controlled by the Anaconda Company. A handout called the *Strike Bulletin* carried strike news. On 27 September it was announced that the Butte *Daily Bulletin,* headed by Burton K. Wheeler, would be a labor paper of general interest. The strike gradually died out, with the main issues largely unresolved. But strike leaders had learned several lessons, one of which was

the importance of a sympathetic daily newspaper. Based on secondary sources; 32 notes.   K. J. Puffer

3893. Hawley, James H. STEVE ADAMS' CONFESSION AND THE STATE'S CASE AGAINST BILL HAYWOOD. *Idaho Yesterdays 1963 7(4): 16-27.* Summary of the confession of Steve Adams in the case of the assassination of Idaho's Governor Frank Steunenberg. Hawley, who was special prosecutor in the case against William D. Haywood for the Steunenberg murder, prepared this summary of Adams' confession on 13 April 1906 for the US Attorney General. The Adams confession, later retracted, was a key factor in the case of the state against Haywood, an alleged accomplice of Adams. In the summary, Hawley sets forth (a year before the trial) the essence of the prosecution's case against Haywood, reviewing the creation of the Western Federation of Miners, the labor troubles in Idaho and Colorado in the 1890's and early 1900's and the assassination of Steunenberg by Harry Orchard, another Adams accomplice, in 1905.   M. Small

3894. Higgs, Robert. RAILROAD RATES AND THE POPULIST UPRISING. *Agric. Hist. 1970 44(3): 291-297.* Shows that, contrary to the beliefs of most recent historians, the Populists probably had good reason to complain of high railroad rates. The important transportation rate for farmers was the carrying cost relative to crop prices, and this did not change substantially during the period 1867-96. Thus, because of declining crop prices, farmers did not benefit from the lower nominal transportation rates during the three decades before 1897. Based primarily on published statistical compilations; 3 graphs, 24 notes.

D. E. Brewster

3895. Hough, Merrill. LEADVILLE AND THE WESTERN FEDERATION OF MINERS. *Colorado Mag. 1972 49(1): 19-34.* From 1878 to the mid-1890's Leadville was Colorado's second largest city and greatest producer of mineral wealth. Traces the history of unionization in Leadville prior to the 1895 establishment of a local of the Western Federation of Miners which, within a year, "organized nearly all the men working in the camp's mines. . . ." In May 1896 the miners began a nine-month strike over wages and union recognition which closed the mines, flared into violence, resulted in occupation by the national guard, and eventually failed in its objectives. No similar conflict occurred in Leadville in the following years. Illus., 37 notes.   O. H. Zabel

3896. Huntoon, Peter. THE NATIONAL BANK NOTE ISSUES OF THE FIRST NATIONAL BANK OF FLAGSTAFF, ARIZONA, 1917-1930. *Plateau 1971 44(1): 18-26.* "The First National Bank of Flagstaff, Arizona, was granted charter number 11120 in 1917 and was liquidated in 1931. During the intervening 14 years, the bank issued national currency as authorized by the National Bank Act. This issuance consisted of [five-, 10-, and 20-dollar] denomination notes in both the Series of 1902 Blue Seal Plain Back and Series of 1929 Type 1 varieties."

J

3897. James, Laurence P. GEORGE TYNG'S LAST ENTERPRISE: A PROMINENT TEXAN AND A RICH MINE IN UTAH. *J. of the West 1969 8(3): 429-437.* Tells of Tyng's involvement with the Miller Mine near Salt Lake City where a rich lode of silver-rich lead carbonate was discovered in 1904. Six hundred thousand dollars worth of ore was taken out of the mine. On 19 January 1906 Tyng was killed by an avalanche while doing paperwork in a little lean-to some distance from the mine.   R. N. Alvis

3898. Jervey, William H. WHEN THE BANKS CLOSED: ARIZONA'S BANK HOLIDAY OF 1933. *Arizona and the West 1968 10(2): 127-152.* In early 1933 the entire banking structure of the country was near collapse. Statewide bank holidays were becoming common. Although bank legislation was progressive in Arizona in the 1920's, the banks of this basically frontier State lacked the capitalization and strength to weather a storm of any consequence. In the wake of the Wall Street collapse of 1929, commodity prices fell for Arizona cattle, cotton, and copper. Copper production declined 95 percent, and the State's per capita income dipped to 263 dollars. Banks became a prime casualty with collapse and preventive mergers resulting. Historical ties bound the banks of California and Arizona together, such as personnel links, California control of some banks in Arizona, the maintenance of significant balances in California institutions by Arizona banks, and the holding of large parts of loans on livestock in Arizona by California banks. When California declared a bank holiday on the evening of 1 March 1933, it was inconceivable that Arizona could keep its banks open. Early the next morning Arizona declared a 3-day moratorium; later in the day an indefinite holiday was legalized by action of the legislature. A national moratorium went into effect on 6 March. Weaker institutions did not survive, but the banking system in the State had fewer and less severe difficulties during the 12-day holiday than in most other States. Arizona had suffered little more than a temporary interruption of business. 2 illus., 57 notes.

D. L. Smith

3899. Johnson, Arthur M. CALIFORNIA AND THE NATIONAL OIL INDUSTRY. *Pacific Hist. R. 1970 39(2): 155-169.* Sketches the history of the relationship between the eastern oil companies and the development of the geographically isolated petroleum industry of California. Although greater independence was possible for both the production and marketing of fuel oil and refined products, the gradual increase of technological progress and the necessities of economic interdependence had practically eliminated the isolation of the California oil industry by 1960. 57 notes.

E. C. Hyslop

3900. Johnson, Arthur M. THE EARLY TEXAS OIL INDUSTRY: PIPELINES AND THE BIRTH OF AN INTEGRATED OIL INDUSTRY, 1901-1911. *J. of Southern Hist. 1966 32(4): 516-528.* Argues that the modern oil industry was created by the influence of the pipeline from the Gulf Coast to tidewater in impressing an integrated form on the leading companies. The Standard Oil pipelines at first were a weapon of near monopoly, but the predominance was challenged by Gulf Oil and the Texas Company, each using the pipeline to gain a firm foothold, operating as competitors of Standard but taking substantially the same attitude toward the use of their pipelines to protect investments. 21 notes.

S. E. Humphreys

3901. Kelly, Daniel T. THE TRINIDAD COAL STRIKE. *Palacio 1968 75(4): 31-34.* The author witnessed many of the events of a strike by coal miners in Trinidad, September 1913. The strike was urged by Mother Jones, a famous strike instigator. A fight between the strikers and the strike-breakers in a tent city at Ludlow resulted in many casualties. Illus.

S. A. Eger

3902. Kesel, Richard H. THE RATON COAL FIELD: AN EVOLVING LANDSCAPE. *New Mexico Hist. R. 1966 41(3): 231-250.* Treats the history of the coal field in four periods: before 1879, 1879-1917, 1917-53, and 1953 to the present. Peak production occurred between 1910 and 1920. Simultaneously the railroads, the population, and economic prosperity reached their highest points. With the decline in production in the 1950's, the mining towns slowly deteriorated. Illus., table, 18 notes.

D. F. Henderson

3903. King, John O. THE EARLY TEXAS OIL INDUSTRY: BEGINNINGS AT CORSICANA, 1894-1901. *J. of Southern Hist. 1966 32(4): 505-515.* The contribution of Corsicana, seat of Navarro County, to the history of oil in Texas has been overshadowed by the 1901 discovery of the prolific Gulf Coast fields around Beaumont. However, Corsicana, where oil was discovered in 1894, saw the oil industry permanently established in Texas and furnished significant patterns in drilling, financing, management, and law which subsequently guided the industry's growth within the State. The State's first "oil town" is not a "curtain raiser" but a fully developed "Act One" of the Texas oil drama. 40 notes.

S. E. Humphreys

3904. Kizer, Benjamin H. ELIZABETH GURLEY FLYNN. *Pacific Northwest Q. 1966 57(3): 110-112.* Biographical sketch of Elizabeth Gurley Flynn who was an eloquent advocate of human rights for unskilled laborers, 1909-64. A major part of the article is devoted to her activities on behalf of the Industrial Workers of the World and her subsequent court trial in Spokane, Washington in 1909.

C. C. Gorchels

3905. Kreienbaum, C. H. and Maunder, Elwood R. THE SIMPSON EXPERIENCE. *Forest Hist. 1968 12(2): 7-19.* When lumber prices dropped 50 percent between 1929 and 1932, Kreienbaum was the sales manager of the Reed Mill, a subsidiary of the Simpson Logging Company, at Shelton. Recalls the impact of the Depression and the way his company

faced that crisis. Following two years of negotiations, the U.S. Forest Service Chief, Lyle F. Watts, signed the Shelton Cooperative Sustained Yield agreement in 1946, but the shift of logging operations into national forest lands was gradual. Cutting was spread out in such a way that regrowth would be as natural as possible. The Shelton agreement is a landmark in the development of industrial forestry.

G. Barrett

3906. Lavender, David. THE PURPLE MOUNTAINS' FADING MAJESTY. *Am. Heritage 1968 19(4): 46-49, 91-96.* Analyzes the economic situation in Colorado since 1929, starting with the acute financial distress of small mining communities. After New Deal legislation devalued the dollar in 1934, small gold-mining operations provided a hand-to-mouth existence until World War II when minerals with wartime priorities were demanded. This war-born need created new mining technology which reduced human labor needs. Automation became the rule, and towns such as Telluride lost their population. The old tax structure increased financial obligations on local residents, but the rapid growth of cities created new life-styles. Mountain residents changed to meet the need. Spas, resorts, and camps began to cater to hunters, skiers, and tourists. Between 1946 and 1964, the visits to Colorado national forests increased tenfold. New towns grew out of this phenomenon, old-time melodrama was revived for tourists, some areas emulated artists' colonies, and the forest service was forced to expand its tourist-related activities. National legislation resulted in the creation of gigantic forest preserves for litter-bearing visitors, new dump sites had to be constructed, and an increased year-round tourist population continued to create a new set of problems. Based on the author's book, *The Rockies*.

J. D. Born, Jr.

3907. Levenstein, Harvey A. THE AFL AND MEXICAN IMMIGRATION IN THE 1920'S: AN EXPERIMENT IN LABOR DIPLOMACY. *Hispanic Am. Hist. R. 1968 48(2): 206-219.* The American Federation of Labor opposed immigration from Europe, the Orient, and Mexico. The author deals with the influence of non-union Mexican labor and the efforts of AFL leader Samuel Gompers and others to restrict, if not eliminate, it. The AFL feared situations such as the Steel Strike of 1919, when large numbers of Mexican strikebreakers were transported from the Southwest to strike companies in the Chicago area. William Green, Gompers' successor, succeeded in organizing an AFL-CROM conference in an attempt to enlist the Confederación Regional Obrera Mexicana in efforts to have the Mexican Government adopt a policy of restricting emigration. Later, a second agreement was arrived at in 1927 when the two groups met at the Fifth Congress of the Pan-American Federation of Labor in Washington, D.C. With the demise of CROM in Mexico in 1928, the idea of voluntary self-restraint died. The AFL recommended endorsement of an ammendment to the National Origins Act (1924), making the quota system applicable to Mexico. Based on AFL archival records and on Mexican and U.S. newspapers; 45 notes.

W. R. Lux

3908. Lindquist, John H. THE JEROME DEPORTATION OF 1917. *Arizona and the West 1969 11(3): 233-246.* The mere presence of the Industrial Workers of the World in a community was cause for near-hysteria in the World War I era. The Wobblies, as these radical labor unionists were generally called, personified all the dangers that Americans believed were inherent in "foreign" ideas. By various means, aroused Federal and local law enforcement machinery and inspired self-styled citizens' groups effectively dealt with the menace throughout the country. The inharmonious labor-management relations in Arizona's mines were seriously worsened by a rash of strikes that threatened to disrupt the economy. The strike that developed at Jerome, Arizona, in mid-1917 also represented a power struggle between the I.W.W. and the Mine, Mill, and Smelter Workers. The I.W.W. gained a temporary advantage in the settlement, but called for a general strike in the district to put down the M.M.S.W. On the morning of 10 July 1917, about half the men in Jerome rounded up over a hundred Wobbly suspects. Nearly 70 were loaded aboard a cattle car attached to the noon freight train. Others with families were ordered out of town. The vigilante action satisfied the competing union, local businessmen who had suffered from economic disruption, mining company operators, and an aroused public. 5 illus., 32 notes.

D. L. Smith

3909. Lindquist, John H. and Fraser, James. A SOCIOLOGICAL INTERPRETATION OF THE BISBEE DEPORTATION. *Pacific*

Hist. R. 1968 37(4): 401-422. By mid-1917, the Industrial Workers of the World were the dominant element among the "faction-ridden" copper miners of Bisbee, Arizona. When a list of demands was rejected by the mine managers, a strike was called to begin 27 June 1917. It seriously crippled copper production and posed a threat to the economy of the area. By surprise on the morning of 12 July 1917, some twelve hundred strikers, sympathizers, and others were forcibly rounded up and deported to Hermanas, New Mexico. While the authors are concerned with the loss of human and constitutional rights, they are surprised that the deportation was so long in coming as the IWW could not be allowed to exist. Because it did not conform to the American pattern of norms, values, and beliefs, it posed a threat to the social order. The prevailing American attitude of that time permitted mass deportation as a solution to irreconcilable differences. 112 notes.   D. L. Smith

3910.   Lonsdale, David L.   THE FIGHT FOR AN EIGHT-HOUR DAY. *Colorado Mag. 1964 43(4): 339-353.* Points out that a movement for labor reform in mining began in the 1890's after mining was taken over by firms from the East. A law was passed in 1890 providing for an eight-hour day, but mining companies decided to cut wages if the workers went on an eight-hour day. A controversy arose over this decision and a strike was threatened. It soon became apparent that the only way to a speedy decision was to have the Colorado Supreme Court rule on the constitutionality of the law. In September 1899 Chief Justice John Campbell handed down the decision that the law providing for an eight-hour day was unconstitutional because it violated the Colorado Bill of Rights. Not until 1913, 20 years after the fight for an eight-hour day had begun, was a true eight-hour law for mine, mill, and smelter workers made and enforced. 38 notes.   I. W. Van Noppen

3911.   MacDonald, Norbert.   SEATTLE, VANCOUVER, AND THE KLONDIKE. *Canadian Hist. R. [Canada] 1968 49(3): 234-246.* Discusses the response of Seattle and Vancouver to the Klondike gold rush of the late 1890's. Revealed is the basic similarity in the way in which Americans and Canadians responded to an economic opportunity. Seattle dominated the gold rush trade, while Federal policies in both nations were shaped to a substantial degree by urban pressure groups. Based on newspapers, reports of government officials and business concerns, personal memoirs, and census data.   A

3912.   Mahar, Franklyn D.   THE MILLIONAIRE AND THE VILLAGE: JESSE WINBURN COMES TO ASHLAND. *Oregon Hist. Q. 1963 64(4): 323-341.* Unusual account of satisfactions and disappointments of a rich man from New York City who moved to Ashland, Oregon, to live in the forest and develop a mineral water spa in a small city, 1921-23.   C. C. Gorchels

3913.   Mayhall, Pamela.   BISBEE'S RESPONSE TO CIVIL DISORDER: A MATTER OF CIRCUMSTANCE. *Am. West 1972 9(3): 22-31.* Bisbee, near the Mexican border, was a booming, patriotic, copper-mining town in 1917. In late June the Industrial Workers of the World, an industrial union of a revolutionary cast, called a strike in Bisbee without going through the formality of a vote. About half of the workers went out on strike and presented demands. The mining companies ignored the IWW's efforts and the strike continued, but more and more miners returned to work. Tempers shortened and violence seemed imminent. The State militia had been mustered into active service for World War I and Federal troops apparently were not available. Bisbee had to handle its own problems and protect itself. On 12 July Bisbee decisively handled its civil disorder. Some 1,200 IWW members and sympathizers were carefully arrested, put in boxcars, and sent to Columbus, New Mexico, where Federal troops were stationed. The Army would not have the strikers, so the train carried them westward to Hermanas, New Mexico, near the Mexican border. The prisoners were released and warned never to return to Bisbee. Despite the storm of controversy and propaganda and legal maneuvering in the wake of the deportation, Bisbee had solved its problem. 5 illus., map, biblio.   D. L. Smith

3914.   McClelland, John M., Jr.   TERROR ON TOWER AVENUE. *Pacific Northwest Q. 1966 57(2): 65-72.* Reexamination of labor difficulties which led to violence in Centralia, Washington taking a toll of five lives on 11 November 1919. Details of the murder trials, the reaction of the public, and analysis of reasons for the decline of Industrial Workers of the World are included.   C. C. Gorchels

3915.   McClurg, Donald J.   THE COLORADO COAL STRIKE OF 1927 - TACTICAL LEADERSHIP OF THE IWW. *Labor Hist. 1963 4(1): 68-92.* Describes the tactical leadership of the Industrial Workers of the World in a strike that was "essentially conservative." The strikers' program involved the traditional bargaining issues of higher wages, shorter hours, better working conditions, and freedom of organization, except for a political Sacco-Vanzetti demonstration.

J. H. Krenkel

3916.   McCoy, Donald R.   ALFRED M. LANDON AND THE OIL TROUBLES OF 1930-'32. *Kansas Hist. Q. 1965 31(2): 113-137.* The independent oil producers were in such a serious financial condition by 1930 that they were compelled to exert pressure on the large companies, state capitols, and Washington to enact legislation protecting their interests. Both the State of Kansas and Alfred Landon are shown to have played an important role in solving this problem. Kansas led the fight to protect independent oilmen by enacting laws to establish production quotas and limit imports, and it was also instrumental in setting the stage for an interstate compact that was to be accepted by a majority of states. Landon got into the fight to save his friends from ruinous price cuts. The battle brought him into prominence and opened the way for a successful gubernatorial career and the presidential nomination in 1936. Based on local newspapers and Landon's papers.   W. F. Zornow

3917.   McDonald, Stephen L.   SOME FACTORS IN THE RECENT ECONOMIC DEVELOPMENT OF THE SOUTHWEST. *Southwestern Soc. Sci. Q. 1965 45(4): 329-339.* Summarizes findings of a two and a half year study of the rapid development of the Southwest in the 1920-62 period in Texas, Louisiana, Arkansas, Oklahoma, and New Mexico. Development means improvement in the average standard of living, i.e., growth of per capita income. Factors assessed include evidence of structural change, patterns of growth of oil and gas production, and reallocations of labor. The growth picture is erratic, with a decline relative to national averages, in the period 1920-30; little change in the 1930's and 1950's; and a sharp rise in the 1940-50 period.

D. F. Henderson

3918.   McGinn, Elinor M.   SIXTY YEARS ON THE DURANGO-AZTEC-FARMINGTON BRANCH 1905-1965. *New Mexico Hist. R. 1967 42(1): 63-74.* A survey of the 49.5 miles of narrow gauge railway of the Denver and Rio Grande from Durango, Colorado, through Aztec, to Farmington, New Mexico. Built in 1905, the line had a mercurial record, with changes from narrow to broad gauge tracks and competition from other lines. Based on newspapers and archival materials in the State Archives and Public Records, Denver; 56 notes.

D. F. Henderson

3919.   McWilliams, Carey.   A MAN, A PLACE, AND A TIME: JOHN STEINBECK AND THE LONG AGONY OF THE GREAT VALLEY IN AN AGE OF DEPRESSION, OPPRESSION, FRUSTRATION, AND HOPE. *Am. West 1970 7(3): 4-8, 38-40, 62-64.* John Steinbeck was "preoccupied with the relationship between man and environment." Steinbeck country stretched from the "preposterous beauty" of the Big Sur-Monterey coast into the harsh and forbidding terrain of the Salinas Valley. He was equally at home with the fish canneries and wharves of the coast and the lettuce sheds and icing plants of Salinas. The dust bowl migration impact on the "salad bowl" area of California in the 1930's inspired Steinbeck's *The Grapes of Wrath* (1939). This and McWilliams' *Factories in the Field*, which appeared a few months later, dramatically sharpened public awareness of the plight of migratory workers in California. The two books were regarded as a part of a subversion conspiracy to bring chaos and revolution to California's fertile farm valleys. McWilliams explains the motivation and impact of the two books. Included are biographical sketches of Steinbeck and the author. 2 illus.   D. L. Smith

3920.   Mergen, Bernard.   DENVER AND THE WAR ON UNEMPLOYMENT. *Colorado Mag. 1970 47(4): 326-337.* Analyzes the Unemployed Citizens' League of Denver, which was formed in 1932 and lasted until the passage in 1933 of the Civilian Conservation Corps Reforestation Relief Act, the Federal Emergency Relief Act, and the National Industrial Recovery Act. Patterned partly on a similar movement in Seattle, although less radical, the Denver League aimed at self-help cooperative ventures in production by the unemployed. It eventually had 25 locals and had chairmen for clothing, food, fuel, health, housing, labor, transportation, publicity, recreation, solicitations, utilities, and wrecking buildings. Probably the main value of the league and others like it was in the self-respect retained by its clients, who felt their efforts paid for their needs. Illus., 35 notes.

O. H. Zabel

3921. Morgan, George T., Jr. NO COMPROMISE - NO RECOGNITION: JOHN HENRY KIRBY, THE SOUTHERN LUMBER OPERATORS' ASSOCIATION, AND UNIONISM IN THE PINEY WOODS, 1906-1916. *Labor Hist. 1969 10(2): 193-204.* Describes the struggle between the Southern Lumber Operators' Association, led by John H. Kirby (1850-1925), and the Brotherhood of Timberworkers in Texas and Louisiana. As Kirby succeeded in organizing the lumber operators in a no-compromise opposition, the unions grew more militant to the point where violent conflict occurred after the Brotherhood amalgamated with the Industrial Workers of the World. The Brotherhood was smashed by 1916, and union organization is still ineffective in the area. Based primarily upon the Kirby MSS of the University of Houston.

L. L. Athey

3922. Morrison, Margaret Darsie. CHARLES ROBINSON ROCKWOOD: DEVELOPER OF THE IMPERIAL VALLEY. *Southern California Q. 1962 44(4): 307-330.* Rockwood was almost a legendary figure in the history of the Imperial Valley in that he was instrumental in forming a vast agricultural empire. The author determines what Rockwood was actually able to achieve in the Imperial Valley from two sources - an autobiography by Rockwood and a study of the history and engineering problems of the Colorado River delta. The financial condition of the California Development Company and the fight for control by Rockwood and George Chaffey were major factors in the purchase of the company in 1905 by the Southern Pacific Railroad. Rockwood is analyzed in three areas: 1) his chosen career of engineering; 2) his work as a financier and promoter; and 3) his ability to visualize the potential of the Imperial Valley, upon which the most value is placed. 21 notes.

D. H. Swift

3923. Murphy, James M. THE TWIN BUTTES RAILROAD. *Arizoniana 1964 5(1): 20-34, and 5(2): 12-25.* A summary account of the Twin Buttes Railroad, which came under ownership and operation of the Southern Pacific in 1909. Extending from Twin Buttes to Tucson via Sahuarita and Preciado, the railroad is examined as a factor in the copper mining and smelting industry of south-central Arizona. Based on printed sources, illus.

W. Unrau

3924. Murphy, Lawrence R. STANLEY R. MC CORMICK: THE YOUNGEST REAPER. *California Hist. Soc. Q. 1969 48(2): 113-123.* A biographical sketch of the youngest son of Cyrus McCormick, inventor of the reaper. The family's wealth provided Stanley with a Princeton University education, a European tour, and a place in the family business. Marriage into a prominent family and land investment in New Mexico suggested a promising future, but McCormick's business career was cut short by a mental disorder. He was taken to the Riven Rock family estate in Santa Barbara, California. Declared an incompetent in 1909, McCormick remained there while his wife crusaded for women's rights. Despite moments of lucidity, McCormick remained permanently insane. His wife, Katherine Dexter McCormick, battled McCormick's relatives for guardianship and estate management, winning a much-publicized court case in 1929. McCormick died in 1947. Ironically, even with vast amounts expended on lawsuits and medical bills, Stanley McCormick's estate increased in value from 10 million dollars to over 36 million dollars. Based on newspaper accounts, documents, and secondary sources; 65 notes.

A. Hoffman

3925. Myatt, William L. DUGGER'S GROCERY. *Colorado Mag. 1965 42(1): 46-54.* From 1895 to 1906 this corner grocery store in Denver prospered. Mr. Dugger introduced the latest technological devices and packaged goods.

I. W. Van Noppen

3926. Myers, Rex. RAILS TO TAYLOR PARK. *Colorado Mag. 1968 45(3): 225-242.* Discusses the interest in a railroad into Taylor Park west of the Continental Divide which came to a climax at the turn of the century with the Taylor Park Railroad Company. Incorporation of the company in 1901 was followed by surveys, a little grading, and slight excavation at a proposed tunnel near Tin Cup Pass. All work stopped in 1904 and the company was declared defunct in 1913. Causes of failure were lack of capital and lack of ore in Taylor Park. Illus., maps, 55 notes.

O. H. Zabel

3927. Norris, James D. THE MISSOURI AND KANSAS ZINC MINERS' ASSOCIATION, 1899-1905. *Business Hist. R. 1966 40(3): 321-334.* A study of the American zinc miners' trade association and its experiments with cooperative price controls. "In spite of the failure of the Association to perfect its exportation schemes or exert effective discipline during shutdowns and thereby control the zinc concentrate market for long periods, its tactics, failures, and successes offer insight into the limitations and possibilities of industrial marketing associations."

J. H. Krenkel

3928. Norvell, James R. THE RAILROAD COMMISSION OF TEXAS: ITS ORIGIN AND HISTORY. *Southwestern Hist. Q. 1965 68(4): 465-480.* The Texas Railroad Commission was created in 1891 after a constitutional amendment made it possible. Its creation and growth are linked inseparably with the public career of James Stephen Hogg who served as attorney general and governor of the State. It became one of the most extensive administrative bodies in the United States. It exercises jurisdiction in five major fields: railroad rates and regulations, oil and gas production and transportation, passenger bus and freight truck regulation, control of gas utility companies, and regulation of propane and butane gases used for public consumption. The commission has been challenged numerous times in the courts but generally has been upheld in its regulatory measures. 31 notes.

D. L. Smith

3929. Oates, Stephen B. FABULOUS SPINDLETOP. *Am. Hist. Illus. 1967 2(7): 12-23.* An account of the search for oil, begun in 1893, at Beaumont, Texas, by Patillo Higgins and, later, by Anthony Lucas. On 10 January 1901 the great Spindletop blew in. The town was never the same—soon there were 214 wells, 120 on one 15-acre tract, and 500 derricks by the end of the year. The once sleepy town soon bulged with 20 to 30 thousand "boomers" but then declined with production in 1902. There was a brief second boom in 1925 but the city of Beaumont was thereafter known for refining and industry—not oil production. Illus.

J. D. Filipiak

3930. Olmsted, Roger. SHIPWRECKED! *Am. West 1966 3(4): 42-49.* More lives were lost during the heyday of Pacific shipping from the time of the 1849 gold rush through World War I than to the Indians in the conquest of the West. Generally, as illustrated by disasters along the Pacific coast of the 1904-18 period, the forces of nature or simple error caused the loss of ships - a frozen harbor, a sudden storm, a breaking sea set up by a harbor entrance bar, a drunken crew. 17 illus.

D. L. Smith

3931. Pentland, H. C. RECENT DEVELOPMENTS IN ECONOMIC HISTORY: SOME IMPLICATIONS FOR LOCAL AND REGIONAL HISTORY. *Tr. of the Hist. and Sci. Soc. of Manitoba [Canada] 1967/68 (24): 7-15.* Considers the interrelation of general and local history. Contrasts traditional and new views of the economic development of the Red River Valley and its contiguous prairies. The importance of railways has recently been called into question, as has the importance of wheat as a factor in the national economy during the years of 1898-1912. Growth of population does not automatically increase per capita wealth, and export statistics are not the only measure of success. 16 notes.

L. F. S. Upton

3932. Plott, Charles R. OCCUPATIONAL SELF-REGULATION: A CASE STUDY OF THE OKLAHOMA DRY CLEANERS. *J. of Law and Econ. 1965 8: 195-222.* Describes and analyzes the establishment in 1939 and operation of a State Dry Cleaning Board since that time, and evaluates the board's influence on the development of the industry. Based on public documents, law reports, the author's master's thesis, trade journals, and articles.

P. J. Coleman

3933. Porter, Kenneth. RACISM IN CHILDREN'S RHYMES AND SAYINGS, CENTRAL KANSAS, 1910-1918. *Western Folklore 1965 24(3): 191-196.* Concerned mainly with the term "nigger." The article is based on the sayings and rhymes which the author heard and used as a child.

J. M. Brady

3934. Prisco, Salvatore, III. JOHN BARRETT AND OREGON COMMERCIAL EXPANSION 1889-1898. *Oregon Hist. Q. 1970 71(2): 141-160.* After being educated at Dartmouth College and Vanderbilt University for the clergy, John Barrett (1866-1938) moved to California and Oregon and soon became an enthusiastic businessman promoting commerce between the Pacific Northwest and East Asian countries. Unsuccessful in getting a post in Japan, Barrett was named diplomatic minister to Siam when he was 28 years old. Barrett's relationship with Oregon is emphasized, although he had worldwide experiences in his long career as diplomat and commercial publicist during the years 1889-1920.
C. C. Gorchels

3935. Ransom, Jay Ellis, ed. TIMBER: LOG DRIVE TO BOISE: 1909. *Montana 1969 19(2): 2-9.* Reminiscences of Jay George Ransom, a participant in a log drive near Boise in 1909. The preceding three years had been spent in cutting trees and piling logs while awaiting a season of favorable high water in Fall Creek and the Boise River. Even at flood, the channels were obstructed by rocks, requiring frequent blasting to keep the logs moving. Of the original nine million board feet of timber, one million arrived undamaged at the mill; this remnant was lost when the retaining dam burst, and the venture brought bankruptcy to the lumber company involved. Considerable detail is supplied regarding the management of this undertaking, in terms of men, equipment, and logistics. Illus.
S. R. Davison

3936. Renshaw, Patrick. THE LOST LEADER, 'BIG BILL' HAYWOOD. *Hist. Today [Great Britain] 1970 20(9): 610-619.* William Dudley Haywood (1869-1928), who assisted in the founding of the Western Federation of Miners, became the Secretary-Treasurer of the Industrial Workers of the World (I.W.W.). He defected to the Soviet Union in 1918. There, after attempting to establish a workers' colony in the Kuznetsk Basin, he returned to Moscow and died as a lost and lonely individual in 1928. An account of his union career in America and Britain precedes the causes of his defection. Describes his volatile oratory and his direction of the syndicalist movement within the I.W.W. from 1912 to 1918, which culminated with his indictment and conviction for conspiracy. Photos.
L. A. Knafla

3937. Rockwell, Arthur E. THE LUMBER TRADE AND THE PANAMA CANAL, 1921-1940. *Econ. Hist. R. [Great Britain] 1971 24(3): 445-462.* What were the external benefits attributable to the Panama Canal on lumber shipments from the United States Pacific Northwest, 1921-40? What was the importance of the canal for the regional economy of the Pacific Northwest? The author analyzes the significance of lumber as a major component of eastbound canal traffic; the Pacific Northwest as producer, consumer, and exporter of lumber; comparative lumber transportation cost of waterborne versus railroad freight to the Atlantic coast market, including direct effects of the canal on waterborne freight rates and the indirect effect on transcontinental freight rates; the external benefits derived from the canal by the United States on lumber shipments; and some theoretical problems concerning the estimates of benefits. 8 appendixes.
B. L. Crapster

3938. Rodnitzky, Jerome L. RECAPTURING THE WEST: THE DUDE RANCH IN AMERICAN LIFE. *Arizona and the West 1968 10(2): 111-126.* Dude or resort ranches probably originated as a result of economic distress in the Dakotas during the 1880's. The collapse of the open range business caused many cattlemen to seek new sources of income. When large corporations moved into the cattle industry, numerous small ranches switched to dude ranching. Some ranches sold out to wealthy Easterners who wanted a few months of ranch life a year. Some ranches were converted to informal lodges to resist encroaching civilization. Others were taken over by associations of sportsmen. The movement spread over the Great Plains and the Rockies. With the establishment of the Dude Ranchers' Association in 1924 the movement took on professional airs. The Great Depression apparently forced many more cattle ranches to cater to dudes. Pseudo-dude ranches soon appeared all over the country. One could even earn a state university (Wyoming) degree in Recreational Ranching. 4 illus., 38 notes.
D. L. Smith

3939. Rose, Gerald A. THE MARCH INLAND: THE STOCKTON CANNERY STRIKE OF 1937. *Southern California Q. 1972 54(1): 67-82, (2): 155-176.* Part I. Discusses important background facets of the labor-management situation in California agriculture which climaxed in

a showdown strike of Stockton cannery workers in April 1937. Background factors included: an interunion struggle between the American Federation of Labor (A.F.L.) and the Congress of Industrial Organizations (C.I.O.) in the effort to organize agricultural workers; an intraunion jurisdictional battle between the Teamsters' Union and the International Longshoremen's Association (I.L.A.), A.F.L. member unions which were attempting to organize cannery warehouse workers and to align cannery workers with their unions; and the Associated Farmers and the California Processors and Growers, Inc. (C.P.G.), who opposed all efforts to unionize farm and cannery workers and who exploited the factional strife among labor organizers. Because the I.L.A. had been so successful in organizing cannery warehousemen in its famous "march inland," the situation within labor's ranks had reached a crisis stage by 1937. Added to this background of rival unions and farmer-processor alignment and giving the situation an explosive character by 1937 were the miserable circumstances of agricultural and cannery laborers who were overworked, underpaid, and neglected by New Deal programs. Based on primary and secondary sources; 73 notes. Part II. Surveys the development of the Stockton cannery strike to the point at which the Associated Farmers and the California Processors and Growers decided to break the strike with force. Stockton became the place for a showdown because it represented the "key to control of the agricultural heartland of the state" to the C.P.G., and the point at which the State leadership of the American Federation of Labor believed it had to stop the "march inland" of the "radical" International Longshoremen's Association. Accordingly, the C.P.G. "were determined to prevent, at any cost, the effective organization of the Stockton canneries" and the California A.F.L. was equally determined to organize the Stockton cannery workers before the I.L.A. could do so. Members of the Stockton Agricultural Workers Union (A.W.U.) which had been established by the A.F.L. in 1936 began the strike on 15 April 1937. They soon faced the mobilization of farmer and canner opposition. Unaided by San Francisco longshoremen who could have made a difference in the outcome, and unable to bring about a general strike in San Joaquin County where Stockton was located, the A.W.U. tried desperately to negotiate a settlement through the Governor's office in Sacramento. The farmers and cannery operators did not want a peaceful settlement and were determined to crush the union once and for all. Based on government documents and contemporary newspaper articles; 101 notes. Article to be continued.
W. L. Bowers

3940. Saloutos, Theodore. ALEXANDER PANTAGES, THEATER MAGNATE OF THE WEST. *Pacific Northwest Q. 1966 57(4): 137-147.* Outlines the career of a Greek immigrant who became a rich and nationally-known theater magnate after a modest entry into show business in Alaska during the gold rush of the 1890's. Success in establishing theaters throughout the western United States followed. As he planned worldwide expansion of his business despite the economic depression of the 1930's, tragedy in his personal life and illness brought death.
C. C. Gorchels

3941. Schonberger, Howard. JAMES J. HILL AND THE TRADE WITH THE ORIENT. *Minnesota Hist. 1968 41(4): 178-190.* Points out a special element in the genius of James J. Hill, the great railroad magnate. Unlike other transcontinental railroad builders, he attempted to develop the area as he went and he scorned most government aid. In line with this view, Hill considered trade with the Orient as little more than a logical extension of his existing transportation system and of the development of US international trade. Hill pushed his plans. He bought a fleet of ships and hired agents to go to China and Japan. The whole scheme ultimately foundered on our export-import rates and their necessary publication. Thus Hill failed to realign US international trade routes.
P. L. Simon

3942. Schonfeld, Robert G. THE EARLY DEVELOPMENT OF CALIFORNIA'S IMPERIAL VALLEY, PART I AND PART II. *Southern California Q. 1968 50(3): 279-307; (4): 395-426.* Part I. An account of the struggle between private enterprise and the Federal Government for control of irrigation development of California's Imperial Valley. Although individuals had advocated an irrigation system for the area as early as 1853, the first water was diverted from the Colorado River to the valley in 1901 by a group of investors organized as the California Development Company. When the Reclamation Service was established by the Newlands Act in the following year, it decided to demonstrate its services and test its authority in the valley. Federal authorities sought to wrest control of irrigation development from private enterprise by arguing that the Colorado River below Yuma, Arizona, where the diversion took place, was a navigable river and therefore not usable as a source of irrigation water. However, the Federal Government's own investigations denied that the Colorado was navigable below Yuma. Moreover, the California Development Company countered with a plan to divert water from the Colorado in Mexico which would cause the Federal Government to get bound up in so much red tape that it would abandon the Imperial Valley project. The company negotiated an agreement with Mexico in 1904 and seemed to emerge victorious in its struggle with the Reclamation Service. Based on letters, public documents, contemporary and secondary sources; 6 illus., map, 23 notes. Part II. In 1905 a sandbar in the Colorado River below the Mexican border deflected the river causing it to cut a new channel where the California Development Company's irrigation canal had been. This caused flooding of the Imperial Valley and the company frantically attempted to close the break. Lacking adequate funds, the company sought help from the Southern Pacific Railroad which had substantial interest in the future of the valley. The Reclamation Service attempted once more to gain control of the irrigation project by urging farmers to file damage suits against the Mexican Government so that it would cancel its concessions to the Development Company, but the scheme failed. The company's attempts to divert the Colorado back to its original channel were unsuccessful and some people thought Government aid was the only solution. However, others insisted that private enterprise could do the job and even raised subscriptions to help defray the costs. The Southern Pacific Railroad then assumed full control of the Project and in February 1907 the break was finally closed. The Development Company was the object of numerous lawsuits and in 1909 was declared bankrupt. After 1907 "the irrigation problems of the valley were in reliable hands" and the struggle between private enterprise and the Federal Government for control ended. In 1911 the Imperial Irrigation District was organized in Southern California and by 1912 it had acquired the water rights of the defunct Development Company. Through the Irrigation District valley farmers were finally able to control their own destiny. Based on letters, public documents, contemporary sources and secondary accounts; 6 illus., 6 maps, 31 notes.   W. L. Bowers

3943. Schruben, Francis W. THE KANSAS STATE REFINERY LAW OF 1905. *Kansas Hist. Q. 1968 34(3): 299-324.* An account of the efforts to establish a state-owned, convict-operated refinery in Kansas during the time that the Standard Oil Company first showed an interest in developing the State's oil reserves. With a long record of protest behind it, Kansas seemed a logical place to carry on the fight against corporate power. Although the plan did not reach fulfillment, it set the stage for such Federal regulation of business as was embodied in the Hepburn Act of 1906, disturbed trusts everywhere, and encouraged the growth of small, independent refineries in Kansas. The plan was admittedly socialistic, but it was quite in line with the popular notion that the consumer is entitled to fair prices. Based on monographs, articles, newspapers, and archives in the Kansas State Historical Society; illus., 120 notes.

W. F. Zornow

3944. Sherman, Richard G. CHARLES G. DAWES, A NEBRASKA BUSINESSMAN, 1887-1894: THE MAKING OF AN ENTREPRENEUR. *Nebraska Hist. 1965 46(3): 193-207.* Examines Dawes' business ventures in Lincoln in real estate, meat packing and banking along with his business practices. Concludes that while Dawes' business interests quickly grew too large for Lincoln, the seven years he spent there were "the crucible period" of his business career.   R. Lowitt

3945. Smith, Richard K. AEROSPACE PROFILE: A DOUGLAS DECISION. *Aerospace Historian 1968 15(3): 4-7.* Discusses the evolution of Donald Willis Douglas as an aeronautical engineer on the west coast, expressed in part by correspondence with Commander Jerome C. Hunsaker, USN. The correspondence also throws light on the state of the aircraft industry on the west coast in 1920. It "illuminates a decision that proved to be of no small import to the development of United States aviation." Trained at the US Naval Academy and the Massachusetts Institute of Technology, Douglas met Hunsaker at the latter institution. After teaching a year, serving as a consultant with the Connecticut Aircraft Company, and producing a significant report on American aviation, Douglas joined the Glenn L. Martin Company and became its chief engineer. In 1920 he left Martin and became the first important aircraft industry migrant to southern California. In letters to his friend, Hunsaker

suggested an alliance with Boeing of Seattle, but Douglas was happy in California where he had allied with the wealthy sportsman pilot and engineer, David R. Davis. The first aircraft of the infant firm, the "Cloudster," was of sound design and the Navy awarded Douglas contracts for DT-1 torpedo bombers in 1921. In 1922 and 1923, contracts were let for DT-2's. The Army ordered four variants of that design for its proposed world flight. During 1924, two of these Douglas "World Cruisers" spent five months making the first circumnavigation of the world by air. Transcontinental isolation from the 80 percent of American aircraft industry found east of Cleveland, Ohio, delayed notice of Douglas and Boeing. The advent of the Boeing B-247 in 1932 and the Douglas DC-1 (1932), DC-2 (1933), and DC-3 (1935) provided the basis for an American air transport boom and fame for an aeronautical engineer who went west in pursuit of what he believed was a better end. 4 photos.   C. W. Ohrvall

3946. Sonnichsen, C. L. COL. W. C. GREENE AND THE COBRE GRANDE COPPER COMPANY. *J. of Arizona Hist. 1971 12(2): 73-100.* William Cornell Greene (1851-1911) was a New York Quaker who became an Arizona rancher and miner and who developed a liking for and the respect of Mexicans from workingmen up to the president of the country. George Mitchell was a transplanted Welsh miner whose inventive aptitude, organizational and developmental ability, and personality brought him considerable success in Arizona and Sonora, Mexico. His invention of the hot-blast furnace was the most advanced contribution to metallurgy at the time. In 1899, with permission of the Mexican Government, Greene and Mitchell formed the Cobre Grande Copper Company to exploit the ore in the Cananea Mountains of Sonora. The company prospered but at the price of constant litigation in the courts of Mexico, Arizona, and the United States. The financial battles and the struggles to control Cobre Grande consumed much of Greene's time, money, and energy. Excerpted from a forthcoming biography. 5 illus., 69 notes.   D. L. Smith

3947. Sonnichsen, C. L. COLONEL WILLIAM C. GREENE AND THE STRIKE AT CANANEA, SONORA, 1906. *Arizona and the West 1971 13(4): 343-368.* Arizona promoter William Cornell Greene (1851-1911) built the operations of the Cananea Consolidated Copper Company into a multimillion-dollar business that paid good dividends to its American stockholders. The city of Cananea and the mining complex constituted an American enclave in northern Mexico a short distance below the Arizona-Sonora border. American employees earned wages which enabled them to maintain their accustomed standard of living. Except for a handful of Mexican officials and professionals, the rest of the employees received minimal wages. Discontent festered and erupted on 1 June 1906 in a walkout which paralyzed the entire mining camp. Demands included minimal pay raises, an eight-hour day, inclusion in promotions, and the end of the company store monopoly. Evidence suggests that discontent was promoted by the Western Federation of Miners. Initial intentions were peaceful, but matters were soon out of control. Finally, ringleaders were jailed and the rank-and-file were back at work on 4 June. An army threat that strikers would be drafted to fight Indians was a potent persuader. The "invasion" from Arizona, the Governor's presence at Greene's summons, and leftist press propaganda inspired Mexican and American legend-makers, whose stories still abound. Greene later proved to his satisfaction that socialist agitators and New York capitalists had inspired the strike. Mexican historians maintain that the Cananea affair was the beginning of the Revolution of 1910. 8 illus., map, 51 notes.   D. L. Smith

3948. Sonnichsen, C. L. INSTANT MILLIONAIRE: COLONEL W. C. GREENE IN FACT AND FOLKLORE. *Am. West 1971 8(6): 4-9, 62-63.* William Cornell Greene (1851-1911) dreamed of employing American capital, machinery, and know-how to make northern Mexico into an industrial-agricultural complex. Not only would Mexico benefit, but Greene and his stockholders would reap rich profits. With the ability to charm Mexican officials (even the chief executive himself), Greene controlled sizable mining, waterpower, and timber concessions in northern Mexico. His great copper mines in the mountains of Sonora alone made him a multimillionaire between 1899 and 1906. His million-acre ranch empire in Sonora and Arizona was a sideline. After knocking about on the western frontier for several years, Greene began to systematize his efforts and activities in 1896. A Mexican revolution, a panic, and an accident terminated his empire and life. Even before his death in 1911, he had become the subject of folklore. He has been portrayed as a rags-to-riches hybrid cowboy capitalist, a crooked promoter, a pathological spender, and a trigger-happy pistoleer. There was an element of truth in all of these images. 8 illus., note.   D. L. Smith

3949. Stanley, Leo L. EARLY RAILROADING. *Noticias 1966 12(4): 8-11.* Describes his work on California railroads just after 1900. Working his way through college, the author sold newspapers on the trains, starting on the San Luis Local. He was promoted by the Dennison News Company to better trains, such as the Sunset Limited and the overnight from San Francisco. The author describes the station "Eating House" in Santa Barbara and mentions the hotel boom there. The new track to the North was not properly settled, and inclement weather often stopped trains. The only competition to the railroad was the stagecoach and "branch lines were necessities." Mentioned are the police watch on trains and the Santa Barbara Mission's fine state of repair. Illus.
T. M. Condon

3950. Stowe, Noel J., ed. PIONEERING LAND DEVELOPMENT IN THE CALIFORNIAS: AN INTERVIEW WITH DAVID OTTO BRANT. *California Hist. Soc. Q. 1968 47(2): 141-155, (3): 237-250.* Continued from previous article. Part II. The interview begins with a discussion of Brant's family background, particularly the life of his father, Otto Freeman Brant. Brant then talks about the founding of the Title Insurance and Trust Company in 1893 and a business venture in the Colorado Desert. He recalls his early years and how he became involved in the real estate business. Lastly he deals with some of the major landholdings he worked with, such as the San Fernando Valley and Tejon Ranch. 33 notes. Part III. Brant relates the experiences of his father in developing properties in southern California and in Mexico, in alliance with Harry Chandler, Harrison Gray Otis, Moses H. Sherman, and other developers. These men frequently supported such projects as the start of Douglas Aircraft and the construction of all-electric homes. Most of this segment of the David Brant interview concerns his recollections of the C-M Ranch in Baja California. In the 1920's an attempt was made to develop the Mexican ranch lands for colonization by Mexican farmers, as a method of negotiating against expropriation by the Mexican Government. Eventually the land was expropriated anyway, with the U.S. Government compensating the Chandler-Brant interests for their losses. The interview with Brant occurred in 1963. 22 notes.
W. A. Buckman and A. Hoffman

3951. Stowe, Noel J., ed. PIONEERING LAND DEVELOPMENT IN THE CALIFORNIAS: AN INTERVIEW WITH DAVID OTTO BRANT. *California Hist. Soc. Q. 1968 47(1): 15-39.* In the early 20th century, Brant was directly involved with the Brant Rancho operation in the San Fernando Valley and represented the family in the Colorado River Land Company. In all, 12 million dollars were spent to open and develop this land in the Imperial Valley over a period of more than 40 years. Brant "offered to explain somewhat the family history and provide background information. . . ." The transcribed interview was taped during the fall of 1963. Illus., maps, 95 notes.   E. P. Stickney

3952. Strite, Daniel D. UP THE KILCHIS. *Oregon Hist. Q. 1971 72(4): 292-314, 1972 73(1): 5-30.* Part I. Reminiscences of a pioneering logger in Tillamook County, 1919-20. Describes the forests, methods of cruising timber resources, construction of lumber camps and mill, and recreational activities. Map, 5 photos. Part II. Details the methods for constructing a logging camp. Emphasizes the use of steam locomotives and the heavy work involved in laying track, constructing trestles, etc. Identifies some of the camp personnel, such as the cook and the warehouse boss. Describes terms used by loggers, such as choker, yarder, whistle punk, and hangup. 13 photos. Article to be continued.
C. C. Gorchels

3953. Suggs, George G., Jr. CATALYST FOR INDUSTRIAL CHANGE: THE W. F. M., 1893-1903. *Colorado Mag. 1968 45(4): 322-339.* In its first decade, ending in 1903, the Western Federation of Miners became a powerful force in Colorado politics. Violence associated with strikes, particularly over wages and hours, gave the federation the popular image of ruthlessness. Moreover, in 1897 president Edward Boyce of the federation took the union out of the American Federation of Labor and from then on publicly advocated socialism as the solution to the miners' problems. While the delegates to the annual conventions gave some support, it is doubtful that the rank and file miners supported

socialism. In any case, political influence, willingness to use force, and increasing socialist orientation prepared the way for two years of industrial warfare (1903-05) which broke the power of the federation in Colorado. Illus., 36 notes.   O. H. Zabel

3954. Suggs, George G., Jr. MILITANT WESTERN LABOR CONFRONTS THE HOSTILE STATE: A CASE STUDY. *Western Hist. Q. 1971 2(4): 385-400.* James H. Peabody, a prominent banker, businessman, and mine owner, became Governor of Colorado in 1903. For a decade Colorado had experienced significant industrial development. Huge industrial combinations had emerged to dominate the economic and political life of the State. When the increasingly powerful and socialist-oriented United Mine Workers of America (U.M.W.) and the Western Federation of Miners (W.F.M.) called a series of strikes, Colorado's fearful businessmen and industrialists believed the time had come to contain or reduce the power of the militant unions. Governor Peabody sympathized with this objective. He blamed the unions for the turmoil of his administration. He deliberately employed military force to remove the "cancerous growths" and received the backing of the State and Federal courts. After that the U.M.W. had to struggle to survive in Colorado's coal fields, and the W.F.M. henceforth was an insignificant force in the mining camps. 54 notes.   D. L. Smith

3955. Suggs, George G., Jr. RELIGION AND LABOR IN THE ROCKY MOUNTAIN WEST: BISHOP NICHOLAS C. MATZ AND THE WESTERN FEDERATION OF MINERS. *Labor Hist. 1970 11(2): 190-206.* Bishop Nicholas C. Matz (1850-1917), head of the Roman Catholic Diocese in Denver, Colorado, was an unrelenting opponent of the Western Federation of Miners. His opposition, when enjoined by that of the State and the employers, was a significant factor in the demise of the W.F.M. Based on the Denver *Catholic Register* and other newspapers; 45 notes.   L. L. Athey

3956. Suggs, George G., Jr. STRIKEBREAKING IN COLORADO: GOVERNOR JAMES H. PEABODY AND THE TELLURIDE STRIKE, 1903-1904. *J. of the West 1966 5(4): 454-476.* During the administration of Governor James H. Peabody (1903-05) a series of strikes by the militant Western Federation of Miners and the United Mine Workers of America occurred in Colorado. One of the most bitter of the strikes was at Telluride, located deep in the San Juan Mountains of southwestern Colorado. A peaceful settlement of issues was made difficult, if not impossible, by the hostile response of corporate and State officials to the demands of the unions. The strikes were broken by the Colorado National Guard. Although the gold mine owners granted an eight-hour day and wage increases, they were successful in breaking the power of the unions. The author concludes that Peabody used the State as an instrument for fostering the objectives of the employer and that his intervention was decisive. Based on material in the Colorado State archives; 93 notes.   D. N. Brown

3957. Taylor, Paul S. MIGRANT MOTHER: 1936. *Am. West 1970 7(3): 41-47.* Dorothea Lange was put on the payroll of a California State relief bureau as a typist. She was really a photographer with an assignment to document a research report the bureau was conducting on rural rehabilitation. A set of poignant photographs which she made in 1936 of starving migrant pea pickers is credited with State action for the construction of camps for migratory laborers. Lange's own account is appended as "The Assignment I'll Never Forget." 7 illus.   D. L. Smith

3958. Tompkins, E. Berkeley. BLACK AHAB: WILLIAM T. SHOREY, WHALING MASTER. *California Hist. Q. 1972 51(1): 75-84.* A native of the West Indies, Shorey pursued a career at sea, rising from the ranks to become master of a whaling ship in 10 years. Although the whaling industry's peak period had passed, whaling voyages continued into the 20th century. For most of his career Shorey operated out of San Francisco, the only black sea captain on the Pacific coast. His crews represented microcosms of society, composed, as they were, of men of all races. After more than 30 years at sea Shorey retired, but he kept his master's license active for the remainder of his life. Based on primary and secondary sources; photos, 28 notes.   A. Hoffman

3959. Torrence, William D. GREAT INDEPENDENT: THE LINCOLN TELEPHONE COMPANY, 1903-1908. *Nebraska Hist. 1970 51(3): 339-358.* Examines the history of the Lincoln Telephone and Telegraph Company of Lincoln, Nebraska, from its founding in 1903 until its consolidation late in 1908 with the Western Telephone Company. Reprinted from *Business History Review* 1959 33(3). 　　　　R. Lowitt

3960. Voeltz, Herman C. COXEY'S ARMY IN OREGON. *Oregon Hist. Q. 1964 65(3): 263-295.* The financial depression in the United States from 1893 to 1897 caused widespread unemployment, reaching a total of four million jobless in 1894. Jacob S. Coxey of Ohio developed a scheme to focus the attention of the nation on the unfortunates who were unemployed. His scheme called for a "petition in boots," a great mass of unemployed workers marching to Washington, D.C. The author recounts the misadventures of the groups of men from the Pacific Northwest who participated in the cross-country trip. Described in detail are clashes with operators of railroads and the courts. Newspapers are footnoted frequently. 　　　　C. C. Gorchels

3961. Wahmann, Russell. RAILROADING IN THE VERDE VALLEY, 1894-1951. *J. of Arizona Hist. 1971 12(3): 153-166.* Copper mining and railroading were inextricably bound together in the Verde Valley of North-central Arizona. Copper ore from the mines of the Jerome area high above the valley floor was rich and accessible but the problems of getting it to established rail lines were physically and economically forbidding. Following completion of the Atlantic and Pacific Railroad across northern Arizona in 1882, proposals and schemes were projected to connect it to the Verde Valley with branch lines. Not until the price of copper dropped in 1891, making the cost of hauling the ore out by mule teams prohibitive, were there any tangible developments. A 26-mile narrow-gauge line to Jerome began in 1895, but the high cost of transloading from it to standard gauge equipment made it too expensive. From then until 1922 other lines and improvements were constructed, dramatically changing the character of the valley, stimulating mining development. The railroads continued to serve this function until 1951. 5 illus., 3 maps, 29 notes. 　　　　D. L. Smith

3962. Ward, James R. ESTABLISHING LAW AND ORDER IN THE OIL FIELDS: THE 1924 RANGER RAIDS IN NAVARRO COUNTY, TEXAS. *Texana 1970 8(1): 38-46.* The Corsicana area of Navarro County experienced an oil boom in the mid-1920's which made Corsicana the per-capita "wealthiest business city in the United States." Its population doubled in a year from 12 thousand to 25 thousand. Since there were many single men working in the oil fields, saloons and brothels sprang up for the oilmen's patronage. These establishments were run openly and attracted many petty criminals. In February 1924, with the help of the Texas Rangers, the local authorities conducted a series of raids which closed many establishments and which resulted in the arrest of 89 suspects. The bootlegging operations were the hardest to control, but further raids in April and May 1924 also curtailed this illegal activity. After these operations, open vice in the Corsicana area virtually disappeared. Based on contemporary newspapers, personal interviews, and local documents; 40 notes. 　　　　R. J. Roske

3963. Watkins, T. H. LION AT BAY. *Am. West 1971 8(1): 30-35, 59-61.* Founded in 1887, Hollywood was located in a watermelon, tomato, green pepper, and sundry fruit producing area. In 1911 a group of film-makers rented a local tavern for a studio and the town was soon overrun by moviemakers. By the close of the 1920's "Hollywood" and "movies" were synonymous terms. The next two decades were Hollywood's golden years. Metro-Goldwyn-Mayer, Paramount, RKO, 20th Century-Fox, and Warner Brothers operated as fiefdoms and dominated the industry. "With all its lunatic extravagances, its pinched meannesses and bloated sentimentality, its greed and venality, this gold rush Hollywood remained a cave of enchantments, a place where only myths were real." The MGM lion, symbolizing the studio system, was increasingly at bay in the post-World War II years. Television, ruinously expensive cinemascope and other super-colossal spectacles, and competition from non-Hollywood producers led to the movie industry's decline. Public auctions have disposed of considerable quantities of the memorabilia and props used in production of the movies. The crippled industry limps on. 6 illus. 　　　　D. L. Smith

3964. White, Gerald T. CALIFORNIA'S OTHER MINERAL. *Pacific Hist. R. 1970 39(2): 135-154.* Although California was the leading oil State during the first quarter of the 20th century, it was isolated by distance and transportation from competition with other U.S. oil areas.

However, it supplied the need for a cheap source of fuel for both the fast-growing western railway system and the marine needs in the Pacific. The State also provided, through the University of California and Stanford, a training ground for scientists who provided leadership in the technological advances of the earth sciences and who were influential both in government and in private petroleum industries, thus affecting the future of the industry throughout the country. 30 notes. 　　　　E. C. Hyslop

3965. Williams, Burton J. MORMONS, MINING, AND THE GOLDEN TRUMPET OF MORONI. *Midwest Q. 1966 8(1): 67-77.* Quotes in entirety a holograph manuscript discovered by the author while gathering material for a biography of the late Senator John J. Ingalls. It is the text of a speech describing in florid oratorical style a visit to Salt Lake City and the silver mine of John J. Daly in 1896. He details dramatically the background and conditions, adulating aspects which he admires and denouncing the "machinations of the brigands and extortioners" who repealed the Sherman Silver Purchase Act in 1893. His colorful vocabulary and verbose expression give us one clear facet of a period and place. 　　　　G. H. G. Jones

3966. Wiprud, Theodore. BUTTE: A TROUBLED LABOR PARADISE. *Montana 1971 21(4): 31-38.* Late in the summer of 1914 martial law was established in Butte to suppress violence committed by the Industrial Workers of the World. State units of the National Guard were stationed in the city from August to mid-October. The author recalls incidents in his own experience as a member of the occupation troops. No outbreaks occurred after the Guard arrived, and it was withdrawn before the onset of winter. 6 photos. 　　　　S. R. Davison

3967. Wollenberg, Charles. *HUELGA*, 1928 STYLE: THE IMPERIAL VALLEY CANTALOUPE WORKERS' STRIKE. *Pacific Hist. R. 1969 38(1): 45-58.* The current conflict between Mexican workers and California farmers has a long heritage. As an example of what previous difficulties can contribute to a better understanding of present problems, a case study is presented of the Imperial Valley cantaloupe workers' strike of 1928. Although it was dwarfed in scope and drama by other strikes, although it was a purely local affair with no outside aid, and although it was broken easily, it is an important event in California labor history. It was the first attempt by Mexican farm laborers to bring about a major work-stoppage. 62 notes. 　　　　D. L. Smith

3968. —. ADOLPH GERMER - UNION ORGANIZER. *Wisconsin Then and Now 1965 11(7): 1-3.* The Ludlow Massacre which climaxed the Colorado mine strike of 1913-14 is only one of the events of a half century of labor history revealed in Adolph Germer's personal correspondence, manuscripts, and diaries recently added to the State Historical Society of Wisconsin. The Germer collection contains 30 letters and telegrams by Eugene V. Debs. Germer reminisces about both Debs and Clarence S. Darrow. Illus. 　　　　E. P. Stickney

3969. —. "THE GRAND CANYON OF ARIZONA": A PANORAMA BY JULES BAUMANN. *J. of Arizona Hist. 1972 13(1): 26-32.* A 1908 promotional curio of the Santa Fe railroad was entitled "*The* Grand Canyon *of* Arizona." The rolled, full-color drawing of various views of the Grand Canyon had accompanying textual material. Four of the pictures, a map, and three of the short articles are herein reproduced. Jules Baumann, the artist, described the setting in "*The* Grand Canyon *of* Arizona." Charles Dudley Warner told of his feelings "On the Brink of the Cañon." C. A. Higgins wrote of "The Titan of Chasms As Seen from the Rim." 　　　　D. L. Smith

Urbanization and Urban Life

3970. Alcorn, Rowena L. and Alcorn, Gordon D. TACOMA SEAMEN'S REST: WATERFRONT MISSION, 1897-1903. *Oregon Hist. Q. 1965 66(2): 101-131.* Collection of diary entries, letters, and descriptive material pertaining to a Tacoma waterfront mission for seafaring men. The role of Mrs. Brigitte Funnemark and daughter, Christine, and experiences of sailors are included.   C. C. Gorchels

3971. Beville, John M. HOW LAS VEGAS PIONEERED A ROTARY CLUB. *Nevada Hist. Soc. Q. 1967 10(3): 29-34.* It was the policy of Rotary International to reject bids from smaller communities that wanted to establish clubs. Persistence of a Las Vegas, Nevada, promoter led Rotary to use Las Vegas as a guinea pig for small-town clubs. Founded in 1923, the experiment was a success. 3 illus.
D. L. Smith

3972. Bitzes, John G. THE ANTI-GREEK RIOT OF 1909 - SOUTH OMAHA. *Nebraska Hist. 1970 51(2): 199-224.* Discusses the murder of an Irish policeman in south Omaha in 1909 by a Greek immigrant and the consequences: rioting and the near extinction (through emigration) of the growing Greek community in the city. Also examines the inflammatory role of the press.   R. Lowitt

3973. DeLorme, Roland L. TURN-OF-THE-CENTURY DENVER: AN INVITATION TO REFORM. *Colorado Mag. 1968 45(1): 1-15.* At the turn of the century, rapidly growing Denver was "notable chiefly for the 'low tone' of its political practices." Corrupt and inefficient government characterized the city. Franchises for such public services as gas, electricity, water, and public transportation had been granted indiscriminately and "effective controls and regulation were surrendered voluntarily." Reformers of the Citizens' Party which won in the municipal elections of 1910 insisted that a financial-political directorate had governed the city. Denver was ripe for reform and sweeping Progressive urban reforms were quickly put into effect. Denver "served as an example, training ground, and power base" for political alignments at the State level and "helped ignite the Colorado Progressive crusade." Illus., 98 notes.   O. H. Zabel

3974. Fahey, John. THE MILLION-DOLLAR CORNER; THE DEVELOPMENT OF DOWNTOWN SPOKANE, 1890-1920. *Pacific Northwest Q. 1971 62(2): 77-85.* Details, building-by-building and house-by-house, the history of the development of the downtown area of Spokane, 1890-1920. Following the fire in 1889 in which 32 blocks of the central city were destroyed, businessmen responded by building larger buildings than those which had burned, using granite and brick to replace the wooden structures. Names many of the city's leaders of commerce and cites their interests. Includes a plat of the area and a table showing the downtown business properties mortgaged, 1884-1900.
C. C. Gorchels

3975. Fergusson, Harvey. TAOS REMEMBERED: RECOLLECTIONS OF A TIME OF INNOCENCE. *Am. West 1971 8(5): 38-41.* The author, who frequently visited Taos for a few days at a time between 1914 and 1941, chats about some of his artist and writer acquaintances who lived there. The town has changed. "Taos today is not the Taos I remember." 3 illus. Prologue and epilogue by T. H. Watkins, associate editor, *The American West.*   D. L. Smith

3976. Gilbert, Vedder M. THE AMERICAN THEATRE: MISSOULA 1910, A CASE HISTORY. *Montana 1968 18(4): 56-68.* Analyzes the theatrical fare at Missoula in 1910 as a sample of small-town entertainment in that decade. The score: 65 shows by touring companies, with casts including big names from Broadway; 30 separate productions by five resident stock companies, and three local amateur offerings. The community of about seven thousand population supported three live theaters, most notably the Harnois, newly opened in November 1909. This building was razed in 1968, after duty as a movie house and as a bowling alley. Illus.   S. R. Davison

3977. Goodwin, H. Marshall, Jr. THE ARROYO SECO: FROM DRY GULCH TO FREEWAY. *Southern California Q. 1965 47(1): 73-102.* In 1895 T. D. Allen of Pasadena surveyed the Arroyo Seco between Los Angeles and Pasadena, but for the next 36 years various plans to build a roadway all failed. Finally in 1931 the Los Angeles City Council recommended work begun "at the earliest possible moment" to help unemployment. After nine years of incessant bickering among real estate men, local politicians, and property owners, the parkway was completed at a cost of over five million dollars. Delays did, however, allow highway engineers to incorporate some of the latest freeway construction techniques being developed in Germany and the eastern United States. Manuscript and published sources.   J. Jensen

3978. Greenleaf, Richard E. THE FOUNDING OF ALBUQUERQUE, 1706: AN HISTORICAL-LEGAL PROBLEM. *New Mexico Hist. R. 1964 39(1): 1-15.* Seldom does a civil suit incite historical research. However, when water is at stake in the southwestern communities that were founded during the Spanish colonial period, such is the case. In 1959 the city of Albuquerque became involved in a dispute with the state engineer over the use of water in the Rio Grande basin of the Albuquerque area. On 14 December 1962 the New Mexico Supreme Court ruled that the city of Albuquerque could not base its claims to unrestricted use of water on the pueblo rights doctrine - unless the city could produce proof that it was founded as a Spanish colonial pueblo, and this meant submission of a certified copy of the instrument of foundation, which the city could not produce. Article discusses briefly pueblo rights doctrine, early history of Albuquerque, and the dispute between the state engineer and the city over the use of waters in the Rio Grande basin of the Albuquerque area.   D. F. Henderson

3979. Harris, Andrew. DEARFIELD, A NEGRO GHOST TOWN IN WELD COUNTY, COLORADO. *Negro Hist. Bull. 1963 27(2): 38-39.* Briefly describes Dearfield, Colorado, a Negro community founded and promoted by O. T. Jackson around the turn of the 20th century and abandoned within a decade after a combination of depression and drought discouraged its settlers. Documented with newspaper material.   L. Gara

3980. Henderson, Robert A. CULTURE IN SPOKANE: 1883-1900. *Idaho Yesterdays 1967 11(4): 14-19.* Lists important cultural developments while Spokane was changing from a crude frontier village to a metropolitan center. A fire in 1889 destroyed most of the business district which was rebuilt. A new library was built and support for kindergartens increased. Reviews literary descriptions of local color and scenic wonders. By 1900 Spokane had achieved cultural attributes; it had an active stage, a strong interest in the fine arts, and a good educational system. Illus., 28 notes.   D. H. Swift

3981. Hernández Álvarez, José. A DEMOGRAPHIC PROFILE OF THE MEXICAN IMMIGRATION TO THE UNITED STATES, 1910-1950. *J. of Inter-Am. Studies 1966 8(3): 471-496.* Mexicans immigrated into the United States after 1910, moving mainly into the Southwest and California, although some did travel into the Northwest. Once in the United States they became urbanized, some intermarried, the education level improved, and many turned from agricultural work to manufacturing in urban centers. Tables included in the text. Based on government census reports.   J. Thomas

3982. Hubbell, Thelma Lee and Lothrop, Gloria R. THE FRIDAY MORNING CLUB, A LOS ANGELES LEGACY. *Southern California Q. 1968 50(1): 59-90.* A narrative history of the Los Angeles Friday Morning Club, a women's organization founded by Caroline M. Severance in 1891. Mrs. Severance, a pioneer in the women's rights movement, started the club as a means of working for female equality and also to give women an opportunity to involve themselves in civic and educational activities. Beginning with only a few women and a modest program in 1891, the club has grown to thousands with a broad program of social, philanthropic, and educational activities. Based on material from the archives of the Los Angeles Friday Morning Club. 2 illus.
W. L. Bowers

3983. Hunt, Rockwell D. FREEPORT: MY BOYHOOD HOMETOWN: REMINISCENCES FROM HIS "BOYHOOD DAYS" OF "CALIFORNIA." *Pacific Historian 1964 8(1): 7-14.* Reminiscences of a boyhood on the Sacramento River, eight miles from Sacramento. Freeport was a town built by the Freeport Railroad Company as a free port of entry. Its early population rapidly rose to four hundred, but the decline of the railroad contributed to its eventual fall to only 125. The author describes the lives of cobblers, blacksmiths, saloon keepers, general merchandisers, and ferrymen. Illus., 2 photos., 2 steel engravings.

T. R. Cripps

3984. Jenkinson, Michael. TYRONE: THE CREATION OF A MODEL GHOST TOWN. *Am. West 1968 5(2): 38-42, 78-79.* Copper mining replaced turquoise mining in the Burro Mountains of southwestern New Mexico in the late 19th century. By 1912 the Phelps-Dodge Corporation bought most of the copper properties in the area. With production soaring and copper prices rising, Phelps-Dodge decided to raze two drab copper camps and to build a model mining city. Hiring the finest architect and spending over a million dollars, Tyrone soon contained comfortable homes for five thousand, a mercantile store, a multipurpose business building (which included a library), a mammoth station to receive a spur of the El Paso and Southwestern Railroad, a hospital, and other amenities, most featuring architectural innovations or stylistic excellence. Within five years of its 1915 creation Tyrone was abandoned. It was the victim of plummeting copper prices and mines that played out. Today, ghost town Tyrone contains a handful of artists, writers, and retired people who enjoy its mild climate. Excerpted from a forthcoming book. 4 illus.

D. L. Smith

3985. McLaird, James D. BUILDING THE TOWN OF CODY: GEORGE T. BECK, 1894-1943. *Ann. of Wyoming 1968 40(1): 73-105.* Traces the career of George T. Beck from 1894 to 1943. During those years Beck organized the Shoshone Land and Irrigation Company which built a canal into the Big Horn Basin and worked to promote immigration into the area. Scandal and continuing litigation over water rights hurt the promoters and slowed settlement. The author stresses his thesis that small-time entrepreneurs such as Beck must be studied to get a better understanding of Western development. Based on Beck's autobiography supplemented by manuscript, newspaper, and published secondary material; 129 notes.

R. L. Nichols

3986. Mitchell, J. Paul. MUNICIPAL REFORM IN DENVER: THE DEFEAT OF MAYOR SPEER. *Colorado Mag. 1968 45(1): 42-60.* Describes the overthrow of Denver's city boss, Robert W. Speer. Opposition of the governing machine, represented by Mayor Speer and pioneer capitalists, to the commission form of city government and to a reforming county assessor, Henry J. Arnold, resulted in victory for the reformers in 1912. Arnold, the candidate for mayor "and the Citizens' party carried every ward and swept every municipal office in tidal wave fashion." Arnold garnered 57.9 percent of the popular vote. "Popular conviction that only the Citizens' party was free of...sinister influences, plus the voters' ability to behold two spectacular victims, commission government and Henry Arnold, produced an overwhelming repudiation of Denver's political status quo in May, 1912." Illus. 57 notes.

O. H. Zabel

3987. Northam, Ray M. DECLINING URBAN CENTERS IN THE UNITED STATES: 1940-1960. *Ann. of the Assoc. of Am. Geographers 1963 53(1): 50-59.* Considers decreases in urban population reflected by data from the *U.S. Census of Population: 1960. Number of Inhabitants.* In the period studied there were 6,034 declining urban centers. Five major concentrations of declining centers were noted: 1) the central section of the Susquehanna River Valley; 2) the Pittsburgh area; 3) southern Illinois; 4) southwestern Iowa, northern Missouri, and eastern Nebraska; 5) northern Utah. "The declining urban center is a small urban center," and "the location of the declining urban center...is typically some distance from a large urbanized area." Illus., maps, tables, 10 notes.

W. R. Boedecker

3988. Orth, Michael. IDEALITY TO REALITY: THE FOUNDING OF CARMEL. *California Hist. Soc. Q. 1969 48(3): 195-210.* The flourishing of Carmel as an art colony coincided with the general renaissance of American fiction that occurred between the 1890's and the 1920's. Carmel, which began as a less than successful venture in real estate investment, earned its reputation in the decade preceding World War I. The chief proponents of Carmel as an artistic residence were poet George Sterling and author Mary Austin. Other noted talents were also attracted to the art colony below San Francisco. Eventually, Sterling and Austin found their friendship strained in a contest for leadership of the colony. After 1910 neither of these figures maintained a regular residence at

Carmel, and so the "first happy period of the colony" came to an end. Based on the writings of Sterling and Austin and on secondary sources; 45 notes.

A. Hoffman

3989. Post, Robert C. THE FAIR FARE FIGHT: AN EPISODE IN LOS ANGELES HISTORY. *Southern California Q. 1970 52(3): 275-298.* Discusses the efforts of the Los Angeles Railway to raise carfare from five cents to seven cents in the face of declining revenue between 1926 and 1930. The California Railroad Commission denied the railway's petition on the basis that the fare hike was unwarranted. The railway appealed the decision which was subsequently reversed by the appellate court. The commission carried the case to the U.S. Supreme Court where the lower court's decision was upheld. The author concludes that the Los Angeles Railway won a pyrrhic victory since it was never able to regain its former level of profits in the face of increasing automobile transportation. Also discusses the unsuccessful attempt to have the city buy and operate the railway, which took place during the struggle over the fare. Based on public documents and secondary sources; 77 notes.

W. L. Bowers

3990. Ripley, Thomas Emerson. ON THE FLOOD TIDE TO FORTUNE. *Am. West 1968 5(5): 25-33.* The 16 photographs of Tacoma, Washington, in the 1890's are interlarded with brief remarks by Ripley, a millwork executive who successfully weathered the panic of 1893. The photographs are from the collections of the Washington State Historical Society. Ripley's comments are taken from his memoirs to be published in a forthcoming book.

D. L. Smith

3991. Romer, Margaret. THE STORY OF LOS ANGELES. *J. of the West 1964 3(1): 1-39, (2): 199-220, (4): 459-488.* Los Angeles grew from a relatively small city in 1900 to a large metropolis in 1930. Contributing factors to this expansion were the advent of the automobile, the development of the motion picture industry, extension of the railroads, and the completion of the Owens River Aqueduct which brought water to the thirsty city. The author details all of this and shows the effect upon government, education, society, and the economic bases of the entire area. Emphasis is placed upon the increasing importance of motion pictures and upon the struggle to secure an adequate supply of water, but the author does not slight social and cultural achievements or the individuals responsible for them. During the years of World War I and the 1920's, not only did the city and the county expand rapidly in population but many notable events occurred. The harbor of Los Angeles became an important port, the people of the city made outstanding contributions to the war effort, Henry Huntington established a renowned library, the Hollywood Bowl and the Coliseum had their inception, the City Hall was constructed, and the meetings of Aimee Semple McPherson became a tourist attraction of almost as great importance as the homes of the movie stars in Beverly Hills. The history of the city from the 1930's to 1960 presents such diverse events as the establishment of the Farmer's Market, labor-management difficulties, construction of the Colorado River Aqueduct, and the effects of World War II on the city. The coming of television and major league baseball, political developments, freeway construction, building of the new civic Center, and natural disasters are detailed. Illus., biblio.

D. N. Brown

3992. Rosenstock, Fred A. RAMBLING RECOLLECTIONS OF A BOOKHUNTER. *Colorado Mag. 1965 42(2): 151-159.* The author came to Denver in 1921, looking for a health spa. In this talk given to the State Historical Society of Colorado in April 1964 he offers amusing recollections about things as they used to be in Denver, concentrating mainly on the bookstores.

R. Sexauer

3993. Shatraw, Milton E. THE TRIP TO TOWN. *Am. West 1967 4(4): 53-54, 75-77.* As a small boy the author lived on a cattle ranch in Teton County in northwestern Montana. Here he reminisces about the 10-mile trips by light buggy or open wagon to the nearest town for supplies and sociability.

D. L. Smith

3994. Sturdivant, Reita. FRANCIS, CHICKASAW NATION, 1894. *Chronicles of Oklahoma 1967 45(2): 143-152.* The town of Francis, Pontotoc County, Oklahoma, was established as Newton in 1894. The change of name was prohibited for some time because there was another Francis post office in the State. Located within the Chickasaw Nation, it prospered with the coming of the Frisco Railroad in 1900. Extensive excerpts from a 1901 special edition of a local newspaper give details of the town at that time. The peak of its history came about 1914-18. From then on it declined and died about the time of World War II. It is now virtually a ghost town. 2 illus., 2 notes.   D. L. Smith

3995. Sweetman, Alice M.   MONDAK: TOWN ON THE LINE. *Montana 1965 15(4): 12-27.* Reminiscences of the author, widow of one of the founders, Luke Sweetman. Mondak was built in 1904 astride the Montana-North Dakota boundary, to take advantage of both liquor and prohibition respectively in the two states. It grew to have stores, a newspaper, lumber yards, schools and grain elevators. Emphasizes the routine, orderly life in this late frontier town, often pictured as rowdy and lawless. Like many small farm towns, Mondak shrank and vanished in the period after World War I. Photo., illus.   S. R. Davison

3996. Thorpe, Elizabeth J.   THE OWLS OF NEWCASTLE. *Montana 1969 19(2): 71-73.* A score of women in a frontier town attempted to offset their isolation by forming a club to encourage cultural and educational interests. On becoming one of the first federated clubs in Wyoming in 1909 its name was changed from the "Owls" to the "Twentieth Century Club." Illus.   S. R. Davison

3997. Wedel, Waldo R.   VISIT TO CARIBOU, 1963.   *Colorado Mag. 1964 41(3): 247-252.* On an annual family visit to the old silver-mining camp of Caribou in Colorado, the author's party explored a trash heap in Caribou, collected and reassembled the parts of an old salt-glazed jug - "a link between Caribou's past and Colorado's present." The jug, they learned, had been sold by the Farmer's Cash Grocery on Blake Street in Denver, a supplier for mining camps, sometime between 1893 and 1903.   I. W. Van Noppen

Minority Groups

3998. Cherny, Robert W.   ISOLATIONIST VOTING IN 1940: A STATISTICAL ANALYSIS. *Nebraska Hist. 1971 52(3): 293-310.* In the 1940 election in Nebraska there was an ethnic response to foreign policy issues with citizens of German stock shifting from the Democratic Party to the Republican Party primarily because of opposition to Franklin D. Roosevelt's handling of foreign affairs.   R. Lowitt

3999. Coletta, Paolo E.   "THE MOST THANKLESS TASK": BRYAN AND THE CALIFORNIA ALIEN LAND LEGISLATION. *Pacific Hist. R. 1967 36(2): 163-187.* Both Secretary of State Bryan and President Wilson hoped to smooth over the strained situation between California and the Japanese by friendly overtures. They were reluctant to challenge the police power of a State with Federal authority, but Bryan was convinced that California's Alien Land Act (known as the Webb Act) violated the Treaty of 1911. Bryan, who was sympathetic to the Japanese, opposed discriminatory laws, but Wilson was too busy with other matters to devote full energy to the matter, so the California law stood, despite Bryan's appeal to the California legislature. Based mainly on Bryan and Wilson papers; 109 notes.   J. McCutcheon

4000. Collins, Dabney Otis.   BATTLE FOR BLUE LAKE: THE TAOS INDIANS FINALLY REGAIN THEIR SACRED LAND. *Am. West 1971 8(5): 32-37.* In 1906 Blue Lake became a part of the newly created Carson National Forest in New Mexico. A few miles from Taos, Blue Lake and nearly 50 thousand acres of surrounding forests and mountains are the ancestral sacred lands of the Taos Pueblo Indians. Symbolically, the sapphire waters of the lake are the source of all Taos life and the retreat of souls after death. Here occurs the annual secret ceremonial rites, witnessed by only two non-Indians. When they felt the implications of what had happened, the Taos Indians began a legal battle for restoration. A 1940 special Federal use permit was substantial progress, but public recreation inroads and pressure from timber interests posed significant threats. After a 1965 Indian Claims Commission ruling the Taos rejected an offer of 300 thousand dollars for their claims. Soon Blue Lake became a national synonym for religious freedom with support from the press and communications media, Congressmen, cabinet officers, and the National Council of Churches. After several bills were introduced in Congress and hearings produced determined opposition as well as support, a White House message broke the stalemate. After signature of a bill

on 15 December 1970, 48 thousand acres of land surrounding Blue Lake were once again owned by the Taos. 3 illus.   D. L. Smith

4001. Daniels, Roger.   WILLIAM JENNINGS BRYAN AND THE JAPANESE.   *Southern California Q. 1966 48(3): 227-240.* Bryan, a moderate racist in an immoderate age, violated his own principles of popular sovereignty in an attempt to maintain peaceful relations between the United States and Japan. His efforts to negotiate the question of Japanese immigration and ownership of land in California were not notably useful, in spite of his sincerity. 53 notes.   H. Kelsey

4002. Davis, William E.   A SWEDISH GEM IN IDAHO'S SHINING MOUNTAINS.   *Idaho Yesterdays 1966 10(3): 2-11.* "A portrait of Dr. Sven Liljeblad, linguist and ethnologist, who has spent a quarter century studying the Indians of Idaho." Liljeblad began his academic career in Sweden, and has been associated with Idaho State College as a professor of sociology since 1940. His major contributions include intensive studies of the language of the Bannock, Shoshoni, and Northern Paiute tribes. 2 illus.   D. H. Swift

4003. DeGraaf, Lawrence B.   THE CITY OF BLACK ANGELS: EMERGENCE OF THE LOS ANGELES GHETTO, 1890-1930. *Pacific Hist. R. 1970 39(3): 323-352.* Studies the origins and growth of the black ghetto, since 1900 the largest in California. Describes the ghetto as it was both before and after the great migration from the South which started in 1915, and the gradual increase of restriction to and deterioration of the area. Covers the housing situation and the relationship with other minorities, both major factors in the distinctive nature of the black ghetto in Los Angeles. 113 notes.   E. C. Hyslop

4004. Diller, Julie Beaver.   A GLANCE AT ROCK SPRINGS. *Ann. of Wyoming 1971 43(1): 91-111.* Details cultural and social life during the 1920's in Rock Springs, a southwestern Wyoming town of six to eight thousand people. Composed mostly of immigrant coal miners and their families, Rock Springs had a widespread reputation for outstanding musical talent and peaceful ethnic coexistence. The inhabitants formed numerous regionally celebrated instrumental and vocal groups and enjoyed frequent performances by touring vaudeville acts, opera companies, and nationally renowned individual artists. Violinist John Brueggemann's School of Music and his voluntary public school teaching inspired much of this enthusiasm for music and supplied most of the townspeople's musical education. Music also contributed immensely to the success of the community's patriotic annual International Night celebrations, which featured ethnic songs and dances performed by representatives of more than 40 nationalities. Illus., 45 notes, biblio., appendix.

G. R. Adams

4005. Ellison, Ralph.   ON BECOMING A WRITER.   *Commentary 1964 38(4): 57-60.* Recollections and comments on growing up as a Negro in Oklahoma in the years between World War I and the Great Depression with some observations on writing, and a certain acerbity toward "friends of the Negro" and others.   E. W. Hathaway

4006. Gatewood, Willard B.   KANSAS NEGROES AND THE SPANISH-AMERICAN WAR.   *Kansas Hist. Q. 1971 37(3): 300-313.* The war with Spain came just as Kansas Negroes faced an uncertain future, but the war seemed to offer some hope that it might lead to better times. Negroes joined the 23d Kansas, an all-black regiment, with expectation that the imperial venture might improve their economic position and demonstrate their willingness to be valuable citizens. The results were far from encouraging; the blacks did not improve their position but learned only that this "is a world of deception." Some Negroes appreciated the new empire as a possible refuge from the oppressive atmosphere at home. Perhaps such a possibility offered the only hope of Negroes to share in the fruits of imperialism. The deteriorating status of blacks in America prompted many schemes for emigration, and probably in no other State did such projects elicit more discussion among Negroes than in Kansas. Based on secondary sources; illus., 66 notes.

W. F. Zornow

4007. Harmon, Ray.   INDIAN SHAKER CHURCH OF THE DALLES.   *Oregon Hist. Q. 1971 72(2): 148-158.* A small wooden church constructed near The Dalles, probably in 1896, was still standing in 1971 and is expected to be preserved as a historic building. The church was established for use primarily by Indians who were Shakers. Describes some features of the religious ceremonies, prominent people associated with the church, and the layout and furnishings of the church. Based on the 1892-93 annual report of the Bureau of American Ethnology, and on interviews; 5 photos.   C. C. Gorchels

4008. Hokanson, Nels. SWEDES AND THE I.W.W. *Swedish Pioneer Hist. Q. 1972 23(1): 25-35.* While the author was a student at the University of Chicago, 1907-11, he heard the Industrial Workers of the World discussed often, and attended a meeting of students with some of its members, led by John Hanson. The author wondered how many Swedish-Americans were involved in the organization, since the majority of Swedish-Americans were strongly opposed to radical groups. Because files have been destroyed, exact figures are not available. It is known that there were many Swedes in locals in Portland and Seattle. Joel Emanuel Hagglund (1879-1915), commonly known as Joe Hill (or Joseph Hillstrom), was a Swedish folk and labor singer. He was executed in 1915 for allegedly taking part in an attempted robbery in which two were killed. He was given an official funeral in Chicago. The article is followed by the text of the song "Workers of the World Awaken," by Hill. Based on primary sources; 8 notes, biblio.   K. J. Puffer

4009. Jensen, Joan M. APARTHEID: PACIFIC COAST STYLE. *Pacific Hist. R. 1969 38(3): 335-340.* Analyzes the role of municipal ordinances and restrictive covenants as a means to maintain racial segregation. These methods started in California at the end of the 19th century (aimed against the Chinese) and culminated in the Proposition 14 battle in 1967. The methods have affected all minority groups. Historians have done little to document the origins of the specific means used to maintain and increase residential discrimination. Based on primary sources; 8 notes.   E. C. Hyslop

4010. Johnke, James. KANSAS MENNONITES DURING THE SPANISH-AMERICAN WAR. *Mennonite Life 1971 26(2): 70-72.* An examination of the factors which influenced the outlook of Mennonites regarding the Spanish-American War. Initially willing to contribute to the American war effort in nonmilitary ways, the Mennonites soon turned in outraged protest when American military expanionism continued. In the election of 1900, however, they failed to offer strong support to the peace candidacy of William Jennings Bryan. Also, their willingness to work as noncombatants helped relieve potential tensions between them and the general American public. 21 notes.   J. A. Casada

4011. Kalisch, Philip A. THE BLACK DEATH IN CHINATOWN: PLAGUE AND POLITICS IN SAN FRANCISCO, 1900-1904. *Arizona and the West 1972 14(2): 113-136.* On 6 March 1900, in San Francisco, a Chinese man died of the black plague, which is usually fatal and appears in epidemic proportions. Chinatown was immediately placed in quarantine while the city fathers, fearful of economic repercussions, endeavored to conceal the discovery. The unbelieving press accused the board of public health of scare tactics so that it could get its "snout and forelegs in the public trough." Before the plague subsided in 1904, 120 cases were reported. Subsequent outbreaks, probably carried by thousands of Chinese who were permitted to leave the city, occurred in several areas throughout the country. The malady still exists in some of the smaller animal population of the West. The efforts at secrecy precipitated a nationwide controversy that embroiled many State and Federal officials as well as numerous journalists. 4 illus., 53 notes.   D. L. Smith

4012. Knowlton, Clark S. CHANGING SPANISH-AMERICAN VILLAGES OF NORTHERN NEW MEXICO. *Sociol. and Social Res. 1969 53(4): 455-474.* "The Spanish Americans of northern New Mexico and southern Colorado living in isolation from other European groups for almost three hundred years developed a unique rural farm village culture based upon subsistence agriculture, pastoral activities, barter, handicrafts, and trade with the Indians. Until very recently each village was a small isolated, selfsufficient, autonomous social cell. The social structure of the village was structured upon four interrelated social systems: (1) the village community, (2) the patriarchal extended family, (3) the patron system, and (4) folk Catholicism. The extension of American control, the massive loss of range and farming land, the emigration of young adults, increasing acculturational and social differences, and finally the breakdown and malfunctioning of the traditional social systems have created a large apathetic poverty-stricken village population

unable to live in the traditional manner or to develop the necessary social mechanisms to adjust to the dominant Anglo American society."   J

4013. Kowert, Art. LBJ'S BOYHOOD AMONG THE GERMAN-AMERICANS IN TEXAS. *Am.-German R. 1968 34(5): 2-6.* An account of the youthful experiences of Lyndon Baines Johnson, with special reference to the German-speaking population around Fredericksburg, Texas, and their influence on Johnson. Illus.   G. H. Davis

4014. LeWarne, Charles P. THE ANARCHIST COLONY AT HOME, WASHINGTON, 1901-1902. *Arizona and the West 1972 14(2): 155-168.* When President William McKinley was assassinated by a self-proclaimed anarchist in 1901, a wave of antianarchist sentiment swept the Nation. The almost forgotten tiny anarchist community of Home, on the other side of Puget Sound from Tacoma, was suddenly remembered. The Tacoma press opened a barrage of assaults and innuendo despite protests of the anarchists that they deplored the assassination. Sunday sermons, civic leaders, and veterans' groups entered the fray, hoping to convince the residents of Home that they were not welcome to continue their residence. There was even the threat of a vigilante raid from Tacoma. Court action against some of the Home newspaper articles and strict enforcement of postal restrictions failed to curb the largely imagined threat posed by the anarchists. The upheaval finally ran its course. Home grew a little, attracting freethinkers and the curious, and it remained undisturbed by the outside world except for a 1911 tempest-in-a-teapot dispute about nude bathing. Today, Home is a peaceful rural community concerned mostly with poultry raising and tourism. 3 illus., map, 25 notes.   D. L. Smith

4015. LeWarne, Charles P. EQUALITY COLONY: THE PLAN TO SOCIALIZE WASHINGTON. *Pacific Northwest Q. 1968 59(3): 137-146.* The rise and fall of the colony of Equality founded in the State of Washington under the auspices of the National Union of the Brotherhood of the Co-operative Commonwealth, 1897-1907. This colony was one of a number of utopian socialistic settlements which sprang up in the State and across the Nation especially in the 19th century. After an industrious beginning, the Equality Colony declined because of disagreements and the latter-day activities of members who allegedly included anarchists, spiritualists, and free lovers.   C. C. Gorchels

4016. Luebke, Frederick C. THE GERMAN-AMERICAN ALLIANCE IN NEBRASKA, 1910-1917. *Nebraska Hist. 1968 49(2): 165-185.* A careful history and analysis of the German-American Alliance from its creation to its demise brought about by the tensions aroused by World War I. Primarily political in its purposes (to stave off prohibition, woman suffrage, and other progressive reforms) the alliance, because of the war, was unable to play a role as an agency mitigating the process whereby German immigrants could be absorbed into American society without losing their cultural identity.   R. Lowitt

4017. Matthews, Fred H. WHITE COMMUNITY AND "YELLOW PERIL." *Mississippi Valley Hist. R. 1964 50(4): 612-633.* Among early radicals whose ideas confronted entrenched conservatism on the Japanese in California were E. A. Ross of Stanford, Josiah Royce, and missionary Sidney Lewis Gulick. Sumner's cultural relativism was used as a weapon in attacking the idea of "assimilation." In 1925 Robert E. Park made a survey of race relations in California. He distinguished between specific racial prejudice, culturally acquired, and the underlying emotions involved, founded "in fundamental human nature." The "objective" world of economic competition and visible racial differences was by the post-World War II period seen as a stage for the acting-out of deeper frustrations lurking within individuals shaped by a fluid social order. "California's Japanese were no longer pictured as independent causes of conflict but as catalysts precipitating impulses held latent in American national character." 67 notes.   E. P. Stickney

4018. Miyamoto, S. Frank. THE JAPANESE MINORITY IN THE PACIFIC NORTHWEST. *Pacific Northwest Q. 1963 54(4): 143-149.* Account of immigration of Japanese to the Pacific Northwest, with particular attention to years of 1900 to 1924. Most of the immigrants were unmarried males who worked in groups in mills and as railroad section hands at first, then became important in the regional economy as salmon-cannery workers, truck farmers, and operators of small businesses. Most recently, Japanese-Americans have become important in art and science.   C. C. Gorchels

4019. O'Neil, Floyd A.   AN ANGUISHED ODYSSEY: THE FLIGHT OF THE UTES, 1906-1908.   *Utah Hist. Q. 1968 36(4): 315-327.* Traces the history of the retreat of the Utes in the face of white advance into their territory and relates how those members of the tribe who were forced to retreat to the Uintah Basin in Utah reacted to invasion of that basin by fleeing in 1906 to South Dakota where they hoped to ally with the Sioux to make a last stand against encroachment on their lands. The Sioux rejected the offer of alliance, the Federal Government refused to provide aid to the Utes at the South Dakota location, and the United States Army brought steady pressure to persuade them to return to Utah, which they did in 1908. Based in the main on Department of the Interior reports and newspaper accounts.   S. L. Jones

4020. Patterson, James.   THE UNASSIMILATED GREEKS OF DENVER.   *Anthropological Q. 1970 43(4): 243-253.* "The Greek community in Denver began around the turn of the century. As it grew and prospered the majority of its members moved out of the original Greek town and today there is only one Greek coffee house left in the area. This *kafeneion* serves the remaining 40 to 50 unassimilated old men and the few younger new arrivals. The old men have been largely unsuccessful financially, maintain strong emotional orientation toward Greece, are ambivalent toward U.S. culture and are a source of embarrassment to the dominant Americanized middle class Greek community. The study focuses on the habitués of the coffee house and their peripheral relationship to the larger Greek community and church. It also looks at the conflicts and factionalism with their group and makes some predictions for the future."   AIA(2:1:136) J

4021. Paulsen, George E.   THE YELLOW PERIL AT NOGALES: THE ORDEAL OF COLLECTOR WILLIAM M. HOEY.   *Arizona and the West 1971 13(2): 113-128.* In 1899, a U.S. Treasury Department investigation implicated the Collector of Customs at Nogales in smuggling Chinese aliens into the country from Nogales, Sonora. He was replaced by William M. Hoey who became a distinguished resident of Nogales. In 1901 Hoey was arrested and charged with the same offense. Added to this sensational news was the suicide of one of his subordinates and the rumor that Hoey had been "framed" by some of his deputies. Another rumor linked these developments with an attempt to gain a presidential nomination from a prominent politician. While the 1902 jury verdict was not guilty, Hoey had lost his job and salary and his reputation had been smeared because of false reports and accusations. Even though he was not reinstated, Hoey remained in Nogales as a respected member of the community and developed his extensive mining properties and investments. Further refinements of the Mexican-American extradition treaties did not solve the problem of illegal entry. When the Mexican Government expelled the Chinese aliens from Sonora in 1936 the problem was finally eliminated in the Nogales district. 3 illus., 34 notes.
D. L. Smith

4022. Philp, Kenneth.   ALBERT B. FALL AND THE PROTEST FROM THE PUEBLOS, 1921-23.   *Arizona and the West 1970 12(3): 237-254.* Although the treaty of Guadalupe Hidalgo (1848) confirmed Pueblo Indian ownership of 700 thousand acres of Spanish land grants in New Mexico, and even though the Federal Supreme Court had upheld Pueblo right to sell these lands as non-wards of the Federal Government, the 1910 enabling act for New Mexico statehood reversed this position. The Pueblo again became wards of the Federal Government. The validity of thousands of non-Indian claims to the lands within the Pueblo grants was at stake. At the request of Secretary of the Interior Albert Bacon Fall, Senator Holm O. Bursum from New Mexico sponsored a bill in Congress to confirm such titles as were held by non-Indians meeting certain conditions. The 1921 Bursum bill met determined opposition in a nationwide protest which resulted in its defeat and new laws to protect Indian rights. Although Fall's resignation in 1923 from his cabinet position is usually explained by his involvement in the Teapot Dome affair, the furor over his sponsorship of the Bursum bill was an important factor in his decision. 5 illus., map, 46 notes.   D. L. Smith

4023. Rossi, Jean L.   ENCHANTED GARDEN.   *Pacific Historian 1969 13(1): 8-13.* Narrates the history of the Japanese Tea Garden at Golden Gate Park in San Francisco since its design by George Turner Marsh for the 1897 Mid-Winter Fair. In 1941, the Hagiwara family, long-time caretakers of the garden, were forced to relocate in Utah by the US Government. The name of the garden was changed to "Oriental Tea Garden" until 1952. The garden was in danger of losing its authenticity, but in 1964 it was relandscaped by Nagao Sakurai, landscape architect at the Japanese Imperial Palace for 20 years. Based on secondary sources; 13 notes.   F. I. Murphy

4024. Servín, Manuel P.   THE PRE-WORLD WAR II MEXICAN-AMERICAN: AN INTERPRETATION.   *California Hist. Soc. Q. 1966 45(4): 325-338.* Explains the historical background for the fact that the Mexican became a "despised minority...when the North American migrated to Mexican Texas and California finding on the whole a poor class of Hispanic settler." After the fall of Díaz in Mexico a new wave of immigrants came into the Southwest. Despite the prejudice against them, the pre-World War II Mexican maintained a good record and made some remarkable achievements. His crime record was remarkably low; he established a good cultural Spanish press and broke into motion pictures and music. Beginning in 1942 the young Mexican encountered entirely different social and economic conditions from those his predecessors had met. Unfortunately, a minority of the wartime Mexican-American youths, the Pachucos, attacked American servicemen in a way that gave the Mexican an undeserved reputation for lawlessness and disloyalty that quickly ended the hard-earned reputation of the prewar Mexican. Based on official documents and church records, 39 notes.
E. P. Stickney

4025. Spaulding, Edward Selden.   AS I KNEW THEM.   *Noticias 1967 13(4): 9-17.* Describes various Santa Barbara Chinese individuals and groups remembered by the author. There were Mr. Fong, a Presbyterian merchant who sold cheap imports, especially firecrackers; hard-working and skillful cooks; and vegetablemen, renting cheap plots of land and selling vegetables door-to-door. The Chinese went to Chinatown every evening possible and walked in single file. Honest, intelligent, and humorous, they nevertheless had to pay 10 percent on bank loans, not the normal five percent. Chinese labor did not undercut American labor; the author's family paid their Chinese cook 75 dollars monthly with board while "the going wage for so-called Americans" was 50 dollars. Gin Chow, who predicted the weather correctly and was known throughout the county for it, was one of 40 ranchers and farmers who opposed the proposed Gibraltar Dam. After seemingly slight injury in an automobile accident, he predicted his imminent death, and died. 4 photos.
T. M. Condon

4026. Stuck, Larry R.   THE CASE AGAINST POPULATION CONTROL: THE PROBABLE CREATION OF THE FIRST AMERICAN INDIAN STATE.   *Human Organization 1971 30(4): 393-399.* The expansion in numbers of the Navajo since the 1930's is the major reason for the Navajo's increased political and economic strength, particularly in comparison with other Amerindian tribes. Cites some of the consequences of this growth, and suggests that the conflict between the Navajo and Arizona, New Mexico, and Utah could result in the creation of a 51st State. Abstracts in English, French, and Spanish. 6 notes, biblio.
E. S. Johnson

4027. Sylvers, Malcolm.   SICILIAN SOCIALISTS IN HOUSTON, TEXAS, 1896-98.   *Labor Hist. 1970 11(1): 77-81.* A brief discussion of the minutes and dues register of the *Unione Socialista dei Lavoratori Italiani "Giuffrida Defelice"* of Houston, Texas, a group of Sicilian Socialists. The author calls for research into the problems posed by small Socialist immigrant groups.   L. L. Athey

4028. Unruh, John D.   THE HUTTERITES DURING WORLD WAR I.   *Mennonite Life 1969 24(3): 130-137.* Describes the experiences of the Hutterian Brethren of South Dakota and Montana during World War I. Because they spoke German and adhered to the principles of pacifism, the Hutterites were subjected to almost continual harassment. The fifty-odd Hutterite men who were drafted into military service absolutely refused to wear the uniform or work. All of these draftees were subjected to more or less harsh treatment. Some were tortured, two died from inhuman treatment at Fort Leavenworth military prison. The Hutterites who remained on the farms were attacked in English-language newspapers, they were pressured into buying Liberty Bonds, their property was stolen, and the South Dakota State Council of Defense brought suit to dissolve the Hutterische Brüder-Gemeinde. Based on interviews and published primary sources; 30 notes.   D. J. Abramoske

4029. Wenzel, Lawrence A. THE RURAL PUNJABIS OF CALIFORNIA: A RELIGIO-ETHNIC GROUP. *Phylon 1968 29(3): 245-256.* Analyzes the social and cultural characteristics of a community of about 900 East Indians living in north central California. The majority came from northwestern Punjab and thus have common linguistic, religious (Sikh), and cultural ties. Discusses the components of the Sikh religion. The Punjabis entered the United States legally between 1898 and 1924, and afterward continued to enter illegally in small numbers. Most are involved in agricultural activities and many have been moderately successful. They maintain their cultural heritage through continuing East Indian religious festivals and joining associations of East Indians. The religious element in their lives (Sikhism) has been the most important factor in maintaining their identity. 44 notes.   R. D. Cohen

4030. Wollenberg, Charles. RACE AND CLASS IN RURAL CALIFORNIA: THE EL MONTE BERRY STRIKE OF 1933. *California Hist. Q. 1972 51(2): 155-164.* One of the more important agricultural strikes in California occurred in El Monte in the summer of 1933. At issue were the wages of berry pickers. The Communist-affiliated Cannery and Agricultural Workers Industrial Union initiated the strike, but was soon displaced by Mexican organizers working in cooperation with the Mexican consulate. The strike attracted special notice, as it pitted Mexican workers against Japanese growers. White growers and property-holders who had leased lands to the Japanese in spite of the State's alien land laws sided with the Japanese, as did the Los Angeles Chamber of Commerce. The workers received support from the Mexican Government. The workers won a hollow victory, for by the time the strike was settled the harvest season had ended. The Japanese growers claimed they won the strike, but the entire affair contributed to tensions in Japanese-white relations in the long run. This form of class-race conflict has not disappeared, for Nisei farm owners have recently organized against attempts by Cesar Chavez's United Farm Workers union to unionize workers on their farms. Note.   A. Hoffman

4031. Woodard, James E. VERNON: AN ALL NEGRO TOWN IN SOUTHEASTERN OKLAHOMA. *Negro Hist. Bull. 1964 27(5): 115-116.* A sketch of the town of Vernon, Oklahoma, which was founded by Negroes from the South in 1911 and which currently contains only a small remnant of its earlier population.   L. Gara

Agriculture

4032. Arrington, Leonard. THE U AND I SUGAR COMPANY IN WASHINGTON. *Pacific Northwest Q. 1966 57(3): 101-109.* Sketch of the growth of the Utah-Idaho Sugar Company in Washington state, with details of the struggle to overcome beet leaf hopper (White Fly) blight and the economic risks of establishing million dollar processing plants in Toppenish, Sunnyside, and Mount Vernon.   C. C. Gorchels

4033. Arrington, Leonard J. WESTERN AGRICULTURE AND THE NEW DEAL. *Agric. Hist. 1970 44(4): 337-353.* Asks what pattern, if any, characterized government agricultural loans and expenditures during the New Deal. Concludes that per capita expenditures "were a function of the absolute and percentage changes in per capita farm income from 1929 to 1932." Funds were not directed primarily to the poorest farm States, but rather to those that experienced the greatest drop in income. The measures sought in practice to provide relief. They were neither reform-oriented nor a move toward greater economic equality. Based mainly on Bureau of the Budget documents; 5 tables, 5 diagrams, 3 notes.   D. E. Brewster

4034. Babson, Sydney G. HOOD RIVER VALLEY WILD NIGHT. *Oregon Hist. Q. 1969 70(1): 50-55.* Reminiscences of pioneering experiences in the Hood River valley of Oregon in 1908, with an account of selecting land in the area after the writer and his brother had given up their jobs in New York City to go west and "buy some wild land, clear it, and plant it to apples." The "wild night" of the title was occasioned by a Chinook, a violent but warm wind from the Pacific, which melted the winter's snow. Illus.   C. C. Gorchels

4035. Bakken, Douglas A., ed. LUNA E. KELLIE AND THE FARMERS' ALLIANCE. *Nebraska Hist. 1969 50(2): 185-205.* An account written in 1926 by Luna E. Kellie recalling her experiences as Secretary of the Farmers' Alliance in Nebraska from 1894 to 1900. Photos, 30 notes.   R. Lowitt

4036. Ballantine, Norman S. CHINOOK. *Colorado Mag. 1964 41(2): 147-153.* The horrifying experiences of eight men driving a herd of 1500 head of cattle through the Colorado River Canyon who were trapped when a melting ice floe blocked road and river. One small aperture in the ice enabled the steers to pass through, single file, to safety.   I. W. Van Noppen

4037. Bowen, Marshall. ENVIRONMENTAL PERCEPTION AND GEOGRAPHIC CHANGE IN SOUTHWEST SHERIDAN COUNTY. *Nebraska Hist. 1970 51(3): 319-338.* Analytical account of a sector of southwest Sheridan County during the 1890's. Stresses that gradual understanding of the environment shifted the economic base of the sector from agriculture to ranching during this critical decade.   R. Lowitt

4038. Brandon, William. BERNALILLO COUNTY. *Am. West 1967 4(1): 28-29, 70-71.* From the ages of seven to 11 the author lived on a four-acre ranch near Albuquerque in Bernalillo County, New Mexico. He reminisces about his horse, playmates, school, and especially how he played cowboy rounding up his family's milk cow.   D. L. Smith

4039. Carlson, Martin E. WILLIAM E. SMYTHE: IRRIGATION CRUSADER. *J. of the West 1968 7(1): 41-47.* Summarizes the activities of Smythe, a promoter of irrigation in the years 1890-95. Smythe believed in irrigation because it would, he felt, compel the adoption of the small-farm unit which would be a bulwark of liberty in an era when great corporations were gaining power and influence. Smythe publicized his views in the *Irrigation Age* (which he founded in 1891) and the *Omaha Bee.* Smythe was also founder and one-time president of the National Irrigation Congress. Based on a book and newspaper articles written by Smythe; 27 notes.   E. A. Erickson

4040. Colley, Charles C. THE CALIFORNIA DATE GROWING INDUSTRY, 1890-1939, PART I AND PART II. *Southern California Q. 1967 49(1): 47-63 and (2): 167-191.* Part I. Date growing as an industry was introduced to California in 1890 when the U.S. Department of Agriculture imported date offshoots from the Middle East. Since the soil of the Imperial and Coachella Valleys was similar to that of the Sahara and since only about half of the irrigable land in those locations could be used to grow ordinary crops, it was concluded that date culture could be important to California. Experimenting with varieties of dates, growing techniques, and ripening processes, California date growers soon surpassed the Old World in scientific date culture. But plant quarantine was not considered during these early years and California date plants became infested by the Parlatoria date scale, an insect pest introduced from the Middle East. It was discovered that torching killed the scale but left the date palms unharmed and an eradication program was started. It required over two decades to eliminate the scale and at great loss to California farmers and much expense to the State and Federal Governments. Passage of quarantine laws and government inspection stopped the introduction of new pests. Illus., 63 notes. Part II. Concerns marketing problems of the California date industry between 1890 and 1939. Competition from foreign imports, inconsistent fruit quality, and failure to effect adequate marketing policies and grower organization were the major problems. During the 1930's tariff duties reduced the amount of competition from abroad and date growing organizations eventually imposed grading standards, but these changes came slowly and generally after several attempts were made and reverses were experienced. As part of the New Deal program the Federal Government attempted to establish marketing controls, but these were struck down by the courts as an unlawful delegation of authority to a trade body. The date growing industry began to diversify during the 1930's, however, and byproducts made from low quality dates helped the industry survive some of the bad years of the depression. Tariff regulation, imposition of grading standards and diversification helped the date growing industry but its economic problems were not completely resolved until World War II eliminated foreign competition. Based on public and organizational documents and reports and on secondary sources, illus., 96 notes.   W. L. Bowers

4041. Dalziel, Hazel Webb. THE WAY IT WAS. *Colorado Mag. 1968 45(2): 101-119.* A nostalgic but perceptive reminiscence about farm life in the last decade of the 19th century in Weld County, Colorado. The author describes the daily tasks, joys, and sorrows of an age now gone forever. Her descriptions of rural home life - sans plumbing, electricity, central heating, and other conveniences now taken for granted - present a valuable commentary on "the way it was." 2 notes.

O. H. Zabel

4042. Danker, Donald F. NEBRASKA'S HOMEMADE WIND-MILLS. *Am. West 3(1): 13-19.* During the summer of 1897, three University of Nebraska students were sent on a round trip from Lincoln to Denver to study and photograph the homemade windmills in the valley of the Platte River. This rather prevalent device was often more than a poor man's substitute for manufactured mills, some were "objects of considerable pride." 11 illus.

D. L. Smith

4043. Day, J. Herold. JOHN SHEPHERD DAY. *Ann. of Wyoming 1964 36(2): 239-241.* Biographical sketch of John Day, owner and operator of the Battle Axe Ranch from the 1890's until the 1940's.

R. L. Nichols

4044. Downing, Charles Oliver and Smith, Sharon Reed. RECOLLECTIONS OF A GOSHEN COUNTY HOMESTEADER. *Ann. of Wyoming. 1971 43(1): 53-72.* A description of homestead living and the social, economic, and political development of Goshen County, Wyoming, to 1920. Downing (b. 1883), a native of New York, arrived in Wyoming in 1910, established a 160-acre homestead 50 miles north of Cheyenne, and supplemented his income by teaching. Later he participated in the creation of Goshen County, served as county school superintendent and county assessor, and founded a real estate firm in Torrington. Despite initial scorn from ranchers, Downing and the other homesteaders of the region enjoyed a warm social life while working together to improve their land. Gradually their healthy effect on the area's economy won them the cattlemen's acceptance. Illus.

G. R. Adams

4045. Fonaroff, L. Schuyler. CONSERVATION AND STOCK REDUCTION ON THE NAVAJO TRIBAL RANGE. *Geographical R. 1963 53(2): 200-223.* Analyzes the livestock reduction program begun as a conservation measure by the Federal government in the 1930's, with reference to some of the human problems involved in the Navajo country in northeastern Arizona. The first attempts to reduce the livestock met with resistance by the Indians who could not comprehend its purpose. The destructive native grazing techniques here described have still not been replaced by the agronomist's rational grazing pattern. In many areas where agriculture or seasonal wages might have produced more income, most Navajos still felt that the traditional sheep raising had a social value that outweighed the economic. The end of the reduction program in most districts was followed by a marked stock increase despite the fact that the range was continually deteriorating. Illus., map, table, 47 notes.

E. P. Stickney

4046. Forbes, Robert Humphrey. THE MAKING OF A PIONEER: A REMINISCENCE. *Arizoniana 1964 5(4): 42-48.* Recalls his arrival in 1894 in Tucson as professor of chemistry at the University of Arizona. Working with the U.S. Department of Agriculture he developed date palm offshoots from North Africa. Another service was a study of the effects of copper compounds on crops. The decision in the litigation favored the farmers whose crops were damaged by tailings from copper mines in irrigating waters; but it benefited "the miners who impounded tailings from which they extracted additional copper by improved methods." After 13 years abroad, in 1931 he became dean of the College of Agriculture and served (1938-54) in the Arizona state legislature. Illus. A bibliography of his writings is included.

E. P. Stickney

4047. Forrest, Earle R. RIDING FOR THE OLD C O BAR. *Arizoniana 1964 5(1): 1-19.*

4048. Friggens, Paul. CHANGE RIDES THE RANGE. *Southwest R. 1964 49(3): 282-289.* Brief survey of the cattle industry in the 20th century, including the beef factories, which can fatten fifty thousand cattle at a time, artificial insemination, and the mechanization of the cowboy through two-way radios and airplanes.

D. F. Henderson

4049. Frost, Melvin J. RECENT HOMESTEADING IN SAN JUAN COUNTY, UTAH. *Southern Q. 1965 3(3): 235-243.* Until quite recently homesteading by wheat farmers in this southeastern county of Utah was feasible; 30,400 acres were granted to settlers by the federal government, 1930-63.

D. A. Stokes

4050. Gillespie, A. S. REMINISCENCES OF A SWAN COMPANY COWBOY. *Ann. of Wyoming 1964 36(2): 198-203.* An illustrated account of the Wyoming cattle industry during the 1890's to the 1950's by a retired ex-cowboy.

R. L. Nichols

4051. Gregor, Howard F. REGIONAL HIERARCHIES IN CALIFORNIA AGRICULTURAL PRODUCTION: 1939-1954. *Ann. of the Assoc. of Am. Geographers 1963 53(1): 27-37.* Portrays the alterations of previously highly stable regional rankings of agriculture resulting from shifting population patterns and intensification of agriculture. Maps, tables, 20 notes.

W. R. Boedecker

4052. Halloran, Arthur F. AN EXPERIMENTAL INTRODUCTION OF BIGHORN SHEEP INTO THE WICHITA MOUNTAINS OF OKLAHOMA. *Great Plains J. 1970 9(2): 85-90.* Describes the attempt, in 1928-29, to transplant Rocky Mountain Bighorn Sheep from Rocky Mountains National Park in Banff, Alberta, to the Wichita Mountains of Oklahoma. Two rams and five ewes sent to Oklahoma quickly died, unable to adjust to the new environment. Illus.

O. H. Zabel

4053. Hardin, Floyd. STAMPEDE: RANGELAND TERROR. *Montana 1964 14(1): 48-52.* Present-tense narrative, expressed in the second person, of a cattle stampede. Derived from the author's experience on the Montana range around 1900.

L. G. Nelson

4054. Heathcote, Leslie M. THE MONTANA ARID LAND COMMISSION, 1895-1903. *Agric. Hist. 1964 38(2): 108-117.* The Montana Arid Land Commission was established in 1895 to carry out the provisions of the Carey Land Act. Under this act, each state of the arid West might obtain one million acres of public land from the Federal government after the state had provided irrigation and settlement of the land. The Commission and all four of its irrigation projects failed. The failures resulted from inadequacies of the reclamation laws, the aversion of the state to putting up funds for reclamation, poor personnel of the Commission, overvaluation of construction work, and fiscal irregularities by the Commission.

W. D. Rasmussen

4055. Hendrickson, Kent. THE SUGAR-BEET LABORER AND THE FEDERAL GOVERNMENT: AN EPISODE IN THE HISTORY OF THE GREAT PLAINS IN THE 1930'S. *Great Plains J. 1964 3(2): 44-59.* Discusses the effect of federal legislation in the 1930's on the growers, laborers and processors in the beet-sugar industry especially in Colorado. Labor, much of it done by migrant Mexicans, was the largest expense of the grower. Poor wages, child labor, noneducational opportunities and poor living conditions were major problems. Although the Jones-Costigan Act of 1934 and the Sugar Act of 1937 improved labor conditions somewhat, they undoubtedly benefited the grower and processor more than the sugar-beet laborer.

O. H. Zabel

4056. Hewes, Leslie. CAUSES OF WHEAT FAILURE IN THE DRY FARMING REGION, CENTRAL GREAT PLAINS, 1939-1957. *Econ. Geography 1965 41(4): 313-330.* The chief crop of the central Great Plains is dry farmed winter wheat. Farming is risky, due primarily to drought, wind, hail. The Federal Crop Insurance Corp. records now permit somewhat quantitative identification of the chief hazards, and the percentage of failure attributable to each, by county. The area covered is western Kansas, eastern Colorado, southwestern Nebraska, and southeastern Wyoming, a total of 70 counties. The most general cause of crop failure is drought. The area of greatest hazard from wind is southwestern Kansas, while hail is the principal menace in 15 out of the 22 most northerly counties studied. In certain years a single cause has been of unusual importance: winterkilling in 1951; wind in 1954. The threats of grasshoppers - common in the 1930's, and of winterkilling have decreased in importance. "Quantitative analyses of the causes of wheat failure should aid materially in charting the progress of the farmer in learning to live with a hazardous natural environment...." 13 maps.

J. E. Caswell

4057. Hosmer, Helen. IMPERIAL VALLEY. *Am. West 1966 3(1): 34-49, 79.* Once part of the Colorado Desert, California's Imperial Valley is now one of the world's richest farming areas. After a half century of attempted private exploitation of the valley's potential, climaxed by the disastrous floods of 1904-06, the basis of today's irrigation system was set forth in the Reclamation Act of 1902 and confirmed in the Boulder Canyon Project Act of 1928. Today the valley is the battlefield where private power challenges public policy over the entire purpose of western reclamation; the confrontation involves "agri-industrialists" pitted against the "family farm" people. Photographic illus., 2 notes, annotated biblio., map. D. L. Smith

4058. Hunter, William C. THE BALDWIN FARMS IN NORTH DAKOTA. *North Dakota Hist. 1966 33(4): 400-419.* These so-called bonanza farms were part of extensive land purchases by George Baldwin, a Wisconsin dealer in real estate. In 1898 Baldwin formed the Baldwin Land Company with a capital of 25 thousand dollars to deal in real estate and to hold mortgages, stocks, and bonds. Upon his death the trustees, one of whom was his son George Baldwin, improved the Dakota holdings by establishing ranches with modern buildings and livestock, and directing their operations. Tenants operated the ranches and received a half share of the earnings. Crops were diversified. Depression in the 1930's resulted in operating losses. Liquidation began in 1947 with the sale of ranches and was completed in 1953, thus ending the day of the huge corporate farming operations in Dickey County. Based chiefly on Baldwin family papers deposited in the Institute of Regional Studies, North Dakota State University; 53 notes. I. W. Van Noppen

4059. Jones, C. Clyde. AN AGRICULTURAL COLLEGE'S RESPONSE TO A CHANGING WORLD. *Agric. Hist. 1968 42(4): 283-295.* Reviews the response of the agricultural experiment station and the extension service of Kansas State University to external change. The continuing trend was the promotion of better farming and the improvement of the economic status of the farmer. From its founding until about 1910, the college assisted Kansans in their struggle to cope with the natural environment. From 1910 to 1940, the emphasis shifted to efficiency in farming. After World War II, concern with marketing, rural sociology, agriculturally-related industries, and international development became noticeable. These shifts were responses to national and international conditions. In its foreign programs, the college has completed a cycle and in many respects is back on the frontier, assisting primitive farmers in their search for new varieties of crops and improved production techniques. Based on reports and bulletins of Kansas State University. W. D. Rasmussen

4060. Kilgour, William Edward. THE NESTER. *Montana 1965 15(1): 37-51.* Anecdotes of a central Montana homestead in the era of World War I. The author and his father attempted to develop a farm in an area now proved to be more suitable for cattle-ranching.
S. R. Davison

4061. Lambert, C. Roger. TEXAS CATTLEMEN AND THE AAA, 1933-1935. *Arizona and the West 1972 14(2): 137-154.* Initially, Texas cattlemen refused with pride the early efforts of New Deal government supervision in 1933. As drought and depression swept the range, however, there was a reluctant reversal of their earlier position. Before any suitable arrangements could be worked out, the Agricultural Adjustment Administration (AAA) began massive emergency beef purchasing to reduce the number of cattle on the drought-blighted ranges. After some two million head of cattle were slaughtered from the Texas herds alone, the emergency program was halted, over the protests of the cattlemen. The AAA urged them to join the New Deal controls program, but they refused. Eventually, as cattle prices began to climb again, Texas cattlemen felt vindicated in their independent stance and untainted by participation in a government-controlled economy. 6 illus., 36 notes. D. L. Smith

4062. Littleton, Betty, ed. TOURING THE SOUTHEAST KANSAS AREA IN 1896: FROM THE DIARY OF THOMAS BUTCHER. *Kansas Hist. Q. 1969 35(2): 143-154.* Thomas Butcher came to Sun City, Barber County, Kansas, in 1875 and developed a profitable 800-acre farm. He lost it during the depression of 1893. The author, Butcher's great-granddaughter, edited the diary which he kept during a trip in 1896 through southeastern Kansas, northeastern Oklahoma, and southwestern Missouri. The daily entries for the period from 1 June to 3 July vary from

a sentence or two in length to nearly half a page. The longer entries contain information on local crop conditions and on material and mechanical progress both on the farms and in the towns through which he passed. The document is reproduced. Illus., photos, 10 notes.
W. F. Zornow

4063. Loeffler, M. John. BEET-SUGAR PRODUCTION ON THE COLORADO PIEDMONT. *Ann. of the Assoc. of Am. Geographers 1963 53(3): 364-389.* A "case study" of the geography of beet sugar production. Considered are beet sugar history, the physical landscape of the region, the agronomy of sugar-beet culture, harvesting, manufacturing, marketing, by-products, basic problems, and recent developments. Illus., maps, tables, 49 notes, selected biblio. W. R. Boedecker

4064. Luebke, Frederick. POLITICAL RESPONSE TO AGRICULTURAL DEPRESSION IN NEBRASKA, 1922. *Nebraska Hist. 1966 47(1): 15-55.* After surveying the depths of the agricultural depression in Nebraska by 1922, the political response of the farmer in seeking solutions to his problems is examined by analyzing all Nebraska parties and their candidates. While the results of the 1922 election cannot exclusively be attributed to agricultural dissatisfaction, it did play a prominent role in the results. R. Lowitt

4065. Lux, Mabel. HONYOCKERS OF HARLEM. *Montana 1963 13(4): 2-14.* As a result of the Great Northern Railroad's promotion of dry-land farming, the land along Montana's Milk River was heavily occupied in the years 1900-15. In an area better suited to grazing, inexperienced newcomers locally called "Honyockers" undertook to establish grain growing, and met some early success when ample rainfall and high prices were the rule. For several years after 1918, droughts and hot winds destroyed the crops, bringing severe hardships and driving out all but the most determined of the settlers. Much of the land was acquired by stockmen, who have turned it back to grazing. Written from family history and personal experience. S. R. Davison

4066. McKeen, Ona Lee. THE COWHAND. *Am. Heritage 1963 14(6): 16-31.* A portfolio of photographs taken by Edwin E. Smith of the life of the cowboy in the early years of the 20th century.
C. R. Allen, Jr.

4067. Meers, John R. THE CALIFORNIA WINE AND GRAPE INDUSTRY AND PROHIBITION. *California Hist. Soc. Q. 1967 46(1): 19-32.* Investigates the efforts of the wine and grape industry to oppose prohibition from 1908 to the ratification of the 18th amendment. During this period the California growers were "reaping the benefits from state to state encroachment of prohibition." Carload shipments East profited by rising prices as the demand for grapes for homemade wine increased. By 1920 the growers were prosperous beyond belief. The overproduction of grapes brought the wine industry into alliance with the liquor and beer forces. 50 notes. E. P. Stickney

4068. Moore, Austin L., ed. THE LAST EDEN. THE DIARY OF ALICE MOORE AT THE XX RANCH. *Ann. of Wyoming 1969 41(1): 63-81.* In addition to giving an account of a teen-age girl's camping on the XX Ranch in southeastern Wyoming during 1912, the editor discusses the ranch and the William R. Williams family which founded it. The diary describes a summer camping vacation of the Frank Moore family of five. It includes comments on the tents, weather, food, hiking, fishing, reading, and general remarks about the bird and animal life then abounding in the Laramie Mountains. The editor participated in the vacation as a boy of eleven and thus uses no annotations. Illus.
R. L. Nichols

4069. Pitzer, Paul C. HAMLIN GARLAND AND BURTON BABCOCK. *Pacific Northwest Q. 1965 56(2): 86-88.* Describes the futile efforts of author Hamlin Garland to aid his friend, Burton Babcock, in retrieving ownership to land which Babcock had lost through failure to observe the provisions of the Forest Homestead Act of 1906.
C. C. Gorchels

4070. Reeve, Frank D., ed. THE SHEEP INDUSTRY IN ARIZONA, 1906. *New Mexico Hist. R. 1964 39(2): 111-156.* Additional excerpts from *The "Old Observer" in Arizona,* and from the *American Shepherd's Bulletin,* vol. 11, no. 3, March 1906. Observations include comment on the towns of Prescott, Williams, Winslow, and Holbrook; schools, Indians, Land Scrip operations, shearing machines, and the Aztec Land and Cattle Company.

D. F. Henderson

4071. Reeve, Frank D. THE SHEEP INDUSTRY IN ARIZONA, 1905-1906. *New Mexico Hist. R. 1964 39(1): 40-79*. Continued from 1963 38(3): 244-252, and 38(4): 323-343. The concluding part of the "Old Observer" in Arizona is as interesting and valuable as the two previous installments. Observations range from type of crops to water conservation, from races at the state fair to the work of the Salvation Army, from the expense of running a band of two thousand sheep to the difficulties of running an Indian industrial school. Reproduced from *The American Shepherd's Bulletin,* vol. 11, no. 1, January 1906.

D. F. Henderson

4072. Reeve, Frank D., ed. THE SHEEP INDUSTRY IN ARIZONA, 1903. *New Mexico Hist. R. 1963 38(3): 244-252, and (4): 323-343*. Part I. Shortly after the American Civil War, enough military pressure was brought to bear on the Apache Indians to allow the reintroduction of sheep into Arizona. The industry developed slowly in the territory. Observations of its pioneer nature were first published in *The American Shepherd's Bulletin,* vol. 8, no. 6, June 1903, reprinted in this article. Part II. The second installment, from *American Shepherd's Bulletin,* vol. 11, no. 1, January 1906, includes observations which range from mineral deposits to the type of vegetation, from the price of wool to the weight of lambs, from the wages of herders to the tax rate on land. Annotated by the editor.

D. F. Henderson

4073. Ridgley, Ronald. THE RAILROADS AND RURAL DEVELOPMENT IN THE DAKOTAS. *North Dakota Hist. 1969 36(2): 164-187*. In 1908 President Theodore Roosevelt formed the Commission on Rural Life to study the position of the farmer in American life. The Commission reported in 1910 with findings that poor schooling and poor roads were chief deficiencies in rural areas. Dakota railroads had started a program in the early 20th century to improve the numbers and conditions of roads in the United States. The railroads held that good highways increased railroad business. Good Roads demonstration trains were operated in the Dakotas to educate the people in the need for better roads. Farmers, however, did not have a deep interest in improved roads. The railroads also helped in raising the level of farmers' agricultural skills. Education away from a single-crop economy and experimental farms were two methods employed by the railroads. The North Dakota Agricultural College was also enlisted in the program. By the time World War I began there were many positive signs that the efforts of the railroads and others were paying dividends. Based mainly on primary source materials; illus., photos, 56 notes.

E. P. Costello

4074. Riley, Paul D. THE NEBRASKA HALL OF AGRICULTURAL ACHIEVEMENT. *Nebraska Hist. 1972 53(1): 87-98*. The movement to honor outstanding leaders in Nebraska agriculture got underway in 1916. Lists the honorees from 1917 to the present, along with pictures of selected members of the hall.

R. Lowitt

4075. Rosentreter, G. W. MY COWBOY EXPERIENCES IN THE 1890'S. *Ann. of Wyoming 1965 37(2): 221-233*. An autobiographical description of ranch life in Wyoming from 1890 to 1895. Rosentreter, a German immigrant, began ranch work as a teen-aged boy, working at such tasks as herding livestock, erecting fences, digging post-holes and ditches, cooking and repairing ranch equipment. In 1895 he took out a homestead claim, and built a farm on which he still lives. Illus.

R. L. Nichols

4076. Saloutos, Theodore. THE NEW DEAL AND FARM POLICY IN THE GREAT PLAINS. *Agric. Hist. 1969 43(3): 345-355*. Those responsible for New Deal farm policies found the Great Plains to be one of the most maladjusted agricultural regions in the country. Thus, that area received an abnormally high percentage of assistance. The Federal Emergency Relief Administraion, the Agricultural Adjustment Administration, and other agencies moved quickly in 1933 and 1934 to aid the area by the purchase of starving cattle, production control of major farm commodities, and the purchase of submarginal land. A program to plant trees as a shelterbelt was one of the more controversial programs, while soil conservation plans were widely accepted. These and other measures were of material assistance to the larger farmers and ranchers, but they

delayed the elimination of small, inefficient farms which lacked capital, managerial talent, and equipment.

W. D. Rasmussen

4077. Schlebecker, John T. AGRICULTURE IN WESTERN NEBRASKA, 1906-1966. *Nebraska Hist. 1967 48(3): 249-266*. Using census data from 37 western counties and contrasting these counties with eastern Nebraska, the author concludes that western Nebraska, settled somewhat later, gained from the experience of eastern Nebraska settlers. They had the advantage of improved technology and developed a type of land use better suited to the area. Crops raised in the 37 western counties fared better in wartime inflation and the farmers relatively less in periods of depression. The value of agricultural production was better and the average mortgage debt was lower in western counties.

R. Lowitt

4078. Scott, Roy V. AMERICAN RAILROADS AND AGRICULTURAL EXTENSION, 1900-1914: A STUDY IN RAILWAY DEVELOPMENTAL TECHNIQUES. *Business Hist. R. 1965 39(1): 74-98*. After having read a cross section of the Granger and Populist literature regarding the railroads, one would suspect that the railroads were the one and only natural enemy of the farmer. The author delineates the fallacy in this by showing that the railroads, while looking out solely for their own interests, not only extended agriculture by establishing model farms and encouraging the germinal county agent idea, but also improved farming methods through their educational trains and financial backing for county fairs and rural youth organizations. Thus it would seem that the railroad man and the farmer were in actuality partners in progress rather than commercial competitors. Based on agricultural quarterlies and the private letters of railroad men and governmental agents.

J. H. Krenkel

4079. Shatraw, Milton E. THRASHIN' TIME. *Am. West 1969 6(4): 32-35*. Reminisces about boyhood experiences on a Montana ranch in the first decade of the century. The annual autumn grain threshing time with horse drawn equipment was the highlight of the year for the lad. Excerpted from a forthcoming book.

D. L. Smith

4080. Shover, John L. THE COMMUNIST PARTY AND THE MIDWEST FARM CRISIS OF 1933. *J. of Am. Hist. 1964 51(2): 248-266*. Describes the rural protest movement of the early 1930's and the attempts of the American Communist Party to infiltrate and take advantage of the farmer's discontent, especially in Iowa, Nebraska, and Minnesota. The party assigned some of its best organizers to the work, and an important debate arose over which agrarian program they should pursue. Party objectives, mainly to build class consciousness in rural areas and create an agrarian wing to the proletarian movement, failed, as the New Deal agricultural program brought the farmers needed assistance.

H. J. Silverman

4081. Snedecor, Marie, ed. THE HOMESTEADERS: THEIR DREAMS HELD NO SHADOWS. *Montana 1969 19(2): 10-27*. The letters of Lillie Klein written to her parents from a homestead in Blaine County, Montana, in 1913. There are details of housebuilding and other phases of pioneering in the dry-land wheat area of Montana's "High Line." Illus.

S. R. Davison

4082. Taylor, Paul S. CALIFORNIA FARM LABOR: A REVIEW. *Agric. Hist. 1968 42(1): 49-53*. Reviews Jerold S. Auerbach's *Labor and Liberty; The La Follette Committee and the New Deal* (Indianapolis: Bobbs-Merrill, 1966). California's farm labor problem was peculiar from an early time because land was accumulated into large holdings, and the demand for laborers was fed by a succession of dispossessed persons of myriad races. The sources for the history of California's agricultural labor remain largely unexploited. The La Follette Committe hearings and other sources mentioned by the author should be drawn upon for research in this field.

W. D. Rasmussen

4083. Taylor, Paul S. HAND LABORERS IN THE WESTERN SUGAR BEET INDUSTRY. *Agric. Hist. 1967 41(1): 19-26*. The participation of hand labor was necessary to the establishment of the sugar beet industry. About the turn of the century, the industry decided to rely primarily upon immigrant laborers. The processing factors took the lead in securing this immigrant labor, first Japanese and then Mexican. The emphasis upon this labor led eventually to government intervention in immigration, the tariff, and legal protections for sugar beet workers. Based largely on congressional hearings.

W. D. Rasmussen

4084.　Tweton, D. Jerome.　THE BORDER FARMER AND THE CANADIAN RECIPROCITY ISSUE, 1911-1912. *Agric. Hist. 1963 37(4): 235-241.* The reciprocity treaty negotiated with Canada in 1911 seemed to favor American manufacturing and newspaper interests, and would permit the Canadian farmer to compete in the United States market on equal terms. The treaty was strongly opposed by North Dakota and Minnesota farmers, who felt that it proved President Taft was not in touch or in sympathy with the agrarian interests. This feeling contributed to Taft's defeat in 1912.　　　　　　　　　　　W. D. Rasmussen

4085.　Tweton, D. Jerome.　THEODORE ROOSEVELT AND LAND LAW REFORM. *Mid-America 1967 49(1): 44-54.* In 1903 President Roosevelt appointed a commission to investigate public land problems. The Public Lands Commission task was to study and recommend changes in the entire system of American land law. By 1905 the commission presented its report which advocated seven basic changes. Congress failed to respond to most of the recommendations by the time Roosevelt left office, although new homestead legislation was enacted. Based primarily on government documents, 41 notes.　　　　　　　L. D. Silveri

4086.　Waage, Wesley A.　THE WHEAT GROWER: A JOURNAL OF THE COMMODITY POOLING MOVEMENT. *North Dakota Q. 1971 39(3): 29-33.* Analyzes *The Wheat Grower,* the official publication of the wheat growers' pool in North Dakota during the years 1923-31. Finds the paper typical in its orientation toward farm life, but too optimistic about the future of pooling as a device for increasing the farmer's income. Overoptimism resulted in disillusionment when the promised results did not materialize. The final decline of the wheat pool, however, is attributed to the disastrous economic conditions of the 1930's, not to the faults of *The Wheat Grower.* Based on secondary sources and files of the Wheat Growers' Association; 9 notes.　　　　J. F. Mahoney

4087.　Walther, Thomas R.　SOME ASPECTS OF ECONOMIC MOBILITY IN BARRETT TOWNSHIP OF THOMAS COUNTY, 1885-1905. *Kansas Hist. Q. 1971 37(3): 281-287.* Examines the success or failure of individual farmers in Kansas by comparing data on 64 farmers found on the 1895 manuscript census of agriculture. There was a pattern of adaptation and industry on the part of the successful farmers of Thomas County. The 10 farm families that had enjoyed the greatest amount of vertical economic and social mobility before 1895 had the highest average in the value of farm machinery, winter and spring wheat acreage, corn acreage, barley acreage, sale of poultry and eggs, and number of cows and cattle. The successful farmer learned to adapt to the plains. Based on secondary sources and Kansas tract books of the General Land Office; 16 notes.　　　　　　　　　W. F. Zornow

4088.　Williams, Elizabeth Evenson.　W. R. RONALD: PRAIRIE EDITOR AND AN AAA ARCHITECT. *South Dakota Hist. 1971 1(3): 272-291.* Summarizes the life and journalistic career of William Roy Ronald, editor of the Mitchell *Daily Republic,* 1909-51. He was a Progressive Republican who sometimes took Democratic positions and became part of an influential group that wrote and promoted farm legislation. Ronald chaired the committee which wrote the bill that enacted the Agriculture Adjustment Act of 1933. Ronald, said an associate, was "'a courageous and dynamic person, and a tower of influence in South Dakota'" Illus., 82 notes.　　　　　　　　　D. H. Swift

4089.　Wilson, James A.　THE ARIZONA CATTLE INDUSTRY: ITS POLITICAL AND PUBLIC IMAGE, 1950-1963. *Arizona and the West 1966 8(4): 339-348.* All but about one-tenth of the land in Arizona is controlled by the State or Federal Government, most of it by the latter. With State and Federal lands available for grazing, many ranchers were encouraged to invest heavily in blooded stock and equipment. At midcentury when governmental policies began to alter the foundations of their industry they objected vociferously. When Federal grazing fees were raised in the name of conservation, the public did not sympathize with the cattlemen who objected that this would force sizable reduction in available grazing land. Most people did not realize that the cattlemen themselves, to maximize profitable beef production, were far-sighted conservationists; they had put in about three-fifths of the fences, dikes, diversion dams, cattleguards, and other improvements on Arizona's public domain. Transferring public domain into a limited use status would also deprive the State of much needed tax revenue. And so it was with regard to several questions: drought relief, the opposition of sports-

men and naturalists, State legislation to change the per acre lease base, and other issues. Although they were openly attacked, ranching interests answered effectively and convincingly but never loud enough to be heard above the chorus of unfavorable opinion. The cattlemen came to be regarded as land-grabbers, political corrupters, and preyers on the natural resources of the State and Nation. 21 notes.　　　　D. L. Smith

4090.　Wright, Carl C.　PRAIRIE SCENES AND MOODS. *Southwestern Hist. Q. 1969 72(3): 385-394.* A reminiscence of the author's childhood days on a farm in the blackland prairies of south central Texas in the 1920's. 12 notes.　　　　　　　D. L. Smith

4091.　Wyman, Walker D. and Hart, John D.　THE LEGEND OF CHARLIE GLASS. *Colorado Mag. 1969 46(1): 40-54.* Charlie Glass was a Negro cowboy and top foreman, in the twenties and thirties, of the Lazy Y Cross Ranch of Oscar L. Turner in western Colorado and eastern Utah. He became involved in the cattlemen-sheepmen wars and killed a Basque sheepherder in 1921. In the trial he was acquitted of the murder charge. However, in 1937 he was killed in a truck accident under peculiar circumstances which suggest foul play by two transient sheepherders. Based largely on newspaper accounts and interviews; illus.
　　　　　　　　　　　　　　　　　　　O. H. Zabel

4092.　Young, Karl.　FIRST CUTTING: A REMEMBRANCE OF THE HIGH PLAINS. *Am. West 1966 3(4): 16-19, 72-74.* When the author graduated from high school in southern Utah in 1924, he bought a packsaddle and a horse and headed for Crow Indian country in Montana. In Cody, Wyoming, he hired out to a farmer to replenish his depleted resources. Haying and the chores were his duties. For the first cutting ever made on one field, the young man was given an unevenly matched team of horses, one of which had never been used for such a purpose. Even though an accident which resulted in the loss of one of the horses relaxed the distant attitude of the farmer toward his hired hand, the young man struck out once more for Crow country. A "remembrance" of the author. Illus.　　　　　　　D. L. Smith

4093.　Zucker, Norman L.　GEORGE W. NORRIS: PROGRESSIVE FROM THE PLAINS. *Nebraska Hist. 1964 45(2): 147-164.* Examines Norris' views on agriculture and agricultural legislation, particularly in the 1920's. Norris' agricultural bias is criticized as unsound and his legislative suggestions as unrealistic.　　　　　　R. Lowitt

Conservation and Reclamation

4094.　Alexander, Thomas G.　SENATOR REED SMOOT AND WESTERN LAND POLICY, 1905-1920. *Arizona and the West 1971 13(3): 245-264.* The senatorial career of Republican Reed Smoot (1862-1941) of Utah is usually associated with staunch conservatism, party regularity, and high protective tariff. Equally important, however, were his contributions to conservation and public land policy. In service on the Committee on Public Lands and Surveys (1905-33), Smoot emerged as a leader of the business-minded conservationists. This group believed that private business and the States in which the resources were located should be included in the conservation consideration. Smoot championed public control of forests, the establishment of national parks, and the use of policies that would discourage wasteful exploitation and encourage businessmen to invest in systematic development. Smoot's role in securing enduring conservation legislation was significant. He was also instrumental in reclamation of arid land and in enlarged homesteads legislation. 4 illus., 35 notes.　　　　　　　　　　　D. L. Smith

4095.　Antrei, Albert.　A WESTERN PHENOMENON, THE ORIGIN AND DEVELOPMENT OF WATERSHED RESEARCH: MANTI, UTAH, 1889. *Am. West 1971 8(2): 42-47, 59.* About 1870 sheep and wool production began to pay off handsomely to the people of Manti, who lived at the foot of a canyon which cut up to the Wasatch Plateau in central Utah. Thousands of tons of wool were produced on the tablelands of the plateau. The plateau was gradually denuded. In 1889, the waters of the canyon "scoured its channel with all the junk of nature and dumped the whole mess in Manti's lap." This became an annual and worsening occurrence. In 1903 the Manti Forest Reserve was created, all grazing was curtailed on the watershed, and the long process of natural repair was begun. As new Federal conservation agencies accumulated experience and knowledge, intelligent management was introduced to the Manti watershed so the area's economy would not suffer. In 1911 an experiment station was established on the Wasatch Plateau and a range survey was made. Here many of the principles of range management were formulated. 9 illus., map.　　　　　D. L. Smith

4096. Arrington, Leonard J. and Dittmer, Lowell. RECLAMATION IN THREE LAYERS: THE OGDEN RIVER PROJECT, 1934-1965. *Pacific Hist. R. 1966 35(1): 15-34*. Traces the construction problems and contributions of the Pine View Dam near Ogden, Utah.

J. McCutcheon

4097. Baldwin, Donald N. WILDERNESS: CONCEPT AND CHALLENGE. *Colorado Mag. 1967 44(3): 224-240*. Traces the development of the U.S. Forest Service's concept of the use of wilderness areas for recreational purposes. When Lyndon B. Johnson signed the Wilderness Bill on 3 September 1964, he brought to a successful culmination a conservation battle that had been fought since 1919, for which Arthur Carhart deserves credit. In May 1919 Carhart became Recreation Engineer throughout the Rocky Mountain Region of the Forest Service. He drafted a plan that became a model for other areas of the national forests stressing preservation and protection of natural features in primitive areas where no roads or cabins were to be built. Aldo Leopold, then assistant forester of District 3 in Albuquerque, New Mexico, has been credited with leading the movement to preserve America's wilderness heritage, but the author maintains that Leopold took up the campaign after conferring with Carhart, and that Carhart should have the title "father of the Wilderness concept." 5 illus., 64 notes.　　　　I. W. Van Noppen

4098. Bandy, William R. GHOSTS TOOK OVER THE TUNNEL. *Ann. of Wyoming 1966 38(1): 76-83*. A reminiscent account of drilling four irrigation tunnels as part of the S. L. Wiley project to bring water from the South Fork of the Shoshone River 30 miles to Dry Creek Valley in the Oregon Basin of Wyoming in 1907-08. Included is a description of the transportation in the area, the camp buildings, camp recreation, and the tunneling activities. The author describes his role as a young engineer and his fear that two of the tunnels might not meet inside the mountain. He also gives his reaction to the tunnel sites while revisiting them 57 years later. Illus.　　　　R. L. Nichols

4099. Bartlett, Richard A. THOSE INFERNAL MACHINES IN YELLOWSTONE. *Montana 1970 20(3): 16-29*. Examines the circumstances of the first sanctioned use of cars in Yellowstone National Park in 1915 after a decade of agitation for their admittance. Poor roads and danger of frightening horses were arguments used against automobiles. Resistance was led by franchised companies who operated horse-drawn stages. The park is shown as a retreat for wealthy vacationers before the use of cars opened the area to the general public. Based on official correspondence; illus., 22 notes.　　　　S. R. Davison

4100. Bergman, H. J. THE RELUCTANT DISSENTER: GOVERNOR HAY OF WASHINGTON AND THE CONSERVATION PROBLEM. *Pacific Northwest Q. 1971 62(1): 27-33*. Marion E. Hay (1865-1933), respected as a man of solid achievements in his term as Governor, was a supporter of conservation who was trapped by the paradoxes of the time, 1908-12. In many ways Hay demonstrated a constructive attitude toward conservation, but his disagreements about the means rather than the ends of Federal control of natural resources made him appear in a bad light. In that day of Gifford Pinchot's energetic activities, a moderate such as Hay, who "recognized the need for protection of the nation's natural resources but believed that it should be balanced by a similar recognition of the need for the continued economic growth of the states affected by the conservation program," was an open target for criticism.　　　　C. C. Gorchels

4101. Buchholz, Curtis W. W. R. LOGAN AND GLACIER NATIONAL PARK. *Montana 1969 19(3): 3-17*. In 1911 Glacier Park's first superintendent William R. Logan confronted the problem which faces all administrators of public lands - to what degree should nature be preserved and to what extent should resources be utilized? Logan saw as his first duty making the park accessible to the public. Building of roads and trails was delayed during the first summer by serious fires in the area and by problems concerning land titles. His policy of recreation at the

expense of total preservation has been followed generally by his successors. Illus., 58 notes.　　　　S. R. Davison

4102. Clepper, Henry. THE FOREST SERVICE BACKLASHED. *Forest Hist. 1968 11(4): 6-15*. Gifford Pinchot was replaced in 1910 as chief of the Forest Service by Henry Graves. The economic enemies of the national forest system in the years 1910-20 included the organized mining interests of the West, stockmen and sheepmen, water power firms, and land speculators. Legislators tried to return the national forests to the States and thereby convert them eventually to private ownership. The Forest Service had to investigate false mining claims made to obtain timberland. Senators Joseph W. Bailey of Texas, William E. Borah and Weldon B. Heyburn of Idaho, and Albert B. Fall of New Mexico attacked the Forest Service. The Forest Service made gains. The National Park Service Act was passed in 1916. 12 photos, notes.　　　B. A. Vatter

4103. Coulter, C. Brewster. THE NEW SETTLERS ON THE YAKIMA PROJECT, 1880-1910. *Pacific Northwest Q. 1970 61(1): 10-21*. Gives the background of the creation in 1906 of the government-sponsored reclamation project in the Yakima Valley in the State of Washington. The author describes the five waves of migration which brought settlers to the area before and after irrigation agriculture was developed. Strife between developers of irrigation facilities and farmers is described, and some political problems are cited.　　　　C. C. Gorchels

4104. Cracroft, Richard H. THROUGH UTAH AND THE WESTERN PARKS: THOMAS WOLFE'S FAREWELL TO AMERICA. *Utah Hist. Q. 1969 37(3): 290-306*. A western trip in 1938, capped by a whirlwind tour of several national parks, confirmed Wolfe's view that a major theme in American life was the tension between the fecund beauty of its landscape and the sterility of its culture. Based primarily on Wolfe's published account, *A Western Journal, A Daily Log of the Great Parks Trip, June 20-July 2, 1938* (Pittsburgh, 1951).　　　　S. L. Jones

4105. Dobbs, Gordon B., ed. H. M. CHITTENDEN'S "NOTES ON FORESTRY PAPER." *Pacific Northwest Q. 1966 57(2): 73-81*. In response to successful organization of conservation forces by Theodore Roosevelt and Gifford Pinchot against waste of forests, Hiram M. Chittenden (civil engineer and historian who lived in the West for most of his career) wrote a dissenting paper which criticized Pinchot as being one-sided, dishonest, and dedicated to scientific fallacies. The paper had substantial impact, 1908-16, but did not divert widespread belief that standing forests prevent floods.　　　　C. C. Gorchels

4106. Dodds, Gordon B., ed. CONSERVATION AND RECLAMATION IN THE TRANS-MISSISSIPPI WEST: A CRITICAL BIBLIOGRAPHY. *Arizona and the West 1971 13(2): 143-171*. This selected bibliography of some 130 annotated items constitutes "the significant secondary works on conservation and reclamation" published from 1917 through 1970. They are listed chronologically by publication dates. Few studies appeared before World War I. Serious attention was given to the subject in the post-War period; and under the influence of the New Deal, historians became concerned with the economic aspects of conservation, especially flood control, forests, irrigation, and reclamation. In the 1950's a shift in emphasis put the focus on the "aesthetic-spiritual" concerns of the "preservationists." In recent years the treatment of history of conservation in the West has been quite uneven. The field is wide open for further scholarly studies.　　　　D. L. Smith

4107. Doerr, Arthur H. DRY CONDITIONS IN OKLAHOMA IN THE 1930'S AND 1950'S AS DELIMITED BY THE ORIGINAL THORNTHWAITE CLIMATIC CLASSIFICATION. *Great Plains J. 1963 2(2): 67-76*. Uses the Thornthwaite Climatic Classification to compare the drought periods of 1930-38 and 1950-58 in Oklahoma, basing conclusions on the reports of 89 stations in the state. Annual maps for the years considered show areas classified as desert, semiarid, subhumid, humid and perhumid. Concludes that the two periods were very similar except that in the 1950's men were better prepared for the dry period by conservation techniques, irrigation and crop insurance. The author insists that "the present humid conditions are simply a pleasant interlude before drought conditions descend again in the 1970's." O. H. Zabel

4108. DuBois, Coert. TRAIL BLAZERS. *Forest Hist. 1965 9(3): 14-22*. A private landowner inside a forest reserve could receive negotiable script for outside land. The big lumber firms bought up the script, so in 1903 Gifford Pinchot, chief of the Forest Service, and Theodore Roosevelt enlarged the reserve area in a countermove. Coert DuBois was assigned to Colorado to survey boundaries for the new reserves covering La Plata Mountains and the San Juan River and to Montana. In 1905 when forest reserves were transferred from the Department of the Interior to the Department of Agriculture, the U.S. Forest Service was formed from the old Bureau of Forestry. The Land Office employees came under the Forest Service, which employed only Civil Service workers, and so the Land Office work had to be reorganized to bring it up to Civil Service standards. To accomplish the reorganization, DuBois was sent to the Gila National Forest and Lincoln National Forest in New Mexico and to the present Sequoia National Forest in California. Excerpted from Coert DuBois' privately printed autobiography, 3 photos.

B. A. Vatter

4109. Elwell, Alcott Farrar. HIS DIARY, WYOMING 1908, AS CAMP COOK, U.S. GEODETIC SURVEY ROOSEVELT LIGNITE CONSERVATION. *Ann. of Wyoming 1966 38(2): 142-172.* Includes portions of the diary kept by Alcott F. Elwell for 2 July-21 October 1908. Elwell, a Harvard College undergraduate, worked on the survey team in Wyoming to help meet his educational expenses. His diary discusses train travel, the diet and living conditions of the survey team, personal friction between team members, the terrain and weather, and infrequent trips into nearby towns. The diary is in the collections of the Wyoming State Archives and Historical Department. Illus.

R. L. Nichols

4110. Flynn, Ted P. FROM BULLS TO BULLDOZERS. *Forest Hist. 1963 7(3): 14-17.* Ted P. Flynn, a French-Canadian logger, became a construction engineer and equipment designer for the U.S. Forest Service in Oregon. He and Ralph B. Moore built a counterbalanced, hand-lift angle blade bulldozer and attached it to a Cletrac tractor in 1923. The appearance of bulldozers at the equipment display of the 1928 forest engineers' meeting at Santa Barbara, California, stimulated their production. Flynn continued to improve the model at the Forest Service Laboratory in Portland, Oregon. 4 illus.

B. A. Vatter

4111. Foster, James C. THE DEER OF KAIBAB: FEDERAL-STATE CONFLICT IN ARIZONA. *Arizona and the West 1970 12(3): 255-268.* In late 1924 three sportsmen were routinely arrested for possession of out-of-season deer in Arizona. The State thus asserted its right to control deer hunting in the Kaibab National Forest in the northern part of the State. Arizona won the first round in the dispute over licensing and establishing game seasons. About a year later the State attempted to extend its jurisdiction, which resulted in a Federal-State showdown. For three years a battle raged between the U.S. Forest Service's wildlife management experts and the politically-appointed State game wardens. The State contended that control over wildlife was legally a State prerogative. The legal definition of Federal property rights within an established State was the crux of the matter. In *Hunt vs. the United States* (1928) the Supreme Court upheld Federal jurisdiction over wildlife in nationally-owned reserves in special situations. Although a precedent decision, all the questions were not resolved because the legal and legislative battles still continue to plague game managers. 33 notes.

D. L. Smith

4112. Foster, Laura. HONEYMOON IN HETCH HETCHY: A 1914 GLIMPSE OF A YOSEMITE VALLEY - FOCAL POINT OF AMERICA'S FIRST MAJOR CONSERVATION CRUSADE. *Am. West 1971 8(3): 10-15.* Hetch Hetchy Valley of the Tuolumne River in the Sierra Nevada of California was said to have rivaled Yosemite Valley a few miles to its southeast. In the 1910's a dam created a reservoir which provides most of the water supply for San Francisco. Hetch Hetchy represents the absolute defeat of one of America's first conservation crusades. In 1914, in the midst of the controversy, two young people, Dorothy Stillman and Robert Duryea, whose families were on opposite sides of the question, married and then spent their two-week honeymoon on a mule-packing trip to the floor of the valley. Their conclusion was a qualified affirmative in favor of construction of the dam. 10 illus.

D. L. Smith

4113. Fritz, Emanuel. RECOLLECTIONS OF FORT VALLEY, 1916-1917. *Forest Hist. 1964 8(3): 2-6.* Emanuel Fritz was a city boy assigned to a forest research station in northern Arizona. In winter there were heavy snowfalls. In summer the small staff was kept busy with data

collection and reforestation studies. Much time was devoted to maintenance work, repairing buildings, plumbing, fencing, and the single-wire telephone line to Flagstaff.

R. S. Burke

4114. Garber, C. Y. FIRE ON PINE CREEK. *Idaho Yesterdays 1967 11(2): 26-30.* The author relates his personal experience of a forest fire on Pine Creek in the Coeur d'Alene district of Northern Idaho. There were several mills and mining companies in the area of the fire, but only one company, the Constitution, escaped damage. The courageous efforts of some 20 men, including the author, who fought the fire continuously for over 36 hours, were the reason the Constitution buildings were unscathed. Illus.

B. B. Swift

4115. Glass, Mary Ellen. THE FIRST NATIONALLY SPONSORED ARID LAND RECLAMATION PROJECT: THE NEWLANDS PROJECT IN CHURCHILL COUNTY, NEVADA. *Nevada Hist. Soc. Q. 1971 14(1): 2-12.* When Francis Griffith Newlands arrived in Nevada in 1889 the mining boom was over and the need for a stable agriculture was apparent. In 1890 Newlands presented to the people of Nevada his scheme to remake the desert into an agricultural paradise. Churchill County in western Nevada was chosen as the area to be converted by a vast system of irrigation canals and ditches. Instead of a vast agricultural utopia, only modest results were achieved. The soils of the area were not adequate to support heavy agriculture, so that only about 70 thousand acres were ever irrigated. Retrospection followed optimistic legislative action and planning and the realities of desert reclamation soon became apparent to all. Photo, 41 notes.

E. P. Costello

4116. Glass, Mary Ellen. THE NEWLANDS RECLAMATION PROJECT: YEARS OF INNOCENCE, 1903-1907. *J. of the West 1968 7(1): 55-63.* The early trials and tribulations (high cost of construction, alkali soils, and floods) of the Truckee-Carson reclamation project of West-central Nevada. Based largely on newspaper articles; 35 notes.

E. A. Erickson

4117. Gressley, Gene M. ARTHUR POWELL DAVIS, RECLAMATION, AND THE WEST. *Agric. Hist. 1968 42(3): 241-257.* The Reclamation Service was under constant political attack and torn by internal dissension almost from its establishment until the mid-1920's. In the early 1920's, the director Arthur Powell Davis, a celebrated civil engineer, was summarily dismissed by Secretary of the Interior Hubert Work. Work announced that a businessman was needed to manage reclamation. Davis, however, had a definite economic and political philosophy drawn from the writings of Henry George and from the Progressive movement. The service represented an attempt to merge the conflicting ideologies of private and public interest, of local decentralization and Federal centralization. The answer lay not in a businessman, but in a compromise of vested interests in a Federal power structure. Based upon manuscripts in the Western History Research Center, Laramie, Wyoming.

W. D. Rasmussen

4118. Hampton, H. Duane. THE ARMY AND THE NATIONAL PARKS. *Forest Hist. 1966 10(3): 3-17.* Yellowstone National Park was established in 1872. Civilian control and a lack of appropriations by Congress failed to preserve the park against depredation by private interests. Captain Moses Harris, US Cavalry, became park superintendent in 1886. The park was preserved and developed. Army control was used subsequently in other parks, especially in California. Civilian control was reinstated when the Army wanted to withdraw from park duty in order to have full force available for the US intervention in the Mexican civil war, and the National Park Service was created in 1916 under President Woodrow Wilson. 5 photos, map, lithograph, 55 notes.

B. A. Vatter

4119. Holsinger, M. Paul. WYOMING V. COLORADO REVISITED. THE UNITED STATES SUPREME COURT AND THE LARAMIE RIVER CONTROVERSY, 1911-1922. *Ann. of Wyoming 1970 42(1): 47-56.* Discusses the significance of irrigation to Wyoming agriculture and the threat posed by the actions of water companies in Colorado which sought to divert the flow of the Laramie River. The Wyoming State government brought suit against Colorado on this issue, and the resulting case *Wyoming v. Colorado* dragged on for a decade. Justice Willis Van Devanter eventually wrote the decision which established the judicial foundation for Federal water policies in the West. This ruling gave Wyoming the bulk of the water in question. Based on court records, manuscript material in the Library of Congress, and printed secondary material; 37 notes.   R. L. Nichols

4120. Johnson, Paul C. TURN OF THE WHEEL: THE MOTOR CAR VERSUS YOSEMITE. *California Hist. Q. 1972 51(3): 205-212.* In 1913, the Department of the Interior allowed automobiles to enter Yosemite National Park. Reproduces a 1914 list of 65 restrictions placed on the automobile. Park restrictions included a speed limit of 10 miles per hour, limitations on times of entry, and granting right of way to pack trains and teams. After 60 years, the rules seem quaintly laughable; but the National Park Service, observing that 10 thousand autos a day can be found in the park on holiday weekends, has plans to return eventually to the original 1901 ban on automobiles. The regulations are reproduced from an original copy at the National Park Service Reference Library in Yosemite. 3 photos, 3 notes.   A. Hoffman

4121. Koch, Elers. LAUNCHING THE U.S.F.S. IN THE NORTH-ERN REGION. *Forest Hist. 1965 9(3): 9-13.* Between 1903 and 1906 western national forests were organized, taking their present regional shape in 1908. Between 1903 and 1905 Koch and several other young foresters set up the national forest system. Koch rode horseback on the Shasta and in the Santa Monica Mountains in California, the Lewis and Clark National Forest of the Gallatin, Tabacco Root Range, and the Castle Mountains; the breaks of the Little Missouri in North Dakota, the Big Horn in Wyoming, and the Lolo in Montana. In 1905 he administered civil service examinations for rangers. A field test showed the applicant's ability to survive in wild country, and literacy was tested in a written examination. Koch began administering the Lolo, Bitterroot, and Missoula Forests in 1906. Trail construction and fire control occupied his attention in 1908. Adapted from reminiscences in *Early Days in the Forest Service,* published by the Northern Region, U.S. Forest Service, Missoula, Montana; photo.   B. A. Vatter

4122. Lillard, Richard G. THE SIEGE AND CONQUEST OF A NATIONAL PARK. *Am. West 1968 5(1): 28-32, 67-72.* The 20th-century years before World War I were momentous in the history of national parks. Through conferences, lobbying, and politics, whether automobiles should be permitted in the parks provoked much agonizing soul-searching and serious debate. Yosemite Valley in California was the test case. A Department of the Interior 1913 decision to make the parks as accessible as possible to the great mass of people opened the floodgates. The automobile, according to the author, has brought more downgrading changes in five decades than five thousand years of the ravages of nature itself. 6 illus., biblio. note.   D. L. Smith

4123. Luten, Daniel B. THE USE AND MISUSE OF A RIVER. *Am. West 1967 4(2): 47-53, 73-75.* After the details of the geography and the geology of the Colorado River, the author traces the history of the use of its water. The Colorado River Compact of 1922 provided for an equal division between upper and lower basins. Later, a treaty with Mexico assured that country of a 10th of the river's flow. More recently the U.S. Supreme Court redefined the shares of California, Arizona, and Nevada. Dams and reservoirs were created and others planned for flood control, power generation, irrigation, and other uses. To concern for the river's usefulness was added, beginning about 1955, an increasing concern for the preservation of its beauty and wildness. The problem is to determine the part of wisdom in resolving conflicts between utility and beauty. The author pessimistically feels that conservationists are fighting a losing battle. 2 maps, 5 charts, biblio. notes.   D. L. Smith

4124. Macinko, George. THE COLUMBIA BASIN PROJECT: EX-PECTATIONS, REALIZATIONS, IMPLICATIONS. *Geographical R. 1963 53(2): 185-199.* Traces the origins, growth, and limited results of the Columbia Basin Project with the purposes of indicating what future developments may be anticipated in the field of reclamation. Grand Coulee Dam, begun in 1934, ushered in the land use period that was marked by the unfolding of the Columbia Basin Project comprising two and a half million acres. The project began operation in 1948, by which date wheat farming had been reestablished over much of the eastern area. Various factors made project costs greatly exceed expectations. Land use that was judged best "scientifically" was not used because the farmers were not able to finance the transition from row crops to livestock operations. Future irrigation, the author predicts, will be more costly than that

of the past. The granting of priority to irrigation precludes the development of industries requiring large quantities of water, despite the fact that industrial uses of water are far more profitable. Greater flexibility and reduction of time lag will be required if reclamation developments are to thrive. Map, graphs, 21 notes.   E. P. Stickney

4125. Martinson, Arthur D. MOUNT RAINIER NATIONAL PARK: FIRST YEARS. *Forest Hist. 1966 10(3): 27-33.* President William McKinley signed the Mount Rainier National Park Act 2 March 1899. Unlike Yellowstone and the California parks, Rainier's problem was not preservation of itself but creation of accessibility through roads and publicity. The Rainier Committee, formed by local Chambers of Commerce and Rotary Clubs, lobbied for Federal funds and publicized the park through the mass media. 3 photos, 29 notes.   B. A. Vatter

4126. Maunder, Elwood R., ed. MEMOIRS OF A FORESTER. *Forest Hist. 1967 10(4): 6-12,29-35.* David T. Mason studied forestry at Yale University. Sam Dana was his classmate; H. H. Chapman and Henry Graves his teachers. Mason worked for the US Forest Service from 1907 to 1915 in Washington, D. C.; Montezuma National Forest at Durango, Colorado; and with Albert W. Cooper in Deerlodge National Forest surrounding Butte and Anaconda, Montana. From 1915 to 1921 he was on the forestry faculty at the University of California. He organized the timber valuation section of the Bureau of Internal Revenue (1919-20). Partly as a result of the contacts he made while working for Internal Revenue, in 1921 he started a forestry consulting firm in Portland, Oregon. 9 photos.   B. A. Vatter

4127. McCarthy, G. Michael. WHITE RIVER FOREST RESERVE: THE CONSERVATION CONFLICT. *Colorado Mag. 1972 49(1): 55-67.* The last two decades of the 19th century saw the first major controversy over conservation in Colorado. The problem centered around the agitation for and the creation of the 1,198,180-acre White River Forest Reserve - Colorado's first - in 1891. The wastefulness of natural resources by the pioneer gave rise to a new idea: the Nation's resources were not inexhaustible and the Federal Government should protect them. Conservationists included sportsmen, tourist promoters, and some settlers who desired protection. Opposition to the reserve was led by H. H. Eddy, Speaker of Colorado's House of Representatives and cattleman, and included community developers, ranchers, the bulk of the settlers, and some exploiters. Opposition to the reserve continued throughout the 1890's, and evasion of the law was widespread; however, "the White River controversy brought into clear relief for the first time the issues of the conservation movement." Illus., 33 notes.   O. H. Zabel

4128. McCloskey, Michael. THE LAST BATTLE OF THE RED-WOODS. *Am. West 1969 6(5): 55-64.* When the Save-the-Redwoods League was founded in 1918, a campaign was launched to establish a redwood national park in California. The prime time for its creation would have been the 1920's and 1930's while some of the best forests were still intact, but the time was not ripe politically. Lumbering, disastrous floods, freeway extension into the region, and other eroding factors decimated the forests. With only about one-seventh of the original Pacific Coast redwood forest remaining uncut, it was the 1960's before monumental opposition was overcome; the Redwood National Park became a reality in 1968. It was the most expensive park ever established. Its creation pioneered new guidelines by repossessing a national asset that had fallen into private hands and by using congressional condemnation of land to create a park. Conservationists regard the park as too small but better than nothing. They are still trying to enlarge the area involved and to further protective guarantees written into legislation. 3 illus.   D. L. Smith

4129. McGee, Gale. WHAT IRRIGATION MEANS TO WYO-MING. *J. of the West 1968 7(1): 6-9.* Surveys the impact of irrigation on the economy of Wyoming. If it were not for irrigation, largely due to the Reclamation Act of 1902, there would be little agriculture in Wyoming today. In 1965 two-thirds of Wyoming farms (one and one-half million acres) were under irrigation. In that same year agriculture, one of the State's primary industries, had a return of 183 million dollars.   E. A. Erickson

4130. Mercer, Duane D. THE COLORADO CO-OPERATIVE COMPANY. *Colorado Mag. 1967 44(4): 293-306.* In 1894 a group of 10 organized the Colorado Co-operative, a utopian or socialistic society. The society bought 2,000 acres in Tabeguache Park. The land had to be irrigated by water from the San Miguel River 15 miles away. Settlers were recruited. Each must own one share of stock in the co-operative. Members worked very hard to dig the ditch and bring water. Private property ownership was permitted. Internal discord occurred but entertainment helped unite the members. The ditch was finished, water reached the park, but members who had water refused further ditch work. Private enterprise caused the failure of the co-operative in 1909. 4 illus., 71 notes.

I. W. Van Noppen

4131. Meredith, Howard L. SMALL DAM POLITICS: THE SANDSTONE CREEK PROJECT. *Great Plains J. 1967 6(2): 97-107.* Describes the development of flood control in the Sandstone Creek area in western Oklahoma, and how the area served as a model for later developments. Clearly portrayed is the struggle between the Corps of Engineers which supported large downstream reservoirs and the Soil Conservation Service which proposed small upstream control dams. The efficiency and added benefits of the latter were demonstrated at Sandstone Creek, but the author concludes that a combination of both produces the best kind of flood control. Based on primary sources, map, 31 notes.

O. H. Zabel

4132. Messing, John. PUBLIC LANDS, POLITICS, AND PROGRESSIVES: THE OREGON LAND FRAUD TRIALS, 1903-1910. *Pacific Hist. R. 1966 35(1): 35-66.* Argues that the land fraud trials, involving the General Land Office, were important in ending abuses involving public lands, helping shape the Roosevelt conservation policy, stirring up public opinion, and making Francis J. Heney, prosecutor during the trials, a radical reformer for land law change.

J. McCutcheon

4133. Nash, Roderick. A HOME FOR THE SPIRIT: A BRIEF HISTORY OF THE WILDERNESS PRESERVATION MOVEMENT - THE STORY OF AN IDEA GIVEN THE STRENGTH OF LAW. *Am. West 1971 8(1): 40-47.* The first major American wilderness controversy was the 1908-13 attempt to keep a part of the Yosemite National Park from being developed as a municipal reservoir. Although the preservationists lost that battle, they learned much from the experience as to method and rationale. By molding public opinion and employing professional lobbyists they were able to mount a broad public protest. In the 1950's a move to secure Federal legislation for a proposed dam that threatened the Dinosaur National Monument on the Colorado-Utah border was defeated. Preservation had prevailed for the first time in a major confrontation, one in which the sanctity of all national monuments and parks seemed at stake. With this encouragement a campaign was mounted that led to the establishment of the National Wilderness Preservation System by Federal law in 1964. The momentum thus generated has carried the wilderness movement to a series of impressive triumphs since then. 5 illus., biblio. note.

D. L. Smith

4134. Neil, J. Meredith. A FORGOTTEN ALTERNATIVE: RECLAMATION BY THE STATES. *Idaho Yesterdays 1965 9(4): 18-21.* Pressure for governmental irrigation programs resulted from the desire to regulate private canal companies. The Carey Act (1894) ceded arid land to the States for reclamation development. Rees Davis argued for irrigation districts. He said that canal companies should recognize the change in popular sentiment and give up their property for a "reasonable consideration." Davis planned for underwriting, by the State, of "the financing of irrigation projects," and repayment "on a long-term basis by the water charges." The "success of the federal Reclamation Bureau in receiving complete repayment for its huge projects from farmer-users" proved that Davis' plan was feasible.

D. H. Swift

4135. Olson, David S. THE SAVENAC NURSERY: A FOREST SERVICE MEMOIR. *Forest Hist. 1967 11(2): 15-21.* After studying forestry at the University of Nebraska, the author worked as a fire lookout scout during the summers in the national forests. After graduation he headed the Savenac Nursery in Lolo National Forest, Idaho, and at first used his personal checking account to meet his payroll, submitting an expense account to the Federal government. In 1920 when promoted to chief of planting, he moved the head office from Missoula, Montana, to

Savenac, then reluctantly moved it back to Missoula in 1927 where he worked until he joined the Shelterbelt Project in 1934. 8 illus.

B. A. Vatter

4136. Penick, James L., Jr. THE AGE OF THE BUREAUCRAT - ANOTHER VIEW OF THE BALLINGER-PINCHOT CONTROVERSY. *Forest Hist. 1963 7(1/2): 15-20.* President William Howard Taft's Secretary of the Interior, Richard Achilles Ballinger, formerly Theodore Roosevelt's Commissioner of the General Land Office, sought to bring conservation back into the political arena and out of the hands of so-called politically disinterested expert bureaucracies such as those of Gifford Pinchot, Chief of the Forest Service in the Department of Agriculture, and Frederick Haynes Newell, Director of the Reclamation Service. Ballinger believed the policies of the bureaucracies underwrote monopoly by maintaining the status quo within natural resources business enterprises. Although grazing licenses conserved grazing lands, for example, and slowed the process of big businesses getting bigger, they virtually prevented the small business from getting big and reduced new entry of businesses on any scale. Based on the author's unpublished doctoral dissertation at the University of California, Berkeley, in 1962; 28 notes.

B. A. Vatter

4137. Polenberg, Richard. CONSERVATION AND REORGANIZATION: THE FOREST SERVICE LOBBY, 1937-1938. *Agric. Hist. 1965 39(4): 230-239.* The President's committee on Administrative Management proposed in 1937 that the Department of the Interior become a Department of Conservation. It was understood that the Forest Service would be transferred from the Department of Agriculture to the new department. The Forest Service lobby used its influence with politicians and organizations to kill the proposal for a Department of Conservation and obtained assurances the service would not be transferred.

W. D. Rasmussen

4138. Reinhardt, Richard. THE CASE OF THE HARD-NOSED CONSERVATIONISTS. *Am. West 1967 4(1): 52, 54, 85-92.* The Sierra Club of San Francisco was founded in 1892 to stave off commercial exploitation of the natural resources and beauty of the Yosemite Valley. This nonprofit, nonpolitical, and tax-exempt organization has been better known for its promotion of outdoor recreation, its nature publications, and its resolutions favoring sound conservation practices. Of late, however, it has become a rather militant lobbyist group, aggressively pressuring defense of America's natural resources. The tax-exempt status of a private organization taking stands on controversial matters of public policy has been questioned. A fight with the lumber industry over the location of a redwood national park in northern California, and an attack on proposed power dams that would affect the Grand Canyon of the Colorado River, both of which brought prominent nationwide newspaper ads, open letters to public officials, pleas for contributions and letters to congressmen and membership in the club, provoked the Internal Revenue Service to question the club's tax status. Pending the outcome, although the membership is not necessarily pleased with the public image the club now has, the hard-nosed militancy continues to prevail, and probably will no matter what the Internal Revenue Service decides. Reproduces one of the recent advertisements of the club.

D. L. Smith

4139. Richardson, Elmo R. OLYMPIC NATIONAL PARK: 20 YEARS OF CONTROVERSY. *Forest Hist. 1968 12(1): 6-15.* The Olympic National Park was created on the Olympic Peninsula in Washington State between 1897 and 1940 around the Olympic National Forest nucleus designated by President Grover Cleveland and administered by the Forest Service in the Department of Agriculture. Impetus came from the Department of Interior, headed by Harold Ickes, and the Emergency Conservation Committee of New York City. Washington Governor Clarence Martin, under pressure from the commercial forest products investors, opposed President Franklin Delano Roosevelt's creation of the park which included the Olympic Mountains, coniferous forests including rain forest corridors, a Pacific coastline, and the rare Olympic elk, but the voters of the four peninsula counties voted for Roosevelt in a landslide in 1940. 6 photos.

B. A. Vatter

4140. Ryan, Marian L. LOS ANGELES NEWSPAPERS FIGHT THE WATER WAR, 1924-1927. *Southern California Q. 1968 50(2): 177-190.* Los Angeles' search for an adequate water supply brought it into conflict with farming and ranching interest in Owens Valley during the

1920's. Having bought water rights and built a 238-mile aqueduct to Owens Valley early in the century, Los Angeles leaders failed to provide reservoirs to store water for the dry cycles. Therefore, when the drought of the 1920's occurred, there was not enough water for the city and the agrarian interests of Owens Valley. The author admits that poor planning created the problem, but she contends that the situation got out of hand between 1924 and 1927 because of the publicity campaign waged by Los Angeles newspapers. Publicists for the valley's position exaggerated valley grievances and the inequities in the city's proposal to buy up agrarian interest in the valley in order to have enough water. The campaign whipped up by the *Record* and other of the city's newspapers precipitated violent acts against the city's aqueduct and water supply, while the *Los Angeles Times* and other defenders of the city devoted so much space to their defense that they let the real issue slip away. Conviction of two of the valley's leaders for embezzlement in 1927 discredited the valley's position since it appeared to many that these men had been motivated by necessity to cover up their criminal acts. After this event, Los Angeles bought the necessary land and Owens Valley slipped into the limbo which the author believes was inevitable in this confrontation. Based chiefly on Los Angeles newspapers editorials; 46 notes.

W. L. Bowers

4141. Sageser, A. Bower. EDITOR BRISTOW AND THE GREAT PLAINS IRRIGATION REVIVAL OF THE 1890'S. *J. of the West 1964 3(1): 75-89.* The farmer on the Great Plains has always been beset by recurring periods of drought. Many individuals have concluded that irrigation was the answer to this problem. One of the most persistent advocates was the Kansas newspaper publisher and political leader, Joseph L. Bristow. In 1896 he began publication of a small monthly journal, *The Irrigation Farmer.* The thesis of this publication was that the Great Plains could and should be irrigated. As early as the 1880's efforts had been made to irrigate the semiarid region, but for a variety of reasons had failed. Bristow helped organize the Interstate Irrigation Association at Salina, Kansas, in 1893 and thereafter traveled extensively promoting its gospel. Due largely to his speeches and the articles in his newspaper, numerous irrigation associations were established and some projects were inaugurated. His greatest contribution was in supplying accurate information, especially to the areas unable to use river irrigation. 35 notes.

D. N. Brown

4142. Sageser, A. Bower. LOS ANGELES HOSTS AN INTERNATIONAL IRRIGATION CONGRESS. *J. of the West 1965 4(3): 411-424.* The first irrigation congress met in Salt Lake City in 1891. Plans for a meeting in Los Angeles were made and a committee pressed President Cleveland to invite foreign delegates. Editors of irrigation journals publicized the project and in October 1893 the congress was assembled in the Grand Opera House. Prominent speakers reviewed the progress of irrigation in the West and tours were made to the irrigated areas of California. On the final day the committee on resolutions presented a platform calling for the irrigation of arid lands by the Federal Government and changes in water laws of the nation. This platform was adopted and an executive committee was elected. As a result of this conference further activity in irrigation matters was stimulated. Subsequent congresses helped to educate the public as to the need for conservation of water resources. Based on newspapers and other printed sources. Illus., tables, 31 notes.

D. N. Brown

4143. Schmalz, Bruce L. HEADGATES AND HEADACHES: THE POWELL TRACT. *Idaho Yesterdays 1965 9(4): 22-25.* Discusses "a Lost River project which failed." The author explains the problems in trying to develop a dam to divert water in Lost River onto the Powell Tract with the use of private capital. The project, organized under the Carey Act (1894), had the indirect support of the State, which set the price charged for water and supervised the project. Inadequate design and the amount of water required to fulfill crop needs was not considered or understood. The lack of adequate State supervision, laws, and regulations was evident.

D. H. Swift

4144. Sorenson, Willis Conner. THE KANSAS NATIONAL FOREST, 1905-1915. *Kansas Hist. Q. 1969 35(4): 386-395.* The Garden City Forest Reserve, which was established by executive order in 1905, became the Kansas National Forest in 1908. At that time it covered an area of more than three hundred thousand acres. The project was abandoned in 1915. The planners, who hoped to create a large forest for beauty, lumber, fuel, and control of the climate, had to admit that their objectives had

failed. The experiment was not a total loss, however, since it provided the New Dealers with much valuable information when they set out to reforest some of the Southern plains after the dust bowl. Based on articles, Government records, and newspapers; illus., 42 notes.

W. F. Zornow

4145. Steele, Annie Laurie. A HISTORY OF THE SANDSTONE CREEK AREA UP-STREAM FLOOD PREVENTION PROJECT. *Chronicles of Oklahoma 1965 43(4): 432-442.* The Sandstone Creek watershed project pioneered flood control programs in Oklahoma and the nation. The Soil Conservation Service and local landowners sought to make the earth a vast sponge. Deep-rooted grasses were planted. Contour plowing and crop rotation were practiced, miles of terrace and a network of small earth dams were built. This was among the first coordinated programs of land treatment and upstream detention reservoirs for flood control. Its success was dramatic, elimination of floods and erosion, irrigation, increased water supply, increased land value, recreational areas, fishing and wildlife benefits. Much credit is due to the landowners. The area, once part of the "Dust Bowl," is now a garden spot. The success of the project has drawn wide attention to western Oklahoma. 4 illus., 32 notes.

I. W. Van Noppen

4146. Stone, Lois C. A LEGACY OF GOOD BREEDING. *Forest Hist. 1968 12(3): 21-29.* James G. Eddy (1881-1964) and Luther Burbank shared a common interest in the breeding of coniferous trees. In 1925 the Eddy Tree Breeding station was established at Placerville, and nursery plantings were started in 1927. In 1952 the American Forestry Association honored Eddy for his contribution to American forestry. Relates his effort to advance the science of forest genetics and his interest in the conservation of forest products.

G. Barrett

4147. Stout, Joe A., Jr. CATTLEMEN, CONSERVATIONISTS, AND THE TAYLOR GRAZING ACT. *New Mexico Hist. R. 1970 45(4): 311-332.* Traces the interplay between cattlemen and conservationists over attempts to control public grazing lands. The conservationists won a partial victory with the passage of the Taylor Grazing Act (1934), which withdrew 173 million acres of unreserved public lands and established grazing districts. Cattlemen, however, had successfully amended the bill to give rights-of-way to stockmen for stock driving and to give preference to previous users in assigning permits. 72 notes.

D. F. Henderson

4148. Strong, Douglas H. THE SIERRA FOREST RESERVE: THE MOVEMENT TO PRESERVE THE SAN JOAQUIN VALLEY WATERSHED. *California Hist. Soc. Q. 1967 46(1): 3-17.* The movement to preserve the Sierra Nevada and its forests began in 1889 and led to the creation of the Sequoia, Yosemite, and General Grant National Parks but did not preserve the watershed as the Tulare County group had proposed. The Forest Reserve Act of 1891 failed to provide for the administration necessary to protect the land set aside, with the result that lumbermen and sheepmen continued to treat it as public domain. In 1907 Gifford Pinchot, chief of the Forest Service, secured funds and personnel. The later history of the Sierra Forest Reserve which has continued to be vital to the farming economy of the San Joaquin Valley is summarized. Illus., 42 notes.

E. P. Stickney

4149. Sutton, Imre. GEOGRAPHICAL ASPECTS OF CONSTRUCTION PLANNING: HOOVER DAM REVISITED. *J. of the West 1968 7(3): 301-344.* Examines from many aspects the impact of the construction of the Hoover Dam. Beginning with a physical description of the area, the author traces the progress of the legislation which made the dam a reality. Among the economic problems which had to be faced was the creation of a town for the workers and the supporting services to inhabitants. Many labor problems had to be solved. The backing up of the Colorado River into an immense lake posed other problems such as the change in the recreational use of the area and the preservation of archaeological sites. There is a summary of the impact of the construction period on southern Nevada. Illus., maps.

R. N. Alvis

4150. Swain, Donald C. THE BUREAU OF RECLAMATION AND THE NEW DEAL, 1933-1940. *Pacific Northwest Q. 1970 61(3): 137-146.* Overcoming serious problems traced as far back as the 1920's, the Bureau of Reclamation under the New Deal 1933-40 became so successful that Harold Ickes called the bureau "a veritable Aladdin's lamp." With the accelerated development of hydroelectric power to provide a financial base, the Depression years saw the completion of such important reclamation projects as Grand Coulee Dam and the Central Valley Project.   C. C. Gorchels

4151. Swain, Donald C. THE FOUNDING OF THE NATIONAL PARK SERVICE. *Am. West 1969 6(5): 6-9.* The National Park Service Act was not enacted until 1916 because of a prolonged debate between practical conservationists (who advocated efficient utilization of forests, mineral deposits, hydroelectric power, grasslands, and reclamation sites) and nature-lover conservationists (who worked for the preservation of scenery for aesthetic reasons). Management had been piecemeal under various executive departments, making policy coordination practically impossible. Described are the details of the well-conceived and skillfully-executed lobbying and political maneuvering that secured the necessary Congressional legislation for creation of the National Park Service. This act established the concept that preservation of natural beauty is a valid and significant aspect of the Federal conservation program. 2 illus.
                                                              D. L. Smith

4152. Tanasoca, Donald and Richardson, Elmo, ed. SIX MONTHS IN GARDEN VALLEY. *Idaho Yesterdays 1967 11(2): 16-24.* Excerpts taken from Donald Tanasoca's recollections of the six months he spent in a Civilian Conservation Corps camp near Banks, Idaho. A young man, Tanasoca faced unemployment at the end of a summer job in 1939 and impulsively joined the CCC's and left New Jersey for a new experience in the West. Everything was foreign to him: "tent life, open air and the empty land." A romantic image was fulfilled, but the realities of hard work, meeting different people, learning to live in a different community, and realizing one's own abilities, all gave Tanasoca experiences that otherwise would not have been obtained.   B. B. Swift

4153. Timmins, William M. THE FAILURE OF THE HATCHTOWN DAM, 1914. *Utah Hist. Q. 1968 36(3): 363-373.* Describes problems which developed at the dam on the Sevier River at Hatch, Utah, prior to its break in May 1914, and also provides accounts of how residents of the area reacted to the disaster. Factors involved in the decision not to reconstruct the dam are also discussed. Based on newspaper accounts; Governor William Spry's papers in the Utah State Archives; Minutes of the Hatch Ward, Panguitch Stake in the Church of Jesus Christ of Latter-Day Saints Historians Library Salt Lake City; and a letter to the author from Mrs. Effel Riggs, who saw the flood which followed the break in the dam. Illus., maps.   S. L. Jones

4154. Tweton, D. Jerome. THEODORE ROOSEVELT AND THE ARID LANDS. *North Dakota Q. 1968 36(2): 21-28.* Traces the background of the Newlands Reclamation Act and its passage in 1902. The author focuses upon the key efforts of Theodore Roosevelt to provide water accessible to actual settlers of arid western lands and cites evidence of sectional opposition from eastern and middle-western farm sources. Without Roosevelt's efforts, the measure could have been lost. Based on Roosevelt's public and private papers and newspaper commentary; 2 illus., 34 notes.   J. F. Mahoney

4155. Vap, Jeanne R. THE "GRAND TETON": FRONTIER NEWSPAPER IN THE TWENTIETH CENTURY. *Ann. of Wyoming 1970 42(2): 149-182.* Discusses the *Grand Teton,* a weekly newspaper published in Jackson from December 1931 to May 1934. It was established to oppose the efforts of John D. Rockefeller, Jr. to purchase land in the Jackson Hole règion and then deed this land to the United States in order to enlarge Grand Teton National Park. Using the tactics of a 19th-century frontier newspaper, the *Grand Teton* attacked the Snake River Land Company, a Rockefeller organization which bought land in the disputed region, and the *Jackson's Hole Courier* which supported national park expansion. The paper failed to sway Congress and ceased publication in May 1934. Based on newspaper files, personal interviews and correspondence, published government documents, and secondary material; illus., 188 notes, biblio.   R. L. Nichols

4156. Wessel, Thomas R. PROLOGUE TO THE SHELTERBELT, 1870 TO 1934. *J. of the West 1967 6(1): 119-134.* In 1935, near Mangum, Oklahoma, the first tree was planted in a massive shelterbelt program for the Great Plains. Actually this was a process which had been going on for 65 years. Early settlers on the plains were encouraged to plant trees. Some farmers did this voluntarily in an effort to duplicate the familiar weather conditions of the East, but others were encouraged by laws enacted by State legislatures and by the Federal government. The author traces the development of this legislation and its effect on the reforestation of some areas of the West. He concludes that shelterbelt planting was sporadic and unplanned and that the value was often lost in the attempts to bring rain to the plains. Based largely on government reports, illus., 46 notes.   D. N. Brown

4157. Wessel, Thomas R. ROOSEVELT AND THE GREAT PLAINS SHELTERBELT. *Great Plains J. 1969 8(2): 57-74.* Discusses "one of the most ambitious and least remembered conservation projects of the thirties.... Dust storms were an old nemesis to settlers on the Great Plains" and in 1933 President Franklin Roosevelt asked the Forest Service to determine the cost of planting rows of tree belts throughout the Great Plains. Beginning in 1934, using drought relief funds, trees were planted. A 1935 report proposed a hundred mile-wide zone from Canada to Texas. Each year tree planting continued in spite of congressional opposition, lack of funds, and continual sniping by opponents. Use of the Works Progress Administration funds, the Norris-Doxey Act, a change of name to Prairie States Forestry Project, and opposition from private nurserymen all played a part in the shelterbelt program. In 1942 the responsibility for planting was transferred to the Soil Conservation Service with "drastically curtailed shelterbelt planting." Roosevelt continued his interest in the project to the time of his death. Illus., 38 notes.
                                                              O. H. Zabel

SUBJECT INDEX

Subject Profile Index (SPIndex) carries both generic and specific index terms. Begin a search at the general term but also look under more specific or related terms. Cross-references are included.

Each string of index descriptors is intended to present a profile of a given article; however, no particular relationship between any two terms in the profile is implied. Terms within the profile are listed alphabetically after the leading term. The variety of punctuation and capitalization reflects production methods and has no intrinsic meaning; e.g., there is no difference in meaning between "History, study of" and "History (study of)."

Cities, towns, and counties are listed following their respective states or provinces; e.g., "Ohio (Columbus)." Terms beginning with an arabic numeral are listed after the letter Z. The chronology of the bibliographic entry follows the index descriptors. In the chronology, "c" stands for "century"; e.g., "19c" means "19th century."

Note that "United States" is not used as a leading index term; if no country is mentioned, the index entry refers to the United States alone. When an entry refers to both Canada and the United States, both "Canada" and "USA" appear in the string of index descriptors, but "USA" is not a leading term. When an entry refers to any other country and the United States, only the other country is indexed.

The last number in the index string, in italics, refers to the bibliographic entry number.

A

Aa Indians. Catholic Church (records). Great Powers. Jumano Indians. Kiowa Indians. New Mexico. Pawnee Indians. 1694-1875. *92*

Abbey, Edward. California. Pacific Northwest. Pennsylvania. Reminiscences. Southwest. Travel account. 1944. *3559*

Aberhart, William. Alberta. Political Leadership. Social Credit. 1935-43. *3413*

—. Canada. Conscription, Military. Elections. Herridge, W. D. New Democracy Movement. Political Reform. Social Credit Party. 1939-40. *3387*

Abolition Movement *See also* Antislavery Sentiments.

—. Andrews, Stephen Pearl. Annexation. Lawyers. Texas. 1839-43. *2670*

—. Andrews, Stephen Pearl. Great Britain. Texas. 1840-44. *2666*

—. Annexation. Democratic Party. Hale, John P. Hill, Isaac. New Hampshire. Pierce, Franklin. Political Attitudes. Texas. Whigs. 1829-45. *2653*

—. Arny, William Frederick Millon. Disciples of Christ. Education. Indians. Morrill Act. New Mexico Territory. Republican Party. Territorial Government. 1862-67. *2857*

—. Brown, John. Fugitive Slave Law. Kansas. Massachusetts. Negroes. Underground Railroad. 1800-59. *2559*

—. Butler, Pardee. Disciples of Christ. Kansas. Reform. Temperance Movements. 1850's-70's. *2333*

—. Clergy. Kansas (Leavenworth). Missouri (Weston). Starr, Frederick. 1854-55. *2433*

—. Mexican War. Parker, Theodore. Political Attitudes. Theology. ca 1840-60. *545*

Aborigines. Australia. Indian-White Relations. Land Tenure. New Guinea. Papuans. 19c. *1488*

Abrahamsohn, Abraham. Australia. California. Gold Rushes. 1849-53. *410*

—. California. Gold Mines and Mining. Westward Movement. 1849. *409*

Abreu, Jesús G. Armijo, Manuel. Beaubien, Carlos. Colorado (southern). Land grants. Maxwell, Lucien Bonaparte. Miranda, Guadalupe. New Mexico (northern). Settlement. 1841-46. *200*

Acculturation *See also* Assimilation.

—. Attitudes. Friends, Society of. Grant, Ulysses S. Indian-White Relations. Trans-Mississippi West. 1869-85. *1487*

Acculturation (problems of). Colorado. New Mexico. Rural Settlements. Social Organizations. Spanish Americans. 17c-20c. *4012*

Acequia Madre Historic Site. Irrigation. New Mexico (Santa Fe). 1610-1970. *178*

Adams, Alva. Adams, Ella Nye. Colorado. First Ladies. 1887-1931. *2769*

—. Colorado. Elections. Peabody, James H. Political Reform. Progressivism. 1904. *3821*

—. Colorado (Leadville). MacIntyre, Albert A. Strikes. 1896-97. *3871*

—. Democratic Party. Elections (gubernatorial). McDonald, Jesse. Peabody, James. Political Corruption. Republican Party. 1904-05. *3765*

Adams, Andy (*Log of a Cowboy*). Authors. Cowboys. Fiction. 1903. *1953*

Adams, Annette Abbott. California. Elections. Law. Politics. Women. 1900-20's. *3768*

Adams, Ansel. National Parks and Reserves. Nature Photography. Wilderness. 20c. *2084*

Adams, Augusta. Massachusetts (Boston). Mormons. Polygamy. Utah. Young, Brigham. 1840's-86. *2243*

Adams, Cassily. Arizona Pioneers' Historical Society. Custer, George A. Little Big Horn (battle). Painting. 1885-1967. *2138*

Adams, Charles Francis, Jr. Antislavery Sentiments. House of Representatives. Massachusetts State Texas Committee. Palfrey, John Gorham. Sumner, Charles. Texas. Wilson, Henry. 1845. *2624*

—. Gould, Jay. Management. Railroads. Senate Judiciary Committee. Union Pacific Railroad. 1870-90. *1334*

Adams, Ella Nye. Adams, Alva. Colorado. First Ladies. 1887-1931. *2769*

Adams, George Washington Joshua. Church of the Messiah. Evangelism. Mormons. Palestine (Jaffa). 1811-80. *2225*

Adams, Grizzly. California. Pioneers. 1850's. *3017*

Adams, John Quincy. Agriculture. Cass, Lewis. Douglas, Stephen A. Federal Policy. Land policies. Webster, Daniel. Westward Movement. 1812-50. *288*

—. California. Diplomacy. France. Great Britain. Jackson, Andrew. Mexico. Polk, James K. Ports. Trade. 1820-45. *12*

Adams, John Quincy (speech). Annexation. Slavery. Texas. 1838. *2672*

Adams, Samuel. Arizona. Callville. Colorado River. *Esmeralda* (vessel). Freight and Freightage. Mormons. 1866. *1410*

Adams, Steve (confession). Assassination. Colorado. Hawley, James H. Haywood, William Dudley ("Big Bill"). Idaho. Labor Disputes. Orchard, Harry. Steunenberg, Frank. Trials. Western Federation of Miners. 1890-1906. *3893*

Addams, Jane. Europe. Ford, Henry. Hanna, L. B. Jordan, David Starr. North Dakota. Pacifism. Schwimmer, Rosika. World War I. 1915-16. *3713*

Administrative Law *See also* Civil Service; Local Government; Public Administration.

—. Alberta. Judicial divisions. Manitoba. Northwest Territories. Ontario. Quebec. Saskatchewan. 1858-1912. *3155*

Adobe Flores. California (southern). Land Tenure. 17c-19c. *1709*

Adobe houses. Colorado (Madrid Plaza). Mexican Americans. Migration, Internal. 1860-1900. *1631*

Adobe Walls (battle). Buffalo Wallow (battle). Cheyenne Indians. Comanche Indians. Indian Wars. Kiowa Indians. Lyman's Wagon Train (battle). Palo Duro Canyon (battle). Price's Fight (battle). Red River Indian War. Texas Panhandle. 1874. *846*

—. California. Carson, Christopher (Kit). Civil War. Comanche Indians. Kiowa Indians. New Mexico. Red River Indian War. Santa Fe Trail. Texas (South Canadian River). Ute Indians. 1862-75. *669*

—. Comanche Indians. Indian Wars. Mackenzie, Ranald S. Miles, Nelson A. Military Campaigns. Texas. 1874-75. *741*

Adolescence. Carver, George Washington. Education. Farms. Kansas. 1870's-80's. *1601*

Adult Education. Buck, Solon J. (review article). Farmers. Grange. Kelley, Oliver H. 1880-1910. *286*

Advertising *See also* Marketing; Propaganda; Public Relations; Publicity; Salesmen and Salesmanship.

—. Arizona. Baumann, Jules. Grand Canyon. Higgins, C. A. Railroads. Santa Fe Railroad. Warner, Charles Dudley. 1908. *3969*

—. Atchison, Topeka and Santa Fe Railroad. Germans, Russian. Kansas. Mennonites. Railroads. Settlement. 1878. *1530*

—. Baker, Charles. Colorado (San Juan Mountains). Settlement (promotion of). 1860-67. *2782*

—. Banking. Cooke, Jay. Great Britain (London). Marketing (bonds). Northern Pacific Railroad. Railroads. 1869-73. *1365*

—. Beck, George T. Irrigation. Settlement. Shoshone Land and Irrigation Company. Wyoming (Big Horn Basin; Cody). 1894-1943. *3985*

—. Cities. Colorado (Colorado Springs, Durango). Denver and Rio Grande Western Railroad. Palmer, William Jackson. Railroads. 1836-73. *1700*

—. Collins, Charles. Gold Mines and Mining. South Dakota (Sioux City). 1874-76. *2505*

—. Colorado. Gilpin, William. Great American Desert (myth of). Trans-Mississippi West. 1843-48. *2475*

—. Custer, George A. Great Plains. Hazen, William B. Northern Pacific Railroad. Railroads. Settlement. 1860's. *2453*

—. Dakota Territory. Donan, Pat. Journalism. Pacific Northwest. 1865-1902. *2418*

—. Entertainment. Folk Medicine. Medicine shows. 1865-1900. *2192*

—. Immigration. Scandinavian Americans. Washington. 1890-1910. *1460*

Aeronautics. *Avitor Hermes, Jr.* (balloon). Marriott, Frederick. Porter, Rufus. Travel. 1849-83. *1328*

—. Balloons. California. 1870-1911. *1308*

Agate Fossil Beds National Monument. Cook family. Frontier and Pioneer Life. Nebraska (Agate Springs). 20c. *1606*

Agrarianism. Ameringer, Oscar. Oklahoma. Socialism. 1907. *2606*

Agricultural Adjustment Act (1933). Agricultural Reform. *Daily Republic* (newspaper). Journalism. Politics. Ronald, William Roy. South Dakota. 1909-51. *4088*

Agricultural Adjustment Administration. Agricultural Policy. Federal Emergency Relief Administration. Great Plains. New Deal. Shelterbelt Program. Soil Conservation. 1933-34. *4076*

—. Cattle Raising. New Deal. Texas. 1930's. *4061*

Agricultural Cooperatives. Beersheba. Hebrew Union Agricultural Society. Jews. Kansas. Settlement. 1882-85. *1470*

—. Beersheba. Hebrew Union Agricultural Society. Jews. Kansas. 1882-86. *1525*

American Cattle Company. Cattle Raising. *Daily Republican* (newspaper). Kansas (Clark County). Perry Ranch. 1890. *2531*

American Civil Liberties Union. California (Los Angeles, San Pedro). Freedom of Speech. Industrial Workers of the World. Sinclair, Upton. Strikes. 1923. *3838*

American Colonization Society. Colonization (attitudes toward). Negroes. Turner, Frederick Jackson. Woolfolk, George R. 19c. *1508*

American Federation of Labor. Agricultural Labor. Associated Farmers. California Processors and Growers, Inc. California (Stockton). Cannery Workers. Congress of Industrial Organizations. International Longshoremen's Association. Strikes. Teamsters' Union. 1937. *3939*

—. Anaconda Copper Mining Company. Copper Mines and Mining. Fire. Industrial Workers of the World. Montana (Butte). Press. State Politics. Strikes. 1917. *3891*

—. Boyce, Edward. Colorado. Labor Unions and Organizations. Mines. Socialism. Strikes. Violence. Western Federation of Miners. 1903-05. *3953*

—. Confederación Regional Obrera Mexicana. Gompers, Samuel. Green, William. Immigration. Mexico. National Origins Act (1924). Pan-American Federation of Labor. 1920's. *3907*

—. Gompers, Samuel. Labor Unions and Organizations. Washington (Seattle). 1919-20. *3882*

American Forestry Association. Botany. Burbank, Luther. Conservation of Natural Resources. Eddy, James G. Eddy Tree Breeding Station. Horticulture. 1925-52. *4146*

American Fur Company. Assiniboin Indians. Campbell, Robert. Deschamps-Rem Feud. Fort Union. Fort William. Fur Trade. Larpenteur, Charles. Mountain Men. Rocky Mountain Fur Company. Sublette, William. 1807-72. *912*

—. Astor, John Jacob. Fur Trade. 1808-34. *902*

—. Beaubien, Carlos. Frémont, John C. Gold Rushes. Maxwell Land Grant. Maxwell, Lucien Bonaparte. Miranda, Guadalupe. New Mexico. Trading posts. 1818-75. *1225*

—. Black Beaver (Sikitomaker, Delaware Chief). Indian-White Relations. Scientific Expeditions. Scouts and Guides. 1806-80. *332*

—. Boller, Henry A. Frost, Todd and Company. Fur Trade. Letters. Missouri River. 1836-60. *904*

—. Bridger, Jim. Miller, Alfred Jacob. Mountain Men. Painting. Rocky Mountains. Stewart, William Drummond. 1837. *2116*

—. Campbell, Robert. Diaries. Fort Union. Fort William. Fur Trade. McKenzie, Kenneth. Sublette and Campbell (firm). 1833. *878*

—. Campbell, Robert. Diaries. Fort William. Fur Trade. Missouri (St. Louis). Sublette, William. 1833. *879*

—. Commerce. Fur Trade. Great Plains. Missouri River. Steamboats. 1831-87. *1413*

—. Crook, Ramsay. Fur Trade. Missouri (St. Louis). 1795-1817. *901*

—. Fort Snelling. Fur Trade. Sibley, Henry H. Stambaugh, Samuel C. Sutlers, US Army. 1830's. *914*

—. Fort Union. Meteorology. North Dakota. Patent Office. Pennsylvania (Philadelphia). Riter, Frederick G. Smithsonian Institution. 1853-88. *920*

—. Fur Trade. Labarge, Joseph. Missouri River. Steamboats. 1820's-30's. *1405*

American Heritage (periodical). Bibliographies (annotated). Trans-Mississippi West. 1949-69. *268*

American Historical Association (Pacific Coast Branch). Bolton, Herbert Eugene. Colorado, University of. Goodykoontz, Colin Brummitt. Historians. Turner, Frederick Jackson. Westward Movement. 1885-1958. *227*

American Institute of Architects. California. Historic Buildings Committee. Historical Sites and Parks. Los Angeles Cultural Heritage Board. Preservation. 1966. *3100*

American Legion. Centralia Massacre. Industrial Workers of the World. Labor Disputes. Pamphlets. Washington (Centralia). 1919. 1920-67. *3637*

American Russian Commercial Company. Alaska. California (San Francisco). Ice (shipping of). Trade. 1850-70. *3499*

American Settler (newspaper). English Americans. Farmers. Immigration. Middle Classes. 1865-1900. *1562*

American Shepherd's Bulletin (journal). Arizona. Sheep Raising. 1903-06. *4072*

American Sugar Refining Company. Agricultural Production. Beet sugar industry. Idaho. Mormons. Sugar. Utah-Idaho Sugar Company. 1891-1950. *3845*

—. Agriculture Department. Beet sugar industry. California (Alvarado). Mormons. Nebraska. Oxnard brothers. Spreckels, Claus. Utah Sugar Company. Wisconsin (Fond du Lac). 1888-1913. *1216*

American Unitarian Association. Kansas Territory (Lawrence). Missions and Missionaries. Nute, Ephraim. Unitarianism. 1854-61. *2321*

Americanization. Canadian west. Immigration. 19c. *3171*

Americas (North and South). Book of Mormon. Culture. Middle East. Mormons. Theology. Prehistory. *2297*

Amerika breva (newspaper). Immigration. Kansas. Republican Party. Swedish Americans. 19c. *1502*

Ameringer, Oscar. Agrarianism. Oklahoma. Socialism. 1907. *2606*

Ames Monument. Ames, Oakes. Ames, Oliver, Jr. Railroads. Richardson, Henry Hobson. Saint-Gaudens, Augustus. Sculpture. Union Pacific Railroad. Wyoming (Sherman). 1800-82. *2098*

Ames, Oakes. Ames Monument. Ames, Oliver, Jr. Railroads. Richardson, Henry Hobson. Saint-Gaudens, Augustus. Sculpture. Union Pacific Railroad. Wyoming (Sherman). 1800-82. *2098*

Ames, Oliver, Jr. Ames Monument. Ames, Oakes. Railroads. Richardson, Henry Hobson. Saint-Gaudens, Augustus. Sculpture. Union Pacific Railroad. Wyoming (Sherman). 1800-82. *2098*

Amézqueta, Joaquín de. Books. Frontier and Pioneer Life. 1800. *171*

Amijo, Manuel. Colorado. Craig, William. Land grants. Vigil and St. Vrain Land Grant. 1843-1900. *1159*

Amon Carter Museum of Western Art. Art Galleries and Museums. Texas (Fort Worth). 1961. *2148*

Amphibious Operations. Civil War. Confederate Army. Galveston Harbor (battle). Texas. 1863. *630*

Anabaptists. Bibliographies. Canada. Europe. Mennonites. Urbanization. USA. 1894-1968. *2349*

Anaconda Copper Mining Company. American Federation of Labor. Copper Mines and Mining. Fire. Industrial Workers of the World. Montana (Butte). Press. State Politics. Strikes. 1917. *3891*

—. Butte *Daily Bulletin* (newspaper). Montana. *Strike Bulletin* (pamphlet). Strikes. Wheeler, Burton K. 1917-24. *3892*

—. Copper Mines and Mining. Industrial Workers of the World. Labor Disputes. Little, Frank. Montana (Butte). Murder. 1917. *3890*

Anarchism and Anarchists *See also* Communism.

—. Canada. Great Britain. Martin, Wallace. *New Age* (newspaper). Orage, A. R. Social Credit (review article). 19c. 1967-69. *3138*

—. McKinley, William (assassination). Washington (Home). 1901-02. *4014*

Ancient Order of United Workmen. Insurance. Kansas. McNall, Webb. Reform. 1890's. *3595*

Anderson, A. J. Armies. Colorado (Trinidad). Indian-White Relations. Ka-ni-ache (chief). Ute Indians (Moache). 1866-80. *823*

Anderson, Bill. Civil War. Clay County Boys. Guerrilla Warfare. James, Jesse. Kansas. Missouri. Quantrill, William C. 1861-64. *603*

Anderson, David. Centennial Celebrations. Institute of Rupert's Land. Northwest Territories. Social Organizations. 1848-64. *3205*

Anderson, John Alvin. Nebraska. Photography. 1870-1900. *2087*

Anderson, Maxwell. Colleges and Universities. Drama. Koch, Frederick Henry. North Dakota, University of. Sock and Buskin Society. Theater Production and Direction. 1905-18. *3601*

Anderson, Robert. Discovery and Exploration. Florida. Fort Sumter. Frémont, John C. Hardee, William. Mexican War. Military. Oregon. Talbot, Theodore. 1823-62. *498*

Andrew Palm Family Memorial Church. Palm, Andrew (family). Texas (Round Rock). Widen, Carl T. (speech). 19c. 1966. *1555*

Andrews, Stephen Pearl. Abolition Movement. Annexation. Lawyers. Texas. 1839-43. *2670*

—. Abolition Movement. Great Britain. Texas. 1840-44. *2666*

Andrus, James. Military Intelligence. Utah (southern). Woolley, Franklin B. (report). 1866. *2813*

Anecdotes. Bank of America. California. Giannini, Amadeo Peter. Giannini, Attilio Henry. Reminiscences. Roosevelt, Franklin D. (administration). Santa Anita Racetrack. Securities and Exchange Commission. Transamerica Corporation. 1920-43. *3861*

—. California. Reminiscences. Sinclair, Upton. 1878-1968. *3597*

—. Crow Indians. Miller, Fred E. Montana. Photography. 1900-36. *2061*

—. Idaho (Santa area). Renfro, John (family). 1888-1965. *1593*

Angeles Crest Highway System. Angeles National Forest. Automobile Club of Southern California. California (San Gabriel Mountains). Highways. 1919-61. *3607*

Angeles National Forest. Angeles Crest Highway System. Automobile Club of Southern California. California (San Gabriel Mountains). Highways. 1919-61. *3607*

Anglo-American Boundary Commission. Boundaries. Canada. Royal Geographical Society. USA. 49th Parallel. 1872. 1967. *3180*

Animal specimens. Fort Mandan. Jefferson, Thomas. Lewis and Clark Expedition. Scientists. 1805. *355*

Animals. Coronado, Francisco. Discovery and Exploration. Plants. 1540-41. *78*

—. Country Life. Fowler, Gene. Reminiscences. Rocky Mountains. Senator (burro). 20c. *3590*

—. Economic History. Fur Trade. 1790-1890. *882*

—. Indians. Lindneux, Robert Ottokar. Painting. Rocky Mountains. 1902-66. *2112*

Animals (domestic, wild). Attitudes. Farmers. Great Plains. Nature. Ranchers. 1963. *1044*

Animas Land Grant. Colorado. Congress. Land Tenure. Mexico. Property rights. 1843-1900. *174*

Ann Arbor Register (newspaper). Geographical Survey West of the One Hundredth Meridian. Idaho. Kintner, Charles Jacob. Letters. Scientific Expeditions. Utah. Wheeler, George Montague. 1877. *327*

Annexation. Abolition Movement. Andrews, Stephen Pearl. Lawyers. Texas. 1839-43. *2670*

—. Abolition Movement. Democratic Party. Hale, John P. Hill, Isaac. New Hampshire. Pierce, Franklin. Political Attitudes. Texas. Whigs. 1829-45. *2653*

—. Adams, John Quincy (speech). Slavery. Texas. 1838. *2672*

—. *Alabama* (vessel). British Columbia. Great Britain. Manitoba (Red River). Nova Scotia. 1865-70. *3130*

—. Antislavery Sentiments. Democratic Party. New York. Polk, James K. Texas. VanBuren, Martin. Wilmot Proviso. 1846. *248*

—. Antislavery Sentiments. Ohio. Political Attitudes. Texas. Whigs. 1836. *2674*

—. Antislavery Sentiments. Old Northwest. Politics. Texas. Whigs. 1836-44. *2675*

—. Canada. Minnesota. Ramsey, Alexander. Taylor, James Wickes. 1868. *3275*

—. Education. Houston, Sam. Lamar, Mirabeau Buonaparte. Nicaragua. Public Lands (sale of). Taylor, Zachary. Texas. 1830's-59. *2681*

—. Mormons. Nevada Territory (Washoe). Territorial Government. Utah Territory. 1827-61. *2842*

Annexation (attempted). Canada. Catholic Church. Great Britain. Métis. Rebellions. Riel, Louis. USA. Wolseley, Garnet Joseph. 1844-85. *3221*

Annexation (proposed). Arizona. New Mexico (Grant County, Silver City). Political Corruption. Santa Fe Ring. State Politics. 1876. *2858*

Annie Laurie Consolidated Gold Mining Company. Gold Mines and Mining. Kimberly gold mine. Pace, Josephine. Reminiscences. Utah. ca 1900's. *985*

Anthropology *See also* Acculturation; Archaeology; Ethnology; Language; Linguistics; Race Relations; Social Change.

—. Archives. Ethnology. Manuscripts (Mexican, Spanish). Mexico. Southwest. -1750. *17*

—. Arizona Archaeological and Historical Society. 1916-66. *2891*
—. Brandon House. Diaries. Fur Trade. Indians. Letters. Manitoba (Souris-Mouth area). Yorstone, William. 1793-1821. *3267*
—. Colorado State Historical Society. Fort Vasquez. Fur Trade. Military Camps and Forts. Platte River (South). 1835-1970. *898*
—. Fort Union. Historical Sites and Parks. New Mexico. 1851-1960. *537*
Archbishops. Church of England. Great Britain (Canterbury, York). Missions and Missionaries. Western Canada Fund. 19c. *3122*
Archbishops' Western Canada Fund. Canada. Church of England. Missions and Missionaries. Railroads. 1910-20. *3121*
Archibald, Adams George. Governors. Manitoba. Nova Scotia. Riel, Louis. 1870-83. *3266*
Architecture *See also* Buildings; Construction.
—. Arizona. Inturralde, Francisco. Letters. San Xavier del Bac (church). 1797. *123*
—. Arizona Territory (southern). Cowboys. Ranch houses. 1863-1912. *2158*
—. Beehive House. Blood, Moroni. Hoyt, Samuel Pierce. Lion House. Mormons. Polygamy. Utah. Watkins, John. Young, Brigham. 1853-68. *2115*
—. B'nai B'rith synagogue. California (Los Angeles). Jews. Kysor, Ezra F. 1873-96. *1516*
—. Brown, Henry Cordes. Capitol building. Colorado (Denver). Myers, Elijah E. State Government. 1876-1908. *2783*
—. Calef, Elmer. Farms. Oregon (Willamette Valley). Reminiscences. Vermont (Washington). 1855-73. *1587*
—. California. Mission San Fernando Rey de España. 1797-1965. *162*
—. California (Folsom). Cohn, Phillip C. Cohn, Simon. Hyman, Jacob. Jews. 1913-16. *2090*
—. California Historical Society. California (San Francisco). The Mansion (building). Whittier, William Franklin. 1894-1969. *2986*
—. California (Los Angeles). Eisen, Percy A. Walker, Albert R. 1920-40. *3673*
—. California (Los Angeles, Watts). Rodilla, Sam. Rodilla Towers. 1921-54. *3572*
—. California (southern). Spain (Cultural influence). Wright, Frank Lloyd. 1895-1930. *3591*
—. Central-hall houses. Mormons. Settlement. 1846-90. *2264*
—. Churches. Coalville Tabernacle. Mormons. Photography. Utah. 1967. *2150*
—. France. Spain. Texas. 1588-1890. *2095*
—. Hewitt, Edgar L. Museum of New Mexico (Fine Arts Building). New Mexico. 1912-17. *2862*
—. Missions. Southwest. 16c-19c. *148*
—. Photography. Texas. Victorianism, American. Webb, Tedd. 1969. *2076*
Architecture (Victorian). California (Alameda). City Planning. 1968. *2135*
Archives *See also* names of individual archives, e.g. Georgetown University Archives; Documents; Manuscripts.
—. Anthropology. Ethnology. Manuscripts (Mexican, Spanish). Mexico. Southwest. -1750. *17*
—. Bolton, Frederick. Bolton, Herbert Eugene. Carnegie Institution (Department of Historical Research). Jameson, J. Franklin. Letters. Mexico. Research. 1913. *2398*
—. California. Catholic Church. Los Angeles Chancery Archives. 1739-1965. *2389*
—. California State Archives. 1966. *3013*
—. Canada. Great Britain (London). Hudson's Bay Company (records). Preservation. Public Archives. 1671-1966. *3127*
—. Canada. United Church. 1965. *3195*
—. Canadian west. Fur Trade. North West Company. 19c. *3149*
—. Colleges and Universities. Floridas. Libraries. Louisiana. Research (sources). Spain. 1576-1803. *11*
—. Federal Records Centers. Historiography. New Deal. Pacific Northwest. 1930's. *3748*
—. Federal Records Centers. Libraries. Research. Washington. 1968. *2953*
—. Federal Records Centers. Research. Western Territorial and State Archives. 1971. *2421*
—. Historians. Mormons. 1968. *2230*
—. Jesuits. St. Louis University (Pius XII Memorial Library). 1968. *2381*
—. Mexico. Saint Mary's University of San Antonio (Spanish Archives of Laredo). Spain. Texas (Laredo). 1749-1868. 1934. *48*

—. New Mexico State Records Center and Archives. Southwest. Texas, University of. 1968. *2409*
—. New Mexico, University of (Zimmerman Library). 1927-72. *2860*
Archives (diocesan). Canada. Catholic Church. Society for the History of the Catholic Church. 1964. *3209*
Archives, National. Colleges and Universities. Documents. Stanford University. Surveying. Wheeler, George Montague. 1871-1964. *358*
—. Imprints. Letters. Printing. Territorial Government. Treasury Department. 1790-1894. *2036*
Archives Nationales. Bibliothèque du Dépôt de la Marine Archives. Bibliothèque Nationale Archives. France (Paris). Louisiana. Maps. 17c-18c. 1965. *2644*
Archives (Soviet). Foreign Relations. Fur Trade. Russian American Company. 1800-1964. *226*
Archives (state). Budge, William. Idaho (Bear Lake County). Stevenson, E. A. 1863-88. *2745*
Archy case (California, 1858). Burnett, Peter Hardeman. California. Slavery. Supreme Court (state). 1858. *3028*
Arcos, Duke of. Aveiro, Duchess of. California. Indians. Kino, Eusebio Francisco. Letters. Mexico (Sonora, Conicari). Missions and Missionaries. Spain. 1687. *94*
Arguello, Concepción. California (Fort Ross, San Francisco). Rezanov, Nikolai. Russia. 1805-41. *3086*
Arikara Indians. Custer, George A. Fort Berthold Reservation. Indian scouts. North Dakota. Sioux Indians. 1866-76. *732*
—. Fort Berthold. Fur Trade. Hidatsa Indians. Mandan Indians. 1700-1884. *883*
Arizona. Adams, Samuel. Callville. Colorado River. *Esmeralda* (vessel). Freight and Freightage. Mormons. 1866. *1410*
—. Advertising. Baumann, Jules. Grand Canyon. Higgins, C. A. Railroads. Santa Fe Railroad. Warner, Charles Dudley. 1908. *3969*
—. Agricultural Industry. Date industry. 1890-1916. *3865*
—. Aguirre, Higinio. Aguirre, Juan Antonio. Aguirre, Pedro. Cattle Raising. New Mexico Territory. Trade. 1850's-1960. *2689*
—. *American Shepherd's Bulletin* (journal). Sheep Raising. 1903-06. *4072*
—. Annexation (proposed). New Mexico (Grant County, Silver City). Political Corruption. Santa Fe Ring. State Politics. 1876. *2858*
—. Apache Indian Mission. Concordia Seminary. Missions and Missionaries. Missouri (St. Louis). Reminiscences. Uplegger, Francis J. 1874-1964. *2379*
—. Apache Indians. Apache Kid. Courts Martial and Courts of Inquiry. Mexico. 1857-1924. *1798*
—. Apache Indians. *Arizona Miner* (newspaper). Camp McDowell. Indian Wars. McDowell, Irvin. Sanford, George B. 1866-73. *738*
—. Apache Indians. Armies. Daily Life. Military Camps and Forts. Reminiscences. Soldiers. 1860's-80's. *529*
—. Apache Indians. Bascom, George N. Cochise (chief). 1858-61. *828*
—. Apache Indians. Baylor, John Paul. Civil War. Confederate States of America. Davis, Jefferson. Indian policy. Texas. 1862-63. *623*
—. Apache Indians. Baylor, John R. Civil War. Confederate Army. Fort Fillmore. Fort Union. Glorieta Pass (battle). Hunter, Sherod. Military Campaigns. New Mexico Territory. Pichacho Peak (battle). Sibley, Henry Hopkins. 1861-65. *616*
—. Apache Indians. Carleton, James H. Civil War. Civil-Military Relations. Gadsden Purchase. Military Government. 1854-65. *579*
—. Apache Indians. Clum, John P. Indian agents. Kautz, August V. San Carlos Reservation. 1877. *856*
—. Apache Indians. Criminal Law. Federal Government. Gardner, Earl. Hanging. *Phoenix Gazette* (newspaper). San Carlos Reservation. 1936. *3639*
—. Apache Indians. Crook, George. Fort Bowie. Geronimo (leader). Indian Wars. *Los Angeles Times* (newspaper). Lummis, Charles Fletcher. 1886. *730*
—. Apache Indians. Crook, George. Indian Wars. McIntosh, Archie. Scouts and Guides. 1834-1902. *769*

—. Apache Indians. Fort Buchanan. Gadsden Purchase. Mexico. Military Camps and Forts. USA. 1853-61. *518*
—. Apache Indians. Fort San Phelipe de Guevavi (Terrenate). Mexico (Sonora). Mission Guevavi. 1742-75. *138*
—. Apache Indians. Indian Wars. Mexico (Sonora). New Mexico. 1831-49. *814*
—. Apache Indians. Indian-White Relations. Scouts and Guides. Sieber, Al. 19c-1970. *2910*
—. Apache Indians. Jesuits. Mission San José de Tumacacori. Missions and Missionaries. New Spain. Pima Indians. Ximeno, Bartholomé. 1772-73. *139*
—. Apache Indians (Chiricahua). Gatewood, Charles B. Geronimo (Chiricahua Apache leader). Indian Wars. Letters. Miles, Nelson A. 1886. *701*
—. Architecture. Inturralde, Francisco. Letters. San Xavier del Bac (church). 1797. *123*
—. Arkansas. California (Los Angeles). Fort Smith. Railroads (transcontinental). Santa Fe Railroad. Surveying. Whipple, Amiel Weeks. 1853-54. *347*
—. Armies. Colorado River. Fort Mojave. Indians. Roads. Westward Movement. 1846-90. *464*
—. Armies. Frontier and Pioneer Life. Indian-White Relations. Kautz, August V. 1874-78. *533*
—. Armies. Indian Wars. Telegraph. 1873-77. *1323*
—. Asplund, Julia. Libraries. New Mexico. Winsor, Mulford. 1912-63. *2694*
—. Atchison, Topeka and Santa Fe Railroad. Fred Harvey Company. Grand Canyon National Park. Railroads. Tourism. 1888-1919. *1209*
—. Attitudes. Grand Canyon. 1540-1966. *2702*
—. Backus, Henry Titus. Courts (territorial). 1865-69. *2883*
—. Banking. California. Depressions. 1933. *3898*
—. Bascom, George N. Cochise, Apache Chief. Congress. Fort Bowie National Historic Site. Goldwater, Barry. Udall, Morris K. 1858-1964. *530*
—. Baylor, John R. Confederate Army. Mexican Americans. Military Occupation. Sibley, Henry Hopkins. Texas. 1861-62. *622*
—. Bentley, Alenson. Crime and Criminals. Fort Defiance. Tevis, James H. *Weekly Arizonian* (newspaper). 1859-61. *1782*
—. Bibliographies. 1969. *2903*
—. Bibliographies. Dissertations. 1965. *2888*
—. Bibliographies. History Teaching. 1963. *2870*
—. Bibliographies. New Mexico. 1846-61. *2709*
—. Bibliographies. New Mexico. 1846-61. *2710*
—. Bibliographies. New Mexico. Printing. 1834-1966. *2012*
—. Bishops. Catholic Church. Salpointe, John Baptiste. 19c. *2871*
—. Bishops. Episcopal Church, Protestant. 1859-94. *2383*
—. Brodie, Alexander O. McClintock, James Harvey. O'Neill, William Owen ("Buckey"). Spanish-American War. Volunteer Armies. 1870-1901. *2887*
—. Buehman, Albert. Henry and Albert Buehman Memorial Collection. Mines. Photography. 1870-1900. *2086*
—. Bull Moose movement. Constitutions, State. Political Reform. Propaganda. Republican Party. Roosevelt, Theodore. Taft, William H. 1910-16. *2890*
—. Business. Copper Mines and Mining. Greene, William Cornell. Mexico (Sonora). 1899-1911. *3948*
—. Business. Drachman, Philip (family). Immigration. Jews. 1863-90's. *1234*
—. C O Bar (ranch). Cowboys. 1904-08. *4047*
—. California. Cattle drives. Diaries. Erskine, Michael H. New Mexico. Texas. 1854. *1122*
—. California. Colorado. Mexico. New Mexico. Plan of San Diego. Revolutionary Movements. Texas. 1915. *3592*
—. California. Colorado River. Conservation of Natural Resources. Mexico. Nevada. Water use. 1922-67. *4123*
—. California. Colorado River. Explorers. Gila River. Kino, Eusebio Francisco. Mexico. 1687-1711. *108*
—. California. DH-4 (aircraft). Macready, John A. Map Drawing. Mather, Stephen. Pacific Northwest. Photography. Stevens, A. W. 1924. *3628*

B

Bank of Italy. Bank of America National Trust and Savings Association. California. Giannini, Amadeo Peter. Italian Americans. 1904-30. *3886*

Bank of North Dakota. *Iconoclast* (newspaper). Martinson, Henry R. North Dakota. Political Reform. Reminiscences. Socialist Party. State Mill and Elevator. 1910-20's. *3782*

Bankhead, S. P. Arkansas. Civil War. Fort Smith. Indian Territory (Confederate). Letters. Steele, Frederick. Texas. 1863. *580*

Banking *See also* Credit; Federal Reserve System; Investments; Money.

—. Advertising. Cooke, Jay. Great Britain (London). Marketing (bonds). Northern Pacific Railroad. Railroads. 1869-73. *1365*

—. Arizona. California. Depressions. 1933. *3898*

—. Arizona (Flagstaff). First National Bank. Money. 1917-30. *3896*

—. Arizona (Tucson). Jacobs, Mark Israel. Jews. Mark I. Jacobs Company. Retail Trade. 1867-75. *1278*

—. Art (illustrations). California (San Francisco). Gold Rushes. Mines. Wells, Fargo and Company. 1848-50's. *2079*

—. Banks, Charles Wells. California (San Francisco). Crime and Criminals. Embezzlement. Hume, John B. Wells, Fargo and Company. 1871-90. *1753*

—. Bohm, S. H. J. & W. Seligman & Co. Montana (Helena). New York. Seligman Family. 1868. *2734*

—. California. Economic Conditions. Gold Rushes. Wells, Fargo and Company. 1852-1972. *1313*

—. California. Nevada. New York. Pony Express. Transportation. Wells, Fargo and Company. 1852-68. *1311*

—. Colorado (Georgetown). Cushman, William H. 1867-83. *1239*

—. Cooke, Jay. Great Northern Railway. Hill, James Jerome. Morgan, J. Pierpont. Northern Pacific Railroad. Northern Securities Company. Railroads. Villard, Henry. 1864-1904. *1350*

—. Dakota Territory (Bismarck). Diaries. Farm loans. Smith, George Watson. 1878. *1271*

—. Depressions. Federal Reserve System. Montana. 1910-25. *3889*

—. Economic Conditions. Money (shortage of). Nebraska Territory. 1854-76. *1222*

—. First National Bank. Idaho (Boise). Money (gold dust, greenbacks). 1867. *1265*

—. Huntley, Chet. Montana (Whitehall). Reminiscences. Robberies. 20c. *3616*

—. Politics. Texas (Austin). Wooldridge, Alexander Penn. 1899-1930. *2660*

Banks, Charles Wells. Banking. California (San Francisco). Crime and Criminals. Embezzlement. Hume, John B. Wells, Fargo and Company. 1871-90. *1753*

Banks, Nathaniel Prentiss. Bayou Bourbeau (battle). Civil War. Green, Thomas. Louisiana (Opelousas). Roberts, Oran Milo. Sabine Pass. Taylor, Richard. Texas. 1863. *585*

—. Blair's Landing (battle). Civil War. Louisiana (Mansfield; Shreveport, Loggy Bayou). Naval Battles. Red River. 1864. *586*

Banning, Phineas. Butterfield Overland Mail. California (Los Angeles). Los Angeles and San Pedro Railroad. Railroads. Shipping. Stagecoaches. Transportation. 1846-61. *1293*

—. California (Los Angeles, San Pedro Bay). Construction. Peck, George H. Ports. White, Stephen M. 1592-1969. *1649*

Banning's Indian Boarding School. California. Engelhardt, Zephyrin. Mission Santa Barbara. St. Joseph's College. Teaching. 1851-1934. *166*

Bannock Indians. California. Indian-White Relations. Military policy. Mormons. Oregon. Shoshoni Indians. Utah. Washington. Westward Movement. 1859-63. *771*

—. Colleges and Universities. Ethnology. Idaho State College. Liljeblad, Sven. Linguistics. Paiute Indians. Shoshoni Indians. 1940-65. *4002*

—. Idaho (Salmon River). Missions and Missionaries. Mormons. Mountain Men. Shoshoni Indians. 1855-58. *2360*

—. Idaho (southeastern). Indian-White Relations. Shoshoni Indians. Violence. Westward Movement. 1841-63. *365*

—. Indian-White Relations. Shoshoni Indians. Utah. Van Orman, Reuban. Van Orman, Zachias. 1860-62. *742*

Bannock Mountain Road. Armies. Fort Hill Hall. Idaho. Roads (military). Utah (Great Salt Lake). 1849-50. *524*

Bannock War. Diaries. Indians. Military Campaigns. Nevada. Oregon. 1878. *694*

Bannon, John Francis. Historians. Philosophy of History. Spanish Borderlands. 17c. 1970. *2*

Baptist Standard (newspaper). Historians (criticism of). Texas State Historical Association. Wooten, Dudley G. 1880-1929. *2638*

Baptiste, Jean. Charbonneau, Toussaint. Discovery and Exploration. Hidatsa Indians. Lewis and Clark Expedition. Sacagawea (Shoshoni Indian). Shoshoni Indians. 1803-84. *344*

Baptists. McCoy, Isaac. Missions and Missionaries. Missouri (Jackson County). Mormons. 1831-33. *2219*

Baranov, Alexsandr A. Alaska. Fur Trade. Russian-American Company. ca 1795-1824. *3523*

Barbed wire. Agricultural settlement. Cattle industry. Farmers. Glidden, Joseph Farwell. Great Plains. Illinois. 19c. *1051*

—. Cattle Raising. Cherokee Strip Livestock Association. Federal Government. Oklahoma. 1879-85. *1125*

—. Cattle Raising. Herd laws. Kansas. Nebraska. 1860's-70's. *1047*

Bard, Thomas Robert. California. Johnson, Hiram. Pardee, George C. Political Reform. Propaganda. Railroads and State. Republican Party. Southern Pacific Railroad. 1899-1905. *3766*

Barker, Eugene Campbell. Colleges and Universities. Organization of American Historians. *Southwestern Historical Quarterly* (periodical). Texas, University of. 1874-1956. *2419*

Barker, William Morris. Episcopal Church, Protestant. Washington (Olympia). 1894-1901. *3618*

Barkhart, Ernest. Brown, Anna. Bureau of Investigation. Crime and Criminals. Hale, W. R. Oil Industry and Trade. Oklahoma. Osage Indians. Roan, Henry. Smith Family. USA. 1906-26. *932*

Barlow, Lew. Collectors and Collecting. Wyoming (Gillette). 1898-1964. *3699*

Barnard, Kate. Labor Unions and Organizations. Oklahoma. Political Reform. Progressivism. 1900's. *2582*

Barnes, J. A. Alberta. Farms. Homesteading and Homesteaders. Reminiscences. 1912. *3366*

Barnett, Graham. Ballads. Folk Songs. Outlaws. Texas. 1890's-1930's. *2159*

Barney, James Mitchell. Arizona (Yuma). Historians. 1860's. *2869*

Barns (round). Folklore. Nebraska. 1970. *2147*

Barr colony. Letters. Saskatchewan (Lloydminster). Settlement. 1903-06. *3346*

Barr, Isaac M. Colonization (attempted). Great Britain. Northwest Territories. Settlement. 1902-03. *3234*

Barrett, John. Asia. Diplomacy. Oregon. Trade. 1889-1920. *3934*

Barron, Joseph. Chouteau, Paul. Indians. Jefferson, Thomas. Peale, Charles Willson. Pennsylvania (Philadelphia). Portraits (silhouettes). Sagessaga (Little Osage Chief). 1806. *2108*

Barrows, David Prescott. California, University of (Berkeley). Colleges and Universities. Gilman, Daniel Coit. Moses, Bernard. Political Science. Teaching. 1872-1951. *1862*

Bartlett, John Russell. Bartlett-Garcia Conde Boundary Line. Boundaries. Guadalupe Hidalgo Treaty. Mexico. Pierce, Franklin. Surveying. 1850-53. *2408*

—. Boundary Commission. California. Camp Yuma. Colorado River. Craig, Louis (murder). 1852. *364*

Bartlett, Washington. Buckley, Chris. California (San Francisco). City Politics. 1883-87. *3079*

Bartlett-Garcia Conde Boundary Line. Bartlett, John Russell. Boundaries. Guadalupe Hidalgo Treaty. Mexico. Pierce, Franklin. Surveying. 1850-53. *2408*

Barton, Benjamin Smith. Ellicott, Andrew. Jefferson, Thomas. Lewis, Meriwether. Patterson, Robert. Rush, Benjamin. Scientists. Wistar, Caspar. 1803. *2187*

Bascom, George N. Apache Indians. Arizona. Cochise (chief). 1858-61. *828*

—. Arizona. Cochise, Apache Chief. Congress. Fort Bowie National Historic Site. Goldwater, Barry. Udall, Morris K. 1858-1964. *530*

Baseball. Frontier and Pioneer Life. Recreation. 1860's-80's. *1739*

—. Montana (Plentywood, Scobey). 1925-26. *3633*

Baseball (Sandlot). California (San Francisco). Language. 1860. *1740*

Bashford, Coles. Arizona Territory (Prescott). Law. Political Corruption (assumed). State Politics. Wisconsin. 1850-78. *2880*

Basinski, Julius. Business. Immigration. Jews. Montana. 1870-1900. *1499*

—. Jews. Merchants. Montana (Miles City). Washington (Tacoma). 1870-1926. *1259*

Basque Americans. Bolívar, Simón. Latin America. Nevada. Sheep Raising. 1870's-1969. *1463*

—. Folklore. Idaho (Boise). Immigration. ca 1900-65. *1448*

Bass, Sam. Black Hills. Folklore. Outlaws. Railroads. South Dakota. Texas Rangers. Union Pacific Railroad. 1877-80's. *1794*

Batoche (battle). Diaries. Métis. Middleton, Frederick Dobson. Minto, 4th Earl of. North West Rebellion. Saskatchewan. 1885. *3340*

Battle Axe Ranch. Day, John. Wyoming. 1890's-1940's. *4043*

Battle cries. Alamo (battle). San Jacinto (battle). Texas (San Antonio). 1836. *2630*

Battles *See also* names of battles, e.g. Harlem Heights (battle); Naval Battles.

—. Arkansas. Civil War. Fort Smith. 1863. *588*

—. California (Weaverville). Chinese Americans. Gold Mining camps. 1854. *1486*

—. Carranza, Venustiano. Foreign Relations. Mexico. Military. New Mexico (Columbus). Pershing, John J. Spilsbury, Lemuel. Villa, Pancho. 1916. *3717*

—. Missouri (Jackson County). Mormons (forced removal). 1833. *2277*

Baum, Lyman Frank *(Wizard of Oz)*. Farmers. Populism. Symbolism in Literature. 1900. *3629*

Baumann, Jules. Advertising. Arizona. Grand Canyon. Higgins, C. A. Railroads. Santa Fe Railroad. Warner, Charles Dudley. 1908. *3969*

Baxter Springs (massacre). Blunt, James G. Civil War. Guerrilla Warfare. Kansas. Quantrill, William C. 1863. *652*

—. Centennial Celebrations. Civil War (raids). Kansas (Lawrence). Mine Creek (battle). Quantrill, William C. Robertson, James I., Jr. 1863-64. 1963-64. *679*

Baylor, George. Civil War. Fort Fillmore (surrender of). Lynde, Isaac. New Mexico Territory. 1861. *594*

Baylor, John Paul. Apache Indians. Arizona. Civil War. Confederate States of America. Davis, Jefferson. Indian policy. Texas. 1862-63. *623*

Baylor, John R. Apache Indians. Arizona. Civil War. Confederate Army. Fort Fillmore. Fort Union. Glorieta Pass (battle). Hunter, Sherod. Military Campaigns. New Mexico Territory. Pichacho Peak (battle). Sibley, Henry Hopkins. 1861-65. *616*

—. Arizona. Confederate Army. Mexican Americans. Military Occupation. Sibley, Henry Hopkins. Texas. 1861-62. *622*

Bayou Bourbeau (battle). Banks, Nathaniel Prentiss. Civil War. Green, Thomas. Louisiana (Opelousas). Roberts, Oran Milo. Sabine Pass. Taylor, Richard. Texas. 1863. *585*

Beachy, William C. ("Hill"). California. Idaho. Mines. Nevada. Stagecoaches. 1864-73. *1303*

Beads, Jacob. Canada. Cook, Thomas. Fort Ellice. Frontier and Pioneer Life. Millar, Henry. 1831-91. *3289*

Beale, Edward Fitzgerald. California. Explorers. 1822-93. *448*

—. California. Federal Government. Public Lands. Surveying. 1861-64. *1140*

Beals, Samuel DeWitt. High Schools. Nebraska (Omaha). Teaching. 1826-1900. *1854*

Bear Flag Revolt. Atherton, Faxon Dean. California Historical Society (Faxon Dean Atherton Collection). California (Monterey). Hammond, George P. *(The Larkin Papers).* Jones, Thomas ap Catesby. Larkin, Thomas Oliver. Letters. 1842-53. 1951-65. *565*

Bear River. Colorado. Lumber and Lumbering. Utah. Wyoming (Evanston). 1872-85. *1226*

Beatte, Alexis Pierre. Great Plains. Mountain Men. 19c. *2476*

—. *Colonist* (newspaper). Immigration. Negro Suffrage. Racism. 1860. *3481*

British Columbia (Victoria). Hudson's Bay Company. Indian-White Relations. Missions and Missionaries. Population. 19c-20c. *3446*

British North America Act (1867). Bill 59. Catholic Church. Education. French (language). Manitoba. Protestantism. Public Schools. 1807-1967. *3282*

Broadwater, Charles A. Hotels. Montana (Helena). 1889-1935. *3850*

Brodie, Alexander O. Arizona. McClintock, James Harvey. O'Neill, William Owen ("Buckey"). Spanish-American War. Volunteer Armies. 1870-1901. *2887*

Brokmeyer, Henry C. Creek Indians. Indians. Literature (German). Oklahoma. ca 1853-1906. *2610*

—. Hunting. Indian Territory. Reminiscences. Young, Thomas Fox. 1880. *1742*

Brooks, Edward C. Clergy. Colorado (Canon City). Methodist Church. Prisons. 1885-87. *1749*

Brooks, Juanita. Lee, John D. Libraries. Mormons. Pioneers. Reminiscences. 1966. *2238*

Brooks, Juanita (review article). China. Diaries. Mormons. Stout, Hosea. Westward Movement. 1837-54. *2289*

Brooks, William. Chinook Indians. Pacific Northwest. 1835-39. *2932*

Brotherhood of Timber Workers. Industrial Workers of the World. Kirby, John Henry. Labor Disputes. Louisiana. Lumber and Lumbering. Southern Lumber Operators' Association. Texas. 1906-16. *3921*

—. Joyce, William. Kirby, John Henry. Kirby Lumber Company. L & M Company. Labor Unions and Organizations. Lumber and Lumbering. Lutcher, Henry J. Moore, G. Bedell. Negroes. Texas (eastern). Trinity County Lumber Company. 1820-1965. *1262*

Brouillet, J. B. A. Beckwith, Paul. Catholic Church. Dakota Territory (Devil's Lake). Indians (agencies). McLaughlin, James. Minnesota. 1871-1923. *2365*

—. Blackfoot Reservation. Catholic Church. Grant, Ulysses S. (administration). Imoda, John Baptist Camillus. Letters. Methodist Church. Missions and Missionaries. Montana. 1874. *2386*

Brown, Anna. Barkhart, Ernest. Bureau of Investigation. Crime and Criminals. Hale, W. R. Oil Industry and Trade. Oklahoma. Osage Indians. Roan, Henry. Smith Family. USA. 1906-26. *932*

Brown, Benjamin. Intermountain Farmers Association. Jews. Poultry. Utah (Clarion colony). 19c-1967. *1227*

Brown, Frank Mason. Colorado River. Denver, Colorado Cañon and Pacific Railroad. Green River. Kendrick, Frank C. Railroads. Stanton, Robert Brewster. Surveying. 1889. *1376*

—. Colorado River. Kendrick, Frank C. (notebook). Railroads. 1889. *445*

Brown, G. W. *Morning Leader* (newspaper). Political Leadership. Saskatchewan. 1910-15. 1919. *3325*

Brown, Henry Cordes. Architecture. Capitol building. Colorado (Denver). Myers, Elijah E. State Government. 1876-1908. *2783*

Brown, James J. Brown, Margaret Tobin. Colorado (Denver). *Titanic* (vessel). 1880's-1920's. *1625*

Brown, John. Abolition Movement. Fugitive Slave Law. Kansas. Massachusetts. Negroes. Underground Railroad. 1800-59. *2559*

—. California (Los Angeles). Flores, José María. Fort Moore Hill. Gillespie, Archibald. Mexican War. Rescue attempts. Stockton, Robert Field. 1846. *569*

—. Guerrilla Warfare. Kansas. Murder. Slavery. 1856. *2560*

—. Humphrey, Heman. Kansas. Letters. Slavery. State Government. 1857. *2543*

Brown, John H. Hillmon, John W. Hillmon, Sallie Quinn. *Insurance Company* v. *Hillmon* (US, 1892). Kansas. Populism. 1878-92. *1424*

Brown, John S. Foster, Daniel. Kansas Territory (Lawrence). Missions and Missionaries. Nute, Ephraim. Unitarianism. Whitman, Edmund. 1854-61. *2322*

Brown, Margaret Tobin. Brown, James J. Colorado (Denver). *Titanic* (vessel). 1880's-1920's. *1625*

Brown, Mrs. Hugh. Celebrations. Nevada (Tonopah). Railroads. Reminiscences. 1904. *3857*

Brown University. Clark University. Colleges and Universities. Harvard University. Hedges, James Blaine. History Teaching. Turner, Frederick Jackson. 1894-1965. *229*

Browne, Charles Farrar. *See* Ward, Artemus.

Browne, J. Ross. California. Haraszthy de Mokcsa, Agoston. Lobbying. Wilson, Benjamin D. Winemaking. 1866. *3068*

Browne, J. Ross. California. Federal Government. Gold Mines and Mining. Political Corruption. Westward Movement. 1850's-60's. *1754*

Brueggemann, John. Celebrations (International Night). City Life. Ethnic Groups. Music. Social Customs. Wyoming (Rock Springs). 1920's. *4004*

Bruguier, Johnnie. Indian-White Relations. Miles, Nelson A. Scouts and Guides. Sioux Indians. Sitting Bull (Chief). 1876-90. *734*

Bruja (vessel). Cocopa Indians. Colorado River. Fishing (oysters). General Pearl and Coral Fishing Association. Great Britain. Hardy, R. W. H. 1826. *74*

Bryan, James Perry. Austin, Stephen F. James Perry Bryan Map Collection. Map Drawing. Texas. 1507-1885. *2633*

Bryan, William Jennings. Attitudes. Kansas. Mennonites. Pacifism. Spanish-American War. 1898-1900. *4010*

—. California. Federal Government. Japanese Americans. State Legislatures. Webb Act (1913). Wilson, Woodrow (administration). 1913-14. *3999*

—. California. Foreign Relations. Immigration. Japan. Land Tenure. Popular sovereignty (principle of). 1901-15. *4001*

—. Callahan, James Yancy. Flynn, Dennis T. Oklahoma Territory. Political Campaigns. Populism. 1890's. *2616*

—. "Cross of Gold" (speech). Political Leadership. 1896-1908. *3836*

—. Dahlman, James O. Democratic Party. Nebraska. Political Campaigns. Temperance Movements. 1910. *3735*

—. Democratic Party. Hitchcock, Gilbert M. Nebraska. Patronage. Politics. Prohibition. Wilson, Woodrow (administration). 1840's-1916. *3736*

—. Destler, Chester McArthur (*American Radicalism, 1865-1901*, 1946). Politics. Populists. Watson, Thomas Edward. 1896. *3744*

—. Economic Reform. Free silver movement. Harvey, William Hope ("Coin"). Panic of 1893. Political Theory. Politics. Sherman Silver Purchase Act. 1893-1936. *3824*

—. Editors and Editing. Nebraska (Omaha). *World-Herald* (newspaper). 1894. *3804*

—. Federal Reserve System. Nebraska. New Deal. Norris, George William. Political Reform. Wherry, Kenneth S. 1900-51. *3740*

—. Historical Sites and Parks. Nebraska. 1965. *2513*

Bryant, Edwin *What I Saw in California*. California. Gold Rushes. 1849-69. *3010*

Bryant, Frank B. Gold Mines and Mining. Idaho (Salmon River Mountains). Railroads. Reminiscences. 1909-11. *3858*

Bryce, James. California. Chinese Americans. Kearney, Denis. Workingmen's Party. 1879-88. *3072*

Bucareli y Ursúa, Antonio María. California. Colonial Government. Letters. Neve, Felipe de. Serra, Junípero. 1776-77. *188*

—. California (Monterey). Fages, Pedro. Letters. Military Camps and Forts. 1773. *112*

—. California (San Diego River). Documents (forged). Mendoza, Julla Ramón. Mission San Diego. New Spain. Private Lands Commission. Serra, Junípero. Water rights. 1773. *119*

Buchanan, James. Calhoun, John C. Corcoran, William W. Democratic Party. Douglas, Stephen A. Lobbying. Webster, Daniel. Whigs. 1840-61. *556*

—. Comanche Indians. Confederate Army. Indian Territory. Leeper, Matthew. Wichita Agency (battle). 1840-62. *624*

Buchanan, James (administration). Armies. Federal Government. Hookaday, John M. Intervention. Magraw, W. M. F. Mormons. Patronage. Utah Territory. 1857. *2825*

Buck (dog). Alaska. Civilization. London, Jack (*Call of the Wild*). Symbolism in Literature. Wilderness. 1903. *3525*

Buck, Royal. Frontier and Pioneer Life. Letters. Nebraska (Red Willow Creek). Settlement. 1872-73. *1428*

Buck, Solon J. (review article). Adult Education. Farmers. Grange. Kelley, Oliver H. 1880-1910. *286*

Buckley, Chris. Bartlett, Washington. California (San Francisco). City Politics. 1883-87. *3079*

Buckley House. Arizona (Tucson). Butterfield Overland Mail. 1858. *2902*

Budd, James Herbert. Economic Reform. Elections (state). Political Parties. Railroads and State. 1894. *3802*

Budge, William. Archives (state). Idaho (Bear Lake County). Stevenson, E. A. 1863-88. *2745*

Buehman, Albert. Arizona. Henry and Albert Buehman Memorial Collection. Mines. Photography. 1870-1900. *2086*

Buena Vista (battle). Clark County Volunteers. Gibson, Thomas Ware. Indiana. Letters. Mexican War. Taylor, Zachary. 1846-48. *577*

—. Elections (presidential). Indiana Volunteers. Mexican War. Taylor, Zachary. Voting and Voting Behavior. 1848. *575*

—. Mexican War. Scott, Winfield. Taylor, Zachary. Texas Rangers. 1846-48. *566*

Buena Vista Vineyard. California (Sonoma Valley). Haraszthy de Mokcsa, Ágoston. Ralston, William C. Winemaking. 1820-69. *1231*

Buffalo. Alexis, Grand Duke. Cody, William F. (Buffalo Bill). Custer, George A. Hunting. Nebraska. Sheridan, Philip. Spotted Tail (Sioux Chief). 1872. *1741*

—. Cabeza de Vaca, Alvar Núñez. Hunting. North America. Railroads. 1521-1889. *312*

—. Cattle Raising. Food. Great Plains. 19c. *2441*

—. Folklore. 19c-20c. *1875*

Buffalo Bill. *See* Cody, William.

Buffalo Bill Historical Center. Cody, William F. (Buffalo Bill). Museums. Wyoming (Cody). 1840's-76. 1969. *2154*

Buffalo Hump (chief). Comanche Indians. Ferdinand, Roemer von. German Americans. Ketumse (chief). Meusebach, J. O. Neighbors, Robert S. Old Owl (chief). Santa Anna (chief). Surveying. Treaties. 1847. *1515*

Buffalo hunts. Artists (illustrators). Great Britain. Houghton, Arthur Boyd. *London Graphic* (newspaper). Mormons. Pawnee Indians. 1869-70. *2122*

—. Diaries. Kansas (Dodge City). Masterson, Bat. Masterson, Edward J. Masterson, James P. Raymond, Henry H. 1872-73. *300*

—. Montana (Black Hills). Reminiscences. Snow storms. Wilson, William E. 1880. *2736*

Buffalo (Republican Herd). Cooke, Lawson. Diaries. Hunting. Kansas (Smoky Hill River). Nebraska. Platte River. 1870-71. *2564*

Buffalo sanctuaries. Alberta. Elk Island Park. Wainwright Park. 1907-09. 1964. *3424*

—. Allard, Charles P. Montana. Pablo, Michel. Walking Coyote, Samuel. Yellowstone National Park. 1885-90. *1185*

Buffalo Trails Museum. Museums. North Dakota (Williams County). 1966-67. *2485*

Buffalo Wallow (battle). Adobe Walls (battle). Cheyenne Indians. Comanche Indians. Indian Wars. Kiowa Indians. Lyman's Wagon Train (battle). Palo Duro Canyon (battle). Price's Fight (battle). Red River Indian War. Texas Panhandle. 1874. *846*

Buildings *See also* Architecture.

—. Auditorium Company. California (Los Angeles). Hazard's Pavilion. Los Angeles Philharmonic Auditorium. Music Center. Temple Baptist Church. 1886-1964. *1818*

—. Bacon, Henry Douglas. California, University of, Berkeley (Bacon Hall). Paleontology. Teachers. 1868-1961. *3093*

—. Bibliographies. Military Camps and Forts. Nevada. 1860-89. *515*

—. Business. City Planning. Washington (Spokane). 1890-1920. *3974*

—. California. Fire. Gold Rushes. Iron shutters. 1849-50's. *2106*

—. California (San Francisco). Churches. Mission San Francisco. 1776-91. *118*

—. Colleges and Universities. Oklahoma State University. Old Central. Stillwater *Gazette* (newspaper). 1894-1964. *1826*

—. Montana (Bozeman). Theater. 1887-1966. *1637*

Buildings (prefabricated). California (San Francisco). Gold Rushes. 1849. *2134*

Buildings (stone). Business. Montana (Helena). 1880's. *2136*

Bukharin, Nikolai Ivanovich. Knutson, Alfred. North Dakota (Bismarck). Red Peasant International (Farmers International). Revolutionary Movements. United Farmers Educational League. 1920's. *3745*

Bull Moose movement. Arizona. Constitutions, State. Political Reform. Propaganda. Republican Party. Roosevelt, Theodore. Taft, William H. 1910-16. *2890*

Bulla, Robert Nelson. California. Separatist Movements. 1907-21. *3056*

Bulletin (newspaper). Alberta (Red Deer). Calgary and Edmonton Railway. Country Life. Railroads. Settlement. 1891-93. *3425*

Bungi (dialect). Cree Indians. Fur Trade. Hudson's Bay Company. Lower Fort Garry. Manitoba. Red River. 19c-1968. *3302*

Bunker Hill and Sullivan Mine. Gold Mines and Mining. Idaho (northern). 1885-1900. *967*

Bunsen, Christian von. California. Colonization. Humboldt, Alexander von. Prussia. Roenne, Friedrich von. 1842. *193*

Burbank, Luther. American Forestry Association. Botany. Conservation of Natural Resources. Eddy, James G. Eddy Tree Breeding Station. Horticulture. 1925-52. *4146*

Bureau of Education. Alaska. Bureau of Indian Affairs. Congress. Eaton, John. Education. Federal Government. Indians. Jackson, Sheldon. Orthodox Eastern Church, Russian. 1884-1931. *3551*

Bureau of Identification and Records. Cattle theft. Department of Public Safety. Fletcher, Joseph Sidney. Law Enforcement. Texas and Southwestern Cattle Raisers' Association. 1906-66. *3683*

Bureau of Indian Affairs. Alaska. Bureau of Education. Congress. Eaton, John. Education. Federal Government. Indians. Jackson, Sheldon. Orthodox Eastern Church, Russian. 1884-1931. *3551*

—. Assimilation. Burke, Charles. Collier, John. Indians. Nativism. Reform. 1921-45. *1544*

—. Assimilation. Cheyenne Indians (southern). Comanche Indians. Indian-White Relations. Kiowa Indians. Pope, John. 1875-83. *716*

—. Civil War. Confederate States of America. Five Civilized Tribes. Indian Territory. Plains Indians. Treaties. Wilson's Creek (battle). 1861. *643*

—. Civil War. Great Plains. Indian-White Relations. Pioneers. 1861-65. *608*

—. Civil War. Indian Territory. Indian-White Relations. Kansas. Refugees. 1861-65. *609*

—. Civilians. Indians (agencies). 19c. *1550*

Bureau of Investigation. Barkhart, Ernest. Brown, Anna. Crime and Criminals. Hale, W. R. Oil Industry and Trade. Oklahoma. Osage Indians. Roan, Henry. Smith Family. USA. 1906-26. *932*

Bureau of the Budget. Economic Aid. New Deal. Roosevelt, Franklin D. 1933-38. *3720*

Bureaucracies. Ballinger, Richard A. Business. Conservation of Natural Resources. Forest Service. Interior Department. Monopolies. Newell, Frederick Haynes. Pinchot, Gifford. Politics. Taft, William H. 1909-26. *4136*

—. Civil Service. Public Policy. Reform. Trans-Mississippi West. 1850-1970. *284*

Burger, James. California. Frontier and Pioneer Life. Gold Rushes. Letters. New York City (Staten Island). Westward Movement. 1850. *1027*

Burke, Charles. Assimilation. Bureau of Indian Affairs. Collier, John. Indians. Nativism. Reform. 1921-45. *1544*

Burke, Frank. Army Signal Corps (Weather Service). Fort Maginnis. Frontier and Pioneer Life. Letters. Montana. Vigilantes. 1880's. *475*

Burke, Thomas. Railroads. Real Estate. Washington (Wenatchee). 1888-93. *1675*

Burleigh, Walter A. Congress. Dakota Territory. Missouri River. Montana Territory. Politics. Sioux Indians. Steamboats. 1861-96. *2499*

Burleson, Edward. Austin, Stephen F. Austin, William T. Gonzales (battle). Houston, Sam. Mexico. Military Campaigns. San Antonio (battle). Texas Revolution. Wharton, William H. 1835. *463*

Burlington and Missouri River Railroad. Immigration. Mennonites. Nebraska (Gage County, Jefferson County). Railroads. Russian Americans. 1873-78. *1551*

Burnett, James. Arizona (Tombstone). Greene, William Cornell. Trials. 1897. *1769*

Burnett, Peter Hardeman. Archy case (California, 1858). California. Slavery. Supreme Court (state). 1858. *3028*

—. California. Catholic Church. Disciples of Christ. Indians. Mission Waiilatpu. 1820's-1909. *2327*

Burnett, Robert. Boundaries. California (Los Angeles area). Land Tenure. Public Domain. Redondo, Sausal. Rosecrans, William Starke. 1848-87. *1158*

Burns, Robert H. Cattle Raising. Cowboys. Great Britain. Investments. Reminiscences. Sheep Raising. Wyoming (Laramie Plains). 1880-1957. *1081*

Burns, Robert I. Discovery and Exploration (review article). Goetzmann, William R. Hollon, W. Eugene. Jones, Holway R. Josephy, Alvin M., Jr. 19c. 1965-66. *309*

Burns, Walter Noble. Arizona (Tombstone). Earp, Wyatt (legend of). Fiction. Hall, Oakley. Kreps, Robert. Lewis, Alfred Henry. OK Corral (gunfight). Wyckoff, James. 1897-1963. *1980*

—. California. Folklore. Murieta, Joaquin. Ridge, John Rollin. 1850's-1967. *2984*

Burnt Ranch Massacre. California. Ethnohistory. Tolowa Indians. 1853-1963. *3033*

Burr, Aaron. Arkansas River. Discovery and Exploration. Mexico. Pike, Zebulon. Rio Grande River. Wilkinson, James. 1806-07. *389*

—. California. Mexican War. Southwest. Yale University, Beinecke Library. 17c-19c. *259*

Burr, Jason F. California. Connecticut Mining and Trading Company. Diaries. *General Morgan* (vessel). Gold Rushes. Lyman, Albert. Voyages. 1848-50. *958*

Burros. Frontier and Pioneer Life. Packsaddles (*aparejo*). 19c. *1306*

Burroughs, Raymond Darwin, ed. (review article). Lewis and Clark Expedition. Natural History. 1804-06. 1961. *440*

Burrowes, Thomas. Burrows, Edward. Burrows, John T. California (Shasta, Trinity Counties). Frontier and Pioneer Life. Gold Mines and Mining. Letters. New Jersey (Middletown). 1854-59. *1003*

Burrows, Edward. Burrowes, Thomas. Burrows, John T. California (Shasta, Trinity Counties). Frontier and Pioneer Life. Gold Mines and Mining. Letters. New Jersey (Middletown). 1854-59. *1003*

Burrows, John T. Burrowes, Thomas. Burrows, Edward. California (Shasta, Trinity Counties). Frontier and Pioneer Life. Gold Mines and Mining. Letters. New Jersey (Middletown). 1854-59. *1003*

Burrows, Julius Caesar. Mormons. Political Leadership. Senate. Smoot, Reed. 1903-07. *3764*

Burrus, Ernest J. California. Humboldt, Alexander von. Kino, Eusebio Francisco. Maps. Mexico. 1681-1710. 1965. *64*

Bursum, Holm O. Fall, Albert Bacon. Land Tenure. New Mexico. Pueblo Indians. 1921-23. *4022*

—. Law Enforcement. New Mexico Territory. Politics. 1894. *1775*

Burton, Richard. Bowles, Samuel. Colfax, Schuyler. Greeley, Horace. Overland Journeys to the Pacific. Stagecoaches. Transportation (transcontinental). Travel accounts. Twain, Mark. 1859-65. *1326*

Bush, Asahel. Democratic Party. Lane, Joseph. Oregon. Political Factions. 1858. *2966*

Bush, Joseph. Catlin, George. Clark, William. Harding, Chester. Jarvis, John W. Lewis, Meriwether. Peale, Charles Willson. Portraits. Saint-Mémin, Charles Balthazar Julien Fevret de. 1880's. *2096*

Bushnell, William. Badger, Joseph E. Cowboys. Ellis, Edward S. Ingraham, Prentiss. Literature. Patten, William G. 1864-1900. *1876*

Business *See also* Advertising; Banking; Corporations; Credit; Management; Manufactures; Marketing; Real Estate Business; Salesmen and Salesmanship.

—. Agricultural Production. Canadian Pacific Railway. Economic Growth. Fort Garry. Manitoba (Winnipeg). Railroads. Urbanization. 1870-90. *3270*

—. Air Forces. Hill Air Force Base (Ogden Air Materiel Area). Utah. 1938-65. *2805*

—. Antislavery Sentiments. Colonization. Kansas. New England Emigrant Aid Company. Thayer, Eli. 1854-56. *2534*

—. Arizona. Copper Mines and Mining. Greene, William Cornell. Mexico (Sonora). 1899-1911. *3948*

—. Arizona. Drachman, Philip (family). Immigration. Jews. 1863-90's. *1234*

—. Arizona (Nogales). Ephraim, Leopold. Mexico. Mines. Nogales Water Company. 1880-1923. *1272*

—. Arizona (Tucson). Mexico (Mesilla). Ochoa, Estevan. 1831-88. *1213*

—. Atchison, Topeka and Santa Fe Railroad. Finance. Gould, Jay. Huntington, Collis P. Railroads. St. Louis and San Francisco Railway Company. 1880-82. *1381*

—. Ballinger, Richard A. Bureaucracies. Conservation of Natural Resources. Forest Service. Interior Department. Monopolies. Newell, Frederick Haynes. Pinchot, Gifford. Politics. Taft, William H. 1909-26. *4136*

—. Basinski, Julius. Immigration. Jews. Montana. 1870-1900. *1499*

—. Beekeeping. California. Harbison, John Steward. Inventions. Langstroth, Lorenzo Lorraine. 1622-1869. *1286*

—. Blue laws. Legislation. Texas. 1871-1961. *3589*

—. Buildings. City Planning. Washington (Spokane). 1890-1920. *3974*

—. Buildings (stone). Montana (Helena). 1880's. *2136*

—. California. Economic Reform. Public Utilities Act (1911). Railroads and State. State regulation. 1911-15. *3852*

—. California (San Bernardino). Jews. Katz, Marcus. Local Politics. Wells, Fargo and Company. 1852-99. *1280*

—. California (Santa Monica). Jews. Mooser, Abraham. 1858-1910. *1279*

—. Canada. Cowboys. Rodeos. USA. 1870-1970. *1735*

—. Cattle Raising. Conrad, Charles Edward. Conrad, William G. Montana (Fort Benton, Great Falls, Kalispell). 1850-1902. *1247*

—. Cattle Raising. Frewen, Moreton. Great Britain. Powder River Cattle Company. Wyoming. 1878-85. *1131*

—. Chicago, Burlington and Quincy Railroad. Ethics. Perkins, Charles Elliott. Public Opinion. Railroads. 1870-81. *1359*

—. Chouteau, Pierre, Jr. Fur Trade (decline of). Indians. Mississippi River region. Rice, Henry M. Sibley, Henry H. Ullman, Joseph. 1830-80. *887*

—. Civil War. Fort Scott. Kansas. Poetry. Ware, Eugene Fitch. 1866-1907. *1941*

—. Cooperative Communities. Snow, Lorenzo. Utah (Brigham City). 1864-96. *2802*

—. Diaries. Frontier and Pioneer Life. McConnell, Robert. Pacific Northwest. 1881. *1223*

—. Economic Conditions. Jews. New Mexico (Santa Fe). Southwest. Spiegelberg Family. 1846-93. *1237*

—. Farmers. Panic of 1893. Politics. Populism. Progressivism. 19c. *3825*

—. Farmers. Texas (New Braunfels). Torrey, John F. 1846-73. *1215*

—. Gold Rushes. Illinois (Chicago). Missouri (St. Louis). Montana (Madison County). Portland-Walla Walla-Mullan Road. Trade Routes. 1862-68. *984*

—. Gronna, Asle J. North Dakota. Republican Party. Territorial Government. 1890-1904. *3805*

—. Buildings (stone). Montana (Helena). 1880's. *2136*

—. Oregon (Ashland). Spas (mineral water). Winburn, Jesse. 1921-23. *3912*

—. Utah. 1850-70. *1270*

Business Cycles *See also* Business History; Depressions.

—. California (San Francisco). Jews. Pacific Coast Stock Exchange. Stock Exchange. 1849-1917. *1255*

—. Idaho (Mineral City). Silver Mining. 1870's-80's. *1642*

Business History. Kansas. Missouri (Kansas City). Settlement. Slavery. 1854-57. *2533*

—. Texas (Brazos River). Torrey Trading Post. 1840's. *1268*

Business ventures. Dawes, Charles G. Nebraska (Lincoln). 1887-94. *3944*

Business ventures (proposed). Diplomacy. Latin America. Montana. Stuart, Granville. 1894-1918. *2721*

Bustamante y Tagle, Bernardo Antonio de. Apache Indians (Gila). Military Campaigns. New Mexico (Cliff). Sáenz, Bartolomé. Spaniards. Vildósola, Gabriel Antonio de. 1756. *31*

—. Attitudes (whites). Chinese Americans (image of). Negroes. Racism. 1848-90. *1451*
—. Attitudes (whites). Mexican Americans. Political Participation. Racism. 20c. *3037*
—. Audubon, John James (*Birds of America*). Grayson, Andrew Jackson. Mexico. Ornithology. Painting. 1846-69. *2143*
—. Audubon, John Woodhouse. El Dorado Trail. Gold Rushes. Hampden Mining Company. Kit Carson Association. Webb, Henry L. 1849. *360*
—. Australian ballot. Political Corruption. Reform. Voting and Voting Behavior. 1891. *3803*
—. Australian ballot. Political Corruption. "Vallejo Tapeworm" (ballot). Voting and Voting Behavior. 1850's-91. *3076*
—. Authority (episcopal). Catholic Church. New Spain. 16c-1964. *158*
—. Automobiles. Interior Department. Yosemite National Park. 1900-67. *4122*
—. *Aviator* (aircraft). Editors and Editing. Marriott, Frederick. 1849-83. *1305*
—. Ballads. Folk Songs. Immigration. Portugese Americans. 1920's-50's. *1964*
—. Ballads. Folk Songs. Portuguese Americans. 19c. *1965*
—. Bancroft, Hubert Howe. Forster, John. Mexico. Pico, Pío. Politics. Savage, Thomas. 1832-47. *214*
—. Bancroft, Hubert Howe. Historians. Hittell, Theodore Henry. Methodology (scientific approach, stylistic approach). 20c. *3077*
—. Bank of America National Trust and Savings Association. Bank of Italy. Giannini, Amadeo Peter. Italian Americans. 1904-30. *3886*
—. Banking. Economic Conditions. Gold Rushes. Wells, Fargo and Company. 1852-1972. *1313*
—. Banking. Nevada. New York. Pony Express. Transportation. Wells, Fargo and Company. 1852-68. *1311*
—. Banning's Indian Boarding School. Engelhardt, Zephyrin. Mission Santa Barbara. St. Joseph's College. Teaching. 1851-1934. *166*
—. Bannock Indians. Indian-White Relations. Military policy. Mormons. Oregon. Shoshoni Indians. Utah. Washington. Westward Movement. 1859-63. *771*
—. Bard, Thomas Robert. Johnson, Hiram. Pardee, George C. Political Reform. Propaganda. Railroads and State. Republican Party. Southern Pacific Railroad. 1899-1905. *3766*
—. Bartlett, John Russell. Boundary Commission. Camp Yuma. Colorado River. Craig, Louis (murder). 1852. *364*
—. Beachy, William C. ("Hill"). Idaho. Mines. Nevada. Stagecoaches. 1864-73. *1303*
—. Beale, Edward Fitzgerald. Explorers. 1822-93. *448*
—. Beale, Edward Fitzgerald. Federal Government. Public Lands. Surveying. 1861-64. *1140*
—. Beekeeping. Business. Harbison, John Steward. Inventions. Langstroth, Lorenzo Lorraine. 1622-1869. *1286*
—. Bekeart, Frank. Bekeart, Philip. Bekeart, Philip Kendall. Gunsmiths. 1849-1965. *1220*
—. Benjamin, Judah P. 1860-65. *3049*
—. Benjamin, Judah P. Black, Jeremiah S. Castillero, Andres. Courts. Frémont, John C. Land claims. Legal Ethics. Mines. *New Almaden Case* (US, 1860). Randolph, Edmund. 1860. *871*
—. Bibliographies. Books (miniature). Printing. 1850's-1970. *2053*
—. Bibliographies. Colorado. Gold Rushes. Guidebooks. Westward Movement. 1848-49. 1858-59. *931*
—. Bibliographies. Ethnic Groups. 1834-1971. *3098*
—. Bibliographies. Missions and Missionaries. Serra, Junípero. 1787-1969. *157*
—. Bibliographies. Taylor, Alexander S. 1863-1967. *3095*
—. Bidwell, John. DeSmet, Pierre Jean. Marsh, John. Oregon Trail. Overland Journeys to the Pacific. 1841. *400*
—. Bierce, Ambrose G. Letters. Miller, Joaquin. Stoddard, Charles W. Twain, Mark. 1870's. *1906*
—. Bingham, John A. Letters. Missouri (Independence). Santa Fe Trail. Travel account. 1848-49. *377*
—. Black Laws. Civil Rights (restrictions). Migration, Internal. Negroes. 1848-60. *1445*
—. Books. Hide and tallow industry. Voyages. 1820's-30's. *39*

—. Branciforte, Marqués de. Colonization (proposed). Costansó, Miguel. Spain. 1794. *150*
—. Brant, David Otto (interview). Brant, Otto Freeman. Chandler, Harry. C-M Ranch. Land development. Mexico. Otis, Harrison Gray. Real Estate Business. Sherman, Moses H. Tejon Ranch. Title Insurance and Trust Company. 1893-1920's. *3950*
—. British Columbia. Fraser River. Gold Rushes. Prospectors. 1858-65. *3431*
—. Browne, J. Ross. Haraszthy de Mokcsa, Agoston. Lobbying. Wilson, Benjamin D. Winemaking. 1866. *3068*
—. Browne, J. Ross. Federal Government. Gold Mines and Mining. Political Corruption. Westward Movement. 1850's-60's. *1754*
—. Bryan, William Jennings. Federal Government. Japanese Americans. State Legislatures. Webb Act (1913). Wilson, Woodrow (administration). 1913-14. *3999*
—. Bryan, William Jennings. Foreign Relations. Immigration. Japan. Land Tenure. Popular sovereignty (principle of). 1901-15. *4001*
—. Bryant, Edwin *What I Saw in California*. Gold Rushes. 1849-69. *3010*
—. Bryce, James. Chinese Americans. Kearney, Denis. Workingmen's Party. 1879-88. *3072*
—. Bucareli y Ursúa, Antonio María. Colonial Government. Letters. Neve, Felipe de. Serra, Junípero. 1776-77. *188*
—. Buildings. Fire. Gold Rushes. Iron shutters. 1849-50's. *2106*
—. Bulla, Robert Nelson. Separatist Movements. 1907-21. *3056*
—. Bunsen, Christian von. Colonization. Humboldt, Alexander von. Prussia. Roenne, Friedrich von. 1842. *193*
—. Burger, James. Frontier and Pioneer Life. Gold Rushes. Letters. New York City (Staten Island). Westward Movement. 1850. *1027*
—. Burnett, Peter Hardeman. Catholic Church. Disciples of Christ. Indians. Mission Waiilatpu. 1820's-1909. *2327*
—. Burns, Walter Noble. Folklore. Murieta, Joaquin. Ridge, John Rollin. 1850's-1967. *2984*
—. Burnt Ranch Massacre. Ethnohistory. Tolowa Indians. 1853-1963. *3033*
—. Burr, Aaron. Mexican War. Southwest. Yale University, Beinecke Library. 17c-19c. *259*
—. Burr, Jason F. Connecticut Mining and Trading Company. Diaries. *General Morgan* (vessel). Gold Rushes. Lyman, Albert. Voyages. 1848-50. *958*
—. Burrus, Ernest J. Humboldt, Alexander von. Kino, Eusebio Francisco. Maps. Mexico. 1681-1710. 1965. *64*
—. Business. Economic Reform. Public Utilities Act (1911). Railroads and State. State regulation. 1911-15. *3852*
—. Cabrillo, Juan Rodríguez. Colorado River. Cortés, Hernán. Discovery and Exploration. Drake, Sir Francis. Mexico. Portolá, Gaspar de. Sovereignty (symbolic claims to). Ulloa, Francisco de. Vizcaíno, Sebastián. 1535-1600. *75*
—. Cabrillo, Juan Rodríguez. Discovery and Exploration. Pacific Coast. 1542-43. *72*
—. Cabrillo National Monument. Historical Sites and Parks. 1968. *67*
—. California Mutual Protective Association. Diaries. Gold Rushes. Kansas. Overland Journeys to the Pacific. Robinson, Charles. 1849-92. *323*
—. *Californian* (periodical). Gold Rushes (stories of). Harte, Bret. Literature. *Overland Monthly* (periodical). 1849-71. *1869*
—. Catalá, Magín. Catholic Church. Indians. Mission Santa Clara de Asís. Music. Viader, José. 17c. *125*
—. Catholic Church. Church Schools. Constitutions, State. State Aid to Education. 1852-78. *1831*
—. Catholic Church. Civil Court Cases. Hague Tribunal. Mexico. Mixed Claims Commission. Pious Fund (charitable trust). 19c-1967. *164*
—. Catholic Church. Courts. Doyle, John Thomas. Mexico. Missions and Missionaries. Pious Fund. 1819-1906. *159*
—. Catholic Church. Gold Rushes. Letters. Phelan, Gregory J. 1848-58. *2354*
—. Catholic Church. Jesuits. Lopez de Santa Anna, Antonio. Mexico. Pious Fund. Spain. 1767-1913. *161*

—. Catholic Church. Journalism. *Serra Bulletin* (periodical). *Western Jesuit* (periodical). 1853-63. *2054*
—. Catholic Church. San Francisco Chancery Archives. 1769-1962. *2390*
—. Cattle Raising. Cowboys. Mexico. Saddles, Mother Hubbard. Spain. Texas. 16c-1966. *46*
—. Central Pacific Railroad. Chinese Americans. Construction. Railroads. Sierra Nevada Mountains. 1865-69. *1528*
—. Central Pacific Railroad. Congress. Crocker, Charles. Hopkins, Mark. Huntington, Collis P. Judah, Theodore D. Lobbying. Railroads (transcontinental). Stanford, Leland. Surveying. 1862. *1373*
—. Chandler, Raymond (*The Long Goodbye*). Editors and Editing. Slang. 1954. *1949*
—. Child Study. Harris, James William. Teachers. ca 1903-57. *3608*
—. China. Expansionism. Jackson, Andrew. Massachusetts (Boston). Ports (Pacific Coast). Trade. 1789-1829. *1228*
—. China. Foreign Relations. Japan. Russia. Trade. 1830's-1917. *305*
—. Chinese. Credit-ticket system. Immigration. Social Customs. 1850's-60's. *1442*
—. Chinese Americans. Discrimination, Housing. Law (county, state). Negroes. Proposition 14 (1967). 1890-1967. *4009*
—. Chinese Americans. Howe, James Wong. Immigration. Kingman, Dong. Labor. 1850-1900. *3009*
—. Chinese Americans. Immigration. Racism. 1840's-70's. *3008*
—. Chinese Americans (exclusion). Kearney, Denis. Labor. Racism. 1870's. *3065*
—. Chinese Exclusion Act (1882). Coolidge, Mary. Immigration. 1852-82. *1510*
—. Christian Science. Health Insurance. Medicine and State. Social Insurance Commission. 1915-18. *3700*
—. Chumash Indians. Engelhardt, Zephyrin. Mission Santa Barbara. Rebellions. Ripoll, Antonio (report). Sarría, Vincente Francisco de. 1824. *114*
—. Church and State. Colonial Government. Croix, Teodoro de. Missions and Missionaries. Neve, Felipe de. Serra, Junípero. 1774-82. *105*
—. Church and State. Courts. Religious Education. Sunday Laws. Taxation (exemption). ca 1880-1964. *2220*
—. Cities. Diaries. Gold Mines and Mining. *Ka Hae Hawaii* (newspaper). Pule, J. Smith, Lowell. Transportation. 1858-59. *955*
—. City Government. Economic Conditions. Military. Spain. 1776-1821. *191*
—. Civil Court Cases. Land Act (1851). Mexican Americans. 1851-53. *1147*
—. Civil Rights. Courts (state). *Mirror of the Times* (newspaper). Negroes. Testimony laws (repeal). 1851-63. *3026*
—. Civil Rights. Education. Negroes. Sanderson, Jeremiah B. 1854-75. *1494*
—. Civil War. Confederate States of America. Kennedy, H. Military Intelligence. Nevada (Virginia City). 1864. *604*
—. Civil War. Low, Frederick F. Military Recruitment. Stanford, Leland. Stoeckl, Baron de. 1861-65. *635*
—. Civil War claims. Federal Government. Military Finance. State Government. 1861-1967. *612*
—. Clar, C. Raymond. Forests and Forestry. History. Pardee, George C. Research. State Government. 18c-1927. *1178*
—. Clay, Henry. Compromise of 1850. Slavery. Statehood movements. 1850. *3031*
—. Climate. Physical Geography. Population. Urbanization. 1840-1960. *1570*
—. Climatotherapy. Diseases. Folk Medicine. 1860-1900. *2212*
—. Colleges and Universities. Junior Colleges. 1907-59. *3663*
—. Colonial Government. Gobernantes. Spain. 1769-1822. *204*
—. Colonialism. Mission San Gabriel Arcangel. Spain. 1771-1971. *160*
—. Colonization law (1824). Land grant titles. 1824-48. *172*
—. Colorado River. Freight and Freightage. Hawaii. Idaho. Montana. Mormons. Railroads. Settlement. Shipping. Trade. Union Pacific Railroad. Utah (Salt Lake City). 1864-69. *861*

California (Fort Ross). Agriculture. Russia. 1841. *3006*

California (Fort Ross, San Francisco). Arguello, Concepción. Rezanov, Nikolai. Russia. 1805-41. *3086*

California (Freeport). Historians. Hunt, Rockwell D. (obituary). 1860's-1966. *3106*

California (Freeport; Sacramento River). City Life. Freeport Railroad Company. Hunt, Rockwell D. Railroads. Reminiscences. 20c. *3983*

California Geological Survey. Geology. Public Policy. Scientific Experiments and Research. State Legislatures. Whitney, Josiah Dwight. 1860-74. *2201*

California (Glendale). Arthur H. Clark Company. Clark, Arthur H. Clark, Arthur H., Jr. Galleher, Paul W. Publishers and Publishing. Rare Books. 1902-62. *2024*

California (Grass Valley). Cornish Americans. Frémont, John C. Grass Valley Cornish Carol Choir. Mines. 1848-1940. *1004*

California (Hetch Hetchy Valley). Camping. Dams. Duryea, Robert. Nature Conservation. Stillman, Dorothy. Yosemite National Park. 1910-14. *4112*

California Historical Society. Architecture. California (San Francisco). The Mansion (building). Whittier, William Franklin. 1894-1969. *2986*

—. Bibliographies. Camp, Charles L. Cowan, Robert E. *Quarterly* (periodical). Wagner, Henry R. 1871-1971. *3023*

—. Bibliographies. Wagner, Henry R. 1887-1957. *2397*

California Historical Society (Faxon Dean Atherton Collection). Atherton, Faxon Dean. Bear Flag Revolt. California (Monterey). Hammond, George P. (*The Larkin Papers*). Jones, Thomas ap Catesby. Larkin, Thomas Oliver. Letters. 1842-53. 1951-65. *565*

California History Foundation. Conference of California Historical Societies. Hunt, Rockwell D. (obituary). Southern California, University of. 1868-1966. *3060*

California History Institute. Hunt, Rockwell D. Jedediah Smith Society. 1947-67. *3001*

California (Hollywood). Film industry. 1887-1970. *3963*

—. Films. Fox, William. Sinclair, Upton. 1915-34. *3822*

California (Humboldt Bay). Bigler, John. Congress. Eel River Indians. Indians (agencies). McKee, Redick. Treaties. 1851-52. *3043*

—. Toponymy. 1968. *3002*

California (Humboldt County). Arcata and Mad River Railroad. Economic Conditions. Lumber and Lumbering. Railroads. Sacramento Valley Railroad. Simpson Logging Company. Union Plank Walk, Rail Track, and Wharf Company Railroad. Washington. 1853-1963. *1345*

California (Imperial Valley). Agricultural Labor. Mexican Americans. Strikes. 1928. *3967*

—. Agricultural Policy. Boulder Canyon Project Act (1928). Farmers. Reclamation Act (1902). 1850-1965. *4057*

—. Agricultural Production. California Development Company. Chaffey, George. Colorado River. Economic Development. Engineering. Railroads. Rockwood, Charles Robinson. Southern Pacific Railroad. 1905. *3922*

—. California Development Company. Colorado River. Federal Government. Imperial Irrigation District. Irrigation. Mexico. Reclamation Service. Southern Pacific Railroad. 1901-12. *3942*

California (Imperial Valley; Coachella Valley). Date industry. Marketing. Tariff. 1890-1939. *4040*

California (Imperial Valley, San Fernando Valley). Brant, David Otto (interview). Colorado River Land Company. Land development. ca 1923-63. *3951*

California Indians (southern). Culture. Horses (use of). Plains Indians. Pueblo Indians. Southwest. Spain. 1541-1850. *199*

California Infantry, 3rd. Civil War. Connor, Patrick E. Mormons. Postal Service (protection of). Utah. Young, Brigham. 1861-65. *634*

California (Irvine). Irvine, James. Railroads. Santa Fe Railroad. Settlement. 1887-1967. *1693*

California (Kern County). Austin, Mary. Frontier and Pioneer Life. Literature. 1888-92. *1969*

California (Klamath County; Humboldt County; Siskiyou County). County Government. Economic Conditions. 1876. *3058*

California Land Grant Act (1851). Civil Court Cases. Land Tenure. Legislation. Mexico. Suscol Principle. USA. 1850's. *1149*

California (Long Beach). City Government. Civil Court Cases. Mallon, Felix. Oil Industry and Trade. State Government. 1930-66. *3875*

California (Long Beach, Los Alamitos). Boascana, Geronimo. Cattle Raising. Fages, Pedro. Indians. Nieto, Manuel Perez. 1784-1952. *209*

California (Los Angeles). Architecture. B'nai B'rith synagogue. Jews. Kysor, Ezra F. 1873-96. *1516*

—. Architecture. Eisen, Percy A. Walker, Albert R. 1920-40. *3673*

—. Arizona. Arkansas. Fort Smith. Railroads (transcontinental). Santa Fe Railroad. Surveying. Whipple, Amiel Weeks. 1853-54. *347*

—. Auditorium Company. Buildings. Hazard's Pavilion. Los Angeles Philharmonic Auditorium. Music Center. Temple Baptist Church. 1886-1964. *1818*

—. Banning, Phineas. Butterfield Overland Mail. Los Angeles and San Pedro Railroad. Railroads. Shipping. Stagecoaches. Transportation. 1846-61. *1293*

—. Boddy, E. Manchester. *Daily News* (newspaper). Democratic Party. Douglas, Helen Gahagan. Political Reform. Press. 1926-54. *3662*

—. Brown, John. Flores, José María. Fort Moore Hill. Gillespie, Archibald. Mexican War. Rescue attempts. Stockton, Robert Field. 1846. *569*

—. Catholic Church. Law. Scott, Joseph. 1867-1958. *3096*

—. Celebrations (religious). Hall, Hiland. Letters. Social Customs. Vermont (North Bennington). 1852. *2309*

—. Cemeteries. Hebrew Benevolent Society of Los Angeles. Jews. 1855-1968. *1454*

—. *Century Magazine* (periodical). Jackson, Helen Hunt. Settlement. 1883. *195*

—. Cleveland, Grover. Irrigation. Water Conservation. 1891-1901. *4142*

—. Climatotherapy. Hospitals (founding of). Sanitation. Settlement. 1850-1900. *2210*

—. Colorado (Denver). Juvenile Courts. Lindsey, Benjamin Barr. Reform. 1894-1943. *3565*

—. Colorado River Aqueduct. Economic Development. Film Industry. Huntington, Henry. McPherson, Aimee Semple. Owens River Aqueduct. Urbanization. Water Supply. 1900-64. *3991*

—. Crespi, Juan. Diaries. Discovery and Exploration. Fages, Pedro. Perez, Juan. Portolá, Gaspar de. 1769-74. *3099*

—. Diaries. Fort Leavenworth. Kansas. Kearny, Stephen Watts. Mexican War. Mormons. New Mexico (Santa Fe). Whitworth, Robert W. 1846-47. *550*

—. Fairfax Temple. Jews. Reminiscences. Sonderling, Jacob. 1923-63. *3681*

—. Federal Government. Huntington, Collis P. Ports. 1870-1964. *1664*

—. Federal Government. Ports. 1871-1934. *1665*

—. Federal Records Centers. Research. 1853-1968. *302*

—. Folk Songs. Lummis, Charles Fletcher. Mexican Americans. Museums. New Mexico. Railroads. Santa Fe Railroad. Southwest Museum. 1880's-1920's. *1902*

—. Food Industry. Japanese American Company Union. Labor Unions and Organizations. Race Relations. Retail Food Clerks' Union. 1930's. *3059*

—. Fort Tejon. Mormons. Mowry, Sylvester. Nevada. Overland Journeys to the Pacific. Utah (Salt Lake City). 1854-55. *322*

—. France (Bordeaux). Hawaii. Trade. Vignes, Jean Louis. Winemaking. 1779-1862. *1254*

—. Friday Morning Club. Severance, Caroline M. Women. 1891-1968. *3982*

—. Ghettos. Housing. Race Relations. 1890-1930. *4003*

—. Harman, Moses. Illinois (Chicago). Journalism. Kansas. Political Protest. Valley Falls Liberal League. 1879-1908. *2055*

—. Historical Sites and Parks. Mexican Culture. Spanish Culture. 1781. *210*

—. Jews. 1850-60. *1547*

—. Kindergarten. Severence, Caroline M. Unitarianism. Woman Suffrage. 1875-1914. *1810*

—. Letters. London, Jack. Lummis, Charles Fletcher. Southwest Archaeological Society. 1905. *1903*

—. Lynchings. Vigilantes. 1835-74. *1748*

—. Murrieta, Joaquin. Myths and Symbols. 16c-20c. *3080*

—. Special Libraries Association. 1968. *2982*

California (Los Angeles area). Boundaries. Burnett, Robert. Land Tenure. Public Domain. Redondo, Sausal. Rosecrans, William Starke. 1848-87. *1158*

California (Los Angeles; Monterey). Dodson, Jacob. Frémont, John C. Kearney, Stephen Watts. Negroes. 1847. *2995*

California (Los Angeles; Owens Valley). Agriculture. Newspapers. Water Supply. 1924-27. *4140*

California (Los Angeles, San Francisco). Assassination. Lincoln, Abraham. Martial Law. McDowell, Irvin. Newspapers. 1865. *3092*

—. Johnson, Hiram. Labor Unions and Organizations. Propaganda. Voting and Voting Behavior. 1914. *3817*

California (Los Angeles, San Pedro). American Civil Liberties Union. Freedom of Speech. Industrial Workers of the World. Sinclair, Upton. Strikes. 1923. *3838*

—. Economic Development. Harbor. Railroads. Santa Fe Railroad. Southern Pacific Railroad. Union Pacific Railroad. 1869-1917. *1404*

California (Los Angeles, San Pedro Bay). Banning, Phineas. Construction. Peck, George H. Ports. White, Stephen M. 1592-1969. *1649*

California (Los Angeles; Santa Barbara). Amat, Thaddeus. Bishops. Cathedrals. Catholic Church. Our Lady of Sorrows Church. Saint Vibiana's Cathedral. 1856-76. *2387*

California (Los Angeles; Santa Clara Valley). California Battalion (route of). Frémont, John C. Historiography. Military Occupation. 1846. *542*

California (Los Angeles, Watts). Architecture. Rodilla, Sam. Rodilla Towers. 1921-54. *3572*

California (Los Angeles-Monterey diocese). Bishops. Cantwell, John Joseph. Catholic Church. 1915-17. *3704*

California (Los Angeles-San Diego Diocese). Cantwell, John Joseph. Catholic Church. Confraternity of Christian Doctrine. Immigrant Welfare Department. Mexican Americans. Social Work. 19c. *1553*

California (Malibu). Folk Songs. Haggerty, Jack (legend of). Michigan (southern). 1872. *1910*

California (Marysville). Frontier and Pioneer Life. Gold Rushes. Letters. Missouri (Fort Leavenworth). Overland Journeys to the Pacific. Travel account. 1850. *335*

California (Mojave Desert). Bevo (beer, sale of). Prohibition. Reminiscences. Shelp, Willard B., Jr. 1918. *3084*

—. Conservation of Natural Resources. Dangermond, Peter. Falconer, Smith, Jr. Parks. Smith, Jedediah Strong. Water Resources, Department of. 1826. 1965. *905*

California (Mokelumne Hill). Fox, P. V. Frontier and Pioneer Life. Gold Mines and Mining. Letters. Newton, Louisa M. 1852-53. *1010*

California (Montecito). Gardens. Gould, William P. La Favorita (residence). 1905. *3105*

California (Monterey). Atherton, Faxon Dean. Bear Flag Revolt. California Historical Society (Faxon Dean Atherton Collection). Hammond, George P. (*The Larkin Papers*). Jones, Thomas ap Catesby. Larkin, Thomas Oliver. Letters. 1842-53. 1951-65. *565*

—. Bucareli y Ursúa, Antonio María. Fages, Pedro. Letters. Military Camps and Forts. 1773. *112*

—. Diaries. Gómez, Rafael. 1831-37. *3*

—. Foreign Relations. France. Great Britain. Jones, Thomas ap Catesby. Mexico. Navies. 1842. *552*

—. Foreign Relations. Great Britain. Jones, Thomas ap Catesby. Mexico. Navies. Upshur, Abel P. 1842. *553*

—. Jones, Thomas ap Catesby. Lake Borgne (battle). Mexico. Navies. Plantations. Virginia (Fairfax County). War of 1812. 1790-1858. *554*

California (Monterey; Los Angeles; Santa Barbara). Amat, Thaddeus. Catholic Church. Mora y Borrell, Francisco. Spain. 1827-1905. 1962. *2388*

California (Monterey, San Diego). Croix, Marqués de. Fages, Pedro. Letters. Missions and Missionaries. Serra, Junípero. 1770-71. *113*

California (San Miguel Island). Cabrillo, Juan Rodríguez. Canaliño Indians. 1542-1946. *58*

California (San Pedro). Army Corps of Engineers. Railroads. Shipping (deep water). Southern Pacific Railroad. 1867-90. *1340*

California (San Pedro Bay). Ports. Trade. 19c. *1708*

California (Santa Barbara). 1893. *3052*

—. Arlington Hotel. Reminiscences. Social Conditions. Storke, Thomas M. Tourism. 1880's-90's. *1432*

—. Art (etchings). Borein, Edward. 20c. *2140*

—. Ballard, Shreve. Railroads. Reminiscences. Southern Pacific Railroad. Transportation. 1910's. *3847*

—. Borein, Edward. Borein, Lucile. Cowboys. Decorative Arts. Poetry. 1872-1947. *2152*

—. Chinese Americans. Chow, Gin. Reminiscences. Spaulding, Edward Selden. 20c. *4025*

—. Civil Court Cases. McCormick, Katherine Dexter. McCormick, Stanley R. Mental Illness. Riven Rock Family Estate. 1900-47. *3924*

—. Dana, Richard Henry, Jr. Diego, García. Fiestas. Social Customs. 1820-1966. *1433*

—. Episcopal Church, Protestant. Furlong, Mary Elizabeth. Furlong, Matthew W. Letters. Voyages. Williams, Thomas George. 1864-69. *3029*

—. Flower Festival. 1895. *3104*

—. Railroads. Reminiscences. Stanley, Leo L. 1900's. *3949*

California (Santa Barbara Channel Islands). Letters. Powell, Laurence Clark. Travel account. Wright, Austin T. 1931. *3102*

California (Santa Barbara Channel; Point Conception). Cabrillo, Juan Rodríguez. Lighthouses. Vizcáino, Sebastián. 1542-1965. *77*

California (Santa Catalina Island). Civil War. Indians (reservations). Military Occupation. 1864. *638*

California (Santa Catalina Island; Avalon). Photography. Resorts. 19c-1972. *2083*

California (Santa Clara Valley). Diaries. Fowler, Matthew Van Benschoten. 1851. *362*

California (Santa Cruz Island). Caire family. Catholic Church. Churches. 1542-1936. *2385*

California (Santa Monica). Business. Jews. Mooser, Abraham. 1858-1910. *1279*

California (Santa Monica Canyon). Celebrations (religious). Fiesta. Marquez, Reye y. 19c. *2334*

California (Santa Paula). Fruit and Fruit Crops (industry). Lemons. Oil Industry and Trade. 1890's-1945. *3851*

California (Santa Ynez Valley). Economic Conditions. Settlement. 1782-1962. *3063*

California (Shasta, Trinity Counties). Burrowes, Thomas. Burrows, Edward. Burrows, John T. Frontier and Pioneer Life. Gold Mines and Mining. Letters. New Jersey (Middletown). 1854-59. *1003*

California (Sierras). Central Pacific Railroad. Pioneer Stage Company. Railroads. Stagecoaches. Wells, Fargo and Company. 1849-60's. *1812*

California (Smith River). Indians. Rites and Ceremonies. Shakers. 1881-1930's. *2330*

California (Sonoma). Haraszthy de Mokcsa, Ágoston. Winemaking. ca 1850's-ca 1910. *1075*

California (Sonoma Valley). Buena Vista Vineyard. Haraszthy de Mokcsa, Ágoston. Ralston, William C. Winemaking. 1820-69. *1231*

California (southern). Adobe Flores. Land Tenure. 17c-19c. *1709*

—. Architecture. Spain (Cultural influence). Wright, Frank Lloyd. 1895-1930. *3591*

—. Bell, Alphonz E. California, University of (Los Angeles). Colleges and Universities. Land development. Occidental. 1875-1947. *3070*

—. Chandler, Raymond. Literature. Local History. 1930's-60's. *3653*

—. Civil War. Democratic Party. Downey, John G. Gwin, William. Hamilton, Henry. Knights of the Golden Circle. *Los Angeles Star* (newspaper). Secret Societies. Sectionalism. Sumner, Edwin Vose. 1860-65. *620*

—. Cooper, Ellwood. Reclamation of Land. Trees (eucalyptus). 1875-1910. *1208*

—. Dawson, Ernest. Miller, George Thomas (*Constructive Socialism*). Social Organizations. Voluntary Cooperative Association. Watson, James. 1913-22. *3677*

—. English Americans. Immigration. Irish Americans. 1850-70. *3000*

—. Goldwater, Barry. Individualism. Morality. Political Culture. Reagan, Ronald. Settlement. 1930-66. *3837*

—. Historians. Jews. Newmark, Marco Ross. 1878-1959. *1548*

—. Johnson, Hiram. LaFollette, Robert Marion. Political Attitudes. Progressivism. Wilson, Woodrow. 1910-20's. *3808*

California (Southern; San Diego). Gold Rushes. Law and Society. 1830's-40's. *206*

California (Southern; San Francisco). Agriculture (experiments). Coffee. Imports. 1870's-92. *1073*

California State Archives. Archives. 1966. *3013*

California State Board of Forestry. Forests and Forestry. Public Policy. 1883-1960. *1194*

California State Geological Survey. Conservation of Natural Resources. Discovery and Exploration. Fages, Pedro. Muir, John. Sequoia National Park. Smith, Jedediah Strong. Tharp, Hale D. Whitney, Josiah Dwight. 1772-1966. *446*

California State Relief Bureau. Lange, Dorothea. Migrant Labor. Photography. 1936. *3957*

California (Stockton). Agricultural Labor. American Federation of Labor. Associated Farmers. California Processors and Growers, Inc. Cannery Workers. Congress of Industrial Organizations. International Longshoremen's Association. Strikes. Teamsters' Union. 1937. *3939*

—. Cemeteries. Jews. Temple Israel Cemetery. 1849-68. *1533*

—. LeDoux, Emma. McVicar, A. N. Murder. Trials. 1906-41. *2997*

—. Restorations. Sperry Flour Mills. 1888. 1968. *1251*

California (Sunnyvale). Fremont High School. Frontier thesis. Students. Turner, Frederick Jackson. 1965. *1855*

California (Tragedy Springs). Mormon Battalion. Murder. 1848. *1756*

California Trail. Diaries. Humbolt Trail. Nevada Territory. Overland Journeys to the Pacific. Yager, James Pressley. 1863. *379*

—. Discovery and Exploration. Hensley, Samuel J. Salt Lake Cutoff. Utah. 1849-50's. *367*

—. Mineral springs. Travel accounts. Wyoming (Soda Springs, Steamboat Springs). ca 19c. *415*

California (Tulare County). Political Parties. Populism. 1892. *3756*

California, University of. Collectors and Collecting. Libraries. 1964. *3020*

—. Colleges and Universities. Oil Industry and Trade. Scientific Experiments and Research. Stanford University. 1900-25. *3964*

—. Kerchen, John L. Labor. Sharrenberg, Paul. Vocational Education. 1921-41. *3582*

California, University of (Bancroft Library). Alaska. Bancroft, Hubert Howe. Diaries. Libraries. Petroff, Ivan. Travel account. 1878. *3535*

—. Bolton, Herbert Eugene. Colleges and Universities. History Teaching. Stanford University. Texas, University of. Turner, Frederick Jackson. 20c. *1*

—. Bolton, Herbert Eugene. Explorers. Historians. Priestley, Herbert Ingram. Spanish borderlands. 1875-1944. *73*

—. Greenwood, Robert. Imprints. Libraries. 1850-62. *2034*

—. Hammond, George P. Scholes, France V. Serra Award. Speeches, Addresses, etc.. 1964. *57*

California, University of (Berkeley). Barrows, David Prescott. Colleges and Universities. Gilman, Daniel Coit. Moses, Bernard. Political Science. Teaching. 1872-1951. *1862*

—. Crespi, Juan. Excavations. Los Angeles County Museum of Natural History. Paleontology. Rancho La Brea. 1769-1968. *128*

California, University of, Berkeley (Bacon Hall). Bacon, Henry Douglas. Buildings. Paleontology. Teachers. 1868-1961. *3093*

California, University of (Los Angeles). Bell, Alphonz E. California (Southern). Colleges and Universities. Land development. Occidental. 1875-1947. *3070*

—. Editors and Editing. Iowa. *Pacific Historical Review* (periodical). Parish, John Carl. 1881-1939. *2929*

California (upper). Colonization (proposed). Foreign Policy. Prussia. 1842. *192*

California (Volcano). Astronomy. Lick, James. Madeira, George. 1860-87. 1969. *2214*

California Volunteers. Arizona (Tucson). Fergusson, David. Map Drawing. Mills, John B., Jr. 1862. *1633*

California (Weaverville). Battles. Chinese Americans. Gold Mining camps. 1854. *1486*

California (Yolo County; Woodland). Hershey, David N. Opera Houses. Theater. 1896-1913. *1730*

California (Yosemite). Letters. Muir, Daniel. Muir, John. 1869-76. *1181*

California (Yosemite Valley). Arizona. Conservation of Natural Resources. Grand Canyon. Internal Revenue Service. Lobbying. Public Policy. Sierra Club. Taxation (exemption). 1892-1966. *4138*

California (Yreka). Cairns, Andrew. Gold Rushes. Letters. Washington (Olympia). 1850-62. *959*

Californian (periodical). California. Gold Rushes (stories of). Harte, Bret. Literature. *Overland Monthly* (periodical). 1849-71. *1869*

Californios. Anza, Juan Bautista de. San Gorgonio Pass. Toponymy. 1774-1850's. *396*

—. Gold Rushes. Social Conditions. 1769-1864. *182*

Callahan, James Yancy. Bryan, William Jennings. Flynn, Dennis T. Oklahoma Territory. Political Campaigns. Populism. 1890's. *2616*

Callville. Adams, Samuel. Arizona. Colorado River. *Esmeralda* (vessel). Freight and Freightage. Mormons. 1866. *1410*

Camacho, Manuel Avila. Agricultural Labor. Braceros Program. California. Defense Policy. Foreign Relations. Mexico. Roosevelt, Franklin D. US-Mexico Defense Board. World War II. 1941-45. *3640*

Camanche (vessel). *Aquila* (vessel). California (San Francisco; Hathaway Wharf). Civil War. Ironclad vessels. 1863-99. *472*

—. California (San Francisco). Civil War. Naval Vessels. New Jersey. Ryan, James T. 1862-1920's. *644*

Camas Prairie (battle). Fred, Munn. Howard, Oliver Otis. Idaho. Military Campaigns. Nez Percé Indians. Reminiscences. Sioux Indians. 1876-77. *781*

Camera (use of). British Columbia. Deville, Edouard Gaston. Map Drawing. Photography. Surveying. 1885-1924. *3480*

Cameron, Colin. Arizona. Cattle Raising. Investments. San Rafael Cattle Company. 1882-1903. *1080*

Cameron, Ralph Henry. Arizona (Flagstaff). Atchison, Topeka and Santa Fe Railroad. Atlantic and Pacific Railway. Bright Angel Trail, formerly Cameron Trail. Mines. Powell, John Wesley. Railroads. Stanton, Robert Brewster. Tourism. 1883. *1281*

Camp Bowie. Apache Indians. Arizona (Chiricahua Pass). Camp Crittenden. Dorr, Levi L. Indian Wars. Letters. Military Campaigns. 1869. *834*

—. Arizona Territory. Armies. Camp Thomas. Diaries. Medicine (practice of). Moran, George H. R. 1878. *2195*

Camp, Charles L. Bibliographies. California Historical Society. Cowan, Robert E. *Quarterly* (periodical). Wagner, Henry R. 1871-1971. *3023*

Camp Crittenden. Apache Indians. Arizona (Chiricahua Pass). Camp Bowie. Dorr, Levi L. Indian Wars. Letters. Military Campaigns. 1869. *834*

Camp Floyd. Historical Sites and Parks. Johnston, Albert Sidney. Mormons. Utah. 1858-1966. *2801*

Camp Groce. Civil War. Confederate States of America. Prisons (military). Texas (Hempstead). 1863-64. *646*

Camp Henderson. Indian Wars. Military Campaigns. Oregon Volunteer Cavalry. Paiute Indians, Northern. 1864. *794*

Camp, Joseph. Diaries. Iowa. Nebraska (Omaha). Travel account. 1859. *336*

Camp Lewis. Economic Conditions. Washington (Tacoma). 1916-17. *2939*

Camp McDowell. Apache Indians. Arizona. *Arizona Miner* (newspaper). Indian Wars. McDowell, Irvin. Sanford, George B. 1866-73. *738*

Camp Missouri. Field, Gabriel. Field's Trace (road). Missouri (Chariton). Nebraska. Yellowstone Expedition. 1819. *418*

Camp Thomas. Arizona Territory. Armies. Camp Bowie. Diaries. Medicine (practice of). Moran, George H. R. 1878. *2195*

Camp Walbach. Army of Utah. Fort Riley-Bridger Pass (military road). Mormon War. Nebraska Territory. Wyoming (Cheyenne Pass). 1858-59. *516*

Camp Williams. Mormons. National Guard. Utah. 1894-1965. *2806*

Camp Wood. Lewis and Clark Expedition. Mississippi River. Missouri. 1803-04. *320*

Camp Yuma. Bartlett, John Russell. Boundary Commission. California. Colorado River. Craig, Louis (murder). 1852. *364*

Campaigns. *See* Military Campaigns.

Campaigns, Political. *See* Political Campaigns.

Campbell, John. Colorado. Courts. Labor Reform (eight-hour day). Mines. 1890-1913. *3910*

Campbell, Prince Lucien. Allen, Eric W. Colleges and Universities. Journalism. Oregon, University of, School of Journalism. Turnbull, George S. (review article). 1912-62. *3570*

Campbell, Robert. American Fur Company. Assiniboin Indians. Deschamps-Rem Feud. Fort Union. Fort William. Fur Trade. Larpenteur, Charles. Mountain Men. Rocky Mountain Fur Company. Sublette, William. 1807-72. *912*

—. American Fur Company. Diaries. Fort Union. Fort William. Fur Trade. McKenzie, Kenneth. Sublette and Campbell (firm). 1833. *878*

—. American Fur Company. Diaries. Fort William. Fur Trade. Missouri (St. Louis). Sublette, William. 1833. *879*

Campbell, Walter Stanley (pseud. Stanley Vestal). Indian-White Relations. Plains Indians. Scholarship. Sioux Indians. 1887-1957. *315*

Campgrounds, municipal. Automobiles. Kansas. Tourist Camp Bureau. 1920's. *3701*

Camping *See also* Outdoor Life.

—. Arizona. Diaries. Grand Canyon National Park. Kitt, Edith Stratton. Travel account. 1914. *3622*

—. California (Hetch Hetchy Valley). Dams. Duryea, Robert. Nature Conservation. Stillman, Dorothy. Yosemite National Park. 1910-14. *4112*

—. Colorado. Diaries. Ghost towns. Rocky Mountains. Schenck, Annie E. 1871. *1738*

—. Diaries. Moore, Alice. Moore, Frank (family). Vacations. Williams, William R. (family). Wyoming (southeastern). XX Ranch. 1912. *4068*

Campsites. Idaho (Salmon River area). Lewis and Clark expedition. Travel account. 1805. 1963. *426*

Camsell, Charles. Fort Simpson. Fur Trade. Northwest Territories (Mackenzie River district). Reminiscences. ca 1900. *3114*

Canada *See also* individual provinces; Atlantic Provinces; North America; Prairie Provinces.

—. Aberhart, William. Conscription, Military. Elections. Herridge, W. D. New Democracy Movement. Political Reform. Social Credit Party. 1939-40. *3387*

—. Agricultural Cooperatives. *Ha-meliz* (newspaper). *Ha-yom* (newspaper). Immigration. Jews. Russia. USA. 1880's. *1474*

—. Alaska. Bond, Marshall, Sr. Gold Rushes. Jack (dog). Klondike region. London, Jack (*Call of the Wild*). 1897-1903. *3487*

—. Alaska. Expansionism. Public Opinion. USA. 1867. *3516*

—. Alaska Boundary Award. Boer War. French Canadians. Great Britain. Nationalism. USA. 1900-03. *3148*

—. Alaska Purchase. Boundary disputes. Diplomacy. North Pacific Sealing Convention. Sealing. USA. 1867-1903. *3529*

—. Anabaptists. Bibliographies. Europe. Mennonites. Urbanization. USA. 1894-1968. *2349*

—. Anarchism and Anarchists. Great Britain. Martin, Wallace. *New Age* (newspaper). Orage, A. R. Social Credit (review article). 19c. 1967-69. *3138*

—. Anglo-American Boundary Commission. Boundaries. Royal Geographical Society. USA. 49th Parallel. 1872. 1967. *3180*

—. Annexation. Minnesota. Ramsey, Alexander. Taylor, James Wickes. 1868. *3275*

—. Annexation (attempted). Catholic Church. Great Britain. Métis. Rebellions. Riel, Louis. USA. Wolseley, Garnet Joseph. 1844-85. *3221*

—. Archbishops' Western Canada Fund. Church of England. Missions and Missionaries. Railroads. 1910-20. *3121*

—. Archives. Great Britain (London). Hudson's Bay Company (records). Preservation. Public Archives. 1671-1966. *3127*

—. Archives. United Church. 1965. *3195*

—. Archives (diocesan). Catholic Church. Society for the History of the Catholic Church. 1964. *3209*

—. Armies. Indian-White Relations. Northwest Mounted Police. USA. 1878. *3182*

—. Assimilation. Immigration. Ukrainians. 1891-1967. *3186*

—. Assiniboin Indians, Council of. Fur Trade. Letters. Orkney Islands. Red River. Sutherland, James. 1814-44. *3237*

—. Beads, Jacob. Cook, Thomas. Fort Ellice. Frontier and Pioneer Life. Millar, Henry. 1831-91. *3289*

—. Bering Sea. Diplomacy. Great Britain. USA. 1890-93. *3530*

—. Bibliographies. Gordon, Arthur Hamilton. Howe, Joseph. Local History. 1850's-1912. 1964. *3219*

—. Bibliographies. Local History. 1965. *3126*

—. Biculturalism. English Canadians. French Canadians. Historical and Scientific Society of Manitoba. Historical Society of St. Boniface. Manitoba, University of. St. Boniface College. 1962. *3293*

—. Blackfoot Indians. Boundary disputes. Indians (forced removal). Montana. USA. 1875-1900. *1127*

—. Boundary disputes. Great Britain. Oregon Treaty (1846). Strait of Juan de Fuca. USA. 1846-71. *3430*

—. British Columbia, University of. Colleges and Universities. Great Britain. Manitoba, University of. Medical Education. Minnesota, University of. Sherrington, Charles. Wesbrook, Frank Fairchild. 1868-1919. *3434*

—. Business. Cowboys. Rodeos. USA. 1870-1970. *1735*

—. Card, Elder. Mormons. Religious Liberty. Settlement. 1887-1902. *3147*

—. Catholic Church. Hudson's Bay Company. Missions and Missionaries. Trade. 1820-60. *3119*

—. *Chief Commissioner* (steamboat). *Northcote* (steamboat). Red River. Saskatchewan River. Steamboats. 1872-74. *3243*

—. Church and State. Hutterites. Pacifism. Persecution. USA. 1553-1969. *3177*

—. Church of England. Fur Trade. Hudson's Bay Company. Indians. Missions and Missionaries. 17c-18c. *3118*

—. Class consciousness. Elections. Independent Labor Party. Liberal Party. Manitoba (Winnipeg). Parliaments. Politics. Puttee, Arthur. Sifton, Clifford. 1899-1904. *3290*

—. Columbia River. Flood Control. USA. Water (power). 1964. *3190*

—. Columbia River Treaty. Flood Control. USA. Water (power). 1964. *3145*

—. Columbia River Treaty. Flood Control. USA. Water (power). 1961. 1964. *3188*

—. Columbia River Treaty (proposed). Flood Control. International Joint Commission (*Report*). USA. Water (power). 1959-63. *3154*

—. Columbia River Treaty (proposed). USA. Water (power). 1961-64. *3189*

—. Confederation. Economic Development. Treaty of Washington (1871). ca 1870's-90's. *3191*

—. Cooperatives. Fishermen's Protective Union. Grain Growers' Grain Company. Union Trading Company. United Grain Growers. 19c-20c. *3159*

—. Cree Indians. Fort Assiniboine. Montana. Negroes. Pershing, John J. 10th Cavalry, US. 1895-96. *523*

—. Culture. Europe. Medieval legacy. Mexico. USA. White, Lynn, Jr. (review article). 19c. *303*

—. Delafield, Joseph. Diaries. Lefroy, John Henry. Simpson, Frances Ramsey. Simpson, George. Simpson, Ramsey. Surveying. USA. Voyages. 1823-44. *3157*

—. Delisle, William. Great Salt Lake (specious map of). Lahontan, Baron of. Map Drawing. USA. 1703. *83*

—. Demography. Polish Canadians. 1900-60. *3453*

—. Dewdney, Edgar. Governors. Indian-White Relations. North West Rebellion. Prairie Provinces. 1879-1916. *3108*

—. Discovery and Exploration. Great Plains. LaVérendrye, Sieur de. 1730's-40's. *3113*

—. Discrimination. Hutterites. Pacifism. 1870-1967. *3169*

—. Economic Conditions. MacDonald, John Alexander. National Development. 19c. *3129*

—. Europe. Green, L. C. Indians. Law. Minority legal rights (review article). Modeen, Tore. Treaties. 1969-70. *3142*

—. Explorers. Great Lakes. Nature Conservation. Olson, Sigurd. Reminiscences. Travel account. 19c. *3158*

—. Farmers. Immigration. Ukrainian Canadians. 1891-1913. *3247*

—. Farmers. Minnesota. North Dakota. Taft, William H. Treaties. 1911-12. *4084*

—. Foreign Relations. Hudson's Bay Company. Royal Canadian Mounted Police. Settlement. USA. 17c-20c. *3255*

—. Fraser River. Mackenzie, Alexander. 1793-1963. *3438*

—. French Canadians. Grant, Ulysses S. Great Britain. Immigration. Irish Americans. Letters. Riel, Louis. USA. 1869-75. *3207*

—. Fur Trade. Great Britain. Hudson's Bay Company. Monopolies. Royal Society. Secrecy. Wegg, Samuel. 1670-1799. *3184*

—. Fur Trade. Great Britain. Letters. Skinning. Sunderland Canadian Lands Company Ltd. 1925. *3426*

—. Fur Trade. Hudson's Bay Company. Mergers. North West Company. 17c-19c. *3240*

—. Fur Trade (competition). Hudson's Bay Company. North West Company. Selkirk, 5th Earl of. 1800-21. *3131*

—. Gleason, Herbert Wendell. Jeffers, LeRoy. Photography. Rocky Mountains. USA. Wilderness. 1875-1937. *3192*

—. Hudson's Bay Company. Medals (commemorative). Money (promissory notes, tokens). Numismatics. 1791-1870. *3140*

—. Immigration. Ukrainians (Ruthenians). 1909. *3144*

—. Irrigation. National Irrigation Congress. USA. Western Canada Irrigation Association. 1907-26. *3455*

—. Jaxon, Joseph. North West Rebellion. Political Protest. Riel, Louis. USA. 19c. *3212*

—. Law Enforcement. Northwest Mounted Police. 1873-1918. *3194*

—. Letters. *Manitoba Free Press* (newspaper). Northwest Mounted Police. 1875-76. *3193*

—. Manitoba Act (1870). Métis. Resistance. Riel, Louis. 1844-85. *3252*

—. Mennonites. Urbanization. 1786-1968. *3136*

—. Military Campaigns. North West Rebellion. Reminiscences. Williams, Milton. 1885. *3422*

—. Rocky Mountains (passes). ca 1800-60. *3173*

Canada (Arctic, Pacific Coasts). Mineral Resources (rights to). Oil and Petroleum Products (exploration for). 1967. *3459*

Canada (Assiniboia, Rupert's Land). Governors. Mactavish, William. Métis. Riel, Louis. 1858-70. *3199*

Canada (Northern). Gold Rushes. Government intervention. Klondike region. Oil Industry and Trade. 1905-69. *3490*

Canada (Peace River). Fort Dunvegan. Fur Trade. Hudson's Bay Company. Land promotion. North West Company. 1805-1918. *3368*

Canada (Rupert's Land). Agriculture. Balance of Power. Economic Conditions. Fur Trade. Hudson's Bay Company. Indians. Métis. 1856-96. *3174*

—. Dennis, John S. Surveying. 19c. *3232*

—. Fur Trade. Hudson's Bay Company. Simpson, George. Travel accounts. 1826-60. *3176*

—. Law. Matheson, Hugh. Thom, Adam. 1850. *3304*

Canada (Saskatchewan River). Steamboats. 19c. *3408*

Canadian Northern Railway. British Columbia. Canadian Pacific Railway. Construction. Railroads. Roads. Rocky Mountains (Fraser Canyon). Trans-Canada Highway. 1861-1945. *3464*

—. Political Corruption (ascribed). Prairie Provinces. Railroads. Transportation. 1900's. *3161*

—. Prairie Provinces. Railroads. Settlement. 1900's. *3244*

Canadian northwest coast. Fur Trade. Hudson's Bay Company. Land Tenure. Overland Telegraph. Russians. Tolmie, William Fraser. 1838-67. *3447*

Canadian Pacific Irrigation Department. Alberta Irrigation Company. Alberta (Palliser Triangle area). Irrigation. 1878-1940. *3370*

Canadian Pacific Railway. Agricultural Production. Business. Economic Growth. Fort Garry. Manitoba (Winnipeg). Railroads. Urbanization. 1870-90. *3270*

—. Alberta. Cattle Raising. Railroads. 1881-83. *3230*

—. Cattle Raising. Centennial Celebrations. *Daily Tribune* (newspaper). Kansas. New York. 1867-80's. *1139*

—. Cattle Raising. Kansas (Abilene). Railroads. Texas. Westward Movement. 1867-71. *1091*

Chisum, John S. Dolan, James J. Lincoln County War. McSween, Alexander A. Murphy, Lawrence G. New Mexico. Riley, John H. 1878-83. *2859*

Chittenden, Hiram Martin. Conservation of Natural Resources. Forests and Forestry. Pinchot, Gifford. Roosevelt, Theodore. 1908-16. *4105*

—. DeSmet, Pierre Jean. Fur Trade. Historians. Missouri River. Steamboats. Yellowstone National Park. 1858-1917. *244*

—. Fur Trade. Historiography. Turner, Frederick Jackson. Webb, Walter Prescott. 1800-50. *906*

—. Fur Trade. Historiography. Turner, Frederick Jackson. Webb, Walter Prescott. 1800-50. *907*

—. Montana. Norris, Philetus W. Roads. Yellowstone National Park. 1870-1915. *1319*

Chivington, John M. Arapaho Indians. Cheyenne Indians. Colorado Volunteer Cavalry, 3rd Regiment. Evans, John. Indian Wars. Politics. Sand Creek Massacre. 1860-63. *859*

—. Cheyenne Indians. Colorado Cavalry, 3rd. Indian-White Relations. Politics. Sand Creek Massacre. 1862-65. *844*

—. Civil War. Colorado. Confederate States of America. Fort Lyons. Fort Wise. Guerrilla Warfare. Mattison, George. New Mexico. Reynolds, James S. Santa Fe Trail. 1861. *665*

—. Colorado. Great Plains. Indian Wars. Tappan, Samuel F. 1862-64. *722*

Choctaw Indians. American Board for Foreign Missions. Christianity. Education. Missions and Missionaries. Oklahoma. 1800-60. *1857*

—. Berry, Mrs. Houston Henry. Colleges and Universities. Frontier and Pioneer Life. Kidd-Key College. Oklahoma (Norman). Oklahoma, University of. Reminiscences. 1888-1966. *1579*

—. Boudinot, Elias C. Cherokee Indians. Oklahoma. Sovereignty (disputed). Supreme Court. Taxation (excise). Tobacco. Watie, Stand. 1860-71. *1250*

—. Cherokee Indians. Missions and Missionaries. Nez Percé Indians. Oneida Indians. Protestant Churches. Seneca Indians. Sioux Indians. Social Change. 1760-1860. *2313*

—. Chickasaw Indians. Freedmen's Oklahoma Association. Indian Territory. Indian-Negro relations. Land Tenure. 1866-89. *1439*

—. Civil War. Confederate States of America. Edwards, John. Indian Territory. Missionaries. Presbyterian Church. Vigilance Committee. 1861. *614*

—. Oklahoma. Presbyterian Church. Schools. Spencer Academy. 1842-1900. *1823*

Cholera epidemic. Indian-White Relations. Kansas. Missouri River. Steamboats. Westward Movement. 1851. *2529*

—. Kansas. 38th Infantry, US. 1866-67. *2563*

Chouteau, Paul. Barron, Joseph. Indians. Jefferson, Thomas. Peale, Charles Willson. Pennsylvania (Philadelphia). Portraits (silhouettes). Sagessaga (Little Osage Chief). 1806. *2108*

Chouteau, Pierre, Jr. Business. Fur Trade (decline of). Indians. Mississippi River region. Rice, Henry M. Sibley, Henry H. Ullman, Joseph. 1830-80. *887*

Chow, Gin. California (Santa Barbara). Chinese Americans. Reminiscences. Spaulding, Edward Selden. 20c. *4025*

Christian Science. California. Health Insurance. Medicine and State. Social Insurance Commission. 1915-18. *3700*

Christianity *See also* Catholic Church; Missions and Missionaries; Protestantism; Theology.

—. American Board for Foreign Missions. Choctaw Indians. Education. Missions and Missionaries. Oklahoma. 1800-60. *1857*

—. Indian religion. Plains Indians. 1970. *2375*

Christmas celebrations. Austrian Americans. Highland Boy Mine. Reminiscences. Richards, Paul. Serbian Americans. US Mining, Smelting, and Refining Company. Utah (Bingham Canyon). 19c. *2829*

—. Frontier and Pioneer Life. Montana Territory. 1854-72. *1585*

Chronicles of Oklahoma (periodical). Bibliographies. Education. *Mid-America* (periodical). *Minnesota History* (periodical). *Nebraska History Magazine. North Dakota History* (periodical). *Northwest Ohio Quarterly. Ohio Historical Quarterly.* Oklahoma. *Wisconsin Magazine of History.* 1968. *1844*

Chumash Indians. California. Engelhardt, Zephyrin. Mission Santa Barbara. Rebellions. Ripoll, Antonio (report). Sarría, Vincente Francisco de. 1824. *114*

Church and Social Problems. Colorado (Denver). Episcopal Church, Protestant. Hart, Henry Martyn. Income Tax. 1879-1920. *2367*

Church and State *See also* Religious Liberty.

—. Arizona. Estelric, Juan Bautista. Liberós, Ramón. Mission San José de Tumacàcori. Perez, Ignacio. 1821-23. *136*

—. California. Colonial Government. Croix, Teodoro de. Missions and Missionaries. Neve, Felipe de. Serra, Junípero. 1774-82. *105*

—. California. Courts. Religious Education. Sunday Laws. Taxation (exemption). ca 1880-1964. *2220*

—. Canada. Hutterites. Pacifism. Persecution. USA. 1553-1969. *3177*

—. Catholic Church. Federal Government. Northwest Territories (Regina). Ontario (Ottawa). Politics. Schools. Territorial Government. 1898-1903. *3233*

—. Local Government. Mormons. Utah. 19c. *2798*

—. Mormons. Political Participation. 19c-1966. *2300*

—. Mormons. Politics. 1835-1966. *2301*

Church bells. Old Colony Church. Oregon (Aurora). 1867. *2393*

Church History. Bibliographies. Drury, Clifford Merrill. Navy Chaplain Corps. San Francisco Theological Seminary. Trans-Mississippi West. 1934-69. *2315*

Church Missionary Society. Alaska. Fort Yukon. Kirkby, William West. Loucheux Indians. *Nor'Wester* (newspaper). Travel account. 1856-62. *3513*

—. Church of England. Cockran, William. Diaries. Manitoba (Red River Settlement). Simpson, George. 1825-65. *3265*

Church of England. Alberta. Country Life. Missions and Missionaries. 1902-16. *3222*

—. Alberta. Creighton, Oswin. Frontier and Pioneer Life. Missions and Missionaries. Travel account. 1910. *3372*

—. Alberta (southern). Blackfoot Indians (Blood). Missions and Missionaries. 1883-86. *3417*

—. Archbishops. Great Britain (Canterbury, York). Missions and Missionaries. Western Canada Fund. 19c. *3122*

—. Archbishops' Western Canada Fund. Canada. Missions and Missionaries. Railroads. 1910-20. *3121*

—. Canada. Fur Trade. Hudson's Bay Company. Indians. Missions and Missionaries. 17c-18c. *3118*

—. Church Missionary Society. Cockran, William. Diaries. Manitoba (Red River Settlement). Simpson, George. 1825-65. *3265*

—. Cree Indians. Diaries. Mackay, J. A. Missions and Missionaries. Saskatchewan. Stanley Mission. 1870-72. *3337*

Church of the Messiah. Adams, George Washington Joshua. Evangelism. Mormons. Palestine (Jaffa). 1811-80. *2225*

Church Schools *See also* Religious Education.

—. California. Catholic Church. Constitutions, State. State Aid to Education. 1852-78. *1831*

Churches *See also* Cathedrals.

—. Architecture. Coalville Tabernacle. Mormons. Photography. Utah. 1967. *2150*

—. Buildings. California (San Francisco). Mission San Francisco. 1776-91. *118*

—. Caire family. California (Santa Cruz Island). Catholic Church. 1542-1936. *2385*

—. German Americans. Texas (Fredericksburg). 1846. 1934-35. *1466*

—. Indians. Oregon (The Dalles). Shakers. 1896. 1971. *4007*

—. Music. New Mexico. 17c. *152*

Churches (spatial distribution). Nebraska. Rural Settlements. 1894-1968. *2376*

Cian, Thomas. Alemany, Joseph. California (San Francisco). Catholic Church. Chinese Americans. Missions and Missionaries. 1853-62. *1506*

Circus stories. Dime novels. Wild West Show Stories. 1890's-1900's. *1937*

Cisneros, José. Artists (illustrators). Bibliographies. Books. Bywaters, Jerry. Mead, Ben Carlton. Texas. 1967. *2104*

Cities *See also* headings beginning with the word city and the word urban; names of cities and towns by state; Housing; Rural-Urban Studies; Urbanization.

—. Advertising. Colorado (Colorado Springs, Durango). Denver and Rio Grande Western Railroad. Palmer, William Jackson. Railroads. 1836-73. *1700*

—. California. Diaries. Gold Mines and Mining. *Ka Hae Hawaii* (newspaper). Pule, J. Smith, Lowell. Transportation. 1858-59. *955*

—. Folklore. Literature. Regionalism. 17c-1966. *1932*

—. Frontier and Pioneer Life. Law Enforcement. Mining camps. 1849-1900. *1707*

—. German Americans. Immigration. Settlement. Texas. 1865-1968. *1490*

—. Gold Rushes. Nevada. 1859-1969. *1711*

—. Mines. Settlement. 19c. *1001*

—. Nebraska. Toponymy. 19c-1966. *1669*

—. Oklahoma. Railroads. 19c. *1646*

—. Population (decline). 1940-60. *3987*

Cities (gateway). Manitoba (Winnipeg). Transportation. USA. Wholesale Trade. 1970. *3269*

Cities (incorporation). Arizona Territory (Tucson). Land Tenure. Territorial Government. 1871-77. *1685*

Citizens' Party. Arnold, Henry J. City Government. Colorado (Denver). Political Reform. Speer, Robert W. 1912. *3986*

—. City Government. Colorado (Denver). Political Corruption. Progressivism. Reform. 1910. *3973*

City Government *See also* Cities; City Politics; Public Administration.

—. Alaska (Sitka). Economic Development. 1867-73. *3540*

—. Arnold, Henry J. Citizens' Party. Colorado (Denver). Political Reform. Speer, Robert W. 1912. *3986*

—. California. Economic Conditions. Military. Spain. 1776-1821. *191*

—. California (Long Beach). Civil Court Cases. Mallon, Felix. Oil Industry and Trade. State Government. 1930-66. *3875*

—. Citizens' Party. Colorado (Denver). Political Corruption. Progressivism. Reform. 1910. *3973*

—. Economic Development. Lumber and Lumbering. Oregon (Prineville). Railroads. 1890-1965. *3873*

—. Photography. Texas (Houston). 1880-1910. *2063*

City Life. Alberta (Edmonton). Toponymy. 19c-20c. *3410*

—. Arizona (Charleston, Milville). Silver Mining. 1878-89. *1644*

—. Arizona (Helvetia, Santa Rita Mountains). Copper Mines and Mining. Helvetia Copper Company. 1870's-1923. *1640*

—. Arizona (Yuma). Cargill, Andrew Hays. Doan, May Cargill. Reminiscences. 1902-20. *2872*

—. Brueggemann, John. Celebrations (International Night). Ethnic Groups. Music. Social Customs. Wyoming (Rock Springs). 1920's. *4004*

—. California (El Monte). Farmers. Settlement. 1851-66. *1662*

—. California (Freeport; Sacramento River). Freeport Railroad Company. Hunt, Rockwell D. Railroads. Reminiscences. 20c. *3983*

—. California (Sacramento, San Francisco). Frontier and Pioneer Life. Gold Mines and Mining. Letters. Thompson, Ephraim. 1850's. *933*

—. California (San Francisco). Cogswell and Rand Company. Cogswell, Moses Pearson. Diaries. 1849. *1636*

—. Chickasaw Indians. Economic Growth. Oklahoma (Ardmore). Roth, Alva. Settlement. 1834-1913. *1696*

—. Civil War. Reconstruction. Texas (Austin). 1861-76. *1647*

—. Colorado (Denver). 1890-1900. *1632*

—. Colorado (Manitou Springs). French. 1815-71. *1656*

—. Culture. Washington (Spokane). 1883-1900. *3980*

—. Far Western States. Urbanization. 1880's. *1667*

—. Fergusson, Harvey. New Mexico (Taos). Reminiscences. 1914-41. *3975*

—. Courts. Coxey, Jacob S. Oregon. Railroads. Unemployment. 1893-97. *3960*

—. Folk Songs. Hoover, Herbert. Public Opinion. Republican Party. Roosevelt, Franklin D. Texas. 1930's. *3706*

—. Great Plains. Religion. 1890's. *1042*

—. Kansas. 1930's. *3611*

—. Photographs. Reminiscences. Ripley, Thomas E. Washington (Tacoma). 1890's. *3990*

Depressions (agricultural). Elections. Farmers. Nebraska. Political Parties. 1922. *4064*

Derbanne, François Dion Deprez. Louisiana. Settlement. Texas. 18c. *175*

Derby, George H. (pseud. Squibob). California (Benicia). Hotels. Satire. 1850. *3015*

Deschamps-Rem Feud. American Fur Company. Assiniboin Indians. Campbell, Robert. Fort Union. Fort William. Fur Trade. Larpenteur, Charles. Mountain Men. Rocky Mountain Fur Company. Sublette, William. 1807-72. *912*

Deseret Alphabet. Mormons. Phonetics. Utah. 1853-68. *2252*

Desert Land Act. Carey, Joseph Maull. Johnson County War. Voting and Voting Behavior. Wyoming. 1891-95. *2760*

Deserts. Arizona (Tucson). Botany. Coville, Frederick V. Forest Service. MacDougal, Daniel T. Research Laboratories. 1903-60. *3710*

DeSmet, Pierre Jean. Alberta. Blackfoot Indians. Jesuits. Plateau Indians. Treaties. 1844-45. *3399*

—. Bidwell, John. California. Marsh, John. Oregon Trail. Overland Journeys to the Pacific. 1841. *400*

—. Bishops. Letters. Missions and Missionaries. Oregon Territory (Saint Paul). Quebec. 1844. *2314*

—. Blackfoot Indians. Fort Rice Treaty (1868). Missions and Missionaries. Montana. Salish Indians. 1830-68. *2304*

—. Chittenden, Hiram Martin. Fur Trade. Historians. Missouri River. Steamboats. Yellowstone National Park. 1858-1917. *244*

—. Fort Rice. Galpin, Charles. Indians. Missions and Missionaries. Montana. North Dakota. Sioux Indians. Sitting Bull (Chief). Travel account. 1868. *799*

DeSoto Expedition Commission. Arkansas. Discovery and Exploration. Louisiana. Moscoso de Alvarado, Luis de. Ouachita River Valley. 1541-43. 1939. *66*

DeSoto, Hernando. Coronado, Francisco. Great Plains. Horses (use of). New Mexico. New Spain. Pacific Northwest. Plains Indians. 1650-19c. *25*

—. Discovery and Exploration. Louisiana. Mississippi River. Moscoso, Luis de. Texas. 1542-43. *84*

Destler, Chester McArthur (*American Radicalism, 1865-1901*, 1946). Bryan, William Jennings. Politics. Populists. Watson, Thomas Edward. 1896. *3744*

Detroit Journal (newspaper). Arizona (Mesa, Tempe). Hill, Edwin Bliss. Michigan. Publishers and Publishing. Reclamation Service. 1866-1949. *2022*

Development *See also* Economic Development; National Development.

—. British Columbia (Kamloops). Cattle Raising. Sheep Raising. Shuswap Indians. 1810-1967. *3427*

—. Environment. Landmarks. Lewis and Clark Trail. 1965. *319*

—. National Characteristics. Natural Resources. Westward Movement. 19c-20c. *249*

Deville, Edouard Gaston. British Columbia. Camera (use of). Map Drawing. Photography. Surveying. 1885-1924. *3480*

Dewdney, Edgar. Canada. Governors. Indian-White Relations. North West Rebellion. Prairie Provinces. 1879-1916. *3108*

Dewey, Will. Indian-White Relations. Letters. Travel accounts. Utah. 19c. *429*

DeWindt, Harry. Alaska. Bering Strait. Cochrane, John Dundas. Ledyard, John. Railroads. Russia (Kamchatka, St. Petersburg). Western Union Telegraph Company. 1788-1900. *3501*

DeWitt, Green. Kerr, James. Settlement. Surveying. Texas. 1825-50. *2631*

DeYoung, Charles. California. Constitutions, State. DeYoung, M. H. Kearney, Denis. Political Reform. San Francisco *Chronicle* (newspaper). 1865-79. *2027*

DeYoung, M. H. California. Constitutions, State. DeYoung, Charles. Kearney, Denis. Political Reform. San Francisco *Chronicle* (newspaper). 1865-79. *2027*

DHS Ranch. Davis, Andrew J. Fort Maginnis. Hauser, Samuel T. Montana. Politics. Stuart, Granville. 1880's. *1113*

DH-4 (aircraft). Arizona. California. Macready, John A. Map Drawing. Mather, Stephen. Pacific Northwest. Photography. Stevens, A. W. 1924. *3628*

Dialects *See also* Linguistics; Speech.

—. California (Boonville). Language. 1880's. *1802*

—. Language. South or Southern States. 19c-20c. *1821*

Diamond Dick (stories). Bibliographies. Dime novels. Frontier and Pioneer Life. Law Enforcement. Wade, Bertrand (fictional character). Wade, Richard (fictional character). 1878-1911. *1934*

Diamond Hunting. Davis, Jackson L. Idaho (Owyhee region). Lyon, Caleb. 1865-92. *973*

Diaries *See also* Reminiscences.

—. Alaska. Bancroft, Hubert Howe. California, University of (Bancroft Library). Libraries. Petroff, Ivan. Travel account. 1878. *3535*

—. Alaska (Anvik). California (San Francisco). Indians. Kuskokwin River. Missions and Missionaries. Parker, Octavius. Travel account. Yukon River. 1888. *3552*

—. Alberta. Allan, Robert K. Big Bear (chief). Cree Indians. Indian Wars. North West Rebellion. Riel, Louis. 1885. *3197*

—. Alberta. British Columbia. Peace River. Surveying. Thompson, David. 1803. *3374*

—. Alberta. Daily Life. 1889-91. *3400*

—. Alberta (Kicking Horse Cache). Canadian Pacific Railway. Columbia River. Railroads. Rocky Mountains. Sheldon, F. E. Surveying. Travel account. 20c. *3167*

—. Alberta (Red Deer River). Bow River. Hudson's Bay Company. Kutenai Indians. McGillivray, Duncan. North West Company. Rocky Mountain House. Thompson, David. Travel accounts. 1800. *3376*

—. Allen, James. California. Egan, Howard. Lee, John D. Mexican War. Mormons. Polk, James K. Travel account. Volunteer Armies. 1846. *558*

—. American Fur Company. Campbell, Robert. Fort Union. Fort William. Fur Trade. McKenzie, Kenneth. Sublette and Campbell (firm). 1833. *878*

—. American Fur Company. Campbell, Robert. Fort William. Fur Trade. Missouri (St. Louis). Sublette, William. 1833. *879*

—. Archaeology. Brandon House. Fur Trade. Indians. Letters. Manitoba (Souris-Mouth area). Yorstone, William. 1793-1821. *3267*

—. Arizona. California. Cattle drives. Erskine, Michael H. New Mexico. Texas. 1854. *1122*

—. Arizona. Camping. Grand Canyon National Park. Kitt, Edith Stratton. Travel account. 1914. *3622*

—. Arizona. Colorado. Huish, David. New Mexico. Photography. Utah. 1898-99. *3598*

—. Arizona (Prescott). *Empire* (newspaper). English, Lydia E. Kansas (Concordia). Santa Fe Trail. Travel account. Westward Movement. 1875-76. *437*

—. Arizona Territory. Armies. Camp Bowie. Camp Thomas. Medicine (practice of). Moran, George H. R. 1878. *2195*

—. Arizona (Whipple Barracks). Bourke, John Gregory. Crook, George. Grand Canyon National Park. Havasupai Indians. Travel account. 1884. *703*

—. Arizona (Yuma). Fages, Pedro. Indian-White Relations. Mexico (Sonora). Military Campaigns. Yuma Indians. 1781. *69*

—. Assiniboin Indians. Boller, Henry A. Fort Atkinson. Frontier and Pioneer Life. Fur Trade. Hidatsa Indians. 1858. *875*

—. Austin, Henry. Bolivar House. Holley, Mary Austin. Texas. 1830's. *2652*

—. Banking. Dakota Territory (Bismarck). Farm loans. Smith, George Watson. 1878. *1271*

—. Bannock War. Indians. Military Campaigns. Nevada. Oregon. 1878. *694*

—. Batoche (battle). Métis. Middleton, Frederick Dobson. Minto, 4th Earl of. North West Rebellion. Saskatchewan. 1885. *3340*

—. Beersheba. Davis, Charles K. Hebrew Union Agricultural Society. Immigration. Jews. Kansas (Cimarron). Russian Emigrants' Aid Society. Wise, Isaac Mayer. 1882. *1461*

—. Blackfoot Indians. Catholic Church. Donnelly, Joseph P. Flathead Indians. Missions and Missionaries. Point, Nicolas. Skitswish Indians. 1840-47. 1967. *2366*

—. Borden, Robert Laird. Canadian West. Northrup, Minnie. Northrup, Will. Travel account. 1902. *3156*

—. Boundaries. Dawson, George Mercer. Great Britain. Saskatchewan. USA. 1873. *3357*

—. Bowen, Edwin A. Colorado. Frontier and Pioneer Life. Gold Rushes. 1859. *1002*

—. Brackett, Albert Gallatin. Fort Ellis. Montana (Bozeman). Wyoming. 1869. *797*

—. Bright, Abbie. Daily Life. Homesteading and Homesteaders. Kansas. 1870-71. *1609*

—. British Columbia (Ashcroft). Cornwall, Clement Francis. Cornwall, Henry Tennant. Political Leadership. Settlement. 1859-1910. *3478*

—. British Columbia (Charlotte Isles). Colnett, James. Great Britain. *Prince of Wales* (vessel). Tsimshian Indians. 1787. *3465*

—. Brooks, Juanita (review article). China. Mormons. Stout, Hosea. Westward Movement. 1837-54. *2289*

—. Buffalo hunts. Kansas (Dodge City). Masterson, Bat. Masterson, Edward J. Masterson, James P. Raymond, Henry H. 1872-73. *300*

—. Buffalo (Republican Herd). Cooke, Lawson. Hunting. Kansas (Smoky Hill River). Nebraska. Platte River. 1870-71. *2564*

—. Burr, Jason F. California. Connecticut Mining and Trading Company. *General Morgan* (vessel). Gold Rushes. Lyman, Albert. Voyages. 1848-50. *958*

—. Business. Frontier and Pioneer Life. McConnell, Robert. Pacific Northwest. 1881. *1223*

—. Butcher, Thomas. Economic Conditions. Farms. Kansas (Barber County; Sun City). Littleton, Betty. Travel account. 1896. *4062*

—. California. California Mutual Protective Association. Gold Rushes. Kansas. Overland Journeys to the Pacific. Robinson, Charles. 1849-92. *323*

—. California. Cities. Gold Mines and Mining. *Ka Hae Hawaii* (newspaper). Pule, J. Smith, Lowell. Transportation. 1858-59. *955*

—. California. Cool, Peter Y. Daily Life. Gold Mines and Mining. 1851-52. *934*

—. California. Country Life. Friends, Society of. Gold Mines and Mining. Lindsey, Robert. Lindsey, Sarah. 1859-60. *392*

—. California. Crespi, Juan. Discovery and Exploration. Mission San Carlos Borromeo. Missions and Missionaries. *Santiago* (vessel). Settlement. 1770-82. *131*

—. California. Crespi, Juan. Franciscans. 1769-74. *91*

—. California. Customs inspectors. Fowler, Matthew Van Benschoten. 1851. *3022*

—. California. Fages, Pedro. Mexico (Sonora). Military Expeditions. Mission San Gabriel Arcangel. Serra, Junipero. Settlement. 1782. *194*

—. California. Forty-Niners. Fourth of July. Gold Rushes. Lorton, William B. Swain, William B. Watson, William J. 1849-51. *946*

—. California. Gold Rushes. Jamison, Samuel M. Overland Journeys to the Pacific. 1850. *394*

—. California. Gold Rushes. Kansas. Overland Journeys to the Pacific. Pioneers. 1849-50. *2525*

—. California. Gold Rushes. Tate, James A. 1849. *1020*

—. California. Indian-White Relations. Military expeditions. Oregon. Piper, Alexander. 1860. *488*

—. California (as an island). Discovery and Exploration. Spaniards. 18c. *62*

—. California Cavalry Column. Civil War. New Mexico. Teal, John W. 1861-65. *670*

—. California (Los Angeles). Crespi, Juan. Discovery and Exploration. Fages, Pedro. Perez, Juan. Portolá, Gaspar de. 1769-74. *3099*

—. California (Los Angeles). Fort Leavenworth. Kansas. Kearny, Stephen Watts. Mexican War. Mormons. New Mexico (Santa Fe). Whitworth, Robert W. 1846-47. *550*

—. California (Monterey). Gómez, Rafael. 1831-37. *3*

—. California (Pennsylvania Gulch). McQuig, John. Mining. Nevada. 1869. *988*

—. California (Sacramento). Gold Rushes. Hillyer, Edwin. Indian-White Relations. Murder. Westward Movement. 1849. *380*

E

G

—. Canada. Hudson's Bay Company. Mergers. North West Company. 17c-19c. *3240*

—. Canada (Peace River). Fort Dunvegan. Hudson's Bay Company. Land promotion. North West Company. 1805-1918. *3368*

—. Canada (Rupert's Land). Hudson's Bay Company. Simpson, George. Travel accounts. 1826-60. *3176*

—. Canadian northwest coast. Hudson's Bay Company. Land Tenure. Overland Telegraph. Russians. Tolmie, William Fraser. 1838-67. *3447*

—. Canadian West. Discovery and Exploration. LaVérendrye, Sieur de. South Dakota (Pierre). 1727-60. *3210*

—. Canadian West. Fort Edmonton. Fort Ellice. Fort Garry. Military Camps and Forts. Red River carts. Touchwood Hills (post). 19c. *3151*

—. Canadian west. Historiography. 18c-19c. *3178*

—. Chaboillez. Chippewa Indians. Diaries. North Dakota (Pembina). 1797-98. *897*

—. Cheyenne Indians. Dougherty, John. Indian-White Relations. Lisa, Manuel. Missouri Fur Company. Osage Indians. 1809-19. *925*

—. Chittenden, Hiram Martin. DeSmet, Pierre Jean. Historians. Missouri River. Steamboats. Yellowstone National Park. 1858-1917. *244*

—. Chittenden, Hiram Martin. Historiography. Turner, Frederick Jackson. Webb, Walter Prescott. 1800-50. *906*

—. Chittenden, Hiram Martin. Historiography. Turner, Frederick Jackson. Webb, Walter Prescott. 1800-50. *907*

—. Civilization (concepts of). Indian-White Relations. Noble Savage (theme). 18c-19c. *917*

—. Colorado River. Explorers. Gila River. Pattie, James Ohio. Southwest. 1826. *899*

—. Discovery and Exploration. Hudson's Bay Company. Prairie Provinces. 1770-1970. *3183*

—. Discovery and Exploration. Smith, Jackson and Sublette (firm). Smith, Jedediah Strong. 1822-31. *911*

—. France. Louisiana Territory. Spain. Vasquez, Benito. 1795-1803. *32*

—. Frontier and Pioneer Life. Menard, Pierre. Mountain Men. St. Louis Missouri Fur Company. Social Customs. 1809-10. *910*

—. Government intervention. Settlement. 1820-30. *915*

—. Great Plains. Historical Sites and Parks. Rocky Mountains. 1800-50's. *2413*

—. Historical Sites and Parks. Nebraska (Bordeaux). 1846-72. 1956-67. *895*

—. Hudson's Bay Company. Idaho (Snake County). Northwest Company. Pacific Fur Company. Pacific Northwest. Payette, François. 1812-44. *893*

—. Hudson's Bay Company. Smith, Jedediah Strong. 1824-29. *436*

—. Humor. *Joe Miller's Joke Book.* Pacific Northwest. 1839. *1967*

—. Mandan Indians. St. Louis Missouri Fur Company. Sheheke (Shahaka, Mandan chief). Thomas (physician). Travel account. 1809. *896*

—. Mexico. New Mexico. Spain. 1540-1821. *219*

—. Missouri River. Navigation. Inland. Steamboats. Yellowstone (vessel). 19c. *1412*

—. Mountain Men. Settlement. 1805-45. *888*

—. Settlement. Wyoming (Teton County, Jackson Hole). 1840-80's. *2747*

Fur Trade (buffalo robes). Arapaho Indians. Cheyenne Indians. Fort Vasquez. Sublette, Andrew. Vasquez, Louis. 1835-40. 1930's. *891*

Fur Trade (competition). Canada. Hudson's Bay Company. North West Company. Selkirk, 5th Earl of. 1800-21. *3131*

Fur Trade (decline of). Business. Chouteau, Pierre, Jr. Indians. Mississippi River region. Rice, Henry M. Sibley, Henry H. Ullman, Joseph. 1830-80. *887*

Furlong, Mary Elizabeth. California (Santa Barbara). Episcopal Church, Protestant. Furlong, Matthew W. Letters. Voyages. Williams, Thomas George. 1864-69. *3029*

Furlong, Matthew W. California (Santa Barbara). Episcopal Church, Protestant. Furlong, Mary Elizabeth. Letters. Voyages. Williams, Thomas George. 1864-69. *3029*

Furnas, Robert W. Arbor Day. Miller, George L. Morton, Julius Sterling. Nebraska. Tree Planting. 1850's-1900. *1195*

Gable, Gilbert E. Jefferson (state of). Oregon (Curry County). Secession. 1941. *2972*

Gadsden Purchase. Apache Indians. Arizona. Carleton, James H. Civil War. Civil-Military Relations. Military Government. 1854-65. *579*

—. Apache Indians. Arizona. Fort Buchanan. Mexico. Military Camps and Forts. USA. 1853-61. *518*

—. Arizona Territory (creation of). Compromise of 1850. Heintzelman, Samuel Peter. Mowry, Sylvester. Poston, Charles D. Sectionalism. Territorial Government. 1848-63. *2906*

—. Guadalupe Hidalgo Treaty (1848). Immigration. Mexico. New Mexico (Refugio; Chamberino). 1848-53. *218*

—. Mexican Americans. Miles, Dixon S. New Mexico Territory (Mesilla). 1854. *2691*

Gage County Council of Defense. German Americans. Lutheran Church. Nebraska (Gage County; Barneston). Nebraska State Council of Defense. Studier, Herman E. ("Some Reminiscences of My Life," 1931). World War I. 1917-18. *3634*

Gage, Thomas. Carter, Clarence Edwin. Colleges and Universities. Editors and Editing. Miami University (Ohio). *Territorial Papers of the United States.* 1910-61. *2411*

Gaines' Mill (battle). Civil War. New York Regiment (Patchogue's Kansas Brigade, Company C). 1861-65. *662*

Gaire, Jean. Canadian west. Colonization. France. Missions and Missionaries. 19c. *3236*

Galbraith, John S. British Columbia. Douglas, James. Expansionism. Gold Rushes. Great Britain. 1850-63. *3435*

Galisteo Pueblo. Marta, Bernardo de. New Mexico. Santo Domingo Reservation. Zia Pueblo. 1597-17c. *95*

Gallatin, Albert. Antiwar Sentiment. Mexico. 1812-49. *562*

Gallegos, José Manuel. Agriculture. Governors. Lane, William Carr (diary). New Mexico Territory. 1852-53. *2845*

Galleher, Paul W. Arthur H. Clark Company. California (Glendale). Clark, Arthur H. Clark, Arthur H., Jr. Publishers and Publishing. Rare Books. 1902-62. *2024*

Gally, Martha James. Daily Life. Diaries. Nevada (Hot Creek). Silver Mining. 1866. *965*

Gaipin, Charles. DeSmet, Pierre Jean. Fort Rice. Indians. Missions and Missionaries. Montana. North Dakota. Sioux Indians. Sitting Bull (Chief). Travel account. 1868. *799*

Galt, Elliot. Alberta Irrigation Company. Canadian Pacific Railway. Canals. Irrigation. Magrath, C. A. Palliser Triangle. Railroads. Settlement. 1882-1901. *3378*

Galveston Custom House. Construction. Texas. Treasury Department. Young, Ammi Burnham. 1857-61. *2685*

Galveston Harbor (battle). Amphibious Operations. Civil War. Confederate Army. Texas. 1863. *630*

Gálvez, José. California. Croix, Teodoro de. Letters. Military conquest. Portolá, Gaspar de. 1769-70. *22*

—. California. Indians. Lanz de Casafonda, Manuel. Letters. Missions and Missionaries. Serra, Junípero. Verger, Rafael. 1771. *115*

Gambling. Boxing. Gans, Joe. Gans-Nelson prizefight. Moore, Jack D. Nevada (Goldfield). Rickard, George Lewis ("Tex"). Wiley, Joseph L. 1906. *3576*

Gambrell, Herbert. Bond, George. Editors and Editing. Hubbell, Jay B. *Southwest Review* (periodical). Texas. 1915-27. *3614*

Game management conflicts. Arizona. Federal Government. Forest Service. *Hunt* v. *United States* (US, 1928). Hunting. Kaibab National Forest. State Government. Wildlife Conservation. 1924-69. *4111*

Gano, Richard M. Cabin Creek Stockade (battle). Civil War. DeMorse, Charles. Hopkins, Henry. Indian Territory. Price, Sterling. Texas Regiment, 29th, 30th. Watie, Stand. 1864. *596*

Gans, Joe. Boxing. Gambling. Gans-Nelson prizefight. Moore, Jack D. Nevada (Goldfield). Rickard, George Lewis ("Tex"). Wiley, Joseph L. 1906. *3576*

Gans-Nelson prizefight. Boxing. Gambling. Gans, Joe. Moore, Jack D. Nevada (Goldfield). Rickard, George Lewis ("Tex"). Wiley, Joseph L. 1906. *3576*

Gantt's Fort. Bent's Fort. Colorado. Fort Cass. Indian trade. 19c. *903*

Garber, C. Y. Constitution (mining company). Fire Fighting. Idaho (Coeur d'Alene, Pine Creek). Reminiscences. 20c. *4114*

Garcés, Francisco Tomás Hermenegildo. Arizona. California. Discovery and Exploration. Mission San Gabriel Arcangel. Mojave River (discovery of). New Mexico. Yuma Massacre (battle). 1775-81. *85*

Garcés, Francisco Tomás Hermenegildo (martyrdom). Mexico (Sonora). New Mexico (Yuma Crossing). Yuma Indians. 1738-81. *137*

Gard, Wayne. Bibliographies. Centennial Celebrations. Chisholm Trail. 1867. 1967. *1106*

Garden of the World (myth of). Discovery and Exploration. Great American Desert (myth of). Great Plains. James, Edwin. Long, Stephen H. Pike, Zebulon. Swift, William Henry. 1805-1930's. *2436*

Gardens. California (Montecito). Gould, William P. La Favorita (residence). 1905. *3105*

Gardiner, James B. Indian-White Relations. Kansas. Ottawa Indians. Settlement. Shawnee Indians. 1832. *2546*

Gardner, Alexander. Brady, Mathew. Kansas. Photography. 1867. *2072*

Gardner, Earl. Apache Indians. Arizona. Criminal Law. Federal Government. Hanging. *Phoenix Gazette* (newspaper). San Carlos Reservation. 1936. *3639*

Garfield, James A. Chinese Americans. Colorado (Denver, Leadville). Democratic Party. Riots. *Rocky Mountain News* (newspaper). 1880. *1565*

Garland, Hamlin. Babcock, Burton. Forest Homestead Act (1906). Land Tenure. 1906. *4069*

—. Cather, Willa. Great Plains. Homestead Act (1862). Homesteading and Homesteaders. Literature. Rølvaag, Ole E. Smith, Martha L. Stewart, Elinore Pruitt. 1860-1967. *1983*

—. Cather, Willa. Great Plains. Literature. Rølvaag, Ole E. 1880's-1930's. *1072*

—. Colorado. Fiction. Rocky Mountains. 1892-1914. *1917*

—. Diaries. 1891-1939. *1915*

—. Great Plains. Literature. 1860-1940. *1919*

—. Indians. Literature. 19c. *1947*

—. Literature. Social Reform. 1887-1917. *2003*

—. North Central States. Rural Settlements. 1899-1940. *1650*

Garra, Antonio. California (San Diego). Indians. Rebellions. 1851. *3024*

Garrard, Lewis H. (*Wah-to-Yah and the Taos Trail*). Cheyenne Indians. Santa Fe Trail. Southwest (Purgatoire River). Travel account. Vi-Po-Na (Chief). 1846-50. 1936-68. *369*

Garrett, Pat. Billy the Kid. Customs collection. Law Enforcement. New Mexico. Roosevelt, Theodore. Texas (El Paso). 1850-1908. *1774*

—. Customs collection. New Mexico. Politics. Roosevelt, Theodore. Texas (El Paso). 1881-1908. *3790*

Garvey, Marcus. Black Nationalism. Fortune, Timothy Thomas. *New York Age* (newspaper). Oklahoma Territory. Republican Party. 1880's. *1464*

Gassaway, Frank H. California (San Francisco, Santa Cruz). Fourth of July. Gold Mines and Mining. 1882. *3075*

Gates, Charles M. Historians. Minnesota Historical Society. National Development. National Park Service. Old Northwest. *Pacific Northwest Quarterly* (periodical). Washington, University of. 1904-63. *2928*

Gates, Guerdon. Diaries. Red River. Settlement. Texas. 1841-42. *374*

Gates, Paul W. (*Fifty Million Acres: Conflicts over Kansas Land Policy, 1854-1890*, 1954). Credit. Kansas. Land. 1854-80. *1168*

Gatewood, Charles B. Apache Indians (Chiricahua). Arizona. Geronimo (Chiricahua Apache leader). Indian Wars. Letters. Miles, Nelson A. 1886. *701*

"Gathering" (social movement). Mormons. Theology. 19c-20c. *2260*

Gay, Jane. Dawes Act (1887). Fletcher, Alice Cunningham. Idaho. McBeth, Kate. Nez Percé Indians. 1889-92. *283*

Geary, John. Commerce. Economic Growth. Missouri (Kansas City). Panic of 1857. 1856-57. *1672*

Geiger, Maynard. California. Historical Sites and Parks. Lacouague, Pierre. Mission San Juan Capistrano. 1776-78. 1967. *146*

—. Colorado (Colorado Springs). Engineering. Florence and Cripple Creek Railroad. Railroads. 1892-1915. *2781*

—. Colorado (Leadville). 1878-82. *1668*

—. Colorado (Pikes Peak area). Frontier thesis. Greeley, Horace. Ingalls, John J. Richardson, Albert Deane. Social Conditions. Turner, Frederick Jackson. Villard, Henry. 1859-61. *2791*

—. Colorado (San Juan Mountains; Telluride). National Guard. Peabody, James H. State Government. Strikes. United Mine Workers of America. Western Federation of Miners. 1903-04. *3956*

—. Congress. Fisk, James Liberty. Montana. 1862-65. *456*

—. DeLaMar, J. R. Delamar Mining District. Nevada (Delamar, Pioche). 1896-1900. *2844*

—. Diaries. Missouri River. Montana. Travel account. Vanmeter, Abel J. 1865-66. *1248*

—. Economic Conditions. Freight and Freightage. Frontier and Pioneer Life. Jews. Salesmen and Salesmanship. 1849-1900. *1221*

—. Farms. Frontier and Pioneer Life. Kirkaldie, Franklin Luther. Letters. Montana. 1860's. *1598*

—. Fire. Hamilton, Gideon Anthony. Letters. Nevada (Virginia City; Comstock Lode). 1875. *928*

—. Fourth of July. Swan, James G. (*Northwest Coast*). Washington (Shoalwater Bay). 1853. 1966. *2934*

—. Gold Rushes. Industrial Technology. South Dakota (Homestake). 1876-1971. *1012*

—. Greiner, John. Montoya, Maraquita. New Mexico Mining Company. Ortiz, José Francisco. Whittlesey, Elisha. 1828-70. *1008*

—. Idaho (Coeur d'Alene). 1860-1964. *940*

—. Klondike region. Treadgold, Arthur N. C. Yukon Gold Company. Yukon Territory (Dawson). 1906-66. *3493*

—. Miner's Delight. Wyoming (South Pass region). 1860-1940. *979*

—. Montana. 1852-65. *1029*

—. Montana. Overland Diamond R Freight Line. Railroads. Trade. Union Pacific Railroad. Utah. 1869. *1314*

—. Montana (Garnet). 1865-90. *937*

—. Montana (Gilt Edge). Mueller, George. Travel account. Wilson, William E. 1881. *458*

—. Ogilvie, William. Yukon Territory. 1887-1912. *3496*

—. Salting. Silver Mining. 19c-20c. *963*

Gold Mines and Mining (lost). Alamo (battle). Bowie, James. Frontier and Pioneer Life. Mission San Saba. Texas (San Antonio). 1796-1836. *2634*

Gold Mining camps. Battles. California (Weaverville). Chinese Americans. 1854. *1486*

Gold Rushes. Abrahamsohn, Abraham. Australia. California. 1849-53. *410*

—. Alaska. Bond, Marshall, Sr. Canada. Jack (dog). Klondike region. London, Jack (*Call of the Wild*). 1897-1903. *3487*

—. Alaska. California. Colorado. Georgia. South Dakota (Black Hills). 1828-97. *986*

—. Alaska. Dime novels. Klondike region. Yukon Territory. 19c. *3491*

—. Alaska (Chilkoot Pass, White Pass). Klondike region. Yukon Territory (Dawson). 1890's. *3488*

—. Alaska (Circle City). Canoe trips. Yukon Territory (Dawson). 1898. 1964. *3489*

—. Alaska (Kauwerak, Mary's Igloo). Cossacks. Russia (Siberia). Settlement. 17c-1898. *3510*

—. Alaska (Nome). Snake River. 1898-1900. *3527*

—. Alberta. British Columbia (Cariboo Gold Fields). Fort Pitt. Ontario (St. Catherine). Overlanders of 1862. Rocky Mountains (Yellowhead Pass). Travel account. 1862. *3153*

—. Alberta (Edmonton). British Columbia (Cariboo). California. "English Charlie.". Homesteading and Homesteaders. Saskatchewan River. 1849-1900. *3172*

—. American Fur Company. Beaubien, Carlos. Frémont, John C. Maxwell Land Grant. Maxwell, Lucien Bonaparte. Miranda, Guadalupe. New Mexico. Trading posts. 1818-75. *1225*

—. Arizona. Clum, John P. Railroads. San Carlos Apache Reservation. Southern Pacific Railroad. Yukon Territory (Klondike). 1874-1932. *296*

—. Arkansas (Little Rock). British Columbia. California. Gibbs, Miflin Wister. Judges. Negroes. Pennsylvania (Philadelphia). 1823-80. *993*

—. Armies. Canadian West. Firearms (function of). Fraser River. Fur Trade. Hudson's Bay Company. Indians. Thompson River. 1670-1967. *3170*

—. Art (illustrations). Banking. California (San Francisco). Mines. Wells, Fargo and Company. 1848-50's. *2079*

—. Audubon, John Woodhouse. California. El Dorado Trail. Hampden Mining Company. Kit Carson Association. Webb, Henry L. 1849. *360*

—. Audubon, John Woodhouse. California Company. Overland Journeys to the Pacific. Simson, Robert. Trask, John B. Webb, Henry L. 1849-50. *325*

—. Australia. Forman, George. Missouri (St. Louis). Montana. Travel account. 1852-64. *961*

—. Banking. California. Economic Conditions. Wells, Fargo and Company. 1852-1972. *1313*

—. Bibliographies. California. Colorado. Guidebooks. Westward Movement. 1848-49. 1858-59. *931*

—. Boomtowns. New Mexico (La Belle). 1880's-1900. *1684*

—. Bowen, Edwin A. Colorado. Diaries. Frontier and Pioneer Life. 1859. *1002*

—. Bridges. Montana (Jefferson River). Parsons Bridge. 1865. 1960. *1292*

—. British Columbia. California. Fraser River. Prospectors. 1858-65. *3431*

—. British Columbia. Douglas, James. Expansionism. Galbraith, John S. Great Britain. 1850-63. *3435*

—. British Columbia (Queen Charlotte Islands; Englefield Bay). Douglas, James. *Georgianna* (vessel). Haida Indians. Indian-White Relations. Prospectors. 1850-53. *3444*

—. British Columbia (Vancouver). Federal Policy. Washington (Seattle). Yukon Territory (Klondike). 1890's. *3911*

—. Bryant, Edwin *What I Saw in California*. California. 1849-69. *3010*

—. Buildings. California. Fire. Iron shutters. 1849-50's. *2106*

—. Buildings (prefabricated). California (San Francisco). 1849. *2134*

—. Burger, James. California. Frontier and Pioneer Life. Letters. New York City (Staten Island). Westward Movement. 1850. *1027*

—. Burr, Jason F. California. Connecticut Mining and Trading Company. Diaries. *General Morgan* (vessel). Lyman, Albert. Voyages. 1848-50. *958*

—. Business. Illinois (Chicago). Missouri (St. Louis). Montana (Madison County). Portland-Walla Walla-Mullan Road. Trade Routes. 1862-68. *984*

—. Cairns, Andrew. California (Yreka). Letters. Washington (Olympia). 1850-62. *959*

—. California. California Mutual Protective Association. Diaries. Kansas. Overland Journeys to the Pacific. Robinson, Charles. 1849-92. *323*

—. California. Catholic Church. Letters. Phelan, Gregory J. 1848-58. *2354*

—. California. Crime and Criminals. Foreign Miner's Tax (1850). Mexicans. Prospectors (white). Racism. 1848-52. *956*

—. California. Diaries. Forty-Niners. Fourth of July. Lorton, William B. Swain, William B. Watson, William J. 1849-51. *946*

—. California. Diaries. Jamison, Samuel M. Overland Journeys to the Pacific. 1850. *394*

—. California. Diaries. Kansas. Overland Journeys to the Pacific. Pioneers. 1849-50. *2525*

—. California. Diaries. Tate, James A. 1849. *1020*

—. California. Documents. Stock Companies. 1849. *978*

—. California. Economic Growth. Nevada. San Francisco Mining Exchange. Silver Mining. 1849-62. *1238*

—. California. Elder, James. Letters. New York. 1851-52. *361*

—. California. Emmet, Thomas Addis (family). Emmet, William J. LeRoy, Herman R. Letters. Voyages. 1849-50. *987*

—. California. "Great Grandma" (song). 1962-68. *2000*

—. California. Guidebooks. Hall, John E. *Missouri Republican* (newspaper). Satire. 1848-51. *318*

—. California. Hawaii. Letters. 1848-50's. *941*

—. California. "Joe Bowers" (folksong). Woodward, John. 1849-50's. *3097*

—. California. Kern, Edward. Letters. Sutter, John A. 1839-53. *943*

—. California. Mental Illness. Stockton State Hospital. 1853-63. *1013*

—. California. Missouri (Independence). Oregon. Overland Journeys to the Pacific. 1849. *438*

—. California. Negroes. 1849-63. *960*

—. California. Sutter, John A. 1848. *945*

—. California. Travel accounts. Wyoming. 1849. *343*

—. California (Columbia). Centennial Celebrations. German Americans. Schiller, Friedrich von. 1859. *1801*

—. California (Marysville). Frontier and Pioneer Life. Letters. Missouri (Fort Leavenworth). Overland Journeys to the Pacific. Travel account. 1850. *335*

—. California (Placerville, San Francisco). Frontier and Pioneer Life. Letters. Mormons. Overland Journeys to the Pacific. Social Customs. Steele, Harriet. 1852-53. *442*

—. California (Sacramento). Diaries. Hillyer, Edwin. Indian-White Relations. Murder. Westward Movement. 1849. *380*

—. California (San Francisco). Daguerre, Louis Jacques. Photography. 1839-49. *2078*

—. California (San Francisco). *Daily Alta California* (newspaper). Daily Life. Idaho (Boise Basin). Social Conditions. 1863. *926*

—. California (San Francisco). Photographs. 1851-56. *2067*

—. California (San Francisco). Robinson, David G. Satire. "Seeing the Elephant" (comedy). Theater. 1850-1906. *1736*

—. California (Southern; San Diego). Law and Society. 1830's-40's. *206*

—. Californios. Social Conditions. 1769-1864. *182*

—. Canada (Northern). Government intervention. Klondike region. Oil Industry and Trade. 1905-69. *3490*

—. *Century Magazine* (periodical). Idaho (Coeur d'Alene). Reminiscences. Smalley, Eugene V. 1884. *998*

—. Cities. Nevada. 1859-1969. *1711*

—. Civil War. Historical sources (need for). Indian Wars. Mexican War. 1870's-80's. 1964. *471*

—. Clemens, Earle. Journalism. Nevada. Rhyolite *Herald* (newspaper). 1905-11. *2028*

—. Colorado. Diaries. Mallory, Samuel. Montana. State Government. 1860-80. *2713*

—. Colorado (Cherry Creek). Frontier and Pioneer Life. Journalism. 1859. *2026*

—. Colorado (Pikes Peak). Greeley, Horace. Gregory Diggings District. Gregory, John Hamilton. Letters. 1859. *995*

—. Colorado (Pikes Peak). Kansas. Newspapers. 1858-59. *2023*

—. Colorado (Pikes Peak). Kansas Territory. Territorial Government. 1855-61. *2775*

—. Colorado Territory. Kansas. Territorial Government. 1858-61. *2774*

—. Crime and Criminals. Frontier and Pioneer Life. Idaho (Baboon Gulch, Lewiston). Miller, Cincinnatus H. Reminiscences. Vigilantes. 1862. *976*

—. Custer, George A. Dakota Territory (Black Hills). Indian-White Relations. Laramie Treaty (1868). Scientific Expeditions. Sheridan, Philip. Sioux Indians. 1874. *397*

—. Daily Life. Forman, George. Idaho (Idaho City). Michigan. Missouri (St. Joseph). 1864. *939*

—. Demography. Frontier and Pioneer Life. Klondike region. Religious affiliations. Yukon Territory (Dawson). 1898-1902. *3495*

—. Diaries. Fish, James W. Indian-White Relations. Larned, William L. 1860's. *405*

—. Diaries. Fisk, Robert E. Harlan, Wilson Barber. Montana. Westward Movement. 1866. *378*

—. Diaries. Nebraska. Overland Journeys to the Pacific. Taylor, Calvin. 1850. *457*

—. Duval, Isaac Harding. Mexico. Passports. Southwest. 1849. *329*

—. Earp, Wyatt. Idaho (Coeur d'Alene; Eagle City). Saloons. 1884. *1671*

—. Fish Expedition of 1864. Larned, Horatio H. Larned, William L. Letters. 1860's. *424*

—. Fort Abercrombie. Montana (Diamond City). North Dakota. Pony Express. Sioux Indians. 1867-68. *1304*

Great Britain (London; Beaver Hall). British Columbia. Fur Trade. Nootka Sound Controversy (1790). Pacific Northwest. Spain. USSR. 1790-1963. *3462*

Great Britain (Stromness Harbour). Cowie, Isaac. Fort Qu'Appelle. Hudson's Bay Company. *Prince Rupert* (vessel). Saskatchewan. Voyages. 1867. *3300*

"Great Grandma" (song). California. Gold Rushes. 1962-68. *2000*

Great Lakes. Canada. Explorers. Nature Conservation. Olson, Sigurd. Reminiscences. Travel account. 19c. *3158*

—. Catlin, George. Kane, Paul. Painting. Rocky Mountains. 1845-48. *3123*

Great Northern Railway. Banking. Cooke, Jay. Hill, James Jerome. Morgan, J. Pierpont. Northern Pacific Railroad. Northern Securities Company. Railroads. Villard, Henry. 1864-1904. *1350*

—. Canadian Pacific Railway. Cascade Mountains. Civil Engineering. Discovery and Exploration. Hill, James Jerome. Montana (Marias Pass). Railroads. Rocky Mountains. Stevens, John Frank. Washington (Stevens Pass). 1889-1943. *1346*

—. Cascade Mountains (Stevens Pass). Civil Engineering. Discovery and Exploration. Hill, James Jerome. Montana (Marias Pass). Oregon Trunk Line. Pacific Northwest. Railroads. Stevens, John Frank. 1889-1911. *1367*

—. Hill, James Jerome. Kennedy, John S. Kittson, Norman Wolfred. Letters. Railroads. Smith, Donald Alexander. Stephen, George. 1878. *1361*

Great Plains. Advertising. Custer, George A. Hazen, William B. Northern Pacific Railroad. Railroads. Settlement. 1860's. *2453*

—. Agricultural Adjustment Administration. Agricultural Policy. Federal Emergency Relief Administration. New Deal. Shelterbelt Program. Soil Conservation. 1933-34. *4076*

—. Agricultural Labor. Beet sugar industry. Jones-Costigan Act (1934). Sugar Act (1937). Working Conditions. 1930's. *4055*

—. Agricultural Organizations. Bristow, Joseph L. Interstate Irrigation Association. *Irrigation Farmer* (periodical). Reclamation of Land. 1890's. *4141*

—. Agricultural settlement. Barbed wire. Cattle industry. Farmers. Glidden, Joseph Farwell. Illinois. 19c. *1051*

—. Agricultural Technology and Research. Homesteading and Homesteaders. 1870-1900. *1146*

—. Agricultural Technology and Research. Irrigation (pump, windmill). 1910-67. *1199*

—. Agriculture. Alaska. Frontier thesis. Geography. Indians. Webb, Walter Prescott. 19c-20c. *3505*

—. Agriculture. Economic Growth. Social Change. 1963. *1050*

—. Agriculture. Legislation. Norris, George William. 1920's. *4093*

—. Alberta. Farmers. Fur Trade. Indians. Settlement. Prehistory-19c. *2465*

—. American Fur Company. Commerce. Fur Trade. Missouri River. Steamboats. 1831-87. *1413*

—. Animals (domestic, wild). Attitudes. Farmers. Nature. Ranchers. 1963. *1044*

—. Armies. California. Mexican War. Painting. Sully, Alfred. 19c. *2144*

—. Armies. Fiction. Indian Wars. King, Charles Bird. 1870-80. *1959*

—. Armies. Long, Stephen H. Scientific Expeditions. 1819-20. *420*

—. Art Galleries and Museums. Benton, Thomas Hart. Joslyn Art Museum. Koerner, W. H. D. Nebraska (Omaha). Painting. 1833-1900. *2126*

—. Beatte, Alexis Pierre. Mountain Men. 19c. *2476*

—. Black Hawk War. Dodge, Henry. First Dragoon Regiment. Indian Wars. Kearny, Stephen Watts. Santa Fe Trail. 1834-46. *747*

—. Blocker, Albert Pickens. Cattle Raising. 1880's-1943. *1084*

—. Boom towns. Cattle drives. Illinois. Kansas. Texas. 1860's-20c. *1093*

—. Boundaries. New Spain. Oconor, Hugo. 1539-1779. *217*

—. Buffalo. Cattle Raising. Food. 19c. *2441*

—. Bureau of Indian Affairs. Civil War. Indian-White Relations. Pioneers. 1861-65. *608*

—. Canada. Discovery and Exploration. LaVérendrye, Sieur de. 1730's-40's. *3113*

—. Cather, Willa. Garland, Hamlin. Homestead Act (1862). Homesteading and Homesteaders. Literature. Rølvaag, Ole E. Smith, Martha L. Stewart, Elinore Pruitt. 1860-1967. *1983*

—. Cather, Willa. Garland, Hamlin. Literature. Rølvaag, Ole E. 1880's-1930's. *1072*

—. Cattle Raising. Climate. Land. 1860-1912. *1095*

—. Cattle Raising. Economic Conditions. Farms. Legislation. Settlement. 19c. *1062*

—. Chivington, John M. Colorado. Indian Wars. Tappan, Samuel F. 1862-64. *722*

—. Cody, William F. (Buffalo Bill). Cowboys. Dime novels. Indians. Myths and Symbols. Outlaws. Wild West shows. 1850-70. *1883*

—. Confederate States of America. Indian-White Relations. Kiowa Indians. Pike, Albert. 1861. *619*

—. Conflict and Conflict Resolution. Land speculation. Local Politics. Violence. 1880's. *2474*

—. Conservation of Natural Resources. Ecology. Grasslands. 19c-20c. *1193*

—. Conservation of Natural Resources. Forest Service. Norris-Doxey Act. Roosevelt, Franklin D. Shelterbelt Program. Soil Conservation Service. Works Progress Administration. 1933-42. *4157*

—. Conservation of Natural Resources. Legislation (federal, state). Oklahoma (Mangum). Shelterbelt Program. 1870-1934. *4156*

—. Constitutions, State. Political Attitudes. Radicals and Radicalism. Webb, Walter Prescott (thesis). 19c. *2434*

—. Coronado, Francisco. DeSoto, Hernando. Horses (use of). New Mexico. New Spain. Pacific Northwest. Plains Indians. 1650-19c. *25*

—. Courts Martial and Courts of Inquiry. Custer, George A. Indian Wars. 1867. *779*

—. Cowboys. Dude Ranchers' Association. Resorts. 1880-1966. *3938*

—. Cowboys. Negroes. 1850-70's. *1088*

—. Crop failures. Federal Crop Insurance Corporation. Wheat. 1939-57. *4056*

—. Depressions. Religion. 1890's. *1042*

—. Diaries. Menefee, Arthur M. Nevada (Carson City). Pioneers. Travel account. 1857. *1316*

—. Discovery and Exploration. Garden of the World (myth of). Great American Desert (myth of). James, Edwin. Long, Stephen H. Pike, Zebulon. Swift, William Henry. 1805-1930's. *2436*

—. Draper, Lyman C. Historical Societies. Massachusetts Historical Society. Minnesota Historical Society. Wisconsin Historical Society. 1790-1967. *2425*

—. Dry farming. Irrigation. Rain and Rainfall. Settlement. 19c-20c. *2432*

—. Economic Development. Environment. Natural Resources. 19c-20c. *2464*

—. Erosion. Gully formation. Southwest. Prehistory-1966. *2480*

—. Explorers. Gilpin, William. Great American Desert (concept of). Long, Stephen H. Pike, Zebulon. 1530-1857. *2456*

—. Explorers. Great American Desert (concept). James, Edwin. Long, James. Pike, Zebulon. Westward Movement. 1803-23. *2454*

—. Farmers. Land (policies, prices). Migration. Prairie Provinces. 1880-1914. *3201*

—. Farmers. Land (policies, prices). Migration. Prairie Provinces. 1880-1914. *3202*

—. Federal Policy. Indians. Public Opinion. 1865-80. *2458*

—. Freight and Freightage (rates). Populism. Railroads. 1867-96. *3894*

—. Frontier and Pioneer Life (definition of). 1860-90. *2481*

—. Frontier thesis. Historians. Turner, Frederick Jackson. Webb, Walter Prescott (works). 1888-1963. *2470*

—. Frontier thesis. Philosophy of History. Texas. Webb, Walter Prescott (works). 19c. 1959-63. *2471*

—. Fur Trade. Historical Sites and Parks. Rocky Mountains. 1800-50's. *2413*

—. Garland, Hamlin. Literature. 1860-1940. *1919*

—. Geography. Great American Desert. James, Edwin. Long, Stephen H. Myths and Symbols. 19c-20c. *2437*

—. Geology. Newberry, John Strong. Trees (absence of). 1873. *2448*

—. Ghost Dance. Paiute Indians. Rocky Mountains. Sects, Religious. South Dakota. Ute Indians. Wounded Knee (battle). Wovoka (Jack Wilson). 1870-90. *737*

—. Historians. Malin, James C. 1930's. *2431*

—. Historiography. Parrish, Randall. Settlement. Webb, Walter Prescott. 1850-1965. *2444*

—. Homesteading and Homesteaders. Sod houses. 1870's-80's. *2118*

—. Horses. Painting. Remington, Frederick ("Horses of the Plains"). Sketches. 1889. *2155*

—. Horses (use of). Plains Indians. Spaniards. 17c-19c. *4*

—. Libraries. Minnesota Historical Society Library (Neill, Pond Papers). Newberry Library (Ayer, Graff Collections). Southern Methodist University (De Golyer Foundation Library). Yale University Library (Beinecke and Coe Collection). 1969. *2459*

—. Photography. Railroads. Russell, Andrew Joseph. Union Pacific Railroad. 1868-69. *2077*

—. Population. Soil Conservation. Urbanization. 1789-1966. *1576*

—. Railroads (transcontinental). Surveying. Whipple, Amiel Weeks. 1852-53. *346*

Great Plains (concept of). Economic Development. Gilpin, William. Settlement. 1836-60. *2457*

Great Plains (image of). Economic Development. Physical Geography. 19c-20c. *2455*

Great Plains Journal. Museum of the Great Plains. Oklahoma, University of. 1963. *2446*

Great Powers. Aa Indians. Catholic Church (records). Jumano Indians. Kiowa Indians. New Mexico. Pawnee Indians. 1694-1875. *92*

Great Salt Lake (specious map of). Canada. Delisle, William. Lahontan, Baron of. Map Drawing. USA. 1703. *83*

Greek Americans. Assimilation. Colorado (Denver). *Kafencion* (coffee shop). 1900-69. *4020*

—. Copper Mines and Mining. Immigration. Strikes. Utah (Brigham Canyon). Utah Copper Company. Western Federation of Labor. 1900-12. *2830*

—. Emigration. Murder. Nebraska (Omaha). Press. Riots. 1909. *3972*

Greeley, Horace. Bowles, Samuel. Burton, Richard. Colfax, Schuyler. Overland Journeys to the Pacific. Stagecoaches. Transportation (transcontinental). Travel accounts. Twain, Mark. 1859-65. *1326*

—. Brier, James. Brier, Juliet Wells. California (Death Valley). Letters. Michigan. Overland Journeys to the Pacific. St. Joseph Company. 1814-49. *3050*

—. California. Railroads. Travel account. 1859. *1402*

—. Colorado (Pikes Peak). Gold Rushes. Gregory Diggings District. Gregory, John Hamilton. Letters. 1859. *995*

—. Colorado (Pikes Peak area). Frontier thesis. Gold Mines and Mining. Ingalls, John J. Richardson, Albert Deane. Social Conditions. Turner, Frederick Jackson. Villard, Henry. 1859-61. *2791*

Green Corn Rebellion (1917). Grandfather Clause (1910). Negro Suffrage. Oklahoma. Socialist Party. 1900-18. *2605*

Green, Duff C. Explorers. Mexico. Rio Grande River. Texas. U.S. Boundary Survey Commission. 1852. *452*

Green, L. C. Canada. Europe. Indians. Law. Minority legal rights (review article). Modeen, Tore. Treaties. 1969-70. *3142*

Green Peach War. Civil War. Negroes. Oklahoma (Muskogee). Reminiscences. Tomm, Jim. 1859-1906. *1437*

Green River. Brown, Frank Mason. Colorado River. Denver, Colorado Cañon and Pacific Railroad. Kendrick, Frank C. Railroads. Stanton, Robert Brewster. Surveying. 1889. *1376*

—. Colorado River. Hayden, Ferdinand Vandeveer. King, Clarence. Monuments. Powell, John Wesley. Scientific Expeditions. Surveying. Toponymy. Wheeler, George Montague. 1867-79. *2216*

Green, Thomas. Banks, Nathaniel Prentiss. Bayou Bourbeau (battle). Civil War. Louisiana (Opelousas). Roberts, Oran Milo. Sabine Pass. Taylor, Richard. Texas. 1863. *585*

Green, Thomas J. Armies. Dyer, Leon. Texas Revolution. 1836-37. *521*

—. Civil War. Confederate Army. Texas. Val Verde (battle). 1861-65. *615*

Houston, University of. Bibliographies. Colleges and Universities. Kunkel, Mike. Literature. McMurtry, Larry. Texas. 20c. *1957*

Howard, Oliver Otis. Camas Prairie (battle). Fred, Munn. Idaho. Military Campaigns. Nez Percé Indians. Reminiscences. Sioux Indians. 1876-77. *781*

—. Continental Army. Indian Wars. Joseph (chief). Miles, Nelson A. Montana. Nez Percé War. White Bird Canyon (battle). 1877. *700*

—. Crook, George. Custer, George A. Grierson, Benjamin Henry. Indian-White Relations. Miles, Nelson A. Military General Staff. Pope, John. 1865-85. *719*

—. Crook, George. Grierson, Benjamin Henry. Indian Wars. Mackenzie, Ranald S. Miles, Nelson A. Military Service, Professional. Pope, John. 19c. *718*

Howard, William Alanson. Biegelow, Martha M. Dakota Territory. Hayes, Rutherford B. Michigan. Political Conventions. 1813-80. *2461*

Howe, Edgar Watson (*The Story of a Country Town*). Country Life. Kansas. Town life. 19c. *1961*

Howe, Frederic (*Privilege and Democracy*). California. Conservation of Natural Resources. Heney, Francis J. Progressivism. Recall (judicial). Smith, J. Allen (*Spirit of American Government*). 1907-11. *3566*

Howe, James Wong. California. Chinese Americans. Immigration. Kingman, Dong. Labor. 1850-1900. *3009*

Howe, Joseph. Bibliographies. Canada. Gordon, Arthur Hamilton. Local History. 1850's-1912. 1964. *3219*

Howell, Charles W. Diaries. Discovery and Exploration. Missouri River. Navigation, Inland. 1867. *395*

Howell, William T. Arizona. Law. Territorial Government. 1864. *2901*

—. Arizona Territory. Courts (federal). Law. 1810-70. *2885*

Howland, Andrew M. Communes. Faithists. Minnesota (Dona Ana, Las Cruces). Newbrough, John B. Publicity. *Republican* (newspaper). Shalam. 1884-91. *1539*

Hoyt, Samuel Pierce. Architecture. Beehive House. Blood, Moroni. Lion House. Mormons. Polygamy. Utah. Watkins, John. Young, Brigham. 1853-68. *2115*

—. Utah (Hoytsville). 1844-89. *1604*

Hubbell, James B. Dakota Territory. Indian-White Relations. Moscow Expedition. Sioux Indians. Thompson, Clark W. 1863. *766*

Hubbell, Jay B. Bond, George. Editors and Editing. Gambrell, Herbert. *Southwest Review* (periodical). Texas. 1915-27. *3614*

Hubbell, John Lorenzo. Navajo Indians. New Mexico (Ganado). Trading posts. 19c. *872*

Huckleberry, E. R. Medicine (practice of). Oregon (Tillamook County). Reminiscences. 1923-45. *3615*

Huddleston, George. Alabama. Attitudes. Bowie, Hamilton. Foreign Relations. Hodgson, Samuel. Mexico. National Guard. Wilson, Woodrow. Wright, Maude Hawk. 1916-17. *3685*

Hudson Bay Railroad. Button, Thomas. Hydraulic Engineering. International Nickel Company. Kelsey Generating Station. Manitoba (Nelson River). Mines (nickel). Railroads. 1612-1957. *3258*

Hudson's Bay Company. Agriculture. Alberta. British Columbia. Economic Conditions. Peace River area. Settlement. Technology. Transportation. Wheat. 1788-1967. *3386*

—. Agriculture. Balance of Power. Canada (Rupert's Land). Economic Conditions. Fur Trade. Indians. Métis. 1856-96. *3174*

—. Agriculture. Fur Trade. Manitoba (Red River settlement). Riel, Louis. Settlement. 1870. *3294*

—. Agriculture. Fur Trade. Pacific Northwest. Russia (Siberia). Russian American Company. 1805-46. *3139*

—. Alaska. Dall, W. H. Fort Yukon. Whymper, Frederick. 1847-68. *3556*

—. Alaska. Fort Yukon. Lower Fort Garry. Murray, Alexander Hunter. Murray, Anne Campbell. 1846-62. *3522*

—. Alberta. Blackfoot Indians. Fort Edmonton. Letters. Rowand, John. Simpson, George. 1840. *3411*

—. Alberta. Daily Life. Fort Edmonton. 1870-73. *3423*

—. Alberta (Edmonton). Land booms. Niddrie, John G. Real Estate Business. Reminiscences. 1911-12. *3405*

—. Alberta (Red Deer River). Bow River. Diaries. Kutenai Indians. McGillivray, Duncan. North West Company. Rocky Mountain House. Thompson, David. Travel accounts. 1800. *3376*

—. Armies. Canadian West. Firearms (function of). Fraser River. Fur Trade. Gold Rushes. Indians. Thompson River. 1670-1967. *3170*

—. Blackfoot Indians. Canadian West. Indian-White Relations. Law Enforcement. Montana. Northwest Mounted Police. Settlement. Trade (whiskey). 1870-98. *3134*

—. Blanket economy. Fort Langley. Fur Trade. Salish Indians. 1820-1966. *3482*

—. British Columbia. Flett, John. Fort Nisqually. Settlement. 1841. *3109*

—. British Columbia (Babine Lake). Copper Mines and Mining. Fort Babine. Fort Kilmaurs. Harmon, Daniel. McDougall, James. 1822-1968. *3457*

—. British Columbia (Prince George, McLeod Lake Trading Post). Fraser, Simon. Fur Trade. North West Company. Simpson, George. 1805-1964. *3450*

—. British Columbia (Vancouver Island; Nanaimo). Canadian Pacific Railway. Coal Mines and Mining. Economic Development. Railroads. 19c-20c. *3471*

—. British Columbia (Victoria). Indian-White Relations. Missions and Missionaries. Population. 19c-20c. *3446*

—. Bungi (dialect). Cree Indians. Fur Trade. Lower Fort Garry. Manitoba. Red River. 19c-1968. *3302*

—. California (San Francisco). Fort Vancouver. Fur Trade. Great Britain. Hawaii (Honolulu). Pacific Northwest. Russia. 1841-60. *916*

—. Canada. Catholic Church. Missions and Missionaries. Trade. 1820-60. *3119*

—. Canada. Church of England. Fur Trade. Indians. Missions and Missionaries. 17c-18c. *3118*

—. Canada. Foreign Relations. Royal Canadian Mounted Police. Settlement. USA. 17c-20c. *3255*

—. Canada. Fur Trade. Great Britain. Monopolies. Royal Society. Secrecy. Wegg, Samuel. 1670-1799. *3184*

—. Canada. Fur Trade. Mergers. North West Company. 17c-19c. *3240*

—. Canada. Fur Trade (competition). North West Company. Selkirk, 5th Earl of. 1800-21. *3131*

—. Canada. Medals (commemorative). Money (promissory notes, tokens). Numismatics. 1791-1870. *3140*

—. Canada (Peace River). Fort Dunvegan. Fur Trade. Land promotion. North West Company. 1805-1918. *3368*

—. Canada (Rupert's Land). Fur Trade. Simpson, George. Travel accounts. 1826-60. *3176*

—. Canadian northwest coast. Fur Trade. Land Tenure. Overland Telegraph. Russians. Tolmie, William Fraser. 1838-67. *3447*

—. Carlton House. Centennial Celebrations. General Winter Express. Historical Sites and Parks. North West Rebellion. Saskatchewan. Simpson, George. 1795-1885. 1964-65. *3359*

—. Cowie, Isaac. Fort Qu'Appelle. Great Britain (Stromness Harbour). *Prince Rupert* (vessel). Saskatchewan. Voyages. 1867. *3300*

—. Daily Life. Diaries. Fort George. Lattie, Alexander. Oregon Territory. 1846. *900*

—. Discovery and Exploration. Fur Trade. Prairie Provinces. 1770-1970. *3183*

—. Discovery and Exploration. Mount Rainier National Park. Rainier, Peter. Tourism. Vancouver, George. Washington. 1792-1899. *2065*

—. Excavations. Historical Sites and Parks. Lower Fort Garry National Historic Park. Manitoba. 1830-1911. 1965-67. *3272*

—. Fort Garry. Manitoba (Red River Valley). Métis. Mulligan, James. Rebellions. Riel, Louis. 1869. *3260*

—. Fort Vancouver. Hawaii (Honolulu). Trade. 1829-59. *3460*

—. Fur Trade. Idaho (Snake County). Northwest Company. Pacific Fur Company. Pacific Northwest. Payette, François. 1812-44. *893*

—. Fur Trade. Smith, Jedediah Strong. 1824-29. *436*

—. Historical Sites and Parks. Lower Fort Garry. Manitoba. Red River. 1831-1969. *3278*

—. Immigration. Irish. Manitoba (Red River Colony). North West Company. Scots. Selkirk, 5th Earl of. 1810-21. *3271*

—. Indian Affairs and Northern Development, Department of. Lower Fort Garry. Manitoba (Selkirk). Quebec Rifles, 2d Battalion. Red River Indian War. Royal First Warwickshire Regiment of Foot. 1831-70. 1965. *3310*

—. Manitoba (Selkirk, Winnipeg). Railroads. Riel, Louis. Trade. 1859-1907. *3200*

—. Oregon. 1846-1900. *1559*

Hudson's Bay Company Archives. Bolton, Herbert Eugene. Clark, Robert Carlton. Colleges and Universities. Frontier thesis. *Oregon Historical Quarterly* (periodical). Oregon, University of. Turner, Frederick Jackson. 1900-39. *3185*

Hudson's Bay Company (records). Archives. Canada. Great Britain (London). Preservation. Public Archives. 1671-1966. *3127*

Huerta, Victoriano. Conspiracies. Foreign Relations. Germany. Mexico. 1915. *3642*

Hughes, Charles Evans. Attitudes. Colorado. Newspapers. Political Campaigns. Progressive Party. Roosevelt, Theodore. 1910-16. *3761*

—. California. Crocker, William H. Elections (presidential). Johnson, Hiram. Wilson, Woodrow. 1916. *3021*

—. Democratic Party. Elections (presidential). Foreign Policy. North Dakota. Republican Party. Wilson, Woodrow. 1916. *3835*

—. Elections (presidential). Kansas. Republican Party. 1916. *2557*

Hughes, H. Stuart. Frontier thesis. Manifest Destiny (reappraisal). Methodology. Philosophy of History. Turner, Frederick Jackson. Webb, Walter Prescott. 19c. 1963. *2404*

Hughes, Robert J. Highland County Historical Museum. Museums. North Dakota. Rosemeade Potteries. 1946-66. *2492*

Hughes, Sam. Arizona Pioneers' Historical Society. Carleton, James H. Documents. Lockwood, Frank Cummins. Pioneers. 1862. *2916*

Huish, David. Arizona. Colorado. Diaries. New Mexico. Photography. Utah. 1898-99. *3598*

Hulbert, Archer Butler. Frontier thesis. Historians. Turner, Frederick Jackson. 1873-1933. *234*

Human Rights. Courts. Flynn, Elizabeth Gurley. Industrial Workers of the World. Labor (unskilled). Washington (Spokane). 1909-64. *3904*

Humanism. Cather, Willa. Literature. London, Jack. Norris, Frank. 20c. *1994*

Humboldt, Alexander von. Bunsen, Christian von. California. Colonization. Prussia. Roenne, Friedrich von. 1842. *193*

—. Burrus, Ernest J. California. Kino, Eusebio Francisco. Maps. Mexico. 1681-1710. 1965. *64*

Humbolt Mountain Range. Alexander, Annie Montague. Nevada. Paleontology. Saurian Expedition of 1905. 1867-1905. *460*

Humbolt Trail. California Trail. Diaries. Nevada Territory. Overland Journeys to the Pacific. Yager, James Pressley. 1863. *379*

Hume, John B. Banking. Banks, Charles Wells. California (San Francisco). Crime and Criminals. Embezzlement. Wells, Fargo and Company. 1871-90. *1753*

Humor *See also* Satire.

—. Arizona. Economic Reform. Hall, DeForest (Dick Wick Hall). Hopi Indians. Literature. *Salome Sun* (news flier). *Saturday Evening Post* (periodical). 1877-1926. *3647*

—. California (Calaveras County). Gold Mines and Mining. Literature. Twain, Mark ("The Celebrated Jumping Frog of Calaveras County"). 1865. *1988*

—. Comic strips. Frontier and Pioneer Life. (*Out Our Way*) (cartoon). Williams, James Robert. 1888-1957. *1421*

—. Cowboys. 19c. *1076*

—. Cowboys. Fiction. Lewis, Alfred Henry. Southwest. 1883-1913. *1943*

—. Daily Life. Pacific Northwest. Pioneers. 19c. *1418*

—. Davis, Harold Lenoir. Fiction. Folklore. Frontier and Pioneer Life. Pacific Northwest. 1935-60. *1879*

—. Folklore. Great Britain. Texas. 17c-1963. *2618*

—. Folklore. Kansas. Youth. 1900-63. *2535*

—. Frontier and Pioneer Life. Pacific Northwest. 1870-95. *1916*

—. Fur Trade. *Joe Miller's Joke Book*. Pacific Northwest. 1839. *1967*

—. Kansas. Lecture tour. Missouri (St. Joseph). Ward, Artemus. 1863-64. *1817*

—. Arizona Territory. Armies. Arthur, Chester A. Crime and Criminals. Mexico (Chihuahua, Sonora). 1882. *1797*

—. Arizona (Tucson). Buttner, Adolph George. 1866-85. *1760*

—. Bibliographies. Diamond Dick (stories). Dime novels. Frontier and Pioneer Life. Wade, Bertrand (fictional character). Wade, Richard (fictional character). 1878-1911. *1934*

—. Billy the Kid. Customs collection. Garrett, Pat. New Mexico. Roosevelt, Theodore. Texas (El Paso). 1850-1908. *1774*

—. Blackfoot Indians. Canadian West. Hudson's Bay Company. Indian-White Relations. Montana. Northwest Mounted Police. Settlement. Trade (whiskey). 1870-98. *3134*

—. Bootlegging. Oil Industry and Trade. Prostitution. Texas (Navarro County, Corsicana). Texas Rangers. 1924. *3962*

—. British Columbia (Steveston, Wellington). Coal Mines and Mining. Fishing industry. Militia. Strikes. 1890-1900. *3476*

—. Bureau of Identification and Records. Cattle theft. Department of Public Safety. Fletcher, Joseph Sidney. Texas and Southwestern Cattle Raisers' Association. 1906-66. *3683*

—. Bursum, Holm O. New Mexico Territory. Politics. 1894. *1775*

—. California. Executions. Forner y Brugada, José. Murder. 1850's. *1778*

—. California (San Francisco). Casey, James P. Deportation. King, James. Political Corruption. Terry, David Smith. Vigilantes. 1851-56. *1779*

—. Canada. Northwest Mounted Police. 1873-1918. *3194*

—. Chickasaw Nation. Dawes Commission. Freedmen. Land policies. Oklahoma. Reconstruction. 1861-94. *629*

—. Cities. Frontier and Pioneer Life. Mining camps. 1849-1900. *1707*

—. Colorado (Animas City). Outlaws. Stockton, Port. 1852-82. *1746*

—. Dogtown Settlement. Murrill, William Bartley. Oklahoma Territory. Outlaws. 1890's. *1770*

—. Earp, Wyatt. Folklore. Gunfighters. *Harper's New Monthly Magazine*. Hickok, Wild Bill. Kansas. Masterson, Bat. 1860's-90's. *1789*

—. Five Civilized Tribes. Indian Territory. Indian-White Relations. Negroes. 1880-1900. *1772*

—. Fort Hays. Hickok, Wild Bill. Kansas (Hays City). 1869. *1792*

—. Fountain, Albert Jennings. New Mexico (Mesilla). Public Schools. Republican Party. Santa Fe Ring. State Politics. 1861-80's. *1845*

—. Germany. Gerstäcker, Friedrich. Texas. Western novels. 1838-45. *1984*

—. Horner, Joseph (alias Frank Canton). Johnson County War. Nebraska. Outlaws. Texas. 1869-1916. *1745*

—. Indian-White Relations. Nevada. Paiute Indians. Washo Indians. Wasson, Warren. 1849-62. *2838*

—. Letters. Mining Camps. Washington Territory. 1862. *1781*

—. Mexico. Mountain Men. Trapping. 1821-28. *922*

—. North West Mounted Police. Rustling (cattle, horses). Saskatchewan. 1890-1910. *3326*

—. Reconstruction. Texas State Police. 1865-76. *1743*

Lawford, Charles H. Alberta. Methodist Church. Missions and Missionaries. Ukrainians. 1898. *3382*

Lawmen. *See* Law Enforcement.

Lawrence and Carbondale Railroad. Alma and Burlingame Railroad. Coal Mines and Mining. Kansas (Osage County). Manhattan Railroad. Missouri Pacific Railroad. Railroads. Santa Fe Railroad. 1869-1910. *942*

Lawrence, Henry W. Foster, Warren. *Inter-Mountain Advocate* (newspaper). Labor Reform. Political Reform. Populism. Utah. 1893-1900. *3753*

Lawyers *See also* Judges; Legal Ethics.

—. Abolition Movement. Andrews, Stephen Pearl. Annexation. Texas. 1839-43. *2670*

—. California. Frontier thesis. State Politics. Turner, Frederick Jackson. 1850-90. *2987*

—. Hawley, James H. Idaho. State Government. Western Federation of Miners. 1890's. *3870*

—. Land disputes. Letters. Maxwell Land Grant. New Mexico. New York *Sun* (newspaper). Newman, Simeon Harrison. Political Corruption. Santa Fe Ring. 1875. *1777*

—. McCarran, Patrick Anthony. Nevada. Political Leadership. Reform. Senate. 1922-54. *3784*

Lay, Henry Champlin. Episcopal Church, Protestant. Southwest. 1859-61. *2348*

Lazy Y Cross Ranch. Cattle wars. Colorado. Cowboys. Glass, Charlie. Negroes. Turner, Oscar L. Utah. 1920's-37. *4091*

Lea, Margaret Moffette. Houston, Sam. Texas. 1819-67. *2643*

Leader (newspaper). Davin, Nicholas Flood. Political Leadership. Saskatchewan (Regina). 1882-1901. *3341*

Leadership *See also* Political Leadership.

—. Agriculture. Nebraska Hall of Agricultural Achievement. 1916-72. *4074*

—. Arizona. Freudenthal, Samuel J. Frontier and Pioneer Life. New Mexico. Reminiscences. Texas (El Paso). 1880's-1932. *1236*

—. Finance. Mining. Wardner, James F. 1871-99. *863*

—. Indian Wars. Peace. Sioux Indians. Spotted Tail (Chief). 1876-77. *684*

—. Mormons. Utah (Salt Lake Valley). Young, Brigham. 1844-47. *2246*

League of Women Voters. California. Edson, Katherine Philips. State Industrial Welfare Commission. Woman Suffrage. 1911-31. *3775*

—. Child Welfare. Nebraska. Women. 1920-70. *3743*

Lease, Mary Elizabeth. Political Leadership. Populism. 1890-94. *3734*

Leatherwood, R. N. Arizona (Prescott, Tucson). Capital cities. Letters. Territorial Government (13th Legislature). 1885. *2915*

Leavell Coal Company. Avery, Cyrus S. Avery Realty Company. Coal Mines and Mining. Eastern Oklahoma Agricultural Association. Oil Industry and Trade. Oklahoma. Real Estate Business. State Politics. Togo Oil Company. 1907-63. *3722*

Leavenworth, Henry. Catlin, George. Fort Gibson. Fort Leavenworth. Museums. Peace medals. Portraits (miniatures). 1801-66. 1971. *708*

—. Indian-White Relations. Kansas (Fort Leavenworth). Military Service, Professional. 1827. *796*

Leavenworth, Jesse Henry. Armies. Comanche Indians. Indian Wars. Kiowa-Comanche Treaty. 1865. *829*

—. Comanche Indians. *Harper's New Monthly Magazine*. Indians (agencies). Kiowa Indians. Political Corruption. 1862-70. *1796*

Lebeck, Peter. California. Excavations. Foxtail Rangers. Historical Sites and Parks. Tombs. 1890. *3083*

Lecture tour. Humor. Kansas. Missouri (St. Joseph). Ward, Artemus. 1863-64. *1817*

Lectures *See also* Speeches, Addresses, etc.

—. Colorado College (summer school). Wilson, Woodrow. 1894. *3693*

—. Davenport, Homer. Oregon (Silverton). 1867-1912. *1806*

—. Education. Kansas. Libraries. 1854-64. *1832*

LeDoux, Emma. California (Stockton). McVicar, A. N. Murder. Trials. 1906-41. *2997*

Ledyard, John. Alaska. Bering Strait. Cochrane, John Dundas. DeWindt, Harry. Railroads. Russia (Kamchatka, St. Petersburg). Western Union Telegraph Company. 1788-1900. *3501*

Lee, Andrew E. Kyle, James Henderson. Loucks, Henry Langford. National Farmers' Alliance. Political Parties. Populism. Reform. South Dakota. State Politics. 1884-96. *3760*

Lee, Jason. Government. Methodist Church. Missions and Missionaries. Oregon. Young, Ewing. 1834-45. *2973*

Lee, John D. Allen, James. California. Diaries. Egan, Howard. Mexican War. Mormons. Polk, James K. Travel account. Volunteer Armies. 1846. *558*

—. Brooks, Juanita. Libraries. Mormons. Pioneers. Reminiscences. 1966. *2238*

—. Diaries. Mexico. Missouri (Atchison County). Mormons. New Mexico (Santa Fe). 1846. *559*

Lee, R. W. Civil War. Confederate States of America. Five Civilized Tribes. Indian-White Relations. Osage Indians. 1864. *581*

Leeper, John Milton. Farmers. Frontier thesis. Rural-Urban Studies. Turner, Frederick Jackson. 1880-1900. *1059*

Leeper, Matthew. Buchanan, James. Comanche Indians. Confederate Army. Indian Territory. Wichita Agency (battle). 1840-62. *624*

Lefroy, John Henry. Canada. Delafield, Joseph. Diaries. Simpson, Frances Ramsey. Simpson, George. Simpson, Ramsey. Surveying. USA. Voyages. 1823-44. *3157*

Leftism *See also* Communism; Radicals and Radicalism; Socialism.

Legal Ethics. Benjamin, Judah P. Black, Jeremiah S. California. Castillero, Andres. Courts. Frémont, John C. Land claims. Mines. *New Almaden Case* (US, 1860). Randolph, Edmund. 1860. *871*

Legal heritage (Spanish). Economic legislation. Law and Society. Pioneers. Southwest. 16c-20c. *185*

Legal history. Common law. Judicial Administration. Territorial Government. 19c. *2692*

Legal traditions. Colorado (Denver). Courts. 1859-61. *2765*

Legislation *See also* Congress; Law; Legislative Bodies.

—. Agricultural Department. Conservation of Natural Resources. Forests and Forestry. Prairie States Forestry Project. South Dakota. 1862-1970. *1177*

—. Agriculture. Great Plains. Norris, George William. 1920's. *4093*

—. Alaska. Congress. Harrison, Benjamin. Jackson, Sheldon. Missions and Missionaries. Presbyterian Church. 1800-92. *3539*

—. Blue laws. Business. Texas. 1871-1961. *3589*

—. California. Discrimination. Indians. ca 1850-1968. *1471*

—. California Land Grant Act (1851). Civil Court Cases. Land Tenure. Mexico. Suscol Principle. USA. 1850's. *1149*

—. Cattle Raising. Economic Conditions. Farms. Great Plains. Settlement. 19c. *1062*

—. Child Welfare. Food and drug standards. Montana. Propaganda. State Politics. 1900-15. *2730*

—. Colorado. Ku Klux Klan. Locke, John Galen. Morley, Clarence J. Politics. 1920's. *3840*

—. Colorado. Political Attitudes. Progressivism. 1900-20. *3820*

—. Construction. Hoover Dam. Nevada (southern). 1936. *4149*

—. Economic Conditions. Forests and Forestry. Oregon and California Railway. Railroads. 1866-1937. *1377*

—. Hutterites. Montana (Hilldale). 1969. *1519*

—. Northern Pacific Railroad. Railroads. 1920-27. *3664*

—. Workmen's Compensation. Wyoming. 1900-15. *3877*

Legislation (direct). Elections. Oklahoma. Politics. State Government. 1907-65. *3758*

Legislation (federal, state). Conservation of Natural Resources. Great Plains. Oklahoma (Mangum). Shelterbelt Program. 1870-1934. *4156*

Legislative Bodies *See also* Congress; House of Representatives; Parliaments; Provincial Legislatures; Senate; State Legislatures.

—. Mitchell, Robert Byington. New Mexico Territory. Territorial Government. 1867-69. *2861*

Lehi factory. Sugar beets. Utah Sugar Company. 1891-1924. *1217*

Leigh, William Robinson. Art Galleries and Museums. New York City. Oklahoma (Tulsa). Thomas Gilcrease Institute of American History and Art. 1896-1964. *2129*

Leland, Cyrus. Elections. Kansas. Politics. Populist Party. 1892-94. *3793*

Lemons. California (Santa Paula). Fruit and Fruit Crops (industry). Oil Industry and Trade. 1890's-1945. *3851*

Lenger, John F. Music (bands). Nebraska. Niobrara Reservation. Sioux Indians (Santee). 1884. *2171*

Leopold, Aldo. Carhart, Arthur H. Forest Service. Johnson, Lyndon B. (administration). Nature Conservation. Recreation. Wilderness Bill (1964). 1919-64. *4097*

LeRoy, Herman R. California. Emmet, Thomas Addis (family). Emmet, William J. Gold Rushes. Letters. Voyages. 1849-50. *987*

Leslie, Frank. Literature. Railroads. Reinhardt, Richard. Travel accounts. 1867. 1967. *1391*

Leslie's Monthly Magazine (periodical). Cowboy Song. Hanson, Joseph Mills. Lomax, John (*Cowboy Songs*, 1910). Music. 1904-10. *3707*

Lesser, Sol. California. Marriage. Political Campaigns (gubernatorial). Sinclair, Upton. 1878-1968. *1991*

Lynching (attempted). Espionage Act. Kansas (Burton). Mennonites. Pacifism. Schrag, John. Trials. World War I. 1918. *3621*

Lynchings. California (Los Angeles). Vigilantes. 1835-74. *1748*

Lynde, Isaac. Baylor, George. Civil War. Fort Fillmore (surrender of). New Mexico Territory. 1861. *594*

Lyon, Caleb. Davis, Jackson L. Diamond Hunting. Idaho (Owyhee region). 1865-92. *973*

—. Idaho Territory. Indian policies. Treaties. 1864-66. *2742*

Lytle, John Thomas. Cattle Raising. Texas Cattle Raisers' Association. 19c. *1130*

M

MacAdams, Roberta Catherine. Alberta. Political Campaigns. Provincial Legislatures. 1917. *3391*

Macdonald, Hugh John. Coyne, James H. Manitoba (Winnipeg). Political Leadership. Red River Expedition (1870). Saskatchewan Rebellion. 1870-1929. *3301*

MacDonald, John Alexander. Blackfoot Indians. Canadian Pacific Railway. Lacombe, Albert. North West Rebellion. Railroads. Riel, Louis. Stephen, George (1st Baron Mount Stephen). VanHorne, William Cornelius. 1880-1912. *3117*

—. Canada. Economic Conditions. National Development. 19c. *3129*

Macdonald Report (1962). British Columbia. Colleges and Universities. Junior Colleges (proposed). 1962-66. *3449*

MacDougal, Daniel T. Arizona (Tucson). Botany. Coville, Frederick V. Deserts. Forest Service. Research Laboratories. 1903-60. *3710*

Macfie, Matthew. British Columbia. Clarke, William F. Colonial Missionary Society. Congregational Unions in Canada and England. Missions and Missionaries. Negroes. Segregation. 1859-60. *3469*

MacGregor, James. Canadian West. *Globe* (newspaper). Great Britain. Lorne, Marquis of. Travel account. 1881. *3235*

Machinery *See also* Inventions.

Machinery (bulldozers). Engineering. Flynn, Ted P. Forest Service. Moore, Ralph B. Oregon. 1923-52. *4110*

MacInnis, Grace. King, William Lyon Mackenzie. Manitoba. Old Age Pension. Political Leadership. Reminiscences. Winnipeg General Strike. Woodsworth, James Shaver. 1919-42. *3285*

MacIntyre, Albert A. Adams, Alva. Colorado (Leadville). Strikes. 1896-97. *3871*

Mackay, Charles (works). Great Britain. Mayhew, Henry. Mormons. Pratt, Orson. Utah. 1830-1957. *2227*

Mackay, J. A. Church of England. Cree Indians. Diaries. Missions and Missionaries. Saskatchewan. Stanley Mission. 1870-72. *3337*

Mackay, John Alexander. Canoe trip. Diaries. Halson, K. Indians. Manitoba (The Pas). Matheson, Canon. Matheson, Eleanor Shepphird. Missions and Missionaries. Saskatchewan (Lac La Ronge). 1920. *3208*

Mackenzie, Alexander. British Columbia (Prince George). Economic Growth. Fraser, Simon. Grand Trunk Pacific Railway. Lumber and Lumbering. Railroads. Transportation. 1793-1967. *3441*

—. Canada. Fraser River. 1793-1963. *3438*

Mackenzie, Ranald S. Adobe Walls (battle). Comanche Indians. Indian Wars. Miles, Nelson A. Military Campaigns. Texas. 1874-75. *741*

—. Comanche Indians. Fort Sill. Indian-White Relations. Kiowa Indians. Oklahoma. 1872-91. *855*

—. Crook, George. Grierson, Benjamin Henry. Howard, Oliver Otis. Indian Wars. Miles, Nelson A. Military Service, Professional. Pope, John. 19c. *718*

—. Indian Wars. Kickapoo Indians. Mexico. Texas. 1873. *838*

Mackie, John. Ballantyne, Robert Michael. Canadian West. Frontier and Pioneer Life. Literature. Saxby, Jessie M. 1841. *3160*

Maclay, Charles. California (San Fernando Valley). Dace, Catherine Hubbard. Diaries. Economic Development. Mission San Fernando Rey de España. Pico, Andres. Porter, Benjamin F. Porter, George K. Settlement. 1861-73. *1638*

Macready, John A. Arizona. California. DH-4 (aircraft). Map Drawing. Mather, Stephen. Pacific Northwest. Photography. Stevens, A. W. 1924. *3628*

Mactavish, William. Canada (Assiniboia, Rupert's Land). Governors. Métis. Riel, Louis. 1858-70. *3199*

Macune, Charles W. Agricultural Organizations. Farmers' Alliance. People's Party. Politics. 1890-1920. *3789*

Madeira, George. Astronomy. California (Volcano). Lick, James. 1860-87. 1969. *2214*

Madero, Francisco I. Mexico. Revolutionary Movements (attempted). Reyes, Bernardo. Texas (San Antonio). 1911. *3650*

—. Mexico (Chihuahua). Mormons. Religious Liberty. Settlement. Young, Brigham. 1852-1912. *2302*

Madstone (use of). Hydrophobia. Medicine (practice of). Oklahoma. 19c. *2198*

Magazines. *See* Periodicals.

Magné, Louis. Belgo-American Company. Oil Industry and Trade. Wyoming. 1900-04. *3864*

Magrath, C. A. Alberta Irrigation Company. Canadian Pacific Railway. Canals. Galt, Elliot. Irrigation. Palliser Triangle. Railroads. Settlement. 1882-1901. *3378*

Magraw, W. M. F. Armies. Buchanan, James (administration). Federal Government. Hookaday, John M. Intervention. Mormons. Patronage. Utah Territory. 1857. *2825*

Mahoney, Mary. Colorado. Nebraska. Travel account. 1901. *402*

Mailer, Norman. Heroes (concept of). Individualism. Novels. Outlaws. Violence. 19c-20c. *1799*

Maine *See also* New England.

—. California. Gold Mines and Mining. Shipping. Trade. Travel account. 1849-52. *1277*

Mair, Charles. Begg, Alexander. Fiction. Manitoba (Red River). Schultz, John Christian. 1871. *3305*

Maksutov, Dmitrii P. Alaska. Russian-American Company. 1832-89. *3518*

Malamud, Bernard (review article). Frontier myth. 1961. *1873*

Malaria. California. Eucalyptus trees. Folk Medicine. 1850's-80's. *2211*

Malheur Indian Agency. Indian raids. Letters. Oregon (Grant County; Canyon City). 1878. *1603*

Malin, James C. Great Plains. Historians. 1930's. *2431*

Mallon, Felix. California (Long Beach). City Government. Civil Court Cases. Oil Industry and Trade. State Government. 1930-66. *3875*

Mallory, Samuel. Colorado. Diaries. Gold Rushes. Montana. State Government. 1860-80. *2713*

—. Missouri River. Missouri (St. Louis). Montana (Fort Benton). Travel accounts. 1864-68. *439*

Maltby, John Rogers. Frontier and Pioneer Life. Nebraska (Clay County). 1868-71. *2514*

Management *See also* Industrial Relations.

—. Adams, Charles Francis, Jr. Gould, Jay. Railroads. Senate Judiciary Committee. Union Pacific Railroad. 1870-90. *1334*

—. Construction. Railroads. 1850-70. *1387*

Manco Curro Pass Massacre. Jicarilla Apache Indians. New Mexico. 1848. *2852*

Mandan Indians. Arikara Indians. Fort Berthold. Fur Trade. Hidatsa Indians. 1700-1884. *883*

—. Blackfoot Indians. Europe. Kiowa Indians. Omaha Indians. Sioux Indians. Social Change. Trade. 19c. *913*

—. Fur Trade. St. Louis Missouri Fur Company. Sheheke (Shahaka, Mandan chief). Thomas (physician). Travel account. 1809. *896*

Manfred, Frederick. Authors. Clark, Walter Van Tilburg. Fisher, Vardis. Guthrie, A. B., Jr. Waters, Frank. Western novels. 19c-1966. *1950*

Mangas Coloradas (chief). Apache Indians (Copper Mine band). Fort McLane. Murder. 1863. *785*

Manhattan Railroad. Alma and Burlingame Railroad. Coal Mines and Mining. Kansas (Osage County). Lawrence and Carbondale Railroad. Missouri Pacific Railroad. Railroads. Santa Fe Railroad. 1869-1910. *942*

Manifest Destiny. Attitudes. Historiography. Mexican War. Polk, James K. (administration). 1846-48. 1964. *551*

—. Benton, Thomas Hart. *Enquirer* (newspaper). Expansionism. Missouri (St. Louis). Oregon. 1818-20. *2927*

—. California. New York (Rochester). Oregon. Settlement. Speeches, Addresses, etc.. Warner, Jonathan Trumbull (Juan José Warner). 1840. *2936*

—. Caribbean. Imperialism. Pacific Ocean. 1800-1914. *285*

—. Fergusson, Harvey. Literature. Mexican Americans. Race Relations. Southwest. 1921-67. *1972*

—. Geography. Louisiana Territory (image of). 1803-04. *2427*

—. Linn, Lewis Fields. Oregon. Senate. 1839-43. *2967*

—. Mexican War. Westward Movement. 1763-1848. *557*

Manifest Destiny (reappraisal). Frontier thesis. Hughes, H. Stuart. Methodology. Philosophy of History. Turner, Frederick Jackson. Webb, Walter Prescott. 19c. 1963. *2404*

Manitoba *See also* Prairie Provinces.

—. Administrative Law. Alberta. Judicial divisions. Northwest Territories. Ontario. Quebec. Saskatchewan. 1858-1912. *3155*

—. Agricultural Reform. Patrons of Industry. 1890-98. *3291*

—. Archibald, Adams George. Governors. Nova Scotia. Riel, Louis. 1870-83. *3266*

—. Bill 59. British North America Act (1867). Catholic Church. Education. French (language). Protestantism. Public Schools. 1807-1967. *3282*

—. Bungi (dialect). Cree Indians. Fur Trade. Hudson's Bay Company. Lower Fort Garry. Red River. 19c-1968. *3302*

—. Cartoons and Caricatures. Dale, Archie. *Winnipeg Free Press* (newspaper). 1910-54. *3283*

—. Civilian Conservation Corps. Federal Emergency Administration of Public Works. Horticulture. International Peace Garden. North Dakota. Peace (symbol of). 1932-64. *3303*

—. Daily Life. Discrimination. Hutterites. Settlement. 1874-1960. *3297*

—. Economic Policy. Emigration. North Dakota. 1870's-90's. *3306*

—. Emigration. Iceland. Settlement. 1870-1900. *3296*

—. Excavations. Historical Sites and Parks. Hudson's Bay Company. Lower Fort Garry National Historic Park. 1830-1911. 1965-67. *3272*

—. Historical Sites and Parks. Hudson's Bay Company. Lower Fort Garry. Red River. 1831-1969. *3278*

—. Immigration. Indians. Jews. Law. Reminiscences. Rosenbaum, Bella W. Washington (Seattle). 1880's-1914. *1524*

—. King, William Lyon Mackenzie. MacInnis, Grace. Old Age Pension. Political Leadership. Reminiscences. Winnipeg General Strike. Woodsworth, James Shaver. 1919-42. *3285*

—. Land. Settlement. 1870-1913. *3309*

—. Lower Fort Garry. 1831. 1963. *3286*

—. Mennonites. Social Change. Sommerfeld Mennonite Church. 1890-1948. *3280*

—. Rural-Urban Studies. Teachers. Ukrainian Canadians. 1891-1921. *3307*

Manitoba Act (1870). Bilingualism. French language (abolition). Politics. Provincial Legislatures. Schools. 1870-90. *3264*

—. Canada. Métis. Resistance. Riel, Louis. 1844-85. *3252*

Manitoba (Arborg, Winnipeg). Icelanders. Immigration. Linguistics. Toponymy. USA. 20c. *3262*

Manitoba Free Press (newspaper). Canada. Letters. Northwest Mounted Police. 1875-76. *3193*

Manitoba (Grand Rapids). Historical Sites and Parks. LaVérendrye, Sieur de. 1727-60. *3211*

Manitoba (Lake of the Woods, Winnipeg). Landscape Painting. Phillips, Walter J. Rocky Mountains. 1914-63. *3257*

Manitoba (Long Plant, Oak Lake, Turtle Mountain). Indians (reservations). Minnesota. Refugees. Saskatchewan (Standing Buffalo, Wood Mountain). Sioux Indians. 1862-1968. *3238*

Manitoba (Minnedosa area). Frontier and Pioneer Life. Settlement. 1870-1928. *3268*

Manitoba (Nelson River). Button, Thomas. Hudson Bay Railroad. Hydraulic Engineering. International Nickel Company. Kelsey Generating Station. Mines (nickel). Railroads. 1612-1957. *3258*

Manitoba (northern). Economic Development. Forests and Forestry. Mines. Nickel industry. Roads. Tourism. 1950's-72. *3298*

Manitoba (Portage La Prairie). Local Government. Settlement. Spence, Thomas. 1738-1967. *3292*

Manitoba (Red River). *Alabama* (vessel). Annexation. British Columbia. Great Britain. Nova Scotia. 1865-70. *3130*

—. Begg, Alexander. Fiction. Mair, Charles. Schultz, John Christian. 1871. *3305*

—. Education (single v. dual system). Settlement. 1811-34. *3281*

—. Military Campaigns. North West Rebellion. Riel, Louis. Wolseley, Garnet Joseph. 1870. *3263*

Manitoba (Red River Colony). Hudson's Bay Company. Immigration. Irish. North West Company. Scots. Selkirk, 5th Earl of. 1810-21. *3271*

Manitoba (Red River settlement). Agriculture. Fur Trade. Hudson's Bay Company. Riel, Louis. Settlement. 1870. *3294*

—. Church Missionary Society. Church of England. Cockran, William. Diaries. Simpson, George. 1825-65. *3265*

—. Cowley, Abraham. Frontier and Pioneer Life. Great Britain. Immigration. Letters. Settlement. 1845-54. *3284*

Manitoba (Red River Valley). Fort Garry. Hudson's Bay Company. Métis. Mulligan, James. Rebellions. Riel, Louis. 1869. *3260*

—. Fort Garry. Military Campaigns. North West Rebellion. Riel, Louis. Wolseley, Garnet Joseph. 1870. *3259*

—. Music (military). North West Rebellion. "Red River Valley". 1869-96. *3274*

Manitoba (Selkirk). Hudson's Bay Company. Indian Affairs and Northern Development, Department of. Lower Fort Garry. Quebec Rifles, 2d Battalion. Red River Indian War. Royal First Warwickshire Regiment of Foot. 1831-70. 1965. *3310*

Manitoba (Selkirk, Winnipeg). Hudson's Bay Company. Railroads. Riel, Louis. Trade. 1859-1907. *3200*

Manitoba (Souris-Mouth area). Archaeology. Brandon House. Diaries. Fur Trade. Indians. Letters. Yorstone, William. 1793-1821. *3267*

Manitoba (St. Boniface). Diaries. Fenian invasion (proposed). Métis. O'Donohue, W. B. Proulx, J.-B. Riel, Louis. 1870. *3299*

Manitoba (Steinbach). Education. Mennonites. 19c. *3277*

Manitoba Telephone System. Bell Telephone Company. Provincial Government. Radio broadcasting. Telephone. 1878-1954. *3295*

Manitoba (The Pas). Canoe trip. Diaries. Halson, K. Indians. Mackay, John Alexander. Matheson, Canon. Matheson, Eleanor Shepphird. Missions and Missionaries. Saskatchewan (Lac La Ronge). 1920. *3208*

Manitoba, University of. Biculturalism. Canada. English Canadians. French Canadians. Historical and Scientific Society of Manitoba. Historical Society of St. Boniface. St. Boniface College. 1962. *3293*

—. British Columbia, University of. Canada. Colleges and Universities. Great Britain. Medical Education. Minnesota, University of. Sherrington, Charles. Wesbrook, Frank Fairchild. 1868-1919. *3434*

Manitoba (Winnipeg). Agricultural Production. Business. Canadian Pacific Railway. Economic Growth. Fort Garry. Railroads. Urbanization. 1870-90. *3270*

—. Black Robe (use). Idaho Territory. Linguistics. Washington Territory. 1821-47. *2344*

—. Borden, Robert Laird. Federal Government. One Big Union. Railroads. Robertson, Gideon. Strikes. 1919. *3261*

—. Canada. Class consciousness. Elections. Independent Labor Party. Liberal Party. Parliaments. Politics. Puttee, Arthur. Sifton, Clifford. 1899-1904. *3290*

—. Cities (gateway). Transportation. USA. Wholesale Trade. 1970. *3269*

—. Coyne, James H. Macdonald, Hugh John. Political Leadership. Red River Expedition (1870). Saskatchewan Rebellion. 1870-1929. *3301*

—. Economic Conditions. Mennonites. Migration, Internal. Rural-Urban Studies. 1945-68. *3276*

—. Franko, Ivan. Genyk, Kyrylo. Immigration. Labor Unions and Organizations. Oles'kiv, Joseph. Ukrainians. 1895-96. *3146*

—. Jews. Schools. 1874-1954. *3279*

—. Local Government. Municipal Enquiry Commission. 1870-1961. *3273*

—. Mennonites. Religious life. Rural-Urban Studies. Social Change. 1964. *3308*

—. North West Company. Red River Valley. Selkirk, 5th Earl of. Semple, Robert. Settlement. Seven Oaks (battle). 1815. *3288*

Manitoban (newspaper). Epidemics. Prairie Provinces. Smallpox. 1869-70. *3256*

Manje, Juan Mateo. Arizona (Yuma County). Mercury Mining. 1697. 1965. *29*

Manogue, Patrick. Catholic Church. Gold Mines and Mining. Nevada (Virginia City). St. Mary in the Mountains Church. 1860-1935. *2353*

—. Catholic Church. Nevada (Virginia City). Social Conditions. 1860-95. *2391*

Manti Forest Reserve. Sheep Raising. Soil Conservation. Utah (Manti). 1870-1911. *4095*

Manuelito (chief). Arizona. Indians (reservations). Navajo Indian Police. New Mexico. 1868-73. *750*

Manufactures *See also* names of articles manufactured, e.g. Furniture, etc.; names of industries, e.g. Steel Industry and Trade, etc.; Corporations; Machinery.

—. Cattle Raising. Economic Conditions. Northern Pacific Railroad. Oregon Pacific Railroad. Pacific Northwest. Railroads. Union Pacific Railroad. Wheat. 19c. *1348*

—. Central Pacific Railroad. Freight and Freightage. Huntington, Collis P. Railroads (rebate policies). Studebaker Brothers Manufacturing Company. Studebaker, Peter. 1881-84. *1388*

—. Colt, Samuel. Inventions. Morse, Samuel. Revolvers. Telegraph. 1839-62. *254*

—. Industrialization. Oil Industry and Trade. Texas. 1900-60. *3859*

—. Industrialization. South or Southern States. Trans-Mississippi West. 1850-60. *1218*

Manuscripts *See also* Documents.

—. Anthropology. Mexico. Southwest. Spain. 1500-1750. *18*

—. Auctions. Mormons. Parke-Bernet Galleries. Southwest. Spain. 1613-19c. 1967. *7*

—. Foreign Relations. France. Texas. 1838-46. *2620*

—. Libraries. Lumber and Lumbering. Stephen F. Austin State College Library (East Texas Room). Texas (East). 1880-1930. *2654*

—. North Dakota State Historical Society (collections). 1963. *2494*

—. Research. Travel accounts (sources). 1968. *407*

Manuscripts (collections). Missouri, University of. Western Americana. 1963. *228*

Manuscripts (Mexican, Spanish). Anthropology. Archives. Ethnology. Mexico. Southwest. -1750. *17*

Manuscripts (minute book). Cattle Raising. Texas and Southwestern Cattle Raisers' Association. 1877-92. *1109*

Map Drawing. Arizona. California. DH-4 (aircraft). Macready, John A. Mather, Stephen. Pacific Northwest. Photography. Stevens, A. W. 1924. *3628*

—. Arizona (Tucson). California Volunteers. Fergusson, David. Mills, John B., Jr. 1862. *1633*

—. Austin, Stephen F. Bryan, James Perry. James Perry Bryan Map Collection. Texas. 1507-1885. *2633*

—. British Columbia. Camera (use of). Deville, Edouard Gaston. Photography. Surveying. 1885-1924. *3480*

—. Canada. Delisle, William. Great Salt Lake (specious map of). Lahontan, Baron of. USA. 1703. *83*

—. Colorado River (Cataract Canyon). Daily Life. Diaries. Kolb, Ellsworth. Scientific Expeditions. 1921. *432*

—. Diaries. Explorers. Notikewin River. Peace River. Thompson, David. 1789-1814. *3132*

—. Discovery and Exploration. Goethals, George W. Pacific Northwest. Washington (Colville Valley). 1882-84. *373*

Maps. Archives Nationales. Bibliothèque du Dépôt de la Marine Archives. Bibliothèque Nationale Archives. France (Paris). Louisiana. 17c-18c. 1965. *2644*

—. Arizona (Nogales, formerly Issacson). Bradford, William, Jr. Mexico. Mines. New Mexico and Arizona Railroad. Railroads. Sonora Railroad. Trade. 1880. *1692*

—. Bancroft, Hubert Howe. California (San Francisco). Sandels, G. M. Waseurtz af. 1843. *1641*

—. Bishop, Francis. Colorado River. Discovery and Exploration. 1871. *431*

—. Burrus, Ernest J. California. Humboldt, Alexander von. Kino, Eusebio Francisco. Mexico. 1681-1710. 1965. *64*

—. California (Oakland). Carpentier, Horace W. Kellersberger, Julius. Portois, Pierre. Squatter settlements. Surveying. 1852. *1701*

—. Colorado State Historical Society. Historical Sites and Parks. 1929-69. *2793*

—. Lafora, Nicholas de. Mexico (Chihuahua, Ciudad Juarez). Texas (El Paso). Urrutia, Joseph de. 1766. *121*

Marble Industry. Colorado (Marble). Meek, Channing F. Osgood, John C. Vermont Marble Company. Yule Creek White Marble Company. 1800-1941. *1011*

March Field. Air Bases. Armies. California (Riverside). Land Tenure. 1917-18. *3603*

Marias River. Discovery and Exploration. Lewis and Clark Expedition. Missouri River. Montana. 1803-05. *317*

Marines *See also* Navies.

—. Great Britain. Mexico. Naval Vessels (capture of). Texas. 1835-46. *503*

Maritime Law *See also* Freight and Freightage.

—. California. Dana, Richard Henry, Jr. (*Two Years before the Mast*). Seamen. 1840. *1924*

Mark I. Jacobs Company. Arizona (Tucson). Banking. Jacobs, Mark Israel. Jews. Retail Trade. 1867-75. *1278*

Marketing. California (Imperial Valley; Coachella Valley). Date industry. Tariff. 1890-1939. *4040*

—. Finance. Oregon (Albany, Salem). Woolen Industry. 1854-1907. *1260*

—. Lamoreaux, Theodore J. Mines. Public Relations. Trans-Mississippi West. 1880's-1920's. *929*

Marketing (bonds). Advertising. Banking. Cooke, Jay. Great Britain (London). Northern Pacific Railroad. Railroads. 1869-73. *1365*

Markey, Joseph J. California. Discovery and Exploration. Historiography. Mexico. Ulloa, Francisco de. Wagner, Henry R. 1540. 1970's. *65*

Marlow, Arthur. Echo Flour Mill. Reminiscences. Utah. Wright, Marguerite J. ca 1900-64. *1290*

Marmaduke, John S. (capture). Civil War (battles). Iowa. Kansas. Missouri (Mine Creek). Price, Sterling. 1864. *650*

Marquez, Reye y. California (Santa Monica Canyon). Celebrations (religious). Fiesta. 19c. *2334*

Marriage *See also* Sex; Women.

—. Attitudes. Harman, Moses. Sects, Religious. Sex. Victorianism, American. 19c. *2295*

—. Caldwell Brotherhood of Bachelors. Idaho (Caldwell). ca 1890. *1698*

—. California. Lesser, Sol. Political Campaigns (gubernatorial). Sinclair, Upton. 1878-1968. *1991*

—. Houston, Sam. Letters. 1845. *2622*

Marriott, Frederick. Aeronautics. *Avitor Hermes, Jr.* (balloon). Porter, Rufus. Travel. 1849-83. *1328*

—. *Aviator* (aircraft). California. Editors and Editing. 1849-83. *1305*

Marsh, Arthur L. Education. Washington Education Association. 1919-51. *2941*

Marsh, George Turner. California (San Francisco). Hagiwara family. Japanese Tea Garden. Sakurai, Nagao. 1897-1969. *4023*

Marsh, John. Bidwell, John. California. DeSmet, Pierre Jean. Oregon Trail. Overland Journeys to the Pacific. 1841. *400*

Marshall Coal Mining Company. Colorado. Denver, Marshall and Boulder Railway Company. Golden, Boulder, and Caribou Railway Company. Kansas Pacific Railroad. Railroads. Union Pacific Railroad. 1878-86. *1362*

Marshall, Verne. *Cedar Rapids Gazette* (newspaper). Editors and Editing. *Emporia Gazette* (newspaper). Intervention. Pacifism. White, William Allen. World War II. 1940. *3694*

Marshes. California (Central Valley). Diseases (theory of). Settlement. 19c. *3091*

Marston, B. W. Civil War. Confederate Army. Cooper, Douglas H. Indian Division. 1864. *583*

Marston, Sylvester Witt. Indian Territory (Muscogee; Union Mission). 1852-78. *2586*

Marta, Bernardo de. Galisteo Pueblo. New Mexico. Santo Domingo Reservation. Zia Pueblo. 1597-17c. *95*

Marti, José. Homesteading and Homesteaders. Land rush. Oklahoma (Guthrie). 1889. *1145*

—. Apache Indians (Chiricahua). Arizona. Gatewood, Charles B. Geronimo (Chiricahua Apache leader). Indian Wars. Letters. 1886. *701*

—. Apache Indians (Chiricahua). Geronimo (leader). Indian Wars. Wood, Leonard. 1876-97. *833*

—. Big Crow (death). Cheyenne Indians. Crazy Horse (chief). Indian Wars. Sioux Indians. Wolf Mountain (battle). 1877. *805*

—. Bruguier, Johnnie. Indian-White Relations. Scouts and Guides. Sioux Indians. Sitting Bull (Chief). 1876-90. *734*

—. Continental Army. Howard, Oliver Otis. Indian Wars. Joseph (chief). Montana. Nez Percé War. White Bird Canyon (battle). 1877. *700*

—. Crook, George. Custer, George A. Grierson, Benjamin Henry. Howard, Oliver Otis. Indian-White Relations. Military General Staff. Pope, John. 1865-85. *719*

—. Crook, George. Grierson, Benjamin Henry. Howard, Oliver Otis. Indian Wars. Mackenzie, Ranald S. Military Service, Professional. Pope, John. 19c. *718*

Military *See also* headings beginning with the words military and paramilitary; Armaments; Armies; Artillery; Battles; Cavalry; Civil-Military Relations; Defense Policy; Guerrilla Warfare; Infantry; Logistics; Navies; Politics and the Military; Uniforms, Military; Veterans; War.

—. Anderson, Robert. Discovery and Exploration. Florida. Fort Sumter. Frémont, John C. Hardee, William. Mexican War. Oregon. Talbot, Theodore. 1823-62. *498*

—. Battles. Carranza, Venustiano. Foreign Relations. Mexico. New Mexico (Columbus). Pershing, John J. Spilsbury, Lemuel. Villa, Pancho. 1916. *3717*

—. California. City Government. Economic Conditions. Spain. 1776-1821. *191*

—. Daily Life. Diaries. Fort Buford. Sanford, Wilmot P. 1874-75. *493*

—. Discovery and Exploration. Fort Mackinac. Fort Snelling. Long, Stephen H. Red River Expedition (1870). Scott, Martin. Vermont (Bennington). Yellowstone River Expedition. 1814-47. *517*

—. Indians. Mexico. Missions and Missionaries. Royal Regulation of Presidios. Southwest. Spain. 1772-86. *106*

Military Bases *See also* names of military bases, e.g. Travis Air Force Base; Air Bases; Navy-yards and Naval Stations.

—. Alaska. Alcan Highway. Bering, Vitus. Chirikov, Alexei. Coast Survey. Congress. Economic Development. Geological Survey. Gold Mines and Mining. Russia. Territorial Government. World War II. 1741-1967. *3509*

Military Biography *See also* names of wars with the subdivision biography, e.g. World War II (biography).

—. Custer, George A. Indian Wars. Little Big Horn (battle). Psychohistory. 1876. *817*

—. Custer, George A. Indian Wars. Psychohistory. Sioux Indians. 1876. *744*

Military Campaigns. Adobe Walls (battle). Comanche Indians. Indian Wars. Mackenzie, Ranald S. Miles, Nelson A. Texas. 1874-75. *741*

—. Alencaster, Real. Baca, Bartolomé. Melgares, Facundo. Navajo Indians. New Mexico. Treaties. Vizcarra, José Antonio. 1795-1846. *207*

—. Anza, Juan Bautista de. Apache Indians. Arizona (Gila River region). Indian Wars. Spain. 1766. *70*

—. Apache Indians. Arizona. Baylor, John R. Civil War. Confederate Army. Fort Fillmore. Fort Union. Glorieta Pass (battle). Hunter, Sherod. New Mexico Territory. Pichacho Peak (battle). Sibley, Henry Hopkins. 1861-65. *616*

—. Apache Indians. Arizona (Chiricahua Pass). Camp Bowie. Camp Crittenden. Dorr, Levi L. Indian Wars. Letters. 1869. *834*

—. Apache Indians (Gila). Bustamante y Tagle, Bernardo Antonio de. New Mexico (Cliff). Sáenz, Bartolomé. Spaniards. Vildósola, Gabriel Antonio de. 1756. *31*

—. Apache Indians (Mescalero). Crime and Criminals. Indians. New Mexico. Price, William Redwood. Texas. 1873. *777*

—. Arizona (Yuma). Diaries. Fages, Pedro. Indian-White Relations. Mexico (Sonora). Yuma Indians. 1781. *69*

—. Arkansas. Blunt, James G. Civil War (battles). Cooper, Douglas H. Elk Creek (battle). Fort Gibson. Fort Smith. Honey Springs (battle). Indian Territory. Old Fort Wayne (battle). Steele, William. 1862-63. *675*

—. Arkansas. Civil War. Fort Smith. Van Buren (battle). 1862. *591*

—. Arkansas (Little Rock). Civil War. Price, Sterling. Steele, Frederick. 1863. *627*

—. Arkansas River. Civil War. Fort Smith. Indian Territory. 1863. *590*

—. Armies. California. Frémont, John C. Kearny, Stephen Watts. Mexican War. Navies. Sloat, John D. Stockton, Robert Field. 1846-47. *555*

—. Austin, Stephen F. Austin, William T. Burleson, Edward. Gonzales (battle). Houston, Sam. Mexico. San Antonio (battle). Texas Revolution. Wharton, William H. 1835. *463*

—. Bannock War. Diaries. Indians. Nevada. Oregon. 1878. *694*

—. Black Kettle (chief). Cheyenne Indians. Crawford, Samuel. Custer, George A. Kansas Volunteer Cavalry, 19th. Sheridan, Philip. 1868-69. *848*

—. Camas Prairie (battle). Fred, Munn. Howard, Oliver Otis. Idaho. Nez Percé Indians. Reminiscences. Sioux Indians. 1876-77. *781*

—. Camp Henderson. Indian Wars. Oregon Volunteer Cavalry. Paiute Indians, Northern. 1864. *794*

—. Canada. North West Rebellion. Reminiscences. Williams, Milton. 1885. *3422*

—. Cavalry. Comanche Indians. Indian Wars. Negroes. New Mexico. Nolan, Nicholas. Texas. 1877. *727*

—. Cheyenne Indians. Custer, George A. Hancock, Winfield S. Kiowa Indians. Sioux Indians. 7th Cavalry, US. 1867. *845*

—. Cheyenne Indians. Duncan, Thomas. Fort McPherson. Indian Wars. Nebraska (Republican River Valley). Royall, William Bedford. Sioux Indians. Summit Springs (battle). 5th Cavalry, US. 1869. *726*

—. Cheyenne Indians. Indian Wars. Sioux Indians. Soldiers (volunteer). 1865. *721*

—. Civil War. 1861-65. *657*

—. Civil War. Confederate Army. Glorieta Pass (battle). Johnson's Ranch (battle). New Mexico. Valverde (battle). 1862. *674*

—. Dakota Territory. Indian Wars. North Dakota (Ellendale). Northwest Indian Expedition. Pope, John. Sibley, Henry H. Sioux Indians. Sully, Alfred. White Stone Hill (battle). 1863. *690*

—. Dakota Territory. Indians. Montana. Sioux Indians. Sully, Alfred. 1864. *688*

—. Diaries. Mexico. Navajo Indians. New Mexico. Vizcarra, José Antonio. 1823. *93*

—. Edmonds, James E. Fort Brown. Mexican War. Pruyn, Robert N. Reminiscences. Taylor, Zachary. Texas. 1846-48. *568*

—. Fauntleroy, Thomas T. Indian Wars. Jicarilla Apache Indians. New Mexican Volunteers. St. Vrain, Ceran. Southwest. Ute Indians (Moache). 1855. *822*

—. Fort Garry. Manitoba (Red River Valley). North West Rebellion. Riel, Louis. Wolseley, Garnet Joseph. 1870. *3259*

—. Indian-White Relations. Kansas. Missions and Missionaries. Surveying. Vital Statistics. 1836-41. *2526*

—. Lamar, Mirabeau Buonaparte. New Mexico (Santa Fe). Texas. 1839-41. *2683*

—. Manitoba (Red River). North West Rebellion. Riel, Louis. Wolseley, Garnet Joseph. 1870. *3263*

Military Campaigns (proposed). Foreign Relations. France. Great Britain. Louisiana. Napoleon. Spain. 1801-03. *2477*

Military Campaigns (raids). Foreign Relations. Germany. Mexico (Santa Isabel). New Mexico (Columbus). Rauschbaum, Lyman B. Sommerfeld, Felix A. Villa, Pancho. 1915-16. *3668*

Military Camps and Forts *See also* names of military camps and forts, e.g. Fort Apache.

—. Apache Indians. Arizona. Armies. Daily Life. Reminiscences. Soldiers. 1860's-80's. *529*

—. Apache Indians. Arizona. Fort Buchanan. Gadsden Purchase. Mexico. USA. 1853-61. *518*

—. Apache Indians. Carleton, James H. Fort Sumner. Indians (reservations). Munroe, John. Navajo Indians. New Mexico (Bosque Redondo). Surveying. 1850-64. *501*

—. Archaeology. Colorado State Historical Society. Fort Vasquez. Fur Trade. Platte River (South). 1835-1970. *898*

—. Arizona. Fort Yuma. McCall, George A. 1851-83. *482*

—. Arizona. Mormons. Pipe Spring National Monument. 1873-1923. *2898*

—. Arizona (Tucson). Ewell, Richard S. Letters. Mission of San Xavier del Bac. 1856. *489*

—. Artillery. Oregon (Columbia River). Washington. 1863-65. *490*

—. Bibliographies. Buildings. Nevada. 1860-89. *515*

—. Bierce, Ambrose G. Bozeman Trail. Colorado. Fort Benton. Hazen, William B. Indians. Montana. Wyoming. 1866. *505*

—. Bucareli y Ursúa, Antonio María. California (Monterey). Fages, Pedro. Letters. 1773. *112*

—. Canadian West. Fort Edmonton. Fort Ellice. Fort Garry. Fur Trade. Red River carts. Touchwood Hills (post). 19c. *3151*

—. Carter, William A., Jr. Fort Bridger. Fort Thornburgh. Railroads. Reminiscences. Roads. Union Pacific Railroad. Utah (Vernal). Ute Indians. Wyoming. 1879-1966. *1325*

—. Comanche Indians. Mission San Saba. Spain. Texas. 1757-70. *167*

—. Diaries. Fort Hays. Fort Leavenworth. Goodale, Ephriam. Kansas. 1878-79. *485*

—. Economic Conditions. Fort Cameron. Fort Duchesne. Fort Thornburgh. Indian-White Relations. Settlement. Utah. War Department. 1872-1912. *683*

—. Families. Frontier and Pioneer Life. 1860's. *470*

—. Fort Logan. Montana (Smith River area). 1869-80. *1706*

—. Fort Pembina. North Dakota. Settlement. 1870-95. *1705*

—. Fort Totten. Historical Sites and Parks. Indians (reservations). North Dakota Historical Society. Sioux Indians. 1867-1967. *841*

—. New Mexico (southwestern). 1851-66. *508*

—. Women. 1860-1900. *519*

Military commanders. Fort Laramie. US Military Academy. Wyoming. 1849-90. *500*

Military conditions. Civil War. Indian Territory. 1865. *582*

Military conquest. California. Croix, Teodoro de. Gálvez, José. Letters. Portolá, Gaspar de. 1769-70. *22*

Military discipline. Armies. Crime and Criminals. Fort Laramie. 19c. *499*

Military expeditions. California. Diaries. Indian-White Relations. Oregon. Piper, Alexander. 1860. *488*

—. California. Diaries. Fages, Pedro. Mexico (Sonora). Mission San Gabriel Arcangel. Serra, Junípero. Settlement. 1782. *194*

—. Expansionism. Kansas (Leavenworth). Martin Cantonment (supply depot). Missouri River. 1818. *510*

Military Finance. California. Civil War claims. Federal Government. State Government. 1861-1967. *612*

Military General Staff. Attitudes. Custer, George A. (image of). Indian Wars. 1867-76. *831*

—. Crook, George. Custer, George A. Grierson, Benjamin Henry. Howard, Oliver Otis. Indian-White Relations. Miles, Nelson A. Pope, John. 1865-85. *719*

Military Government *See also* Military Occupation.

—. Apache Indians. Arizona. Carleton, James H. Civil War. Civil-Military Relations. Gadsden Purchase. 1854-65. *579*

—. California. Frémont, John C. Kearney, Stephen Watts. Kentucky (Owensboro). Mason, Richard Barnes. 1817-47. *3073*

Military Intelligence. Andrus, James. Utah (southern). Woolley, Franklin B. (report). 1866. *2813*

—. Austria. Germany. Mexico. Texas (San Antonio). Visser, Olga. World War I. Zimmermann Note. 1917. *3569*

—. California. Civil War. Confederate States of America. Kennedy, H. Nevada (Virginia City). 1864. *604*

Military Occupation *See also* Military Government; Resistance.

—. Alaska (Sitka). Economic Conditions. Russian-American Company. Social Conditions. 1804-84. *3554*

—. Arizona. Baylor, John R. Confederate Army. Mexican Americans. Sibley, Henry Hopkins. Texas. 1861-62. *622*

National Wilderness Preservation System. Dinosaur National Monument. Lobbying. Nature Conservation. Public Opinion. Yellowstone National Park. 1908-1970. *4133*

Nationalism *See also* Independence Movements; Minorities; Patriotism; Separatist Movements.
—. Alaska Boundary Award. Boer War. Canada. French Canadians. Great Britain. USA. 1900-03. *3148*
—. Expansionism. Frontier thesis. Philosophy. Turner, Frederick Jackson. Westward Movement. 1830's. *252*
—. Fiction. Germany. May, Karl. Old Shatterhand (fictional character). Romanticism. Winnetou (Apache Chief, fictional). 19c. *1885*

Nativism. Assimilation. Bureau of Indian Affairs. Burke, Charles. Collier, John. Indians. Reform. 1921-45. *1544*
—. Assimilation. Cherokee Indians. Indian-White Relations. Oklahoma. Racism. 19c-20c. *2613*
—. Catholic Church. Freemasonry. Ideology. Mormons. Prejudice. ca 1800-60. *2253*
—. Chinese Americans. Gold Mines and Mining. Immigration. Montana. 1860's-70's. *1522*
—. Far Western States. Literary Criticism. Myths and Symbols. 1967. *1985*
—. Ku Klux Klan. Oregon. *Pierce* v. *Society of Sisters* (US, 1925). Public Schools. Scottish Rite Masons. 1922-25. *3610*
—. Lutheran Church (Missouri Synod). Nebraska State Council of Defense. World War I. 1917-18. *3638*

Nativity Plays. *Los Pastores* (play). Music. New Mexico. 19c. *213*

Natural History *See also* Botany; Geology; Museums.
—. Burroughs, Raymond Darwin, ed. (review article). Lewis and Clark Expedition. 1804-06. 1961. *440*
—. California. Santa Barbara Natural History Society. Scientific Expeditions. Yates, Lorenzo Gordin. 1864-1900. *2181*
—. Coues, Elliott. Geological Survey. Hayden Survey. Ornithology. Travel accounts (editing of). 1842-99. *2180*
—. Lewis and Clark expedition. Lewis, Meriwether. 1804-06. *354*

Natural Resources *See also* Conservation of Natural Resources; Fishing; Forests and Forestry; Mineral Resources; Reclamation of Land; Soil Conservation; Wilderness.
—. Alaska. Economic Development. 1867-1967. *3498*
—. Development. National Characteristics. Westward Movement. 19c-20c. *249*
—. Economic Development. Environment. Great Plains. 19c-20c. *2464*
—. Montana. 1965. *2727*

Natural Resources (exploitation of). Economic Conditions. Federal Programs (public acceptance of). Mines. New Deal. Oil Industry and Trade. Wyoming. 1930's. *3774*

Nature *See also* Ecology; Wilderness.
—. Animals (domestic, wild). Attitudes. Farmers. Great Plains. Ranchers. 1963. *1044*
—. Cather, Willa. Myths and Symbols. Novels. 1900-47. *1913*

Nature Conservation *See also* Wildlife Conservation.
—. Alberta (Bow River Valley). Canadian Pacific Railway. Fire. Floods. Railroads. 1881-1964. *3404*
—. Bailey, Joseph W. Borah, William E. Fall, Albert Bacon. Forest Service. Graves, Henry. Heyburn, Weldon B. Mines. National Park Service Act (1916). Pinchot, Gifford. 1910-20. *4102*
—. California. Eminent Domain. Redwood National Park (founding of). Save-the-Redwoods League. 1918-68. *4128*
—. California (Hetch Hetchy Valley). Camping. Dams. Duryea, Robert. Stillman, Dorothy. Yosemite National Park. 1910-14. *4112*
—. Canada. Explorers. Great Lakes. Olson, Sigurd. Reminiscences. Travel account. 19c. *3158*
—. Carhart, Arthur H. Forest Service. Johnson, Lyndon B. (administration). Leopold, Aldo. Recreation. Wilderness Bill (1964). 1919-64. *4097*
—. Colorado-Big Thompson Water Project. Mills, Enos. Mission 66. Rocky Mountain National Park. 1891-1965. *1196*
—. Dinosaur National Monument. Lobbying. National Wilderness Preservation System. Public Opinion. Yellowstone National Park. 1908-1970. *4133*

—. DuBois, Coert. Far Western States. Forest Service. Land Office. National Parks and Reserves. Pinchot, Gifford. Roosevelt, Theodore. 1899-1917. *4108*
—. Forest Service. National Park Service. Sequoia National Park. 1876-1926. *1203*
—. Grand Teton National Park. *Grand Teton* (newspaper). *Jackson's Hole Courier* (newspaper). Rockefeller, John D., Jr. Snake River Land Company. Wyoming (Jackson Hole). 1931-34. *4155*
—. Historic Sites Act. National Park Service. Preservation. Yellowstone National Park. 1872-1966. *1212*
—. Lobbying. National Park Service Act (1916). 1916. *4151*
—. National Park Service. Utah (Glen Canyon). 1957-65. *2822*

Nature Photography. Adams, Ansel. National Parks and Reserves. Wilderness. 20c. *2084*
—. Arizona. Colorado River. Grand Canyon. 1871-1966. *2080*

Nauvoo Legion. Arizona. Lincoln, Abraham. Mormons. Navajo Indians. Smith, Lot. Utah War (1857). 1830-92. *2294*
—. Cummings, Benjamin Franklin. Fort Limhi. Indian Wars. Mormons. Oregon Territory. Utah. 1858. *693*

Nava, Pedro de. Azanza, Miguel Joseph de. Comanche Indians. Indian-White Relations. Lipan Apache Indians. Treaty of 1785. 1785. *107*

Navajo Indian Police. Arizona. Indians (reservations). Manuelito (chief). New Mexico. 1868-73. *750*

Navajo Indians. Alencaster, Real. Baca, Bartolomé. Melgares, Facundo. Military Campaigns. New Mexico. Treaties. Vizcarra, José Antonio. 1795-1846. *207*
—. Apache Indians. Carleton, James H. Fort Sumner. Indians (reservations). Military Camps and Forts. Munroe, John. New Mexico (Bosque Redondo). Surveying. 1850-64. *501*
—. Apache Indians. Civil War. Fort Fillmore. Indian Wars. Mesilla (battle). New Mexico. 1851-62. *504*
—. Apache Indians. Comanche Indians. Indian raids. Kiowa Indians. Mexico (northern). Southwest. Ute Indians. 1830's-40's. *51*
—. Apache Indians (Mescalero). Fort Sumner. Indian-White Relations. New Mexico. Wallen, Henry Davies (report). 1863. *849*
—. Arizona. Federal Government. Sheep Raising (reduction program). Soil Conservation. Values. 1930's-60. *4045*
—. Arizona. Indian-White Relations. New Mexico. Population growth (consequences). States (51st, creation of). Utah. 1930's-71. *4026*
—. Arizona. Lincoln, Abraham. Mormons. Nauvoo Legion. Smith, Lot. Utah War (1857). 1830-92. *2294*
—. Arizona (Canyon de Chelly region). Carson, Christopher (Kit). Indian Wars. Pfeiffer, Albert H. 1864. *745*
—. Arizona (Saint Michaels). Bibliographies. Indian languages. Missions and Missionaries. Printing. Translating and Interpreting. Wycliffe Bible Translators, Inc. 18c-20c. *2020*
—. Arizona (St. Michaels). Franciscans. Language. Missions and Missionaries. Printing. 1898-1910. *2911*
—. Colorado (Pueblo). Fort Canby. Fort Defiance. New Mexico. 1863-64. *754*
—. Diaries. Mexico. Military Campaigns. New Mexico. Vizcarra, José Antonio. 1823. *93*
—. Grant, Ulysses S. Missions and Missionaries. New Mexico. Presbyterian Church. Quaker Peace Policy. 1890-1912. *2864*
—. Hubbell, John Lorenzo. New Mexico (Ganado). Trading posts. 19c. *872*
—. Indians (reservations). Land Tenure. Oil and Petroleum Products. 1868-1934. *954*
—. Indian-White Relations. New Mexico. Newby, Edward W. B. Walker, Robert. 1847-48. *776*

Naval Battles *See also* names of battles, e.g. Lake Erie (battle); etc.; Battles.
—. Banks, Nathaniel Prentiss. Blair's Landing (battle). Civil War. Louisiana (Mansfield; Shreveport, Loggy Bayou). Red River. 1864. *586*

Naval Recruiting and Enlistment. *See* Conscription, Military; Military Recruiting.

Naval Strategy. *America* (warship). Gordon, John. Great Britain. Oregon territory. 1844-48. *2926*

—. Gulf of Mexico. Jackson, Andrew (administration). Texas Revolution. 1835-38. *2621*

Naval Vessels. California (San Francisco). *Camanche* (vessel). Civil War. New Jersey. Ryan, James T. 1862-1920's. *644*

Naval Vessels (capture of). Great Britain. Marines. Mexico. Texas. 1835-46. *503*

Navies *See also* headings beginning with the word naval; Military; Navigation.
—. Armies. California. Frémont, John C. Kearny, Stephen Watts. Mexican War. Military Campaigns. Sloat, John D. Stockton, Robert Field. 1846-47. *555*
—. British Columbia. Discovery and Exploration. Great Britain. Nootka Island. Painting. 18c. *3442*
—. California. Kendrick, John, Jr. O'Cain, Joseph Burling. Smuggling. Spain. 1790's. *13*
—. California (Monterey). Foreign Relations. France. Great Britain. Jones, Thomas ap Catesby. Mexico. 1842. *552*
—. California (Monterey). Foreign Relations. Great Britain. Jones, Thomas ap Catesby. Mexico. Upshur, Abel P. 1842. *553*
—. California (Monterey). Jones, Thomas ap Catesby. Lake Borgne (battle). Mexico. Plantations. Virginia (Fairfax County). War of 1812. 1790-1858. *554*
—. California (Monterey, San Diego, San Francisco). Colonization. *San Antonio* (vessel). *San Carlos* (vessel). Spain. Surveying. 1769-75. *222*
—. Independence Movements. Texas. 1836-45. *494*
—. Metcalfe, Theodore W. Nebraska. 1930-66. *3578*

Navigation *See also* Lighthouses; Navies.
—. Commerce. Lamme, Archilles. Missouri River. Montana (Miles City; Yellowstone River). Steamboats. *Yellowstone* (steamboat). 1876-79. *1407*

Navigation, Inland. Armies. Atkinson, Henry. Missouri River. Steamboats. Technology. *Western Engineer* (vessel). 1818-25. *1414*
—. Diaries. Discovery and Exploration. Howell, Charles W. Missouri River. 1867. *395*
—. Fur Trade. Missouri River. Steamboats. Yellowstone (vessel). 19c. *1412*
—. *Independence* (vessel). Missouri River. *Missouri* (vessel). Steamboats. Trans-Mississippi West. *Western Engineer* (vessel). Yellowstone River. 1819-85. *1411*
—. Texas. Transportation. 19c. *1417*

Navy Chaplain Corps. Bibliographies. Church History. Drury, Clifford Merrill. San Francisco Theological Seminary. Trans-Mississippi West. 1934-69. *2315*

Near East. *See* Middle East.

Nebraska *See also* Western States.
—. Agriculture. Armies. Fort Atkinson. Missouri Valley. 1818-27. *1068*
—. Agriculture. Federal Government. Paddock, Algernon S. Political Attitudes. Populism. 19c. *1064*
—. Agriculture. Land use. Settlement. 1906-66. *4077*
—. Agriculture Department. American Sugar Refining Company. Beet sugar industry. California (Alvarado). Mormons. Oxnard brothers. Spreckels, Claus. Utah Sugar Company. Wisconsin (Fond du Lac). 1888-1913. *1216*
—. Alexis, Grand Duke. Buffalo. Cody, William F. (Buffalo Bill). Custer, George A. Hunting. Sheridan, Philip. Spotted Tail (Sioux Chief). 1872. *1741*
—. Anderson, John Alvin. Photography. 1870-1900. *2087*
—. Anthropology. Dawes Act (1887). Fletcher, Alice Cunningham. Indians. Land Tenure. Omaha Allotment Act (1882). Reform. South Dakota. 1881-1923. *1503*
—. Anti-Saloon League. Politics. Propaganda. Temperance Movements. 1898-1910. *3832*
—. Antiwar Sentiment. Norris, George William. Political Campaigns. Republican Party. Senate. World War I. 1917-18. *3777*
—. Arbor Day. Furnas, Robert W. Miller, George L. Morton, Julius Sterling. Tree Planting. 1850's-1900. *1195*
—. Assimilation. Catholic Church. German Americans. Lutheran Church. Political Parties (affiliation). Rural-Urban Studies. 1889-1915. *2350*
—. Aughey, Samuel. Climate. Myths and Symbols. Settlement. 1871-80. *1065*

New York Age (newspaper). Black Nationalism. Fortune, Timothy Thomas. Garvey, Marcus. Oklahoma Territory. Republican Party. 1880's. *1464*

New York City. Art Galleries and Museums. Leigh, William Robinson. Oklahoma (Tulsa). Thomas Gilcrease Institute of American History and Art. 1896-1964. *2129*

New York City (Staten Island). Burger, James. California. Frontier and Pioneer Life. Gold Rushes. Letters. Westward Movement. 1850. *1027*

New York (Cooper Union). Kansas (Atchison). Lincoln, Abraham. Political Speeches. 1859. *2550*

New York (Finger Lakes district). California. Rhine wines. Winemaking. 19c-20c. *1066*

New York Foundling Hospital. Arizona (Clifton, Morenci). Children. Supreme Court. Vigilantes. 1904-05. *3644*

New York Herald (newspaper). Custer, George A. Little Big Horn (battle). Montana. Sioux Indians. Sitting Bull (Chief, interview). 1876. *860*

New York Regiment (Patchogue's Kansas Brigade, Company C). Civil War. Gaines' Mill (battle). 1861-65. *662*

New York (Rochester). California. Manifest Destiny. Oregon. Settlement. Speeches, Addresses, etc.. Warner, Jonathan Trumbull (Juan José Warner). 1840. *2936*

New York *Sun* (newspaper). Land disputes. Lawyers. Letters. Maxwell Land Grant. New Mexico. Newman, Simeon Harrison. Political Corruption. Santa Fe Ring. 1875. *1777*

New York Volunteers. California. Mexican War. 1846-48. *3062*

Newberry, John Strong. Geology. Great Plains. Trees (absence of). 1873. *2448*

Newberry Library (Ayer, Graff Collections). Great Plains. Libraries. Minnesota Historical Society Library (Neill, Pond Papers). Southern Methodist University (De Golyer Foundation Library). Yale University Library (Beinecke and Coe Collection). 1969. *2459*

Newbrough, John B. Communes. Faithists. Howland, Andrew M. Minnesota (Dona Ana, Las Cruces). Publicity. *Republican* (newspaper). Shalam. 1884-91. *1539*

Newby, Edward W. B. Indian-White Relations. Navajo Indians. New Mexico. Walker, Robert. 1847-48. *776*

Newcomb, James P. Coke, Richard. Know-Nothing Party. Reconstruction. Republican Party. Texas. 1865-74. *2669*

Newell, Frederick Haynes. Ballinger, Richard A. Bureaucracies. Business. Conservation of Natural Resources. Forest Service. Interior Department. Monopolies. Pinchot, Gifford. Politics. Taft, William H. 1909-26. *4136*

Newell, Robert. Idaho. Mountain Men. Nez Percé Indians. ca 1840's. *892*

Newlands, Francis Griffith. Irrigation. Newlands Reclamation Act (1902). Political Attitudes. 1878-1902. *1189*

—. Nevada (Churchill County). Newlands Reclamation Project. Reclamation of Land (attempted). 1889-1900. *4115*

Newlands Reclamation Act (1902). Byers, William Newton. Carey Act (1894). Federal Government (aid). Irrigation. *Rocky Mountain News* (newspaper). 1859-1902. *1183*

—. Irrigation. Newlands, Francis Griffith. Political Attitudes. 1878-1902. *1189*

—. Roosevelt, Theodore. Settlement. Water Supply. 1902. *4154*

Newlands Reclamation Project. Nevada. Reclamation of Land. 1903-07. *4116*

—. Nevada (Churchill County). Newlands, Francis Griffith. Reclamation of Land (attempted). 1889-1900. *4115*

Newman, Simeon Harrison. Land disputes. Lawyers. Letters. Maxwell Land Grant. New Mexico. New York *Sun* (newspaper). Political Corruption. Santa Fe Ring. 1875. *1777*

—. Las Vegas *Weekly Mail* (newspaper). New Mexico. Publishers and Publishing. Upson, M. A. "Ash". 1872. *2044*

Newmark, Marco Ross. California (Southern). Historians. Jews. 1878-1959. *1548*

Newspaper Collections. Canadian West History. Research (sources). 1968. *3179*

Newspapers *See also* Editors and Editing; Journalism; Periodicals; Press; Reporters and Reporting.

—. Agriculture. California (Los Angeles; Owens Valley). Water Supply. 1924-27. *4140*

—. Arapaho *Arrow* (newspaper). Arapaho *Bee* (newspaper). Boosterism. El Reno *Democrat* (newspaper). Kingfisher *Free Press* (newspaper). Oklahoma Territory. Watonga *Republican* (newspaper). 1890's. *2033*

—. Assassination. California (Los Angeles, San Francisco). Lincoln, Abraham. Martial Law. McDowell, Irvin. 1865. *3092*

—. *Atlanta Constitution* (newspaper). Georgia. Styles, Carey Wentworth. Temperance Movements. Texas. 1840-97. *2038*

—. Attitudes. Canadian West. Regionalism. 1870-96. *3166*

—. Attitudes. Colorado. Hughes, Charles Evans. Political Campaigns. Progressive Party. Roosevelt, Theodore. 1910-16. *3761*

—. Boosterism. Kansas. *Wichita Eagle* (newspaper). 1872-92. *2015*

—. California. Editors and Editing. *Herald-Examiner* (newspaper). Los Angeles *Daily Express* (newspaper). Los Angeles *Star* (newspaper). Lummis, Charles Fletcher. Otis, Harrison Gray. 1851-1900. *2051*

—. Cattle Raising. Sheep Raising. Women. Wyoming Territory (Cheyenne, Douglas, Laramie). 1869-89. *2037*

—. Celebrations. Fourth of July. Gold Mines and Mining. 1880. *968*

—. *Cheyenne Transporter* (newspaper). Frontier and Pioneer Life. Indian Territory (Darlington). 1879-86. *2008*

—. Chinese Americans. Discrimination. Europeans (southern). Immigration. Nevada. 1870-1910. *1535*

—. Colorado. Elections (state). Free Silver. Patterson, Thomas. Populism. *Rocky Mountain News* (newspaper). 1892. *3833*

—. Colorado (Pikes Peak). Gold Rushes. Kansas. 1858-59. *2023*

—. Congregationalism. *Daily Capital* (newspaper). Kansas (Topeka). Sheldon, Charles Monroe (*In His Steps*, 1896). 1896-1900. *3660*

—. Custer, George A. Grant, Frederick Dent. Grant, Ulysses S. Little Big Horn (battle). Public Opinion. South or Southern States. 1876. *709*

—. Discovery and Exploration. Foreign Relations. Louisiana Purchase. Public Opinion. 1802-03. *2452*

—. *Eureka Sentinel* (newspaper). *Nevada State Journal* (newspaper). *Pioche Record* (newspaper). 1860-1969. *2019*

—. Frontier and Pioneer Life. Idaho Territory. Ruby City *Owyhee Avalanche* (newspaper). Social Change. 1863-72. *2040*

—. Germany. Japan. Mexico. Public Opinion. South or Southern States. Southwest. World War I. Zimmermann Note. 1917. *3567*

—. Homesteading and Homesteaders. Nonpartisan League. North Dakota. 1880-1919. *2049*

—. Kansas (Great Bend). Nonpartisan League. Political Attitudes. 1921. *2549*

Newspapers (editorials). California. Elections. 1948-62. *3034*

Newspapers (prospectuses of). Attitudes. Texas. 1830's-40's. *2039*

Newton General Massacre. Atchison and Topeka Railroad. Atchison, Topeka and Santa Fe Railroad. Finance. Government. Indian-White Relations. Kansas. Railroads. 1859-72. *1396*

Newton, Harold D. Diaries. National Guard. Texas. Vermont. 1916. *3649*

Newton, Louisa M. California (Mokelumne Hill). Fox, P. V. Frontier and Pioneer Life. Gold Mines and Mining. Letters. 1852-53. *1010*

Nez Percé Indians. Armies. Congress. Hayes, Rutherford B. Indian Wars. Politics and the Military (pay suspension). 1877. *836*

—. Big Hole (battle). Indian Wars. Tourists. Wyoming. Yellowstone National Park. 1877. *699*

—. Camas Prairie (battle). Fred, Munn. Howard, Oliver Otis. Idaho. Military Campaigns. Reminiscences. Sioux Indians. 1876-77. *781*

—. Cherokee Indians. Choctaw Indians. Missions and Missionaries. Oneida Indians. Protestant Churches. Seneca Indians. Sioux Indians. Social Change. 1760-1860. *2313*

—. Costa Rica. Daily Life. Diaries. Idaho Territory. Indian-White Relations. Moses (chief). Washington Territory. Wilbur, James Harvey. Wood, C. E. S. Yakima Indians. 1878-79. *539*

—. Dawes Act (1887). Fletcher, Alice Cunningham. Gay, Jane. Idaho. McBeth, Kate. 1889-92. *283*

—. Fort Leavenworth. Indians (agencies). Jones, Hiram. Joseph (chief). Kansas. Oklahoma. Sherman, William T. 1877-78. *791*

—. Idaho. Indian Claims Commission Act (1946). Indian-White Relations. Treaties. 1855-1957. *257*

—. Idaho. Mountain Men. Newell, Robert. ca 1840's. *892*

—. Idaho (Lewiston). Indian-White Relations. 1877-85. *710*

—. Indian Wars. Joseph (Chief). Montana. Redwolf, Josiah. 1877. *681*

—. Indian Wars. Steptoe Massacre. Timothy (Chief). Washington (Spokane). 1858. *746*

—. Indian Wars. Tilden, Sam (Suhm-keen, interview). 1877. 1962. *682*

—. Indian-White Relations. Moses (chief). Pacific Northwest. ca 1830-79. *2924*

Nez Percé Trail. Indians. Montana. Parker, Samuel. 1835. *428*

Nez Percé War. Continental Army. Howard, Oliver Otis. Indian Wars. Joseph (chief). Miles, Nelson A. Montana. White Bird Canyon (battle). 1877. *700*

—. Indian Wars. Montana (Cow Island). 1877. *780*

—. Indian-White Relations. 1877. *840*

—. Joseph (chief). Montana. Speeches, Addresses, etc.. 1877. *698*

Nicaragua. Annexation. Education. Houston, Sam. Lamar, Mirabeau Buonaparte. Public Lands (sale of). Taylor, Zachary. Texas. 1830's-59. *2681*

Nicholas, Wilson Cary. Constitutions (interpretation of). Jefferson, Thomas. Louisiana Purchase. Taylor, John. Tracy, Uriah. 1803. *2435*

Nickel industry. Economic Development. Forests and Forestry. Manitoba (northern). Mines. Roads. Tourism. 1950's-72. *3298*

Niddrie, John G. Alberta (Edmonton). Hudson's Bay Company. Land booms. Real Estate Business. Reminiscences. 1911-12. *3405*

Nieto, Manuel Perez. Boascana, Geronimo. California (Long Beach, Los Alamitos). Cattle Raising. Fages, Pedro. Indians. 1784-1952. *209*

Nims, Frederick A. Colorado River. Denver, Colorado Cañon and Pacific Railroad. *Denver Republican* (newspaper). *Denver Times* (newspaper). Press coverage. Railroads. *Rocky Mountain News* (newspaper). Stanton, Robert Brewster. Surveying. 1889-90. *2050*

Niobrara Reservation. Lenger, John F. Music (bands). Nebraska. Sioux Indians (Santee). 1884. *2171*

No. 119 (locomotive). *Jupiter* (locomotive). Railroads (transcontinental). Utah (Promontory). 1869. *1342*

Noble, Kate Y. Jones, John E. Letters. Pioneers. Utah (Great Salt Lake; Frémont Island). Wenner, Uriah J. (family). 1886-1942. *2826*

Noble Savage (theme). Civilization (concepts of). Fur Trade. Indian-White Relations. 18c-19c. *917*

Nock, George W. Arizona (Yuma). Colorado River Indian Reservation. Indians (agencies). Mohave Indians. Teaching. 1887-90. *2913*

Nogales Water Company. Arizona (Nogales). Business. Ephraim, Leopold. Mexico. Mines. 1880-1923. *1272*

Nolan, Nicholas. Cavalry. Comanche Indians. Indian Wars. Military Campaigns. Negroes. New Mexico. Texas. 1877. *727*

Nonpartisan League. Agriculture. Economic Policy. Federal Government. Isolationism. North Dakota. Political Attitudes. War. 1916-60. *3712*

—. Dubois, Fred T. Elections. Idaho. Pressure Groups. 1918. *3831*

—. Farmers. Political Parties. Saskatchewan. 1885-1914. *3351*

—. Homesteading and Homesteaders. Newspapers. North Dakota. 1880-1919. *2049*

—. Kansas (Great Bend). Newspapers. Political Attitudes. 1921. *2549*

Nootka Convention (1795). British Columbia (Vancouver Island, Nootka Sound). Cook, James. Fur Trade. Great Britain. Spain. Spanish Armament Crisis (1790). Vancouver, George. 1774-1965. *3484*

Nootka Island. British Columbia. Discovery and Exploration. Great Britain. Navies. Painting. 18c. *3442*

Nootka Sound Controversy (1790). British Columbia. Fur Trade. Great Britain (London; Beaver Hall). Pacific Northwest. Spain. USSR. 1790-1963. *3462*

P

Pachucos. Assimilation. California. Immigration. Mexican Americans. Texas. 1840's-1942. *4024*

Pacific Alaska Airways. Airplanes, Military. Alaska. DeHavillard Liberty (airplane). Eielson, Ben. 1920. *3547*

Pacific Coast. Cabrillo, Juan Rodríguez. California. Discovery and Exploration. 1542-43. *72*

—. Civilians (evacuation of). Japanese Americans. World War II. 1942. *2923*

—. Disasters. Shipwrecks. 1849-1918. *3930*

Pacific Coast Stock Exchange. Business Cycles. California (San Francisco). Jews. Stock Exchange. 1849-1917. *1255*

Pacific Fur Company. Fur Trade. Hudson's Bay Company. Idaho (Snake County). Northwest Company. Pacific Northwest. Payette, François. 1812-44. *893*

Pacific Historical Review (periodical). California, University of (Los Angeles). Editors and Editing. Iowa. Parish, John Carl. 1881-1939. *2929*

Pacific Junction Railway (proposed). Edgar, James D. Ontario (Toronto). Railroads. 19c. *3175*

Pacific Northwest. 1783-1889. *2930*

—. Abbey, Edward. California. Pennsylvania. Reminiscences. Southwest. Travel account. 1944. *3559*

—. Advertising. Dakota Territory. Donan, Pat. Journalism. 1865-1902. *2418*

—. Agriculture. Fur Trade. Hudson's Bay Company. Russia (Siberia). Russian American Company. 1805-46. *3139*

—. Alaska. Bibliographies. Dissertations. Social Sciences. 1964-70. *2920*

—. Alaska. Bibliographies. Dissertations. Theses. 1958-63. *2919*

—. Alaska. British Columbia (Vancouver Island). Fuller, Frank. Jesuits. Missions and Missionaries. Murder. Protestant Churches. Seghers, Charles John. 1880's. *2933*

—. Archives. Federal Records Centers. Historiography. New Deal. 1930's. *3748*

—. Arizona. California. DH-4 (aircraft). Macready, John A. Map Drawing. Mather, Stephen. Photography. Stevens, A. W. 1924. *3628*

—. Artists (Spanish). Cardero, José. Echeverría, Atanasio. Surfa, Tomás de. 1783-1802. *63*

—. Balfour, Guthrie and Company. Economic Development. Great Britain. 1869-1914. *1273*

—. Bibliographies. 1971. *2410*

—. British Columbia. Fur Trade. Great Britain (London; Beaver Hall). Nootka Sound Controversy (1790). Spain. USSR. 1790-1963. *3462*

—. British Columbia (Nootka Island). Colonization. Discovery and Exploration. Foreign Relations. Great Britain. Spain. Treaties. 16c-17c. *59*

—. British Columbia (Tofino). Columbia River. Discovery and Exploration. Fort Defiance. Gray, Robert. 1791-92. *3433*

—. Brooks, William. Chinook Indians. 1835-39. *2932*

—. Business. Diaries. Frontier and Pioneer Life. McConnell, Robert. 1881. *1223*

—. California (Sacramento, San Francisco). Diaries. Friends, Society of. Gold Mines and Mining. Hawaii. Lindsey, Sarah. 1859-60. *391*

—. California (San Francisco). Fort Vancouver. Fur Trade. Great Britain. Hawaii (Honolulu). Hudson's Bay Company. Russia. 1841-60. *916*

—. Cascade Mountains (Stevens Pass). Civil Engineering. Discovery and Exploration. Great Northern Railway. Hill, James Jerome. Montana (Marias Pass). Oregon Trunk Line. Railroads. Stevens, John Frank. 1889-1911. *1367*

—. Cattle Raising. Economic Conditions. Manufactures. Northern Pacific Railroad. Oregon Pacific Railroad. Railroads. Union Pacific Railroad. Wheat. 19c. *1348*

—. Cattle Raising. Prairie Provinces. 1969. *3225*

—. Coronado, Francisco. DeSoto, Hernando. Great Plains. Horses (use of). New Mexico. New Spain. Plains Indians. 1650-19c. *25*

—. Courts (territorial). McFadden, Obadiah B. Politics. 1853-75. *2935*

—. Daily Life. Humor. Pioneers. 19c. *1418*

—. Davis, Harold Lenoir. Fiction. Folklore. Frontier and Pioneer Life. Humor. 1935-60. *1879*

—. Davis, Harold Lenoir. Literature. Mencken, H. L. Sandburg, Carl. Stevens, James. 1926-27. *1884*

—. Discovery and Exploration. Goethals, George W. Map Drawing. Washington (Colville Valley). 1882-84. *373*

—. Downing, Alfred. Land surveys. Sketches. 1873-83. *2130*

—. Economic status. Oregon (Roseburg). Population turnover. Settlement. 1880-1900. *1574*

—. Episcopal Church, Protestant. 19c-1967. *2342*

—. Exports. Lumber and Lumbering. Photography. Ships. William Hester Collection. 1893-1915. *2082*

—. Folk Songs. "I'll Take You Home Again, Kathleen" (song). 1969. *2161*

—. Free African Society. Medicare (history of). Pennsylvania (Philadelphia). Voluntary Associations. Workmen's Compensation. 1787-1929. *3674*

—. Freight and Freightage. Lumber and Lumbering. Panama Canal. Railroads. Shipping. 1921-40. *3937*

—. Frontier and Pioneer Life. Humor. 1870-95. *1916*

—. Fur seal (description). Sealing. Terajima, Ryoan. 1715. *889*

—. Fur Trade. Hudson's Bay Company. Idaho (Snake County). Northwest Company. Pacific Fur Company. Payette, François. 1812-44. *893*

—. Fur Trade. Humor. *Joe Miller's Joke Book.* 1839. *1967*

—. Geography. Meinig, D. W. (review article). Missions and Missionaries. Pioneers. 1805-1910. 1969. *2922*

—. Gingerbread (shipment of). 1796-1830's. *865*

—. Immigration. Japanese Americans. Labor. 1900-24. *4018*

—. Indians. Shakers. Slocum, John. 1882-1966. *2368*

—. Indian-White Relations. Moses (chief). Nez Percé Indians. ca 1830-79. *2924*

—. Lorain, Lorenzo. Photography. 1856-61. *2066*

—. McElroy, Thornton Fleming. Printing. 1852-85. *2007*

—. Mercer, Asa Shinn. Women. 1864-66. *2921*

Pacific Northwest Quarterly (periodical). Gates, Charles M. Historians. Minnesota Historical Society. National Development. National Park Service. Old Northwest. Washington, University of. 1904-63. *2928*

Pacific Ocean. Caribbean. Imperialism. Manifest destiny. 1800-1914. *285*

Pacific Squadron. Apache Canyon (battle). Army of the Pacific. Civil War. Glorieta Pass (battle). 1862-65. *628*

Pacifism. Addams, Jane. Europe. Ford, Henry. Hanna, L. B. Jordan, David Starr. North Dakota. Schwimmer, Rosika. World War I. 1915-16. *3713*

—. Attitudes. Bryan, William Jennings. Kansas. Mennonites. Spanish-American War. 1898-1900. *4010*

—. Canada. Church and State. Hutterites. Persecution. USA. 1553-1969. *3177*

—. Canada. Discrimination. Hutterites. 1870-1967. *3169*

—. *Cedar Rapids Gazette* (newspaper). Editors and Editing. *Emporia Gazette* (newspaper). Intervention. Marshall, Verne. White, William Allen. World War II. 1940. *3694*

—. Eggleston, C. V. Harriman, Job. Nevada (Nevada City). Reclamation of Land. Settlement. Socialism. 1916-18. *3676*

—. Elections. Foreign Policy. Isolationism. North Dakota. Political Attitudes. Wilson, Woodrow. 1914. *3834*

—. Espionage Act. Kansas (Burton). Lynching (attempted). Mennonites. Schrag, John. Trials. World War I. 1918. *3621*

—. Fort Leavenworth (prison). Hutterites. Montana. Persecution. South Dakota. World War I. 1917-18. *4028*

Packsaddles *(aparejo)*. Burros. Frontier and Pioneer Life. 19c. *1306*

Paddock, Algernon S. Agriculture. Federal Government. Nebraska. Political Attitudes. Populism. 19c. *1064*

Paddock, John Adams. Episcopal Church, Protestant. Northern Pacific Railroad. Railroads. Washington (Tacoma). 1870-1900. *2343*

Painting *See also* Landscape Painting.

—. Adams, Cassily. Arizona Pioneers' Historical Society. Custer, George A. Little Big Horn (battle). 1885-1967. *2138*

—. American Fur Company. Bridger, Jim. Miller, Alfred Jacob. Mountain Men. Rocky Mountains. Stewart, William Drummond. 1837. *2116*

—. Animals. Indians. Lindneux, Robert Ottokar. Rocky Mountains. 1902-66. *2112*

—. Arizona. Dixon, Maynard. Indians. Mexican Americans. Pioneers. Utah. 1920-46. *2088*

—. Arizona. Explorers. Grand Canyon. Moran, Thomas. Photography. Powell, John Wesley. 1870's. *2149*

—. Armies. California. Great Plains. Mexican War. Sully, Alfred. 19c. *2144*

—. Art Galleries and Museums. Benton, Thomas Hart. Great Plains. Joslyn Art Museum. Koerner, W. H. D. Nebraska (Omaha). 1833-1900. *2126*

—. Artists. Dallas, Jacob A. Frémont, John C. Kyle, Joseph. Panoramas, Moving. Skirving, John. 1849-51. *321*

—. Audubon, John James *(Birds of America)*. California. Grayson, Andrew Jackson. Mexico. Ornithology. 1846-69. *2143*

—. Beecher's Island (battle). Cheyenne Indians. Colorado (Yuma County). Forsyth, George A. Indian Wars. Lindneux, Robert Ottokar. Sioux Indians. 1868. *2151*

—. Blackfoot Indians. Point, Nicolas. Religion. 1846-47. *2110*

—. Bodmer, Karl. 1830's. *357*

—. British Columbia. Discovery and Exploration. Great Britain. Navies. Nootka Island. 18c. *3442*

—. California. Grayson, Andrew Jackson. Mexico. Ornithology. 1846-60's. *3088*

—. Catlin, George. Great Lakes. Kane, Paul. Rocky Mountains. 1845-48. *3123*

—. Collectors and Collecting. Michener, James A. Texas, University of (Austin). 1969. *2114*

—. Gollings, Elling William (Bill). Wyoming (Sheridan). 1912-32. *2139*

—. Great Plains. Horses. Remington, Frederick ("Horses of the Plains"). Sketches. 1889. *2155*

—. Holzhuber, Franz (sketchbooks). Mississippi River. 1850's. *2123*

—. Horses. Idaho. Mines. Ostner, Charles Leopold. 1828-1913. *2132*

—. Letters. Leutze, Emanuel (sketch books). Meigs, Montgomery C. *Westward the Course of Empire Takes Its Way* (mural). 1841-63. *2141*

—. Leutze, Emanuel. *Westward the Course of Empire Takes Its Way* (mural). 1862. *2145*

—. Miller, Alfred Jacob. Mountain Men. Scotland. Stewart, William Drummond. 1837. *2133*

—. Montana. Paxson, Edgar S. 1879-1919. *2142*

Paiute Indians. Bannock Indians. Colleges and Universities. Ethnology. Idaho State College. Liljeblad, Sven. Linguistics. Shoshoni Indians. 1940-65. *4002*

—. California. Irrigation. Nevada (Pyramid Lake). Truckee-Carson Irrigation District. 1900-72. *1200*

—. Fort Churchill. Indian Wars. Nevada. Silver Mining. 1860-69. *479*

—. Ghost Dance. Great Plains. Rocky Mountains. Sects, Religious. South Dakota. Ute Indians. Wounded Knee (battle). Wovoka (Jack Wilson). 1870-90. *737*

—. Ghost Dance. Sects, Religious. Sioux Indians. Wilson, Jack (Wovoka). 1888-90. *773*

—. Indian-White Relations. Law Enforcement. Nevada. Washo Indians. Wasson, Warren. 1849-62. *2838*

Paiute Indians, Northern. Camp Henderson. Indian Wars. Military Campaigns. Oregon Volunteer Cavalry. 1864. *794*

Paleontology. Alexander, Annie Montague. Humbolt Mountain Range. Nevada. Saurian Expedition of 1905. 1867-1905. *460*

—. Bacon, Henry Douglas. Buildings. California, University of, Berkeley (Bacon Hall). Teachers. 1868-1961. *3093*

—. California, University of, Berkeley. Crespi, Juan. Excavations. Los Angeles County Museum of Natural History. Rancho La Brea. 1769-1968. *128*

—. Geology. Hayden, Ferdinand Vandeveer. Scientific Expeditions. South Dakota (Black Hills). Trans-Mississippi West. 1853-66. *447*

Palestine (Jaffa). Adams, George Washington Joshua. Church of the Messiah. Evangelism. Mormons. 1811-80. *2225*

Peale, Charles Willson. Barron, Joseph. Chouteau, Paul. Indians. Jefferson, Thomas. Pennsylvania (Philadelphia). Portraits (silhouettes). Sagessaga (Little Osage Chief). 1806. *2108*

—. Bush, Joseph. Catlin, George. Clark, William. Harding, Chester. Jarvis, John W. Lewis, Meriwether. Portraits. Saint-Mémin, Charles Balthazar Julien Fevret de. 1880's. *2096*

—. Jefferson, Thomas. Lewis and Clark Expedition. Wildlife specimens. ca 1805. *2202*

Pease, Elisha Marshall. Foreign Relations. Letters. Texas Revolution. 1836-41. *2628*

Peck, George H. Banning, Phineas. California (Los Angeles, San Pedro Bay). Construction. Ports. White, Stephen M. 1592-1969. *1649*

Pedagogy. *See* Teaching.

Peffer, William Alfred. Democratic Party. Elections. Kansas. People's Party. Republican Party. Senate. 1891. *3719*

Pemberton, J. N. ("Pete"). Arizona (Winslow). Giles, William Joe. Murder. 1905. *2868*

Pembina State Museum (Barry Collection). Fort Daer. Fort Pembina. Museums. North Dakota. 1960. *2483*

Penitentes. Folk Art. Indians. New Mexico. Santos. 17c-20c. *220*

Pennsylvania. Abbey, Edward. California. Pacific Northwest. Reminiscences. Southwest. Travel account. 1944. *3559*

—. California. Local Government. Political Recruitment. State Government. Training-ground thesis. 1900-62. *3728*

Pennsylvania Germans. Kansas. Westward Movement. 19c. *1447*

Pennsylvania (Philadelphia). American Fur Company. Fort Union. Meteorology. North Dakota. Patent Office. Riter, Frederick G. Smithsonian Institution. 1853-88. *920*

—. Arkansas (Little Rock). British Columbia. California. Gibbs, Miflin Wister. Gold Rushes. Judges. Negroes. 1823-80. *993*

—. Barron, Joseph. Chouteau, Paul. Indians. Jefferson, Thomas. Peale, Charles Willson. Portraits (silhouettes). Sagessaga (Little Osage Chief). 1806. *2108*

—. Free African Society. Medicare (history of). Pacific Northwest. Voluntary Associations. Workmen's Compensation. 1787-1969. *3674*

Pennsylvania Railroad. Colorado. Denver and Rio Grande Western Railroad. Kansas Pacific Railroad. Palmer, William Jackson. Railroads. Royal Gorge War. Thompson, J. Edgar. 1871-80. *1399*

People v. *Hall* (Calif., 1854). California Criminal Act. Civil Rights. Racism. Testimony laws. 1854. *3040*

People's Independent Party. Antitrust. California. International Workingmen's Association. Political Factions. Populist Party. Railroads. San Francisco Nationalist Club. Southern Pacific Railroad. 1873-98. *3035*

People's Party. Agricultural Organizations. Farmers' Alliance. Macune, Charles W. Politics. 1890-1920. *3789*

—. Democratic Party. Elections. Kansas. Peffer, William Alfred. Republican Party. Senate. 1891. *3719*

Peralta Grant. Arizona. Land Grants (Spanish). Real Estate Business. Reavis, James Addison. 1890-96. *1174*

Perez, Ignacio. Arizona. Church and State. Estelric, Juan Bautista. Liberós, Ramón. Mission San José de Tumacàcori. 1821-23. *136*

Perez, Juan. California (Los Angeles). Crespi, Juan. Diaries. Discovery and Exploration. Fages, Pedro. Portolá, Gaspar de. 1769-74. *3099*

Periodicals *See also* Editors and Editing; Newspapers; Press.

—. Boundaries. Great Britain. Oregon Territory. Political Attitudes. 1820-46. *2942*

—. Great American Desert. Myths and Symbols. 1864-1964. *2466*

—. Kansas. 1854-1904. *2567*

Periodicals (religious). Editors and Editing. Oregon. 1846-55. *2359*

Periodization of History. Mexican American history (status of). 1848-1969. *1514*

Perkins, Charles Elliott. Business. Chicago, Burlington and Quincy Railroad. Ethics. Public Opinion. Railroads. 1870-81. *1359*

—. Chicago, Burlington and Quincy Railroad. Colorado (Denver). Gould, Jay. Iowa Pool. Railroads. Union Pacific Railroad. 1870's-80's. *1386*

—. Chicago, Burlington and Quincy Railroad. Gould, Jay. Hannibal and St. Joseph Railroad. Illinois (Chicago). Kansas (Kansas City). Railroads. Santa Fe Railroad. 1869-88. *1395*

—. Colleges and Universities. Harvard University, Mormon Collection. Hooper, Alice Forbes Perkins. Mormons. Turner, Frederick Jackson. Utah. 1910. *2233*

Perkins, Henry Kirk White. Indians. Methodist Church. Missions and Missionaries. Oregon (Dalles). 1841-84. *2331*

Perkins, Jacob R. Dodge, Greenville (memoirs). Historical legends. Railroads. Union Pacific Railroad. 1866-70. *1356*

Perry Ranch. American Cattle Company. Cattle Raising. *Daily Republican* (newspaper). Kansas (Clark County). 1890. *2531*

Perryman, George. Oklahoma (Tulsa). Pony Express. Postal Service. Star route mail. Yeargain, Green. 1878-83. *1329*

Persecution *See also* Anti-Semitism; Civil Rights; Religious Liberty.

—. Canada. Church and State. Hutterites. Pacifism. USA. 1553-1969. *3177*

—. Edmunds, George Franklin. Edmunds-Tucker Act (1887). Mormons. Polygamy. Teller, Henry Moore. Utah Territory. 1887-90. *2272*

—. Fort Leavenworth (prison). Hutterites. Montana. Pacifism. South Dakota. World War I. 1917-18. *4028*

—. Mormons. Nevada (Meadow Valley). Settlement. 1858. *2240*

—. Mormons. Senate. Smoot, Reed. Utah. 1903-07. *3763*

Pershing, John J. Battles. Carranza, Venustiano. Foreign Relations. Mexico. Military. New Mexico (Columbus). Spilsbury, Lemuel. Villa, Pancho. 1916. *3717*

—. Canada. Cree Indians. Fort Assiniboine. Montana. Negroes. 10th Cavalry, US. 1895-96. *523*

—. Cavalry. Frontier and Pioneer Life. 1893-98. *522*

Peters, DeWitt. Chacon, Rafael. Colorado (southern). Fort Massachusetts. Indian Wars. Jicarilla Apache Indians. Ute Indians (Moache). 1855. *820*

Peterson, H. G. Border Aerial Patrol. Cavalry. Davis, P. H. Mexico (Juarez). Texas (El Paso). Villa, Pancho. 1919. *3606*

Petitions. California (San Francisco). Congressional Union. Constitutional Amendments (19th). Field, Sara Bard. Panama Pacific International Exposition. Wilson, Woodrow. Woman Suffrage. 1915-20. *3749*

Petitot, Emile. Bibliographies. Indians. Missions and Missionaries. Northwest Territories. Philosophy of History. ca 1868-1916. *3168*

Petroff, Ivan. Alaska. Bancroft, Hubert Howe. California, University of (Bancroft Library). Diaries. Libraries. Travel account. 1878. *3535*

—. Alaska. Bancroft, Hubert Howe. Russia. 1842-91. *3517*

—. Alaska. Bancroft, Hubert Howe (*History of Alaska, 1730-1885*). Historiography. Pierce, Richard A. 1730-1885. *3520*

Petroff, Ivan (writings). Alaska. Bancroft, Hubert Howe. Historians. 19c. *3508*

Petroleum. *See also* Oil and Petroleum Products.

Petty, John D. Durant, Thomas C. Frémont, John C. Hallett, Samuel. Railroads. Scott, Thomas A. Union Pacific Railroad (Eastern Division). 1860's. *1390*

Pfeiffer, Albert H. Arizona (Canyon de Chelly region). Carson, Christopher (Kit). Indian Wars. Navajo Indians. 1864. *745*

Pfeiffer, Joe (interview). Frontier and Pioneer Life. Homesteading and Homesteaders. Wyoming (Jackson Hole). ca 1900-62. *3687*

Phantom coach (legend). Folklore. Great Britain. Ireland. Texas. 19c. *1867*

Pheasant breeding. China. Denny, Gertrude. Denny, Owen. Oregon. Poultry. 1852-1933. *1596*

Phelan, Gregory J. California. Catholic Church. Gold Rushes. Letters. 1848-58. *2354*

Phelps, John Wolcott. Catholic Church. Utah. 19c. *2377*

Phelps, William Wines. *Evening and Morning Star* (newspaper). Missouri (Jackson County). Mormons. 1833. *2278*

Phelps-Dodge Corporation. Arizona. Capital. Economic Development. Livestock. Railroads. Santa Fe Railroad. Southern Pacific Railroad. United Verde Company. 1854-94. *1261*

—. Copper Mines and Mining. Ghost Towns. New Mexico (Tyrone). 1890-1968. *3984*

Philanthropy. Art Galleries and Museums. California (Sacramento). Crocker, Edwin Bryant. Crocker, Margaret Ellen. 1821-1901. *3054*

—. Hutton, May. Idaho. Mines. Orphanages. Washington (Spokane). 1860-1915. *2951*

Philippines. Armies (volunteer units). Attitudes. Cuba. Racism. Spanish-American War. 1898-99. *3670*

—. Nebraska Regiment, 1st. Spanish-American War. Stotsenburg, John Miller. 1898-99. *3619*

Phillips, John ("Portugee"). Fetterman Massacre (battle). Fort Laramie. Fort Phil Kearny. Indian Wars. Rescue attempts. 1866. *687*

—. Folklore. Fort Laramie. Fort Phil Kearny. Wyoming. 1866. *1954*

Phillips, Leon C. Governors. Oklahoma Historical Society. 1939-43. *3729*

Phillips, Ulrich Bonnell. Cattle Raising. Farmers. Historiography. Owsley, Frank L. Phillips-Gray-Dodd (planter-poor white thesis). Racism. Schafer, Joseph. South or Southern States. Turner, Frederick Jackson. 1800-1962. *1045*

Phillips, Walter J. Landscape Painting. Manitoba (Lake of the Woods, Winnipeg). Rocky Mountains. 1914-63. *3257*

Phillips, Walter Shelley. Artists (illustrators). Bibliographies. Books. Muller, Dan. 1967. *2105*

Phillips-Gray-Dodd (planter-poor white thesis). Cattle Raising. Farmers. Historiography. Owsley, Frank L. Phillips, Ulrich Bonnell. Racism. Schafer, Joseph. South or Southern States. Turner, Frederick Jackson. 1800-1962. *1045*

Philosophy *See also* Ethics; Rationalism.

—. Expansionism. Frontier thesis. Nationalism. Turner, Frederick Jackson. Westward Movement. 1830's. *252*

Philosophy of History *See also* Historiography.

—. Bannon, John Francis. Historians. Spanish Borderlands. 17c. 1970. *2*

—. Bibliographies. Indians. Missions and Missionaries. Northwest Territories. Petitot, Emile. ca 1868-1916. *3168*

—. Bolton, Herbert Eugene. Spanish borderlands. 1920-53. *8*

—. Frontier thesis. Great Plains. Texas. Webb, Walter Prescott (works). 19c. 1959-63. *2471*

—. Frontier thesis. Hughes, H. Stuart. Manifest Destiny (reappraisal). Methodology. Turner, Frederick Jackson. Webb, Walter Prescott. 19c. 1963. *2404*

—. Frontier thesis. Tennessee (Cumberland Gap). Turner, Frederick Jackson. Wyoming (South Pass). 1972. *232*

—. Guthrie, A. B., Jr. Novels (historical). Westward Movement. 1971. *1966*

—. Historians. Webb, Walter Prescott (obituary). 1918-63. *2445*

Philosophy of History (hemispheric unity). Bolton, Herbert Eugene. Local History. 20c. *54*

Phoenix Gazette (newspaper). Apache Indians. Arizona. Criminal Law. Federal Government. Gardner, Earl. Hanging. San Carlos Reservation. 1936. *3639*

Phonetics *See also* Linguistics; Speech.

—. Deseret Alphabet. Mormons. Utah. 1853-68. *2252*

Photographic essay. Colorado. Roosevelt, Theodore. 1896-1912. *2792*

—. Lewis and Clark Expedition (reenactment). 1804-06. 1965. *404*

Photographs. Boomtowns. California (San Diego). 1880's. *2058*

—. California (San Francisco). Gold Rushes. 1851-56. *2067*

—. Depressions. Reminiscences. Ripley, Thomas E. Washington (Tacoma). 1890's. *3990*

Photography *See also* Films; Nature Photography.

—. Anderson, John Alvin. Nebraska. 1870-1900. *2087*

—. Anecdotes. Crow Indians. Miller, Fred E. Montana. 1900-36. *2061*

—. Architecture. Churches. Coalville Tabernacle. Mormons. Utah. 1967. *2150*

—. Architecture. Texas. Victorianism, American. Webb, Tedd. 1969. *2076*

—. Arizona. Buehman, Albert. Henry and Albert Buehman Memorial Collection. Mines. 1870-1900. *2086*

—. Arizona. California. DH-4 (aircraft). Macready, John A. Map Drawing. Mather, Stephen. Pacific Northwest. Stevens, A. W. 1924. *3628*

—. Calhoun, John C. Cass, Lewis. Douglas, Stephen A. *Dred Scott* v. *Sanford* (US 1857). Federal Government. Free Soil Doctrine. Slavery. Sovereignty. Squatter Sovereignty Doctrine. States' Rights. 1789-1860. *1526*

—. California (Tulare County). Populism. 1892. *3756*

—. Colorado. Elections. State Politics. Teller, Henry Moore. Waite, Davis H. Wolcott, Edward O. 1892-1902. *3772*

—. Depressions (agricultural). Elections. Farmers. Nebraska. 1922. *4064*

—. Farmers. Nonpartisan League. Saskatchewan. 1885-1914. *3351*

—. Indian Territory. Oklahoma Territory. Statehood movements. 1890-1906. *2590*

—. Kyle, James Henderson. Lee, Andrew E. Loucks, Henry Langford. National Farmers' Alliance. Populism. Reform. South Dakota. State Politics. 1884-96. *3760*

—. Lewelling, Seth. Oregon. Politics. Progressive movement. Reform. State Government. U'Ren, William S. 1892-98. *2970*

—. Political Conventions. Utah. 1912. *3829*

Political Parties (affiliation). Assimilation. Catholic Church. German Americans. Lutheran Church. Nebraska. Rural-Urban Studies. 1889-1915. *2350*

—. Foreign Policy. German Americans. Nebraska. Roosevelt, Franklin D. Voting and Voting Behavior. 1940. *3998*

Political Protest *See also* Riots.

—. Calhoun, John C. Emerson, Ralph Waldo. Lowell, James Russell. Mexican War. Polk, James K. Thoreau, Henry David. 1846-48. *563*

—. California (Los Angeles). Harman, Moses. Illinois (Chicago). Journalism. Kansas. Valley Falls Liberal League. 1879-1908. *2055*

—. Canada. Jaxon, Joseph. North West Rebellion. Riel, Louis. USA. 19c. *3212*

—. Communist Party. Folk Songs. Industrial Workers of the World. Music (religious). 19c-20c. *2163*

—. Folk Songs. Mexican Americans. Poetry. Southwest. 18c-1971. *1882*

Political Recruitment. California. Local Government. Pennsylvania. State Government. Training-ground thesis. 1900-62. *3728*

Political Reform *See also* names of reform movements, e.g. Progressivism, etc.; Lobbying; Political Corruption.

—. Aberhart, William. Canada. Conscription, Military. Elections. Herridge, W. D. New Democracy Movement. Social Credit Party. 1939-40. *3387*

—. Adams, Alva. Colorado. Elections. Peabody, James H. Progressivism. 1904. *3821*

—. Agricultural Reform. Grand Forks *Daily Herald* (newspaper). Journalism. LaFollette, Robert Marion. North Dakota. Winship, George B. 1879-1911. *2010*

—. Arizona. Bull Moose movement. Constitutions, State. Propaganda. Republican Party. Roosevelt, Theodore. Taft, William H. 1910-16. *2890*

—. Arnold, Henry J. Citizens' Party. City Government. Colorado (Denver). Speer, Robert W. 1912. *3986*

—. Bank of North Dakota. *Iconoclast* (newspaper). Martinson, Henry R. North Dakota. Reminiscences. Socialist Party. State Mill and Elevator. 1910-20's. *3782*

—. Bard, Thomas Robert. California. Johnson, Hiram. Pardee, George C. Propaganda. Railroads and State. Republican Party. Southern Pacific Railroad. 1899-1905. *3766*

—. Barnard, Kate. Labor Unions and Organizations. Oklahoma. Progressivism. 1900's. *2582*

—. Boddy, E. Manchester. California (Los Angeles). *Daily News* (newspaper). Democratic Party. Douglas, Helen Gahagan. Press. 1926-54. *3662*

—. Bryan, William Jennings. Federal Reserve System. Nebraska. New Deal. Norris, George William. Wherry, Kenneth S. 1900-51. *3740*

—. California. Colorado River Project. Johnson, Hiram. Senate. State Politics. 1911-41. *3747*

—. California. Constitutions, State. DeYoung, Charles. DeYoung, M. H. Kearney, Denis. San Francisco *Chronicle* (newspaper). 1865-79. *2027*

—. California. Elections (state). Farmers. Johnson, Hiram. Lincoln-Roosevelt Republican League. Railroads. Southern Pacific Railroad. 1910. *3796*

—. Colorado. Fiscal Policy. Public Welfare. State Government. 1918-41. *3709*

—. Colorado (Denver). Constitutions, State. Home rule. Local Politics. 1861-1911. *1657*

—. Colorado (Denver). Costigan, Edward P. Law and Society. Status revolution. 20c. *3741*

—. Colorado (Denver). Progressive Party. State Government. 1906. *3752*

—. Congress. Populism. Simpson, Jerry. 1880-1900. *3727*

—. Constitutions, State. Farmers' Union. Labor Unions and Organizations. Oklahoma. Propaganda. 1904-10. *2583*

—. Doster, Frank. Kansas. Liberalism. 1920's. *2532*

—. Elections. Washington (Seattle). 1900-20. *2938*

—. Foster, Warren. *Inter-Mountain Advocate* (newspaper). Labor Reform. Lawrence, Henry W. Populism. Utah. 1893-1900. *3753*

—. Gill, Hiram C. Progressivism. Reporters and Reporting. Smith, Joe E. Washington (Seattle). 1900-20. *3769*

—. Hay, Marion E. Impeachment. Schively, John H. Washington. 1909-12. *3726*

—. Jim Crow Laws. Kansas. Progressivism. Roosevelt, Theodore. White, William Allen. 1890-1912. *3716*

—. Provincial Government. Salcedo y Quiroga, Manuel María de (report). Spain. Texas. 1809. *173*

Political satire. Humor (regional). Twain, Mark. 1865. *1927*

Political Science *See also* Government; Imperialism; Law; Legislation; Nationalism; Politics; Public Administration; Utopias.

—. Barrows, David Prescott. California, University of (Berkeley). Colleges and Universities. Gilman, Daniel Coit. Moses, Bernard. Teaching. 1872-1951. *1862*

Political Speeches *See also* names of political figures and groups with the subdivision addresses, e.g. Churchill, Winston (addresses); Debates.

—. California. Loeb, William. Moody, William H. Pardee, George C. Roosevelt, Theodore. Travel account. 1903. *3654*

—. Kansas (Atchison). Lincoln, Abraham. NY (Cooper Union). 1859. *2550*

Political Surveys *See also* Public Opinion.

Political Systems (party structures). Political Factions. Territorial Government. 19c. *2415*

Political Theory *See also* kinds of political theory, e.g. Democracy; Political Science.

—. Bryan, William Jennings. Economic Reform. Free silver movement. Harvey, William Hope ("Coin"). Panic of 1893. Politics. Sherman Silver Purchase Act. 1893-1936. *3824*

Political Violence. *See* Violence; Terrorism.

Politics *See also* headings beginning with the word political; City Politics; Elections; Geopolitics; Government; Intergovernmental Relations; Legislative Bodies; Lobbying; Local Politics; State Politics.

—. Adams, Annette Abbott. California. Elections. Law. Women. 1900-20's. *3768*

—. Agricultural Adjustment Act (1933). Agricultural Reform. *Daily Republic* (newspaper). Journalism. Ronald, William Roy. South Dakota. 1909-51. *4088*

—. Agricultural Organizations. Farmers' Alliance. Macune, Charles W. People's Party. 1890-1920. *3789*

—. Agricultural Reform. Democratic Party. Idaho. New Deal. Reform. Ross, Charles Ben. 1933-38. *3781*

—. Annexation. Antislavery Sentiments. Old Northwest. Texas. Whigs. 1836-44. *2675*

—. Anti-Saloon League. Nebraska. Propaganda. Temperance Movements. 1898-1910. *3832*

—. Arapaho Indians. Cheyenne Indians. Chivington, John M. Colorado Volunteer Cavalry, 3rd Regiment. Evans, John. Indian Wars. Sand Creek Massacre. 1860-63. *859*

—. Arizona. Courts (federal district). Taft, William Howard. Wilson, Woodrow. 1912-13. *2884*

—. Arizona. Economic Development. Federal Government. Historiography. 20c. *3584*

—. Arizona. Frémont, John C. McCormick, Richard C. Safford, Anson P. K. 1860's-90's. *2892*

—. Arizona. Judges (territorial). 1863-1912. *2879*

—. Arizona. New Mexico. Roosevelt, Theodore. Statehood movements. Taft, William H. 1908. *2703*

—. Ballinger, Richard A. Bureaucracies. Business. Conservation of Natural Resources. Forest Service. Interior Department. Monopolies. Newell, Frederick Haynes. Pinchot, Gifford. Taft, William H. 1909-26. *4136*

—. Bancroft, Hubert Howe. California. Forster, John. Mexico. Pico, Pío. Savage, Thomas. 1832-47. *214*

—. Banking. Texas (Austin). Wooldridge, Alexander Penn. 1899-1930. *2660*

—. Beveridge, Albert J. Senate Committee on Territories. Southwest. Statehood movements. 1902-12. *2693*

—. Bilingualism. French language (abolition). Manitoba Act (1870). Provincial Legislatures. Schools. 1870-90. *3264*

—. Borah, William E. Idaho. Idaho (Coeur d'Alene). Johnson, Claudius O. Labor Unions and Organizations. Mines. Populism. Senate. Wells, Merle W. 1884-1940. 1892-99. *2739*

—. Bossism. California (San Francisco). Ruef, Abraham. Schmitz, Eugene E. Union Labor Party. 1890-1906. *3830*

—. Bratton, Sam G. Chavez, Dennis. Hatch, Carl. New Mexico. Public Opinion. Roosevelt, Franklin D. (administration). Supreme Court. VanDevanter, Willis. 1937. *3739*

—. Brindle, William. Calhoun, John C. Democratic Party. General Land Office. Kansas. Moore, Ely. Public Lands (transfer of). Shoemaker, Thomas C. Surveying. 1850's. *1142*

—. Bristow, Joseph L. Editors and Editing. Irrigation. Kansas (Salina). ca 1880-1908. *2048*

—. Bryan, William Jennings. Democratic Party. Hitchcock, Gilbert M. Nebraska. Patronage. Prohibition. Wilson, Woodrow (administration). 1840's-1916. *3736*

—. Bryan, William Jennings. Destler, Chester McArthur (*American Radicalism, 1865-1901*, 1946). Populists. Watson, Thomas Edward. 1896. *3744*

—. Bryan, William Jennings. Economic Reform. Free silver movement. Harvey, William Hope ("Coin"). Panic of 1893. Political Theory. Sherman Silver Purchase Act. 1893-1936. *3824*

—. Burleigh, Walter A. Congress. Dakota Territory. Missouri River. Montana Territory. Sioux Indians. Steamboats. 1861-96. *2499*

—. Bursum, Holm O. Law Enforcement. New Mexico Territory. 1894. *1775*

—. Business. Farmers. Panic of 1893. Populism. Progressivism. 19c. *3825*

—. California. Democratic Party. Republican Party. State Government. Warren, Earl. 1943-53. *3759*

—. California. Gwin, William. Slavery. 1849-65. *3087*

—. California (San Diego). Cubberley, Ellwood Patterson. Jordan, David Starr. Public Schools. 1896-98. *3686*

—. Canada. Class consciousness. Elections. Independent Labor Party. Liberal Party. Manitoba (Winnipeg). Parliaments. Puttee, Arthur. Sifton, Clifford. 1899-1904. *3290*

—. Capital sites. Nebraska Territory (Lincoln, Omaha). Territorial Government. 1856-67. *2508*

—. Carey, Joseph Maull. Congress. Letters. Statehood movements. VanDevanter, Willis. Wyoming. 1890. *2749*

—. Catholic Church. Church and State. Federal Government. Northwest Territories (Regina). Ontario (Ottawa). Schools. Territorial Government. 1898-1903. *3233*

—. Cattle barons. Johnson County War. Mercer, Asa Shinn. *Northwestern Live Stock Journal*. Wyoming State Growers Association. 1877-94. *2750*

—. Cattle trail (national). Cowboys. Texas. 1883-86. *1112*

—. Chadwick, Stephen James. Daily Life. Oregon (Roseburg). Reminiscences. 1855-83. *2962*

—. Chaffee, Jerome B. Colorado. Elbert, Sam. Grant, Ulysses S. McCook, Edward M. Republican Party. 1869-75. *2790*

—. Cherokee Neutral Land League. Fort Scott and Gulf Railroad. Homesteading and Homesteaders. Joy, James F. Kansas (Kansas City, Topeka). Land Tenure. Railroads. Texas (Galveston). 1868-70. *1380*

—. Cheyenne Indians. Chivington, John M. Colorado Cavalry, 3rd. Indian-White Relations. Sand Creek Massacre. 1862-65. *844*

—. Church and State. Mormons. 1835-1966. *2301*

—. Arizona. Capital. Economic Development. Livestock. Phelps-Dodge Corporation. Santa Fe Railroad. Southern Pacific Railroad. United Verde Company. 1854-94. *1261*

—. Arizona. Clum, John P. Gold Rushes. San Carlos Apache Reservation. Southern Pacific Railroad. Yukon Territory (Klondike). 1874-1932. *296*

—. Arizona. Copper Mines and Mining. Southern Pacific Railroad. Twin Buttes Railroad. 1903-09. *3923*

—. Arizona. Henry and Albert Buehman Memorial Collection. New Mexico. Photography. 1880's. *2064*

—. Arizona (Flagstaff). Atchison, Topeka and Santa Fe Railroad. Atlantic and Pacific Railway. Bright Angel Trail, formerly Cameron Trail. Cameron, Ralph Henry. Mines. Powell, John Wesley. Stanton, Robert Brewster. Tourism. 1883. *1281*

—. Arizona (Globe). Arizona Mineral Belt Railroad. Atlantic and Pacific Railroad. Eddy, James W. Mines. 1880-93. *1401*

—. Arizona (Nogales, formerly Issacson). Bradford, William, Jr. Maps. Mexico. Mines. New Mexico and Arizona Railroad. Sonora Railroad. Trade. 1880. *1692*

—. Arizona (Tombstone). Scott, Thomas A. 19c-1960. *1383*

—. Arizona (Verde Valley). Atlantic and Pacific Railroad. Copper Mines and Mining. 1894-1951. *3961*

—. Armies. Indians. Interior Department. Montana (Bozeman). North Dakota (Bismarck). Northern Pacific Railroad. Surveying. 1873. *1393*

—. Army Corps of Engineers. California (San Pedro). Shipping (deep water). Southern Pacific Railroad. 1867-90. *1340*

—. Associated Oil Company. California. Oil Industry and Trade. Southern Pacific Railroad. Standard Oil Company. Union Oil Company. 1895-1911. *3844*

—. Atchison and Topeka Railroad. Atchison, Topeka and Santa Fe Railroad. Finance. Government. Indian-White Relations. Kansas. Newton General Massacre. 1859-72. *1396*

—. Atchison, Topeka and Santa Fe Railroad. 1911-17. *3563*

—. Atchison, Topeka and Santa Fe Railroad. Business. Finance. Gould, Jay. Huntington, Collis P. St. Louis and San Francisco Railway Company. 1880-82. *1381*

—. Atchison, Topeka and Santa Fe Railroad. Colorado (El Moro, Trinidad). Denver and Rio Grande Western Railroad. Southern Colorado Coal and Town Company. 1876-88. *1704*

—. Atchison, Topeka and Santa Fe Railroad. Economic Development. Kansas (Cheney, Marshall, Spivey, Zenda). 19c. *2569*

—. Atchison, Topeka and Santa Fe Railroad. Food Industry. Harvey, Frederick Henry. Harvey Houses. Kansas (Florence, Topeka). Kansas Pacific Railroad. Missouri (St. Louis). Restaurant Chains. 1876-1901. *1249*

—. Atchison, Topeka and Santa Fe Railroad. Missouri Pacific Railroad. Trade Routes. Union Pacific Railroad. 1889-1910. *1332*

—. Atlantic and Pacific Railroad. Indian Territory. Indian-White Relations. 1870-1907. *1382*

—. Automobiles. Oregon (Deschutes Canyon). 1909. *3643*

—. Ballard, Shreve. California (Santa Barbara). Reminiscences. Southern Pacific Railroad. Transportation. 1910's. *3847*

—. Banking. Cooke, Jay. Great Northern Railway. Hill, James Jerome. Morgan, J. Pierpont. Northern Pacific Railroad. Northern Securities Company. Villard, Henry. 1864-1904. *1350*

—. Banning, Phineas. Butterfield Overland Mail. California (Los Angeles). Los Angeles and San Pedro Railroad. Shipping. Stagecoaches. Transportation. 1846-61. *1293*

—. Bass, Sam. Black Hills. Folklore. Outlaws. South Dakota. Texas Rangers. Union Pacific Railroad. 1877-80's. *1794*

—. Beecher's Island (battle). Cheyenne Indians. Forsyth, George A. Indian Wars. Kansas Pacific Railroad. Roman Nose (Chief). 1868. *696*

—. Bethany College. Carlson, C. R. Colleges and Universities. Immigration. Kansas (Lindsborg). Kansas Pacific Railroad. Olsson, Olof. Swedish Americans. 1868-1941. *1501*

—. Blackfoot Indians. Canadian Pacific Railway. Lacombe, Albert. MacDonald, John Alexander. North West Rebellion. Riel, Louis. Stephen, George (1st Baron Mount Stephen). VanHorne, William Cornelius. 1880-1912. *3117*

—. Boosterism. Colorado. Freeman, Frederick Kemper. Freeman, Legh (Leigh) Richmond. *Frontier Index* (newspaper). Nebraska. Union Pacific Railroad. Wyoming. 1865-84. *2041*

—. Borden, Robert Laird. Federal Government. Manitoba (Winnipeg). One Big Union. Robertson, Gideon. Strikes. 1919. *3261*

—. Bridges. Idaho (Lewiston). Snake River Valley. Washington (Clarkston). 1925-30. *3579*

—. British Columbia. Canadian Northern Railway. Canadian Pacific Railway. Construction. Roads. Rocky Mountains (Fraser Canyon). Trans-Canada Highway. 1861-1945. *3464*

—. British Columbia (Prince George). Economic Growth. Fraser, Simon. Grand Trunk Pacific Railway. Lumber and Lumbering. Mackenzie, Alexander. Transportation. 1793-1967. *3441*

—. British Columbia (Vancouver Island; Nanaimo). Canadian Pacific Railway. Coal Mines and Mining. Economic Development. Hudson's Bay Company. 19c-20c. *3471*

—. British Columbia (Vancouver Island; Victoria). Canadian Pacific Railway. Esquimalt and Nanaimo Railway. 1880's. *3451*

—. Brown, Frank Mason. Colorado River. Denver, Colorado Cañon and Pacific Railroad. Green River. Kendrick, Frank C. Stanton, Robert Brewster. Surveying. 1889. *1376*

—. Brown, Frank Mason. Colorado River. Kendrick, Frank C. (notebook). 1889. *445*

—. Brown, Mrs. Hugh. Celebrations. Nevada (Tonopah). Reminiscences. 1904. *3857*

—. Bryant, Frank B. Gold Mines and Mining. Idaho (Salmon River Mountains). Reminiscences. 1909-11. *3858*

—. Buffalo. Cabeza de Vaca, Alvar Núñez. Hunting. North America. 1521-1889. *312*

—. Burke, Thomas. Real Estate. Washington (Wenatchee). 1888-93. *1675*

—. Burlington and Missouri River Railroad. Immigration. Mennonites. Nebraska (Gage County, Jefferson County). Russian Americans. 1873-78. *1551*

—. Business. Chicago, Burlington and Quincy Railroad. Ethics. Perkins, Charles Elliott. Public Opinion. 1870-81. *1359*

—. Button, Thomas. Hudson Bay Railroad. Hydraulic Engineering. International Nickel Company. Kelsey Generating Station. Manitoba (Nelson River). Mines (nickel). 1612-1957. *3258*

—. California. Central Pacific Railroad. Chinese Americans. Construction. Sierra Nevada Mountains. 1865-69. *1528*

—. California. Colorado River. Freight and Freightage. Hawaii. Idaho. Montana. Mormons. Settlement. Shipping. Trade. Union Pacific Railroad. Utah (Salt Lake City). 1864-69. *861*

—. California. Economic Development. Land grants. Myths and Symbols. Settlement. Southern Pacific Railroad. 19c. *1368*

—. California. Economic Growth. George, Henry. Reminiscences. 1868. *1360*

—. California. Elections (state). Farmers. Johnson, Hiram. Lincoln-Roosevelt Republican League. Political Reform. Southern Pacific Railroad. 1910. *3796*

—. California. Greeley, Horace. Travel account. 1859. *1402*

—. California. Migrant Labor. 1870's-1941. *1431*

—. California (Freeport; Sacramento River). City Life. Freeport Railroad Company. Hunt, Rockwell D. Reminiscences. 20c. *3983*

—. California (Irvine). Irvine, James. Santa Fe Railroad. Settlement. 1887-1967. *1693*

—. California (Los Angeles). Folk Songs. Lummis, Charles Fletcher. Mexican Americans. Museums. New Mexico. Santa Fe Railroad. Southwest Museum. 1880's-1920's. *1902*

—. California (Los Angeles, San Pedro). Economic Development. Harbor. Santa Fe Railroad. Southern Pacific Railroad. Union Pacific Railroad. 1869-1917. *1404*

—. California (Pomona). Tourism. 1880's-90's. *1291*

—. California Railroad Commission. Constitutions, State. Monopolies. Rate regulation. Reform. Southern Pacific Railroad. 1879-1911. *1378*

—. California (Santa Barbara). Reminiscences. Stanley, Leo L. 1900's. *3949*

—. California (Sierras). Central Pacific Railroad. Pioneer Stage Company. Stagecoaches. Wells, Fargo and Company. 1849-60's. *1312*

—. Canadian Northern Railway. Political Corruption (ascribed). Prairie Provinces. Transportation. 1900's. *3161*

—. Canadian Northern Railway. Prairie Provinces. Settlement. 1900's. *3244*

—. Canadian Pacific Railway. Canadian West. Economic Development. Great Britain. *Truth* (newspaper). 1881. *3187*

—. Canadian Pacific Railway. Canadian West. *Emigrant* (periodical). Frontier and Pioneer Life. 1880's. *3164*

—. Canadian Pacific Railway. Cascade Mountains. Civil Engineering. Discovery and Exploration. Great Northern Railway. Hill, James Jerome. Montana (Marias Pass). Rocky Mountains. Stevens, John Frank. Washington (Stevens Pass). 1889-1943. *1346*

—. Canadian Pacific Railway. Discovery and Exploration. Horetzky, Charles. Photography. Rocky Mountains. 19c. *3110*

—. Canadian Pacific Railway. Lacombe, Albert. Shaughnessy, Thomas. 1892-1916. 1967. *3115*

—. Canadian Pacific Railway. Reminiscences. Saskatchewan (Maple Creek). Settlement. 1882-1907. *3338*

—. Carter, William A., Jr. Fort Bridger. Fort Thornburgh. Military Camps and Forts. Reminiscences. Roads. Union Pacific Railroad. Utah (Vernal). Ute Indians. Wyoming. 1879-1966. *1325*

—. Cascade Mountains (Stevens Pass). Civil Engineering. Discovery and Exploration. Great Northern Railway. Hill, James Jerome. Montana (Marias Pass). Oregon Trunk Line. Pacific Northwest. Stevens, John Frank. 1889-1911. *1367*

—. Cattle Raising. Chisholm Trail. Kansas (Abilene). Texas. Westward Movement. 1867-71. *1091*

—. Cattle Raising. Economic Conditions. Manufactures. Northern Pacific Railroad. Oregon Pacific Railroad. Pacific Northwest. Union Pacific Railroad. Wheat. 19c. *1348*

—. Cattle Raising. Freight and Freightage. Mores, Marquis de. New York. North Dakota (Medora). Northern Pacific Railroad. Northern Pacific Refrigerator Car Company. 1882-87. *1284*

—. Central Pacific Railroad. Chinese Americans. 19c. *1372*

—. Central Pacific Railroad. Colorado. Federal Government. Kansas Pacific Railroad. Lobbying. Missouri (Kansas City). Union Pacific Railroad. 1865-69. *1389*

—. Central Pacific Railroad. Colorado Territory (Strasburg). Kansas Pacific Railroad. Union Pacific Railroad. 1870. *1374*

—. Central Pacific Railroad. Construction. Federal subsidies. Fraud. Sierra Nevada Mountains. 1860's. *1352*

—. Central Pacific Railroad. Economic Conditions. Land grants. Public Welfare. Union Pacific Railroad. 19c. *1379*

—. Central Pacific Railroad. Federal Government. Local Government. Nebraska (Omaha). Political Corruption. Union Pacific Railroad. 19c. *1357*

—. Central Pacific Railroad. *Herald* (newspaper). Miller, George L. Nebraska (Omaha). Publicity. Settlement. Union Pacific Railroad. 1865-85. *1630*

—. Cherokee Neutral Land League. Fort Scott and Gulf Railroad. Homesteading and Homesteaders. Joy, James F. Kansas (Kansas City, Topeka). Land Tenure. Politics. Texas (Galveston). 1868-70. *1380*

—. Cheyenne Indians. Fort David A. Russell. Indian-White Relations. Union Pacific Railroad. Wyoming (Cheyenne). 1867-90. *1663*

—. Chicago, Burlington and Quincy Railroad. Colorado (Denver). Gould, Jay. Iowa Pool. Perkins, Charles Elliott. Union Pacific Railroad. 1870's-80's. *1386*

—. Chicago, Burlington and Quincy Railroad. Gould, Jay. Hannibal and St. Joseph Railroad. Illinois (Chicago). Kansas (Kansas City). Perkins, Charles Elliott. Santa Fe Railroad. 1869-88. *1395*

—. Chicago, Burlington and Quincy Railroad. Great Britain. Immigration (recruitment). Nebraska. 1871-75. *1505*

—. China. Hill, James Jerome. Japan. Shipping. Trade. 1878-1916. *3941*

—. Cities. Oklahoma. 19c. *1646*

—. Douglas, Stephen A. Lincoln, Abraham. Morality. Popular sovereignty. 1850's. *1529*

—. Foreign Relations. Indians. Letters. Mexico. Milan, Benjamin Rush. Outlaws. Poinsett, Joel. Refugees. Texas. 1825. *203*

—. Kansas Territory. Platte County Self-Defensive Association. Stringfellow, Benjamin F. 1830's-60's. *2523*

—. Mormons. Negroes. Smith, Joseph. Young, Brigham. 19c. *2283*

Slavery (expansion of). Congress. Debates. Kansas. Nebraska. Public Opinion. 1854. *2449*

Slavery (extension). New Mexico. Smith, Truman (speech). Utah. 1850. *1480*

Slavery (extension of). Compromise of 1850. Democratic Party. Free Soil Party. Geopolitics. Whigs. 1850. *311*

—. Far Western States. Labor (white). Racism. Republican Party. 1815-60. *1446*

Sloat, John D. Armies. California. Frémont, John C. Kearny, Stephen Watts. Mexican War. Military Campaigns. Navies. Stockton, Robert Field. 1846-47. *555*

Slocum, John. Indians. Pacific Northwest. Shakers. 1882-1966. *2368*

Slums. *See* Cities.

Smalley, Eugene V. *Century Magazine* (periodical). Gold Rushes. Idaho (Coeur d'Alene). Reminiscences. 1884. *998*

Smalley, Flora. Arizona. Letters. Travel accounts. 1902. *2909*

Smallpox. Epidemics. *Manitoban* (newspaper). Prairie Provinces. 1869-70. *3256*

Smith, Al. Anti-evolution movement. Education. Oklahoma. State Legislatures. 1923-28. *1861*

—. California. Democratic Party. Elections (presidential). 1928-32. *3818*

Smith, Benjamin F. Fort Phil Kearny. Indian Wars. Powell, James. Wagon Box Fight (battle). Wyoming. 1867. *783*

Smith, Donald Alexander. Great Northern Railway. Hill, James Jerome. Kennedy, John S. Kittson, Norman Wolfred. Letters. Railroads. Stephen, George. 1878. *1361*

Smith, Edwin E. Cowboys. Photography. ca 1900-30. *4066*

Smith, Elmer Boyd. Artists (illustrators). Bibliographies. Books. Schiewetz, E. M. Schoonover, Frank E. Schreyvogel, Charles. Stoops, Herbert Morton. Suydam, Edward Howard. Thomason, John William, Jr. 19c-1966. *2102*

Smith, Erwin Evans. Cowboys. Photography. Texas. 1886-1947. *2059*

Smith Family. Barkhart, Ernest. Brown, Anna. Bureau of Investigation. Crime and Criminals. Hale, W. R. Oil Industry and Trade. Oklahoma. Osage Indians. Roan, Henry. USA. 1906-26. *932*

Smith, Francis. Francis Smith and Company. Great Britain. Investments. Texas. 1875-90's. *1246*

Smith, George M. Letters. Montana. Reminiscences. 1904-17. *2731*

Smith, George Watson. Banking. Dakota Territory (Bismarck). Diaries. Farm loans. 1878. *1271*

Smith, Henry Nash *(Virgin Land)*. Social Psychology. Waters, Frank *(The Colorado)*. Western novels. Wyatt Earp Syndrome. 19c-20c. *1981*

Smith, Hoke. Cherokee Indians. Chicago, Kansas and Nebraska Railway. Chicago, Rock Island and Pacific Railway. Oklahoma (Round Pond, South Enid). Railroads and State. Sabotage. 1893-94. *2584*

Smith, Ira Gilbert (family). Ashley, William H. Pioneers. Smith, Jedediah Strong. Wills. ca 1800-49. *264*

Smith, J. Allen *(Spirit of American Government)*. California. Conservation of Natural Resources. Heney, Francis J. Howe, Frederic *(Privilege and Democracy)*. Progressivism. Recall (judicial). 1907-11. *3566*

Smith, Jackson and Sublette (firm). Ashley, William H. Fitzpatrick, Thomas. Fort Laramie. Fur Trade. Sublette, Milton. Wyeth, Nathaniel. 1830's. *909*

—. Discovery and Exploration. Fur Trade. Smith, Jedediah Strong. 1822-31. *911*

Smith, Jedediah Strong. Ashley, William H. Comanche Indians. Discovery and Exploration. Far Western States. Fur Trade. Henry, Andrew. Mountain Men. Rocky Mountains. 1822-31. *880*

—. Ashley, William H. Pioneers. Smith, Ira Gilbert (family). Wills. ca 1800-49. *264*

—. California (Mojave Desert). Conservation of Natural Resources. Dangermond, Peter. Falconer, Smith, Jr. Parks. Water Resources, Department of. 1826. 1965. *905*

—. California State Geological Survey. Conservation of Natural Resources. Discovery and Exploration. Fages, Pedro. Muir, John. Sequoia National Park. Tharp, Hale D. Whitney, Josiah Dwight. 1772-1966. *446*

—. Colter, John. Glass, Hugh. Johnson, John. Literature. Mountain Men. 1803-46. *1993*

—. Discovery and Exploration. 1823-31. *433*

—. Discovery and Exploration. Fur Trade. Smith, Jackson and Sublette (firm). 1822-31. *911*

—. Fur Trade. Hudson's Bay Company. 1824-29. *436*

—. Historiography. 1798-1831. 1967. *908*

Smith, Joe E. Gill, Hiram C. Political Reform. Progressivism. Reporters and Reporting. Washington (Seattle). 1900-20. *3769*

Smith, Joseph. Boggs, Lilburn W. Douglas, Stephen A. Extradition. Missouri. Mormons. Trials. 1841-43. *2265*

—. Calhoun, John C. Civil Rights. Courts. Dunklin, Daniel. Federal Government. Jackson, Andrew. Missouri (Jackson County). Mormons. 1833-44. *2280*

—. Historical Sites and Parks. Missouri (Liberty). Mormons. Prisons. 1838. 1963. *2256*

—. Historiography. Mormons. 1966. *2255*

—. Historiography. Mormons. Utah. Young, Brigham. 1966. *2261*

—. Mormons. 1820-1965. *2249*

—. Mormons. 1827-1965. *2282*

—. Mormons. Negroes. Slavery. Young, Brigham. 19c. *2283*

—. Mormons. Political Attitudes. Texas. Theology. 1844. *2266*

—. Mormons. Polygamy. Young, Brigham. 19c. *2275*

—. Mormons. Utah. Westward Movement. Young, Brigham. 1830's-40's. *2248*

Smith, Kirby. Civil War. Confederate Army. Cooper, Douglas H. Fort Gibson. Fort Smith. Honey Springs (battle). Indian Territory. Maxey, Samuel Bell. Steele, William. Watie, Stand. 1863-64. *626*

—. Civil War. Confederate States of America. Indian Territory. Postal Service. Reagan, John. 1861-65. *660*

Smith, Lot. Arizona. Lincoln, Abraham. Mormons. Nauvoo Legion. Navajo Indians. Utah War (1857). 1830-92. *2294*

Smith, Lowell. California. Cities. Diaries. Gold Mines and Mining. *Ka Hae Hawaii* (newspaper). Pule, J. Transportation. 1858-59. *955*

Smith, Marcus Aurelius. Arizona (Tombstone). Democratic Party. Political Leadership. 1886-1924. *2874*

Smith, Martha L. Cather, Willa. Garland, Hamlin. Great Plains. Homestead Act (1862). Homesteading and Homesteaders. Literature. Rølvaag, Ole E. Stewart, Elinore Pruitt. 1860-1967. *1983*

Smith, Robert Pearsal. Mines. New Mexico (Lake Valley). Sierra Grande Mining Company. Stocks and Bonds. Whitman, Walt. 19c. *1019*

Smith, Thomas L. California. Idaho (Bear River). Oregon. Ostner, Charles Leopold. Trading posts. 19c. *1252*

Smith, Truman (speech). New Mexico. Slavery (extension). Utah. 1850. *1480*

Smith, Victor. Chase, Salmon P. Customs collection. Lincoln, Abraham. Political Corruption. State Politics. Washington Territory (Port Townsend, Puget Sound). 1860's. *2943*

Smith, William. California. Gold Mines and Mining. State Politics. Virginia. 1797-1887. *944*

Smithsonian Institution. American Fur Company. Fort Union. Meteorology. North Dakota. Patent Office. Pennsylvania (Philadelphia). Riter, Frederick G. 1853-88. *920*

Smoot, Reed. Burrows, Julius Caesar. Mormons. Political Leadership. Senate. 1903-07. *3764*

—. Conservation of Natural Resources. Public Lands. Senate Public Lands and Surveys Committee. 1905-33. *4094*

—. Democratic Party. Elections. Political Factions. Republican Party. Utah. 1916. *3816*

—. Foreign Policy. Mexico (northern). Mormons. 1909-21. *2245*

—. Mormons. Persecution. Senate. Utah. 1903-07. *3763*

Smuggling. Aliens. Arizona (Nogales). Chinese. Customs collection. Hoey, William M. Mexico (Sonora, Nogales). Political Corruption. 1899-1902. *4021*

—. California. Kendrick, John, Jr. Navies. O'Cain, Joseph Burling. Spain. 1790's. *13*

—. California. Massachusetts (Boston). Spain. 1797-1821. *180*

Smythe, William E. *Irrigation Age* (periodical). National Irrigation Congress. Nebraska. *Omaha Bee* (newspaper). 1890-95. *4039*

Snake Indians. Diaries. Hebard, Grace Raymond *(Sacajawea)*. Luttig, John. North Dakota. Sacagawea (Shoshoni Indian). Shoshoni Indians. South Dakota. Wyoming. 1811-84. *430*

Snake River. Alaska (Nome). Gold Rushes. 1898-1900. *3527*

Snake River Land Company. Grand Teton National Park. *Grand Teton* (newspaper). *Jackson's Hole Courier* (newspaper). Nature Conservation. Rockefeller, John D., Jr. Wyoming (Jackson Hole). 1931-34. *4155*

Snake River Valley. Bridges. Idaho (Lewiston). Railroads. Washington (Clarkston). 1925-30. *3579*

Snively, Jacob. Cooke, Philip St. George. Mexico. Santa Fe Trail. Texas. 1843-44. *2658*

Snow. Cattle Raising. Livestock (loss of). Montana. 1886-87. *1118*

Snow, Eliza R. Blackburn, Abner. Literature. Meeks, Pridley. Mormons. Pratt, Parley P. Stout, Hosea. Turner, Anne Clark. 19c-20c. *2288*

Snow, Leslie. Daily Life. Kansas. Letters. Snow, Susan Currier. 1887-89. *1577*

Snow, Lorenzo. Brigham City Dramatic Association. Theater. Utah. 1855-56. *2823*

—. Business. Cooperative Communities. Utah (Brigham City). 1864-96. *2802*

Snow storms. Buffalo hunts. Montana (Black Hills). Reminiscences. Wilson, William E. 1880. *2736*

Snow, Susan Currier. Daily Life. Kansas. Letters. Snow, Leslie. 1887-89. *1577*

Sobaipuri Indians. Arizona (Calabasas; Guebabi). Kino, Eusebio Francisco. Settlement. 16c-1927. *16*

Social Change *See also* Economic Growth; Industrialization; Modernization.

—. Agriculture. Economic Growth. Great Plains. 1963. *1050*

—. Art. Indian-White Relations. Pueblo Indians (villages). Science. Southwest. 1530-1972. *33*

—. Attitudes. Conservatism. Mennonites. Saskatchewan (Martensville). Urbanization. 1870's. 1968. *3345*

—. Blackfoot Indians. Europe. Kiowa Indians. Mandan Indians. Omaha Indians. Sioux Indians. Trade. 19c. *913*

—. California (Orange County). Martin, Glenn. Transportation. 1870's-1955. *2988*

—. Cherokee Indians. Choctaw Indians. Missions and Missionaries. Nez Percé Indians. Oneida Indians. Protestant Churches. Seneca Indians. Sioux Indians. 1760-1860. *2313*

—. Colorado. Democratic Party. New Deal. Reform. State Politics. 1930's. *3708*

—. Frontier and Pioneer Life. Idaho Territory. Newspapers. Ruby City *Owyhee Avalanche* (newspaper). 1863-72. *2040*

—. Manitoba. Mennonites. Sommerfeld Mennonite Church. 1890-1948. *3280*

—. Manitoba (Winnipeg). Mennonites. Religious life. Rural-Urban Studies. 1964. *3308*

—. Mennonites. Urbanization. 1968. *3143*

—. Populism. 1890-1900. *291*

Social Classes *See also* Class Struggle; Middle Classes; Social Mobility.

—. Alberta. Explorers. Fort Chipewyan. Fur Trade. 18c. *3369*

—. Isolationism. Liberalism. North Dakota. Political Attitudes. 1914-63. *3711*

Social Conditions *See also* Cities; Cost of Living; Country Life; Daily Life; Economic Conditions; Labor; Marriage; Migration, Internal; Popular Culture; Social Classes; Social Mobility; Social Problems; Social Reform; Social Surveys.

—. Agriculture. Population. Texas (Cross Timbers). 1890-1960. *3884*

—. Alaska (Sitka). Economic Conditions. Military Occupation. Russian-American Company. 1804-84. *3554*

—. Alberta Coal Branch. Coal Mines and Mining. Frontier and Pioneer Life. 1968. *3379*

—. Arlington Hotel. California (Santa Barbara). Reminiscences. Storke, Thomas M. Tourism. 1880's-90's. *1432*

State Government See also Constitutions, State; Governors; State Legislatures; State Politics; States' Rights; Territorial Government.
—. Agriculture. Colorado. Irrigation. Laramie River. Supreme Court. VanDevanter, Willis. Water policy. Wyoming v. Colorado (1911-22). 1911-22. 4119
—. Anti-Saloon League. Oklahoma. Temperance Movements. Women's Christian Temperance Union. 1907-11. 2595
—. Architecture. Brown, Henry Cordes. Capitol building. Colorado (Denver). Myers, Elijah E. 1876-1908. 2783
—. Arizona. Cattle industry. Economic Conditions. Federal Government. Land Tenure. Political Attitudes. Public Opinion. 1950-63. 4089
—. Arizona. Federal Government. Forest Service. Game management conflicts. Hunt v. United States (US, 1928). Hunting. Kaibab National Forest. Wildlife Conservation. 1924-69. 4111
—. Arizona (Prescott). Gold Mines and Mining. Letters. McCormick, Richard C. Political Campaigns. 1864. 972
—. Boundary disputes. Debt reduction. Henderson, James Pinckney. New Mexico. Public Lands (sale of). Texas. 1845-50. 2686
—. Bradley, Lewis Rice. Cattle Raising. Nevada. 1871-78. 2839
—. Brown, John. Humphrey, Heman. Kansas. Letters. Slavery. 1857. 2543
—. California. Civil War claims. Federal Government. Military Finance. 1861-1967. 612
—. California. Clar, C. Raymond. Forests and Forestry. History. Pardee, George C. Research. 18c-1927. 1178
—. California. Democratic Party. Politics. Republican Party. Warren, Earl. 1943-53. 3759
—. California. Local Government. Pennsylvania. Political Recruitment. Training-ground thesis. 1900-62. 3728
—. California (Long Beach). City Government. Civil Court cases. Mallon, Felix. Oil Industry and Trade. 1930-66. 3875
—. Coal Mines and Mining. Colorado. Labor Disputes. Peabody, James H. United Mine Workers of America. Western Federation of Miners. 1903-13. 3954
—. Coke, Richard. Davis, Edmund Jackson. Letters. Maxey, Samuel Bell. Reconstruction. Texas. 1874. 2645
—. Colorado. Diaries. Gold Rushes. Mallory, Samuel. Montana. 1860-80. 2713
—. Colorado. Federal Government. Indian-White Relations. Judicial Administration. Murder. Ute Indians. 1870's-80's. 1766
—. Colorado. Fiscal Policy. Political Reform. Public Welfare. 1918-41. 3709
—. Colorado (Denver). Political Reform. Progressive Party. 1906. 3752
—. Colorado (San Juan Mountains; Telluride). Gold Mines and Mining. National Guard. Peabody, James H. Strikes. United Mine Workers of America. Western Federation of Miners. 1903-04. 3956
—. Congress. Frantz, Frank. Oklahoma. Warren amendment. 1906-07. 2601
—. Congress. Hearrell, Alice. Murray, William H. ("Alfalfa Bill"). Oklahoma. 1912-38. 2612
—. Congress. Kansas. Reform. 1866-1900. 2552
—. Conservation of Natural Resources. Federal Government. Historians. Land policies. Public Domain (use of). 1789-1965. 1187
—. Constitutional convention (state). North Dakota (Bismarck). Spalding, Burleigh F. 1861-89. 2497
—. Constitutions, State. Harrison, Benjamin (administration). North Dakota (Bismarck). South Dakota. Statehood movements. 1889. 2447
—. County commissioners (role). Local Government. Oklahoma. Politics. 1927-63. 3757
—. Davis, Jonathan M. Elections. Kansas. 1924-43. 3746
—. Dry Cleaning Board. Industry. Oklahoma. 1939-64. 3932
—. Elections. Legislation (direct). Oklahoma. Politics. 1907-65. 3758
—. Hawley, James H. Idaho. Lawyers. Western Federation of Miners. 1890's. 3870
—. Kansas. Landon, Alfred M. Oil Industry and Trade. 1930-32. 3916

—. Lewelling, Seth. Oregon. Political Parties. Politics. Progressive movement. Reform. U'Ren, William S. 1892-98. 2970
—. Miller, John. North Dakota. Politics. 1878-1908. 2486
—. Miller, John. North Dakota (Bismarck). 1889. 2489
State Historical Society of Wisconsin. American Association for State and Local History. Draper, Lyman C. Scholars. Thwaites, Reuben Gold. Wisconsin. 1853-1913. 276
State histories. Bibliographies. 1970. 2424
State Industrial Welfare Commission. California. Edson, Katherine Philips. League of Women Voters. Woman Suffrage. 1911-31. 3775
State Land Office. California. Public Domain. 1858-98. 1154
State Legislatures. Anti-evolution movement. Education. Oklahoma. Smith, Al. 1923-28. 1861
—. Arizona. Governors. Vetoes. 1912-63. 2895
—. Bryan, William Jennings. California. Federal Government. Japanese Americans. Webb Act (1913). Wilson, Woodrow (administration). 1913-14. 3999
—. California. Constitutional convention (state). Debts. 1879. 3046
—. California. Hall, William Hammond. Water resources. 1878-88. 1186
—. California. Land reserves. Parks. Redwoods. 1852-1967. 1190
—. California Geological Survey. Geology. Public Policy. Scientific Experiments and Research. Whitney, Josiah Dwight. 1860-74. 2201
—. Elections. Kansas. Populist Party. Republican Party. 1892-93. 2561
—. Lobbying. Oklahoma. 1961. 3799
—. Politics. Texas. 1935-61. 3795
State Legislatures (special sessions). Arizona. 1912-63. 2896
State Legislatures (unicameral). Nebraska. Norris, George William. Progressivism. 1890-1934. 2520
State Mill and Elevator. Bank of North Dakota. Iconoclast (newspaper). Martinson, Henry R. North Dakota. Political Reform. Reminiscences. Socialist Party. 1910-20's. 3782
State Politics See also Elections; Governors; Political Campaigns; Political Parties; State Government.
—. American Federation of Labor. Anaconda Copper Mining Company. Copper Mines and Mining. Fire. Industrial Workers of the World. Montana (Butte). Press. Strikes. 1917. 3891
—. Annexation (proposed). Arizona. New Mexico (Grant County, Silver City). Political Corruption. Santa Fe Ring. 1876. 2858
—. Arizona Territory (Prescott). Bashford, Coles. Law. Political Corruption (assumed). Wisconsin. 1850-78. 2880
—. Avery, Cyrus S. Avery Realty Company. Coal Mines and Mining. Eastern Oklahoma Agricultural Association. Leavell Coal Company. Oil Industry and Trade. Oklahoma. Real Estate Business. Togo Oil Company. 1907-63. 3722
—. California. Colorado River Project. Johnson, Hiram. Political Reform. Senate. 1911-41. 3747
—. California. Education. Hyatt, Edward. Public Schools. 1894-1919. 1841
—. California. Educational Reform. Fisher Bill (1961). Fisher, Hugo. Teacher certification requirements. 1850-1962. 1836
—. California. Frontier thesis. Lawyers. Turner, Frederick Jackson. 1850-90. 2987
—. California. Gold Mines and Mining. Smith, William. Virginia. 1797-1887. 944
—. California. Ide, William Brown. Mexican War. 1796-1852. 544
—. California (Oakland). Knowland, Joseph Russell. Tribune (newspaper). Warren, Earl. 1914-30. 3751
—. Cattle Raising. Judges. Republican Party. Van Devanter, Willis. Wyoming. 1884-97. 2755
—. Chase, Salmon P. Customs collection. Lincoln, Abraham. Political Corruption. Smith, Victor. Washington Territory (Port Townsend, Puget Sound). 1860's. 2943
—. Child Welfare. Food and drug standards. Legislation. Montana. Propaganda. 1900-15. 2730
—. Colorado. Democratic Party. New Deal. Reform. Social Change. 1930's. 3708
—. Colorado. Elections. Political Parties. Teller, Henry Moore. Waite, Davis H. Wolcott, Edward O. 1892-1902. 3772

—. Colorado. First Ladies. Populism. Waite, Celia O. Crane. Waite, David Hanson. 1893-95. 2767
—. Colorado. Populism. Rogers, John Rankin. Waite, David Hanson. Washington. 1892-1901. 3754
—. Colorado. Waite, Davis H. Woman Suffrage. 1892-94. 2784
—. Conservation of Natural Resources. Economic Growth. Hay, Marion E. Pinchot, Gifford. Washington. 1908-12. 4100
—. Constitutional convention (state). States' Rights. Stewart, Charles Bellinger. Texas. 1830-61. 2671
—. Democratic Party. Montana. New Deal. Political Factions. Wheeler, Burton K. 1933-36. 3780
—. Elections (federal). Electoral College. Hayes, Rutherford B. Oregon. Tilden, Samuel J. 1876. 2969
—. Fountain, Albert Jennings. Law Enforcement. New Mexico (Mesilla). Public Schools. Republican Party. Santa Fe Ring. 1861-80's. 1845
—. Johnson County War. Populism. Stock Growers' Association. Wyoming. 1890's. 2752
—. Kyle, James Henderson. Lee, Andrew E. Loucks, Henry Langford. National Farmers' Alliance. Political Parties. Populism. Reform. South Dakota. 1884-96. 3760
State regulation. Business. California. Economic Reform. Public Utilities Act (1911). Railroads and State. 1911-15. 3852
—. Hogg, James Stephen. Oil Industry and Trade. Railroads. Texas Railroad Commission. Transportation. 1891-1965. 3928
State songs. Korn, Anna Lee Brosius. Missouri (Hamilton). Oklahoma. 1869-1965. 2591
State Voters' League. Colorado (Denver). Lindsey, Benjamin Barr. Progressivism. 1905-06. 2772
Statehood. Government. Judges. Montana Territory. Political Attitudes. 1864-89. 2733
Statehood Day. Clyde, George D. (speech). Utah. 1964. 2811
Statehood (issue of). Congress. Elections (federal). Kansas. Politics. Slavery. 1860. 2570
Statehood movements. Arizona. New Mexico. Politics. Roosevelt, Theodore. Taft, William H. 1908. 2703
—. Beveridge, Albert J. Politics. Senate Committee on Territories. Southwest. 1902-12. 2693
—. Boundaries. Kansas Territory. 1858-59. 2541
—. California. Clay, Henry. Compromise of 1850. Slavery. 1850. 3031
—. Carey, Joseph Maull. Congress. Letters. Politics. VanDevanter, Willis. Wyoming. 1890. 2749
—. Celebrations. Cheyenne Daily Sun (newspaper). Wyoming. 1890. 2761
—. Congress. Democratic Party. Indian Territory. Oklahoma Territory. Republican Party. 1889-1906. 2589
—. Constitutional convention (state). Territorial Government. Wyoming. 1880's. 2757
—. Constitutions, State. Harrison, Benjamin (administration). North Dakota (Bismarck). South Dakota. State Government. 1889. 2447
—. Economic Conditions. Social Conditions. Utah. 1896. 2831
—. Federal Government. Governors. Oklahoma Territory. Population. Public Opinion. 1891-99. 2599
—. Indian Territory. Oklahoma Territory. Political Parties. 1890-1906. 2590
—. Mormons. Polygamy. Utah. 1846-96. 1963. 2816
—. Nebraska. Politics. 1859-67. 2506
—. Politics. Senate. Texas. 1845. 2625
States' Rights See also Secession.
—. Calhoun, John C. Cass, Lewis. Douglas, Stephen A. Dred Scott v. Sanford (US 1857). Federal Government. Free Soil Doctrine. Political Parties. Slavery. Sovereignty. Squatter Sovereignty Doctrine. 1789-1860. 1526
—. Constitutional convention (state). State Politics. Stewart, Charles Bellinger. Texas. 1830-61. 2671
States (51st, creation of). Arizona. Indian-White Relations. Navajo Indians. New Mexico. Population growth (consequences). Utah. 1930's-71. 4026

—. Annexation. Education. Houston, Sam.
Lamar, Mirabeau Buonaparte. Nicaragua.
Public Lands (sale of). Taylor, Zachary.
1830's-59. *2681*

—. Antilabor legislation. Labor Law. 1897-1947.
3856

—. Apache Indians. Arizona. Baylor, John Paul.
Civil War. Confederate States of America.
Davis, Jefferson. Indian policy. 1862-63.
623

—. Apache Indians (Mescalero). Crime and
Criminals. Indians. Military Campaigns.
New Mexico. Price, William Redwood. 1873.
777

—. Appalachia. Culture. Mountain Men.
Westward Movement. 1800-80. *2650*

—. Architecture. France. Spain. 1588-1890.
2095

—. Architecture. Photography. Victorianism,
American. Webb, Tedd. 1969. *2076*

—. Arizona. Baylor, John R. Confederate Army.
Mexican Americans. Military Occupation.
Sibley, Henry Hopkins. 1861-62. *622*

—. Arizona. California. Cattle drives. Diaries.
Erskine, Michael H. New Mexico. 1854.
1122

—. Arizona. California. Colorado. Mexico.
New Mexico. Plan of San Diego.
Revolutionary Movements. 1915. *3592*

—. Arkansas. Bankhead, S. P. Civil War. Fort
Smith. Indian Territory (Confederate). Letters.
Steele, Frederick. 1863. *580*

—. Arkansas. Folklore (oral). Louisiana. 1968.
1868

—. Arkansas. Louisiana. Rice. 1880-1910. *1049*

—. Armies. Courts Martial and Courts of Inquiry.
Flipper, Henry Ossian. Fort Davis. Negroes.
1881. *1755*

—. Armies. Daily Life. Dungan, Hugh P. Fort
Brown. Letters. 1851-52. *484*

—. Armies. Fort Davis. Medicine (practice of).
Weisel, Daniel. 1869-72. *2182*

—. Armies. Kramer, Adam. Letters. Military
Service, Professional. 1866-67. *525*

—. Art. Florida (St. Augustine). Fort Marion.
Indian Wars. Kiowa Indians. Oklahoma.
Pratt, Richard Henry. Zo-tom (Kiowa Indian,
sketchbook). 1869-75. *2156*

—. Artists (illustrators). Bibliographies. Books.
Bywaters, Jerry. Cisneros, José. Mead, Ben
Carlton. 1967. *2104*

—. Assimilation. California. Immigration.
Mexican Americans. Pachucos. 1840's-1942.
4024

—. *Atlanta Constitution* (newspaper). Georgia.
Newspapers. Styles, Carey Wentworth.
Temperance Movements. 1840-97. *2038*

—. Attitudes. Newspapers (prospectuses of).
1830's-40's. *2039*

—. Austin, Henry. Bolivar House. Diaries.
Holley, Mary Austin. 1830's. *2652*

—. Austin, Stephen F. Cotton. Economic
Conditions. Farmers. 1820's-61. *1058*

—. Austin, Stephen F. Bryan, James Perry. James
Perry Bryan Map Collection. Map Drawing.
1507-1885. *2633*

—. Ballads. Barnett, Graham. Folk Songs.
Outlaws. 1890's-1930's. *2159*

—. Bangs, Samuel. Mexico. Pioneers. Printing.
1817-47. *212*

—. Banks, Nathaniel Prentiss. Bayou Bourbeau
(battle). Civil War. Green, Thomas. Louisiana
(Opelousas). Roberts, Oran Milo. Sabine Pass.
Taylor, Richard. 1863. *585*

—. Bee, Hamilton Prioleau. Civil War.
Confederate Army. Fort Brown. Mexico.
Trade. 1861-65. *672*

—. Bibliographies. Colleges and Universities.
Houston, University of. Kunkel, Mike.
Literature. McMurtry, Larry. 20c. *1957*

—. Bibliographies. Genealogy. Research (sources).
1968. *2680*

—. Bibliographies. Oil Industry and Trade.
1963-64. *994*

—. Blue laws. Business. Legislation. 1871-1961.
3589

—. Bond, George. Editors and Editing. Gambrell,
Herbert. Hubbell, Jay B. *Southwest Review*
(periodical). 1915-27. *3614*

—. Boom towns. Cattle drives. Great Plains.
Illinois. Kansas. 1860's-20c. *1093*

—. Boundary disputes. Courts. Federal
Government. Oklahoma. Red River.
Surveying. 1859-1927. *2428*

—. Boundary disputes. Debt reduction.
Henderson, James Pinckney. New Mexico.
Public Lands (sale of). State Government.
1845-50. *2686*

—. Brotherhood of Timber Workers. Industrial
Workers of the World. Kirby, John Henry.
Labor Disputes. Louisiana. Lumber and
Lumbering. Southern Lumber Operators'
Association. 1906-16. *3921*

—. Cabet, Etienne. Icaria. Settlement. Utopias.
1848. *1469*

—. Cabeza de Vaca, Alvar Núñez. Indian-White
Relations. Karankawa Indians. 1528-1858.
56

—. California. Cattle Raising. Cowboys. Mexico.
Saddles, Mother Hubbard. Spain. 16c-1966.
46

—. California. Frontier customs. Great Britain.
Law (development of). 1607-1967. *267*

—. California. Stereotypes. 1968. *3044*

—. Cattle Raising. Chisholm Trail. Kansas
(Abilene). Railroads. Westward Movement.
1867-71. *1091*

—. Cattle Raising. Colorado. Cowboys. Dobie, J.
Frank. Goodnight, Charles. Iliff, John Wesley.
1836-1929. *1089*

—. Cattle Raising. Hunter, John Marvin. 1865-80.
1129

—. Cattle Raising. Louisiana. 18c-19c. *2649*

—. Cattle Raising. Mexican Americans. Ranching
techniques. South or Southern States. 1820-50.
1107

—. Cattle Raising. Montana Range Riders'
Association Museum. Museums.
Reminiscences. Stockyards. Wilder, Dale.
1899-1957. *1128*

—. Cattle Raising. Pryor, Ike T. Reminiscences.
Tennessee. 1861-70's. *1086*

—. Cattle Raising. Spaniards. 18c-19c. *202*

—. Cattle trail (national). Cowboys. Politics.
1883-86. *1112*

—. Cavalry. Comanche Indians. Indian Wars.
Military Campaigns. Negroes. New Mexico.
Nolan, Nicholas. 1877. *727*

—. Census. Demography. Ethnic Groups.
Religion. Rural-Urban Studies. 1850. *1572*

—. Cities. German Americans. Immigration.
Settlement. 1865-1968. *1490*

—. Civil Rights. Judges. Negroes. Supreme Court
(state). 1845-60. *1513*

—. Civil War. 1861-65. *649*

—. Civil War. Confederate Army. Green, Thomas
J. Val Verde (battle). 1861-65. *615*

—. Civil War. Confederate Army. Military
Recruitment. Polish Brigade. Sulakowski,
Valery. Virginia. 1862-63. *631*

—. Civil War. Confederate Army (Rocket Battery).
1864. *632*

—. Civil War. Confederate States of America.
France. Houston, Sam. Letters. Lubbock,
Francis Richard. Napoleon III. Théron,
Benjamin. 1862. *606*

—. Civil War (antecedents). Comanche Indians.
Fort Cooper (surrender of). Letters. Militia.
1861. *642*

—. Clothing. Hat styles. Johnson, Lyndon B.
16c-1964. *1435*

—. Coke, Richard. Davis, Edmund Jackson.
Letters. Maxey, Samuel Bell. Reconstruction.
State Government. 1874. *2645*

—. Coke, Richard. Know-Nothing Party.
Newcomb, James P. Reconstruction.
Republican Party. 1865-74. *2669*

—. "Cole Younger" (ballad). Folk Songs.
Outlaws. Younger, Coleman. 1869-1916.
1962. *1866*

—. Colonization. Independence Movements.
Mexico. Ortíz de Ayala, Tadeo. 1833. *215*

—. Comanche Indians. Indians (tribal warfare).
Oklahoma (Red River; Taovayas). Ortiz
Parrilla, Diego. 1759. *14*

—. Comanche Indians. Mexico. 1743-1836.
184

—. Comanche Indians. Military Camps and Forts.
Mission San Saba. Spain. 1757-70. *167*

—. Comfort, John W. Indian Wars. Military
Service, Professional. Uniforms, Military.
5th Cavalry, US. 1865-92. *792*

—. Communes. Icaria. Illinois. Iowa (Adams
County; New Icaria). 1848-95. *1430*

—. Considérant, Victor Prosper. Immigration.
Réunion. Utopias. Wolski, Kalikst. 1855-76.
1456

—. Constitutional Convention (state). 1875. *2636*

—. Constitutional convention (state). State Politics.
States' Rights. Stewart, Charles Bellinger.
1830-61. *2671*

—. Construction. Galveston Custom House.
Treasury Department. Young, Ammi Burnham.
1857-61. *2685*

—. Cooke, Philip St. George. Mexico. Santa Fe
Trail. Snively, Jacob. 1843-44. *2658*

—. Cooley, Elizabeth Ann. Daily Life. Diaries.
McClure, James W. Missouri. 1842-48. *1597*

—. Cordero y Bustamante, Manuel Antonio.
Spain. Territorial Government. 1805-08.
15

—. Cotton. Economic Conditions. Farmers.
Industrialization. 1865-1900. *1224*

—. Cotton. Industrial Revolution. Trade.
1865-85. *1232*

—. Cowboys. Photography. Smith, Erwin Evans.
1886-1947. *2059*

—. Cuney, Norris Wright. Negroes. Political
Leadership. Republican Party. 1883-96. *2627*

—. Cushing, E. H. Houston *Telegraph*
(newspaper). Printing. Schools. Textbooks.
1863-65. *2016*

—. Czechoslovakian Americans. Oklahoma
(Ardmore). Stolfa, John, Sr. 1889-1966. *1450*

—. *Décimas.* Folk Songs. Mexico. 18c-20c.
40

—. *Décimas.* Folk Songs. Mexico. 1749-1850.
41

—. Depressions. Folk Songs. Hoover, Herbert.
Public Opinion. Republican Party. Roosevelt,
Franklin D. 1930's. *3706*

—. Derbanne, François Dion Deprez. Louisiana.
Settlement. 18c. *175*

—. DeSoto, Hernando. Discovery and Exploration.
Louisiana. Mississippi River. Moscoso, Luis de.
1542-43. *84*

—. DeWitt, Green. Kerr, James. Settlement.
Surveying. 1825-50. *2631*

—. Diaries. Gates, Guerdon. Red River.
Settlement. 1841-42. *374*

—. Diaries. National Guard. Newton, Harold D.
Vermont. 1916. *3649*

—. Diplomacy. Foreign Relations. France.
Mexico. Saligny, Alphonse Dubois de. ca
1820's-50's. *2400*

—. Diplomacy. France. Pig War. Saligny,
Alphonse Dubois de. ca 1836-45. *2619*

—. Discovery and Exploration. Mexico. Vaca,
Cabeza de. 1527-36. *71*

—. Diseases. Folk Medicine. 19c-1968. *2177*

—. Dobie, J. Frank. Literature. 1888-1964.
1898

—. Dobie, J. Frank (portrait). 1931. *3609*

—. Economic Conditions. Labor Unions and
Organizations. Railroads. Strikes. 1838-76.
1039

—. Economic Development. Louisiana. Red River.
Reminiscences. Scovell, M. L. Steamboats.
Transportation. 1815-1915. *1409*

—. Edmonds, James E. Fort Brown. Mexican
War. Military Campaigns. Pruyn, Robert N.
Reminiscences. Taylor, Zachary. 1846-48.
568

—. Elections (federal). Whigs. 1848-52. *2626*

—. Explorers. Green, Duff C. Mexico. Rio
Grande River. U.S. Boundary Survey
Commission. 1852. *452*

—. Farms. Reminiscences. Wright, Carl C.
1920's. *4090*

—. Folklore. 1968. *1914*

—. Folklore. Great Britain. Humor. 17c-1963.
2618

—. Folklore. Great Britain. Ireland. Phantom
coach (legend). 19c. *1867*

—. Folklore. Maverick, Samuel A. Pioneers.
1828-70. *2677*

—. Foreign Relations. France. Great Britain.
Henderson, James Pinckney. Houston, Sam.
Irion, Robert Anderson. Letters. 1830's-40's.
2673

—. Foreign Relations. France. Manuscripts.
1838-46. *2620*

—. Foreign Relations. Houston, Sam. Mexico.
1842-43. *2688*

—. Foreign Relations. Indians. Letters. Mexico.
Milan, Benjamin Rush. Outlaws. Poinsett, Joel.
Refugees. Slavery. 1825. *203*

—. Fort Brown. Fort Clark. Fort Duncan. Fort
McIntosh. Military Service, Professional
(inspector-general). San Antonio Arsenal. San
Antonio Arsenal. Schriver, Edmund (report).
1872-73. *477*

—. Fort Davis. Frontier and Pioneer Life.
Negroes. 1867-85. *528*

—. Francis Smith and Company. Great Britain.
Investments. Smith, Francis. 1875-90's. *1246*

—. Freedman's Bureau. Historiography. Ku Klux
Klan. Reconstruction. 1865-76. *2668*

—. Frontier and Pioneer Life. 1836-45. *2640*

—. Frontier and Pioneer Life. Mexico. New
Mexico. Spain. ca 1700-50. *100*

—. Frontier thesis. Great Plains. Philosophy of
History. Webb, Walter Prescott (works).
19c. 1959-63. *2471*

V

Waite, Celia O. Crane. Colorado. First Ladies. Populism. State Politics. Waite, David Hanson. 1893-95. *2767*

Waite, David Hanson. Colorado. First Ladies. Populism. State Politics. Waite, Celia O. Crane. 1893-95. *2767*

—. Colorado. Populism. Rogers, John Rankin. State Politics. Washington. 1892-1901. *3754*

Waite, Davis H. Colorado. Elections. Political Parties. State Politics. Teller, Henry Moore. Wolcott, Edward O. 1892-1902. *3772*

—. Colorado. State Politics. Woman Suffrage. 1892-94. *2784*

Wakamatsu Tea and Silk Farm Colony. California (El Dorado County; Gold Hill). Immigration. Japanese Americans. 1869-71. *1545*

Waldner, Michael. Communes. Hutterites. Immigration. Russian Americans. South Dakota (Bon Homme County). 1874-75. *1473*

Waldo, David. Land speculation. Missouri. New Mexico (Taos). Southwest. Trade. 1820-78. *1243*

Waldorf, John Taylor. Gold Rushes. Nevada (Virginia City). Reminiscences. 1873-86. *1616*

Walker, Albert R. Architecture. California (Los Angeles). Eisen, Percy A. 1920-40. *3673*

Walker, "Big Jim". Crime and Criminals. Oklahoma. Wilson, Hank. 1894-95. *1117*

Walker, Paul Atlee. Corporate Commission. Federal Communications Commission. Oklahoma. 1881-1965. *2609*

Walker, Robert. Indian-White Relations. Navajo Indians. New Mexico. Newby, Edward W. B. 1847-48. *776*

Walker, Robert J. Alaska Purchase. Foreign Relations. Polk, James K. Russian-American Company. Seward, William Henry. Stoeckl, Edouard de. 1845-67. *3514*

Walking Coyote, Samuel. Allard, Charles P. Buffalo sanctuaries. Montana. Pablo, Michel. Yellowstone National Park. 1885-90. *1185*

Walking trips. Arizona. Lummis, Charles Fletcher. New Mexico. 1884. 1963. *372*

Wallace, William (Henson). Idaho. Political Leadership. Territorial Government. ca 1841-79. *2737*

Wallen, Henry Davies (report). Apache Indians (Mescalero). Fort Sumner. Indian-White Relations. Navajo Indians. New Mexico. 1863. *849*

Walsh, Thomas J. Courts. Democratic Party. Montana. Senate. 1890-1918. *3724*

—. Dakota Territory (Redfield). Politics. 1884-90. *2504*

Walter Prescott Webb Memorial Lecture Series. Colleges and Universities. Historians. Texas, University of (Arlington). Webb, Walter Prescott. 1888-1963. *2430*

Walters, Archer. Diaries. English Americans. Illinois (Nauvoo). Iowa. Mormons. Westward Movement. 1846-56. *2293*

Walters, Theodore A. Ickes, Harold. Idaho. New Deal. Politics. Roosevelt, Franklin D. 1933-37. *3807*

Walther, Theobald F. Kansas (Humbolt). Nebraska. 1862-1917. *1591*

Walton, John Calloway. Farmer-Labor Reconstruction League. Farmers (white tenant). Ku Klux Klan. Oklahoma (Marshall County). Pine, William. Politics. Radicals and Radicalism. Socialism. Voting and Voting Behavior. 1910-24. *3731*

—. Governors. Impeachment. Ku Klux Klan. Oklahoma. 1923-24. *3792*

War See also names of wars, battles, etc., e.g. American Revolution, Gettysburg (battle), etc.; Antiwar Sentiment; Battles; Civil War; Guerrilla Warfare; Military; Military Strategy; Naval Strategy; Peace; Refugees.

—. Agriculture. Economic Policy. Federal Government. Isolationism. Nonpartisan League. North Dakota. Political Attitudes. 1916-60. *3712*

War Department. Arkansas. Curtis, Samuel Ryan. Fort Smith. Indian Territory. Kansas. Steele, Frederick. 1863-64. *589*

—. Economic Conditions. Fort Cameron. Fort Duchesne. Fort Thornburgh. Indian-White Relations. Military Camps and Forts. Settlement. Utah. 1872-1912. *683*

War of 1812. California (Monterey). Jones, Thomas ap Catesby. Lake Borgne (battle). Mexico. Navies. Plantations. Virginia (Fairfax County). 1790-1858. *554*

—. Foreign Relations. France. French Revolution. Great Britain. Louisiana Purchase. Napoleon. Washington, George (administration). XYZ Affair. 1783-1812. *274*

Ward, Allen T. Indians. Letters. Methodist Church. Missions and Missionaries. Schools. 1842-51. *2308*

Ward, Artemus. Humor. Kansas. Lecture tour. Missouri (St. Joseph). 1863-64. *1817*

Wardner, James F. Finance. Leadership. Mining. 1871-99. *863*

Ware, Eugene Fitch. Business. Civil War. Fort Scott. Kansas. Poetry. 1866-1907. *1941*

—. Civil War (personal narratives). Fort Kearney. Iowa Cavalry, 7th. Nebraska. 1864. *492*

—. Fort Scott. Kansas. Law. Poetry. 1867-71. *1940*

—. Kansas. Literature. Poetry. 1841-1911. *1942*

Warner, Charles Dudley. Advertising. Arizona. Baumann, Jules. Grand Canyon. Higgins, C. A. Railroads. Santa Fe Railroad. 1908. *3969*

Warner, Glenn ("Pop"). Carlisle Indian School. Colleges and Universities. Exendine, Albert Andrew. Football. Indians. Oklahoma. Thorpe, James. 1879-1962. *1843*

Warner, Jonathan Trumbull (Juan José Warner). California. Manifest Destiny. New York (Rochester). Oregon. Settlement. Speeches, Addresses, etc.. 1840. *2936*

Warner, Luna. Diaries. Frontier and Pioneer Life. Homesteading and Homesteaders. Kansas (Downs). Lewis, Frank. Warner, Walter. 1870-74. *1580*

Warner, Walter. Diaries. Frontier and Pioneer Life. Homesteading and Homesteaders. Kansas (Downs). Lewis, Frank. Warner, Luna. 1870-74. *1580*

Warren amendment. Congress. Frantz, Frank. Oklahoma. State Government. 1906-07. *2601*

Warren, Earl. California. Democratic Party. Politics. Republican Party. State Government. 1943-53. *3759*

—. California (Oakland). Knowland, Joseph Russell. State Politics. *Tribune* (newspaper). 1914-30. *3751*

Warren, Francis E. Cattle Raising. Democratic Party. Johnson County War. Republican Party. Territorial Government. Wyoming. 1892. *1097*

Warren, John L. L. Agriculture. California. Colleges and Universities. Federal Aid to Education. Letters. 1853. *1849*

Warren, Kemble. Discovery and Exploration. Nebraska Territory. 1855-57. *366*

Washakie (Chief). Indian-White Relations. Letters. Shoshoni Indians. Young, Brigham. 1854-57. *748*

—. Indian-White Relations. Ray, Patrick Henry. Reminiscences. Shoshoni Indians. 1851-90's. *728*

Washburn-Doane Expedition. Diaries. Everts, Truman C. Gillette, Warren C. Montana (Helena). 1870. *2719*

—. Everts, Truman C. Survival account. Yellowstone National Park. 1870. *2753*

Washington. Advertising. Immigration. Scandinavian Americans. 1890-1910. *1460*

—. Agricultural Cooperatives. Fruit and Fruit Crops (industry). Yakima Valley Fruit Growers' Association. 1900-20. *3869*

—. Agriculture. Cattle Raising. Indian-White Relations. Sheep Raising. 1864-1964. *1096*

—. Alaska. Communications Technology. Telegraph. 1867-1914. *3544*

—. Arcata and Mad River Railroad. California (Humboldt County). Economic Conditions. Lumber and Lumbering. Railroads. Sacramento Valley Railroad. Simpson Logging Company. Union Plank Walk, Rail Track, and Wharf Company Railroad. 1853-1963. *1345*

—. Archives. Federal Records Centers. Libraries. Research. 1968. *2953*

—. Artillery. Military Camps and Forts. Oregon (Columbia River). 1863-65. *490*

—. Bannock Indians. California. Indian-White Relations. Military policy. Mormons. Oregon. Shoshoni Indians. Utah. Westward Movement. 1859-63. *771*

—. British Columbia (Vancouver). Immigration. Japanese Canadians. Labor Disputes. Racism. Riots. 1887-1907. *3483*

—. California. Lumber and Lumbering. Oregon. Shipping. Simpson, Asa Mead. 1826-1915. *1219*

—. Colorado. Populism. Rogers, John Rankin. State Politics. Waite, David Hanson. 1892-1901. *3754*

—. Columbia Basin Project. Grand Coulee Dam. Land use. Reclamation of Land. Water use. 1930-63. *4124*

—. Conservation of Natural Resources. Economic Growth. Hay, Marion E. Pinchot, Gifford. State Politics. 1908-12. *4100*

—. Discovery and Exploration. Hudson's Bay Company. Mount Rainier National Park. Rainier, Peter. Tourism. Vancouver, George. 1792-1899. *2065*

—. Emergency Conservation Committee of New York City. Ickes, Harold. Lumber and Lumbering. Martin, Clarence. Olympic National Park. Roosevelt, Franklin D. 1897-1940. *4139*

—. Equality Colony. National Union of the Brotherhood of the Co-operative Commonwealth. Utopias. 1897-1907. *4015*

—. Governors. Territorial Government. 1853-89. *2955*

—. Hay, Marion E. Impeachment. Political Reform. Schively, John H. 1909-12. *3726*

—. Idaho. Indian-White Relations. Methodism. Missions and Missionaries. Wilbur, James Harvey. Yakima Reservation. 1859-87. *2337*

—. Kansas. Kingsbury, John Adams. Social Work. 1876-1908. *3661*

—. Museums. Seattle Museum of History and Industry. 1968. *2946*

—. Panama Canal (construction). Railroads. Stevens, John Frank. Surveying. 1890-1925. *1369*

—. Poindexter, Miles. Political Leadership. Progressive Party. Roosevelt, Theodore. 1910-12. *3771*

—. Politics. Real Estate Business. Winston, Patrick Henry. 1886-1903. *2950*

—. Prohibition. Voting and Voting Behavior. 1914. *3574*

Washington (Centralia). American Legion. Centralia Massacre. Industrial Workers of the World. Labor Disputes. Pamphlets. 1919. 1920-67. *3637*

—. Industrial Workers of the World. Labor Disputes. Murder. Trials. 1919. *3914*

—. Negroes. Pioneers. Washington, George (1817-1902). 1842-1902. *1689*

Washington (Clarkston). Bridges. Idaho (Lewiston). Railroads. Snake River Valley. 1925-30. *3579*

Washington (Colville Valley). Discovery and Exploration. Goethals, George W. Map Drawing. Pacific Northwest. 1882-84. *373*

Washington Education Association. Education. Marsh, Arthur L. 1919-51. *2941*

Washington (Everett). "Bloody Sunday.". Industrial Workers of the World. Labor Disputes. 1916-17. *3862*

—. Haywood, William Dudley ("Big Bill"). Industrial Workers of the World. Labor Disputes. Literature. 1916. *3848*

Washington, George. Arizona. Excavations. Fillmore, Millard. Pierce, Franklin. Pipes (clay). 1967. *2878*

Washington, George (administration). Foreign Relations. France. French Revolution. Great Britain. Louisiana Purchase. Napoleon. War of 1812. XYZ Affair. 1783-1812. *274*

Washington, George (statue of). Idaho (Boise). Ostner, Charles Leopold. Sculpture. 1869-1965. *2131*

Washington, George (1817-1902). Negroes. Pioneers. Washington (Centralia). 1842-1902. *1689*

Washington (Guide to). Communism. Federal Writers' Project. 1935-41. *2956*

Washington (Home). Anarchism and Anarchists. McKinley, William (assassination). 1901-02. *4014*

Washington (Mount Vernon, Sunnyside, Toppenish). Sugar. Utah-Idaho Sugar Company. White Fly (beet leaf hopper). 1899-1966. *4032*

Washington (Nisqually). Indians. Methodist Church. Missions and Missionaries. Richmond, John P. 1840-42. *2338*

Washington (Nisqually; Mt. Rainier). Diaries. Tolmie, William Fraser. Travel account. 1833. *326*

Washington (northern). Cascade Mountains. Construction. Roads (wagon). 1880-96. *1317*

Washington (Ocosta). 19c. *1626*

Washington (Olympia). Barker, William Morris. Episcopal Church, Protestant. 1894-1901. *3618*

—. Arizona (Yuma). Diaries. Fages, Pedro. Indian-White Relations. Mexico (Sonora). Military Campaigns. 1781. *69*

—. Garcés, Francisco Tomás Hermenegildo (martyrdom). Mexico (Sonora). New Mexico (Yuma Crossing). 1738-81. *137*

Yuma Massacre (battle). Arizona. California. Discovery and Exploration. Garcés, Francisco Tomás Hermenegildo. Mission San Gabriel Arcangel. Mojave River (discovery of). New Mexico. 1775-81. *85*

Yuman Indians. California. *Hartford Courant* (newspaper). Letters. Overland Journeys to the Pacific. Travel account. 1850. *981*

Z

ZA ranch. Cattle Raising. Codwise, Charles W. Colorado. Cowboys. Daily Life. Hayes, Edward. Letters. Roundups. 1887. *1103*

Zacualtipan (battle). Hays, John Coffee. Jarauta, Padre. Mexican War. Polk, William H. Texas Rangers. Truett, Alfred M. 1848. *574*

Zalvidea, José María de. California (San Marino). Franciscans. Mission San Gabriel Arcangel. Old Mill State Monument. ca 1816-1965. *102*

Zan Hicklan's Ranch. Carson, Christopher (Kit). Colorado. Hunting. Indians. Military Recruitment. Reminiscences. Wilmot, Luther Perry. 1860-61. *1620*

Zane, Charles S. Judges. Mormons. Utah. 1884-93. *2794*

Zarate, Asencio de. Catholic Church. Historical Sites and Parks. Llana, Geronimo de la. New Mexico. Tombs. 17c-18c. *9*

Zia Pueblo. Galisteo Pueblo. Marta, Bernardo de. New Mexico. Santo Domingo Reservation. 1597-17c. *95*

Zimmermann Note. Austria. Germany. Mexico. Military Intelligence. Texas (San Antonio). Visser, Olga. World War I. 1917. *3569*

—. Germany. Japan. Mexico. Newspapers. Public Opinion. South or Southern States. Southwest. World War I. 1917. *3567*

Zinc Miners' Association. Industrial organizations. Kansas. Missouri. Price controls. 1899-1905. *3927*

Zion National Park. Harding, Warren G. Larson, A. Karl. Reminiscences. Utah. 1923. *3624*

Zion's Camp. Missouri (Jackson County). Mormons. Ohio (Kirtland). 1830's. *2276*

Zogbaum, Rufus Fairchild. Artists (illustrators). Bibliographies. Books. ca 1872-1925. *2101*

Zo-tom (Kiowa Indian, sketchbook). Art. Florida (St. Augustine). Fort Marion. Indian Wars. Kiowa Indians. Oklahoma. Pratt, Richard Henry. Texas. 1869-75. *2156*

Zuñi Indians. Discovery and Exploration. Dorantes, Estevancio de. Southwest. Spain. 1528-39. *60*

1

10th Cavalry, US. Canada. Cree Indians. Fort Assiniboine. Montana. Negroes. Pershing, John J. 1895-96. *523*

10th Cavalry, US (Troop E). Arizona (Bear Valley). Negroes. Reminiscences. Ryder, Frederick H. L. Yaqui Indians. 1918. *3705*

101 Ranch Wild West Show. Cowboys. Mexico (Mexico City). Pickett, William (Bill). 1908. *3697*

—. Entertainment. Miller Brothers. Popular Culture. 1904-32. *3665*

3

3d Cavalry, US. Fort Cummings. Mutinies. Negroes. New Mexico. 1867. *509*

38th Infantry, US. Cholera epidemic. Kansas. 1866-67. *2563*

4

49th Parallel. Anglo-American Boundary Commission. Boundaries. Canada. Royal Geographical Society. USA. 1872. 1967. *3180*

5

5th Cavalry, US. Cheyenne Indians. Duncan, Thomas. Fort McPherson. Indian Wars. Military Campaigns. Nebraska (Republican River Valley). Royall, William Bedford. Sioux Indians. Summit Springs (battle). 1869. *726*

—. Comfort, John W. Indian Wars. Military Service, Professional. Texas. Uniforms, Military. 1865-92. *792*

7

7th Cavalry, US. *Army and Navy Journal.* Indian Wars. Little Big Horn (battle, survivors). Relief funds. 1876. *815*

—. Benteen, Frederick W. Little Big Horn (battle). Montana (Yankton). Recreation (baseball team). 1876. *462*

—. Big Foot (Chief). Ghost Dance. Indian Wars. Plains Indians. Sioux Indians. South Dakota. Wounded Knee (battle). 1890. *697*

—. Cheyenne Indians. Custer, George A. Hancock, Winfield S. Kiowa Indians. Military Campaigns. Sioux Indians. 1867. *845*

—. Custer Battlefield National Monument. Custer, George A. National Parks and Reserves. Sioux Indians. 1876-1940. *806*

—. Custer, George A. Diaries. Indian-White Relations. North Dakota. Sioux Indians. Sitting Bull (Chief). 1876. *691*

—. Custer, George A. Hamilton, Louis McLane (death). Indian Wars. Letters. Washita (Battle). 1868-69. *858*

8

8th Cavalry, US. Arizona Territory. Fort Whipple. Gregg, J. Irvin. Indian-White Relations. Nevada (Churchill Barracks). 1867. *695*

AUTHOR INDEX

LIST OF PERIODICALS

A

Ábside [Mexico]
Aerospace Historian
Agricultural History
Air Power Historian (old title, see Aerospace Historian)
Alabama Historical Quarterly
Alabama Review
Alberta Historical Review [Canada]
American Archivist
American Bar Association Journal
American Benedictine Review
American Book Collector
American Heritage
American Historical Review
American History Illustrated
American Jewish Archives
American Jewish Historical Quarterly
American Journal of Economics and Sociology
American Journal of Legal History
American Literature
American Neptune
American Quarterly
American Scandinavian Review
American Scholar
American Speech
American West
American West Review (old title, see American West)
American-German Review
Americas: A Quarterly Review of Inter-American Cultural History (Academy of American Franciscan History) [old title, see Americas (Academy of Franciscan History)]
Annales: Économies, Sociétés, Civilisations [France]
Annals of Iowa
Annals of the American Academy of Political and Social Science
Annals of the Association of American Geographers
Annals of Wyoming
Anthropologica (AIA)
Anthropological Quarterly (AIA)
Arctic [Canada]
Arizona and the West
Arizona Quarterly
Arizoniana (old title, see Journal of Arizona History)
Arkansas Historical Quarterly
Army Quarterly and Defence Journal [Great Britain]
Art in America
Australian Journal of Politics and History [Australia]
Aztlán

B

Beaver [Canada]
Boletín del Archivo General de la Nación [Mexico]
Bulletin of the History of Medicine
Bulletin of the Missouri Historical Society (old title, see Missouri Historical Society Bulletin)
Bulletin of the School of Oriental and African Studies [Great Britain]
Bulletin of the United Church of Canada (old title, see Bulletin of the Committee on Archives of the United Church of Canada) [Canada]
Business History Review

C

Cahiers d'Histoire Mondiale (superseded by Cultures) [France]
California Anthropologist
California Historian
California Historical Quarterly
California Historical Society Quarterly (old title, see California Historical Quarterly)
Canadian Catholic Historical Association Annual Report [Canada]
Canadian Dimension [Canada]
Canadian Geographical Journal [Canada]
Canadian Historic Sites [Canada]
Canadian Historical Association Annual Report [Canada]
Canadian Historical Review [Canada]
Canadian Journal of Economics and Political Science [Canada]
Canadian Library [Canada]
Canadian Review of American Studies [Canada]
Catholic Historical Review

D

Dalhousie Review [Canada]
Daughters of the American Revolution Magazine
Dialogue: A Journal of Mormon Thought

E

Economic Geography
Encounter
Essex Institute Historical Collections
Estudios Centro Americanos [El Salvador]
Ethnohistory
External Affairs [Canada]

F

Film Heritage
Florida Historical Quarterly
Forest History

G

Geographical Journal [Great Britain]
Geographical Review
Geography [Great Britain]
Georgia Review
Great Plains Journal

H

Harvard Library Bulletin
Hawaiian Historical Society Annual Reports
Hawaiian Journal of History
Hidalguía (IHE) [Spain]
Hispanic American Historical Review
Historia Mexicana [Mexico]
Historia y Vida (IHE) [Spain]
Historian
Historic Preservation
Historical and Scientific Society of Manitoba Papers (old title, see Transactions of the Historical and Scientific Society of Manitoba) [Canada]
Historical Magazine of the Protestant Episcopal Church
Historical New Hampshire
Historiska och Litteraturhistoriska Studier [Finland]
History of Education Quarterly
History Today [Great Britain]
Human Organization
Humánitas [Mexico]
Huntington Library Quarterly

I

Idaho Yesterdays
Indian Journal of Social Research (suspended pub 1967) [India]
Indian Sociological Bulletin [India]
Indiana Magazine of History
Inland Seas
International Journal [Canada]
International Migration Review
Internationale Spectator [Netherlands]
Irish Sword [Republic of Ireland]
Isis

J

Jahrbuch für Amerikastudien [German Federal Republic]
Journal of American Folklore
Journal of American History
Journal of American Studies [Great Britain]

Journal of Arizona History
Journal of Canadian Studies [Canada]
Journal of Church and State
Journal of Conflict Resolution
Journal of Economic History
Journal of Human Relations (suspended pub 1973)
Journal of Inter-American Studies
Journal of Law and Economics
Journal of Library History, Philosophy, and Comparative Librarianship
Journal of Mexican American History
Journal of Negro History
Journal of Politics
Journal of Popular Culture
Journal of Presbyterian History
Journal of Southern History
Journal of the Folklore Institute
Journal of the History of Medicine and Allied Sciences
Journal of the Illinois State Historical Society
Journal of the Royal Australian Historical Society [Australia]
Journal of the Society of Architectural Historians
Journal of the West
Journal of Transport History [Great Britain]
Journalism Quarterly

K

Kansas Historical Quarterly (superseded by Kansas History)
Kansas Quarterly
Kentucky Folklore Record
Kiva
Kroeber Anthropological Society Papers

L

Labor History
Library Chronicle of the University of Texas
Library Quarterly
Lincoln Herald
Long Island Forum
Louisiana History
Louisiana Studies
Lutheran Quarterly (ceased pub 1977)

M

Mankind
Manuscripta
Manuscripts
Massachusetts Historical Society Proceedings
Masterkey
Mennonite Life
Mennonite Quarterly Review
Methodist History
Mid-America
MidContinent American Studies Journal (old title, see American Studies: An Interdisciplinary Journal)
Midwest Journal of Political Science
Midwest Quarterly
Military Affairs
Military Collector and Historian
Military Review
Minnesota History
Minority of One
Mississippi Valley Historical Review (old title, see Journal of American History)
Missouri Historical Review
Missouri Historical Society Bulletin
Montana Magazine of History (old title, see Montana: Magazine of Western History)

N

Names
Nebraska History
Negro History Bulletin
Nevada Historical Society Quarterly
New England Quarterly
New Jersey History
New Mexico Historical Review
New York Historical Society Quarterly
New York History
New-England Galaxy
North Dakota History
North Dakota Quarterly
Northwest Ohio Quarterly: a Journal of History and Civilization
Noticias

C (center column, continued)

Centaurus [Denmark]
Chesopiean (AIA)
Chronicles of Oklahoma
Church History
Civil War History
Civil War Times Illustrated
Colorado Magazine
Colorado Quarterly
Commentary
Concordia Historical Institute Quarterly
Connecticut Historical Society Bulletin
Contemporary Review [Great Britain]
Cooperation and Conflict [Denmark]
Cry California

O

Ohio History
Ontario History [Canada]
Oregon Historical Quarterly
Organon (ceased pub 1972)

P

Pacific Historian
Pacific Historical Review
Pacific Northwest Quarterly
Paedagogica Historica [Belgium]
Palacio
Palimpsest
Papers of the Bibliographical Society of America
Past and Present [Great Britain]
Pennsylvania History
Phylon
Plains Anthropologist
Plateau
Polar Record [Great Britain]
Polish American Studies
Polish Review
Proceedings of the American Philosophical Society
Prologue: the Journal of the National Archives

Q

Quarterly Journal of Speech
Quarterly Journal of Studies on Alcohol (old title,
    see Journal of Studies on Alcohol)
Quarterly Journal of the Library of Congress
Quarterly Review of Economics and Business
Queen's Quarterly [Canada]

R

Rapport: Société Canadienne d'Histoire de l'Église
    Catholique [Canada]
Records of the American Catholic Historical Society
    of Philadelphia
Register of the Kentucky Historical Society
Rendezvous
Research Studies
Revista de la Sociedad Bolivariana de Venezuela
    [Venezuela]
Revue de l'Université d'Ottawa [Canada]
Revue de Paris (ceased pub 1970) [France]
Revue d'Histoire de l'Amérique Française [Canada]
Rocky Mountain Social Science Journal

S

Saskatchewan History [Canada]

Scholarly Publishing [Canada]
Seiyōshigaku [Japan]
Slavonic and East European Review [Great Britain]
Smithsonian
Smithsonian Journal of History (ceased pub 1968)
Social Science
Social Science Quarterly
Social Studies
Societas
Sociological Analysis
Sociology and Social Research
South Dakota History
Southern California Quarterly
Southern Folklore Quarterly
Southern Quarterly
Southern Speech Journal
Southwest Review
Southwestern Historical Quarterly
Southwestern Journal of Anthropology (AIA)
Southwestern Lore (AIA)
Southwestern Social Science Quarterly (old title, see
    Social Science Quarterly)
Special Libraries
Speech Monographs
Spiegel Historiael [Netherlands]
Staten Island Historian
Stirpes
Studies [Republic of Ireland]
Studies in History and Society
Swedish Pioneer Historical Quarterly

T

Technology and Culture
Tennessee Historical Quarterly
Texana
Trans-Action: Social Science and Modern Society
    (old title, see Society)
Transactions of the Historical and Scientific Society
    of Manitoba [Canada]
Transactions of the Royal Historical Society [Great
    Britain]
Transactions of the Royal Society of Canada
    [Canada]
Turun Historiallinen Arkisto [Finland]

U

Új Látóhatár [German Federal Republic]
Ukrainian Quarterly
Ukraïns'kyi Istorychnyi Zhurnal [Union of Soviet
    Socialist Republic]
United States Naval Institute Proceedings
University of Birmingham Journal [Great Britain]
University of Toronto Quarterly [Canada]
University of Wyoming Publications

Utah Historical Quarterly

V

Ventures (ceased pub 1971)
Vermont History
Virginia Cavalcade
Virginia Magazine of History and Biography
Virginia Quarterly Review

W

Warship International
West Virginia History
Western American Literature
Western Explorer (ceased pub 1968)
Western Folklore
Western Historical Quarterly
Western Humanities Review
Western Political Quarterly
Western Review (ceased pub 1973)
Western States Jewish Historical Quarterly
Wilson Library Bulletin
Wisconsin Magazine of History
Wisconsin Then and Now

Y

Yale University Library Gazette
Yivo Annual of Jewish Social Science

FESTSCHRIFTEN

Essays on American Literature in Honor of Jay B.
    Hubbell (Durham: Duke U. Press, 1967)
Essays on the American Civil War (Austin: U. of
    Texas Press, 1968)
Festschrift Percy Ernst Schramm zu seinem
    siebzigsten Geburtstag von Schülern und
    Freunden zugeeignet (Wiesbaden: Franz Steiner
    Verlag GMBH, 1964)
Folklore International: Essays in Honor of Wayland
    Debs Hand (Hatboro: Folklore Associates, Inc.,
    1967)
In the Trek of the Immigrants: Essays Presented to
    Carl Wittke (Rock Island, Illinois: Augustana
    Coll. Lib., 1964)
The Swedish Immigrant Community in Transition:
    Essays in Honor of Dr. Conrad Bergendoff
    (Rock Island, Illinois: Augustana Hist. Soc.,
    1963)
Writing Southern History: Essays in Historiography
    in honor of Fletcher M. Green (Baton Rouge:
    Louisiana State U. Pr., 1965)

LIST OF ABSTRACTERS

A

Abramoske, D. J.
Abrash, M.
Adams, G. R.
Allard, C. J.
Allen, C. R., Jr.
Allen, R. F.
Altmann, B.
Alvis, R. N.
Andrusiak, N.
Anness, D.
Aptheker, H.
Athey, L. L.

B

Baldelli, G.
Barbato, B. A.
Barrett, G.
Bassett, T. D. S.
Bassler, G.
Bauer, K. J.
Beauchamp, E. R.
Bedford, H. F.
Beezley, W. H.
Berman, M.
Birkos, A. S.
Bishop, C. A.
Boedecker, W. R.
Boles, J. B.
Born, J. D.
Bottorff, W. K.
Bowers, W. L.
Boyd, C. L.
Brady, J. M.
Brandes, J.
Brescia, A. M.
Brewster, D. E.
Brockman, N. C.
Brockway, D.
Brooks, W. J.
Brown, D. N.
Brown, E.
Brown, L.
Buckman, W. A.
Bumsted, J. M.
Burke, R. S.
Burns, H. M.
Bushnell, D.
Byrum, J. D.

C

Calkin, H. L.
Calvert, R. V.
Cameron, D. D.
Casada, J. A.
Cashman, L.
Caswell, J. E.
Chappell, K.
Chauvin, K. A.
Chauvin, W. D.
Cherno, M.
Clarke, J.
Clifton, P. O.
Coats, A. W.
Cohen, R. D.
Coleman, P. J.
Condon, T. M.
Corbitt, D. C.
Costello, E. P.
Crapster, B. L.
Cripps, T. R.

Crowe, J. C.
Curl, D. W.

D

Davidson, S. R.
Davis, G. H.
Davis, K. P.
Davis, T. B.
Davison, S. R.
Delaney, R. W.
Dodd, D. B.
Dodds, G. B.
Drummond, B. A.
Duff, J. B.
Duniway, D. C.

E

Earnhart, H. G.
Eger, S. A.
Eichelberger, C. L.
Eilerman, R. J.
Ekrut, V. S.
Elkins, W.
Emery, G.
Eminhizer, E. E.
Engler, D. J.
Erickson, E. A.
Erlebacher, A.

F

Farnham, T. J.
Feldman, E.
Fiala, R. D.
Filipiak, J. D.
Filler, L.
Findlay, J. F.
Findling, J. E.
Flack, J. K.
Ford, R. J. C.
Fox, M. B.
Fox, W. L.
Frank, W. C.
Frazier, C. E.
Freedman, A. S.

G

Gagnon, G. O.
Gara, L.
Gorchels, C. C.
Graham, H. J.
Grant, C. L.
Grattan, W. J.
Griffin, W. R.
Grob, G. N.

H

Hamilton, A. J.
Hamilton, C. G.
Hanks, R. J.
Hathaway, E. W.
Hawes, J. M.
Hayes, M. A.
Henderson, D. F.
Henry, B. W.
Herbst, J.
Hofeling, L. P.
Hoffman, A.

Horacek, M. J.
Horn, D. E.
Hough, M.
Howell, R.
Hubbard, L. L.
Hudson, J. A.
Hudson, R. O.
Hudspeth, R. N.
Hull, G. W.
Humphreys, S. E.
Hyslop, E. C.

J

James, K.
Jensen, J.
Johnson, B. D.
Johnson, E. S.
Jones, G. H. G.
Jones, S. L.
Jordan, H. D.

K

Keiser, J. H.
Kelsey, H.
Kennedy, P. W.
Knafla, L. A.
Krenkel, J. H.
Kroeger, M.
Kubicek, R. V.
Kurland, G.

L

Lange, R. B.
Lawrance, A. H.
Layton, R. V.
Leonard, I. M.
Levinson, R. E.
Lindsey, D.
Lohof, B. A.
Lovin, H. T.
Lowitt, R.
Lux, W. R.
Lydon, J. G.

M

Machan, M. W.
Mahoney, J. F.
Main, A. K.
Malyon, H. F.
McAuley, M.
McBaine, M. J.
McBaine, R. V.
McBane, R. L.
McCain, P. M.
McCarthy, J. M.
McClure, P.
McCusker, J. J.
McCutcheon, J.
McGinty, G. W.
McIntyre, D.
McNeel, S. L.
McNiff, W. J.
Melamed, R. S.
Metz, W. D.
Miller, O. L.
Miller, W. B.
Moen, N. W.
Moore, R. J.
Moore, W. P.
Morgan, W. G.

Morrison, B. M.
Mulligan, W. H.
Murdoch, D. H.
Murdock, E. C.
Murphy, F. I.
Murphy, L. R.

N

Negaard, H. A.
Nelson, L. G.
Newman, B.
Newton, C. A.
Nichols, R. L.
Noppen, I. W. Van

O

Oberholzer, E.
O'Brien, E. J.
Ogilvie, C. F.
Ohrvall, C. W.
Oliver, D. C.
Orr, A.

P

Panting, G. E.
Parkinson, R. J.
Paul, J. F.
Paulston, R. G.
Pearson, S. C.
Peterson, N. L.
Peterson, W. F.
Petrie, M.
Picht, D. R.
Pickett, R. S.
Pliska, S. R.
Powell, H. B.
Puffer, K. J.
Pusateri, C. J.

R

Raife, L. R.
Rasmussen, J. L.
Rasmussen, W. D.
Reid, W. S.
Rex, M. B.
Richardson, D. R.
Righter, R.
Roddy, E. G.
Rollins, A. B.
Roon, K. B. van
Rosenthal, F.
Roske, R. J.
Rossi, F. J.
Rotondaro, F.

S

Sagara, M.
Scaccia, J. F.
Seligmann, G. L.
Selleck, R. G.
Sexauer, R.
Shapiro, E. S.
Sherter, S. R.
Shoemaker, R. W.
Silveri, L. D.
Silverman, H. J.
Simon, P. L.

Skau, G. H.
Slavutych, Y.
Sloan, D. A.
Small, M.
Smart, J. H.
Smith, C. O.
Smith, D. L.
Smith, G. P.
Smith, W. D.
Smoot, J. G.
Snow, G. E.
Solnick, B. B.
Spencer, W. F.
Stanndard, J.
Stelzner, H. G.
Stickney, E. P.
Stifflear, A. J.
Stokes, D. A.
Storey, B. A.
Susskind, J. L.
Swanson, B. E.
Swift, B. B.
Swift, D. C.
Swift, D. H.

T

Tallman, R. D.
Tennyson, B. D.
Thacker, J. W.
Thibault, C.
Thomas, J.
Thomas, P. D.
Trennert, R. A.
Turner, A.
Tutorow, N. E.

U

Unrau, W.
Upton, L. F. S.
Usher, J. M. E.

V

Várkonyi, P.
Vatter, B. A.
Visser, D.

W

Ward, H. M.
Warren, C. N.
Wechman, R. J.
Weltsch, R. E.
West, K. B.
White, L. J.
Whitham, W. B.
Wilkins, B.
Williamson, R. L.
Willigan, W. L.
Wilson, R. E.
Woodward, R. L.
Wurtz, R. J.

Y

Yanchisin, D. A.
Young, A. P.

Z

Zabel, O. H.
Zilversmit, A.
Zornow, W. F.

THE AMERICAN
AND
CANADIAN WEST